ACTIVITY-BASED COSTING (Chapter 4)

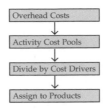

Activity-based costing involves the following four steps:
1. Identify and classify the major activities involved in the manufacture of specific products, and allocate the manufacturing overhead costs to the appropriate cost pools.
2. Identify the cost driver that has a strong correlation to the costs accumulated in the cost pool.
3. Compute the overhead rate for each cost driver.
4. Assign manufacturing overhead costs for each cost pool to products, using the overhead rates (cost per driver).

COST-VOLUME-PROFIT (Chapter 5)

Types of Costs

Variable costs	Vary in total directly and proportionately with changes in activity level
Fixed costs	Remain the same in total regardless of change in activity level
Mixed costs	Contain both a fixed and a variable element

CVP Income Statement Format

	Total	Per Unit
Sales	$xx	$xx
Variable costs	xx	xx
Contribution margin	xx	$xx
Fixed costs	xx	
Net income	$xx	

Breakeven Point

$$\text{Breakeven point in units} = \text{Fixed costs} \div \text{Contribution margin per unit}$$

Target Net Income

$$\text{Required sales in units} = (\text{Fixed costs} + \text{Target net income}) \div \frac{\text{Contribution}}{\text{margin per unit}}$$

INCREMENTAL ANALYSIS (Chapter 6)

1. Identify the relevant costs associated with each alternative. Relevant costs are those costs and revenues that differ across alternatives. Choose the alternative that maximizes net income.
2. Opportunity costs are those benefits that are given up when one alternative is chosen instead of another one. Opportunity costs are relevant costs.
3. Sunk costs have already been incurred and will not be changed or avoided by any future decision. Sunk costs are not relevant costs.

VARIABLE COSTING (Chapter 7)

Absorption Costing		Variable Costing
Product Cost	← Fixed Manufacturing Overhead →	Period Cost

Absorption Costing Income Statement

Sales		$X
Cost of goods sold		X
Gross profit		X
Variable selling and administrative expenses	$X	
Fixed selling and administrative expenses	X	X
Net income		$X

Variable Costing Income Statement

Sales		$X
Variable cost of goods sold	$X	
Variable selling and administrative expenses	X	X
Contribution margin		X
Fixed manufacturing overhead	X	
Fixed selling and administrative expenses	X	X
Net income		$X

Break-even Point with Multiple Products

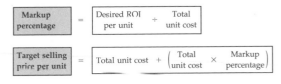

$$\text{Break-even point in units} = \frac{\text{Fixed costs}}{\text{Weighted-average unit contribution margin}}$$

$$\text{Break-even point in dollars} = \frac{\text{Fixed costs}}{\text{Weighted-average contribution margin ratio}}$$

$$\text{Degree of operating leverage} = \frac{\text{Contribution margin}}{\text{Net income}}$$

PRICING (Chapter 8)

External Pricing

$$\text{Markup percentage} = \frac{\text{Desired ROI per unit}}{\text{Total unit cost}}$$

$$\text{Target selling price per unit} = \text{Total unit cost} + \left(\text{Total unit cost} \times \text{Markup percentage} \right)$$

Transfer Pricing

$$\text{Minimum transfer price} = \text{Variable cost} + \text{Opportunity cost}$$

eGrade Plus

with EduGen

www.wiley.com/college/weygandt

Based on the Activities You Do Every Day

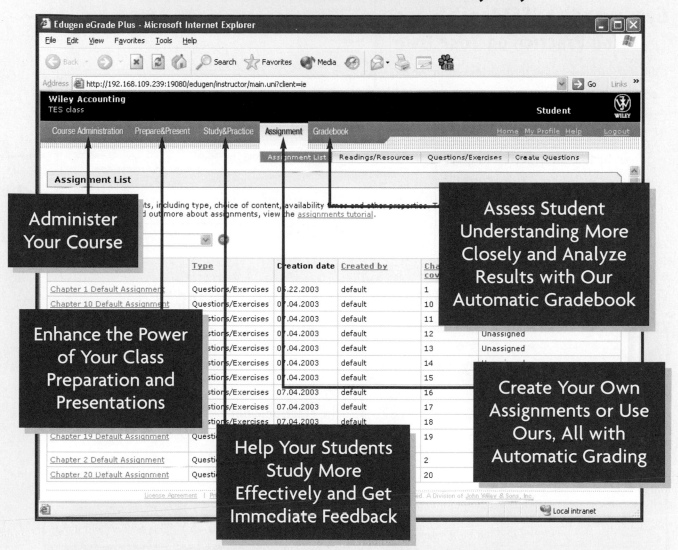

Administer Your Course

Enhance the Power of Your Class Preparation and Presentations

Help Your Students Study More Effectively and Get Immediate Feedback

Assess Student Understanding More Closely and Analyze Results with Our Automatic Gradebook

Create Your Own Assignments or Use Ours, All with Automatic Grading

All the content and tools you need, all in one location, in an easy-to-use browser format.

Choose the resources you need, or rely on the arrangement supplied by us.

Now, many of Wiley's Book Companion Sites are available with EduGen, allowing you to create your own teaching and learning environment. Upon adoption of EduGen, you can begin to customize your course with the resources shown here. eGrade Plus with EduGen integrates text and media and keeps all of a book's online resources in one easily accessible location. eGrade Plus integrates two resources: homework problems for students and a multimedia version of this Wiley text. With eGrade Plus, each problem is linked to the relevant section of the multimedia book.

Students,
eGrade Plus with EduGen Allows You to:

Study More Effectively

Get Immediate Feedback When You Practice on Your Own

Our website links directly to **electronic book content**, so that you can review the text while you study and complete homework online. Additional resources include **interactive chapter reviews, web-based tutorials**, and **self-assessment quizzing**.

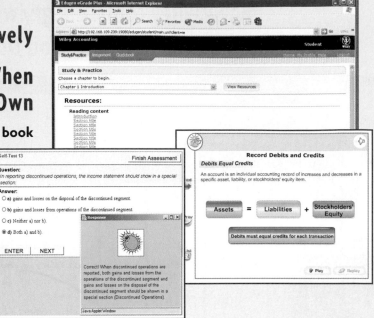

Complete Assignments / Get Help with Problem Solving

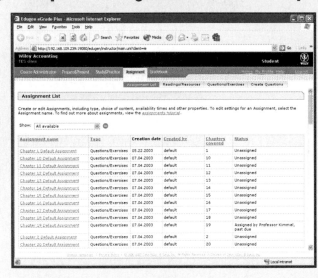

An **"Assignment"** area keeps all your assigned work in one location, making it easy for you to stay on task. In addition, many homework problems contain a **link** to the relevant section of the **electronic book**, providing you with a text explanation to help you conquer problem-solving obstacles as they arise.

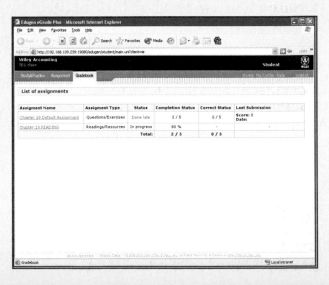

Keep Track of How You're Doing

A **Personal Gradebook** allows you to view your results from past assignments at any time.

MANAGERIAL ACCOUNTING

Tools for Business Decision Making

3 RD EDITION

JERRY J. WEYGANDT PhD, CPA
Arthur Andersen Alumni Professor of Accounting
University of Wisconsin
Madison, Wisconsin

DONALD E. KIESO PhD, CPA
KPMG Emeritus Professor of Accounting
Northern Illinois University
DeKalb, Illinois

PAUL D. KIMMEL PhD, CPA
Associate Professor of Accounting
University of Wisconsin—Milwaukee
Milwaukee, Wisconsin

WILEY

JOHN WILEY & SONS, INC.

Dedicated to
our former students and our colleagues, past and present,
and to
our wives Enid, Donna, and Merlynn

PUBLISHER: Susan Elbe
ASSOCIATE PUBLISHER: Jay O'Callaghan
MARKETING MANAGER: Steve Herdegen
DEVELOPMENT EDITOR: Ann Torbert
ASSOCIATE EDITOR: Ed Brislin
PRODUCTION SERVICES MANAGER: Jeanine Furino
MEDIA EDITOR: Allison Morris
PRODUCTION MANAGEMENT SERVICES: Ingrao Associates
PROJECT EDITOR: David Kear
PHOTO EDITOR: Sara Wight
SENIOR ILLUSTRATION EDITOR: Sandra Rigby
ART STUDIO: Precision Graphics
COVER PHOTO: © Gamma Ray Studio, Inc./The Image Bank/Getty Images
TEXT DESIGNER: Dawn L. Stanley
COVER DESIGN: Norm Christensen

This book was set in New Aster by TECHBOOKS and printed and bound by Von Hoffmann Press. The cover was printed by Von Hoffmann Press.

This book is printed on acid-free paper.

Library of Congress Cataloging-in-Publication Data

Weygandt, Jerry J.
  Managerial accounting: tools for business decision making/Jerry J. Weygandt, Donald E. Kieso, Paul D. Kimmel.—3rd ed.
      p. cm.
  Various muti-media instructional aids are available to supplement the text.
  Includes bibliographical references and index.
  ISBN 0-471-661783-3 (cloth)
    1. Managerial accounting. I. Kieso, Donald E. II. Kimmel, Paul D. III. Title.
  HF5657.4.W49 2004
  658.15'11—dc22

                                                            2004059588

ISBN US Edition 0471-66178-3
ISBN WIE 0471-66182-1
Printed in the United States of America

10 9 8 7 6 5 4 3

Jerry J. Weygandt, PhD, CPA, is Arthur Andersen Alumni Professor of Accounting at the University of Wisconsin—Madison. He holds a Ph.D. in accounting from the University of Illinois. Articles by Professor Weygandt have appeared in the *Accounting Review, Journal of Accounting Research, Accounting Horizons, Journal of Accountancy*, and other academic and professional journals. These articles have examined such financial reporting issues as accounting for price-level adjustments, pensions, convertible securities, stock option contracts, and interim reports. Professor Weygandt is author of other accounting and financial reporting books and is a member of the American Accounting Association, the American Institute of Certified Public Accountants, and the Wisconsin Society of Certified Public Accountants. He has served on numerous committees of the American Accounting Association and as a member of the editorial board of the *Accounting Review*; he also has served as President and Secretary-Treasurer of the American Accounting Association. In addition, he has been actively involved with the American Institute of Certified Public Accountants and has been a member of the Accounting Standards Executive Committee (AcSEC) of that organization. He has served on the FASB task force that examined the reporting issues related to accounting for income taxes and is presently a trustee of the Financial Accounting Foundation. Professor Weygandt has received the Chancellor's Award for Excellence in Teaching and the Beta Gamma Sigma Dean's Teaching Award. He is on the board of directors of M & I Bank of Southern Wisconsin. He is the recipient of the Wisconsin Institute of CPA's Outstanding Educator's Award and the Lifetime Achievement Award. In 2001 he received the American Accounting Association's Outstanding Accounting Educator Award.

Donald E. Kieso, PhD, CPA, received his bachelor's degree from Aurora University and his doctorate in accounting from the University of Illinois. He has served as chairman of the Department of Accountancy and is currently the KPMG Emeritus Professor of Accountancy at Northern Illinois University. He has public accounting experience with Price Waterhouse & Co. (San Francisco and Chicago) and Arthur Andersen & Co. (Chicago) and research experience with the Research Division of the American Institute of Certified Public Accountants (New York). He has done postdoctorate work as a Visiting Scholar at the University of California at Berkeley and is a recipient of NIU's Teaching Excellence Award and four Golden Apple Teaching Awards. Professor Kieso is the author of other accounting and business books and is a member of the American Accounting Association, the American Institute of Certified Public Accountants, and the Illinois CPA Society. He has served as a member of the Board of Directors of the Illinois CPA Society, the AACSB's Accounting Accreditation Committees, the State of Illinois Comptroller's Commission, as Secretary-Treasurer of the Federation of Schools of Accountancy, and as Secretary-Treasurer of the American Accounting Association. Professor Kieso is currently serving on the Board of Trustees and Executive Committee of Aurora University, as a member of the Board of Directors of Kishwaukee Community Hospital, and as Treasurer and Director of Valley West Community Hospital. From 1989 to 1993 he served as a charter member of the national Accounting Education Change Commission. He is the recipient of the Outstanding Accounting Educator Award from the Illinois CPA Society, the FSA's Joseph A. Silvoso Award of Merit, the NIU Foundation's Humanitarian Award for Service to Higher Education, a Distinguished Service Award from the Illinois CPA Society, and in 2003 an honorary doctorate from Aurora University.

Paul D. Kimmel, PhD, CPA, received his bachelor's degree from the University of Minnesota and his doctorate in accounting from the University of Wisconsin. He is an Associate Professor at the University of Wisconsin—Milwaukee, and has public accounting experience with Deloitte & Touche (Minneapolis). He was the recipient of the UWM School of Business Advisory Council Teaching Award, the Reggie Taite Excellence in Teaching Award, and a three-time winner of the Outstanding Teaching Assistant Award at the University of Wisconsin. He is also a recipient of the Elijah Watts Sells Award for Honorary Distinction for his results on the CPA exam. He is a member of the American Accounting Association and the Institute of Management Accountants and has published articles in *Accounting Review, Accounting Horizons, Advances in Management Accounting, Managerial Finance, Issues in Accounting Education, Journal of Accounting Education*, as well as other journals. His research interests include accounting for financial instruments and innovation in accounting education. He has published papers and given numerous talks on incorporating critical thinking into accounting education, and helped prepare a catalog of critical thinking resources for the Federated Schools of Accountancy.

In this Third Edition of *Managerial Accounting: Tools for Business Decision Making*, we strove to build on those things that made the earlier editions a success in the classroom. Our goals are straightforward: We want this book to present the fundamental concepts of managerial accounting in an easy-to-understand fashion. We want to present only those concepts that students need to know. And we want students to leave the course confident that they will be able to apply the basic decision skills that they learned in this course when they enter the work-force. As a result, as you read through the list of changes to this edition and review the text, the common theme you will notice is that these changes were made to simplify and clarify our presentation of basic concepts or to strengthen the students' decision-making skills. We are very excited about this edition of the text. As in the earlier editions, our efforts were driven by the following key beliefs:

"Less is more."

Our instructional objective is to provide students with an understanding of those concepts that are fundamental to the use of managerial accounting. Most students will forget procedural details within a short period of time. On the other hand, concepts, if well taught, should be remembered for a lifetime. Concepts are especially important in a world where the details are constantly changing.

"Don't just sit there— do something."

Students learn best when they are actively engaged. The overriding pedagogical objective of this book is to provide students with continual opportunities for active learning. One of the best tools for active learning is strategically placed questions. Our discussions are framed by questions, often beginning with rhetorical questions and ending with review questions. Even our selection of analytical devices, called *Decision Tools*, is referenced using key questions to emphasize the purpose of each. In addition, technology offers many opportunities to enhance the learning environment. Through the use of interactive activities at our Website at http://www.wiley.com/college/weygandt, we offer many opportunities for active learning. In addition, both in the homework and at the Website, we offer more opportunities to employ spreadsheet templates.

"I'll believe it when I see it."

Students will be most willing to commit time and energy to a topic when they believe that it is relevant to their future careers. There is no better way to demonstrate relevance than to ground discussion in the real world. By using high-profile companies like **Starbucks**, **Microsoft**, **Ben & Jerry's**, and **Intel** to frame our discussion of accounting issues, we demonstrate the relevance of accounting while teaching students about companies with which they are familiar. In addition, because the economy has shifted toward service industries, many of the companies used as examples are service based. This shift is emphasized by our new homework feature which emphasizes more service-company exercises. In addition, we provide many references to service companies such as **American Express**, **Federal Express**, and **Union Pacific Railroad** throughout the text.

"You'll need to make a decision."

All business people must make decisions. Decision making involves critical evaluation and analysis of the information at hand, and this takes practice. We have integrated important analytical tools throughout the book. After each new decision tool is presented, we summarize the key features of that tool in a *Decision Toolkit*. At the end of each chapter, the *Using the Decision Toolkit* activity provides a comprehensive demonstration of an analysis of a real-world problem using the decision tools presented in the chapter. The *Broadening Your Perspective* homework activities require the student to employ these decision tools. Finally, seven *Cases for Management Decision Making*, provided at the end of the text, require students to employ decision-making skills in rich, realistic business settings.

Key Features of Each Chapter

CHAPTER 1, Managerial Accounting

- Compares and contrasts managerial accounting with financial accounting.
- Identifies three broad functions of management.
- Defines three classes of manufacturing costs, organizational structure, and business ethics issues.
- Distinguishes between product costs and period costs.
- Presents the costs of goods manufactured section of the income statement.
- Presents an overview of trends in managerial accounting including shift toward service industries, value chain management, enterprise resource planning, just-in-time inventory, activity-based costing, theory of constraints, and the balanced scorecard.

CHAPTER 2, Job Order Cost Accounting

- Provides an overview of cost accounting systems.
- Illustrates flow of costs in a job order cost system.
- Presents use of job cost sheets.
- Demonstrates use of predetermined overhead rate.
- Illustrates basic entries for job order cost system.
- Provides simple presentation of overapplied and underapplied overhead.

CHAPTER 3, Process Cost Accounting

- Explains the difference between job order and process costing systems.
- Illustrates the flow of costs and end-of-period accounting procedures for process costing.
- Demonstrates computation of physical units of production, equivalent units of production, and unit costs.
- Shows how to assign costs to units of output and prepare a production cost report.

CHAPTER 4, Activity-Based Costing

- Explains the need for activity-based costing (ABC).
- Contrasts ABC to traditional costing systems.
- Identifies numerous activities, activity cost pools, and cost drivers.
- Discusses implications of value-added and non-value-added activities.
- Illustrates use of ABC in service industries.
- Reviews the benefits and limitations of ABC.
- Discusses the implications of activity levels.
- Appendix illustrates use of just-in-time inventory systems.

CHAPTER 5, Cost-Volume-Profit

- Distinguishes between variable and fixed costs, and explains relevant range and mixed costs.
- Identifies components and assumptions of CVP analysis.
- Discusses concept of contribution margin and illustrates CVP income statement.
- Illustrates calculation of break-even point.
- Discusses margin of safety and target net income.

CHAPTER 6, Incremental Analysis

- Presents the concept of incremental analysis through a simple example.
- Explains the concepts of relevant cost, opportunity cost, and sunk cost.
- Applies incremental analysis in the following decision settings:
  - Accept an order at a special price
  - Make or buy
  - Sell or process further, including discussion of joint costs
  - Retain or replace equipment
  - Eliminate an unprofitable segment
  - Allocate limited resources across multiple products

CHAPTER 7, Variable Costing: A Decision-Making Perspective

We created an entirely new chapter that:

- Explains the difference between absorption costing and variable costing.
- Discusses the effect that changes in production level and sales level have on net income measured under absorption costing versus variable costing.
- Discusses the relative merits of absorption costing versus variable costing for management decision making.
- Explains sales mix and its effect on break-even analysis.
- Promotes understanding of how operating leverage affects profitability.

CHAPTER 8, Pricing

- Demonstrates how to compute target cost when a product's price is determined by the market.
- Illustrates how to compute target selling price using cost-plus pricing.

- Demonstrates how to use time and materials pricing when services are provided.
- Discusses the objective of transfer pricing.
- Illustrates how to determine a transfer price using the cost-based, market-based, and negotiated approaches.
- Explains the issues involved when goods are transferred between countries with different tax rates.

CHAPTER 9, Budgetary Planning

- Discusses benefits of budgeting.
- Illustrates the process of assembling information for a master budget.
- Prepares budgeted income statement, balance sheet, and cash budget.
- Discusses use of budgets in merchandising, service, and not-for-profit enterprises.

CHAPTER 10, Budgetary Control and Responsibility Accounting

- Explains how budgets are used to control costs and operations.
- Contrasts static budgets and flexible budgets.
- Uses a case study to illustrate usefulness of flexible budgets.
- Illustrates responsibility reporting systems.
- Defines cost centers, profit centers, and investment centers.
- Illustrates the computation and use of return on investment and (in a chapter appendix) residual income.

CHAPTER 11, Standard Costs and Balanced Scorecard

- Differentiates between a standard and a budget.
- Discusses advantages of standard costs and methods of computing.
- Illustrates computation of direct materials variance, direct labor variance, and manufacturing overhead variance.

- Demonstrates analysis through comparison of actual with standard.
- Discusses basic features and usefulness of the balanced scorecard.
- Appendix illustrates the journal entries for a standard cost system.

CHAPTER 12, Planning for Capital Investments

- Discusses nature of capital budgeting decisions.
- Describes and illustrates four methods of evaluating capital expenditures:
  - Cash payback technique
  - Net present value method
  - Internal rate of return method
  - Annual rate of return technique
- Discusses the profitability index, post audits, and the implications of intangible benefits when making capital budgeting decisions.

CHAPTER 13, Statement of Cash Flows

- Discusses the purpose and usefulness of the statement of cash flows.
- Discusses the implications of the product life-cycle for analysis of the statement of cash flows.
- Illustrates preparation of the statement of cash flows using one year of transactions for both the indirect and direct methods. The presentation is designed to allow the instructor to focus exclusively on either the indirect approach or the direct approach, or to cover both.
- Presents ratio analysis of the statement of cash flows using free cash flow, capital expenditure ratio, current cash debt coverage, and cash debt coverage.

CHAPTER 14, Financial Analysis: The Big Picture

- Provides a comprehensive discussion of analytical tools and their interrelationships.
- Illustrates horizontal and vertical analysis.
- Provides thorough analysis of the actual financial statements of Kellogg Company using ratio analysis.

New in This Edition

Textual Changes

The Second Edition of Managerial Accounting was very well received. In the spirit of continuous improvement, we have made many changes to the Third Edition. The most significant changes are summarized as follows.

- **Reorganization of chapters into four sections**: Cost Concepts (Chapters 1–4), Decision-Making Concepts (Chapters 5–8), Planning and Control Concepts (Chapters 9–12), Performance Evaluation Concepts (Chapters 13 and 14).

- **Addition of new Chapter 7**, Variable Costing: A Decision-Making Perspective.
- Introduction of **more end-of-chapter material using service-company examples**.
- **Introduction of new concepts** such as operating leverage, balanced scorecard, and theory of constraints.
- **Increased emphasis on the use of spreadsheets**, by employing spreadsheets in our illustrations and significantly increasing the amount of end-of-chapter material that is supported by spreadsheets.
- An additional set of **C Problems** appears at the book's Website to complement the set of A and B problems in the textbook.

Improvements in Technology—eGrade Plus

Technology offers many opportunities to enrich the learning environment. With this edition of the text we have expanded the materials provided on our Website, which now includes tutorials. The most exciting technological development of this edition is **eGrade Plus**. eGrade Plus is a Web-based product that provides an integrated suite of learning resources via a unique class homepage. Through this homepage students can access the following: the full content of the textbook, assignments, selected solutions, exams created by the instructor, and an online gradebook to monitor progress.

Changes Made In The Third Edition

CHAPTER 1, Basic Cost Concepts for Managers
- New discussion of the changing role of managerial accountants.
- New section on organizational structure.
- New section on business ethics.
- New material on the value chain, theory of constraints, and balanced scorecard.
- Revised and added exercises and problems.

CHAPTER 2, Job Order Cost Accounting
- Two new Business Insight boxes on job order costing software and use of job order costing by service companies.
- Revised and added exercises and problems.

CHAPTER 3, Process Cost Accounting
- Illustrations 3-5 and 3-12 revised for clarity.
- Illustrations presented as spreadsheets where appropriate.
- Revised and added exercises and problems.

CHAPTER 4, Activity-Based Costing
- Illustration 4-13 revised for clarity.
- Illustrations presented as spreadsheets where appropriate.

- Section on classification of activity levels moved from the appendix into the chapter.
- Section on just-in-time inventory moved into a chapter-end appendix.
- Revised and added exercises and problems.

CHAPTER 5, Cost-Volume-Profit
- Section on target net income moved forward to better integrate with discussion on break-even analysis.
- Appendix on variable costing replaced by new chapter on variable costing (Chapter 7).
- Illustrations presented as spreadsheets where appropriate.
- Revised and added new exercises and problems.

CHAPTER 6, Incremental Analysis
- Chapter on incremental analysis moved from Chapter 9 to Chapter 6 to reinforce concepts of cost-volume-profit.
- Added discussion on theory of constraints.
- New Business Insight box on make-or-buy decision by Superior Industries.
- Illustrations presented as spreadsheets where appropriate.
- Revised and added new exercises and problems.

CHAPTER 7, Variable Costing: A Decision-Making Perspective
Entirely new chapter, created to:
- Explain the difference between absorption costing and variable costing.
- Discuss the effect that changes in production level and sales levels have on net income measured under absorption costing versus variable costing.
- Discuss the relative merits of absorption costing versus variable costing for management decision making.
- Explain sales mix and its effect on break-even analysis.
- Understand how operating leverage affects profitability.

CHAPTER 8, Pricing
- Chapter on pricing moved from Chapter 11 to Chapter 8 to reinforce concepts of cost-volume-profit.
- New formula added for target cost.
- New discussion of the use of variable cost pricing.
- New Business Insight box on the pricing of Levi's jeans sold to Wal-Mart.
- Illustrations presented as spreadsheets where appropriate.
- Revised and added exercises and problems.

CHAPTER 9, Budgetary Planning

- New discussions of participative budgeting and budgetary slack.
- Two new Business Insight boxes on participative budgeting at Time Warner and cash budgeting by engineering firm Alstom.
- Illustrations presented as spreadsheets where appropriate.
- Revised and added exercises and problems.

CHAPTER 10, Budgetary Control and Responsibility Accounting

- Illustrations presented as spreadsheets where appropriate.
- Revised and added exercise and problems.

CHAPTER 11, Standard Costs and Balanced Scorecard

- New section added on balanced scorecard.
- Two new Business Insight boxes on the development of shared industrial standards and the use of balanced scorecard at United Airlines.
- Illustrations presented as spreadsheets where appropriate.
- Revised and added exercises and problems.

CHAPTER 12, Planning for Capital Investments

- Revised explanation on how to estimate net annual cash flow.
- New explanation of cash payback when cash flows are uneven.
- Internal rate of return discussion revised to show trial-and-error procedure.

- New Business Insight box on purchase of information technology for managing investments by mutual fund American Century.
- Revised and added exercises and problems.

CHAPTER 13, Statement of Cash Flows

- Coverage of the indirect and direct methods of preparing the operating activities section revised, shortened, and edited.
- Coverage of transactions for both the indirect and direct methods condensed from two years' of transactions to one year.
- New Business Insight box on misguided cash flow reporting by WorldCom, Inc. and Dynegy, Inc.
- Revised and added exercises and problems.

CHAPTER 14, Financial Analysis: The Big Picture

- Material on sustainable income deleted.
- Corporate data updated.
- Illustrations presented as spreadsheets where appropriate.
- Revised and added exercises and problems.

APPENDIX A: Time Value of Money

APPENDIX B: Ethical Standards

Cases for Management Decision Making

- Cases 3 and 4 have been switched to reflect new chapter sequence.
- New Case 6 added for use with Chapters 5 and 9.
- New Case 7 added for use with Chapters 5, 9, and 11.

Proven Pedagogical Framework

In this book we have used many proven pedagogical tools to help students learn accounting concepts and apply them to decision making in the business world. This pedagogical framework emphasizes the *processes* students undergo as they learn.

Learning How to Use the Text

- The text begins with a **Student Owner's Manual**, which helps students understand the value of the text's learning aids and how to use them. After becoming familiar with the pedagogy, students can take a *Learning Styles Quiz* (p. xxvii) to help them identify how they learn best—visually, aurally, through reading and writing, kinesthetically, or through a combination of these styles. They then will find tips on in-class and at-home learning strategies,

as well as help in identifying the text features that would be most useful to them based on their learning style.

- Additionally, Chapter 1 contains notes (printed in blue) that explain each learning aid the first time it appears.
- **The Navigator** pulls all the learning aids together into a learning system. It is designed to guide students through each chapter and help them succeed in learning the material. The Navigator consists of (1) a checklist at the beginning of the chapter, which outlines text features and study aids students will need in order to master the topics, and (2) a series of check boxes that prompt students to use the learning aids and set priorities as they study. At the end of the chapter, students are reminded to return to The

Navigator to check off their completed work. The Navigator from Chapter 2 is shown below.

```
THE NAVIGATOR ✔

▶ Scan Study Objectives            [  ]
▶ Read Feature Story               [  ]
▶ Read Preview                     [  ]
▶ Read text and answer Before You Go On
     p. 53 [ ]    p. 64 [ ]    p. 70 [ ]
▶ Work Using the Decision Toolkit  [  ]
▶ Review Summary of Study Objectives [  ]
▶ Work Demonstration Problem       [  ]
▶ Answer Self-Study Questions      [  ]
▶ Complete Assignments             [  ]
```

Understanding the Context

- **Study Objectives**, listed at the beginning of each chapter, form a learning framework throughout the text. Each objective is repeated in the margin at the appropriate place in the main body of the chapter and again in the **Summary of Study Objectives**. Also, end-of-chapter assignment materials are linked to the Study Objectives.

- A chapter-opening **Feature Story** presents a scenario that helps students picture how the chapter topic relates to the real world of accounting and business situations. It also serves as a recurrent example in the chapter. Each story that focuses on a well-known company ends with the company's Web address to encourage students to go online for more information about these companies.

- A chapter **Preview** links the chapter-opening Feature Story to the major topics of the chapter. First, an introductory paragraph explains how the story relates to the topics to be discussed, and then a graphic outline of the chapter provides a "road map," useful for seeing the big picture as well as the connections between subtopics.

Learning the Material

- This book emphasizes the accounting experiences of **real companies and business situations throughout**, from chapter-opening Feature Stories to the chapter's last item of homework material. Details on these many features follow. In addition, every chapter uses accounting practices of real companies. Names of real companies are highlighted in red, and many of these real-world examples and illustrations are identified by a company logo.

- Continuing the real-world flavor of the book, **Business Insight** boxes in each chapter give students glimpses into how real companies make decisions using accounting information. The boxes, highlighted with striking photographs, focus on four different accounting perspectives—those of managers, international business, service companies, and e-business.

- Color **illustrations** support and reinforce the concepts of the text. **Infographics** help students visualize and apply accounting concepts to the real world. These infographics often portray important concepts in entertaining and memorable ways. A number of illustrations demonstrate **spreadsheet format** for computations that lend themselves to that format. When illustrations present financial statements or computations, numbers or categories are highlighted in colored type to draw students' attention to key information.

- **Before You Go On** sections occur at the end of each key topic and consists of two parts: *Review It* serves as a learning check within the chapter by asking students to stop and answer knowledge and comprehension questions about the material just covered. *Do It* is a brief demonstration problem that gives immediate practice using the material just covered. An **Action Plan** lists the steps necessary to complete the task, and a **Solution** is provided to help students understand the reasoning involved in reaching an answer. The *Do It* exercises are keyed to related homework exercises.

- **Helpful Hints** in the margins expand upon or help clarify concepts under discussion in the nearby text. This feature actually makes the book an Annotated *Student* Edition.

- **Key terms** and concepts are printed in blue where they are first explained in the text and are defined again in the end-of-chapter glossary. **Alternative Terminology** notes in the margins present synonymous terms that students may come across in subsequent accounting courses and in business.

- Each chapter presents **decision tools** that are useful for analyzing and solving the business problems discussed in that chapter. At the end of the text discussion relating to the decision tool, a **Decision Toolkit** summarizes the key features of that decision tool and reinforces its purpose.

- A **Using the Decision Toolkit** exercise, which follows the final Before You Go On section in the chapter, shows students how to use the decision tools presented in that chapter.

Putting It Together

At the end of each chapter, between the body of the text material and the homework materials, are several features useful for review and reference:

- A **Summary of Study Objectives** reviews the main points of the chapter; the **Decision Toolkit—A Summary** presents in one place the decision tools used throughout the chapter; and a **Glossary** of important terms gives definitions with page references to the text.

- Next, a **Demonstration Problem** gives students another opportunity to refer to a detailed solution to a representative problem before they do homework assignments. An **Action Plan** presented in the margin lists strategies to assist students in understanding the solution and help establish a logic for approaching similar problems. A *Web icon* tells students that there is an Interactive Demonstration Problem they can work on the book's Website.

Developing Skills through Practice

Questions, exercises, and problems throughout the homework material make use of the decision tools presented in the chapter.

- **Self-Study Questions** comprise a practice test to enable students to check their understanding of important concepts. These questions are keyed to the Study Objectives, so students can go back and review sections of the chapter in which they find they need further work. Answers appear on the last page of the chapter. A *Web icon* tells students that they can answer the Self-Study Questions in an interactive format on the text's Website. They can also take an additional Self-Test on the Website to further help them master the material.

- **Questions** provide a full review of chapter content and help students prepare for class discussions and testing situations.

- **Brief Exercises** build students' confidence and test their basic skills. Each exercise focuses on a single *Study Objective*.

- Each of the **Exercises** focuses on one or more of the *Study Objectives*. These tend to take a little longer to complete and present more of a challenge to students than Brief Exercises. The Exercises help instructors and students make a manageable transition to more challenging problems. Certain exercises, marked with a pencil icon ✏️➤, help students practice business writing skills. Exercises relating to service companies are marked with an identifying icon.

- **Problems** stress the application of the concepts presented in the chapter. Two sets of problems—A and B—have corresponding problems keyed to the same *Study Objectives*, thus giving instructors greater flexibility in assigning homework. A new set of **C Problems** is available online at the book's Website. Problems marked with a pencil icon ✏️➤, help build business writing skills. The *Web icon* indicates that students can complete certain problems in an interactive format on the text's Website.

- Each Brief Exercise, Exercise, and Problem has a **description of the concept** covered and is keyed to the Study Objectives.

- **Spreadsheet Exercises and Problems**, identified by an icon, can be solved using Excel templates available on the textbook's Website.

Expanding and Applying Knowledge

Broadening Your Perspective is a unique section at the end of each chapter that offers a wealth of resources to help instructors and students pull together the learning for the chapter. This section offers problems and projects for those instructors who want to broaden the learning experience by bringing in more real-world decision making, analysis, and critical thinking activities. The elements of the **Broadening Your Perspective** section are as follows.

- **Group Decision Cases** help students build decision-making skills by analyzing accounting information in a less structured situation. These cases either require evaluation of a manager's decision, or lead to a decision among alternative courses of action. As group activities, these cases promote teamwork and help prepare students for the business world, where they will be working with teams of people.

- Like the decision cases, the **Managerial Analysis** assignments build analytical and decision-making skills in problematic situations encountered by business managers. They also require the application of business communication skills.

- The **Real-World Focus** problems ask students to apply techniques and concepts presented in the chapter to specific situations faced by actual companies.

- **Exploring the Web** exercises guide students to Websites where they can find and analyze information related to the chapter topic. These sites can be reached directly or by linking through the text's Website.

- **Communication Activities** give students practice in communicating to different audiences in varying modes—letters, reports, memos, explanations, and analyses. These are skills much in demand by employers.

- Since the ability to read and understand business publications is an asset used over the span of one's career, **Research Assignments** direct students to annual reports or articles published in the *Wall Street Journal* and other popular business periodicals for further study and analysis of key topics.

- **Ethics Cases** contain ethical dilemmas and ask students to analyze the situation, identify the stakeholders affected, describe the ethical issues involved, and decide on an appropriate course of action.

- **Cases for Management Decision Making**, provided at the end of the text, require students to use the decision tools presented in the chapters in realistic business situations. The cases can be used as a comprehensive capstone activity at the end of the course, or as a recurring activity during the course. They are intended to be richer and more challenging than a traditional problem but are still targeted at an introductory-level student.

Active Teaching and Learning Supplementary Material

Managerial Accounting, *Third Edition, features a full range of teaching and learning resources. Driven by the same principles as the textbook, these materials provide a consistent and well-integrated learning system. This hands-on, real-world package guides **instructors** through the process of active learning and gives them the tools to* *create an interactive learning environment. With its emphasis on activities, exercises, and the Internet, the package encourages **students** to take an active role in the course and prepares them for decision making in a real-world context.*

 # Weygandt's Integrated Technology Solutions

Helping Teachers Teach and Students Learn
www.wiley.com/college/weygandt

For Instructors

The *Managerial Accounting* **companion Website** at www.wiley.com/college/weygandt provides a seamless integration of text and media and keeps all of the book's online resources in one easily accessible location. On this Website instructors will find electronic versions of the **Solutions Manual, Instructor's Manual, Test Bank, Computerized Test Bank, PowerPoint presentations**, and other resources.

In addition, portions of the *Managerial Accounting* Website are available with **eGradePlus**, a new online resource that integrates text and media and allows you to customize your course with the following tools:

- A **Course Administration** tool helps instructors manage their course and integrate Wiley Website resources with course-management systems, thereby helping instructors keep all class materials in one location.

- A **Prepare and Present** tool contains all instructor resources. Instructors can easily adapt, customize, and add to this content to meet the needs of their particular course.

- An **Assignment** area is one of the most powerful features of the *Managerial Accounting* Website. It allows instructors to assign online homework and quizzes comprised of end-of-chapter textbook questions, and it automatically grades the submitted materials and records the results in an instructor gradebook, thus

saving valuable instructor time. Students benefit from the option to receive immediate feedback on their work, allowing them to quickly determine their understanding of course content.

- An **Instructor's Gradebook** keeps track of student progress and allows instructors to analyze individual and overall class understanding of course concepts.

For Students

The *Managerial Accounting* **Student Website** provides a wealth of support materials that will help students develop their conceptual understanding of class material and improve their ability to solve problems. On this Website students will find **Excel templates, PowerPoint presentations, Web quizzing**, and other resources.

In addition, portions of the Student Website are available in a premium version where students will find the following resources:

- **"Study and Practice"** resources that can include select interactive, end-of-chapter problems linked directly to the text e-book. Additional resources include interactive chapter reviews, demonstration problem tutorials, and other problem-solving resources.

- An **"Assignment"** area that contains all homework assignments in one location. Many homework problems contain a link to the relevant sections of the e-book, providing students with context-sensitive help.

- A **"Personal Gradebook"** allows each student to view results from past assignments at any time.

Instructor's Active Teaching Aids

An extensive support package, including print and technology tools, helps you maximize your teaching effectiveness. We offer useful supplements for instructors with varying levels of experience and instructional circumstances.

Instructor's Resource System on CD-ROM The Instructor's Resource CD (*IR CD*) provides all instructor support material in an electronic format that is easy to navigate and use. The IR CD contains an electronic version of instructor print supplements that can be used in the classroom, for printing out material, for uploading to your own Website, or for downloading and modifying. The IR CD gives you the flexibility to access and prepare instructional material based on your individual needs.

Solutions Manual The Solutions Manual contains detailed solutions to all exercises and problems in the textbook and suggested answers to the questions and cases. Each chapter includes an *assignment classification table*, an *assignment characteristics table*, and a *Bloom's taxonomy table*. Print is large and bold for easy readability in lecture settings, and instructors may duplicate portions of the manual without paying a permissions fee. A team of independent accuracy checkers has carefully verified the accuracy of the Solutions Manual. (The Solutions Manual is also available at www.wiley.com/college/weygandt and on the IR CD.)

Solutions Transparencies Packaged in an organizer box with chapter file folders, these transparencies feature detailed solutions to all exercises and problems in the textbook as well as suggested answers to the Broadening Your Perspectives activities. They feature large, bold type for better projection and easy readability in large classroom settings.

Instructor's Manual The Instructor's Manual is a comprehensive set of resources for preparing and presenting an active learning course. Included in each chapter are chapter reviews and lecture outlines with teaching tips. In addition to an assignment classification table, an assignment characteristics table, and a list of study objectives, each chapter contains a 20-minute quiz. Illustrations at the end of each chapter include diagrams, graphs, and exercises that can be used as classroom handouts or overhead transparencies. (Also available at www.wiley.com/college/weygandt and on the IR CD.)

Teaching Transparencies Designed to support and clarify concepts in the text, these acetate transparencies contain illustrations that are also found in the Instructor's Manual.

Test Bank The Test Bank is a comprehensive testing package that allows instructors to tailor examinations according to study objectives, learning skills, and con-

tent. The Text Bank contains over 2,200 examination questions and exercises. Examination questions focus on computations, concepts, decision-making, and the real-world environment. Actual financial statements are used throughout to provide a relevant context for questions.

Each chapter of the Test Bank includes a *Summary of Questions by Study Objectives* and a *Summary of Objectives by Questions* (linking test items to study objectives), and an indication of question placement according to Bloom's taxonomy. Exercises are identified by estimated completion time. New to this edition are brief exercises and more computational multiple-choice questions.

In addition to a *final exam*, the Test Bank provides an *Achievement Test for every two chapters* in the textbook and a *Comprehensive Exam for every four chapters* of the text. The tests, which are easy to photocopy and distribute to students, consist of problems and exercises as well as multiple-choice, matching, and true/false questions. (Also available at www.wiley.com/college/weygandt and on the IR CD.)

Computerized Test Bank The Test Bank is also available in a computerized version, for use with IBM and IBM compatible computers running Windows 3.1 or higher. This Computerized Test Bank offers a number of valuable options that allow instructors to create multiple versions of the same test. For example, instructors can scramble the order of questions and the order of answers within a multiple-choice question. The computerized test bank also allows instructors to customize test questions by modifying existing problems or by adding new questions. (Also available at www.wiley.com/college/weygandt and on the IR CD.)

PowerPoint Presentations The PowerPoint lecture aid contains a combination of key concepts, images, and problems from the textbook for use in the classroom. Designed according to the organization of the material in the textbook, this series of electronic transparencies can be used to visually reinforce important managerial accounting principles. (Available at www.wiley.com/college/weygandt and on the IR CD.)

WebCT and Blackboard The course-management systems WebCT and Blackboard offer an integrated set of course-management tools that enable instructors to easily design, develop, and manage Web-based and Web-enhanced courses.

The Wiley *Managerial Accounting* WebCT and Blackboard courses contain the basic course-management shell with all online resources for students. It allows the professor to present all or part of a course online and helps students organize the course material, understand key concepts, and access additional tools. The Wiley WebCT and Blackboard course can be customized to fit an individual professor's needs. For more information, see www.wiley.com/college/ solutions.

Business Extra Select Wiley's Business Extra Select program contains copyright-cleared content from XanEdu's premier databases of leading business resources such as Harvard Business School Cases, *Fortune*, *The Economist*, the *Wall Street Journal*, and more.

Creating a Business Extra Select CoursePack is easy! You can combine the content from this title with your Business Extra Select choices in a single custom-published CoursePack in just a few simple steps. No other custom publishing program is this seamless and easy to use!

For more information about Business Extra Select, please contact your Wiley representative or go to www.wiley.com/college/bxs.

 Faculty Resource Network The Faculty Resource Network is a group of peers ready to support the use of online course management tools and discipline specific software/learning systems in the classroom. They will help you apply innovative classroom techniques, implement specific software packages, and tailor the technology experience to the specific needs of each individual class. The Faculty Resource Network also provides you with virtual training sessions led by faculty for faculty. All you need to participate in a virtual seminar is a high-speed internet access and a phone line. For more information about the Faculty Resource Network please contact your Wiley representative or go to www.FacultyResourceNetwork.com.

Students' Active Learning Aids

The Weygandt *Managerial Accounting Student Website* at www.wiley.com/college/weygandt provides a wealth of support materials that will help students develop their understanding of course concepts and increase their ability to solve problems. On this Website students will find **Web Quizzing, Excel Files, PowerPoint presentations**, and other resources.

In addition, portions of the Student Website are available with **eGradePlus**, an online study aid where students will find **Interactive Homework Questions** assigned by their instructors, a personal gradebook, and much more.

Take Action! CD-ROM Available as a supplement to accompany the main text, this dynamic CD contains study tools such as interactive chapter reviews and self-tests for every chapter of the textbook. This CD is an excellent resource for class preparation and review.

Study Guide The Study Guide is a comprehensive review of *Managerial Accounting* and a powerful tool when used in the classroom and in preparation for exams. Each chapter of the Study Guide includes a chapter review consisting of 20 to 30 key points; a demonstration problem linked to study objectives in the textbook; and additional opportunities for students to practice their knowledge and skills through true/false, multiple-choice, matching, and exercises linked to study objectives. Detailed solutions and

explanations to all exercises provide students with immediate feedback.

Working Papers Working Papers are templates customized for each end-of-chapter exercise, problem, and case. A convenient resource for organizing and completing homework assignments, these printed templates demonstrate how to correctly set up solution formats.

Excel Working Papers Available on CD-ROM, these Excel-formatted forms can be used for all end-of-chapter exercises, problems, and cases. A convenient resource for organizing and completing homework assignments, these electronic templates demonstrate how to correctly set up solution formats. The Excel Working Papers provide students with the option of printing forms and completing them manually, or entering data electronically and then printing out a completed form. By entering data electronically, students can paste homework to a new file and e-mail the worksheet to their instructor.

***Managerial Accounting* Excel Templates** Available online, the Excel workbook and templates allow students to complete select end-of-chapter exercises and problems identified by a spreadsheet icon in the margin of the main text. A useful introduction to computers, the electronic spreadsheets also enhance students' accounting skills. Templates are available on the book companion site.

Acknowledgments

In the course of developing *Managerial Accounting*, we have benefited greatly from the input of focus group participants, manuscript reviewers, users of the first and second editions, ancillary authors, and proofers and problem checkers. We greatly appreciate the constructive suggestions and innovative ideas of the reviewers and the creativity and accuracy of the ancillary authors and checkers. We wish to express our ongoing gratitude to the following people.

Reviewers and Focus Group Participants for
Prior Editions of *Managerial Accounting*

Victoria Beard, *University of North Dakota*

Kelly A. Blacker, *Mercy College*

Nancy Boyd, *Middle Tennessee State University*

Joan Cook, *Milwaukee Area Technical College*

Ken Coubillion, *San Joaquin Delta College*

Linda Denning, *Jefferson Community College*

Denise M. English, *Boise State University*

Cecelia Fewox, *Trident Technical College*

Albert Fisher, *Community College of Southern Nevada*

Jeannie Folk, *College of DuPage*

George Gardner, *Bemidji State University*

Jane Grange, *Chicago State University*

Marc Giullian, *University of Louisiana—Lafayette*

John J. Goetz, *University of Texas—Arlington*

Thomas Hofmeister, *Northwestern Business School*

Kathy Horton, *College of DuPage*

Sharon Johnson, *Kansas City Community College*

David Karmon, *Central Michigan University*

J. Suzanne King, *University of Charleston*

Shirly Kleiner, *Johnson County Community College*

Terry Kubichan, *Old Dominion University*

Chor Lau, *California State University—Los Angeles*

Robyn Lawrence, *University of Scranton*

Melanie Mackey, *Ocean County College*

Jamie O'Brien, *South Dakota State University*

Shelly Ota, *Leeward Community College*

Deanne Pannell, *Pellissippi State Technical College*

Kenneth R. Pelfrey, *Ohio State University*

Peter J. Poznanski, *Cleveland State University*

David Ravetch, *University of California—Los Angeles*

Jill Russell, *Camden County College*

Paul J. Shinal, *Cayuga Community College*

Jerome Spallino, *Westmoreland County Community College*

Ellen Sweatt, *Georgia Perimeter College*

Cynthia Tomes, *Des Moines Area Community College*

Michael F. van Breda, *Southern Methodist University*

Chris Widmer, *Tidewater Community College*

Reviewers and Focus Group Participants for
Third Edition of *Managerial Accounting*

Dawn Addington, *St. Louis University*

Peter Aghimien, *Indiana University—South Bend*

Walter Baggett, *Manhattan College*

Kevan Bloomgrem, *Fairleigh Dickinson University*

Angela Brandt, *University of Wisconsin—Madison*

Christy Burge, *University of Louisville*

Jacqueline Calderone, *Monmouth University*

Charles Carmen, *Delso Community College*

D. Constable, *Georgia Perimeter College*

Constance Cooper, *University of Cincinnati*

Patti Fedje, *Minot State University*

Ron Flinn, *Creighton University*

Lisa Gillespie, *Loyola University of Chicago*

Linda Graves, *John A. Logan College*

Kevin Green, *Washington and Lee University*

Mary Haley, *Cumberland University*

Kermit Keeling, *Loyola College*

Mehmet Kocakulah, *University of Southern Indiana*

Laura Jean Kreissl, *University of Wisconsin—Parkside*

Mike Labalokie, *Penn State—Mt. Alto*

Ira Landis, *University of Judaism*

Adena LeJuene, *Louisiana State University—Alexandria*

Bernard McNeal, *Bowie State University*

Mike Metzcar, *Indiana Wesleyan University*

Lee Nicholas, *University of Northern Iowa*

Roger Reynolds, *University of Dayton*

Martin Rudoff, *Community College of Philadelphia*

Karen Senecal, *Washington College*

William Serafin, *Community College of Allegheny*

Robbie Sheffy, *Tarrant County Junior College NW*

Jeff Storm, *Lincolnland Community College*

Paul Swanson, *Bradley University*

Leslie Vaughan, *St. Louis University*

Lin Zheng, *Northeastern Illinois University*

Ancillary Authors, Contributors, and Proofers

John Borke, *University of Wisconsin—Platteville:*
   Text and Solutions Manual Proofer

James M. Emig, *Villanova University:*
   Solutions Manual, Test Bank, and Study Guide proofer

Larry R. Falcetto, *Emporia State University:*
   Instructor's Manual and Check Figures author, Text and Solutions Manual Proofer

Douglas W. Kieso, *Aurora University:*
   Study Guide author

Laura McNally:
eGrade author and proofer

Charles J. Russo, *Bloomsburg University*:
Test Bank author

Rex Schildhouse, *University of Phoenix, San Diego*:
Excel Templates and Workbook author

Teresa Speck, *St. Mary's University*:
Text and Solutions Manual proofer

Diane Tanner, *University of North Florida*:
Test Bank author

Sheila Viel, *University of Wisconsin—Milwaukee*:
Problem material contributor and text proofer

Dan R. Ward, *University of Louisiana—Lafayette*:
PowerPoint author

Suzanne Ward, *University of Louisiana—Lafayette*:
PowerPoint author

Dick D. Wasson, *Southwestern College*:
Working Papers and Excel Working Papers author,
Text and Solutions Manual proofer

We appreciate the exemplary support and professional commitment given to us by our publisher Susan Elbe, associate publisher Jay O'Callaghan, marketing manager Steve Herdegen, development editor Ann Torbert, project editor Ed Brislin, assistant editor Brian Kamins, program assistant Kristen Babroski, media editor Allie Morris, vice president of higher education production and manufacturing Ann Berlin, designer Dawn Stanley, illustration editor Sandra Rigby, photo editor Sara Wight, production manager Jeanine Furino, supplements production editor Lenore Belton, project editor Suzanne Ingrao of Ingrao Associates, product manager Carole Kuhn at TechBooks, and project manager Karin Vonesh at Elm Street Publishing Services. We also appreciate the skills of David Kear, whose excellent work got him promoted into another position. All of these professionals provided innumerable services that helped this project take shape.

Finally, our thanks for the support provided by Will Pesce, president and chief executive officer, and Bonnie Lieberman, senior vice president of the College Division.

Suggestions and comments from users—instructors and students alike—will be appreciated.

JERRY J. WEYGANDT

DONALD E. KIESO

PAUL D. KIMMEL

CHAPTER 7

Variable Costing: A Decision-Making Perspective

Study Objectives at the beginning of each chapter give you a framework for learning the specific concepts covered in the chapter. Each study objective reappears in the margin where the concept is discussed. Finally, you can review the study objectives in the **Summary** at the end of the chapter text.

The Navigator is a learning system designed to guide you through each chapter and help you succeed in learning the material. It consists of (1) a checklist at the beginning of the chapter, which outlines text features and study aids you will need, and (2) a series of check boxes that prompt you to use the learning aids in the chapter and set priorities as you study.

STUDY OBJECTIVES

After studying this chapter,
you should be able to:

1 Explain the difference between absorption costing and variable costing.

2 Discuss the effect that changes in production level and sales level have on net income measured under absorption costing versus variable costing.

3 Discuss the relative merits of absorption costing versus variable costing for management decision making.

4 Explain the term sales mix and its effects on break-even sales.

5 Understand how operating leverage affects profitability.

☑ THE NAVIGATOR

THE NAVIGATOR ✔

▶ Scan *Study Objectives* ☐

▶ Read *Feature Story* ☐

▶ Read *Preview* ☐

▶ Read text and answer *Before You Go On* ☐
   p. 275 ☐   p. 279 ☐   p. 282 ☐

▶ Work *Using the Decision Toolkit* ☐

▶ Review *Summary of Study Objectives* ☐

▶ Work *Demonstration Problem* ☐

▶ Answer *Self-Study Questions* ☐

▶ Complete *Assignments* ☐

FEATURE STORY

What Goes Up (*fast*), Must Come Down (*fast*)

During the late 1990s many people marveled at the efficiency of the so-called "New Economy," which uses digital technologies to improve business processes. Some managers were actually startled by their own success. The New Economy had created a new formula for profit. For example, David Peterschmidt, chief executive at software developer **Inktomi**, noted that the company had incurred considerable fixed costs in developing new software, but its variable costs were minor. As a consequence, once sales had covered the fixed costs, every additional sale was basically pure profit. When sales were booming, he happily stated, "Next to the federal government, this is the only business that's allowed to print money." But that was then. When the economy lagged, the new profit formula went sour. The company's sales disappeared, but its fixed costs did not. In no time, Inktomi went from record profits to staggering losses.

Many other companies have had similar experiences. As their manufacturing plants have become more automated, their fixed costs have become increasingly high. For example, during a 5-year period, the average cost of a typical **Intel** semiconductor

The **Feature Story** helps you picture how the chapter topic relates to the real world of accounting and business. References to the Feature Story throughout the chapter will help you put new ideas in context, organize them, and remember them.

PREVIEW OF CHAPTER 7

As the opening story about **Inktomi** and **Intel** suggests, the relationship between a company's fixed and variable costs can have a huge impact on its profitability. In particular, the trend toward cost structures dominated by fixed costs has significantly increased the volatility of many companies' net income. In order to better track and understand the impact of cost structure on corporate profitability, some companies use an approach called *variable costing*. The purpose of this chapter is to show how variable costing can be helpful in making sound business decisions. The content and organization of this chapter are as follows.

VARIABLE COSTING: A DECISION-MAKING PERSPECTIVE

Absorption Costing versus Variable Costing	Sales Mix	Cost Structure and Operating Leverage
• Illustration comparing absorption and variable costing	• Break-even sales in units	• Effect on contribution margin ratio
• Extended example	• Break-even sales in dollars	• Degree of operating leverage
• Decision-making concerns		• Effect on break-even point
• Potential advantages of variable costing		• Effect on margin of safety ratio

☑ THE NAVIGATOR

The **Preview** links the Feature Story with the major topics of the chapter and describes the purpose of the chapter. It then outlines the topics that are discussed. This narrative and visual preview helps you organize the information you are learning.

Absorption Costing versus Variable Costing

In the earlier chapters, both variable and fixed manufacturing costs were classified as product costs. In job order costing, for example, a job is assigned the costs of direct materials, direct labor, and **both** variable and fixed manufacturing overhead. This costing approach is referred to as **full** or **absorption costing**. It is so named because all manufacturing costs are charged to, or absorbed by, the product. Absorption costing is the approach used for external reporting un-

STUDY OBJECTIVE 1

Explain the difference between absorption costing and variable costing.

Study Objectives reappear in the margins where the related topic is discussed. End-of-chapter assignments are keyed to study objectives.

JOB ORDER COST SYSTEM

Under a job order cost system, costs are assigned to each **job** or to each **batch** of goods. An example of a job would be the manufacture of a mainframe computer by **IBM**, the production of a movie by **Disney**, or the making of a fire truck by **Western States**. An example of a batch would be the printing of 225 wedding invitations by a local print shop, or the printing of a weekly issue of *Fortune* magazine by a hi-tech printer such as **Quad Graphics**. Jobs or batches may be completed to fill a specific customer order or to replenish inventory.

An important feature of job order costing is that each job (or batch) has its own distinguishing characteristics. For example, each house is custom built, each consulting engagement by a CPA firm is unique, and each printing job is different. **The objective is to compute the cost per job.** At each point in the manufacturing of a product or the providing of a service, the job and its associated costs can be identified. A job order cost system measures costs for each completed job, rather than for set time periods. The recording of costs in a job order cost system is shown in Illustration 2-1.

Illustration 2-1 Job order cost system

Job Order Cost System
Two jobs: Wedding Invitations and Menus

Black ink — Typesetting — 225 Invitations — 225 Envelopes — Vellum stock, pure white — **Job # 9501**

Typesetting — Lamination — Colored ink — Yellow stock — 50 Copies — **Job # 9502**

Each job has distinguishing characteristics and related costs.

PROCESS COST SYSTEM

A process cost system is used when a large volume of similar products are manufactured. Production is continuous to ensure that adequate inventories of the finished product(s) are on hand. A process cost system is used in the manufacture of cereal by **Kellogg**, the refining of petroleum by **ExxonMobil**, and the production of automobiles by **General Motors**. Process costing accumulates product-related costs **for a period of time** (such as a week or a month) instead of assigning costs to specific products or job orders. In process costing, the costs are assigned to departments or processes for a set period of time. The recording of costs in a process cost system is shown in Illustration 2-2. The process cost system will be discussed further in Chapter 3.

Illustration 2-2 Process cost system

Process Cost System
Compact Disc Production

1. Oil is pumped. 2. Benzene is removed. 3. The benzene is made into pellets... 4. ...from which compact discs are produced.

Similar products are produced over a specified time period.

Key terms and concepts are printed in blue where they are first explained in the text. They are listed and defined again in the end-of-chapter **Glossary**.

Color illustrations, such as this **infographic**, help you visualize and apply information as you study. They reinforce important concepts and therefore often contain material that may appear on exams.

Names of **real companies** used as examples in the text are shown in red.

Helpful Hints in the margins are like having an instructor with you as you read. They further clarify concepts being discussed.

Preparing the Operating Budgets

A case study of Hayes Company will be used in preparing the operating budgets. Hayes manufactures and sells a single product, Kitchen-mate. The budgets will be prepared by quarters for the year ending December 31, 2005. Hayes Company begins its annual budgeting process on September 1, 2004, and it completes the budget for 2005 by December 1, 2004.

SALES BUDGET

As shown in the master budget in Illustration 9-2, **the sales budget is the first budget prepared**. Each of the other budgets depends on the sales budget. The sales budget is derived from the sales forecast. It represents management's best estimate of sales revenue for the budget period. An inaccurate sales budget may adversely affect net income. For example, an overly optimistic sales budget may result in excessive inventories that may have to be sold at reduced prices. In contrast, an unduly conservative budget may result in loss of sales revenue due to inventory shortages.

The sales budget is prepared by multiplying the expected unit sales volume for each product by its anticipated unit selling price. For Hayes Company, sales volume is expected to be 3,000 units in the first quarter, with 500-unit increments in each succeeding quarter. Based on a sales price of $60 per unit, the sales budget for the year, by quarters, is shown in Illustration 9-3.

Helpful Hint For a retail or manufacturing company, what is the starting point in preparing the master budget, and why? Answer: Preparation of the sales budget is the starting point for the master budget. It sets the level of activity for other functions such as production and purchasing.

Illustration 9-3 Sales budget

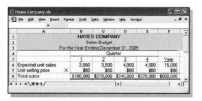

HAYES COMPANY
Sales Budget
For the Year Ending December 31, 2005

	Quarter				
---	1	2	3	4	Year
Expected unit sales	3,000	3,500	4,000	4,500	15,000
Unit selling price	$60	$60	$60	$60	$60
Total sales	$180,000	$210,000	$240,000	$270,000	$900,000

Some companies classify the anticipated sales revenue as cash or credit sales and by geographical regions, territories, or salespersons.

PRODUCTION BUDGET

The production budget shows the units that must be produced to meet anticipated sales. Production requirements are determined from the following formula.[1]

Illustration 9-4 Production requirements formula

Budgeted Sales Units	+	Desired Ending Finished Goods Units	−	Beginning Finished Goods Units	=	Required Production Units

---

Some schedules and tabular displays are presented as **spreadsheets**. The purpose of these spreadsheets is to get you accustomed to reading computations in this format popular in the business world.

Key formulas that you will need to know and use are boxed off.

Business Insight
Service Company Perspective

Frequently when we think of service companies we think of specific, nonroutine tasks, such as rebuilding an automobile engine, providing consulting services on a business acquisition, or working on a major lawsuit. Clearly, such nonroutine situations would call for job order costing.

However, many service companies specialize in performing repetitive, routine aspects of a particular business. For example, auto-care vendors such as **Jiffy Lube** focus on the routine aspects of car care. **H&R Block** focuses on the routine aspects of basic tax practice, and many large law firms focus on routine legal services, such as uncomplicated divorces. For service companies that perform routine, repetitive services, process costing provides a simple solution to their accounting needs. In fact, since in many instances there is little or no work in process at the end of the period, applying process costing in this setting can be even easier than for a manufacturer.

Business Insight examples demonstrate how actual companies make decisions using accounting information. These high-interest boxes are classified by four different points of view—management perspectives, international perspectives, service-company perspectives, and e-business perspectives.

BEFORE YOU GO ON . . .

▶**Review It**

1. In what circumstances would a manufacturer use operations costing instead of process costing?
2. Describe the cost-benefit tradeoff in deciding what costing system to use.

DECISION TOOLKIT

Decision Checkpoints	Info Needed for Decision	Tool to Use for Decision	How to Evaluate Results
What costing method should be used?	Type of product produced	Cost of accounting system; benefits of additional information	The benefits of providing the additional information should exceed the costs of the accounting system needed to develop the information.

Each chapter presents **decision tools** that help decision makers analyze and solve business problems. At the end of the text discussion, a **Decision Toolkit** summarizes the key features of a decision tool and reviews why and how you would use it.

Alternative Terminology notes present synonymous terms that you may come across in practice.

Helpful Hint Fixed costs that may be changeable include research, such as new product development, and management training programs.

Total fixed costs also do not have a straight-line relationship over the entire range of activity. Some fixed costs will not change. But it is possible for management to change other fixed costs. For example, in the Feature Story the dance studio's rent was originally variable and then became fixed at a certain amount. It then increased to a new fixed amount when the size of the studio increased beyond a certain point. An example of the behavior of total fixed costs through all potential levels of activity is shown in part (b) of Illustration 5-3.

For most companies, operating at almost zero or at 100 percent capacity is the exception rather than the rule. Instead, companies often operate over a somewhat narrower range, such as 40–80 percent of capacity. The range over which a company expects to operate during a year is called the relevant range of the activity index. Within the relevant range, as shown in both diagrams in Illustration 5-4, a straight-line relationship generally exists for both variable and fixed costs.

Alternative Terminology The relevant range is also called the *normal* or *practical range*.

BEFORE YOU GO ON . . .

▶**Review It**

1. How do physical units differ from equivalent units of production?
2. What are the formulas for computing unit costs of production?
3. How are costs assigned to units transferred out and in process?
4. What are the four steps in preparing a production cost report?

▶**Do It**

In March, Rodayo Manufacturing had the following unit production costs: materials $6 and conversion costs $9. On March 1, it had zero work in process. During March, 12,000 units were transferred out, and 800 units that were 25 percent completed as to conversion costs and 100 percent complete as to materials were in ending work in process at March 31. Assign the costs to the units transferred out and in process.

Action Plan

• Assign the total manufacturing cost of $15 per unit to the 12,000 units transferred out.
• Assign the materials cost and conversion costs based on equivalent units of production to units in process.

Solution The assignment of costs is as follows.

Costs accounted for		
Transferred out (12,000 × $15)		$180,000
Work in process, March 31		
Materials (800 × $6)	$4,800	
Conversion costs (200ᵃ × $9)	1,800	6,600
Total costs		$186,600

ᵃ800 × 25%

Related exercise material: BE3-4, BE3-5, BE3-6, BE3-7, BE3-8, BE 3-10, E3-3, E3-4, E3-6, E3-8, E3-11, and E3-12.

Before You Go On sections follow each key topic.

Review It questions prompt you to stop and review the key points you have just studied. If you cannot answer these questions, you should go back and read the section again.

Brief *Do It* exercises ask you to put to work your newly acquired knowledge. They outline an **Action Plan** necessary to complete the exercise, and they show a **Solution**.

COSTING SYSTEMS—FINAL COMMENTS

Companies often use a combination of a process cost and a job order cost system, called **operations costing**. Operations costing is similar to process costing in that standardized methods are used to manufacture the product. At the same time, the product may have some customized, individual

A **Using the Decision Toolkit** exercise follows the final set of *Review It* questions in the chapter. It asks you to use business information and the decision tools presented in the chapter. You should think through the questions related to the decision before you study the printed **Solution**.

Using the Decision Toolkit

Martinez Building Products Company is one of the largest manufacturers and marketers of unique, custom-made residential garage doors in the U.S. as well as a major supplier of industrial and commercial doors, grills, and counter shutters for the new construction, repair, and remodel markets. Martinez has developed plans for continued expansion of a network of service operations that sell, install, and service manufactured fireplaces, garage doors, and related products.

Martinez uses a job cost system and applies overhead to production on the basis of direct labor cost. In computing a predetermined overhead rate for the year 2005, the company estimated manufacturing overhead to be $24 million and direct labor costs to be $20 million. In addition the following information is provided.

Actual costs incurred during 2005

Direct materials used	$30,000,000
Direct labor cost incurred	21,000,000
Insurance, factory	500,000
Indirect labor	7,500,000
Maintenance	1,000,000
Rent on building	11,000,000
Depreciation on equipment	2,000,000

Instructions

Answer each of the following.
(a) Why is Martinez Building Products Company using a job order costing system?
(b) On what basis does Martinez allocate its manufacturing overhead? Compute the predetermined overhead rate for the current year.
(c) Compute the amount of the under- or overapplied overhead for 2005.
(d) Martinez had balances in the beginning and ending work in process and finished goods accounts as follows.

	1/1/05	12/31/05
Work in process	$ 5,000,000	$ 4,000,000
Finished goods	13,000,000	11,000,000

Determine the (1) cost of goods manufactured and (2) cost of goods sold for Martinez during 2005. Assume that any under- or overapplied overhead should be included in the cost of goods sold.
(e) During 2005, Job G408 was started and completed. Its cost sheet showed a total cost of $100,000, and the company prices its product at 50% above its cost. What is the price to the customer if the company follows this pricing strategy?

Solution

(a) The company is using a job order system because each job (or batch) must have its own distinguishing characteristics. For example, each type of garage door would be different, and therefore a different cost per garage door should be assigned.
(b) The company allocates its overhead on the basis of direct labor cost. The predetermined overhead rate is 120%, computed as follows.

$$\$24,000,000 \div \$20,000,000 = 120\%$$

(c)	Actual manufacturing overhead	$22,000,000
	...d cost ($21,000,000 × 120%)	25,200,000
	...head	$ 3,200,000

Summary of Study Objectives

1 *Indicate the benefits of budgeting.* The primary advantages of budgeting are that it (a) requires management to plan ahead, (b) provides definite objectives for evaluating performance, (c) creates an early warning system for potential problems, (d) facilitates coordination of activities, (e) results in greater management awareness, and (f) motivates personnel to meet planned objectives.

2 *State the essentials of effective budgeting.* The essentials of effective budgeting are (a) sound organizational structure, (b) research and analysis, and (c) acceptance by all levels of management.

3 *Identify the budgets that comprise the master budget.* The master budget consists of the following budgets: (a) sales, (b) production, (c) direct materials, (d) direct labor, (e) manufacturing overhead, (f) selling and administrative expense, (g) budgeted income statement, (h) capital expenditure budget, (i) cash budget, and (j) budgeted balance sheet.

4 *Describe the sources for preparing the budgeted income statement.* The budgeted income statement is prepared from (a) the sales budget, (b) the budgets for direct materials, direct labor, and manufacturing overhead, and (c) the selling and administrative expense budget.

5 *Explain the principal sections of a cash budget.* The cash budget has three sections (receipts, disbursements, and financing) and the beginning and ending cash balances.

6 *Indicate the applicability of budgeting in non-manufacturing companies.* Budgeting may be used by merchandisers for development of a master budget. In service enterprises budgeting is a critical factor in coordinating staff needs with anticipated services. In not-for-profit organizations, the starting point in budgeting is usually expenditures, not receipts.

The **Summary of Study Objectives** reviews the main points related to the Study Objectives. It provides you with another opportunity to review what you have learned as well as to see how the key topics within the chapter fit together.

DECISION TOOLKIT—A SUMMARY

Decision Checkpoints	Info Needed for Decision	Tool to Use for Decision	How to Evaluate Results
Has the company met its targets for sales, production expenses, selling and administrative expenses, and net income?	Sales forecasts, inventory levels, projected materials, labor, overhead, and selling and administrative requirements	Master budget—a set of interrelated budgets including sales, production, materials, labor, overhead, and selling and administrative budgets	Results are favorable if revenues exceed budgeted amounts, or if expenses are less than budgeted amounts.
Is the company going to need to borrow funds in the coming quarter?	Beginning cash balance, cash receipts, cash disbursements, and desired cash balance	Cash budget	The company will need to borrow money if the cash budget indicates a projected cash deficiency of available cash over cash disbursements for the quarter.

At the end of each chapter, the **Decision Toolkit—A Summary** reviews the context and techniques useful for decision making that were covered in the chapter.

Glossary

Budget A formal written statement of management's plans for a specified future time period, expressed in financial terms. (p. •••)

Budgetary slack The amount by which a manager intentionally underestimates budgeted revenues or overestimates budgeted expenses in order to make it easier to achieve budgetary goals. (p. •••)

Budget committee A group responsible for coordinating the preparation of the budget. (p. •••)

Budgeted balance sheet A projection of financial position at the end of the budget period. (p. •••)

Budgeted income statement An estimate of the expected profitability of operations for the budget period. (p. •••)

The **Glossary** defines all the **key terms** and **concepts** introduced in the chapter. Page references help you find any terms you need to study further. The **Web icon** tells you that you can review these terms interactively on the Website.

APPENDIX
FIFO METHOD

In Chapter 3, we demonstrated the weighted-average method of computing equivalent units. Some companies use a different method to compute equivalent units, which is referred to as the **first-in, first-out (FIFO) method**. The purpose of this appendix is to illustrate how the FIFO method is used in practice.

Equivalent Units Under FIFO

STUDY OBJECTIVE
8
Compute equivalent units using the FIFO method.

Helpful Hint The computation of unit production costs and the assignment of costs to units transferred out and in process also are done on the same basis.

Under the FIFO method, the computation of equivalent units is done on a first-in, first-out basis. Some companies favor the FIFO method because the FIFO cost assumption usually corresponds to the actual physical flow of the goods. Under the FIFO method, it is assumed therefore that the beginning work in process is completed before new work is started.

Using the FIFO method, equivalent units are the sum of the work performed to:

1. Finish the units of beginning work in process inventory.
2. Complete the units started into production during the period (referred to as the **units started and completed**).
3. Start, but only partially complete, the units in ending work in process inventory.

Normally, in a process costing system, some units will always be in process at both the beginning and end of the period.

> In some chapters, **Appendixes** that follow the Decision Toolkit Summary offer expanded coverage of accounting procedures or further discussion of certain topics.

> A **Demonstration Problem** is the final step before you begin homework. These sample problems provide you with an **Action Plan** in the margin that lists the strategies needed to approach and solve the problem. The **Solution** demonstrates both the form and content of complete answers. A **Web icon** tells you that there is an *additional Demonstration Problem* on the book's Website, for added practice.

Demonstration Problem

Spreadwell Paint Company manufactures two high-quality base paints: an **oil-based** paint and a **latex** paint. Both paints are housepaints and are manufactured in neutral white color only. The white base paints are sold to franchised retail paint and decorating stores where pigments are added to tint (color) the paint as desired by the customer. The oil-based paint is made from, thinned, and cleaned with organic solvents (petroleum products) such as mineral spirits or turpentine. The latex paint is made from, thinned, and cleaned with water; synthetic resin particles are suspended in the water and dry and harden when exposed to the air.

Spreadwell uses the same processing equipment to produce both paints in different production runs. Between batches, the vats and other processing equipment must be washed and cleaned.

After analyzing the company's entire operations, Spreadwell's accountants and production managers have identified activity cost pools and accumulated annual budgeted overhead costs by pool as follows.

Activity Cost Pools	Estimated Overhead
Purchasing	$ 240,000
Processing (weighing and mixing, grinding, thinning and drying, straining)	1,400,000
Packaging (quarts, gallons, and 5-gallons)	580,000
Testing	240,000
Storage and inventory control	180,000
Washing and cleaning equipment	560,000
Total annual budgeted overhead	$3,200,000

Following further analysis, activity cost drivers were identified and their expected use by product and activity were scheduled as follows.

Activity Cost Pool	Cost Drivers	Expected Cost Drivers per Activity	Expected Use of Drivers per Product	
			Oil-based	Latex
Purchasing	Purchase orders	1,500 orders	800	700
Processing	Gallons processed	1,000,000 gals.	400,000	600,000
Packaging	Containers filled	400,000 containers	180,000	220,000
	er of tests	4,000 tests	2,100	1,900
	on hand	18,000 gals.	10,400	7,600
	of batches	800 batches	350	450

000 gallons of oil-based paint and 600,000 gallons of
g the year.

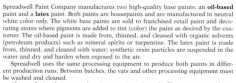

Self-Study Questions

Answers are at the end of the chapter.

(SO 1) 1. Three of the steps in management's decision making process are (1) review results of decision, (2) determine and evaluate possible courses of action, and (3) make the decision. The steps are prepared in the following order:
(a) (1), (2), (3).
(b) (3), (2), (1).
(c) (2), (1), (3).
(d) (2), (3), (1).

(SO 2) 2. Incremental analysis is the process of identifying the financial data that:
(a) do not change under alternative courses of action.
(b) change under alternative courses of action.
(c) are mixed under alternative courses of action.
(d) No correct answer is given.

(SO 3) 3. It costs a company $14 of variable costs and $6 of fixed costs to produce product A that sells for $30. A foreign buyer offers to purchase 3,000 units at $18 each. If the special offer is accepted and produced with unused capacity, net income will:
(a) decrease $6,000.
(b) increase $6,000.
(c) increase $12,000.
(d) increase $9,000.

(SO 3) 4. It costs a company $14 of variable costs and $6 of fixed costs to produce product A at full capacity. Product A sells for $30. A buyer offers to purchase 3,000 units at $18 each. If the special offer is accepted and produced when capacity is fully utilized, net income will:
(a) increase $6,000.
(b) increase $36,000.
(c) decrease $6,000.
(d) decrease $36,000.

(SO 4) 5. In a make-or-buy decision, relevant costs are:
(a) manufacturing costs that will be saved.
(b) the purchase price of the units.
(c) opportunity costs.
(d) all of the above.

(SO 5) 6. The decision rule in a sell-or-process-further decision is: process further as long as the incremental revenue from processing exceeds:
(a) incremental processing costs.
(b) variable processing costs.
(c) fixed processing costs.
(d) No correct answer is given.

(SO 6) 7. In a decision to retain or replace equipment, the book value of the old equipment is a (an):
(a) opportunity cost.
(b) sunk cost.
(c) incremental cost.
(d) marginal cost.

(SO 7) 8. If an unprofitable segment is eliminated:
(a) net income will always increase.
(b) variable expenses of the eliminated segment will have to be absorbed by other segments.
(c) fixed expenses allocated to the eliminated segment will have to be absorbed by other segments.
(d) net income will always decrease.

(SO 8) 9. If the contribution margin per unit is $15 and it takes 3.0 machine hours to produce the unit, the contribution margin per unit of limited resource is:
(a) $25.
(b) $5.
(c) $4.
(d) No correct answer is given.

Self-Study/Self-Test

> **Self-Study Questions** provide a practice test, keyed to Study Objectives, that gives you an opportunity to check your knowledge of important topics. Answers appear at the end of the chapter. The **Web icon** tells you that you can answer these **Self-Study Questions** interactively on the book's Website. There is an additional **Self-Test** at the Website that can further help you master the material.

THE NAVIGATOR

Questions allow you to explain your understanding of concepts and relationships from the chapter. Use them to help prepare for class discussion and tests.

Questions

1. What steps are frequently involved in management's decision-making process?
2. Your roommate, Mike Myer, contends that accounting contributes to most of the steps in management's decision-making process. Is your roommate correct? Explain.
3. "Incremental analysis involves the accumulation of information concerning a single course of action." Do you agree? Why?
4. Sara Gura asks for your help concerning the relevance of variable and fixed costs in incremental analysis. Help Sara with her problem.
5. What data are relevant in deciding whether to accept an order at a special price?
6. Son Ly Company has an opportunity to buy parts at $7 each that currently cost $10 to make. What manufacturing costs are relevant to this make-or-buy decision?
7. Define the term "opportunity cost." How may this cost be relevant in a make-or-buy decision?
8. What is the decision rule in deciding whether to sell a product or process it further?

---

170   **CHAPTER 4**   Activity-Based Costing

Brief Exercises

Identify differences between costing systems.
(SO 1)

BE4-1   Infotrac Inc. sells a high-speed retrieval system for mining information. It provides the following information for the year.

	Budgeted	Actual
Overhead cost	$1,000,000	$950,000
Machine hours	50,000	45,000
Direct labor hours	100,000	90,000

Overhead is applied on the basis of direct labor hours. (a) Compute the predetermined overhead rate. (b) Determine the amount of overhead applied for the year. (c) Explain how an activity-based costing system might differ in terms of computing a predetermined overhead rate.

Identify differences between costing systems.
(SO 1)

BE4-2   Sassafras Inc. has conducted an analysis of overhead costs related to one of its product lines using a traditional costing system (volume-based) and an activity-based costing system. Here are its results.

	Traditional Costing	ABC
Sales revenues	$600,000	$600,000
Overhead costs:		
Product RX3	$ 34,000	$ 50,000
Product Y12	36,000	20,000
	$ 70,000	$ 70,000

Explain how a difference in the overhead costs between the two systems may have occurred.

Identify cost drivers.
(SO 4)

BE4-3   Altex Co. identifies the following activities that pertain to manufacturing overhead: Materials Handling, Machine Setups, Factory Machine Maintenance, Factory Supervision, and Quality Control. For each activity, identify an appropriate cost driver.

Identify cost drivers.
(SO 4)

BE4-4   Ayala Company manufactures four products in a s____ production facility. The company uses activity-based costing. The following activities ____ the company's activity analysis: (a) inventory control, (b) ____ training, (d) quality inspections, (e) material ordering, (f ____ building maintenance.
     For each activity, name a cost driver that might be use____ products.

Brief Exercises help you focus on one Study Objective at a time and thus help you build confidence in your basic skills and knowledge.

---

126   **CHAPTER 3**   Process Cost Accounting

conversion cost is $12, determine the costs to be assigned to the units transferred out and the units in ending work in process. The total costs to be assigned are $664,000.

Prepare a partial production cost report.
(SO 7, 8)

*BE3-12   Using the data in BE3-11, prepare the cost section of the production cost report for Mora Company.

Compute unit costs.
(SO 8)

*BE3-13   Production costs chargeable to the Finishing Department in May at Bell Company are materials $8,000, labor $20,000, overhead $18,000, and transferred-in costs $62,000. Equivalent units of production are materials 20,000 and conversion costs 19,000. Bell uses the FIFO method to compute equivalent units. Compute the unit costs for materials and conversion costs. Transferred-in costs are considered materials costs.

Exercises

Journalize transactions.
(SO 3, 4)

E3-1   Sally May Company manufactures pizza sauce through two production departments: Cooking and Canning. In each process, materials and conversion costs are incurred evenly throughout the process. For the month of March, the work in process accounts show the following debits.

	Cooking	Canning
Beginning work in process	$ –0–	$ 4,000
Materials	14,000	6,000
Labor	8,500	7,000
Overhead	29,500	22,000
Costs transferred in		45,000

Instructions
Journalize the March transactions.

Journalize transactions for two processes.
(SO 4)

E3-2   Greenleaf Manufacturing Company has two production departments: Cutting and Assembly. August 1 inventories are Raw Materials $4,200, Work in Process—Cutting $3,900, Work in Process—Assembly $10,600, and Finished Goods $31,900. During August, the following transactions occurred.

1. Purchased $56,300 of raw materials on account.
2. Incurred $55,000 of factory labor. (Credit Wages Payable.)
3. Incurred $70,000 of manufacturing overhead; $36,000 was paid and the remainder is ____id.
4. ____ioned materials for Cutting $15,700 and Assembly $8,900.
5. ____ctory labor for Cutting $28,000 and Assembly $27,000.
6. ____ overhead at the rate of $20 per machine hour. Machine hours were Cutting ____ d Assembly 1,720.
7. ____red goods costing $77,600 from the Cutting Department to the Assembly ____ment.
8. ____red goods costing $135,000 from Assembly to Finished Goods.
9. ____ods costing $130,000 for $200,000 on account.

Exercises, which are more difficult than Brief Exercises, help you continue to build confidence in your ability to use the material learned in the chapter.

Certain Exercises and Problems, marked with a pencil icon ▭▭▭▭▷ help you practice **business writing skills**, which are much in demand among employers.

---

478   **CHAPTER 11**   Standard Costs and Balanced Scorecard

Instructions
(a) Compute the total, price, and quantity variances for materials and labor.
(b) ▭▭▭▭▷ Provide two possible explanations for each of the unfavorable variances calculated above, and suggest where responsibility for the unfavorable result might be placed.

Compute manufacturing overhead variances and interpret findings.
(SO 5)

E11-7   The following information was taken from the annual manufacturing overhead cost budget of Fernetti Company.

Variable manufacturing overhead costs	$33,000
Fixed manufacturing overhead costs	$21,450
Normal production level in labor hours	16,500
Normal production level in units	4,125
Standard labor hours per unit	4

During the year, 4,000 units were produced, 16,100 hours were worked, and the actual manufacturing overhead was $54,000. Actual fixed manufacturing overhead costs equaled budgeted fixed manufacturing overhead costs. Overhead is applied on the basis of direct labor hours.

Instructions
(a) Compute the total, fixed, and variable predetermined manufacturing overhead rates.
(b) Compute the total, controllable, and volume overhead variances.
(c) ▭▭▭▭▷ Briefly interpret the overhead controllable and volume variances computed in (b).

Compute overhead variances.
(SO 5)

E11-8   The loan department of Local Bank uses standard costs to determine the overhead cost of processing loan applications. During the current month a fire occurred, and the accounting records for the department were mostly destroyed. The following data were salvaged from the ashes.

Standard variable overhead rate per hour	$ 9.00
Standard hours per application	2
Standard hours allowed	2,000
Standard fixed overhead rate per hour	____
Actual fixed over____ ____	____

Some Exercises and Problems focus on accounting situations faced by **Service Companies**. The *service-company icon* highlights these homework materials.

Each **Problem** helps you pull together and apply several concepts from the chapter. Two sets of **PROBLEMS—A** and **B**—are keyed to the same Study Objectives and provide additional opportunities for practice.

Spreadsheet Exercises and **Problems**, identified by an icon, are selected problems that can be solved using the spreadsheet software *Solving Principles of Accounting Problems Using Excel.*

Check Figures in the margin provide key numbers to let you know you're on the right track.

The **Broadening Your Perspective** section helps you pull together various concepts from the chapter and apply them to real-world business situations.

Group Decision Cases help you build decision-making skills by analyzing accounting information in a less structured situation. These cases require teams of students to evaluate a manager's decision, or they lead to a decision among alternative courses of action. These group activities help prepare you for the business world, where you will work with teams of colleagues to solve problems.

Managerial Analysis assignments build analytical and decision-making skills in situations encountered by managers. They also will require you to apply and practice business communication skills.

---

178 **CHAPTER 4** Activity-Based Costing

Problems: Set A

Assign overhead using traditional costing and ABC; compute unit costs; classify activities as value- or non-value-added.
(SO 1, 4, 6)

P4-1A FireOut, Inc. manufactures steel cylinders and nozzles for two models of fire extinguishers: (1) a home fire extinguisher and (2) a commercial fire extinguisher. The **home model** is a high-volume (54,000 units), half-gallon cylinder that holds $2\frac{1}{2}$ pounds of multipurpose dry chemical at 480 PSI. The **commercial model** is a low-volume (10,200 units), two-gallon cylinder that holds 10 pounds of multi-purpose dry chemical at 390 PSI. Both products require 1.5 hours of direct labor for completion. Therefore, total annual direct labor hours are 96,300 or [1.5 hrs. × (54,000 + 10,200)]. Expected annual manufacturing overhead is $1,502,280. Thus, the predetermined overhead rate is $15.60 or ($1,502,280 ÷ 96,300) per direct labor hour. The direct materials cost per unit is $18.50 for the home model and $26.50 for the commercial model. The direct labor cost is $19 per unit for both the home and the commercial models.

The company's managers identified six activity cost pools and related cost drivers and accumulated overhead by cost pool as follows.

Activity Cost Pools	Cost Drivers	Estimated Overhead	Expected Use of Cost Drivers	Expected Use of Drivers by Product	
				Home	Commercial
Receiving	Pounds	$ 70,350	335,000	215,000	120,000
Forming	Machine hours	150,500	35,000	27,000	8,000
Assembling	Number of parts	390,600	217,000	165,000	52,000
Testing	Number of tests	51,000	25,500	15,500	10,000
Painting	Gallons	52,580	5,258	3,680	1,578
Packing and shipping	Pounds	787,250	335,000	215,000	120,000
		$1,502,280			

Instructions

(a) Under traditional product costing, compute the total unit cost of each product. Prepare a simple comparative schedule of the individual costs by product (similar to Illustration 4-4).

(b) Under ABC, prepare a schedule showing the computations of the activity-based overhead rates (per cost driver).

(c) Prepare a schedule assigning each activity's overhead cost pool to each product based on the use of cost drivers. (Include a computation of overhead cost per unit, rounding to the nearest cent.)

(d) Compute the total cost per unit for each product under ABC.

(e) Classify each of the activities as a value-added activity or a non-value-added activity.

(f) Comment on (1) the comparative overhead cost per unit for the two products under ABC, and (2) the comparative total costs per unit under traditional costing and ABC.

---

182 **CHAPTER 4** Activity-Based Costing

Problems: Set B

Assign overhead using traditional costing and ABC; compute unit costs; classify activities as value- or non-value-added.
(SO 1, 4, 6)

P4-1B Waves Galore, Inc. ma[...] hair curler is Waves Galore's hi[...] barrel," 20-watt, triple-heat app[...] with its glow-in-the-dark handle[...] product (40,000 units annually)[...] ting" and a removable filter. It [...]

Both products require one[...] annual direct labor hours are [...] turing overhead is $438,000. [...] rect labor hour. The direct mat[...] for the blow-dryer. The direct [...] blow-dryer.

Waves Galore purchases mo[...] product at its Fargo, North Dako[...] after this year-end will totally [...] system. Waves Galore has ident[...] drivers and has assembled the f[...]

(a) Unit cost—H.M. $60.90

Activity Cost Pool	Cost [...]
Purchasing	Ord[...]
Receiving	Pou[...]
Assembling	Pa[...]
Testing	Te[...]
Finishing	Units
Packing and shipping	Cartons

| | 60,500 | 12,100 |
| $438,000 | | |

Instructions

(a) Under traditional product costing, compute the total unit cost of [...] pare a simple comparative schedule of the individual costs by pr[...] lustration 4-4).

(b) Under ABC, prepare a schedule showing the computations of the [...] head rates (per cost driver).

(c) Prepare a schedule assigning [...] on the use of cost drivers. ([...] ing to the nearest cent.)

(c) Cost assigned—H.M. $1,031,300

(d) Cost/unit—H.M. $56.60

An additional **C Problem Set** is available at the textbook's Website.

---

138 **CHAPTER 3** Process Cost Accounting

Problems: Set C

Problem Set C is provided at the book's Web site, www.wiley.com/college/weygandt.

▶ BROADENING YOUR PERSPECTIVE

Group Decision Case

BYP 3-1 British Beach Company manufactures suntan lotion, called Surtan, in 11-ounce plastic bottles. Surtan is sold in a competitive market. As a result, management is very cost-conscious. Surtan is manufactured through two processes: mixing and filling. Materials are entered at the beginning of each process, and labor and manufacturing overhead occur uniformly throughout each process. Unit costs are based on the cost per gallon of Surtan using the weighted-average costing approach.

On June 30, 2005, Sara Simmons, the chief accountant for the past 20 years, opted to take early retirement. Her replacement, Joe Jacobs, had extensive accounting experience with motels in the area but only limited contact with manufacturing accounting.

During July, Joe correctly accumulated the following production quantity and cost data for the Mixing Department.

Production quantities: Work in process, July 1, 8,000 gallons 75% complete; started into production 100,000 gallons; work in process, July 31, 5,000 gallons 20% complete. Materials are added at the beginning of the process.

Production costs: Beginning work in process $88,000, comprised of $21,000 of materials costs and $67,000 of conversion costs; incurred in July: materials $600,000, conversion costs $785,800.

Joe then prepared a production cost report on the basis of physical units started into production. His report showed a production cost of $14.738 per gallon of Surtan. The management of British Beach was surprised at the high unit cost. The president comes to you, as Sara's top assistant, to review Joe's report and prepare a correct report if necessary.

Instructions

With the class divided into groups, answer the following questions.

(a) Show how Joe arrived at the unit cost of $14.738 per gallon of Surtan.

(b) What error(s) did Joe make in preparing his production cost report?

(c) Prepare a correct production cost report for July.

Managerial Analysis

BYP 3-2 Harris Furniture Company manufactures living room furniture through two departments: Framing and Upholstering. Materials are entered at the beginning of each process. Costs transferred in should be treated as materials cost. For May, the following cost data are obtained from the two work in process accounts.

	Framing	Upholstering
Work in process, May 1	$ -0-	$?
Materials	420,000	?
Conversion costs	210,000	330,000
Costs transferred in	-0-	550,000
Costs transferred out	550,000	?
Work in process, May 31	80,000	?

Instructions

Answer the following questions.

(a) If 3,000 sofas were started into production on May 1 and 2,500 sofas were transferred to Upholstering, what was the unit cost of materials for May in the Framing Department?

Real-World Focus problems ask
you to apply techniques and concepts
presented in the chapter to specific
situations faced by actual companies.
These problems often have a global
focus.

Exploring the Web exercises guide
you to Websites where you can find
and analyze information related to
the chapter topic.

Communication Activities help
you build business communication
skills by asking you to engage in real-
world business situations using writing, speaking, or presentation skills.

(b) Using the data in (a) above, what was the per unit conversion cost of the sofas transferred to Upholstering?
(c) Continuing the assumptions in (a) above, what is the percentage of completion of the
units in process at May 31 in the Framing Department?

Real-World Focus

BYP 3-3 **General Microwave Corp.** is engaged primarily in the design, development,
manufacture, and marketing of microwave, electronic, and fiber-optic test equipment,
components, and subsystems. A substantial portion of the company's microwave product
is sold to manufacturers and users of microwave systems and equipment for applications
in the defense electronics industry.
General Microwave Corp. reports the following information in one of the notes to its
financial statements.

GENERAL MICROWAVE CORPORATION
Notes to the Financial Statement
Work in process inventory reflects all accumulated production costs, which are comprised of direct production costs and overhead, reduced by amounts attribut- able to units delivered. Work in process inventory is reduced to its estimated net realizable value by a charge to cost of sales in the period [in which] excess costs are identified. Raw materials and finished goods inventories are reflected at the lower of cost or market.

Instructions
(a) What types of manufacturing costs are accumulated in the work in process inventory
account?
(b) What types of information must General Microwave have to be able to compute equivalent units of production?
(c) How does General Microwave assign costs to the units transferred out of work in
process that are completed?

Exploring the Web

BYP 3-4 Search the Internet and find the Web sites of two manufacturers that you think
are likely to use process costing. Are there any specifics included in their Web sites that
confirm the use of process costing for each of these companies?

Communication Activity

BYP 3-5 Jenna Haines was a good friend of yours in high school and is from your home
town. While you chose to major in accounting when you both went away to college, she
majored in marketing and management. You have recently been promoted to accounting
manager for the Snack Foods Division of Clark Enterprises, and your friend was promoted to regional sales manager for the same division of Clark. Jenna recently telephoned
you. She explained that she was familiar with job cost sheets, which had been used by
the Special Projects division where she had formerly worked. She was, however, very un-
[...]ction cost reports prepared by your division. She faxed you
[...]s. These included the following.

[...]epares snack foods for special orders in the Snack Foods
[...]k costs of the orders separately?

[...]uction cost reports? Isn't there only one Work in Process

---

140 **CHAPTER 3** Process Cost Accounting

Instructions
Prepare a memo to Jenna. Answer her questions, and include any additional information
you think would be helpful. You may write informally, but be careful to use proper grammar and punctuation.

Research Assignment

BYP 3-6 The May 10, 2004, edition of the *Wall Street Journal* includes an article by
Evan Ramstad titled "A Tight Squeeze" (p. R9).

Instructions
Read the article and answer the following questions.
(a) What is **Proview**'s profit margin on computer monitors? Why is the profit margin so
thin on computer monitors?
(b) What are some of the steps that Proview International has taken to control costs?
(c) Why does the company continue to build tube-based monitors even as many consumers are moving away from them?
(d) Mr. Wang's final comment is, "Every aspect of the business is important, but the most
important is cost." Why does he feel this way?

Ethics Case

BYP 3-7 C. C. Daibo Company manufactures a high-tech component that passes through
two production processing departments, Molding and Assembly. Department managers
are partially compensated on the basis of units of products completed and transferred
out relative to units of product put into production. This was intended as encouragement
to be efficient and to minimize waste.
Barb Crusmer is the department head in the Molding Department, and Wayne Terrago is her quality control inspector. During the month of June, Barb had three new employees who were not yet technically skilled. As a result, many of the units produced in
June had minor molding defects. In order to maintain the department's normal high rate
of completion, Barb told Wayne to pass through inspection and on to the Assembly Department all units that had defects nondetectable to the human eye. "Company and industry tolerances on this product are too high anyway," says Barb. "Less than 2% of the
units we produce are subjected in the market to the stress tolerance we've designed into
them. The odds of those 2% being any of this month's units are even less. Anyway, we're
saving the company money."

Instructions
(a) Who are the potential stakeholders involved in this situation?
(b) What alternatives does Wayne have in this situation? What might the company do to
prevent this situation from occurring?

Answers to Self-Study Questions
1. b   2. d   3. d   4. b   5. b   6. a   7. c   8. a   9. b   10. b
11. b   12. a   13. b

A **Research Assignment** directs
you to published articles in business periodicals for further study
and analysis of key topics.

In the **Ethics Cases**, you will
reflect on typical ethical dilemmas,
analyze the stakeholders and the
issues involved, and decide on an
appropriate course of action.

Answers to Self-Study
Questions provide feedback on
your understanding of concepts.

After you complete your homework
assignments, it's a good idea to go
back to **The Navigator** checklist at
the start of the chapter to see if you
have used all the chapter's study aids.

✓ Remember to go back to the Navigator box on the chapter-opening page
and check off your completed work.

Case 1

Greetings *Inc.*

Greetings Inc. Swims in the Dot-Com Sea: Job Order Costing

Developed by Thomas L. Zeller, Loyola University Chicago and Paul D. Kimmel, University of Wisconsin– Milwaukee

The Business Situation

Greetings Inc. has operated for many years as a nationally recognized retailer of greeting cards and small gift items. It has 1,500 stores throughout the United States located in high-traffic malls.

During the late 1990s, as the stock price of many other companies soared, Greetings' stock price remained flat. As a result of a heated 1998 shareholders' meeting, the president of Greetings, Robert Burns, came under pressure from shareholders to grow Greetings' stock value. As a consequence of this pressure, in 1999 Mr. Burns called for a formal analysis of the company's options with regard to business opportunities.

Location was the first issue considered in the analysis. Greetings stores are located in high-traffic malls where rental costs are high. The additional rental cost was justified, however, by the revenue that resulted from these highly visible locations. In recent years, though, the intense competition from other stores in the mall selling similar merchandise has become a disadvantage of the mall locations.

Mr. Burns felt that to increase revenue in the mall locations, Greetings would need to attract new customers and sell more goods to repeat customers. In order to do this, the company would need to add a new product line. However, to keep costs down, the product line should be one that would not require much additional store space. In order to improve earnings, rather than just increase revenues, Greetings would have to carefully manage the costs of this new product line.

After careful consideration of many possible products, the company's management found a product that seemed to be a very good strategic f[...] existing products: high-quality unframed and framed prints. The crit[...] ment of this plan was that customers would pick out prints by viewi[...] on wide-screen computer monitors in each store. Orders would be p[...] and shipped from a central location. Thus, store size would not hav[...] crease at all. To offer these products, Greetings established a new b[...] unit called WallDécor.com. WallDécor is a "profit center"; that is, th[...] ager of the new business unit is responsible for decisions affecting b[...] enues and costs.

Cases For Management Decision Making, provided at the end of the text, ask you to use the decision tools presented in the chapters in realistic business situations. Your instructor can assign cases as a comprehensive capstone activity at the end of the course or as a recurring activity during the course.

Case 6

Sweats Galore

Developed by Jessica Johnson Frazier, Eastern Kentucky University, and Patricia H. Mounce, Mississippi College

The Business Situation

After graduating with a degree in business from Eastern University in Campus Town, USA, Michael Woods realized that he wanted to remain in Campus Town. After a number of unsuccessful attempts at getting a job in his discipline, Michael decided to go into business for himself. In thinking about his business venture, Michael determined that he had four criteria for the new business:

1. He wanted to do something that he would enjoy.
2. He wanted a business that would give back to the community.
3. He wanted a business that would grow and be more successful every year.
4. Realizing that he was going to have to work very hard, Michael wanted a business that would generate a minimum net income of $25,000 annually.

While reflecting on the criteria he had outlined, Michael, who had been president of his fraternity and served as an officer in several other student organizations, realized that there was no place in Campus Town to have custom sweatshirts made using a silk-screen process. When student organizations wanted sweatshirts to give to their members or to market on campus, the officers had to make a trip to a city 100 miles away to visit "Shirts and More."

Michael had worked as a part-time employee at Shirts and More while he was in high school and had envisioned owning such a shop. He realized that a sweatshirt shop in Campus Town had the potential to meet all four of his criteria. Michael set up an appointment with Jayne Stoll, the owner of Shirts and More, to obtain information useful in getting his shop started. Because Jayne liked Michael and was intrigued by his entrepreneurial spirit, she answered many of Michael's questions.

In addition, Jayne provided information concerning the type of equipment Michael would need for his business and its average useful life. Jayne knows a competitor who is retiring and would like to sell his equipment. Michael can purchase the equipment at the beginning of 2006, and the owner is willing to give him terms of 50 percent due upon purchase and 50 percent due the quarter following the purchase. Michael decided to purchase the following equipment as of January 1, 2006.

This questionnaire aims to find out something about your preferences for the way you work with information. You will have a preferred learning style, and one part of that learning style is your preference for the intake and the output of ideas and information.

Circle the letter of the answer that best explains your preference. Circle more than one if a single answer does not match your perception. Leave blank any question that does not apply.

1. You are about to give directions to a person who is standing with you. She is staying in a hotel in town and wants to visit your house later. She has a rental car. Would you
   a. draw a map on paper?
   b. tell her the directions?
   c. write down the directions (without a map)?
   d. pick her up at the hotel in your car?

2. You are not sure whether a word should be spelled "dependent" or "dependant." Do you
   c. look it up in the dictionary?
   a. see the word in your mind and choose by the way it looks?
   b. sound it out in your mind?
   d. write both versions down on paper and choose one?

3. You have just received a copy of your itinerary for a world trip. This is of interest to a friend. Would you
   b. call her immediately and tell her about it?
   c. send her a copy of the printed itinerary?
   a. show her on a map of the world?
   d. share what you plan to do at each place you visit?

4. You are going to cook something as a special treat for your family. Do you
   d. cook something familiar without the need for instructions?
   a. thumb through the cookbook looking for ideas from the pictures?
   c. refer to a specific cookbook where there is a good recipe?

5. A group of tourists has been assigned to you to find out about wildlife reserves or parks. Would you
   d. drive them to a wildlife reserve or park?
   a. show them slides and photographs?
   c. give them pamphlets or a book on wildlife reserves or parks?
   b. give them a talk on wildlife reserves or parks?

6. You are about to purchase a new CD player. Other than price, what would most influence your decision?
   b. The salesperson telling you what you want to know.
   c. Reading the details about it.
   d. Playing with the controls and listening to it.
   a. Its fashionable and upscale appearance.

7. Recall a time in your life when you learned how to do something like playing a new board game. Try to avoid choosing a very physical skill, e.g., riding a bike. How did you learn best? By
   a. visual clues—pictures, diagrams, charts?
   c. written instructions?
   b. listening to somebody explaining it?
   d. doing it or trying it?

8. You have an eye problem. Would you prefer that the doctor
   b. tell you what is wrong?
   a. show you a diagram of what is wrong?
   d. use a model to show what is wrong?

9. You are about to learn to use a new program on a computer. Would you
   d. sit down at the keyboard and begin to experiment with the program's features?
   c. read the manual that comes with the program?
   b. call a friend and ask questions about it?

10. You are staying in a hotel and have a rental car. You would like to visit friends whose address/location you do not know. Would you like them to
    a. draw you a map on paper?
    b. tell you the directions?
    c. write down the directions (without a map)?
    d. pick you up at the hotel in their car?

11. Apart from price, what would most influence your decision to buy a particular book?
    d. You have used a copy before.
    b. A friend talking about it.
    c. Quickly reading parts of it.
    a. The appealing way it looks.

12. A new movie has arrived in town. What would most influence your decision to go (or not go)?
    b. You heard a radio review about it.
    c. You read a review about it.
    a. You saw a preview of it.

13. Do you prefer a lecturer or teacher who likes to use
    c. a textbook, handouts, readings?
    a. flow diagrams, charts, graphs?
    d. field trips, labs, practical sessions?
    b. discussion, guest speakers?

Count your choices:	a.	b.	c.	d.
	❑	❑	❑	❑
	V	A	R	K

Now match the letter or letters you have recorded most to the same letter or letters in the Learning Styles Chart. You may have more than one learning style preference—many people do. Next to each letter in the chart are suggestions that will refer you to different learning aids throughout this text.

LEARNING STYLES CHART

VISUAL

INTAKE: TO TAKE IN THE INFORMATION	TO MAKE A STUDY PACKAGE	TEXT FEATURES THAT MAY HELP YOU THE MOST	OUTPUT: TO DO WELL ON EXAMS
• Pay close attention to charts, drawings, and handouts your instructor uses. • Underline. • Use different colors. • Use symbols, flow charts, graphs, different arrangements on the page, white space.	Convert your lecture notes into "page pictures." To do this: • Use the "Intake" strategies. • Reconstruct images in different ways. • Redraw pages from memory. • Replace words with symbols and initials. • Look at your pages.	**The Navigator** **Feature Story** **Preview** **Infographics/Illustrations** **Photos** **Business Insight boxed examples** **Accounting Equation Analyses** **Key Terms in blue** **Words in bold** **Demonstration Problem/Action Plan** **Questions/Exercises/ Problems** **Real-World Focus** **Research Assignment** **Exploring the Web**	• Recall your "page pictures." • Draw diagrams where appropriate. • Practice turning your visuals back into words.

AURAL

INTAKE: TO TAKE IN THE INFORMATION	TO MAKE A STUDY PACKAGE	TEXT FEATURES THAT MAY HELP YOU THE MOST	OUTPUT: TO DO WELL ON EXAMS
• Attend lectures and tutorials. • Discuss topics with students and instructors. • Explain new ideas to other people. • Use a tape recorder. • Leave spaces in your lecture notes for later recall. • Describe overheads, pictures, and visuals to somebody who was not in class.	You may take poor notes because you prefer to listen. Therefore: • Expand your notes by talking with others and with information from your textbook. • Tape record summarized notes and listen. • Read summarized notes out loud. • Explain your notes to another "aural" person.	**Preview** **Infographics/Illustrations** **Review It/Do It/Action Plan** **Summary of Study Objectives** **Glossary** **Demonstration Problem/Action Plan** **Self-Study Questions** **Questions/Exercises/ Problems** **Managerial Analysis** **Exploring the Web** **Group Decision Cases** **Communication Activity** **Ethics Cases**	• Talk with the instructor. • Spend time in quiet places recalling the ideas. • Practice writing answers to old exam questions. • Say your answers out loud.

READING/WRITING

INTAKE: TO TAKE IN THE INFORMATION	TO MAKE A STUDY PACKAGE	TEXT FEATURES THAT MAY HELP YOU THE MOST	OUTPUT: TO DO WELL ON EXAMS
• Use lists and headings. • Use dictionaries, glossaries, and definitions. • Read handouts, textbooks, and supplementary library readings. • Use lecture notes.	• Write out words again and again. • Reread notes silently. • Rewrite ideas and principles into other words. • Turn charts, diagrams, and other illustrations into statements.	**The Navigator** **Feature Story** **Study Objectives** **Preview** **Review It/Do It/Action Plan** **Summary of Study Objectives** **Glossary** **Self-Study Questions** **Questions/Exercises/ Problems** **Writing Problems** **Managerial Analysis** **Real-World Focus** **Exploring the Web** **Group Decision Cases** **Communication Activity** **Research Assignment**	• Write exam answers. • Practice with multiple-choice questions. • Write paragraphs, beginnings and endings. • Write your lists in outline form. • Arrange your words into hierarchies and points.

KINESTHETIC

INTAKE: TO TAKE IN THE INFORMATION	TO MAKE A STUDY PACKAGE	TEXT FEATURES THAT MAY HELP YOU THE MOST	OUTPUT: TO DO WELL ON EXAMS
• Use all your senses. • Go to labs, take field trips. • Listen to real-life examples. • Pay attention to applications. • Use hands-on approaches. • Use trial-and-error methods.	You may take poor notes because topics do not seem concrete or relevant. Therefore: • Put examples in your summaries. • Use case studies and applications to help with principles and abstract concepts. • Talk about your notes with another "kinesthetic" person. • Use pictures and photographs that illustrate an idea.	**The Navigator** **Feature Story** **Preview** **Infographics/Illustrations** **Review It/Do It/Action Plan** **Summary of Study Objectives** **Demonstration Problem/ Action Plan** **Self-Study Questions** **Questions/Exercises/ Problems** **Research Assignment** **Exploring the Web** **Group Decision Cases** **Communication Activity**	• Write practice answers. • Role-play the exam situation.

For all learning styles: Be sure to use the book's Website to enhance your understanding of the concepts and procedures of the text.

BRIEF CONTENTS

CONTENTS

PLANNING AND CONTROL CONCEPTS

CHAPTER 1

Managerial Accounting

Study Objectives gives you a framework for learning the specific concepts covered in the chapter.

STUDY OBJECTIVES

After studying this chapter, you should be able to:

1 Explain the distinguishing features of managerial accounting.
2 Identify the three broad functions of management.
3 Define the three classes of manufacturing costs.
4 Distinguish between product and period costs.
5 Explain the difference between a merchandising and a manufacturing income statement.
6 Indicate how cost of goods manufactured is determined.
7 Explain the difference between a merchandising and a manufacturing balance sheet.
8 Identify trends in managerial accounting.

 ☑ THE NAVIGATOR

THE NAVIGATOR ✔

▶ Scan *Study Objectives* ☐
▶ Read *Feature Story* ☐
▶ Read *Preview* ☐
▶ Read text and answer *Before You Go On*
　 p. 9 ☐ p. 11 ☐ p. 17 ☐ p. 22 ☐
▶ Work *Using the Decision Toolkit* ☐
▶ Review *Summary of Study Objectives* ☐
▶ Work *Demonstration Problem* ☐
▶ Answer *Self-Study Questions* ☐
▶ Complete *Assignments* ☐

The **Navigator** is a learning system designed to prompt you to use the learning aids in the chapter and to help you set priorities as you study.

FEATURE STORY

What a Difference a Day Makes

In January 1998 **Compaq Computer** had just become the largest seller of personal computers, and it was *Forbes* magazine's "company of the year." Its chief executive, Eckhard Pfeiffer, was riding high. But during the next two years Compaq lost $2 billion. The company was in chaos, and Mr. Pfeiffer was out of a job. What happened?

First, Dell happened. **Dell Computer** pioneered a new way of making and selling personal computers. Its customers "custom design" their computer over the Internet or phone. Dell reengineered its "supply chain": It coordinated its efforts with its suppliers and streamlined its order-taking and production process. It can ship a computer within two days of taking an order. Personal computers lose 1 percent of their value every week they sit on a shelf. Thus, having virtually no inventory is a great advantage to Dell. Compaq tried to adopt Dell's approach, but with limited success.

The second shock to Compaq came when it acquired a company even larger than itself—**Digital Equipment**. Digital was famous as much for its technical service as it was for its products. Mr. Pfeiffer believed that the purchase of Digital, with its huge and respected technical sales force, opened new opportunities for Compaq as a global service company. Now it could sell to and service high-end corporate customers. But combining the two companies proved to be hugely expensive and extremely complicated.

Ultimately Compaq decided to merge with **Hewlett-Packard** in order to survive.

But now Hewlett-Packard is looking over its shoulder for Dell. Why? Because in 2003 Dell moved into the computer printer business—a segment that Hewlett-Packard has long dominated. Dell currently sells only 2 million printers per year, compared to Hewlett-Packard's 42 million. But many analysts predict that by employing the same techniques that it used in its PC business, Dell will soon take a major share of the printer business—and in the process drive down prices and force some less-nimble competitors out of business.

☑ THE NAVIGATOR

www.compaq.com
www.dell.com
www.hp.com

The **Feature Story** helps you picture how the chapter topic relates to the real world of business and accounting. You will find references to the story throughout the chapter. Many Feature Stories end with the Internet addresses of the companies cited in the story, to help you connect with these real businesses.

This book focuses on issues illustrated in the Feature Story about **Compaq Computer** and **Dell**. These include determining and controlling the costs of material, labor, and overhead and the relationship between costs and profits. In a previous financial accounting course, you learned about the form and content of **financial statements for external users** of financial information, such as stockholders and creditors. These financial statements represent the principal product of financial accounting. Managerial accounting focuses primarily on the preparation of **reports for internal users** of financial information, such as the managers and officers of a company. Managers are evaluated on the results of their decisions. In today's rapidly changing global environment, managers often make decisions that determine their company's fate—and their own fate. Managerial accounting provides tools for assisting management in making decisions and for evaluating the effectiveness of those decisions.

The content and organization of this chapter are as follows.

The **Preview** describes the purpose of the chapter and outlines the major topics and subtopics you will find in it.

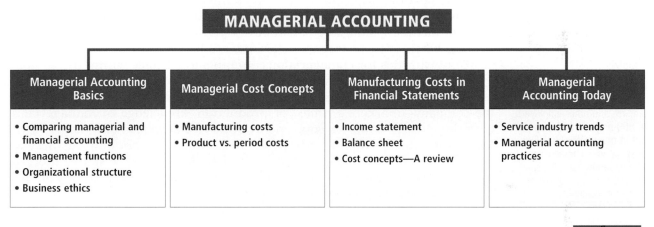

Managerial Accounting Basics

Managerial accounting, also called **management accounting**, is a field of accounting that provides economic and financial information for managers and other internal users. The activities that are part of managerial accounting (and the chapters in which they are discussed in this textbook) are as follows.

Essential terms and concepts are printed in blue where they first appear and are defined in the end-of-chapter Glossary.

1. Explaining manufacturing and nonmanufacturing costs and how they are reported in the financial statements (Chapter 1).
2. Computing the cost of providing a service or manufacturing a product (Chapters 2, 3, and 4).
3. Determining the behavior of costs and expenses as activity levels change and analyzing cost–volume–profit relationships within a company (Chapter 5).
4. Accumulating and presenting relevant data for management decision making (Chapter 6).

5. Evaluating the impact on decision making of alternative approaches for costing inventory (Chapter 7).

6. Determining prices for external and internal transactions (Chapter 8).

7. Assisting management in profit planning and formalizing these plans in the form of budgets (Chapter 9).

8. Providing a basis for controlling costs and expenses by comparing actual results with planned objectives and standard costs (Chapters 10 and 11).

9. Accumulating and presenting data for capital expenditure decisions (Chapter 12).

Managerial accounting applies to all types of businesses—service, merchandising, and manufacturing. It also applies to all forms of business organizations—proprietorships, partnerships, and corporations. Managerial accounting is needed in not-for-profit entities as well as in profit-oriented enterprises.

In the past, managerial accountants were primarily engaged in cost accounting—collecting and reporting costs to management. Recently that role changed significantly. First as the business environment has become more automated, methods to determine the amount and type of cost in a product have changed. Second, managerial accountants are now more responsible for strategic cost management; that is, assisting in evaluating how well the company is employing its resources. As a result, managerial accountants now serve as team members alongside personnel from production, marketing, and engineering when critical strategic decisions are being made.

Opportunities for managerial accountants to advance within the company are considerable. Financial executives must have a background that includes an understanding of managerial accounting concepts. Whatever your position in the company—marketing, sales, or production, knowledge of managerial accounting greatly improves your opportunities for advancement. As the CEO of **Microsoft** noted: "If you're supposed to be making money in business and supposed to be satisfying customers and building market share, there are numbers that characterize those things. And if somebody can't sort of speak to me quantitatively about it, then I'm nervous."

Helpful Hints clarify concepts being discussed.

Helpful Hint According to the U.S. Department of Labor's Bureau of Labor Statistics (BLS) more than one million accountants and auditors currently work for accounting firms, companies, governmental agencies, and other employers. The BLS projects that employment in the profession will increase 10 to 20 percent by 2008, ensuring that accountants will continue to play a vital role in business.

COMPARING MANAGERIAL AND FINANCIAL ACCOUNTING

STUDY OBJECTIVE
1
Explain the distinguishing features of managerial accounting.

There are both similarities and differences between managerial and financial accounting. First, each field of accounting deals with the economic events of a business. Thus, their interests overlap. For example, determining the unit cost of manufacturing a product is part of managerial accounting. Reporting the total cost of goods manufactured and sold is part of financial accounting. In addition, both managerial and financial accounting require that a company's economic events be quantified and communicated to interested parties.

The principal differences between financial accounting and managerial accounting are summarized in Illustration 1-1. The need for various types of economic data is responsible for many of the differences.

MANAGEMENT FUNCTIONS

STUDY OBJECTIVE
2
Identify the three broad functions of management.

Management's activities and responsibilities can be classified into three broad functions. They are:

1. Planning.
2. Directing.
3. Controlling.

Financial Accounting		Managerial Accounting
• External users: stockholders, creditors, and regulators.	**Primary Users of Reports**	• Internal users: officers and managers.
• Financial statements. • Quarterly and annually.	**Types and Frequency of Reports**	• Internal reports. • As frequently as needed.
• General-purpose.	**Purpose of Reports**	• Special-purpose for specific decisions.
• Pertains to business as a whole. • Highly aggregated (condensed). • Limited to double-entry accounting and cost data. • Generally accepted accounting principles.	**Content of Reports**	• Pertains to subunits of the business. • Very detailed. • Extends beyond double-entry accounting to any relevant data. • Standard is relevance to decisions.
• Audit by CPA.	**Verification Process**	• No independent audits.

Illustration 1-1 Differences between financial and managerial accounting

In performing these functions, managers make decisions that have a significant impact on the organization.

Planning requires management to look ahead and to establish objectives. These objectives are often diverse: maximizing short-term profits and market share, maintaining a commitment to environmental protection, and contributing to social programs. For example, **Hewlett-Packard** in an attempt to gain a stronger foothold in the computer industry has greatly reduced its prices to compete with **Dell**. A key objective of management is to add **value** to the business under its control. Value is usually measured by the trading price of the company's stock and by the potential selling price of the company.

Directing involves coordinating a company's diverse activities and human resources to produce a smooth-running operation. This function relates to implementing planned objectives and providing necessary incentives to motivate employees. For example, manufacturers such as **Campbell Soup Company**, **General Motors**, and **Dell** must coordinate purchasing, manufacturing, warehousing, and selling. Service corporations such as **American Airlines**, **Federal Express**, and **AT&T** must coordinate scheduling, sales, service, and acquisitions of equipment and supplies. Directing also involves selecting executives, appointing managers and supervisors, and hiring and training employees.

The third management function, **controlling**, is the process of keeping the company's activities on track. In controlling operations, managers determine whether planned goals are being met. When there are deviations from targeted objectives, they must decide what changes are needed to get back on track. Recent scandals at companies like **Enron**, **Lucent**, and **Xerox** attest to the fact that companies must have adequate controls to ensure that accurate information is developed.

How do managers achieve control? A smart manager in a small operation can make personal observations, ask good questions, and know how to evaluate the answers. But using this approach in a large organization would result in chaos. Imagine the president of **Dell** attempting to determine whether planned objectives are being met without some record of what has happened and what is expected to occur. Thus, a formal system of evaluation is typically used in large businesses. These systems include such features as budgets, responsibility centers, and performance evaluation reports.

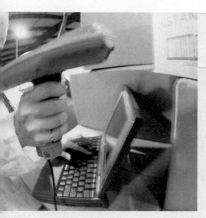

Business Insight
e-Business Perspective

The trend toward more automated and computerized factories has changed the way managers and employees interact. For one thing, managers have fewer direct labor employees to supervise because fewer are needed on the line. Instead of standing in one spot all day, employees and managers have become more mobile, monitoring the computers that control production, and involving themselves in a variety of jobs.

Recently, two technology giants, **General Electric** and **Cisco Systems**, joined forces to build computerized infrastructures for manufacturers. Their goal is to improve productivity by making better use of data generated by factory-automation equipment. Ultimately their systems should provide a closer link between the factory and corporate offices.

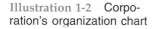

Business Insight examples illustrate interesting situations in real companies and show how managers make decisions using accounting information. Examples labeled **e-Business Perspectives** describe how e-business technology is being used in accounting applications.

Decision making is not a separate management function. Rather, it is the outcome of the exercise of good judgment in planning, directing, and controlling.

ORGANIZATIONAL STRUCTURE

In order to assist in carrying out management functions, most companies prepare **organization charts** to show the interrelationships of activities and the delegation of authority and responsibility within the company. A typical organization chart showing the delegation of responsibility is shown in Illustration 1-2.

Illustration 1-2 Corporation's organization chart

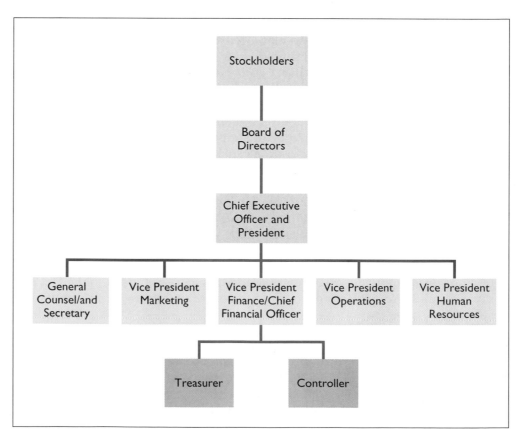

Stockholders own the corporation, but they manage it indirectly through a **board of directors** they elect. Even not-for-profit organizations have a board of directors. The board formulates the operating policies for the company. The board also selects officers, such as a president and one or more vice presidents, to execute policy and to perform daily management functions.

The **chief executive officer (CEO)** has overall responsibility for managing the business. Obviously, even in a small business, in order to accomplish organizational objectives, the company relies on delegation of responsibilities. As the organization chart on page 6 shows, the CEO delegates responsibility to other officers. Each member of the organization has a clearly defined role to play.

Responsibilities within the company are frequently classified as either line or staff positions. Employees with **line positions** are directly involved in the company's primary revenue-generating operating activities. Examples of line positions include the vice president of operations, vice president of marketing, plant managers, supervisors, and production personnel. Employees with **staff positions** are involved in activities that support the efforts of the line employees. In a firm like **General Electric** or **ExxonMobil**, employees in finance, legal, purchasing, and human resources have staff positions. While activities of staff employees are vital to the company, these employees are nonetheless there to serve the line employees that engage in the company's primary operations.

The **chief financial officer (CFO)** is responsible for all of the accounting and finance issues the company faces. The CFO is supported by the **controller** and the **treasurer**. The controller's responsibilities include (1) maintaining the accounting records, (2) maintaining an adequate system of internal control, and (3) preparing financial statements, tax returns, and internal reports. The treasurer has custody of the corporation's funds and is responsible for maintaining the company's cash position.

Also serving the CFO would be the **internal audit staff**. The staff's responsibilities include reviewing the reliability and integrity of financial information provided by the controller and treasurer. Staff members also ensure that internal control systems are functioning properly to safeguard corporate assets. In addition, they investigate compliance with policies and regulations, and in many companies they determine whether resources are being used in the most economical and efficient fashion.

The vice president of operations oversees employees with line positions. For example, the company might have multiple plant managers, each of whom would report to the vice president of operations. Each plant would also have department managers, such as fabricating, painting, and shipping, each of whom would report to the plant manager.

BUSINESS ETHICS

All employees within an organization are expected to act ethically in their business activities. Given the importance of ethical behavior to corporations and their owners (stockholders), an increasing number of organizations provide codes of business ethics for their employees.

Despite these efforts, recent business scandals have resulted in massive investment losses and numerous employee layoffs. A 2003 survey of fraud by international accounting firm KPMG reported a 13 percent increase in instances of corporate fraud compared to five years earlier. It noted that while employee fraud (such things as expense-account abuse, payroll fraud, and theft of assets) represented 60 percent of all instances of fraud, financial reporting fraud (the intentional misstatement of financial reports) was the most costly to companies. That should not be surprising given the long list of companies such as **Enron,**

Global Crossing, **WorldCom**, and others that engaged in massive financial frauds, which have led to huge financial losses and thousands of lost jobs.

Creating Proper Incentives

Complex systems within companies like **Motorola**, **IBM**, and **Nike** are used to control and evaluate the actions of managers. Substantial resources are dedicated to ensure that the actions of employees are monitored and effectively evaluated. Unfortunately, these systems and controls sometimes unwittingly create incentives for managers to take unethical actions. For example, budgets (plans of actions) are prepared by companies to provide future direction. Because the budget is also used as an evaluation tool, some managers try to "game" the budgeting process by underestimating their division's predicted performance so that it will be easier to meet their performance targets. On the other hand, if the budget is set at unattainable levels, managers sometimes take unethical actions to meet the targets in order to receive higher compensation or in some cases to keep their jobs.

For example, in recent years, airline manufacturer **Boeing** has been plagued by a series of scandals including charges of over-billing, corporate espionage, and illegal conflicts of interest. Some long-time employees of Boeing blame the decline in ethics on a change in the corporate culture that took place after Boeing merged with **McDonnell Douglas**. They suggest that evaluation systems implemented after the merger to monitor results and evaluate employee performance made employees believe they needed to succeed no matter what.

As another example, manufacturing companies need to establish production goals for their processes. Again, if controls are not effective and realistic, problems develop. To illustrate, **Schering-Plough**, a pharmaceutical manufacturer, found that employees were so concerned with meeting production standards that they failed to monitor the quality of the product, and as a result the dosages were often wrong.

New Legislation

As a result of the breakdown of controls at a number of large companies, the U.S. Congress enacted legislation to help prevent lapses in internal control from occurring. This legislation, referred to as the Sarbanes-Oxley Act of 2002 (SOX) has important implications for the financial community. One result of SOX was to clarify top management's responsibility for the company's financial statements. CEOs and CFOs must now certify that financial statements give a fair presentation of the company's operating results and its financial condition. In addition, top management must certify that the company maintains an adequate system of internal controls to safeguard the company's assets and ensure accurate financial reports.

Another result of SOX is that more attention is now paid to the composition of the company's board of directors. In particular, the audit committee of the board of directors must be comprised entirely of independent members (that is, non-employees) and must contain at least one financial expert.

Finally, to increase the likelihood of compliance with these and other new rules that are part of the new legislation, the penalties for misconduct were substantially increased.

To provide guidance for managerial accountants, the Institute of Management Accountants (IMA) has developed a code of ethical standards, entitled *Standards of Ethical Conduct for Practitioners of Management Accounting and Financial Management*. The code states that management accountants should not commit acts in violation of these standards. Nor should they condone such acts by others within their organizations. The IMA code of ethical standards is provided in Appendix B at the end of the book. Throughout this course we will address various ethical issues faced by managers.

BEFORE YOU GO ON . . .

▶**Review It**

1. Compare financial accounting and managerial accounting, identifying the principal differences.
2. Identify and discuss the three broad functions of management.
3. What are staff positions? What are line positions? Give examples.
4. What were some of the regulatory changes enacted under the Sarbanes-Oxley Act?

☑ THE NAVIGATOR

Managerial Cost Concepts

For managers at companies like **Dell** or **Hewlett-Packard** to plan, direct, and control operations effectively, good information is needed. One very important type of information is related to costs. Questions such as the following should be asked.

1. What costs are involved in making a product or providing a service?
2. If production volume is decreased, will costs decrease?
3. What impact will automation have on total costs?
4. How can costs best be controlled?

To answer these questions, management needs reliable and relevant cost information. We now explain and illustrate the various cost categories that management uses.

MANUFACTURING COSTS

Manufacturing consists of activities and processes that convert raw materials into finished goods. Contrast this type of operation with merchandising, which sells merchandise in the form in which it is purchased. Manufacturing costs are typically classified as shown in Illustration 1-3.

STUDY OBJECTIVE
3
Define the three classes of manufacturing costs.

Illustration 1-3 Classifications of manufacturing costs

Illustrations like this one convey information in pictorial form to help you visualize and apply the ideas as you study.

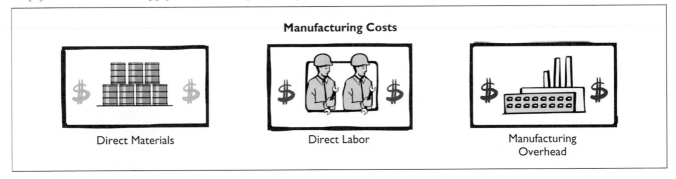

Manufacturing Costs

Direct Materials   Direct Labor   Manufacturing Overhead

Direct Materials

To obtain the materials that will be converted into the finished product, the manufacturer purchases raw materials. **Raw materials** are the basic materials and parts used in the manufacturing process. For example, auto manufacturers such as **General Motors**, **Ford**, and **DaimlerChrysler** use steel, plastics, and tires as raw materials in making cars.

Raw materials that can be physically and directly associated with the finished product during the manufacturing process are called **direct materials**.

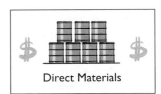

Direct Materials

Examples include flour in the baking of bread, syrup in the bottling of soft drinks, and steel in the making of automobiles. In the Feature Story, direct materials for **Hewlett-Packard** and **Dell Computer** include plastic, glass, hard drives, and processing chips.

But some raw materials cannot be easily associated with the finished product. These are called indirect materials. **Indirect materials** have one of two characteristics. Either (1) they do not physically become part of the finished product, such as lubricants and polishing compounds. Or (2) they cannot be traced because their physical association with the finished product is too small in terms of cost, such as cotter pins and lock washers. Indirect materials are accounted for as part of **manufacturing overhead**.

Direct Labor

Direct Labor

The work of factory employees that can be physically and directly associated with converting raw materials into finished goods is called **direct labor**. Bottlers at **Coca-Cola**, bakers at **Sara Lee**, and typesetters at **TechBooks** are employees whose activities are usually classified as direct labor. **Indirect labor** refers to the work of factory employees that has no physical association with the finished product, or for which it is impractical to trace costs to the goods produced. Examples include wages of maintenance people, time-keepers, and supervisors. Like indirect materials, indirect labor is classified as **manufacturing overhead**.

Business Insight
Management Perspective

Recently a closely watched study of productivity in the automobile industry reported some encouraging improvements for U.S. auto manufacturers. For example, the U.S. unit of **DaimlerChrysler** improved its overall productivity 8.3 percent. But a **Nissan Motor** plant in Tennessee set the standard for least amount of labor hours per vehicle. It produced Altima automobiles using only 15.74 labor hours per vehicle. Chrysler assembly plants required 28 hours per vehicle, and **Ford** took 26 hours.

SOURCE: Ann Keeton, "Chrysler Leads Big Three in Productivity Gains," *Wall Street Journal Online* (June 18, 2003).

Manufacturing Overhead

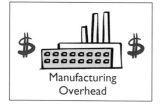

Manufacturing Overhead

Manufacturing overhead consists of costs that are indirectly associated with the manufacture of the finished product. These costs may also be manufacturing costs that cannot be classified as direct materials or direct labor. Manufacturing overhead includes indirect materials, indirect labor, depreciation on factory buildings and machines, and insurance, taxes, and maintenance on factory facilities.

One study found the following magnitudes of the three different product costs as a percentage of the total product cost: direct materials 54 percent, direct labor 13 percent, and manufacturing overhead 33 percent. Note that the direct labor component is the smallest. This component of product cost is dropping substantially because of automation. In some companies, direct labor has become as little as 5 percent of the total cost.

Allocating materials and labor costs to specific products is fairly straightforward. Good record keeping can tell a company how much plastic is used in making each type of gear, or how many hours of factory labor were used to assemble a part. But allocating overhead costs to specific products presents problems. How much of the purchasing agent's salary is attributable to the hun-

Alternative Terminology notes present synonymous terms used in practice.

Alternative Terminology
Terms such as *factory overhead, indirect manufacturing costs,* and *burden* are sometimes used instead of manufacturing overhead.

dreds of different products made in the same plant? What about the grease that keeps the machines humming, or the computers that make sure paychecks come out on time? Boiled down to its simplest form, the question becomes: Which products cause the incurrence of which costs? In subsequent chapters we show various methods of allocating overhead to products.

PRODUCT VERSUS PERIOD COSTS

Each of the manufacturing cost components (direct materials, direct labor, and manufacturing overhead) are product costs. As the term suggests, **product costs** are costs that are a necessary and integral part of producing the finished product. Product costs are recorded as inventory when incurred. Under the matching principle, these costs do not become expenses until the finished goods inventory is sold. The expense is cost of goods sold.

Period costs are costs that are matched with the revenue of a specific time period rather than included as part of the cost of a salable product. These are nonmanufacturing costs. Period costs include selling and administrative expenses. They are deducted from revenues in the period in which they are incurred in order to determine net income.

The foregoing relationships and cost terms are summarized in Illustration 1-4. Our main concern in this chapter is with product costs.

STUDY OBJECTIVE
4
Distinguish between product and period costs.

Alternative Terminology
Product costs are also called *inventoriable costs.*

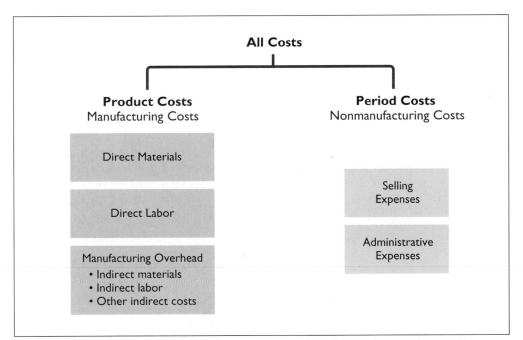

Illustration 1-4   Product versus period costs

BEFORE YOU GO ON . . .

▶**Review It**

1. What are the major cost classifications involved in manufacturing a product?
2. What are product and period costs, and what is their relationship to the manufacturing process?

▶**Do It**

A bicycle company has these costs: tires, salaries of employees who put tires on the wheels, factory building depreciation, wheel nuts, spokes, salary of factory manager, handle bars, and salaries of factory maintenance employees. Classify each cost as direct materials, direct labor, or overhead.

Before You Go On . . . Do it exercises ask you to put to work newly acquired knowledge. The **Action Plan** (next page) outlines the reasoning necessary to complete the exercise. The accompanying **Solution** (next page) shows how the exercise should be solved.

Action Plan

- Classify as direct materials any raw materials that can be physically and directly associated with the finished product.
- Classify as direct labor the work of factory employees that can be physically and directly associated with the finished product.
- Classify as manufacturing overhead any costs that are indirectly associated with the finished product.

Solution

Tires, spokes, and handle bars are direct materials. Salaries of employees who put tires on the wheels are direct labor. All of the other costs are manufacturing overhead.

Related exercise material: BE1-4, BE1-5, BE1-7, E1-2, E1-3, and E1-4.

Manufacturing Costs in Financial Statements

The financial statements of a manufacturer are very similar to those of a merchandiser. The principal differences pertain to the cost of goods sold section in the income statement and the current assets section in the balance sheet.

STUDY OBJECTIVE

5

Explain the difference between a merchandising and a manufacturing income statement.

INCOME STATEMENT

Under a periodic inventory system, the income statements of a merchandiser and a manufacturer differ in the cost of goods sold section. For a merchandiser, cost of goods sold is computed by adding the beginning merchandise inventory to the **cost of goods purchased** and subtracting the ending merchandise inventory. For a manufacturer, cost of goods sold is computed by adding the beginning finished goods inventory to the **cost of goods manufactured** and subtracting the ending finished goods inventory. (See Illustration 1-5.)

Illustration 1-5 Cost of goods sold components

Helpful Hint A periodic inventory system is assumed here.

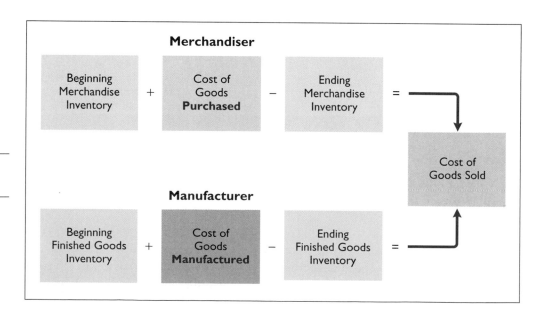

The cost of goods sold sections for merchandising and manufacturing companies in Illustration 1-6 show the different presentations. The other sections of an income statement are similar for merchandisers and manufacturers.

MERCHANDISING COMPANY Income Statement (partial) For the Year Ended December 31, 2005			MANUFACTURING COMPANY Income Statement (partial) For the Year Ended December 31, 2005		
Cost of goods sold			Cost of goods sold		
Merchandise inventory, January 1		$ 70,000	**Finished goods inventory, January 1**		$ 90,000
Cost of goods purchased		650,000	**Cost of goods manufactured** (see Illustration 1-8)		370,000
Cost of goods available for sale		720,000	Cost of goods available for sale		460,000
Merchandise inventory, December 31		400,000	**Finished goods inventory, December 31**		80,000
Cost of goods sold		$320,000	Cost of goods sold		$380,000

A number of accounts are involved in determining the cost of goods manufactured. To eliminate excessive detail, income statements typically show only the total cost of goods manufactured. The details are presented in a Cost of Goods Manufactured Schedule. The form and content of this schedule are shown in Illustration 1-8 (page 14).

Determining the Cost of Goods Manufactured

An example may help show how the cost of goods manufactured is determined. Assume that **Dell** has a number of computers in various stages of production on January 1. In total, these partially completed units are called **beginning work in process inventory**. The costs assigned to beginning work in process inventory are based on the **manufacturing costs incurred in the prior period**.

The manufacturing costs incurred in the current year are used first to complete the work in process on January 1. They then are used to start the production of other computers. The sum of the direct materials costs, direct labor costs, and manufacturing overhead incurred in the current year is the total manufacturing costs for the current period.

We now have two cost amounts: (1) the cost of the beginning work in process and (2) the total manufacturing costs for the current period. The sum of these costs is the total cost of work in process for the year.

At the end of the year, some computers may be only partially completed. The costs of these units become the cost of the **ending work in process inventory**. To find the cost of goods manufactured, we subtract this cost from the total cost of work in process. The determination of the cost of goods manufactured is shown graphically in Illustration 1-7.

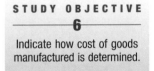

STUDY OBJECTIVE
—— **6** ——
Indicate how cost of goods manufactured is determined.

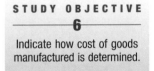

Illustration 1-7 Cost of goods manufactured formula

Cost of Goods Manufactured Schedule

An internal report shows each of the cost elements presented in Illustration 1-7. This report is called the **cost of goods manufactured schedule**. The schedule for Olsen Manufacturing Company (using assumed data) is shown in Illustration 1-8. Note that the schedule presents detailed data for direct materials and for manufacturing overhead.

Review Illustration 1-7 and then examine the cost of goods manufactured schedule in Illustration 1-8. You should be able to distinguish between "Total manufacturing costs" and "Cost of goods manufactured." The difference is the effect of the change in work in process during the period.

Illustration 1-8 Cost of goods manufactured schedule

Often, numbers or categories in the financial statements are highlighted in **red type** to draw your attention to key information.

OLSEN MANUFACTURING COMPANY			
Cost of Goods Manufactured Schedule			
For the Year Ended December 31, 2005			
Work in process, January 1			$ 18,400
Direct materials			
Raw materials inventory, January 1	$ 16,700		
Raw materials purchases	152,500		
Total raw materials available for use	169,200		
Less: Raw materials inventory, December 31	22,800		
Direct materials used		$146,400	
Direct labor		175,600	
Manufacturing overhead			
Indirect labor	14,300		
Factory repairs	12,600		
Factory utilities	10,100		
Factory depreciation	9,440		
Factory insurance	8,360		
Total manufacturing overhead		54,800	
Total manufacturing costs			376,800
Total cost of work in process			395,200
Less: Work in process, December 31			25,200
Cost of goods manufactured			$370,000

Each chapter presents useful information about how decision makers analyze and solve business problems. **Decision Toolkits** summarize the key features of a decision tool and review why and how to use it.

DECISION TOOLKIT

Decision Checkpoints	Info Needed for Decision	Tool to Use for Decision	How to Evaluate Results
Is the company maintaining control over the costs of production?	Cost of material, labor, and overhead	Cost of goods manufactured schedule	Compare the cost of goods manufactured to revenue expected from product sales.

BALANCE SHEET

The balance sheet for a merchandising company shows just one category of inventory. In contrast, the balance sheet for a manufacturer may have three inventory accounts. They are shown in Illustration 1-9.

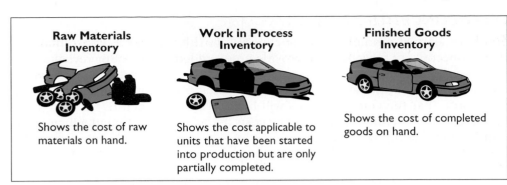

Raw Materials Inventory	Work in Process Inventory	Finished Goods Inventory
Shows the cost of raw materials on hand.	Shows the cost applicable to units that have been started into production but are only partially completed.	Shows the cost of completed goods on hand.

> **STUDY OBJECTIVE**
>
> **7**
>
> Explain the difference between a merchandising and a manufacturing balance sheet.

Finished Goods Inventory is to a manufacturer what Merchandise Inventory is to a merchandiser. It represents the goods that are available for sale.

The current assets sections presented in Illustration 1-10 contrast the presentations of inventories for merchandising and manufacturing companies. Manufacturing inventories are generally listed in the order of their liquidity—the order in which they are expected to be realized in cash. Thus, finished goods inventory is listed first. The remainder of the balance sheet is similar for the two types of companies.

Illustration 1-10 Current assets sections of merchandising and manufacturing balance sheets

MERCHANDISING COMPANY Balance Sheet December 31, 2005		MANUFACTURING COMPANY Balance Sheet December 31, 2005		
Current assets		Current assets		
Cash	$100,000	Cash		$180,000
Receivables (net)	210,000	Receivables (net)		210,000
Merchandise inventory	**400,000**	**Inventories**		
Prepaid expenses	22,000	**Finished goods**	**$80,000**	
Total current assets	$732,000	**Work in process**	**25,200**	
		Raw materials	**22,800**	128,000
		Prepaid expenses		18,000
		Total current assets		$536,000

Each step in the accounting cycle for a merchandiser applies to a manufacturer. For example, prior to preparing financial statements, adjusting entries are required. The adjusting entries are essentially the same as those of a merchandiser. The closing entries are also similar for manufacturers and merchandisers. (For more detail, see the appendix at the end of the chapter.)

DECISION TOOLKIT

Decision Checkpoints	Info Needed for Decision	Tool to Use for Decision	How to Evaluate Results
What is the composition of a manufacturing company's inventory?	Amount of raw materials, work in process, and finished goods inventories	Balance sheet	Determine whether there are sufficient finished goods, raw materials, and work in process inventories to meet forecasted demand.

COST CONCEPTS—A REVIEW

You have learned a number of cost concepts in this chapter. Because many of these concepts are new, here we provide an extended example for review.

Assume that Northridge Company manufactures and sells pre-hung metal doors. Recently, it also has decided to start selling pre-hung wood doors. An old warehouse that the company owns will be used to manufacture the new product. Northridge identifies the following costs associated with manufacturing and selling the pre-hung wood doors.

1. The material cost (wood) for each door is $10.
2. Labor costs required to construct a wood door are $8 per door.
3. Depreciation on the factory equipment used to make the wood doors is $25,000 per year.
4. Property taxes on the factory building used to make the wood doors are $6,000 per year.
5. Advertising costs for the pre-hung wood doors total $2,500 per month or $30,000 per year.
6. Sales commissions related to pre-hung wood doors sold are $4 per door.
7. Salaries for employees who maintain the factory facilities are $28,000.
8. The salary of the plant manager in charge of pre-hung wood doors is $70,000.
9. The cost of shipping pre-hung wood doors is $12 per door sold.

These manufacturing and selling costs can be assigned to the various categories shown in Illustration 1-11.

Illustration 1-11 Assignment of costs to cost categories

	Product Costs			
Cost Item	Direct Materials	Direct Labor	Manufacturing Overhead	Period Costs
1. Material cost ($10) per door	X			
2. Labor costs ($8) per door		X		
3. Depreciation on factory equipment ($25,000 per year)			X	
4. Property taxes on factory building ($6,000 per year)			X	
5. Advertising costs ($30,000 per year)				X
6. Sales commissions ($4 per door)				X
7. Maintenance salaries (factory facilities) ($28,000 per year)			X	
8. Salary of plant manager ($70,000)			X	
9. Cost of shipping pre-hung doors ($12 per door)				X

Remember that total manufacturing costs are the sum of the **product costs—** direct materials, direct labor, and manufacturing overhead. If Northridge Company produces 10,000 pre-hung wood doors the first year, the total manufacturing costs would be $309,000 as shown in Illustration 1-12.

Illustration 1-12
Computation of total
manufacturing costs

Cost Number and Item	Manufacturing Cost
1. Material cost ($10 × 10,000)	$100,000
2. Labor cost ($8 × 10,000)	80,000
3. Depreciation on factory equipment	25,000
4. Property taxes on factory building	6,000
7. Maintenance salaries (factory facilities)	28,000
8. Salary of plant manager	70,000
Total manufacturing costs	**$309,000**

Knowing the total manufacturing costs, Northridge can compute the manufacturing cost per unit. Assuming 10,000 units, the cost to produce one pre-hung wood door is $30.90 ($309,000 ÷ 10,000 units).

The cost concepts discussed in this chapter will be used extensively in subsequent chapters. Study Illustration 1-11 carefully. If you do not understand any of these classifications, go back and reread the appropriate section in this chapter.

BEFORE YOU GO ON . . .

▶**Review It**

1. How does the content of an income statement for a merchandiser differ from that for a manufacturer?
2. How are the work in process inventories reported in the cost of goods manufactured schedule?
3. How does the content of the balance sheet for a merchandiser differ from that for a manufacturer?

☑ THE NAVIGATOR

Managerial Accounting Today

In recent years, the competitive environment for U.S. business has changed significantly. For example, the airline, financial services, and telecommunications industries have been deregulated. Global competition has intensified. The world economy now has the European Union, NAFTA, and ASEAN. Countries like China and India are becoming economic powerhouses. As indicated earlier, managerial accountants must be forward-looking, acting as advisors and information providers to different parts of the organization. Some of the issues they face are discussed below.

SERVICE INDUSTRY TRENDS

The Feature Story notes that at the peak of its success as a personal computer manufacturer, **Compaq** purchased **Digital Equipment**. Its management believed that the future of computing was in providing computer services, rather than in manufacturing computer hardware. In fact, during the most recent decade, the U.S. economy in general shifted toward an emphasis on providing services, rather than goods. Today over 50 percent of U.S. workers are employed by service companies, and that percentage is projected to increase in coming years. Much of this chapter focused on manufacturers. But most of the techniques that you will learn in this course are equally applicable to service entities.

Managers of service companies look to managerial accounting to answer many questions. Illustration 1-13 presents examples of such questions. In some instances the managerial accountant may need to develop new systems for measuring the cost of serving individual customers. In others, companies may need new operating controls to improve the quality and efficiency of specific services. Many of the examples we present in subsequent chapters will be based on service companies.

Illustration 1-13 Service industries and companies and the managerial accounting questions they face

	Industry/Company	Questions Faced by Service-Company Managers
	Transportation **(American Airlines, Amtrak)**	Whether to buy new or used planes? Whether to service a new route?
	Package delivery services **(FedEx, UPS)**	What fee structure to use? What mode of transportation to use?
	Telecommunications **(AT&T, Time Warner)**	What fee structure to use? Whether to service a new community? How many households will it take to break even? Whether to invest in a new satellite or lay new cable?
	Professional services (attorneys, accountants, physicians)	How much to charge for particular services? How much office overhead to allocate to particular jobs? How efficient and productive are individual staff members?
	Financial institutions **(Wells Fargo, Merrill Lynch)**	Which services to charge for, and which to provide for free? Whether to build a new branch office or to install a new ATM? Should fees vary depending on the size of the customers' accounts?
	Health care **(Blue Cross-Blue Shield, HMOs)**	Whether to invest in new equipment? How much to charge for various services? How to measure the quality of services provided?

MANAGERIAL ACCOUNTING PRACTICES

As discussed earlier, the practice of managerial accounting has changed significantly in recent years to better address the needs of managers. The following sections explain some recent managerial accounting practices.

The Value Chain

The **value chain** refers to all activities associated with providing a product or service. For a manufacturer these include research and development, product design, acquisition of raw materials, production, sales and marketing, delivery, customer relations, and subsequent service. Illustration 1-14 depicts the value chain for a manufacturer. In recent years, companies have made huge strides in analyzing all stages of the value chain in an effort to improve productivity and eliminate waste. Japanese automobile manufacturer **Toyota** pioneered many of these innovations.

Illustration 1-14   A manufacturer's value chain

| Research & development and product design | Acquisition of raw materials | Production | Sales & marketing | Delivery | Customer relations and subsequent services |

In the 1980s many companies purchased giant machines to replace humans in the manufacturing process. These machines were designed to produce large batches of products. In recent years these large-batch manufacturing processes have been recognized as very wasteful. They require vast amounts of inventory storage capacity and considerable movement of materials. Consequently, many companies have reengineered their manufacturing processes. As one example, the manufacturing company **Pratt and Whitney** has replaced many large machines with smaller, more flexible ones and has begun reorganizing its plants for more efficient flow of goods. Pratt and Whitney was able to reduce the time that its turbine engine blades spend in the grinding section of its factory from 10 days down to 2 hours. It cut the total amount of time spent making a blade from 22 days to 7 days. The improvements that have resulted from analysis of the value chain have made companies far more responsive to customer needs and have improved profitability.

Technological Change

Technology has played a large role in affecting the value chain. The computerization and automation that have occurred have permitted companies to be much more effective in streamlining production and thus enhancing the value chain. For example, many companies now employ **enterprise resource planning (ERP)** software systems to manage their value chain. ERP systems provide a comprehensive, centralized, integrated source of information used to manage all major business processes, from purchasing to manufacturing to recording human resources.

In large companies, an ERP system might replace as many as 200 individual software packages. For example, an ERP system can eliminate the need for individual software packages for personnel, inventory management, receivables, and payroll. Because the value chain extends beyond the walls of the company, ERP systems both collect from and provide information to the company's major suppliers, customers, and business partners. The largest ERP provider, German corporation **SAP**, has more than 22,000 customers worldwide.

Another example of technological change is **computer-integrated manufacturing (CIM)**. Using CIM, many companies can now manufacture products that are untouched by human hands. An example is the use of robotic equipment in the steel and automobile industries. Automation significantly reduces direct labor costs in many cases. The worker simply monitors the manufacturing process by watching instrument panels.

Also, the widespread use of computers has greatly reduced the cost of accumulating, storing, and reporting managerial accounting information. Computers now make it possible to do more detailed costing of products, processes, and services than was possible under manual processing.

Technology is also affecting the value chain through business-to-business (B2B) e-commerce on the Internet. The Internet has dramatically changed the way corporations do business with one another. Interorganizational information systems connected over the Internet enable customers and suppliers to share information nearly instantaneously. In addition, the Internet has changed the marketplace, often having the effect of cutting out intermediaries (the "middle man"). Industries such as the automobile, airline, hotel, and electronics industries have made commitments to purchase some or all of their supplies and raw materials in the huge B2B electronic marketplaces. For example, **Hilton Hotels** recently committed to purchase as much as $1.5 billion of bed sheets, pest control services, and other items from an online supplier, **PurchasePro.com**.

Just-in-Time Inventory Methods

Many companies have significantly lowered inventory levels and costs using **just-in-time (JIT) inventory** methods. Under a just-in-time method, goods are manufactured or purchased just in time for use. As noted in the Feature Story, **Dell** is famous for having developed a system for making computers in response to individual customer requests. Even though each computer is custom-made to meet each customer's particular specifications, it takes Dell less than 48 hours to assemble the computer and put it on a truck. By integrating its information systems with those of its suppliers, Dell reduced its inventories to nearly zero. This is a huge advantage in an industry where products become obsolete nearly overnight. JIT is discussed further in the appendix to Chapter 4.

Quality

JIT inventory systems require an increased emphasis on product quality. If products are produced only as they are needed, it is very costly for the company to have to stop production because of defects or machine breakdowns. Many companies have installed **total quality management (TQM)** systems to reduce defects in finished products. The goal is to achieve zero defects. These systems require timely data on defective products, rework costs, and the cost of honoring warranty contracts. Often this information is used to help redesign the product in a way that makes it less prone to defect. Or it may be used to reengineer the production process to reduce setup time and decrease the potential for error. TQM systems also provide information on nonfinancial measures such as customer satisfaction, number of service calls, and time to generate reports. Attention to these measures, which employees can control, leads to increased profitability.

Activity-Based Costing

As discussed earlier, overhead costs have become an increasingly large component of product and service costs. By definition, overhead costs cannot be directly traced to individual products. But to determine each product's cost, overhead must be **allocated** to the various products. In order to obtain more accurate product costs, many companies now allocate overhead using **activity-based costing (ABC)**. Under ABC, overhead is allocated based on each product's use of activities in making the product. For example, the company can keep track of the cost of setting up machines for each batch of a production process. Then a particular product can be allocated part of the total set-up cost based on the number of set-ups that product required.

Activity-based costing is beneficial because it results in more accurate product costing and in more careful scrutiny of all activities in the value chain. For example, if a product's cost is high because it requires a high number of set-ups, management will be motivated to determine how to produce the product using the optimal number of machine set-ups. ABC is now widely used by both manufacturing and service companies. **Allied Signal** and **Coca-Cola** have both enjoyed improved results from ABC. **Fidelity Investments** uses ABC to identify which customers are actually costing it money. Chapter 4 discusses ABC further.

Business Insight
Management Perspective

When it comes to total quality management, few companies can compare with **Chiquita Brands International**. Grocery store customers are very picky about bananas—bad bananas are consistently the number one grocery store complaint. Because bananas often account for up to 3 percent of a grocery store's sales, Chiquita goes to great lengths to protect the popular fruit. While bananas are in transit from Central America, "black box" recording devices attached to shipping crates ensure that they are kept in an environment of 90 percent humidity and an unvarying 55-degree temperature. Upon arrival in the U.S., bananas are ripened in airtight warehouses that use carefully monitored levels of ethylene gas. Regular checks are made of each warehouse using ultrasonic detectors that can detect leaks the size of a pinhole. Says one grocery store executive, "No other item in the store has this type of attention and resources devoted to it."

SOURCE: Devon Spurgeon, "When Grocers in U.S. Go Bananas Over Bad Fruit, They Call Laubenthal," *Wall Street Journal* (August 14, 2000), p. A1.

Theory of Constraints

All companies have certain aspects of their business that create "bottlenecks"—constraints that limit the company's potential profitability. An important aspect of managing the value chain is identifying these constraints. The **theory of constraints** is a specific approach used to identify and manage constraints in order to achieve the company goals. Automobile manufacturer **General Motors** has implemented the theory of constraints in all of its North American plants. GM has found that it is most profitable when it focuses on fixing bottlenecks, rather than worrying about whether all aspects of the company are functioning at full capacity. It has greatly improved the company's ability to effectively use overtime labor while meeting customer demand. Chapter 6 discusses an application of the theory of constraints.

Balanced Scorecard

As various business practice innovations have been implemented, managers sometimes focus too enthusiastically on the latest innovation, to the detriment of other areas of the business. For example, in focusing on improving quality, companies sometimes lost sight of cost/benefit considerations. Similarly, in focusing on reducing inventory levels through just-in-time, companies sometimes lost sales due to inventory shortages. The **balanced scorecard** is a performance-measurement approach that uses both financial and nonfinancial measures to evaluate all aspects of a company's operations in an **integrated** fashion. The performance measures are linked in a cause-and-effect fashion to ensure that they all tie to the company's overall objectives.

For example, the company may desire to increase its return on assets, a common financial performance measure (calculated as net income divided by average total assets). It will then identify a series of linked goals that, if each is accomplished, will ultimately result in an increase in return on assets. For example, in order to increase return on assets, sales must increase. In order to increase sales, customer satisfaction must be increased. In order to increase customer satisfaction, product defects must be reduced. In order to reduce product defects, employee training must be increased. Note the linkage, which starts with employee training and ends with return on assets. Each objective will have associated performance measures.

The use of the balanced scorecard is widespread among well-known and respected companies. For example, **Hilton Hotels Corporation** uses the balanced scorecard to evaluate the performance of employees at all of its hotel chains. **Wal-Mart** employs the balanced scorecard, and actually extends its use to evaluation of its suppliers. For example, Wal-Mart recently awarded **Welch Company** the "Dry Grocery Division Supplier of the Year Award" for its balanced scorecard results. The balanced scorecard is discussed further in Chapter 11.

BEFORE YOU GO ON . . .

▶Review It

1. Describe, in sequence, the main components of a manufacturer's value chain.
2. What is an enterprise resource planning (ERP) system? What are its primary benefits?
3. Why is product quality important for companies that implement a just-in-time inventory system?
4. Explain what is meant by "balanced" in the balanced scorecard approach.

☑ THE NAVIGATOR

Using the Decision Toolkit

Using the Decision Toolkit exercises, which follow the final set of Review It questions in the chapter, ask you to use business information and the decision tools presented in the chapter. We encourage you to think through the questions related to the decision before you study the **Solution** (next page).

Giant Manufacturing Co. Ltd. specializes in manufacturing many different models of bicycles. Assume that a new model, the Jaguar, has been well accepted. As a result, the company has established a separate manufacturing facility to produce these bicycles. The company produces 1,000 bicycles per month. Giant's monthly manufacturing cost and other expenses data related to these bicycles are as follows.

1. Rent on manufacturing equipment (lease cost) $2,000/month
2. Insurance on manufacturing building $750/month
3. Raw materials (frames, tires, etc.) $80/bicycle
4. Utility costs for manufacturing facility $1,000/month
5. Supplies for administrative office $800/month
6. Wages for assembly line workers in manufacturing facility $30/bicycle
7. Depreciation on office equipment $650/month
8. Miscellaneous materials (lubricants, solders, etc.) $1.20/bicycle
9. Property taxes on manufacturing building $2,400/year
10. Manufacturing supervisor's salary $3,000/month
11. Advertising for bicycles $30,000/year
12. Sales commissions $10/bicycle
13. Depreciation on manufacturing building $1,500/month

Instructions

(a) Prepare an answer sheet with the following column headings.

	Product Costs			
Cost Item	**Direct Materials**	**Direct Labor**	**Manufacturing Overhead**	**Period Costs**

Enter each cost item on your answer sheet, placing an "X" mark under the appropriate headings.

(b) Compute total manufacturing costs for the month.

Solution

(a)

	Product Costs			
Cost Item	Direct Materials	Direct Labor	Manufacturing Overhead	Period Costs
1. Rent on manufacturing equipment ($2,000/month)			X	
2. Insurance on manufacturing building ($750/month)			X	
3. Raw materials ($80/bicycle)	X			
4. Manufacturing utilities ($1,000/month)			X	
5. Office supplies ($800/month)				X
6. Wages for workers ($30/bicycle)		X		
7. Depreciation on office equipment ($650/month)				X
8. Miscellaneous materials ($1.20/bicycle)			X	
9. Property taxes on manufacturing building ($2,400/year)			X	
10. Manufacturing supervisor's salary ($3,000/month)			X	
11. Advertising cost ($30,000/ycar)				X
12. Sales commissions ($10/bicycle)				X
13. Depreciation on manufacturing building ($1,500/month)			X	

(b)

Cost Item	Manufacturing Cost
Rent on manufacturing equipment	$ 2,000
Insurance on manufacturing building	750
Raw materials ($80 × 1,000)	80,000
Manufacturing utilities	1,000
Labor ($30 × 1,000)	30,000
Miscellaneous materials ($1.20 × 1,000)	1,200
Property taxes on manufacturing building ($2,400 ÷ 12)	200
Manufacturing supervisor's salary	3,000
Depreciation on manufacturing building	1,500
Total manufacturing costs	$119,650

THE NAVIGATOR

The **Summary of Study Objectives** reiterates the main points related to the Study Objectives. It provides you with an opportunity to review what you have learned.

Summary of Study Objectives

1 *Explain the distinguishing features of managerial accounting.* The distinguishing features of managerial accounting are:

Primary users of reports—internal users, who are officers, department heads, managers, and supervisors in the company.

Type and frequency of reports—internal reports that are issued as frequently as the need arises.

Purpose of reports—to provide special-purpose information for a particular user for a specific decision.

Content of reports—pertains to subunits of the business and may be very detailed; may extend beyond double-entry accounting system; the reporting standard is relevance to the decision being made.

Verification of reports—no independent audits.

2 *Identify the three broad functions of management.* The three functions are planning, directing, and controlling. Planning requires management to look ahead and to establish objectives. Directing involves coordinating the diverse activities and human resources of a company to produce a smooth-running operation. Controlling is the process of keeping the activities on track.

3 *Define the three classes of manufacturing costs.* Manufacturing costs are typically classified as either (1) direct materials, (2) direct labor, or (3) manufacturing overhead. Raw materials that can be physically and directly associated with the finished product during the manufacturing process are called direct materials. The work of factory employees that can be physically and directly associated with converting raw materials into finished goods is considered direct labor. Manufacturing overhead consists of costs that are indirectly associated with the manufacture of the finished product.

4 *Distinguish between product and period costs.* Product costs are costs that are a necessary and integral part of producing the finished product. Product costs are also called inventoriable costs. Under the matching principle, these costs do not become

expenses until the inventory to which they attach is sold. Period costs are costs that are identified with a specific time period rather than with a salable product. These costs relate to nonmanufacturing costs and therefore are not inventoriable costs.

5 *Explain the difference between a merchandising and a manufacturing income statement.* The difference between a merchandising and a manufacturing income statement is in the cost of goods sold section. A manufacturing cost of goods sold section shows beginning and ending finished goods inventories and the cost of goods manufactured.

6 *Indicate how cost of goods manufactured is determined.* The cost of the beginning work in process is added to the total manufacturing costs for the current year to arrive at the total cost of work in process for the year. The ending work in process is then subtracted from the total cost of work in process to arrive at the cost of goods manufactured.

7 *Explain the difference between a merchandising and a manufacturing balance sheet.* The difference between a merchandising and a manufacturing balance sheet is in the current assets section. In the current assets section of a manufacturing company's balance sheet, three inventory accounts are presented: finished goods inventory, work in process inventory, and raw materials inventory.

8 *Identify trends in managerial accounting.* Managerial accounting has experienced many changes in recent years. Among these are a shift toward addressing the needs of service companies and improving practices to better meet the needs of managers. Improved practices include a focus on managing the value chain through techniques such as just-in-time inventory, and technological applications such as enterprise resource planning (ERP). In addition, techniques have been developed to improve decision making, such as the theory of constraints and activity-based costing (ABC). Finally, the balanced scorecard is now used by many companies in order to attain a more comprehensive view of the company's operations.

The Decision Toolkit—A Summary reviews the contexts and techniques useful for decision making that were covered in the chapter.

DECISION TOOLKIT—A SUMMARY

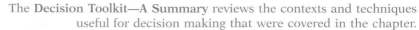

Decision Checkpoints	Info Needed for Decision	Tool to Use for Decision	How to Evaluate Results
Is the company maintaining control over the costs of production?	Cost of material, labor, and overhead	Cost of goods manufactured schedule	Compare the cost of goods manufactured to revenue expected from product sales.
What is the composition of a manufacturing company's inventory?	Amount of raw materials, work in process, and finished goods inventories	Balance sheet	Determine whether there are sufficient finished goods, raw materials, and work in process inventories to meet forecasted demand.

APPENDIX
ACCOUNTING CYCLE FOR A MANUFACTURING COMPANY

The accounting cycle for a manufacturing company is the same as for a merchandising company when a periodic inventory system is used. The journalizing and posting of transactions is the same, except for the additional manufacturing inventories and manufacturing cost accounts. Similarly, the preparation of a trial balance and the journalizing and posting of adjusting entries are the same. Some changes, however, occur in the use of a work sheet and in preparing closing entries.

To illustrate the changes in the work sheet, we will use the cost of goods manufactured schedule for Olsen Manufacturing presented in Illustration 1-8, along with other assumed data. For convenience, the cost of goods manufactured schedule is reproduced in Illustration 1A-1.

STUDY OBJECTIVE
9
Prepare a work sheet and closing entries for a manufacturing company.

OLSEN MANUFACTURING COMPANY
Cost of Goods Manufactured Schedule
For the Year Ended December 31, 2005

Work in process, January 1			$ 18,400
Direct materials			
Raw materials inventory, January 1	$ 16,700		
Raw materials purchases	152,500		
Total raw materials available for use	169,200		
Less: Raw materials inventory, December 31	22,800		
Direct materials used		$146,400	
Direct labor		175,600	
Manufacturing overhead			
Indirect labor	14,300		
Factory repairs	12,600		
Factory utilities	10,100		
Factory depreciation	9,440		
Factory insurance	8,360		
Total manufacturing overhead		54,800	
Total manufacturing costs			376,800
Total cost of work in process			395,200
Less: Work in process, December 31			25,200
Cost of goods manufactured			$370,000

Illustration 1A-1   Cost of goods manufactured schedule

Work Sheet

When a work sheet is used in preparing financial statements, two additional columns are needed for the cost of goods manufactured schedule. As illustrated in the work sheet in Illustration 1A-2, debit and credit columns for this schedule are inserted before the income statement columns.

Illustration 1A-2 Partial work sheet

	Adjusted Trial Balance		Cost of Goods Manufactured		Income Statement		Balance Sheet	
	Dr.	Cr.	Dr.	Cr.	Dr.	Cr.	Dr.	Cr.
Cash	42,500						42,500	
Accounts Receivable (Net)	71,900						71,900	
Finished Goods Inv.	24,600				24,600	19,500	19,500	
Work in Process Inv.	18,400		18,400	25,200			25,200	
Raw Material Inv.	16,700		16,700	22,800			22,800	
Plant Assets	724,000						724,000	
Accumulated Depr.		278,400						278,400
Notes Payable		100,000						100,000
Accounts Payable		40,000						40,000
Income Taxes Payable		5,000						5,000
Common Stock		200,000						200,000
Retained Earnings		205,100						205,100
Sales		680,000				680,000		
Raw Materials Purchases	152,500		152,500					
Direct Labor	175,600		175,600					
Indirect Labor	14,300		14,300					
Factory Repairs	12,600		12,600					
Factory Utilities	10,100		10,100					
Factory Depreciation	9,440		9,440					
Factory Insurance	8,360		8,360					
Selling Expenses	114,900				114,900			
Administrative Exp.	92,600				92,600			
Income Tax Exp.	20,000				20,000			
Totals	1,508,500	1,508,500	418,000	48,000				
Cost of Goods Manufactured				370,000	370,000			
Totals			418,000	418,000	622,100	699,500	905,900	828,500
Net Income					77,400			77,400
Totals					699,500	699,500	905,900	905,900

In the cost of goods manufactured columns, the beginning inventories of raw materials and work in process are entered as debits. In addition, all of the manufacturing costs are entered as debits. The reason is that each of these amounts increases cost of goods manufactured. Ending inventories for raw materials and work in process are entered as credits in the cost of goods manufactured columns because they have the opposite effect—they decrease cost of goods manufactured. The balancing amount for these columns is the cost of goods manufactured. Note that the amount ($370,000) agrees with the amount reported for cost of goods manufactured in Illustration 1A-1. This amount is also entered in the income statement debit column.

The income statement and balance sheet columns for a manufacturing company are basically the same as for a merchandising company. For example, the treatment of the finished goods inventories is identical with the treatment of merchandise inventory. That is, the beginning inventory is entered in the debit column of the income statement, and the ending finished goods inventory is entered in the income statement credit column as well as in the balance sheet debit column.

As in the case of a merchandising company, financial statements for a manufacturing company can be prepared from the statement columns of the work sheet. In addition, the cost of goods manufactured schedule can also be prepared directly from the work sheet.

Closing Entries

The closing entries are different for manufacturing and merchandising companies. **A Manufacturing Summary account is used to close all accounts that appear in the cost of goods manufactured schedule.** The balance of the Manufacturing Summary account is the Cost of Goods Manufactured for the period. Manufacturing Summary is then closed to Income Summary.

The closing entries can be prepared from the work sheet. As illustrated below, the closing entries for the manufacturing accounts are prepared first. The closing entries for Olsen Manufacturing are as follows.

Dec. 31	Work in Process Inventory (Dec. 31)	25,200	
	Raw Materials Inventory (Dec. 31)	22,800	
	Manufacturing Summary		**48,000**
	(To record ending raw materials and work in process inventories)		
31	**Manufacturing Summary**	**418,000**	
	Work in Process Inventory (Jan. 1)		18,400
	Raw Materials Inventory (Jan. 1)		16,700
	Raw Materials Purchases		152,500
	Direct Labor		175,600
	Indirect Labor		14,300
	Factory Repairs		12,600
	Factory Utilities		10,100
	Factory Depreciation		9,440
	Factory Insurance		8,360
	(To close beginning raw materials and work in process inventories and manufacturing cost accounts)		
31	Finished Goods Inventory (Dec. 31)	19,500	
	Sales	680,000	
	Income Summary		699,500
	(To record ending finished goods inventory and close sales account)		
31	Income Summary	622,100	
	Finished Goods Inventory (Jan. 1)		24,600
	Manufacturing Summary		**370,000**
	Selling Expenses		114,900
	Administrative Expenses		92,600
	Income Tax Expense		20,000
	(To close beginning finished goods inventory, manufacturing summary, and expense accounts)		

(*The closing entries continue on the next page.*)

31	Income Summary	77,400	
	Retained Earnings		77,400
	(To close net income to retained earnings)		

After posting, the summary accounts will show the following.

Illustration 1A-3 Summary accounts for a manufacturing company, after posting

Manufacturing Summary

| Dec. 31 | Close | 418,000 | Dec. 31 | Close | 48,000 |
| | | | 31 | Close | 370,000 |

Income Summary

| Dec. 31 | Close | 622,100 | Dec. 31 | Close | 699,500 |
| 31 | Close | 77,400 | | | |

It also would be possible to post each account balance to the Manufacturing Summary account.

Summary of Study Objective for Appendix

9 *Prepare a work sheet and closing entries for a manufacturing company.* Two additional columns are needed in the work sheet for the cost of goods manufactured. In these columns, the beginning inventories of raw materials and work in process are entered as debits, and the ending inventories are entered as credits. All manufacturing costs are entered as debits. To close all of the accounts that appear in the cost of goods manufactured schedule, a Manufacturing Summary account is used.

Glossary

Activity-based costing (ABC) A method of allocating overhead based on each product's use of activities in making the product. (p. 20)

Balanced scorecard A performance-measurement approach that uses both financial and nonfinancial measures, tied to company objectives, to evaluate a company's operations in an integrated fashion. (p. 21)

Board of directors The group of officials elected by the stockholders of a corporation to formulate operating policies, select officers, and otherwise manage the company. (p. 7)

Chief executive officer (CEO) Corporate officer who has overall responsibility for managing the business and delegates that responsibility to other corporate officers. (p. 7)

Chief financial officer (CFO) Corporate officer who is responsible for all of the accounting and finance issues of the company. (p. 7)

Controller Financial officer responsible for a company's accounting records, system of internal control, and preparation of financial statements, tax returns, and internal reports. (p. 7)

Cost of goods manufactured Total cost of work in process less the cost of the ending work in process inventory. (p. 13)

Direct labor The work of factory employees that can be physically and directly associated with converting raw materials into finished goods. (p. 10)

Direct materials Raw materials that can be physically and directly associated with manufacturing the finished product. (p. 9)

Enterprise resource planning (ERP) system Software that provides a comprehensive, centralized, integrated source of information used to manage all major business processes. (p. 19)

Indirect labor Work of factory employees that has no physical association with the finished product, or for which it is impractical to trace the costs to the goods produced. (p. 10)

Indirect materials Raw materials that do not physically become part of the finished product or cannot be traced because their physical association with the finished product is too small. (p. 10)

Just-in-time (JIT) inventory Inventory system in which goods are manufactured or purchased just in time for use. (p. 20)

Line positions Jobs that are directly involved in a company's primary revenue-generating operating activities. (p. 7)

Managerial accounting A field of accounting that provides economic and financial information for managers and other internal users. (p. 3)

Manufacturing overhead Manufacturing costs that are indirectly associated with the manufacture of the finished product. (p. 10)

Period costs Costs that are matched with the revenue of a specific time period and charged to expense as incurred. (p. 11)

Product costs Costs that are a necessary and integral part of producing the finished product. (p. 11)

Staff positions Jobs that support the efforts of line employees. (p. 7)

Theory of constraints A specific approach used to identify and manage constraints in order to achieve the company's goals. (p. 21)

Total cost of work in process Cost of the beginning work in process plus total manufacturing costs for the current period. (p. 13)

Total manufacturing costs The sum of direct materials, direct labor, and manufacturing overhead incurred in the current period. (p. 13)

Total quality management (TQM) Systems implemented to reduce defects in finished products with the goal of achieving zero defects. (p. 20)

Treasurer Financial officer responsible for custody of a company's funds and for maintaining its cash position. (p. 7)

Value chain All activities associated with providing a product or service. (p. 19)

Demonstration Problem

Superior Manufacturing Company has the following cost and expense data for the year ending December 31, 2005.

Raw materials, 1/1/05	$ 30,000	Insurance, factory	$ 14,000
Raw materials, 12/31/05	20,000	Property taxes, factory building	6,000
Raw materials purchases	205,000	Sales (net)	1,500,000
Indirect materials	15,000	Delivery expenses	100,000
Work in process, 1/1/05	80,000	Sales commissions	150,000
Work in process, 12/31/05	50,000	Indirect labor	90,000
Finished goods, 1/1/05	110,000	Factory machinery rent	40,000
Finished goods, 12/31/05	120,000	Factory utilities	65,000
Direct labor	350,000	Depreciation, factory building	24,000
Factory manager's salary	35,000	Administrative expenses	300,000

Instructions
(a) Prepare a cost of goods manufactured schedule for Superior Company for 2005.
(b) Prepare an income statement for Superior Company for 2005.
(c) Assume that Superior Company's ledgers show the balances of the following current asset accounts: Cash $17,000, Accounts Receivable (net) $120,000, Prepaid Expenses $13,000, and Short-term Investments $26,000. Prepare the current assets section of the balance sheet for Superior Company as of December 31, 2005.

Demonstration Problems are a final review before you begin homework. An **Action Plan** that appears in the margin (next page) gives you tips about how to approach the problem, and the **Solution** provided (next page) demonstrates both the form and content of complete answers.

The Web icon (on the left, above) indicates there is an additional Demonstration Problem at the book's Web site.

The spreadsheet icon (on the right, above) indicates there is an Excel spreadsheet template for this problem at the book's Web site.

Action Plan

• Start with beginning work in process as the first item in the cost of goods manufactured schedule.

• Sum direct materials used, direct labor, and total manufacturing overhead to determine total manufacturing costs.

• Sum beginning work in process and total manufacturing costs to determine total cost of work in process.

• Cost of goods manufactured is the total cost of work in process less ending work in process.

• In the cost of goods sold section of the income statement, show beginning and ending finished goods inventory and cost of goods manufactured.

• In the balance sheet, list manufacturing inventories in the order of their expected realization in cash, with finished goods first.

Solution to Demonstration Problem

(a)

SUPERIOR MANUFACTURING COMPANY
Cost of Goods Manufactured Schedule
For the Year Ended December 31, 2005

Work in process, 1/1			$ 80,000
Direct materials			
Raw materials inventory, 1/1	$ 30,000		
Raw materials purchases	205,000		
Total raw materials available for use	235,000		
Less: Raw materials inventory, 12/31	20,000		
Direct materials used		$215,000	
Direct labor		350,000	
Manufacturing overhead			
Indirect labor	90,000		
Factory utilities	65,000		
Factory machinery rent	40,000		
Factory manager's salary	35,000		
Depreciation on building	24,000		
Indirect materials	15,000		
Factory insurance	14,000		
Property taxes	6,000		
Total manufacturing overhead		289,000	
Total manufacturing costs			854,000
Total cost of work in process			934,000
Less: Work in process, 12/31			50,000
Cost of goods manufactured			$884,000

(b)

SUPERIOR MANUFACTURING COMPANY
Income Statement
For the Year Ended December 31, 2005

Sales (net)		$1,500,000
Cost of goods sold		
Finished goods inventory, January 1	$110,000	
Cost of goods manufactured	884,000	
Cost of goods available for sale	994,000	
Less: Finished goods inventory, December 31	120,000	
Cost of goods sold		874,000
Gross profit		626,000
Operating expenses		
Administrative expenses	300,000	
Sales commissions	150,000	
Delivery expenses	100,000	
Total operating expenses		550,000
Net income		$ 76,000

(c)
SUPERIOR MANUFACTURING COMPANY
Balance Sheet (partial)
December 31, 2005

Current assets

Cash		$ 17,000
Short-term investments		26,000
Accounts receivable (net)		120,000
Inventories		
Finished goods	$120,000	
Work in process	50,000	
Raw materials	20,000	190,000
Prepaid expenses		13,000
Total current assets		$366,000

☑ THE NAVIGATOR

This would be a good time to return to the **Student Owner's Manual** at the beginning of the book (or look at it for the first time if you skipped it before) to read about the various types of homework materials that appear at the ends of chapters. Knowing the purpose of different assignments will help you appreciate what each contributes to your accounting skills and competencies.

Note: All asterisked Questions, Exercises, and Problems relate to material in the appendix to the chapter.

Self-Study Questions

Self-Study/Self-Test

(SO 1)   Answers are at the end of the chapter.

1. Managerial accounting:
   (a) is governed by generally accepted accounting principles.
   (b) places emphasis on special-purpose information.
   (c) pertains to the entity as a whole and is highly aggregated.
   (d) is limited to cost data.

(SO 2)   2. The management of an organization performs several broad functions. They are:
   (a) planning, directing, and selling.
   (b) planning, directing, and controlling.
   (c) planning, manufacturing, and controlling.
   (d) directing, manufacturing, and controlling.

(SO 3)   3. Direct materials are a:

	Product Cost	Manufacturing Overhead	Period Cost
(a)	Yes	Yes	No
(b)	Yes	No	No
(c)	Yes	Yes	Yes
(d)	No	No	No

(SO 4)   4. Indirect labor is a:
   (a) nonmanufacturing cost.
   (b) raw material cost.
   (c) product cost.
   (d) period cost.

(SO 3)   5. Which of the following costs would be included in manufacturing overhead of a computer manufacturer?

   (a) The cost of the disk drives.
   (b) The wages earned by computer assemblers.
   (c) The cost of the memory chips.
   (d) Depreciation on testing equipment.

(SO 3)   6. Which of the following is *not* an element of manufacturing overhead?
   (a) Sales manager's salary.
   (b) Plant manager's salary.
   (c) Factory repairman's wages.
   (d) Product inspector's salary.

(SO 5)   7. For the year, Redder Company has cost of goods manufactured of $600,000, beginning finished goods inventory of $200,000, and ending finished goods inventory of $250,000. The cost of goods sold is:
   (a) $450,000.
   (b) $500,000.
   (c) $550,000.
   (d) $600,000.

(SO 6)   8. A cost of goods manufactured schedule shows beginning and ending inventories for:
   (a) raw materials and work in process only.
   (b) work in process only.
   (c) raw materials only.
   (d) raw materials, work in process, and finished goods.

(SO 7)   9. In a manufacturer's balance sheet, three inventories may be reported: (1) raw materials, (2) work in process, and (3) finished goods. Indicate

in what sequence these inventories generally appear on a balance sheet.
(a) (1), (2), (3)
(b) (2), (3), (1)
(c) (3), (1), (2)
(d) (3), (2), (1)

10. Which of the following managerial accounting techniques attempts to allocate manufacturing overhead in a more meaningful fashion? (SO 8)
(a) Just-in-time inventory.
(b) Total-quality management.
(c) Theory of constraints.
(d) Activity-based costing.

Questions

1. (a) "Managerial accounting is a field of accounting that provides economic information for all interested parties." Do you agree? Explain.
   (b) Tina Turner believes that managerial accounting serves only manufacturing firms. Is Tina correct? Explain.

2. Distinguish between managerial and financial accounting as to (a) primary users of reports, (b) types and frequency of reports, and (c) purpose of reports.

3. How does the content of reports and the verification of reports differ between managerial and financial accounting?

4. In what ways can the budgeting process create incentives for unethical behavior?

5. Kent Krause is studying for the next accounting midterm examination. Summarize for Kent what he should know about management functions.

6. "Decision making is management's most important function." Do you agree? Why or why not?

7. Explain the primary difference between line positions and staff positions, and give examples of each.

8. What new rules were enacted under the Sarbanes-Oxley Act to address unethical accounting practices?

9. Alan Bruski is studying for his next accounting examination. Explain to Alan what he should know about the differences between the income statements for a manufacturing and for a merchandising company.

10. Sandy Cesska is unclear as to the difference between the balance sheets of a merchandising company and a manufacturing company. Explain the difference to Sandy.

11. How are manufacturing costs classified?

12. Tony Siebers claims that the distinction between direct and indirect materials is based entirely on physical association with the product. Is Tony correct? Why?

13. Trenton Hipp is confused about the differences between a product cost and a period cost. Explain the differences to Trenton.

14. Identify the differences in the cost of goods sold section of an income statement between a merchandising company and a manufacturing company.

15. The determination of the cost of goods manufactured involves the following factors: (A) beginning work in process inventory, (B) total manufacturing costs, and (C) ending work in process inventory. Identify the meaning of x in the following formulas:
(a) $A + B = x$
(b) $A + B - C = x$

16. Gruber Manufacturing has beginning raw materials inventory $12,000, ending raw materials inventory $15,000, and raw materials purchases $180,000. What is the cost of direct materials used?

17. Jelk Manufacturing Inc. has beginning work in process $26,000, direct materials used $240,000, direct labor $200,000, total manufacturing overhead $150,000, and ending work in process $32,000. What are total manufacturing costs?

18. Using the data in Q17, what are (a) the total cost of work in process and (b) the cost of goods manufactured?

19. In what order should manufacturing inventories be listed in a balance sheet?

20. What is the value chain? Describe, in sequence, the main components of a manufacturer's value chain.

21. What is an enterprise resource planning (ERP) system? What are its primary benefits?

22. Why is product quality important for companies that implement a just-in-time inventory system?

23. Explain what is meant by "balanced" in the balanced scorecard approach.

24. What is activity-based costing, and what are its potential benefits?

*25. How, if at all, does the accounting cycle differ between a manufacturing company and a merchandising company?

*26. What typical account balances are carried into the cost of goods manufactured columns of the manufacturing work sheet?

*27. Prepare the closing entries for (a) ending work in process and raw materials inventories and (b) manufacturing summary. Use XXXs for amounts.

Brief Exercises

BE1-1 Complete the following comparison table between managerial and financial accounting.

	Financial Accounting	Managerial Accounting
Primary users		
Types of reports		
Frequency of reports		
Purpose of reports		
Content of reports		
Verification		

Distinguish between managerial and financial accounting.
(SO 1)

BE1-2 The Sarbanes Oxley Act of 2002 (SOX) has important implications for the financial community. Explain two implications of SOX.

Identify important regulatory changes.
(SO 2)

BE1-3 Listed below are the three functions of the management of an organization.

1. Planning   2. Directing   3. Controlling

Identify the three management functions.
(SO 2)

Identify which of the following statements best describes each of the above functions.
(a) ____ require(s) management to look ahead and to establish objectives. A key objective of management is to add value to the business.
(b) ____ involve(s) coordinating the diverse activities and human resources of a company to produce a smooth-running operation. This function relates to the implementation of planned objectives.
(c) ____ is the process of keeping the activities on track. Management must determine whether goals are being met and what changes are necessary when there are deviations.

BE1-4 Determine whether each of the following costs should be classified as direct materials (DM), direct labor (DL), or manufacturing overhead (MO).
(a) ____Frames and tires used in manufacturing bicycles.
(b) ____Wages paid to production workers.
(c) ____Insurance on factory equipment and machinery.
(d) ____Depreciation on factory equipment.

Classify manufacturing costs.
(SO 3)

BE1-5 Indicate whether each of the following costs of an automobile manufacturer would be classified as direct materials, direct labor, or manufacturing overhead.
(a) ____Windshield.   (e) ____Factory machinery lubricants.
(b) ____Engine.   (f) ____Tires.
(c) ____Wages of assembly line worker.   (g) ____Steering wheel.
(d) ____Depreciation of factory machinery. (h) ____Salary of painting supervisor.

Classify manufacturing costs.
(SO 3)

BE1-6 Identify whether each of the following costs should be classified as product costs or period costs.
(a) ____Manufacturing overhead.   (d) ____Advertising expenses.
(b) ____Selling expenses.   (e) ____Direct labor.
(c) ____Administrative expenses.   (f) ____Direct material.

Identify product and period costs.
(SO 4)

BE1-7 Presented below are Apex Company's monthly manufacturing cost data related to its personal computer products.
(a) Utilities for manufacturing equipment $116,000
(b) Raw material (CPU, chips, etc.) $85,000
(c) Depreciation on manufacturing building $880,000
(d) Wages for production workers $191,000

Classify manufacturing costs.
(SO 3)

Enter each cost item in the following table, placing an "X" under the appropriate headings.

	Product Costs		
	Direct Materials	Direct Labor	Factory Overhead
(a)			
(b)			
(c)			
(d)			

Compute total manufacturing costs and total cost of work in process.
(SO 6)

BE1-8 Sielert Manufacturing Company has the following data: direct labor $249,000, direct materials used $180,000, total manufacturing overhead $208,000, and beginning work in process $25,000. Compute (a) total manufacturing costs and (b) total cost of work in process.

Prepare current assets section.
(SO 7)

BE1-9 In alphabetical order below are current asset items for Osgood Company's balance sheet at December 31, 2005. Prepare the current assets section (including a complete heading).

Accounts receivable	$200,000
Cash	62,000
Finished goods	71,000
Prepaid expenses	38,000
Raw materials	68,000
Work in process	87,000

Determine missing amounts in computing total manufacturing costs.
(SO 6)

BE1-10 Presented below are incomplete manufacturing cost data. Determine the missing amounts for three different situations.

	Direct Materials Used	Direct Labor Used	Factory Overhead	Total Manufacturing Costs
(1)	$35,000	$61,000	$ 50,000	?
(2)	?	$75,000	$140,000	$296,000
(3)	$55,000	?	$111,000	$300,000

Determine missing amounts in computing cost of goods manufactured.
(SO 6)

BE1-11 Use the same data from BE1–10 above and the data below. Determine the missing amounts.

	Total Manufacturing Costs	Work in Process (1/1)	Work in Process (12/31)	Cost of Goods Manufactured
(1)	?	$120,000	$82,000	?
(2)	$296,000	?	$98,000	$321,000
(3)	$300,000	$463,000	?	$715,000

Identify work sheet columns for selected accounts.
(SO 8)

*BE1-12 A work sheet is used in preparing financial statements for Table Manufacturing Company. The following accounts are included in the adjusted trial balance: Finished Goods Inventory $28,000, Work in Process Inventory $21,600, Raw Materials Purchases $175,000, and Direct Labor $140,000. Indicate the work sheet column(s) to which each account should be extended.

Exercises

Identify positions within organizational structure.
(SO 2)

E1-1 The following is a list of terms related to a company's organizational structure.

1. Board of directors.
2. Chief financial officer.
3. Treasurer.
4. Controller.
5. Line position.
6. Chief executive officer.
7. Staff position.

Instructions
Match each of the above terms with the statement below that best describes the term.

(a) ____ Employee who has overall responsibility for managing the business.
(b) ____ Employees who are directly involved in the company's primary revenue-generating activities.
(c) ____ Employee with overall responsibility for all accounting and finance issues.

(d) ____ Group of people elected by the shareholders that selects and oversees company officers and formulates operating policies.

(e) ____ Employees who provide support services to those employees who are directly involved in the company's primary revenue-generating activities.

(f) ____ Employee who maintains accounting records and system of internal controls and prepares financial statements, tax returns, and internal reports.

(g) ____ Employee who has custody of the company's funds and maintains company's cash position.

E1-2 Presented below is a list of costs and expenses usually incurred by Burrand Corporation, a manufacturer of furniture, in its factory.

Classify costs into three classes of manufacturing costs.
(SO 3)

1. Salaries for assembly line inspectors.
2. Insurance on factory machines.
3. Property taxes on the factory building.
4. Factory repairs.
5. Upholstery used in manufacturing furniture.
6. Wages paid to assembly line workers.
7. Factory machinery depreciation.
8. Glue, nails, paint, and other small parts used in production.
9. Factory supervisors' salaries.
10. Wood used in manufacturing furniture.

Instructions
Classify the above items into the following categories: (a) direct materials, (b) direct labor, and (c) manufacturing overhead.

E1-3 Caroline Company reports the following costs and expenses in May.

Determine the total amount of various types of costs.
(SO 3, 4)

Factory utilities	$ 8,500	Direct labor	$69,100
Depreciation on factory equipment	12,650	Sales salaries	49,400
Depreciation on delivery trucks	3,800	Property taxes on factory building	2,500
Indirect factory labor	48,900	Repairs to office equipment	1,300
Indirect materials	80,800	Factory repairs	2,000
Direct materials used	137,600	Advertising	18,000
Factory manager's salary	8,000	Office supplies used	2,640

Instructions
From the information, determine the total amount of:
(a) Manufacturing overhead.
(b) Product costs.
(c) Period costs.

E1-4 Sota Company is a manufacturer of personal computers. Various costs and expenses associated with its operations are as follows.

Classify various costs into different cost categories.
(SO 3, 4)

1. Property taxes on the factory building.
2. Production superintendents' salaries.
3. Memory boards and chips used in assembling computers.
4. Depreciation on the factory equipment.
5. Salaries for assembly line quality control inspectors.
6. Sales commissions paid to sell personal computers.
7. Electrical components used in assembling computers.
8. Wages of workers assembling personal computers.
9. Soldering materials used on factory assembly lines.
10. Salaries for the night security guards for the factory building.

The company intends to classify these costs and expenses into the following categories:
(a) direct materials, (b) direct labor, (c) manufacturing overhead, and (d) period costs.

Classify various costs into different cost categories.
(SO 3)

Homework materials related to **service companies** are indicated by this icon.

Instructions
List the items (1) through (10). For each item, indicate the cost category to which it belongs.

E1-5   The administrators of San Diego County's Memorial Hospital are interested in identifying the various costs and expenses that are incurred in producing a patient's X-ray. A list of such costs and expenses in presented below.

1. Salaries for the X-ray machine technicians.
2. Wages for the hospital janitorial personnel.
3. Film costs for the X-ray machines.
4. Property taxes on the hospital building.
5. Salary of the X-ray technicians' supervisor.
6. Electricity costs for the X-ray department.
7. Maintenance and repairs on the X-ray machines.
8. X-ray department supplies.
9. Depreciation on the X-ray department equipment.
10. Depreciation on the hospital building.

The administrators want these costs and expenses classified as: (a) direct materials, (b) direct labor, or (c) service overhead.

Instructions
List the items (1) through (10). For each item, indicate the cost category to which the item belongs.

Classify various costs into different cost categories.
(SO 4)

E1-6   Rapid Delivery Service reports the following costs and expenses in June 2005.

Indirect materials	$ 5,400	Drivers' salaries	$ 8,000
Depreciation on delivery		Advertising	1,600
equipment	11,200	Delivery equipment	
Dispatcher's salary	5,000	repairs	300
Property taxes on office		Office supplies	650
building	870	Office utilities	990
CEO's salary	10,000	Repairs on office	
Gas and oil for delivery trucks	2,200	equipment	180

Instructions
Determine the total amount of (a) delivery service (product) costs and (b) period costs.

Determine missing amounts in cost of goods manufactured schedule.
(SO 6)

E1-7   An incomplete cost of goods manufactured schedule is presented below.

MADLOCK MANUFACTURING COMPANY
Cost of Goods Manufactured Schedule
For the Year Ended December 31, 2005

Work in process (1/1)			$210,000
Direct materials			
Raw materials inventory (1/1)	$?		
Add: Raw materials purchases	158,000		
Total raw materials available for use	?		
Less: Raw materials inventory (12/31)	7,500		
Direct materials used		$190,000	
Direct labor		?	
Manufacturing overhead			
Indirect labor	$ 18,000		
Factory depreciation	36,000		
Factory utilities	68,000		
Total overhead		122,000	
Total manufacturing costs			?
Total cost of work in process			?
Less: Work in process (12/31)			81,000
Cost of goods manufactured			$530,000

Instructions
Complete the cost of goods manufactured schedule for Madlock Manufacturing Company.

E1-8 Manufacturing cost data for Darlinda Company are presented below.

Determine the missing amount of different cost items.
(SO 6)

	Case A	Case B	Case C
Direct materials used	(a)	$68,400	$130,000
Direct labor	$ 57,000	86,000	(g)
Manufacturing overhead	46,500	81,600	102,000
Total manufacturing costs	180,650	(d)	253,700
Work in process 1/1/05	(b)	16,500	(h)
Total cost of work in process	221,500	(e)	327,000
Work in process 12/31/05	(c)	11,000	70,000
Cost of goods manufactured	185,275	(f)	(i)

Instructions

Indicate the missing amount for each letter (a) through (i).

E1-9 Incomplete manufacturing cost data for Motta Company for 2005 are presented as follows for four different situations.

Determine the missing amount of different cost items, and prepare a condensed cost of goods manufactured schedule.
(SO 6)

	Direct Materials Used	Direct Labor Used	Manufacturing Overhead	Total Manufacturing Costs	Work in Process 1/1	Work in Process 12/31	Cost of Goods Manufactured
(1)	$117,000	$140,000	$ 77,000	(a)	$33,000	(b)	$360,000
(2)	(c)	200,000	132,000	$440,000	(d)	$40,000	470,000
(3)	80,000	100,000	(e)	255,000	60,000	80,000	(f)
(4)	70,000	(g)	75,000	288,000	45,000	(h)	270,000

Instructions

(a) Indicate the missing amount for each letter.
(b) Prepare a condensed cost of goods manufactured schedule for situation (1) for the year ended December 31, 2005.

E1-10 Berger Corporation has the following cost records for June 2005.

Prepare a cost of goods manufactured schedule and a partial income statement.
(SO 5, 6)

Indirect factory labor	$ 4,500	Factory utilities	$ 400
Direct materials used	20,000	Depreciation, factory equipment	1,400
Work in process, 6/1/05	3,000	Direct labor	25,000
Work in process, 6/30/05	3,800	Maintenance, factory equipment	1,800
Finished goods, 6/1/05	5,000	Indirect materials	2,200
Finished goods, 6/30/05	7,500	Factory manager's salary	3,000

Instructions

(a) Prepare a cost of goods manufactured schedule for June 2005.
(b) Prepare an income statement through gross profit for June 2005 assuming net sales are $97,100.

E1-11 Jill Blinton, the bookkeeper for Dewey, Cheatum, and Howe, a political consulting firm, has recently completed a managerial accounting course at her local college. One of the topics covered in the course was the cost of goods manufactured schedule. Jill wondered if such a schedule could be prepared for her firm. She realized that, as a service-oriented company, it would have no Work-in-Process inventory to consider.

Classify various costs into different categories and prepare cost of services provided schedule.
(SO 4, 5, 6)

Listed below are the costs her firm incurred for the month ended August 31, 2005.

Supplies used on consulting contracts	$ 1,200
Supplies used in the administrative offices	1,500
Depreciation on equipment used for contract work	900
Depreciation used on administrative office equipment	1,050
Salaries of professionals working on contracts	12,600
Salaries of administrative office personnel	7,700
Janitorial services for professional offices	400
Janitorial services for administrative offices	500
Insurance on contract operations	800
Insurance on administrative operations	900
Utilities for contract operations	1,100
Utilities for administrative offices	1,300

Instructions
(a) Prepare a schedule of cost of contract services provided (similar to a cost of goods manufactured schedule) for the month.
(b) For those costs not included in (a), explain how they would be classified and reported in the financial statements.

Indicate in which schedule or financial statement(s) different cost items will appear.
(SO 5, 6, 7)

E1-12 Marla Manufacturing Company produces blankets. From its accounting records it prepares the following schedule and financial statements on a yearly basis.
(a) Cost of goods manufactured schedule.
(b) Income statement.
(c) Balance sheet.

The following items are found in its ledger and accompanying data.

1. Direct labor
2. Raw materials inventory, 1/1
3. Work in process inventory, 12/31
4. Finished goods inventory, 1/1
5. Indirect labor
6. Depreciation on factory machinery
7. Work in process, 1/1
8. Finished goods inventory, 12/31
9. Factory maintenance salaries
10. Cost of goods manufactured
11. Depreciation on delivery equipment
12. Cost of goods available for sale
13. Direct materials used
14. Heat and electricity for factory
15. Repairs to roof of factory building
16. Cost of raw materials purchases

Instructions
List the items (1)–(16). For each item, indicate by using the appropriate letter or letters, the schedule and/or financial statement(s) in which the item will appear.

Prepare a cost of goods manufactured schedule, and present the ending inventories of the balance sheet.
(SO 6, 7)

E1-13 An analysis of the accounts of Yellow Knife Manufacturing reveals the following manufacturing cost data for the month ended June 30, 2005.

Inventories	Beginning	Ending
Raw materials	$9,000	$13,100
Work in process	5,000	8,000
Finished goods	9,000	6,000

Costs incurred: Raw materials purchases $64,000, direct labor $57,000, manufacturing overhead $19,900. The specific overhead costs were: indirect labor $5,500, factory insurance $4,000, machinery depreciation $4,000, machinery repairs $1,800, factory utilities $3,100, miscellaneous factory costs $1,500. Assume that all raw materials used were direct materials.

Instructions
(a) Prepare the cost of goods manufactured schedule for the month ended June 30, 2005.
(b) Show the presentation of the ending inventories on the June 30, 2005, balance sheet.

Determine the amount of cost to appear in various accounts, and indicate in which financial statements these accounts would appear.
(SO 5, 6, 7)

E1-14 Kam Motor Company manufactures automobiles. During September 2005 the company purchased 5,000 head lamps at a cost of $9 per lamp. Kam withdrew 4,650 lamps from the warehouse during the month. Fifty of these lamps were used to replace the head lamps in autos used by traveling sales staff. The remaining 4,600 lamps were put in autos manufactured during the month.

Of the autos put into production during September 2005, 90% were completed and transferred to the company's storage lot. Of the cars completed during the month, 75% were sold by September 30.

Instructions
(a) Determine the cost of head lamps that would appear in each of the following accounts at September 30, 2005: Raw Materials, Work in Process, Finished Goods, Cost of Goods Sold, and Selling Expenses.
(b) ▭▭▭▷ Write a short memo to the chief accountant, indicating whether and where each of the accounts in (a) would appear on the income statement or on the balance sheet at September 30, 2005.

Identify various managerial accounting practices.
(SO 8)

E1-15 The following is a list of terms related to managerial accounting practices.

1. Theory of constraints.
2. Activity-based costing.
3. Just-in-time inventory.

4. Balanced scorecard.
5. Value chain.
6. Enterprise resource planning (ERP).

Instructions
Match each of the terms with the statement below that best describes the term.

(a) ____ A system that provides a comprehensive, centralized, integrated source of information used to manage all major business processes.
(b) ____ The group of activities associated with providing a product or service.
(c) ____ An approach used to reduce the cost associated with handling and holding inventory by reducing the amount of inventory on hand.
(d) ____ A method used to allocate overhead to products based on each product's use of the activities that cause the incurrence of the overhead cost.
(e) ____ An approach used to identify those factors that limit a company's productive capacity and to address those limitations so as to maximize profitability.
(f) ____ A performance-measurement technique that attempts to consider and evaluate all aspects of performance using financial and nonfinancial measures in an integrated fashion.

*E1-16 Data for Yellowknife Manufacturing are presented in E1-13.

Prepare a partial worksheet for a manufacturing firm. (SO 9)

Instructions
Beginning with the adjusted trial balance, prepare a partial work sheet for Yellowknife Manufacturing using the format shown in Illustration 1A-2.

Problems: Set A

P1-1A Lair Company specializes in manufacturing motorcycle helmets. The company has enough orders to keep the factory production at 1,000 motorcycle helmets per month. Lair's monthly manufacturing cost and other expense data are as follows.

Classify manufacturing costs into different categories and compute the unit cost. (SO 3, 4)

Maintenance costs on factory building	$ 300
Factory manager's salary	4,000
Advertising for helmets	10,000
Sales commissions	3,000
Depreciation on factory building	700
Rent on factory equipment	6,000
Insurance on factory building	3,000
Raw materials (plastic, polystyrene, etc.)	20,000
Utility costs for factory	800
Supplies for general office	200
Wages for assembly line workers	44,000
Depreciation on office equipment	500
Miscellaneous materials (glue, thread, etc.)	2,000

Instructions
(a) Prepare an answer sheet with the following column headings.

(a) DM $20,000
DL $44,000
MO $16,800
PC $13,700

		Product Costs		
Cost Item	**Direct Materials**	**Direct Labor**	**Manufacturing Overhead**	**Period Costs**

Enter each cost item on your answer sheet, placing the dollar amount under the appropriate headings. Total the dollar amounts in each of the columns.
(b) Compute the cost to produce one motorcycle helmet.

P1-2A Tomlin Company, a manufacturer of tennis rackets, started production in November 2005. For the preceding 5 years Tomlin had been a retailer of sports equipment. After a thorough survey of tennis racket markets, Tomlin decided to turn its retail store into a tennis racket factory.

Classify manufacturing costs into different categories and compute the unit cost. (SO 3, 4)

Raw materials cost for a tennis racket will total $23 per racket. Workers on the production lines are paid on average $13 per hour. A racket usually takes 2 hours to complete. In addition, the rent on the equipment used to produce rackets amounts to $1,300 per month. Indirect materials cost $3 per racket. A supervisor was hired to oversee production; her monthly salary is $3,500.

Janitorial costs are $1,400 monthly. Advertising costs for the rackets will be $6,000 per month. The factory building depreciation expense is $8,400 per year. Property taxes on the factory building will be $4,320 per year.

Instructions

(a) DM $46,000
DL $52,000
MO $13,260
PC $ 6,000

(a) Prepare an answer sheet with the following column headings.

	Product Costs			
Cost Item	Direct Materials	Direct Labor	Manufacturing Overhead	Period Costs

Assuming that Tomlin manufactures, on average, 2,000 tennis rackets per month, enter each cost item on your answer sheet, placing the dollar amount per month under the appropriate headings. Total the dollar amounts in each of the columns.
(b) Compute the cost to produce one racket.

Indicate the missing amount of different cost items, and prepare a condensed cost of goods manufactured schedule, an income statement, and a partial balance sheet.
(SO 5, 6, 7)

P1-3A Incomplete manufacturing costs, expenses, and selling data for two different cases are as follows.

	Case	
	1	2
Direct Materials Used	$ 8,300	$ (g)
Direct Labor	3,000	4,000
Manufacturing Overhead	6,000	5,000
Total Manufacturing Costs	(a)	20,000
Beginning Work in Process Inventory	1,000	(h)
Ending Work in Process Inventory	(b)	2,000
Sales	22,500	(i)
Sales Discounts	1,500	1,200
Cost of Goods Manufactured	15,800	21,000
Beginning Finished Goods Inventory	(c)	4,000
Goods Available for Sale	17,300	(j)
Cost of Goods Sold	(d)	(k)
Ending Finished Goods Inventory	1,200	2,500
Gross Profit	(e)	6,000
Operating Expenses	2,700	(l)
Net Income	(f)	3,200

Instructions

(a) Indicate the missing amount for each letter.
(b) Prepare a condensed cost of goods manufactured schedule for Case 1.

(c) Current assets $17,600

(c) Prepare an income statement and the current assets section of the balance sheet for Case 1. Assume that in Case 1 the other items in the current assets section are as follows: Cash $3,000, Receivables (net) $10,000, Raw Materials $700, and Prepaid Expenses $200.

Prepare a cost of goods manufactured schedule, a partial income statement, and a partial balance sheet.
(SO 5, 6, 7)

P1-4A The following data were taken from the records of Cruz Manufacturing Company for the year ended December 31, 2005.

Raw Materials		Factory Insurance	$ 7,400
Inventory 1/1/05	$ 47,000	Factory Machinery	
Raw Materials		Depreciation	7,700
Inventory 12/31/05	44,200	Factory Utilities	12,900
Finished Goods		Office Utilities Expense	8,600
Inventory 1/1/05	85,000	Sales	475,000
Finished Goods			
Inventory 12/31/05	77,800		

(Data continue on next page.)

Work in Process		Sales Discounts	2,500
Inventory 1/1/05	9,500	Plant Manager's Salary	30,000
Work in Process		Factory Property Taxes	6,100
Inventory 12/31/05	8,000	Factory Repairs	800
Direct Labor	145,100	Raw Materials Purchases	67,500
Indirect Labor	18,100	Cash	28,000
Accounts Receivable	27,000		

Instructions

(a) Prepare a cost of goods manufactured schedule. (Assume all raw materials used were direct materials.)

(b) Prepare an income statement through gross profit.

(c) Prepare the current assets section of the balance sheet at December 31.

(a) CGM $299,900
(b) Gross profit $165,400
(c) Current assets $185,000

P1-5A   Agler Company is a manufacturer of toys. Its controller, Joyce Rotzen, resigned in August 2005. An inexperienced assistant accountant has prepared the following income statement for the month of August 2005.

Prepare a cost of goods manufactured schedule and a correct income statement.
(SO 5, 6)

AGLER COMPANY
Income Statement
For the Month Ended August 31, 2005

Sales (net)		$675,000
Less: Operating expenses		
Raw materials purchases	$200,000	
Direct labor cost	160,000	
Advertising expense	75,000	
Selling and administrative salaries	70,000	
Rent on factory facilities	60,000	
Depreciation on sales equipment	50,000	
Depreciation on factory equipment	35,000	
Indirect labor cost	20,000	
Utilities expense	10,000	
Insurance expense	5,000	685,000
Net loss		$ (10,000)

Prior to August 2005 the company had been profitable every month. The company's president is concerned about the accuracy of the income statement. As her friend, you have been asked to review the income statement and make necessary corrections. After examining other manufacturing cost data, you have acquired additional information as follows.

1. Inventory balances at the beginning and end of August were:

	August 1	August 31
Raw materials	$19,500	$30,000
Work in process	25,000	21,000
Finished goods	40,000	64,000

2. Only 60% of the utilities expense and 70% of the insurance expense apply to factory operations; the remaining amounts should be charged to selling and administrative activities.

Instructions

(a) Prepare a cost of goods manufactured schedule for August 2005.

(b) Prepare a correct income statement for August 2005.

(a) CGM $478,000
(b) NI $ 20,500

*P1-6A   Medina Manufacturing Company uses a simple manufacturing accounting system. At the end of its fiscal year on August 31, 2005, the adjusted trial balance contains the following accounts.

*Complete a work sheet;
prepare a cost of goods
manufactured schedule, an
income statement, and a
balance sheet; journalize and
post the closing entries.*
(SO 9)

Debits			Credits	
Cash	$	16,700	Accumulated Depreciation	$353,000
Accounts Receivable (net)		62,900	Notes Payable	45,000
Finished Goods Inventory		56,000	Accounts Payable	36,200
Work in Process Inventory		27,800	Income Taxes Payable	9,000
Raw Materials Inventory		37,200	Common Stock	352,000
Plant Assets		890,000	Retained Earnings	205,300
Raw Materials Purchases		236,500	Sales	998,000
Direct Labor		283,900		$1,998,500
Indirect Labor		27,400		
Factory Repairs		17,200		
Factory Depreciation		16,000		
Factory Manager's Salary		40,000		
Factory Insurance		11,000		
Factory Property Taxes		14,900		
Factory Utilities		13,300		
Selling Expenses		96,500		
Administrative Expenses		115,200		
Income Tax Expense		36,000		
		$1,998,500		

Physical inventory accounts on August 31, 2005, show the following inventory amounts:
Finished Goods $50,600, Work in Process $23,400, and Raw Materials $44,500.

Instructions
(a) Enter the adjusted trial balance data on a work sheet in financial statement order
and complete the work sheet.

(b) CGM $657,300
(c) NI $ 87,600

(b) Prepare a cost of goods manufactured schedule for the year.
(c) Prepare an income statement for the year and a balance sheet at August 31, 2005.
(d) Journalize the closing entries.
(e) Post the closing entries to Manufacturing Summary and to Income Summary.

Problems: Set B

*Classify manufacturing costs
into different categories and
compute the unit cost.*
(SO 3, 4)

P1-1B Bjerg Company specializes in manufacturing a unique model of bicycle helmet. The model is well accepted by consumers, and the company has enough orders
to keep the factory production at 10,000 helmets per month (80% of its full capacity). Bjerg's monthly manufacturing cost and other expense data are as follows.

Rent on factory equipment	$ 7,000
Insurance on factory building	1,500
Raw materials (plastics, polystyrene, etc.)	75,000
Utility costs for factory	900
Supplies for general office	300
Wages for assembly line workers	43,000
Depreciation on office equipment	800
Miscellaneous materials (glue, thread, etc.)	1,100
Factory manager's salary	5,700
Property taxes on factory building	400
Advertising for helmets	14,000
Sales commissions	7,000
Depreciation on factory building	1,500

Instructions

(a) DM $75,000
   DL $43,000
   MO $18,100
   PC $22,100

(a) Prepare an answer sheet with the following column headings.

	Product Costs			
Cost Item	Direct Materials	Direct Labor	Manufacturing Overhead	Period Costs

Enter each cost item on your answer sheet, placing the dollar amount under the appropriate headings. Total the dollar amounts in each of the columns.

(b) Compute the cost to produce one helmet

P1-2B Copa Company, a manufacturer of stereo systems, started its production in October 2005. For the preceding 3 years Copa had been a retailer of stereo systems. After a thorough survey of stereo system markets, Copa decided to turn its retail store into a stereo equipment factory.

Classify manufacturing costs into different categories and compute the unit cost.
(SO 3, 4)

Raw materials cost for a stereo system will total $74 per unit. Workers on the production lines are on average paid $12 per hour. A stereo system usually takes 5 hours to complete. In addition, the rent on the equipment used to assemble stereo systems amounts to $4,900 per month. Indirect materials cost $5 per system. A supervisor was hired to oversee production; her monthly salary is $3,000.

Janitorial costs are $1,300 monthly. Advertising costs for the stereo system will be $8,500 per month. The factory building depreciation expense is $7,200 per year. Property taxes on the factory building will be $9,000 per year.

Instructions

(a) Prepare an answer sheet with the following column headings.

(a) DM $96,200
    DL $78,000
    MO $17,050
    PC $ 8,500

	Product Costs			
Cost Item	**Direct Materials**	**Direct Labor**	**Manufacturing Overhead**	**Period Costs**

Assuming that Copa manufactures, on average, 1,300 stereo systems per month, enter each cost item on your answer sheet, placing the dollar amount per month under the appropriate headings. Total the dollar amounts in each of the columns.

(b) Compute the cost to produce one stereo system.

P1-3B Incomplete manufacturing costs, expenses, and selling data for two different cases are as follows.

Indicate the missing amount of different cost items, and prepare a condensed cost of goods manufactured schedule, an income statement, and a partial balance sheet.
(SO 5, 6, 7)

	Case	
	1	**2**
Direct Materials Used	$ 7,600	$ (g)
Direct Labor	5,000	8,000
Manufacturing Overhead	8,000	4,000
Total Manufacturing Costs	(a)	18,000
Beginning Work in Process Inventory	1,000	(h)
Ending Work in Process Inventory	(b)	3,000
Sales	24,500	(i)
Sales Discounts	2,500	1,400
Cost of Goods Manufactured	17,000	22,000
Beginning Finished Goods Inventory	(c)	3,300
Goods Available for Sale	18,000	(j)
Cost of Goods Sold	(d)	(k)
Ending Finished Goods Inventory	3,400	2,500
Gross Profit	(e)	7,000
Operating Expenses	2,500	(l)
Net Income	(f)	5,000

Instructions

(a) Indicate the missing amount for each letter.

(b) Prepare a condensed cost of goods manufactured schedule for Case 1.

(c) Prepare an income statement and the current assets section of the balance sheet for Case 1. Assume that in Case 1 the other items in the current assets section are as follows: Cash $4,000, Receivables (net) $15,000, Raw Materials $600, and Prepaid Expenses $400.

(c) Current assets $28,000

P1-4B The following data were taken from the records of Stellar Manufacturing Company for the fiscal year ended June 30, 2005.

Prepare a cost of goods manufactured schedule, a partial income statement, and a partial balance sheet.
(SO 5, 6, 7)

Raw Materials		Factory Insurance	$ 4,600
Inventory 7/1/04	$ 48,000	Factory Machinery	
Raw Materials		Depreciation	16,000
Inventory 6/30/05	39,600	Factory Utilities	27,600
Finished Goods		Office Utilities Expense	8,650
Inventory 7/1/04	96,000	Sales	554,000
Finished Goods		Sales Discounts	4,200
Inventory 6/30/05	95,900	Plant Manager's Salary	29,000
Work in Process		Factory Property Taxes	9,600
Inventory 7/1/04	19,800	Factory Repairs	1,400
Work in Process		Raw Materials Purchases	96,400
Inventory 6/30/05	18,600	Cash	32,000
Direct Labor	149,250		
Indirect Labor	24,460		
Accounts Receivable	27,000		

Instructions

(a) CGM $367,910

(a) Prepare a cost of goods manufactured schedule. (Assume all raw materials used were direct materials.)

(b) Gross profit $181,790
(c) Current assets $213,100

(b) Prepare an income statement through gross profit.

(c) Prepare the current assets section of the balance sheet at June 30, 2005.

Prepare a cost of goods manufactured schedule and a correct income statement.
(SO 5, 6)

P1-5B   Tombert Company is a manufacturer of computers. Its controller resigned in October 2005. An inexperienced assistant accountant has prepared the following income statement for the month of October 2005.

TOMBERT COMPANY
Income Statement
For the Month Ended October 31, 2005

Sales (net)		$780,000
Less: Operating expenses		
Raw materials purchases	$264,000	
Direct labor cost	190,000	
Advertising expense	90,000	
Selling and administrative salaries	75,000	
Rent on factory facilities	60,000	
Depreciation on sales equipment	45,000	
Depreciation on factory equipment	31,000	
Indirect labor cost	28,000	
Utilities expense	12,000	
Insurance expense	8,000	803,000
Net loss		$(23,000)

Prior to October 2005 the company had been profitable every month. The company's president is concerned about the accuracy of the income statement. As his friend, you have been asked to review the income statement and make necessary corrections. After examining other manufacturing cost data, you have acquired additional information as follows.

1. Inventory balances at the beginning and end of October were:

	October 1	October 31
Raw materials	$18,000	$34,000
Work in process	16,000	14,000
Finished goods	30,000	48,000

2. Only 70% of the utilities expense and 60% of the insurance expense apply to factory operations. The remaining amounts should be charged to selling and administrative activities.

Instructions

(a) CGM $572,200
(b) NI $ 9,000

(a) Prepare a schedule of cost of goods manufactured for October 2005.

(b) Prepare a correct income statement for October 2005.

Problems: Set C

Problem Set C is provided at the book's Web site, www.wiley.com/college/weygandt.

▷ B R O A D E N I N G   Y O U R   P E R S P E C T I V E

Group Decision Case

BYP 1-1 Mismatch Manufacturing Company specializes in producing fashion outfits. On July 31, 2005, a tornado touched down at its factory and general office. The inventories in the warehouse and the factory were completely destroyed as was the general office nearby. Next morning, through a careful search of the disaster site, however, Ross Clarkson, the company's controller, and Catherine Harper, the cost accountant, were able to recover a small part of manufacturing cost data for the current month.

"What a horrible experience," sighed Ross. "And the worst part is that we may not have enough records to use in filing an insurance claim."

"It was terrible," replied Catherine. "However, I managed to recover some of the manufacturing cost data that I was working on yesterday afternoon. The data indicate that our direct labor cost in July totaled $240,000 and that we had purchased $345,000 of raw materials. Also, I recall that the amount of raw materials used for July was $350,000. But I'm not sure this information will help. The rest of our records are blown away."

"Well, not exactly," said Ross. "I was working on the year-to-date income statement when the tornado warning was announced. My recollection is that our sales in July were $1,260,000 and our gross profit ratio has been 40% of sales. Also, I can remember that our cost of goods available for sale was $770,000 for July."

"Maybe we can work something out from this information!" exclaimed Catherine. "My experience tells me that our manufacturing overhead is usually 60% of direct labor."

"Hey, look what I just found," cried Catherine. "It's a copy of this June's balance sheet, and it shows that our inventories as of June 30 are Finished goods $38,000, Work in process $25,000, and Raw materials $19,000."

"Super," yelled Ross. "Let's go work something out."

In order to file an insurance claim, Mismatch Company must determine the amount of its inventories as of July 31, 2005, the date of the tornado touchdown.

Instructions
With the class divided into groups, determine the amount of cost in the Raw Materials, Work in Process, and Finished Goods inventory accounts as of the date of the tornado touchdown.

Managerial Analysis

BYP 1-2 Love All is a fairly large manufacturing company located in the southern United States. The company manufactures tennis rackets, tennis balls, tennis clothing, and tennis shoes, all bearing the company's distinctive logo, a large green question mark on a white flocked tennis ball. The company's sales have been increasing over the past 10 years.

The tennis racket division has recently implemented several advanced manufacturing techniques. Robot arms hold the tennis rackets in place while glue dries, and machine vision systems check for defects. The engineering and design team uses computerized drafting and testing of new products. The following managers work in the tennis racket division.

Andre Agassi, Sales Manager (supervises all sales representatives).
Serena Williams, technical specialist (supervises computer programmers).
Pete Sampras, cost accounting manager (supervises cost accountants).
Andy Roddick, production supervisor (supervises all manufacturing employees).
Venus Williams, engineer (supervises all new-product design teams).

Instructions
(a) What are the primary information needs of each manager?
(b) Which, if any, financial accounting report(s) is each likely to use?
(c) Name one special-purpose management accounting report that could be designed for each manager. Include the name of the report, the information it would contain, and how frequently it should be issued.

Real-World Focus

BYP 1-3   Anchor Glass Container Corporation, the third largest manufacturer of glass containers in the U.S., supplies beverage and food producers and consumer products manufacturers nationwide. Parent company **Consumers Packaging Inc.** *(Toronto Stock Exchange:* CGC) is a leading international designer and manufacturer of glass containers.

The following management discussion appeared in a recent annual report of Anchor Glass.

ANCHOR GLASS CONTAINER CORPORATION
Management Discussion

Cost of Products Sold Cost of products sold as a percentage of net sales was 89.3% in the current year compared to 87.6% in the prior year. The increase in cost of products sold as a percentage of net sales principally reflected the impact of operational problems during the second quarter of the current year at a major furnace at one of the Company's plants, higher downtime, and costs and expenses associated with an increased number of scheduled capital improvement projects, increases in labor, and certain other manufacturing costs (with no corresponding selling price increases in the current year). Reduced fixed costs from the closing of the Streator, Illinois, plant in June of the current year and productivity and efficiency gains partially offset these cost increases.

Instructions
What factors affect the costs of products sold at Anchor Glass Container Corporation?

Exploring the Web

BYP 1-4   The Institute of Management Accountants (IMA) is the largest organization of its kind in the world, dedicated to excellence in the practice of management accounting and financial management.

Address: **www.imanet.org**, *or go to* **www.wiley.com/college/weygandt**

Instructions
At the IMA's home page, locate the answers to the following questions.
(a) How many members does the IMA have, and what are their job titles?
(b) What are some of the benefits of joining the IMA as a student?
(c) Use the chapter locator function to locate the IMA chapter nearest you, and find the name of the chapter president.

Communication Activity

BYP 1-5   Refer to Problem 1–5A and add the following requirement.
Prepare a letter to the president of the company, Sue Agler, describing the changes you made. Explain clearly why net income is different after the changes. Keep the following points in mind as you compose your letter.

1. This is a letter to the president of a company, who is your friend. The style should be generally formal, but you may relax some requirements. For example, you may call the president by her first name.

2. Executives are very busy. Your letter should tell the president your main results first (for example, the amount of net income).
3. You should include brief explanations so that the president can understand the changes you made in the calculations.

Research Assignment

BYP 1-6 The March 26, 2004, issue of the *Wall Street Journal* includes an article by Gabriel Kahn titled "Tiger's New Threads." The article discusses a unique approach employed by a company in the textile industry.

Instructions
Read the article and answer the following questions.
(a) Why is **Esquel Group** able to produce a new product faster than its competitors?
(b) Why did Esquel's client list change as it adopted this new approach?
(c) Are there any risks associated with this approach?

Ethics Case

BYP 1-7 Wayne Terrago, controller for Robbin Industries, was reviewing production cost reports for the year. One amount in these reports continued to bother him—advertising. During the year, the company had instituted an expensive advertising campaign to sell some of its slower-moving products. It was still too early to tell whether the advertising campaign was successful.

There had been much internal debate as how to report advertising cost. The vice president of finance argued that advertising costs should be reported as a cost of production, just like direct materials and direct labor. He therefore recommended that this cost be identified as manufacturing overhead and reported as part of inventory costs until sold. Others disagreed. Terrago believed that this cost should be reported as an expense of the current period, based on the conservatism principle. Others argued that it should be reported as Prepaid Advertising and reported as a current asset.

The president finally had to decide the issue. He argued that these costs should be reported as inventory. His arguments were practical ones. He noted that the company was experiencing financial difficulty and expensing this amount in the current period might jeopardize a planned bond offering. Also, by reporting the advertising costs as inventory rather than as prepaid advertising, less attention would be directed to it by the financial community.

Instructions
(a) Who are the stakeholders in this situation?
(b) What are the ethical issues involved in this situation?
(c) What would you do if you were Wayne Terrago?

Answers to Self-Study Questions
1. b   2. b   3. b   4. c   5. d   6. a   7. c   8. a   9. d   10. d

✓ Remember to go back to the Navigator box on the chapter-opening page and check off your completed work.

CHAPTER 2

Job Order Cost Accounting

After studying this chapter,
you should be able to:

1 Explain the characteristics and purposes of cost accounting.

2 Describe the flow of costs in a job order cost accounting system.

3 Explain the nature and importance of a job cost sheet.

4 Indicate how the predetermined overhead rate is determined and used.

5 Prepare entries for jobs completed and sold.

6 Distinguish between under- and over-applied manufacturing overhead.

 THE NAVIGATOR

THE NAVIGATOR ✔

▶ Scan *Study Objectives* ☐

▶ Read *Feature Story* ☐

▶ Read *Preview* ☐

▶ Read text and answer *Before You Go On*
       p. 53 ☐   p. 64 ☐   p. 70 ☐

▶ Work *Using the Decision Toolkit* ☐

▶ Review *Summary of Study Objectives* ☐

▶ Work *Demonstration Problem* ☐

▶ Answer *Self-Study Questions* ☐

▶ Complete *Assignments* ☐

" . . . And We'd Like It in Red"

Western States Fire Apparatus, Inc., of Cornelius, Oregon, is one of the few U.S. companies that makes fire trucks. The company builds about 25 trucks per year. Founded in 1941, the company is run by the children and grand-children of the original founder.

"We buy the chassis, which is the cab and the frame," says Susan Scott, the company's bookkeeper. "In our computer, we set up an account into which all of the direct material that is purchased for that particular job is charged." Other direct materials include the water pump—which can cost $10,000—the lights, the siren, ladders, and hoses.

As for direct labor, the production workers fill out time tickets that tell what jobs they worked on. Usually, the company is building four trucks at any one time. On payday, the controller allocates the pay-roll to the appropriate job record.

Indirect materials, such as nuts and bolts, wiring, lubricants, and abrasives, are allocated to each job in proportion to direct material dollars. Other costs, such as insurance and supervisors' salaries, are allo-cated based on direct labor hours. "We need to allocate overhead in order to know what kind of price we have to charge when we submit our bids," she says.

Western gets orders through a "blind-bidding" process. That is, Western submits its bid without knowing the bid prices made by its competitors. "If we bid too low, we won't make a profit. If we bid too high, we don't get the job."

Regardless of the final price for the truck, the quality had better be first-rate. "The fire

departments let you know if they don't like what you did, and you usually end up fixing it."

THE NAVIGATOR

The Feature Story about **Western States Fire Apparatus** described the manufacturing costs used in making a fire truck. It demonstrated that accurate costing is critical to the company's success. For example, in order to submit accurate bids on new jobs and to know whether it profited from past jobs, the company needs a good costing system. This chapter illustrates how these manufacturing costs would be assigned to specific jobs, such as the manufacture of individual fire trucks. We begin the discussion in this chapter with an overview of the flow of costs in a job order cost accounting system. We then use a case study to explain and illustrate the documents, entries, and accounts in this type of cost accounting system.

The content and organization of Chapter 2 are as follows.

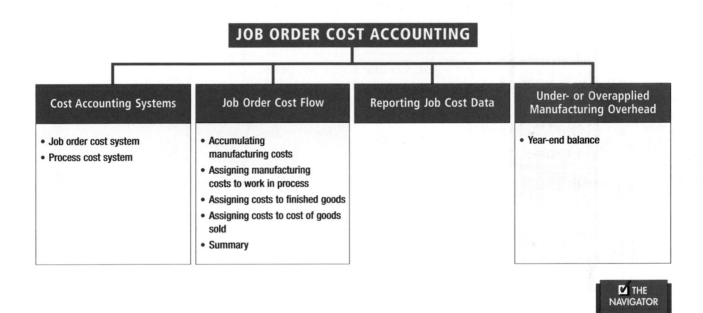

JOB ORDER COST ACCOUNTING

Cost Accounting Systems	Job Order Cost Flow	Reporting Job Cost Data	Under- or Overapplied Manufacturing Overhead
• Job order cost system • Process cost system	• Accumulating manufacturing costs • Assigning manufacturing costs to work in process • Assigning costs to finished goods • Assigning costs to cost of goods sold • Summary		• Year-end balance

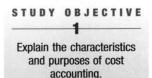

✓ THE NAVIGATOR

Cost Accounting Systems

Cost accounting involves the measuring, recording, and reporting of product costs. From the data accumulated, both the total cost and the unit cost of each product are determined. The accuracy of the product cost information produced by the cost accounting system is critical to the success of the company. As you will see in later chapters, this information is used to determine which products to produce, what price to charge, and the amounts to produce. Accurate product cost information is also vital for effective evaluation of employee performance.

A **cost accounting system** consists of accounts for the various manufacturing costs. These accounts are fully integrated into the general ledger of a company. **An important feature of a cost accounting system is the use of a perpetual inventory system.** Such a system **provides immediate, up-to-date information on the cost of a product**. There are two basic types of cost accounting systems: (1) a job order cost system and (2) a process cost system. Although cost accounting systems differ widely from company to company, most are based on one of these two traditional product costing systems.

STUDY OBJECTIVE

1

Explain the characteristics and purposes of cost accounting.

JOB ORDER COST SYSTEM

Under a job order cost system, costs are assigned to each **job** or to each **batch** of goods. An example of a job would be the manufacture of a mainframe computer by **IBM**, the production of a movie by **Disney**, or the making of a fire truck by **Western States**. An example of a batch would be the printing of 225 wedding invitations by a local print shop, or the printing of a weekly issue of *Fortune* magazine by a hi-tech printer such as **Quad Graphics**. Jobs or batches may be completed to fill a specific customer order or to replenish inventory.

An important feature of job order costing is that each job (or batch) has its own distinguishing characteristics. For example, each house is custom built, each consulting engagement by a CPA firm is unique, and each printing job is different. **The objective is to compute the cost per job.** At each point in the manufacturing of a product or the providing of a service, the job and its associated costs can be identified. A job order cost system measures costs for each completed job, rather than for set time periods. The recording of costs in a job order cost system is shown in Illustration 2-1.

Illustration 2-1 Job order cost system

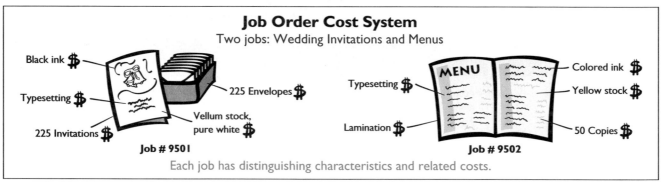

Job Order Cost System
Two jobs: Wedding Invitations and Menus

Black ink $ — Typesetting $ — 225 Invitations $ — 225 Envelopes $ — Vellum stock, pure white $ — **Job # 9501**

Typesetting $ — Lamination $ — Colored ink $ — Yellow stock $ — 50 Copies $ — **Job # 9502**

Each job has distinguishing characteristics and related costs.

PROCESS COST SYSTEM

A process cost system is used when a large volume of similar products are manufactured. Production is continuous to ensure that adequate inventories of the finished product(s) are on hand. A process cost system is used in the manufacture of cereal by **Kellogg**, the refining of petroleum by **ExxonMobil**, and the production of automobiles by **General Motors**. Process costing accumulates product-related costs **for a period of time** (such as a week or a month) instead of assigning costs to specific products or job orders. In process costing, the costs are assigned to departments or processes for a set period of time. The recording of costs in a process cost system is shown in Illustration 2-2. The process cost system will be discussed further in Chapter 3.

Illustration 2-2 Process cost system

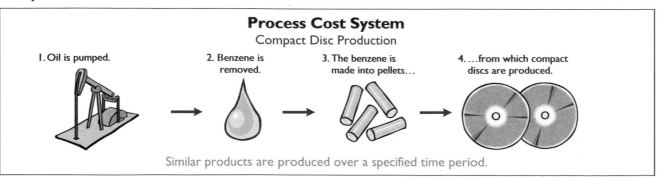

Process Cost System
Compact Disc Production

1. Oil is pumped. → 2. Benzene is removed. → 3. The benzene is made into pellets... → 4. ...from which compact discs are produced.

Similar products are produced over a specified time period.

A company may use both types of cost systems. For example, **General Motors** uses process cost accounting for its standard model cars, such as Saturns and Corvettes, and job order cost accounting for a custom-made limousine for the President of the United States. The objective of both systems is to provide unit cost information for product pricing, cost control, inventory valuation, and financial statement presentation. End-of-period inventory values are computed by using unit cost data.

Business Insight
Management Perspective

Many companies suffer from poor cost accounting. As a result, they sometimes make products they ought not to be selling at all and buy others that they could more profitably make themselves. Also, inaccurate cost data lead companies to misallocate capital and frustrate efforts by plant managers to improve efficiency.

For example, consider the case of a diversified company in the business of rebuilding diesel locomotives. The managers thought they were making money, but a consulting firm found that costs had been seriously underestimated. The company bailed out of the business, and not a moment too soon. Says the consultant who advised the company, "The more contracts it won, the more money it lost." Given that situation, a company cannot stay in business very long!

BEFORE YOU GO ON . . .

▶**Review It**

1. What is cost accounting?
2. What does a cost accounting system consist of?
3. How does a job order cost system differ from a process cost system?

☑ **THE NAVIGATOR**

Job Order Cost Flow

The flow of costs (direct materials, direct labor, and manufacturing overhead) in job order cost accounting parallels the physical flow of the materials as they are converted into finished goods. As shown in Illustration 2-3 (page 54), manufacturing costs are assigned to the Work in Process Inventory account. When a job is completed, the cost of the job is transferred to Finished Goods Inventory. Later when the goods are sold, their cost is transferred to Cost of Goods Sold.

Illustration 2-3 provides a basic overview of the flow of costs in a manufacturing setting. A more detailed presentation of the flow of costs is shown in Illustration 2-4 (page 54). It indicates that there are two major steps in the flow of costs: (1) *accumulating* the manufacturing costs incurred and (2) *assigning* the accumulated costs to the work done. As shown, manufacturing costs incurred are accumulated in entries 1–3 by debits to Raw Materials Inventory, Factory Labor, and Manufacturing Overhead. When these costs are incurred, no attempt is made to associate the costs with specific jobs. The remaining entries (entries 4–8) assign manufacturing costs incurred. In the remainder of this chapter (pages 55–70), we will use a case study to explain how a job order system operates.

STUDY OBJECTIVE

2

Describe the flow of costs in a job order cost accounting system.

Illustration 2-3   Flow of costs in job order cost accounting

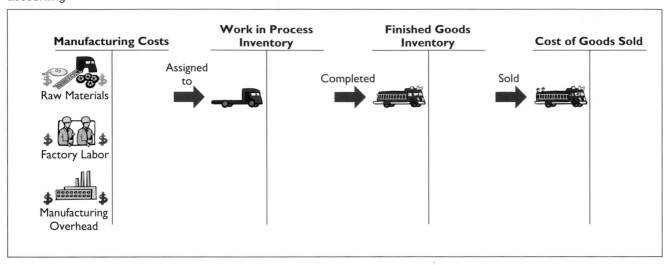

Illustration 2-4   Job order cost accounting system

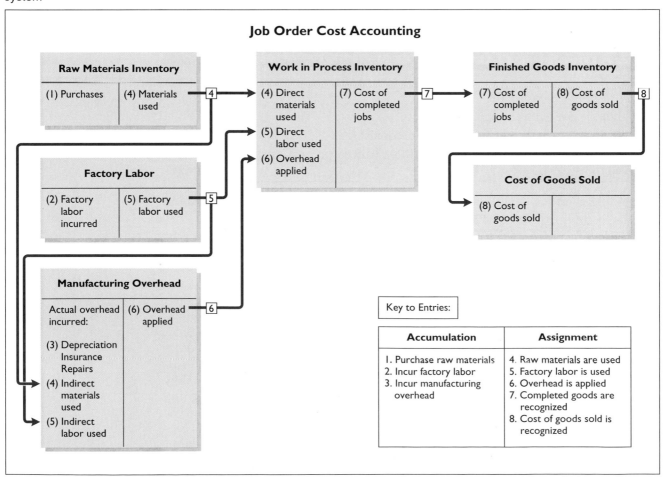

ACCUMULATING MANUFACTURING COSTS

In a job order cost system, manufacturing costs are recorded in the period in which they are incurred. To illustrate, we will use the January transactions of Wallace Manufacturing Company, which makes machine tools.

Raw Materials Costs

The costs of raw materials purchased are debited to Raw Materials Inventory when the materials are received. This account is debited for the invoice cost and freight costs chargeable to the purchaser. It is credited for purchase discounts taken and purchase returns and allowances. **No effort is made at this point to associate the cost of materials with specific jobs or orders.** The procedures for ordering, receiving, recording, and paying for raw materials are similar to the purchasing procedures of a merchandising company.

To illustrate, assume that Wallace Manufacturing purchases 2,000 handles (Stock No. AA2746) at $5 per unit ($10,000) and 800 modules (Stock No. AA2850) at $40 per unit ($32,000) for a total cost of $42,000 ($10,000 + $32,000). The entry to record this purchase on January 4 is:

(1)

Jan. 4	Raw Materials Inventory	42,000	
	Accounts Payable		42,000
	(Purchase of raw materials on account)		

Raw Materials Inventory is a general ledger account. It is also referred to as a **control account** because it summarizes the detailed data regarding specific inventory accounts in the subsidiary ledger. The subsidiary ledger consists of individual records for each item of raw materials. The records may take the form of accounts (or cards) that are manually or mechanically prepared. Or the records may be kept as computer data files. The records are referred to as **materials inventory records** (or **stores ledger cards**). The card for Stock No. AA2746 following the purchase is shown in Illustration 2-5.

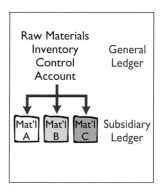

Postings are made daily to the subsidiary ledger. After all postings have been completed, the sum of the balances in the raw materials subsidiary ledger should equal the balance in the Raw Materials Inventory control account.

Illustration 2-5 Materials inventory card

Item: Handles								Part No: AA2746		
	Receipts			Issues			Balance			
Date	Units	Cost	Total	Units	Cost	Total	Units	Cost	Total	
1/4	2,000	$5	$10,000				2,000	$5	$10,000	

Factory Labor Costs

The procedures for accumulating factory labor costs are similar to those for computing the payroll for a merchandising company. Time clocks and time cards are used to determine total hours worked; gross and net earnings for each employee are listed in a payroll register; and individual employee earnings records are maintained. To help ensure the accuracy of data, a company should follow the principles of internal control.

In a manufacturing company, the cost of factory labor consists of (1) gross earnings of factory workers, (2) employer payroll taxes on these earnings, and (3) fringe benefits (such as sick pay, pensions, and vacation pay) incurred by the employer. **Labor costs are debited to Factory Labor when they are incurred.**

To illustrate, assume that Wallace Manufacturing incurs $32,000 of factory labor costs. Of that amount, $27,000 relates to wages payable and $5,000 relates to payroll taxes payable in January. The entry is:

(2)

Jan. 31	Factory Labor	32,000	
	Factory Wages Payable		27,000
	Employer Payroll Taxes Payable		5,000
	(To record factory labor costs)		

Factory labor is subsequently assigned to work in process and manufacturing overhead, as explained later in the chapter.

Manufacturing Overhead Costs

A company may have many types of overhead costs. These costs may be recognized **daily**, as in the case of machinery repairs and the use of indirect materials and indirect labor. Or overhead costs may be recorded **periodically** through adjusting entries. Property taxes, depreciation, and insurance are recorded periodically, for example. This is done using a summary entry, which summarizes the totals from multiple transactions. Using assumed data, the summary entry for manufacturing overhead in Wallace Manufacturing Company is:

(3)

Jan. 31	Manufacturing Overhead	13,800	
	Utilities Payable		4,800
	Prepaid Insurance		2,000
	Accounts Payable (for repairs)		2,600
	Accumulated Depreciation		3,000
	Property Taxes Payable		1,400
	(To record overhead costs)		

Manufacturing Overhead is a control account. The subsidiary ledger consists of individual accounts for each type of cost, such as Factory Utilities, Factory Insurance, and Factory Repairs.

ASSIGNING MANUFACTURING COSTS TO WORK IN PROCESS

STUDY OBJECTIVE
3
Explain the nature and importance of a job cost sheet.

As shown in Illustration 2-4, assigning manufacturing costs to work in process results in the following entries:

1. **Debits** are made to Work in Process Inventory.
2. **Credits** are made to Raw Materials Inventory, Factory Labor, and Manufacturing Overhead.

Journal entries to assign costs to work in process are usually made and posted **monthly**.

An essential accounting record in assigning costs to jobs is a **job cost sheet** shown in Illustration 2-6. A job cost sheet is a form used to record the costs chargeable to a specific job and to determine the total and unit costs of the completed job.

Illustration 2-6   Job cost sheet

Job Cost Sheet

Job No. _____   Quantity _____

Item _____   Date Requested _____

For _____   Date Completed _____

Date	Direct Materials	Direct Labor	Manufacturing Overhead

Cost of completed job
  Direct materials $ _____
  Direct labor   _____
  Manufacturing overhead   _____
Total cost $ _____
Unit cost (total dollars ÷ quantity) $ _____

Helpful Hint In today's electronic environment, job cost sheets are maintained as computer files.

Postings to job cost sheets are made daily, directly from supporting documents.

A separate job cost sheet is kept for each job. The job cost sheets constitute the subsidiary ledger for the Work in Process Inventory account. **Each entry to Work in Process Inventory must be accompanied by a corresponding posting to one or more job cost sheets.**

Business Insight
e-Business Perspective

General Motors recently launched a new Internet-based ordering system intended to deliver custom vehicles in 15 to 20 days instead of the 55 to 60 days it previously took. Customers interested in a GM car can search online to see if any dealers have a car with the options they want. If not, the customer uses an online program to configure a car with the desired options and then places the order. While this online approach could potentially provide savings for automakers by reducing inventory costs, some people are skeptical. One auto analyst stated, "I don't think it's going to lead to a massive change in the way vehicles are built and sold in the next 10 years."

SOURCE: Karen Lundegaard, "GM Tests Web-Based Ordering System, Seeking to Slash Custom-Delivery Time," *Wall Street Journal* (November 17, 2000).

Raw Materials Costs

Raw materials costs are assigned when the materials are issued by the storeroom. To achieve effective internal control over the issuance of materials, the storeroom worker should receive a written authorization before materials are released to production. Such authorization for issuing raw materials is made on a prenumbered materials requisition slip. This form is signed by an

Helpful Hint Approvals are an important part of a materials requisition slip because they help to establish individual accountability over inventory.

authorized employee such as a department supervisor. The materials issued may be used directly on a job, or they may be considered indirect materials. As shown in Illustration 2-7, the requisition should indicate the quantity and type of materials withdrawn and the account to be charged. Direct materials will be charged to Work in Process Inventory, and indirect materials to Manufacturing Overhead.

Illustration 2-7 **Materials requisition slip**

Wallace Manufacturing Company
Materials Requisition Slip

Deliver to: _____Assembly Department_____   Req. No. ___R247___
Charge to: __Work in Process—Job No. 101__   Date: __1/6/05__

Quantity	Description	Stock No.	Cost per Unit	Total
200	Handles	AA2746	$5.00	$1,000

Requested by _Bruce Howart_   Received by _Herb Crowley_
Approved by _Kap Shin_   Costed by _Heather Remmers_

Helpful Hint The internal control principle of documentation includes prenumbering to enhance accountability.

The requisition is prepared in duplicate. A copy is retained in the storeroom as evidence of the materials released. The original is sent to Accounting, where the cost per unit and total cost of the materials used are determined. Any of the inventory costing methods (FIFO, LIFO, or average cost) may be used in costing the requisitions. After the requisition slips have been costed, they are posted daily to the materials inventory records. Also, **requisitions for direct materials are posted daily to the individual job cost sheets**.

Periodically, the requisitions are sorted, totaled, and journalized. For example, if $24,000 of direct materials and $6,000 of indirect materials are used in Wallace Manufacturing in January, the entry is:

	(4)		
Jan. 31	Work in Process Inventory	24,000	
	Manufacturing Overhead	6,000	
	Raw Materials Inventory		30,000
	(To assign materials to jobs and overhead)		

The requisition slips show total direct materials costs of $12,000 for Job No. 101, $7,000 for Job No. 102, and $5,000 for Job No. 103. The posting of requisition slip R247 and other assumed postings to the job cost sheets for materials are shown in Illustration 2-8. After all postings have been completed, the sum of the direct materials columns of the job cost sheets should equal the direct materials debited to Work in Process Inventory.

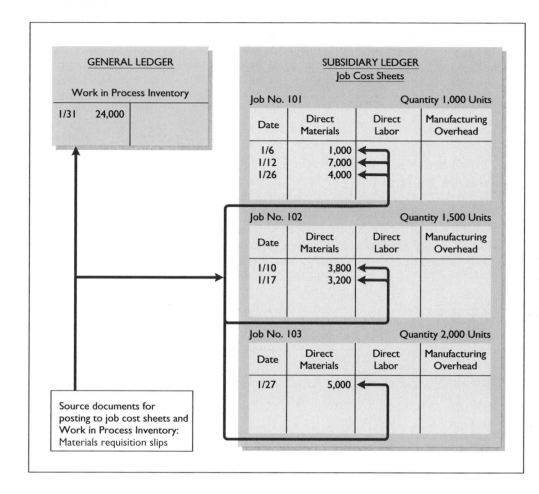

Illustration 2-8   Job cost sheets—direct materials

Helpful Hint Postings to control accounts are made monthly, and postings to job cost sheets are made daily.

The materials inventory record for Part No. AA2746 is shown in Illustration 2-9. It shows the posting of requisition slip R247 for 200 handles and an assumed requisition slip for 760 handles costing $3,800 on January 10 for Job 102.

Illustration 2-9   Materials inventory card following issuances

Item: Handles									Part No: AA2746	
	Receipts			Issues			Balance			
Date	Units	Cost	Total	Units	Cost	Total	Units	Cost	Total	
1/4	2,000	$5	$10,000				2,000	$5	$10,000	
1/6				200	$5	$1,000	1,800	$5	9,000	
1/10				760	$5	3,800	1,040	$5	5,200	

Factory Labor Costs

Factory labor costs are assigned to jobs on the basis of time tickets prepared when the work is performed. The time ticket indicates the employee, the hours worked, the account and job to be charged, and the total labor cost. In many companies these data are accumulated through the use of bar coding and scanning devices. When they start and end work, employees scan bar codes on their identification badges and bar codes associated with each job they work on. When direct labor is involved, the job number must be indicated, as shown in Illustration 2-10. All time tickets should be approved by the employee's supervisor.

Illustration 2-10 Time ticket

Helpful Hint In some companies, different colored time tickets are used for direct and indirect labor.

Wallace Manufacturing Company				
Time Ticket				

Date: 1/6/05

Employee: John Nash   Employee No. 124
Charge to: Work in Process   Job No. 101

Time			Hourly Rate	Total Cost
Start	Stop	Total Hours		
0800	1200	4	10.00	40.00

Approved by _Bob Kadler_   Costed by _M. Cher_

The time tickets are later sent to the payroll department. There, the total time reported for an employee for a pay period is reconciled with total hours worked, as shown on the employee's time card. Then the employee's hourly wage rate is applied, and the total labor cost is computed. Finally, the time tickets are sorted, totaled, and journalized. The account Work in Process Inventory is debited for direct labor, and Manufacturing Overhead is debited for indirect labor. For example, if the $32,000 total factory labor cost consists of $28,000 of direct labor and $4,000 of indirect labor, the entry is:

(5)

Jan. 31	Work in Process Inventory	28,000	
	Manufacturing Overhead	4,000	
	Factory Labor		32,000
	(To assign labor to jobs and overhead)		

As a result of this entry, Factory Labor is left with a zero balance, and gross earnings are assigned to the appropriate manufacturing accounts.

Let's assume that the labor costs chargeable to Wallace's three jobs are $15,000, $9,000, and $4,000. The Work in Process Inventory and job cost sheets after posting are shown in Illustration 2-11. As in the case of direct materials, the postings to the direct labor columns of the job cost sheets should equal the posting of direct labor to Work in Process Inventory.

Illustration 2-11   Job cost sheets—direct labor

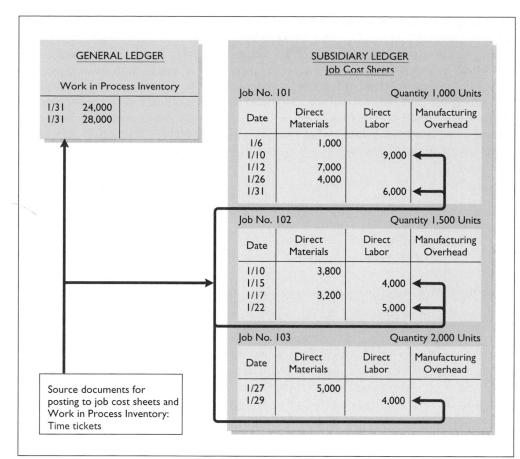

Manufacturing Overhead Costs

We've seen that the actual costs of direct materials and direct labor can be charged to specific jobs. In contrast, manufacturing overhead relates to production operations **as a whole**. As a result, overhead costs cannot be assigned to specific jobs on the basis of actual costs incurred. Instead, manufacturing overhead is assigned to work in process and to specific jobs **on an estimated basis through the use of a predetermined overhead rate**.

STUDY OBJECTIVE 4

Indicate how the predetermined overhead rate is determined and used.

Business Insight
e-Business Perspective

What do companies like **Noratek Solutions**, **Business Systems of America**, **Foundation Software, Inc.**, and **R.C. Systems, Inc.** have in common? All of them provide software to help in recording job order costing information. For example, Noratek Solutions software analyzes every job from every angle, and it supports reporting of estimated and actual costs and revenues for any number of jobs. The system is integrated with purchasing, accounts payable, payroll, and receivables so that a complete cross-reference into all transactions can be easily developed. Users have a complete audit trail so that they can examine the details of any job.

A manual system is provided in this chapter so that the major concepts related to a job order cost system are understood. In practice, sophisticated job order cost software packages frequently are used.

The **predetermined overhead rate** is based on the relationship between estimated annual overhead costs and expected annual operating activity. This relationship is expressed in terms of a common **activity base**. The activity may be stated in terms of direct labor costs, direct labor hours, machine hours, or any other measure that will provide an equitable basis for applying overhead costs to jobs. The predetermined overhead rate is established at the beginning of the year. Small companies often will have a single, company-wide predetermined overhead rate. Large companies, however, often have rates that vary from department to department. The formula for a predetermined overhead rate is as follows.

Illustration 2-12 Formula for predetermined overhead rate

$$\begin{array}{c} \textbf{Estimated Annual} \\ \textbf{Overhead Costs} \end{array} \div \begin{array}{c} \textbf{Expected Annual} \\ \textbf{Operating Activity} \end{array} = \begin{array}{c} \textbf{Predetermined} \\ \textbf{Overhead Rate} \end{array}$$

We indicated earlier that overhead relates to production operations as a whole. In order to know what "the whole" is, the logical thing would be to wait until the end of the year's operations, when all costs for the period would be available. But as a practical matter, that wouldn't work: Managers could not wait that long before having information about product costs of specific jobs completed during the year in order to price products accurately. Instead, using a predetermined overhead rate enables a cost to be determined for the job immediately. Illustration 2-13 indicates how manufacturing overhead is assigned to work in process.

Helpful Hint In contrast to overhead, actual costs for direct materials and direct labor are used to assign costs to Work in Process.

Illustration 2-13 Using predetermined overhead rates

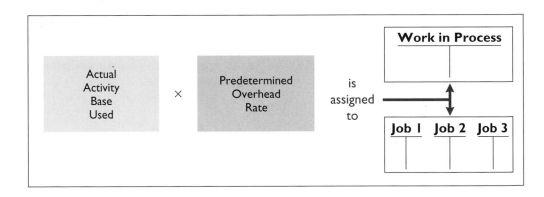

Wallace Manufacturing uses direct labor cost as the activity base. Assuming that annual overhead costs are expected to be $280,000 and that $350,000 of direct labor costs are anticipated for the year, the overhead rate is 80 percent, computed as follows:

$$\$280,000 \div \$350,000 = 80\%$$

This means that for every dollar of direct labor, 80 cents of manufacturing overhead will be assigned to a job. The use of a predetermined overhead rate enables the company to determine the approximate total cost of each job **when the job is completed**.

Historically, direct labor costs or direct labor hours have often been used as the activity base. The reason was the relatively high correlation between direct labor and manufacturing overhead. In recent years, **there has been a trend toward use of machine hours as the activity base, due to increased reliance on automation in manufacturing operations**. Or, as mentioned in Chapter 1, many companies have implemented activity-based costing in an attempt to more accurately allocate overhead costs based on the activities that give rise to the costs.

A company may use more than one activity base. For example, if a job order is manufactured in more than one factory department, each department may have its own overhead rate. In the Feature Story about fire trucks, two bases were used in assigning overhead to jobs: direct materials dollars for indirect materials, and direct labor hours for such costs as insurance and supervisors' salaries.

Manufacturing overhead is applied to work in process when direct labor costs are assigned. It also is applied to specific jobs at the same time. For Wallace Manufacturing, overhead applied for January is $22,400 ($28,000 × 80%). This application is recorded through the following entry.

	(6)		
Jan. 31	Work in Process Inventory	22,400	
	Manufacturing Overhead		22,400
	(To assign overhead to jobs)		

The overhead applied to each job will be 80 percent of the direct labor cost of the job for the month. After posting, the Work in Process Inventory account and the job cost sheets will appear as shown in Illustration 2-14. Note that the debit

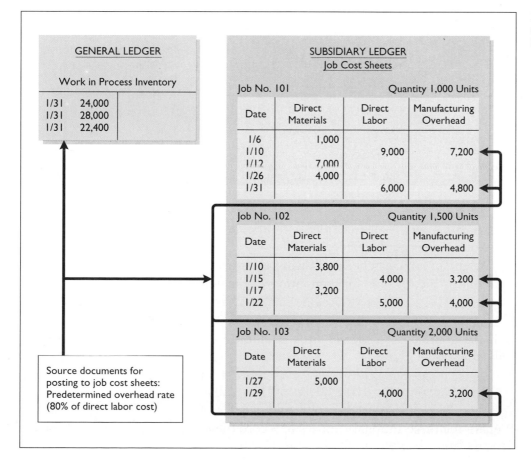

Illustration 2-14 Job cost sheets—manufacturing overhead applied

of $22,400 to Work in Process Inventory equals the sum of the overhead applied to jobs: Job 101 $12,000 + Job 102 $7,200 + Job 103 $3,200.

At the end of each month, **the balance in Work in Process Inventory should equal the sum of the costs shown on the job cost sheets of unfinished jobs**. Assuming that all jobs are unfinished, proof of the agreement of the control and subsidiary accounts in Wallace Manufacturing is shown below.

Illustration 2-15 Proof of job cost sheets to work in process inventory

Work in Process Inventory		Job Cost Sheets	
Jan. 31	24,000	No. 101	$39,000
31	28,000	102	23,200
31	22,400	103	12,200
	74,400 ←	———————	**$74,400**

DECISION TOOLKIT

Decision Checkpoints	Info Needed for Decision	Tool to Use for Decision	How to Evaluate Results
What is the cost of a job?	Cost of material, labor, and overhead assigned to a specific job	Job cost sheet	Compare costs to those of previous periods and to those of competitors to ensure that costs are in line. Compare costs to expected selling price or service fees charged to determine overall profitability.

BEFORE YOU GO ON . . .

▶**Review It**

1. What source documents are used in assigning manufacturing costs to Work in Process Inventory?
2. What is a job cost sheet, and what is its primary purpose?
3. What is the formula for computing a predetermined overhead rate?

▶**Do It**

Danielle Company is working on two job orders. The job cost sheets show the following:

    Direct materials — Job 120 $6,000, Job 121 $3,600
    Direct labor — Job 120 $4,000, Job 121 $2,000
    Manufacturing overhead — Job 120 $5,000, Job 121 $2,500

Prepare the three summary entries to record the assignment of costs to Work in Process from the data on the job cost sheets.

Action Plan

* Recognize that Work in Process Inventory is the control account for all unfinished job cost sheets.
* Debit Work in Process Inventory for the materials, labor, and overhead charged to the job cost sheets.
* Credit the accounts that were debited when the manufacturing costs were accumulated.

Solution

The three summary entries are:

Work in Process Inventory ($6,000 + $3,600)	9,600	
Raw Materials Inventory		9,600
(To assign materials to jobs)		
Work in Process Inventory ($4,000 + $2,000)	6,000	
Factory Labor		6,000
(To assign labor to jobs)		
Work in Process Inventory ($5,000 + $2,500)	7,500	
Manufacturing Overhead		7,500
(To assign overhead to jobs)		

Related exercise material: BE2-3, BE2-4, BE2-7, E2-2, E2-3, E2-7, and E2-8.

☑ THE NAVIGATOR

ASSIGNING COSTS TO FINISHED GOODS

When a job is completed, the costs are summarized and the lower portion of the applicable job cost sheet is completed. For example, if we assume that Job No. 101 is completed on January 31, the job cost sheet will show the following.

STUDY OBJECTIVE

5

Prepare entries for jobs completed and sold.

Illustration 2-16 Completed job cost sheet

Job Cost Sheet

Job No. 101   Quantity 1,000
Item Magnetic Sensors   Date Requested February 5
For Tanner Company   Date Completed January 31

Date	Direct Materials	Direct Labor	Manufacturing Overhead
1/6	$ 1,000		
1/10		$ 9,000	$ 7,200
1/12	7,000		
1/26	4,000		
1/31		6,000	4,800
	$12,000	$15,000	$12,000

Cost of completed job		
Direct materials	$	12,000
Direct labor		15,000
Manufacturing overhead		12,000
Total cost	$	39,000
Unit cost ($39,000 ÷ 1,000)	$	39.00

When a job is finished, an entry is made to transfer its total cost to finished goods inventory. The entry for Wallace Manufacturing is:

(7)

Jan. 31	Finished Goods Inventory	39,000	
	Work in Process Inventory		39,000
	(To record completion of Job No. 101)		

Finished Goods Inventory is a control account. It controls individual finished goods records in a finished goods subsidiary ledger. Postings to the receipts columns are made directly from completed job cost sheets. The finished goods inventory record for Job No. 101 is shown in Illustration 2-17 below.

ASSIGNING COSTS TO COST OF GOODS SOLD

Cost of goods sold is recognized when each sale occurs. To illustrate the entries when a completed job is sold, assume that on January 31 Wallace Manufacturing sells on account Job 101, costing $39,000, for $50,000. The entries to record the sale and recognize cost of goods sold are:

(8)

Jan. 31	Accounts Receivable	50,000	
	Sales		50,000
	(To record sale of Job No. 101)		
31	Cost of Goods Sold	39,000	
	Finished Goods Inventory		39,000
	(To record cost of Job No. 101)		

The units sold, the cost per unit, and the total cost of goods sold for each job sold are recorded in the issues section of the finished goods record, as shown in Illustration 2-17.

Illustration 2-17
Finished goods record

Item: Magnetic Sensors									Job No: 101
	Receipts			Issues			Balance		
Date	Units	Cost	Total	Units	Cost	Total	Units	Cost	Total
1/31	1,000	$39	$39,000				1,000	$39	$39,000
1/31				1,000	$39	$39,000			–0–

SUMMARY OF JOB ORDER COST FLOWS

A completed flow chart for a job order cost accounting system is shown in Illustration 2-18. All postings are keyed to entries 1–8 in Wallace Manufacturing's accounts presented in the cost flow graphic in Illustration 2-4. Illustration 2-19 provides a summary of the flow of documents in a job order cost system.

Illustration 2-18   Flow of costs in a job order cost system

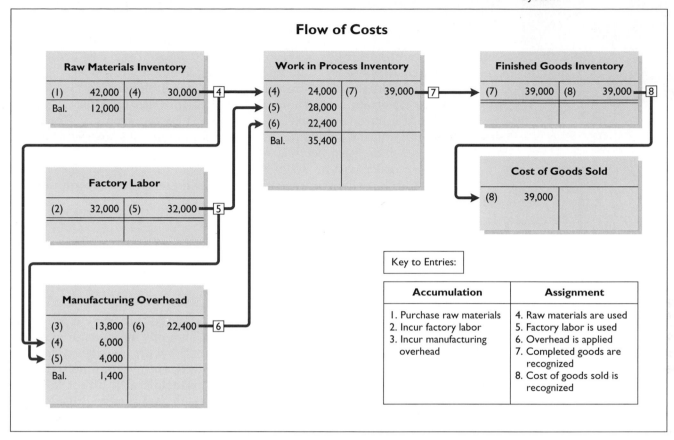

Illustration 2-19   Flow of documents in a job order cost system

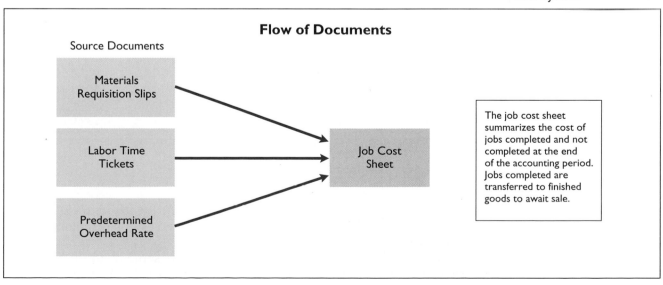

Business Insight
Service Company Perspective

Service companies like the **Mayo Clinic** (health care), **PriceWaterhouse-Coopers** (accounting firm), and **Merrill Lynch** (financial services firm) also use job order costing systems. The major difference in a job order costing system between a manufacturing company such as **Coca-Cola** and a service company such as **Massachusetts General Hospital** involves inventory. Service companies do not have raw materials nor finished goods inventory. However, similar to manufacturing companies, many service companies have substantial overhead costs, which must be allocated.

Because job order costing systems are used extensively in service industries, exercises are provided in the end-of-chapter material to help you understand how to cost various types of services.

Reporting Job Cost Data

Helpful Hint Monthly financial statements are usually prepared for management use only.

At the end of a period, financial statements are prepared that present aggregate data on all jobs manufactured and sold. The cost of goods manufactured schedule in job order costing is the same as in Chapter 1 with one exception: **The schedule shows manufacturing overhead applied, rather than actual overhead costs. This amount is added to direct materials and direct labor to determine total manufacturing costs.** The schedule is prepared directly from the Work in Process Inventory account. A condensed schedule for Wallace Manufacturing Company for January is as follows.

Illustration 2-20 Cost of goods manufactured schedule

WALLACE MANUFACTURING COMPANY		
Cost of Goods Manufactured Schedule		
For the Month Ended January 31, 2005		
Work in process, January 1		$ –0–
Direct materials used	$24,000	
Direct labor	28,000	
Manufacturing overhead applied	**22,400**	
Total manufacturing costs		74,400
Total cost of work in process		74,400
Less: Work in process, January 31		35,400
Cost of goods manufactured		$39,000

Note that the cost of goods manufactured ($39,000) agrees with the amount transferred from Work in Process Inventory to Finished Goods Inventory in journal entry no. 7 in Illustration 2-18.

The income statement and balance sheet are the same as those illustrated in Chapter 1. For example, the partial income statement for Wallace Manufacturing for the month of January is shown in Illustration 2-21.

Illustration 2-21   Partial income statement

WALLACE MANUFACTURING COMPANY Income Statement (partial) For the Month Ending January 31, 2005		
Sales		$50,000
Cost of goods sold		
Finished goods inventory, January 1	$ –0–	
Cost of goods manufactured (See Illustration 2-20)	**39,000**	
Cost of goods available for sale	39,000	
Less: Finished goods inventory, January 31	–0–	
Cost of goods sold		39,000
Gross profit		$11,000

Under- or Overapplied Manufacturing Overhead

When Manufacturing Overhead has a **debit balance**, overhead is said to be underapplied. **Underapplied overhead** means that the overhead assigned to work in process is less than the overhead incurred. Conversely, when manufacturing overhead has a **credit balance**, overhead is overapplied. **Overapplied overhead** means that the overhead assigned to work in process is greater than the overhead incurred. These concepts are shown in Illustration 2-22.

Illustration 2-22   Under- and overapplied overhead

Manufacturing Overhead	
Actual (Costs incurred)	Applied (Costs assigned)

If actual is *greater* than applied, manufacturing overhead is underapplied.

If actual is *less* than applied, manufacturing overhead is overapplied.

YEAR-END BALANCE

At the end of the year, all manufacturing overhead transactions are complete. There is no further opportunity for offsetting events to occur. Accordingly, any balance in Manufacturing Overhead is eliminated by an adjusting entry. Usually, under- or overapplied overhead is considered to be an **adjustment to cost of goods sold**. Thus, **underapplied overhead is debited to Cost of Goods Sold**. **Overapplied overhead is credited to Cost of Goods Sold.** To illustrate, assume that Wallace Manufacturing has a $2,500 credit balance in Manufacturing Overhead at December 31. The adjusting entry for the overapplied overhead is:

Dec. 31	Manufacturing Overhead	2,500	
	Cost of Goods Sold		2,500
	(To transfer overapplied overhead to cost of goods sold)		

After this entry is posted, Manufacturing Overhead will have a zero balance. In preparing an income statement for the year, the amount reported for cost of goods sold will be the account balance **after the adjustment** for either under- or overapplied overhead.

Business Insight
Management Perspective

Overhead also applies in nonmanufacturing companies. The State of Michigan found that auto dealers were charging documentary and service fees ranging from $18 to $445 per automobile and inspection fees from $88 to $360. These fees often were charged auto buyers after a base sales price for the car had been negotiated. The Attorney General of the State of Michigan ruled that auto dealers cannot charge customers additional fees for routine overhead costs. The attorney general said: "Overhead is part of the sales price of a motor vehicle. Processing paper work, dealer incurred costs, and inspection fees to qualify cars for extended warranty plans are ordinary overhead expenses."

Conceptually, it can be argued that under- or overapplied overhead at the end of the year should be allocated among ending work in process, finished goods, and cost of goods sold. The discussion of this possible allocation approach is left to more advanced courses.

DECISION TOOLKIT

Decision Checkpoints	Info Needed for Decision	Tool to Use for Decision	How to Evaluate Results
Has the company over- or underapplied overhead for the period?	Actual overhead costs and overhead applied	Manufacturing overhead account	If the account balance is a credit, overhead applied exceeded actual overhead costs. If the account balance is a debit, overhead applied was less than actual overhead costs.

BEFORE YOU GO ON . . .

▶Review It

1. When are entries made to record the completion and sale of a job?
2. What costs are included in total manufacturing costs in the cost of goods manufactured schedule?

☑ THE NAVIGATOR

Using the Decision Toolkit

Martinez Building Products Company is one of the largest manufacturers and marketers of unique, custom-made residential garage doors in the U.S. as well as a major supplier of industrial and commercial doors, grills, and counter shutters for the new construction, repair, and remodel markets. Martinez has developed plans for continued expansion of a network of service operations that sell, install, and service manufactured fireplaces, garage doors, and related products.

Martinez uses a job cost system and applies overhead to production on the basis of direct labor cost. In computing a predetermined overhead rate for the year 2005, the company estimated manufacturing overhead to be $24 million and direct labor costs to be $20 million. In addition the following information is provided.

Actual costs incurred during 2005

Direct materials used	$30,000,000
Direct labor cost incurred	21,000,000
Insurance, factory	500,000
Indirect labor	7,500,000
Maintenance	1,000,000
Rent on building	11,000,000
Depreciation on equipment	2,000,000

Instructions
Answer each of the following.
(a) Why is Martinez Building Products Company using a job order costing system?
(b) On what basis does Martinez allocate its manufacturing overhead? Compute the predetermined overhead rate for the current year.
(c) Compute the amount of the under- or overapplied overhead for 2005.
(d) Martinez had balances in the beginning and ending work in process and finished goods accounts as follows.

	1/1/05	12/31/05
Work in process	$ 5,000,000	$ 4,000,000
Finished goods	13,000,000	11,000,000

Determine the (1) cost of goods manufactured and (2) cost of goods sold for Martinez during 2005. Assume that any under- or overapplied overhead should be included in the cost of goods sold.
(e) During 2005, Job G408 was started and completed. Its cost sheet showed a total cost of $100,000, and the company prices its product at 50% above its cost. What is the price to the customer if the company follows this pricing strategy?

Solution

(a) The company is using a job order system because each job (or batch) must have its own distinguishing characteristics. For example, each type of garage door would be different, and therefore a different cost per garage door should be assigned.
(b) The company allocates its overhead on the basis of direct labor cost. The predetermined overhead rate is 120%, computed as follows.

$$\$24,000,000 \div \$20,000,000 = 120\%$$

(c)	Actual manufacturing overhead	$22,000,000
	Applied overhead cost ($21,000,000 × 120%)	25,200,000
	Overapplied overhead	$ 3,200,000

(d) (1) Work in process, 1/1/05		$ 5,000,000
Direct materials used	$30,000,000	
Direct labor	21,000,000	
Manufacturing overhead applied	25,200,000	
Total manufacturing costs		76,200,000
Total cost of work in process		81,200,000
Less: Work in process, 12/31/05		4,000,000
Cost of goods manufactured		$77,200,000
(2) Finished goods inventory, 1/1/05	$13,000,000	
Cost of goods manufactured (see above)	77,200,000	
Cost of goods available for sale	90,200,000	
Finished goods inventory, 12/31/05	11,000,000	
Cost of goods sold (unadjusted)	79,200,000	
Less: Overapplied overhead	3,200,000	
Cost of goods sold	$76,000,000	
(e) G408 cost	$ 100,000	
Markup percentage	× 50%	
Profit	$ 50,000	

Price to customer: $150,000 ($100,000 + $50,000)

Summary of Study Objectives

1 *Explain the characteristics and purposes of cost accounting.* Cost accounting involves the procedures for measuring, recording, and reporting product costs. From the data accumulated, the total cost and the unit cost of each product is determined. The two basic types of cost accounting systems are job order cost and process cost.

2 *Describe the flow of costs in a job order cost accounting system.* In job order cost accounting, manufacturing costs are first accumulated in three accounts: Raw Materials Inventory, Factory Labor, and Manufacturing Overhead. The accumulated costs are then assigned to Work in Process Inventory and eventually to Finished Goods Inventory and Cost of Goods Sold.

3 *Explain the nature and importance of a job cost sheet.* A job cost sheet is a form used to record the costs chargeable to a specific job and to determine the total and unit costs of the completed job. Job cost sheets constitute the subsidiary ledger for the Work in Process Inventory control account.

4 *Indicate how the predetermined overhead rate is determined and used.* The predetermined overhead rate is based on the relationship between estimated annual overhead costs and expected annual operating activity. This is expressed in terms of a common activity base, such as direct labor cost. The rate is used in assigning overhead costs to work in process and to specific jobs.

5 *Prepare entries for jobs completed and sold.* When jobs are completed, the cost is debited to Finished Goods Inventory and credited to Work in Process Inventory. When a job is sold the entries are: (a) Debit Cash or Accounts Receivable and credit Sales for the selling price. And (b) debit Cost of Goods Sold and credit Finished Goods Inventory for the cost of the goods.

6 *Distinguish between under- and overapplied manufacturing overhead.* Underapplied manufacturing overhead means that the overhead assigned to work in process is less than the overhead incurred. Overapplied overhead means that the overhead assigned to work in process is greater than the overhead incurred.

DECISION TOOLKIT—A SUMMARY

Decision Checkpoints	Info Needed for Decision	Tool to Use for Decision	How to Evaluate Results
What is the cost of a job?	Cost of material, labor, and overhead assigned to a specific job	Job cost sheet	Compare costs to those of previous periods and to those of competitors to ensure that costs are in line. Compare costs to expected selling price or service fees charged to determine overall profitability.
Has the company over- or underapplied overhead for the period?	Actual overhead costs and overhead applied	Manufacturing overhead account	If the account balance is a credit, overhead applied exceeded actual overhead costs. If the account balance is a debit, overhead applied was less than actual overhead costs.

Glossary

Cost accounting An area of accounting that involves measuring, recording, and reporting product costs. (p. 51)

Cost accounting system Manufacturing cost accounts that are fully integrated into the general ledger of a company. (p. 51)

Job cost sheet A form used to record the costs chargeable to a job and to determine the total and unit costs of the completed job. (p. 56)

Job order cost system A cost accounting system in which costs are assigned to each job or batch. (p. 52)

Materials requisition slip A document authorizing the issuance of raw materials from the storeroom to production. (p. 57)

Overapplied overhead A situation in which overhead assigned to work in process is greater than the overhead incurred. (p. 69)

Predetermined overhead rate A rate based on the relationship between estimated annual overhead costs and expected annual operating activity, expressed in terms of a common activity base. (p. 62)

Process cost system A system of accounting used when a large volume of similar products are manufactured. (p. 52)

Summary entry A journal entry that summarizes the totals from multiple transactions. (p. 56)

Time ticket A document that indicates the employee, the hours worked, the account and job to be charged, and the total labor cost. (p. 60)

Underapplied overhead A situation in which overhead assigned to work in process is less than the overhead incurred. (p. 69)

Demonstration Problem

During February, Cardella Manufacturing works on two jobs: A16 and B17. Summary data concerning these jobs are as follows.

Manufacturing Costs Incurred

Purchased $54,000 of raw materials on account.
Factory labor $76,000, plus $4,000 employer payroll taxes.
Manufacturing overhead exclusive of indirect materials and indirect labor $59,800.

Assignment of Costs

Direct materials: Job A16 $27,000, Job B17 $21,000
Indirect materials: $3,000
Direct labor: Job A16 $52,000, Job B17 $26,000
Indirect labor: $2,000
Manufacturing overhead rate: 80% of direct labor costs.

Job A16 was completed and sold on account for $150,000. Job B17 was only partially completed.

Instructions

(a) Journalize the February transactions in the sequence followed in the chapter.
(b) What was the amount of under- or overapplied manufacturing overhead?

Solution to Demonstration Problem

Action Plan

- In accumulating costs, debit three accounts: Raw Materials Inventory, Factory Labor, and Manufacturing Overhead.
- When Work in Process Inventory is debited, credit one of the three accounts listed above.
- Debit Finished Goods Inventory for the cost of completed jobs. Debit Cost of Goods Sold for the cost of jobs sold.
- Overhead is underapplied when Manufacturing Overhead has a debit balance.

(a)

1.

Feb. 28	Raw Materials Inventory	54,000	
	Accounts Payable		54,000
	(Purchase of raw materials on account)		

2.

28	Factory Labor	80,000	
	Factory Wages Payable		76,000
	Employer Payroll Taxes Payable		4,000
	(To record factory labor costs)		

3.

28	Manufacturing Overhead	59,800	
	Accounts Payable, Accumulated		
	Depreciation, and Prepaid Insurance		59,800
	(To record overhead costs)		

4.

28	Work in Process Inventory	48,000	
	Manufacturing Overhead	3,000	
	Raw Materials Inventory		51,000
	(To assign raw materials to production)		

5.

28	Work in Process Inventory	78,000	
	Manufacturing Overhead	2,000	
	Factory Labor		80,000
	(To assign factory labor to production)		

6.

28	Work in Process Inventory	62,400	
	Manufacturing Overhead		62,400
	(To assign overhead to jobs—		
	80% × $78,000)		

7.

28	Finished Goods Inventory	120,600	
	Work in Process Inventory		120,600
	(To record completion of Job A16: direct		
	materials $27,000, direct labor $52,000,		
	and manufacturing overhead $41,600)		

8.

Feb 28	Accounts Receivable		150,000	
	Sales			150,000
	(To record sale of Job A16)			
28	Cost of Goods Sold		120,600	
	Finished Goods Inventory			120,600
	(To record cost of sale for Job A16)			

(b) Manufacturing Overhead has a debit balance of $2,400 as shown below.

Manufacturing Overhead

(3)	59,800	(6)	62,400
(4)	3,000		
(5)	2,000		
Bal.	2,400		

Thus, manufacturing overhead is underapplied for the month.

Self-Study Questions

college/weygandt
www.wiley.com/

Self-Study/Self-Test

Answers are at the end of the chapter.

(SO 1) 1. Cost accounting involves the measuring, recording, and reporting of:
  (a) product costs.
  (b) future costs.
  (c) manufacturing processes.
  (d) managerial accounting decisions.

(SO 2) 2. In accumulating raw materials costs, the cost of raw materials purchased in a perpetual system is debited to:
  (a) Raw Materials Purchases.
  (b) Raw Materials Inventory.
  (c) Purchases.
  (d) Work in Process.

(SO 2) 3. When incurred, factory labor costs are debited to:
  (a) Work in Process.
  (b) Factory Wages Expense.
  (c) Factory Labor.
  (d) Factory Wages Payable.

(SO 3) 4. The source documents for assigning costs to job cost sheets are:
  (a) invoices, time tickets, and the predetermined overhead rate.
  (b) materials requisition slips, time tickets, and the actual overhead costs.
  (c) materials requisition slips, payroll register, and the predetermined overhead rate.
  (d) materials requisition slips, time tickets, and the predetermined overhead rate.

(SO 3) 5. In recording the issuance of raw materials in a job order cost system, it would be *incorrect* to:
  (a) debit Work in Process Inventory.
  (b) debit Finished Goods Inventory.
  (c) debit Manufacturing Overhead.
  (d) credit Raw Materials Inventory.

(SO 3) 6. The entry when direct factory labor is assigned to jobs is a debit to:
  (a) Work in Process Inventory and a credit to Factory Labor.
  (b) Manufacturing Overhead and a credit to Factory Labor.
  (c) Factory Labor and a credit to Manufacturing Overhead.
  (d) Factory Labor and a credit to Work in Process Inventory.

(SO 4) 7. The formula for computing the predetermined manufacturing overhead rate is estimated annual overhead costs divided by an expected annual operating activity, expressed as:
  (a) direct labor cost.
  (b) direct labor hours.
  (c) machine hours.
  (d) any of the above.

(SO 4) 8. In Crawford Company, the predetermined overhead rate is 80% of direct labor cost. During the month, $210,000 of factory labor costs are incurred, of which $180,000 is direct labor and $30,000 is indirect labor. Actual overhead

incurred was $200,000. The amount of overhead debited to Work in Process Inventory should be:
(a) $120,000.
(b) $144,000.
(c) $168,000.
(d) $160,000.

(SO 5)   9. In Mynex Company, Job No. 26 is completed at a cost of $4,500 and later sold for $7,000 cash. A correct entry is:
(a) Debit Finished Goods Inventory $7,000 and credit Work in Process Inventory $7,000.
(b) Debit Cost of Goods Sold $7,000 and credit Finished Goods Inventory $7,000.

(c) Debit Finished Goods Inventory $4,500 and credit Work in Process Inventory $4,500.
(d) Debit Accounts Receivable $7,000 and credit Sales $7,000.

10. Manufacturing overhead is underapplied if: (SO 6)
(a) actual overhead is less than applied.
(b) actual overhead is greater than applied.
(c) the predetermined rate equals the actual rate.
(d) actual overhead equals applied overhead.

Questions

1. (a) Kent Krause is not sure about the difference between cost accounting and a cost accounting system. Explain the difference to Kent. (b) What is an important feature of a cost accounting system?

2. (a) Distinguish between the two types of cost accounting systems. (b) May a company use both types of cost accounting systems?

3. What type of industry is likely to use a job order cost system? Give some examples.

4. What type of industry is likely to use a process cost system? Give some examples.

5. Your roommate asks your help in understanding the major steps in the flow of costs in a job order cost system. Identify the steps for your roommate.

6. There are three inventory control accounts in a job order system. Identify the control accounts and their subsidiary ledgers.

7. What source documents are used in accumulating direct labor costs?

8. "Entries to Manufacturing Overhead normally are only made daily." Do you agree? Explain.

9. Alan Bruski is confused about the source documents used in assigning materials and labor costs. Identify the documents and give the entry for each document.

10. What is the purpose of a job cost sheet?

11. Indicate the source documents that are used in charging costs to specific jobs.

12. Differentiate between a "materials inventory record" and a "materials requisition slip" as used in a job order cost system.

13. Joe Gruber believes actual manufacturing overhead should be charged to jobs. Do you agree? Why or why not?

14. What relationships are involved in computing a predetermined overhead rate?

15. How can the agreement of Work in Process Inventory and job cost sheets be verified?

16. Jane Jelk believes that the cost of goods manufactured schedule in job order cost accounting is the same as shown in Chapter 1. Is Jane correct? Explain.

17. Alex Cesska is confused about under- and overapplied manufacturing overhead. Define the terms for Alex, and indicate the balance in the manufacturing overhead account applicable to each term.

18. "At the end of the year, under- or overapplied overhead is closed to Income Summary." Is this correct? If not, indicate the customary treatment of this amount.

Brief Exercises

Prepare a flowchart of a job order cost accounting system, and identify transactions.
(SO 2)

BE2-1   Sandy Tool & Die begins operations on January 1. Because all work is done to customer specifications, the company decides to use a job order cost accounting system. Prepare a flow chart of a typical job order system with arrows showing the flow of costs. Identify the eight transactions.

Prepare entries in accumulating manufacturing costs.
(SO 2)

BE2-2   During the first month of operations, Sandy Tool & Die accumulated the following manufacturing costs: raw materials $3,000 on account, factory labor $5,000 of which $4,500 relates to factory wages payable and $500 relates to payroll taxes payable, and utilities payable $2,000. Prepare separate journal entries for each type of manufacturing cost.

BE2-3   In January, Sandy Tool & Die requisitions raw materials for production as follows: Job 1 $900, Job 2 $1,200, Job 3 $500, and general factory use $600. Prepare a summary journal entry to record raw materials used.

Prepare entry for the assignment of raw materials costs.
(SO 2)

BE2-4   Factory labor data for Sandy Tool & Die is given in BE2-2. During January, time tickets show that the factory labor of $5,000 was used as follows: Job 1 $1,200, Job 2 $1,600 Job 3 $1,700, and general factory use $500. Prepare a summary journal entry to record factory labor used.

Prepare entry for the assignment of factory labor costs.
(SO 2)

BE2-5   Data pertaining to job cost sheets for Sandy Tool & Die are given in BE2-3 and BE2-4. Prepare the job cost sheets for each of the three jobs. (*Note:* You may omit the column for Manufacturing Overhead.)

Prepare job cost sheets.
(SO 3)

BE2-6   Burrand Company estimates that annual manufacturing overhead costs will be $600,000. Estimated annual operating activity bases are: direct labor cost $500,000, direct labor hours 50,000, and machine hours 100,000. Compute the predetermined overhead rate for each activity base.

Compute predetermined overhead rates.
(SO 4)

BE2-7   During the first quarter, Sota Company incurs the following direct labor costs: January $40,000, February $30,000, and March $50,000. For each month, prepare the entry to assign overhead to production using a predetermined rate of 120% of direct labor cost.

Assign manufacturing overhead to production.
(SO 4)

BE2-8   In March, Caroline Company completes Jobs 10 and 11. Job 10 cost $25,000 and Job 11 $32,000. On March 31, Job 10 is sold to the customer for $35,000 in cash. Journalize the entries for the completion of the two jobs and the sale of Job 10.

Prepare entries for completion and sale of completed jobs.
(SO 5)

BE2-9   At December 31, balances in Manufacturing Overhead are: Apex Company— debit $1,200, Lopez Company—credit $900. Prepare the adjusting entry for each company at December 31, assuming the adjustment is made to cost of goods sold.

Prepare adjusting entries for under- and overapplied overhead.
(SO 6)

Exercises

E2-1   The gross earnings of the factory workers for Darlinda Company during the month of January are $80,000. The employer's payroll taxes for the factory payroll are $8,000. The fringe benefits to be paid by the employer on this payroll are $4,000. Of the total accumulated cost of factory labor, 85% is related to direct labor and 15% is attributable to indirect labor.

Prepare entries for factory labor.
(SO 2)

Instructions
(a) Prepare the entry to record the factory labor costs for the month of January.
(b) Prepare the entry to assign factory labor to production.

E2-2   Dooley Manufacturing uses a job order cost accounting system. On May 1, the company has a balance in Work in Process Inventory of $3,200 and two jobs in process: Job No. 429 $2,000, and Job No. 430 $1,200. During May, a summary of source documents reveals the following.

Prepare journal entries for manufacturing costs.
(SO 2, 3, 4, 5)

Job Number	Materials Requisition Slips		Labor Time Tickets	
429	$2,500		$2,400	
430	3,500		3,000	
431	4,400	$10,400	7,600	$13,000
General use		800		1,200
		$11,200		$14,200

Dooley Manufacturing applies manufacturing overhead to jobs at an overhead rate of 90% of direct labor cost. Job No. 429 is completed during the month.

Instructions
(a) Prepare summary journal entries to record: (i) the requisition slips, (ii) the time tickets, (iii) the assignment of manufacturing overhead to jobs, and (iv) the completion of Job No. 429.
(b) Post the entries to Work in Process Inventory, and prove the agreement of the control account with the job cost sheets.

Analyze a job cost sheet and prepare entries for manufacturing costs.
(SO 2, 3, 4, 5)

E2-3 A job order cost sheet for Bjerg Company is shown below.

Job No. 92			For 2,000 Units
Date	Direct Materials	Direct Labor	Manufacturing Overhead
Beg. bal. Jan. 1	5,000	6,000	4,200
8	6,000		
12		8,000	6,400
25	2,000		
27		4,000	3,200
	13,000	18,000	13,800

Cost of completed job:	
Direct materials	$13,000
Direct labor	18,000
Manufacturing overhead	13,800
Total cost	$44,800
Unit cost ($44,800 ÷ 2,000)	$22.40

Instructions
(a) ▭▭▭▭▷ On the basis of the foregoing data answer the following questions.
   (1) What was the balance in Work in Process Inventory on January 1 if this was the only unfinished job?
   (2) If manufacturing overhead is applied on the basis of direct labor cost, what overhead rate was used in each year?
(b) Prepare summary entries at January 31 to record the current year's transactions pertaining to Job No. 92.

Analyze costs of manufacturing and determine missing amounts.
(SO 2, 5)

E2-4 Manufacturing cost data for Copa Company, which uses a job order cost system, are presented below.

	Case A	Case B	Case C
Direct materials used	$ (a)	$ 83,000	$ 63,150
Direct labor	50,000	100,000	(h)
Manufacturing overhead applied	42,500	(d)	(i)
Total manufacturing costs	165,650	(e)	250,000
Work in process 1/1/05	(b)	15,500	18,000
Total cost of work in process	201,500	(f)	(j)
Work in process 12/31/05	(c)	11,800	(k)
Cost of goods manufactured	192,300	(g)	262,000

Instructions
Indicate the missing amount for each letter. Assume that in all cases manufacturing overhead is applied on the basis of direct labor cost and the rate is the same.

Compute the manufacturing overhead rate and under- or overapplied overhead.
(SO 4, 6)

E2-5 Rodriquez Company applies manufacturing overhead to jobs on the basis of machine hours used. Overhead costs are expected to total $300,000 for the year, and machine usage is estimated at 125,000 hours.
   For the year, $322,000 of overhead costs are incurred and 130,000 hours are used.

Instructions

(a) Compute the manufacturing overhead rate for the year.
(b) What is the amount of under- or overapplied overhead at December 31?
(c) Assuming the under- or overapplied overhead for the year is not allocated to inventory accounts, prepare the adjusting entry to assign the amount to cost of goods sold.

E2-6 A job cost sheet of Battle Company is given below.

Analyze job cost sheet and prepare entry for completed job.
(SO 2, 3, 4, 5)

Job Cost Sheet

JOB NO. 469   Quantity 2,000
ITEM White Lion Cages   Date Requested 7/2
FOR Tesla Company   Date Completed 7/31

Date	Direct Materials	Direct Labor	Manufacturing Overhead
7/10	828		
12	900		
15		440	528
22		380	456
24	1,600		
27	1,500		
31		540	648

Cost of completed job:
  Direct materials   ———
  Direct labor   ———
   Manufacturing overhead   ———
Total cost   ════
Unit cost   ════

Instructions

(a) ▭▭▭▷ Answer the following questions.
  (1) What are the source documents for direct materials, direct labor, and manufacturing overhead costs assigned to this job?
  (2) What is the predetermined manufacturing overhead rate?
  (3) What are the total cost and the unit cost of the completed job?
(b) Prepare the entry to record the completion of the job.

E2-7 Laird Corporation incurred the following transactions.

Prepare entries for manufacturing costs.
(SO 2, 4, 5)

1. Purchased raw materials on account $46,300.
2. Raw Materials of $36,000 were requisitioned to the factory. An analysis of the materials requisition slips indicated that $8,800 was classified as indirect materials.
3. Factory labor costs incurred were $53,900, of which $49,000 pertained to factory wages payable and $4,900 pertained to employer payroll taxes payable.
4. Time tickets indicated that $50,000 was direct labor and $3,900 was indirect labor.
5. Overhead costs incurred on account were $80,500.
6. Manufacturing overhead was applied at the rate of 150% of direct labor cost.
7. Goods costing $88,000 were completed and transferred to finished goods.
8. Finished goods costing $75,000 to manufacture were sold on account for $103,000.

Instructions

Journalize the transactions. (Omit explanations.)

E2-8 Tombert Printing Corp. uses a job order cost system. The following data summarize the operations related to the first quarter's production.

Prepare entries for manufacturing costs.
(SO 2, 3, 4, 5)

1. Materials purchased on account $192,000, and factory wages incurred $87,300.
2. Materials requisitioned and factory labor used by job:

Job Number	Materials	Factory Labor
A20	$ 32,240	$18,000
A21	42,920	22,000
A22	36,100	15,000
A23	39,270	25,000
General factory use	4,470	7,300
	$155,000	$87,300

3. Manufacturing overhead costs incurred on account $39,500.
4. Depreciation on machinery and equipment $14,550.
5. Manufacturing overhead rate is 70% of direct labor cost.
6. Jobs completed during the quarter: A20, A21, and A23.

Instructions
Prepare entries to record the operations summarized above. (Prepare a schedule showing the individual cost elements and total cost for each job in item 6.)

Prepare a cost of goods manu-factured schedule and partial financial statements.
(SO 2, 5)

E2-9 At May 31, 2005, the accounts of Yellow Knife Manufacturing Company show the following.

1. May 1 inventories—finished goods $12,600, work in process $14,700, and raw materials $8,200.
2. May 31 inventories—finished goods $11,500, work in process $17,900, and raw materials $7,100.
3. Debit postings to work in process were: direct materials $62,400, direct labor $32,000, and manufacturing overhead applied $48,000.
4. Sales totaled $200,000.

Instructions
(a) Prepare a condensed cost of goods manufactured schedule.
(b) Prepare an income statement for May through gross profit.
(c) Indicate the balance sheet presentation of the manufacturing inventories at May 31, 2005.

Compute work in process and finished goods from job cost sheets.
(SO 3, 5)

E2-10 Tomlin Company begins operations on April 1. Information from job cost sheets shows the following.

Job Number		Manufacturing Costs Assigned		Month Completed
	April	May	June	
10	$5,200	$4,400		May
11	6,100	3,900	$3,000	June
12	1,200			April
13		4,700	4,500	June
14		3,900	3,600	Not complete

Job 12 was completed in April. Job 10 was completed in May. Jobs 11 and 13 were completed in June. Each job was sold for 50% above its cost in the month following completion.

Instructions
(a) What is the balance in Work in Process Inventory at the end of each month?
(b) What is the balance in Finished Goods Inventory at the end of each month?
(c) What is the gross profit for May, June, and July?

Prepare entries for costs of services provided.
(SO 2, 4, 5)

E2-11 Shown at the top of the next page are the job cost related accounts for the law firm of Chan, King, and Lou and their manufacturing equivalents:

Law Firm Accounts	Manufacturing Firm Accounts
Supplies	Raw Materials
Direct Attorney Cost	Direct Labor
Operating Overhead	Manufacturing Overhead
Work in Process	Work in Process
Cost of Completed Work	Cost of Goods Sold

Cost data for the month of March follow.

1. Purchased supplies on account $1,500.
2. Issued supplies $1,200 (60% direct and 40% indirect).
3. Time cards for the month indicated labor costs of $75,000 (80% direct and 20% indirect).
4. Operating overhead costs incurred for cash totaled $40,000.
5. Operating overhead is applied at a rate of 90% of direct attorney cost.
6. Work completed totaled $100,000.

Instructions
(a) Journalize the transactions for March. Omit explanations.
(b) Determine the balance of the Work in Process account. Use a T account.

E2-12 Armando Ortiz and Associates, a C.P.A. firm, uses job order costing to capture the costs of its audit jobs. There were no audit jobs in process at the beginning of November. Listed below are data concerning the three audit jobs conducted during November.

Determine cost of jobs and ending balance in work in process and overhead accounts.
(SO 3, 4, 6)

	Hernandez	Navarro	Vallejo
Direct materials	$600	$400	$200
Auditor labor costs	$5,400	$6,600	$3,375
Auditor hours	72	88	45

Overhead costs are applied to jobs on the basis of auditor hours, and the predetermined overhead rate is $50 per auditor hour. The Hernandez job is the only incomplete job at the end of November. Actual overhead for the month was $11,000.

Instructions
(a) Determine the cost of each job.
(b) Indicate the balance of the Work in Process account at the end of November.
(c) Calculate the ending balance of the Manufacturing Overhead account for November.

E2-13 Deco Decorating uses a job order costing system to collect the costs of its interior decorating business. Each client's consultation is treated as a separate job. Overhead is applied to each job based on the number of decorator hours incurred. Listed below are data for the current year.

Determine predetermined overhead rate, apply overhead and determine whether balance under- or overapplied.
(SO 4, 6)

Budgeted overhead	$960,000
Actual overhead	$982,800
Budgeted decorator hours	38,400
Actual decorator hours	39,000

The company uses Operating Overhead in place of Manufacturing Overhead.

Instructions
(a) Compute the predetermined overhead rate.
(b) Prepare the entry to apply the overhead for the year.
(c) Determine whether the overhead was under- or overapplied and by how much.

Problems: Set A

P2-1A Elite Manufacturing uses a job order cost system and applies overhead to production on the basis of direct labor hours. On January 1, 2005, Job No. 25 was the only job in process. The costs incurred prior to January 1 on this job were as follows: direct materials $10,000; direct labor $6,000; and manufacturing overhead $9,000. Job No. 23 had been completed at a cost of $45,000 and was part of finished goods inventory. There was a $5,000 balance in the Raw Materials Inventory account.

Prepare entries in a job cost system and job cost sheets.
(SO 2, 3, 4, 5, 6)

During the month of January, the company began production on Jobs 26 and 27, and completed Jobs 25 and 26. Jobs 23 and 25 were sold on account during the month for $67,000 and $74,000, respectively. The following additional events occurred during the month.

1. Purchased additional raw materials of $45,000 on account.
2. Incurred factory labor costs of $35,500. Of this amount $6,500 related to employer payroll taxes.
3. Incurred manufacturing overhead costs as follows: indirect materials $10,000; indirect labor $7,500; depreciation expense $12,000; and various other manufacturing overhead costs on account $6,000.
4. Assigned direct materials and direct labor to jobs as follows.

Job No.	Direct Materials	Direct Labor
25	$ 5,000	$ 3,000
26	20,000	12,000
27	15,000	9,000

5. The company uses direct labor hours as the activity base to assign overhead. Direct labor hours incurred on each job were as follows: Job No. 25, 200; Job No. 26, 800; and Job No. 27, 600.

Instructions
(a) Calculate the predetermined overhead rate for the year 2005, assuming Elite Manufacturing estimates total manufacturing overhead costs of $400,000, direct labor costs of $300,000, and direct labor hours of 20,000 for the year.
(b) Open job cost sheets for Jobs 25, 26, and 27. Enter the January 1 balances on the job cost sheet for Job No. 25.
(c) Prepare the journal entries to record the purchase of raw materials, the factory labor costs incurred, and the manufacturing overhead costs incurred during the month of January.
(d) Prepare the journal entries to record the assignment of direct materials, direct labor, and manufacturing overhead costs to production. In assigning manufacturing overhead costs, use the overhead rate calculated in (a). Post all costs to the job cost sheets as necessary.

(e) Job 25, $37,000
Job 26, $48,000

(e) Total the job cost sheets for any job(s) completed during the month. Prepare the journal entry (or entries) to record the completion of any job(s) during the month.
(f) Prepare the journal entry (or entries) to record the sale of any job(s) during the month.
(g) What is the balance in the Work in Process Inventory account at the end of the month? What does this balance consist of?
(h) What is the amount of over- or underapplied overhead?

Prepare entries in a job cost system and partial income statement.
(SO 2, 3, 4, 5, 6)

P2-2A   For the year ended December 31, 2005, the job cost sheets of Sprague Company contained the following data.

Job Number	Explanation	Direct Materials	Direct Labor	Manufacturing Overhead	Total Costs
7650	Balance 1/1	$18,000	$20,000	$25,000	$ 63,000
	Current year's costs	27,000	30,000	37,500	94,500
7651	Balance 1/1	12,000	18,000	22,500	52,500
	Current year's costs	28,000	40,000	50,000	118,000
7652	Current year's costs	40,000	64,000	80,000	184,000

Other data:

1. Raw materials inventory totaled $20,000 on January 1. During the year, $100,000 of raw materials were purchased on account.
2. Finished goods on January 1 consisted of Job No. 7648 for $98,000 and Job No. 7649 for $62,000.

3. Job No. 7650 and Job No. 7651 were completed during the year.
4. Job Nos. 7648, 7649, and 7650 were sold on account for $490,000.
5. Manufacturing overhead incurred on account totaled $120,000.
6. Other manufacturing overhead consisted of indirect materials $12,000, indirect labor $18,000 and depreciation on factory machinery $19,500.

Instructions

(a) Prove the agreement of Work in Process Inventory with job cost sheets pertaining to unfinished work. (*Hint*: Use a single T account for Work in Process Inventory.) Calculate each of the following, then post each to the T account: (1) beginning balance, (2) direct materials, (3) direct labor, (4) manufacturing overhead, and (5) completed jobs.

(b) Prepare the adjusting entry for manufacturing overhead, assuming the balance is allocated entirely to cost of goods sold.

(c) Determine the gross profit to be reported for 2005.

(a) (1) $115,500
(4) $167,500
Unfinished job 7652, $184,000

(b) Amount = $2,000

(c) $170,500

P2-3A Steve Taylor is a contractor specializing in custom-built jacuzzis. On May 1, 2005, his ledger contains the following data.

Prepare entries in a job cost system and cost of goods manufactured schedule. (SO 2, 3, 4, 5)

Raw Materials Inventory	$30,000
Work in Process Inventory	12,600
Manufacturing Overhead	2,500 (dr.)

The Manufacturing Overhead account has debit totals of $12,500 and credit totals of $10,000. Subsidiary data for Work in Process Inventory on May 1 include:

Job Cost Sheets

Job by Customer	Direct Materials	Direct Labor	Manufacturing Overhead
Farley	$2,500	$2,000	$1,600
Hendricks	2,000	1,200	960
Minor	900	800	640
	$5,400	$4,000	$3,200

During May, the following costs were incurred: (a) raw materials purchased on account $5,000, (b) labor paid $8,000, (c) manufacturing overhead paid $1,400.

A summary of materials requisition slips and time tickets for the month of May reveals the following.

Job by Customer	Materials Requisition Slips	Time Tickets
Farley	$ 500	$ 400
Hendricks	600	1,000
Minor	2,300	1,300
Bennett	2,400	3,300
	5,800	6,000
General use	1,500	2,000
	$7,300	$8,000

Overhead was charged to jobs on the basis of $0.80 per dollar of direct labor cost.

The jacuzzis for customers Farley, Hendricks, and Minor were completed during May. Each jacuzzi was sold for $12,500 cash.

Instructions

(a) Prepare journal entries for the May transactions: (i) for purchase of raw materials, factory labor costs incurred, and manufacturing overhead costs incurred; (ii) assignment of direct materials, labor, and overhead to production; and (iii) completion of jobs and sale of goods.

(b) Post the entries to Work in Process Inventory.

(c) Reconcile the balance in Work in Process Inventory with the costs of unfinished jobs.

(d) Prepare a cost of goods manufactured schedule for May.

(d) Cost of goods manufactured $20,860

*Compute predetermined over-
head rates, apply overhead,
and calculate under- or overapplied overhead.*
(SO 4, 6)

P2-4A   Acquatic Manufacturing uses a job order cost system in each of its three manufacturing departments. Manufacturing overhead is applied to jobs on the basis of direct
labor cost in Department A, direct labor hours in Department B, and machine hours in
Department C.

In establishing the predetermined overhead rates for 2005 the following estimates
were made for the year.

	Department		
	A	**B**	**C**
Manufacturing overhead	$930,000	$800,000	$750,000
Direct labor cost	$600,000	$100,000	$600,000
Direct labor hours	50,000	40,000	40,000
Machine hours	100,000	120,000	150,000

During January, the job cost sheets showed the following costs and production data.

	Department		
	A	**B**	**C**
Direct materials used	$92,000	$86,000	$64,000
Direct labor cost	$48,000	$35,000	$50,400
Manufacturing overhead incurred	$76,000	$74,000	$61,500
Direct labor hours	4,000	3,500	4,200
Machine hours	8,000	10,500	12,600

Instructions

(a) 155%, $20, $5
(b) $214,400, $191,000
  $177,400
(c) $1,600, $4,000, $(1,500)

(a) Compute the predetermined overhead rate for each department.
(b) Compute the total manufacturing costs assigned to jobs in January in each depart-
    ment.
(c) Compute the under- or overapplied overhead for each department at January 31.

*Analyze manufacturing
accounts and determine
missing amounts.*
(SO 2, 3, 4, 5, 6)

P2-5A   Freedo Company's fiscal year ends on June 30. The following accounts are found
in its job order cost accounting system for the first month of the new fiscal year.

Raw Materials Inventory

July 1	Beginning balance	19,000	July 31	Requisitions	(a)
31	Purchases	90,400			
July 31	Ending balance	(b)			

Work in Process Inventory

July 1	Beginning balance	(c)	July 31	Jobs completed	(f)
31	Direct materials	80,000			
31	Direct labor	(d)			
31	Overhead	(e)			
July 31	Ending balance	(g)			

Finished Goods Inventory

July 1	Beginning balance	(h)	July 31	Cost of goods sold	(j)
31	Completed jobs	(i)			
July 31	Ending balance	(k)			

Factory Labor

July 31	Factory wages	(l)	July 31	Wages assigned	(m)

Manufacturing Overhead

July 31	Indirect materials	8,900	July 31	Overhead applied	117,000
31	Indirect labor	16,000			
31	Other overhead	(n)			

Other data:

1. On July 1, two jobs were in process: Job No. 4085 and Job No. 4086, with costs of
   $19,000 and $8,200, respectively.

2. During July, Job Nos. 4087, 4088, and 4089 were started. On July 31, only Job No. 4089 was unfinished. This job had charges for direct materials $2,000 and direct labor $1,000, plus manufacturing overhead. Manufacturing overhead was applied at the rate of 130% of direct labor cost.

(d) $90,000
(f) $309,000
(l) $106,000

3. On July 1, Job No. 4084, costing $135,000, was in the finished goods warehouse. On July 31, Job No. 4088, costing $143,000, was in finished goods.
4. Overhead was $3,000 underapplied in July.

Instructions

List the letters (a) through (n) and indicate the amount pertaining to each letter. Show computations.

Problems: Set B

P2-1B   Medina Manufacturing uses a job order cost system and applies overhead to production on the basis of direct labor costs. On January 1, 2005, Job No. 50 was the only job in process. The costs incurred prior to January 1 on this job were as follows: direct materials $20,000, direct labor $12,000, and manufacturing overhead $16,000. As of January 1, Job No. 49 had been completed at a cost of $90,000 and was part of finished goods inventory. There was a $15,000 balance in the Raw Materials Inventory account.

Prepare entries in a job cost system and job cost sheets.
(SO 2, 3, 4, 5, 6)

During the month of January, Medina Manufacturing began production on Jobs 51 and 52, and completed Jobs 50 and 51. Jobs 49 and 50 were also sold on account during the month for $122,000 and $158,000, respectively. The following additional events occurred during the month.

1. Purchased additional raw materials of $90,000 on account.
2. Incurred factory labor costs of $65,000. Of this amount $13,000 related to employer payroll taxes.
3. Incurred manufacturing overhead costs as follows: indirect materials $14,000; indirect labor $15,000; depreciation expense $19,000, and various other manufacturing overhead costs on account $20,000.
4. Assigned direct materials and direct labor to jobs as follows.

Job No.	Direct Materials	Direct Labor
50	$10,000	$ 5,000
51	39,000	25,000
52	30,000	20,000

Instructions

(a) Calculate the predetermined overhead rate for 2005, assuming Medina Manufacturing estimates total manufacturing overhead costs of $980,000, direct labor costs of $700,000, and direct labor hours of 20,000 for the year.
(b) Open job cost sheets for Jobs 50, 51, and 52. Enter the January 1 balances on the job cost sheet for Job No. 50.
(c) Prepare the journal entries to record the purchase of raw materials, the factory labor costs incurred, and the manufacturing overhead costs incurred during the month of January.
(d) Prepare the journal entries to record the assignment of direct materials, direct labor, and manufacturing overhead costs to production. In assigning manufacturing overhead costs, use the overhead rate calculated in (a). Post all costs to the job cost sheets as necessary.
(e) Total the job cost sheets for any job(s) completed during the month. Prepare the journal entry (or entries) to record the completion of any job(s) during the month.

(e) Job 50, $70,000
    Job 51, $99,000

(f) Prepare the journal entry (or entries) to record the sale of any job(s) during the month.
(g) What is the balance in the Finished Goods Inventory account at the end of the month? What does this balance consist of?
(h) What is the amount of over- or underapplied overhead?

Prepare entries in a job cost system and partial income statement.
(SO 2, 3, 4, 5, 6)

P2-2B For the year ended December 31, 2005, the job cost sheets of Amend Company contained the following data.

Job Number	Explanation	Direct Materials	Direct Labor	Manufacturing Overhead	Total Costs
7640	Balance 1/1	$25,000	$24,000	$28,800	$ 77,800
	Current year's costs	30,000	36,000	43,200	109,200
7641	Balance 1/1	11,000	18,000	21,600	50,600
	Current year's costs	40,000	48,000	57,600	145,600
7642	Current year's costs	48,000	50,000	60,000	158,000

Other data:

1. Raw materials inventory totaled $15,000 on January 1. During the year, $140,000 of raw materials were purchased on account.
2. Finished goods on January 1 consisted of Job No. 7638 for $87,000 and Job No. 7639 for $92,000.
3. Job No. 7640 and Job No. 7641 were completed during the year.
4. Job Nos. 7638, 7639, and 7641 were sold on account for $530,000.
5. Manufacturing overhead incurred on account totaled $115,000.
6. Other manufacturing overhead consisted of indirect materials $14,000, indirect labor $20,000, and depreciation on factory machinery $8,000.

Instructions

(a) $158,000; Job 7642:
$158,000

(a) Prove the agreement of Work in Process Inventory with job cost sheets pertaining to unfinished work. *Hint:* Use a single T account for Work in Process Inventory. Calculate each of the following, then post each to the T account: (1) beginning balance, (2) direct materials, (3) direct labor, (4) manufacturing overhead, and (5) completed jobs.

(b) Amount = $3,800

(b) Prepare the adjusting entry for manufacturing overhead, assuming the balance is allocated entirely to Cost of Goods Sold.

(c) $158,600

(c) Determine the gross profit to be reported for 2005.

Prepare entries in a job cost system and cost of goods manufactured schedule.
(SO 2, 3, 4, 5)

P2-3B Zion Inc. is a construction company specializing in custom patios. The patios are constructed of concrete, brick, fiberglass, and lumber, depending upon customer preference. On June 1, 2005, the general ledger for Zion Inc. contains the following data.

Raw Materials Inventory	$4,200	Manufacturing Overhead Applied	$32,640
Work in Process Inventory	$5,540	Manufacturing Overhead Incurred	$31,650

Subsidiary data for Work in Process Inventory on June 1 are as follows.

Job Cost Sheets

Cost Element	Customer Job		
	Powell	Aurora	Hayden
Direct materials	$ 600	$ 800	$ 900
Direct labor	320	540	580
Manufacturing overhead	400	675	725
	$1,320	$2,015	$2,205

During June, raw materials purchased on account were $3,900, and all wages were paid. Additional overhead costs consisted of depreciation on equipment $700 and miscellaneous costs of $400 incurred on account.

A summary of materials requisition slips and time tickets for June shows the following.

Customer Job	Materials Requisition Slips	Time Tickets
Powell	$ 800	$ 450
Elgin	2,000	800
Aurora	500	360
Hayden	1,300	800
Powell	300	390
	4,900	2,800
General use	1,500	1,200
	$6,400	$4,000

Overhead was charged to jobs at the same rate of $1.25 per dollar of direct labor cost. The patios for customers Powell, Aurora, and Hayden were completed during June and sold for a total of $18,900. Each customer paid in full.

Instructions
(a) Journalize the June transactions: (i) for purchase of raw materials, factory labor costs incurred, and manufacturing overhead costs incurred; (ii) assignment of direct materials, labor, and overhead to production; and (iii) completion of jobs and sale of goods.
(b) Post the entries to Work in Process Inventory.
(c) Reconcile the balance in Work in Process Inventory with the costs of unfinished jobs.
(d) Prepare a cost of goods manufactured schedule for June.

(d) Cost of goods manufactured $12,940

P2-4B Stein Manufacturing Company uses a job order cost system in each of its three manufacturing departments. Manufacturing overhead is applied to jobs on the basis of direct labor cost in Department D, direct labor hours in Department E, and machine hours in Department K.

In establishing the predetermined overhead rates for 2006 the following estimates were made for the year.

Compute predetermined overhead rates, apply overhead and calculate under- or overapplied overhead.
(SO 4, 6)

	Department		
	D	**E**	**K**
Manufacturing overhead	$1,200,000	$1,500,000	$900,000
Direct labor costs	$1,500,000	$1,250,000	$450,000
Direct labor hours	100,000	125,000	40,000
Machine hours	400,000	500,000	120,000

During January, the job cost sheets showed the following costs and production data.

	Department		
	D	**E**	**K**
Direct materials used	$140,000	$126,000	$78,000
Direct labor costs	$120,000	$110,000	$37,500
Manufacturing overhead incurred	$ 98,000	$129,000	$74,000
Direct labor hours	8,000	11,000	3,500
Machine hours	34,000	45,000	10,400

(a) 80%, $12, $7.50
(b) $356,000, $368,000 $193,500
(c) $2,000, $(3,000), $(4,000)

Instructions
(a) Compute the predetermined overhead rate for each department.
(b) Compute the total manufacturing costs assigned to jobs in January in each department.
(c) Compute the under- or overapplied overhead for each department at January 31.

P2-5B Vargas Corporation's fiscal year ends on November 30. The following accounts are found in its job order cost accounting system for the first month of the new fiscal year.

Analyze manufacturing accounts and determine missing amounts.
(SO 2, 3, 4, 5, 6)

Raw Materials Inventory

Dec. 1	Beginning balance	(a)	Dec. 31	Requisitions	16,850
31	Purchases	19,225			
Dec. 31	Ending balance	7,975			

Work in Process Inventory

Dec. 1	Beginning balance	(b)	Dec. 31	Jobs completed	(f)
31	Direct materials	(c)			
31	Direct labor	8,800			
31	Overhead	(d)			
Dec. 31	Ending balance	(e)			

Finished Goods Inventory

Dec. 1	Beginning balance	(g)	Dec. 31	Cost of goods sold	(i)
31	Completed jobs	(h)			
Dec. 31	Ending balance	(j)			

Factory Labor

Dec. 31	Factory wages	12,025	Dec. 31	Wages assigned	(k)

Manufacturing Overhead

Dec. 31	Indirect materials	1,900	Dec. 31	Overhead applied	(m)
31	Indirect labor	(l)			
31	Other overhead	1,245			

Other data:

1. On December 1, two jobs were in process: Job No. 154 and Job No. 155. These jobs had combined direct materials costs of $9,750 and direct labor costs of $15,000. Overhead was applied at a rate that was 75% of direct labor cost.
2. During December, Job Nos. 156, 157, and 158 were started. On December 31, Job No. 158 was unfinished. This job had charges for direct materials $3,800 and direct labor $4,800, plus manufacturing overhead. All jobs, except for Job No. 158, were completed in December.
3. On December 1, Job No. 153 was in the finished goods warehouse. It had a total cost of $5,000. On December 31, Job No. 157 was the only job finished that was not sold. It had a cost of $4,000.
4. Manufacturing overhead was $230 overapplied in December.

(c) $14,950
(f) $54,150
(i) $55,150

Instructions

List the letters (a) through (m) and indicate the amount pertaining to each letter.

Problems: Set C

Problem Set C is provided at the book's Web site, www.wiley.com/college/weygandt.

▶ **BROADENING YOUR PERSPECTIVE**

Group Decision Case

BYP 2-1 Wang Products Company uses a job order cost system. For a number of months there has been an ongoing rift between the sales department and the production department concerning a special-order product, TC-1. TC-1 is a seasonal product that is manufactured in batches of 1,000 units. TC-1 is sold at cost plus a markup of 40% of cost.

The sales department is unhappy because fluctuating unit production costs significantly affect selling prices. Sales personnel complain that this has caused excessive customer complaints and the loss of considerable orders for TC-1.

The production department maintains that each job order must be fully costed on the basis of the costs incurred during the period in which the goods are produced. Production personnel maintain that the only real solution to the problem is for the sales department to increase sales in the slack periods.

Sandra Devona, president of the company, asks you as the company accountant to collect quarterly data for the past year on TC-1. From the cost accounting system, you accumulate the following production quantity and cost data.

	Quarter			
Costs	1	2	3	4
Direct materials	$100,000	$220,000	$ 80,000	$200,000
Direct labor	60,000	132,000	48,000	120,000
Manufacturing overhead	105,000	153,000	97,000	125,000
Total	$265,000	$505,000	$225,000	$445,000
Production in batches	5	11	4	10
Unit cost (per batch)	$ 53,000	$ 45,909	$ 56,250	$ 44,500

Instructions
With the class divided into groups, answer the following questions.

(a) What manufacturing cost element is responsible for the fluctuating unit costs? Why?
(b) What is your recommended solution to the problem of fluctuating unit cost?
(c) Restate the quarterly data on the basis of your recommended solution.

Managerial Analysis

BYP 2-2   In the course of routine checking of all journal entries prior to preparing year-end reports, Sally Yount discovered several strange entries. She recalled that the president's son Ken had come in to help out during an especially busy time and that he had recorded some journal entries. She was relieved that there were only a few of his entries, and even more relieved that he had included rather lengthy explanations. The entries Ken made were:

1.

Work in Process Inventory	25,000	
Cash		25,000

(This is for materials put into process. I don't find the record that we paid for these, so I'm crediting Cash, because I know we'll have to pay for them sooner or later.)

2.

Manufacturing Overhead	12,000	
Cash		12,000

(This is for bonuses paid to salespeople. I know they're part of overhead, and I can't find an account called "Non-factory Overhead" or "Other Overhead" so I'm putting it in Manufacturing Overhead. I have the check stubs, so I know we paid these.)

3.

Wages Expense	120,000	
Cash		120,000

(This is for the factory workers' wages. I have a note that payroll taxes are $12,000. I still think that's part of wages expense, and that we'll have to pay it all in cash sooner or later, so I credited Cash for the wages and the taxes.)

4.

Work in Process Inventory	3,000	
Raw Materials Inventory		3,000

(This is for the glue used in the factory. I know we used this to make the products, even though we didn't use very much on any one of the products. I got it out of inventory, so I credited an inventory account.)

Instructions
(a) How should Ken have recorded each of the four events?
(b) If the entry was not corrected, which financial statements (income statement or balance sheet) would be affected? What balances would be overstated or understated?

Real-World Focus

BYP 2-3   Founded in 1970, **Parlex Corporation** is a world leader in the design and manufacture of flexible interconnect products. Utilizing proprietary and patented technologies, Parlex produces custom flexible interconnects including flexible circuits, polymer thick film, laminated cables, and value-added assemblies for sophisticated electronics used in automotive, telecommunications, computer, diversified electronics, and aerospace applications. In addition to manufacturing sites in Methuen, Massachusetts; Salem, New Hampshire; Cranston, Rhode Island; San Jose, California; Shanghai, China; Isle of Wight, UK; and Empalme, Mexico, Parlex has logistic support centers and strategic alliances throughout North America, Asia, and Europe.

The following information was provided in the company's annual report.

PARLEX COMPANY
Notes to the Financial Statements

The Company's products are manufactured on a job order basis to customers' specifications. Customers submit requests for quotations on each job, and the Company prepares bids based on its own cost estimates. The Company attempts to reflect the impact of changing costs when establishing prices. However, during the past several years, the market conditions for flexible circuits and the resulting price sensitivity haven't always allowed this to transpire. Although still not satisfactory, the Company was able to reduce the cost of products sold as a percentage of sales to 85% this year versus 87% that was experienced in the two immediately preceding years. Management continues to focus on improving operational efficiency and further reducing costs.

Instructions
(a) Parlex management discusses the job order cost system employed by their company. What are several advantages of using the job order approach to costing?
(b) Contrast the products produced in a job order environment, like Parlex, to those produced when process cost systems are used.

Exploring the Web

BYP 2-4   The Institute of Management Accountants sponsors a certification for management accountants, allowing them to obtain the title of Certified Management Accountant.

Address: **www.imanet.org,** *or go to* **www.wiley.com/college/weygandt**

Steps
1. Go to the site shown above.
2. Choose **Certification**, and then, **Become Certified**.

Instructions
(a) What are the objectives of the certification program?
(b) What is the "experience requirement"?
(c) How many hours of continuing education are required, and what types of courses qualify?

Communication Activity

BYP 2-5   You are the management accountant for Clemente Manufacturing. Your company does custom carpentry work and uses a job order cost accounting system. Clemente sends detailed job cost sheets to its customers, along with an invoice. The job cost sheets show the date materials were used, the dollar cost of materials, and the hours and cost of labor. A predetermined overhead application rate is used, and the total overhead applied is also listed.

Cindy Stein is a customer who recently had custom cabinets installed. Along with her check in payment for the work done, she included a letter. She thanked the company for including the detailed cost information but questioned why overhead was estimated. She stated that she would be interested in knowing exactly what costs were included in overhead, and she thought that other customers would, too.

Instructions
Prepare a letter to Ms. Stein (address: 123 Cedar Lane, Altoona, Kansas 66651) and tell her why you did not send her information on exact costs of overhead included in her job. Respond to her suggestion that you provide this information.

Research Assignment

BYP 2-6 The April 19, 2004, edition of the *Wall Street Journal* contains an article by Andy Pasztor and Jonathan Karp titled "**Northrop** Papers Indicate Coverup."

Instructions
Read the article and answer the following questions.

(a) What type of costing system would Northrop use for these government contracts? Explain your answer.
(b) These contracts were billed on a "cost-plus" basis, meaning that the contract allowed the company simply to keep track of its costs and then bill the government for the costs it incurred, plus a profit. In what ways did Northrop abuse this arrangement?
(c) What systems were in place to try to ensure that the company did not violate the terms of the contract?

Ethics Case

BYP 2-7 ESU Printing provides printing services to many different corporate clients. Although ESU bids most jobs, some jobs, particularly new ones, are negotiated on a "cost-plus" basis. Cost-plus means that the buyer is willing to pay the actual cost plus a return (profit) on these costs to ESU.

Clara Biggio, controller for ESU, has recently returned from a meeting where ESU's president stated that he wanted her to find a way to charge most costs to any project that was on a cost-plus basis. The president noted that the company needed more profits to meet its stated goals this period. By charging more costs to the cost-plus projects and therefore fewer costs to the jobs that were bid, the company should be able to increase its profit for the current year.

Clara knew why the president wanted to take this action. Rumors were that he was looking for a new position and if the company reported strong profit, the president's opportunities would be enhanced. Clara also recognized that she could probably increase the cost of certain jobs by changing the basis used to allocate manufacturing overhead.

Instructions
(a) Who are the stakeholders in this situation?
(b) What are the ethical issues in this situation?
(c) What would you do if you were Clara Biggio?

Answers to Self-Study Questions
1. a **2.** b **3.** c **4.** d **5.** b **6.** a **7.** d **8.** b **9.** c **10.** b

Remember to go back to the Navigator box on the chapter-opening page and check off your completed work.

CHAPTER 3

Process Cost Accounting

STUDY OBJECTIVES

After studying this chapter, you should be able to:

1 Understand who uses process cost systems.

2 Explain the similarities and differences between job order cost and process cost systems.

3 Explain the flow of costs in a process cost system.

4 Make the journal entries to assign manufacturing costs in a process cost system.

5 Compute equivalent units.

6 Explain the four steps necessary to prepare a production cost report.

7 Prepare a production cost report.

☑ THE NAVIGATOR

THE NAVIGATOR ✔

▶ Scan *Study Objectives* ☐

▶ Read *Feature Story* ☐

▶ Read *Preview* ☐

▶ Read text and answer *Before You Go On*
  p. 100 ☐   p. 109 ☐   p. 110 ☐

▶ Work *Using the Decision Toolkit* ☐

▶ Review *Summary of Study Objectives* ☐

▶ Work *Demonstration Problem* ☐

▶ Answer *Self-Study Questions* ☐

▶ Complete *Assignments* ☐

FEATURE STORY

Ben & Jerry's Tracks Its Mix-Ups

At one time, one of the fastest growing companies in the nation was **Ben & Jerry's Homemade, Inc.**, based in Waterbury, Vermont. The ice cream company that started out of a garage in 1978 is now a public company.

Making ice cream is a process—a movement of product from a mixing department to a prepping department to a pint department. The mixing department is where the ice cream is created. The prep area is where extras such as cherries and walnuts are added to make plain ice cream into "Cherry Garcia." And the pint department is where the ice cream is actually put into containers. As the product is processed from one department to the next, the appropriate materials, labor, and overhead are added to it.

"The incoming ingredients from the shipping and receiving departments are stored in certain locations, either in a freezer or dry warehouse," says Beecher Eurich, staff accountant. "As ingredients get added, so do the costs associated with them." How much ice cream is actually produced? Running the plants around the clock, 18 million gallons are produced each year.

Using a process costing system, Eurich can tell you how much a certain batch of ice cream costs to make—its materials, labor, and overhead in each of the production departments. She generates reports for the production department heads, but makes sure not to overdo it. "You can get bogged down in

numbers," says Eurich. "If you're generating a report that no one can use, then that's a waste of time." More likely, though, Ben & Jerry's production people want to know how efficient they are. Why? Many own stock in the company.

THE NAVIGATOR

www.benjerry.com

The cost accounting system used by companies such as **Ben & Jerry's** is called a **process cost accounting** system. In contrast to job order cost accounting, which focuses on the individual job, process cost accounting focuses on the processes involved in mass-producing products that are identical or very similar in nature. The primary objective of the chapter is to explain and illustrate process cost accounting.

The content and organization of this chapter are as follows.

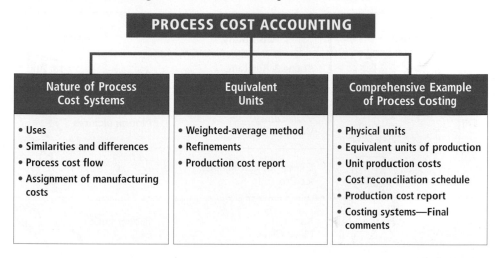

PROCESS COST ACCOUNTING

Nature of Process Cost Systems	Equivalent Units	Comprehensive Example of Process Costing
• Uses • Similarities and differences • Process cost flow • Assignment of manufacturing costs	• Weighted-average method • Refinements • Production cost report	• Physical units • Equivalent units of production • Unit production costs • Cost reconciliation schedule • Production cost report • Costing systems—Final comments

☑ THE NAVIGATOR

The Nature of Process Cost Systems

USES OF PROCESS COST SYSTEMS

Process cost systems are used to apply costs to similar products that are mass-produced in a continuous fashion. **Ben & Jerry's** uses a process cost system: Production of the ice cream, once it begins, continues until the ice cream emerges, and the processing is the same for the entire run—with precisely the same amount of materials, labor, and overhead. Each finished pint of ice cream is indistinguishable from another.

A company such as **USX** uses process costing in the manufacturing of steel. **Kellogg** and **General Mills** use process costing for cereal production; **Exxon-Mobil** uses process costing for its oil refining. And **Sherwin Williams** uses process costing for its paint products. At a bottling company like **Coca-Cola**, the manufacturing process begins with the blending of ingredients. Next the beverage is dispensed into bottles that are moved into position by automated machinery. The bottles are then capped, packaged, and forwarded to the finished goods warehouse. This process is shown in Illustration 3-1.

STUDY OBJECTIVE

1

Understand who uses process cost systems.

Illustration 3-1   Manufacturing processes

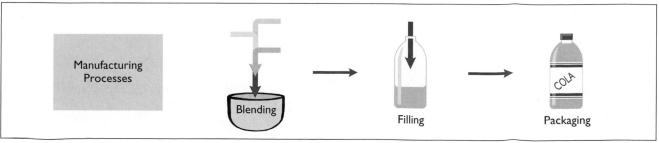

Manufacturing Processes — Blending → Filling → Packaging

For Coca-Cola, as well as the other companies just mentioned, once the production begins, it continues until the finished product emerges, and each unit of finished product is like every other unit.

In comparison, costs in a job order cost system are assigned to a *specific job*. Examples are the construction of a customized home, the making of a motion picture, or the manufacturing of a specialized machine. Illustration 3-2 provides examples of companies that primarily use either a process cost system or a job order cost system.

Illustration 3-2 Process cost and job order cost companies and products

Process Cost System Company	Product		Job Order Cost System Company	Product	
Coca-Cola, PepsiCo	Soft drinks		Young & Rubicam, J. Walter Thompson	Advertising	
ExxonMobil, Royal Dutch Shell	Oil		Walt Disney, Warner Brothers	Motion pictures	
Intel, Advanced Micro Devices	Computer chips		Center Ice Consultants, Ice Pro	Ice rinks	
Dow Chemical, DuPont	Chemicals		Kaiser, Mayo Clinic	Patient health care	

STUDY OBJECTIVE

2

Explain the similarities and differences between job order cost and process cost systems.

SIMILARITIES AND DIFFERENCES BETWEEN JOB ORDER COST AND PROCESS COST SYSTEMS

In a job order cost system, costs are assigned to each job. In a process cost system, costs are tracked through a series of connected manufacturing processes or departments, rather than by individual jobs. Thus, process cost systems are used when a large volume of uniform or relatively homogeneous products is produced. The basic flow of costs in these two systems is shown in Illustration 3-3.

Illustration 3-3 Job order cost and process cost flow

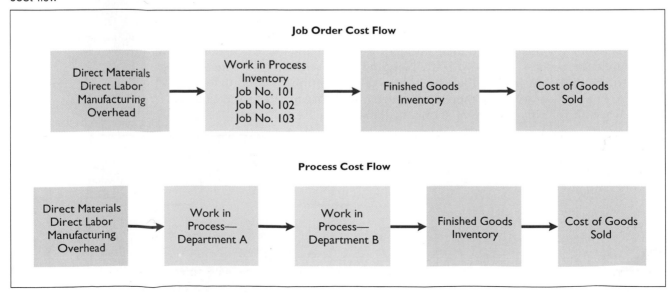

The basic similarities and differences between these two systems are highlighted in the following analysis.

Similarities

Job order cost and process cost systems are similar in three ways:

1. **The manufacturing cost elements.** Both costing systems track three manufacturing cost elements—direct materials, direct labor, and manufacturing overhead.
2. **The accumulation of the costs of materials, labor, and overhead.** In both costing systems, raw materials are debited to Raw Materials Inventory; factory labor is debited to Factory Labor; and manufacturing overhead costs are debited to Manufacturing Overhead.
3. **The flow of costs.** As noted above, all manufacturing costs are accumulated by debits to Raw Materials Inventory, Factory Labor, and Manufacturing Overhead. These costs are then assigned to the same accounts in both costing systems—Work in Process, Finished Goods Inventory, and Cost of Goods Sold. **The methods of assigning costs, however, differ significantly.** These differences are explained and illustrated later in the chapter.

Differences

The differences between a job order cost and a process cost system are as follows.

1. **The number of work in process accounts used.** In a job order cost system, only one work in process account is used. In a process cost system, multiple work in process accounts are used.
2. **Documents used to track costs.** In a job order cost system, costs are charged to individual jobs and summarized in a job cost sheet. In a process cost system, costs are summarized in a production cost report for each department.
3. **The point at which costs are totaled.** In a job order cost system, total costs are determined when the job is completed. In a process cost system, total costs are determined at the end of a period of time.
4. **Unit cost computations.** In a job order cost system, the unit cost is the total cost per job divided by the units produced. In a process cost system, the unit cost is total manufacturing costs for the period divided by the units produced during the period.

The major differences between a job order cost and a process cost system are summarized in Illustration 3-4.

Features	Job Order Cost System	Process Cost System
Work in process accounts	• One work in process account	• Multiple work in process accounts
Documents used	• Job cost sheets	• Production cost reports
Determination of total manufacturing costs	• Each job	• Each period
Unit-cost computations	• Cost of each job ÷ Units produced for the job	• Total manufacturing costs ÷ Units produced during the period

Illustration 3-4   Job order versus process cost systems

PROCESS COST FLOW

Illustration 3-5 shows the flow of costs in the process cost system for Tyler Company. Tyler Company manufactures automatic can openers that are sold to retail outlets. Manufacturing consists of two processes: machining and assembly.

STUDY OBJECTIVE
3
Explain the flow of costs in a process cost system.

In the Machining Department, the raw materials are shaped, honed, and drilled. In the Assembly Department, the parts are assembled and packaged.

Illustration 3-5 Flow of costs in process cost system

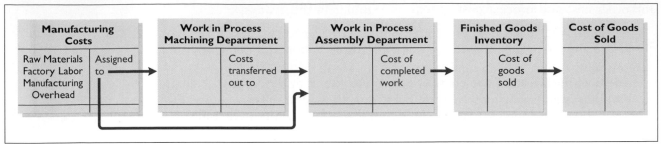

As the flow of costs indicates, materials, labor, and manufacturing overhead can be added in both the Machining and Assembly Departments. When the Machining Department finishes its work, the partially completed units are transferred to the Assembly Department. In the Assembly Department, the goods are finished and are then transferred to the finished goods inventory. Upon sale, the goods are removed from the finished goods inventory. Within each department, a similar set of activities is performed on each unit processed.

ASSIGNMENT OF MANUFACTURING COSTS— JOURNAL ENTRIES

STUDY OBJECTIVE
——— 4 ———
Make the journal entries to assign manufacturing costs in a process cost system.

As indicated earlier, the accumulation of the costs of materials, labor, and manufacturing overhead is the same in a process cost system as in a job order cost system. All raw materials are debited to Raw Materials Inventory when the materials are purchased. All factory labor is debited to Factory Labor when the labor costs are incurred. And overhead costs are debited to Manufacturing Overhead as they are incurred. However, the assignment of the three manufacturing cost elements to Work in Process in a process cost system is different from a job order cost system. Here we'll look at how these manufacturing cost elements are assigned in a process cost system.

Materials Costs

Materials

All raw materials issued for production are a materials cost to the producing department. Materials requisition slips may be used in a process cost system, but **fewer requisitions are generally required than in a job order cost system, because the materials are used for processes rather than for specific jobs.** Requisitions are issued less frequently in a process cost system because the requisitions are for larger quantities.

Materials are usually added to production at the beginning of the first process. However, in subsequent processes, other materials may be added at various points. For example, in the manufacture of **Hershey** candy bars, the chocolate and other ingredients are added at the beginning of the first process, and the wrappers and cartons are added at the end of the packaging process. At Tyler Company, materials are entered at the beginning of each process. The entry to record the materials used is:

Work in Process—Machining	XXXX	
Work in Process—Assembly	XXXX	
Raw Materials Inventory		XXXX
(To record materials used)		

At ice cream maker **Ben & Jerry's**, materials are added in three departments: milk and flavoring in the mixing department; extras such as cherries and walnuts in the prepping department; and cardboard containers in the pinting (packaging) department.

Factory Labor Costs

In a process cost system, as in a job order cost system, time tickets may be used to determine the cost of labor assignable to production departments. Since labor costs are assigned to a process rather than a job, the labor cost chargeable to a process can be obtained from the payroll register or departmental payroll summaries.

Labor costs for the Machining Department will include the wages of employees who shape, hone, and drill the raw materials. The entry to assign these costs for Tyler Company is:

Factory Labor

Work in Process—Machining	XXXX	
Work in Process—Assembly	XXXX	
Factory Labor		XXXX
(To assign factory labor to production)		

Manufacturing Overhead Costs

The objective in assigning overhead in a process cost system is to allocate the overhead costs to the production departments on an objective and equitable basis. That basis is the activity that "drives" or causes the costs. A primary driver of overhead costs in continuous manufacturing operations is **machine time used**, not direct labor. Thus, **machine hours are widely used** in allocating manufacturing overhead costs. The entry to allocate overhead to the two processes is:

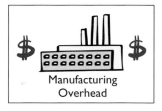
Manufacturing Overhead

Work in Process—Machining	XXXX	
Work in Process—Assembly	XXXX	
Manufacturing Overhead		XXXX
(To assign overhead to production)		

Business Insight
Management Perspective

In one of **Caterpillar's** automated cost centers, work is fed into the cost center, processed by robotic machines, and transferred to the next cost center without human intervention. One person tends all of the machines and spends more time maintaining machines than operating them. In such cases, overhead rates based on direct labor hours may be misleading. Surprisingly, some companies continue to assign manufacturing overhead on the basis of direct labor despite the fact that there is no cause-and-effect relationship between labor and overhead.

Transfer to Next Department

At the end of the month, an entry is needed to record the cost of the goods transferred out of the department. In this case, the transfer is to the Assembly Department, and the following entry is made.

Work in Process—Assembly	XXXXX	
Work in Process—Machining		XXXXX
(To record transfer of units to the Assembly		
Department)		

Transfer to Finished Goods

The units completed in the Assembly Department are transferred to the finished goods warehouse. The entry for this transfer is as follows.

Finished Goods Inventory	XXXXX	
Work in Process—Assembly		XXXXX
(To record transfer of units to finished goods)		

Transfer to Cost of Goods Sold

When finished goods are sold, the entry to record the cost of goods sold is as follows.

Cost of Goods Sold	XXXXX	
Finished Goods Inventory		XXXXX
(To record cost of units sold)		

BEFORE YOU GO ON . . .

▶Review It

1. What type of manufacturing companies might use a process cost accounting system?
2. What are the principal similarities and differences between a job order cost system and a process cost system?

▶Do It

Ruth Company manufactures ZEBO through two processes: Blending and Bottling. In June, raw materials used were Blending $18,000 and Bottling $4,000; factory labor costs were Blending $12,000 and Bottling $5,000; manufacturing overhead costs were Blending $6,000 and Bottling $2,500. Units completed at a cost of $19,000 in the Blending Department are transferred to the Bottling Department. Units completed at a cost of $11,000 in the Bottling Department are transferred to Finished Goods. Journalize the assignment of these costs to the two processes and the transfer of units as appropriate.

Action Plan

- In process cost accounting, keep separate work in process accounts for each process.
- When the costs are assigned to production, debit the separate work in process accounts.
- Transfer cost of completed units to the next process or to Finished Goods.

Solution The entries are:

Work in Process—Blending	18,000	
Work in Process—Bottling	4,000	
Raw Materials Inventory		22,000
(To record materials used)		
Work in Process—Blending	12,000	
Work in Process—Bottling	5,000	
Factory Labor		17,000
(To assign factory labor to production)		
Work in Process—Blending	6,000	
Work in Process—Bottling	2,500	
Manufacturing Overhead		8,500
(To assign overhead to production)		
Work in Process—Bottling	19,000	
Work in Process—Blending		19,000
(To record transfer of units to the Bottling		
Department)		
Finished Goods Inventory	11,000	
Work in Process—Bottling		11,000
(To record transfer of units to finished goods)		

Related exercise material: BE3-1, BE3-2, BE3-3, E3-1, and E3-2.

Equivalent Units

Suppose you were asked to compute the cost of instruction per full-time equivalent student at your college. You are provided the following information.

STUDY OBJECTIVE
5
Compute equivalent units.

Illustration 3-6 Information for full-time student example

Costs:	
Total cost of instruction	$9,000,000
Student population:	
Full-time students	900
Part-time students	1,000

Part-time students take 60 percent of the classes of a full-time student during the year. To compute the number of full-time equivalent students per year, you would make the following computation.

Illustration 3-7 Full-time equivalent unit computation

Full-time Students	+	Equivalent Units of Part-time Students	=	Full-time Equivalent Students
900	+	(60% × 1,000)	=	1,500

The cost of instruction per full-time equivalent student is therefore the total cost of instruction ($9,000,000) divided by the number of full-time equivalent students (1,500), which is $6,000 ($9,000,000 ÷ 1,500).

In a process cost system, the same idea, called equivalent units of production, is used. **Equivalent units of production** measure the work done during the period, expressed in fully completed units. This concept is used to determine the cost per unit of completed product.

WEIGHTED-AVERAGE METHOD

The formula to compute equivalent units of production is as follows.

Illustration 3-8 Equivalent units of production formula

Units Completed and Transferred Out	+	Equivalent Units of Ending Work in Process	=	Equivalent Units of Production

To better understand this concept of equivalent units, consider the following two separate examples.

Example 1: The Blending Department's entire output during the period consists of ending work in process of 4,000 units which are 60 percent complete as to materials, labor, and overhead. The equivalent units of production for the Blending Department are therefore 2,400 units (4,000 × 60%).

Example 2: The Packaging Department's output during the period consists of 10,000 units completed and transferred out, and 5,000 units in ending work in process which are 70 percent completed. The equivalent units of production are therefore 13,500 [10,000 + (5,000 × 70%)].

This method of computing equivalent units is referred to as the **weighted-average method**. It considers the degree of completion (weighting) of the units completed and transferred out and the ending work in process. An alternative method, called the FIFO method, is discussed in the appendix to this chapter.

REFINEMENTS ON THE WEIGHTED-AVERAGE METHOD

Kellogg Company has produced Eggo® Waffles since 1970. Three departments are used to produce these waffles: Mixing, Baking, and Freezing/Packaging. In the Mixing Department dry ingredients, including flour, salt, and baking powder, are mixed with liquid ingredients, including eggs and vegetable oil, to make waffle batter. Information related to the Mixing Department at the end of June is provided in Illustration 3-9.

Illustration 3-9 Information for Mixing Department

MIXING DEPARTMENT		Percentage Complete	
	Physical Units	**Materials**	**Conversion Costs**
Work in process, June 1	100,000	100%	70%
Started into production	800,000		
Total units	900,000		
Units transferred out	700,000		
Work in process, June 30	200,000	100%	60%
Total units	900,000		

Illustration 3-9 indicates that the beginning work in process is 100 percent complete as to materials cost and 70 percent complete as to conversion costs. Conversion costs **refers to the sum of labor costs and overhead costs.** In other words, both the dry and liquid ingredients (materials) are added at the beginning of the process to make Eggo® Waffles. The conversion costs (labor and overhead) related to the mixing of these ingredients were incurred uniformly and are 70 percent complete. The ending work in process is 100 percent complete as to materials cost and 60 percent complete as to conversion costs.

We then use the Mixing Department information to determine equivalent units. **In computing equivalent units, the beginning work in process is not part of the equivalent units of production formula.** The units transferred out to the Baking Department are fully complete as to both materials and conversion costs. The ending work in process is fully complete as to materials, but only 60 percent complete as to conversion costs. **Two equivalent unit computations are therefore necessary:** one for materials and the other for conversion costs. Illustration 3-10 shows these computations.

Helpful Hint Question: When are separate unit cost computations needed for materials and conversion costs? Answer: Whenever the two types of costs do not occur in the process at the same time.

	Equivalent Units	
	Materials	**Conversion Costs**
Units transferred out	700,000	700,000
Work in process, June 30		
200,000 × 100%	200,000	
200,000 × 60%		120,000
Total equivalent units	900,000	820,000

Illustration 3-10 Computation of equivalent units—Mixing Department

The earlier formula used to compute equivalent units of production can be refined to show the computations for materials and for conversion costs, as follows.

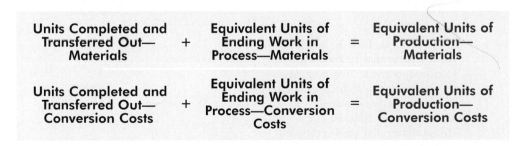

Illustration 3-11 Refined equivalent units of production formula

PRODUCTION COST REPORT

As mentioned earlier, a production cost report is prepared for each department in a process cost system. A production cost report is the key document used by management to understand the activities in a department; it shows the production quantity and cost data related to that department. For example, in producing Eggo® Waffles, **Kellogg Company** would have three production cost reports: Mixing, Baking, and Freezing/Packaging. Illustration 3-12 (page 104) shows the flow of costs to make an Eggo® Waffle and the related production cost reports for each department.

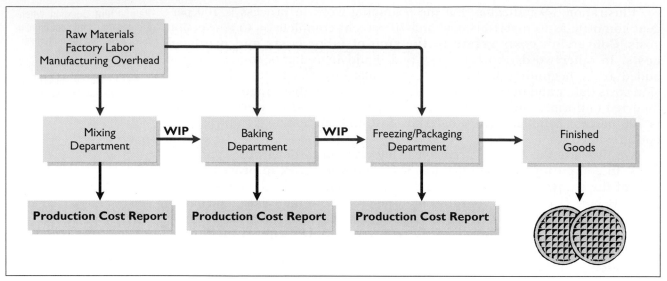

Illustration 3-12   Flow of costs in making Eggo® Waffles

In order to complete a production cost report, the company must perform four steps, which as a whole, make up the process costing system.

STUDY OBJECTIVE

6

Explain the four steps necessary to prepare a production cost report.

1. Compute the physical unit flow.
2. Compute the equivalent units of production.
3. Compute unit production costs.
4. Prepare a cost reconciliation schedule.

The next section explores these steps in an extended example.

Comprehensive Example of Process Costing

Assumed data for the Mixing Department at **Kellogg Company** for the month of June are shown in Illustration 3-13. We will use this information to complete a production cost report for the Mixing Department.

Illustration 3-13   Unit and cost data—Mixing Department

MIXING DEPARTMENT	
Units	
Work in process, June 1	100,000
Direct materials: 100% complete	
Conversion costs: 70% complete	
Units started into production during June	800,000
Units completed and transferred out to Baking Department	700,000
Work in process, June 30	200,000
Direct materials: 100% complete	
Conversion costs: 60% complete	
Costs	
Work in process, June 1	
Direct materials: 100% complete	$ 50,000
Conversion costs: 70% complete	35,000
Cost of work in process, June 1	$ 85,000
Costs incurred during production in June	
Direct materials	$400,000
Conversion costs	170,000
Costs incurred in June	$570,000

COMPUTE THE PHYSICAL UNIT FLOW (STEP 1)

Physical units are the actual units to be accounted for during a period, irrespective of any work performed. To keep track of these units, it is necessary to add the units started (or transferred) into production during the period to the units in process at the beginning of the period. This amount is referred to as the **total units to be accounted for.**

The total units then are accounted for by the output of the period. The output consists of units transferred out during the period and any units in process at the end of the period. This amount is referred to as the **total units accounted for.** Illustration 3-14 shows the flow of physical units for Kellogg Company for the month of June for the Mixing Department.

MIXING DEPARTMENT	
	Physical Units
Units to be accounted for	
Work in process, June 1	100,000
Started (transferred) into production	800,000
Total units	**900,000**
Units accounted for	
Completed and transferred out	700,000
Work in process, June 30	200,000
Total units	**900,000**

Illustration 3-14 Physical unit flow—Mixing Department

The records indicate that 900,000 units must be accounted for in the Mixing Department. Of this sum, 700,000 units were transferred to the Baking Department and 200,000 units were still in process.

COMPUTE EQUIVALENT UNITS OF PRODUCTION (STEP 2)

Once the physical flow of the units is established, it is necessary to measure the Mixing Department's productivity in terms of equivalent units of production. In the Mixing Department, materials are added at the beginning of the process, and conversion costs are incurred uniformly during the process. Thus, two computations of equivalent units are required: one for materials, and one for conversion costs. The equivalent unit computation is as follows.

Helpful Hint Materials are not always added at the beginning of the process. For example, materials are sometimes added uniformly during the process.

	Equivalent Units	
	Materials	**Conversion Costs**
Units transferred out	700,000	700,000
Work in process, June 30		
200,000 × 100%	200,000	
200,000 × 60%		120,000
Total equivalent units	**900,000**	**820,000**

Illustration 3-15 Computation of equivalent units—Mixing Department

Helpful Hint Remember that the beginning work in process is ignored in this computation.

COMPUTE UNIT PRODUCTION COSTS (STEP 3)

Armed with the knowledge of the equivalent units of production, we can now compute the unit production costs. **Unit production costs** are costs expressed in terms of equivalent units of production. When equivalent units of production are different for materials and conversion costs, three unit costs are computed: (1) materials, (2) conversion, and (3) total manufacturing.

The computation of total materials cost related to Eggo® Waffles is as follows.

Illustration 3-16 Total materials cost computation

Work in process, June 1	
Direct materials cost	$ 50,000
Costs added to production during June	
Direct materials cost	400,000
Total materials cost	**$450,000**

The computation of unit materials cost is as follows.

Illustration 3-17 Unit materials cost computation

Total Materials Cost	÷	Equivalent Units of Materials	=	Unit Materials Cost
$450,000	÷	900,000	=	$0.50

The computation of total conversion costs is shown in Illustration 3-18.

Illustration 3-18 Total conversion costs computation

Work in process, June 1	
Conversion costs	$ 35,000
Costs added to production during June	
Conversion costs	170,000
Total conversion costs	**$205,000**

The computation of unit conversion cost is as follows.

Illustration 3-19 Unit conversion cost computation

Total Conversion Costs	÷	Equivalent Units of Conversion Costs	=	Unit Conversion Cost
$205,000	÷	820,000	=	$0.25

Total manufacturing cost per unit is therefore computed as shown in Illustration 3-20 (next page).

Unit Materials Cost	+	Unit Conversion Cost	=	Total Manufacturing Cost per Unit
$0.50	+	$0.25	=	$0.75

Illustration 3-20 Total manufacturing cost per unit

PREPARE A COST RECONCILIATION SCHEDULE (STEP 4)

We are now ready to determine the cost of goods transferred out of the Mixing Department to the Baking Department and the costs in ending work in process. The total costs that were charged to the Mixing Department in June are as follows.

Costs to be accounted for	
Work in process, June 1	$ 85,000
Started into production	570,000
Total costs	**$655,000**

Illustration 3-21 Costs charged to Mixing Department

The total costs charged to the Mixing Department in June are therefore $655,000.

A cost reconciliation schedule is then prepared to assign these costs to (1) units transferred out to the Baking Department and (2) ending work in process.

MIXING DEPARTMENT
Cost Reconciliation Schedule

Costs accounted for		
Transferred out (700,000 × $0.75)		$ 525,000
Work in process, June 30		
Materials (200,000 × $0.50)	$100,000	
Conversion costs (120,000 × $0.25)	30,000	130,000
Total costs		**$655,000**

Illustration 3-22 Cost reconciliation schedule— Mixing Department

The total manufacturing cost per unit, $0.75, is used in costing the units completed and transferred to the Baking Department. In contrast, the unit cost of materials and the unit cost of conversion are needed in costing units in process. The **cost reconciliation schedule** shows that the **total costs accounted for** (Illustration 3-22) equal the **total costs to be accounted for** (see Illustration 3-21).

PREPARING THE PRODUCTION COST REPORT

At this point, we are ready to prepare the production cost report for the Mixing Department. As indicated earlier, this report is an internal document for management that shows production quantity and cost data for a production department.

There are four steps in preparing a production cost report. They are: (1) Prepare a physical unit schedule. (2) Compute equivalent units. (3) Compute unit costs. (4) Prepare a cost reconciliation schedule. The production cost report for the Mixing Department is shown in Illustration 3-23 (page 108). The four steps are identified in the report.

STUDY OBJECTIVE
7
Prepare a production cost report.

Illustration 3-23   Production cost report

	A	B	C	D	E	F
				Mixing Department		
1				Production Cost Report		
2				For the Month Ended June 30, 2005		
3						
4				Equivalent Units		
5			Physical Units	Materials	Conversion Costs	
6	QUANTITIES		Step 1	Step 2		
7	Units to be accounted for					
8	Work in process, June 1		100,000			
9	Started into production		800,000			
10	Total units		900,000			
11	Units accounted for					
12	Transferred out		700,000	700,000	700,000	
13	Work in process, June 30		200,000	200,000	120,000	(200,000 X 60%)
14	Total units		900,000	900,000	820,000	
15	COSTS Unit costs		Step 3	Materials	Conversion Costs	Total
16	Costs in June			$450,000	$205,000	$655,000
17	Equivalent units		(a)	900,000	820,000	
18	Unit costs [(a) ÷ (b)]		(b)	$0.50	$0.25	$0.75
19	Costs to be accounted for					
20	Work in process, June 1					$85,000
21	Started into production					570,000
22	Total costs					$655,000
23	**Cost Reconciliation Schedule**		Step 4			
24	Costs accounted for					
25	Transferred out (700,000 X $0.75)					$525,000
26	Work in process, June 30					
27	Materials (200,000 X $0.50)				$100,000	
28	Conversion costs (120,000 X $0.25)				30,000	130,000
29	Total costs					$655,000

Production cost reports provide a basis for evaluating the productivity of a department. In addition, the cost data can be used to assess whether unit costs and total costs are reasonable. By comparing the quantity and cost data with predetermined goals, top management can also judge whether current performance is meeting planned objectives.

DECISION TOOLKIT

Decision Checkpoints	Info Needed for Decision	Tool to Use for Decision	How to Evaluate Results
What is the cost of a product?	Costs of materials, labor, and overhead assigned to processes used to make the product	Production cost report	Compare costs to previous periods, to competitors, and to expected selling price to evaluate overall profitability.

BEFORE YOU GO ON . . .

▶**Review It**

1. How do physical units differ from equivalent units of production?
2. What are the formulas for computing unit costs of production?
3. How are costs assigned to units transferred out and in process?
4. What are the four steps in preparing a production cost report?

▶**Do It**

In March, Rodayo Manufacturing had the following unit production costs: materials $6 and conversion costs $9. On March 1, it had zero work in process. During March, 12,000 units were transferred out, and 800 units that were 25 percent completed as to conversion costs and 100 percent complete as to materials were in ending work in process at March 31. Assign the costs to the units transferred out and in process.

Action Plan

• Assign the total manufacturing cost of $15 per unit to the 12,000 units transferred out.
• Assign the materials cost and conversion costs based on equivalent units of production to units in process.

Solution The assignment of costs is as follows.

Costs accounted for		
Transferred out (12,000 × $15)		$180,000
Work in process, March 31		
Materials (800 × $6)	$4,800	
Conversion costs (200[a] × $9)	1,800	6,600
Total costs		$186,600

[a]800 × 25%

Related exercise material: BE3-4, BE3-5, BE3-6, BE3-7, BE3-8, BE3-10, E3-3, E3-4, E3-6, E3-8, E3-11, and E3-12.

☑ THE NAVIGATOR

COSTING SYSTEMS—FINAL COMMENTS

Companies often use a combination of a process cost and a job order cost system, called **operations costing**. Operations costing is similar to process costing in that standardized methods are used to manufacture the product. At the same time, the product may have some customized, individual features that require the use of a job order cost system.

Consider, for example, the automobile manufacturer **Ford Motor Company**. Each vehicle at a given plant goes through the same assembly line, but different materials (such as seat coverings, paint, and tinted glass) may be used for different vehicles. Similarly, **Kellogg's** Pop-Tarts Toaster Pastries® go through numerous processes—mixing, filling, baking, frosting, and packaging. The pastry dough, though, comes in three flavors—plain, chocolate, and graham—and fillings include Smucker's® real fruit, chocolate fudge, vanilla creme, brown sugar cinnamon, and S'mores.

A cost-benefit tradeoff occurs as a company decides which costing system to use. A job order system, for example, provides detailed information related to the cost of the product. Because each job has its own distinguishing characteristics, an accurate cost per job can be provided. This information is useful in controlling costs and pricing products. However, the cost of implementing a job order cost system is often expensive because of the accounting costs involved.

On the other hand, for a company like **Intel**, which makes computer chips, is there a benefit in knowing whether the cost of the one hundredth chip produced is different from the one thousandth chip produced? Probably not. An average cost of the product will suffice for control and pricing purposes. In summary, when deciding to use one of these systems, or a combination system, a company must weigh the costs of implementing the system against the benefits from the additional information provided.

Business Insight
Service Company Perspective

Frequently when we think of service companies we think of specific, nonroutine tasks, such as rebuilding an automobile engine, providing consulting services on a business acquisition, or working on a major lawsuit. Clearly, such nonroutine situations would call for job order costing.

However, many service companies specialize in performing repetitive, routine aspects of a particular business. For example, auto-care vendors such as **Jiffy Lube** focus on the routine aspects of car care. **H&R Block** focuses on the routine aspects of basic tax practice, and many large law firms focus on routine legal services, such as uncomplicated divorces. For service companies that perform routine, repetitive services, process costing provides a simple solution to their accounting needs. In fact, since in many instances there is little or no work in process at the end of the period, applying process costing in this setting can be even easier than for a manufacturer.

BEFORE YOU GO ON . . .

▶**Review It**

1. In what circumstances would a manufacturer use operations costing instead of process costing?
2. Describe the cost-benefit tradeoff in deciding what costing system to use.

☑ THE NAVIGATOR

DECISION TOOLKIT

Decision Checkpoints	Info Needed for Decision	Tool to Use for Decision	How to Evaluate Results
✔			👍👎
What costing method should be used?	Type of product produced	Cost of accounting system; benefits of additional information	The benefits of providing the additional information should exceed the costs of the accounting system needed to develop the information.

Using the Decision Toolkit

Essence Company manufactures a high-end after-shave lotion, called Eternity, which is sold in 10-ounce shaped glass bottles. Because the market for after-shave lotion is highly competitive, the company is very concerned about keeping its costs under control. Eternity is manufactured through three processes: mixing, filling, and corking. Materials are added at the beginning of the process, and labor and overhead are incurred uniformly throughout each process. The company uses a weighted-average method to cost its product.

A partially completed production cost report for the month of May for the Mixing Department is shown below.

ESSENCE COMPANY
Mixing Department
Production Cost Report
For the Month Ended May 31, 2005

	Physical Units	Equivalent Units Materials	Conversion Costs
Quantities	Step 1		Step 2
Units to be accounted for			
Work in process, May 1	1,000		
Started into production	2,000		
Total units	3,000		
Units accounted for			
Transferred out	2,200	?	?
Work in process, May 31	800	?	?
Total units	3,000	?	?

Costs		Materials	Conversion Costs	Total
Unit costs Step 3				
Costs in May	(a)	?	?	?
Equivalent units	(b)	?	?	
Unit costs [(a) ÷ (b)]		?	?	?
Costs to be accounted for				
Work in process, May 1				$ 56,300
Started into production				119,320
Total costs				$175,620

Cost Reconciliation Schedule Step 4

Costs accounted for		
Transferred out		?
Work in process, May 31		
Materials	?	
Conversion costs	?	?
Total costs		?

Additional information:
Work in process, May 1, 1000 units

Materials cost, 1,000 units (100% complete)	$49,100	
Conversion costs, 1,000 units (70% complete)	7,200	$ 56,300
Materials cost for May, 2,000 units		$100,000
Conversion costs for May		$ 19,320

Work in process, May 31, 800 units, 100% complete as to materials and 50% complete as to conversion costs.

(*continued from page 111*)

Instructions

(a) Prepare a production cost report for the Mixing Department for the month of May.

(b) Prepare the journal entry to record the transfer of goods from the Mixing Department to the Filling Department.

(c) Explain why Essence Company is using a process cost system to account for its costs.

Solution

(a) A completed production cost report for the Mixing Department is shown below. Computations to support the amounts reported follow the report.

ESSENCE COMPANY
Mixing Department
Production Cost Report
For the Month Ended May 31, 2005

	Physical Units	Equivalent Units	
		Materials	Conversion Costs
Quantities	Step 1		Step 2
Units to be accounted for			
Work in process, May 1	1,000		
Started into production	2,000		
Total units	3,000		
Units accounted for			
Transferred out	2,200	2,200	2,200
Work in process, May 31	800	800	400 (800 × 50%)
Total units	3,000	3,000	2,600

Costs		Materials	Conversion Costs	Total
Unit costs Step 3				
Costs in May	(a)	$149,100	$26,520	$175,620
Equivalent units	(b)	3,000	2,600	
Unit costs [(a) ÷ (b)]		$49.70	$10.20	$59.90
Costs to be accounted for				
Work in process, May 1				$ 56,300
Started into production				119,320
Total costs				$175,620

Cost Reconciliation Schedule Step 4

Costs accounted for		
Transferred out (2,200 × $59.90)		$131,780
Work in process, May 31		
Materials (800 × $49.70)	$39,760	
Conversion costs (400 × $10.20)	4,080	43,840
Total costs		$175,620

Additional computations to support production cost report data:
Materials cost—$49,100 + $100,000
Conversion costs—$7,200 + $19,320

(b) Work in Process—Filling   131,780
      Work in Process—Mixing   131,780

(c) Process cost systems are used to apply costs to similar products that are mass-produced in a continuous fashion. Essence Company uses a process cost system: production of the after-shave lotion, once it begins, continues until the after-shave lotion emerges. The processing is the same for the entire run—with precisely the same amount of materials, labor, and overhead. Each bottle of Eternity after-shave lotion is indistinguishable from another.

☑ THE NAVIGATOR

Summary of Study Objectives

1 *Understand who uses process cost systems.* Process cost systems are used by companies that mass-produce similar products in a continuous fashion. Once production begins, it continues until the finished product emerges. Each unit of finished product is indistinguishable from every other unit.

2 *Explain the similarities and differences between job order cost and process cost systems.* Job order cost systems are similar to process cost systems in three ways: (1) Both systems track the same cost elements—direct materials, direct labor, and manufacturing overhead. (2) Costs are accumulated in the same accounts—Raw Materials Inventory, Factory Labor, and Manufacturing Overhead. (3) Accumulated costs are assigned to the same accounts—Work in Process, Finished Goods Inventory, and Cost of Goods Sold. However, the method of assigning costs differs significantly.

There are four main differences between the two cost systems: (1) A process cost system uses separate accounts for each production department or manufacturing process, rather than only one work in process account used in a job order cost system. (2) In a process cost system, costs are summarized in a production cost report for each department; in a job cost system, costs are charged to individual jobs and summarized in a job cost sheet. (3) Costs are totaled at the end of a time period in a process cost system and at the completion of a job in a job cost system. (4) In a process cost system, unit cost is calculated as: Total manufacturing costs for the period ÷ Units produced during the period. Unit cost in a job cost system is: Total cost per job ÷ Units produced.

3 *Explain the flow of costs in a process cost system.* Manufacturing costs for raw materials, labor, and overhead are assigned to work in process accounts for various departments or manufacturing processes, and the costs of units completed in a department are transferred from one department to another as those units move through the manufacturing process. The costs of completed work are transferred to Finished Goods Inventory. When inventory is sold, costs are transferred to Cost of Goods Sold.

4 *Make the journal entries to assign manufacturing costs in a process cost system.* Entries to assign the costs of raw materials, labor, and overhead consist of a credit to Raw Materials Inventory, Factory Labor, and Manufacturing Overhead, and a debit to Work in Process for each of the departments doing the processing.

Entries to record the cost of goods transferred to another department are a credit to Work in Process for the department whose work is finished and a debit to the department to which the goods are transferred.

The entry to record units completed and transferred to the warehouse is a credit for the department whose work is finished and a debit to Finished Goods Inventory.

Finally, the entry to record the sale of goods is a credit to Finished Goods Inventory and a debit to Cost of Goods Sold.

5 *Compute equivalent units.* Equivalent units of production measure work done during a period, expressed in fully completed units. This concept is used to determine the cost per unit of completed product. Equivalent units are the sum of units completed and transferred out plus equivalent units of ending work in process.

6 *Explain the four steps necessary to prepare a production cost report.* The four steps to complete a production cost report are: (1) Compute the physical unit flow—that is, the total units to be accounted for. (2) Compute the equivalent units of production. (3) Compute the unit production costs, expressed in terms of equivalent units of production. (4) Prepare a cost reconciliation schedule, which shows that the total costs accounted for equal the total costs to be accounted for.

7 *Prepare a production cost report.* The production cost report contains both quantity and cost data for a production department. There are four sections in the report: (1) number of physical units, (2) equivalent units determination, (3) unit costs, and (4) cost reconciliation schedule.

☑ THE NAVIGATOR

DECISION TOOLKIT—A SUMMARY

Decision Checkpoints	Info Needed for Decision	Tool to Use for Decision	How to Evaluate Results
What is the cost of a product?	Costs of materials, labor, and overhead assigned to processes used to make the product	Production cost report	Compare costs to previous periods, to competitors, and to expected selling price to evaluate overall profitability.
Which costing method should be used?	Type of product produced	Cost of accounting system; benefits of additional information	The benefits of providing the additional information should exceed the costs of the accounting system needed to develop the information.

APPENDIX
FIFO METHOD

In Chapter 3, we demonstrated the weighted-average method of computing equivalent units. Some companies use a different method to compute equivalent units, which is referred to as the **first-in, first-out (FIFO) method**. The purpose of this appendix is to illustrate how the FIFO method is used in practice.

Equivalent Units Under FIFO

STUDY OBJECTIVE

8

Compute equivalent units using the FIFO method.

Under the FIFO method, the computation of equivalent units is done on a first-in, first-out basis. Some companies favor the FIFO method because the FIFO cost assumption usually corresponds to the actual physical flow of the goods. Under the FIFO method, it is assumed therefore that the beginning work in process is completed before new work is started.

Using the FIFO method, equivalent units are the sum of the work performed to:

Helpful Hint The computation of unit production costs and the assignment of costs to units transferred out and in process also are done on the same basis.

1. Finish the units of beginning work in process inventory.
2. Complete the units started into production during the period (referred to as the **units started and completed**).
3. Start, but only partially complete, the units in ending work in process inventory.

Normally, in a process costing system, some units will always be in process at both the beginning and end of the period.

ILLUSTRATION

Illustration 3A-1 shows the physical flow of units for the Assembly Department of Shutters Inc. In addition, the illustration indicates the degree of completion of the work in process accounts in regard to conversion costs.

ASSEMBLY DEPARTMENT	
	Physical Units
Units to be accounted for	
Work in process, June 1 (40% complete)	500
Started (transferred) into production	8,000
Total units	**8,500**
Units accounted for	
Completed and transferred out	8,100
Work in process, June 30 (75% complete)	400
Total units	**8,500**

In Illustration 3A-1, the units completed and transferred out (8,100) plus the units in ending work in process (400) equal the total units to be accounted for (8,500). We then compute equivalent units using FIFO as follows.

1. The 500 units of beginning work in process were 40 percent complete. Thus, 300 equivalent units (60% × 500 units) were required to complete the beginning inventory.
2. The units started and completed during the current month are the units transferred out minus the units in beginning work in process. For the Assembly Department, units started and completed are 7,600 (8,100 − 500).
3. The 400 units of ending work in process were 75 percent complete. Thus, equivalent units were 300 (400 × 75%).

Thus, equivalent units for the Assembly Department are 8,200, computed as follows.

ASSEMBLY DEPARTMENT			
Production Data	**Physical Units**	**Work Added This Period**	**Equivalent Units**
Work in process, June 1	500	60%	300
Started and completed	7,600	100%	7,600
Work in process, June 30	400	75%	300
Total	8,500		8,200

Comprehensive Example

To provide a complete illustration of the FIFO method, we will use the data for the Mixing Department at **Kellogg Company** for the month of June, as shown in Illustration 3A-3 (page 116).

COMPUTE THE PHYSICAL UNIT FLOW (STEP 1)

Illustration 3A-4 (page 116) shows the physical flow of units for **Kellogg Company** for the month of June for the Mixing Department.

Under the FIFO method, the physical units schedule is often expanded (as shown in Illustration 3A-5, page 116) to explain the transferred-out section. As a result, in this section the beginning work in process and the units started and completed are reported. These two items further explain the completed and transferred out section.

Illustration 3A-3 Unit and cost data—Mixing Department

MIXING DEPARTMENT	
Units	
Work in process, June 1	100,000
Direct materials: 100% complete	
Conversion costs: 70% complete	
Units started into production during June	800,000
Units completed and transferred out to Baking Department	700,000
Work in process, June 30	200,000
Direct materials: 100% complete	
Conversion costs: 60% complete	
Costs	
Work in process, June 1	
Direct materials: 100% complete	$ 50,000
Conversion costs: 70% complete	35,000
Cost of work in process, June 1	$ 85,000
Costs incurred during production in June	
Direct materials	$400,000
Conversion costs	170,000
Costs incurred in June	$570,000

Illustration 3A-4 Physical unit flow—Mixing Department

MIXING DEPARTMENT	Physical Units
Units to be accounted for	
Work in process, June 1	100,000
Started (transferred) into production	800,000
Total units	**900,000**
Units accounted for	
Completed and transferred out	700,000
Work in process, June 30	200,000
Total units	**900,000**

Illustration 3A-5 Physical unit flow (FIFO)—Mixing Department

MIXING DEPARTMENT	Physical Units
Units to be accounted for	
Work in process, June 1	100,000
Started (transferred) into production	800,000
Total units	**900,000**
Units accounted for	
Completed and transferred out	
Work in process, June 1	**100,000**
Started and completed	**600,000**
	700,000
Work in process, June 30	200,000
Total units	**900,000**

The records indicate that 900,000 units must be accounted for in the Mixing Department. Of this sum, 700,000 units were transferred to the Baking Department and 200,000 units were still in process.

COMPUTE EQUIVALENT UNITS OF PRODUCTION (STEP 2)

As with the method presented in the chapter, once the physical flow of the units is established, it is necessary to determine equivalent units of production. In the Mixing Department, materials are added at the beginning of the process, and conversion costs are incurred uniformly during the process. Thus, two computations of equivalent units are required: one for materials and one for conversion costs.

Helpful Hint Materials are not always added at the beginning of the process. For example, materials are sometimes added uniformly during the process.

Equivalent Units for Materials

Since materials are entered at the beginning of the process, no additional materials costs are required to complete the beginning work in process. In addition, 100 percent of the materials costs has been incurred on the ending work in process. Thus, the computation of equivalent units for materials is as follows.

MIXING DEPARTMENT—MATERIALS			
Production Data	Physical Units	Materials Added This Period	Equivalent Units
Work in process, June 1	100,000	–0–	–0–
Started and finished	600,000	100%	600,000
Work in process, June 30	200,000	100%	200,000
Total	900,000		800,000

Illustration 3A-6 Computation of equivalent units—materials

Equivalent Units for Conversion Costs

The 100,000 units of beginning work in process were 70 percent complete in terms of conversion costs. Thus, 30,000 equivalent units (30% × 100,000 units) of conversion costs were required to complete the beginning inventory. In addition, the 200,000 units of ending work in process were 60 percent complete in terms of conversion costs. Thus, the equivalent units for conversion costs is 750,000, computed as follows.

MIXING DEPARTMENT—CONVERSION COSTS			
Production Data	Physical Units	Work Added This Period	Equivalent Units
Work in process, June 1	100,000	30%	30,000
Started and finished	600,000	100%	600,000
Work in process, June 30	200,000	60%	120,000
Total	900,000		750,000

Illustration 3A-7 Computation of equivalent units—conversion costs

COMPUTE UNIT PRODUCTION COSTS (STEP 3)

Armed with the knowledge of the equivalent units of production, we can now compute the unit production costs. Unit production costs are costs expressed in terms of equivalent units of production. When equivalent units of production are different for materials and conversion costs, three unit costs are computed: (1) materials, (2) conversion, and (3) total manufacturing.

Under the FIFO method, the unit costs of production are based entirely on the production costs incurred during the month. Thus, the costs in the beginning work in process are not relevant, because they were incurred on work done in the preceding month. As indicated from Illustration 3A-3, the costs incurred during production in June were:

Illustration 3A-8 Costs incurred during production in June

Direct materials	$400,000
Conversion costs	170,000
Total costs	$570,000

The computation of unit materials cost, unit conversion costs, and total unit cost related to Eggo® Waffles is as follows.

Illustration 3A-9 Unit cost formulas and computations—Mixing Department

(1) | **Total Materials Cost** | ÷ | **Equivalent Units of Materials** | = | **Unit Materials Cost** |

$400,000 ÷ 800,000 = $0.50

(2) | **Total Conversion Costs** | ÷ | **Equivalent Units of Conversion Costs** | = | **Unit Conversion Cost** |

$170,000 ÷ 750,000 = $0.227 (rounded)*

(3) | **Unit Materials Cost** | + | **Unit Conversion Cost** | = | **Total Manufacturing Cost per Unit** |

$0.50 + $0.227 = $0.727

*For homework problems, round unit costs to three decimal places.

As shown, the unit costs are $0.50 for materials, $0.227 for conversion costs, and $0.727 for total manufacturing costs.

PREPARE A COST RECONCILIATION SCHEDULE (STEP 4)

We are now ready to determine the cost of goods transferred out of the Mixing Department to the Baking Department and the costs in ending work in process. The total costs that were charged to the Mixing Department in June are as follows.

Illustration 3A-10 Costs charged to Mixing Department

Costs to be accounted for	
Work in process, June 1	$ 85,000
Started into production	570,000
Total costs	$655,000

The total costs charged to the Mixing Department in June are $655,000. A cost reconciliation is then prepared to assign these costs to (1) units transferred out to the Baking Department and (2) ending work in process. Under the FIFO method, the first goods to be completed during the period are the units in beginning work in process. Thus, the cost of the beginning work in process is always assigned to the goods transferred to finished goods (or the next department). The FIFO method also means that ending work in process will be assigned only production costs that are incurred in the current period. Illustration 3A-11 shows a cost reconciliation schedule for the Mixing Department.

Illustration 3A-11   Cost reconciliation report

MIXING DEPARTMENT Cost Reconciliation Schedule		
Costs accounted for		
Transferred out		
Work in process, June 1		$ 85,000
Costs to complete beginning work in process		
Conversion costs (30,000 × $0.227)		6,810
Total costs		91,810
Units started and completed (600,000 × $0.727)		435,950*
Total costs transferred out		527,760
Work in process, June 30		
Materials (200,000 × $0.50)	$100,000	
Conversion costs (120,000 × $0.227)	27,240	127,240
Total costs		**$655,000**

*Any rounding errors should be adjusted in the "Units started and completed" calculation.

As you can see, the total costs accounted for ($655,000 from Illustration 3A-11) equal the total costs to be accounted for ($655,000 from Illustration 3A-10).

PREPARING THE PRODUCTION COST REPORT

At this point, we are ready to prepare the production cost report for the Mixing Department. This report is an internal document for management that shows production quantity and cost data for a production department.

There are four steps in preparing a production cost report. They are: (1) Prepare a physical unit schedule. (2) Compute equivalent units. (3) Compute unit costs. (4) Prepare a cost reconciliation schedule. The production cost report for the Mixing Department is shown in Illustration 3A-12 (page 120), with the four steps identified in the report.

As indicated in the chapter, production cost reports provide a basis for evaluating the productivity of a department. In addition, the cost data can be used to assess whether unit costs and total costs are reasonable. By comparing the quantity and cost data with predetermined goals, top management can also judge whether current performance is meeting planned objectives.

FIFO and Weighted Average

The weighted-average method of computing equivalent units has **one major advantage:** It is simple to understand and apply. In cases where prices do not fluctuate significantly from period to period, the weighted-average method will be very similar to the FIFO method. In addition, companies that have been using just-in-time procedures effectively for inventory control purposes will have minimal inventory balances, and therefore differences between the weighted-average and the FIFO methods will not be material.

Conceptually, the FIFO method is superior to the weighted-average method because **current performance is measured** using only costs incurred in the

Illustration 3A-12   Production cost report

			Mixing Department					
	A	**B**	**C**	**D**	**E**	**F**	**G**	
1		**Mixing Department**						
2		Production Cost Report						
3		For the Month Ended June 30, 2005						
4			**Equivalent Units**					
5		Physical Units	Materials	Conversion Costs				
6	**QUANTITIES**	**Step 1**		**Step 2**				
7	Units to be accounted for							
8	Work in process, June 1	100,000						
9	Started into production	800,000						
10	Total units	900,000						
11								
12	Units accounted for							
13	Completed and transferred out							
14	Work in process, June 1	100,000	0	30,000				
15	Started and completed	600,000	600,000	600,000				
16	Work in process, June 30	200,000	200,000	120,000				
17	Total units	900,000	800,000	750,000				
18								
19	**COSTS**							
20	Unit costs **Step 3**	Materials	Conversion Costs	Total				
21	Costs in June (excluding beginning WIP) (a)	$400,000	$170,000	$570,000	(WIP - Work in Process)			
22	Equivalent units (b)	800,000	750,000					
23	Unit costs [(a) ÷ (b)]	$0.50	$0.227	$0.727				
24								
25	Costs to be accounted for							
26	Work in process, June 1			$85,000				
27	Started into production			570,000				
28	Total costs			$655,000				
29								
30	**Cost Reconciliation Schedule** **Step 4**							
31	Costs accounted for							
32	Transferred out							
33	Work in process, June 1			$85,000				
34	Costs to complete beginning work in process							
35	Conversion costs (30,000 X $0.227)			6,810				
36	Total costs			91,810				
37	Units started and completed (600,000 X $0.727)**			435,950	** Any rounding errors			
38	Total costs transferred out			527,760	should be adjusted in the			
39	Work in process, June 30				"Units started and			
40	Materials (200,000 X $0.50)		$100,000		completed"			
41	Conversion costs (120,000 X $0.227)		27,240	127,240				
42	Total costs			$655,000				
43								

Helpful Hint What are the two self-checks in the report? Answer: (1) Total physical units accounted for must equal the total units to be accounted for. (2) Total costs accounted for must equal the total costs to be accounted for.

current period. Managers are, therefore, not held responsible for costs from prior periods over which they may not have any control. In addition, the FIFO method **provides current cost information**, which can be used to establish **more accurate pricing strategies** for goods manufactured and sold in the current period.

Summary of Study Objective for Appendix

8 *Compute equivalent units using the FIFO method.* Equivalent units under the FIFO method are the sum of the work performed to: (1) Finish the units of beginning work in process inventory, if any; (2) complete the units started into production during the period; and (3) start, but only partially complete, the units in ending work in process inventory.

Glossary

Conversion costs The sum of labor costs and overhead costs. (p. 103)

Cost reconciliation schedule A schedule that shows that the total costs accounted for equal the total costs to be accounted for. (p. 107)

Equivalent units of production A measure of the work done during the period, expressed in fully completed units. (p. 102)

Operations costing A combination of a process cost and a job order cost system, in which products are manufactured primarily by standardized methods, with some customization. (p. 109)

Physical units Actual units to be accounted for during a period, irrespective of any work performed. (p. 105)

Process cost system An accounting system used to apply costs to similar products that are mass-produced in a continuous fashion. (p. 95)

Production cost report An internal report for management that shows both production quantity and cost data for a production department. (p. 103)

Total units (costs) accounted for The sum of the units (costs) transferred out during the period plus the units (costs) in process at the end of the period. (pp. 105, 107)

Total units (costs) to be accounted for The sum of the units (costs) started (or transferred) into production during the period plus the units (costs) in process at the beginning of the period. (pp. 105, 107)

Unit production costs Costs expressed in terms of equivalent units of production. (p. 106)

Weighted-average method Method used to compute equivalent units of production which considers the degree of completion (weighting) of the units completed and transferred out and the ending work in process. (p. 102)

Demonstration Problem

Karlene Industries produces plastic ice cube trays in two processes: heating and stamping. All materials are added at the beginning of the Heating Department. Karlene uses the weighted-average method to compute equivalent units.

On November 1, 1,000 trays that were 70% complete were in process in the Heating Department. During November 12,000 trays were started into production. On November 30, 2005, 2,000 trays that were 60% complete were in process.

The following cost information for the Heating Department was also available.

Work in process, November 1:		Costs incurred in November:	
Materials	$ 640	Material	$3,000
Conversion costs	360	Labor	2,300
Cost of work in process, Nov. 1	$1,000	Overhead	4,050

Instructions

(a) Prepare a production cost report for the Heating Department for the month of November 2005, using the weighted-average method.

(b) Journalize the transfer of costs to the Stamping Department.

Solution to Demonstration Problem

(a)

KARLENE INDUSTRIES
Heating Department
Production Cost Report
For the Month Ended November 30, 2005

	Physical Units	Equivalent Units	
		Materials	Conversion Costs
Quantities	Step 1		Step 2
Units to be accounted for			
Work in process, November 1	1,000		
Started into production	12,000		
Total units	13,000		
Units accounted for			
Transferred out	11,000	11,000	11,000
Work in process, November 30	2,000	2,000	1,200
Total units	13,000	13,000	12,200

Costs		Materials	Conversion Costs	Total
Unit costs Step 3				
Costs in November	(a)	$ 3,640	$ 6,710	$10,350
Equivalent units	(b)	13,000	12,200	
Unit costs [(a) ÷ (b)]		$0.28	$0.55	$0.83
Costs to be accounted for				
Work in process, November 1				$ 1,000
Started into production				9,350
Total costs				$10,350

Cost Reconciliation Schedule Step 4

Costs accounted for		
Transferred out (11,000 × $0.83)		$ 9,130
Work in process, November 30		
Materials (2,000 × $0.28)	$ 560	
Conversion costs (1,200 × $0.55)	660	1,220
Total costs		$10,350

(b) Work in Process—Stamping	9,130	
Work in Process—Heating		9,130
(To record transfer of units to the Stamping Department)		

THE NAVIGATOR

Note: All asterisked Questions, Exercises, and Problems relate to material in the appendix to the chapter.

Self-Study Questions

Self-Study/Self-Test

Answers are at the end of the chapter.

(SO 1) 1. Which of the following items is *not* a characteristic of a process cost system?

(a) Once production begins, it continues until the finished product emerges.

(b) The products produced are heterogeneous in nature.

(c) The focus is on continually producing homogeneous products.

(d) When the finished product emerges, all units have precisely the same amount of materials, labor, and overhead.

(SO 2) 2. Indicate which of the following statements is *not* correct.

(a) Both a job order and a process cost system track the same three manufacturing cost elements—direct materials, direct labor, and manufacturing overhead.

(b) In a job order cost system, only one work in process account is used, whereas in a process cost system, multiple work in process accounts are used.

(c) Manufacturing costs are accumulated the same way in a job order and in a process cost system.

(d) Manufacturing costs are assigned the same way in a job order and in a process cost system.

(SO 3) 3. In a process cost system, the flow of costs is:

(a) work in process, cost of goods sold, finished goods.

(b) finished goods, work in process, cost of goods sold.

(c) finished goods, cost of goods sold, work in process.

(d) work in process, finished goods, cost of goods sold.

(SO 4) 4. In making the journal entry to assign raw materials costs:

(a) the debit is to Finished Goods Inventory.

(b) the debit is often to two or more work in process accounts.

(c) the credit is generally to two or more work in process accounts.

(d) the credit is to Finished Goods Inventory.

(SO 5) 5. The Mixing Department's output during the period consists of 20,000 units completed and transferred out, and 5,000 units in ending work in process 60% complete as to materials and conversion costs. Beginning inventory is 1,000 units, 40% complete as to materials and conversion costs. The equivalent units of production are:

(a) 22,600.   (c) 24,000.

(b) 23,000.   (d) 25,000.

(SO 6) 6. In the RYZ Company, there are zero units in beginning work in process, 7,000 units started into production, and 500 units in ending work in process 20% completed. The physical units to be accounted for are:

(a) 7,000.   (c) 7,500.

(b) 7,360.   (d) 7,340.

(SO 6) 7. Mora Company has 2,000 units in beginning work in process, 20% complete as to conversion costs, 23,000 units transferred out to finished goods, and 3,000 units in ending work in process $33\frac{1}{3}\%$ complete as to conversion costs.

The beginning and ending inventory is fully complete as to materials costs. Equivalent units for materials and conversion costs are, respectively:

(a) 22,000, 24,000.

(b) 24,000, 26,000.

(c) 26,000, 24,000.

(d) 26,000, 26,000.

(SO 6) 8. Fortner Company has no beginning work in process; 9,000 units are transferred out and 3,000 units in ending work in process are one-third finished as to conversion costs and fully complete as to materials cost. If total materials cost is $60,000, the unit materials cost is:

(a) $5.00.

(b) $5.45 rounded.

(c) $6.00.

(d) No correct answer is given.

(SO 6) 9. Largo Company has unit costs of $10 for materials and $30 for conversion costs. If there are 2,500 units in ending work in process, 40% complete as to conversion costs, and fully complete as to materials cost, the total cost assignable to the ending work in process inventory is:

(a) $45,000.

(b) $55,000.

(c) $75,000.

(d) $100,000.

(SO 7) 10. A production cost report

(a) is an external report.

(b) shows both the production quantity and cost data related to a department.

(c) shows equivalent units of production but not physical units.

(d) contains six steps.

(SO 8) *11. Hollins Company uses the FIFO method to compute equivalent units. It has 2,000 units in beginning work in process, 20% complete as to conversion costs, 25,000 units started and completed, and 3,000 units in ending work in process, 30% complete as to conversion costs. All units are 100% complete as to materials. Equivalent units for materials and conversion costs are, respectively:

(a) 28,000 and 26,600.

(b) 28,000 and 27,500.

(c) 27,000 and 26,200.

(d) 27,000 and 29,600.

(SO 8) *12. KLM Company uses the FIFO method to compute equivalent units. It has no beginning work in process; 9,000 units are started and completed and 3,000 units in ending work in process are one-third completed. All material is added at the beginning of the process. If total materials cost is $60,000, the unit materials cost is:

(a) $5.00.
(b) $6.00.
(c) $6.67 (rounded).
(d) No correct answer given.

(SO 8) *13. Toney Company uses the FIFO method to compute equivalent units. It has unit costs of $10 for materials and $30 for conversion costs. If there are 2,500 units in ending work in process,

100% complete as to materials and 40% complete as to conversion costs, the total cost assignable to the ending work in process inventory is:
(a) $45,000.   (c) $75,000.
(b) $55,000.   (d) $100,000.

Questions

1. Identify which costing system—job order or process cost—the following companies would use: (a) **Quaker Oats**, (b) **Ford Motor Company**, (c) **Kinko's Print Shop**, and (d) **Warner Bros. Motion Pictures**.

2. Contrast the primary focus of job order cost accounting and of process cost accounting.

3. What are the similarities between a job order and a process cost system?

4. Your roommate is confused about the features of process cost accounting. Identify and explain the distinctive features for your roommate.

5. Tina Turner believes there are no significant differences in the flow of costs between job order cost accounting and process cost accounting. Is Turner correct? Explain.

6. (a) What source documents are used in assigning (1) materials and (2) labor to production?
   (b) What criterion and basis are commonly used in allocating overhead to processes?

7. At Cale Company, overhead is assigned to production departments at the rate of $15 per machine hour. In July, machine hours were 3,000 in the Machining Department and 2,400 in the Assembly Department. Prepare the entry to assign overhead to production.

8. Ben Bratt is uncertain about the steps used to prepare a production cost report. State the procedures that are required, in the sequence in which they are performed.

9. Aaron Carter is confused about computing physical units. Explain to Aaron how physical units to be accounted for and physical units accounted for are determined.

10. What is meant by the term "equivalent units of production"?

11. How are equivalent units of production computed?

12. Clay Company had zero units of beginning work in process. During the period, 9,000 units were completed, and there were 600 units of ending work in process. What were the units started into production?

13. Gia Co. has zero units of beginning work in process. During the period 12,000 units were completed, and there were 600 units of ending work in process 20% complete as to conversion cost and 100% complete as to materials cost. What were the equivalent units

of production for (a) materials and (b) conversion costs?

14. Hall Co. started 3,000 units during the period. Its beginning inventory is 800 units 25% complete as to conversion costs and 100% complete as to materials costs. Its ending inventory is 400 units 20% complete as to conversion costs and 100% complete as to materials costs. How many units were transferred out this period?

15. Grael Company transfers out 14,000 units and has 2,000 units of ending work in process that are 25% complete. Materials are entered at the beginning of the process and there is no beginning work in process. Assuming unit materials costs of $3 and unit conversion costs of $9, what are the costs to be assigned to units (a) transferred out and (b) in ending work in process?

16. (a) Jim Jain believes the production cost report is an external report for stockholders. Is Jim correct? Explain.
    (b) Identify the sections in a production cost report.

17. What purposes are served by a production cost report?

18. At Adan Company, there are 800 units of ending work in process that are 100% complete as to materials and 40% complete as to conversion costs. If the unit cost of materials is $4 and the costs assigned to the 800 units is $6,600, what is the per-unit conversion cost?

19. What is the difference between operations costing and a process costing system?

20. How does a company decide whether to use a job order or a process cost system?

*21. Silva Co. started and completed 2,000 units for the period. Its beginning inventory is 600 units 25% complete and its ending inventory is 400 units 20% complete. Silva uses the FIFO method to compute equivalent units. How many units were transferred out this period?

*22. Ortiz Company transfers out 12,000 units and has 2,000 units of ending work in process that are 25% complete. Materials are entered at the beginning of the process and there is no beginning work in process. Ortiz uses the FIFO method to compute equivalent units. Assuming unit materials costs of $3 and unit conversion costs of $9, what are the costs to be assigned to units (a) transferred out and (b) in ending work in process?

Brief Exercises

BE3-1 Turner Manufacturing purchases $60,000 of raw materials on account, and it incurs $40,000 of factory labor costs. Journalize the two transactions on May 31 assuming the labor costs are not paid until June.

Journalize entries for accumulating costs.
(SO 4)

BE3-2 Data for Turner Manufacturing are given in BE3-1. Supporting records show that (a) the Assembly Department used $29,000 of raw materials and $28,000 of the factory labor, and (b) the Finishing Department used the remainder. Journalize the assignment of the costs to the processing departments on May 31.

Journalize the assignment of materials and labor costs.
(SO 4)

BE3-3 Factory labor data for Turner Manufacturing are given in BE3-2. Manufacturing overhead is assigned to departments on the basis of 150% of labor costs. Journalize the assignment of overhead to the Assembly and Finishing Departments.

Journalize the assignment of overhead costs.
(SO 4)

BE3-4 Barclay Manufacturing Company has the following production data for selected months.

Compute physical units of production.
(SO 6)

| | | | Ending Work in Process | |
Month	Beginning Work in Process	Units Transferred Out	Units	% Complete as to Conversion Cost
January	–0–	20,000	5,000	40%
March	–0–	30,000	4,000	75
July	–0–	50,000	10,000	25

Compute the physical unit flow for each month.

BE3-5 Using the data in BE3-4, compute equivalent units of production for materials and conversion costs, assuming materials are entered at the beginning of the process.

Compute equivalent units of production.
(SO 5)

BE3-6 In Georgia Company, total material costs are $52,000, and total conversion costs are $60,000. Equivalent units of production are materials 10,000 and conversion costs 12,000. Compute the unit costs for materials, conversion costs, and total manufacturing costs.

Compute unit costs of production.
(SO 6)

BE3-7 Sosa Company has the following production data for March: units transferred out 40,000, and ending work in process 5,000 units that are 100% complete for materials and 40% complete for conversion costs. If unit materials cost is $8 and unit conversion cost is $15, determine the costs to be assigned to the units transferred out and the units in ending work in process.

Assign costs to units transferred out and in process.
(SO 6)

BE3-8 Production costs chargeable to the Finishing Department in July in Murdock Company are materials $9,000, labor $23,800, overhead $18,000. Equivalent units of production are materials 20,000 and conversion costs 19,000. Compute the unit costs for materials and conversion costs.

Compute unit costs.
(SO 6)

BE3-9 Data for Murdock Company are given in BE3-8. Production records indicate that 18,000 units were transferred out, and 2,000 units in ending work in process were 50% complete as to conversion cost and 100% complete as to materials. Prepare a cost reconciliation schedule.

Prepare cost reconciliation schedule.
(SO 6)

BE3-10 The Smelting Department of Dewey Manufacturing Company has the following production and cost data for October.

Production: Beginning work in process 2,000 units that are 100% complete as to materials and 20% complete as to conversion costs; units transferred out 8,000 units; and ending work in process 3,000 units that are 100% complete as to materials and 40% complete as to conversion costs.

Compute the equivalent units of production for (a) materials and (b) conversion costs for the month of October.

Compute equivalent units of production.
(SO 5)

*BE3-11 Mora Company has the following production data for March: no beginning work in process, units started and completed 30,000, and ending work in process 5,000 units that are 100% complete for materials and 40% complete for conversion costs. Mora uses the FIFO method to compute equivalent units. If unit materials cost is $8 and unit

Assign costs to units transferred out and in process.
(SO 8)

conversion cost is $12, determine the costs to be assigned to the units transferred out and the units in ending work in process. The total costs to be assigned are $664,000.

Prepare a partial production cost report.
(SO 7, 8)
Compute unit costs.
(SO 8)

*BE3-12 Using the data in BE3-11, prepare the cost section of the production cost report for Mora Company.

*BE3-13 Production costs chargeable to the Finishing Department in May at Bell Company are materials $8,000, labor $20,000, overhead $18,000, and transferred-in costs $62,000. Equivalent units of production are materials 20,000 and conversion costs 19,000. Bell uses the FIFO method to compute equivalent units. Compute the unit costs for materials and conversion costs. Transferred-in costs are considered materials costs.

Exercises

Journalize transactions.
(SO 3, 4)

E3-1 Sally May Company manufactures pizza sauce through two production departments: Cooking and Canning. In each process, materials and conversion costs are incurred evenly throughout the process. For the month of March, the work in process accounts show the following debits.

	Cooking	**Canning**
Beginning work in process	$ –0–	$ 4,000
Materials	14,000	6,000
Labor	8,500	7,000
Overhead	29,500	22,000
Costs transferred in		45,000

Instructions
Journalize the March transactions.

Journalize transactions for two processes.
(SO 4)

E3-2 Greenleaf Manufacturing Company has two production departments: Cutting and Assembly. August 1 inventories are Raw Materials $4,200, Work in Process—Cutting $3,900, Work in Process—Assembly $10,600, and Finished Goods $31,900. During August, the following transactions occurred.

1. Purchased $56,300 of raw materials on account.
2. Incurred $55,000 of factory labor. (Credit Wages Payable.)
3. Incurred $70,000 of manufacturing overhead; $36,000 was paid and the remainder is unpaid.
4. Requisitioned materials for Cutting $15,700 and Assembly $8,900.
5. Used factory labor for Cutting $28,000 and Assembly $27,000.
6. Applied overhead at the rate of $20 per machine hour. Machine hours were Cutting 1,640 and Assembly 1,720.
7. Transferred goods costing $77,600 from the Cutting Department to the Assembly Department.
8. Transferred goods costing $135,000 from Assembly to Finished Goods.
9. Sold goods costing $130,000 for $200,000 on account.

Instructions
Journalize the transactions. (Omit explanations.)

Compute physical units and equivalent units of production.
(SO 5, 6)

E3-3 In Bing Company, materials are entered at the beginning of each process. Work in process inventories, with the percentage of work done on conversion costs, and production data for its Sterilizing Department in selected months during 2005 are as follows.

	Beginning Work in Process		**Units Transferred Out**	**Ending Work in Process**	
Month	**Units**	**Conversion Cost %**		**Units**	**Conversion Cost %**
January	–0–	—	7,000	2,000	70
March	–0–	—	12,000	3,000	30
May	–0–	—	16,000	5,000	80
July	–0–	—	10,000	1,500	40

Instructions
(a) Compute the physical unit flow for January and May.
(b) Compute the equivalent units of production for (1) materials and (2) conversion costs for each month.

E3-4   The Cutting Department of Behan Manufacturing has the following production and cost data for July.

Determine equivalent units, unit costs, and assignment of costs.
(SO 5, 6)

Production	Costs	
1. Transferred out 9,000 units.	Beginning work in process	$ –0–
2. Started 1,000 units that are 40%	Materials	45,000
complete as to conversion	Labor	14,940
costs and 100% complete as	Manufacturing overhead	18,900
to materials at July 31.		

Materials are entered at the beginning of the process. Conversion costs are incurred uniformly during the process.

Instructions
(a) Determine the equivalent units of production for (1) materials and (2) conversion costs.
(b) Compute unit costs and prepare a cost reconciliation schedule.

E3-5   The Sanding Department of Han Furniture Company has the following production and manufacturing cost data for April 2005.

Prepare a production cost report.
(SO 5, 6, 7)

Production: 12,000 units finished and transferred out; 3,000 units started that are 100% complete as to materials and 40% complete as to conversion costs.

Manufacturing costs: Materials $36,000; labor $30,000; overhead $37,320.

Instructions
Prepare a production cost report. There is no beginning work in process.

E3-6   The Blending Department of Ceja Company has the following cost and production data for the month of May.

Determine equivalent units, unit costs, and assignment of costs.
(SO 5, 6)

Work in process, May 1	
Direct materials: 100% complete	$100,000
Conversion costs: 20% complete	75,000
Cost of work in process, May 1	$175,000
Costs incurred during production in May	
Direct materials	$ 800,000
Conversion costs	350,000
Costs incurred in May	$1,150,000

Units transferred out totaled 8,000. Ending work in process was 2,000 units that are 100% complete as to materials and 25% complete as to conversion costs.

Instructions
(a) Compute the equivalent units of production for (1) materials and (2) conversion costs for the month of May.
(b) Compute the unit costs for the month.
(c) Determine the costs to be assigned to the units transferred out and in ending work in process.

E3-7   The ledger of Liu Company has the following work in process account.

Answer questions on costs and production.
(SO 3, 5, 6)

Work in Process—Painting

7/1	Balance	4,450	7/31	Transferred out	?
7/31	Materials	6,100			
7/31	Labor	2,500			
7/31	Overhead	1,650			
7/31	Balance	?			

Production records show that there were 700 units in the beginning inventory, 30% complete, 1,100 units started, and 1,300 units transferred out. The beginning work in process had materials cost of $2,900 and conversion costs of $1,550. The units in ending inventory were 40% complete. Materials are entered at the beginning of the painting process.

Instructions
(a) How many units are in process at July 31?
(b) What is the unit materials cost for July?
(c) What is the unit conversion cost for July?
(d) What is the total cost of units transferred out in July?
(e) What is the cost of the July 31 inventory?

Compute equivalent units, unit costs, and costs assigned.
(SO 5, 6)

E3-8 The Polishing Department of Dimetry Manufacturing Company has the following production and manufacturing cost data for October. Materials are entered at the beginning of the process.

Production: Beginning inventory 1,600 units that are 100% complete as to materials and 30% complete as to conversion costs; units started during the period are 11,000; ending inventory of 2,000 units 10% complete as to conversion costs.

Manufacturing costs: Beginning inventory costs, comprised of $20,000 of materials and $43,180 of conversion costs; materials costs added in Polishing during the month, $162,700; labor and overhead applied in Polishing during the month, $100,080 and $250,940, respectively.

Instructions
(a) Compute the equivalent units of production for materials and conversion costs for the month of October.
(b) Compute the unit costs for materials and conversion costs for the month.
(c) Determine the costs to be assigned to the units transferred out and in process.

Explain the production cost report.
(SO 7)

E3-9 Mary Mahr has recently been promoted to production manager, and so she has just started to receive various managerial reports. One of the reports she has received is the production cost report that you prepared. It showed that her department had 1,000 equivalent units in ending inventory. Her department has had a history of not keeping enough inventory on hand to meet demand. She has come to you, very angry, and wants to know why you credited her with only 1,000 units when she knows she had at least twice that many on hand.

Instructions
▭▭▭▶ Explain to her why her production cost report showed only 1,000 equivalent units in ending inventory. Write an informal memo. Be kind and explain very clearly why she is mistaken.

Prepare a production cost report.
(SO 5, 6, 7)

E3-10 The Welding Department of Marlin Manufacturing Company has the following production and manufacturing cost data for February 2005. All materials are added at the beginning of the process.

Manufacturing Costs		Production Data	
Beginning work in process		Beginning work in process	15,000 units,
Materials	$15,000		10% complete
Conversion costs	30,435 $ 45,435	Units transferred out	49,000
Materials	180,000	Units started	60,000
Labor	35,100	Ending work in process	26,000,
Overhead	64,545		20% complete

Instructions
Prepare a production cost report for the Welding Department for the month of February.

Compute physical units and equivalent units of production.
(SO 5, 6)

E3-11 Container Shipping, Inc. is contemplating the use of process costing to track the costs of its operations. The operation consists of three segments (departments): receiving, shipping, and delivery. Containers are received at Container's docks and sorted according to the ship they will be carried on. The containers are loaded onto a ship, which carries them to the appropriate port of destination. The containers are then off-loaded and delivered to the receiving company.

Container Shipping wants to begin using process costing in the shipping department. Direct materials represent the fuel costs to run the ship, and "Containers in transit" represents work in process. Listed below is information about the shipping department's first month's activity.

Containers in transit, April 1	0
Containers loaded	800
Containers in transit, April 30	350, 40% of direct materials and 30% of conversion costs

Instructions
(a) Determine the physical flow of containers for the month.
(b) Calculate the equivalent units for direct materials and conversion costs.

E3-12 Hi-Tech Mortgage Company uses a process costing system to accumulate costs in its loan application department. When an application is completed it is forwarded to the loan department for final processing. The following processing and cost data pertain to September.

Determine equivalent units, unit costs, and assignment of costs.
(SO 5, 6)

1. Applications in process on September 1, 100	Beginning WIP:	
	Direct materials	$ 1,000
2. Applications started in September, 900	Conversion costs	4,000
	September costs:	
3. Completed applications during September, 800	Direct materials	$ 4,000
	Direct labor	12,000
4. Applications still in process at September 30 were 100% complete as to materials (forms) and 60% complete as to conversion costs.	Overhead	9,400

Materials are the forms used in the application process, and these costs are incurred at the beginning of the process. Conversion costs are incurred uniformly during the process.

Instructions
(a) Determine the equivalent units of service (production) for materials and conversion costs.
(b) Compute the unit costs and prepare a cost reconciliation schedule.

*E3-13 Using the data in E3-12, assume Hi-Tech Mortgage Company uses the FIFO method. Also assume that the applications in process on September 1 were 100% complete as to materials (forms) and 40% complete as to conversion costs.

Compute equivalent units, unit costs, and costs assigned.
(SO 4, 5, 6, 8)

Instructions
(a) Determine the equivalent units of service (production) for materials and conversion costs.
(b) Compute the unit costs and prepare a cost reconciliation schedule.

*E3-14 The Cutting Department of Chan Manufacturing has the following production and cost data for August.

Determine equivalent units, unit costs, and assignment of costs.
(SO 4, 5, 6, 8)

Production	Costs	
1. Started and completed 8,000 units.	Beginning work in process	$ –0–
2. Started 1,000 units that are 40% completed at August 31.	Materials	45,000
	Labor	14,700
	Manufacturing overhead	18,900

Materials are entered at the beginning of the process. Conversion costs are incurred uniformly during the process. Chan Manufacturing uses the FIFO method to compute equivalent units.

Instructions
(a) Determine the equivalent units of production for (1) materials and (2) conversion costs.
(b) Compute unit costs and show the assignment of manufacturing costs to units transferred out and in work in process.

Compute equivalent units, unit costs, and costs assigned.
(SO 4, 5, 6, 8)

*E3-15 The Smelting Department of Amber Manufacturing Company has the following production and cost data for September.

Production: Beginning work in process 2,000 units that are 100% complete as to materials and 20% complete as to conversion costs; units started and finished 11,000 units; and ending work in process 1,000 units that are 100% complete as to materials and 40% complete as to conversion costs.

Manufacturing costs: Work in process, September 1, $15,200; materials added $60,000; labor and overhead $143,000.

Amber uses the FIFO method to compute equivalent units.

Instructions
(a) Compute the equivalent units of production for (1) materials and (2) conversion costs for the month of September.
(b) Compute the unit costs for the month.
(c) Determine the costs to be assigned to the units transferred out and in process.

Answer questions on costs and production.
(SO 3, 4, 5, 6, 8)

*E3-16 The ledger of Platt Company has the following work in process account.

Work in Process—Painting

3/1	Balance	3,680	3/31	Transferred out	?
3/31	Materials	6,600			
3/31	Labor	2,500			
3/31	Overhead	1,280			
3/31	Balance	?			

Production records show that there were 800 units in the beginning inventory, 30% complete, 1,000 units started, and 1,300 units transferred out. The units in ending inventory were 40% complete. Materials are entered at the beginning of the painting process. Platt uses the FIFO method to compute equivalent units.

Instructions
Answer the following questions.
(a) How many units are in process at March 31?
(b) What is the unit materials cost for March?
(c) What is the unit conversion cost for March?
(d) What is the total cost of units started in February and completed in March?
(e) What is the total cost of units started and finished in March?
(f) What is the cost of the March 31 inventory?

Prepare a production cost report for a second process.
(SO 8)

*E3-17 The Welding Department of Hirohama Manufacturing Company has the following production and manufacturing cost data for February 2005. All materials are added at the beginning of the process. Hirohama uses the FIFO method to compute equivalent units.

Manufacturing Costs		**Production Data**	
Beginning work in process	$ 32,175	Beginning work in process	15,000 units,
Costs transferred in	135,000		10% complete
Materials	57,000	Units transferred out	50,000
Labor	35,100	Units transferred in	60,000
Overhead	71,900	Ending work in process	25,000,
			20% complete

Instructions
Prepare a production cost report for the Welding Department for the month of February. Transferred-in costs are considered materials costs.

Problems: Set A

Journalize transactions.
(SO 3, 4)

P3-1A Vargas Company manufactures a nutrient, Everlife, through two manufacturing processes: Blending and Packaging. All materials are entered at the beginning of each process. On August 1, 2005, inventories consisted of Raw Materials $5,000, Work in Process—Blending $0, Work in Process—Packaging $3,945, and Finished Goods $7,500. The beginning inventory for Packaging consisted of 500 units, two-fifths complete as to conversion costs and fully complete as to materials. During August, 9,000 units were started into production in Blending, and the following transactions were completed.

1. Purchased $25,000 of raw materials on account.
2. Issued raw materials for production: Blending $16,800 and Packaging $7,200.
3. Incurred labor costs of $18,770.
4. Used factory labor: Blending $12,230 and Packaging $6,540.
5. Incurred $41,300 of manufacturing overhead on account.
6. Applied manufacturing overhead at the rate of $35 per machine hour. Machine hours were Blending 900 and Packaging 300.
7. Transferred 8,200 units from Blending to Packaging at a cost of $54,940.
8. Transferred 8,600 units from Packaging to Finished Goods at a cost of $74,490.
9. Sold goods costing $62,000 for $85,000 on account.

Instructions
Journalize the August transactions.

P3-2A   Zion Corporation manufactures water skis through two processes: Molding and Packaging. In the Molding Department fiberglass is heated and shaped into the form of a ski. In the Packaging Department, the skis are placed in cartons and sent to the finished goods warehouse. Materials are entered at the beginning of both processes. Labor and manufacturing overhead are incurred uniformly throughout each process. Production and cost data for the Molding Department for January 2005 are presented below.

Complete four steps necessary to prepare a production cost report.
(SO 5, 6, 7)

Production Data	January
Beginning work in process units	–0–
Units started into production	43,000
Ending work in process units	3,000
Percent complete—ending inventory	40%

Cost Data	
Materials	$550,400
Labor	126,640
Overhead	170,000
Total	$847,040

Instructions
(a) Compute the physical unit flow.
(b) Determine the equivalent units of production for materials and conversion costs.
(c) Compute the unit costs of production.
(d) Determine the costs to be assigned to the units transferred out and in process.
(e) Prepare a production cost report for the Molding Department for the month of January.

(c) Materials $12.80
(d) Transferred out $800,000
      WIP $47,040

P3-3A   Stein Corporation manufactures in separate processes refrigerators and freezers for homes. In each process, materials are entered at the beginning and conversion costs are incurred uniformly. Production and cost data for the first process in making two products in two different manufacturing plants are as follows.

Complete four steps necessary to prepare a production cost report.
(SO 5, 6, 7)

	Stamping Department	
	Plant A	Plant B
Production Data—June	R12 Refrigerators	F24 Freezers
Work in process units, June 1	–0–	–0–
Units started into production	20,000	20,000
Work in process units, June 30	2,000	3,000
Work in process percent complete	70%	50%
Cost Data—June		
Work in process, June 1	$ –0–	$ –0–
Materials	840,000	700,000
Labor	200,800	236,000
Overhead	420,000	319,000
Total	$1,460,800	$1,255,000

(a) Plant A:
(1) Transferred out   18,000
     WIP   2,000
(2) Materials   20,000
     CC   19,400
(3) Materials $42
     CC $32
(4) Transferred out $1,332,000
     WIP $128,800

Instructions

(a) For each plant:

(1) Compute the physical unit flow.

(2) Compute equivalent units of production for materials and for conversion costs.

(3) Determine the unit costs of production.

(4) Show the assignment of costs to units transferred out and in process.

(b) Prepare the production cost report for Plant A for June 2005.

Assign costs and prepare pro-
duction cost report.
(SO 5, 6, 7)

P3-4A Elite Company has several processing departments. Costs charged to the Assembly Department for October 2005 totaled $1,328,400 as follows.

Work in process, October 1		
Materials	$ 9,000	
Conversion costs	27,400	$ 36,400
Materials added		1,071,000
Labor		90,000
Overhead		131,000

Production records show that 35,000 units were in beginning work in process 40% complete as to conversion cost, 415,000 units were started into production, and 45,000 units were in ending work in process 20% complete as to conversion costs. Materials are entered at the beginning of each process.

Instructions

(a) Determine the equivalent units of production and the unit costs for the Assembly Department.

(b) Transferred out $1,215,000
WIP $113,400

(b) Determine the assignment of costs to goods transferred out and in process.

(c) Prepare a production cost report for the Assembly Department.

Determine equivalent units
and unit costs and assign
costs.
(SO 5, 6, 7)

P3-5A Sprague Company manufactures bicycles and tricycles. For bicycles, materials are added at the beginning of the production process, and conversion costs are incurred uniformly. Production and cost data for the month of July are as follows.

Production Data—Bicycles	Units	Percent Complete
Work in process units, July 1	400	80%
Units started in production	1,100	
Work in process units, July 31	500	10%

Cost Data—Bicycles		
Work in process, July 1		
Materials	$10,000	
Conversion costs	9,300	$19,300
Direct materials		50,000
Direct labor		23,700
Manufacturing overhead		30,000

Instructions

(a) (1) Materials 1,500
(2) Materials $40
(3) Transferred
out $100,000
WIP $23,000

(a) Calculate the following.

(1) The equivalent units of production for materials and conversion.

(2) The unit costs of production for materials and conversion costs.

(3) The assignment of costs to units transferred out and in process at the end of the accounting period.

(b) Prepare a production cost report for the month of July.

Compute equivalent units
and complete production
cost report.
(SO 5, 7)

P3-6A Taylor Cleaner Company uses a weighted-average process cost system and manufactures a single product—an all-purpose liquid cleaner. The manufacturing activity for the month of May has just been completed. A partially completed production cost report for the month of May for the Mixing and Blending Department is shown on the next page.

TAYLOR CLEANER COMPANY
Mixing and Blending Department
Production Cost Report
For the Month Ended May 31

		Equivalent Units	
	Physical		Conversion
Quantities	**Units**	**Materials**	**Costs**
Units to be accounted for			
Work in process, May 1			
(40% materials, 20%			
conversion costs)	7,000		
Started into production	100,000		
Total units	107,000		
Units accounted for			
Transferred out	95,000	?	?
Work in process, May 31			
(3/4 materials, 1/4			
conversion costs)	12,000	?	?
Total units accounted for	107,000	?	?

Costs		Conversion	
Unit costs	**Materials**	**Costs**	**Total**
Costs in May	$166,400	$98,000	$264,400
Equivalent units	?	?	
Unit costs	$? +	$? =	$?
Costs to be accounted for			
Work in process, May 1			$ 12,000
Started into production			252,400
Total costs			$264,400

Cost Reconciliation Schedule

Costs accounted for			
Transferred out			$?
Work in process, May 31			
Materials		$?	
Conversion costs		?	$?
Total costs			$?

Instructions

(a) Prepare a schedule that shows how the equivalent units were computed so that you can complete the "Quantities: Units accounted for" equivalent units section shown in the production cost report above.
(b) Compute May unit costs.
(c) Complete the "Cost Reconciliation Schedule" part of the production cost report above.

(a)	Materials	104,000
(b)	Materials	$1.60
(c)	Transferred	
	out	$247,000
	WIP	$17,400

P3-7A Nicholas Company manufactures bicycles and tricycles. For both products, materials are added at the beginning of the production process, and conversion costs are incurred uniformly. Nicholas Company uses the FIFO method to compute equivalent units. Production and cost data for the month of March are as follows.

Determine equivalent units and unit costs and assign costs for processes; prepare production cost report.
(SO 8)

		Percent
Production Data—Bicycles	**Units**	**Complete**
Work in process units, March 1	200	80%
Units started into production	1,000	
Work in process units, March 31	200	40%

Cost Data—Bicycles	Units	Percent Complete
Work in process, March 1	$19,280	
Direct materials	50,000	
Direct labor	25,200	
Manufacturing overhead	30,000	

Production Data—Tricycles	Units	Percent Complete
Work in process units, March 1	100	75%
Units started into production	800	
Work in process units, March 31	60	25%

Cost Data—Tricycles	
Work in process, March 1	$ 6,125
Direct materials	38,400
Direct labor	15,100
Manufacturing overhead	20,000

Instructions

(a) Bicycles:
(1) Materials   1,000
(2) Materials $50
(3) Transferred out $109,680
     WIP $14,800

(a) Calculate the following for both the bicycles and the tricycles.
  (1) The equivalent units of production for materials and conversion.
  (2) The unit costs of production for materials and conversion costs.
  (3) The assignment of costs to units transferred out and in process at the end of the accounting period.
(b) Prepare a production cost report for the month of March for the bicycles only.

Problems: Set B

Journalize transactions.
(SO 3, 4)

P3-1B Pepi Company manufactures its product, Vitadrink, through two manufacturing processes: Mixing and Packaging. All materials are entered at the beginning of each process. On October 1, 2005, inventories consisted of Raw Materials $26,000, Work in Process—Mixing $0, Work in Process—Packaging $250,000, and Finished Goods $89,000. The beginning inventory for Packaging consisted of 10,000 units that were 50% complete as to conversion costs and fully complete as to materials. During October, 50,000 units were started into production in the Mixing Department and the following transactions were completed.

1. Purchased $500,000 of raw materials on account.
2. Issued raw materials for production: Mixing $210,000 and Packaging $45,000.
3. Incurred labor costs of $238,900.
4. Used factory labor: Mixing $182,000 and Packaging $56,900.
5. Incurred $800,000 of manufacturing overhead on account.
6. Applied manufacturing overhead on the basis of $24 per machine hour. Machine hours were 28,000 in Mixing and 7,000 in Packaging.
7. Transferred 45,000 units from Mixing to Packaging at a cost of $999,000.
8. Transferred 53,000 units from Packaging to Finished Goods at a cost of $1,455,000.
9. Sold goods costing $1,500,000 for $2,500,000 on account.

Instructions
Journalize the October transactions.

Complete four steps neces-
sary to prepare a production
cost report.
(SO 5, 6, 7)

P3-2B Aquatic Company manufactures bowling balls through two processes: Molding and Packaging. In the Molding Department, the urethane, rubber, plastics, and other materials are molded into bowling balls. In the Packaging Department, the balls are placed in cartons and sent to the finished goods warehouse. All materials are entered at the beginning of each process. Labor and manufacturing overhead are incurred uniformly throughout each process. Production and cost data for the Molding Department during June 2005 are presented below.

Production Data	June
Beginning work in process units	–0–
Units started into production	20,000
Ending work in process units	5,000
Percent complete—ending inventory	40%

Cost Data	
Materials	$286,000
Labor	114,000
Overhead	101,900
Total	$501,900

Instructions
(a) Prepare a schedule showing physical unit flow.
(b) Determine the equivalent units of production for materials and conversion costs.
(c) Compute the unit costs of production.
(d) Determine the costs to be assigned to the units transferred and in process for June.
(e) Prepare a production cost report for the Molding Department for the month of June.

(c) Materials $14.30
CC $12.70
(d) Transferred out $405,000
WIP $96,900

P3-3B Freedo Industries Inc. manufactures in separate processes furniture for homes. In each process, materials are entered at the beginning, and conversion costs are incurred uniformly. Production and cost data for the first process in making two products in two different manufacturing plants are as follows.

Complete four steps necessary to prepare a production cost report.
(SO 5, 6, 7)

	Cutting Department	
	Plant 1	**Plant 2**
Production Data—August	**T12-Tables**	**C10-Chairs**
Work in process units, August 1	–0–	–0–
Units started into production	20,000	15,000
Work in process units, August 31	2,000	500
Work in process percent complete	50%	80%

Cost Data—August		
Work in process, August 1	$ –0–	$ –0–
Materials	380,000	225,000
Labor	190,000	118,100
Overhead	76,000	60,700
Total	$646,000	$403,800

(a) Plant 1:
(1) Transferred out 18,000
    WIP   2,000
(2) Materials   20,000
    CC   19,000
(3) Materials $19
    CC $14
(4) Transferred out $594,000
    WIP $52,000

Instructions
(a) For each plant:
   (1) Compute the physical unit flow.
   (2) Compute equivalent units of production for materials and for conversion costs.
   (3) Determine the unit costs of production.
   (4) Show the assignment of costs of units transferred out and in process.
(b) Prepare the production cost report for Plant 1 for August 2005.

P3-4B Wang Company has several processing departments. Costs charged to the Assembly Department for November 2005 totaled $2,126,000 as follows.

Assign costs and prepare production cost report.
(SO 5, 6, 7)

Work in process, November 1		
Materials	$70,000	
Conversion costs	48,000	$ 118,000
Materials added		1,270,000
Labor		358,000
Overhead		380,000

Production records show that 30,000 units were in beginning work in process 30% complete as to conversion costs, 640,000 units were started into production, and 25,000 units were in ending work in process 40% complete as to conversion costs. Materials are entered at the beginning of each process.

Instructions

(a) Determine the equivalent units of production and the unit costs for the Assembly Department.

(b) Transferred out $2,064,000
    WIP $62,000

(b) Determine the assignment of costs to goods transferred out and in process.

(c) Prepare a production cost report for the Assembly Department.

Determine equivalent units and unit costs and assign costs.
(SO 5, 6, 7)

P3-5B Clemente Company manufactures basketballs. Materials are added at the beginning of the production process and conversion costs are incurred uniformly. Production and cost data for the month of July 2005 are as follows.

Production Data—Basketballs	Units	Percent Complete
Work in process units, July 1	500	60%
Units started into production	1,600	
Work in process units, July 31	600	40%

Cost Data—Basketballs		
Work in process, July 1		
Materials	$540	
Conversion costs	500	$1,040
Direct materials		2,400
Direct labor		1,600
Manufacturing overhead		1,380

Instructions

(a) (1) Materials   2,100
    (2) Materials $1.40
    (3) Transferred
        out $5,100
        WIP $1,320

(a) Calculate the following.

  (1) The equivalent units of production for materials and conversion costs.

  (2) The unit costs of production for materials and conversion costs.

  (3) The assignment of costs to units transferred out and in process at the end of the accounting period.

(b) Prepare a production cost report for the month of July for the basketballs.

Compute equivalent units and complete production cost report.
(SO 5, 7)

P3-6B Magic Processing Company uses a weighted-average process cost system and manufactures a single product—a premium rug shampoo and cleaner. The manufacturing activity for the month of November has just been completed. A partially completed production cost report for the month of November for the Mixing and Cooking Department is shown below and on the next page.

MAGIC PROCESSING COMPANY
Mixing and Cooking Department
Production Cost Report
For the Month Ended November 30

		Equivalent Units	
Quantities	Physical Units	Materials	Conversion Costs
Units to be accounted for			
Work in process, November 1			
(all materials, 70%			
conversion costs)	10,000		
Started into production	160,000		
Total units	170,000		
Units accounted for			
Transferred out	130,000	?	?
Work in process, November 30			
(50% materials, 25%			
conversion costs)	40,000	?	?
Total units accounted for	170,000	?	?

Costs

Unit costs	Materials	Conversion Costs	Total
Costs in November	$240,000	$98,000	$338,000
Equivalent units	?	?	
Unit costs	$? +	$? =	$?

Costs to be accounted for			
Work in process, November 1			$ 38,000
Started into production			300,000
Total costs			$338,000

Cost Reconciliation Schedule

Costs accounted for			
Transferred out			$?
Work in process, November 30			
Materials		$?	
Conversion costs		?	?
Total costs			$?

Instructions

(a) Prepare a schedule that shows how the equivalent units were computed so that you can complete the "Quantities: Units accounted for" equivalent units section shown in the production cost report above.

(b) Compute November unit costs.

(c) Complete the "Cost Reconciliation Schedule" part of the production cost report above.

(a) Materials   150,000
(b) Materials $1.60
(c) Transferred out $299,000
    WIP $39,000

*P3-7B Jessica Company manufactures basketballs and soccer balls. For both products, materials are added at the beginning of the production process and conversion costs are incurred uniformly. Jessica uses the FIFO method to compute equivalent units. Production and cost data for the month of August are as follows.

Determine equivalent units and unit costs and assign costs for processes; prepare production cost report.
(SO 8)

Production Data—Basketballs	Units	Percent Complete
Work in process units, August 1	500	60%
Units started into production	1,600	
Work in process units, August 31	600	50%

Cost Data—Basketballs	
Work in process, August 1	$1,125
Direct materials	1,600
Direct labor	1,175
Manufacturing overhead	1,000

Production Data—Soccer Balls	Units	Percent Complete
Work in process units, August 1	200	80%
Units started into production	2,000	
Work in process units, August 31	150	70%

Cost Data—Soccer Balls	
Work in process, August 1	$ 450
Direct materials	2,600
Direct labor	1,000
Manufacturing overhead	995

Instructions

(a) Calculate the following for both the basketballs and the soccer balls.

(1) The equivalent units of production for materials and conversion.

(2) The unit costs of production for materials and conversion costs.

(3) The assignment of costs to units transferred out and in process at the end of the accounting period.

(b) Prepare a production cost report for the month of August for the basketballs only.

(a) Basketballs:
(1) Materials   1,600
(2) Materials $1
(3) Transferred out $3,865
    WIP $1,035

Problems: Set C

Problem Set C is provided at the book's Web site, www.wiley.com/college/weygandt.

▶ BROADENING YOUR PERSPECTIVE

Group Decision Case

BYP 3-1 British Beach Company manufactures suntan lotion, called Surtan, which is sold in 11-ounce plastic bottles. Surtan is sold in a competitive market. As a result, management is very cost-conscious. Surtan is manufactured through two processes: mixing and filling. Materials are entered at the beginning of each process, and labor and manufacturing overhead occur uniformly throughout each process. Unit costs are based on the cost per gallon of Surtan using the weighted-average costing approach.

On June 30, 2005, Sara Simmons, the chief accountant for the past 20 years, opted to take early retirement. Her replacement, Joe Jacobs, had extensive accounting experience with motels in the area but only limited contact with manufacturing accounting.

During July, Joe correctly accumulated the following production quantity and cost data for the Mixing Department.

> Production quantities: Work in process, July 1, 8,000 gallons 75% complete; started into production 100,000 gallons; work in process, July 31, 5,000 gallons 20% complete. Materials are added at the beginning of the process.

> Production costs: Beginning work in process $88,000, comprised of $21,000 of materials costs and $67,000 of conversion costs; incurred in July: materials $600,000, conversion costs $785,800.

Joe then prepared a production cost report on the basis of physical units started into production. His report showed a production cost of $14.738 per gallon of Surtan. The management of British Beach was surprised at the high unit cost. The president comes to you, as Sara's top assistant, to review Joe's report and prepare a correct report if necessary.

Instructions
With the class divided into groups, answer the following questions.
(a) Show how Joe arrived at the unit cost of $14.738 per gallon of Surtan.
(b) What error(s) did Joe make in preparing his production cost report?
(c) Prepare a correct production cost report for July.

Managerial Analysis

BYP 3-2 Harris Furniture Company manufactures living room furniture through two departments: Framing and Upholstering. Materials are entered at the beginning of each process. Costs transferred in should be treated as materials cost. For May, the following cost data are obtained from the two work in process accounts.

	Framing	Upholstering
Work in process, May 1	$ –0–	$?
Materials	420,000	?
Conversion costs	210,000	330,000
Costs transferred in	–0–	550,000
Costs transferred out	550,000	?
Work in process, May 31	80,000	?

Instructions
Answer the following questions.
(a) If 3,000 sofas were started into production on May 1 and 2,500 sofas were transferred to Upholstering, what was the unit cost of materials for May in the Framing Department?

(b) Using the data in (a), what was the per unit conversion cost of the sofas transferred to Upholstering?

(c) Continuing the assumptions in (a), what is the percentage of completion of the units in process at May 31 in the Framing Department?

Real-World Focus

BYP 3-3   General Microwave Corp. is engaged primarily in the design, development, manufacture, and marketing of microwave, electronic, and fiber-optic test equipment, components, and subsystems. A substantial portion of the company's microwave product is sold to manufacturers and users of microwave systems and equipment for applications in the defense electronics industry.

General Microwave Corp. reports the following information in one of the notes to its financial statements.

GENERAL MICROWAVE CORPORATION
Notes to the Financial Statements

Work in process inventory reflects all accumulated production costs, which are comprised of direct production costs and overhead, reduced by amounts attributable to units delivered. Work in process inventory is reduced to its estimated net realizable value by a charge to cost of sales in the period [in which] excess costs are identified. Raw materials and finished goods inventories are reflected at the lower of cost or market.

Instructions

(a) What types of manufacturing costs are accumulated in the work in process inventory account?

(b) What types of information must General Microwave have to be able to compute equivalent units of production?

(c) How does General Microwave assign costs to the completed units transferred out of work in process?

Exploring the Web

BYP 3-4   Search the Internet and find the Web sites of two manufacturers that you think are likely to use process costing. Are there any specifics included in their Web sites that confirm the use of process costing for each of these companies?

Communication Activity

BYP 3-5   Jenna Haines was a good friend of yours in high school and is from your home town. While you chose to major in accounting when you both went away to college, she majored in marketing and management. You have recently been promoted to accounting manager for the Snack Foods Division of Clark Enterprises, and your friend was promoted to regional sales manager for the same division of Clark. Jenna recently telephoned you. She explained that she was familiar with job cost sheets, which had been used by the Special Projects division where she had formerly worked. She was, however, very uncomfortable with the production cost reports prepared by your division. She faxed you a list of her particular questions. These included the following.

1. Since Clark occasionally prepares snack foods for special orders in the Snack Foods Division, why don't we track costs of the orders separately?

2. What is an equivalent unit?

3. Why am I getting four production cost reports? Isn't there only one Work in Process account?

Instructions

Prepare a memo to Jenna. Answer her questions, and include any additional information you think would be helpful. You may write informally, but be careful to use proper grammar and punctuation.

Research Assignment

BYP 3-6   The May 10, 2004, edition of the *Wall Street Journal* includes an article by Evan Ramstad titled "A Tight Squeeze" (p. R9).

Instructions

Read the article and answer the following questions.

(a) What is **Proview**'s profit margin on computer monitors? Why is the profit margin so thin on computer monitors?
(b) What are some of the steps that Proview International has taken to control costs?
(c) Why does the company continue to build tube-based monitors even as many consumers are moving away from them?
(d) Mr. Wang's final comment is, "Every aspect of the business is important, but the most important is cost." Why does he feel this way?

Ethics Case

BYP 3-7   C. C. Daibo Company manufactures a high-tech component that passes through two production processing departments, Molding and Assembly. Department managers are partially compensated on the basis of units of products completed and transferred out relative to units of product put into production. This was intended as encouragement to be efficient and to minimize waste.

Barb Crusmer is the department head in the Molding Department, and Wayne Terrago is her quality control inspector. During the month of June, Barb had three new employees who were not yet technically skilled. As a result, many of the units produced in June had minor molding defects. In order to maintain the department's normal high rate of completion, Barb told Wayne to pass through inspection and on to the Assembly Department all units that had defects nondetectable to the human eye. "Company and industry tolerances on this product are too high anyway," says Barb. "Less than 2% of the units we produce are subjected in the market to the stress tolerance we've designed into them. The odds of those 2% being any of this month's units are even less. Anyway, we're saving the company money."

Instructions

(a) Who are the potential stakeholders involved in this situation?
(b) What alternatives does Wayne have in this situation? What might the company do to prevent this situation from occurring?

Answers to Self-Study Questions

1. b   **2.** d   **3.** d   **4.** b   **5.** b   **6.** a   **7.** c   **8.** a   **9.** b   **10.** b
*11. b   ***12.** a   ***13.** b

CHAPTER 4

Activity-Based Costing

STUDY OBJECTIVES

After studying this chapter,
you should be able to:

1 Recognize the difference between traditional costing and activity-based costing.

2 Identify the steps in the development of an activity-based costing system.

3 Know how companies identify the activity cost pools used in activity-based costing.

4 Know how companies identify and use cost drivers in activity-based costing.

5 Understand the benefits and limitations of activity-based costing.

6 Differentiate between value-added and non-value-added activities.

7 Understand the value of using activity levels in activity-based costing.

8 Apply activity-based costing to service industries.

THE NAVIGATOR

THE NAVIGATOR ✔

▶ Scan *Study Objectives* ☐

▶ Read *Feature Story* ☐

▶ Read *Preview* ☐

▶ Read text and answer *Before You Go On*
     p. 150 ☐   p. 158 ☐   p. 161 ☐

▶ Work *Using the Decision Toolkit* ☐

▶ Review *Summary of Study Objectives* ☐

▶ Work *Demonstration Problem* ☐

▶ Answer *Self-Study Questions* ☐

▶ Complete *Assignments* ☐

FEATURE STORY

The ABCs of Donut Making—Virtual-Reality Style

Super Bakery, Inc., created in 1990 by former Pittsburgh Steelers' running back Franco Harris, is a nationwide supplier of mineral-, vitamin-, and protein-enriched donuts and other baked goods to the institutional food market, primarily school systems. Super Bakery is a *virtual corporation*, in which only the core, strategic functions of the business are performed inside the company. The remaining activities—selling, manufacturing, warehousing, and shipping—are outsourced to a network of external companies.

Super Bakery draws these cooperating companies together and organizes the work flow. The goal is to add maximum value to the company while making the minimum investment in permanent staff, fixed assets, and working capital. The results are notable: Super Bakery's sales have grown at an average annual rate of approximately 20 percent during most of its existence.

One of Super Bakery's challenges has been to control the cost of the outsourced activities. Management suspected a wide variation in the cost of serving customers in different parts of the country. Yet its traditional costing methods were spreading costs over the entire customer base. Each customer's order *appeared* to cost the same amount to complete. In actuality, orders with high profit margins were subsidizing orders with low profit margins. Super Bakery

desired a system that would more accurately assign the costs of each order. With such a system, pricing could be improved.

The company looked at and eventually changed to a system that could identify the costs associated with the *activities* performed in the business—manufacturing, sales, warehousing, and shipping. The new activity-based costing system showed that the costs and profit margins on each sale vary significantly. Super Bakery is now able to track the profitability of each customer's account and the performance of outsourced activities. This donut maker, as a result, even knows the cost of the donut holes!

Source: Tom R.V. Davis and Bruce L. Darling, "ABC in a Virtual Corporation," *Management Accounting* (October 1996), pp. 18–26.

As indicated in our Feature Story about **Super Bakery, Inc.**, the traditional costing systems described in earlier chapters are not the best answer for every company. Because Super Bakery suspected that the traditional system was masking significant differences in its real cost structure, it sought a new method of assigning costs. Similar searches by other companies for ways to improve operations and gather more accurate data for decision-making have resulted in the development of powerful new management tools, including **activity-based costing (ABC)**. The primary objective of this chapter is to explain and illustrate this concept.

The content and organization of this chapter are as follows.

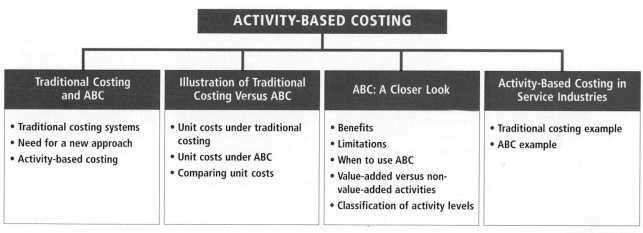

ACTIVITY-BASED COSTING

Traditional Costing and ABC	Illustration of Traditional Costing Versus ABC	ABC: A Closer Look	Activity-Based Costing in Service Industries
• Traditional costing systems • Need for a new approach • Activity-based costing	• Unit costs under traditional costing • Unit costs under ABC • Comparing unit costs	• Benefits • Limitations • When to use ABC • Value-added versus non-value-added activities • Classification of activity levels	• Traditional costing example • ABC example

☑ THE NAVIGATOR

Traditional Costing and Activity-Based Costing

TRADITIONAL COSTING SYSTEMS

It is probably impossible to determine the **exact** cost of a product or service. However, in order to achieve improved management decisions, every effort to provide decision makers with the most accurate cost estimates must be made. The most accurate estimate of product cost occurs when the costs are traceable directly to the product produced or the service provided. Direct material and direct labor costs are the easiest to trace directly to the product through the use of material requisition forms and payroll time sheets. Overhead costs, on the other hand, are an indirect or common cost that generally cannot be easily or directly traced to individual products or services. Instead, we use estimates to assign overhead costs to products and services.

Often the most difficult part of computing accurate unit costs is determining the proper amount of **overhead cost** to assign to each product, service, or job. In our coverage of job order costing in Chapter 2 and of process costing in Chapter 3, we used a single or plantwide overhead rate throughout the year for the entire factory operation. That rate was called the **predetermined overhead rate**. For job order costing we assumed that **direct labor cost** was the relevant activity base for assigning all overhead costs to jobs. For process costing, we assumed that **machine hours** was the relevant activity base for assigning all overhead to the process or department.

STUDY OBJECTIVE

1

Recognize the difference between traditional costing and activity-based costing.

The use of direct labor as the activity base made sense when overhead cost allocation systems were first developed. At that time, direct labor made up a large portion of total manufacturing cost. Therefore, it was widely accepted that there was a high correlation between direct labor and the incurrence of overhead cost. As a result, direct labor became the most popular basis for allocating overhead.

Even in today's increasingly automated environment, direct labor is sometimes the appropriate basis for assigning overhead cost to products. It is appropriate to use direct labor when (a) direct labor constitutes a significant part of total product cost, and (b) a high correlation exists between direct labor and changes in the amount of overhead costs. A simplified (one-stage) traditional costing system relying on direct labor to assign overhead is displayed in Illustration 4-1.

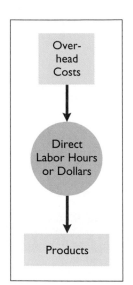

Illustration 4-1 Traditional one-stage costing system

THE NEED FOR A NEW APPROACH

In recent years manufacturers and service providers have experienced tremendous change. Advances in computerized systems, technological innovation, global competition, and automation have changed the manufacturing environment drastically. As a result, the amount of direct labor used in many industries has greatly decreased, and total overhead costs resulting from depreciation on expensive equipment and machinery, utilities, repairs, and maintenance have significantly increased. When there is not a correlation between direct labor and overhead, it is inappropriate to use plantwide predetermined overhead rates based on direct labor. Companies that use overhead rates based on direct labor, when this correlation does not exist, experience significant product cost distortions.

To avoid such distortions, many companies now use machine hours as the basis on which to allocate overhead in an automated manufacturing environment. But even machine hours may not suffice as the only plantwide basis for allocating all overhead. If the manufacturing process is complex, then only multiple allocation bases can result in more accurate product-cost computations. In such situations, managers need to consider an overhead cost allocation method that uses multiple bases. That method is **activity-based costing**.

ACTIVITY-BASED COSTING

Broadly, **activity-based costing (ABC)** is an approach for allocating overhead costs. More specifically, ABC allocates overhead to multiple activity cost pools, and it then assigns the activity cost pools to products and services by means of cost drivers. To understand more clearly what that means, you need to apply some new meanings to the rather common-sounding words that make up the definition. In activity-based costing, an **activity** is any event, action, transaction, or work sequence that incurs cost when producing a product or providing a service. An **activity cost pool** is a distinct type of activity (e.g., ordering materials or setting up machines). A **cost driver** is any factor or activity that has a direct cause-effect relationship with the resources consumed. The reasoning behind ABC cost allocation is simple: **Products consume activities, and activities consume resources**.

These definitions of terms will become clearer as we look more closely at how ABC works. ABC allocates overhead in a two-stage process. In the first stage, overhead costs are allocated to activity cost pools. (In traditional costing systems, in contrast, these costs are allocated to departments or to jobs.) Examples of overhead cost pools are ordering materials, setting up machines, assembling products, inspecting products.

In the second stage, the overhead allocated to the activity cost pools is assigned to products using cost drivers. The cost drivers measure the number of individual activities undertaken or performed to produce products or provide services. Examples are number of purchase orders, number of setups, labor hours, or number of inspections. Illustration 4-2 shows examples of activities, and possible cost drivers to measure them, for a company that manufactures two products—axles and steering wheels.

Illustration 4-2 Activities and related cost drivers

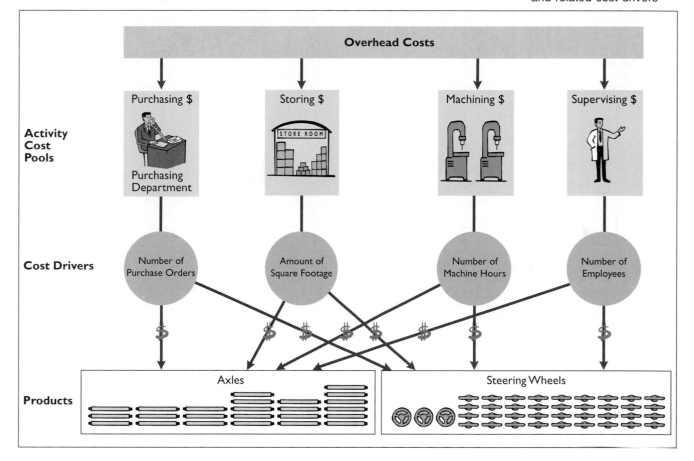

In the first step (as shown at the top of Illustration 4-2), the company's overhead costs are allocated to activity cost pools. In this simplified example, four activity cost pools have been identified: purchasing, storing, machining, and supervising. After the costs are allocated to the activity cost pools, the company uses cost drivers to determine the costs to be assigned to the individual products (either axles or steering wheels) based on each product's use of each activity. For example, if axles require more activity by the purchasing department, as measured by the number of required purchase orders, then more of the overhead cost from the purchasing pool will be allocated to the axles.

The more complex a product's manufacturing operation, the more activities and cost drivers it is likely to have. If there is little or no correlation between changes in the cost driver and consumption of the overhead cost, inaccurate product costs are inevitable.

The design of a more complex activity-based costing system with seven activity cost pools is graphically shown in Illustration 4-3 (page 146) for Lift Jack Company. Lift Jack Company manufactures two automotive jacks—an automobile scissors jack and a truck hydraulic jack.

Illustration 4-3   ABC
system design—Lift Jack
Company

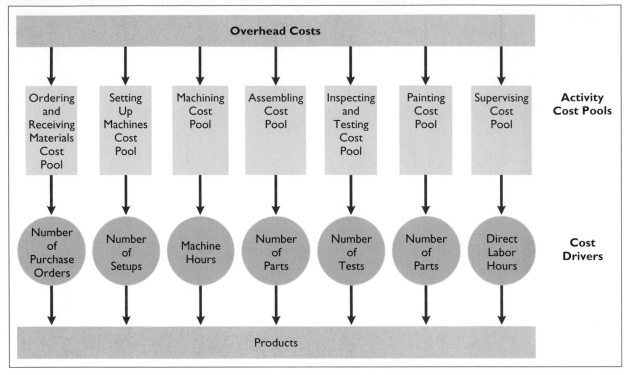

The Lift Jack Company illustration contains seven activity cost pools. In some companies the number of activities related to a cost pool can be substantial. For example, at **Clark-Hurth** (a division of **Clark Equipment Company**), a manufacturer of axles and transmissions, over 170 activities were identified. At **Compumotor** (a division of **Parker Hannifin**) over 80 activities were identified in just the procurement function of its Material Control Department.

Illustration of
Traditional Costing versus ABC

In this section we present a simple case example that compares traditional costing and activity-based costing. It illustrates how ABC eliminates the distortion that can occur in traditional overhead cost allocation. You should understand that ABC does not replace an existing job order or process costing system. What ABC does is to segregate overhead into various cost pools in an effort to provide more accurate cost information. As a result, ABC supplements—not replaces—the traditional cost systems.

Assume that Atlas Company produces two automobile antitheft devices, The Boot and The Club. The Boot is a high-volume item totaling 25,000 units annually. The Club is a low-volume item totaling only 5,000 units per year. Each product requires one hour of direct labor for completion. Therefore, total annual direct labor hours are 30,000 (25,000 + 5,000). Expected annual manufacturing overhead costs are $900,000. Thus, the predetermined overhead rate is $30 ($900,000 ÷ 30,000) per direct labor hour.

The direct materials cost per unit is $40 for The Boot and $30 for The Club. The direct labor cost is $12 per unit for each product.

UNIT COSTS UNDER TRADITIONAL COSTING

The computation of the unit cost for The Boot and The Club under traditional costing is shown in Illustration 4-4.

	Products	
Manufacturing Costs	**The Boot**	**The Club**
Direct materials	$0	$30
Direct labor	12	12
Overhead	30*	30*
Total unit cost	**$82**	**$72**

*Predetermined overhead rate times direct labor hours ($30 × 1hr. = $30).

Illustration 4-4   Computation of unit costs—traditional costing

UNIT COSTS UNDER ABC

Let's now calculate unit costs under ABC, in order to compare activity-based costing with a traditional costing system. Activity-based costing involves the following four steps.

1. Identify and classify the major activities involved in the manufacture of specific products, and allocate manufacturing overhead costs to the appropriate cost pools.
2. Identify the cost driver that has a strong correlation to the costs accumulated in the cost pool.
3. Compute the overhead rate for each cost driver.
4. Assign manufacturing overhead costs for each cost pool to products, using the overhead rates (cost per driver).

STUDY OBJECTIVE
2
Identify the steps in the development of an activity-based costing system.

Identify and Classify Activities and Allocate Overhead to Cost Pools (Step 1)

A well-designed activity-based costing system starts with an analysis of the activities performed to manufacture a product or provide a service. This analysis should identify all resource-consuming activities. It requires a detailed, step by step walk-through of each operation, documenting every activity undertaken to accomplish a task. Atlas Company identified three activity-cost pools: setting up machines, machining, and inspecting.

Next, overhead costs are assigned directly to the appropriate activity cost pool. For example, all overhead costs directly associated with Atlas Company's machine setups (such as salaries, supplies, and depreciation) would be assigned to the machine setup cost pool. The three cost pools, along with the estimated overhead allocated to each cost pool, are shown in Illustration 4-5.

STUDY OBJECTIVE
3
Know how companies identify the activity cost pools used in activity-based costing.

Activity Cost Pools	**Estimated Overhead**
Setting up machines	$300,000
Machining	500,000
Inspecting	100,000
Total	$ 900,000

Illustration 4-5   Activity cost pools and estimated overhead

Identify Cost Drivers (Step 2)

After costs are allocated to the activity cost pools, the cost drivers for each cost pool must be identified. The cost driver must accurately measure the actual consumption of the activity by the various products. To achieve accurate costing, a **high degree of correlation** must exist between the cost driver and the actual consumption of the overhead costs in the cost pool.

The cost drivers identified by Atlas and their total expected use per activity cost pool are shown in Illustration 4-6.

Illustration 4-6 Cost drivers and their expected use

Activity Cost Pools	Cost Drivers	Expected Use of Cost Drivers per Activity
Setting up machines	Number of setups	**1,500** setups
Machining	Machine hours	**50,000** machine hours
Inspecting	Number of inspections	**2,000** inspections

Availability and ease of obtaining data relating to the cost driver is an important factor that must be considered in its selection.

Compute Overhead Rates (Step 3)

Next, an **activity-based overhead rate** per cost driver is computed by dividing the estimated overhead per activity by the number of cost drivers expected to be used per activity. The formula for this computation is shown in Illustration 4-7.

Illustration 4-7 Formula for computing activity-based overhead rate

$$\frac{\textbf{Estimated Overhead Per Activity}}{\textbf{Expected Use of Cost Drivers Per Activity}} = \textbf{Activity-Based Overhead Rate}$$

Atlas Company computes its activity-based overhead rates by using estimated overhead per activity cost pool, shown in Illustration 4-5, and the expected use of cost drivers per activity, shown in Illustration 4-6. The computations are presented in Illustration 4-8.

Illustration 4-8 Computation of activity-based overhead rates

Activity Cost Pools	Estimated ÷ Overhead	Expected Use of Cost Drivers per Activity	=	Activity-Based Overhead Rates
Setting up machines	$300,000	1,500 setups		**$200** per setup
Machining	500,000	50,000 machine hours		**$10** per machine hour
Inspecting	100,000	2,000 inspections		**$50** per inspection
Total	$900,000			

Assign Overhead Costs to Products (Step 4)

In assigning overhead costs, it is necessary to know the expected use of cost drivers **for each product**. Because of its low volume, The Club requires more setups and inspections than The Boot. The expected use of cost drivers per product for each of Atlas's products is shown in Illustration 4-9.

Illustration 4-9
Expected use of cost drivers per product

Activity Cost Pools	Cost Drivers	Expected Use of Cost Drivers per Activity	Expected Use of Cost Drivers per Product	
			The Boot	The Club
Setting up machines	Number of setups	1,500 setups	500	1,000
Machining	Machine hours	50,000 machine hours	30,000	20,000
Inspecting	Number of inspections	2,000 inspections	500	1,500

To assign overhead costs to each product, the activity-based overhead rates per cost driver (Illustration 4-8) are multiplied by the number of cost drivers expected to be used per product (Illustration 4-9). The amount of overhead cost assigned to each product for Atlas Company is shown in Illustration 4-10.

Illustration 4-10   Assignment of activity cost pools to products

ATLAS COMPANY

	The Boot				The Club			
Activity Cost Pools	Expected Use of Cost Drivers per Product	X	Activity-Based Overhead Rates	=	Cost Assigned	Expected Use of Cost Drivers per Product	X	Activity-Based Overhead Rates	=	Cost Assigned
Setting up machines	500		$200		$100,000	1,000		$200		$200,000
Machining	30,000		10		300,000	20,000		10		200,000
Inspecting	500		50		25,000	1,500		50		75,000
Total costs assigned [(a)]					$425,000					$475,000
Units produced [(b)]					25,000					5,000
Overhead cost per unit [(a) ÷ (b)]					$17					$95

These data show that under ABC, overhead costs are shifted from the high-volume product (The Boot) to the low-volume product (The Club). This shift results in more accurate costing for two reasons:

1. Low-volume products often require more special handling, such as more machine setups and inspections, than high-volume products. This is true for Atlas Company. Thus, the low-volume product frequently is responsible for more overhead costs per unit than is a high-volume product.[1]

2. Assigning overhead using ABC will usually increase the cost per unit for low-volume products as compared to a traditional overhead allocation. Therefore, traditional cost drivers such as direct labor hours are usually not appropriate for assigning overhead costs to low-volume products.

COMPARING UNIT COSTS

A comparison of unit manufacturing costs under traditional costing and ABC shows the following significant differences.

[1]Robin Cooper and Robert S. Kaplan, "How Cost Accounting Distorts Product Costs," *Management Accounting* 69, No. 10 (April 1988), pp. 20–27.

Illustration 4-11 Comparison of unit product costs

Manufacturing Costs	The Boot		The Club	
	Traditional Costing	ABC	Traditional Costing	ABC
Direct materials	$40	$40	$30	$30
Direct labor	12	12	12	12
Overhead	30	17	30	95
Total cost per unit	$82	$69	$72	$137

Overstated $13   Understated $65

The comparison shows that unit costs under traditional costing are significantly distorted. The cost of producing The Boot is overstated $13 per unit ($82 – $69), and the cost of producing The Club is understated $65 per unit ($137 – $72). These differences are attributable entirely to how manufacturing overhead is assigned. A likely consequence of the differences in assigning overhead is that Atlas Company has been overpricing The Boot and possibly losing market share to competitors. Moreover, it has been sacrificing profitability by underpricing The Club.

Business Insight
International Perspective

Activity-based costing was pioneered in the United States: **John Deere Company** coined the term less than 25 years ago. ABC has been adopted by numerous well-known U.S. companies including **IBM, AT&T, Hewlett-Packard, Procter and Gamble, Tektronix, Hughes Aircraft, Caterpillar,** and **American Express**. Its use outside the United States is limited. The cost of implementation may discourage some foreign companies.

In Japan, where activity-based costing is less used, companies prefer volume measures such as direct labor hours to assign overhead cost to products. Japanese managers are convinced that reducing direct labor is essential to continuous cost reduction. And, using direct labor as the basis for overhead allocation forces Japanese companies to watch direct labor more closely. Possibly, labor cost reduction is more of a priority than developing more accurate product costs.

BEFORE YOU GO ON . . .

▶ **Review It**

1. Historically, why has direct labor hours been the most popular basis for allocating overhead costs to products?
2. What changes have occurred in the industrial environment to diminish the appeal of traditional volume-based overhead allocation systems?
3. What four steps are involved in developing an ABC system?

▶**Do It**

Lift Jack Company, as shown in Illustration 4-3, page 146, has seven activity cost pools and two products. It expects to produce 200,000 units of its automobile scissors jack, and 80,000 units of its truck hydraulic jack. Having identified its activity cost pools and the cost drivers for each cost pool, Lift Jack Company accumulated the following data relative to those activity cost pools and cost drivers.

	Annual Overhead Data			**Expected Use of Cost Drivers per Product**	
Activity Cost Pools	**Cost Drivers**	**Estimated Overhead**	**Expected Use of Cost Drivers per Activity**	**Scissors Jacks**	**Hydraulic Jacks**
Ordering and receiving	Purchase orders	$ 200,000	2,500 orders	1,000	1,500
Machine setup	Setups	600,000	1,200 setups	500	700
Machining	Machine hours	2,000,000	800,000 hours	300,000	500,000
Assembling	Parts	1,800,000	3,000,000 parts	1,800,000	1,200,000
Inspecting and testing	Tests	700,000	35,000 tests	20,000	15,000
Painting	Parts	300,000	3,000,000 parts	1,800,000	1,200,000
Supervising	Direct labor hours	1,200,000	200,000 hours	130,000	70,000
		$6,800,000			

Using the above data, do the following:
(a) Prepare a schedule showing the computations of the activity-based overhead rates per cost driver.
(b) Prepare a schedule assigning each activity's overhead cost to the two products.
(c) Compute the overhead cost per unit for each product.
(d) Comment on the comparative overhead cost per unit.

Action Plan

• Determine the activity-based overhead rate by dividing the estimated overhead per activity by the expected use of cost drivers per activity.

• Assign the overhead of each activity cost pool to the individual products by multiplying the expected use of cost driver per product times the activity-based overhead rate.

• Determine overhead cost per unit by dividing the overhead assigned to each product by the number of units of that product.

Solution

(a) Computations of activity-based overhead rates per cost driver:

Activity Cost Pools	**Estimated Overhead**	÷	**Expected Use of Cost Drivers per Activity**	=	**Activity-Based Overhead Rates**
Ordering and receiving	$ 200,000		2,500 purchase orders		$80 per order
Machine setup	600,000		1,200 setups		$500 per setup
Machining	2,000,000		800,000 machine hours		$2.50 per machine hour
Assembling	1,800,000		3,000,000 parts		$0.60 per part
Inspecting and testing	700,000		35,000 tests		$20 per test
Painting	300,000		3,000,000 parts		$0.10 per part
Supervising	1,200,000		200,000 direct labor hours		$6 per direct labor hour
	$6,800,000				

(b) Assignment of each activity's overhead cost to products using ABC:

| Activity Cost Pools | Scissors Jacks | | | Hydraulic Jacks | | |
	Expected Use of Cost Drivers per Product ×	Activity-Based Overhead Rates	= Cost Assigned	Expected Use of Cost Drivers per Product ×	Activity-Based Overhead Rates	= Cost Assigned
Ordering and receiving	1,000	$80	$ 80,000	1,500	$80	$ 120,000
Machine setup	500	$500	250,000	700	$500	350,000
Machining	300,000	$2.50	750,000	500,000	$2.50	1,250,000
Assembling	1,800,000	$0.60	1,080,000	1,200,000	$0.60	720,000
Inspecting and testing	20,000	$20	400,000	15,000	$20	300,000
Painting	1,800,000	$0.10	180,000	1,200,000	$0.10	120,000
Supervising	130,000	$6	780,000	70,000	$6	420,000
Total assigned costs			$3,520,000			$3,280,000

(c) Computation of overhead cost per unit:

	Scissors Jack	Hydraulic Jack
Total costs assigned	$3,520,000	$3,280,000
Total units produced	200,000	80,000
Overhead cost per unit	$17.60	$41.00

(d) These data show that the total overhead assigned to 80,000 hydraulic jacks is nearly as great as the overhead assigned to 200,000 scissors jacks. However, the overhead cost per hydraulic jack is $41.00. It is only $17.60 per scissors jack.

Related exercise material: BE4-1, BE4-2, BE4-3, BE4-4, BE4-5, BE4-6, BE4-7, E4-1, E4-2, E4-3, E4-4, E4-5, E4-6, E4-7, E4-8, E4-9, E4-10, and E4-11.

☑ THE NAVIGATOR

Activity-Based Costing: A Closer Look

As the use of activity-based costing has grown, both its practical benefits and its limitations have become apparent.

BENEFITS OF ABC

The primary benefit of ABC is **more accurate product costing**. Here's why:

STUDY OBJECTIVE
5
Understand the benefits and limitations of activity-based costing.

1. **ABC leads to more cost pools** used to assign overhead costs to products. Instead of one plantwide pool (or even departmental pools) and a single cost driver, numerous activity cost pools with more relevant cost drivers are utilized. Costs are assigned more directly on the basis of the number of cost drivers used to produce each product.

2. **ABC leads to enhanced control over overhead costs.** Under ABC, many overhead costs can be traced directly to activities—allowing some indirect costs to be identified as direct costs. Thus, managers have become more aware of their responsibility to control the activities that generate those costs.

3. **ABC leads to better management decisions.** More accurate product costing should contribute to setting selling prices that can help achieve desired product profitability levels. In addition, more accurate cost data could be helpful in deciding whether to make or buy a product part or component, and sometimes even whether to eliminate a product.

In fact, identification of what activities drive costs can result in some indirect costs being accounted for as direct costs. This is because, under ABC, these costs are traceable to specific activities.

Activity-based costing does not change the amount of overhead costs. What it does do is to allocate those overhead costs in a more accurate manner. Furthermore, if the score-keeping is more realistic and more accurate, managers should be able to better understand cost behavior and overall profitability.

LIMITATIONS OF ABC

Although ABC systems often provide better product cost data than traditional volume-based systems, there are limitations:

1. **ABC can be expensive to use.** Many companies are discouraged from using ABC by the increased cost of identifying multiple activities and applying numerous cost drivers. Activity-based costing systems are more complex than traditional costing systems—sometimes significantly more complex. So companies must ask, is the cost of implementation greater than the benefits of greater accuracy? Sometimes it may be. For some companies there may be no need to consider ABC at all because their existing system is sufficient. If the costs of ABC outweigh the benefits, then the company should not implement ABC.

2. **Some arbitrary allocations continue.** Even though more overhead costs can be assigned directly to products through ABC's multiple activity cost pools, certain overhead costs remain to be allocated by means of some arbitrary volume-based cost driver such as labor or machine hours.

Business Insight
Service Company Perspective

Although most publicized ABC applications are in manufacturing companies or large service firms, ABC can be applied in a very small service business. **Mahany Welding Supply**, a small family-run welding service business in Rochester, N.Y., applied ABC to determine the cost of servicing customers and to identify feasible cost reduction opportunities.

Application of ABC at Mahany Welding's operations provided information about the five employees who were involved in different activities of revenue generation—i.e., delivery of supplies (rural versus city), welding services, repairs, telephone sales, field or door-to-door sales, repeat business sales, and cold-call sales. Activity cost pools were assigned to the five revenue-producing employees using relevant cost drivers. ABC revealed annual net income (loss) by employee as follows: Employee #1, $65,431; Employee #2, $35,154; Employee #3, $13,731; Employee #4, ($10,957); Employee #5, ($46,180). This comparative information was an eye-opener to the owner of Mahany Welding—who was Employee #5!

SOURCE: Michael Krupnicki and Thomas Tyson, "Using ABC to Determine the Cost of Servicing Customers," *Management Accounting* (December 31, 1997), pp. 40–46.

WHEN TO USE ABC

How does a company know when to use ABC? The presence of one or more of the following factors would point to possibly using ABC:

1. Product lines differ greatly in volume and manufacturing complexity.
2. Product lines are numerous, diverse, and require differing degrees of support services.
3. Overhead costs constitute a significant portion of total costs.
4. The manufacturing process or the number of products has changed significantly—for example, from labor-intensive to capital-intensive due to automation.
5. Production or marketing managers are ignoring data provided by the existing system and are instead using "bootleg" costing data or other alternative data when pricing or making other product decisions.

The redesign and installation of a product-costing system is a significant decision that requires considerable cost and a major effort to accomplish. Therefore, financial managers need to be very cautious and deliberate when initiating changes in costing systems. A key factor in implementing a successful ABC system is the support of top management.

DECISION TOOLKIT

Decision Checkpoints	Info Needed for Decision	Tool to Use for Decision	How to Evaluate Results
When should we use ABC?	Knowledge of the products or product lines, the manufacturing process, and overhead costs.	A detailed and accurate cost accounting system; cooperation between accountants and operating managers	Compare the results under both costing systems. If managers are better able to understand and control their operations using ABC, and the costs are not prohibitive, use of ABC would be beneficial.

VALUE-ADDED VERSUS NON-VALUE-ADDED ACTIVITIES

Some companies that have experienced the benefits of activity-based costing have applied it to a broader range of management activities. **Activity-based management (ABM)** extends the use of ABC from product costing to a comprehensive management tool that focuses on reducing costs and improving processes and decision making. A refinement of activity-based costing used in ABM is the classification of activities as either value-added or non-value-added.

Value-added activities increase the worth of a product or service to customers; they involve resource usage and related costs that customers are willing to pay for. Value-added activities are the activities of actually manufacturing a product or performing a service—they increase the worth of the product or service. Examples of value-added activities in a manufacturing operation are engineering design, machining, assembly, painting, and packaging. Examples of value-added activities in a service company would be performing surgery, providing legal research for legal services, or delivering packages by a delivery service.

Non-value-added activities are production- or service-related activities that simply **add cost to, or increase the time spent on, a product or service without increasing its market value**. Examples of non-value-added activities in a manufacturing operation include the repair of machines; the storage of inventory; the moving of raw materials, assemblies, and finished product within the factory; building maintenance; inspections; and inventory control. Examples of non-value-added activities in service enterprises might include taking appointments, reception, bookkeeping, billing, traveling, ordering supplies, advertising, cleaning, and computer repair.

Activity flowcharts are often used to help identify the activities that will be used in ABC costing. Illustration 4-12 shows an activity flowchart.

Illustration 4-12 Flowchart showing value-added and non-value-added activities

HEARTLAND MANUFACTURING COMPANY
Activity Flowchart

Activities

NVA	NVA	NVA	NVA	VA		NVA	NVA	VA	NVA	NVA	NVA	VA
Receive and Inspect Materials	Move and Store Materials	Move Materials to Production and Wait	Set up Machines	Machining: Drill	Lathe	Inspect	Move and Wait	Assembly	Inspect and Test	Move to Storage	Store Finished Goods	Package and Ship

| Current Days | 1 | 12 | 2.5 | 1.5 | 2 | 1 | 0.2 | 6 | 2 | 0.3 | 0.5 | 14 | 1 |

Total Current Average Time = 44 days

| Proposed Days | 1 | 4 | 1.5 | 1.5 | 2 | 1 | 0.2 | 2 | 2 | 0.3 | 0.5 | 10 | 1 |

*Total Proposed Average Time = **27** days*

Proposed reduction in nonvalue-added time = 17 days

VA = Value-added   NVA = Non-value-added

In the top part of this flowchart, activities are identified as value-added or non-value-added. The value-added activities are highlighted in red. In the lower part of the flowchart are two rows showing the number of days spent on each activity. The first row shows the number of days spent on each activity under the current manufacturing process. The second row shows the number of days expected to be spent on each activity under management's proposed reengineered manufacturing process.

The proposed changes would reduce time spent on non-value-added activities by 17 days. This 17-day improvement would be due entirely to moving inventory more quickly through the non-value-added processes—that is, by reducing inventory time in moving, storage, and waiting. The appendix at the end of this chapter discusses a just-in-time inventory system, which is used to eliminate non-value-added activities related to inventory.

Not all activities labeled non-value-added are totally wasteful, nor can they be totally eliminated. For example, although inspection time is a non-value-added activity from a customer's perspective, few companies would eliminate their quality control functions. Similarly, moving and waiting time is non-value-added, but it would be impossible to completely eliminate. Nevertheless, when managers recognize the non-value-added characteristic of these activities, they are motivated to minimize them as much as possible. Attention to such matters is part of the growing practice of activity-based management which helps managers concentrate on **continuous improvement** of operations and activities.

Business Insight
Management Perspective

Often the best way to improve a process is to learn from observing a different process. At the giant food producer **General Mills**, production line technicians were flown to North Carolina to observe first-hand how race-car pit crews operate. In a NASCAR car race, the value-added activity is driving toward the finish-line; any time spent in the pit is non-value-added. Every split second saved in the pit increases the chances of winning. From what the General Mills technicians learned at the car race, as well as other efforts, they were able to reduce set-up time from 5 hours to just 20 minutes.

DECISION TOOLKIT

Decision Checkpoints	Info Needed for Decision	Tool to Use for Decision	How to Evaluate Results
How can activity-based-management help managers manage the business?	Activities classified as value-added and non-value-added	The activity analysis flowchart extended to identify each activity as value-added or non-value-added	The flowchart should motivate managers to minimize non-value-added activities. Managers should better understand the relationship between activities and the resources they consume.

CLASSIFICATION OF ACTIVITY LEVELS

STUDY OBJECTIVE

7

Understand the value of using activity levels in activity-based costing.

As mentioned earlier, traditional costing systems are volume-driven—driven by unit-based cost drivers such as direct labor or machine hours. Some activity costs are strictly variable and are caused by the production or acquisition of a single unit of product or the performance of a single unit of service. However, the recognition that other activity costs are not driven by unit-based cost drivers has led to the development of a classification of ABC activities, consisting of four levels. The four levels of activities are classified and defined as follows.

1. **Unit-level activities.** Activities performed for each unit of production.
2. **Batch-level activities.** Activities performed for each batch of products rather than each unit.
3. **Product-level activities.** Activities performed in support of an entire product line, but not always performed every time a new unit or batch of products is produced.
4. **Facility-level activities.** Activities required to support or sustain an entire production process.

Greater accuracy in overhead cost allocation may be achieved by recognizing these four different levels of activities and, from them, developing specific activity cost pools and their related cost drivers. Illustration 4-13 graphically displays this four-level activity hierarchy, along with the types of activities and examples of cost drivers for those activities at each level.

Four Levels	Types of Activities	Examples of Cost Drivers
Unit-Level Activities		
	Machine-related Drilling, cutting, milling, trimming, pressing	Machine hours
	Labor-related Assembling, painting, sanding, sewing	Direct labor hours or cost
Batch-Level Activities		
	Equipment setups	Number of setups or setup time
	Purchase ordering	Number of purchase orders
	Inspection	Number of inspections or inspection time
	Material handling	Number of material moves
Product-Level Activities		
	Product design	Number of product designs
	Engineering changes	Number of changes
Facility-Level Activities		
	Plant management salaries	Number of employees managed
	Plant depreciation	Square footage
	Property taxes	Square footage
	Utilities	Square footage

Illustration 4-13 Hierarchy of activity levels

This classification provides managers a structured way of thinking about the relationships between activities and the resources they consume. In contrast, traditional volume-based costing recognizes only unit-level costs. **Failure to recognize this classification of activities is one of the reasons that volume-based cost allocation causes distortions in product costing.**

As indicated earlier, allocating all overhead costs by unit-based cost drivers can send false signals to managers: Dividing batch-, product-, or facility-level costs by the number of units produced gives the mistaken impression that these costs vary with the number of units. **The resources consumed by batch-, product-, and facility-level supporting activities do not vary at the unit level**, nor can they be controlled at the unit level. The number of activities performed at the batch level goes up as the number of batches rises—not as the number of units within the batches changes. Similarly, the number of product-level activities performed depends on the number of different products—not on how many units or batches are produced. Furthermore, facility-sustaining activity costs are not dependent upon the number of products, batches, or units produced. Batch-, product-, and facility-level costs can be controlled only by modifying batch-, product-, and facility-level activities.

BEFORE YOU GO ON . . .

▶Review It

1. What are the benefits of activity-based costing?
2. What are the limitations of activity-based costing?
3. What company factors would indicate ABC as the superior costing system?
4. What is the benefit of classifying activities as value-added and non-value-added?
5. How is the classification of activities into unit-level, batch-level, product-level, and facility-level important to managers?

▶Do It

Morgan Toy Company manufactures six primary product lines in its Morganville plant. As a result of an activity analysis, the accounting department has identified eight activity cost pools. Each of the toy products is produced in large batches, with the whole plant devoted to one product at a time. Classify each of the following activities as either unit-level, batch-level, product-level, or facility-level: (a) engineering design, (b) machine setup, (c) inventory management, (d) plant cafeteria, (e) inspections after each setup, (f) polishing parts, (g) assembling parts, (h) health and safety.

Action Plan

• Recall that:
  Unit-level activities are performed for each individual unit of product.
  Batch-level activities are performed each time a batch of a product is produced.
  Product-level activities are performed to support an entire product line.
  Facility-level activities support the production process across the entire range of products.

Solution (a) Product-level, (b) batch-level, (c) product-level, (d) facility-level, (e) batch-level, (f) unit-level, (g) unit-level, (h) facility-level.

Related exercise material: BE4-10, BE4-11, BE4-12, E4-17, and E4-18.

☑ THE NAVIGATOR

Activity-Based Costing in Service Industries

STUDY OBJECTIVE

8

Apply activity-based costing to service industries.

Although initially developed and implemented by manufacturers, activity-based costing has been widely adopted in service industries as well. ABC has been a useful tool in such diverse industries as airlines, railroads, hotels, hospitals, banks, insurance companies, telephone companies, and financial services firms. The overall objective of ABC in service firms is no different than it is in a manufacturing company. That objective is to identify the key activities that generate costs and to keep track of how many of those activities are performed for each service provided (by job, service, contract, or customer).

The general approach to identifying activities, activity cost pools, and cost drivers is the same for service companies and for manufacturers. Also, the labeling of activities as value-added and non-value-added, and the attempt to reduce or eliminate non-value-added activities as much as possible, is just as valid in service industries as in manufacturing operations. What sometimes makes implementation of activity-based costing difficult in service industries is that **a larger proportion of overhead costs are company-wide costs** that cannot be directly traced to specific services provided by the company.

To illustrate the application of activity-based costing to a service enterprise, contrasted to traditional costing, we use a public accounting firm. This illustration is equally applicable to a law firm, consulting firm, architect, or any service firm that performs numerous services for a client as part of a job.

TRADITIONAL COSTING EXAMPLE

Assume that the public accounting firm of Check and Doublecheck prepares the following condensed annual budget (see Illustration 4-14).

Illustration 4-14   Condensed annual budget of a service firm under traditional costing

CHECK AND DOUBLECHECK, CPAs
Annual Budget

Revenue		$2,000,000
Direct labor	$ 600,000	
Overhead (expected)	1,200,000	
Total costs		1,800,000
Operating income		$ 200,000

$$\frac{\text{Estimated overhead}}{\text{Direct labor cost}} = \text{Predetermined overhead rate}$$

$$\frac{\$1,200,000}{\$600,000} = 200\%$$

Under traditional costing, direct labor is the professional service performed, and it is the basis for overhead application to each audit job. To determine the operating income earned on any job, Check and Doublecheck applies overhead at the rate of 200 percent of actual direct professional labor costs incurred. For example, assume that Check and Doublecheck records $70,000 of actual direct professional labor cost during its audit of Plano Molding Company, which was billed an audit fee of $260,000. Under traditional costing, using 200 percent as the rate for applying overhead to the job, applied overhead and operating income related to the Plano Molding Company audit would be computed as shown in Illustration 4-15.

Illustration 4-15   Overhead applied under traditional costing system

CHECK AND DOUBLECHECK, CPAs
Plano Molding Company Audit

Revenue		$260,000
Less: Direct professional labor	$ 70,000	
Applied overhead (200% × $70,000)	140,000	210,000
Operating income		$ 50,000

In this example, only one direct cost item and one overhead application rate are used under traditional costing.

ACTIVITY-BASED COSTING EXAMPLE

Under activity-based costing, Check and Doublecheck's estimated annual overhead costs of $1,200,000 are distributed to several activity cost pools. Activity-based overhead rates per cost driver are computed by dividing each activity overhead cost pool by the expected number of cost drivers used per activity. Illustration 4-16 shows an annual overhead budget using an ABC system.

Illustration 4-16 Condensed annual budget of a service firm under activity-based costing

CHECK AND DOUBLECHECK, CPAs
Annual Overhead Budget

Activity Cost Pools	Cost Drivers	Estimated Overhead	$\div$ Expected Use of Cost Drivers per Activity	$=$ Activity-Based Overhead Rates
Secretarial support	Direct professional hours	$ 210,000	30,000	$7 per hour
Direct labor fringe benefits	Direct labor cost	240,000	$ 600,000	$0.40 per $1 labor cost
Printing and photocopying	Working paper pages	20,000	20,000	$1 per page
Computer support	CPU minutes	200,000	50,000	$4 per minute
Telephone and postage	None (Traced directly)	71,000	N/A	Based on usage
Legal support	Hours used	129,000	860	$150 per hour
Insurance (professional liability, etc.)	Revenue billed	120,000	$2,000,000	$0.06 per $1 revenue
Recruiting and training	Direct professional hours	210,000	30,000	$7 per hour
		$1,200,000		

Note that some of the overhead costs can be directly assigned (see telephone and postage).

The assignment of the individual overhead activity rates to the actual number of activities used in the performance of the Plano Molding audit results in total overhead assigned of $165,100 as shown in Illustration 4-17.

Illustration 4-17 Assigning overhead in a service company

Check and DoubleCheck CPAS
Plano Molding Company Audit

Activity Cost Pools	Cost Drivers	Actual Use of Drivers	Activity-Based Overhead Rates	Cost Assigned
Secretarial support	Direct professional hours	3,800	$7.00	$26,600
Direct labor fringe benefits	Direct labor cost	$70,000	$0.40	28,000
Printing and photocopying	Working paper pages	1,800	$1.00	1,800
Computer support	CPU minutes	8,600	$4.00	34,400
Telephone and postage	None (Traced directly)			8,700
Legal support	Hours used	156	$150.00	23,400
Insurance (professional liability, etc.)	Revenue billed	$260,000	$0.06	15,600
Recruiting and training	Direct professional hours	3,800	$7.00	26,600
				$165,100

Under activity-based costing, overhead costs of $165,100 are assigned to the Plano Molding Company audit, as compared to $140,000 under traditional costing. A comparison of total costs and operating margins is shown in Illustration 4-18.

CHECK AND DOUBLECHECK, CPAs Plano Molding Company Audit				
	Traditional Costing		**ABC**	
Revenue		$260,000		$260,000
Expenses				
Direct professional labor	$ 70,000		$ 70,000	
Applied overhead	140,000		165,100	
Total expenses		210,000		235,100
Operating income		**$ 50,000**		**$ 24,900**
Profit margin		**19.2%**		**9.6%**

Illustration 4-18   Comparison of traditional costing with ABC in a service company

The comparison shows that the assignment of overhead costs under traditional costing is distorted. The total cost assigned to performing the audit of Plano Molding Company is greater under activity-based costing by $25,100, or 12 percent higher, and the profit margin is only half as great. Traditional costing gives the false impression of an operating profit of $50,000. This is more than double the operating income of $24,900 using ABC.

BEFORE YOU GO ON . . .

▶**Review It**

1. What is the primary barrier to effectively implementing ABC in a service-company environment?
2. What is the main advantage to be gained by using ABC in a service-company environment?

☑ THE NAVIGATOR

Using the Decision Toolkit

Precor Company manufactures a line of high-end exercise equipment of commercial quality. Assume that the chief accountant has proposed changing from a traditional costing system to an activity-based costing system. The financial vice-president is not convinced, so she requests that the next large order for equipment be costed under both systems for purposes of comparison and analysis. An order from Slim-Way Salons, Inc., for 150 low-impact treadmills is received and is identified as the order to be subjected to dual costing. The following cost data relate to the Slim-Way order.

Data relevant to both costing systems

Direct materials	$55,500
Direct labor hours	820
Direct labor rate per hour	$ 18.00

Data relevant to the traditional costing system

Predetermined overhead rate is 300% of direct labor cost.

(continued from page 161)

Data relevant to the activity-based costing system

Activity Cost Pools	Cost Drivers	Activity-Based Overhead Rate	Expected Use of Cost Drivers per Treadmill
Engineering design	Engineering hours	$30 per hour	330
Machine setup	Setups	$200 per setup	22
Machining	Machine hours	$25 per hour	732
Assembly	Number of subassemblies	$8 per subassembly	1,450
Packaging and shipping	Packaging/shipping hours	$15 per hour	152
Building occupancy	Machine hours	$6 per hour	732

Instructions

Compute the total cost of the Slim-Way Salons, Inc. order under (a) the traditional costing system and (b) the activity-based costing system. (c) As a result of this comparison, which costing system is Precor likely to adopt? Why?

Solution

(a) Traditional costing system:

Direct materials	$ 55,500
Direct labor (820 × $18)	14,760
Overhead assigned ($14,760 × 300%)	44,280
Total costs assigned to Slim-Way order	$114,540
Number of low-impact treadmills	150
Cost per unit	$763.60

(b) Activity-based costing system:

Direct materials		$ 55,500
Direct labor (820 × $18)		14,760
Overhead activities costs:		
Engineering design (330 hours @ $30)	$ 9,900	
Machine setup (22 setups @ $200)	4,400	
Machining (732 machine hours @ $25)	18,300	
Assembly (1,450 subassemblies @ $8)	11,600	
Packaging and shipping (152 hours @ $15)	2,280	
Building occupancy (732 hours @ $6)	4,392	50,872
Total costs assigned to Slim-Way order		$121,132
Number of low-impact treadmills		150
Cost per unit		$807.55

(c) Precor Company will likely adopt ABC because of the difference in the cost per unit (which ABC found to be higher). More importantly, ABC provides greater insight into the sources and causes of the cost per unit. Managers are given greater insight into which activities to control in order to reduce costs. ABC will provide better product costing and greater profitability for the company.

THE NAVIGATOR

Summary of Study Objectives

1 *Recognize the difference between traditional costing and activity-based costing.* A traditional costing system allocates overhead to products on the basis of predetermined plantwide or departmentwide volume of unit-based output rates such as direct labor or machine hours. An ABC system allocates overhead to identified activity cost pools, and costs are then assigned to products using related cost drivers that measure the activities (resources) consumed.

2 *Identify the steps in the development of an activity-based costing system.* The development of an activity-based costing system involves four steps: (1) Identify and classify the major activities involved in the manufacture of specific products, and allocate manufacturing overhead costs to the appropriate cost pools. (2) Identify the cost driver that has a strong correlation to the costs accumulated in the cost pool. (3) Compute the overhead rate per cost driver. (4) Assign manufacturing overhead costs for each cost pool to products or services using the overhead rates.

3 *Know how companies identify the activity cost pools used in activity-based costing.* To identify activity cost pools, a company must perform an analysis of each operation or process, documenting and timing every task, action, or transaction.

4 *Know how companies identify and use cost drivers in activity-based costing.* Cost drivers identified for assigning activity cost pools must (a) accurately measure the actual consumption of the activity by the various products, and (b) have related data easily available.

5 *Understand the benefits and limitations of activity-based costing.* Features of ABC that make it a more accurate product costing system include: (1) the increased number of cost pools used to assign overhead, (2) the enhanced control over overhead costs, and (3) the better management decisions it makes possible. The limitations of ABC are: (1) the higher analysis and measurement costs that accompany multiple activity centers and cost drivers, and (2) the necessity still to allocate some costs arbitrarily.

6 *Differentiate between value-added and non-value-added activities.* Value-added activities increase the worth of a product or service. Non-value-added activities simply add cost to, or increase the time spent on, a product or service without increasing its market value. Awareness of these classifications encourages managers to reduce or eliminate the time spent on the non-value-added activities.

7 *Understand the value of using activity levels in activity-based costing.* Activities may be classified as unit-level, batch-level, product-level, and facility-level. Overhead costs at unit-, batch-, product-, and facility-levels are controlled by modifying unit-, batch-, product-, and facility-level activities, respectively. Failure to recognize this classification of levels can result in distorted product costing.

8 *Apply activity-based costing to service industries.* The overall objective of using ABC in service industries is no different than for manufacturing industries, that is, improved costing of services provided (by job, service, contract, or customer). The general approach to costing is the same: analyze operations, identify activities, accumulate overhead costs by activity cost pools, and identify and use cost drivers to assign the cost pools to the services.

DECISION TOOLKIT—A SUMMARY

Decision Checkpoints	Info Needed for Decision	Tool to Use for Decision	How to Evaluate Results
When should we use ABC?	Knowledge of the products or product lines, the manufacturing process, and overhead costs.	A detailed and accurate cost accounting system; cooperation between accountants and operating managers	Compare the results under both costing systems. If managers are better able to understand and control their operations using ABC, and the costs are not prohibitive, the use of ABC would be beneficial.
How can activity-based management help managers manage the business?	Activities classified as value-added and non-value-added	The activity analysis flowchart extended to identify each activity as value-added or non-value-added	The flowchart should motivate managers to minimize non-value-added activities. Managers should better understand the relationship between activities and the resources they consume.

APPENDIX
JUST-IN-TIME PROCESSING

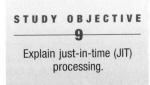

STUDY OBJECTIVE

9

Explain just-in-time (JIT) processing.

Traditionally, continuous process manufacturing has been based on a **just-in-case** philosophy: Inventories of raw materials are maintained *just in case* some items are of poor quality or a key supplier is shut down by a strike. Similarly, subassembly parts are manufactured and stored *just in case* they are needed later in the manufacturing process. Finished goods are completed and stored *just in case* unexpected and rush customer orders are received. This philosophy often results in a **push approach**, in which raw materials and subassembly parts are pushed through each process. Traditional processing often results in the buildup of extensive manufacturing inventories.

Primarily in response to foreign competition, many U.S. firms have switched to **just-in-time (JIT) processing**. JIT manufacturing is dedicated to having the right amount of materials, parts, or products at the time they are needed. Under JIT processing, raw materials are received **just in time** for use in production, subassembly parts are completed **just in time** for use in finished goods, and finished goods are completed **just in time** to be sold. Illustration 4A-1 shows the sequence of activities in just-in-time processing.

Illustration 4A-1   Just-in-time processing

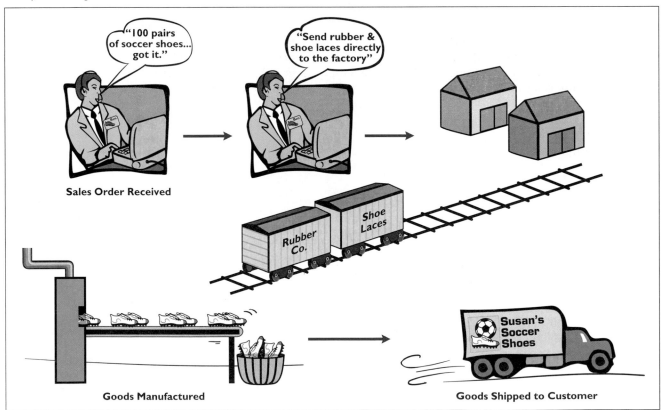

Objective of JIT Processing

The primary objective of JIT is to eliminate all manufacturing inventories. Inventories are considered to have an adverse effect on net income because they tie up funds and storage space that could be made available for more productive purposes. JIT strives to eliminate inventories by using a **demand-pull approach** in manufacturing. This approach begins with the customer placing an order with the company. This order, which indicates product demand, starts the process of pulling the product through the manufacturing process. A signal is sent via a computer to the next preceding work station indicating the exact materials (parts and sub-assemblies) needed for a time period, such as an eight-hour shift, to complete the production of a specified product. The preceding process, in turn, sends its signal to other preceding processes. The goal is a smooth continuous flow in the manufacturing process, with no buildup of inventories at any point.

Elements of JIT Processing

There are three important elements in JIT processing:

1. A company must have **dependable suppliers** who are willing to deliver on short notice exact quantities of raw materials according to precise quality specifications. (This may even include multiple deliveries within the same day.) Suppliers must also be willing to deliver the raw materials at specified work stations rather than at a central receiving department. This type of purchasing requires constant and direct communication with suppliers, which is facilitated by an online computer linkage between the company and its suppliers.

2. A **multiskilled work force** must be developed. Under JIT, machines are often strategically grouped into work cells or centers and much of the work is automated. As a result, one worker may have the responsibility to operate and maintain several different types of machines.

3. A **total quality control system** must be established throughout the manufacturing operations. Total quality control means **no defects**. Since only required quantities are signaled by the demand-pull approach, any defects at a work station will shut down operations at subsequent work stations. Total quality control requires continuous monitoring by both employees and supervisors at each work station.

Helpful Hint Buyer leverage is important in finding dependable suppliers. Companies like GM and GE have more success than smaller companies.

Business Insight
Management Perspective

JIT first hit the USA in the early 1980s when it was adopted by automobile companies to help compete with foreign competition. It is now being successfully used in many companies, including **Dell**, **Caterpillar**, and **Harley-Davidson**. The effects in many cases have been dramatic. For example, after using JIT for two years, a major division of **Hewlett-Packard** found that work-in-process inventories (in dollars) were down 82 percent, scrap/rework costs were down 30 percent, space utilization was down 40 percent, and labor efficiency improved 50 percent. As indicated, JIT not only reduces inventory but also enables a manufacturer to produce a better product faster and with less waste.

Benefits of JIT Processing

The major benefits of implementing JIT processing are:

1. Manufacturing inventories are significantly reduced or eliminated.
2. Product quality is enhanced.

Helpful Hint Without its emphasis on quality control, JIT would be impractical or even impossible. In JIT, quality is engineered into the production process.

Helpful Hint JIT is easier said than done. JIT requires a total commitment by management and employees, a complete change in philosophy, and significant changes in the way production is organized. JIT takes time to implement.

3. Rework costs and inventory storage costs are reduced or eliminated.
4. Production cost savings are realized from the improved flow of goods through the processes.

One of the major accounting benefits of JIT is the elimination of separate raw materials and work-in-process inventory accounts. These accounts are replaced by one account called Raw and In-Process Inventory. All materials and conversion costs are charged to this account. Due to the reduction (or elimination) of in-process inventories, the computation of equivalent units of production is simplified.

BEFORE YOU GO ON . . .

▶Review It

1. What is the difference between the push approach and the demand-pull approach to handling inventories in a manufacturing operation?
2. What are the major benefits of implementing JIT?
3. What are the principal accounting effects of just-in-time processing?

Summary of Study Objective for Appendix

9 *Explain just-in-time (JIT) processing.* JIT is a processing system that is dedicated to having on hand the right materials and products at the time they are needed, thereby reducing the amount of inventory and the time inventory is held. One of the principal accounting effects is that one account, Raw and In-Process Inventory, replaces both the raw materials and work-in-process inventory accounts.

Glossary

Activity Any event, action, transaction, or work sequence that causes a cost to be incurred in producing a product or providing a service. (p. 144)

Activity-based costing (ABC) An overhead cost allocation system that allocates overhead to multiple activity cost pools and assigns the activity cost pools to products or services by means of cost drivers that represent the activities used. (p. 144)

Activity-based management (ABM) Extends ABC from product costing to a comprehensive management tool that focuses on reducing costs and improving processes and decision making. (p. 154)

Activity cost pool The overhead cost attributed to a distinct type of activity or related activities. (p. 144)

Batch-level activities Activities performed for each batch of products. (p. 156)

Cost driver Any factor or activity that has a direct cause–effect relationship with the resources consumed. In ABC cost drivers are used to assign activity cost pools to products or services. (p. 144)

Facility-level activities Activities required to support or sustain an entire production process and not dependent on number of products, batches, or units produced. (p. 156)

Just-in-time (JIT) processing A processing system dedicated to having the right amount of materials, parts, or products arrive as they are needed, thereby reducing the amount of inventory. (p. 164)

Non-value-added activity An activity that adds cost to, or increases the time spent on, a product or service without increasing its market value. (p. 155)

Product-level activities Activities performed for and identifiable with an entire product line. (p. 156)

Unit-level activities Activities performed for each unit of production. (p. 156)

Value-added activity An activity that increases the worth of a product or service. (p. 154)

Demonstration Problem

Spreadwell Paint Company manufactures two high-quality base paints: an **oil-based** paint and a **latex** paint. Both paints are housepaints and are manufactured in neutral white color only. The white base paints are sold to franchised retail paint and decorating stores where pigments are added to tint (color) the paint as desired by the customer. The oil-based paint is made from, thinned, and cleaned with organic solvents (petroleum products) such as mineral spirits or turpentine. The latex paint is made from, thinned, and cleaned with water; synthetic resin particles are suspended in the water and dry and harden when exposed to the air.

Spreadwell uses the same processing equipment to produce both paints in different production runs. Between batches, the vats and other processing equipment must be washed and cleaned.

After analyzing the company's entire operations, Spreadwell's accountants and production managers have identified activity cost pools and accumulated annual budgeted overhead costs by pool as follows.

Activity Cost Pools	Estimated Overhead
Purchasing	$ 240,000
Processing (weighing and mixing, grinding, thinning and drying, straining)	1,400,000
Packaging (quarts, gallons, and 5-gallons)	580,000
Testing	240,000
Storage and inventory control	180,000
Washing and cleaning equipment	560,000
Total annual budgeted overhead	$3,200,000

Following further analysis, activity cost drivers were identified and their expected use by product and activity were scheduled as follows.

Activity Cost Pools	Cost Drivers	Expected Cost Drivers per Activity	Expected Use of Drivers per Product	
			Oil-based	Latex
Purchasing	Purchase orders	1,500 orders	800	700
Processing	Gallons processed	1,000,000 gals.	400,000	600,000
Packaging	Containers filled	400,000 containers	180,000	220,000
Testing	Number of tests	4,000 tests	2,100	1,900
Storing	Avg. gals. on hand	18,000 gals.	10,400	7,600
Washing	Number of batches	800 batches	350	450

Spreadwell has budgeted 400,000 gallons of oil-based paint and 600,000 gallons of latex paint for processing during the year.

Instructions

(a) Prepare a schedule showing the computations of the activity-based overhead rates.
(b) Prepare a schedule assigning each activity's overhead cost pool to each product.
(c) Compute the overhead cost per unit for each product.
(d) Classify each activity cost pool as value-added or non-value-added.

Solution to Demonstration Problem

(a) Computations of activity-based overhead rates:

Activity Cost Pools	Estimated Overhead ÷	Expected Use of Cost Drivers =	Activity-Based Overhead Rates
Purchasing	$ 240,000	1,500 orders	$160 per order
Processing	1,400,000	1,000,000 gallons	$1.40 per gallon
Packaging	580,000	400,000 containers	$1.45 per container
Testing	240,000	4,000 tests	$60 per test
Storing	180,000	18,000 gallons	$10 per gallon
Washing	560,000	800 batches	$700 per batch
	$3,200,000		

(b) Assignment of activity cost pools to products:

Activity Cost Pools	Oil-Based Paint Expected Use of Drivers	Overhead Rates	Cost Assigned	Latex Paint Expected Use of Drivers	Overhead Rates	Cost Assigned
Purchasing	800	$160	$ 128,000	700	$160	$ 112,000
Processing	400,000	$1.40	560,000	600,000	$1.40	840,000
Packaging	180,000	$1.45	261,000	220,000	$1.45	319,000
Testing	2,100	$60	126,000	1,900	$60	114,000
Storing	10,400	$10	104,000	7,600	$10	76,000
Washing	350	$700	245,000	450	$700	315,000
Total overhead assigned			$1,424,000			$1,776,000

(c) Computation of overhead cost assigned per unit:

	Oil-Based Paint	Latex Paint
Total overhead cost assigned	$1,424,000	$1,776,000
Total gallons produced	400,000	600,000
Overhead cost per gallon	$3.56	$2.96

(d) Value-added activities: processing and packaging.
Non-value-added activities: purchasing, testing, storing, and washing.

Note: All asterisked Questions, Exercises, and Problems relate to material in the appendix to the chapter.

Self-Study Questions

Self-Study/Self-Test

Answers are at the end of the chapter.

(SO 1) 1. Activity-based costing (ABC):
    (a) can be used only in a process cost system.
    (b) focuses on units of production.
    (c) focuses on activities performed to produce a product.
    (d) uses only a single basis of allocation.

(SO 1) 2. Activity-based costing:
    (a) is the initial phase of converting to a just-in-time operating environment.
    (b) can be used only in a job order costing system.

    (c) is a two-stage overhead cost allocation system that identifies activity cost pools and cost drivers.
    (d) uses direct labor as its primary cost driver.

(SO 1, 4) 3. Any activity that causes resources to be consumed is called a:
    (a) just-in-time activity.
    (b) facility-level activity.
    (c) cost driver.
    (d) non-value-added activity.

(SO 4) 4. The overhead rate for Machine Setups is $100 per setup. Products A and B have 80 and 60

setups, respectively. The overhead assigned to each product is:
(a) Product A $8,000, Product B $8,000.
(b) Product A $8,000, Product B $6,000.
(c) Product A $6,000, Product B $6,000.
(d) Product A $6,000, Product B $8,000.

(SO 4) 5. Donna Crawford Co. has identified an activity cost pool to which it has allocated estimated overhead of $1,920,000. It has determined the expected use of cost drivers per that activity to be 160,000 inspections. Widgets require 40,000 inspections, Gadgets 30,000 inspections, and Targets, 90,000 inspections. The overhead assigned to each product is:
(a) Widgets $40,000, Gadgets $30,000, Targets $90,000.
(b) Widgets $480,000, Gadgets $360,000, Targets $108,000.
(c) Widgets $360,000, Gadgets $480,000, Targets $1,080,000.
(d) Widgets $480,000, Gadgets $360,000, Targets $1,080,000.

(SO 6) 6. An activity that adds costs to the product but does not increase its market value is a:
(a) value-added activity.
(b) cost driver.
(c) cost–benefit activity.
(d) non-value-added activity.

7. The following activity is value-added: (SO 6)
(a) Storage of raw materials.
(b) Moving parts from machine to machine.
(c) Shaping a piece of metal on a lathe.
(d) All of the above.

8. A relevant facility-level cost driver for heating (SO 7) costs is:
(a) machine hours.
(b) direct material.
(c) floor space.
(d) direct labor cost.

*9. Under just-in-time processing: (SO 9)
(a) raw materials are received just in time for use in production.
(b) subassembly parts are completed just in time for use in assembling finished goods.
(c) finished goods are completed just in time to be sold.
(d) All of the above.

*10. The primary objective of just-in-time process- (SO 9) ing is to:
(a) accumulate overhead in activity cost pools.
(b) eliminate or reduce all manufacturing inventories.
(c) identify relevant activity cost drivers.
(d) identify value-added activities.

Questions

1. Under what conditions is direct labor a valid basis for allocating overhead?

2. What has happened in recent industrial history to reduce the usefulness of direct labor as the primary basis for allocating overhead to products?

3. In an automated manufacturing environment, what basis of overhead allocation is frequently more relevant than direct labor hours?

4. What is generally true about overhead allocation to high-volume products versus low-volume products under a traditional costing system?

5. (a) What are the principal differences between activity-based costing (ABC) and traditional product costing?
   (b) What assumptions must be met for ABC costing to be useful?

6. What is the formula for computing activity-based overhead rates?

7. What steps are involved in developing an activity-based costing system?

8. Explain the preparation and use of a value-added/non-value-added activity flowchart in an ABC system.

9. What is an activity cost pool?

10. What is a cost driver?

11. What makes a cost driver accurate and appropriate?

12. What is the formula for assigning activity cost pools to products?

13. What are the benefits of activity-based costing?

14. What are the limitations of activity-based costing?

15. Under what conditions is ABC generally the superior overhead costing system?

16. What refinement has been made to enhance the efficiency and effectiveness of ABC for use in managing costs?

17. Of what benefit is classifying activities as value-added and non-value-added?

18. In what ways is the application of ABC to service industries the same as its application to manufacturing companies?

19. What is the relevance of the classification of levels of activity to ABC?

*20. (a) Describe the philosophy and approach of just-in-time processing.
    (b) Identify the major elements of JIT processing.

Brief Exercises

Identify differences between costing systems.
(SO 1)

BE4-1 Infotrac Inc. sells a high-speed retrieval system for mining information. It provides the following information for the year.

	Budgeted	Actual
Overhead cost	$1,000,000	$950,000
Machine hours	50,000	45,000
Direct labor hours	100,000	90,000

Overhead is applied on the basis of direct labor hours. (a) Compute the predetermined overhead rate. (b) Determine the amount of overhead applied for the year. (c) Explain how an activity-based costing system might differ in terms of computing a predetermined overhead rate.

Identify differences between costing systems.
(SO 1)

BE4-2 Sassafras Inc. has conducted an analysis of overhead costs related to one of its product lines using a traditional costing system (volume-based) and an activity-based costing system. Here are its results.

	Traditional Costing	ABC
Sales revenues	$600,000	$600,000
Overhead costs:		
Product RX3	$ 34,000	$ 50,000
Product Y12	36,000	20,000
	$ 70,000	$ 70,000

Explain how a difference in the overhead costs between the two systems may have occurred.

Identify cost drivers.
(SO 4)

BE4-3 Altex Co. identifies the following activities that pertain to manufacturing overhead: Materials Handling, Machine Setups, Factory Machine Maintenance, Factory Supervision, and Quality Control. For each activity, identify an appropriate cost driver.

Identify cost drivers.
(SO 4)

BE4-4 Ayala Company manufactures four products in a single production facility. The company uses activity-based costing. The following activities have been identified through the company's activity analysis: (a) inventory control, (b) machine setups, (c) employee training, (d) quality inspections, (e) material ordering, (f) drilling operations, and (g) building maintenance.

For each activity, name a cost driver that might be used to assign overhead costs to products.

Compute activity-based overhead rates.
(SO 4)

BE4-5 Gomez Company identifies three activities in its manufacturing process: machine setups, machining, and inspections. Estimated annual overhead cost for each activity is $180,000, $325,000, and $87,500, respectively. The cost driver for each activity and the expected annual usage are: number of setups 2,500, machine hours 25,000, and number of inspections 1,750. Compute the overhead rate for each activity.

Compute activity-based overhead rates.
(SO 4)

BE4-6 Coats Galore, Inc. uses activity-based costing as the basis for information to set prices for its six lines of seasonal coats. Compute the activity-based overhead rates using the following budgeted data for each of the activity cost pools.

Activity Cost Pools	Estimated Overhead	Expected Use of Cost Drivers per Activity
Designing	$ 450,000	12,000 designer hours
Sizing and cutting	4,000,000	160,000 machine hours
Stitching and trimming	1,440,000	80,000 labor hours
Wrapping and packing	336,000	32,000 finished units

Compute activity-based overhead rates.
(SO 4)

BE4-7 Computer Parts, Inc., a manufacturer of computer chips, employs activity-based costing. The following budgeted data for each of the activity cost pools is provided below for the year 2005.

Activity Cost Pools	Estimated Overhead	Expected Use of Cost Drivers per Activity
Ordering and receiving	$ 90,000	15,000 orders
Etching	480,000	60,000 machine hours
Soldering	1,760,000	440,000 labor hours

For 2005, the company had 11,000 orders and used 50,000 machine hours, and labor hours totaled 500,000. What is the total overhead applied?

BE4-8 Jerry Lewis Novelty Company identified the following activities in its production and support operations. Classify each of these activities as either value added or non value-added.

Classify activities as value- or non-value-added. (SO 6)

(a) Purchasing.
(b) Receiving.
(c) Design engineering.
(d) Storing inventory.
(e) Cost accounting.
(f) Moving work-in-process.
(g) Inspecting and testing.
(h) Painting and packing.

BE4-9 Rowan and Martin is an architectural firm that is contemplating the installation of activity-based costing. The following activities are performed daily by staff architects. Classify these activities as value-added or non-value-added: (1) designing and drafting, 3 hours; (2) staff meetings, 1 hour; (3) on-site supervision, 2 hours; (4) lunch, 1 hour; (5) consultation with client on specifications, 1.5 hours; (6) entertaining a prospective client for dinner, 2 hours.

Classify service company activities as value- or non-value-added. (SO 6, 8)

BE4-10 Quick Pix is a large film developing and processing center that serves 130 outlets in grocery stores, service stations, camera and photo shops, and drug stores in 16 nearby towns. Quick Pix operates 24 hours a day, 6 days a week. Classify each of the following activity costs of Quick Pix as either unit-level, batch-level, product-level, or facility-level.

Classify activities according to level. (SO 7, 8)

(a) Developing fluids.
(b) Photocopy paper.
(c) Depreciation of machinery.
(d) Setups for enlargements.
(e) Supervisor's salary.
(f) Ordering materials.
(g) Pickup and delivery.
(h) Commission to dealers.
(i) Insurance on building.
(j) Loading developing machines.

BE4-11 Tool Time, Inc. operates 20 injection molding machines in the production of tool boxes of four different sizes, named the Apprentice, the Handyman, the Journeyman, and the Professional. Classify each of the following costs as unit-level, batch-level, product-level, or facility-level.

Classify activities according to level. (SO 7)

(a) First-shift supervisor's salary.
(b) Powdered raw plastic.
(c) Dies for casting plastic components.
(d) Depreciation on injection molding machines.
(e) Changing dies on machines.
(f) Moving components to assembly department.
(g) Engineering design.
(h) Employee health and medical insurance coverage.

BE4-12 Trek Cycle Company uses three activity pools to apply overhead to its products. Each activity has a cost driver used to allocate the overhead costs to the product. The activities and related overhead costs are as follows: Product design $50,000; Machining $300,000; and Material handling $100,000. The cost drivers and expected use are as follows.

Compute rates and activity levels. (SO 4, 7)

Activities	Cost Drivers	Expected Use of Cost Drivers per Activity
Product design	Number of product changes	10
Machining	Machine hours	150,000
Material handling	Number of set ups	100

(a) Compute the predetermined overhead rate for each activity. (b) Classify each of these activities as unit-level, batch-level, product-level, or facility-level.

Exercises

E4-1 Elle Inc. has two types of handbags: standard and custom. The controller has decided to use a plantwide overhead rate based on direct labor costs. The president has heard of activity-based costing and wants to see how the results would differ if this system

Assign overhead using traditional costing and ABC. (SO 1, 4)

were used. Two activity cost pools were developed: machining and machine setup. Presented below is information related to the company's operations.

	Standard	Custom
Direct labor costs	$50,000	$100,000
Machine hours	1,000	1,000
Setup hours	100	400

Total estimated overhead costs are $300,000. Overhead cost allocated to the machining activity cost pool is $200,000, and $100,000 is allocated to the machine setup activity cost pool.

Instructions
(a) Compute the overhead rate using the traditional (plantwide) approach.
(b) Compute the overhead rates using the activity-based costing approach.
(c) Determine the difference in allocation between the two approaches.

Explain difference between traditional and activity-based costing.
(SO 1)

E4-2   Perdon Inc. has conducted the following analysis related to its product lines, using a traditional costing system (volume-based) and an activity-based costing system. Both the traditional and the activity-based costing systems include direct materials and direct labor costs.

		Total Costs	
Products	Sales Revenue	Traditional	ABC
Product 540X	$200,000	$55,000	$50,000
Product 137Y	160,000	50,000	35,000
Product 249S	80,000	15,000	35,000

Instructions
(a) For each product line, compute operating income using the traditional costing system.
(b) For each product line, compute operating income using the activity-based costing system.
(c) Using the following formula, compute the percentage difference in operating income for each of the product lines of Perdon: Operating Income (ABC) − Operating Income (traditional cost) ÷ Operating Income (traditional cost). (Round the percentage to two decimals.)
(d) Provide a rationale as to why the costs for Product 540X are approximately the same using either the traditional or activity-based costing system.

Assign overhead using traditional costing and ABC.
(SO 1, 4)

E4-3   International Fabrics has budgeted overhead costs of $900,000. It has allocated overhead on a plantwide basis to its two products (wool and cotton) using direct labor hours which are estimated to be 450,000 for the current year. The company has decided to experiment with activity-based costing and has created two activity cost pools and related activity cost drivers. These two cost pools are: Cutting (cost driver is machine hours) and Design (cost driver is number of setups). Overhead allocated to the Cutting cost pool is $300,000 and $600,000 is allocated to the Design cost pool. Additional information related to these pools is as follows.

	Wool	Cotton	Total
Machine hours	100,000	100,000	200,000
Number of setups	1,000	500	1,500

Instructions
(a) Determine the amount of overhead allocated to the wool product line and the cotton product line using activity-based costing.
(b) What is the difference between the allocation of overhead to the wool and cotton product lines using activity-based costing versus the traditional approach, assuming direct labor hours were incurred evenly between the cutting and design activities?

Assign overhead using traditional costing and ABC.
(SO 1, 4)

E4-4   Alonzo Inc. manufactures two products: car and truck wheels. To determine the amount of overhead to assign to each product line, the controller, YuYu Ortega, has developed the following information.

	Car	Truck
Estimated wheels produced	40,000	10,000
Direct labor hours per wheel	1	3

Total estimated overhead costs for the two product lines are $700,000.

Instructions

(a) Compute the overhead cost assigned to the car and truck wheels, assuming that direct labor hours is used to allocate overhead costs.

(b) Ortega is not satisfied with the traditional method of allocating overhead because he believes that most of the overhead costs relate to the truck wheel product line because of its complexity. He therefore develops the following three activity cost pools and related cost drivers to better understand these costs.

Activity Cost Pools	Expected Use of Cost Drivers	Estimated Overhead Costs
Setting up machines	1,000 setups	$180,000
Assembling	70,000 labor hours	280,000
Inspection	1,200 inspections	240,000

Compute the activity-based overhead rates for these three cost pools.

(c) Compute the cost that is assigned to the car and truck product lines using an activity-based costing system, given the following information.

Expected Use of Cost Drivers per Product

	Car	Truck
Number of setups	200	800
Direct labor hours	40,000	30,000
Number of inspections	100	1,100

(d) What do you believe Ortega should do?

E4-5 Shady Lady sells window coverings to both commercial and residential customers. The following information relates to its budgeted operations for the current year.

Assign overhead using traditional costing and ABC.
(SO 1, 4)

	Commercial		Residential	
Revenues		$300,000		$480,000
Direct material costs	$ 30,000		$ 50,000	
Direct labor costs	100,000		300,000	
Overhead costs	50,000	180,000	150,000	500,000
Operating income (loss)		$120,000		($ 20,000)

The controller, Wanda Lewis, is concerned about the residential product line. She cannot understand why this line is not more profitable given that the installations of window coverings are less complex to install for residential customers. In addition, the residential client base resides in close proximity to the company office, so travel costs are not as expensive on a per client visit for residential customers. As a result, she has decided to take a closer look at the overhead costs assigned to the two product lines to determine whether a more accurate product costing model can be developed. Here are the three activity cost pools and related information she developed:

Activity Cost Pools	Estimated Overhead	Cost Drivers
Scheduling and travel	$90,000	Hours of travel
Setup time	70,000	Number of setups
Supervision	40,000	Direct labor cost

Expected Use of Cost Drivers per Product

	Commercial	Residential
Scheduling and travel	1,000	500
Setup time	450	250

Instructions

(a) Compute the activity-based overhead rates for each of the three cost pools, and determine the overhead cost assigned to each product line.

(b) Compute the operating income for the each product line, using the activity-based overhead rates.

(c) What do you believe Wanda Lewis should do?

Assign overhead using traditional costing and ABC.
(SO 1, 4)

E4-6 Wilkins Corporation manufactures safes—large mobile safes, and large walk-in stationary bank safes. As part of its annual budgeting process, Wilkins is analyzing the profitability of its two products. Part of this analysis involves estimating the amount of overhead to be allocated to each product line. The following information relates to overhead.

	Mobile Safes	Walk-in Safes
Units planned for production	200	50
Material moves per product line	300	200
Purchase orders per product line	450	350
Direct labor hours per product line	800	1,700

Instructions

(a) The total estimated manufacturing overhead was $235,000. Under traditional costing (which assigns overhead on the basis of direct-labor hours), what amount of manufacturing overhead costs are assigned to:
  (1) One mobile safe?
  (2) One walk-in safe?

(b) The total estimated manufacturing overhead of $235,000 was comprised of $150,000 for material-handling costs and $85,000 for purchasing activity costs. Under activity-based costing (ABC):
  (1) What amount of material handling costs are assigned to:
    (a) One mobile safe?
    (b) One walk-in safe?
  (2) What amount of purchasing activity costs are assigned to:
    (a) One mobile safe?
    (b) One walk-in safe?

(c) Compare the amount of overhead allocated to one mobile safe and to one walk-in safe under the traditional costing approach versus under ABC.

Identify activity cost pools.
(SO 3)

E4-7 Quik Prints Company is a small printing and copying firm with three high-speed offset printing presses, five copiers (two color and three black and white), one collator, one cutting and folding machine, and one fax machine. To improve its pricing practices, owner-manager Damon Hastings is installing activity-based accounting. Additionally, Damon employs five employees: two printers/designers, one receptionist/bookkeeper, one sales and copy-machine operator, and one janitor/delivery clerk. Damon can operate any of the machines and, in addition to managing the entire operation, he performs the training, designing, selling, and marketing functions.

Instructions

As Quik Prints' independent accountant who prepares tax forms and quarterly financial statements, you have been asked to identify the activities that would be used to accumulate overhead costs for assignment to jobs and customers. Using your knowledge of a small printing and copying firm (and some imagination), identify at least twelve activity cost pools as the start of an activity-based costing system for Quik Prints Company.

Identify activity cost pools and cost drivers.
(SO 3, 4)

E4-8 Galavic Corporation manufactures snowmobiles in its Blue Mountain, Wisconsin plant. The following costs are budgeted for the first quarter's operations.

Machine setup, indirect materials	$ 4,000
Inspections	16,000
Tests	4,000
Insurance, plant	110,000
Engineering design	140,000
Depreciation, machinery	520,000
Machine setup, indirect labor	20,000
Property taxes	29,000
Oil, heating	19,000
Electricity, plant lighting	21,000
Engineering prototypes	60,000
Depreciation, plant	210,000
Electricity, machinery	36,000
Custodial (machine maintenance) wages	19,000

Instructions

Classify the above costs of Galavic Corporation into activity cost pools using the following: engineering, machinery, machine setup, quality control, factory utilities, maintenance. Next, identify a cost driver that may be used to assign each cost pool to each line of snowmobiles.

E4-9 Peter Catalano's Verde Vineyards in Oakville, California produces three varieties of wine: Merlot, Viognier, and Pinot Noir. His winemaster, Kyle Ward, has identified the following activities as cost pools for accumulating overhead and assigning it to products.

Identify activity cost drivers.
(SO 4)

1. Culling and replanting. Dead or overcrowded vines are culled, and new vines are planted or relocated. (Separate vineyards by variety.)
2. Tying. The posts and wires are reset, and vines are tied to the wires for the dormant season.
3. Trimming. At the end of the harvest the vines are cut and trimmed back in preparation for the next season.
4. Spraying. The vines are sprayed with chemicals for protection against insects and fungi.
5. Harvesting. The grapes are hand-picked, placed in carts, and transported to the crushers.
6. Stemming and crushing. Cartfuls of bunches of grapes of each variety are separately loaded into machines which remove stems and gently crush the grapes.
7. Pressing and filtering. The crushed grapes are transferred to presses which mechanically remove the juices and filter out bulk and impurities.
8. Fermentation. The grape juice, by variety, is fermented in either stainless-steel tanks or oak barrels.
9. Aging. The wines are aged in either stainless-steel tanks or oak barrels for one to three years depending on variety.
10. Bottling and corking. Bottles are machine-filled and corked.
11. Labeling and boxing. Each bottle is labeled, as is each nine-bottle case, with the name of the vintner, vintage, and variety.
12. Storing. Packaged and boxed bottles are stored awaiting shipment.
13. Shipping. The wine is shipped to distributors and private retailers.
14. Heating and air-conditioning of plant and offices.
15. Maintenance of buildings and equipment. Printing, repairs, replacements, and general maintenance are performed in the off-season.

Instructions

For each of Verde's fifteen activity cost pools, identify a probable cost driver that might be used to assign overhead costs to its three wine varieties.

E4-10 Anna Bellatorre, Inc. manufactures five models of kitchen appliances at its Mesa plant. The company is installing activity-based costing and has identified the following activities performed at its Mesa plant.

Identify activity cost drivers.
(SO 4)

1. Designing new models.
2. Purchasing raw materials and parts.
3. Storing and managing inventory.
4. Receiving and inspecting raw materials and parts.
5. Interviewing and hiring new personnel.
6. Machine forming sheet steel into appliance parts.
7. Manually assembling parts into appliances.
8. Training all employees of the company.
9. Insuring all tangible fixed assets.
10. Supervising production.
11. Maintaining and repairing machinery and equipment.
12. Painting and packaging finished appliances.

Having analyzed its Mesa plant operations for purposes of installing activity-based costing, Anna Bellatorre, Inc. identified its activity cost centers. It now needs to identify relevant activity cost drivers in order to assign overhead costs to its products.

Instructions

Using the activities listed above, identify for each activity one or more cost drivers that might be used to assign overhead to Anna Bellatorre's five products.

E4-11 Fontillas Instrument, Inc. manufactures two products: missile range instruments and space pressure gauges. During April, 50 range instruments and 300 pressure gauges

Compute overhead rates and assign overhead using ABC.
(SO 4, 5)

were produced, and overhead costs of $89,500 were estimated. An analysis of estimated overhead costs reveals the following activities.

Activities	Cost Drivers	Total Cost
1. Materials handling	Number of requisitions	$35,000
2. Machine setups	Number of setups	27,500
3. Quality inspections	Number of inspections	27,000

The cost driver volume for each product was as follows.

Cost Drivers	Instruments	Gauges	Total
Number of requisitions	400	600	1,000
Number of setups	200	300	500
Number of inspections	200	400	600

Instructions
(a) Determine the overhead rate for each activity.
(b) Assign the manufacturing overhead costs for April to the two products using activity-based costing.
(c) ▷ Write a memorandum to the president of Fontillas Instrument explaining the benefits of activity-based costing.

Assign overhead using traditional costing and ABC; classify activities as value- or non-value-added.
(SO 1, 4, 6)

E4-12 Lim Clothing Company manufactures its own designed and labeled sports attire and sells its products through catalog sales and retail outlets. While Lim has for years used activity-based costing in its manufacturing activities, it has always used traditional costing in assigning its selling costs to its product lines. Selling costs have traditionally been assigned to Lim's product lines at a rate of 70% of direct material costs. Its direct material costs for the month of March for Lim's "high intensity" line of attire are $400,000. The company has decided to extend activity-based costing to its selling costs. Data relating to the "high intensity" line of products for the month of March are as follows.

Activity Cost Pools	Cost Drivers	Overhead Rate	Number of Cost Drivers Used per Activity
Sales commissions	Dollar sales	$0.05 per dollar sales	$930,000
Advertising—TV/Radio	Minutes	$300 per minute	250
Advertising—Newspaper	Column inches	$10 per column inch	2,000
Catalogs	Catalogs mailed	$2.50 per catalog	60,000
Cost of catalog sales	Catalog orders	$1 per catalog order	9,000
Credit and collection	Dollar sales	$0.03 per dollar sales	$930,000

Instructions
(a) Compute the selling costs to be assigned to the "high-intensity" line of attire for the month of March: (1) using the traditional product costing system (direct material cost is the cost driver), and (2) using activity-based costing.
(b) By what amount does the traditional product costing system undercost or overcost the "high-intensity" product line?
(c) Classify each of the activities as value-added or non-value-added.

Assign overhead using traditional costing and ABC; classify activities as value- or non-value-added.
(SO 1, 4, 6)

E4-13 Healthy Products, Inc., uses a traditional product costing system to assign overhead costs uniformly to all products. To meet Food and Drug Administration requirements and to assure its customers of safe, sanitary, and nutritious food, Healthy engages in a high level of quality control. Healthy assigns its quality-control overhead costs to all products at a rate of 17% of direct-labor costs. Its direct-labor cost for the month of June for its low-calorie dessert line is $55,000. In response to repeated requests from its financial vice president, Healthy's management agrees to adopt activity-based costing. Data relating to the low-calorie dessert line for the month of June are as follows.

Activity Cost Pools	Cost Drivers	Overhead Rate	Number of Cost Drivers Used per Activity
Inspections of material received	Number of pounds	$0.60 per pound	6,000 pounds
In-process inspections	Number of servings	$0.33 per serving	10,000 servings
FDA certification	Customer orders	$12.00 per order	420 orders

Instructions
(a) Compute the quality-control overhead cost to be assigned to the low-calorie dessert product line for the month of June: (1) using the traditional product costing system (direct labor cost is the cost driver), and (2) using activity-based costing.
(b) By what amount does the traditional product costing system undercost or overcost the low-calorie dessert line?
(c) Classify each of the activities as value-added or non-value-added.

E4-14 In an effort to expand the usefulness of its activity-based costing system, Peter Catalano's Verde Vineyards decides to adopt activity-based management techniques. One of these ABM techniques is qualifying its activities as either value-added or non-value-added.

Classify activities as value-added or non-value-added.
(SO 6)

Instructions
Using Verde's list of fifteen activity cost pools in Exercise 4-9, classify each of the activities as either value-added or non-value-added.

E4-15 Anna Bellatorre, Inc. is interested in using its activity-based costing system to improve its operating efficiency and its profit margins by applying activity-based management techniques. As part of this undertaking, you have been asked to classify its Mesa plant activities as value-added or non-value-added.

Classify activities as value-added or non-value-added.
(SO 6)

Instructions
Using the list of activities identified in Exercise 4-10, classify each activity as either value-added or non-value-added.

E4-16 Dewey and Cheatam is a law firm that is initiating an activity-based costing system. Jim Dewey, the senior partner and strong supporter of ABC, has prepared the following list of activities performed by a typical attorney in a day at the firm.

Classify service company activities as value-added or non-value-added.
(SO 6, 8)

Activities	Hours
Writing contracts and letters	1.0
Attending staff meetings	0.5
Taking depositions	1.0
Doing research	1.0
Traveling to/from court	1.0
Contemplating legal strategy	1.0
Eating lunch	1.0
Litigating a case in court	2.5
Entertaining a prospective client	2.0

Instructions
Classify each of the activities listed by Jim Dewey as value-added or non-value-added and defend your classification. How much was value-added time and how much was non-value-added?

E4-17 Having itemized its costs for the first quarter of next year's budget, Galavic Corporation desires to install an activity-based costing system. First it identified the activity cost pools in which to accumulate factory overhead; second, it identified the relevant cost drivers. (This was done in Exercise 4-8.)

Classify activities by level.
(SO 7)

Instructions
Using the activity cost pools identified in Exercise 4-8, classify each of those cost pools as either unit-level, batch-level, product-level, or facility-level.

E4-18 Otto Dieffenbach & Sons, Inc. is a small manufacturing company in La Jolla that uses activity-based costing. Dieffenbach & Sons accumulates overhead in the following activity cost pools.

Classify activities by level.
(SO 7)

1. Hiring personnel.
2. Managing parts inventory.
3. Purchasing.
4. Testing prototypes.
5. Designing products.
6. Setting up equipment.
7. Training employees.
8. Inspecting machined parts.
9. Machining.
10. Assembling.

Instructions
For each activity cost pool, indicate whether the activity cost pool would be unit-level, batch-level, product-level, or facility-level.

Problems: Set A

Assign overhead using traditional costing and ABC; compute unit costs; classify activities as value- or non-value-added.
(SO 1, 4, 6)

P4-1A   FireOut, Inc. manufactures steel cylinders and nozzles for two models of fire extinguishers: (1) a home fire extinguisher and (2) a commercial fire extinguisher. The **home model** is a high-volume (54,000 units), half-gallon cylinder that holds $2\frac{1}{2}$ pounds of multipurpose dry chemical at 480 PSI. The **commercial model** is a low-volume (10,200 units), two-gallon cylinder that holds 10 pounds of multi-purpose dry chemical at 390 PSI. Both products require 1.5 hours of direct labor for completion. Therefore, total annual direct labor hours are 96,300 or [1.5 hrs. × (54,000 + 10,200)]. Expected annual manufacturing overhead is $1,502,280. Thus, the predetermined overhead rate is $15.60 or ($1,502,280 ÷ 96,300) per direct labor hour. The direct materials cost per unit is $18.50 for the home model and $26.50 for the commercial model. The direct labor cost is $19 per unit for both the home and the commercial models.

The company's managers identified six activity cost pools and related cost drivers and accumulated overhead by cost pool as follows.

Activity Cost Pools	Cost Drivers	Estimated Overhead	Expected Use of Cost Drivers	Expected Use of Drivers by Product	
				Home	Commercial
Receiving	Pounds	$ 70,350	335,000	215,000	120,000
Forming	Machine hours	150,500	35,000	27,000	8,000
Assembling	Number of parts	390,600	217,000	165,000	52,000
Testing	Number of tests	51,000	25,500	15,500	10,000
Painting	Gallons	52,580	5,258	3,680	1,578
Packing and shipping	Pounds	787,250	335,000	215,000	120,000
		$1,502,280			

Instructions

(a) Unit cost—H.M. $60.90

(a) Under traditional product costing, compute the total unit cost of each product. Prepare a simple comparative schedule of the individual costs by product (similar to Illustration 4-4).

(b) Under ABC, prepare a schedule showing the computations of the activity-based overhead rates (per cost driver).

(c) Cost assigned—H.M.
$1,031,300

(c) Prepare a schedule assigning each activity's overhead cost pool to each product based on the use of cost drivers. (Include a computation of overhead cost per unit, rounding to the nearest cent.)

(d) Cost/unit—H.M. $56.60

(d) Compute the total cost per unit for each product under ABC.

(e) Classify each of the activities as a value-added activity or a non-value-added activity.

(f) Comment on (1) the comparative overhead cost per unit for the two products under ABC, and (2) the comparative total costs per unit under traditional costing and ABC.

Assign overhead to products using ABC and evaluate decision.
(SO 4)

P4-2A   Jacobson Electronics manufactures two large-screen television models: the Royale which sells for $1,600, and a new model, the Majestic, which sells for $1,300. The production cost computed per unit under traditional costing for each model in 2005 was as follows.

Traditional Costing	Royale	Majestic
Direct materials	$ 700	$420
Direct labor ($20 per hour)	120	100
Manufacturing overhead ($38 per DLH)	228	190
Total per unit cost	$1,048	$710

In 2005, Jacobson manufactured 25,000 units of the Royale and 10,000 units of the Majestic. The overhead rate of $38 per direct labor hour was determined by dividing total expected manufacturing overhead of $7,600,000 by the total direct labor hours (200,000) for the two models.

Under traditional costing, the gross profit on the models was: Royale $552 or ($1,600 − $1,048), and Majestic $590 or ($1,300 − $710). Because of this difference, management is considering phasing out the Royale model and increasing the production of the Majestic model.

Before finalizing its decision, management asks Jacobson's controller to prepare an analysis using activity-based costing (ABC). The controller accumulates the following information about overhead for the year ended December 31, 2005.

Activities	Cost Drivers	Estimated Overhead	Expected Use of Cost Drivers	Activity-Based Overhead Rate
Purchasing	Number of orders	$1,200,000	40,000	$30
Machine setups	Number of setups	900,000	18,000	50
Machining	Machine hours	4,800,000	120,000	40
Quality control	Number of inspections	700,000	28,000	25

The cost drivers used for each product were:

Cost Drivers	Royale	Majestic	Total
Purchase orders	15,000	25,000	40,000
Machine setups	5,000	13,000	18,000
Machine hours	75,000	45,000	120,000
Inspections	9,000	19,000	28,000

Instructions

(a) Assign the total 2005 manufacturing overhead costs to the two products using activity-based costing (ABC).

(b) What was the cost per unit and gross profit of each model using ABC costing?

(c) ▭▭▭▷ Are management's future plans for the two models sound? Explain.

(a) Royale $3,925,000

(b) Cost/unit—Royale $977

P4-3A   Stellar Stairs Co. of Poway designs and builds factory-made premium wooden stairs for homes. The manufactured stair components (spindles, risers, hangers, hand rails) permit installation of stairs of varying lengths and widths. All are of white oak wood. Its budgeted manufacturing overhead costs for the year 2006 are as follows.

Assign overhead costs using traditional costing and ABC; compare results.
(SO 1, 4)

Overhead Cost Pools	Amount
Purchasing	$ 57,000
Handling materials	82,000
Production (cutting, milling, finishing)	210,000
Setting up machines	85,000
Inspecting	90,000
Inventory control (raw materials and finished goods)	126,000
Utilities	180,000
Total budget overhead costs	$830,000

For the last 4 years, Stellar Stairs Co. has been charging overhead to products on the basis of machine hours. For the year 2006, 100,000 machine hours are budgeted.

Heather Fujar, owner-manager of Stellar Stairs Co., recently directed her accountant, Lindsay Baker, to implement the activity-based costing system that she has repeatedly proposed. At Heather Fujar's request, Lindsay and the production foreman identify the following cost drivers and their usage for the previously budgeted overhead cost pools.

Activity Cost Pools	Cost Drivers	Expected Use of Cost Drivers
Purchasing	Number of orders	600
Handling materials	Number of moves	8,000
Production (cutting, milling, finishing)	Direct labor hours	100,000
Setting up machines	Number of setups	1,250
Inspecting	Number of inspections	6,000
Inventory control (raw materials and finished goods)	Number of components	168,000
Utilities	Square feet occupied	90,000

Jason Dion, sales manager, has received an order for 280 stairs from Community Builders, Inc., a large housing development contractor. At Jason's request, Lindsay prepares cost estimates for producing components for 280 stairs so Jason can submit a contract price per stair to Community Builders. She accumulates the following data for the production of 280 stairways.

Direct materials	$103,600
Direct labor	$112,000
Machine hours	14,500
Direct labor hours	5,000
Number of purchase orders	60
Number of material moves	800
Number of machine setups	100
Number of inspections	450
Number of components	16,000
Number of square feet occupied	8,000

Instructions

(a) Compute the predetermined overhead rate using traditional costing with machine hours as the basis.

(b) Cost/stair $1,199.82

(c) Cost/stair $1,055.54

(b) What is the manufacturing cost per stairway under traditional costing?

(c) What is the manufacturing cost per stairway under the proposed activity-based costing? (Prepare all of the necessary schedules.)

(d) ▭▭▭▭▷ Which of the two costing systems is preferable in pricing decisions and why?

Assign overhead costs using traditional costing and ABC; compare results.
(SO 1, 4)

P4-4A Mendocino Corporation produces two grades of wine from grapes that it buys from California growers. It produces and sells roughly 3,000,000 liters per year of a low-cost, high-volume product called CoolDay. It sells this in 600,000 5-liter jugs. Mendocino also produces and sells roughly 300,000 liters per year of a low-volume, high-cost product called LiteMist. LiteMist is sold in 1-liter bottles. Based on recent data, the CoolDay product has not been as profitable as LiteMist. Management is considering dropping the inexpensive CoolDay line so it can focus more attention on the LiteMist product. The LiteMist product already demands considerably more attention than the CoolDay line.

Tyler Silva, president and founder of Mendocino, is skeptical about this idea. He points out that for many decades the company produced only the CoolDay line, and that it was always quite profitable. It wasn't until the company started producing the more complicated LiteMist wine that the profitability of CoolDay declined. Prior to the introduction of LiteMist, the company had simple equipment, simple growing and production procedures, and virtually no need for quality control. Because LiteMist is bottled in 1-liter bottles, it requires considerably more time and effort, both to bottle and to label and box than does CoolDay. The company must bottle and handle 5 times as many bottles of LiteMist to sell the same quantity as CoolDay. CoolDay requires 1 month of aging; LiteMist requires 1 year. CoolDay requires cleaning and inspection of equipment every 10,000 liters; LiteMist requires such maintenance every 600 liters.

Tyler has asked the accounting department to prepare an analysis of the cost per liter using the traditional costing approach and using activity-based costing. The following information was collected.

	CoolDay	LiteMist
Direct materials per liter	$0.40	$1.20
Direct labor cost per liter	$0.25	$0.50
Direct labor hours per liter	0.05	0.09
Total direct labor hours	120,000	25,000

Activity Cost Pools	Cost Drivers	Estimated Overhead	Expected Use of Cost Drivers	Expected Use of Cost Drivers per Product	
				CoolDay	LiteMist
Grape processing	Cart of grapes	$ 145,860	6,600	6,000	600
Aging	Total months	396,000	6,600,000	3,000,000	3,600,000
Bottling and corking	Number of bottles	270,000	900,000	600,000	300,000
Labeling and boxing	Number of bottles	189,000	900,000	600,000	300,000
Maintain and in-spect equipment	Number of inspections	240,800	800	350	450
		$1,241,660			

Instructions

Answer each of the following questions. (Round all calculations to three decimal places.)

(a) Under traditional product costing using direct labor hours, compute the total man-ufacturing cost per **liter** of both products.

(b) Under ABC, prepare a schedule showing the computation of the activity-based overhead rates (per cost driver).

(c) Prepare a schedule assigning each activity's overhead cost pool to each product, based on the use of cost drivers. Include a computation of overhead cost per liter.

(d) Compute the total manufacturing cost per liter for both products under ABC.

(e) ▰▰▰▭▷ Write a memo to Tyler Silva discussing the implications of your analysis for the company's plans. In this memo provide a brief description of ABC, as well as an explanation of how the traditional approach can result in distortions.

(a) Cost/liter—C.D. $1.078

(c) Cost/liter—C.D. $.241

P4-5A Hy and Lowe is a public accounting firm that offers two primary services, au-diting and tax return preparation. A controversy has developed between the partners of the two service lines as to who is contributing the greater amount to the bottom line. The area of contention is the assignment of overhead. The tax partners argue for assigning overhead on the basis of 40% of direct labor dollars, while the audit partners argue for implementing activity-based costing. The partners agree to use next year's budgeted data for purposes of analysis and comparison. The following overhead data are collected to develop the comparison.

Assign overhead costs to services using traditional costing and ABC; compute overhead rates and unit costs; compare results. (SO 1, 4, 6, 8)

Activity Cost Pools	Cost Drivers	Estimated Overhead	Expected Use of Cost Drivers	Expected Use of Cost Drivers per Service	
				Audit	Tax
Employee training	Direct labor dollars	$216,000	$1,800,000	$1,000,000	$800,000
Typing and secretarial	Number of reports/forms	76,200	2,500	600	1,900
Computing	Number of minutes	204,000	60,000	25,000	35,000
Facility rental	Number of employees	142,500	40	22	18
Travel	Per expense reports	81,300	Direct	56,000	25,300
		$720,000			

Instructions

(a) Using traditional product costing as proposed by the tax partners, compute the total overhead cost assigned to both services (audit and tax) of Hy and Lowe.

(b) (1) Using activity-based costing, prepare a schedule showing the computations of the activity-based overhead rates (per cost driver).

    (2) Prepare a schedule assigning each activity's overhead cost pool to each service based on the use of the cost drivers.

(c) Classify each of the activities as a value-added activity or a non-value-added activity.

(d) ▰▰▰▭▷ Comment on the comparative overhead cost per unit for the two products under both traditional costing and ABC.

(b) (2) Cost assigned—Tax $362,337

(d) Difference—Audit $42,337

Problems: Set B

Assign overhead using traditional costing and ABC; compute unit costs; classify activities as value- or non-value-added.
(SO 1, 4, 6)

P4-1B Waves Galore, Inc. manufactures hair curlers and blow-dryers. The handheld hair curler is Waves Galore's high volume product (80,000 units annually). It is a "large barrel," 20-watt, triple-heat appliance designed to appeal to the teenage market segment with its glow-in-the-dark handle. The handheld blow-dryer is Waves Galore's lower-volume product (40,000 units annually). It is a three-speed, 2,000 watt appliance with a "cool setting" and a removable filter. It also is designed for the teen market.

Both products require one hour of direct labor for completion. Therefore, total annual direct labor hours are 120,000, (80,000 + 40,000). Expected annual manufacturing overhead is $438,000. Thus, the predetermined overhead rate is $3.65 per direct labor hour. The direct materials cost per unit is $5.25 for the hair curler and $9.75 for the blow-dryer. The direct labor cost is $8.00 per unit for the hair curler and the blow-dryer.

Waves Galore purchases most of the parts from suppliers and assembles the finished product at its Fargo, North Dakota plant. It recently adopted activity-based costing, which after this year-end will totally replace its traditional direct labor-based cost accounting system. Waves Galore has identified the following six activity cost pools and related cost drivers and has assembled the following information.

Activity Cost Pools	Cost Drivers	Estimated Overhead	Expected Use of Cost Drivers	Expected Use of Cost Drivers per Product Curlers	Expected Use of Cost Drivers per Product Dryers
Purchasing	Orders	$ 57,500	500	170	330
Receiving	Pounds	42,000	140,000	58,000	82,000
Assembling	Parts	166,000	830,000	415,000	415,000
Testing	Tests	52,000	130,000	82,000	48,000
Finishing	Units	60,000	120,000	80,000	40,000
Packing and shipping	Cartons	60,500	12,100	8,040	4,060
		$438,000			

Instructions

(a) Unit cost—Dryer $21.40

(a) Under traditional product costing, compute the total unit cost of each product. Prepare a simple comparative schedule of the individual costs by product (similar to Illustration 4-4).

(b) Under ABC, prepare a schedule showing the computations of the activity-based overhead rates (per cost driver).

(c) Cost assigned—Dryer $205,050

(c) Prepare a schedule assigning each activity's overhead cost pool to each product based on the use of cost drivers. (Include a computation of overhead cost per unit, rounding to the nearest cent.)

(d) Cost/unit—Dryer $22.88

(d) Compute the total cost per unit for each product under ABC.

(e) Classify each of the activities as a value-added activity or a non-value-added activity.

(f) Comment on (1) the comparative overhead cost per unit for the two products under ABC, and (2) the comparative total costs per unit under traditional costing and ABC.

Assign overhead to products using ABC and evaluate decision.
(SO 4)

P4-2B Tough Thermos, Inc. manufactures two plastic thermos containers at its plastic molding facility in Bend, Oregon. Its large container, called the Ice House, has a volume of 5 gallons, side carrying handles, a snap-down lid, and a side drain and plug. Its smaller container, called the Cool Chest, has a volume of 2 gallons, an over-the-top carrying handle which is part of a tilting lid, and a removable shelf. Both containers and their parts are made entirely of hard-molded plastic. The Ice House sells for $35 and the Cool Chest sells for $24. The production costs computed per unit under traditional costing for each model in 2005 were as follows.

Traditional Costing	Ice House	Cool Chest
Direct materials	$ 9.50	$ 6.00
Direct labor ($10 per hour)	8.00	5.00
Manufacturing overhead ($17.08 per DLH)	13.66	8.54
Total per unit cost	$31.16	$19.54

In 2005, Tough Thermos manufactured 50,000 units of the Ice House and 20,000 units of the Cool Chest. The overhead rate of $17.08 per direct labor hour was determined by dividing total expected manufacturing overhead of $854,000 by the total direct labor hours (50,000) for the 2 models.

Under traditional costing, the gross profit on the two containers was: Ice House $3.84 or ($35 − $31.16), and Cool Chest $4.46 or ($24 − $19.54). The gross margin rates on cost are: Ice House 12% or ($3.84 ÷ $31.16), and Cool Chest 23% or ($4.46 ÷ $19.54). Because Tough Thermos can earn a gross margin rate on the Cool Chest that is nearly twice as great as that earned on the Ice House, with less investment in inventory and labor costs, its management is urging its sales staff to put its efforts into selling the Cool Chest over the Ice House.

Before finalizing its decision, management asks the controller Sven Meza to prepare a product costing analysis using activity-based costing (ABC). Meza accumulates the following information about overhead for the year ended December 31, 2005.

Activities	Cost Drivers	Estimated Overhead	Expected Use of Cost Drivers	Activity-Based Overhead Rate
Purchasing	Number of orders	$179,000	4,475	$40 per order
Machine setups	Number of setups	195,000	780	$250 per setup
Extruding	Machine hours	320,000	80,000	$4 per machine hour
Quality control	Tests and inspections	160,000	8,000	$20 per test

The cost drivers used for each product were:

Cost Drivers	Ice House	Cool Chest	Total
Purchase orders	2,500	1,975	4,475
Machine setups	480	300	780
Machine hours	60,000	20,000	80,000
Tests and inspections	5,000	3,000	8,000

Instructions

(a) Assign the total 2005 manufacturing overhead costs to the two products using activity-based costing (ABC).

(b) What was the cost per unit and gross profit of each model using ABC costing?

(c) ✏️▶ Are management's future plans for the two models sound?

(a) Ice House $560,000

(b) Cost/unit—Ice $28.70

P4-3B Kitchen Kabinets Company designs and builds upscale kitchen cabinets for luxury homes. Many of the kitchen cabinet and counter arrangements are custom made, but occasionally the company does mass production on order. Its budgeted manufacturing overhead costs for the year 2006 are as follows.

Assign overhead costs using traditional costing and ABC; compare results.
(SO 1, 4)

Overhead Cost Pools	Amount
Purchasing	$ 114,400
Handling materials	164,320
Production (cutting, milling, finishing)	500,000
Setting up machines	174,480
Inspecting	184,800
Inventory control (raw materials and finished goods)	252,000
Utilities	360,000
Total budget overhead costs	$1,750,000

For the last 3 years, Kitchen Kabinets Company has been charging overhead to products on the basis of machine hours. For the year 2006, 100,000 machine hours are budgeted.

Ben Chen, the owner-manager, recently directed his accountant, John Kandy, to implement the activity-based costing system he has repeatedly proposed. At Ben's request, John and the production foreman identify the following cost drivers and their usage for the previously budgeted overhead cost pools.

Activity Cost Pools	Activity Cost Drivers	Expected Use of Cost Drivers
Purchasing	Number of orders	650
Handling materials	Numbers of moves	8,000
Production (cutting, milling, finishing)	Direct labor hours	100,000
Setting up machines	Number of setups	1,200
Inspecting	Number of inspections	6,000
Inventory control (raw materials and finished goods)	Number of components	36,000
Utilities	Square feet occupied	90,000

Sara Sosa, sales manager, has received an order for 50 kitchen cabinet arrangements from Bitty Builders, a housing development contractor. At Sara's request, John prepares cost estimates for producing components for 50 cabinet arrangements so Sara can submit a contract price per kitchen arrangement to Bitty Builders. He accumulates the following data for the production of 50 kitchen cabinet arrangements.

Direct materials	$180,000
Direct labor	$200,000
Machine hours	15,000
Direct labor hours	12,000
Number of purchase orders	50
Number of material moves	800
Number of machine setups	100
Number of inspections	450
Number of components (cabinets and accessories)	3,000
Number of square feet occupied	8,000

Instructions

(a) Compute the predetermined overhead rate using traditional costing with machine hours as the basis. (Round to the nearest cent.)

(b) Cost/Kitchen $12,850

(b) What is the manufacturing cost per complete kitchen arrangement under traditional costing?

(c) Cost/Kitchen $10,932.64

(c) What is the manufacturing cost per kitchen arrangement under the proposed activity-based costing? (Prepare all of the necessary schedules.)

(d) ▭▭▭▶ Which of the two costing systems is preferable in pricing decisions and why?

Assign overhead costs using traditional costing and ABC; compare results.
(SO 1, 4)

P4-4B Vino Verite Corporation produces two grades of wine from grapes that it buys from California growers. It produces and sells, in 1-gallon jugs, roughly 800,000 gallons per year of a low-cost, high-volume product called StarDew. It also produces and sells roughly 200,000 gallons per year of a low-volume, high-cost product called VineRose. VineRose is sold in 1-liter bottles; thus 200,000 gallons results in roughly 800,000 bottles. Based on recent data, the StarDew product has not been as profitable as VineRose. Management is considering dropping the inexpensive StarDew so it can focus more attention on the VineRose line product. VineRose already demands considerably more attention than StarDew.

Jorge Rojo, president and founder of Vino Verite, is skeptical about this idea. He points out that for many decades the company produced only the StarDew line, and that it was always quite profitable. It wasn't until the company started producing the more complicated VineRose wine that the profitability of StarDew declined. Prior to the introduction of VineRose the company had simple equipment, simple growing and production procedures, and virtually no need for quality control. Because VineRose is bottled in 1-liter bottles it requires considerably more time and effort, both to bottle and to label and box, than does StarDew. (There are roughly 4 liters in a gallon; thus the company must bottle and handle 4 bottles of VineRose to sell the same amount of wine as StarDew.) StarDew requires 1 month of aging; VineRose requires 1 year. StarDew requires cleaning and inspection of equipment every 5,000 gallons; VineRose requires such maintenance every 500 gallons.

Jorge has asked the accounting department to prepare an analysis of the cost per gallon using the traditional costing approach and using activity-based costing. The following information was collected.

	StarDew	VineRose
Direct materials per gallon	$1.10	$2.40
Direct labor cost per gallon	$0.50	$1.00
Direct labor hours per gallon	0.075	0.15
Total direct labor hours	60,000	30,000

				Expected Use of Cost Drivers per Product	
Activity Cost Pools	Cost Drivers	Estimated Overhead	Expected Use of Cost Drivers	StarDew	VineRose
Grape processing	Cart of grapes	$ 189,000	10,000	8,000	2,000
Aging	Total months	416,000	10,400,000	800,000	9,600,000
Bottling and corking	Number of bottles	360,000	1,600,000	800,000	800,000
Labeling and boxing	Number of bottles	240,000	1,600,000	800,000	800,000
Maintain and inspect equipment	Number of inspections	280,000	560	160	400
		$1,485,000			

Instructions

Answer each of the following questions. (Round all calculations to three decimal places.)

(a) Under traditional product costing using direct labor hours, compute the total manufacturing cost per **gallon** of both products.

(b) Under ABC, prepare a schedule showing the computation of the activity-based overhead rates (per cost driver).

(c) Prepare a schedule assigning each activity's overhead cost pool to each product, based on the use of cost drivers. Include a computation of overhead cost per unit.

(d) Compute the total manufacturing cost per gallon for both products under ABC.

(e) ▬▬▬▶ Write a memo to Jorge Rojo discussing the implications of your analysis for the company's plans. In this memo provide a brief description of ABC, as well as an explanation of how the traditional approach can result in distortions.

(a) Cost/gal.—S.D. $2.838

(c) Cost/gal.—S.D. $0.704

P4-5B Farm and Home Veterinary Clinic is a small-town partnership that offers two primary services, farm animal services and pet care services. Providing veterinary care to farm animals requires travel to the farm animal (house calls), while veterinary care to pets generally requires that the pet be brought into the clinic. As part of an investigation to determine the contribution that each of these two types of services makes to overall profit, one partner argues for allocating overhead using activity-based costing while the other partner argues for a more simple overhead cost allocation on the basis of direct labor hours. The partners agree to use next year's budgeted data, as prepared by their public accountant, for analysis and comparison purposes. The following overhead data are collected to develop the comparison.

Assign overhead costs to services using traditional costing and ABC; compute overhead rates and unit costs; compare results.
(SO 1, 4, 6, 8)

				Expected Use of Cost Drivers by Service	
Activity Cost Pools	Cost Drivers	Estimated Overhead	Expected Use of Cost Drivers	Farm Animals	Pets
Drug treatment	Treatments	$ 64,000	4,000	1,700	2,300
Surgery	Operations	70,000	800	200	600
Travel	Mileage	28,000	28,000	26,000	2,000
Consultation	Appointment/Calls	33,000	3,000	600	2,400
Accounting/office	Direct labor hours	30,000	5,000	2,000	3,000
Boarding and grooming	100% pets	40,000			
		$265,000			

Instructions

(a) Using traditional product costing as proposed by the one partner, compute the total overhead cost assigned to both services of Farm and Home Veterinary Clinic.

(b) (1) Using activity-based costing, prepare a schedule showing the computations of the activity-based overhead rates (per cost driver).

(b) Cost assigned—Farm Animals $89,300

(2) Prepare a schedule assigning each activity's overhead cost pool to each service based on the use of the cost drivers.

(c) Classify each of the activities as a value-added activity or a non-value-added activity.

(d) ABC—Pets 66%

(d) Comment on the comparative overhead cost assigned to the two services under both traditional costing and ABC.

Problems: Set C

Problem Set C is provided at the book's Web site, www.wiley.com/college/weygandt.

▷ BROADENING YOUR PERSPECTIVE

Group Decision Case

BYP 4-1 **East Valley Hospital** is a primary medical health care facility and trauma center that serves 11 small, rural midwestern communities within a 40-mile radius. The hospital offers all the medical/surgical services of a typical small hospital. It has a staff of 18 full-time doctors and 20 part-time visiting specialists. East Valley has a payroll of 150 employees consisting of technicians, nurses, therapists, managers, directors, administrators, dieticians, secretaries, data processors, and janitors.

Instructions
With the class divided into groups, discuss and answer the following.
(a) Using your (limited, moderate, or in-depth) knowledge of a hospital's operations, identify as many **activities** as you can that would serve as the basis for implementing an activity-based costing system.
(b) For each of the activities listed in (a), identify a **cost driver** that would serve as a valid measure of the resources consumed by the activity.

Managerial Analysis

BYP 4-2 **Ideal Manufacturing Company** of Sycamore, Illinois has supported a research and development (R&D) department that has for many years been the sole contributor to the company's new farm machinery products. The R&D activity is an overhead cost center that provides services only to in-house manufacturing departments (four different product lines), all of which produce agricultural/farm/ranch related machinery products.

The department has never sold its services outside, but because of its long history of success, larger manufacturers of agricultural products have approached Ideal to hire its R&D department for special projects. Because the costs of operating the R&D department have been spiraling uncontrollably, Ideal's management is considering entertaining these outside approaches to absorb the increasing costs. But, (1) management doesn't have any cost basis for charging R&D services to outsiders, and (2) it needs to gain control of its R&D costs. Management decides to implement an activity-based costing system in order to determine the charges for both outsiders and the in-house users of the department's services.

R&D activities fall into four pools with the following annual costs.

Market analysis	$1,050,000
Product design	2,280,000
Product development	3,600,000
Prototype testing	1,400,000

Activity analysis determines that the appropriate cost drivers and their usage for the four activities are:

Activities	Cost Drivers	Total Estimated Drivers
Market analysis	Hours of analysis	15,000 hours
Product design	Number of designs	2,500 designs
Product development	Number of products	90 products
Prototype testing	Number of tests	700 tests

Instructions
(a) Compute the activity-based overhead rate for each activity cost pool.
(b) How much cost would be charged to an in-house manufacturing department that consumed 1,800 hours of market analysis time, was provided 280 designs relating to 10 products, and requested 92 engineering tests?
(c) How much cost would serve as the basis for pricing an R&D bid with an outside company on a contract that would consume 800 hours of analysis time, require 178 designs relating to 3 products, and result in 70 engineering tests?
(d) What is the benefit to Ideal Manufacturing of applying activity-based costing to its R&D activity for both in-house and outside charging purposes?

Real-World Focus

BYP 4-3   Hewlett-Packard (H-P) is considered one of the best managed and most innovative companies in the world. It continually has shown an ability to adapt to global competitive challenges through technical innovation and continual reassessment of its management and control mechanisms. Most applications of activity-based costing by Hewlett-Packard have been successful.

But, over the period August 1988 to August 1989, the Colorado Springs Division of Hewlett-Packard designed an activity-based costing system with the goal of providing for better product costing and inventory valuation. It began implementation in November 1989 but halted the process in the summer of 1992. Since then, the Colorado Springs Division has made no further attempts to re-implement a more expansive ABC approach.

Instructions
The March 1997 issue of *Management Accounting* contains an article by Steven P. Landry, Larry M. Wood, and Tim M. Linquist about the Colorado Springs Division titled "Can ABC Bring Mixed Results?" Read the article and answer the following questions.
(a) What went wrong at H-P's Colorado Springs Division in the design, development, and implementation of its activity-based costing system?
(b) What conclusions were drawn from H-P's Colorado Springs Division experience? What does successful ABC implementation require?

Exploring the Web

BYP 4-4   Cost Technology describes itself as a "global consulting company specializing in profit management." The company helps manufacturing, service, and government organizations implement methods, such as activity-based costing and activity-based management, that will improve corporate profitability. The home page of Cost Technology includes information about the company, its markets, and products. The following exercise investigates the company in more depth.

Address: **http://costechnology.com**
        (*or go to* **www.wiley.com/college/weygandt**)

Instructions
Answer the following questions.
(a) Under the "services" section of Cost Technology's Web page, the company provides a definition of activity-based costing. What is this definition, and how does it differ from the one provided in the textbook?
(b) Under the "knowledgebase" section of its Web page, Cost Technology identifies a number of seminars related to activity-based costing. Explain the contents of these two seminars: (1) "The ABC Assessment: Obtaining the Highest Value from Your Implementation" and (2) "The Drivers of Successful ABC Implementation."

Communication Activity

BYP 4-5   In our Feature Story about **Super Bakery, Inc.**, we described a virtual corporation as one that consists of a core unit that is supported by a network of outsourced activities. A virtual corporation minimizes investment in human resources, fixed assets, and working capital. The application of ABC to Super Bakery, Inc. is described in an article titled "ABC in a Virtual Corporation" by Tom Davis and Bruce Darling, in the October 1996 issue of *Management Accounting*.

Instructions

Assume you are the controller of a virtual corporation. Using the article as a basis for your communication, write a summary that answers the following questions.

(a) What unique strategies and tactics did Super Bakery's management implement that caused sales to take off and continue to grow at an average rate of 20%?

(b) Why did Super Bakery's management feel that it was necessary to install an ABC system?

(c) What is the main difference between Super Bakery's ABC system and other manufacturers' ABC systems?

Research Assignment

BYP 4-6   The April 1998 issue of *Management Accounting* includes an article by Kip R. Krumwiede titled "ABC: Why It's Tried and How It Succeeds."

Instructions

Read the article and answer the following questions.

(a) What is the adoption and implementation status of ABC according to the survey conducted in 1996 by the Cost Management Group of the Institute of Management Accountants?

(b) What did Krumwiede's survey attempt to determine?

(c) In Krumwiede's survey, what factors appeared to separate those companies that adopted ABC from those that did not adopt ABC?

(d) Identify at least five "Basic ABC Implementation Tips" recommended in the article.

Ethics Case

BYP 4-7   Marcus Lim, the cost accountant for Hi-Power Mower Company, recently installed activity-based costing at Hi-Power's St. Louis lawn tractor (riding mower) plant where three models—the 8-horsepower Bladerunner, the 12-horsepower Quickcut, and the 18-horsepower Supercut—are manufactured. Marcus's new product costs for these three models show that the company's traditional costing system had been significantly undercosting the 18-horsepower Supercut. This was due primarily to the lower sales volume of the Supercut compared to the Bladerunner and the Quickcut.

Before completing his analysis and reporting these results to management, Marcus is approached by his friend Ray Pon, who is the production manager for the 18-horsepower Supercut model. Ray has heard from one of Marcus's staff about the new product costs and is upset and worried for his job because the new costs show the Supercut to be losing, rather than making, money.

At first Ray condemns the new cost system, whereupon Marcus explains the practice of activity-based costing and why it is more accurate than the company's present system. Even more worried now, Ray begs Marcus, "Massage the figures just enough to save the line from being discontinued. You don't want me to lose my job do you? Anyway, nobody will know."

Marcus holds firm but agrees to recompute all his calculations for accuracy before submitting his costs to management.

Instructions

(a) Who are the stakeholders in this situation?

(b) What, if any, are the ethical considerations in this situation?

(c) What are Marcus's ethical obligations to the company? To his friend?

Answers to Self-Study Questions

1. c   2. c   3. c   4. b   5. d   6. d   7. c   8. c   *9. d   *10. b

   Remember to go back to the Navigator box on the chapter-opening page and check off your completed work.

CHAPTER 5

Cost-Volume-Profit

STUDY OBJECTIVES

After studying this chapter,
you should be able to:

1 Distinguish between variable and fixed costs.

2 Explain the significance of the relevant range.

3 Explain the concept of mixed costs.

4 List the five components of cost-volume-profit analysis.

5 Indicate what contribution margin is and how it can be expressed.

6 Identify the three ways to determine the break-even point.

7 Give the formulas for determining sales required to earn target net income.

8 Define margin of safety, and give the formulas for computing it.

 ☑ THE NAVIGATOR

THE NAVIGATOR ✔

▶ Scan *Study Objectives* ☐

▶ Read *Feature Story* ☐

▶ Read *Preview* ☐

▶ Read text and answer *Before You Go On*
    p. 198 ☐   p. 205 ☐   p. 210 ☐

▶ Work *Using the Decision Toolkit* ☐

▶ Review *Summary of Study Objectives* ☐

▶ Work *Demonstration Problem* ☐

▶ Answer *Self-Study Questions* ☐

▶ Complete *Assignments* ☐

FEATURE STORY

Growing by Leaps and Leotards

When the last of her three children went off to school, Amy began looking for a job. At this same time, her daughter asked to take dance classes. The nearest dance studio was over 20 miles away, and Amy didn't know how she would balance a new job and drive her daughter to dance class. Suddenly it hit her—why not start her own dance studio?

Amy sketched out a business plan: A local church would rent its basement for $6 per hour. The size of the basement limited the number of students she could teach, but the rent was low. Insurance for a small studio was $50 per month. Initially she would teach classes only for young kids since that was all she felt qualified to do. She thought she could charge $2.50 for a one-hour class. There was room for 8 students per class. She wouldn't get rich—but at least it would be fun, and she didn't have much at risk.

Amy soon realized that the demand for dance classes far exceeded her capacity. She considered renting a bigger space that could serve 15 students per class. But her rent would also increase significantly. Also, rather than paying rent by the hour, she would have to pay $600 per month, even during the summer months when demand for dance classes was low. She also would have to pay utilities—roughly $70 per month.

However, with a bigger space Amy could offer classes for teens and adults. Teens and adults would pay a higher fee—$5 per hour—though the number of students per class would have to be smaller,

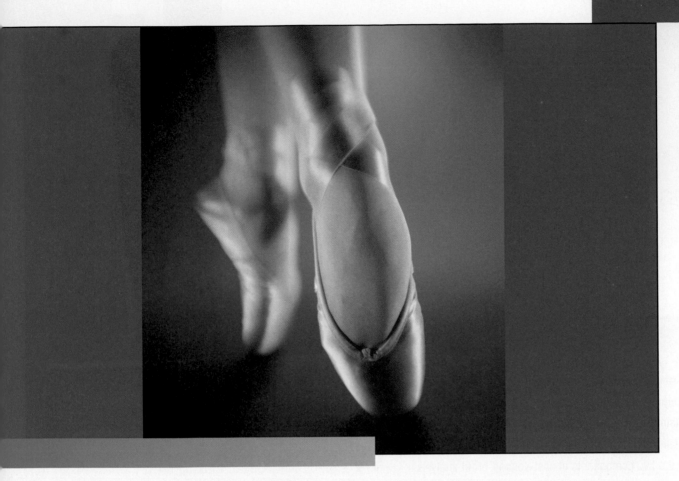

probably only 8 per class. She could hire a part-time instructor at about $18 per hour to teach advanced classes. Insurance costs could increase to $100 per month. In addition, she would need a part-time administrator at $100 per month to keep records. Amy also realized she could increase her income by selling dance supplies such as shoes, towels, and leotards.

Amy laid out a new business plan based on these estimates. If she failed, she stood to lose real money. Convinced she could make a go of it, she made the big plunge.

Her planning paid off: Within 10 years of starting her business in a church basement Amy had over 800 students, seven instructors, two administrators, and a facility with three separate studios.

As the Feature Story indicates, to manage any size business you must understand how costs respond to changes in sales volume and the effect of costs and revenues on profits. A prerequisite to understanding cost-volume-profit (CVP) relationships is knowledge of how costs behave. In this chapter, we first explain the considerations involved in cost behavior analysis. Then we discuss and illustrate CVP analysis.

The content and organization of Chapter 5 are as follows.

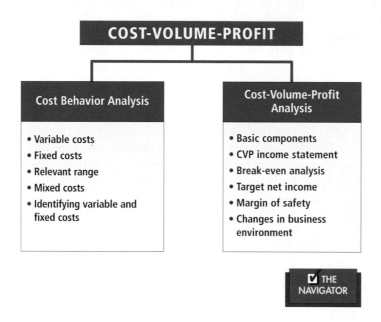

Cost Behavior Analysis

Cost behavior analysis is the study of how specific costs respond to changes in the level of business activity. As you might expect, some costs change, and others remain the same. For example, for an airline company such as **Southwest** or **United**, the longer the flight the higher the fuel costs. On the other hand, **Massachusetts General Hospital**'s employee costs to run the emergency room on any given night are relatively constant regardless of the number of patients serviced. A knowledge of cost behavior helps management plan operations and decide between alternative courses of action. Cost behavior analysis applies to all types of entities, as the Feature Story about Amy's dance studio indicates.

The starting point in cost behavior analysis is measuring the key business activities. Activity levels may be expressed in terms of sales dollars (in a retail company), miles driven (in a trucking company), room occupancy (in a hotel), or dance classes taught (by a dance studio). Many companies use more than one measurement base. A manufacturer, for example, may use direct labor hours or units of output for manufacturing costs and sales revenue or units sold for selling expenses.

For an activity level to be useful in cost behavior analysis, changes in the level or volume of activity should be correlated with changes in costs. The activity level selected is referred to as the activity (or volume) index. The **activity index** identifies the activity that causes changes in the behavior of costs.

With an appropriate activity index, it is possible to classify the behavior of costs in response to changes in activity levels into three categories: variable, fixed, or mixed.

VARIABLE COSTS

Variable costs are costs that vary **in total** directly and proportionately with changes in the activity level. If the level increases 10 percent, total variable costs will increase 10 percent. If the level of activity decreases by 25 percent, variable costs will decrease 25 percent. Examples of variable costs include direct materials and direct labor for a manufacturer; cost of goods sold, sales commissions, and freight-out for a merchandiser; and gasoline in airline and trucking companies. A variable cost may also be defined as a cost that **remains the same *per unit* at every level of activity**.

To illustrate the behavior of a variable cost, assume that Damon Company manufactures radios that contain a $10 digital clock. The activity index is the number of radios produced. As each radio is manufactured, the total cost of the clocks increases by $10. As shown in part (a) of Illustration 5-1, total cost of the clocks will be $20,000 if 2,000 radios are produced, and $100,000 when 10,000 radios are produced. We also can see that a variable cost remains the same per unit as the level of activity changes. As shown in part (b) of Illustration 5-1, the unit cost of $10 for the clocks is the same whether 2,000 or 10,000 radios are produced.

Illustration 5-1 Behavior of total and unit variable costs

Helpful Hint True or false: Variable cost per unit changes directly and proportionately with changes in activity. Answer: False. Per unit cost remains constant at all levels of activity.

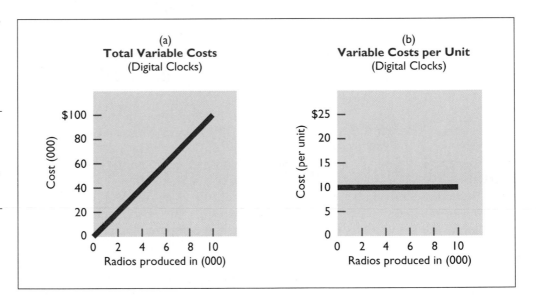

Companies that rely heavily on labor to manufacture a product, such as **Nike** or **Reebok**, or to provide a service, such as **Hilton** or **Marriott**, are likely to have many variable costs. In contrast, companies that use a high proportion of machinery and equipment in producing revenue, such as **AT&T** or **Duke Energy Co.**, may have few variable costs.

FIXED COSTS

Fixed costs are costs that **remain the same in total** regardless of changes in the activity level. Examples include property taxes, insurance, rent, supervisory salaries, and depreciation on buildings and equipment. Because total fixed costs

remain constant as activity changes, it follows that **fixed costs *per unit* vary inversely with activity: As volume increases, unit cost declines, and vice versa**.

To illustrate the behavior of fixed costs, assume that Damon Company leases its productive facilities at a cost of $10,000 per month. Total fixed costs of the facilities will remain constant at every level of activity, as shown in part (a) of Illustration 5-2. But, on a per unit basis, the cost of rent will decline as activity increases, as shown in part (b) of Illustration 5-2. At 2,000 units, the unit cost is $5 ($10,000 ÷ 2,000). When 10,000 radios are produced, the unit cost is only $1 ($10,000 ÷ 10,000).

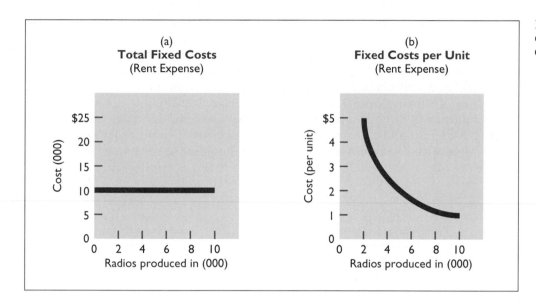

Illustration 5-2 Behavior of total and unit fixed costs

The trend for many manufacturers is to have more fixed costs and fewer variable costs. This trend is the result of increased use of automation and less use of employee labor. As a result, depreciation and lease charges (fixed costs) increase, whereas direct labor costs (variable costs) decrease.

Business Insight
Management Perspective

When Thomas Moser quit teaching communications at Bates College 25 years ago, he turned to what he loved doing—furniture woodworking. Today he has over 120 employees. In a business where profit margins are seldom thicker than wood shavings, cost control is everything. Moser keeps no inventory; a 50 percent deposit buys the wood. Because computer-driven machines cut most of the standardized parts and joints, "we're free to be inefficient in assembly and finishing work, where the craft is most obviously expressed," says Moser. Direct labor costs are a manageable 30 percent of revenues. By keeping a tight lid on costs and running an efficient operation, Moser is free to spend most of his time doing what he enjoys most—designing furniture.

SOURCE: Excerpts from "Out of the Woods," *Forbes* (April 5, 1999), p. 74.

RELEVANT RANGE

In Illustration 5-1, a straight line was drawn throughout the entire range of the activity index for total variable costs. In essence, the assumption was made that the costs were **linear**. If a relationship is linear (that is straight-line), then changes in the activity index will result in a direct, proportional change in the variable cost. For example, if the activity level doubles, the cost will double.

It is now necessary to ask: Is the straight-line relationship realistic? Does the linear assumption produce useful data for CVP analysis?

In most business situations, a straight-line relationship **does not exist** for variable costs throughout the entire range of possible activity. At abnormally low levels of activity, it may be impossible to be cost-efficient. Small-scale operations may not allow the company to obtain quantity discounts for raw materials or to use specialized labor. In contrast, at abnormally high levels of activity, labor costs may increase sharply because of overtime pay. Also at high activity levels, materials costs may jump significantly because of excess spoilage caused by worker fatigue. As a result, in the real world, the relationship between the behavior of a variable cost and changes in the activity level is often **curvilinear**, as shown in part (a) of Illustration 5-3. In the curved sections of the line, a change in the activity index will not result in a direct, proportional change in the variable cost. That is, a doubling of the activity index will not result in an exact doubling of the variable cost. The variable cost may more than double, or it may be less than double.

Illustration 5-3   Nonlinear behavior of variable and fixed costs

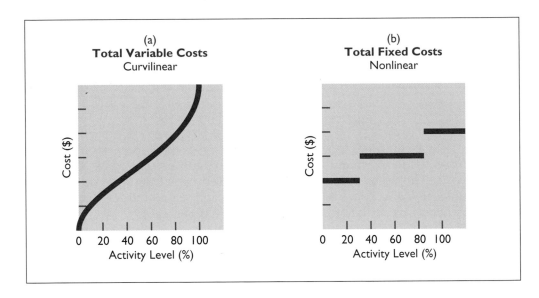

Helpful Hint Fixed costs that may be changeable include research, such as new product development, and management training programs.

Total fixed costs also do not have a straight-line relationship over the entire range of activity. Some fixed costs will not change. But it is possible for management to change other fixed costs. For example, in the Feature Story the dance studio's rent was originally variable and then became fixed at a certain amount. It then increased to a new fixed amount when the size of the studio increased beyond a certain point. An example of the behavior of total fixed costs through all potential levels of activity is shown in part (b) of Illustration 5-3.

For most companies, operating at almost zero or at 100 percent capacity is the exception rather than the rule. Instead, companies often operate over a somewhat narrower range, such as 40–80 percent of capacity. The range over which a company expects to operate during a year is called the **relevant range** of the activity index. Within the relevant range, as shown in both diagrams in Illustration 5-4, a straight-line relationship generally exists for both variable and fixed costs.

Alternative Terminology The relevant range is also called the *normal* or *practical range.*

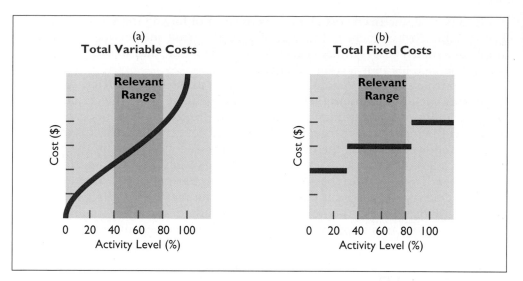

Illustration 5-4 Linear behavior within relevant range

As you can see, although the linear (straight-line) relationship may not be completely realistic, **the linear assumption produces useful data for CVP analysis as long as the level of activity remains within the relevant range**.

MIXED COSTS

Mixed costs are costs that contain both a variable element and a fixed element. Sometimes called **semivariable costs, mixed costs change in total but not proportionately with changes in the activity level**.

The rental of a **U-Haul** truck is a good example of a mixed cost. Assume that local rental terms for a 17-foot truck, including insurance, are $50 per day plus 50 cents per mile. When determining the cost of a one-day rental, the per day charge is a fixed cost (with respect to miles driven), whereas the mileage charge is a variable cost. The graphic presentation of the rental cost for a one-day rental is as follows.

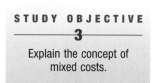

STUDY OBJECTIVE
3
Explain the concept of mixed costs.

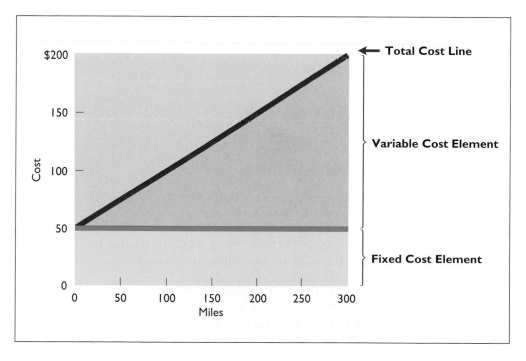

Illustration 5-5 Behavior of a mixed cost

In this case, the fixed cost element is the cost of having the service available. The variable cost element is the cost of actually using the service. Another example of a mixed cost is utility costs (electric, telephone, and so on), where there is a flat service fee plus a usage charge.

For purposes of CVP analysis, **mixed costs must be classified into their fixed and variable elements**. How does management make the classification? One possibility is to determine the variable and fixed components each time a mixed cost is incurred. But because of time and cost constraints, this approach is rarely followed. Instead, the usual approach is to collect data on the behavior of the mixed costs at various levels of activity. An analysis is then performed to identify the fixed and variable cost components. Various types of analysis can be used. One type of analysis, called the **high-low method**, is discussed below. Other methods, such as the scatter diagram method and least squares regression analysis, are more appropriately explained in cost accounting courses.

High-Low Method

The high-low method uses the total costs incurred at the high and low levels of activity to classify mixed costs into fixed and variable components. The difference in costs between the high and low levels represents variable costs, since only the variable cost element can change as activity levels change. The steps in computing fixed and variable costs under this method are as follows.

1. **Determine variable cost per unit from the following formula.**

Illustration 5-6 Formula for variable cost per unit using high-low method

Change in Total Costs	÷	**High minus Low Activity Level**	=	**Variable Cost per Unit**

To illustrate, assume that Metro Transit Company has the following maintenance costs and mileage data for its fleet of buses over a 4-month period.

Illustration 5-7 Assumed maintenance costs and mileage data

Month	**Miles Driven**	**Total Cost**	**Month**	**Miles Driven**	**Total Cost**
January	20,000	$30,000	March	35,000	$49,000
February	40,000	48,000	April	50,000	63,000

The high and low levels of activity are 50,000 miles in April and 20,000 miles in January. The maintenance costs at these two levels are $63,000 and $30,000, respectively. The difference in maintenance costs is $33,000 ($63,000 − $30,000) and the difference in miles is 30,000 (50,000 − 20,000). Therefore, for Metro Transit, variable cost per unit is $1.10, computed as follows.

$$\$33,000 \div 30,000 = \$1.10$$

2. **Determine the fixed cost by subtracting the total variable cost at either the high or the low activity level from the total cost at that activity level.**

For Metro Transit, the computations are shown in Illustration 5-8.

Illustration 5-8 High-low method computation of fixed costs

		METRO TRANSIT	
		Activity Level	
		High	**Low**
Total cost		$63,000	$30,000
Less:	Variable costs		
	50,000 X $1.10	55,000	
	20,000 X $1.10		22,000
Total fixed costs		$8,000	$8,000

Maintenance costs are therefore $8,000 per month plus $1.10 per mile. This is represented by the following formula:

$$\text{Maintenance costs} = \text{Fixed costs} + (\$1.10 \times \text{miles driven})$$

For example, at 45,000 miles, estimated maintenance costs would be $8,000 fixed and $49,500 variable ($1.10 × 45,000) for a total of $57,500.

The high-low method generally produces a reasonable estimate for analysis. However, it does not produce a precise measurement of the fixed and variable elements in a mixed cost because other activity levels are ignored in the computation.

IMPORTANCE OF IDENTIFYING VARIABLE AND FIXED COSTS

Why is it important to segregate costs into variable and fixed elements? The answer may become apparent if we look at the following four business decisions.

1. If **American Airlines** is to make a profit when it reduces all domestic fares by 30 percent, what reduction in costs or increase in passengers will be required? **Answer**: To make a profit when it cuts domestic fares by 30 percent, American Airlines will have to increase the number of passengers or cut its variable costs for those flights. Its fixed costs will not change.

2. If **Ford Motor Company** meets the United Auto Workers' demands for higher wages, what increase in sales revenue will be needed to maintain current profit levels? **Answer**: Higher wages to UAW members at Ford Motor Company will increase the variable costs of manufacturing automobiles. To maintain present profit levels, Ford will have to cut other variable costs or increase the price of its automobiles.

3. If **USX Corp.**'s program to modernize plant facilities through significant equipment purchases reduces the work force by 50 percent, what will be the effect on the cost of producing one ton of steel? **Answer**: The modernizing of plant facilities at USX Corp. changes the proportion of fixed and variable costs of producing one ton of steel. Fixed costs increase because of higher depreciation charges, whereas variable costs decrease due to the reduction in the number of steelworkers.

4. What happens if **Kellogg Company** increases its advertising expenses but cannot increase prices because of competitive pressure? **Answer**: Sales volume must be increased to cover the increase in fixed advertising costs.

BEFORE YOU GO ON . . .

▶Review It

1. What are the effects on (a) a variable cost and (b) a fixed cost due to a change in activity?
2. What is the relevant range, and how do costs behave within this range?
3. What are the steps in applying the high-low method to mixed costs?

▶Do It

Helena Company reports the following total costs at two levels of production.

	10,000 units	20,000 units
Direct materials	$20,000	$40,000
Maintenance	8,000	10,000
Depreciation	4,000	4,000

Classify each cost as either variable, fixed, or mixed.

Action Plan

- Recall that a variable cost varies in total directly and proportionately with each change.
- Recall that a fixed cost remains the same in total with each change.
- Recall that a mixed cost changes in total but not proportionately with each change.

Solution   Direct materials is a variable cost. Maintenance is a mixed cost. Depreciation is a fixed cost.

Related exercise material: BE5-1, BE5-2, BE5-3, E5-1, E5-2, and E5-3.

☑ THE NAVIGATOR

Cost-Volume-Profit Analysis

Cost-volume-profit (CVP) analysis is the study of the effects of changes in costs and volume on a company's profits. CVP analysis is important in profit planning. It also is a critical factor in such management decisions as setting selling prices, determining product mix, and maximizing use of production facilities.

BASIC COMPONENTS

CVP analysis considers the interrelationships among the components shown in Illustration 5-9.

Illustration 5-9   Components of CVP analysis

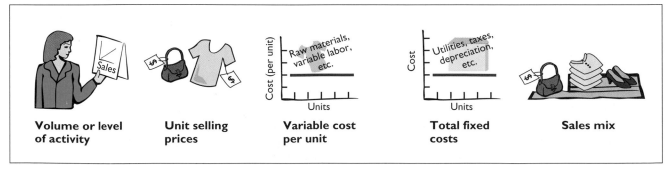

| Volume or level of activity | Unit selling prices | Variable cost per unit | Total fixed costs | Sales mix |

The following assumptions underlie each CVP analysis.

1. The behavior of both costs and revenues is linear throughout the relevant range of the activity index.
2. Costs can be classified accurately as either variable or fixed.
3. Changes in activity are the only factors that affect costs.
4. All units produced are sold.
5. When more than one type of product is sold, the sales mix will remain constant. That is, the percentage that each product represents of total sales will stay the same. Sales mix complicates CVP analysis because different products will have different cost relationships. In this chapter we assume a single product. Sales mix issues are addressed in Chapter 7.

When these assumptions are not valid, the CVP analysis may be inaccurate.

CVP INCOME STATEMENT

Because CVP is so important for decision making, management often wants this information reported in a **CVP income statement** format. The CVP income statement classifies costs as variable or fixed and computes a contribution margin. **Contribution margin** is the amount of revenue remaining after deducting variable costs. It is often stated both as a total amount and on a per unit basis.

We will use Vargo Video Company to illustrate a CVP income statement. Vargo Video produces a high-end, progressive-scan DVD player/recorder with up to 160-hour recording capacity and MP3 playback capability. Relevant data for the DVD players sold by this company in June 2005 are as follows.

STUDY OBJECTIVE

5

Indicate what contribution margin is and how it can be expressed.

Unit selling price of DVD player	$500
Unit variable costs	$300
Total monthly fixed costs	$200,000
Units sold	1,600

Illustration 5-10
Assumed selling and cost data for Vargo Video

The CVP income statement for Vargo Video therefore would be reported as follows.

VARGO VIDEO COMPANY
CVP Income Statement
For the Month Ended June 30, 2005

	Total	Per Unit
Sales (1,600 DVD players)	$ 800,000	$ 500
Variable costs	480,000	300
Contribution margin	**320,000**	**$200**
Fixed costs	200,000	
Net income	**$120,000**	

Illustration 5-11 CVP income statement, with net income

A traditional income statement and a CVP income statement both report the same bottom-line net income of $120,000. However a traditional income statement does not classify costs as variable or fixed, and therefore a contribution margin would not be reported. In addition, both a total and a per unit amount are often shown on a CVP income statement to facilitate CVP analysis.

In the applications of CVP analysis that follow, we will assume that the term "cost" includes all costs and expenses pertaining to production and sale of the product. That is, cost includes manufacturing costs plus selling and administrative expenses. An expanded format for the CVP income statement is discussed in Chapter 7.

Contribution Margin Per Unit

Vargo Video's CVP income statement shows a contribution margin of $320,000, and a contribution margin per unit of $200 ($500 − $300). The formula for **contribution margin per unit** and the computation for Vargo Video are:

Illustration 5-12 Formula for contribution margin per unit

Unit Selling Price	−	Unit Variable Costs	=	Contribution Margin per Unit
$500	−	$300	=	$200

Contribution margin per unit indicates that for every DVD player sold, Vargo will have $200 to cover fixed costs and contribute to net income. Because Vargo Video has fixed costs of $200,000, it must sell 1,000 DVD players ($200,000 ÷ $200) before it earns any net income. Vargo's CVP income statement, assuming a zero net income, would report the following.

Illustration 5-13 CVP income statement, with zero net income

VARGO VIDEO COMPANY
CVP Income Statement
For the Month Ended June 30, 2005

	Total	Per Unit
Sales (1,000 DVD players)	$500,000	$ 500
Variable costs	300,000	300
Contribution margin	**200,000**	**$200**
Fixed costs	200,000	
Net income	$ –0–	

It follows that for every DVD player sold above 1,000 units, net income is increased $200. For example, assume that Vargo sold one more DVD player, for a total of 1,001 DVD players sold. In this case it would report net income of $200 as shown in Illustration 5-14.

Illustration 5-14 CVP income statement, with net income

VARGO VIDEO COMPANY
CVP Income Statement
For the Month Ended June 30, 2005

	Total	Per Unit
Sales (1,001 DVD players)	$500,500	$ 500
Variable costs	300,300	300
Contribution margin	**200,200**	**$200**
Fixed costs	200,000	
Net income	$ 200	

Contribution Margin Ratio

Some managers prefer to use a contribution margin ratio in CVP analysis. The **contribution margin ratio** is the contribution margin per unit divided by the unit selling price. For Vargo Video, the ratio is as follows.

Contribution Margin per Unit	÷	Unit Selling Price	=	Contribution Margin Ratio
$200	÷	$500	=	40%

Illustration 5-15   Formula for contribution margin ratio

The contribution margin ratio of 40 percent means that $0.40 of each sales dollar ($1 × 40%) is available to apply to fixed costs and to contribute to net income.

This expression of contribution margin is very helpful in determining the effect of changes in sales on net income. For example, if sales increase $100,000, net income will increase $40,000 (40% × $100,000). Thus, by using the contribution margin ratio, managers can quickly determine increases in net income from any change in sales.

We can also see this effect through a CVP income statement. Assume that Vargo Video's current sales are $500,000 and it wants to know the effect of a $100,000 increase in sales. It could prepare a comparative CVP income statement analysis as follows.

Illustration 5-16   Comparative CVP income statements

VARGO VIDEO COMPANY
CVP Income Statements
For the Month Ended June 30, 2005

	No Change		With Change	
	Total	**Per Unit**	**Total**	**Per Unit**
Sales	$500,000	$ 500	$600,000	$ 500
Variable costs	300,000	300	360,000	300
Contribution margin	**200,000**	**$200**	**240,000**	**$200**
Fixed costs	200,000		200,000	
Net income	**$ –0–**		**$ 40,000**	

Study these CVP income statements carefully. The concepts presented in these statements will be used extensively in this and later chapters.

DECISION TOOLKIT

Decision Checkpoints	Info Needed for Decision	Tool to Use for Decision	How to Evaluate Results
What was the contribution toward fixed costs and income from each unit sold?	Selling price per unit and variable cost per unit	$\text{Contribution margin per unit} = \text{Unit selling price} - \text{Unit variable cost}$	Every unit sold will increase income by the contribution margin.
What was the increase in income as a result of an increase in sales?	Contribution margin per unit and unit selling price	$\text{Contribution margin ratio} = \text{Contribution margin per unit} \div \text{Unit selling price}$	Every dollar of sales will increase income by the contribution margin ratio.

BREAK-EVEN ANALYSIS

A key relationship in CVP analysis is the level of activity at which total revenues equal total costs (both fixed and variable). This level of activity is called the **break-even point**. At this volume of sales, the company will realize no income and will suffer no loss. The process of finding the break-even point is called **break-even analysis**. Knowledge of the break-even point is useful to management when it decides whether to introduce new product lines, change sales prices on established products, or enter new market areas.

The break-even point can be:

1. Computed from a mathematical equation.
2. Computed by using contribution margin.
3. Derived from a cost-volume-profit (CVP) graph.

The break-even point can be expressed **either in sales units or sales dollars**.

Mathematical Equation

A common equation used for CVP analysis is shown in Illustration 5-17.

Illustration 5-17 Basic CVP equation

$$\text{Sales} = \text{Variable Costs} + \text{Fixed Costs} + \text{Net Income}$$

Identifying the break-even point is a special case of CVP analysis. Because at the break-even point net income is zero, **break-even occurs where total sales equal variable costs plus fixed costs**.

The break-even point **in units** can be computed directly from the equation by **using unit selling prices** and **unit variable costs**. The computation for Vargo Video is:

Illustration 5-18 Computation of break-even point in units

$$\text{Sales} = \text{Variable Costs} + \text{Fixed Costs} + \text{Net Income}$$

$$\$500Q = \$300Q + \$200,000 + \$0$$

$$\$200Q = \$200,000$$

$$Q = 1,000 \text{ units}$$

where

$$Q = \text{sales volume in units}$$
$$\$500 = \text{selling price}$$
$$\$300 = \text{variable cost per unit}$$
$$\$200,000 = \text{total fixed costs}$$

Thus, Vargo Video must sell 1,000 units to break even.

To find **sales dollars** required to break even, we multiply the units sold at the break-even point times the selling price per unit, as shown below.

$$1,000 \times \$500 = \$500,000 \text{ (break-even sales dollars)}$$

Contribution Margin Technique

We know that contribution margin equals total revenues less variable costs. It follows that at the break-even point, **contribution margin must equal total fixed costs**. On the basis of this relationship, we can compute the break-even point using either the contribution margin per unit or the contribution margin ratio.

When the contribution margin per unit is used, the formula to compute break-even point in units is fixed costs divided by contribution margin per unit. For Vargo Video the computation is as follows.

Fixed Costs	÷	Contribution Margin per Unit	=	Break-even Point in Units
$200,000	÷	$200	=	1,000 units

Illustration 5-19 Formula for break-even point in units using contribution margin

One way to interpret this formula is that Vargo Video generates $200 of contribution margin with each unit that it sells. This $200 is used to pay off fixed costs. Therefore, the company must sell 1,000 units to pay off $200,000 in fixed costs.

When the contribution margin ratio is used, the formula to compute break-even point in dollars is fixed costs divided by the contribution margin ratio. We know that the contribution margin ratio for Vargo Video is 40 percent ($200 ÷ $500), which means that every dollar of sales generates 40¢ to pay off fixed costs. Thus, the break-even point in dollars is:

Fixed Costs	÷	Contribution Margin Ratio	=	Break-even Point in Dollars
$200,000	÷	40%	=	$500,000

Illustration 5-20 Formula for break-even point in dollars using contribution margin ratio

Business Insight
e-Business Perspective

The Internet is wringing inefficiencies out of nearly every industry. While commercial aircraft spend roughly 4,000 hours a year in the air, chartered aircraft spend only 500 hours flying. That means that they are sitting on the ground—not making any money—nearly 90 percent of the time. Enter **flightserve.com**. For about the same cost as a first-class ticket, flightserve.com matches up executives with charter flights in small "private jets." The executive gets a more comfortable ride and can avoid the hassle of big airports. Flightserve.com says that the average charter jet has eight seats. When all eight seats are full, the company has an 80 percent profit margin. It breaks even at an average of 3.3 full seats per flight.

SOURCE: "Jet Set Go," *The Economist* (March 18, 2000), p. 68.

Graphic Presentation

An effective way to find the break-even point is to prepare a break-even graph. Because this graph also shows costs, volume, and profits, it is referred to as a **cost-volume-profit (CVP) graph.**

As shown in the CVP graph in Illustration 5-21 (page 204), sales volume is recorded along the horizontal axis. This axis should extend to the maximum level of expected sales. Both total revenues (sales) and total costs (fixed plus variable) are recorded on the vertical axis.

Illustration 5-21 CVP graph

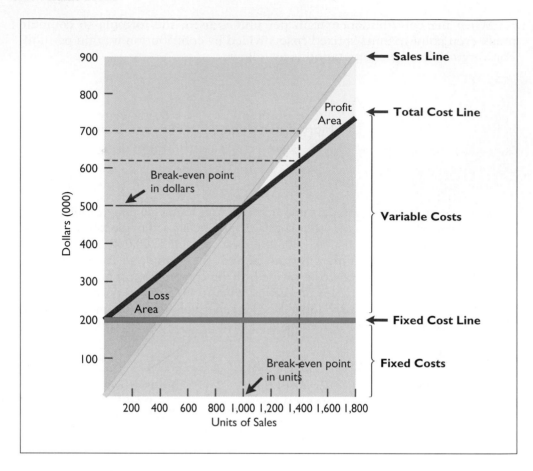

The construction of the graph, using the data for Vargo Video, is as follows.

1. Plot the total-sales line, starting at the zero activity level. For every DVD player sold, total revenue increases by $500. For example, at 200 units, sales are $100,000. At the upper level of activity (1,800 units), sales are $900,000. The revenue line is assumed to be linear through the full range of activity.

2. Plot the total fixed cost using a horizontal line. For the DVD players, this line is plotted at $200,000. The fixed cost is the same at every level of activity.

3. Plot the total cost line. This starts at the fixed-cost line at zero activity. It increases by the variable cost at each level of activity. For each DVD player, variable costs are $300. Thus, at 200 units, total variable cost is $60,000, and the total cost is $260,000. At 1,800 units total variable cost is $540,000, and total cost is $740,000. On the graph, the amount of the variable cost can be derived from the difference between the total cost and fixed cost lines at each level of activity.

4. Determine the break-even point from the intersection of the total cost line and the total revenue line. The break-even point in dollars is found by drawing a horizontal line from the break-even point to the vertical axis. The break-even point in units is found by drawing a vertical line from the break-even point to the horizontal axis. For the DVD players, the break-even point is $500,000 of sales, or 1,000 units. At this sales level, Vargo Video will cover costs but make no profit.

The CVP graph also shows both the net income and net loss areas. Thus, the amount of income or loss at each level of sales can be derived from the total sales and total cost lines.

A CVP graph is useful because the effects of a change in any element in the CVP analysis can be quickly seen. For example, a 10 percent increase in selling price will change the location of the total revenue line. Likewise, the effects on total costs of wage increases can be quickly observed.

Business Insight
Management Perspective

Computer graphics are a valuable companion to many computer software packages. Color graphs can be instantly changed to provide visual "what if" analysis.
Current technology allows for stunning graphs in a variety of different formats (pie charts, bar, stacked bar, two-dimensional, three-dimensional, etc.). In the appropriate situation, a graph can literally be worth a thousand words.

DECISION TOOLKIT

Decision Checkpoints	Info Needed for Decision	Tool to Use for Decision	How to Evaluate Results
At what amount of sales does a company cover its costs?	Unit selling price, unit variable cost, and total fixed costs	Break-even point analysis *In units:* $$\text{Break-even point} = \frac{\text{Fixed costs}}{\text{Unit contribution margin}}$$ *In dollars:* $$\text{Break-even point} = \frac{\text{Fixed costs}}{\text{Contribution margin ratio}}$$	Below the break-even point, the company is unprofitable.

BEFORE YOU GO ON . . .

▶Review It

1. What are the assumptions that underlie each CVP application?
2. What is contribution margin, and how can it be expressed?
3. How can the break-even point be determined?

▶Do It

Lombardi Company has a unit selling price of $400, variable costs per unit of $240, and fixed costs of $180,000. Compute the break-even point in units using (a) a mathematical equation and (b) contribution margin per unit.

Action Plan

• Apply the formula: Sales = Variable costs + Fixed costs + Net income.
• Apply the formula: Fixed costs ÷ Contribution margin per unit = Break-even point in units.

Solution (a) The formula is $400Q = $240Q + $180,000. The break-even point in units is 1,125 ($180,000 ÷ $160). (b) The contribution margin per unit is $160 ($400 − $240). The formula therefore is $180,000 ÷ $160, and the break-even point in units is 1,125.

Related exercise material: BE5-6, BE5-8, BE5-9, E5-4, E5-5, E5-6, E5-9, and E5-10.

✓ THE NAVIGATOR

STUDY OBJECTIVE

7

Give the formulas for determining sales required to earn target net income.

TARGET NET INCOME

Rather than simply "breaking even," management usually sets an income objective for individual product lines. This objective is called **target net income**. It indicates the sales necessary to achieve a specified level of income. The sales necessary to achieve target net income can be determined from each of the approaches used to determine break-even sales.

Mathematical Equation

We know that at the break-even point no profit or loss results for the company. By adding an amount for target net income to the same basic equation, we obtain the following formula for determining required sales.

Illustration 5-22 Formula for required sales to meet target net income

$$
\text{Required Sales} = \text{Variable Costs} + \text{Fixed Costs} + \text{Target Net Income}
$$

Required sales may be expressed in **either sales units or sales dollars**. Assuming that target net income is $120,000 for Vargo Video, the computation of required sales in units is as follows.

Illustration 5-23 Computation of required sales

$$
\text{Required Sales} = \text{Variable Costs} + \text{Fixed Costs} + \text{Target Net Income}
$$

$$
\$500Q = \$300Q + \$200,000 + \$120,000
$$

$$
\$200Q = \$320,000
$$

$$
Q = 1,600
$$

where

Q = sales volume
$\$500$ = selling price
$\$300$ = variable costs per unit
$\$200,000$ = total fixed costs
$\$120,000$ = target net income

The sales dollars required to achieve the target net income is found by multiplying the units sold by the unit selling price [(1,600 × $500) = $800,000].

Contribution Margin Technique

As in the case of break-even sales, the sales required to meet a target net income can be computed in either units or dollars. The formula to compute required sales in units for Vargo Video using the contribution margin per unit is as follows.

Illustration 5-24 Formula for required sales in units using contribution margin per unit

$$
\frac{\text{Fixed Costs} + \text{Target Net Income}} \div \text{Contribution Margin Per Unit} = \text{Required Sales in Units}
$$

$$
(\$200,000 + \$120,000) \div \$200 = 1,600 \text{ units}
$$

This computation tells Vargo that to achieve its desired target net income of $120,000, it must sell 1,600 DVD players.

The formula to compute the required sales in dollars for Vargo Video using the contribution margin ratio is as follows.

Fixed Costs + Target Net Income	÷	Contribution Margin Ratio	=	Required Sales in Dollars
($200,000 + $120,000)	÷	40%	=	$800,000

Illustration 5-25 Formula for required sales in dollars using contribution margin ratio

This computation tells Vargo that to achieve its desired target net income of $120,000, it must generate sales of $800,000.

Graphic Presentation

The CVP graph in Illustration 5-21 (on page 204) can also be used to find the sales required to meet target net income. In the profit area of the graph, the distance between the sales line and the total cost line at any point equals net income. Required sales are found by analyzing the differences between the two lines until the desired net income is found.

For example, suppose Vargo Video sells 1,400 DVD players. Illustration 5-21 shows that a vertical line drawn at 1,400 units intersects the sales line at $700,000 and the total cost line at $620,000. The difference between the two amounts represents the net income (profit) of $80,000.

MARGIN OF SAFETY

The margin of safety is another relationship that may be calculated in CVP analysis. **Margin of safety** is the difference between actual or expected sales and sales at the break-even point. This relationship measures the "cushion" that management has, allowing it to still break even if expected sales fail to materialize. The margin of safety may be expressed in dollars or as a ratio.

The formula for stating the **margin of safety in dollars** is actual (or expected) sales minus break-even sales. Assuming that actual (expected) sales for Vargo Video are $750,000, the computation is:

> **STUDY OBJECTIVE**
> ─────── 8 ───────
> Define margin of safety, and give the formulas for computing it.

Actual (Expected) Sales	−	Break-even Sales	=	Margin of Safety in Dollars
$750,000	−	$500,000	=	$250,000

Illustration 5-26 Formula for margin of safety in dollars

This means that the company's sales could fall by $250,000 before it would be operating at a loss.

The **margin of safety ratio** is computed by dividing the margin of safety in dollars by actual (or expected) sales. The formula and computation for determining the margin of safety ratio are:

Margin of Safety in Dollars	÷	Actual (Expected) Sales	=	Margin of Safety Ratio
$250,000	÷	$750,000	=	33%

Illustration 5-27 Formula for margin of safety ratio

This means that the company's sales could fall by 33 percent before it would be operating at a loss.

The higher the dollars or the percentage, the greater the margin of safety. Management should evaluate the adequacy of the margin of safety in terms of such factors as the vulnerability of the product to competitive pressures and to downturns in the economy.

Business Insight
Service Company Perspective

Computation of break-even and margin of safety is important for service companies as well. Consider how the promoter for the Rolling Stones' tour used the break-even point and margin of safety. For example, one outdoor show should bring 70,000 individuals for a gross of $2.45 million. The promoter guarantees $1.2 million to the Rolling Stones. In addition, 20 percent of gross, or approximately $500,000, goes to the stadium in which the performance is staged. Add another $400,000 for other expenses such as ticket takers, parking attendants, advertising, and so on. This leaves $350,000 to the promoter per show, if it sells out. At 75 percent, the promoter breaks about even. At 50 percent, the promoter loses hundreds of thousands of dollars. However, the promoter also shares in sales of T-shirts and memorabilia for which the promoter will net over $7 million during the tour. From a successful Rolling Stones' tour, the promoter could make $35 million!

CVP AND CHANGES IN THE BUSINESS ENVIRONMENT

When the **IBM** personal computer (PC) was introduced, it sold for $2,500. Today the same type of computer sells for much less. Recently, when oil prices rose, the break-even point for airline companies such as **American**, **Southwest**, and **United** rose dramatically. Because of lower prices for imported steel, the demand for domestic steel dropped significantly. The point should be clear: Business conditions change rapidly, and management must respond intelligently to these changes. CVP analysis can help.

To illustrate how CVP analysis can be used in responding to change, we will look at three independent situations that might occur at Vargo Video. Each case is based on the original DVD player sales and cost data, which were:

Illustration 5-28 Original DVD player sales and cost data

Unit selling price	$500
Unit variable cost	$300
Total fixed costs	$200,000
Break-even sales	$500,000 or 1,000 units

CASE 1. A competitor is offering a 10 percent discount on the selling price of its DVD players. Management must decide whether to offer a similar discount. **Question**: What effect will a 10 percent discount on selling price have on the break-even point for DVD players? **Answer**: A 10 percent discount on selling price reduces the selling price per unit to $450 [$500 − ($500 × 10%)]. Variable costs per unit remain unchanged at $300. Thus, the contribution margin per unit is $150. Assuming no change in fixed costs, break-even sales are 1,333 units, computed as follows.

Fixed Costs	÷	Contribution Margin per Unit	=	Break-even Sales
$200,000	÷	$150	=	1,333 units (rounded)

Illustration 5-29 Computation of break-even sales in units

For Vargo Video, this change would require monthly sales to increase by 333 units, or 33⅓ percent, in order to break even. In reaching a conclusion about offering a 10 percent discount to customers, management must determine how likely it is to achieve the increased sales. Also, management should estimate the possible loss of sales if the competitor's discount price is not matched.

CASE II. To meet the threat of foreign competition, management invests in new robotic equipment that will lower the amount of direct labor required to make DVD players. It is estimated that total fixed costs will increase 30 percent and that variable cost per unit will decrease 30 percent. **Question**: What effect will the new equipment have on the sales volume required to break even? **Answer**: Total fixed costs become $260,000 [$200,000 + (30% × $200,000)]. The variable cost per unit becomes $210 [$300 − (30% × $300)]. The new break-even point is approximately 900 units, computed as follows.

Fixed Costs	÷	Contribution Margin per Unit	=	Break-even Sales
$260,000	÷	($500 − $210)	=	900 units (rounded)

Illustration 5-30 Computation of break-even sales in units

These changes appear to be advantageous for Vargo Video. The break-even point is reduced by 10 percent, or 100 units.

CASE III. Vargo's principal supplier of raw materials has just announced a price increase. The higher cost is expected to increase the variable cost of DVD players by $25 per unit. Management would like to hold the line on the selling price of the DVD players. It plans a cost-cutting program that will save $17,500 in fixed costs per month. Vargo is currently realizing monthly net income of $80,000 on sales of 1,400 DVD players. **Question**: What increase in units sold will be needed to maintain the same level of net income? **Answer**: The variable cost per unit increases to $325 ($300 + $25). Fixed costs are reduced to $182,500 ($200,000 − $17,500). Because of the change in variable cost, the contribution margin per unit becomes $175 ($500 − $325). The required number of units sold to achieve the target net income is computed as follows.

Fixed Costs + Target Net Income	÷	Contribution Margin per Unit	=	Required Sales in Units
($182,500 + $80,000)	÷	$175	=	1,500

Illustration 5-31 Computation of required sales

To achieve the required sales, 1,500 DVD players will have to be sold, an increase of 100 units. If this does not seem to be a reasonable expectation, management will either have to make further cost reductions or accept less net income if the selling price remains unchanged.

Business Insight
e-Business Perspective

When analyzing an Internet business, the so-called "conversion rate" is closely watched. It is calculated by dividing the number of people who actually take action at an Internet site (e.g., buy something) by the total number of people who visit the site. Average conversion rates are from 3 to 5 percent. A rate below 2 percent is poor, while a rate above 10 percent is great.

Conversion rates have an obvious effect on break-even point. Suppose you spend $10,000 on your site, and you attract 5,000 visitors. If you get a 2 percent conversion rate (100 purchases), your site costs $100 per purchase ($10,000 ÷ 100). A 4 percent conversion rate gets you down to a cost of $50 per transaction, and an 8 percent conversion rate gets you down to $25. Studies have shown that conversion rates increase if the site has an easy-to-use interface, fast-performing screens, a convenient ordering process, and advertising that is both clever and clear.

SOURCE: J. William Gurley, "The One Internet Metric That Really Counts," *Fortune* (March 6, 2000), p. 392.

DECISION TOOLKIT

Decision Checkpoints	Info Needed for Decision	Tool to Use for Decision	How to Evaluate Results
How can a company use CVP analysis to improve profitability?	Data on what effect a price change, a fixed-cost change, or a trade-off between fixed and variable costs would have on volume and costs	Measurement of income at new volume levels	If profitability increases under proposed change, adopt change.

BEFORE YOU GO ON . . .

▶**Review It**

1. What is the formula for computing the margin of safety (a) in dollars and (b) as a ratio?
2. What is the equation to compute target net income?

✓ THE NAVIGATOR

Using the Decision Toolkit

B.T. Hernandez Company, maker of high-quality flashlights, has experienced steady growth over the last 6 years. However, increased competition has led Mr. Hernandez, the president, to believe that an aggressive campaign is needed next year to maintain the company's present growth. The company's accountant has presented Mr. Hernandez with the following data for the current year, 2005, for use in preparing next year's advertising campaign.

Cost Schedules

Variable costs	
Direct labor per flashlight	$ 8.00
Direct materials	4.00
Variable overhead	3.00
Variable cost per flashlight	$15.00

Fixed costs		
Manufacturing		$ 25,000
Selling		40,000
Administrative		70,000
Total fixed costs		$135,000
Selling price per flashlight		$ 25.00
Expected sales, 2005 (20,000 flashlights)		$500,000

Mr. Hernandez has set the sales target for the year 2006 at a level of $550,000 (22,000 flashlights).

Instructions

(Ignore any income tax considerations.)

(a) What is the projected operating income for 2005?

(b) What is the contribution margin per unit for 2005?

(c) What is the break-even point in units for 2005?

(d) Mr. Hernandez believes that to attain the sales target in the year 2006, the company must incur an additional selling expense of $10,000 for advertising in 2006, with all other costs remaining constant. What will be the break-even point in dollar sales for 2006 if the company spends the additional $10,000?

(e) If the company spends the additional $10,000 for advertising in 2006, what is the sales level in dollars required to equal 2005 operating income?

Solution

(a)

Expected sales		$500,000
Less:		
Variable cost (20,000 flashlights × $15)		300,000
Fixed costs		135,000
Projected operating income		$ 65,000

(b)

Selling price per flashlight	$25
Variable cost per flashlight	15
Contribution margin per unit	$10

(c) Fixed costs ÷ Contribution margin per unit = Break-even point in units
$135,000 ÷ $10 = 13,500 units

(d) Fixed costs ÷ Contribution margin ratio = Break-even point in dollars
$145,000 ÷ 40% = $362,500

Fixed costs (from 2005)	$135,000
Additional advertising expense	10,000
Fixed costs (2006)	$145,000

Contribution margin = Sales − Variable costs

Expected sales	$550,000
Variable costs (22,000 × $15)	330,000
Contribution margin	$220,000

Contribution margin ratio = Contribution margin ÷ Sales
40% = $220,000 ÷ $550,000

(e) Required sales = (Fixed costs + Target net income) ÷ Contribution margin ratio

$525,000 = ($145,000 + $65,000) ÷ 40%

☑ THE NAVIGATOR

Summary of Study Objectives

1 *Distinguish between variable and fixed costs.* Variable costs are costs that vary in total directly and proportionately with changes in the activity index. Fixed costs are costs that remain the same in total regardless of changes in the activity index.

2 *Explain the significance of the relevant range.* The relevant range is the range of activity in which a company expects to operate during a year. It is important in CVP analysis because the behavior of costs is assumed to be linear throughout the relevant range.

3 *Explain the concept of mixed costs.* Mixed costs increase in total but not proportionately with changes in the activity level. For purposes of CVP analysis, mixed costs must be classified into their fixed and variable elements. One method that management may use to classify these costs is the high-low method.

4 *List the five components of cost-volume-profit analysis.* The five components of CVP analysis are (a) volume or level of activity, (b) unit selling prices, (c) variable cost per unit, (d) total fixed costs, and (e) sales mix.

5 *Indicate what contribution margin is and how it can be expressed.* Contribution margin is the amount of revenue remaining after deducting variable costs. It is identified in a CVP income statement, which classifies

costs as variable or fixed. It can be expressed as a per unit amount or as a ratio.

6 *Identify the three ways to determine the break-even point.* The break-even point can be (a) computed from a mathematical equation, (b) computed by using a contribution margin technique, and (c) derived from a CVP graph.

7 *Give the formulas for determining sales required to earn target net income.* The general formula is: Required sales = Variable costs + Fixed costs + Target net income. Two other formulas are: Required sales in units = (Fixed costs + Target net income) ÷ Contribution margin per unit, and Required sales in dollars = (Fixed costs + Target net income) ÷ Contribution margin ratio.

8 *Define margin of safety, and give the formulas for computing it.* Margin of safety is the difference between actual or expected sales and sales at the break-even point. The formulas for margin of safety are: Actual (expected) sales − Break-even sales = Margin of safety in dollars; Margin of safety in dollars ÷ Actual (expected) sales = Margin of safety ratio.

DECISION TOOLKIT—A SUMMARY

Decision Checkpoints	Info Needed for Decision	Tool to Use for Decision	How to Evaluate Results
What was the contribution toward fixed costs and income from each unit sold?	Selling price per unit and variable cost per unit	$$\frac{\text{Contribution margin}}{\text{per unit}} = \frac{\text{Unit}}{\text{selling price}} - \frac{\text{Unit}}{\text{variable cost}}$$	Every unit sold will increase income by the contribution margin.
What was the increase in income as a result of an increase in sales?	Contribution margin per unit and unit selling price	$$\frac{\text{Contribution margin ratio}}{} = \frac{\text{Contribution margin per unit}}{} \div \frac{\text{Unit selling price}}{}$$	Every dollar of sales will increase income by the contribution margin ratio.
At what amount of sales does a company cover its costs?	Unit selling price, unit variable cost, and total fixed costs	Break-even point analysis *In units:* $$\frac{\text{Break-even point}}{} = \frac{\text{Fixed costs}}{\text{Unit contribution margin}}$$ *In dollars:* $$\frac{\text{Break-even point}}{} = \frac{\text{Fixed costs}}{\text{Contribution margin ratio}}$$	Below the break-even point, the company is unprofitable.
How can a company use CVP analysis to improve profitability?	Data on what effect a price change, a fixed-cost change, or a trade-off between fixed and variable costs would have on volume and costs	Measurement of income at new volume levels	If profitability increases under proposed change, adopt change.

Glossary

Activity index   The activity that causes changes in the behavior of costs. (p. 191)

Break-even point   The level of activity at which total revenues equal total costs. (p. 202)

Contribution margin (CM)   The amount of revenue remaining after deducting variable costs. (p. 199)

Contribution margin per unit   The amount of revenue remaining per unit after deducting variable costs; calculated as unit selling price minus unit variable cost. (p. 200)

Contribution margin ratio   The percentage of each dollar of sales that is available to apply to fixed costs and to contribute to net income; calculated as contribution margin per unit divided by unit selling price. (p. 201)

Cost behavior analysis   The study of how specific costs respond to changes in the level of business activity. (p. 191)

Cost-volume-profit (CVP) analysis   The study of the effects of changes in costs and volume on a company's profits. (p. 198)

Cost-volume-profit (CVP) graph   A graph showing the relationship between costs, volume, and profits. (p. 203)

Cost-volume-profit (CVP) income statement   A statement for internal use that classifies costs as fixed or variable and reports contribution margin in the body of the statement. (p. 199)

Fixed costs   Costs that remain the same in total regardless of changes in the activity level. (p. 192)

High-low method   A mathematical method that uses the total costs incurred at the high and low levels of activity to classify mixed costs into fixed and variable components. (p. 196)

Margin of safety   The difference between actual or expected sales and sales at the break-even point. (p. 207)

Mixed costs   Costs that contain both a variable and a fixed cost element and change in total but not proportionately with changes in the activity level. (p. 195)

Relevant range   The range of the activity index over which the company expects to operate during the year. (p. 194)

Target net income   The income objective for individual product lines. (p. 206)

Variable costs   Costs that vary in total directly and proportionately with changes in the activity level. (p. 192)

Demonstration Problem

Mabo Company makes calculators that sell for $20 each. For the coming year, management expects fixed costs to total $220,000 and variable costs to be $9 per unit.

Instructions
(a) Compute break-even point in units using the mathematical equation.
(b) Compute break-even point in dollars using the contribution margin (CM) ratio.
(c) Compute the margin of safety percentage assuming actual sales are $500,000.
(d) Compute the sales required in dollars to earn net income of $165,000 using the mathematical equation.

Solution to Demonstration Problem

(a) Sales = Variable costs + Fixed costs + Net income
  $\$20Q = \$9Q + \$220{,}000 + \$0$
  $\$11Q = \$220{,}000$
    $Q = 20{,}000$ units

(b) Contribution margin per unit = Unit selling price − Unit variable costs
        $\$11 = \$20 − \$9$
   Contribution margin ratio = Contribution margin per unit ÷ Unit selling price
         $55\% = \$11 ÷ \$20$
   Break-even point in dollars = Fixed cost ÷ Contribution margin ratio
            $= \$220{,}000 ÷ 55\%$
            $= \$400{,}000$

Action Plan
- Know the formulas.
- Recognize that variable costs change with sales volume; fixed costs do not.
- Avoid computational errors.

(c) Margin of safety = $\dfrac{\text{Actual sales} - \text{Break-even sales}}{\text{Actual sales}}$

$$= \dfrac{\$500,000 - \$400,000}{\$500,000}$$

$$= 20\%$$

(d) Required sales = Variable costs + Fixed costs + Net income

$$\$20Q = \$9Q + \$220,000 + \$165,000$$
$$\$11Q = \$385,000$$
$$Q = 35,000 \text{ units}$$
$$35,000 \text{ units} \times \$20 = \$700,000 \text{ required sales}$$

Self-Study Questions

Self-Study/Self-Test

Answers are at the end of the chapter.

(SO 1) 1. Variable costs are costs that:
   (a) vary in total directly and proportionately with changes in the activity level.
   (b) remain the same per unit at every activity level.
   (c) Neither of the above.
   (d) Both (a) and (b) above.

(SO 2) 2. The relevant range is:
   (a) the range of activity in which variable costs will be curvilinear.
   (b) the range of activity in which fixed costs will be curvilinear.
   (c) the range over which the company expects to operate during a year.
   (d) usually from zero to 100% of operating capacity.

(SO 3) 3. Mixed costs consist of a:
   (a) variable cost element and a fixed cost element.
   (b) fixed cost element and a controllable cost element.
   (c) relevant cost element and a controllable cost element.
   (d) variable cost element and a relevant cost element.

(SO 3) 4. Kendra Corporation's total utility costs during the past year were $1,200 during its highest month and $600 during its lowest month. These costs corresponded with 10,000 units of production during the high month and 2,000 units during the low month. What are the fixed and variable components of its utility costs using the high-low method?
   (a) $0.075 variable and $450 fixed.
   (b) $0.120 variable and $0 fixed.
   (c) $0.300 variable and $0 fixed.
   (d) $0.060 variable and $600 fixed.

(SO 4) 5. One of the following is *not* involved in CVP analysis. That factor is:
   (a) sales mix.
   (b) unit selling prices.
   (c) fixed costs per unit.
   (d) volume or level of activity.

(SO 5) 6. Contribution margin:
   (a) is revenue remaining after deducting variable costs.
   (b) may be expressed as contribution margin per unit.
   (c) is selling price less cost of goods sold.
   (d) Both (a) and (b) above.

(SO 5) 7. Cournot Company sells 100,000 wrenches for $12 a unit. Fixed costs are $300,000, and net income is $200,000. What should be reported as variable expenses in the CVP income statement?
   (a) $700,000.   (c) $500,000.
   (b) $900,000.   (d) $1,000,000.

(SO 6) 8. Gossen Company is planning to sell 200,000 pliers for $4 per unit. The contribution margin ratio is 25%. If Gossen will break even at this level of sales, what are the fixed costs?
   (a) $100,000.   (c) $200,000.
   (b) $160,000.   (d) $300,000.

(SO 7) 9. Gabriel Corporation has fixed costs of $180,000 and variable costs of $8.50 per unit. It has a target income of $268,000. How many units must it sell at $12 per unit to achieve its target net income?
   (a) 51,429 units.   (c) 76,571 units.
   (b) 128,000 units.   (d) 21,176 units.

(SO 8) 10. Marshall Company had actual sales of $600,000 when break-even sales were $420,000. What is the margin of safety ratio?
   (a) 25%.   (c) 33⅓%.
   (b) 30%.   (d) 45%.

Questions

1. (a) What is cost behavior analysis?
   (b) Why is cost behavior analysis important to management?

2. (a) Jenny Beason asks your help in understanding the term "activity index." Explain the meaning and importance of this term for Jenny.
   (b) State the two ways that variable costs may be defined.

3. Contrast the effects of changes in the activity level on total fixed costs and on unit fixed costs.

4. E.L. Dion claims that the relevant range concept is important only for variable costs.
   (a) Explain the relevant range concept.
   (b) Do you agree with E.L.'s claim? Explain.

5. "The relevant range is indispensable in cost behavior analysis." Is this true? Why or why not?

6. Shawn Grace is confused. He does not understand why rent on his apartment is a fixed cost and rent on a Hertz rental truck is a mixed cost. Explain the difference to Shawn.

7. How should mixed costs be classified in CVP analysis? What approach is used to effect the appropriate classification?

8. At the high and low levels of activity during the month, direct labor hours are 90,000 and 40,000, respectively. The related costs are $185,000 and $100,000. What are the fixed and the unit variable costs at any level of activity?

9. "Cost-volume-profit (CVP) analysis is based entirely on unit data." Do you agree? Explain.

10. Andrea Dubois defines contribution margin as the amount of profit available to cover operating expenses. Is there any truth in this definition? Discuss.

11. The traditional income statement for Rice Company shows sales $900,000, cost of goods sold $500,000, and operating expenses $200,000. Assuming all costs and expenses are 70% variable and 30% fixed, prepare a CVP income statement through contribution margin.

12. Darosa Company's Speedo pocket calculator sells for $40. Variable costs per unit are estimated to be $25. What are the contribution margin per unit and the contribution margin ratio?

13. "Break-even analysis is of limited use to management because a company cannot survive by just breaking even." Do you agree? Explain.

14. Total fixed costs are $22,000 for Forrest Inc. It has a contribution margin per unit of $15, and a contribution margin ratio of 25%. Compute the break-even sales in dollars.

15. Luz Foly asks your help in constructing a CVP graph. Explain to Luz (a) how the break-even point is plotted, and (b) how the level of activity and dollar sales at the break-even point are determined.

16. Jain Company's break-even sales are $600,000. Assuming fixed costs are $240,000, what sales volume is needed to achieve a target net income of $60,000?

17. Define the term "margin of safety." If Harold Company expects to sell 1,600 units of its product at $12 per unit, and break-even sales for the product are $13,440, what is the margin of safety ratio?

Brief Exercises

BE5-1 Monthly production costs in Ogden Company for two levels of production are as follows.

Classify costs as variable, fixed, or mixed.
(SO 1, 3)

Cost	2,000 units	4,000 units
Indirect labor	$10,000	$20,000
Supervisory salaries	5,000	5,000
Maintenance	2,500	4,000

Indicate which costs are variable, fixed, and mixed, and give the reason for each answer.

BE5-2 For Leahy Company, the relevant range of production is 40–80% of capacity. At 40% of capacity, a variable cost is $2,000 and a fixed cost is $5,000. Diagram the behavior of each cost within the relevant range assuming the behavior is linear.

Diagram the behavior of costs within the relevant range.
(SO 2)

BE5-3 For Stork Company, a mixed cost is $40,000 plus $6 per direct labor hour. Diagram the behavior of the cost using increments of 1,000 hours up to 5,000 hours on the horizontal axis and increments of $10,000 up to $70,000 on the vertical axis.

Diagram the behavior of a mixed cost.
(SO 3)

Determine variable and fixed cost elements using the high-low method.
(SO 3)

BE5-4 Spitz Company accumulates the following data concerning a mixed cost, using miles as the activity level.

	Miles Driven	Total Cost		Miles Driven	Total Cost
January	8,000	$14,100	March	8,500	$15,000
February	7,500	13,500	April	8,200	14,400

Compute the variable and fixed cost elements using the high-low method.

Determine variable and fixed cost elements using the high-low method.
(SO 3)

BE5-5 Westerville Corp. has collected the following data concerning its maintenance costs for the past 6 months.

	Units produced	Total cost
July	18,000	$32,000
August	32,000	48,000
September	36,000	55,000
October	22,000	38,000
November	40,000	65,000
December	38,000	62,000

Compute the variable and fixed cost elements using the high-low method.

Determine missing amounts for contribution margin.
(SO 5)

BE5-6 Determine the missing amounts.

	Unit Selling Price	Unit Variable Costs	Contribution Margin per Unit	Contribution Margin Ratio
1.	$260	$160	(a)	(b)
2.	$500	(c)	$140	(d)
3.	(e)	(f)	$360	30%

Prepare CVP income statement.
(SO 5)

BE5-7 Fontillas Manufacturing Inc. has sales of $1,800,000 for the first quarter of 2005. In making the sales, the company incurred the following costs and expenses.

	Variable	Fixed
Cost of goods sold	$750,000	$540,000
Selling expenses	95,000	60,000
Administrative expenses	79,000	70,000

Prepare a CVP income statement for the quarter ended March 31, 2005.

Compute the break-even point.
(SO 6)

BE5-8 Lehi Company has a unit selling price of $400, variable costs per unit of $250, and fixed costs of $150,000. Compute the break-even point in units using (a) the mathematical equation and (b) contribution margin per unit.

Compute the break-even point.
(SO 6)

BE5-9 Wesland Corp. had total variable costs of $170,000, total fixed costs of $120,000, and total revenues of $250,000. Compute the required sales in dollars to break even.

Compute sales for target net income.
(SO 7)

BE5-10 For Biswell Company, variable costs are 75% of sales, and fixed costs are $180,000. Management's net income goal is $60,000. Compute the required sales in dollars needed to achieve management's target net income of $60,000. (Use the contribution margin approach.)

Compute the margin of safety and the margin of safety ratio.
(SO 8)

BE5-11 For Korb Company actual sales are $1,200,000 and break-even sales are $840,000. Compute (a) the margin of safety in dollars and (b) the margin of safety ratio.

Compute the required sales in units for target net income.
(SO 7)

BE5-12 PCB Corporation has fixed costs of $480,000. It has a unit selling price of $6, unit variable cost of $4.50, and a target net income of $1,500,000. Compute the required sales in units to achieve its target net income.

Exercises

E5-1   Fowler Company manufactures a single product. Annual production costs incurred in the manufacturing process are shown below for two levels of production.

Define and classify variable, fixed, and mixed costs.
(SO 1, 3)

	Costs Incurred			
Production in Units	**5,000**		**10,000**	
Production Costs	**Total Cost**	**Cost/ Unit**	**Total Cost**	**Cost/ Unit**
Direct materials	$8,250	$1.65	$16,500	$1.65
Direct labor	9,400	1.88	18,800	1.88
Utilities	1,400	0.28	2,300	0.23
Rent	4,000	0.80	4,000	0.40
Maintenance	800	0.16	1,200	0.12
Supervisory salaries	1,000	0.20	1,000	0.10

Instructions
(a) Define the terms variable costs, fixed costs, and mixed costs.
(b) Classify each cost above as either variable, fixed, or mixed.

E5-2   The owner/operator of Toledo Taxi Company is interested in determining the cost equation for his one-vehicle taxi service, based on the number of miles driven. To that end he has collected the following volume and cost data.

Determine fixed and variable costs using the high-low method and use cost equation.
(SO 1, 3)

Month	Total Operating Costs	Number of Miles Driven
July	$16,000	13,000
August	17,800	14,250
September	12,400	9,750
October	15,100	12,500
November	13,250	10,500
December	11,500	9,000

Instructions
(a) Use the high-low method to calculate the variable and fixed cost components.
(b) The owner feels that the maximum level of operating costs that the company can sustain, because of cash flow concerns, is $14,500. Determine the number of miles that correspond to that level of costs.

E5-3   The controller of Gutierrez Industries has collected the following monthly expense data for use in analyzing the cost behavior of maintenance costs.

Determine fixed and variable costs using the high-low method and prepare graph.
(SO 1, 3)

Month	Total Maintenance Costs	Total Machine Hours
January	$2,800	3,000
February	3,000	4,000
March	3,600	6,000
April	4,500	7,900
May	3,200	5,000
June	5,000	8,000

Instructions
(a) Determine the fixed and variable cost components using the high-low method.
(b) Prepare a graph showing the behavior of maintenance costs, and identify the fixed and variable cost elements. Use 2,000 unit increments and $1,000 cost increments.

Compute break-even point and margin of safety.
(SO 5, 6, 8)

E5-4 The San Marcos Inn is trying to determine its break-even point. The inn has 75 rooms that are rented at $50 a night. Operating costs are as follows.

Salaries	$8,500 per month
Utilities	2,000 per month
Depreciation	1,000 per month
Maintenance	500 per month
Maid service	5 per room
Other costs	33 per room

Instructions
(a) Determine the inn's break-even point in (1) number of rented rooms per month and (2) dollars.
(b) If the inn plans on renting an average of 50 rooms per day (assuming a 30-day month), what is (1) the monthly margin of safety in dollars and (2) the margin of safety ratio?

Compute variable cost per unit, contribution margin ratio, and increase in fixed costs.
(SO 5)

E5-5 In 2005, Demuth Company had a break-even point of $320,000 based on a selling price of $8 per unit and fixed costs of $140,000. In 2006, the selling price and the variable cost per unit did not change, but the break-even point increased to $450,000.

Instructions
(a) Compute the variable cost per unit and the contribution margin ratio for 2005.
(b) Compute the increase in fixed costs for 2006.

Compute contribution margin, break-even point, and margin of safety.
(SO 5, 6, 8)

E5-6 In the month of June, Angela's Beauty Salon gave 3,500 haircuts, shampoos, and permanents at an average price of $30. During the month, fixed costs were $16,800 and variable costs were 80% of sales.

Instructions
(a) Determine the contribution margin in dollars, per unit, and as a ratio.
(b) Using the contribution margin technique, compute the break-even point in dollars and in units.
(c) Compute the margin of safety in dollars and as a ratio.

Compute various components to derive target net income under different assumptions.
(SO 6, 7)

E5-7 Johansen Company had $150,000 of net income in 2005 when the selling price per unit was $150, the variable costs per unit were $100, and the fixed costs were $750,000. Management expects per unit data and total fixed costs to remain the same in 2006. The president of Johansen Company is under pressure from stockholders to increase net income by $90,000 in 2006.

Instructions
(a) Compute the number of units sold in 2005.
(b) Compute the number of units that would have to be sold in 2006 to reach the stockholders' desired profit level.
(c) Assume that Johansen Company sells the same number of units in 2006 as it did in 2005. What would the selling price have to be in order to reach the stockholders' desired profit level?

Compute net income under different alternatives.
(SO 8)

E5-8 Ger Company reports the following operating results for the month of August: Sales $300,000 (units 5,000); variable costs $210,000; and fixed costs $70,000. Management is considering the following independent courses of action to increase net income.

1. Increase selling price by 10% with no change in total variable costs.
2. Reduce variable costs to 58% of sales.
3. Reduce fixed costs by $20,000.

Instructions
Compute the net income to be earned under each alternative. Which course of action will produce the highest net income?

Compute break-even point and prepare CVP income statement.
(SO 5, 6, 8)

E5-9 Regional Airways, Inc., a small two-plane passenger airline, has asked for your assistance in some basic analysis of its operations. Both planes seat 10 passengers each, and they fly commuters from Regional's base airport to the major city in the state, Metropolis. Each month 40 round-trip flights are made. Shown on page 219 is a recent month's activity in the form of a cost-volume-profit income statement.

Fare revenues (300 fares)		$45,000
Variable costs		
Fuel	$14,000	
Snacks and drinks	800	
Landing fees	2,000	
Supplies and forms	1,200	18,000
Contribution margin		27,000
Fixed costs		
Depreciation	3,000	
Salaries	15,000	
Advertising	500	
Airport hanger fees	1,750	20,250
Net income		$ 6,750

Instructions
(a) Calculate the break-even point in (1) dollars and (2) number of fares.
(b) Without calculations, determine the contribution margin at the break-even point.
(c) If fares were decreased by 10%, an additional 100 fares could be generated. However, variable costs would increase by 35%. Should the fare decrease be adopted?

E5-10 Embleton Company estimates that variable costs will be 40% of sales, and fixed costs will total $900,000. The selling price of the product is $5.

Prepare a CVP graph and compute break-even point and margin of safety. (SO 6, 8)

Instructions
(a) Prepare a CVP graph, assuming maximum sales of $4,000,000. (*Note*: Use $500,000 increments for sales and costs and 100,000 increments for units.)
(b) Compute the break-even point in (1) units and (2) dollars.
(c) Compute the margin of safety in (1) dollars and (2) as a ratio, assuming actual sales are $2 million.

E5-11 Hall Company had sales in 2005 of $1,500,000 on 60,000 units. Variable costs totaled $720,000, and fixed costs totaled $400,000.

A new raw material is available that will decrease the variable costs per unit by 25% (or $3.00). However, to process the new raw material, fixed operating costs will increase by $150,000. Management feels that one-half of the decline in the variable costs per unit should be passed on to customers in the form of a sales price reduction. The marketing department expects that this sales price reduction will result in a 5% increase in the number of units sold.

Prepare a CVP income statement before and after changes in business environment. (SO 5)

Instructions
Prepare a CVP income statement for 2005, (a) assuming the changes have not been made, and (b) assuming that changes are made as described.

Problems: Set A

P5-1A The Peace Barber Shop employs four barbers. One barber, who also serves as the manager, is paid a salary of $1,800 per month. The other barbers are paid $1,300 per month. In addition, each barber is paid a commission of $4 per haircut. Other monthly costs are: store rent $800 plus 60 cents per haircut, depreciation on equipment $500, barber supplies 40 cents per haircut, utilities $300, and advertising $200. The price of a haircut is $11.

Determine variable and fixed costs, compute break-even point, prepare a CVP graph, and determine net income. (SO 1, 3, 5, 6)

Instructions
(a) Determine the variable cost per haircut and the total monthly fixed costs.
(b) Compute the break-even point in (1) units and (2) dollars.
(c) Prepare a CVP graph, assuming a maximum of 1,500 haircuts in a month. Use increments of 300 haircuts on the horizontal axis and $3,300 increments on the vertical axis.
(d) Determine the net income, assuming 1,500 haircuts are given in a month.

(a) VC $5

(d) NI $1,500

Prepare a CVP income statement, compute break-even point, contribution margin ratio, margin of safety ratio, and sales for target net income.
(SO 5, 6, 7, 8)

P5-2A Tyson Company bottles and distributes LO-KAL, a fruit drink. The beverage is sold for 50 cents per 16-ounce bottle to retailers, who charge customers 70 cents per bottle. Management estimates the following revenues and costs.

Net sales	$2,500,000	Selling expenses—variable	$ 90,000
Direct materials	360,000	Selling expenses—fixed	200,000
Direct labor	650,000	Administrative expenses—	
Manufacturing overhead—		variable	30,000
variable	370,000	Administrative expenses—	
Manufacturing overhead—		fixed	140,000
fixed	260,000		

Instructions
(a) Compute (1) the contribution margin and (2) the fixed costs.
(b) Compute the break-even point in (1) units and (2) dollars.
(c) Compute the contribution margin ratio and the margin of safety ratio.
(d) Determine the sales dollars required to earn net income of $240,000.

(b) 3,000,000 units

Compute break-even point under alternative courses of action.
(SO 5, 6)

P5-3A Cruz Manufacturing had a bad year in 2005. For the first time in its history it operated at a loss. The company's income statement showed the following results from selling 80,000 units of product: Net sales $1,600,000; total costs and expenses $1,740,000; and net loss $140,000. Costs and expenses consisted of the following.

	Total	Variable	Fixed
Cost of goods sold	$1,200,000	$780,000	$420,000
Selling expenses	420,000	75,000	345,000
Administrative expenses	120,000	45,000	75,000
	$1,740,000	$900,000	$840,000

Management is considering the following independent alternatives for 2006.

1. Increase unit selling price 25% with no change in costs and expenses.
2. Change the compensation of salespersons from fixed annual salaries totaling $200,000 to total salaries of $40,000 plus a 5% commission on net sales.
3. Purchase new high-tech factory machinery that will change the proportion between variable and fixed cost of goods sold to 50:50.

Instructions
(a) Compute the break-even point in dollars for 2005.
(b) Compute the break-even point in dollars under each of the alternative courses of action. (Round to the nearest dollar.) Which course of action do you recommend?

(b) (2) $1,754,839

Compute break-even point and margin of safety ratio, and prepare a CVP income statement before and after changes in business environment.
(SO 5, 6, 7, 8)

P5-4A Lois Baiser is the advertising manager for Value Shoe Store. She is currently working on a major promotional campaign. Her ideas include the installation of a new lighting system and increased display space that will add $27,000 in fixed costs to the $225,000 currently spent. In addition, Lois is proposing that a 6⅔% price decrease (from $30 to $28) will produce an increase in sales volume from 17,000 to 20,000 units. Variable costs will remain at $10 per pair of shoes. Management is impressed with Lois's ideas but concerned about the effects that these changes will have on the break-even point and the margin of safety.

Instructions
(a) Compute the current break-even point in units, and compare it to the break-even point in units if Lois's ideas are used.
(b) Compute the margin of safety ratio for current operations and after Lois's changes are introduced. (Round to nearest full percent.)
(c) Prepare a CVP income statement for current operations and after Lois's changes are introduced. Would you make the changes suggested?

(b) current 34%
new 30%

Compute break-even point and margin of safety ratio, and prepare a CVP income statement before and after changes in business environment.
(SO 5, 6, 7, 8)

P5-5A Poole Corporation has collected the following information after its first year of sales. Net sales were $1,600,000 on 100,000 units; selling expenses $240,000 (40% variable and 60% fixed); direct materials $511,000; direct labor $285,000; administrative expenses $280,000 (20% variable and 80% fixed); manufacturing overhead $360,000 (70% variable and 30% fixed). Top management has asked you to do a CVP analysis so that it can make plans for the coming year. It has projected that unit sales will increase by 10% next year.

Instructions

(a) Compute (1) the contribution margin for the current year and the projected year, and (2) the fixed costs for the current year. (Assume that fixed costs will remain the same in the projected year.)

(b) Compute the break-even point in units and sales dollars.

(c) The company has a target net income of $310,000. What is the required sales in dollars for the company to meet its target?

(d) If the company meets its target net income number, by what percentage could its sales fall before it is operating at a loss? That is, what is its margin of safety ratio?

(e) The company is considering a purchase of equipment that would reduce its direct labor costs by $104,000 and would change its manufacturing overhead costs to 30% variable and 70% fixed (assume total manufacturing overhead cost is $360,000, as above). It is also considering switching to a pure commission basis for its sales staff. This would change selling expenses to 90% variable and 10% fixed (assume total selling expense is $240,000, as above). Compute (1) the contribution margin and (2) the contribution margin ratio, and recompute (3) the break-even point in sales dollars. Comment on the effect each of management's proposed changes has on the break-even point.

Problems: Set B

P5-1B   Hung Van owns the College Barber Shop. He employs five barbers and pays each a base rate of $1,200 per month. One of the barbers serves as the manager and receives an extra $600 per month. In addition to the base rate, each barber also receives a commission of $3.50 per haircut.

Determine variable and fixed costs, compute break-even point, prepare a CVP graph, and determine net income.
(SO 1, 3, 5, 6)

Other costs are as follows.

Advertising	$200 per month
Rent	$1,000 per month
Barber supplies	$0.30 per haircut
Utilities	$175 per month plus $0.20 per haircut
Magazines	$25 per month

Hung currently charges $12 per haircut.

Instructions

(a) Determine the variable cost per haircut and the total monthly fixed costs.

(b) Compute the break-even point in (1) units and (2) dollars.

(c) Prepare a CVP graph, assuming a maximum of 2,000 haircuts in a month. Use increments of 400 haircuts on the horizontal axis and $4,000 on the vertical axis.

(d) Determine net income, assuming 1,500 haircuts are given in a month.

P5-2B   Corbin Company bottles and distributes NO-KAL, a diet soft drink. The beverage is sold for 40 cents per 16-ounce bottle to retailers, who charge customers 60 cents per bottle. Management estimates the following revenues and costs.

Prepare a CVP income statement, compute break-even point, contribution margin ratio, margin of safety ratio, and sales for target net income.
(SO 5, 6, 7, 8)

Net sales	$1,500,000	Selling expenses—variable	$80,000
Direct materials	400,000	Selling expenses—fixed	65,000
Direct labor	250,000	Administrative expenses—	
Manufacturing overhead—		variable	20,000
variable	300,000	Administrative expenses—	
Manufacturing overhead—		fixed	52,000
fixed	93,000		

Instructions

(a) Compute (1) the contribution margin and (2) the fixed costs.

(b) Compute the break-even point in (1) units and (2) dollars.

(c) Compute the contribution margin ratio and the margin of safety ratio. (Round to full percents.)

(d) Determine the sales dollars required to earn net income of $120,000.

Compute break-even point under alternative courses of action.
(SO 5, 6)

P5-3B   Griffey Manufacturing's sales slumped badly in 2005. For the first time in its history, it operated at a loss. The company's income statement showed the following results from selling 500,000 units of product: Net sales $2,500,000; total costs and expenses $2,600,000; and net loss $100,000. Costs and expenses consisted of the following.

	Total	Variable	Fixed
Cost of goods sold	$2,100,000	$1,440,000	$ 660,000
Selling expenses	300,000	72,000	228,000
Administrative expenses	200,000	48,000	152,000
	$2,600,000	$1,560,000	$1,040,000

Management is considering the following independent alternatives for 2006.

1. Increase unit selling price 20% with no change in costs and expenses.
2. Change the compensation of salespersons from fixed annual salaries totaling $210,000 to total salaries of $70,000 plus a 4% commission on net sales.
3. Purchase new automated equipment that will change the proportion between variable and fixed cost of goods sold to 60% variable and 40% fixed.

Instructions
(a) Compute the break-even point in dollars for 2005.

(b) (1) $2,166,667

(b) Compute the break-even point in dollars under each of the alternative courses of action. (Round to the nearest dollar.) Which course of action do you recommend?

Compute break-even point and margin of safety ratio, and prepare a CVP income statement before and after changes in business environment.
(SO 5, 6)

P5-4B Barb Tsai is the advertising manager for Thrifty Shoe Store. She is currently working on a major promotional campaign. Her ideas include the installation of a new lighting system and increased display space that will add $25,000 in fixed costs to the $300,000 currently spent. In addition, Barb is proposing that a 5% price decrease ($40 to $38) will produce a 20% increase in sales volume (30,000 to 36,000). Variable costs will remain at $25 per pair of shoes. Management is impressed with Barb's ideas but concerned about the effects that these changes will have on the break-even point and the margin of safety.

Instructions
(a) Compute the current break-even point in units, and compare it to the break-even point in units if Barb's ideas are used.

(b) current 33%
    new 31%

(b) Compute the margin of safety ratio for current operations and after Barb's changes are introduced. (Round to nearest full percent.)
(c) Prepare a CVP income statement for current operations and after Barb's changes are introduced. Would you make the changes suggested?

Compute break-even point and margin of safety ratio, and prepare a CVP income statement before and after changes in business environment.
(SO 5, 6, 7, 8)

P5-5B Washington Corporation has collected the following information after its first year of sales. Net sales were $2,400,000 on 200,000 units; selling expenses $360,000 (30% variable and 70% fixed); direct materials $626,500; direct labor $507,500; administrative expenses $420,000 (40% variable and 60% fixed); manufacturing overhead $540,000 (50% variable and 50% fixed). Top management has asked you to do a CVP analysis so that it can make plans for the coming year. It has projected that unit sales will increase by 20% next year.

Instructions
(a) Compute (1) the contribution margin for the current year and the projected year, and (2) the fixed costs for the current year. (Assume that fixed costs will remain the same in the projected year.)

(b) 215,000 units

(b) Compute the break-even point in units and sales dollars.
(c) The company has a target net income of $620,000. What is the required sales in dollars for the company to meet its target?
(d) If the company meets its target net income number, by what percentage could its sales fall before it is operating at a loss? That is, what is its margin of safety ratio?

(e) (3) $1,897,297

(e) The company is considering a purchase of equipment that would reduce its direct labor costs by $240,000 and would change its manufacturing overhead costs to 30% variable and 70% fixed (assume total manufacturing overhead cost is $540,000, as above). It is also considering switching to a pure commission basis for its sales staff. This would change selling expenses to 80% variable and 20% fixed (assume total selling expense is $360,000, as above). Compute (1) the contribution margin and (2) the contribution margin ratio, and recompute (3) the break-even point in sales dollars. Comment on the effect each of management's proposed changes has on the break-even point.

Problems: Set C

Problem Set C is provided at the book's Web site, www.wiley.com/college/weygandt.

▷ BROADENING YOUR PERSPECTIVE

Group Decision Case

BYP 5-1   Clay Company has decided to introduce a new product. The new product can be manufactured by either a capital-intensive method or a labor-intensive method. The manufacturing method will not affect the quality of the product. The estimated manufacturing costs by the two methods are as follows.

	Capital-Intensive	Labor-Intensive
Direct materials	$5 per unit	$5.50 per unit
Direct labor	$6 per unit	$7.20 per unit
Variable overhead	$3 per unit	$4.80 per unit
Fixed manufacturing costs	$2,440,000	$1,390,000

Clay's market research department has recommended an introductory unit sales price of $30. The incremental selling expenses are estimated to be $500,000 annually plus $2 for each unit sold, regardless of manufacturing method.

Instructions
With the class divided into groups, answer the following.
(a) Calculate the estimated break-even point in annual unit sales of the new product if Clay Company uses the:
   (1) capital-intensive manufacturing method.
   (2) labor-intensive manufacturing method.
(b) Determine the annual unit sales volume at which Clay Company would be indifferent between the two manufacturing methods.
(c) Explain the circumstance under which Clay should employ each of the two manufacturing methods.

(CMA adapted)

Managerial Analysis

BYP 5-2   The condensed income statement for the Phan and Nguyen partnership for 2005 is as follows.

PHAN AND NGUYEN COMPANY
Income Statement
For the Year Ended December 31, 2005

Sales (200,000 units)		$1,200,000
Cost of goods sold		800,000
Gross profit		400,000
Operating expenses		
Selling	$320,000	
Administrative	160,000	480,000
Net loss		($80,000)

A cost behavior analysis indicates that 75% of the cost of goods sold are variable, 50% of the selling expenses are variable, and 25% of the administrative expenses are variable.

Instructions

(Round to nearest unit, dollar, and percentage, where necessary.)

(a) Compute the break-even point in units and in total sales dollars for 2005.

(b) Phan has proposed a plan to get the partnership "out of the red" and improve its profitability. She feels that the quality of the product could be substantially improved by spending $0.55 more per unit on better raw materials. The selling price per unit could be increased to only $6.50 because of competitive pressures. Phan estimates that sales volume will increase by 30%. What effect would Phan's plan have on the profits and the break-even point in dollars of the partnership?

(c) Nguyen was a marketing major in college. He believes that sales volume can be increased only by intensive advertising and promotional campaigns. He therefore proposed the following plan as an alternative to Phan's. (1) Increase variable selling expenses to $0.85 per unit, (2) lower the selling price per unit by $0.20, and (3) increase fixed selling expenses by $20,000. Nguyen quoted an old marketing research report that said that sales volume would increase by 50% if these changes were made. What effect would Nguyen's plan have on the profits and the break-even point in dollars of the partnership?

(d) Which plan should be accepted? Explain your answer.

Real-World Focus

BYP 5-3 The **Coca-Cola Company** hardly needs an introduction. A line taken from the cover of a recent annual report says it all: If you measured time in servings of Coca-Cola, "a billion Coca-Cola's ago was yesterday morning." On average, every U.S. citizen drinks 363 8-ounce servings of Coca-Cola products each year. Coca-Cola's primary line of business is the making and selling of syrup to bottlers. These bottlers then sell the finished bottles and cans of Coca-Cola to the consumer.

In the annual report of Coca-Cola, the following information was provided.

THE COCA-COLA COMPANY
Management Discussion

Our gross margin declined to 61 percent this year from 62 percent in the prior year, primarily due to costs for materials such as sweeteners and packaging.

The increases [in selling expenses] in the last two years were primarily due to higher marketing expenditures in support of our Company's volume growth.

We measure our sales volume in two ways: (1) gallon shipments of concentrates and syrups and (2) unit cases of finished product (bottles and cans of Coke sold by bottlers).

Instructions

Answer the following questions.

(a) Are sweeteners and packaging a variable cost or a fixed cost? What is the impact on the contribution margin of an increase in the per unit cost of sweeteners or packaging? What are the implications for profitability?

(b) In your opinion, are marketing expenditures a fixed cost, variable cost, or mixed cost to The Coca-Cola Company? Give justification for your answer.

(c) Which of the two measures cited for measuring volume represents the activity index as defined in this chapter? Why might Coca-Cola use two different measures?

Exploring the Web

BYP 5-4   Ganong Bros. Ltd., located in St. Stephen, New Brunswick, is Canada's oldest independent candy company. Its products are distributed worldwide. In 1885, Ganong invented the popular "chicken bone," a cinnamon flavored, pink, hard candy jacket over a chocolate center. The home page of Ganong, listed below, includes information about the company and its products.

Address: www.ganong.com/index.cfm?section=3&page=10
            ***(or go to* www.wiley.com/college/weygandt)**

Instructions
Read the description of "chicken bones," and answer the following.
(a) Describe the steps in making "chicken bones."
(b) Identify at least two variable and two fixed costs that are likely to affect the production of "chicken bones."

Communication Activity

BYP 5-5   Your roommate asks your help on the following questions about CVP analysis formulas.
(a) How can the mathematical equation for break-even sales show both sales units and sales dollars?
(b) How do the formulas differ for contribution margin per unit and contribution margin ratio?
(c) How can contribution margin be used to determine break-even sales in units and in dollars?

Instructions
Write a memo to your roommate stating the relevant formulas and answering each question.

Research Assignment

BYP 5-6   The June 2, 2003, issue of the *Wall Street Journal* includes an article by Anna Wilde Mathews and Jennifer Ordonez titled "Clear Channel Revamps Its Concert Strategy."

Instructions
Read the article and answer the following questions.
(a) The article notes that Clear Channel cut performer Peter Gabriel's upfront per concert fee in half (from $600,000 down to approximately $300,000). Discuss the impact this change would have on the company's cost structure.
(b) Clear Channel also cut the average ticket price of the Peter Gabriel shows from $91 to $43. This will increase the number of tickets the company must sell to break-even. Why might it be desirable for Clear Channel to lower its ticket price?
(c) Clear Channel owns many of the arenas and amphitheatres that it books concerts in. How does this impact its cost structure and its corporate strategy?
(d) Why did Clear Channel choose not to book some "big-name" acts in the current year that it did book in the past?

Ethics Case

BYP 5-7   Ronnie Drake is an accountant for Benson Company. Early this year Ronnie made a highly favorable projection of sales and profits over the next 3 years for Benson's hot-selling computer PLEX. As a result of the projections Ronnie presented to senior management, they decided to expand production in this area. This decision led to dislocations of some plant personnel who were reassigned to one of the company's newer plants in another state. However, no one was fired, and in fact the company expanded its work force slightly.

Unfortunately, Ronnie rechecked his computations on the projections a few months later and found that he had made an error that would have reduced his projections substantially. Luckily, sales of PLEX have exceeded projections so far, and management is satisfied with its decision. Ronnie, however, is not sure what to do. Should he confess his honest mistake and jeopardize his possible promotion? He suspects that no one will catch the error because sales of PLEX have exceeded his projections, and it appears that profits will materialize close to his projections.

Instructions

(a) Who are the stakeholders in this situation?

(b) Identify the ethical issues involved in this situation.

(c) What are the possible alternative actions for Ronnie? What would you do in Ronnie's position?

Answers to Self-Study Questions

1. d   2. c   3. a   4. a   5. c   6. d   7. a   8. c   9. b   10. b

Remember to go back to the Navigator box on the chapter-opening page and check off your completed work.

CHAPTER 6

Incremental Analysis

After studying this chapter, you should be able to:

1 Identify the steps in management's decision-making process.

2 Describe the concept of incremental analysis.

3 Identify the relevant costs in accepting an order at a special price.

4 Identify the relevant costs in a make-or-buy decision.

5 Identify the relevant costs in determining whether to sell or process materials further.

6 Identify the relevant costs to be considered in retaining or replacing equipment.

7 Identify the relevant costs in deciding whether to eliminate an unprofitable segment.

8 Determine sales mix when a company has limited resources.

THE NAVIGATOR

THE NAVIGATOR ✔

▶ Scan *Study Objectives* ☐

▶ Read *Feature Story* ☐

▶ Read *Preview* ☐

▶ Read text and answer *Before You Go On*
      p. 240 ☐   p. 243 ☐

▶ Work *Using the Decision Toolkit* ☐

▶ Review *Summary of Study Objectives* ☐

▶ Work *Demonstration Problem* ☐

▶ Answer *Self-Study Questions* ☐

▶ Complete *Assignments* ☐

Make It or Buy It?

When is a manufacturer not a manufacturer? When it outsources. An extension of the classic "make or buy" decision, outsourcing involves hiring other companies to make all or part of a product or to perform services. Who is outsourcing? **Nike**, **General Motors**, **Sara Lee**, and **Hewlett-Packard**, to name a few. Even a recent trade journal article for small cabinet makers outlined the pros and cons of building cabinet doors and drawers internally, or outsourcing them to other shops.

Gibson Greetings, Inc., one of the country's largest sellers of greeting cards, has experienced both the pros and cons of outsourcing. In April one year it announced it would outsource the manufacturing of all of its cards and gift wrap. Gibson's stock price shot up quickly because investors believed the strategy could save the company $10 million a year, primarily by reducing manufacturing costs. But later in the same year Gibson got a taste of the negative side of outsourcing: When one of its suppliers was unable to meet its production schedule, about $20 million of Christmas cards went to stores a month later than scheduled.

Outsourcing is often a point of dispute in labor negotiations. Although many of the jobs lost to outsourcing go overseas, that is not always the case. In fact, a recent trend is to hire out work to vendors located close to the company. This reduces shipping costs and can improve coordination of efforts.

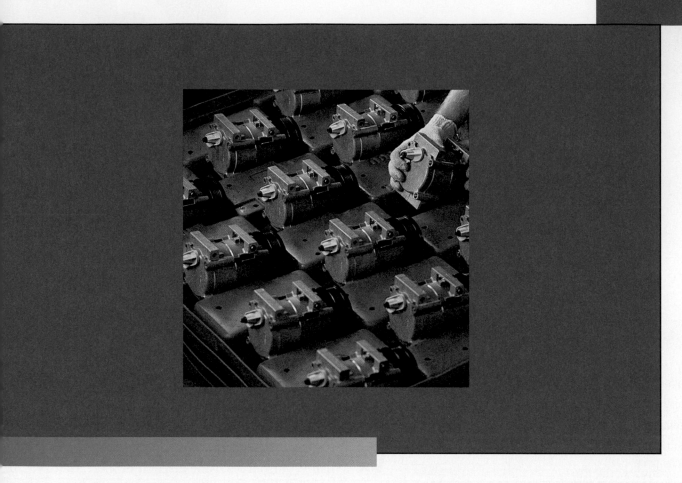

One company that has benefited from local outsourcing is **Solectron Corporation** in Silicon Valley. It makes things like cell phones, printers, and computers for high-tech companies in the region. To the surprise of many, it has kept thousands of people employed in California, rather than watching those jobs go overseas. What is its secret? It produces high-quality products efficiently. Solectron has to be efficient because it operates on a very thin profit margin—that is, it makes a tiny amount of money on each part—but it makes millions and millions of parts. It has proved the logic of outsourcing as a management decision, both for the companies for whom it makes parts and for its owners and employees.

THE NAVIGATOR

An important purpose of management accounting is to provide managers with relevant information for decision making. Companies of all sorts must make product decisions. **Philip Morris** decided to cut prices to raise market share. **Oral-B Laboratories** opted to produce a new, higher priced ($5) toothbrush. **General Motors** discontinued making the Buick Riviera and announced the closure of its Oldsmobile Division. **Quaker Oats** decided to sell a line of beverages, at a price more than one billion dollars less than it paid for that product line only a few years before. Ski manufacturers like **Dynastar** had to decide whether to use their limited resources to make snowboards instead of downhill skis.

This chapter explains management's decision-making process and a decision-making approach called incremental analysis. The use of incremental analysis is demonstrated in a variety of situations.

The content and organization of this chapter are as follows.

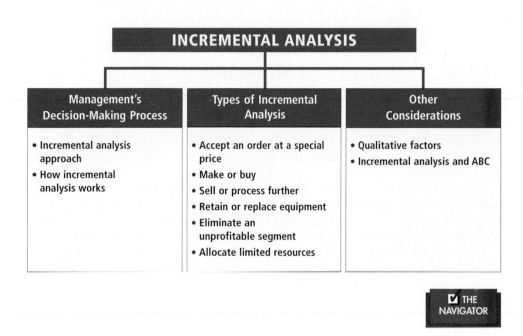

INCREMENTAL ANALYSIS

Management's Decision-Making Process	Types of Incremental Analysis	Other Considerations
• Incremental analysis approach • How incremental analysis works	• Accept an order at a special price • Make or buy • Sell or process further • Retain or replace equipment • Eliminate an unprofitable segment • Allocate limited resources	• Qualitative factors • Incremental analysis and ABC

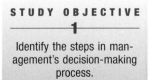

THE NAVIGATOR

Management's Decision-Making Process

Making decisions is an important management function. Management's decision-making process does not always follow a set pattern, because decisions vary significantly in their scope, urgency, and importance. It is possible, though, to identify some steps that are frequently involved in the process. These steps are shown in Illustration 6-1 (on page 230).

Accounting's contribution to the decision-making process occurs primarily in Steps 2 and 4—evaluating possible courses of action, and reviewing results. In Step 2, for each possible course of action, relevant revenue and cost data are provided. These show the expected overall effect on net income. In Step 4, internal reports are prepared that review the actual impact of the decision.

STUDY OBJECTIVE

1

Identify the steps in management's decision-making process.

229

Illustration 6-1 Manage-
ment's decision-
making process

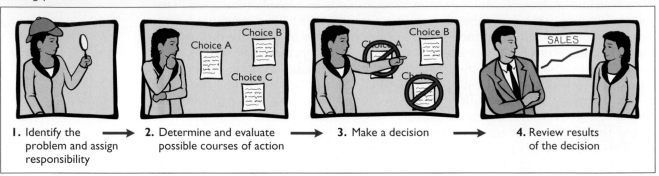

1. Identify the problem and assign responsibility → 2. Determine and evaluate possible courses of action → 3. Make a decision → 4. Review results of the decision

In making business decisions, management ordinarily considers both financial and nonfinancial information. **Financial** information is related to revenues and costs and their effect on the company's overall profitability. **Nonfinancial** information relates to such factors as the effect of the decision on employee turnover, the environment, or the overall image of the company in the community. Although nonfinancial information can be as important as the financial information, we will focus primarily on financial information that is relevant to the decision.

INCREMENTAL ANALYSIS APPROACH

STUDY OBJECTIVE
2
Describe the concept of incremental analysis.

Decisions involve a choice among alternative courses of action. Suppose that you were deciding whether to purchase or lease a computer for use in doing your accounting homework. The financial data relate to the cost of leasing versus the cost of purchasing. For example, leasing would involve periodic lease payments; purchasing would require "up-front" payment of the purchase price. In other words, the financial data relevant to the decision are the data that would vary in the future among the possible alternatives. The process used to identify the financial data that change under alternative courses of action is called incremental analysis. In some cases, you will find that when you use incremental analysis, both costs **and** revenues will vary. In other cases, only costs **or** revenues will vary.

Just as your decision to buy or lease a PC will affect your future, similar decisions, on a larger scale, will affect a company's future. Incremental analysis identifies the probable effects of those decisions on future earnings. Such analysis inevitably involves estimates and uncertainty. Gathering data for incremental analyses may involve market analysts, engineers, and accountants. In quantifying the data, the accountant is expected to produce the most reliable information available at the time the decision must be made.

Alternative Terminology Incremental analysis is also called *differential analysis* because the analysis focuses on differences.

HOW INCREMENTAL ANALYSIS WORKS

The basic approach in incremental analysis is illustrated in the following example.

Illustration 6-2 Basic approach in incremental analysis

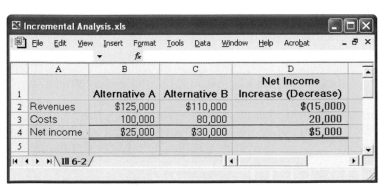

	Alternative A	Alternative B	Net Income Increase (Decrease)
Revenues	$125,000	$110,000	$(15,000)
Costs	100,000	80,000	20,000
Net income	$25,000	$30,000	$5,000

In this example, alternative B is being compared with alternative A. The net income column shows the differences between the alternatives. In this case, incremental revenue will be $15,000 less under alternative B than under alternative A. But a $20,000 incremental cost saving will be realized.[1] Thus, alternative B will produce $5,000 more net income than alternative A.

In the following pages you will encounter three important cost concepts used in incremental analysis, as defined and discussed in Illustration 6-3.

Illustration 6-3   Key cost concepts in incremental analysis

- **Relevant cost**   In incremental analysis, the only factors to be considered are those costs and revenues that differ across alternatives. Those factors are called relevant costs. Costs and revenues that do not differ across alternatives can be ignored when trying to choose between alternatives.

- **Opportunity cost**   Often in choosing one course of action, the company must give up the opportunity to benefit from some other course of action. For example, if a machine is used to make one type of product, the benefit of making another type of product with that machine is lost. This lost benefit is referred to as opportunity cost.

- **Sunk cost**   Costs that have already been incurred and will not be changed or avoided by any future decision are referred to as sunk costs. For example, if you have already purchased a machine, and now a new, more efficient machine is available, the book value of the original machine is a sunk cost. It should have no bearing on your decision whether to buy the new machine. **Sunk costs are not relevant costs**.

Incremental analysis sometimes involves changes that at first glance might seem contrary to your intuition. For example, sometimes variable costs **do not** change under the alternative courses of action. Also, sometimes fixed costs **do** change. For example, direct labor, normally a variable cost, is not an incremental cost in deciding between two new factory machines if each asset requires the same amount of direct labor. In contrast, rent expense, normally a fixed cost, is an incremental cost in a decision whether to continue occupancy of a building or to purchase or lease a new building.

---

[1]Although income taxes are sometimes important in incremental analysis, they are ignored in the chapter for simplicity's sake.

Types of Incremental Analysis

A number of different types of decisions involve incremental analysis. The more common types of decisions are whether to:

1. Accept an order at a special price.
2. Make or buy component parts or finished products.
3. Sell products or process them further.
4. Retain or replace equipment.
5. Eliminate an unprofitable business segment.
6. Allocate limited resources.

We will consider each of these types of decisions in the following pages.

ACCEPT AN ORDER AT A SPECIAL PRICE

Sometimes a company may have an opportunity to obtain additional business if it is willing to make a major price concession to a specific customer. To illustrate, assume that Sunbelt Company produces 100,000 automatic blenders per month, which is 80 percent of plant capacity. Variable manufacturing costs are $8 per unit. Fixed manufacturing costs are $400,000, or $4 per unit. The blenders are normally sold directly to retailers at $20 each. Sunbelt has an offer from Mexico Co. (a foreign wholesaler) to purchase an additional 2,000 blenders at $11 per unit. Acceptance of the offer would not affect normal sales of the product, and the additional units can be manufactured without increasing plant capacity. What should management do?

Helpful Hint This is a good example of different costs for different purposes. In the long run all costs are relevant, but for this decision only costs that change are relevant.

If management makes its decision on the basis of the total cost per unit of $12 ($8 + $4), the order would be rejected, because costs ($12) would exceed revenues ($11) by $1 per unit. However, since the units can be produced within existing plant capacity, the special order **will not increase fixed costs**. Let's identify the relevant data for the decision. First, the variable manufacturing costs will increase $16,000, ($8 × 2,000). Second, the expected revenue will increase $22,000, ($11 × 2,000). Thus, as shown in Illustration 6-4, Sunbelt will increase its net income by $6,000 by accepting this special order.

Illustration 6-4 Incremental analysis—accepting an order at a special price

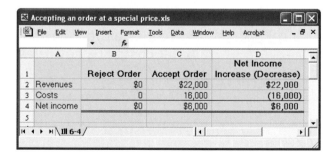

	Reject Order	Accept Order	Net Income Increase (Decrease)
Revenues	$0	$22,000	$22,000
Costs	0	16,000	(16,000)
Net income	$0	$6,000	$6,000

Two points should be emphasized: First, it is assumed that sales of the product in other markets **would not be affected by this special order**. If other sales were affected, then Sunbelt would have to consider the lost sales in making the decision. Second, if Sunbelt is operating **at full capacity**, it is likely that the special order would be rejected. Under such circumstances, the company would have to expand plant capacity. In that case, the special order would have to absorb these additional fixed manufacturing costs, as well as the variable manufacturing costs.

MAKE OR BUY

When a manufacturer assembles component parts in producing a finished product, management must decide whether to make or buy the components. The decision to buy parts or services is often referred to as outsourcing. For example, as discussed in the *Feature Story,* a company such as **General Motors Corpo-**

ration may either make or buy the batteries, tires, and radios used in its cars. Similarly, **Hewlett-Packard Corporation** may make or buy the electronic circuitry, cases, and printer heads for its printers. The decision to make or buy components should be made on the basis of incremental analysis.

To illustrate the analysis, assume that Baron Company incurs the following annual costs in producing 25,000 ignition switches for motor scooters.

Direct materials	$ 50,000
Direct labor	75,000
Variable manufacturing overhead	40,000
Fixed manufacturing overhead	60,000
Total manufacturing costs	$225,000
Total cost per unit ($225,000 ÷ 25,000)	**$9.00**

Illustration 6-5 Annual product cost data

Or, instead of making its own switches, Baron Company might purchase the ignition switches from Ignition, Inc. at a price of $8 per unit. The question again is, "What should management do?"

At first glance, it appears that management should purchase the ignition switches for $8, rather than make them at a cost of $9. However, a review of operations indicates that if the ignition switches are purchased from Ignition, Inc., *all* of Baron's variable costs but only $10,000 of its fixed manufacturing costs will be eliminated (avoided). Thus, $50,000 of the fixed manufacturing costs will remain if the ignition switches are purchased. The relevant costs for incremental analysis, therefore, are as follows.

Illustration 6-6 Incremental analysis—make or buy

	Make	Buy	Net Income Increase (Decrease)
Direct materials	$50,000	$0	$50,000
Direct labor	75,000	0	75,000
Variable manufacturing costs	40,000	0	40,000
Fixed manufacturing costs	60,000	50,000	10,000
Purchase price (25,000 × $8)	0	200,000	(200,000)
Total annual cost	$225,000	$250,000	$(25,000)

This analysis indicates that Baron Company will incur $25,000 of additional cost by buying the ignition switches. Therefore, Baron should continue to make the ignition switches, even though the total manufacturing cost is $1 higher than the purchase price. The reason is that if the company purchases the ignition switches, it will still have fixed costs of $50,000 to absorb.

Helpful Hint In the make-or-buy decision it is important for management to take into account the social impact of the choice. For instance, buying may be the most economically feasible solution, but such action could result in the closure of a manufacturing plant that employs many good workers.

Opportunity Cost

The foregoing make-or-buy analysis is complete only if it is assumed that the productive capacity used to make the ignition switches cannot be converted to another purpose. If there is an opportunity to use this productive capacity in some other manner, then this opportunity cost must be considered. As indicated earlier, **opportunity cost** is the potential benefit that may be obtained by following an alternative course of action.

To illustrate, assume that through buying the switches, Baron Company can use the released productive capacity to generate additional income of $28,000 from producing a different product. This lost income is an additional cost of continuing to make the switches in the make-or-buy decision. This opportunity cost therefore is added to the "Make" column, for comparison. As shown, it is now advantageous to buy the ignition switches.

Illustration 6-7 Incremental analysis—make or buy, with opportunity cost

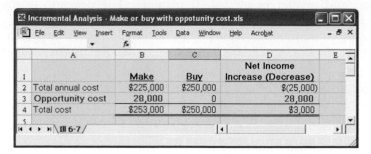

	A	B	C	D	E
1		**Make**	**Buy**	**Net Income Increase (Decrease)**	
2	Total annual cost	$225,000	$250,000	$(25,000)	
3	Opportunity cost	28,000	0	28,000	
4	Total cost	$253,000	$250,000	$3,000	
5					

The qualitative factors in this decision include the possible loss of jobs for employees who produce the ignition switches. In addition, management must assess how well the supplier will be able to satisfy the company's quality control standards at the quoted price per unit.

Business Insight
International Perspective

Consider the make-or-buy decision faced by **Superior Industries International, Inc.**, a big aluminum-wheel maker in Van Nuys, California. For years, president Steve Borick had ignored the possibility of Chinese manufacturing. Then Mr. Borick started getting a blunt message from **General Motors** and **Ford**, with whom Superior does 85 percent of its business: Match the prices that they were seeing at Chinese wheel suppliers. If Superior did not want to agree to new terms at those lower prices, both auto makers said separately that they could go directly to Chinese manufacturers or could turn to another North American wheel-maker that would.

Stories like this, repeated in various industries, illustrate why manufacturers engage in overseas outsourcing. (Some refer to this as *off-shoring*.) For example, compare the relative labor costs in major auto-producing nations, in dollars per hour, to see why incremental analysis often leads to outsourcing production to countries like China.

Germany	$33.00
United States	$22.50
France	$22.10
Japan	$20.20
Canada	$19.40
United Kingdom	$18.60
South Korea	$8.40
Taiwan	$5.20
Mexico	$2.70
China	$0.90

SOURCE: Norihiko Shirouzu, "Big Three's Outsourcing Plan: Make Parts Suppliers Do It," *Wall Street Journal* (June 10, 2004), p. A1.

SELL OR PROCESS FURTHER

Many manufacturers have the option of selling products at a given point in the production cycle or continuing to process with the expectation of selling them at a later point at a higher price. For example, a bicycle manufacturer such as **Schwinn** could sell its 10-speed bicycles to retailers either unassembled or assembled. A furniture manufacturer such as **Ethan Allen** could sell its dining room sets to furniture stores either unfinished or finished. The sell-or-process-further decision should be made on the basis of incremental analysis. The basic decision rule is: **Process further as long as the incremental revenue from such processing exceeds the incremental processing costs.**

STUDY OBJECTIVE

5

Identify the relevant costs in determining whether to sell or process materials further.

Single-Product Case

Assume, for example, that Woodmasters Inc. makes tables. The cost to manufacture an unfinished table is $35, computed as follows.

Illustration 6-8 Per unit cost of unfinished table

Direct materials	$15
Direct labor	10
Variable manufacturing overhead	6
Fixed manufacturing overhead	4
Manufacturing cost per unit	**$35**

The selling price per unfinished unit is $50. Woodmasters currently has unused productive capacity that is expected to continue indefinitely. What are the relevant costs? Management concludes that some of this capacity may be used to finish the tables and sell them at $60 per unit. For a finished table, direct materials will increase $2 and direct labor costs will increase $4. Variable manufacturing overhead costs will increase by $2.40 (60% of direct labor). No increase is anticipated in fixed manufacturing overhead.

The incremental analysis on a per unit basis is as follows.

Illustration 6-9 Incremental analysis—sell or process further

Incremental Analysis - Sell or process further.xls			
	A	B	C	D

	A	B (Sell)	C (Process Further)	D (Net Income Increase (Decrease))
2	Sales per unit	$50.00	$60.00	$10.00
3	Cost per unit			
4	Direct materials	15.00	17.00	(2.00)
5	Direct labor	10.00	14.00	(4.00)
6	Variable manufacturing overhead	6.00	8.40	(2.40)
7	Fixed manufacturing overhead	4.00	4.00	0.00
8	Total	35.00	43.40	(8.40)
9	Net income per unit	$15.00	$16.60	$1.60

It would be advantageous for Woodmaster to process the tables further. The incremental revenue of $10.00 from the additional processing is $1.60 higher than the incremental processing costs of $8.40.

Multiple-Product Case

Sell-or-process-further decisions are particularly applicable to production processes that produce multiple products simultaneously. In many industries, a number of end-products are produced from a single raw material and a common production process. These multiple end-products are commonly referred to as **joint products**. For example, in the meat-packing industry, a single sheep

Helpful Hint Current net income is known. Net income from processing further is an estimate. In making its decision, management could add a "risk" factor for the estimate.

produces meat, internal organs, hides, wool, bones, and fat. In the petroleum industry, crude oil is refined to produce gasoline, lubricating oil, kerosene, paraffin, and ethylene.

Illustration 6-10 presents a joint product situation for Marais Creamery involving a decision **to sell or process further** cream and skim milk. Cream and skim milk are products that result from the processing of raw milk.

Illustration 6-10 Joint production process—Creamery

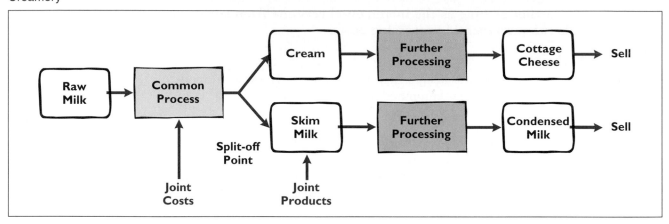

Marais incurs many costs prior to the manufacture of the cream and skim milk. All costs incurred prior to the point at which the two products are separately identifiable (the *split-off point*) are called **joint costs**. For purposes of determining the cost of each product, joint product costs must be allocated to the individual products. This is frequently done based on the relative sales value of the joint products. While this allocation is important for determination of product cost, it is irrelevant for any sell-or-process-further decisions. The reason is that these joint product costs are **sunk costs**. That is, they have already been incurred, and they cannot be changed or avoided by any subsequent decision.

The daily cost and revenue data for Marais Creamery are shown in Illustration 6-11.

Illustration 6-11 Cost and revenue data per day

Costs (per day)	
Joint cost allocated to cream	$ 9,000
Joint cost allocated to skim milk	5,000
Processing cream into cottage cheese	10,000
Processing skim milk into condensed milk	8,000

Expected Revenues from Products (per day)	
Cream	$19,000
Skim milk	11,000
Cottage cheese	27,000
Condensed milk	26,000

From this information we can determine whether the company should simply sell the cream and skim milk, or process them further into cottage cheese and condensed milk. Illustration 6-12 (page 237) provides the analysis necessary to determine whether to sell the cream or process it further into cottage cheese.

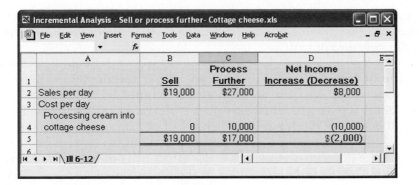

From this analysis we can see that Marais should not process the cream further because it will sustain an incremental loss of $2,000. Illustration 6-13, however, shows that Marais Company should process the skim milk into condensed milk, as it will increase net income by $7,000.

	Sell	Process Further	Net Income Increase (Decrease)
1			
2 Sales per day	$11,000	$26,000	$15,000
3 Cost per day			
4 Processing skim milk into condensed milk	0	8,000	(8,000)
5	$11,000	$18,000	$7,000

Note that the amount of joint costs allocated to each product ($9,000 to the cream and $5,000 to the skim milk) is irrelevant in deciding whether to sell or process further. Why? The joint costs remain the same whether or not further processing is performed.

RETAIN OR REPLACE EQUIPMENT

Management often has to decide whether to continue using an asset or replace it. To illustrate, assume that Jeffcoat Company has a factory machine with a book value of $40,000 and a remaining useful life of 4 years. It is considering replacing this machine with a new machine. A new machine is available that costs $120,000. It is expected to have zero salvage value at the end of its 4-year useful life. If the new machine is acquired, variable manufacturing costs are expected to decrease from $160,000 to $125,000 annually, and the old unit will be scrapped. The incremental analysis for the **4-year period** is as follows.

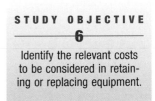

STUDY OBJECTIVE 6

Identify the relevant costs to be considered in retaining or replacing equipment.

Illustration 6-14 Incremental analysis—retain or replace equipment

	Retain Equipment		Replace Equipment		Net Income Increase (Decrease)
1					
2 Variable manufacturing costs	$640,000	a	$500,000	b	$140,000
3 New machine cost	0		120,000		(120,000)
4 Total	$640,000		$620,000		$20,000
5					
6 a(4 years × $160,000)					
7 b(4 years × $125,000)					

In this case, it would be to the company's advantage to replace the equipment. The lower variable manufacturing costs due to replacement more than offset the cost of the new equipment.

One other point should be mentioned regarding Jeffcoat's decision: **The book value of the old machine does not affect the decision.** Book value is a **sunk cost,** which is a cost that cannot be changed by any present or future decision. **Sunk costs are not relevant in incremental analysis.** In this example, if the asset is retained, book value will be depreciated over its remaining useful life. Or, if the new unit is acquired, book value will be recognized as a loss of the current period. Thus, the effect of book value on current and future earnings is the same regardless of the replacement decision. **Any trade-in allowance or cash disposal value of the existing asset, however, is relevant** to the decision, because this value will not be realized if the asset is continued in use.

ELIMINATE AN UNPROFITABLE SEGMENT

STUDY OBJECTIVE

7

Identify the relevant costs in deciding whether to eliminate an unprofitable segment.

Management sometimes must decide whether to eliminate an unprofitable business segment. Again, the key is to **focus on the relevant costs—the data that change under the alternative courses of action**. To illustrate, assume that Martina Company manufactures tennis racquets in three models: Pro, Master, and Champ. Pro and Master are profitable lines. Champ (highlighted in color in the table below) operates at a loss. Condensed income statement data are as follows.

Illustration 6-15 Segment income data

	Pro	Master	Champ	Total
Sales	$800,000	$300,000	**$100,000**	$1,200,000
Variable costs	520,000	210,000	**90,000**	820,000
Contribution margin	280,000	90,000	**10,000**	380,000
Fixed costs	80,000	50,000	**30,000**	160,000
Net income	$200,000	$ 40,000	**$ (20,000)**	$ 220,000

Helpful Hint A decision to discontinue a segment based solely on the bottom line—net loss—is inappropriate.

It might be expected that total net income will increase by $20,000, to $240,000, if the unprofitable Champ line of racquets is eliminated. However, **net income may actually decrease if the Champ line is discontinued**. The reason is that the fixed costs allocated to the Champ racquets will have to be absorbed by the other products. To illustrate, assume that the $30,000 of fixed costs applicable to the unprofitable segment are allocated ⅔ to the Pro model and ⅓ to the Master model if the Champ model is eliminated. Fixed costs will increase to $100,000 ($80,000 + $20,000) in the Pro line and to $60,000 ($50,000 + $10,000) in the Master line. The revised income statement is:

Illustration 6-16 Income data after eliminating unprofitable product line

	Pro	Master	Total
Sales	$800,000	$300,000	$1,100,000
Variable costs	520,000	210,000	730,000
Contribution margin	280,000	90,000	370,000
Fixed costs	**100,000**	**60,000**	160,000
Net income	$180,000	$ 30,000	**$ 210,000**

Total net income has decreased $10,000 ($220,000 − $210,000). This result is also obtained in the following incremental analysis of the Champ racquets.

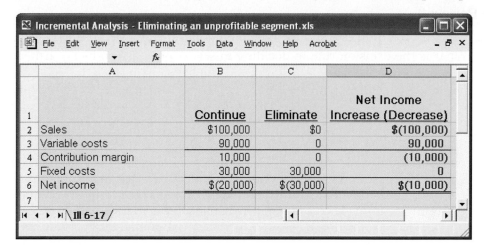

	Continue	Eliminate	Net Income Increase (Decrease)
2 Sales	$100,000	$0	$(100,000)
3 Variable costs	90,000	0	90,000
4 Contribution margin	10,000	0	(10,000)
5 Fixed costs	30,000	30,000	0
6 Net income	$(20,000)	$(30,000)	$(10,000)

Illustration 6-17   Incremental analysis—eliminating an unprofitable segment

The loss in net income is attributable to the Champ line's contribution margin ($10,000) that will not be realized if the segment is discontinued.

In deciding on the future status of an unprofitable segment, management should consider the effect of elimination on related product lines. It may be possible for continuing product lines to obtain some or all of the sales lost by the discontinued product line. In some businesses, services or products may be linked—for example, free checking accounts at a bank, or coffee at a donut shop. In addition, management should consider the effect of eliminating the product line on employees who may have to be discharged or retrained.

Business Insight
Management Perspective

In 1994 **Quaker Oats** paid $1.7 billion for one of America's hottest new beverage companies. While some observers thought that Quaker Oats had overpaid, Quaker's management believed it was an exciting purchase because it would make a great strategic partner for Quaker Oats' famous sport drink—Gatorade.

But for a variety of reasons, the acquisition didn't work out. One of the reasons was that at about the same time, several other major beverage manufacturers decided to begin producing and selling competing fruit and tea drinks. Worse yet, the processing methods used by these other manufacturers appeared to allow them to produce their drinks much more inexpensively.

Only a few years after purchasing the beverage company, Quaker Oats sold it and took a $1.4 billion loss. Management stated that by selling this division, the company could reduce its debt burden and focus its remaining assets on its cereal brands and Gatorade.

DECISION TOOLKIT

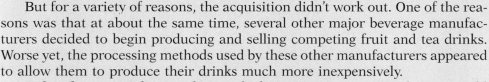

Decision Checkpoints	Info Needed for Decision	Tool to Use for Decision	How to Evaluate Results
Which alternative should the company choose?	All relevant costs and opportunity costs	Compare relevant cost of each alternative.	Choose the alternative that maximizes net income.

BEFORE YOU GO ON . . .

▶**Review It**

1. Give three examples of how incremental analysis might be used.
2. What is the decision rule in deciding to sell or process products further?
3. How may the elimination of an unprofitable segment decrease the overall net income of a company?

▶**Do It**

Cobb Company incurs a cost of $28 per unit, of which $18 is variable, to make a product that normally sells for $42. A foreign wholesaler offers to buy 5,000 units at $25 each. Cobb will incur shipping costs of $1 per unit. Compute the increase or decrease in net income Cobb will realize by accepting the special order, assuming Cobb has excess operating capacity.

Action Plan

• Identify all revenues that will change as a result of accepting the order.
• Identify all costs that will change as a result of accepting the order, and net this amount against the change in revenues.

Solution

	Reject	**Accept**	**Net Income Increase (Decrease)**
Revenues	$-0-	$125,000	$125,000
Costs	-0-	95,000*	(95,000)
Net income	$-0-	$ 30,000	$ 30,000

*(5,000 × $18) + (5,000 × $1)

Given the result of the analysis, Cobb Company should accept the special order.

Related exercise material: BE6-3, E6-1, and E6-2.

ALLOCATE LIMITED RESOURCES

STUDY OBJECTIVE
8
Determine sales mix when a company has limited resources.

Everyone's resources are limited. For a company, the limited resource may be floor space in a retail department store, or raw materials, direct labor hours, or machine capacity in a manufacturing company. When a company has limited resources, management must decide which products to make and sell in order to maximize net income.

To illustrate, assume that Collins Company manufactures deluxe and standard pen and pencil sets. The limiting resource is machine capacity, which is 3,600 hours per month. Relevant data consist of the following.

Illustration 6-18 Contribution margin and machine hours

	Deluxe Sets	**Standard Sets**
Contribution margin per unit	$8	$6
Machine hours required per unit	0.4	0.2

The deluxe sets may appear to be more profitable since they have a higher contribution margin ($8) than the standard sets ($6). However, the standard sets take fewer machine hours to produce than the deluxe sets. Therefore, it is necessary to find the **contribution margin per unit of limited resource**, in this case, contribution margin per machine hour. This is obtained by dividing the contribution margin per unit of each product by the number of units of the limited resource required for each product, as shown in Illustration 6-19.

	Deluxe Sets	Standard Sets
Contribution margin per unit (a)	$8	$6
Machine hours required (b)	0.4	0.2
Contribution margin per unit of limited resource [(a) ÷ (b)]	$20	$30

Illustration 6-19 Contribution margin per unit of limited resource

The computation shows that the standard sets have a higher contribution margin per unit of limited resource. This would suggest that, given sufficient demand for standard sets, the company should shift the sales mix to standard sets or increase machine capacity.

If Collins Company is able to increase machine capacity from 3,600 hours to 4,200 hours, the additional 600 hours could be used to produce either the standard or deluxe pen and pencil sets. The total contribution margin under each alternative is found by multiplying the machine hours by the contribution margin per unit of limited resource, as shown below.

	Produce Deluxe Sets	Produce Standard Sets
Machine hours (a)	600	600
Contribution margin per unit of limited resource (b)	$20	$30
Contribution margin [(a) × (b)]	$12,000	$18,000

Illustration 6-20 Incremental analysis—computation of total contribution margin

From this analysis, we can see that to maximize net income, all of the increased capacity should be used to make and sell the standard sets.

As indicated in Illustration 6-19, the constraint for the production of the Deluxe sets is the larger number of machine hours needed to produce these pens. In addressing this problem, we have taken the limited number of machine hours as a given, and have attempted to maximize the contribution margin given the constraint. One question that Collins should ask, however, is whether this constraint can be reduced or eliminated. For example, the constraint might be due to a bottleneck in production or to poorly trained machine operators. In addition, other possible solutions, such as outsourcing part of the production, acquiring additional new equipment (discussed in Chapter 12), or striving to eliminate any non-value-added activities, should be considered.

As discussed in Chapter 1, this approach to evaluating constraints is referred to as the theory of constraints. The **theory of constraints** is a specific approach used to identify and manage constraints in order to achieve the company's goals. According to this theory, a company must continually identify its constraints and find ways to reduce or eliminate them, where appropriate.

Helpful Hint CM alone is not enough to make this decision. The key factor is CM per limited resource.

Business Insight
Management Perspective

When fragrance sales recently went flat, retailers turned up the heat on fragrance manufacturers. The amount of floor space devoted to fragrances was reduced, leaving fragrance manufacturers fighting each other for a smaller space. The retailer doesn't just choose the fragrance with the highest contribution margin. Instead, it chooses the fragrance with the highest contribution margin per square foot. In this game, a product with a lower contribution margin, but a higher turnover, could well be the winner.

DECISION TOOLKIT

Decision Checkpoints	Info Needed for Decision	Tool to Use for Decision	How to Evaluate Results
How many units of product A and B should we produce in light of a limited resource?	Contribution margin per unit, limited resource required per unit	$$\text{Contribution margin per unit of limited resource} = \frac{\text{Contribution margin per unit}}{\text{Limited resource per unit}}$$	Any additional capacity of limited resource should be applied toward the product with higher contribution margin per unit of limited resource.

Other Considerations in Decision Making

QUALITATIVE FACTORS

In this chapter we have focused primarily on the quantitative factors that affect a decision—those attributes that can be easily expressed in terms of numbers or dollars. However, many of the decisions involving incremental analysis have important qualitative features; though not easily measured, they should not be ignored.

Consider, for example, the potential effects of the make-or-buy decision or of the decision to eliminate a line of business on existing employees and the community in which the plant is located. The cost savings that may be obtained from outsourcing or from eliminating a plant should be weighed against these qualitative attributes. One example would be the cost of lost morale that might result. Al "Chainsaw" Dunlap was a so-called "turnaround" artist who went into many companies, identified inefficiencies (using incremental analysis techniques), and tried to correct these problems to improve corporate profitability. Along the way he laid off thousands of employees at numerous companies. As head of **Sunbeam**, it was Al Dunlap who lost his job because his Draconian approach failed to improve Sunbeam's profitability. It was widely reported that Sunbeam's employees openly rejoiced for days after his departure. Clearly, qualitative factors can matter.

RELATIONSHIP OF INCREMENTAL ANALYSIS AND ACTIVITY-BASED COSTING

In Chapter 4 we noted that many companies have shifted to activity-based costing to allocate overhead costs to products. The primary reason for using activity-based costing is that it results in a more accurate allocation of overhead. The concepts presented in this chapter are completely consistent with the use of activity-based costing. In fact, activity-based costing will result in better identification of relevant costs and, therefore, better incremental analysis.

Business Insight
Management Perspective

The existence of excess plant capacity is frequently the incentive for management to add new products. Adding one new product may not add much incremental cost. But continuing to add products will at some point create new constraints, perhaps requiring additional investments in people, equipment, and facilities.

The effects of product and product line proliferation are generally understood. But the effect on incremental overhead costs of *changes in servicing customers* is less understood. For example, if a company newly offers its customers the option of product delivery by case or by pallet, the new service may appear to be simple and low in cost. But, if the manufacturing process must be realigned to package in two different forms; if two sets of inventory records must be maintained; and if warehousing, handling, and shipping require two different arrangements or sets of equipment, the additional costs of this new option could be as high as a whole new product. If the customer service option were adopted for all products, the product line could effectively be doubled—but so might many overhead costs.

SOURCE: Elizabeth Haas Edersheim and Joan Wilson, "Complexity at Consumer Goods Companies: Naming and Taming the Beast," *Journal of Cost Management*.

BEFORE YOU GO ON . . .

▶Review It

1. What is the critical factor in allocating limited resources to various product lines?
2. What are some qualitative factors that should be considered in an incremental analysis decision?
3. What is the theory of constraints?

☑ THE NAVIGATOR

Using the Decision Toolkit

Suppose **Hewlett-Packard Company** must decide whether to make or buy some of its components from **Solectron Corp**. The cost of producing 50,000 electrical connectors for its printers is $110,000, broken down as follows.

Direct materials	$60,000	Variable manufacturing overhead	$12,000
Direct labor	30,000	Fixed manufacturing overhead	8,000

Instead of making the electrical connectors at an average cost per unit of $2.20 ($110,000 ÷ 50,000), the company has an opportunity to buy the connectors at $2.15 per unit. If the connectors are purchased, all variable costs and one-half of the fixed costs will be eliminated.

Instructions

(a) Prepare an incremental analysis showing whether the company should make or buy the electrical connectors.

(b) Will your answer be different if the released productive capacity resulting from the purchase of the connectors will generate additional income of $25,000?

Solution

(a)

	Make	Buy	Net Income Increase (Decrease)
Direct materials	$ 60,000	$ –0–	$ 60,000
Direct labor	30,000	–0–	30,000
Variable manufacturing costs	12,000	–0–	12,000
Fixed manufacturing costs	8,000	4,000	4,000
Purchase price	–0–	107,500	(107,500)
Total cost	$110,000	$111,500	$ (1,500)

This analysis indicates that Hewlett-Packard will incur $1,500 of additional costs if it buys the electrical connectors. H-P therefore would choose to make the connectors.

(b)

	Make	Buy	Net Income Increase (Decrease)
Total cost	$110,000	$111,500	$(1,500)
Opportunity cost	25,000	–0–	25,000
Total cost	$135,000	$111,500	$23,500

Yes, the answer is different. The analysis shows that if additional capacity is released, net income will be increased by $23,500 if the electrical connectors are purchased. In this case, H-P would choose to purchase the connectors.

THE
NAVIGATOR

Summary of Study Objectives

1 *Identify the steps in management's decision-making process.* Management's decision-making process consists of (a) identifying the problem and assigning responsibility for the decision, (b) determining and evaluating possible courses of action, (c) making the decision, and (d) reviewing the results of the decision.

2 *Describe the concept of incremental analysis.* Incremental analysis is the process that is used to identify financial data that change under alternative courses of action. These data are relevant to the decision because they will vary in the future among the possible alternatives.

3 *Identify the relevant costs in accepting an order at a special price.* The relevant costs are those that change if the order is accepted. These are typically variable manufacturing costs. The relevant information in accepting an order at a special price is the difference between the variable manufacturing costs to produce the special order and expected revenues.

4 *Identify the relevant costs in a make-or-buy decision.* In a make-or-buy decision, the relevant costs are (a) the variable manufacturing costs that will be saved, (b) the purchase price, and (c) opportunity costs.

5 *Identify the relevant costs in determining whether to sell or process materials further.* The decision rule for whether to sell or process materials further is: Process further as long as the incremental revenue from processing exceeds the incremental processing costs.

6 *Identify the relevant costs to be considered in retaining or replacing equipment.* The relevant costs to be considered in determining whether equipment should be retained or replaced are the effects on variable costs and the cost of the new equipment. Also, any disposal value of the existing asset must be considered.

7 *Identify the relevant costs in deciding whether to eliminate an unprofitable segment.* In deciding whether to eliminate an unprofitable segment, the relevant costs arc the variable costs that drive the contribution margin, if any, produced by the segment. Disposition of the segment's fixed expenses must also be considered.

8 *Determine sales mix when a company has limited resources.* When a company has limited resources, it is necessary to find the contribution margin per unit of limited resource. This amount is then multiplied by the units of limited resource to determine which product maximizes net income.

DECISION TOOLKIT—A SUMMARY

Decision Checkpoints	Info Needed for Decision	Tool to Use for Decision	How to Evaluate Results
Which alternative should the company choose?	All relevant costs and opportunity costs	Compare the relevant cost of each alternative.	Choose the alternative that maximizes net income.
How many units of product A and B should we produce in light of a limited resource?	Contribution margin per unit, limited resource required per unit	$$\text{Contribution margin per unit of limited resource} = \frac{\text{Contribution margin per unit}}{\text{Limited resource per unit}}$$	Any additional capacity of limited resource should be applied toward the product with higher contribution margin per unit of limited resource.

Glossary

Incremental analysis The process of identifying the financial data that change under alternative courses of action. (p. 230)

Joint costs For joint products, all costs incurred prior to the point at which the two products are separately identifiable (known as the *split-off point*). (p. 236)

Joint products Multiple end-products produced from a single raw material and a common production process. (p. 235)

Opportunity cost The potential benefit that may be obtained from following an alternative course of action. (p. 231)

Relevant costs Those costs and revenues that differ across alternatives. (p. 231)

Sunk cost A cost that cannot be changed by any present or future decision. (p. 231)

Theory of constraints A specific approach used to identify and manage constraints in order to achieve the company's goals. (p. 241)

Demonstration Problem

Carolina Corporation manufactures and sells three different types of high-quality sealed ball bearings. The bearings vary in terms of their quality specifications—primarily with respect to their smoothness and roundness. They are referred to as Fine, Extra-Fine, and Super-Fine bearings. Machine time is limited. More machine time is required to manufacture the Extra-Fine and Super-Fine bearings. Additional information is provided below.

	Product		
	Fine	**Extra-Fine**	**Super-Fine**
Selling price	$6.00	$10.00	$16.00
Variable costs and expenses	4.00	6.50	11.00
Contribution margin	$2.00	$ 3.50	$ 5.00
Machine hours required	0.02	0.04	0.08

Total fixed costs: $234,000

Instructions

Answer each of the following questions.

(a) Ignoring the machine time constraint, what strategy would appear optimal?

(b) What is the contribution margin per unit of limited resource for each type of bearing?

(c) If additional machine time could be obtained, how should the additional capacity be used?

Action Plan

- To determine how best to use a limited resource, calculate the contribution margin per unit of limited resource for each product type.

Solution to Demonstration Problem

(a) The Super-Fine bearings have the highest contribution margin per unit. Thus, ignoring any manufacturing constraints, it would appear that the company should shift toward production of more Super-Fine units.

(b) The contribution margin per unit of limited resource is calculated as:

	Fine	**Extra-Fine**	**Super-Fine**
$\dfrac{\text{Contribution margin per unit}}{\text{Limited resource consumed per unit}}$	$\dfrac{\$2}{.02} = \$100$	$\dfrac{\$3.5}{.04} = \$87.50$	$\dfrac{\$5}{.08} = \$62.50$

(c) The Fine bearings have the highest contribution margin per limited resource, even though they have the lowest contribution margin per unit. Given the resource constraint, any additional capacity should be used to make Fine bearings.

THE NAVIGATOR

Self-Study Questions

Answers are at the end of the chapter.

(SO 1) 1. Three of the steps in management's decision making process are (1) review results of decision, (2) determine and evaluate possible courses of action, and (3) make the decision. The steps are prepared in the following order:
(a) (1), (2), (3).
(b) (3), (2), (1).
(c) (2), (1), (3).
(d) (2), (3), (1).

(SO 2) 2. Incremental analysis is the process of identifying the financial data that:
(a) do not change under alternative courses of action.
(b) change under alternative courses of action.
(c) are mixed under alternative courses of action.
(d) No correct answer is given.

(SO 3) 3. It costs a company $14 of variable costs and $6 of fixed costs to produce product Z200 that sells for $30. A foreign buyer offers to purchase 3,000 units at $18 each. If the special offer is accepted and produced with unused capacity, net income will:
(a) decrease $6,000.
(b) increase $6,000.
(c) increase $12,000.
(d) increase $9,000.

(SO 3) 4. It costs a company $14 of variable costs and $6 of fixed costs to produce product Z200 at full capacity. Product Z200 sells for $30. A buyer offers to purchase 3,000 units at $18 each. The seller will incur special shipping costs of $5 per unit. If the special offer is accepted and produced with unused capacity, net income will:
(a) increase $3,000.
(b) increase $12,000.
(c) decrease $12,000.
(d) decrease $3,000.

(SO 4) 5. In a make-or-buy decision, relevant costs are:
(a) manufacturing costs that will be saved.
(b) the purchase price of the units.
(c) opportunity costs.
(d) all of the above.

(SO 5) 6. The decision rule in a sell-or-process-further decision is: process further as long as the incremental revenue from processing exceeds:
(a) incremental processing costs.
(b) variable processing costs.
(c) fixed processing costs.
(d) No correct answer is given.

(SO 6) 7. In a decision to retain or replace equipment, the book value of the old equipment is a (an):
(a) opportunity cost.
(b) sunk cost.
(c) incremental cost.
(d) marginal cost.

(SO 7) 8. If an unprofitable segment is eliminated:
(a) net income will always increase.
(b) variable expenses of the eliminated segment will have to be absorbed by other segments.
(c) fixed expenses allocated to the eliminated segment will have to be absorbed by other segments.
(d) net income will always decrease.

(SO 8) 9. If the contribution margin per unit is $15 and it takes 3.0 machine hours to produce the unit, the contribution margin per unit of limited resource is:
(a) $25.
(b) $5.
(c) $4.
(d) No correct answer is given.

Questions

1. What steps are frequently involved in management's decision-making process?

2. Your roommate, Mike Myer, contends that accounting contributes to most of the steps in management's decision-making process. Is your roommate correct? Explain.

3. "Incremental analysis involves the accumulation of information concerning a single course of action." Do you agree? Why?

4. Sara Gura asks for your help concerning the relevance of variable and fixed costs in incremental analysis. Help Sara with her problem.

5. What data are relevant in deciding whether to accept an order at a special price?

6. Son Ly Company has an opportunity to buy parts at $7 each that currently cost $10 to make. What manufacturing costs are relevant to this make-or-buy decision?

7. Define the term "opportunity cost." How may this cost be relevant in a make-or-buy decision?

8. What is the decision rule in deciding whether to sell a product or process it further?

9. What are joint products? What accounting issue results from the production process that creates joint products?

10. How are allocated joint costs treated when making a sell-or-process-further decision?

11. Your roommate, Vanessa Hunt, is confused about sunk costs. Explain to your roommate the meaning of sunk costs and their relevance to a decision to retain or replace equipment.

12. Erm Paris Inc. has one product line that is unprofitable. What circumstances may cause overall company net income to be lower if the unprofitable product line is eliminated?

13. How is the contribution margin per unit of limited resource computed?

14. What is the theory of constraints? Provide some examples of possible constraints for a manufacturer.

Brief Exercises

Identify the steps in management's decision-making process.
(SO 1)

BE6-1 The steps in management's decision-making process are listed in random order below. Indicate the order in which the steps should be executed.

____ Make a decision
____ Identify the problem and assign responsibility

____ Review results of the decision
____ Determine and evaluate possible courses of action

Determine incremental changes.
(SO 2)

BE6-2 Anna Company is considering two alternatives. Alternative A will have revenues of $150,000 and costs of $100,000. Alternative B will have revenues of $185,000 and costs of $125,000. Compare Alternative A to Alternative B showing incremental revenues, costs, and net income.

Determine whether to accept a special order.
(SO 3)

BE6-3 In Sydney Company it costs $30 per unit ($20 variable and $10 fixed) to make a product at full capacity that normally sells for $45. A foreign wholesaler offers to buy 3,000 units at $24 each. Sydney will incur special shipping costs of $2 per unit. Assuming that Sydney has excess operating capacity, indicate the net income (loss) Sydney would realize by accepting the special order.

Determine whether to make or buy a part.
(SO 4)

BE6-4 Emil Manufacturing incurs unit costs of $7.50 ($4.50 variable and $3 fixed) in making a sub-assembly part for its finished product. A supplier offers to make 10,000 of the assembly part at $5 per unit. If the offer is accepted, Emil will save all variable costs but no fixed costs. Prepare an analysis showing the total cost saving, if any, Emil will realize by buying the part.

Determine whether to sell or process further.
(SO 5)

BE6-5 Green Inc. makes unfinished bookcases that it sells for $60. Production costs are $35 variable and $10 fixed. Because it has unused capacity, Green is considering finishing the bookcases and selling them for $70. Variable finishing costs are expected to be $8 per unit with no increase in fixed costs. Prepare an analysis on a per unit basis showing whether Green should sell unfinished or finished bookcases.

Determine whether to sell or process further, joint products.
(SO 5)

BE6-6 Each day, Dunham Corporation processes 1 ton of a secret raw material into two resulting products, AB1 and XY1. When it processes 1 ton of the raw material the company incurs joint processing costs of $60,000. It allocates $25,000 of these costs to AB1 and $35,000 of these costs to XY1. The resulting AB1 can be sold for $90,000. Alternatively, it can be processed further to make AB2 at an additional processing cost of $50,000, and sold for $150,000. Each day's batch of XY1 can be sold for $90,000. Alternatively, it can be processed further to create XY2, at an additional processing cost of $50,000, and sold for $130,000. Discuss what products Dunham Corporation should make.

Determine whether to retain or replace equipment.
(SO 6)

BE6-7 Chudzick Company has a factory machine with a book value of $90,000 and a remaining useful life of 4 years. A new machine is available at a cost of $250,000. This machine will have a 4-year useful life with no salvage value. The new machine will lower annual variable manufacturing costs from $600,000 to $500,000. Prepare an analysis showing whether the old machine should be retained or replaced.

BE6-8 Bitterman, Inc., manufactures golf clubs in three models. For the year, the Big Bart line has a net loss of $5,000 from sales $200,000, variable costs $175,000, and fixed costs $30,000. If the Big Bart line is eliminated, $15,000 of fixed costs will remain. Prepare an analysis showing whether the Big Bart line should be eliminated.

Determine whether to eliminate an unprofitable segment.
(SO 7)

BE6-9 In Astoria Company, data concerning two products are: Contribution margin per unit—Product A $10, Product B $12; machine hours required for one unit—Product A 2, Product B 3. Compute the contribution margin per unit of limited resource for each product.

Show allocation of limited resources.
(SO 8)

Exercises

E6-1 Quick Company manufactures toasters. For the first 8 months of 2005, the company reported the following operating results while operating at 75% of plant capacity:

Use incremental analysis for special order.
(SO 3)

Sales (350,000 units)	$4,375,000
Cost of goods sold	2,500,000
Gross profit	1,875,000
Operating expenses	875,000
Net income	$1,000,000

Cost of goods sold was 70% variable and 30% fixed; operating expenses were also 70% variable and 30% fixed.

In September, Quick Company receives a special order for 15,000 toasters at $7.50 each from Ortiz Company of Mexico City. Acceptance of the order would result in $3,000 of shipping costs but no increase in fixed operating expenses.

Instructions
(a) Prepare an incremental analysis for the special order.
(b) ▣▣▣▶ Should Quick Company accept the special order? Why or why not?

E6-2 Hardy Fiber Company is the creator of Y-Go, a technology that weaves silver into its fabrics to kill bacteria and odor on clothing while managing heat. Y-Go has become very popular as an undergarment for sports activities. Operating at capacity, the company can produce 1,000,000 undergarments of Y-Go a year. The per unit and the total costs for an individual garment when the company operates at full capacity are as follows.

Use incremental analysis for special order.
(SO 3)

	Per Undergarment	Total
Direct materials	$2.00	$2,000,000
Direct labor	0.50	500,000
Variable manufacturing overhead	1.00	1,000,000
Fixed manufacturing overhead	1.50	1,500,000
Variable selling expenses	0.25	250,000
Totals	$5.25	$5,250,000

The U.S. Army has approached Hardy Fiber and expressed an interest in purchasing 200,000 Y-Go undergarments for soldiers in extremely warm climates. The Army would pay the unit cost for direct materials, direct labor, and variable manufacturing overhead costs. In addition, the Army has agreed to pay an additional $1 per undergarment to cover all other costs and provide a profit. Presently, Hardy Fiber is operating at 70 percent capacity and does not have any other potential buyers for Y-Go. If Hardy Fiber accepts the Army's offer, it will not incur any variable selling expenses related to this order.

Instructions
Using incremental analysis, determine whether Hardy Fiber should accept the Army's offer.

Use incremental analysis for make-or-buy decision.
(SO 4)

E6-3 Stahl Inc. has been manufacturing its own shades for its table lamps. The company is currently operating at 100% of capacity, and variable manufacturing overhead is charged to production at the rate of 70% of direct labor cost. The direct materials and direct labor cost per unit to make the lamp shades are $5 and $6, respectively. Normal production is 30,000 table lamps per year.

A supplier offers to make the lamp shades at a price of $15.50 per unit. If Stahl Inc. accepts the supplier's offer, all variable manufacturing costs will be eliminated, but the $45,000 of fixed manufacturing overhead currently being charged to the lamp shades will have to be absorbed by other products.

Instructions
(a) Prepare the incremental analysis for the decision to make or buy the lamp shades.
(b) ▭▭▭▷ Should Stahl Inc. buy the lamp shades?
(c) ▭▭▭▷ Would your answer be different in (b) if the productive capacity released by not making the lamp shades could be used to produce income of $35,000?

Use incremental analysis for make-or-buy decision.
(SO 4)

E6-4 SY Telc has recently started the manufacture of RecRobo, a three-wheeled robot that can scan a home for fires and gas leaks and then transmit this information to a mobile phone. The cost structure to manufacture 20,000 RecRobo's is as follows.

	Cost
Direct materials ($40 per robot)	$ 800,000
Direct labor ($30 per robot)	600,000
Variable overhead ($6 per robot)	120,000
Allocated fixed overhead ($25 per robot)	500,000
Total	$2,020,000

SY Telc is approached by Chen Inc. which offers to make RecRobo for $90 per unit or $1,800,000.

Instructions
(a) Using incremental analysis, determine whether SY Telc should accept this offer under each of the following independent assumptions.
  (1) Assume that $300,000 of the fixed overhead cost can be reduced (avoided).
  (2) Assume that none of the fixed overhead can be reduced (avoided). However, if the robots are purchased from Chen Inc., SY Telc can use the released productive resources to generate additional income of $300,000.
(b) Describe the qualitative factors that might affect the decision to purchase the robots from an outside supplier.

Use incremental analysis for further processing of materials decision.
(SO 5)

E6-5 Wanda Sublette recently opened her own basketweaving studio. She sells finished baskets in addition to the raw materials needed by customers to weave baskets of their own. Wanda has put together a variety of raw material kits, each including materials at various stages of completion. Unfortunately, owing to space limitations, Wanda is unable to carry all varieties of kits originally assembled and must choose between two basic packages.

The basic introductory kit includes undyed, uncut reeds (with dye included) for weaving one basket. This basic package costs Wanda $14 and sells for $28. The second kit, called Stage 2, includes cut reeds that have already been dyed. With this kit the customer need only soak the reeds and weave the basket. Wanda is able to produce the second kit by using the basic materials included in the first kit and adding one hour of her own time, which she values at $20 per hour. Because she is more efficient at cutting and dying reeds than her average customer, Wanda is able to make two kits of the dyed reeds, in one hour, from one kit of undyed reeds. The Stage 2 kit sells for $35.

Instructions
Determine whether Wanda's basketweaving shop should carry the basic introductory kit with undyed and uncut reeds or the Stage 2 kit with reeds already dyed and cut. Prepare an incremental analysis to support your answer.

Determine whether to sell or process further, joint products.
(SO 5)

E6-6 Benson, Inc. produces three separate products from a common process costing $100,000. Each of the products can be sold at the split-off point or can be processed further and then sold for a higher price. Shown on the next page are cost and selling price data for a recent period.

P6-4A Last year (2005) Calway Condos installed a mechanized elevator for its tenants. *Compute gain or loss, and* The owner of the company, Cab Calway, recently returned from an industry equipment *determine if equipment* exhibition where he watched a computerized elevator demonstrated. He was impressed *should be replaced.* with the elevator's speed, comfort of ride, and cost efficiency. Upon returning from the (SO 6) exhibition, he asked his purchasing agent to collect price and operating cost data on the new elevator. In addition, he asked the company's accountant to provide him with cost data on the company's elevator. This information is presented below.

	Old Elevator	New Elevator
Purchase price	$120,000	$180,000
Estimated salvage value	0	0
Estimated useful life	6 years	5 years
Depreciation method	Straight-line	Straight-line
Annual operating costs other than depreciation:		
Variable	$ 35,000	$ 12,000
Fixed	23,000	8,400

Annual revenues are $240,000, and selling and administrative expenses are $29,000, regardless of which elevator is used. If the old elevator is replaced now, at the beginning of 2006, Calway Condos will be able to sell it for $25,000.

Instructions
(a) Determine any gain or loss if the old elevator is replaced.
(b) Prepare a 5-year summarized income statement for each of the following assumptions:
  (1) The old elevator is retained.
  (2) The old elevator is replaced.   (b)(2) NI $698,000
(c) Using incremental analysis, determine if the old elevator should be replaced.   (c) NI increase $33,000
(d) ▭▭▭▭▷ Write a memo to Cab Calway explaining why any gain or loss should be ignored in the decision to replace the old elevator.

P6-5A Lewis Manufacturing Company has four operating divisions. During the first *Compute contribution mar-* quarter of 2005, the company reported aggregate income from operations of $176,000 *gin and prepare incremental* and the following divisional results. *analysis concerning elimina-*
tion of divisions.
(SO 7)

	Division			
	I	II	III	IV
Sales	$250,000	$200,000	$500,000	$400,000
Cost of goods sold	200,000	189,000	300,000	250,000
Selling and administrative expenses	65,000	60,000	60,000	50,000
Income (loss) from operations	$ (15,000)	$ (49,000)	$140,000	$100,000

Analysis reveals the following percentages of variable costs in each division.

	I	II	III	IV
Cost of goods sold	70%	90%	80%	75%
Selling and administrative expenses	40	70	50	60

Discontinuance of any division would save 50% of the fixed costs and expenses for that division.

Top management is very concerned about the unprofitable divisions (I and II). Consensus is that one or both of the divisions should be discontinued.

Instructions
(a) Compute the contribution margin for Divisions I and II.   (a) I $84,000
(b) Prepare an incremental analysis concerning the possible discontinuance of (1) Division I and (2) Division II. What course of action do you recommend for each division?
(c) Prepare a columnar condensed income statement for Lewis Manufacturing, assum-   (c) Income III $133,850 ing Division II is eliminated. Use the CVP format. Division II's unavoidable fixed costs are allocated equally to the continuing divisions.
(d) Reconcile the total income from operations ($176,000) with the total income from operations without Division II.

Problems: Set B

Make incremental analysis for special order and identify nonfinancial factors in the decision.
(SO 3)

P6-1B Oakbrook Company is currently producing 18,000 units per month, which is 80% of its production capacity. Variable manufacturing costs are currently $13.20 per unit, and fixed manufacturing costs are $72,000 per month. Oakbrook pays a 9% sales commission to its sales people, has $30,000 in fixed administrative expenses per month, and is averaging $432,000 in sales per month.

A special order received from a foreign company would enable Oakbrook Company to operate at 100% capacity. The foreign company offered to pay 80% of Oakbrook's current selling price per unit. If the order is accepted, Oakbrook will have to spend an extra $2.00 per unit to package the product for overseas shipping. Also, Oakbrook Company would need to lease a new stamping machine to imprint the foreign company's logo on the product, at a monthly cost of $5,000. The special order would require a sales commission of $4,000.

Instructions

(a) Compute the number of units involved in the special order and the foreign company's offered price per unit.

(b) What is the manufacturing cost of producing one unit of Oakbrook's product for regular customers?

(c) NI increase $9,000

(c) Prepare an incremental analysis of the special order. Should management accept the order?

(d) What is the lowest price that Oakbrook could accept for the special order to earn net income of $1.20 per unit?

(e) What nonfinancial factors should management consider in making its decision?

Make incremental analysis related to make or buy, consider opportunity cost, and identify nonfinancial factors.
(SO 4)

P6-2B The management of Dunham Manufacturing Company has asked for your assistance in deciding whether to continue manufacturing a part or to buy it from an outside supplier. The part, called Tropica, is a component of Dunham's finished product.

An analysis of the accounting records and the production data revealed the following information for the year ending December 31, 2005.

1. The Machinery Department produced 35,000 units of Tropica.

2. Each Tropica unit requires 10 minutes to produce. Three people in the Machinery Department work full time (2,000 hours per year) producing Tropica. Each person is paid $12 per hour.

3. The cost of materials per Tropica unit is $2.20.

4. Manufacturing costs directly applicable to the production of Tropica are: indirect labor, $6,000; utilities, $1,500; depreciation, $1,800; property taxes and insurance, $1,000. All of the costs will be eliminated if Tropica is purchased.

5. The lowest price for a Tropica from an outside supplier is $4 per unit. Freight charges will be $0.50 per unit, and a part-time receiving clerk at $8,500 per year will be required.

6. If Tropica is purchased, the excess space will be used to store Dunham's finished product. Currently, Dunham rents storage space at approximately $0.80 per unit stored per year. Approximately 5,000 units per year are stored in the rented space.

Instructions

(a) NI decrease $2,700

(a) Prepare an incremental analysis for the make or buy decision. Should Dunham make or buy the part? Why?

(b) NI increase $9,300

(b) Prepare an incremental analysis, assuming the released facilities can be used to produce $12,000 of net income in addition to the savings on the rental of storage space. What decision should now be made?

(c) What nonfinancial factors should be considered in the decision?

Determine if product should be sold or processed further.
(SO 5)

P6-3B Bonita Household Products Co. is a diversified household cleaner processing company. The company's Poway plant produces two products: a glass cleaner and a metal cleaner from a common set of chemical inputs, (TLC). Each week 1,000,000 ounces of chemical input are processed at a cost of $200,000 into 750,000 ounces of metal cleaner and 250,000 ounces of glass cleaner. The metal cleaner has no market value until it is converted into a polish with the trade name MetalShine. The additional processing costs for this conversion amount to $270,000. MetalShine sells at $15 per 25-ounce bottle.

The glass cleaner can be sold for $24 per 25-ounce bottle. However, the glass cleaner can be converted into two other products by adding 250,000 ounces of another compound (MST) to the 250,000 ounces of glass cleaner. This joint process will yield 250,000 ounces each of plastic cleaner (PC) and plastic polish (PP). The additional processing costs for this process amount to $140,000. Both plastic products can be sold for $20 per 25-ounce bottle.

The company decided not to process the glass cleaner into PC and PP based on the following analysis.

| | Glass Cleaner | Process Further | | |
		Plastic Cleaner (PC)	Plastic Polish (PP)	Total
Production in ounces	(250,000)	(250,000)	(250,000)	
Revenue	$240,000	$200,000	$200,000	$400,000
Costs:				
TLC costs	50,000*	40,000	40,000	80,000**
MST costs	0	70,000	70,000	140,000
Total costs	50,000	110,000	110,000	220,000
Weekly gross profit	$190,000	$ 90,000	$ 90,000	$180,000

*If glass cleaner is not processed further it is allocated ¼ of the $200,000 of TLC cost, which is equal to ¼ of the total physical output.
**If glass cleaner is processed further, total physical output is 1,250,000 ounces. PC and PP combined account for 40% of the total physical output and are each allocated 20% of the TLC cost.

Instructions
(a) Determine if management made the correct decision to not process the glass cleaner further by doing the following.
   (1) Calculate the company's total weekly gross profit assuming the glass cleaner is not processed further.
   (2) Calculate the company's total weekly gross profit assuming the glass cleaner is processed further.
   (3) Compare the resulting net incomes and comment on management's decision.
(b) Using incremental analysis, determine if the glass cleaner should be processed further.

(2) Gross profit $240,000

(CMA adapted)

P6-4B Quik Press Inc. offers one-day dry cleaning. At the beginning of 2005, the company purchased a mechanized pressing machine. The owner of the company, Jill Jabowski, recently returned from an industry equipment exhibition where she watched a computerized press demonstrated. She was impressed with the machine's speed, efficiency, and quality of output. Upon returning from the exhibition, she asked her purchasing agent to collect price and operating cost data on the new press. In addition, she asked the company's accountant to provide her with cost data on the company's press. This information is presented below.

Compute gain or loss, and determine if equipment should be replaced.
(SO 6)

	Old Press	New Press
Purchase price	$120,000	$150,000
Estimated salvage value	0	0
Estimated useful life	6 years	5 years
Depreciation method	Straight-line	Straight-line
Annual operating expenses other than depreciation:		
Variable	$30,000	$10,000
Fixed	20,000	7,000

Annual revenues are $200,000, and selling and administrative expenses are $24,000, regardless of which press is used. If the old press is replaced now, at the beginning of 2006, Quik Press will be able to sell it for $10,000.

Instructions
(a) Determine any gain or loss if the old press is replaced.
(b) Prepare a 5-year summarized income statement for each of the following assumptions:
    (1) The old press is retained.
    (2) The old press is replaced.

(b)(2) NI $555,000
(c) NI increase $25,000

(c) Using incremental analysis, determine if the old press should be replaced.
(d) Write a memo to Jill Jabowski explaining why any gain or loss should be ignored in the decision to replace the old press.

Compute contribution margin and prepare incremental analysis concerning elimination of divisions.
(SO 7)

P6-5B Hindu Manufacturing Company has four operating divisions. During the first quarter of 2005, the company reported total income from operations of $36,000 and the following results for the divisions.

	Division			
	Taos	**Boseman**	**Salem**	**Olympia**
Sales	$405,000	$730,000	$920,000	$500,000
Cost of goods sold	400,000	480,000	576,000	390,000
Selling and administrative expenses	100,000	207,000	246,000	120,000
Income (loss) from operations	$ (95,000)	$ 43,000	$ 98,000	$(10,000)

Analysis reveals the following percentages of variable costs in each division.

	Taos	**Boseman**	**Salem**	**Olympia**
Cost of goods sold	90%	80%	90%	95%
Selling and administrative expenses	60	60	70	80

Discontinuance of any division would save 70% of the fixed costs and expenses for that division.

Top management is deeply concerned about the unprofitable divisions (Taos and Olympia). The consensus is that one or both of the divisions should be eliminated.

Instructions

(a) Olympia $33,500

(a) Compute the contribution margin for the two unprofitable divisions.
(b) Prepare an incremental analysis concerning the possible elimination of (1) the Taos Division and (2) the Olympia Division. What course of action do you recommend for each division?

(c) Income Salem $86,000

(c) Prepare a columnar condensed income statement using the CVP format for Hindu Manufacturing Company, assuming (1) the Taos Division is eliminated, and (2) the unavoidable fixed costs and expenses of the Taos Division are allocated 30% to Boseman, 50% to Salem, and 20% to Olympia.
(d) Compare the total income from operations with the Taos Division ($36,000) to total income from operations without this division.

Problems: Set C

Problem Set C is provided at the book's Web site, www.wiley.com/college/weygandt.

BROADENING YOUR PERSPECTIVE

Group Decision Case

BYP6-1 Castle Company is considering the purchase of a new machine. The invoice price of the machine is $125,000, freight charges are estimated to be $4,000, and installation costs are expected to be $6,000. Salvage value of the new equipment is expected to be zero after a useful life of 4 years. Existing equipment could be retained and used for an additional 4 years if the new machine is not purchased. At that time, the salvage value of the equipment would be zero. If the new machine is purchased now, the existing machine would have to be scrapped. Castle's accountant, Shaida Fang, has accumulated the following data regarding annual sales and expenses with and without the new machine.

1. Without the new machine, Castle can sell 12,000 units of product annually at a per unit selling price of $100. If the new machine is purchased, the number of units produced and sold would increase by 20%, and the selling price would remain the same.
2. The new machine is faster than the old machine, and it is more efficient in its usage of materials. With the old machine the gross profit rate will be 25% of sales, whereas the rate will be 30% of sales with the new machine.
3. Annual selling expenses are $180,000 with the current equipment. Because the new equipment would produce a greater number of units to be sold, annual selling expenses are expected to increase by 10% if it is purchased.
4. Annual administrative expenses are expected to be $100,000 with the old machine, and $113,000 with the new machine.
5. The current book value of the existing machine is $36,000. Castle uses straight-line depreciation.

Instructions
With the class divided into groups, prepare an incremental analysis for the 4 years showing whether Castle should keep the existing machine or buy the new machine. (Ignore income tax effects.)

Managerial Analysis

BYP6-2 Technology Plus manufactures private-label small electronic products, such as alarm clocks, calculators, kitchen timers, stopwatches, and automatic pencil sharpeners. Some of the products are sold as sets, and others are sold individually. Products are studied as to their sales potential, and then cost estimates are made. The Engineering Department develops production plans, and then production begins. The company has generally had very successful product introductions. Only two products introduced by the company have been discontinued.

One of the products currently sold is a multi-alarm alarm clock. The clock has four alarms that can be programmed to sound at various times and for varying lengths of time. The company has experienced a great deal of difficulty in making the circuit boards for the clocks. The production process has never operated smoothly. The product is unprofitable at the present time, primarily because of warranty repairs and product recalls. Two models of the clocks were recalled, for example, because they sometimes caused an electric shock when the alarms were being shut off. The Engineering Department is attempting to revise the manufacturing process, but the revision will take another 6 months at least.

The clocks were very popular when they were introduced, and since they are private-label, the company has not suffered much from the recalls. Presently, the company has a very large order for several items from Kmart Stores. The order includes 5,000 of the multi-alarm clocks. When the company suggested that Kmart purchase the clocks from another manufacturer, Kmart threatened to rescind the entire order unless the clocks were included.

The company has therefore investigated the possibility of having another company make the clocks for them. The clocks were bid for the Kmart order based on an estimated $6.65 cost to manufacture:

Circuit board, 1 each @ $2.00	$2.00
Plastic case, 1 each @ $0.75	0.75
Alarms, 4 @ $0.10 each	0.40
Labor, 15 minutes @ $12/hour	3.00
Overhead, $2.00 per labor hour	0.50

Technology Plus could purchase clocks to fill the Kmart order for $11 from Silver Star, a Korean manufacturer with a very good quality record. Silver Star has offered to reduce the price to $7.50 after Technology Plus has been a customer for 6 months, placing an order of at least 1,000 units per month. If Technology Plus becomes a "preferred customer" by purchasing 15,000 units per year, the price would be reduced still further to $4.50.

Alpha Products, a local manufacturer, has also offered to make clocks for Technology Plus. They have offered to sell 5,000 clocks for $4 each. However, Alpha Products has been in business for only 6 months. They have experienced significant turnover in their labor force, and the local press has reported that the owners may face tax evasion charges soon. The owner of Alpha Products is an electronic engineer, however, and the quality of the clocks is likely to be good.

If Technology Plus decides to purchase the clocks from either Silver Star or Alpha, all the costs to manufacture could be avoided, except a total of $5,000 in overhead costs for machine depreciation. The machinery is fairly new, and has no alternate use.

Instructions
(a) What is the difference in profit under each of the alternatives if the clocks are to be sold for $14.50 each to Kmart?
(b) What are the most important nonfinancial factors that Technology Plus should consider when making this decision?
(c) What do you think Technology Plus should do in regard to the Kmart order? What should it do in regard to continuing to manufacture the multi-alarm alarm clocks? Be prepared to defend your answer.

Real-World Focus

BYP6-3   Founded in 1983, **Beverly Hills Fan Company** is located in Woodland Hills, California. With 23 employees and sales of less than $10 million, the company is relatively small. Management feels that there is potential for growth in the upscale market for ceiling fans and lighting. They are particularly optimistic about growth in Mexican and Canadian markets.

Presented below is information from the president's letter in the company's annual report.

BEVERLY HILLS FAN COMPANY
President's Letter

An aggressive product development program was initiated during the past year resulting in new ceiling fan models planned for introduction this year. Award winning industrial designer Ron Rezek created several new fan models for the Beverly Hills Fan and L.A. Fan lines, including a new Showroom Collection, designed specifically for the architectural and designer markets. Each of these models has received critical acclaim, and order commitments for this year have been outstanding. Additionally, our Custom Color and special order fans continued to enjoy increasing popularity and sales gains as more and more customers desire fans that match their specific interior decors. Currently, Beverly Hills Fan Company offers a product line of over 100 models of contemporary, traditional, and transitional ceiling fans.

Instructions
(a) What points did the company management need to consider before deciding to offer the special-order fans to customers?
(b) How would incremental analysis be employed to assist in this decision?

Exploring the Web

BYP6-4   Outsourcing by both manufacturers and service companies is becoming increasingly common. There are now many firms that specialize in outsourcing consulting.

Address: **www.trowbridgegroup.net/value.htm (*or go to* www.wiley.com/college/weygandt)**

Instructions

Go to the Web page of **The Trowbridge Group** at the address shown above, and answer the following questions.

(a) What are some of the ways that outsourcing can "strengthen the overall performance of the company"?

(b) What are some of the potential problems that arise when companies outsource?

Communication Activity

BYP6-5   Jeff Howell is a production manager at a metal fabricating plant. Last night he read an article about a new piece of equipment that would dramatically reduce his division's costs. Jeff was very excited about the prospect, and the first thing he did this morning was to bring the article to his supervisor, Nathan Peas, the plant manager. The following conversation occurred:

> *Jeff:* Nathan, I thought you would like to see this article on the new PDD1130; they've made some fantastic changes that could save us millions of dollars.

> *Nathan:* I appreciate your interest Jeff, but I actually have been aware of the new machine for two months. The problem is that we just bought a new machine last year. We spent $2 million on that machine, and it was supposed to last us 12 years. If we replace it now we would have to write its book value off of the books for a huge loss. If I go to top management now and say that I want a new machine, they will fire me. I think we should use our existing machine for a couple of years, and then when it becomes obvious that we have to have a new machine, I will make the proposal.

Instructions

Jeff just completed a course in managerial accounting, and he believes that Nathan is making a big mistake. Write a memo from Jeff to Nathan explaining Nathan's decision-making error.

Research Assignment

BYP6-6   The December 2003 issue of *Inc.* magazine includes an article by Norm Brodsk titled "Street Smart."

Instructions

Read the article and answer the following questions.

(a) What is the "capacity trap" discussed in this article?

(b) What are three problems discussed in the article in not selling at full price even if a company has excess capacity?

(c) As indicated in the article, when might it make sense to discount price given excess capacity?

Ethics Case

BYP6-7   Robert Buey became Chief Executive Officer of Phelps Manufacturing two years ago. At the time, the company was reporting lagging profits, and Robert was brought in to "stir things up." The company has three divisions, electronics, fiber optics, and plumbing supplies. Robert has no interest in plumbing supplies, and one of the first things he did was to put pressure on his accountants to reallocate some of the company's fixed costs away from the other two divisions to the plumbing division. This had the effect of causing the plumbing division to report losses during the last two years; in the past it had always reported low, but acceptable, net income. Robert felt that this reallocation would shine a favorable light on him in front of the board of directors because it meant that the electronics and fiber optics divisions would look like they were improving. Given that these are "businesses of the future," he believed that the stock market would react favorably to these increases, while not penalizing the poor results of the plumbing division. Without this shift in the allocation of fixed costs, the profits of the electronics and fiber optics divisions would not have improved. But now the board of directors has suggested that the plumbing division be closed because it is reporting losses. This would mean that nearly 500 employees, many of whom have worked for Phelps their whole lives, would lose their jobs.

Instructions
(a) If a division is reporting losses, does that necessarily mean that it should be closed?
(b) Was the reallocation of fixed costs across divisions unethical?
(c) What should Robert do?

_____

Answers to Self-Study Questions
1. d   2. b   3. c   4. d   5. d   6. a   7. b   8. c   9. b

Variable Costing: A Decision-Making Perspective

STUDY OBJECTIVES

After studying this chapter, you should be able to:

1 Explain the difference between absorption costing and variable costing.

2 Discuss the effect that changes in production level and sales level have on net income measured under absorption costing versus variable costing.

3 Discuss the relative merits of absorption costing versus variable costing for management decision making.

4 Explain the term sales mix and its effects on break-even sales.

5 Understand how operating leverage affects profitability.

 THE NAVIGATOR

THE NAVIGATOR ✔

▶ Scan *Study Objectives* ☐

▶ Read *Feature Story* ☐

▶ Read *Preview* ☐

▶ Read text and answer *Before You Go On*
    p. 275 ☐   p. 279 ☐   p. 282 ☐

▶ Work *Using the Decision Toolkit* ☐

▶ Review *Summary of Study Objectives* ☐

▶ Work *Demonstration Problem* ☐

▶ Answer *Self-Study Questions* ☐

▶ Complete *Assignments* ☐

FEATURE STORY

What Goes Up (*fast*), Must Come Down (*fast*)

During the late 1990s many people marveled at the efficiency of the so-called "New Economy," which uses digital technologies to improve business processes. Some managers were actually startled by their own success. The New Economy had created a new formula for profit. For example, David Peterschmidt, chief executive at software developer **Inktomi**, noted that the company had incurred considerable fixed costs in developing new software, but its variable costs were minor. As a consequence, once sales had covered the fixed costs, every additional sale was basically pure profit. When sales were booming, he happily stated, "Next to the federal government, this is the only business that's allowed to print money." But that was then. When the economy lagged, the new profit formula went sour. The company's sales disappeared, but its fixed costs did not. In no time, Inktomi went from record profits to staggering losses.

Many other companies have had similar experiences. As their manufacturing plants have become more automated, their fixed costs have become increasingly high. For example, during a 5-year period, the average cost of a typical **Intel** semiconductor plant rose from $500 million to $2 billion as its manufacturing processes became increasingly sophisticated. These high fixed costs have made Intel very dependent on producing a high volume of computer

chips. It needs high volume so that it can spread its fixed costs across a lot of units, thereby reducing the fixed cost per unit. As one Intel employee put it, "You have high fixed costs, so you want to minimize those fixed costs and keep factories running 24 hours a day."

However, when management focuses too heavily on keeping volume high to reduce fixed costs per unit, it sometimes produces more inventory than the market wants. When this happens, companies have to cut prices sharply. High-tech firms, like Intel, whose products become rapidly obsolete, have occasionally been stuck with inventory that nobody wanted. Thus, while the huge outlays

for new equipment have made these companies exceptionally efficient, such outlays have also increased their exposure to economic swings. In fact, because so many companies now have cost structures that rely heavily on fixed costs, many economists worry that swings in the entire economy will be more volatile than in the past.

Source: Greg Ip, "As Profits Swoon, Companies Blame A Marked Change in Cost Structure," *Wall Street Journal Online* (May 16, 2001).

As the Feature Story about **Inktomi** and **Intel** suggests, the relationship between a company's fixed and variable costs can have a huge impact on its profitability. In particular, the trend toward cost structures dominated by fixed costs has significantly increased the volatility of many companies' net income. In order to better track and understand the impact of cost structure on corporate profitability, some companies use an approach called *variable costing*. The purpose of this chapter is to show how variable costing can be helpful in making sound business decisions. The content and organization of this chapter are as follows.

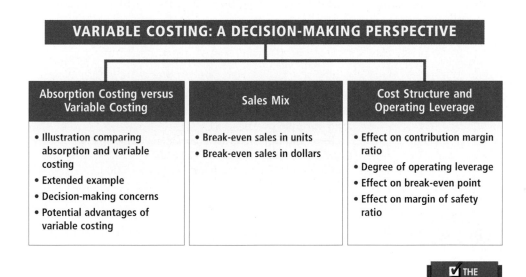

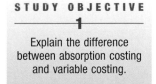

Absorption Costing versus Variable Costing

In the earlier chapters, both variable and fixed manufacturing costs were classified as product costs. In job order costing, for example, a job is assigned the costs of direct materials, direct labor, and **both** variable and fixed manufacturing overhead. This costing approach is referred to as **full** or **absorption costing**. It is so named because all manufacturing costs are charged to, or absorbed by, the product. Absorption costing is the approach used for external reporting under generally accepted accounting principles.

An alternative approach is to use variable costing. Under **variable costing**, only direct materials, direct labor, and variable manufacturing overhead costs are considered product costs. Fixed manufacturing overhead costs are recognized as period costs (expenses) when incurred. The difference between absorption costing and variable costing is graphically shown as follows.

STUDY OBJECTIVE

1

Explain the difference between absorption costing and variable costing.

Illustration 7-1 Difference between absorption costing and variable costing

Selling and administrative expenses are period costs under both absorption and variable costing.

Variable costing may not be used for external financial reports because generally accepted accounting principles require that fixed manufacturing overhead be accounted for as a product cost.

ILLUSTRATION COMPARING ABSORPTION COSTING AND VARIABLE COSTING

To illustrate absorption and variable costing, assume that Premium Products Corporation manufactures a polyurethane sealant, called Fix-it, for car windshields. Relevant data for Fix-it in January 2005, the first month of production, are as follows.

Illustration 7-2   Sealant sales and cost data for Premium Products Corporation

Selling price	$20 per unit.
Units	Produced 30,000; sold 20,000; beginning inventory zero.
Variable unit costs	Manufacturing $9 (direct materials $5, direct labor $3, and variable overhead $1).
	Selling and administrative expenses $2.
Fixed costs	Manufacturing overhead $120,000.
	Selling and administrative expenses $15,000.

The per unit manufacturing cost under each costing approach is computed in Illustration 7-3.

Illustration 7-3   Computation of per unit manufacturing cost

Type of Cost	Absorption Costing	Variable Costing
Direct materials	$ 5	$ 5
Direct labor	3	3
Variable manufacturing overhead	1	1
Fixed manufacturing overhead		
($120,000 ÷ 30,000 units produced)	4	0
Manufacturing cost per unit	**$13**	**$9**

The manufacturing cost per unit is $4 ($13 − $9) higher for absorption costing. This occurs because fixed manufacturing overhead costs are a product cost under absorption costing. Under variable costing, they are, instead, a period cost, and so they are expensed. Based on these data, each unit sold and each unit remaining in inventory is costed at $13 under absorption costing and at $9 under variable costing.

Absorption Costing Illustration

The income statement for Premium Products using absorption costing is shown in Illustration 7-4 (page 267). It shows that cost of goods manufactured is $390,000, computed by multiplying the 30,000 units produced times the manufacturing cost per unit of $13 (see Illustration 7-3). Cost of goods sold is $260,000, after subtracting ending inventory of $130,000. Under absorption costing, $40,000 (10,000 units × $4) of the fixed overhead is deferred to a future period as part of the cost of ending inventory.

Illustration 7-4   Absorption costing income statement

PREMIUM PRODUCTS CORPORATION
Income Statement
For the Month Ended January 31, 2005
Absorption Costing

Sales (20,000 units × $20)		$400,000
Cost of goods sold		
Inventory, January 1	$ –0–	
Cost of goods manufactured (30,000 units × $13)	390,000	
Cost of goods available for sale	390,000	
Inventory, January 31 (10,000 units × $13)	**130,000**	
Cost of goods sold (20,000 units × $13)		260,000
Gross profit		140,000
Variable selling and administrative expenses		
(20,000 × $2)	40,000	
Fixed selling and administrative expenses	15,000	55,000
Net income		**$ 85,000**

Helpful Hint The income statement in Illustration 7-4 is the same as that used under generally accepted accounting principles and the same as that used previously in Chapter 2.

Variable Costing Illustration

As shown in Illustration 7-5, the cost–volume–profit format is used in preparing a variable costing income statement. The variable manufacturing cost of $270,000 is computed by multiplying the 30,000 units produced times variable manufacturing cost of $9 per unit (see Illustration 7-3). As in absorption costing, both variable and fixed selling and administrative expenses are treated as period costs.

Illustration 7-5   Variable costing income statement

PREMIUM PRODUCTS CORPORATION
Income Statement
For the Month Ended January 31, 2005
Variable Costing

Sales (20,000 units × $20)		$400,000
Variable cost of goods sold		
Inventory, January 1	$ –0–	
Variable cost of goods manufactured		
(30,000 units × $9)	270,000	
Variable cost of goods available for sale	270,000	
Inventory, January 31 (10,000 units × $9)	**90,000**	
Variable cost of goods sold	180,000	
Variable selling and administrative expenses		
(20,000 units × $2)	40,000	220,000
Contribution margin		180,000
Fixed manufacturing overhead	120,000	
Fixed selling and administrative expenses	15,000	135,000
Net income		**$ 45,000**

Helpful Hint Note the difference in the computation of the ending inventory: $9 per unit here, $13 per unit above.

There is one primary difference between variable and absorption costing: Under variable costing, the fixed manufacturing overhead is charged as an expense in the current period. Fixed manufacturing overhead costs of the current period, therefore, are not deferred to future periods through the ending inventory. As a result, absorption costing will show a higher net income number than variable costing whenever units produced exceed units sold. This difference can be seen in the income statements in Illustrations 7-4 and 7-5. There is a $40,000 difference in the ending inventories ($130,000 under absorption costing versus $90,000 under variable costing). Under absorption costing, $40,000 of the fixed overhead costs (10,000 units × $4) has been deferred to a future period as part of inventory. In contrast, under variable costing, all fixed manufacturing costs are expensed in the current period.

As shown, when units produced exceed units sold, income under absorption costing is **higher**. When units produced are less than units sold, income under absorption costing is **lower**. When units produced and sold are the same, net income will be **equal** under the two costing approaches. In this case, there is no increase in ending inventory. So fixed overhead costs of the current period are not deferred to future periods through the ending inventory.

AN EXTENDED EXAMPLE

To further illustrate the concepts underlying absorption and variable costing, an extended example using Overbay Inc., a manufacturer of small airplane drones, is provided below. We assume that production volume stays the same each year over the three-year period, but the number of units sold varies each year.

2005 Results

As indicated in Illustration 7-6 below, the variable manufacturing cost per drone is $240,000, and the fixed manufacturing cost per drone is $60,000. Total manufacturing cost per drone is therefore $300,000 ($240,000 + $60,000). Overbay also has variable selling and administrative expenses of $5,000 per drone, or $50,000 per year ($5,000 × 10 drones sold). The fixed selling and administrative expenses are $80,000.

Illustration 7-6   Information for Overbay Inc.

	2005	2006	2007
Volume information			
Drones in beginning inventory	0	0	2
Drones produced	10	10	10
Drones sold	10	8	12
Drones in ending inventory	0	2	0
Financial information			
Selling price per drone	$400,000		
Variable manufacturing cost per drone	$240,000		
Fixed manufacturing overhead for the year	$600,000		
Fixed manufacturing overhead per drone	$ 60,000 ($600,000 ÷ 10)		
Variable selling and administrative expenses per drone	$ 5,000		
Fixed selling and administrative expenses	$ 80,00 0		

An absorption costing income statement for 2005 for Overbay Inc. is shown in Illustration 7-7.

Illustration 7-7   Absorption costing income statement—2005

OVERBAY INC.
Income Statement
For the Year Ended 2005
Absorption Costing

Sales (10 drones × $400,000)		$4,000,000
Cost of goods sold (10 drones × $300,000)		3,000,000
Gross profit		1,000,000
Variable selling and administrative expenses (10 drones × $5,000)	$50,000	
Fixed selling and administrative expenses	80,000	130,000
Net income		$ 870,000

Overbay reports net income of $870,000 under absorption costing.

Under a variable costing system the income statement follows a cost–volume–profit (CVP) format. In this case, the manufacturing cost is comprised solely of the variable manufacturing costs of $240,000 per drone. The fixed manufacturing costs of $600,000 for the year are expensed in 2005. As in absorption costing, the fixed and variable selling and administrative expenses are period costs expensed in 2005. A variable costing income statement for Overbay Inc. for 2005 is shown in Illustration 7-8.

OVERBAY INC.
Income Statement
For the Year Ended 2005
Variable Costing

Sales (10 drones × $400,000)		$4,000,000
Variable cost of goods sold		
(10 drones × $240,000)	$2,400,000	
Variable selling and administrative expenses		
(10 drones × $5,000)	50,000	2,450,000
Contribution margin		1,550,000
Fixed manufacturing overhead	600,000	
Fixed selling and administrative expenses	80,000	680,000
Net income		$ 870,000

Illustration 7-8   Variable costing income statement—2005

As shown in Illustration 7-8, the variable costing net income of $870,000 is the same as the absorption costing net income computed in Illustration 7-7. **When the numbers of units produced and sold are the same, net income is equal under the two costing approaches.** Because no increase in ending inventory occurs, no fixed manufacturing overhead costs incurred in 2005 are deferred to future periods using absorption costing.

2006 Results

In 2006, Overbay produced ten drones but sold only eight drones. As a result, there are two drones in ending inventory. The absorption costing income statement for 2006 is shown in Illustration 7-9.

OVERBAY INC.
Income Statement
For the Year Ended 2006
Absorption Costing

Sales (8 drones × $400,000)		$3,200,000
Cost of goods sold (8 drones × $300,000)		2,400,000
Gross profit		800,000
Variable selling and administrative expenses		
(8 drones × $5,000)	$40,000	
Fixed selling and administrative expenses	80,000	120,000
Net income		$ 680,000

Illustration 7-9   Absorption costing income statement—2006

Under absorption costing, the ending inventory of two drones is $600,000 ($300,000 × 2). Each unit of ending inventory includes $60,000 of fixed manufacturing overhead. Therefore, fixed manufacturing overhead costs of $120,000 ($60,000 × 2 drones) are deferred until a future period.

The variable costing income statement for 2006 is shown in Illustration 7-10.

Illustration 7-10 Variable costing income statement—2006

OVERBAY INC. Income Statement For the Year Ended 2006 Variable Costing		
Sales (8 drones × $400,000)		$3,200,000
Variable cost of goods sold (8 drones × $240,000)	$1,920,000	
Variable selling and administrative expenses (8 drones × $5,000)	40,000	1,960,000
Contribution margin		1,240,000
Fixed manufacturing overhead	600,000	
Fixed selling and administrative expenses	80,000	680,000
Net income		$ 560,000

As shown, when units produced (10) exceeds units sold (8), net income under absorption costing ($680,000) is higher than net income under variable costing ($560,000). The reason: The cost of the ending inventory is higher under absorption costing than under variable costing. In 2006, under absorption costing, fixed manufacturing overhead of $120,000 is deferred and carried to future periods as part of inventory. Under variable costing, the $120,000 is expensed in the current period and, therefore the difference in the two net income numbers is $120,000 ($680,000 − $560,000).

2007 Results

In 2007, Overbay produced ten drones and sold twelve (10 drones from the current year's production and 2 drones from the beginning inventory). As a result, there are no drones in ending inventory. The absorption costing income statement for 2007 is shown in Illustration 7-11.

Illustration 7-11 Absorption costing income statement—2007

OVERBAY INC. Income Statement For the Year Ended 2007 Absorption Costing		
Sales (12 drones × $400,000)		$4,800,000
Cost of goods sold (12 drones × $300,000)		3,600,000
Gross profit		1,200,000
Variable selling and administrative expenses (12 drones × $5,000)	$60,000	
Fixed selling and administrative expenses	80,000	140,000
Net income		$1,060,000

Fixed manufacturing costs of $720,000 are expensed as part of cost of goods sold in 2007. This $720,000 includes $120,000 of fixed manufacturing costs incurred during 2006 and included in beginning inventory, plus $600,000 of fixed manufacturing costs incurred during 2007. Given this result for the absorption costing statement, what would you now expect the result to be under variable costing? Let's take a look.

The variable costing income statement for 2007 is shown in Illustration 7-12.

OVERBAY INC.		
Income Statement		
For the Year Ended 2007		
Variable Costing		
Sales (12 drones × $400,000)		$4,800,000
Variable cost of goods sold		
(12 drones × $240,000)	$2,880,000	
Variable selling and administrative expenses		
(12 drones × $5,000)	60,000	2,940,000
Contribution margin		1,860,000
Fixed manufacturing overhead	600,000	
Fixed selling and administrative expenses	80,000	680,000
Net income		$1,180,000

Illustration 7-12   Variable costing income statement—2007

When Drones produced (10) are less than Drones sold (12), net income under absorption costing ($1,060,000) is less than net income under variable costing ($1,180,000). This difference of $120,000 ($1,180,000 − $1,060,000) results because $120,000 of fixed manufacturing overhead costs in beginning inventory are charged to 2007 under absorption costing. Under variable costing, there is no fixed manufacturing overhead cost in beginning inventory.

The results of the three years are summarized in Illustration 7-13.

	Net Income under Two Costing Approaches		
	2005	**2006**	**2007**
	Production = Sales	**Production > Sales**	**Production < Sales**
Absorption costing	$ 870,000	$ 680,000	$1,060,000
Variable costing	870,000	560,000	1,180,000
Difference	$ –0–	$120,000	$(120,000)

Illustration 7-13   Comparison of net income under two costing approaches

This relationship between production and sales and its effect on net income under the two costing approaches is shown graphically in Illustration 7-14.

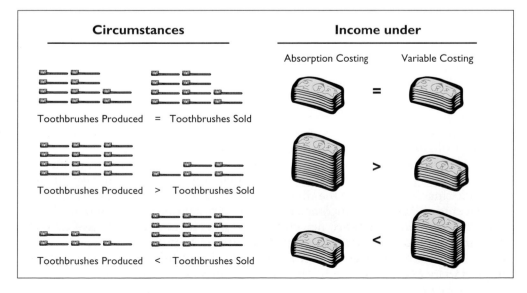

Illustration 7-14   Summary of income effects under absorption costing and variable costing

DECISION-MAKING CONCERNS

STUDY OBJECTIVE

3

Discuss the relative merits of absorption costing versus variable costing for management decision making.

Generally accepted accounting principles (GAAP) requires that absorption costing be used for the costing of inventory for external reporting purposes. Net income measured under GAAP (absorption costing) is often used internally to evaluate performance, justify cost reductions, or evaluate new projects. Some companies, however, have recognized that net income calculated using GAAP does not highlight differences between variable and fixed costs and may lead to poor business decisions. Consequently, these companies use variable costing for internal reporting purposes. The following discussion and example highlight a significant problem related to the use of absorption costing for decision-making purposes.

When production exceeds sales, absorption costing reports a higher net income than variable costing. The reason is that some fixed manufacturing costs are not expensed in the current period, but are deferred to future periods as part of inventory. As a result, management may be tempted to overproduce in a given period in order to increase net income. Although net income will increase, this decision to overproduce may not be in the company's best interest.

Suppose, for example, a division manager's compensation is based upon the division's net income. In such a case the manager may decide to meet the net income targets by increasing production. While this overproduction may increase the manager's compensation, the buildup of inventories in the long run will lead to additional costs to the company. This situation is avoided under variable costing, because net income under variable costing is unaffected by changes in production levels. This is shown in the following illustration.

Warren Lund, a division manager of Walker Enterprises, is under pressure to boost the performance of the Lighting Division in 2005. Unfortunately, recent profits have not met expectations. The expected sales for this year are 20,000 units. As he plans for the year, Warren has to decide whether to produce 20,000 or 30,000 units. The following facts are available for the division.

Illustration 7-15 Facts for Lighting Division— 2005

Beginning inventory	0
Expected sales in units	20,000
Selling price per unit	$15
Variable manufacturing cost per unit	$6
Fixed manufacturing overhead cost (total)	$60,000
Fixed manufacturing overhead costs per unit	
Based on 20,000 units	$3 per unit ($60,000 ÷ 20,000 units)
Based on 30,000 units	$2 per unit ($60,000 ÷ 30,000 units)
Total manufacturing cost per unit	
Based on 20,000 units	$9 per unit ($6 variable + $3 fixed)
Based on 30,000 units	$8 per unit ($6 variable + $2 fixed)
Variable selling and administrative expenses per unit	$1
Fixed selling and administrative expenses	$15,000

The division's results based upon the two possible levels of output are presented in Illustration 7-16 (page 273) under absorption costing.

If the Lighting Division produces 20,000 units, its net income under absorption costing is $85,000. If it produces 30,000 units, its net income is $105,000. By producing 30,000 units, the division has inventory of 10,000 units. This excess inventory causes net income to increase $20,000 because $20,000 of fixed costs (10,000 units × $2) are not charged to the current year, but are deferred to future periods. What do you think Warren Lund might do in this situation? Given his concern about the profit numbers of the Lighting Division, he may be tempted to increase production. Although this increased production will increase 2005 net income, it may be costly to the company in the long run.

Illustration 7-16 Absorption costing income statement—2005

	20,000 Produced	30,000 Produced
LIGHTING DIVISION		
Income Statement		
For the Year Ended 2005		
Absorption Costing		
Sales (20,000 units × $15)	$300,000	$ 300,000
Cost of goods sold	180,000*	160,000**
Gross profit	120,000	140,000
Variable selling and administrative expenses (20,000 units × $1)	20,000	20,000
Fixed selling and administrative expenses	15,000	15,000
Net income	$ 85,000	$105,000

*(20,000 units × $9)
**(20,000 units × $8)

Now let's evaluate the same situation under variable costing. A variable costing income statement is shown for production at both 20,000 and 30,000 units, using the information in Illustration 7-15.

Illustration 7-17 Variable costing income statement—2005

	20,000 Produced	30,000 Produced
LIGHTING DIVISION		
Income Statement		
For the Year Ended 2005		
Variable Costing		
Sales (20,000 units × $15)	$300,000	$300,000
Variable cost of goods sold (20,000 units × $6)	120,000	120,000
Variable selling and administrative expenses (20,000 units × $1)	20,000	20,000
Contribution margin	160,000	160,000
Fixed manufacturing overhead	60,000	60,000
Fixed selling and administrative expenses	15,000	15,000
Net income	$ 85,000	$ 85,000

From this example we see that under variable costing, net income is not affected by the number of units produced. Net income is $85,000 whether 20,000 or 30,000 units are produced. Why? Because fixed manufacturing overhead is treated as a period expense. Unlike absorption costing, no fixed manufacturing overhead is deferred through inventory buildup. Therefore, under variable costing, production does not increase income; sales do. As a result, managers like Warren Lund cannot affect profitability by increasing production if variable costing is used.

POTENTIAL ADVANTAGES OF VARIABLE COSTING

Variable costing has a number of potential advantages relative to absorption costing:

1. Net income computed under variable costing is unaffected by changes in production levels. As a result, it is much easier to understand the impact of fixed and variable costs on the computation of net income when variable costing is used.

2. The use of variable costing is consistent with the cost–volume–profit material presented in Chapter 5 and the incremental analysis material presented in Chapter 6. Later in this chapter you will see other situations where the variable costing approach would be beneficial.

3. Net income computed under variable costing is closely tied to changes in sales levels (not production levels), and therefore provides a more realistic assessment of the company's success or failure during a period.

4. The presentation of fixed and variable cost components on the face of the variable costing income statement makes it easier to identify these costs and understand their effect on the business. Under absorption costing, the allocation of fixed costs to inventory makes it difficult to evaluate the impact of fixed costs on the company's results.

Companies that use just-in-time processing techniques to minimize their inventories will not have significant differences between absorption and variable costing net income.

Business Insight
Service Company Perspective

Although most service companies don't have inventory, the distinction between absorption costing and variable costing is still relevant to them. For example, many shipping companies have begun to rely more heavily on variable costing for decision making, especially for pricing decisions. For shipping companies, the problems with absorption costing become most apparent when operations are below full capacity. If they set their price based on absorption cost, they will spread their full fixed costs over their existing jobs—resulting in a high fixed cost charge per shipment. This will make their price too high relative to competitors, and they will lose business—thus operating even further below capacity, and consequently charging an even higher fixed charge per job. This cycle continues until they are out of business. If, instead, they set their prices using variable costing, they can avoid this dangerous cycle.

DECISION TOOLKIT

Decision Checkpoints	Info Needed for Decision	Tool to Use for Decision	How to Evaluate Results

What is the company's composition of fixed versus variable costs?	Variable cost of goods sold; variable selling and administrative expenses, fixed manufacturing overhead, fixed selling and administrative expenses	**Variable costing income statement**
		Sales
		Less:
		  Variable cost of goods sold
		  Variable selling and administrative expenses
		Contribution margin
		Less:
		  Fixed manufacturing overhead
		  Fixed selling and administrative expenses
		Net income
			Variable costing income statement provides information about variable and fixed costs that is needed for CVP analysis and incremental analysis.

BEFORE YOU GO ON . . .

▶**Review It**

1. What is the primary distinction between absorption costing and variable costing?
2. Explain how a difference between the amount produced and amount sold creates a difference between net income under absorption costing and net income under variable costing.
3. What are the potential advantages of variable costing for decision making?

▶**Do It**

Justin and Andrea Doll Company produces and sells tennis balls. The following costs are available for the year ended December 31, 2005. The company has no beginning inventory. In 2005, 8,000,000 units were produced, but only 7,500,000 units were sold. The unit selling price was $0.50 per ball. Costs and expenses were:

Variable costs per unit	
Direct materials	$0.10
Direct labor	0.05
Variable manufacturing overhead	0.08
Variable selling and administrative expenses	0.02
Annual fixed costs and expenses	
Manufacturing overhead	$500,000
Selling and administrative expenses	100,000

(a) Compute the manufacturing cost of one unit of product using variable costing. (b) Prepare a 2005 income statement for Justin and Andrea Doll Company using variable costing.

Action Plan

• Recall that under variable costing, only variable manufacturing costs are treated as manufacturing (product) costs.
• Subtract all fixed costs, both manufacturing overhead and selling and administrative expenses, as period costs.

Solution

(a) The cost of one unit of product under variable costing would be:

Direct materials	$0.10
Direct labor	0.05
Variable manufacturing overhead	0.08
	$0.23

(b) The variable costing income statement would be as follows.

JUSTIN AND ANDREA DOLL COMPANY
Income Statement
For the Year Ended December 31, 2005
Variable Costing

Sales (7,500,000 × $0.50)		$3,750,000
Variable cost of goods sold (7,500,000 × $0.23)	$1,725,000	
Variable selling and administrative expenses	150,000	1,875,000
Contribution margin		1,875,000
Fixed manufacturing overhead	500,000	
Fixed selling and administrative expenses	100,000	600,000
Net income		$1,275,000

Related exercise material: BE7-1, BE7-3, BE7-5, BE7-6, BE7-8, E7-1, E7-2, E7-3, and E7-4.

☑ THE
NAVIGATOR

Sales Mix

The information provided by a variable costing income statement is very useful for management decision making. One of the most important considerations a company must face is evaluation of the mix of products that it sells. Most companies sell more than one product. **Sales mix** is the relative percentage in which each product is sold when a company sells more than one product. For example, if 75 percent of **Hewlett Packard**'s sales are printers and if the other 25 percent are PCs, its sales mix is 75 percent to 25 percent.

Sales mix is important to managers because different products often have substantially different contribution margins. For example, **Ford**'s SUVs and F150 pickups have higher contribution margins compared to its economy cars. Similarly, first-class tickets sold by **United Airlines** provide substantially higher contribution margins than coach-class tickets.

In this section we discuss how sales mix affects decision making using break-even analysis. The information needed for this analysis is readily available on variable costing income statements. This analysis is illustrated below for both sales in units and sales in dollars.

BREAK-EVEN SALES IN UNITS

Break-even sales can be computed for a mix of two or more products by determining the **weighted-average unit contribution margin of all the products**. To illustrate, we will assume that Vargo Video sells both DVD players and television sets with the per unit data shown in Illustration 7-18. It also incurs $200,000 in fixed costs.

Illustration 7-18 Per unit data—sales mix

Unit Data	DVD Players	TVs
Selling price	$500	$800
Variable costs	300	400
Contribution margin	$200	$400
Sales mix	75%	25%

Illustration 7-19 Weighted-average unit contribution margin

The weighted-average unit contribution margin for the sales mix of 75 percent DVD players and 25 percent TVs is $250, which is computed as follows.

DVD Players				**TVs**				
(Unit Contribution Margin	×	Sales Mix Percentage)	+	(Unit Contribution Margin	×	Sales Mix Percentage)	=	Weighted-Average Unit Contribution Margin
($200	×	.75)	+	($400	×	.25)	=	$250

We then use the weighted-average unit contribution margin to compute the break-even point in unit sales. The computation of break-even sales in units for Vargo Video, assuming $200,000 of fixed costs, is as follows.

Illustration 7-20 Break-even point in units

Fixed Costs	÷	Weighted-Average Unit Contribution Margin	=	Break-even Point in Units
$200,000	÷	$250	=	800 units

Note that with the sales mix of 75 percent to 25 percent, 75 percent of the units sold will be DVD players and 25 percent will be TVs. Therefore, in order to break even, Vargo Video must sell 600 DVD players (.75 × 800 units) and 200 TVs (.25 × 800 units). This can be verified by the following.

Product	Unit Sales	×	Unit Contribution Margin	=	Total Contribution Margin
DVD players	600	×	$200	=	$ 120,000
TVs	200	×	400	=	80,000
	800				**$200,000**

Illustration 7-21 Break-even proof—sales mix

Management should continually review the company's sales mix. At any level of units sold, **net income will be greater if higher contribution margin units are sold than lower contribution margin units**. For Vargo Video, the television sets produce the higher contribution margin. Consequently, if 300 TVs and 500 DVD players are sold, net income would be higher than in the current sales mix, even though total units sold has not changed.

An analysis of these relationships shows that a shift from low-margin sales to high-margin sales may increase net income, even though there is a decline in total units sold. Likewise, a shift from high- to low-margin sales may result in a decrease in net income, even though there is an increase in total units sold.

DECISION TOOLKIT

Decision Checkpoints ✔	Info Needed for Decision	Tool to Use for Decision	How to Evaluate Results
How many units of product A and product B do we need to sell to break even?	Fixed costs, weighted-average contribution margin, sales mix	Break-even point in units $=$ $\dfrac{\text{Fixed costs}}{\text{Weighted-average unit contribution margin}}$	To determine number of units of product A and B, allocate total units based on sales mix.

BREAK-EVEN SALES IN DOLLARS

The calculation of the break-even point presented for Vargo Video in the previous section works well if the company has **only a small number of products**. In contrast, consider **3M**, the maker of Post-it Notes, which has more than 30,000 products. In order to calculate the break-even point for 3M using a weighted-average unit contribution margin, we would need to calculate 30,000 different contribution margins. That is not realistic. For a company like 3M we calculate the break-even point using sales information for divisions or product lines, rather than for individual products.

To illustrate, suppose that Kale Garden Supply Company has two divisions—Indoor Plants and Outdoor Plants. Each division has hundreds of different types of plants and plant-care products. During the last year, 20 percent of the company's sales were from the Indoor Plant Division, and 80 percent were from the Outdoor Plant Division. The Indoor Plant Division has a contribution margin ratio of 40 percent, while the Outdoor Plant Division has a contribution margin ratio of 30 percent. Total fixed costs are $300,000.

The formula for computing the **break-even point in dollars is fixed costs divided by the weighted-average contribution margin ratio**. To compute the company's weighted-average contribution margin ratio, we multiply each division's

Illustration 7-22 Calculation of weighted-average contribution margin

contribution margin ratio by its sales mix percentage and then sum these amounts, as shown in Illustration 7-22.

Indoor Plant Division				Outdoor Plant Division				
(Contribution Margin Ratio	×	Sales Mix Percentage)	+	(Contribution Margin Ratio	×	Sales Mix Percentage)	=	Weighted-Average Contribution Margin Ratio
(.40	×	.20)	+	(.30	×	.80)	=	.32

We then can use the weighted-average contribution margin ratio of 32 percent to compute the company's break-even point in dollars.

Illustration 7-23 Calculation of break-even point in dollars

Fixed Costs	÷	Weighted-Average Contribution Margin Ratio	=	Break-even Point in Dollars
$300,000	÷	.32	=	$937,500

The break-even point is based on the sales mix of 20 percent to 80 percent. Of the company's total break-even sales of $937,500, a total of $187,500 (.20 × $937,500) will come from the Indoor Plant Division and $750,000 (.80 × $937,500) will come from the Outdoor Plant Division.

This break-even point is based on the sales mix of 20 percent to 80 percent. What would be the impact on the break-even point if a higher percentage of the company's sales were to come from the Indoor Plant Division? Because the Indoor Plant Division enjoys a higher contribution margin ratio, this change in the sales mix would result in a higher weighted-average contribution margin ratio, and consequently a lower break-even point in dollars. The opposite would occur if a higher percentage of sales were expected from the Outdoor Plant Division. As you can see, the information provided under variable costing can help managers better understand the impact of sales mix on profitability.

Business Insight
Management Perspective

Zoom Kitchen, a chain of four restaurants in the Chicago area, is known for serving sizable portions of meat and potatoes. But the company's management is quite pleased with the fact that during the past four years salad sales have increased from 18 percent of its sales mix to 40 percent. Why are they pleased? Because the contribution margin on salads is much higher than on meat. The restaurant made a conscious effort to encourage people to buy more salads by offering an interesting assortment of salad ingredients including jicama, beets, marinated mushrooms, grilled tuna, and carved turkey. Management has to be very sensitive to contribution margin—it costs about $600,000 to open up a new Zoom Kitchen restaurant.

SOURCE: Amy Zuber, "Salad Sales 'Zoom' at Meat-and-Potatoes Specialist," *Nation's Restaurant News* (November 12, 2001), p. 26.

DECISION TOOLKIT

Decision Checkpoints	Info Needed for Decision	Tool to Use for Decision	How to Evaluate Results
How many dollars of sales are required from each division in order to break even?	Fixed costs, weighted-average contribution margin ratio, sales mix	$$\text{Break-even point in dollars} = \frac{\text{Fixed costs}}{\text{Weighted-average contribution margin ratio}}$$	To determine the sales dollars required from each division, allocate the total break-even sales using the sales mix.

BEFORE YOU GO ON . . .

▶Review It

1. What is meant by the term sales mix?
2. Why is sales mix important for break-even analysis?
3. How does the number of products that a company sells affect the method that is used to determine the break-even point?
4. What information is needed to compute break-even sales in units? Break-even sales in dollars?

☑ THE NAVIGATOR

Cost Structure and Operating Leverage

Cost structure refers to the relative proportion of fixed versus variable costs that a company incurs. Cost structure can have a significant effect on profitability.

Consider the following example of two separate companies that make wooden croquet mallets. Old English Mallet Company uses a traditional, labor-intensive approach to form, sand, and apply a protective finish to the mallets. New Wave Mallet Company has invested in a completely automated system. The factory employees are involved only in setting up, adjusting, and maintaining the machinery. Variable cost income statements for each company are shown in Illustration 7-24.

STUDY OBJECTIVE
5
Understand how operating leverage affects profitability.

	Old English Company	New Wave Company
Sales	$300,000	$300,000
Variable costs	255,000	120,000
Contribution margin	45,000	180,000
Fixed costs	15,000	150,000
Net income	$ 30,000	$ 30,000

Illustration 7-24 Variable costing income statements for two companies

Both companies have the same sales and the same net income. However, because of the differences in their cost structures, they differ greatly in the way they would be managed. Let's evaluate the impact of cost structure on the profitability of the two companies.

EFFECT ON CONTRIBUTION MARGIN RATIO

First let's look at the contribution margin ratio. Illustration 7-25 shows the computation of the contribution margin ratio for each company.

Illustration 7-25 Contribution margin ratio for two companies

	Contribution Margin	÷	Sales	=	Contribution Margin Ratio
Old English	$45,000	÷	$300,000	=	.15
New Wave	$180,000	÷	$300,000	=	.60

New Wave has a contribution margin ratio of 60 percent versus only 15 percent for Old English. That means that with every dollar of sales, New Wave generates 60 cents of contribution margin (and thus a 60 cent increase in net income), versus only 15 cents for Old English. However, it also means that for every dollar that sales decline, New Wave loses 60 cents in net income, whereas Old English will lose only 15 cents. New Wave's cost structure, which relies more heavily on fixed costs, makes it more sensitive to changes in sales revenue.

Operating leverage refers to the extent to which a company's net income reacts to a given change in sales. Companies that have higher fixed costs relative to variable costs have higher operating leverage. When a company's sales revenue is increasing, high operating leverage is a good thing because it means that profits will increase rapidly. But when sales are declining, too much operating leverage can have devastating consequences.

DEGREE OF OPERATING LEVERAGE

How can we compare operating leverage across two companies? The **degree of operating leverage** provides a measure of a company's earnings volatility and can be used to compare companies. Degree of operating leverage is computed by dividing total contribution margin by net income. This formula is presented in Illustration 7-26, and applied to our two mallet manufacturers.

Illustration 7-26 Computation of degree of operating leverage

	Contribution Margin	÷	Net Income	=	Degree of Operating Leverage
Old English	$45,000	÷	$30,000	=	1.5
New Wave	$180,000	÷	$30,000	=	6

New Wave's earnings would go up (or down) by 4.0 times (6 ÷ 1.5) as much as Old English Company's with an equal increase (or decrease) in sales. For example, suppose both companies experience a 5 percent decrease in sales. Old English's net income will decrease by 7.5 percent (1.5 × 5%), while New Wave's will decrease by 30 percent (6 × 5%). Thus, New Wave's higher operating leverage exposes it to greater earnings volatility risk.

EFFECT ON BREAK-EVEN POINT

The difference in operating leverage also affects the break-even point. The break-even point for each company is calculated in Illustration 7-27.

	Fixed Costs	÷	Contribution Margin Ratio	=	Break-even Point in Dollars
Old English	$15,000	÷	.15	=	$100,000
New Wave	$150,000	÷	.60	=	$250,000

Illustration 7-27 Computation of break-even point for two companies

New Wave needs to generate $150,000 ($250,000 − $100,000) more in sales than Old English before it breaks even. This makes New Wave riskier than Old English because a company cannot survive for very long unless it at least breaks even.

EFFECT ON MARGIN OF SAFETY RATIO

We can also evaluate the relative impact that changes in sales would have on the two companies by computing the margin of safety ratio (see Chapter 5, p. 207). Illustration 7-28 shows the computation of the **margin of safety ratio** for the two companies.

	(Actual Sales	−	Break-even Sales)	÷	Actual Sales	=	Margin of Safety Ratio
Old English	($300,000	−	$100,000)	÷	$300,000	=	.67
New Wave	($300,000	−	$250,000)	÷	$300,000	=	.17

Illustration 7-28 Computation of margin of safety ratio for two companies

The difference in the margin of safety ratio also reflects the difference in risk between the two companies. Old English could sustain a 67 percent decline in sales before it would be operating at a loss. New Wave could sustain only a 17 percent decline in sales before it would be "in the red."

You should be careful not to conclude from this analysis that a cost structure that relies on higher fixed costs, and consequently has higher operating leverage, is necessarily bad. When used carefully, operating leverage can add considerably to a company's profitability. Computer equipment manufacturer **Komag** enjoyed a 66 percent increase in net income when its sales increased by only 8 percent. As one commentator noted, "Komag's fourth quarter illustrates the company's significant operating leverage; a small increase in sales leads to a big profit rise." However, as our illustration demonstrates, increased reliance on fixed costs increases a company's risk. In recent years, computer equipment manufacturer **Cisco Systems** has substantially reduced its operating leverage by choosing to outsource much of its production. While this has made the company less susceptible to economic swings, it has also reduced its ability to experience the incredible profitability that it used to have during economic booms.

The choice of cost structure must be carefully considered. There are many ways that companies can influence their cost structure. For example, by acquiring sophisticated robotic equipment, many companies have reduced their use of manual labor. Similarly, some brokerage firms, such as **E*Trade**, have reduced their reliance on human brokers and have instead invested heavily in computers and online technology. In so doing, they have increased their reliance on fixed costs (through depreciation on the robotic equipment or computer equipment) and reduced their reliance on variable costs (the variable employee labor cost). Alternatively, some companies such as **Cisco Systems**, have reduced their fixed costs and increased their variable costs by outsourcing their production. **Nike**, for example, does very little manufacturing, but instead outsources the manufacture of nearly all of its shoes. It has consequently converted many of its fixed costs into variable costs and therefore reduced its operating leverage.

Business Insight
Management Perspective

Cost structures vary considerably across industries, but they also vary considerably across companies within industries. For example, the airline industry is characterized by two types of companies—low-cost, low-fare airlines such as **Southwest Airlines** and **JetBlue Airways**, and the high-cost, high-fare airline giants such as **United Airlines** and **American Airlines**. One reason that airline giants have higher costs is that they are trapped in a flight system that they invented—the hub-and-spoke approach. Under this approach, passengers are flown from their city of origination to centralized hub cities and then flown to their ultimate destination. This results in high-fixed costs and high operating leverage. When air traffic was at peak volumes during the late 1990s, the large carriers enjoyed record profits. But in recent years this same cost structure has resulted in massive losses and a series of bankruptcy declarations.

DECISION TOOLKIT

Decision Checkpoints	Info Needed for Decision	Tool to Use for Decision	How to Evaluate Results
How sensitive is the company's net income to changes in sales?	Contribution margin and net income	Degree of operating leverage $= \dfrac{\text{Contribution margin}}{\text{Net income}}$	Reports the change in net income that will occur with a given change in sales. A high degree of operating leverage means that the company's net income is very sensitive to changes in sales.

BEFORE YOU GO ON . . .

▶ **Review It**

1. What is operating leverage?
2. What are the benefits of operating leverage? What are the drawbacks of operating leverage?
3. How can operating leverage be measured?
4. What impact does an increase in operating leverage have on a company's break-even point? On a company's margin of safety ratio?

☑ THE NAVIGATOR

Using the Decision Toolkit

Rexfield Corp. is contemplating a huge investment in automated mass-spectrometers for its medical laboratory testing services. Its current process relies heavily on the expertise of a high number of lab technicians. The new equipment would employ a computer expert system that integrates much of the decision process and knowledge base that is used by a skilled lab technician.

Rex Field, the company's CEO, has requested that an analysis of projected results using the old technology versus the new technology be done for the coming year. The accounting department has prepared the following variable costing income statements for use in your analysis.

	Old	**New**
Sales revenue	$2,000,000	$2,000,000
Variable costs	1,400,000	600,000
Contribution margin	600,000	1,400,000
Fixed costs	400,000	1,200,000
Net income	$ 200,000	$ 200,000

Instructions

Use the information provided above to do the following.

(a) Compute the degree of operating leverage for the company under each scenario, and discuss your results.

(b) Compute the break-even point in dollars and margin of safety ratio for the company under each scenario, and discuss your results.

(c) The company's sales, like most companies in healthcare-related fields, have been nearly unaffected by economic swings. Jason Wells, the head of the sales department, is on the verge of closing a deal with a nationwide chain of hospitals that would increase sales by $1,000,000 per year. Prepare new variable costing income statements under both the old and new approaches. Discuss your conclusions regarding what actions management should take.

Solution

(a)

	Contribution Margin	÷	Net Income	=	Degree of Operating Leverage
Old	$600,000	÷	$200,000	=	3
New	$1,400,000	÷	$200,000	=	7

The degree of operating leverage measures the company's sensitivity to changes in sales. By switching to a cost structure dominated by fixed costs, the company would significantly increase its operating leverage. As a result, with a percentage change in sales, its percentage change in net income would be 2.33 as much (7 ÷ 3) under the new structure as it would under the old.

(b) To compute the break-even point in sales dollars, we need first to compute the contribution margin ratio under each scenario. Under the old structure the contribution margin ratio would be .30 ($600,000 ÷ $2,000,000), and under the new it would be .70 ($1,400,000 ÷ $2,000,000).

	Fixed Costs	÷	Contribution Margin Ratio	=	Break-even point in dollars
Old	$400,000	÷	.30	=	$1,333,333
New	$1,200,000	÷	.70	=	$1,714,286

Because the company's fixed costs would be substantially higher under the new cost structure, its break-even point would increase significantly, from $1,333,333 to $1,714,286. A higher break-even point is riskier because it means that the company must generate higher sales to be profitable.

The margin of safety ratio tells how far sales can fall before the company is operating at a loss.

	(Actual Sales − Break-even Sales)	÷	Actual Sales	=	Margin of Safety Ratio
Old	($2,000,000 − $1,333,333)	÷	$2,000,000	=	.33
New	($2,000,000 − $1,714,286)	÷	$2,000,000	=	.14

Under the old structure, sales could fall by 33 percent before the company would be operating at a loss. Under the new structure, sales could fall by only 14 percent.

(c)

	Old	New
Sales	$3,000,000	$3,000,000
Variable costs	2,100,000*	900,000**
Contribution margin	900,000	2,100,000
Fixed costs	400,000	1,200,000
Net income	$ 500,000	$ 900,000

*$3,000,000 × ($1,400,000 ÷ $2,000,000)
**$3,000,000 × ($600,000 ÷ $2,000,000)

If sales increase by $1,000,000, net income under the old cost structure will increase to $500,000. Under the new cost structure, net income will increase to $900,000. Because of the high degree of operating leverage under the new cost structure, the company's net income would be much more sensitive to changes in sales. Given the fact that the company's sales are not very susceptible to economic swings, switching to the new cost structure would appear to make sense. It would result in a significant increase in net income compared to the amount of incremental risk that it would incur.

☑ THE NAVIGATOR

Summary of Study Objectives

1 *Explain the difference between absorption costing and variable costing.* Under absorption costing, fixed manufacturing costs are product costs. Under variable costing, fixed manufacturing costs are period costs.

2 *Discuss the effect that changes in production level and sales level have on net income measured under absorption costing versus variable costing.* If production volume exceeds sales volume, net income under absorption costing will exceed net income under variable costing by the amount of fixed manufacturing costs included in ending inventory that results from units produced but not sold during the period. If production volume is less than sales volume, net income under absorption costing will be less than under variable costing by the amount of fixed manufacturing costs included in the units sold during the period that were not produced during the period.

3 *Discuss the relative merits of absorption costing versus variable costing for management decision making.* The use of variable costing is consistent with cost–volume–profit analysis and incremental analysis. Net income under variable costing is unaffected by changes in production levels. Instead, it is closely tied to changes in sales. The presentation of fixed costs in the variable costing approach makes it easier

to identify fixed costs and to evaluate their impact on the company's profitability.

4 *Explain the term sales mix and its effects on break-even sales.* Sales mix is the relative proportion in which each product is sold when a company sells more than one product. For a company with a small number of products, break-even sales in units is determined by using the weighted-average unit contribution margin of all the products. If the company sells many different products, then calculating the break-even point using unit information is not practical. Instead, in a company with many products, break-even sales in dollars is calculated using the weighted-average contribution margin ratio.

5 *Understand how operating leverage affects profitability.* Operating leverage refers to the degree to which a company's net income reacts to a change in sales. Operating leverage is determined by a company's relative use of fixed versus variable costs. Companies with high fixed costs relative to variable costs have high operating leverage. A company with high operating leverage will experience a sharp increase (decrease) in net income with a given increase (decrease) in sales. The degree of operating leverage can be measured by dividing contribution margin by net income.

☑ THE NAVIGATOR

DECISION TOOLKIT—A SUMMARY

Decision Checkpoints	Info Needed for Decision	Tool to Use for Decision	How to Evaluate Results

What is the company's composition of fixed versus variable costs?	Variable cost of goods sold; variable selling and administrative expenses, fixed manufacturing overhead, fixed selling and administrative expenses	**Variable costing income statement**
		Sales
		Less:
		  Variable cost of goods sold
		  Variable selling and administrative expenses
		Contribution margin
		Less:
		  Fixed manufacturing overhead
		  Fixed selling and administrative expenses
		Net income
			Variable costing income statement provides information about variable and fixed costs that is needed for CVP analysis and incremental analysis.

How many units of product A and product B do we need to sell to break even?	Fixed costs, weighted-average contribution margin, sales mix	Break-even point in units $=\dfrac{\text{Fixed costs}}{\text{Weighted-average unit contribution margin}}$	To determine number of units of product A and B, allocate total units based on sales mix
How many dollars of sales are required from each division in order to break even?	Fixed costs, weighted-average contribution margin ratio, sales mix	Break-even point in dollars $=\dfrac{\text{Fixed costs}}{\text{Weighted-average contribution margin ratio}}$	To determine the sales dollars required from each division, allocate the total break-even sales using the sales mix.
How sensitive is the company's net income to changes in sales?	Contribution margin and net income	Degree of operating leverage $=\dfrac{\text{Contribution margin}}{\text{Net income}}$	Reports the change in net income that will occur with a given change in sales. A high degree of operating leverage means that the company's net income is very sensitive to changes in sales.

Glossary

Absorption costing A costing approach in which all manufacturing costs are charged to the product. (p. 265)

Cost structure The relative proportion of fixed versus variable costs that a company incurs. (p. 279)

Degree of operating leverage A measure of the extent to which a company's net income reacts to a change in sales. It is calculated by dividing contribution margin by net income. (p. 280)

Operating leverage The extent to which a company's net income reacts to a given change in sales. Operating leverage is determined by a company's relative use of fixed versus variable costs. (p. 280)

Sales mix The relative percentage in which each product is sold when a company sells more than one product. (p. 276)

Variable costing A costing approach in which only variable manufacturing costs are product costs, and fixed manufacturing costs are period costs (expenses). (p. 265)

Demonstration Problem

Taylor Enterprises produces birdhouses. In 2005 it began the year with no beginning inventory. During the year it produced 10,000 birdhouses and sold 8,000 for $30 per house. Variable manufacturing costs were $9 per house produced; variable selling and administrative expenses were $4 per unit sold; fixed manufacturing costs were $70,000 in total and $7 ($70,000 ÷ 10,000) per unit; fixed selling and administrative costs were $20,000.

Action Plan

- Recall that under variable costing, only variable manufacturing costs are treated as manufacturing costs.

- For variable costing, subtract all fixed costs, both manufacturing overhead and selling and administrative expenses as period costs.

- For absorption costing, manufacturing costs include variable materials and labor and overhead, as well as an allocated per unit charge for fixed manufacturing overhead.

Instructions

(a) Prepare an income statement using absorption costing.
(b) Prepare an income statement using variable costing.
(c) Show a computation that explains the difference in net income under the two costing approaches.

Solution to Demonstration Problem

(a)

TAYLOR ENTERPRISES
Income Statement
For the Year Ended 2005
Absorption Costing

Sales (8,000 units × $30)		$240,000
Cost of goods sold [8,000 units × ($9 + $7)]		128,000
Gross profit		112,000
Variable selling and administrative expenses (8,000 units × $4)	$32,000	
Fixed selling and administrative expenses	20,000	52,000
Net income		$ 60,000

(b)

TAYLOR ENTERPRISES
Income Statement
For the Year Ended 2005
Variable Costing

Sales (8,000 units × $30)		$240,000
Variable cost of goods sold (8,000 units × $9)	$72,000	
Variable selling and administrative expenses (8,000 units × $4)	32,000	104,000
Contribution margin		136,000
Fixed manufacturing overhead	70,000	
Fixed selling and administrative expenses	20,000	90,000
Net income		$ 46,000

(c) The difference in net income of $14,000 can be explained by the 2,000-unit difference between the number of *units sold* (8,000) versus the number of *units produced* (10,000). The company deferred $7 per unit of fixed manufacturing costs in the 2,000 units of ending inventory. This represents the total difference of $14,000 ($7 × 2,000 units) in net income under variable costing ($46,000) versus absorption costing ($60,000).

Self-Study Questions

Answers are at the end of the chapter.

(SO 1) 1. Fixed manufacturing overhead costs are recognized as:
   (a) period costs under absorption costing.
   (b) product costs under absorption costs.
   (c) product costs under variable costing.
   (d) part of ending inventory costs under both absorption and variable costing.

(SO 1, 2) 2. Net income computed under absorption costing will be:
   (a) higher than net income under variable costing in all cases.
   (b) equal to net income under variable costing in all cases.
   (c) higher than net income under variable costing when units produced are greater than units sold.
   (d) higher than net income under variable costing when units produced are less than units sold.

(SO 2) 3. A company will be in compliance with GAAP when it prepares financial statements in accordance with:
   (a) cost-volume-profit principles.
   (b) absorption costing principles.
   (c) variable costing principles.
   (d) All of the above methods.

(SO 2) 4. A manager can increase reported income by:
   (a) producing more units than units sold under absorption costing.
   (b) producing fewer units than sold under absorption costing.
   (c) producing more units than sold under variable costing.
   (d) producing fewer units than sold under variable costing.

(SO 2) 5. Gross profit is disclosed on an income statement prepared using:
   (a) CVP analysis.
   (b) absorption costing.
   (c) variable costing.
   (d) All costing methods.

(SO 3) 6. When preparing internal reports, service companies:
   (a) cannot benefit from variable costing because they have no inventory.
   (b) cannot use variable costing.
   (c) can benefit from variable costing because they have both fixed and variable costs.
   (d) Both (a) and (b) are correct.

(SO 3) 7. Using variable costing rather than absorption costing is an advantage to a company because:
   (a) variable costing is consistent with cost-volume-profit and incremental analysis used by managers for decision making.
   (b) it agrees with the income information released to external users under GAAP.
   (c) it always produces higher net income.
   (d) it focuses on gross profit, which is the best indicator of a company's ability to meet income goals.

(SO 4) 8. Sales mix is:
   (a) important to sales managers but not to accountants.
   (b) easier to analyze on absorption costing income statements.
   (c) a measure of the relative percentage of a company's variable costs to its fixed costs.
   (d) a measure of the relative percentage in which a company's products are sold.

(SO 4) 9. Net income will be:
   (a) greater if more higher-contribution margin units are sold than lower-contribution margin units.
   (b) greater if more lower-contribution margin units are sold than higher-contribution margin units.
   (c) equal as long as total sales remain equal, regardless of which products are sold.
   (d) unaffected by changes in the mix of products sold.

(SO 5) 10. The degree of operating leverage:
   (a) can be computed by dividing total contribution margin by net income.
   (b) provides a measure of the company's earnings volatility.
   (c) affects a company's break-even point.
   (d) All of the above.

(SO 5) 11. A high degree of operating leverage:
   (a) indicates that a company has a larger percentage of variable costs relative to its fixed costs.
   (b) is computed by dividing fixed costs by contribution margin.
   (c) exposes a company to greater earnings volatility risk.
   (d) exposes a company to less earnings volatility risk.

THE NAVIGATOR

Questions

1. What is variable costing? What is absorption costing?

2. What costs are considered as product costs in a variable costing system?

3. How are fixed manufacturing overhead costs treated in a variable costing system?

4. Under absorption costing, what happens to fixed manufacturing overhead costs if ending inventories increase during the period?

5. What is the main difference between absorption and variable costing approaches?

6. Flygt Corporation sells one product, its waterproof hiking boot. It began operations in the current year and had an ending inventory of 10,500 units. The company sold 20,000 units throughout the year. Fixed manufacturing overhead is $5 per unit, and total manufacturing cost per unit is $20 (including fixed manufacturing overhead costs). What is the difference in net income between absorption and variable costing?

7. If production equals sales, what, if any, is the difference between net income under absorption costing versus under variable costing?

8. If production is greater than sales, how does absorption costing net income differ from variable costing net income?

9. In the long run, will net income be higher or lower under variable costing compared to absorption costing?

10. Brunow Company uses an absorption costing system for internal reporting. If its production exceeds sales by 5,000 units, how will fixed manufacturing overhead be affected?

11. Can variable costing be used for external financial statements? Why or why not?

12. What are some of the benefits to a manager of using variable costing instead of absorption costing?

13. How might the use of just-in-time inventory techniques affect the difference in net income computed under variable costing and under absorption costing?

14. Which method, absorption or variable costing, is better for a company to use as its costing system? Explain. Why do those firms that use variable costing also maintain absorption costing systems?

15. What is meant by the term sales mix? How does sales mix affect the calculation of the break-even point?

16. Radial Company sells two types of radial tires. The lower-priced model is guaranteed for only 40,000 miles; the higher-priced model is guaranteed for 100,000 miles. The unit contribution margin on the higher-priced tire is twice as high as that of the lower-priced tire. If the sales mix shifts so that the company begins to sell more units of the lower-priced tire, explain how the company's break-even point in units will change.

17. What approach should be used to calculate the break-even point of a company that has many products?

18. What is meant by "cost structure?" Explain how a company's cost structure affects its break-even point.

19. What is operating leverage? How does a company increase its operating leverage?

20. How does the replacement of manual labor with automated equipment affect a company's cost structure? What implications does this have for its operating leverage and break-even point?

21. What is a measure of operating leverage, and how is it calculated?

22. Acorn Company has a degree of operating leverage of 8. Oak Company has a degree of operating leverage of 4. Interpret these measures.

Brief Exercises

Identify costs as product costs or period costs under variable costing.
(SO 1)

BE7-1 Determine whether each of the following costs would be classified as product costs or period costs under a variable costing system.

	Product Cost	Period Cost
Commission fees for salespersons		
Glue for wooden chairs—variable		
Fabric for T-shirts		
Labor costs for producing TVs		
Factory rent expense—fixed		
Factory utility costs—variable		
Car mileage costs for salespersons		
Administrative expenses—fixed		
Administrative Internet connection fees		
Wages—assembly line		

Identify costs as product costs or period costs under absorption costing.
(SO 1)

BE7-2 Determine whether each of the costs shown at the top of page 289 would be classified as product costs or period costs under an absorption costing system.

	Product Cost	Period Cost
Commission fees for salespersons		
Glue for wooden chairs—variable		
Fabric for T-shirts		
Labor costs for producing TVs		
Factory rent expense—fixed		
Factory utility costs—variable		
Car mileage costs for salespersons		
Administrative expenses—fixed		
Administrative Internet connection fees		
Wages—assembly line		

BE7-3 Large Orange Company produces basketballs. It incurred the following costs during the year.

Direct materials	$14,490
Direct labor	$25,530
Fixed manufacturing overhead	$10,000
Variable manufacturing overhead	$32,420
Selling costs	$21,000

Compute product costs under variable costing. (SO 1)

What are the total product costs for the company under variable costing?

BE7-4 Information concerning Large Orange Company is provided in BE7-3. What are the total product costs for the company under absorption costing?

Compute product costs under absorption costing. (SO 1)

BE7-5 Burns Manufacturing incurred the following costs during the year: direct materials $20 per unit; direct labor $12 per unit; variable manufacturing overhead $15 per unit; variable selling and administrative costs $8 per unit; fixed manufacturing overhead $120,000; and fixed selling and administrative costs $10,000. Burns produced 12,000 units and sold 10,000 units. Determine the manufacturing cost per unit under (a) absorption costing and (b) variable costing.

Determine manufacturing cost per unit under absorption and variable costing. (SO 1)

BE7-6 During 2005 Rafael Corp. produced 40,000 units and sold 30,000 units for $12 per unit. Variable manufacturing costs were $4 per unit. Annual fixed manufacturing overhead was $80,000 ($2 per unit). Variable selling and administrative costs were $1 per unit sold, and fixed selling and administrative expenses were $10,000. Prepare a variable costing income statement.

Prepare a variable costing income statement. (SO 1)

BE7-7 Information for Rafael Corp. is given in BE7-6. (a) Prepare an absorption costing income statement. (b) Reconcile the difference between net income under variable costing and net income under absorption costing. That is, show a calculation that explains what causes the difference in net income between the two approaches.

Prepare an absorption costing income statement and reconcile difference between variable costing and absorption costing net income. (SO 1, 2)

BE7-8 Caspian Company produced 20,000 units and sold 18,000 units during the current year. Under absorption costing, net income was $25,000. Fixed overhead was $190,000. Determine the net income under variable costing.

Determine net income under variable costing. (SO 1, 2)

BE7-9 Russell Corporation sells three different models of mosquito "zapper." Model A12 sells for $50 and has variable costs of $40. Model B22 sells for $100 and has variable costs of $70. Model C124 sells for $400 and has variable costs of $300. The sales mix of the three models is: A12, 60%; B22, 25%; and C124, 15%. What is the weighted-average unit contribution margin?

Compute weighted-average unit contribution margin based on sales mix. (SO 4)

BE7-10 Information for Russell Corporation is given in BE7-9. If the company has fixed costs of $199,500, how many units of each model must the company sell in order to break even?

Compute break-even point in units for company with multiple products. (SO 4)

BE7-11 Presto Candle Supply makes candles. The sales mix (as a percent of total dollar sales) of its three product lines is: birthday candles 30%, standard tapered candles 50%, and large scented candles 20%. The contribution margin ratio of each candle type is shown on the top of page 290.

Compute break-even point in dollars for company with multiple product lines. (SO 4)

Candle Type	Contribution Margin Ratio
Birthday	10%
Standard tapered	20%
Large scented	45%

If the company's fixed costs are $440,000 per year, what is the dollar amount of each type of candle that must be sold to break even?

Determine weighted-average contribution margin.
(SO 4)

BE7-12 Family Furniture Co. consists of two divisions, Bedroom Division and Dining Room Division. The results of operations for the most recent quarter are:

	Bedroom Division	Dining Room Division
Sales	$500,000	$750,000
Variable costs	250,000	450,000
Contribution margin	$250,000	$300,000

Determine the company's weighted-average contribution margin ratio.

Compute degree of operating leverage.
(SO 5)

BE7-13 Ron's Shingle Corporation is considering the purchase of a new automated shingle-cutting machine. The new machine will reduce variable labor costs but will increase depreciation expense. Contribution margin is expected to increase from $160,000 to $240,000. Net income is expected to be the same at $40,000. Compute the degree of operating leverage before and after the purchase of the new equipment. Interpret your results.

Compute break-even point with change in operating leverage.
(SO 5)

BE7-14 Presented below are variable costing income statements for Finch Company and Sparrow Company. They are in the same industry, with the same net incomes, but different cost structures.

	Finch Co.	Sparrow Co.
Sales	$150,000	$150,000
Variable costs	60,000	15,000
Contribution margin	90,000	135,000
Fixed costs	50,000	95,000
Net income	$ 40,000	$ 40,000

Compute the break-even point in dollars for each company and comment on your findings.

Determine contribution margin from degree of operating leverage.
(SO 5)

BE7-15 The degree of operating leverage for Delta Corp. and Epsilon Co. are 1.4 and 5.6, respectively. Both have net incomes of $50,000. Determine their respective contribution margins.

Exercises

Compute total product cost, and prepare an income statement using variable costing.
(SO 1)

E7-1 Wu Equipment Company manufactures and distributes industrial air compressors. The following costs are available for the year ended December 31, 2005. The company has no beginning inventory. In 2005, 1,500 units are produced, but only 1,200 units are sold. The unit selling price was $4,500. Costs and expenses were as follows.

Variable cost per unit:	
Direct materials	$ 800
Direct labor	$1,500
Variable manufacturing overhead	$ 300
Variable selling and administrative expenses	$ 70
Annual fixed costs and expenses:	
Manufacturing overhead	$1,200,000
Selling and administrative expenses	$ 100,000

Instructions
(a) Compute the manufacturing cost of one unit of product using variable costing.

Prepare income statements under absorption costing and variable costing.
(SO 1)

(b) Prepare a 2005 income statement for Wu Company using variable costing.

E7-2 Asian Windows manufactures a hand-painted bamboo window shade for standard-size windows. Production and sales data for 2005 are shown at the top of page 291.

Variable manufacturing costs	$40 per shade
Fixed manufacturing overhead costs	$100,000
Variable selling and administrative expenses	$9 per shade
Fixed selling and administrative expenses	$250,000
Selling price	$90 per shade
Units produced	10,000 shades
Units sold	8,500 shades

Instructions
(a) Prepare an income statement using absorption costing.
(b) Prepare an income statement using variable costing.

E7-3 Bob's Company builds custom fishing lures for sporting goods stores. In its first year of operations, 2005, the company incurred the following costs.

Compute product cost and prepare an income statement under variable costing.
(SO 1)

Variable cost per unit

Direct materials	$7.50
Direct labor	$2.45
Variable manufacturing overhead	$5.75
Variable selling and administrative expenses	$3.90

Fixed costs per year

Fixed manufacturing overhead	$234,650
Fixed selling and administrative expenses	$240,100

Bob's Company sells the fishing lures for $25. During 2005, the company sold 80,000 lures and produced 95,000 lures.

Instructions
(a) Assuming the company uses variable costing, calculate Bob's manufacturing cost per unit for 2005.
(b) Prepare a variable costing income statement for 2005.

E7-4 Information for Bob's Company is provided in E7-3.

Compute product cost and prepare an income statement under absorption costing.
(SO 1)

Instructions
(a) Assuming the company uses absorption costing, calculate Bob's manufacturing cost per unit for 2005.
(b) Prepare an absorption costing income statement for 2005.

E7-5 Empey Manufacturing produces towels to be sold as souvenirs to sporting events throughout the world. Assume that units produced equaled units sold in 2005. Here is the company's variable costing income statement.

Compute product cost under absorption costing and variable costing; prepare an absorption costing income statement; compare usefulness of variable costing format versus absorption costing format.
(SO 1, 2, 3)

EMPEY MANUFACTURING
Income Statement
For the Year Ended December 31, 2005
Variable Costing

Sales (260,700 units)		$521,400
Variable cost of goods sold	$255,486	
Variable selling expenses	31,284	
Variable administrative expenses	36,498	323,268
Contribution margin		198,132
Fixed manufacturing overhead	96,459	
Fixed selling expenses	38,500	
Fixed administrative expenses	42,625	177,584
Net income		$ 20,548

Unit selling price:	$2.00
Variable costs per unit:	
Direct materials	$0.26
Direct labor	$0.34
Variable manufacturing overhead	$0.38
Variable selling	$0.12
Variable administrative	$0.14

Instructions
(a) Under variable costing, what was the manufacturing cost per unit for each towel?
(b) Under absorption costing, what was the manufacturing cost per unit for each towel?
(c) Prepare an absorption costing income statement for Empey Manufacturing.
(d) Can you explain why there is or is not a difference in net income numbers for the two types of income statements?
(e) Why might Empey Manufacturing want to prepare both an absorption costing income statement and a variable costing income statement?

Determine ending inventory under variable costing and determine whether absorption or variable costing would result in higher net income.
(SO 1, 2)

E7-6   Ortiz Company produced 10,000 units during the past year, but only 9,000 of the units were sold. The following additional information is also available.

Direct materials used	$90,000
Direct labor incurred	$30,000
Variable manufacturing overhead	$24,000
Fixed manufacturing overhead	$50,000
Fixed selling and administrative expenses	$70,000
Variable selling and administrative expenses	$10,000

There was no work-in-process inventory at the beginning of the year, nor did Ortiz have any beginning finished goods inventory.

Instructions
(a) What would be Ortiz Company's finished goods inventory cost on December 31 under variable costing?
(b) Which costing method, absorption or variable costing, would show a higher net income for the year? By what amount?

Compute manufacturing cost under absorption and variable costing and explain difference.
(SO 2)

E7-7   Hardwood Inc. produces wooden crates used for shipping products by ocean liner. In 2005, Hardwood incurred the following costs.

Wood used in crate production	$54,000
Nails (considered insignificant and a variable expense)	$ 340
Direct labor	$37,000
Utilities for the plant:	
$2,000 each month,	
plus $0.45 for each kilowatt-hour used each month	
Rent expense for the plant for the year	$21,400

Assume Hardwood used an average 500 kilowatt-hours each month over the past year.

Instructions
(a) What is Hardwood's total manufacturing cost if it uses a variable costing approach?
(b) What is Hardwood's total manufacturing cost if it uses an absorption costing approach?
(c) What accounts for the difference in manufacturing costs between these two costing approaches?

Compute break-even point in units for a company with more than one product.
(SO 4)

E7-8   Grass King manufactures lawnmowers, weed-trimmers, and chainsaws. Its sales mix and contribution margin per unit are as follows.

	Sales Mix	Contribution Margin per Unit
Lawnmowers	30%	$30
Weed-trimmers	50%	$20
Chainsaws	20%	$40

Grass King has fixed costs of $4,600,000.

Instructions
Compute the number of units of each product that Grass King must sell in order to break even under this product mix.

Compute service line break-even point and target net income in dollars for a company with more than one service.
(SO 4)

E7-9   Rapid Auto has over 200 auto-maintenance service outlets nationwide. It provides primarily two lines of service: oil changes and brake repair. Oil change–related services represent 65% of its sales and provide a contribution margin ratio of 20%. Brake repair represents 35% of its sales and provides a 60% contribution margin ratio. The company's fixed costs are $16,000,000 (that is, $80,000 per service outlet).

Instructions

(a) Calculate the dollar amount of each type of service that the company must provide in order to break even.

(b) The company has a desired net income of $60,000 per service outlet. What is the dollar amount of each type of service that must be provided by each service outlet to meet its target net income per outlet?

E7-10 Blazer Delivery is a rapidly growing delivery service. Last year 80% of its revenue came from the delivery of mailing "pouches" and small, standardized delivery boxes (which provides a 10% contribution margin). The other 20% of its revenue came from delivering non-standardized boxes (which provides a 60% contribution margin). With the rapid growth of Internet retail sales, Blazer believes that there are great opportunities for growth in the delivery of non-standardized boxes. The company has fixed costs of $12,000,000.

Compute break-even point in dollars for a company with more than one service.
(SO 4)

Instructions

(a) What is the company's break-even point in total sales dollars? At the break-even point, how much of the company's sales are provided by each type of service?

(b) The company's management would like to hold its fixed costs constant, but shift its sales mix so that 60% of its revenue comes from the delivery of non-standardized boxes and the remainder from pouches and small boxes. If this were to occur, what would be the company's break-even sales, and what amount of sales would be provided by each service type?

E7-11 Tiger Golf Accessories sells golf shoes, gloves, and a laser-guided range-finder that measures distance. Shown below are unit cost and sales data.

Compute break-even point in units for a company with multiple products.
(SO 4)

	Pairs of Shoes	**Pairs of Gloves**	**Range-Finder**
Unit sales price	$100	$30	$250
Unit variable costs	60	10	200
Unit contribution margin	$ 40	$20	$ 50
Sales mix	40%	50%	10%

Fixed costs are $620,000.

Instructions

(a) Compute the break-even point in units for the company.

(b) Determine the number of units to be sold at the break-even point for each product line.

(c) Verify that the mix of sales units determined in (b) will generate a zero net income.

E7-12 Mega Electronix sells television sets and DVD players. The business is divided into two divisions along product lines. Variable costing income statements for a recent quarter's activity are presented below.

Determine break-even point in dollars for two divisions.
(SO 4)

	TV Division	**DVD Division**	**Total**
Sales	$600,000	$400,000	$1,000,000
Variable costs	450,000	240,000	690,000
Contribution margin	$150,000	$160,000	310,000
Fixed costs			124,000
Net income			$ 186,000

Instructions

(a) Determine sales mix percentage and contribution margin ratio for each division.

(b) Calculate the company's weighted-average contribution margin ratio.

(c) Calculate the company's break-even point in dollars.

(d) Determine the sales level in dollars for each division at the break-even point.

E7-13 The variable costing income statements shown on page 294 are available for Billings Company and Bozeman Company.

Compute degree of operating leverage and evaluate impact of alternative cost structures on net income.
(SO 5)

	Billings Co.	Bozeman Co.
Sales revenue	$600,000	$600,000
Variable costs	280,000	80,000
Contribution margin	320,000	520,000
Fixed costs	170,000	370,000
Net income	$150,000	$150,000

Instructions

(a) Compute the degree of operating leverage for each company and interpret your results.

(b) Assuming that sales revenue increases by 10%, prepare a variable costing income statement for each company.

(c) Discuss how the cost structure of these two companies affects their operating leverage and profitability.

Compute degree of operating leverage and evaluate impact of alternative cost structures on net income and margin of safety.
(SO 5)

E7-14 Imagen Arquitectonica of Tijuana, B.C., Mexico is contemplating a major change in its cost structure. Currently, all of its drafting work is performed by skilled draftsmen. Alfredo Ayala, Imagen's owner, is considering replacing the draftsmen with a computerized drafting system. However, before making the change Alfredo would like to know the consequences of the change, since the volume of business varies significantly from year to year. Shown below are variable costing income statements for each alternative.

	Manual System	Computerized System
Sales	$1,500,000	$1,500,000
Variable costs	1,200,000	600,000
Contribution margin	300,000	900,000
Fixed costs	60,000	660,000
Net income	$ 240,000	$ 240,000

Instructions

(a) Determine the degree of operating leverage for each alternative.

(b) Which alternative would produce the higher net income if sales increased by $100,000?

(c) Using the margin of safety ratio, determine which alternative could sustain the greater decline in sales before operating at a loss.

Compute degree of operating leverage and impact on net income of alternative cost structures.
(SO 5)

E7-15 An investment banker is analyzing two companies that specialize in the production and sale of candied apples. Old-Fashion Apples uses a labor-intensive approach, and Mech-Apple uses a mechanized system. Variable costing income statements for the two companies are shown below.

	Old-Fashion Apples	Mech-Apple
Sales	$400,000	$400,000
Variable costs	320,000	160,000
Contribution margin	80,000	240,000
Fixed costs	20,000	180,000
Net income	$ 60,000	$ 60,000

The investment banker is interested in acquiring one of these companies. However, she is concerned about the impact that each company's cost structure might have on its profitability.

Instructions

(a) Calculate each company's degree of operating leverage. Determine which company's cost structure makes it more sensitive to changes in sales volume.

(b) Determine the effect on each company's net income if sales decrease by 10% and if sales increase by 5%. Do not prepare income statements.

(c) Which company should the investment banker acquire? Discuss.

Problems: Set A

P7-1A   Blue Mountain Products manufactures and sells a variety of camping products. Recently the company opened a new plant to manufacture a light-weight, self-standing tent. Cost and sales data for the first month of operations are shown below.

Calculate product cost; prepare income statements under variable costing and absorption costing and reconcile difference.
(SO 1, 2)

Manufacturing costs:	
Fixed overhead	$200,000
Variable overhead	$4 per tent
Direct labor	$16 per tent
Direct materials	$40 per tent
Beginning inventory	0 tents
Tents produced	10,000
Tents sold	9,000
Selling and administrative costs:	
Fixed	$400,000
Variable	$6 per tent sold

The tent sells for $150. Management is interested in the opening month's results and has asked for an income statement.

Instructions
(a) Assuming the company uses absorption costing, do the following.
   (i) Calculate the manufacturing cost per unit.
   (ii) Prepare an absorption costing income statement for the month of June 2005.
(b) Assuming the company uses variable costing, do the following.
   (i) Calculate the manufacturing cost per unit.
   (ii) Prepare a variable costing income statement for the month of June 2005.
(c) Reconcile the difference in net income between the two methods.

(a) (i) $80

(b) (i) $60

P7-2A   AFN Company produces plastic that is used for injection-molding applications such as gears for small motors. In 2005, the first year of operations, AFN produced 4,000 tons of plastic and sold 3,000 tons. In 2006, the production and sales results were exactly reversed. In each year, the selling price per ton was $2,000, variable manufacturing costs were 15% of the sales price of units produced, variable selling expenses were 10% of the selling price of units sold, fixed manufacturing costs were $2,400,000, and fixed administrative expenses were $600,000.

Prepare income statements under absorption costing and variable costing for a company with beginning inventory, and reconcile difference.
(SO 1, 2, 3)

Instructions
(a) Prepare income statements for each year using variable costing. (Use the format from Illustration 7-5.)
(b) Prepare income statements for each year using absorption costing. (Use the format from Illustration 7-4.)
(c) Reconcile the differences each year in net income under the two costing approaches.
(d) ▭▭▭▷ Comment on the effects of production and sales on net income under the two costing approaches.

(a) 2005 NI $1,500,000

(b) 2005 NI $2,100,000

P7-3A   Basic Electric Motors is a division of Basic Electric Products Corporation. The division manufactures and sells an electric motor used in a wide variety of applications. During the coming year it expects to sell 50,000 units for $30 per unit. Esther Madonna is the division manager. She is considering producing either 50,000 or 80,000 units during the period. Other information is presented in the schedule.

Prepare absorption and variable costing income statements and reconcile differences between absorption and variable costing income statements when sales level and production level change. Discuss relative usefulness of absorption costing versus variable costing.
(SO 1, 2, 3)

Division Information for 2005

Beginning inventory	0
Expected sales in units	50,000
Selling price per unit	$30
Variable manufacturing costs per unit	$12
Fixed manufacturing overhead costs (total)	$400,000

Fixed manufacturing overhead costs per unit:
Based on 50,000 units	$8 per unit ($400,000 ÷ 50,000)
Based on 80,000 units	$5 per unit ($400,000 ÷ 80,000)

Manufacturing cost per unit:
Based on 50,000 units	$20 per unit ($12 variable + $8 fixed)
Based on 80,000 units	$17 per unit ($12 variable + $5 fixed)
Variable selling and administrative expenses	$2
Fixed selling and administrative expenses (total)	$40,000

Instructions

(a) 80,000 produced:
NI $510,000

(b) 80,000 produced:
NI $360,000

(a) Prepare an absorption costing income statement, with one column showing the results if 50,000 units are produced and one column showing the results if 80,000 units are produced.

(b) Prepare a variable costing income statement, with one column showing the results if 50,000 units are produced and one column showing the results if 80,000 units are produced.

(c) Reconcile the difference in net incomes under the two approaches and explain what accounts for this difference.

(d) ▰▰▰▶ Discuss the relative usefulness of the variable costing income statements versus the absorption costing income statements for decision making and for evaluating the manager's performance.

Determine break-even sales under alternative sales strategies and evaluate results.
(SO 4)

P7-4A The Creekside Inn is a restaurant in Tucson, Arizona. It specializes in southwestern style meals in a moderate price range. Terry Wilson, the manager of Creekside, has determined that during the last 2 years the sales mix and contribution margin ratio of its offerings are as follows.

	Percent of Total Sales	Contribution Margin Ratio
Appetizers	10%	60%
Main entrees	60%	30%
Desserts	10%	50%
Beverages	20%	80%

Terry is considering a variety of options to try to improve the profitability of the restaurant. Her goal is to generate a target net income of $150,000. The company has fixed costs of $1,200,000 per year.

Instructions

(a) Total sales $3,000,000

(b) Total sales $3,750,000

(a) Calculate the total restaurant sales and the sales of each product line that would be necessary to achieve the desired target net income.

(b) Terry believes the restaurant could greatly improve its profitability by reducing the complexity and selling price of its entrees to increase the number of clients that it serves. It would then more heavily market its appetizers and beverages. She is proposing to drop the contribution margin ratio on the main entrees to 10% by dropping the average selling price. She envisions an expansion of the restaurant that would increase fixed costs by 50%. At the same time, she is proposing to change the sales mix to the following.

	Percent of Total Sales	Contribution Margin Ratio
Appetizers	20%	60%
Main entrees	30%	10%
Desserts	10%	50%
Beverages	40%	80%

Compute the total restaurant sales, and the sales of each product line that would be necessary to achieve the desired target net income.

(c) Total sales $5,909,091

(c) Suppose that Terry drops the selling price on entrees and increases fixed costs as proposed in part (b), but customers are not swayed by the marketing efforts and the sales mix remains what it was in part (a). Compute the total restaurant sales and the sales of each product line that would be necessary to achieve the desired target net income. Comment on the potential risks and benefits of this strategy.

P7-5A The following variable costing income statements are available for Old Company and New Company.

Compute degree of operating leverage and evaluate impact of operating leverage on financial results.
(SO 5)

	Old Company	New Company
Sales	$400,000	$400,000
Variable costs	180,000	80,000
Contribution margin	220,000	320,000
Fixed costs	170,000	270,000
Net income	$ 50,000	$ 50,000

Instructions

(a) Compute the break-even point in dollars and the margin of safety ratio for each company.

(b) Compute the degree of operating leverage for each company and interpret your results.

(c) Assuming that sales revenue increases by 20%, prepare a variable costing income statement for each company.

(d) Assuming that sales revenue decreases by 20%, prepare a variable costing income statement for each company.

(e) ▰▰▰▶ Discuss how the cost structure of these two companies affects their operating leverage and profitability.

(a) BE, Old $309,091
    BE, New $337,500

(b) DOL, Old 4.4
    DOL, New 6.4

Problems: Set B

P7-1B Spongebob Products manufactures and sells a variety of swimming products. Recently the company opened a new plant to manufacture a light-weight, inflatable boat. Cost and sales data for the first month of operations are shown below.

Calculate product cost; prepare income statements under variable costing and absorption costing and reconcile difference.
(SO 1, 2)

Manufacturing costs:	
Fixed overhead costs	$150,000
Variable overhead	$5 per boat
Direct labor	$10 per boat
Direct materials	$10 per boat
Beginning inventory	0 boats
Boats produced	50,000
Boats sold	46,000
Selling and administrative costs:	
Fixed	$300,000
Variable	$8 per boat sold

The boat sells for $60. Management is interested in the opening month's results and has asked for an income statement.

Instructions

(a) Assuming the company uses absorption costing, do the following.
   (i) Calculate the production cost per unit.
   (ii) Prepare an income statement for the month of July 2005.

(b) Assuming the company uses variable costing, do the following.
   (i) Calculate the production cost per unit.
   (ii) Prepare an income statement for the month of July 2005.

(c) Reconcile the difference in net income between the two methods.

(a) (i) $28

(b) (i) $25

P7-2B Zaki Metal Company produces the steel wire that is used for the production of paper clips. In 2005, the first year of operations, Zaki produced 40,000 miles of wire and sold 30,000 miles. In 2006, the production and sales results were exactly reversed. In each year, the selling price per mile was $80, variable manufacturing costs were 25% of the sales price of units produced, variable selling expenses were $6 per mile sold, fixed manufacturing costs were $1,200,000, and fixed administrative expenses were $200,000.

Prepare income statements under absorption costing and variable costing for a company with beginning inventory, and reconcile difference.
(SO 1, 2, 3)

Instructions

(a) Prepare income statements for each year using variable costing. (Use the format from Illustration 7-5.)
(b) Prepare income statements for each year using absorption costing. (Use the format from Illustration 7-4.)
(c) Reconcile the differences each year in net income under the two costing approaches.
(d) Comment on the effects of production and sales on net income under the two costing approaches.

Prepare absorption and variable costing income statements and reconcile differences between absorption and variable costing income statements when sales level and production level change. Discuss relative usefulness of absorption costing versus variable costing.
(SO 1, 2, 3)

P7-3B   Harrison Pumps is a division of Liverpool Controls Corporation. The division manufactures and sells a pump used in a wide variety of applications. During the coming year it expects to sell 60,000 units for $20 per unit. Richard Starkey manages the division. He is considering producing either 60,000 or 100,000 units during the period. Other information is presented in the following schedule.

Division Information for 2005

Beginning inventory	0
Expected sales in units	60,000
Selling price per unit	$20.00
Variable manufacturing costs per unit	$9.00
Fixed manufacturing overhead costs (total)	$240,000

Fixed manufacturing overhead costs per unit:
  Based on 60,000 units $4.00 per unit ($240,000 ÷ 60,000)
  Based on 100,000 units $2.40 per unit ($240,000 ÷ 100,000)

Manufacturing cost per unit:
  Based on 60,000 units $13.00 per unit ($9.00 variable + $4.00 fixed)
  Based on 100,000 units $11.40 per unit ($9.00 variable + $2.40 fixed)

Variable selling and administrative expenses	$1
Fixed selling and administrative expenses (total)	$30,000

Instructions

(a) Prepare an absorption costing income statement, with one column showing the results if 60,000 units are produced and one column showing the results if 100,000 units are produced.
(b) Prepare a variable costing income statement, with one column showing the results if 60,000 units are produced and one column showing the results if 100,000 units are produced.
(c) Reconcile the difference in net incomes under the two approaches and explain what accounts for this difference.
(d) Discuss the relative usefulness of the variable costing income statements versus the absorption costing income statements for decision making and for evaluating the manager's performance.

Determine break-even sales under alternative sales strategies and evaluate results.
(SO 4)

P7-4B   The Bricktown Pub is a restaurant in Platteville, Wisconsin. It specializes in classic American fare in a moderate price range. Ben Borke, the manager of Bricktown, has determined that during the last 2 years the sales mix and contribution margin of its offerings are as follows.

	Percent of Total Sales	Contribution Margin Ratio
Appetizers	10%	50%
Main entrees	55%	30%
Desserts	10%	60%
Beverages	25%	75%

Ben is considering a variety of options to try to improve the profitability of the restaurant. His goal is to generate a target net income of $155,000. The company has fixed costs of $400,000 per year.

Instructions

(a) Calculate the total restaurant sales and the sales of each product line that would be necessary to achieve the desired target net income.

(b) Ben believes the restaurant could greatly improve its profitability by reducing the complexity and selling price of its entrees to increase the number of clients that it serves, and then more heavily marketing its appetizers and beverages. He is proposing to drop the contribution margin on the main entrees to 15% by dropping the average selling price. He envisions an expansion of the restaurant that would increase fixed costs by 50%. At the same time, he is proposing to change the sales mix to the following.

(b) Total sales $1,480,392

	Percent of Total Sales	Contribution Margin Ratio
Appetizers	15%	50%
Main entrees	30%	15%
Desserts	15%	60%
Beverages	40%	75%

Compute the total restaurant sales, and the sales of each product line that would be necessary to achieve the desired target net income.

(c) Suppose that Ben drops the selling price on entrees, and increases fixed costs as proposed in part (b), but customers are not swayed by his marketing efforts, and the sales mix remains what it was in part (a). Compute the total restaurant sales and the sales of each product line that would be necessary to achieve the desired target net income. Comment on the potential risks and benefits of this strategy.

(c) Total sales $1,986,842

P7-5B The following variable costing income statements are available for Retro Company and Modern Company.

Compute degree of operating leverage and evaluate impact of operating leverage on financial results.
(SO 5)

	Retro Company	Modern Company
Sales	$500,000	$500,000
Variable costs	300,000	100,000
Contribution margin	200,000	400,000
Fixed costs	140,000	340,000
Net income	$ 60,000	$ 60,000

Instructions

(a) Compute the break-even point in dollars and the margin of safety ratio for each company.

(a) BE, Retro $350,000

(b) Compute the degree of operating leverage for each company and interpret your results.

(b) DOL, Retro 3.3

(c) Assuming that sales revenue increases by 25%, prepare a variable costing income statement for each company.

(d) Assuming that sales revenue decreases by 25%, prepare a variable costing income statement for each company.

(e) ▭▭▭▷ Discuss how the cost structure of these two companies affects their operating leverage and profitability.

Problems: Set C

Problem Set C is provided at the book's Web site, www.wiley.com/college/weygandt.

▷ BROADENING YOUR PERSPECTIVE

Group Decision Case

BYP 7-1 ComfortCraft manufactures swivel seats for customized vans. It currently manufactures 10,000 seats per year, which it sells for $480 per seat. It incurs variable costs of $180 per seat and fixed costs of $2,200,000. It is considering automating the upholstery process, which is now largely manual. It estimates that if it does so, its fixed costs will be $3,200,000, and its variable costs will decline to $80 per seat.

Instructions

With the class divided into groups, answer the following questions.

(a) Prepare a variable costing income statement based on current activity.

(b) Compute contribution margin ratio, break-even point in dollars, margin of safety ratio, and degree of operating leverage based on current activity.

(c) Prepare a variable costing income statement assuming that the company invests in the automated upholstery system.

(d) Compute contribution margin ratio, break-even point in dollars, margin of safety ratio, and degree of operating leverage assuming the new upholstery system is implemented.

(e) Discuss the implications of adopting the new system.

Managerial Analysis

BYP 7-2 Big Brick Manufacturing produces basketballs used for indoor or outdoor games. The company has been having significant troubles over the past few years, as the number of competitors in the basketball market has increased dramatically. Recently, the company has been forced to cut back production, in order to decrease its rising inventory level. The following is a list of costs for the company in 2005.

Variable Cost Per Unit:	
Rubber	$2.75
Other materials—indirect	1.40
Ball makers—direct labor	5.60
Factory electricity usage	0.50
Factory water usage	0.15
Other labor—indirect	0.27
Selling and administrative expense	0.40

Fixed Costs Per Year:	
Factory property taxes	$120,000
Factory sewer usage	50,000
Factory electricity usage	40,000
Selling and administrative expense	83,000

Big Brick Manufacturing had ending inventories of 85,000 basketballs in 2004. For these units, fixed manufacturing overhead cost was $4.00 per unit, and variable manufacturing cost per unit was $9.67. In 2005, the company produced 35,000 basketballs; it sold 90,000 basketballs and had an ending inventory of 30,000 units. The basketballs sold for $18 each. Assume that Big Brick uses the FIFO method for computing cost of goods sold.

Instructions

(a) Compute Brick Manufacturing's 2005 manufacturing cost per unit under a variable costing system.

(b) Prepare a variable costing income statement for 2005. (Use the format from Illustration 7-5.)

(c) Compute Brick Manufacturing's 2005 manufacturing cost per unit under absorption costing.

(d) Prepare an absorption costing income statement for 2005. (Use the format from Illustration 7-4.)

(e) Big Brick Manufacturing's chief financial officer, Mr. Swish, is contemplating the benefits of using absorption and variable costing approaches. He has asked you to perform a variety of tasks to help him analyze the difference between the two approaches.

 (i) Reconcile the differences between the net income values of the two approaches.

(ii) Mr. Swish has been very impressed with the variable costing techniques that he has seen so far. He has been contemplating doing away with absorption costing for the company. What do you think about this suggestion?

Real-World Focus

BYP 7-3 In its 2003 annual report the **Del Monte Foods Company** reported three separate operating segments: consumer products (which includes a variety of canned foods including tuna, fruit, and vegetables); pet products (which includes pet food and snacks and veterinary products); and soup and infant-feeding products (which includes soup, broth, and infant feeding and pureed products).

In its annual report Del Monte uses absorption costing. As a result, information regarding the relative composition of its fixed and variable costs is not available. We have assumed that $860.3 million of its total operating expenses of $1,920.3 million are fixed and have allocated the remaining variable costs across the three divisions. Sales data, along with assumed expense data, are provided below.

| | (in millions) | |
	Sales	Variable Costs
Consumer products	$1,031.8	$ 610
Pet products	837.3	350
Soup and infant-feeding products	302.0	100
	$2,171.1	$1,060

Instructions

(a) Compute each segment's contribution margin ratio and the sales mix.
(b) Using the information computed in part (a), compute the company's break-even point in dollars, and then determine the amount of sales that would be generated by each division at the break-even point.

Exploring the Web

BYP 7-4 The external financial statements published by publicly traded companies are based on absorption cost accounting. As a consequence, it is very difficult to gain an understanding of the relative composition of the companies' fixed and variable costs. It is possible, however, to learn about a company's sales mix and the relative profitability of its various divisions. This exercise looks at the financial statements of **FedEx Corporation**.

Address: **www.fedex.com/us/investorrelations/,** *or go to*
www.wiley.com/college/weygandt

Steps

1. Go to the site above.
2. Choose "Financial Downloads."
3. Choose "2003 Annual Report."

Instructions

(a) Read page 37 of the report under the heading "General." What are the three primary product lines of the company? What does the company identify as the key factors affecting operating results?
(b) Page 43 of the report lists the operating expenses of FedEx Ground. Assuming that rentals, depreciation, and "other" are all fixed costs, prepare a variable costing income statement for 2003, and compute the division's contribution margin ratio and the break-even point in dollars.
(c) Page 71, Note 13, ("Business segment information") provides additional information regarding the relative profitability of the three business segments.
   (i) Calculate the sales mix for 2001 and 2003. (Note: Exclude "other" among your categories, and deduct it from the total revenue.)
   (ii) The company does not provide the contribution margin for each division, but it does provide "operating margin" (operating income divided by revenues) on pages 41, 43, and 44. List these for each division for 2001 and 2003.
   (iii) Assuming that the "operating margin" (operating income divided by revenues) moves in parallel with each division's contribution margin, how has the shift in sales mix affected the company's profitability from 2001 to 2003?

Communication Activity

BYP 7-5 Gigliuto Company's fixed overhead costs are $4 per unit, and its variable overhead costs are $8 per unit. In the first month of operations, 50,000 units are produced and 45,000 units are sold.

Instructions

Write a short memo to the chief financial officer explaining which costing approach will produce the higher income and what the difference will be. Also, explain what potential benefits the company might obtain by supplementing its absorption costing system with a variable costing system. Finally, explain why the company probably needs to continue to maintain an absorption costing system, even if it decides to adopt a variable costing system.

Research Assignment

BYP 7-6 The May 12, 2004, edition of the *Wall Street Journal* has an article by David Bank and Gary McWilliams titled "Squeeze Play: Picking a Big Fight With Dell, H-P Cuts PC Profits Razor-Thin" (page A1).

Instructions

Read the article and answer the following questions.

(a) How is HP using its sales mix as a strategic weapon in its battle with Dell?
(b) What are some of the reasons that Dell's PC division has higher profit margins than the PC division of HP?
(c) Why is HP willing to sell its PCs at prices that enable it to just break even, rather than to make a profit? What are some of the advantages of this approach? What are some of the disadvantages?
(d) Dell has recently entered the market for computer printers. It hopes to apply the same just-in-time techniques to the manufacture and sale of printers that it has used so successfully for PCs. HP is currently the largest seller of printers, and its printer division has a high contribution margin ratio. If Dell is successful in moving into the printer business, what implications might this have for HP's corporate break-even point and its corporate profitability?

Ethics Case

BYP 7-7 Scott Bestor was hired during January 2005 to manage the home products division of Advanced Techno. As part of his employment contract, he was told that he would get $5,000 of additional bonus for every 1% increase that the division's profits exceeded those of the previous year.

Soon after coming on board, Scott met with his plant managers and explained that he wanted the plants to be run at full capacity. Previously the plant had employed just-in-time inventory practices and had consequently produced units only as they were needed. Scott stated that under previous management the company had missed out on too many sales opportunities because it didn't have enough inventory on hand. Because previous management had employed just-in-time inventory practices, when Scott came on board there was virtually no beginning inventory. The selling price and variable cost per unit remained the same from 2004 to 2005. Additional information is provided below.

	2004	2005
Net income	$ 400,000	$ 600,000
Units produced	20,000	25,000
Units sold	20,000	20,000
Fixed manufacturing overhead costs	$1,000,000	$1,000,000
Fixed manufacturing overhead costs per unit	$ 50	$ 40

Instructions

(a) Calculate Scott's bonus based upon the net income shown above.
(b) Recompute the 2004 and 2005 results using variable costing.
(c) Recompute Scott's 2005 bonus under variable costing.
(d) Were Scott's actions unethical? Do you think any actions need to be taken by the company?

CHAPTER 8

Pricing

STUDY OBJECTIVES

After studying this chapter,
you should be able to:

1 Compute a target cost when a product price is determined by the market.

2 Compute a target selling price using cost-plus pricing.

3 Use time and material pricing to determine the cost of services provided.

4 Determine a transfer price using the negotiated, cost-based, and market-based approaches.

5 Explain the issues that arise when transferring goods between divisions located in countries with different tax rates.

THE NAVIGATOR

FEATURE STORY

"I'll Call Your Bluff, and Raise You 43 Percent"

If you own a PC, then there is a roughly 85 percent chance that the microprocessor chip that runs your machine was made by **Intel**. That's because for as long as most people can remember, Intel has had at least an 85 percent share of the market for PC computer chips. It isn't that nobody else makes computer chips; it's just that the competition can't seem to get a foothold.

Intel's primary competition comes from a scrappy company called **Advanced Micro Devices (AMD)**. Recently, Intel made a couple of missteps that caused it to lose a few points of market share to AMD. First, Intel had two product recalls on its chips. Then it had problems meeting demand. In the meantime, AMD was boasting that it had a chip that was more powerful than Intel's, and that it had plenty of supply to meet demand. The result was that Intel's market share fell—to 82 percent.

To those familiar with Intel, its response was easily predicted. It cut prices by up to 26 percent. One analyst noted, "When Intel screws up, they can't send flowers, so they cut prices." Said another analyst, "Intel has drawn a line in the sand at 85 percent market share, and they will use price to regain that share."

AMD had little choice but to respond with price cuts of its own. It cut prices by up to 46 percent on some of its chips. In the past, price wars have

THE NAVIGATOR ✔

▶ Scan *Study Objectives* ☐
▶ Read *Feature Story* ☐
▶ Read *Preview* ☐
▶ Read text and answer *Before You Go On*
    p. 311 ☐   p. 314 ☐   p. 323 ☐
▶ Work *Using the Decision Toolkit* ☐
▶ Review *Summary of Study Objectives* ☐
▶ Work *Demonstration Problem* ☐
▶ Answer *Self-Study Questions* ☐
▶ Complete *Assignments* ☐

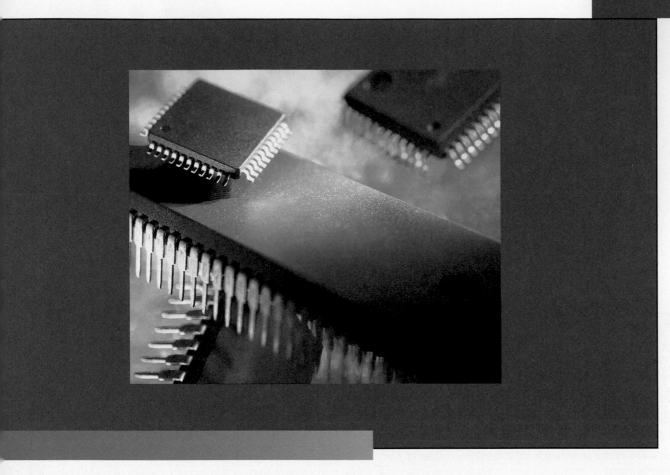

typically hurt AMD worse since Intel's massive volume allows it to produce chips at a lower cost. In 2003 Intel's gross profit rate was 56.7 percent, while AMD's was only 33.9 percent. An all-out price war, however, would leave both companies battered and bruised. The stock price of both companies fell on the news of the price cuts.

Source: Molly Williams, "Intel Cuts Prices, Prompts AMD to Answer the Call," *Wall Street Journal* (October 17, 2000).

As the Feature Story about **Intel** and **AMD** indicates, few management decisions are more important than setting prices. Intel, for example, must sell computer chips at a price that is high enough to cover its costs and ensure a reasonable profit. But if the price is too high, the chips will not sell. In this chapter, two types of pricing situations are examined. The first part of the chapter addresses pricing for goods sold or services provided to external parties. The second part of the chapter addresses pricing decisions faced when goods are sold to other divisions within the same company.

The content and organization of the chapter are as follows.

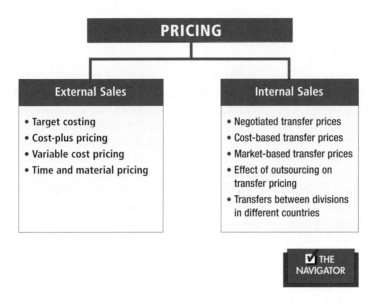

PRICING

External Sales
- Target costing
- Cost-plus pricing
- Variable cost pricing
- Time and material pricing

Internal Sales
- Negotiated transfer prices
- Cost-based transfer prices
- Market-based transfer prices
- Effect of outsourcing on transfer pricing
- Transfers between divisions in different countries

☑ THE NAVIGATOR

SECTION 1
EXTERNAL SALES

Establishing the price for any good or service is affected by many factors. Take the pharmaceutical industry as an example. Its approach to profitability has been to spend heavily on research and development in an effort to find and patent a few new drugs, price them high, and market them aggressively. Due to the AIDS crisis in Africa, the drug industry has been under considerable pressure recently to lower prices on drugs used to treat AIDS. For example, **Merck Co.** lowered the price of its AIDS drug Crixivan to $600 per patient in these countries. This compares with the $6,016 it typically charges in the United States.[1] As a consequence, individuals in the United States are questioning whether prices in the U.S. market are too high. The drug companies counter that to cover their substantial financial risks to develop these products, they need to set the prices high. Illustration 8-1 indicates the many factors that can affect pricing decisions.

---

[1]"AIDS Gaffes in Africa Come Back to Haunt Drug Industry at Home," *Wall Street Journal* (April 23, 2001), p. 1.

Illustration 8-1 Pricing factors

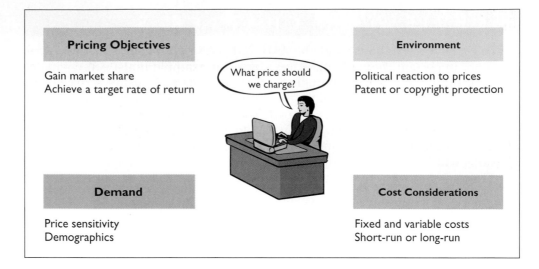

Pricing Objectives	Environment
Gain market share Achieve a target rate of return	Political reaction to prices Patent or copyright protection

What price should we charge?

Demand	Cost Considerations
Price sensitivity Demographics	Fixed and variable costs Short-run or long-run

In the long run a company must price its product to cover its costs and earn a reasonable profit. But to price its product appropriately, it must have a good understanding of market forces at work. In most cases, a company does not set the prices. Instead the price is set by the competitive market (the laws of supply and demand). For example, a company such as **ChevronTexaco** or **Exxon-Mobil** cannot set the price of gasoline by itself. These companies are called **price takers** because the price of gasoline is set by market forces (the supply of oil and the demand by customers). This is the case for any product that is not easily differentiated from competing products, such as farm products (corn or wheat) or minerals (coal or sand).

In other situations the company sets the prices. This would be the case where the product is specially made for a customer, as in a one-of-a-kind product such as a designer dress by **Zoran** or **Armani**. This also occurs when there are few or no other producers capable of manufacturing a similar item. An example would be a company that has a patent or copyright on a unique process, such as the case of computer chips by **Intel**. However, it is also the case when a company can effectively differentiate its product or service from others. Even in a competitive market like coffee, **Starbucks** has been able to differentiate its product and charge a premium for a cup of java.

Business Insight
e-Business Perspective

How has e-business affected pricing? The answer isn't simple, because of two conflicting forces. On the one hand, the Internet allows customers to easily compare prices, thus driving prices down. In fact, many companies feared that the Internet would squeeze all profits out of their businesses. However, e-business has also allowed many businesses to more effectively target their customers and differentiate their products, thus allowing them to avoid severe price competition by striving to create customer-focused "markets of one." E-business technology conveniently provides up-to-date information about "buying behaviors and the level of real-time local demand. Also, e-businesses are able to customize offerings by rebundling related services and products—often from a number of different companies—into attractive 'baskets'."

SOURCE: M. V. Deise et al., *Executive's Guide to E-Business: From Tactics to Strategy* (New York: John Wiley & Sons, Inc., 2000), p. 195.

Target Costing

Automobile manufacturers like **Ford** or **Toyota** face a competitive market. The price of an automobile is affected greatly by the laws of supply and demand, so no company in this industry can affect the price to a significant degree. Therefore, to earn a profit, companies in the auto industry must focus on controlling costs. This requires setting a target cost that provides a desired profit. The relationship and importance of a target cost to the price and desired profit are shown in Illustration 8-2.

STUDY OBJECTIVE

1

Compute a target cost when a product price is determined by the market.

Market Price   −   Desired Profit   =   Target Cost

Illustration 8-2 Target cost as related to price and profit

If **General Motors**, for example, can produce its automobiles for the target cost (or less), it will meet its profit goal. If it cannot achieve its target cost, it will fail to produce the desired profit (and will most likely "get hammered" by stockholders and the market). In a competitive market, a company chooses the segment of the market it wants to compete in—that is, its market niche. For example, it may choose between selling luxury goods or economy goods in order to focus its efforts on one segment or the other.

Once the company has identified its segment of the market, it does market research to determine the target price. This target price is the price that the company believes would place it in the optimal position for its target audience. Once the company has determined this target price, it can determine its target cost by setting a desired profit. The difference between the target price and the desired profit is the target cost of the product. (This computation is shown in Illustration 8-2.) After the company determines the target cost, a team of employees with expertise in a variety of areas (production and operations, marketing, and finance) is assembled. The team's task is to design and develop a product that can meet quality specifications while not exceeding the target cost. The target cost includes all product and period costs necessary to make and market the product or service.

Business Insight
Management Perspective

"And the price should be $19 per pair of jeans instead of $23," said the retailer **Wal-Mart** to jean maker **Levi Strauss**. What happened to Levi Strauss is what happens to many manufacturers who deal with Wal-Mart. Wal-Mart often sets the price, and the manufacturer has to find out how to make a profit, given that price. In Levi Strauss's case, it revamped its distribution and production to serve Wal-Mart and improve its overall record of timely deliveries. Producing a season of new jeans styles, from conception to store shelves, used to take Levi 12 to 15 months. Today it takes just 10 months for Levi Strauss signature jeans; for regular Levi's, the time is down to 7 1/2 months. As the chief executive of Levi Strauss noted, "We had to change people and practice. It's been somewhat of a D-Day invasion approach."

SOURCE: "In Bow to Retailers' New Clout, Levi Strauss Makes Alterations," *Wall Street Journal* (June 17, 2004), pA1.

DECISION TOOLKIT

Decision Checkpoints	Info Needed for Decision	Tool to Use for Decision	How to Evaluate Results
✔			👍👎
How does management use target costs to make decisions about manufacturing products or providing services?	Target selling price, desired profit, target cost	Target selling price less desired profit equals target cost	If target cost is too high, company will not earn desired profit. If desired profit is not achieved, company must evaluate whether to manufacture the product or provide the service.

Cost-Plus Pricing

STUDY OBJECTIVE

2

Compute a target selling price using cost-plus pricing.

As discussed, in a competitive, common-product environment the market price is already set, and the company instead must set a target cost. But, in a less competitive or noncompetitive environment, the company may be faced with the task of setting its own price. When the price is set by the company, price is commonly a function of the cost of the product or service. That is, the typical approach is to use **cost-plus pricing**. This approach involves establishing a cost base and adding to this cost base a **markup** to determine a **target selling price**. The size of the markup (the "plus") depends on the desired return on investment (ROI = net income ÷ invested assets) for the product line, product, or service. In determining the proper markup, the company must also consider competitive and market conditions, political and legal issues, and other relevant risk factors. The cost-plus pricing formula is expressed as follows.

Illustration 8-3 Cost-plus pricing formula

$$\text{Cost} + \frac{\text{Markup Percentage}}{\times} = \frac{\text{Target Selling}}{\text{Price}}$$
$$\text{Cost}$$

To illustrate, assume that Cleanmore Products, Inc. is in the process of setting a selling price on its new top-of-the-line, 3-horsepower, 16-gallon, variable-speed wet/dry shop vacuum. The per unit variable cost estimates for the new shop vacuum are as follows.

Illustration 8-4 Variable costs per unit

	Per Unit
Direct materials	$23
Direct labor	17
Variable manufacturing overhead	12
Variable selling and administrative expenses	8
Variable cost per unit	**$60**

In addition, Cleanmore has the following fixed costs per unit at a budgeted sales volume of 10,000 units.

	Total Costs	÷	Budgeted Volume	=	Cost Per Unit
Fixed manufacturing overhead	$280,000	÷	10,000	=	$28
Fixed selling and administrative expenses	240,000	÷	10,000	=	24
Fixed cost per unit					**$52**

Illustration 8-5   Fixed cost per unit, 10,000 units

Cleanmore has decided to price its new shop vacuum to earn a 20 percent return on its investment (ROI) of $1,000,000. Therefore, Cleanmore expects to receive income of $200,000 (20% × $1,000,000) on its investment. On a per unit basis, the desired ROI is $20 ($200,000 ÷ 10,000). Given the per unit costs shown above, we then compute the sales price to be $132, as follows.

	Per Unit
Variable cost	$ 60
Fixed cost	52
Total cost	112
Desired ROI	20
Selling price per unit	**$132**

Illustration 8-6   Computation of selling price, 10,000 units

In most cases, companies like Cleanmore will use a percentage markup on cost to determine the selling price. The formula to compute the markup percentage to achieve a desired ROI of $20 per unit is as follows.

Desired ROI Per Unit	÷	Total Unit Cost	=	Markup Percentage
$20	÷	$112	=	17.86%

Illustration 8-7   Computation of markup percentage

Using a 17.86 percent markup on cost, Cleanmore Products would compute the target selling price as follows.

Total Unit Cost	+	(Total Unit Cost	×	Markup Percentage)	=	Target Selling Price Per Unit
$112	+	($112	×	17.86%)	=	$132

Illustration 8-8   Computation of selling price— markup approach

Cleanmore should set the price for its wet/dry vacuum at $132 per unit.

LIMITATIONS OF COST-PLUS PRICING

The cost-plus pricing approach has a major advantage: It is simple to compute. However, the cost model does not give consideration to the demand side. That is, will customers pay the price Cleanmore computed for its vacuums? In addition, sales volume plays a large role in determining per unit costs. The lower the sales volume, for example, the higher the price Cleanmore must charge to meet its desired ROI. To illustrate, if the budgeted sales volume was 8,000 instead of 10,000, Cleanmore's variable cost per unit would remain the same. However, the fixed cost per unit would change as follows.

Illustration 8-9 Fixed cost per unit, 8,000 units

	Total Costs	÷	Budgeted Volume	=	Cost Per Unit
Fixed manufacturing overhead	$280,000	÷	8,000	=	$35
Fixed selling and administrative expenses	240,000	÷	8,000	=	30
Fixed cost per unit					**$65**

As indicated in Illustration 8-5, fixed costs per unit for 10,000 units were $52. However, at a lower sales volume of 8,000 units, fixed costs per unit increase to $65. Cleanmore's desired 20% ROI now results in a $25 ROI per unit [(20% × $1,000,000) ÷ 8,000]. The selling price can be computed as follows.

Illustration 8-10 Computation of selling price, 8,000 units

	Per Unit
Variable cost	$ 60
Fixed cost	65
Total cost	125
Desired ROI	25
Selling price per unit	**$150**

As shown, the lower the budgeted volume, the higher the per unit price. The reason: Fixed costs and ROI are spread over fewer units, and therefore the fixed cost and ROI per unit increase. In this case, at 8,000 units, Cleanmore would have to mark up its total unit costs 20 percent to earn a desired ROI of $25 per unit, as shown below.

$$20\% = \frac{\$25 \text{ (desired ROI)}}{\$125 \text{ (total unit cost)}}$$

The target selling price would then be $150, as indicated earlier:

$$\$125 + (\$125 \times 20\%) = \$150$$

The opposite effect will occur if budgeted volume is higher (say, at 12,000 units) because fixed costs and ROI can be spread over more units. As a result, the cost-plus model of pricing will achieve its desired ROI only when Cleanmore sells the quantity it budgeted. If actual volume is much less than budgeted volume, Cleanmore may sustain losses unless it can raise its prices.

Variable Cost Pricing

In determining the target price for Cleanmore's shop vacuum, we calculated the cost base by including all costs incurred. This approach is referred to as **full cost pricing**. Instead of using full costs to set prices, some companies simply add a markup to their variable costs. Using **variable cost pricing** as the basis for setting prices avoids the problem of using poor cost information (as shown in Illustration 8-9) related to fixed cost per unit computations. Variable cost pricing also is helpful in pricing special orders or when excess capacity exists.

The major disadvantage of variable cost pricing is that managers may set the price too low to cover their fixed costs. In the long run, failure to cover fixed costs will lead to losses. As a result companies that use variable cost pricing must adjust their markups to make sure that the price set will provide a fair return. An example of how variable costs are used as the basis for setting prices is discussed in the appendix to this chapter.

Business Insight
Service Company Perspective

Did you ever wonder what is the real cost of an expensive meal? The answer might make you lose your appetite. On average, most restaurants shoot for a 300 percent markup above the cost of the basic ingredients. The actual markup differs across food items because a 300 percent markup on some items (such as expensive seafood or choice cuts of meat) would result in prices that no diner would be willing to pay. As a consequence, to achieve an average 300 percent markup, some items are marked up much more than 300 percent. For example, pasta and vegetables typically are marked up 500 percent, mussels 650 percent, and salmon 900 percent.

To be fair, focusing on the cost of a restaurant meal's raw ingredients is like "calculating the value of a Picasso based on the cost of the paint." The price of your meal has to cover the labor necessary to prepare and deliver the meal, the facility the meal is served in, and overhead, plus a profit.

SOURCE: Eileen Daspin, "What Do Restaurants Really Pay for Meals?" *Wall Street Journal* (March 10, 2000).

DECISION TOOLKIT

Decision Checkpoints	Info Needed for Decision	Tool to Use for Decision	How to Evaluate Results
What factors should be considered in determining selling price in a less competitive environment?	Total cost per unit and desired profit (cost-plus pricing)	Total cost per unit plus desired profit equals target selling price	Does company make its desired profit? If not, does it result from less volume?

BEFORE YOU GO ON . . .

▶Review It

1. What is a target cost, and how is it used by management?
2. What is the general formula for determining the target selling price with cost-plus pricing?
3. How is the per unit return on investment determined?

▶Do It

Air Corporation produces air purifiers. The following per unit cost information is available: direct materials $16; direct labor $18; variable manufacturing overhead $11; fixed manufacturing overhead $10; variable selling and administrative expenses $6; and fixed selling and administrative expenses $10. Using a 45 percent markup percentage on total per unit cost, compute the target selling price.

Action Plan

• Calculate the total cost per unit.
• Multiply the total cost per unit by the markup percentage, then add this amount to the total cost per unit to determine the target selling price.

Solution

Direct materials	$16
Direct labor	18
Variable manufacturing overhead	11
Fixed manufacturing overhead	10
Variable selling and administrative expenses	6
Fixed selling and administrative expenses	10
Total unit cost	$71

$$\begin{pmatrix} \text{Total} \\ \text{unit cost} \end{pmatrix} + \begin{pmatrix} \text{Total} \\ \text{unit cost} \times \begin{matrix} \text{Markup} \\ \text{percentage} \end{matrix} \end{pmatrix} = \begin{matrix} \text{Target} \\ \text{selling price} \end{matrix}$$

$$\$71 \quad + \quad (\$71 \quad \times \quad 45\%) \quad = \quad \$102.95$$

Related exercise material: BE8-2, BE8-3, BE8-4, BE8-5, E8-3, E8-4, E8-5, E8-6, and E8-7.

☑ THE NAVIGATOR

Time and Material Pricing

STUDY OBJECTIVE

3

Use time and material pricing to determine the cost of services provided.

Another variation on cost-plus pricing is called **time and material pricing**. Under this approach, the company sets two pricing rates—one for the **labor** used on a job and another for the **material**. The labor rate includes direct labor time and other employee costs. The material charge is based on the cost of direct parts and materials used and a **material loading charge** for related overhead costs. Time and material pricing is widely used in service industries, especially professional firms such as public accounting, law, engineering, and consulting firms, as well as construction companies, repair shops, and printers.

To illustrate a time and material pricing situation, assume the following data for Lake Holiday Marina, a boat and motor repair shop.

Illustration 8-11 Total annual budgeted time and material costs

LAKE HOLIDAY MARINA **Budgeted Costs for the Year 2005**		
	Time **Charges**	**Material** **Loading** **Charges***
Mechanics' wages and benefits	$103,500	–
Parts manager's salary and benefits	–	$11,500
Office employee's salary and benefits	20,700	2,300
Other overhead (supplies, depreciation, property taxes, advertising, utilities)	26,800	14,400
Total budgeted costs	$151,000	$28,200

*The invoice cost of the materials is excluded from the material loading charges.

Using time and material pricing involves three steps: (1) calculate the per hour labor charge, (2) calculate the charge for obtaining and holding materials, and (3) calculate the charges for a particular job.

STEP 1: CALCULATE THE LABOR CHARGE.   The first step for time and material pricing is to determine a charge for labor time. The charge for labor time is expressed as a rate per hour of labor. This rate includes: (1) the direct labor cost of the employee, including hourly rate or salary and fringe benefits; (2) selling, administrative, and similar overhead costs; and (3) an allowance for a desired profit or ROI per hour of employee time. In some industries, such as auto, boat, and farm equipment repair shops, the same hourly labor rate is charged regardless of which employee performs the work. In other industries, the rate charged is according to classification or level of the employee. In a public accounting firm, for example, the services of an assistant, senior, manager, or partner would be charged at different rates, as would those of a paralegal, associate, or partner in a law firm.

Computation of the hourly charges for Lake Holiday Marina during 2005 is shown in Illustration 8-12. The marina budgets 5,000 hours of repair time in 2005, and it desires a profit margin of $8 per hour of labor.

Lake Holiday Marina III 8-12.xls

	A	B	C	D	E	F
1	Per Hour	Total Cost	÷	Total Hours	=	Per Hour Charge
2	Hourly labor rate for repairs					
3	Mechanics' wages and benefits	$103,500	÷	5,000	=	$20.70
4	Overhead costs					
5	Office employee's salary and benefits	20,700	÷	5,000	=	4.14
6	Office overhead	26,800	÷	5,000	=	5.36
7	Total hourly cost	$151,000	÷	5,000	=	30.20
8	Profit margin					8.00
9	Rate charged per hour of labor					$38.20

Illustration 8-12   Computation of hourly time-charge rate

This rate of $38.20 is multiplied by the number of hours of labor used on any particular job to determine the labor charge for that job.

STEP 2: CALCULATE THE MATERIAL LOADING CHARGE.   The charge for materials typically includes the invoice price of any materials used on the job plus a material loading charge. The **material loading charge** covers the costs of purchasing, receiving, handling, and storing materials, plus any desired profit margin on the materials themselves. The material loading charge is expressed as a **percentage** of the total estimated costs of parts and materials for the year. To determine this percentage, the company does the following: (1) It estimates its total annual costs for purchasing, receiving, handling, and storing materials. (2) It divides this amount by the total estimated cost of parts and materials. And (3) it adds a desired profit margin on the materials themselves.

Computation of the material loading charge used by Lake Holiday Marina during 2005 is shown in Illustration 8-13. The marina estimates that the total invoice cost of parts and materials used in 2005 will be $120,000. The marina desires a 20 percent profit margin on the invoice cost of parts and materials.

Lake Holiday Marina.xls

	A	B	C	D	E	F
1		Material Loading Charges	÷	Total Invoice Cost, Parts and Materials	=	Material Loading Percentage
2	Overhead costs					
3	Parts manager's salary and benefits	$11,500				
4	Office employee's salary	2,300				
5		13,800	÷	$120,000	=	11.50%
6						
7	Other overhead	14,400	÷	120,000	=	12.00%
8		$28,200	÷	120,000	=	23.50%
9	Profit margin					20.00%
10	Material loading percentage					43.50%

Illustration 8-13   Computation of material loading charge

The material loading charge on any particular job is 43.50 percent multiplied by the cost of materials used on the job. For example, if $100 of parts were used, the additional material loading charge would be $43.50.

STEP 3: CALCULATE CHARGES FOR A PARTICULAR JOB. The charges for any particular job are the sum of (1) the labor charge, (2) the charge for the materials, and (3) the material loading charge. For example, suppose that Lake Holiday Marina prepares a price quotation to estimate the cost to refurbish a used 28-foot pontoon boat. Lake Holiday Marina estimates the job will require 50 hours of labor and $3,600 in parts and materials. The marina's price quotation is shown in Illustration 8-14.

Illustration 8-14 Price quotation for time and material

LAKE HOLIDAY MARINA Time and Material Price Quotation		
Job: Marianne Perino, repair of 28-foot pontoon boat		
Labor charges: 50 hours @ $38.20		$1,910
Material charges		
Cost of parts and materials	$3,600	
Material loading charge (43.5% × $3,600)	1,566	5,166
Total price of labor and material		$7,076

Included in the $7,076 price quotation for the boat repair and refurbishment are charges for labor costs, overhead costs, materials costs, materials handling and storage costs, and a profit margin on both labor and parts. Lake Holiday Marina used labor hours as a basis for computing the time rate. Other companies, such as machine shops, plastic molding shops, and printers, might use machine hours.

DECISION TOOLKIT

Decision Checkpoints	Info Needed for Decision	Tool to Use for Decision	How to Evaluate Results
How do we set prices when it is difficult to estimate total cost per unit?	Two pricing rates needed: one for labor use and another for materials	Compute labor rate charge and material rate charge. In each of these calculations, add a profit margin.	Is the company profitable under this pricing approach? Are employees earning reasonable wages?

BEFORE YOU GO ON . . .

▶**Review It**

1. What is time and material pricing? Where is it often used?
2. What is a material loading charge?

▶**Do It**

Presented below are data for Harmon Electrical Repair Shop for next year.

Repair-technicians' wages	$130,000
Fringe benefits	30,000
Overhead	20,000

The desired profit margin per labor hour is $10. The material loading charge is 40 percent of invoice cost. It is estimated that 8,000 labor hours will be worked next year. If Harmon repairs a TV that takes 4 hours to repair and uses parts of $50, compute the bill for this job.

Action Plan

• Calculate the labor charge.

• Calculate the material loading charge.

• Compute the bill for specific repair.

Solution

	Total Cost	÷	Total Hours	=	Per Hour Charge
Repair-technician's wages	$130,000	÷	8,000	=	$16.25
Fringe benefits	30,000	÷	8,000	=	3.75
Overhead	20,000	÷	8,000	=	2.50
	$180,000	÷	8,000	=	22.50
Profit margin					10.00
Rate charged per hour of labor					$32.50

Materials cost	$50
Materials loading charge ($50 × 40%)	20
Total materials cost	$70

Cost of TV repair	
Labor costs ($32.50 × 4)	$130
Materials cost	70
Total repair cost	$200

Related exercise material: BE8-6, E8-8, E8-9, and E8-10.

☑ THE NAVIGATOR

SECTION 2
INTERNAL SALES

In today's global economy, growth is vital to survival. Frequently growth is "vertical," meaning the company expands in the direction of either its suppliers or its customers. For example, a manufacturer of bicycles, like **Trek**, may acquire a chain of bicycle shops. A movie production company like **Walt Disney** or **Time Warner** may acquire a movie theater chain or a cable television company.

Divisions within vertically integrated companies normally transfer goods or services to other divisions within the same company, as well as make sales to customers outside the company. When goods are transferred internally, the price used to record the transfer between the two divisions is the transfer price. Illustration 8-15 (page 316) highlights these transactions for Aerobic Bicycle Company. Aerobic Bicycle has a Bicycle Assembly Division and a Bicycle Component Division.

The pricing issues presented by transfer pricing are similar to those related to outside pricing issues. The objective is to maximize the return to the whole company. In addition, in the transfer pricing situation, it is important that divisional performance should not decline because of internal transfers. As a result, setting a transfer price is complicated because of competing interests among divisions within the company. For example, setting the transfer price high will benefit the Bicycle Component Division (the selling division), but will hurt the Bicycle Assembly Division (the purchasing division).

Illustration 8-15 Transfer pricing illustration

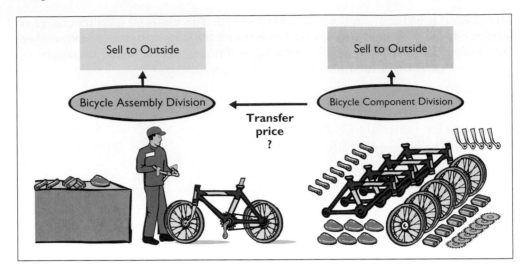

There are three possible approaches for determining a transfer price:

STUDY OBJECTIVE
4
Determine a transfer price using the negotiated, cost-based, and market-based approaches.

1. Negotiated transfer prices.
2. Cost-based transfer prices.
3. Market-based transfer prices.

Conceptually, a negotiated transfer price should work best, but due to practical considerations, the other two methods are often used.

Negotiated Transfer Prices

The **negotiated transfer price** is determined through agreement of division managers. To illustrate the negotiated transfer pricing approach, we will examine Alberta Company. Until recently Alberta focused exclusively on making rubber soles for work boots and hiking boots. These rubber soles were sold to boot manufacturers. However, last year the company decided to take advantage of its strong reputation by expanding into the business of making hiking boots. As a consequence of this expansion, the company is now structured as two independent divisions, the Boot Division and the Sole Division. The manager of each division is compensated based on achievement of profitability targets for his or her division.

The Sole Division continues to make rubber soles for both hiking boots and work boots and to sell these soles to other boot manufacturers. The Boot Division manufactures leather uppers for hiking boots and attaches these uppers to rubber soles. During its first year the Boot Division purchased its rubber soles from outside suppliers so as not to disrupt the operations of the Sole Division. However, top management now wants the Sole Division to provide at least some of the soles used by the Boot Division. Illustration 8-16 shows the computation of the contribution margin per unit for each division when the Boot Division purchases soles from an outside supplier.

Illustration 8-16 Basic information for Alberta Company

Boot Division		Sole Division	
Selling price of hiking boots	$90	Selling price of sole	$18
Variable cost of manufacturing boot (not including sole)	35	Variable cost per sole	11
Cost of sole purchased from outside suppliers	17		
Contribution margin per unit	**$38**	**Contribution margin per unit**	**$ 7**
Total contribution margin per unit		**$45** ($38 + $7)	

This information indicates that the Boot Division has a contribution margin per unit of $38 and the Sole Division $7. The total contribution margin per unit is $45 ($38 + $7). Now let's ask the question, "What would be a fair transfer price if the Sole Division sold 10,000 soles to the Boot Division?"

NO EXCESS CAPACITY

As indicated in Illustration 8-16, the Sole Division charges $18 and derives a contribution margin of $7 per sole. The Sole Division has no excess capacity and produces and sells 80,000 units (soles) to outside customers. Therefore, the Sole Division must receive from the Boot Division a payment that will at least cover its variable cost per sole **plus** its lost contribution margin per sole (often referred to as **opportunity cost**). Otherwise, the Sole Division should not sell its soles to the Boot Division. The minimum transfer price that would be acceptable to the Sole Division is $18, as shown below.

Variable Cost	+	Opportunity Cost	=	Minimum Transfer Price
$11	+	$7	=	$18

Illustration 8-17 Minimum transfer price—no excess capacity

From the perspective of the Boot Division (the buyer), the most it will pay is what the sole would cost from an outside supplier. In this case, therefore, the Boot Division would pay no more than $17. As shown in Illustration 8-18, an acceptable transfer price is not available in this situation.

Illustration 8-18 Transfer price negotiations—no deal

EXCESS CAPACITY

What happens if the Sole Division **has excess capacity?** For example, assume the Sole Division can produce 80,000 soles but can sell only 70,000 soles in the open market. As a result, it has available capacity of 10,000 units. In this situation, the Sole Division does not lose its contribution margin of $7 per unit and, therefore, the minimum price it would now accept is $11, as shown below.

Variable Cost	+	Opportunity Cost	=	Minimum Transfer Price
$11	+	$0	=	$11

Illustration 8-19 Minimum transfer price formula—excess capacity

In this case, the Boot Division and the Sole Division should negotiate a transfer price within the range of $11 to $17, as shown in Illustration 8-20.

Illustration 8-20 Transfer pricing negotiations—deal

Given excess capacity, Alberta Company will increase its overall net income if the 10,000 soles are purchased internally. This is true as long as the Sole Division's variable cost is less than the outside price of $17. The Sole Division will receive a positive contribution margin from any transfer price above its variable cost of $11. The Boot Division will benefit from any price below $17. At any transfer price above $17 the Boot Division will go to an outside supplier, a solution that would be undesirable to both divisions, as well as to the company as a whole.

VARIABLE COSTS

In the minimum transfer price formula, **variable cost is defined as the variable cost of units sold *internally***. In some instances the variable cost of units sold internally will differ from the variable cost of units sold externally. For example, variable selling expenses often are reduced when units are sold internally. In this case, the variable cost of units sold internally will be lower than that of units sold externally.

Alternatively, the variable cost of units sold internally could be higher if the internal division requests a special order that requires more expensive materials or additional labor. For example, assume that the Boot Division would like to make 5,000 new high-margin, heavy-duty boots. The sole required for this boot will be made of a denser rubber and an intricate lug design. Alberta Company is not aware of any supplier that currently makes such a sole, nor do they feel that any other supplier can meet the quality expectations. As a consequence, there is no available market price to use as the transfer price.

We can, however, still employ the formula for the minimum transfer price to assist in arriving at a reasonable solution. After evaluating the special sole, the Sole Division determines that its variable cost would be $19 per sole. The Sole Division is at full capacity. The Sole Division's opportunity cost at full capacity is the $7 ($18 − $11) per sole that it earns producing the standard sole and selling it to an outside customer. Therefore, the minimum transfer price that the Sole Division would be willing to accept would be:

Illustration 8-21 Minimum transfer price formula—special order

Variable Cost	+	Opportunity Cost	=	Minimum Transfer Price
$19	+	$7	=	$26

The transfer price of $26 provides the Sole Division with enough revenue to cover its increased variable cost and its opportunity cost (contribution margin on its standard sole).

SUMMARY OF NEGOTIATED TRANSFER PRICING APPROACH

Under the negotiated transfer pricing approach, a minimum transfer price is established by the selling division, and a maximum transfer price is established by the purchasing division. This system provides a sound basis for establishing a transfer price because both divisions are better off if the proper decision rules are used. However, negotiated transfer pricing often is not used because:

- Market price information is sometimes not easily obtainable.
- A lack of trust between the two negotiating divisions may lead to a breakdown in the negotiations.
- Negotiations often lead to different pricing strategies from division to division which is cumbersome and sometimes costly to implement.

Many companies, therefore, often use more objective and simple systems based on cost or market information to develop transfer prices.

Cost-Based Transfer Prices

One method of determining transfer prices is to base the transfer price on the costs incurred by the division producing the goods or services. If a **cost-based transfer price** is used, the transfer price may be based on variable costs alone, or on variable costs plus fixed costs. A markup may be added to these cost numbers.

Unfortunately, under a cost-based approach, divisions sometimes use improper transfer prices. This leads to a loss of profitability for the company and unfair evaluations of division performance. To illustrate, assume that Alberta Company requires the division to use a transfer price based on the variable cost of the sole. With no excess capacity, here is what happens to the contribution margin per unit of the two divisions.

Boot Division		Sole Division	
Selling price of hiking boots	$90	Selling price of sole	$11
Variable cost of manufacturing boot (not including sole)	35	Variable cost per sole	11
Cost of sole purchased from Sole Division	11	Contribution margin per unit	$ 0
Contribution margin per unit	**$44**		
Total contribution margin per unit		**$44** ($44 + $0)	

Illustration 8-22   Cost-based transfer price— 10,000 units

This cost-based transfer system is a bad deal for the Sole Division, as it reports no profit on the transfer of 10,000 soles to the Boot Division. If the Sole Division could sell these soles to an outside customer, it would make $70,000 [10,000 × ($18 − $11)]. The Boot Division, on the other hand, is delighted, as its contribution margin per unit increases from $38 to $44, or $6 per boot. The Sole Division lost a contribution margin per unit of $7 (Illustration 8-16, page 316), and the Boot Division experienced only a $6 increase in its contribution margin per unit. Overall, Alberta Company loses $10,000 [10,000 boots × ($7 − $6)]. Illustration 8-23 (page 320) illustrates this deficiency.

The overall results change if the Sole Division **has excess capacity**. In this case, the Sole Division continues to report a zero profit on these 10,000 units but does not lose the $7 per unit (because it had excess capacity). The Boot Division gains $6. So overall, the company is better off by $60,000 (10,000 × $6). However, with a cost-based system, the Sole Division continues to report a zero profit on these 10,000 units.

Illustration 8-23   Cost-based transfer price results—no excess capacity

From this analysis, we can see that a cost-based system does not reflect the division's true profitability. What's more, it does not even provide adequate incentive for the Sole Division to control costs. Whatever the division's costs are, these costs are passed on to the next division. Notwithstanding these disadvantages, the cost system is simple to understand and easy to use because the information is already available in the accounting system. In addition, market information is sometimes not available, so the only alternative is some type of cost-based system. As a result, it is the most common method used by companies to establish transfer prices.

Market-Based Transfer Prices

The **market-based transfer price** is based on existing market prices of competing goods or services. A market-based system is often considered the best approach because it is objective and generally provides the proper economic incentives. For example, if the Sole Division can charge the market price, it is indifferent as to whether soles are sold to outside customers or internally to the Boot Division—it does not lose any contribution margin. Similarly, the Boot Division pays a price for the soles that is at or reasonably close to market.

When the Sole Division has no excess capacity, the market-based system works reasonably well. The Sole Division receives market price and the Boot Division pays market price. If the Sole Division has excess capacity, however, the market-based system can lead to actions that are not in the best interest of the company. For example, the minimum transfer price that the Sole Division should receive is its variable cost plus opportunity cost. Given that the Sole Division has excess capacity, its opportunity cost is zero. However, under the market-based system, the Sole Division transfers the goods at the market price of $18, for a contribution margin per unit of $7. The Boot Division manager then has to accept the $18 sole price. The Boot Division must recognize, however, that this price is not the cost of the sole, given that the Sole Division had excess capacity. As a result, the Boot Division may overprice its boots in the market if it uses the market price of the sole plus a markup in setting the price of the boot. This action can lead to losses for Alberta overall.

As indicated earlier, in many cases, there simply is not a well-defined market for the good or service being transferred. As a result, a reasonable market value cannot be developed, and therefore companies resort to a cost-based system.

Effect of Outsourcing on Transfer Pricing

An increasing number of companies rely on **outsourcing**. Outsourcing involves contracting with an external party to provide a good or service, rather than performing the work internally. Some companies have taken outsourcing to the extreme by outsourcing all of their production. These so-called **virtual companies** have well-established brand names, but they don't manufacture any of their own products. Incremental analysis (Chapter 6) is used to determine whether outsourcing is profitable. As companies increasingly rely on outsourcing, it means that fewer components are transferred internally between divisions.

Transfers Between Divisions in Different Countries

As more companies "globalize" their operations, an increasing number of transfers are between divisions that are located in different countries. For example, one estimate suggests that 60 percent of trade between countries is simply transfers between divisions. Differences in tax rates across countries can complicate the determination of the appropriate transfer price.

Companies must pay income tax in the country where income is generated. In order to maximize income and minimize income tax, many companies prefer to report more income in countries with low tax rates, and less income in countries with high tax rates. This is accomplished by adjusting the transfer prices they use on internal transfers between divisions located in different countries. The division in the low-tax-rate country is allocated more contribution margin, and the division in the high-tax-rate country is allocated less.

To illustrate, suppose that Alberta's Boot Division is located in a country with a corporate tax rate of 10 percent, and the Sole Division is located in a country with a tax rate of 30 percent. Illustration 8-24 demonstrates the after-tax contribution margin to the company as a whole assuming first, that the soles are transferred at a transfer price of $18, and second, that the soles are transferred at a transfer price of $11.

STUDY OBJECTIVE

5

Explain the issues that arise when transferring goods between divisions located in countries with different tax rates.

Illustration 8-24 After-tax contribution margin per unit under alternative transfer prices

$18 Transfer Price

Boot Division		Sole Division	
Selling price of hiking boots	$90.00	Selling price of sole	$18.00
Variable cost of manufacturing boot (not including sole)	35.00	Variable cost per sole	11.00
Cost of sole purchased internally	18.00		
Before-tax contribution margin	37.00	Before-tax contribution margin	7.00
Tax at 10%	3.70	Tax at 30%	2.10
After-tax contribution margin	$33.30	After-tax contribution margin	$ 4.90

Before-tax total contribution margin per unit to company = $37 + $7 = **$44**
After-tax total contribution margin per unit to company = $33.30 + $4.90 = **$38.20**

$11 Transfer Price

Boot Division		Sole Division	
Selling price of hiking boots	$90.00	Selling price of sole	$11.00
Variable cost of manufacturing boot (not including sole)	35.00	Variable cost per sole	11.00
Cost of sole purchased internally	11.00		
Before-tax contribution margin	44.00	Before-tax contribution margin	0.00
Tax at 10%	4.40	Tax at 30%	0.00
After-tax contribution margin	$39.60	After-tax contribution margin	$ 0.00

Before-tax total contribution margin per unit to company = $44 + $0 = **$44**
After-tax total contribution margin per unit to company = $39.60 + $0 = **$39.60**

Note that the before-tax total contribution margin to Alberta Company is $44 regardless of whether the transfer price is $18 or $11. However, the after-tax total contribution margin to Alberta Company is $38.20 using the $18 transfer price, and $39.60 using the $11 transfer price. The reason: When the $11 transfer price is used, more of the contribution margin is attributed to the division that is in the country with the lower tax rate.

As this analysis shows, Alberta Company would be better off using the $11 transfer price. However, this presents some concerns. First, the Sole Division manager won't be happy with an $11 transfer price. This price may lead to unfair evaluations of the Sole Division's manager. Second, the company must ask whether it is legal and ethical to use an $11 transfer price when the market price clearly is higher than that.

Additional consideration of international transfer pricing is presented in advanced accounting texts.

Business Insight
International Perspective

International transfer pricing issues create a huge headache for the Internal Revenue Service. Some estimates suggest that the United States loses over $25 billion in underpaid taxes due to transfer price abuses. Occasionally violators are caught. **Toyota**, for example, reportedly paid a $1 billion dollar settlement. But enforcement is complicated and time-consuming, and many foreign firms are reluctant to give access to their records.

U.S. companies have also been accused of abuse of transfer pricing. It has been noted that at one time U.S. giant **Westinghouse** booked over 25 percent of its profit in the tiny island of Puerto Rico. At the time, the corporate tax rate there was zero. The rules require that the transfer price be based on the current market price that a nonrelated party would pay for the goods. But often this is difficult to determine.

DECISION TOOLKIT

Decision Checkpoints	Info Needed for Decision	Tool to Use for Decision	How to Evaluate Results
What price should be charged for transfer of goods between divisions of a company?	Variable costs, opportunity costs, market prices	Variable cost plus opportunity cost provides minimum transfer price for seller.	If income of division provides fair evaluation of managers, then transfer price is useful. Also, income of the company overall should not be reduced due to the transfer pricing approach.

▶**Review It**

1. What are the objectives of transfer pricing?
2. What are the three approaches to transfer pricing? What are the advantages and disadvantages of each?
3. How do some companies reduce their tax payments through their choice of transfer price?

☑ THE NAVIGATOR

Using the Decision Toolkit

Cedarburg Lumber specializes in building "high-end" playhouses for kids. It builds the components in its factory, then ships the parts to the customer's home. It has contracted with carpenters across the country to do the final assembly. Each year it comes out with a new model. This year's model looks like a miniature castle, complete with spires and drawbridge. The following cost estimates for this new product have been provided by the accounting department for a budgeted volume of 1,000 units.

	Per Unit	Total
Direct materials	$ 840	
Direct labor	$1,600	
Variable manufacturing overhead	$ 400	
Fixed manufacturing overhead		$540,000
Variable selling and administrative expenses	$ 510	
Fixed selling and administrative expenses		$320,000

Cedarburg Lumber uses cost-plus pricing to set its selling price. Management also directs that the target price be set to provide a 25% return on investment (ROI) on invested assets of $4,200,000.

Instructions
(a) Compute the markup percentage and target selling price on this new playhouse.
(b) Assuming that the volume is 1,500 units instead of 1,000 units, compute the markup percentage and target selling price that will allow Cedarburg Lumber to earn its desired ROI of 25%.

Solution
(a)
Variable cost per unit

	Per Unit
Direct materials	$ 840
Direct labor	1,600
Variable manufacturing overhead	400
Variable selling and administrative expenses	510
Variable cost per unit	$3,350

Fixed cost per unit

	Total Costs	÷	Budgeted Volume	=	Cost Per Unit
Fixed manufacturing overhead	$540,000	÷	1,000	=	$540
Fixed selling and administrative expenses	320,000	÷	1,000	=	320
Fixed cost per unit	$860,000				$860

Computation of selling price (1,000 units)

Variable cost per unit	$3,350
Fixed cost per unit	860
Total unit cost	4,210
Desired ROI per unit*	1,050
Selling price	$5,260

*($4,200,000 × .25) ÷ 1,000

The markup percentage is:

$$\frac{\text{Desired ROI per unit}}{\text{Total unit cost}} = \frac{\$1,050}{\$4,210} = 24.9\%$$

(b) If the company produces 1,500 units, its selling price and markup percentage would be:

Computation of selling price (1,500 units)

Variable cost per unit	$3,350
Fixed cost per unit ($860,000 ÷ 1,500)	573
Total unit cost	3,923
Desired ROI per unit*	700
Selling price	$4,623

*($4,200,000 × .25) ÷ 1,500

The markup percentage would be:

$$\frac{\text{Desired ROI per unit}}{\text{Total unit cost}} = \frac{\$700}{\$3,923} = 17.8\%$$

Summary of Study Objectives

1 *Compute a target cost when a product price is determined by the market.* To compute a target cost, the company determines its target selling price. Once the target selling price is set, it determines its target cost by setting a desired profit. The difference between the target price and desired profit is the target cost of the product.

2 *Compute a target selling price using cost-plus pricing.* Cost-plus pricing involves establishing a cost base and adding to this cost base a markup to determine a target selling price. The cost-plus pricing formula is expressed as follows: Target selling price = Cost + (Markup percentage × Cost).

3 *Use time and material pricing to determine the cost of services provided.* Under time and material pricing, two pricing rates are set—one for the labor used on a job and another for the material. The labor rate includes direct labor time and other employee costs.

The material charge is based on the cost of direct parts and materials used and a material loading charge for related overhead costs.

4 *Determine a transfer price using the negotiated, cost-based, and market-based approaches.* The negotiated price is determined through agreement of division managers. Under a cost-based approach, the transfer price may be based on variable cost alone or on variable cost plus fixed costs. A markup may be added to these numbers. The cost-based approach often leads to poor performance evaluations and purchasing decisions. The advantage of the cost-based system is its simplicity. A market-based transfer price is based on existing competing market prices and services. A market-based system is often considered the best approach because it is objective and generally provides the proper economic incentives.

5 *Explain the issues that arise when transferring goods between divisions located in countries with different tax rates.* Companies must pay income tax in the country where income is generated. In order to maximize income and minimize income tax, many companies prefer to report more income in countries with low tax rates, and less income in countries with high tax rates. This is accomplished by adjusting the transfer prices they use on internal transfers between divisions located in different countries.

☑ THE NAVIGATOR

DECISION TOOLKIT—A SUMMARY

Decision Checkpoints	Info Needed for Decision	Tool to Use for Decision	How to Evaluate Results
How does management use target costs to make decisions about manufacturing products or providing services?	Target selling price, desired profit, target cost	Target selling price less desired profit equals target cost	If target cost is too high, company will not earn desired profit. If desired profit is not achieved, company must evaluate whether to manufacture the product or provide the service.
What factors should be considered in determining selling price in a less competitive environment?	Total cost per unit and desired profit (cost-plus pricing)	Total cost per unit plus desired profit equals target selling price	Does company make its desired profit? If not, does it result from less volume?
How do we set prices when it is difficult to estimate total cost per unit?	Two pricing rates needed: one for labor use and another for materials	Compute labor rate charge and materials rate charge. In each of these calculations, add a profit margin.	Is the company profitable under this pricing approach? Are employees earning reasonable wages?
What price should be charged for transfer of goods between divisions of a company?	Variable costs, opportunity costs, market prices	Variable cost plus opportunity cost provides minimum transfer price for seller.	If income of division provides fair evaluation of managers, then transfer price is useful. Also, income of the company overall should not be reduced due to the transfer pricing approach.

APPENDIX
OTHER COST APPROACHES TO PRICING

In determining the target price for Cleanmore's shop vacuum in the chapter, we calculated the cost base by **including all costs incurred**. This approach is referred to as **full cost pricing**. Using total cost as the basis of the markup makes sense conceptually because in the long run the price must cover all costs and provide a reasonable profit. However, total cost is difficult to determine in practice. This is because period costs (selling and administrative expenses) are difficult to trace to a specific product. Activity-based-costing can be used to overcome this difficulty to some extent.

In practice, two other cost approaches are used: (1) absorption cost pricing, and (2) variable cost pricing. Absorption cost pricing is more popular than

STUDY OBJECTIVE
6
Determine prices using absorption cost pricing and variable cost pricing.

variable cost pricing.[2] We will illustrate both of them, though, because both have merit.

Absorption Cost Pricing

Absorption cost pricing is consistent with generally accepted accounting principles (GAAP). The reason: It includes both variable and fixed manufacturing costs as product costs. **Both variable and fixed selling and administrative costs are excluded from this cost base.** Thus, selling and administrative costs plus the target ROI must be provided for through the markup.

The **first step** in absorption cost pricing is to compute the unit **manufacturing cost**. For Cleanmore Products, Inc., this amounts to $80 per unit at a volume of 10,000 units, as shown in Illustration 8A-1.

Illustration 8A-1 Computation of unit manufacturing cost

	Per Unit
Direct materials	$23
Direct labor	17
Variable manufacturing overhead	12
Fixed manufacturing overhead ($280,000 ÷ 10,000)	28
Total unit manufacturing cost (absorption cost)	$80

In addition, Cleanmore provided the following information regarding selling and administrative expenses per unit and desired ROI per unit.

Illustration 8A-2 Other information

Variable selling and administrative expenses	$ 8
Fixed selling and administrative expenses ($240,000 ÷ 10,000)	24
Desired ROI per unit	20

The **second step** in absorption cost pricing is to compute the markup percentage using the formula in Illustration 8A-3. Note that when manufacturing cost per unit is used as the cost base to compute the markup percentage, the **percentage must cover the desired ROI and also the selling and administrative expenses**.

Illustration 8A-3 Markup percentage—absorption cost pricing

Desired ROI Per Unit	+	Selling and Administrative Expenses Per Unit	=	Markup Percentage	×	Manufacturing Cost Per Unit
$20	+	$32	=	MP	×	$80

Solving we find:

$$MP = (\$20 + \$32) \div \$80 = 65\%$$

The **third** and final **step** is to set the target selling price. Using a markup percentage of 65 percent and absorption cost pricing, we compute the target selling price as shown in Illustration 8A-4.

---

[2]For a discussion of cost-plus pricing, see Eunsup Skim and Ephraim F. Sudit, "How Manufacturers Price Products," *Management Accounting* (February 1995), pp. 37–39; and V. Govindarajan and R.N. Anthony, "How Firms Use Cost Data in Pricing Decisions," *Management Accounting*, 65, no. 1, pp. 30–36.

Manufacturing Cost per Unit	+	(Markup Percentage	×	Manufacturing Cost Per Unit)	=	Target Selling Price
$80	+	(65%	×	$80)	=	$132

Using a target price of $132 will produce the desired 20 percent return on investment for Cleanmore Products on its 3-horsepower, wet/dry shop vacuum at a volume level of 10,000 units, as shown in Illustration 8A-5.

CLEANMORE PRODUCTS, INC.
Budgeted Absorption Cost Income Statement

Revenue (10,000 units × $132)	$1,320,000
Cost of goods sold (10,000 units × $80)	800,000
Gross profit	520,000
Selling and administrative expenses [10,000 units × ($8 + $24)]	320,000
Net income	**$ 200,000**

Budgeted ROI

$$\frac{\text{Net income}}{\text{Invested assets}} = \frac{\$200,000}{\$1,000,000} = \textbf{20\%}$$

Markup Percentage

$$\frac{\text{Net income} + \text{Selling and administrative expenses}}{\text{Cost of goods sold}} = \frac{\$200,000 + \$320,000}{\$800,000} = \textbf{65\%}$$

Because of the fixed cost element, if more than 10,000 units are sold, the ROI will be greater than 20 percent. And, if fewer than 10,000 units are sold, the ROI will be less than 20 percent. The markup percentage is also verified by adding $200,000 (the net income) and $320,000 (selling and administrative expenses) and then dividing by $800,000 (the cost of goods sold or the cost base).

Most companies that use cost-plus pricing use either absorption cost or full cost as the basis. The reasons for this tendency are as follows.

1. Absorption cost information is most readily provided by a company's cost accounting system. Because absorption cost data already exists in general ledger accounts, it is cost effective to use it for pricing.
2. Basing the cost-plus formula on only variable costs could encourage managers to set too low a price to boost sales. There is the fear that if only variable costs are used, they will be substituted for full costs and lead to suicidal price cutting.
3. Absorption cost or full cost provides the most defensible base for justifying prices to all interested parties—managers, customers, and government.

Variable Cost Pricing

Under **variable cost pricing**, the cost base consists of all of the **variable costs** associated with a product, including variable selling and administrative costs. **Because fixed costs are not included in the base, the markup must provide for fixed costs (manufacturing, and selling and administrative) and the target ROI.** Variable cost pricing is more useful for making short-run decisions because it considers variable cost and fixed cost behavior patterns separately.

The **first step** in variable cost pricing is to compute the unit variable cost. For Cleanmore Products, Inc., this amounts to $60 per unit as shown in Illustration 8A-6.

	Per Unit
Direct materials	$23
Direct labor	17
Variable manufacturing overhead	12
Variable selling and administrative expense	8
Total unit variable cost	$60

The **second step** in variable cost pricing is to compute the markup percentage. The formula for the markup percentage is shown in Illustration 8A-7. For Cleanmore, fixed costs include fixed manufacturing overhead of $28 per unit ($280,000 ÷ 10,000) and fixed selling and administrative expenses of $24 per unit ($240,000 ÷ 10,000).

Desired ROI Per Unit	+	Fixed Costs Per Unit	=	Markup Percentage	×	Variable Cost Per Unit
$20	+	($28 + $24)	=	MP	×	$60

Solving, we find:

$$MP = \frac{\$20 + (\$28 + \$24)}{\$60} = 120\%$$

The **third step** is to set the target selling price. Using a markup percentage of 120 percent and the contribution approach, the selling price is computed in Illustration 8A-8.

Variable Cost Per Unit	+	(Markup Percentage	×	Variable Cost Per Unit)	=	Target Selling Price
$60	+	(120%	×	$60)	=	$132

Using a target price of $132 will produce the desired 20 percent return on investment for Cleanmore Products on its 3-horse power, wet/dry shop vacuum at a volume level of 10,000 units, as shown in Illustration 8A-9.

Under any of the three pricing approaches we have looked at (full cost, absorption cost, and variable cost), the desired ROI will be attained only if the budgeted sales volume for the period is attained. None of these approaches guarantees a profit or a desired ROI. Achieving a desired ROI is the result of many factors, some of which are beyond the company's control, such as market conditions, political and legal issues, customers' tastes, and competitive actions.

Because absorption cost pricing includes allocated fixed costs, it does not make clear how the company's costs will change as volume changes. To avoid blurring the effects of cost behavior on net income, some managers therefore prefer variable cost pricing. The specific reasons for using variable cost

CLEANMORE PRODUCTS, INC.
Budgeted Variable Cost Income Statement

Revenue (10,000 vacuums × $132)		$1,320,000
Variable costs (10,000 vacuums × $60)		600,000
Contribution margin		720,000
Fixed manufacturing overhead (10,000 vacuums × $28)	$280,000	
Fixed selling and administrative expenses (10,000 vacuums × $24)	240,000	520,000
Net income		**$ 200,000**

Budgeted ROI

$$\frac{\text{Net income}}{\text{Invested assets}} = \frac{\$200,000}{\$1,000,000} = \underline{\underline{\textbf{20\%}}}$$

Markup Percentage

$$\frac{\text{Net income} + \text{Fixed costs}}{\text{Variable costs}} = \frac{\$200,000 + \$520,000}{\$600,000} = \underline{\underline{\textbf{120\%}}}$$

pricing, even though the basic accounting data are less accessible, are as follows.

1. Variable cost pricing, being based on variable cost, is more consistent with cost-volume-profit analysis used by managers to measure the profit implications of changes in price and volume.

2. Variable cost pricing provides the type of data managers need for pricing special orders. It shows the incremental cost of accepting one more order.

3. Variable cost pricing avoids arbitrary allocation of common fixed costs (such as executive salaries) to individual product lines.

Summary of Study Objective for Appendix

6 *Determine prices using absorption cost pricing and variable cost pricing.* Absorption cost pricing uses total manufacturing cost as the cost base and provides for selling and administrative costs plus the target ROI through the markup. The target selling price is computed as: Manufacturing cost per unit + (Markup percentage × Manufacturing cost per unit).

Variable cost pricing uses all of the variable costs, including selling and administrative costs, as the cost base and provides for fixed costs and target ROI through the markup. The target selling price is computed as: Variable cost per unit + (Markup percentage × Variable cost per unit).

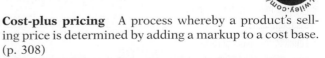

Glossary

Absorption cost pricing An approach to pricing that defines the cost base as the manufacturing cost; it excludes both variable and fixed selling and administrative costs. (p. 326)

Cost-based transfer price A transfer price that uses as its foundation the costs incurred by the division producing the goods. (p. 319)

Cost-plus pricing A process whereby a product's selling price is determined by adding a markup to a cost base. (p. 308)

Full cost pricing An approach to pricing that defines the cost base as all costs incurred. (p. 310)

Market-based transfer price A transfer price that is based on existing market prices of competing products. (p. 320)

Markup The percentage applied to a product's cost to determine the product's selling price. (p. 308)

Material loading charge A charge added to cover the cost of purchasing, receiving, handling, and storing materials, plus any desired profit margin on the materials themselves. (p. 313)

Negotiated transfer price A transfer price that is determined by the agreement of the division managers. (p. 316)

Outsourcing Contracting with an external party to provide a good or service, rather than performing the work internally. (p. 320)

Target cost The cost that will provide the desired profit on a product when the seller does not have control over the product's price. (p. 307)

Target selling price The selling price that will provide the desired profit on a product when the seller has the ability to determine the product's price. (p. 308)

Time and material pricing An approach to cost-plus pricing in which the company uses two pricing rates, one for the labor used on a job and another for the material. (p. 312)

Transfer price The price used to record the transfer of goods between two divisions of a company. (p. 315)

Variable cost pricing An approach to pricing that defines the cost base as all variable costs; it excludes both fixed manufacturing and fixed selling and administrative costs. (pp. 310, 327)

Demonstration Problem

Revco Electronics is a division of International Motors, an automobile manufacturer. Revco produces car radio/CD players. Revco sells its products to International Motors, as well as to other car manufacturers and electronics distributors. The following information is available regarding Revco's car radio/CD player.

Selling price of car radio/CD player to external customers	$49
Variable cost per unit	$28
Capacity	200,000 units

Instructions

Determine whether the goods should be transferred internally or purchased externally and what the appropriate transfer price should be under each of the following **independent** situations.

(a) Revco Electronics is operating at full capacity. There is a saving of $4 per unit for variable cost if the car radio is made for internal sale. International Motors can purchase a comparable car radio from an outside supplier for $47.

(b) Revco Electronics has sufficient existing capacity to meet the needs of International Motors. International Motors can purchase a comparable car radio from an outside supplier for $47.

(c) International Motors wants to purchase a special-order car radio/CD player that also includes a tape deck. It needs 15,000 units. Revco Electronics has determined that the additional variable cost would be $12 per unit. Revco Electronics has no spare capacity. It will have to forgo sales of 15,000 units to external parties in order to provide this special order.

Action Plan

- Determine whether company is at full capacity or not.
- Find the minimum transfer price, using formulas.
- Compare maximum price the buyer would pay to the minimum price for the seller.
- Determine if a deal can be made.

Solution to Demonstration Problem

(a) Revco Electronics' opportunity cost (its lost contribution margin) would be $21 ($49 − $28). Using the formula for minimum transfer price, we determine:

$$\text{Minimum transfer price} = \text{Variable cost} + \text{Opportunity cost}$$
$$\$45 \quad\quad = (\$28 - \$4) + \quad \$21$$

Since this minimum transfer price is less than the $47 it would cost if International Motors purchases from an external party, internal transfer should take place. Revco Electronics and International Motors should negotiate a transfer price between $45 and $47.

(b) Since Revco Electronics has available capacity, its opportunity cost (its lost contribution margin) would be $0. Using the formula for minimum transfer price, we determine the following.

$$\underset{\$28}{\text{Minimum transfer price}} = \underset{\$28}{\text{Variable cost}} + \underset{\$0}{\text{Opportunity cost}}$$

Since International Motors can purchase the unit for $47 from an external party, the most it would be willing to pay would be $47. It is in the best interest of the company as a whole, as well as the two divisions, for a transfer to take place. The two divisions must reach a negotiated transfer price between $28 and $47 that recognizes the costs and benefits to each party and is acceptable to both.

(c) Revco Electronics' opportunity cost (its lost contribution margin per unit) would be $21 ($49 − $28). Its variable cost would be $40 ($28 + $12). Using the formula for minimum transfer price, we determine the following.

$$\underset{\$61}{\text{Minimum transfer price}} = \underset{\$40}{\text{Variable cost}} + \underset{\$21}{\text{Opportunity cost}}$$

Note that in this case Revco Electronics has no available capacity. Its management may decide that it does not want to provide this special order because to do so will require that it cut off the supply of the standard unit to some of its existing customers. This may anger those customers and result in the loss of customers.

☑ THE NAVIGATOR

Note: All asterisked Questions, Exercises, and Problems relate to material in the appendix to the chapter.

Self-Study Questions

Self-Study/Self-Test

Answers are at the end of the chapter.

(SO 2)   1. Cost-plus pricing means that:
  (a) Selling price = Variable cost + (Markup percentage + Variable cost).
  (b) Selling price = Cost + (Markup percentage × Cost).
  (c) Selling price = Manufacturing cost + (Markup percentage + Manufacturing cost).
  (d) Selling price = Fixed cost + (Markup percentage × Fixed cost).

(SO 1)   2. Target cost related to price and profit means that:
  (a) cost and desired profit must be determined before selling price.
  (b) cost and selling price must be determined before desired profit.
  (c) price and desired profit must be determined before costs.
  (d) costs can be achieved only if the company is at full capacity.

(SO 1)   3. Classic Toys has examined the market for toy train locomotives. It believes there is a market niche in which it can sell locomotives at $80 each. It estimates that 10,000 of these locomotives could be sold annually. Variable costs to make a locomotive are expected to be $25. Classic anticipates a profit of $15 per locomotive. The target cost for the locomotive is:
  (a) $80.   (c) $40.
  (b) $65.   (d) $25.

(SO 2)   4. Adler Company is considering developing a new product. The company has gathered the following information on this product.

Expected total unit cost	$25
Estimated investment for new product	$500,000
Desired ROI	10%
Expected number of units to be produced and sold	1,000

The desired markup percentage and selling price given this information is:
  (a) markup percentage 10%; selling price $55.
  (b) markup percentage 200%; selling price $75.
  (c) markup percentage 10%; selling price $50.
  (d) markup percentage 100%; selling price $55.

(SO 2)   5. The following information is provided for Mystique Co. for the new product it recently introduced.

Total unit cost	$30
Desired ROI per unit	$10
Target selling price	$40

What would be Mystique Co.'s percentage markup on cost?
(a) 125%.   (c) 33 ⅓%.
(b) 75%.   (d) 25%.

(SO 3)   6. Crescent Electrical Repair has decided to price its work on a time and material basis. It estimates the following costs for the year related to labor.

Technician wages and benefits	$100,000
Office employee's salary and benefits	$ 40,000
Other overhead	$ 80,000

Crescent desires a profit margin of $10 per labor hour and budgets 5,000 hours of repair time for the year. The office employee's salary, benefits, and other overhead costs should be divided evenly between time charges and material loading charges. Crescent labor charge per hour would be:
(a) $42.   (c) $32.
(b) $34.   (d) $30.

(SO 4)   7. The Plastics Division of Weston Company manufactures plastic molds and then sells them to customers for $70 per unit. Its variable cost is $30 per unit, and its fixed cost per unit is $10. Management would like the Plastics Division to transfer 10,000 of these molds to another division within the company at a price of $40. The Plastics Division is operating at full capacity.

What is the minimum transfer price that the Plastics Division should accept?
(a) $10.   (c) $40.
(b) $30.   (d) $70.

(SO 4)   8. Assume the same information as question 7, except that the Plastics Division has available capacity of 10,000 units for plastic moldings. What is the minimum transfer price that the Plastics Division should accept?
(a) $10.   (c) $40.
(b) $30.   (d) $70.

(SO 6)   *9. AST Electrical provides the following cost information related to its production of electronic circuit boards.

	Per Unit
Variable manufacturing cost	$40
Fixed manufacturing cost	$30
Variable selling and administrative expenses	$ 8
Fixed selling and administrative expenses	$12
Desired ROI per unit	$15

What is its markup percentage assuming that AST Electrical uses absorption cost pricing?
(a) 16.67%.   (c) 54.28%.
(b) 50%.   (d) 118.75%.

(SO 6)   *10. Assume the same information as question 9 and determine AST Electrical's markup percentage using variable cost pricing.
(a) 16.67%.   (c) 54.28%.
(b) 50%.   (d) 118.75%.

THE NAVIGATOR

Questions

1. What are the two types of pricing environments for sales to external parties?

2. In what situation does a company place the greatest focus on its target cost? How is the target cost determined?

3. What is the basic formula to determine the target selling price in cost-plus pricing?

4. Stine Corporation produces a filter that has a per unit cost of $17. The company would like a 30% markup. Using cost-plus pricing, determine the per unit selling price.

5. What is the basic formula for the markup percentage?

6. What are some of the factors that affect a company's target ROI?

7. Livingston Corporation manufactures an electronic switch for dishwashers. The cost base per unit, excluding selling and administrative expenses, is $60.

The per unit cost of selling and administrative expenses is $20. The company's desired ROI per unit is $6. Calculate its markup percentage on total unit cost.

8. Estevan manufactures a standard cabinet for a DVD player. The variable cost per unit is $15. The fixed cost per unit is $9. The desired ROI per unit is $6. Compute the markup percentage on total unit cost and the target selling price for the cabinet.

9. In what circumstances is time and material pricing most often used?

10. What is the material loading charge? How is it expressed?

11. What is a transfer price? Why is determining a fair transfer price important to division managers?

12. When setting a transfer price, what objective(s) should the company have in mind?

13. What are the three approaches for determining transfer prices?

14. Describe the cost-based approach to transfer pricing. What is the strength of this approach? What are the weaknesses of this approach?

15. What is the general formula for determining the minimum transfer price that the selling division should be willing to accept?

16. When determining the minimum transfer price, what is meant by the "opportunity cost"?

17. In what circumstances will a negotiated transfer price be used instead of a market-based price?

18. Explain how transfer pricing between divisions located in different countries is used to reduce tax payments, and discuss the propriety of this approach.

*19. What costs are excluded from the cost base when the absorption cost pricing is used to determine the markup percentage?

*20. Kay Corporation manufactures a fiber optic connector. The variable cost per unit is $15. The fixed cost per unit is $9. The company's desired ROI per unit is $3. Compute the markup percentage using variable cost pricing.

Brief Exercises

BE8-1 Russell Company manufactures computer hard drives. The market for hard drives is very competitive. The current market price for a computer hard drive is $45. Russell would like a profit of $14 per drive. How can Russell Company accomplish this objective?

Compute target cost. (SO 1)

BE8-2 Gruner Corporation produces snowboards. The following per unit cost information is available: direct materials $12; direct labor $8; variable manufacturing overhead $6; fixed manufacturing overhead $14; variable selling and administrative expenses $4; and fixed selling and administrative expenses $12. Using a 32% markup percentage on total per unit cost, compute the target selling price.

Use cost-plus pricing to determine selling price. (SO 2)

BE8-3 Travis Corporation produces high-performance rotors. It expects to produce 50,000 rotors in the coming year. It has invested $10,000,000 to produce rotors. The company has a required return on investment of 18%. What is its ROI per unit?

Compute ROI per unit. (SO 2)

BE8-4 Shandling Corporation produces microwave units. The following per unit cost information is available: direct materials $36; direct labor $24; variable manufacturing overhead $18; fixed manufacturing overhead $42; variable selling and administrative expenses $14; and fixed selling and administrative expenses $28. Its desired ROI per unit is $30. Compute its markup percentage using a total cost approach.

Compute markup percentage. (SO 2)

BE8-5 During the current year Bierko Corporation expects to produce 10,000 units and has budgeted the following: net income $300,000; variable costs $1,100,000; and fixed costs $100,000. It has invested assets of $1,500,000. The company's budgeted ROI was 20%. What was its budgeted markup percentage using a full cost approach?

Compute ROI and markup percentage. (SO 2)

BE8-6 Swayze Small Engine Repair charges $45 per hour of labor. It has a material loading percentage of 40%. On a recent job replacing the engine of a riding lawnmower, Swayze worked 10.5 hours and used parts with a cost of $700. Calculate Swayze's total bill.

Use time and material pricing to determine bill. (SO 3)

BE8-7 The Heating Division of ITA International produces a heating element that it sells to its customers for $42 per unit. Its variable cost per unit is $19, and its fixed cost per unit is $10. Top management of ITA International would like the Heating Division to transfer 15,000 heating units to another division within the company at a price of $29. The Heating Division is operating at full capacity. What is the minimum transfer price that the Heating Division should accept?

Determine minimum transfer price. (SO 4)

BE8-8 Use the data from BE8-7, but assume that the Heating Division has sufficient excess capacity to provide the 15,000 heating units to the other division. What is the minimum transfer price that the Heating Division should accept?

Determine minimum transfer price with excess capacity. (SO 4)

BE8-9 Use the data from BE8-7, but assume that the units being requested are special high-performance units, and that the division's variable cost would be $24 per unit. What is the minimum transfer price that the Heating Division should accept?

Determine minimum transfer price for special order. (SO 4)

***BE8-10** Using the data in BE8-4, compute the markup percentage using absorption cost pricing.

Compute markup percentage using absorption cost pricing. (SO 6)

***BE8-11** Using the data in BE8-4, compute the markup percentage using variable cost pricing.

Compute markup percentage using variable cost pricing. (SO 6)

Exercises

Compute target cost.
(SO 1)

E8-1 Culver Cheese Company has developed a new cheese slicer called Slim Slicer. The company plans to sell this slicer through its catalog which is issued monthly. Given market research, Culver believes that it can charge $15 for the Slim Slicer. Prototypes of the Slim Slicer, however, are costing $22. By using cheaper materials and gaining efficiencies in mass production Culver believes it can reduce Slim Slicer's cost substantially. Culver wishes to earn a return of 30% of the selling price.

Instructions
(a) Compute the target cost for the Slim Slicer.
(b) When is target costing particularly helpful in deciding whether to produce a given product?

Compute target cost.
(SO 1)

E8-2 LasikLook is involved in producing and selling high-end golf equipment. The company has recently been involved in developing various types of laser guns to measure yardages on the golf course. One small laser gun, called LittleLasik, appears to have a very large potential market. Because of competition, LasikLook does not believe that it can charge more than $90 for LittleLasik. At this price, LasikLook believes it can sell 100,000 of these laser guns. LittleLasik will require an investment of $8,500,000 to manufacture, and the company wants an ROI of 20%.

Instructions
Determine the target cost for one LittleLasik.

Compute target cost and cost-plus pricing.
(SO 1, 2)

E8-3 Mucky Duck makes swimsuits and sells these suits directly to retailers. Although Mucky Duck has a variety of suits, it does not make the All-Body suit used by highly-skilled swimmers. The market research department believes that a strong market exists for this type of suit. The department indicates that the All-Body suit would sell for approximately $110. Given its experience, Mucky Duck believes the All-Body suit would have the following manufacturing costs.

Direct materials	$ 25
Direct labor	30
Manufacturing overhead	45
Total costs	$100

Instructions
(a) Assume that Mucky Duck uses cost-plus pricing, setting the selling price 25% above its costs. (1) What would be the price charged for the All-Body swimsuit? (2) Under what circumstances might Mucky Duck consider manufacturing the All-Body swimsuit given this approach?
(b) Assume that Mucky Duck uses target costing. What is the price that Mucky Duck would charge the retailer for the All-Body swimsuit?
(c) What is the highest acceptable manufacturing cost Mucky Duck would be willing to incur to produce the All-Body swimsuit, if it desired a profit of $25 per unit?

Use cost-plus pricing to determine selling price.
(SO 2)

E8-4 Selleck Corporation makes a commercial-grade cooking griddle. The following information is available for Selleck Corporation's anticipated annual volume of 30,000 units.

	Per Unit	Total
Direct materials	$17	
Direct labor	$ 8	
Variable manufacturing overhead	$11	
Fixed manufacturing overhead		$360,000
Variable selling and administrative expenses	$ 4	
Fixed selling and administrative expenses		$150,000

The company uses a 40% markup percentage on total cost.

Instructions
(a) Compute the total cost per unit.
(b) Compute the target selling price.

E8-5   Marlowe Corporation makes a mechanical stuffed alligator that sings the Martian national anthem. The following information is available for Marlowe Corporation's anticipated annual volume of 500,000 units.

Use cost-plus pricing to determine various amounts.
(SO 2)

	Per Unit	Total
Direct materials	$ 7	
Direct labor	$ 9	
Variable manufacturing overhead	$15	
Fixed manufacturing overhead		$3,300,000
Variable selling and administrative expenses	$14	
Fixed selling and administrative expenses		$1,500,000

The company has a desired ROI of 25%. It has invested assets of $24,000,000.

Instructions
(a) Compute the total cost per unit.
(b) Compute the desired ROI per unit.
(c) Compute the markup percentage using total cost per unit.
(d) Compute the target selling price.

E8-6   Roxy's Recording Studio rents studio time to musicians in 2-hour blocks. Each session includes the use of the studio facilities, a digitally recorded tape of the performance, and a professional music producer/mixer. Anticipated annual volume is 1,000 sessions. The company has invested $2,058,000 in the studio and expects a return on investment (ROI) of 20%. Budgeted costs for the coming year are as follows.

Use cost-plus pricing to determine various amounts.
(SO 2)

	Per Session	Total
Direct materials (tapes, CDs, etc)	$ 20	
Direct labor	400	
Variable overhead	50	
Fixed overhead		$950,000
Variable selling and administrative expenses	40	
Fixed selling and administrative expenses		500,000

Instructions
(a) Determine the total cost per session.
(b) Determine the desired ROI per session.
(c) Calculate the mark-up percentage on the total cost per session.
(d) Calculate the target price per session.

E8-7   Caan Corporation produces industrial robots for high-precision manufacturing. The following information is given for Caan Corporation.

Use cost-plus pricing to determine various amounts.
(SO 2)

	Per Unit	Total
Direct materials	$380	
Direct labor	$290	
Variable manufacturing overhead	$ 72	
Fixed manufacturing overhead		$1,800,000
Variable selling and administrative expenses	$ 55	
Fixed selling and administrative expenses		$ 327,000

The company has a desired ROI of 20%. It has invested assets of $49,600,000. It anticipates production of 3,000 units per year.

Instructions
(a) Compute the cost per unit of the fixed manufacturing overhead and the fixed selling and administrative expenses.
(b) Compute the desired ROI per unit. (Round to the nearest dollar.)
(c) Compute the target selling price.

Use time and material pricing to determine bill.
(SO 3)

E8-8   Padong Remanufacturing rebuilds spot welders for manufacturers. The following budgeted cost data for 2006 is available for Padong.

	Time Charges	Material Loading Charges
Technicians' wages and benefits	$228,000	–
Parts manager's salary and benefits	–	$42,500
Office employee's salary and benefits	38,000	9,000
Other overhead	15,200	24,000
Total budgeted costs	$281,200	$75,500

The company desires a $35 profit margin per hour of labor and a 25% profit margin on parts. It has budgeted for 7,600 hours of repair time in the coming year, and estimates that the total invoice cost of parts and materials in 2006 will be $400,000.

Instructions
(a) Compute the rate charged per hour of labor.
(b) Compute the material loading percentage. (Round to three decimal places.)
(c) Lindy Corporation has requested an estimate to rebuild its spot welder. Padong estimates that it would require 40 hours of labor and $2,500 of parts. Compute the total estimated bill.

Use time and material pricing to determine bill.
(SO 3)

E8-9 Justin's Custom Electronics (JCE) sells and installs complete security, computer, audio, and video systems for homes. On newly constructed homes it provides bids using time and material pricing. The following budgeted cost data are available.

	Time Charges	Material Loading Charges
Technicians' wages and benefits	$150,000	–
Parts manager's salary and benefits	–	$34,000
Office employee's salary and benefits	28,000	12,000
Other overhead	15,000	42,000
Total budgeted costs	$193,000	$88,000

The company has budgeted for 6,000 hours of technician time during the coming year. It desires a $38 profit margin per hour of labor and a 100% profit on parts. It estimates the total invoice cost of parts and materials in 2006 will be $700,000.

Instructions
(a) Compute the rate charged per hour of labor. (Round to 2 decimal places.)
(b) Compute the material loading percentage. (Round to 2 decimal places.)
(c) JCE has just received a request for a bid from R.J. Builders on a $1,200,000 new home. The company estimates that it would require 80 hours of labor and $40,000 of parts. Compute the total estimated bill.

Use time and material pricing to determine bill.
(SO 3)

E8-10 Karl's Klassic Kars restores classic automobiles to showroom status. Budgeted data for the current year are:

	Time Charges	Material Loading Charges
Restorers' wages and fringe benefits	$270,000	
Purchasing agent's salary and fringe benefits		$ 67,500
Administrative salaries and fringe benefits	54,000	21,960
Other overhead costs	21,600	75,600
Total budgeted costs	$345,600	$165,060

The company anticipated that the restorers would work a total of 12,000 hours this year. Expected parts and materials were $1,260,000.

In late January, the company experienced a fire in its facilities that destroyed most of the accounting records. The accountant remembers that the hourly labor rate was $68.80 and that the material loading charge was 93.10%.

Instructions
(a) Determine the profit margin per hour on labor.
(b) Determine the profit margin on materials.
(c) Determine the total price of labor and materials on a job that was completed after the fire that required 150 hours of labor and $60,000 in parts and materials.

E8-11 Allied Company's Small Motor Division manufactures a number of small motors used in household and office appliances. The Household Division of Allied then assembles and packages such items as blenders and juicers. Both divisions are free to buy and sell any of their components internally or externally. The following costs relate to small motor LN233 on a per unit basis.

Determine minimum transfer price.
(SO 4)

Fixed cost per unit	$ 5
Variable cost per unit	8
Selling price per unit	30

Instructions
(a) Assuming that the Small Motor Division has excess capacity, compute the minimum acceptable price for the transfer of small motor LN233 to the Household Division.
(b) Assuming that the Small Motor Division does not have excess capacity, compute the minimum acceptable price for the transfer of the small motor to the Household Division.
(c) ▭▭▭▶ Explain why the level of capacity in the Small Motor Division has an effect on the transfer price.

E8-12 The Cycle Division of TravelVelocity Company has the following per unit cost data related to its most recent cycle called Roadbuster.

Determine effect on income from transfer price.
(SO 4)

Selling price		$2,200
Variable cost of goods sold		
Body frame	$300	
Other variable costs	900	1,200
Contribution margin		$1,000

Presently, the Cycle Division buys its body frames from an outside supplier. However TravelVelocity has another division, FrameBody, that makes body frames for other cycle companies. The Cycle Division believes that FrameBody's product is suitable for its new Roadbuster cycle. Presently, FrameBody sells its frames for $350 per frame. The variable cost for FrameBody is $250. The Cycle Division is willing to pay $275 to purchase the frames from FrameBody.

Instructions
(a) Assume that FrameBody has excess capacity and is able to meet all of the Cycle Division's needs. If the Cycle Division buys 1,000 frames from FrameBody, determine the following: (1) effect on the income of the Cycle Division; (2) effect on the income of FrameBody; and (3) effect on the income of TravelVelocity.
(b) Assume that FrameBody does not have excess capacity and therefore would lose sales if the frames were sold to the Cycle Division. If the Cycle Division buys 1,000 frames from FrameBody, determine the following: (1) effect on the income of the Cycle Division; (2) effect on the income of FrameBody; and (3) effect on the income of TravelVelocity.

E8-13 NuVox Corporation manufactures car stereos. It is a division of RustBucket Motors, which manufactures vehicles. NuVox sells car stereos to RustBucket, as well as to other vehicle manufacturers and retail stores. The following information is available for NuVox's standard unit: variable cost per unit $34; fixed cost per unit $23; and selling price to outside customer $85. RustBucket currently purchases a standard unit from an outside supplier for $80. Because of quality concerns and to ensure a reliable supply, the top management of RustBucket has ordered NuVox to provide 200,000 units per year at a transfer price of $34 per unit. NuVox is already operating at full capacity. NuVox can avoid $4 per unit of variable selling costs by selling the unit internally.

Determine minimum transfer price.
(SO 4)

Instructions
Answer each of the following questions.
(a) What is the minimum transfer price that NuVox should accept?
(b) What is the potential loss to the corporation as a whole resulting from this forced transfer?
(c) How should this situation be resolved?

Compute minimum transfer price.
(SO 4)

E8-14   The Faucet Division of Korey Plumbing Corporation has recently been approached by the Bathtub Division with a proposal. The Bathtub Division would like to make a special "ivory" tub with gold-plated fixtures for the company's 50-year anniversary. It would make only 5,000 of these units. It would like the Faucet Division to make the fixtures and provide them to the Bathtub Division at a transfer price of $160. The estimated variable cost per unit would be $135. However, by selling internally the Faucet Division would save $6 per unit on variable selling expenses. The Faucet Division is currently operating at full capacity. Its standard unit sells for $50 per unit and has variable costs of $29.

Instructions
Compute the minimum transfer price that the Faucet Division should be willing to accept, and discuss whether it should accept this offer.

Determine minimum transfer price.
(SO 4)

E8-15   The Appraisal Department of Mega-Mortgage Bank performs appraisals of business properties for loans being considered by the bank and appraisals for home buyers that are financing their purchase through some other financial institution. The department charges $160 per home appraisal, and its variable costs are $126 per appraisal.

Recently, Mega-Mortgage Bank has opened its own Home-Loan Department and wants the Appraisal Department to perform 1,200 appraisals on all Mega-Mortgage Bank–financed home loans. Bank management feels that the cost of these appraisals to the Home-Loan Department should be $150. The variable cost per appraisal to the Home-Loan Department would be $6 less than those performed for outside customers due to savings in administrative costs.

Instructions
(a) Determine the minimum transfer price, assuming the Appraisal Department has excess capacity.
(b) Determine the minimum transfer price, assuming the Appraisal Department has no excess capacity.
(c) Assuming the Appraisal Department has no excess capacity, should management force the department to charge the Home-Loan Department only $150? Discuss.

Compute total cost per unit, ROI, and markup percentages using absorption cost pricing and variable cost pricing.
(SO 6)

*E8-16   Information for Marlowe Corporation is given in E8-5.

Instructions
Using the information given in E8-5, answer the following.
(a) Compute the total cost per unit.
(b) Compute the desired ROI per unit.
(c) Using absorption cost pricing, compute the markup percentage.
(d) Using variable cost pricing, compute the markup percentage.

Compute markup percentage using absorption cost pricing and variable cost pricing.
(SO 6)

*E8-17   Firefly Corporation produces outdoor portable fireplace units. The following per unit cost information is available: direct materials $21; direct labor $26; variable manufacturing overhead $16; fixed manufacturing overhead $22; variable selling and administrative expenses $9; and fixed selling and administrative expenses $15. The company's ROI per unit is $20.

Instructions
Compute Firefly Corporation's markup percentage using (1) absorption cost pricing and (2) variable cost pricing.

Compute various amounts using absorption cost pricing and variable cost pricing.
(SO 6)

*E8-18   Information for Caan Corporation is given in E8-7.

Instructions
Using the information given in E8-7, answer the following.
(a) Compute the cost per unit of the fixed manufacturing overhead and the fixed selling and administrative expenses.
(b) Compute the desired ROI per unit. (Round to the nearest dollar.)

(c) Compute the markup percentage and target selling price using absorption cost pricing. (Round the markup percentage to 3 decimal places.)

(d) Compute the markup percentage and target selling price using variable cost pricing. (Round the markup percentage to 3 decimal places.)

Problems: Set A

P8-1A Lafluer Corporation needs to set a target price for its newly designed product M14–M16. The following data relate to this new product.

Use cost-plus pricing to determine various amounts.
(SO 2)

	Per Unit	Total
Direct materials	$20	
Direct labor	$42	
Variable manufacturing overhead	$10	
Fixed manufacturing overhead		$1,440,000
Variable selling and administrative expenses	$ 5	
Fixed selling and administrative expenses		$1,040,000

These costs are based on a budgeted volume of 80,000 units produced and sold each year. Lafluer uses cost-plus pricing methods to set its target selling price. The markup on total unit cost is 30%.

Instructions

(a) Compute the total variable cost per unit, total fixed cost per unit, and total cost per unit for M14–M16.

(b) Compute the desired ROI per unit for M14–M16.

(c) Compute the target selling price for M14–M16.

(d) Compute variable cost per unit, fixed cost per unit, and total cost per unit assuming that 60,000 M14–M16s are sold during the year. (Round to 2 decimal places.)

(a) Variable cost per unit $77

P8-2A Bolus Computer Parts Inc. is in the process of setting a selling price on a new component it has just designed and developed. The following cost estimates for this new component have been provided by the accounting department for a budgeted volume of 50,000 units.

Use cost-plus pricing to determine various amounts.
(SO 2)

	Per Unit	Total
Direct materials	$50	
Direct labor	$25	
Variable manufacturing overhead	$20	
Fixed manufacturing overhead		$600,000
Variable selling and administrative expenses	$18	
Fixed selling and administrative expenses		$400,000

Bolus Computer Parts management requests that the total cost per unit be used in cost-plus pricing its products. On this particular product, management also directs that the target price be set to provide a 25% return on investment (ROI) on invested assets of $1,200,000.

Instructions

(Round all calculations to two decimal places.)

(a) Compute the markup percentage and target selling price that will allow Bolus Computer Parts to earn its desired ROI of 25% on this new component.

(b) Assuming that the volume is 40,000 units, compute the markup percentage and target selling price that will allow Bolus Computer Parts to earn its desired ROI of 25% on this new component.

(b) Target selling price $145.50

Use time and material pricing to determine bill.
(SO 3)

P8-3A Hawks Electronic Repair Shop has budgeted the following time and material for 2005.

HAWKS ELECTRONIC REPAIR SHOP
Budgeted Costs for the Year 2005

	Time Charges	Material Loading Charges
Shop employees' wages and benefits	$108,000	–
Parts manager's salary and benefits	–	$25,400
Office employee's salary and benefits	20,000	13,600
Overhead (supplies, depreciation, advertising, utilities)	26,000	18,000
Total budgeted costs	$154,000	$57,000

Hawks budgets 5,000 hours of repair time in 2005 and will bill a profit of $5 per labor hour along with a 30% profit markup on the invoice cost of parts. The estimated invoice cost for parts to be used is $100,000.

On January 5, 2005 Hawks is asked to submit a price estimate to fix a 72″ big-screen TV. Hawks estimates that this job will consume 20 hours of labor and $500 in parts.

Instructions

(a) Compute the labor rate for Hawks Electronic Repair Shop for the year 2005.

(b) Compute the material loading charge percentage for Hawks Electronic Repair Shop for the year 2005.

(c) $1,651

(c) Prepare a time and material price quotation for fixing the big-screen TV.

Determine minimum transfer price with no excess capacity and with excess capacity.
(SO 4)

P8-4A Wordsmith is a publishing company with a number of different book lines. Each line has contracts with a number of different authors. The company also owns a printing operation called Pronto Press. The book lines and the printing operation each operate as a separate profit center. The printing operation earns revenue by printing books by authors under contract with the book lines owned by Wordsmith, as well as authors under contract with other companies. The printing operation bills out at $0.01 per page, and a typical book requires 500 pages of print. A manager from Business Books, one of the Wordsmith's book lines, has approached the manager of the printing operation offering to pay $0.007 per page for 1,200 copies of a 500-page book. The book line pays outside printers $0.009 per page. The printing operation's variable cost per page is $0.006.

Instructions

Determine whether the printing should be done internally or externally, and the appropriate transfer price, under each of the following situations.

(a) Assume that the printing operation is booked solid for the next two years, and it would have to cancel an obligation with an outside customer in order to meet the needs of the internal division.

(b) Assume that the printing operation has available capacity.

(c) ✏️▶ The top management of Wordsmith believes that the printing operation should always do the printing for the company's authors. On a number of occasions it has forced the printing operation to cancel jobs with outside customers in order to meet the needs of its own lines. Discuss the pros and cons of this approach.

(d) loss to company $600

(d) Calculate the change in contribution margin to each division, and to the company as a whole, if top management forces the printing operation to accept the $0.007 per page transfer price when it has no available capacity.

Determine minimum transfer price with no excess capacity.
(SO 4)

P8-5A Zapp Manufacturing Company makes various electronic products. The company is divided into a number of autonomous divisions that can either sell to internal units or sell externally. All divisions are located in buildings on the same piece of property. The Board Division has offered the Chip Division $20 per unit to supply it with chips for 40,000 boards. It has been purchasing these chips for $21 per unit from outside suppliers. The Chip Division receives $22.50 per unit for sales made to outside customers on this type of chip. The variable cost of chips sold externally by the Chip Division is $14. It estimates that it will save $4 per chip of selling expenses on units sold internally to the Board Division. The Chip Division has no excess capacity.

Instructions

(a) Calculate the minimum transfer price that the Chip Division should accept. Discuss whether it is in the Chip Division's best interest to accept the offer.

(b) Total loss to company $100,000

(b) Suppose that the Chip Division decides to reject the offer. What are the financial implications for each division, and for the company as a whole, of this decision?

P8-6A Commcenter Manufacturing (CM) is a division of Worldwide Communications, Inc. CM produces pagers and other personal communication devices. These devices are sold to other Worldwide divisions, as well as to other communication companies. CM was recently approached by the manager of the Personal Communications Division regarding a request to make a special pager designed to receive signals from anywhere in the world. The Personal Communications Division has requested that CM produce 10,000 units of this special pager. The following facts are available regarding the Commcenter Manufacturing Division.

Determine minimum transfer price under different situations.
(SO 4)

Selling price of standard pager	$95
Variable cost of standard pager	50
Additional variable cost of special pager	35

Instructions

For each of the following independent situations, calculate the minimum transfer price, and discuss whether the internal transfer should take place or whether the Personal Communications Division should purchase the pager externally.

(a) The Personal Communications Division has offered to pay the CM Division $105 per pager. The CM Division has no available capacity. The CM Division would have to forgo sales of 10,000 pagers to existing customers in order to meet the request of the Personal Communications Division.

(b) The Personal Communications Division has offered to pay the CM Division $160 per pager. The CM Division has no available capacity. The CM Division would have to forgo sales of 14,000 pagers to existing customers in order to meet the request of the Personal Communications Division.

(b) Minimum price $148

(c) The Personal Communications Division has offered to pay the CM Division $105 per pager. The CM Division has available capacity.

*P8-7A Fast Buck Corporation needs to set a target price for its newly designed product EverReady. The following data relate to this new product.

Compute the target price using absorption cost pricing and variable cost pricing.
(SO 6)

	Per Unit	Total
Direct materials	$20	
Direct labor	$40	
Variable manufacturing overhead	$10	
Fixed manufacturing overhead		$1,400,000
Variable selling and administrative expenses	$ 5	
Fixed selling and administrative expenses		$1,120,000

The costs above are based on a budgeted volume of 80,000 units produced and sold each year. Fast Buck uses cost-plus pricing methods to set its target selling price. Because some managers prefer absorption cost pricing and others prefer variable cost pricing, the accounting department provides information under both approaches using a markup of 50% on absorption cost and a markup of 75% on variable cost.

Instructions

(a) Compute the target price for one unit of EverReady using absorption cost pricing.

(b) Compute the target price for one unit of EverReady using variable cost pricing.

(a) Markup $43.75
(b) Markup $56.25

*P8-8A Weather Guard Windows Inc. is in the process of setting a target price on its newly designed tinted window. Cost data relating to the window at a budgeted volume of 4,000 units are as follows.

Compute various amounts using absorption cost pricing and variable cost pricing.
(SO 6)

	Per Unit	Total
Direct materials	$100	
Direct labor	$ 70	
Variable manufacturing overhead	$ 20	
Fixed manufacturing overhead		$120,000
Variable selling and administrative expenses	$ 10	
Fixed selling and administrative expenses		$102,000

Weather Guard Windows uses cost-plus pricing methods that are designed to provide the company with a 30% ROI on its tinted window line. A total of $700,000 in assets is committed to production of the new tinted window.

Instructions

(a) 40%

(a) Compute the markup percentage under absorption cost pricing that will allow Weather Guard Windows to realize its desired ROI.

(b) Compute the target price of the window under absorption cost pricing, and show proof that the desired ROI is realized.

(c) Compute the markup percentage under variable cost pricing that will allow Weather Guard Windows to realize its desired ROI. (Round to 3 decimal places.)

(d) Compute the target price of the window under variable cost pricing, and show proof that the desired ROI is realized.

(e) Since both absorption cost pricing and variable cost pricing produce the same target price and provide the same desired ROI, why do both methods exist? Isn't one method clearly superior to the other?

Problems: Set B

Use cost-plus pricing to determine various amounts.
(SO 2)

P8-1B   Wamser Corporation needs to set a target price for its newly designed product E2-D2. The following data relate to this new product.

	Per Unit	Total
Direct materials	$18	
Direct labor	$30	
Variable manufacturing overhead	$ 8	
Fixed manufacturing overhead		$1,440,000
Variable selling and administrative expenses	$ 4	
Fixed selling and administrative expenses		$1,080,000

These costs are based on a budgeted volume of 90,000 units produced and sold each year. Wamser uses cost-plus pricing methods to set its target selling price. The markup on total unit cost is 25%.

Instructions

(a) Variable cost per unit $60

(a) Compute total variable cost per unit, total fixed cost per unit, and total cost per unit for E2-D2.

(b) Compute the desired ROI per unit for E2-D2.

(c) Compute the target selling price for E2-D2.

(d) Compute variable cost per unit, fixed cost per unit, and total cost per unit assuming that 80,000 E2-D2s are sold during the year.

Use cost-plus pricing to determine various amounts.
(SO 2)

P8-2B   Bosworth Electronics Inc. is in the process of setting a selling price on a new CDL component it has just developed. The following cost estimates for this component have been provided by the accounting department for a budgeted volume of 50,000 units.

	Per Unit	Total
Direct materials	$38	
Direct labor	$24	
Variable manufacturing overhead	$18	
Fixed manufacturing overhead		$450,000
Variable selling and administrative expenses	$12	
Fixed selling and administrative expenses		$360,000

Bosworth's management uses cost-plus pricing to set its selling price. Management also directs that the target price be set to provide a 20% return on investment (ROI) on invested assets of $1,500,000.

Instructions

(Round all calculations to two decimal places.)

(a) Compute the markup percentage and target selling price on this new CDL component.

(b) Target selling price $119.75

(b) Assuming that the volume is 40,000 units, compute the markup percentage and target selling price that will allow Bosworth Electronics to earn its desired ROI of 20%.

P8-3B   Zip's Auto Body Shop has budgeted the following time and material for 2005.

ZIP'S AUTO BODY SHOP
Budgeted Costs for the Year 2005

Use time and material pricing to determine bill.
(SO 3)

	Time Charges	Material Loading Charges
Shop employees' wages and benefits	$111,000	–
Parts manager's salary and benefits	–	$26,600
Office employee's salary and benefits	21,000	12,000
Overhead (supplies, depreciation, advertising, utilities)	24,600	15,000
Total budgeted costs	$156,600	$53,600

Zip's budgets 6,000 hours of repair time in 2005. It will bill a profit of $7 per labor hour along with a 40% profit markup on the invoice cost of parts. Zip's anticipates using $200,000 of parts in 2005.

On January 10, 2005, Zip's is asked to submit a price estimate for the repair of a 2002 Chevrolet Blazer that was damaged in a head-on collision. Zip's estimates that this repair will consume 61 hours of labor and $4,200 in parts and materials.

Instructions
(a) Compute the labor rate for Zip's Auto Body Shop for the year 2005.
(b) Compute the material loading charge percentage for Zip's Auto Body Shop for the year 2005. (Round to 3 decimal places.)
(c) Prepare a time and material price quotation for the repair of the 2002 Blazer.

(c) $9,024.70

P8-4B Cosmic Sounds is a record company with a number of record labels. Each record label has contracts with a number of recording artists. It also owns a recording studio called Blast Off. The record labels and the recording studio operate as separate profit centers. The studio earns revenue by recording artists under contract with the labels owned by Cosmic Sounds, as well as artists under contract with other companies. The studio bills out at $1,100 per hour, and a typical CD requires 80 hours of studio time. A manager from Big Bang, one of the Cosmic Sounds' record labels, has approached the manager of the recording studio offering to pay $800 per hour for an 80-hour session. The record label pays outside studios $1,000 per hour. The recording studio's variable cost per hour is $600.

Determine minimum transfer price with no excess capacity and with excess capacity.
(SO 4)

Instructions
Determine whether the recording should be done internally or hired externally, and the appropriate transfer price, under each of the following situations.
(a) Assume that the recording studio is booked solid for the next 3 years, and it would have to cancel an obligation with an outside customer in order to meet the needs of the internal division.
(b) Assume that the recording studio has available capacity.
(c) ▰▰▰▰▷ The top management of Cosmic Sounds believes that the recording studio should always do the recording for the company's artists. On a number of occasions it has forced the recording studio to cancel jobs with outside customers in order to meet the needs of its own labels. Discuss the pros and cons of this approach.
(d) Calculate the change in contribution margin to each division, and to the company as a whole, if top management forces the recording studio to accept the $800 transfer price when it has no available capacity.

(d) Loss to company $8,000

P8-5B Chula Vista Pump Company makes irrigation pump systems. The company is divided into a number of autonomous divisions that can either sell to internal units or sell externally. All divisions are located in buildings on the same piece of property. The Pump Division has offered the Washer Division $4 per unit to supply it with the washers for 50,000 units. It has been purchasing these washers for $4.30 per unit from outside suppliers. The Washer Division receives $4.60 per unit for sales made to outside customers on this type of washer. The variable cost of units sold externally by the Washer Division is $3.20. It estimates that it will save 70 cents per unit of selling expenses on units sold internally to the Pump Division. The Washer Division has no excess capacity.

Determine minimum transfer price with no excess capacity.
(SO 4)

Instructions
(a) Calculate the minimum transfer price that the Washer Division should accept. Discuss whether it is in the Washer Division's best interest to accept the offer.
(b) Suppose that the Washer Division decides to reject the offer. What are the financial implications for each division, and the company as a whole, of the decision to reject the offer?

(b) Total loss to company $20,000

Determine minimum transfer price under different situations.
(SO 4)

P8-6B Heartland Engines is a division of EverGreen Lawn Equipment Company. Heartland makes engines for lawn mowers, snow blowers, and other types of lawn and garden equipment. It sells its engines to the Lawn Mower Division and the Snow Blower Division of the company, as well as to other lawn equipment companies. It was recently approached by the manager of the Lawn Mower Division with a request to make a special, high-performance engine for a lawn mower designed to mow heavy brush. The Lawn Mower Division has requested that Heartland produce 8,500 units of this special engine. The following facts are available regarding the Heartland Engine Division.

Selling price of standard lawn mower engine	$88
Variable cost of standard lawn mower engine	$55
Additional variable cost of special engine	$41

Instructions

For each of the following independent situations, calculate the minimum transfer price, and discuss whether the internal transfer should take place or whether the Lawn Mower Division should purchase its goods externally.

(a) $129

(a) The Lawn Mower Division has offered to pay the Heartland Engine Division $110 per engine. Heartland Engine has no available capacity. Heartland Engine would have to forgo sales of 8,500 units to existing customers in order to meet the request of the Lawn Mower Division.

(b) $142.59

(b) The Lawn Mower Division has offered to pay the Heartland Engine Division $170 per engine. Heartland has no available capacity. Heartland Engine would have to forgo sales of 12,000 units to existing customers in order to meet the request of the Lawn Mower Division. (Round to 2 decimal places.)

(c) $96

(c) The Lawn Mower division has offered to pay the Heartland Engine Division $110 per engine. Heartland Engine Division has available capacity.

Compute the target price using absorption cost pricing and variable cost pricing.
(SO 6)

*P8-7B Wamser Corporation needs to set a target price for its newly designed product E2-D2. The following data relate to this new product.

	Per Unit	Total
Direct materials	$18	
Direct labor	$30	
Variable manufacturing overhead	$ 8	
Fixed manufacturing overhead		$1,440,000
Variable selling and administrative expenses	$ 4	
Fixed selling and administrative expenses		$1,080,000

The above costs are based on a budgeted volume of 90,000 units produced and sold each year. Wamser uses cost-plus pricing methods to set its target selling price. Because some managers prefer to work with absorption cost pricing and other managers prefer variable cost pricing, the accounting department provides information under both approaches using a markup of 50% on absorption cost and a markup of 80% on variable cost.

Instructions

(a) Markup $36
(b) Markup $48

(a) Compute the target price for one unit of E2-D2 using absorption cost pricing.
(b) Compute the target price for one unit of E2-D2 using variable cost pricing.

Compute various amounts using absorption cost pricing and variable cost pricing.
(SO 6)

*P8-8B Santana Furniture Inc. is in the process of setting a target price on its newly designed leather recliner sofa. Cost data relating to the sofa at a budgeted volume of 3,000 units are as follows.

	Per Unit	Total
Direct materials	$140	
Direct labor	$ 80	
Variable manufacturing overhead	$ 40	
Fixed manufacturing overhead		$180,000
Variable selling and administrative expenses	$ 20	
Fixed selling and administrative expenses		$ 90,000

Santana Furniture uses cost-plus pricing methods that are designed to provide the company with a 30% ROI on its stuffed furniture line. A total of $700,000 in assets are committed to production of the new leather recliner sofa.

Instructions

(a) Compute the markup percentage under absorption cost pricing that will allow Santana Furniture to realize its desired ROI.   (a) 37.5%

(b) Compute the target price of the sofa under absorption cost pricing, and show proof that the desired ROI is realized.

(c) Compute the markup percentage under variable cost pricing that will allow Santana Furniture to realize its desired ROI. (Round to 3 decimal places.)

(d) Compute the target price of the sofa under variable cost pricing, and show proof that the desired ROI is realized.

(e) Since both absorption cost pricing and variable cost pricing produce the same target price and provide the same desired ROI, why do both methods exist? Isn't one method clearly superior to the other?

Problems: Set C

Problem Set C is provided at the book's Web site, www.wiley.com/college/weygandt.

▷ BROADENING YOUR PERSPECTIVE

Group Decision Case

BYP 8-1 Aurora Manufacturing has multiple divisions that make a wide variety of products. Recently the Bearing Division and the Wheel Division got into an argument over a transfer price. The Wheel Division needed bearings for garden tractor wheels. It normally buys its bearings from an outside supplier for $24 per set. The company's top management recently initiated a campaign to persuade the different divisions to buy their materials from within the company whenever possible. As a result, Steve Hamblin, the purchasing manager for the Wheel Division, received a letter from the vice president of Purchasing, ordering him to contact the Bearing Division to discuss buying bearings from this division.

To comply with this request, Steve from the Wheel Division called Terry Tompkin of the Bearing Division, and asked the price for 15,000 bearings. Terry responded that the bearings normally sell for $35 per set. However, Terry noted that the Bearing Division would save $3 on marketing costs by selling internally, and would pass this cost savings on to the Wheel Division. He further commented that they were at full capacity, and therefore would not be able to provide any bearings presently. In the future, if they had available capacity, they would be happy to provide bearings.

Steve responded indignantly, "Thanks but no thanks." He said, "We can get all the bearings we need from Falk Manufacturing for $24 per set." Terry snorted back, "Falk makes junk. It costs us $22 per set just to make our bearings. Our bearings can withstand heat of 2,000 degrees centigrade, and are good to within .00001 centimeters. If you guys are happy buying junk, then go ahead and buy from Falk."

Two weeks later, Steve's boss from the central office stopped in to find out whether he had placed an order with the Bearing Division. Steve responded that he would sooner buy his bearings from his worst enemy than from the Bearing Division.

Instructions

With the class divided into groups, prepare answers to the following questions.

(a) Why might the company's top management want the divisions to start doing more business with one another?

(b) Under what conditions should a buying division be forced to buy from an internal supplier? Under what conditions should a selling division be forced to sell to an internal division, rather than to an outside customer?

(c) The Vice President of Purchasing thinks that this problem should be resolved by forcing the Bearing Division to sell to the Wheel Division at its cost of $22. Is this a good solution for the Wheel Division? Is this a good solution for the Bearing Division? Is this a good solution for the company?

(d) Provide at least two other possible solutions to this problem. Discuss the merits and drawbacks of each.

Managerial Analysis

BYP 8-2　Construction on the Atlantis Full-Service Car Wash is nearing completion. The owner is Jay Leer, a retired accounting professor. The car wash is strategically located on a busy street that separates an affluent suburban community from a middle-class community. It has two state-of-the-art stalls. Each stall can provide anything from a basic two-stage wash and rinse to a five-stage luxurious bath. It is all "touch-less," that is, there are no brushes to potentially damage the car. Outside each stall there is also a 400 horsepower vacuum. Jay likes to joke that these vacuums are so strong that they will pull the carpet right out of your car if you aren't careful.

Jay has some important decisions to make before he can open the car wash. First, he knows that there is one drive-through car wash only a 10-minute drive away. It is attached to a gas station; it charges $5 for a basic wash, and $4 if you also buy at least 8 gallons of gas. It is a "brush"-type wash with rotating brush heads. There is also a self-serve "stand outside your car and spray until you are soaked" car wash a 15-minute drive away from Jay's location. He went over and tried this out. He went through $3 in quarters to get the equivalent of a basic wash. He knows that both of these locations always have long lines, which is one reason why he decided to build a new car wash.

Jay is planning to offer three levels of wash service—Basic, Deluxe, and Premium. The Basic is all automated; it requires no direct intervention by employees. The Deluxe is all automated except that at the end an employee will wipe down the car and will put a window treatment on the windshield that reduces glare and allows rainwater to run off more quickly. The Premium level is a "pampered" service. This will include all the services of the Deluxe, plus a special wax after the machine wax, and an employee will vacuum the car, wipe down the entire interior, and wash the inside of the windows. To provide the Premium service, Jay will have to hire a couple of "car wash specialists" to do the additional pampering.

Jay has pulled together the following estimates, based on data he received from the local Chamber of Commerce and information from a trade association.

	Per Unit	Total
Direct materials per Basic wash	$0.25	
Direct materials per Deluxe wash	0.75	
Direct materials per Premium wash	1.05	
Direct labor per Basic wash	na	
Direct labor per Deluxe wash	0.40	
Direct labor per Premium wash	2.40	
Variable overhead per Basic wash	0.10	
Variable overhead per Deluxe and Premium washes	0.20	
Fixed overhead		$112,500
Variable selling and administrative expenses all washes	0.10	
Fixed selling and administrative expenses		121,500

The total estimated number of washes of any type is 45,000. Jay has invested assets of $324,000. He would like a return on investment (ROI) of 25%.

Instructions
Answer each of the following questions.
(a) Identify the issues that Jay must consider in deciding on the price of each level of service of his car wash. Also discuss what issues he should consider in deciding on what levels of service to provide.
(b) Jay estimates that of the total 45,000 washes, 20,000 will be Basic, 20,000 will be Deluxe, and 5,000 will be Premium. Calculate the selling price, using cost-plus pricing, that Jay should use for each type of wash to achieve his desired ROI of 25%.
(c) During the first year, instead of selling 45,000 washes, Jay sold 43,000 washes. He was quite accurate in his estimate of first-year sales, but he was way off on the types of washes that he sold. He sold 3,000 Basic, 31,000 Deluxe, and 9,000 Premium. His actual total fixed expenses were as he expected, and his variable cost per unit was as estimated. Calculate Jay's actual net income and his actual ROI. (Round to 2 decimal places.)
(d) Jay is using a traditional approach to allocate overhead. As a consequence, he is allocating overhead equally to all three types of washes, even though the Basic wash

is considerably less complicated and uses very little of the technical capabilities of the machinery. What should Jay do to determine more accurate costs per unit? How will this affect his pricing and, consequently, his sales?

Real-World Focus

BYP 8-3 Merck & Co., Inc. is a global, research-driven pharmaceutical company that discovers, develops, manufactures, and markets a broad range of human and animal health products. The following are excerpts from the financial review section of the company's annual report.

MERCK & CO., INC.
Financial Review Section (partial)

In the United States, the Company has been working with private and governmental employers to slow the increase of health care costs.

Outside of the United States, in difficult environments encumbered by government cost containment actions, the Company has worked with payers to help them allocate scarce resources to optimize health care outcomes, limiting potentially detrimental effects of government actions on sales growth.

Several products face expiration of product patents in the near term.

The Company, along with other pharmaceutical manufacturers, received a notice from the Federal Trade Commission (FTC) that it was conducting an investigation into pricing practices.

Instructions
Answer each of the following questions.
(a) In light of the above excerpts from Merck's annual report, discuss some unique pricing issues faced by companies that operate in the pharmaceutical industry.
(b) What are some reasons why identical drugs sold by the same company often are sold for dramatically different prices in different countries? And how can the same drug used for both humans and animals cost significantly different prices?
(c) Suppose that Merck has just developed a revolutionary new drug for the treatment of arthritis. Discuss the steps it would go through in setting a price. Include a discussion of the information it would need to gather, and the issues it would need to consider.

Exploring the Web

BYP 8-4 Shopping "robots" have become very popular on the Web. These are sites that will find the price of a specified product that is listed by retailers on the Web ("e-tailers"). This allows the customer to search for the lowest possible price.

Address: **www.dealtime.com** *or go to* **www.wiley.com/college/weygandt**

Steps
1. Go to the Web page of DealTime.
2. Under the heading "**Electronics**," click on **DVD players**.
3. Choose one of the models under the heading "**Top Picks**."

Instructions
(a) Write down the name of the retailer and the price of the two lowest-priced units and the two highest-priced units.
(b) As a consumer, what concerns might you have in clicking on the "buy" button?
(c) Why might a consumer want to purchase a unit from a retailer that isn't offering the lowest price?
(d) What implications does the existence of these sites have for retailers?

Communication Activity

BYP 8-5 Judy Prest recently graduated from college with a degree in landscape architecture. Her father runs a tree, shrub, and perennial-flower nursery, and her brother has a business delivering topsoil, mulch, and compost. Judy has decided that she would like to start a landscape business. She believes that she can generate a nice profit for herself, while providing an opportunity for both her brother's and father's businesses to grow.

One potential problem that Judy is concerned about is that her father and brother tend to charge the highest prices of any local suppliers for their products. She is hoping that she can demonstrate that it would be in her interest, as well as theirs, for them to sell to her at a discounted price.

Instructions

Write a memo to Judy explaining what information she must gather, and what issues she must consider in working out an arrangement with her father and brother. In your memo, discuss how this situation differs from a "standard" transfer pricing problem, but also, how it has many of the characteristics of a transfer pricing problem.

Research Assignment

BYP 8-6 The June 17, 2004, issue of the *Wall Street Journal* includes an article titled "In Bow to Retailers' New Clout, Levi Strauss Makes Alterations."

Instructions

Read the article and answer the following questions.
(a) How has the selling of Levi's changed for **Levi Strauss**?
(b) Explain the market power of **Wal-Mart** and how it affected the price of Levi's.
(c) What did Levi Strauss do to revitalize its jeans business?

Ethics Case

BYP 8-7 Giant Airlines operates out of three main "hub" airports in the United States. Recently Mosquito Airlines began operating a flight from Reno, Nevada, into Giant's Metropolis hub for $190. Giant Airlines offers a price of $425 for the same route. The management of Giant is not happy about Mosquito invading its turf. In fact, Giant has driven off nearly every other competing airline from its hub, so that today 90% of flights into and out of Metropolis are Giant Airline flights. Mosquito is able to offer a lower fare because its pilots are paid less, it uses older planes, and it has lower overhead costs. Mosquito has been in business for only 6 months, and it services only two other cities. It expects the Metropolis route to be its most profitable.

Giant estimates that it would have to charge $210 just to break even on this flight. It estimates that Mosquito can break even at a price of $160. Within one day of Mosquito's entry into the market, Giant dropped its price to $140, whereupon Mosquito matched its price. They both maintained this fare for a period of 9 months, until Mosquito went out of business. As soon as Mosquito went out of business, Giant raised its fare back to $425.

Instructions

Answer each of the following questions.
(a) Who are the stakeholders in this case?
(b) What are some of the reasons why Mosquito's breakeven point is lower than that of Giant?
(c) What are the likely reasons why Giant was able to offer this price for this period of time, while Mosquito couldn't?
(d) What are some of the possible courses of action available to Mosquito in this situation?
(e) Do you think that this kind of pricing activity is ethical? What are the implications for the stakeholders in this situation?

Answers to Self-Study Questions

1. b   2. c   3. b   4. b   5. c   6. a   7. d   8. b   9. b   10. d

Remember to go back to the Navigator box on the chapter-opening page and check off your completed work.

CHAPTER 9

Budgetary Planning

STUDY OBJECTIVES

After studying this chapter, you should be able to:

1 Indicate the benefits of budgeting.

2 State the essentials of effective budgeting.

3 Identify the budgets that comprise the master budget.

4 Describe the sources for preparing the budgeted income statement.

5 Explain the principal sections of a cash budget.

6 Indicate the applicability of budgeting in nonmanufacturing companies.

☑ THE
NAVIGATOR

THE NAVIGATOR ✔

▶ Scan *Study Objectives* ☐

▶ Read *Feature Story* ☐

▶ Read *Preview* ☐

▶ Read text and answer *Before You Go On*
   p. 356 ☐ p. 360 ☐ p. 368 ☐ p. 371 ☐

▶ Work *Using the Decision Toolkit* ☐

▶ Review *Summary of Study Objectives* ☐

▶ Work *Demonstration Problem* ☐

▶ Answer *Self-Study Questions* ☐

▶ Complete *Assignments* ☐

FEATURE STORY

The Next Amazon.com? Not Quite

The bursting of the dot-com bubble resulted in countless stories of dot-com failures. Many of these ventures were half-baked, get-rich-quick schemes, rarely based on sound business practices. Initially they saw money flowing in faster than they knew what to do with—which was precisely the problem. Without proper planning and budgeting, much of the money went to waste. In some cases, failure was actually brought on by rapid, uncontrolled growth.

One such example was online discount bookseller, **www.Positively-You.com**. One of the Web site's co-founders, Lyle Bowline, had never run a business. However, his experience as an assistant director of an entrepreneurial center had provided him with knowledge about the do's and don'ts of small business. To minimize costs, he started the company off small and simple. He invested $5,000 in computer equipment and ran the business out of his basement. In the early months, even though sales were only about $2,000 a month, the company actually made a profit because it kept its costs low (a feat few other dot-coms could boast of).

Things changed dramatically when the company received national publicity in the financial press. Suddenly the company's sales increased to $50,000 a month—fully 25 times the previous level. The "simple" little business suddenly needed a business

plan, a strategic plan, and a budget. It needed to rent office space and to hire employees.

Initially, members of a local book club donated time to help meet the sudden demand. But quickly the number of paid employees ballooned. The sudden growth necessitated detailed planning and budgeting. The need for a proper budget was accentuated by the fact that the company's gross profit was only 16 cents on each dollar of goods sold. This meant that after paying for its inventory, the company had only 16 cents of every dollar to cover its remaining operating costs.

Unfortunately, the company never got things under control. Within a few months, sales had plummeted to $12,000 per month. At this level of sales the company could not meet the mountain of monthly expenses that it had accumulated in trying to grow. Ironically, the company's sudden success, and the turmoil it created, appears to have been what eventually caused the company to fail.

THE NAVIGATOR

As the Feature Story about **Positively-You.com** indicates, budgeting is critical to financial well-being. As a student, you budget your study time and your money. Families budget income and expenses. Governmental agencies budget revenues and expenditures. Business enterprises use budgets in planning and controlling their operations.

Our primary focus in this chapter is budgeting—specifically, how budgeting is used as a **planning tool** by management. Through budgeting, it should be possible for management to maintain enough cash to pay creditors, to have sufficient raw materials to meet production requirements, and to have adequate finished goods to meet expected sales.

The content and organization of Chapter 9 are as follows.

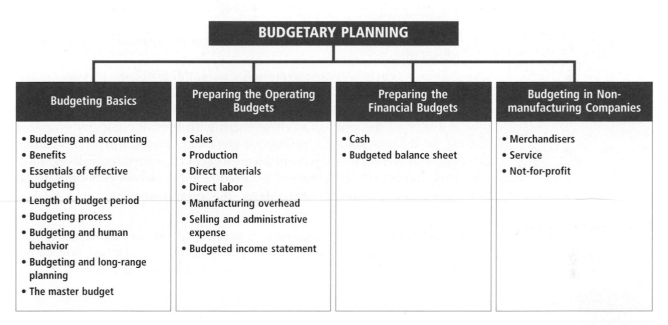

BUDGETARY PLANNING

Budgeting Basics	Preparing the Operating Budgets	Preparing the Financial Budgets	Budgeting in Non-manufacturing Companies
• Budgeting and accounting • Benefits • Essentials of effective budgeting • Length of budget period • Budgeting process • Budgeting and human behavior • Budgeting and long-range planning • The master budget	• Sales • Production • Direct materials • Direct labor • Manufacturing overhead • Selling and administrative expense • Budgeted income statement	• Cash • Budgeted balance sheet	• Merchandisers • Service • Not-for-profit

☑ THE NAVIGATOR

Budgeting Basics

One of management's major responsibilities is planning. As explained in Chapter 1, **planning** is the process of establishing enterprise-wide objectives. A successful organization makes both long-term and short-term plans. These plans set forth the objectives of the company and the proposed way of accomplishing them.

A **budget** is a formal written statement of management's plans for a specified future time period, expressed in financial terms. It normally represents the primary method of communicating agreed-upon objectives throughout the organization. Once adopted, a budget becomes an important basis for evaluating performance. It promotes efficiency and serves as a deterrent to waste and inefficiency. We consider the role of budgeting as a **control device** in Chapter 10.

BUDGETING AND ACCOUNTING

Accounting information makes major contributions to the budgeting process. From the accounting records, historical data on revenues, costs, and expenses can be obtained. These data are helpful in formulating future budget goals.

Normally, accountants have the responsibility for presenting management's budgeting goals in financial terms. In this role, they translate management's plans and communicate the budget to employees throughout the company. Periodic budget reports are prepared that provide the basis for measuring performance and comparing actual results with planned objectives. The budget itself, and the administration of the budget, however, are entirely management responsibilities.

THE BENEFITS OF BUDGETING

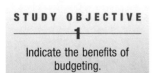

STUDY OBJECTIVE
1
Indicate the benefits of budgeting.

The primary benefits of budgeting are:

1. It requires all levels of management to **plan ahead** and to formalize goals on a recurring basis.
2. It provides **definite objectives** for evaluating performance at each level of responsibility.
3. It creates an **early warning system** for potential problems so that management can make changes before things get out of hand.
4. It facilitates the **coordination of activities** within the business. It does this by correlating the goals of each segment with overall company objectives. Thus, production and sales promotion can be integrated with expected sales.
5. It results in greater **management awareness** of the entity's overall operations and the impact on operations of external factors, such as economic trends.
6. It **motivates personnel** throughout the organization to meet planned objectives.

A budget is an aid to management; it is not a substitute for management. A budget cannot operate or enforce itself. The benefits of budgeting will be realized only when budgets are carefully administered by management.

ESSENTIALS OF EFFECTIVE BUDGETING

STUDY OBJECTIVE
2
State the essentials of effective budgeting.

Effective budgeting depends on a **sound organizational structure**. In such a structure, authority and responsibility for all phases of operations are clearly defined. Budgets based on **research and analysis** should result in realistic goals that will contribute to the growth and profitability of a company. And, the effectiveness of a budget program is directly related to its **acceptance by all levels of management**.

Once the budget has been adopted, it should be an important tool for evaluating performance. Variations between actual and expected results should be systematically and periodically reviewed to determine their cause(s). However, individuals should not be held responsible for variations that are beyond their control.

LENGTH OF THE BUDGET PERIOD

The budget period is not necessarily one year in length. **A budget may be prepared for any period of time**. Various factors influence the length of the budget period. These factors include the type of budget, the nature of the organization, the need for periodic appraisal, and prevailing business conditions. For example, cash may be budgeted monthly, whereas a plant expansion budget may cover a 10-year period.

The budget period should be long enough to provide an attainable goal under normal business conditions. Ideally, the time period should minimize the impact of seasonal or cyclical fluctuations. On the other hand, the budget period should not be so long that reliable estimates are impossible.

The **most common budget period is one year**. The annual budget, in turn, is often supplemented by monthly and quarterly budgets. Many companies use **continuous 12-month budgets**. These budgets drop the month just ended and add a future month. One advantage of continuous budgeting is that it keeps management planning a full year ahead.

THE BUDGETING PROCESS

The development of the budget for the coming year generally starts several months before the end of the current year. The budgeting process usually begins with the collection of data from each organizational unit of the company. Past performance is often the starting point from which future budget goals are formulated.

The budget is developed within the framework of a **sales forecast**. This forecast shows potential sales for the industry and the company's expected share of such sales. Sales forecasting involves a consideration of various factors: (1) general economic conditions, (2) industry trends, (3) market research studies, (4) anticipated advertising and promotion, (5) previous market share, (6) changes in prices, and (7) technological developments. The input of sales personnel and top management are essential to the sales forecast.

In small companies like **Positively-You.com**, the budgeting process is often informal. In larger companies, responsibility for coordinating the preparation of the budget is assigned to a **budget committee**. The committee ordinarily includes the president, treasurer, chief accountant (controller), and management personnel from each of the major areas of the company, such as sales, production, and research. The budget committee serves as a review board where managers can defend their budget goals and requests. Differences are reviewed, modified if necessary, and reconciled. The budget is then put in its final form by the budget committee, approved, and distributed.

Business Insight
Management Perspective

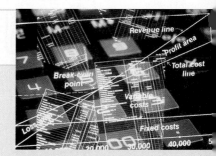

A recent study by Willard & Shullman Group Ltd. found that fewer than 14 percent of businesses with fewer than 500 employees do an annual budget or have a written business plan. In all, nearly 60 percent of these businesses have no plans on paper at all. For many small businesses the basic assumption is that, "As long as I sell as much as I can, and keep my employees paid, I'm doing OK." A few small business owners even say that they see no need for budgeting and planning. Most small business owners, though, say that they understand that budgeting and planning are critical for survival and growth. But given the long hours that they already work addressing day-to-day challenges, they also say that they are "just too busy to plan for the future."

BUDGETING AND HUMAN BEHAVIOR

A budget can have a significant impact on human behavior. It may inspire a manager to higher levels of performance. Or, it may discourage additional effort and pull down the morale of a manager. Why do these diverse effects occur? The answer is found in how the budget is developed and administered.

In developing the budget, each level of management should be invited to participate. This "bottom-to-top" approach is referred to as **participative budgeting**. The advantages of participative budgeting are, first, that lower-level managers have more detailed knowledge of their specific area and thus should be able to provide more accurate budgetary estimates. Second, by inviting lower-level managers to participate in the budgeting process, they are more likely to perceive the resulting budget as fair. The overall goal is to reach agreement on a budget that the managers consider fair and achievable, but which also meets the corporate goals set by top management. When this goal is met, the budget will provide positive motivation for the managers. In contrast, if the managers view the budget as being unfair and unrealistic, they may feel discouraged and uncommitted to budget goals. The risk of having unrealistic budgets is generally greater when the budget is developed from top management down to lower management than vice versa.

Participative budgeting does, however, have potential disadvantages. First, it can be far more time-consuming (and thus more costly) than a "top-down" approach, in which the budget is simply dictated to lower-level managers. A second disadvantage of participative budgeting is that it can foster budgetary "gaming" through budgetary slack. **Budgetary slack** occurs when managers intentionally underestimate budgeted revenues or overestimate budgeted expenses in order to make it easier to achieve budgetary goals. To minimize budgetary slack, higher-level managers must carefully review and thoroughly question the budget projections provided to them by employees whom they supervise. Illustration 9-1 graphically displays the appropriate flow of budget data from bottom to top in an organization.

Illustration 9-1 Flow of budget data from lower levels of management to top levels

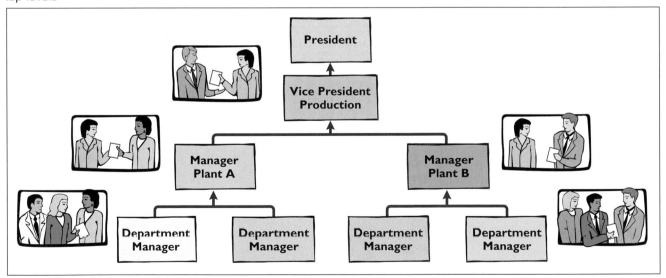

President

Vice President Production

Manager Plant A

Manager Plant B

Department Manager

Department Manager

Department Manager

Department Manager

Helpful Hint Unrealistic budgets can lead to unethical employee behavior such as cutting corners on the job or distorting internal financial reports.

Administering the budget relates to how the budget is used by top management. As explained earlier, the budget should have the complete support of top management. The budget also should be an important basis for evaluating performance. The effect of an evaluation will be positive when top management tempers criticism with advice and assistance. In contrast, a manager is likely to respond negatively if the budget is used exclusively to assess blame.

A budget may be used improperly as a pressure device to force improved performance. Or, it can be used as a positive aid in achieving projected goals. In sum, a budget can become a manager's friend or a foe.

Business Insight
Management Perspective

The merits of participative budgeting are not lost on the employees of **Time Warner**. In 2000, in an effort to revive its plummeting stock, the company's top management determined and publicly announced (without consulting middle managers) bold new financial goals for the coming year. The company's middle-level managers felt that the 2001 budgets were based on top management's growth aspirations, and that those budgetary goals were unattainable. At the end of the year they were proven correct.

The next year the company got a new CEO who promised in 2002, "We will not over promise, and we will deliver." The 2002 budgets were developed from the bottom up, with each operating unit setting what it felt were optimistic but attainable goals. In the words of one manager, using this approach created a sense of teamwork: "We're all going forward with our arms locked together."

SOURCE: Carol J. Loomis, "AOL Time Warner's New Math," *Fortune* (February 4, 2002), pp. 98–102.

BUDGETING AND LONG-RANGE PLANNING

In business, you may hear talk about the need for long-range planning. Budgeting and long-range planning are not the same. One important difference is the **time period involved**. The maximum length of a budget is usually one year, and budgets are often prepared for shorter periods of time, such as a month or a quarter. In contrast, long-range planning usually encompasses a period of at least five years.

A second significant difference is in **emphasis**. Budgeting focuses on achieving specific short-term goals, such as meeting annual profit objectives. **Long-range planning**, on the other hand, identifies long-term goals, selects strategies to achieve those goals, and develops policies and plans to implement the strategies. In long-range planning, management also considers anticipated trends in the economic and political environment and how the company should cope with them.

The final difference between budgeting and long-range planning pertains to the **amount of detail presented**. Budgets, as you will see in this chapter, can be very detailed. Long-range plans contain considerably less detail. The data in long-range plans are intended more for a review of progress toward long-term goals than as a basis of control for achieving specific results. The primary objective of long-range planning is to develop the best strategy to maximize the company's performance over an extended future period.

> **Helpful Hint** In comparing a budget with a long-range plan: (1) Which has more detail? (2) Which is done for a longer period of time? (3) Which is more concerned with short-term goals?
> Answers: (1) Budget. (2) Long-range plan. (3) Budget.

THE MASTER BUDGET

The term "budget" is actually a shorthand term to describe a variety of budget documents. All of these documents are combined into a master budget. The **master budget** is a set of interrelated budgets that constitutes a plan of action for a specified time period. The individual budgets included in a master budget are pictured in Illustration 9-2.

> **STUDY OBJECTIVE**
> **3**
> Identify the budgets that comprise the master budget.

Illustration 9-2 Components of the master budget

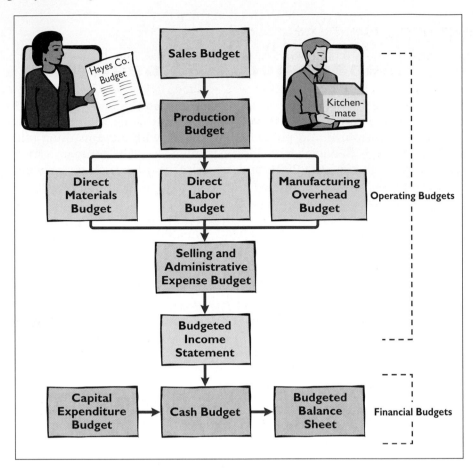

As the illustration shows, the master budget contains two classes of budgets. **Operating budgets** are the individual budgets that result in the preparation of the budgeted income statement. These budgets establish goals for the company's sales and production personnel. In contrast, **financial budgets** are the capital expenditure budget, the cash budget, and the budgeted balance sheet. These budgets focus primarily on the cash resources needed to fund expected operations and planned capital expenditures.

The master budget is prepared in the sequence shown in Illustration 9-2. The operating budgets are developed first, beginning with the sales budget. Then the financial budgets are prepared. We will explain and illustrate each budget shown in Illustration 9-2 except the capital expenditure budget. This budget is discussed under the topic of capital budgeting in Chapter 12.

BEFORE YOU GO ON . . .

▶**Review It**

1. What are the benefits of budgeting?
2. What are the factors essential to effective budgeting?
3. How does the budget process work?
4. How does budgeting differ from long-range planning?
5. What is a master budget?

Preparing the Operating Budgets

A case study of Hayes Company will be used in preparing the operating budgets. Hayes manufactures and sells a single product, Kitchen-mate. The budgets will be prepared by quarters for the year ending December 31, 2005. Hayes Company begins its annual budgeting process on September 1, 2004, and it completes the budget for 2005 by December 1, 2004.

SALES BUDGET

As shown in the master budget in Illustration 9-2, **the sales budget is the first budget prepared**. Each of the other budgets depends on the sales budget. The sales budget is derived from the sales forecast. It represents management's best estimate of sales revenue for the budget period. An inaccurate sales budget may adversely affect net income. For example, an overly optimistic sales budget may result in excessive inventories that may have to be sold at reduced prices. In contrast, an unduly conservative budget may result in loss of sales revenue due to inventory shortages.

The sales budget is prepared by multiplying the expected unit sales volume for each product by its anticipated unit selling price. For Hayes Company, sales volume is expected to be 3,000 units in the first quarter, with 500-unit increments in each succeeding quarter. Based on a sales price of $60 per unit, the sales budget for the year, by quarters, is shown in Illustration 9-3.

Helpful Hint For a retail or manufacturing company, what is the starting point in preparing the master budget, and why? Answer: Preparation of the sales budget is the starting point for the master budget. It sets the level of activity for other functions such as production and purchasing.

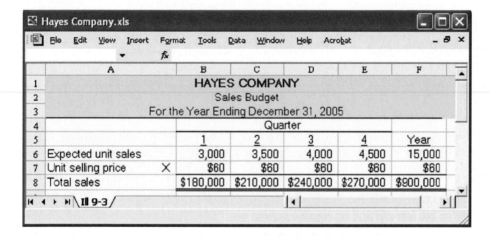

Illustration 9-3 Sales budget

HAYES COMPANY
Sales Budget
For the Year Ending December 31, 2005

	Quarter				
	1	**2**	**3**	**4**	**Year**
Expected unit sales	3,000	3,500	4,000	4,500	15,000
Unit selling price ✕	$60	$60	$60	$60	$60
Total sales	$180,000	$210,000	$240,000	$270,000	$900,000

Some companies classify the anticipated sales revenue as cash or credit sales and by geographical regions, territories, or salespersons.

PRODUCTION BUDGET

The production budget shows the units that must be produced to meet anticipated sales. Production requirements are determined from the following formula.[1]

Illustration 9-4 Production requirements formula

$$\text{Budgeted Sales Units} + \text{Desired Ending Finished Goods Units} - \text{Beginning Finished Goods Units} = \text{Required Production Units}$$

A realistic estimate of ending inventory is essential in scheduling production requirements. Excessive inventories in one quarter may lead to cutbacks in production and employee layoffs in a subsequent quarter. On the other

---

[1]This formula ignores any work in process inventories, which are assumed to be nonexistent in Hayes Company.

hand, inadequate inventories may result either in added costs for overtime work or in lost sales. Hayes Company believes it can meet future sales requirements by maintaining an ending inventory equal to 20 percent of the next quarter's budgeted sales volume. For example, the ending finished goods inventory for the first quarter is 700 units (20% × anticipated second-quarter sales of 3,500 units). The production budget is shown in Illustration 9-5.

Illustration 9-5 Production budget

HAYES COMPANY					
Production Budget					
For the Year Ending December 31, 2005					
	Quarter				
	1	2	3	4	Year
Expected unit sales (Illustration 9-3)	3,000	3,500	4,000	4,500	
Add: Desired ending finished goods units [a]	700	800	900	1,000 [b]	
Total required units	3,700	4,300	4,900	5,500	
Less: Beginning finished goods units	600 [c]	700	800	900	
Required production units	3,100	3,600	4,100	4,600	15,400

[a] 20% of next quarter's sales

[b] Expected 2006 first-quarter sales, 5,000 units × 20%

[c] 20% of estimated first-quarter 2005 sales units

The production budget, in turn, provides the basis for determining the budgeted costs for each manufacturing cost element, as explained in the following pages.

Business Insight
Management Perspective

Wrong move, wrong time, poor planning. When **Fruit of the Loom Inc.** saw underwear and apparel sales slowing, it cut back production sharply. Too sharply, in fact: almost overnight, demand soared. Caught with its shorts down, the company hired back thousands of workers and frantically increased production. The mistimed production cuts contributed to a 43 percent fall in first-quarter profits. For the year, Fruit stood to lose $200 million in sales, and analysts expected an 11 percent drop in profits for the year.

DIRECT MATERIALS BUDGET

The **direct materials budget** shows both the quantity and cost of direct materials to be purchased. The quantities of direct materials are derived from the following formula.

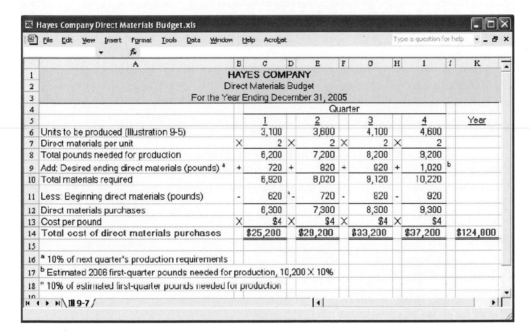

Illustration 9-6 Formula for direct materials quantities

The budgeted cost of direct materials to be purchased is then computed by multiplying the required units of direct materials by the anticipated cost per unit.

The desired ending inventory is again a key component in the budgeting process. For example, inadequate inventories could result in temporary shutdowns of production. Because of its close proximity to suppliers, Hayes Company has found that an ending inventory of raw materials equal to 10 percent of the next quarter's production requirements is sufficient. The manufacture of each Kitchen-mate requires 2 pounds of raw materials, and the expected cost per pound is $4. The direct materials budget is shown in Illustration 9-7.

Illustration 9-7 Direct materials budget

Hayes Company Direct Materials Budget.xls

File Edit View Insert Format Tools Data Window Help Acrobat

HAYES COMPANY
Direct Materials Budget
For the Year Ending December 31, 2005

	Quarter				
	1	2	3	4	Year
Units to be produced (Illustration 9-5)	3,100	3,600	4,100	4,600	
Direct materials per unit	× 2	× 2	× 2	× 2	
Total pounds needed for production	6,200	7,200	8,200	9,200	
Add: Desired ending direct materials (pounds) [a]	+ 720	+ 820	+ 920	+ 1,020 [b]	
Total materials required	6,920	8,020	9,120	10,220	
Less: Beginning direct materials (pounds)	- 620 [c]	- 720	- 820	- 920	
Direct materials purchases	6,300	7,300	8,300	9,300	
Cost per pound	× $4	× $4	× $4	× $4	
Total cost of direct materials purchases	$25,200	$29,200	$33,200	$37,200	$124,800

[a] 10% of next quarter's production requirements
[b] Estimated 2006 first-quarter pounds needed for production, 10,200 × 10%
[c] 10% of estimated first-quarter pounds needed for production

DIRECT LABOR BUDGET

Like the direct materials budget, the **direct labor budget** contains the quantity (hours) and cost of direct labor necessary to meet production requirements. The total direct labor cost is derived from the following formula.

Illustration 9-8 Formula for direct labor cost

$$\text{Units to be Produced} \times \text{Direct Labor Time per Unit} \times \text{Direct Labor Cost per Hour} = \text{Total Direct Labor Cost}$$

Direct labor hours are determined from the production budget. At Hayes Company, two hours of direct labor are required to produce each unit of finished goods. The anticipated hourly wage rate is $10. These data are shown in Illustration 9-9. The direct labor budget is critical in maintaining a labor force that can meet the expected levels of production.

Illustration 9-9 Direct labor budget

HAYES COMPANY
Direct Labor Budget
For the Year Ending December 31, 2005

	Quarter				Year
	1	2	3	4	
Units to be produced (Illustration 9-5)	3,100	3,600	4,100	4,600	
Direct labor time (hours) per unit	× 2	× 2	× 2	× 2	
Total required direct labor hours	6,200	7,200	8,200	9,200	
Direct labor cost per hour	× $10	× $10	× $10	× $10	
Total direct labor cost	$62,000	$72,000	$82,000	$92,000	$308,000

Helpful Hint An important assumption in Illustration 9-9 is that the company can add to and subtract from its work force as needed so that the $10 per hour labor cost applies to a wide range of possible production activity.

BEFORE YOU GO ON . . .

▶ **Review It**

1. What is the formula to determine required production units?
2. What are the inputs necessary to prepare the direct labor budget?
3. Which budget must be prepared before the direct materials budget?

▶ **Do It**

Becker Company estimates that unit sales in quarter 1 will be 12,000, 16,000 in quarter 2, and 20,000 in quarter 3, at a unit selling price of $30. Management desires to have ending finished goods inventory equal to 15% of the next quarter's expected unit sales. Prepare a production budget by quarter for the first 6 months of 2005.

Action Plan

• Begin with budgeted sales in units.
• Add desired finished goods inventory.
• Subtract beginning finished goods inventory.

Solution

BECKER COMPANY
Production Budget
For the Six Months Ending June 30, 2005

	Quarter		Six
	1	2	Months
Expected unit sales	12,000	16,000	28,000
Add: Desired ending finished goods	2,400	3,000	3,000
Total required units	14,400	19,000	31,000
Less: Beginning finished goods inventory	1,800	2,400	1,800
Required production units	12,600	16,600	29,200

Related exercise material: BE9-3, E9-3, and E9-5.

☑ THE NAVIGATOR

MANUFACTURING OVERHEAD BUDGET

The **manufacturing overhead budget** shows the expected manufacturing overhead costs for the budget period. As shown in Illustration 9-10, **this budget distinguishes between variable and fixed overhead costs**. Hayes Company expects variable costs to fluctuate with production volume on the basis of the following rates per direct labor hour: indirect materials $1.00, indirect labor $1.40, utilities $0.40, and maintenance $0.20. Thus, for the 6,200 direct labor hours to produce 3,100 units, budgeted indirect materials are $6,200 (6,200 × $1), and budgeted indirect labor is $8,680 (6,200 × $1.40). Hayes also recognizes that some maintenance is fixed. The amounts reported for fixed costs are assumed for our example. The accuracy of budgeted fixed overhead cost estimates can be greatly improved by employing activity-based costing.

At Hayes Company, overhead is applied to production on the basis of direct labor hours. Thus, as shown in Illustration 9-10, the annual rate is $8 per hour ($246,400 ÷ 30,800).

Illustration 9-10   Manufacturing overhead budget

	HAYES COMPANY Manufacturing Overhead Budget For the Year Ending December 31, 2005					
	A	B	C	D	E	F
		Quarter				
		1	2	3	4	Year
6	Variable costs					
7	Indirect materials ($1.00 / hour)	$6,200	$7,200	$8,200	$9,200	$30,800
8	Indirect labor ($1.40 / hour)	8,680	10,080	11,480	12,880	43,120
9	Utilities ($0.40 / hour)	2,480	2,880	3,280	3,680	12,320
10	Maintenance ($0.20 / hour)	1,240	1,440	1,640	1,840	6,160
11	Total variable costs	18,600	21,600	24,600	27,600	92,400
12	Fixed costs					
13	Supervisory salaries	20,000	20,000	20,000	20,000	80,000
14	Depreciation	3,800	3,800	3,800	3,800	15,200
15	Property taxes and insurance	9,000	9,000	9,000	9,000	36,000
16	Maintenance	5,700	5,700	5,700	5,700	22,800
17	Total fixed costs	38,500	38,500	38,500	38,500	154,000
18	Total manufacturing overhead	$57,100	$60,100	$63,100	$66,100	$246,400
19	Direct labor hours (Illustration 9-9)	6,200	7,200	8,200	9,200	30,800
20	Manufacturing overhead rate per direct labor hour ($246,400 ÷ 30,800)					$8

SELLING AND ADMINISTRATIVE EXPENSE BUDGET

Hayes Company combines its operating expenses into one budget, the **selling and administrative expense budget**. This budget projects anticipated selling and administrative expenses for the budget period. In this budget, as in the preceding one, expenses are classified as either variable or fixed. In this case, the variable expense rates per unit of sales are sales commissions $3 and freight-out $1. Variable expenses per quarter are based on the unit sales from the sales budget (Illustration 9-3). For example, sales in the first quarter are expected to be 3,000 units. Thus, Sales Commissions Expense is $9,000 (3,000 × $3), and Freight-out is $3,000 (3,000 × $1). Fixed expenses are based on assumed data. The selling and administrative expense budget is shown in Illustration 9-11.

Illustration 9-11 Selling and administrative expense budget

	HAYES COMPANY Selling and Administrative Expense Budget For the Year Ending December 31, 2005				
	Quarter				
	1	2	3	4	Year
Budgeted sales in units	3,000	3,500	4,000	4,500	15,000
Variable expenses					
Selling commissions ($3 per unit)	$9,000	$10,500	$12,000	$13,500	$45,000
Freight-out ($1 per unit)	3,000	3,500	4,000	4,500	15,000
Total variable expenses	12,000	14,000	16,000	18,000	60,000
Fixed expenses					
Advertising	5,000	5,000	5,000	5,000	20,000
Sales salaries	15,000	15,000	15,000	15,000	60,000
Office salaries	7,500	7,500	7,500	7,500	30,000
Depreciation	1,000	1,000	1,000	1,000	4,000
Property taxes and insurance	1,500	1,500	1,500	1,500	6,000
Total fixed expenses	30,000	30,000	30,000	30,000	120,000
Total selling and administrative expenses	$42,000	$44,000	$46,000	$48,000	$180,000

Business Insight
℮-Business Perspective

Good budgeting depends on good information. And good information is what e-business is all about. As manufacturers, suppliers, and customers become electronically linked, each benefits by being better informed. **Dell Computer** not only is directly linked to **Solectron**, one of its main suppliers, but also to **Texas Instruments**, one of the main suppliers of parts to Solectron. This linking takes a lot of guesswork out of planning and budgeting for all three companies.

To further improve planning and budgeting, Dell hopes that some day everyone in its industry will anonymously provide their up-to-the-minute production and sales information at a central, electronic exchange. A centralized database such as this would provide valuable information about the supply and demand of computer goods in the marketplace. This information might dramatically improve sales projections, leading to significant improvements in the budgeting process.

SOURCE: "E-Management," *The Economist* (November 11, 2000).

BUDGETED INCOME STATEMENT

STUDY OBJECTIVE
4

Describe the sources for preparing the budgeted income statement.

The **budgeted income statement** is the important end-product of the operating budgets. This budget indicates the expected profitability of operations for the budget period. The budgeted income statement provides the basis for evaluating company performance.

As you would expect, this budget is prepared from the various operating budgets. For example, to find the cost of goods sold, it is first necessary to determine the total unit cost of producing one Kitchen-mate, as follows.

Illustration 9-12 Computation of total unit cost

Cost of One Kitchen-mate

Cost Element	Illustration	Quantity	Unit Cost	Total
Direct materials	9-7	2 pounds	$ 4.00	$ 8.00
Direct labor	9-9	2 hours	$10.00	20.00
Manufacturing overhead	9-10	2 hours	$ 8.00	16.00
Total unit cost				**$44.00**

Cost of goods sold can then be determined by multiplying the units sold by the unit cost. For Hayes Company, budgeted cost of goods sold is $660,000 (15,000 × $44). All data for the statement are obtained from the individual operating budgets except the following: (1) interest expense is expected to be $100, and (2) income taxes are estimated to be $12,000. The budgeted income statement is shown in Illustration 9-13.

Illustration 9-13 Budgeted income statement

HAYES COMPANY
Budgeted Income Statement
For the Year Ending December 31, 2005

Sales (Illustration 9-3)	$900,000
Cost of goods sold (15,000 × $44)	660,000
Gross profit	240,000
Selling and administrative expenses (Illustration 9-11)	180,000
Income from operations	60,000
Interest expense	100
Income before income taxes	59,900
Income tax expense	12,000
Net income	$ 47,900

DECISION TOOLKIT

Decision Checkpoints	Info Needed for Decision	Tool to Use for Decision	How to Evaluate Results
Has the company met its targets for sales, production expenses, selling and administrative expenses, and net income?	Sales forecasts, inventory levels, projected materials, labor, overhead, and selling and administrative requirements	Master budget—a set of interrelated budgets including sales, production, materials, labor, overhead, and selling and administrative budgets	Results are favorable if revenues exceed budgeted amounts, or if expenses are less than budgeted amounts.

Preparing the Financial Budgets

As shown in Illustration 9-2, the financial budgets consist of the capital expenditure budget, the cash budget, and the budgeted balance sheet. The capital expenditure budget is discussed in Chapter 12; the other budgets are explained in the following sections.

CASH BUDGET

The **cash budget** shows anticipated cash flows. Because cash is so vital, this budget is often considered to be the most important output in preparing financial budgets.

The cash budget contains three sections (cash receipts, cash disbursements, and financing) and the beginning and ending cash balances, as shown in Illustration 9-14.

Illustration 9-14   Basic form of a cash budget

ANY COMPANY Cash Budget	
Beginning cash balance	$X,XXX
Add: Cash receipts (Itemized)	X,XXX
Total available cash	X,XXX
Less: Cash disbursements (Itemized)	X,XXX
Excess (deficiency) of available cash over cash disbursements	X,XXX
Financing	X,XXX
Ending cash balance	$X,XXX

The **cash receipts section** includes expected receipts from the company's principal source(s) of revenue. These are usually cash sales and collections from customers on credit sales. This section also shows anticipated receipts of interest and dividends, and proceeds from planned sales of investments, plant assets, and the company's capital stock.

The **cash disbursements section** shows expected cash payments. Such payments include direct materials, direct labor, manufacturing overhead, and selling and administrative expenses. This section also includes projected payments for income taxes, dividends, investments, and plant assets.

The **financing section** shows expected borrowings and the repayment of the borrowed funds plus interest. This section is needed when there is a cash deficiency or when the cash balance is below management's minimum required balance.

Data in the cash budget must be prepared in sequence. The ending cash balance of one period becomes the beginning cash balance for the next period. Data for preparing the cash budget are obtained from other budgets and from information provided by management. In practice, cash budgets are often prepared for the year on a monthly basis.

To minimize detail, we will assume that Hayes Company prepares an annual cash budget by quarters. The cash budget for Hayes Company is based on the following assumptions.

1. The January 1, 2005, cash balance is expected to be $38,000.
2. Sales (Illustration 9-3): 60 percent are collected in the quarter sold and 40 percent are collected in the following quarter. Accounts receivable of $60,000 at December 31, 2004, are expected to be collected in full in the first quarter of 2005.
3. Short-term investments are expected to be sold for $2,000 cash in the first quarter.
4. Direct materials (Illustration 9-7): 50 percent are paid in the quarter purchased and 50 percent are paid in the following quarter. Accounts payable

of $10,600 at December 31, 2004, are expected to be paid in full in the first quarter of 2005.

5. Direct labor (Illustration 9-9): 100 percent is paid in the quarter incurred.
6. Manufacturing overhead (Illustration 9-10) and selling and administrative expenses (Illustration 9-11): All items except depreciation are paid in the quarter incurred.
7. Management plans to purchase a truck in the second quarter for $10,000 cash.
8. Hayes makes equal quarterly payments of its estimated annual income taxes.
9. Loans are repaid in the earliest quarter in which there is sufficient cash (that is, when the cash on hand exceeds the $15,000 minimum required balance).

In preparing the cash budget, it is useful to prepare schedules for collections from customers (assumption No. 2, above) and cash payments for direct materials (assumption No. 4, above). These schedules are shown in Illustrations 9-15 and 9-16.

Illustration 9-15   Collections from customers

SCHEDULE OF EXPECTED COLLECTIONS FROM CUSTOMERS

| | Quarter | | | |
	1	2	3	4
Accounts receivable, 12/31/04	$ 60,000			
First quarter ($180,000)	108,000	$ 72,000		
Second quarter ($210,000)		126,000	$ 84,000	
Third quarter ($240,000)			144,000	$ 96,000
Fourth quarter ($270,000)				162,000
Total collections	$168,000	$198,000	$228,000	$258,000

Illustration 9-16   Payments for direct materials

SCHEDULE OF EXPECTED PAYMENTS FOR DIRECT MATERIALS

| | Quarter | | | |
	1	2	3	4
Accounts payable, 12/31/04	$10,600			
First quarter ($25,200)	12,600	$12,600		
Second quarter ($29,200)		14,600	$14,600	
Third quarter ($33,200)			16,600	$16,600
Fourth quarter ($37,200)				18,600
Total payments	$23,200	$27,200	$31,200	$35,200

The cash budget for Hayes Company is shown in Illustration 9-17 (page 366). The budget indicates that $3,000 of financing will be needed in the second quarter to maintain a minimum cash balance of $15,000. Since there is an excess of available cash over disbursements of $22,500 at the end of the third quarter, the borrowing, plus $100 interest, is repaid in this quarter.

Illustration 9-17 Cash budget

		HAYES COMPANY							
		Cash Budget							
		For the Year Ending December 31, 2005							
					Quarter				
	Assumption	1		2		3		4	
Beginning cash balance	1	$38,000		$25,500		$15,000		$19,400	
Add: Receipts									
Collections from customers	2	168,000		198,000		228,000		258,000	
Sale of securities	3	2,000		0		0		0	
Total receipts		170,000		198,000		228,000		258,000	
Total available cash		208,000		223,500		243,000		277,400	
Less: Disbursements									
Direct materials	4	23,200		27,200		31,200		35,200	
Direct labor	5	62,000		72,000		82,000		92,000	
Manufacturing overhead	6	53,300 a		56,300		59,300		62,300	
Selling and administrative expenses	6	41,000 b		43,000		45,000		47,000	
Purchase of truck	7	0		10,000		0		0	
Income tax expense	8	3,000		3,000		3,000		3,000	
Total disbursements		182,500		211,500		220,500		239,500	
Excess (deficiency) of available cash over cash disbursements		25,500		12,000		22,500		37,900	
Financing									
Borrowings		0		3,000		0		0	
Repayments - plus $100 interest	9	0		0		3,100		0	
Ending cash balance		$25,500		$15,000		$19,400		$37,900	
a $57,100 - $3,800 depreciation									
b $42,000 - $1,000 depreciation									

Business Insight
Management Perspective

Douglas Roberson, president of **Atlantic Network**, woke up one morning to find that his company was out of cash. At that point, Roberson realized that managing cash flow is different from simply accumulating sales. He says: "If you don't do serious projections about how much cash you will need to handle sales—and how long it will take to collect on invoices—you can end up out of business no matter how fast you are growing." In fact, Roberson says, fast growth makes cash flow problems worse because the company can be spending cash on supplies and payroll at an accelerated pace while waiting 45 days or longer to collect receivables.

A cash budget contributes to more effective cash management. It can show managers when additional financing will be necessary well before the actual need arises. And, it can indicate when excess cash will be available for investments or other purposes.

DECISION TOOLKIT

Decision Checkpoints	Info Needed for Decision	Tool to Use for Decision	How to Evaluate Results
Is the company going to need to borrow funds in the coming quarter?	Beginning cash balance, cash receipts, cash disbursements, and desired cash balance	Cash budget	The company will need to borrow money if the cash budget indicates a projected cash deficiency of available cash over cash disbursements for the quarter.

BUDGETED BALANCE SHEET

The **budgeted balance sheet** is a projection of financial position at the end of the budget period. This budget is developed from the budgeted balance sheet for the preceding year and the budgets for the current year. Pertinent data from the budgeted balance sheet at December 31, 2004, are as follows.

Buildings and equipment	$182,000	Common stock	$225,000
Accumulated depreciation	$ 28,800	Retained earnings	$ 46,480

The budgeted balance sheet at December 31, 2005, is shown below.

Illustration 9-18   Budgeted balance sheet

HAYES COMPANY
Budgeted Balance Sheet
December 31, 2005

Assets

Cash		$ 37,900
Accounts receivable		108,000
Finished goods inventory		44,000
Raw materials inventory		4,080
Buildings and equipment	$192,000	
Less: Accumulated depreciation	48,000	144,000
Total assets		$337,980

Liabilities and Stockholders' Equity

Accounts payable	$ 18,600
Common stock	225,000
Retained earnings	94,380
Total liabilities and stockholders' equity	$337,980

The computations and sources of the amounts are explained below.

Cash: Ending cash balance $37,900, shown in the cash budget (Illustration 9-17).

Accounts receivable: 40 percent of fourth-quarter sales $270,000, shown in the schedule of expected collections from customers (Illustration 9-15).

Finished goods inventory: Desired ending inventory 1,000 units, shown in the production budget (Illustration 9-5) times the total unit cost $44 (shown in Illustration 9-12).

Raw materials inventory: Desired ending inventory 1,020 pounds, times the cost per pound $4, shown in the direct materials budget (Illustration 9-7).

Buildings and equipment: December 31, 2004, balance $182,000, plus purchase of truck for $10,000.

Accumulated depreciation: December 31, 2004, balance $28,800, plus $15,200 depreciation shown in manufacturing overhead budget (Illustration 9-10) and $4,000 depreciation shown in selling and administrative expense budget (Illustration 9-11).

Accounts payable: 50 percent of fourth-quarter purchases $37,200, shown in schedule of expected payments for direct materials (Illustration 9-16).

Common stock: Unchanged from the beginning of the year.

Retained earnings: December 31, 2004, balance $46,480, plus net income $47,900, shown in budgeted income statement (Illustration 9-13).

After the budgeting data are entered into the computer, the various budgets (sales, cash, etc.) can be prepared, as well as the budgeted financial statements. Management can also manipulate the budgets in "what if" (sensitivity) analyses based on different hypothetical assumptions. For example, suppose that sales were budgeted to be 10 percent higher in the coming quarter. What impact would the change have on the rest of the budgeting process and the financing needs of the business? The computer can quickly "play out" the impact of the various assumptions on the budgets. Armed with these analyses, management can make more informed decisions about the impact of various projects. They also can anticipate future problems and business opportunities. As seen in this chapter, budgeting is an excellent use of electronic spreadsheets.

BEFORE YOU GO ON . . .

▶**Review It**

1. What are the two classifications of the individual budgets in the master budget?
2. What is the sequence for preparing the budgets that comprise the operating budgets?
3. Identify some of the source documents that would be used in preparing each of the operating budgets.
4. What are the three principal sections of the cash budget?

▶**Do It**

Martian Company management wants to maintain a minimum monthly cash balance of $15,000. At the beginning of March, the cash balance is $16,500, expected cash receipts for March are $210,000, and cash disbursements are expected to be $220,000. How much cash, if any, must be borrowed to maintain the desired minimum monthly balance?

Action Plan

• Write down the basic form of the cash budget, starting with the beginning cash balance, adding cash receipts for the period, deducting cash disbursements, and identifying the needed financing to achieve the desired minimum ending cash balance.

• Insert the data given into the outlined form of the cash budget.

Brief Exercises

BE9-1   Russo Manufacturing Company uses the following budgets: Balance Sheet, Capital Expenditure, Cash, Direct Labor, Direct Materials, Income Statement, Manufacturing Overhead, Production, Sales, and Selling and Administrative. Prepare a diagram of the interrelationships of the budgets in the master budget. Indicate whether each budget is an operating or a financial budget.

Prepare a diagram of a master budget.
(SO 3)

BE9-2   Maltz Company estimates that unit sales will be 10,000 in quarter 1; 12,000 in quarter 2; 14,000 in quarter 3; and 18,000 in quarter 4. Using a sales price of $70 per unit, prepare the sales budget by quarters for the year ending December 31, 2005.

Prepare a sales budget.
(SO 3)

BE9-3   Sales budget data for Maltz Company are given in BE9-2. Management desires to have an ending finished goods inventory equal to 25% of the next quarter's expected unit sales. Prepare a production budget by quarters for the first 6 months of 2005.

Prepare a production budget for 2 quarters.
(SO 3)

BE9-4   Gomez Company has 1,600 pounds of raw materials in its December 31, 2005, ending inventory. Required production for January and February of 2006 are 4,000 and 5,500 units, respectively. Two pounds of raw materials are needed for each unit, and the estimated cost per pound is $6. Management desires an ending inventory equal to 20% of next month's materials requirements. Prepare the direct materials budget for January.

Prepare a direct materials budget for 1 month.
(SO 3)

BE9-5   For Tracey Company, units to be produced are 5,000 in quarter 1 and 6,000 in quarter 2. It takes 1.8 hours to make a finished unit, and the expected hourly wage rate is $14 per hour. Prepare a direct labor budget by quarters for the 6 months ending June 30, 2005.

Prepare a direct labor budget for 2 quarters.
(SO 3)

BE9-6   For Savage Inc. variable manufacturing overhead costs are expected to be $20,000 in the first quarter of 2005 with $2,000 increments in each of the remaining three quarters. Fixed overhead costs are estimated to be $35,000 in each quarter. Prepare the manufacturing overhead budget by quarters and in total for the year.

Prepare a manufacturing overhead budget.
(SO 3)

BE9-7   Rado Company classifies its selling and administrative expense budget into variable and fixed components. Variable expenses are expected to be $25,000 in the first quarter, and $3,000 increments are expected in the remaining quarters of 2005. Fixed expenses are expected to be $40,000 in each quarter. Prepare the selling and administrative expense budget by quarters and in total for 2005.

Prepare a selling and administrative expense budget.
(SO 3)

BE9-8   Stoker Company has completed all of its operating budgets. The sales budget for the year shows 50,000 units and total sales of $2,000,000. The total unit cost of making one unit of sales is $24. Selling and administrative expenses are expected to be $300,000. Income taxes are estimated to be $150,000. Prepare a budgeted income statement for the year ending December 31, 2005.

Prepare a budgeted income statement for the year.
(SO 4)

BE9-9   Chow Industries expects credit sales for January, February, and March to be $200,000, $260,000, and $310,000, respectively. It is expected that 70% of the sales will be collected in the month of sale, and 30% will be collected in the following month. Compute cash collections from customers for each month.

Prepare data for a cash budget.
(SO 5)

BE9-10   Reebles Wholesalers is preparing its merchandise purchases budget. Budgeted sales are $400,000 for April and $450,000 for May. Cost of goods sold is expected to be 60% of sales. The company's desired ending inventory is 20% of the following month's cost of goods sold. Compute the required purchases for April.

Determine required merchandise purchases for 1 month.
(SO 6)

Exercises

E9-1   Vosser Electronics Inc. produces and sells two models of pocket calculators, XQ-103 and XQ-104. The calculators sell for $12 and $25, respectively. Because of the intense competition Vosser faces, management budgets sales semiannually. Its projections for the first 2 quarters of 2005 are as follows.

Prepare a sales budget for 2 quarters.
(SO 3)

| | **Unit Sales** | |
Product	Quarter 1	Quarter 2
XQ-103	30,000	25,000
XQ-104	12,000	13,000

No changes in selling prices are anticipated.

Instructions
Prepare a sales budget for the 2 quarters ending June 30, 2005. List the products and show for each quarter and for the 6 months, units, selling price, and total sales by product and in total.

Prepare a sales budget for four quarters.
(SO 3)

E9-2 Roche and Young, CPAs, are preparing their service revenue (sales) budget for the coming year (2005). The practice is divided into three departments: auditing, tax, and consulting. Billable hours for each department, by quarter, are provided below.

Department	Quarter 1	Quarter 2	Quarter 3	Quarter 4
Auditing	2,200	1,600	2,000	2,400
Tax	3,000	2,400	2,000	2,500
Consulting	1,500	1,500	1,500	1,500

Average hourly billing rates are: auditing $80, tax $90, and consulting $100.

Instructions
Prepare the service revenue (sales) budget for 2005 by listing the departments and showing for each quarter and the year in total, billable hours, billable rate, and total revenue.

Prepare quarterly production budgets.
(SO 3)

E9-3 Wayans Company produces and sells automobile batteries, the heavy-duty HD-240. The 2005 sales budget is as follows.

Quarter	HD-240
1	5,000
2	7,000
3	8,000
4	10,000

The January 1, 2005, inventory of HD-240 is 2,000 units. Management desires an ending inventory each quarter equal to 40% of the next quarter's sales. Sales in the first quarter of 2006 are expected to be 30% higher than sales in the same quarter in 2005.

Instructions
Prepare quarterly production budgets for each quarter and in total for 2005.

Prepare a direct materials purchases budget.
(SO 3)

E9-4 Samano Industries has adopted the following production budget for the first 4 months of 2006.

Month	Units	Month	Units
January	10,000	March	5,000
February	8,000	April	4,000

Each unit requires 5 pounds of raw materials costing $2 per pound. On December 31, 2005, the ending raw materials inventory was 15,000 pounds. Management wants to have a raw materials inventory at the end of the month equal to 30% of next month's production requirements.

Instructions
Prepare a direct materials purchases budget by month for the first quarter.

Prepare production and direct materials budgets by quarters for 6 months.
(SO 3)

E9-5 On January 1, 2006 the Sanchez Company budget committee has reached agreement on the following data for the 6 months ending June 30, 2006.

Sales units:	First quarter 5,000; second quarter 8,000; third quarter 7,000
Ending raw materials inventory:	50% of the next quarter's production requirements
Ending finished goods inventory:	30% of the next quarter's expected sales units
Third-quarter production:	7,250 units

The ending raw materials and finished goods inventories at December 31, 2005, follow the same percentage relationships to production and sales that occur in 2006. Three pounds of raw materials are required to make each unit of finished goods. Raw materials purchased are expected to cost $4 per pound.

Instructions
(a) Prepare a production budget by quarters for the 6-month period ended June 30, 2006.
(b) Prepare a direct materials budget by quarters for the 6-month period ended June 30, 2006.

E9-6   Pacer, Inc., is preparing its direct labor budget for 2005 from the following production budget based on a calendar year.

Prepare a direct labor budget.
(SO 3)

Quarter	Units	Quarter	Units
1	20,000	3	35,000
2	25,000	4	30,000

Each unit requires 1.2 hours of direct labor.

Instructions
Prepare a direct labor budget for 2005. Wage rates are expected to be $15 for the first 2 quarters and $16 for quarters 3 and 4.

E9-7   Keyser Company is preparing its manufacturing overhead budget for 2005. Relevant data consist of the following.

Prepare a manufacturing overhead budget for the year.
(SO 3)

Units to be produced (by quarters): 10,000, 12,000, 14,000, 16,000.

Direct labor: Time is 1.5 hours per unit.

Variable overhead costs per direct labor hour: Indirect materials $0.70; indirect labor $1.20; and maintenance $0.30.

Fixed overhead costs per quarter: Supervisory salaries $35,000; depreciation $16,000; and maintenance $12,000.

Instructions
Prepare the manufacturing overhead budget for the year, showing quarterly data.

E9-8   Lockwood Company combines its operating expenses for budget purposes in a selling and administrative expense budget. For the first 6 months of 2005, the following data are available.

Prepare a selling and administrative expense budget for 2 quarters.
(SO 3)

1. Sales: 20,000 units quarter 1; 24,000 units quarter 2.
2. Variable costs per dollar of sales: Sales commissions 5%, delivery expense 2%, and advertising 3%.
3. Fixed costs per quarter: Sales salaries $10,000, office salaries $6,000, depreciation $4,200, insurance $1,500, utilities $800, and repairs expense $600.
4. Unit selling price: $20.

Instructions
Prepare a selling and administrative expense budget by quarters for the first 6 months of 2005.

E9-9   Haven Company has accumulated the following budget data for the year 2005.

Prepare a budgeted income statement for the year.
(SO 3, 4)

1. Sales: 40,000 units, unit selling price $80.
2. Cost of one unit of finished goods: Direct materials 2 pounds at $5 per pound, direct labor 3 hours at $12 per hour, and manufacturing overhead $6 per direct labor hour.
3. Inventories (raw materials only): Beginning, 10,000 pounds; ending, 15,000 pounds.
4. Raw materials cost: $5 per pound.
5. Selling and administrative expenses: $200,000.
6. Income taxes: 30% of income before income taxes.

Instructions
(a) Prepare a schedule showing the computation of cost of goods sold for 2005.
(b) Prepare a budgeted income statement for 2005.

E9-10   Nunez Company expects to have a cash balance of $46,000 on January 1, 2005. Relevant monthly budget data for the first 2 months of 2005 are as follows.

Prepare a cash budget for 2 months.
(SO 5)

Collections from customers: January $75,000, February $150,000.

Payments for direct materials: January $45,000, February $70,000.

Direct labor: January $30,000, February $45,000. Wages are paid in the month they are incurred.

Manufacturing overhead: January $21,000, February $30,000. These costs include depreciation of $1,000 per month. All other overhead costs are paid as incurred.

Selling and administrative expenses: January $15,000, February $20,000. These costs are exclusive of depreciation. They are paid as incurred.

Sales of marketable securities in January are expected to realize $10,000 in cash. Nunez Company has a line of credit at a local bank that enables it to borrow up to $25,000. The company wants to maintain a minimum monthly cash balance of $20,000.

Instructions

Prepare a cash budget for January and February.

Prepare schedules for cash receipts and cash payments, and determine ending balances for balance sheet.
(SO 5, 6)

E9-11   Environmental Landscaping Inc. is preparing its budget for the first quarter of 2005. The next step in the budgeting process is to prepare a cash receipts schedule and a cash payments schedule. To that end the following information has been collected.

Clients usually pay 60% of their fee in the month that service is provided, 30% the month after, and 10% the second month after receiving service.

Actual service revenue for 2004 and expected service revenues for 2005 are: November 2004, $90,000; December 2004, $80,000; January 2005, $100,000; February 2005, $120,000; March 2005, $130,000.

Purchases on landscaping supplies (direct materials) are paid 40% in the month of purchase and 60% the following month. Actual purchases for 2004 and expected purchases for 2005 are: December 2004, $14,000; January 2005, $12,000; February 2005, $15,000; March 2005, $18,000.

Instructions

(a) Prepare the following schedules for each month in the first quarter of 2005 and for the quarter in total:
  (1) Expected collections from clients.
  (2) Expected payments for landscaping supplies.
(b) Determine the following balances at March 31, 2005:
  (1) Accounts receivable.
  (2) Accounts payable.

Prepare a cash budget for two quarters.
(SO 5, 6)

E9-12   Donnegal Dental Clinic is a medium-sized dental service specializing in family dental care. The clinic is currently preparing the master budget for the first 2 quarters of 2005. All that remains in this process is the cash budget. The following information has been collected from other portions of the master budget and elsewhere.

Beginning cash balance	$ 30,000
Required minimum cash balance	25,000
Payment of income taxes (2nd quarter)	4,000
Professional salaries:	
1st quarter	140,000
2nd quarter	140,000
Interest from investments (2nd quarter)	5,000
Overhead costs:	
1st quarter	75,000
2nd quarter	100,000
Selling and administrative costs, including	
$3,000 depreciation:	
1st quarter	50,000
2nd quarter	70,000
Purchase of equipment (2nd quarter)	50,000
Sale of equipment (1st quarter)	15,000
Collections from clients:	
1st quarter	230,000
2nd quarter	380,000
Interest on repayments (2nd quarter)	300

Instructions

Prepare a cash budget for each of the first two quarters of 2005.

E9-13   In May 2005, the budget committee of Loebs Stores assembles the following data in preparation of budgeted merchandise purchases for the month of June.

1. Expected sales: June $550,000, July $600,000.
2. Cost of goods sold is expected to be 70% of sales.
3. Desired ending merchandise inventory is 40% of the following (next) month's cost of goods sold.
4. The beginning inventory at June 1 will be the desired amount.

Prepare a purchases budget and budgeted income statement for a merchandiser.
(SO 6)

Instructions
(a) Compute the budgeted merchandise purchases for June.
(b) Prepare the budgeted income statement for June through gross profit.

Problems: Set A

P9-1A   Tilger Farm Supply Company manufactures and sells a fertilizer called Basic II. The following data are available for preparing budgets for Basic II for the first 2 quarters of 2005.

Prepare budgeted income statement and supporting budgets.
(SO 3, 4)

1. Sales: Quarter 1, 40,000 bags; quarter 2, 55,000 bags. Selling price is $60 per bag.
2. Direct materials: Each bag of Basic II requires 6 pounds of Crup at a cost of $3 per pound and 10 pounds of Dert at $1.50 per pound.
3. Desired inventory levels:

Type of Inventory	January 1	April 1	July 1
Basic II (bags)	10,000	15,000	20,000
Crup (pounds)	9,000	12,000	15,000
Dert (pounds)	15,000	20,000	25,000

4. Direct labor: Direct labor time is 15 minutes per bag at an hourly rate of $12 per hour.
5. Selling and administrative expenses are expected to be 10% of sales plus $150,000 per quarter.
6. Income taxes are expected to be 30% of income from operations.

   Your assistant has prepared two budgets: (1) The manufacturing overhead budget shows expected costs to be 100% of direct labor cost. (2) The direct materials budget for Dert which shows the cost of Dert to be $682,500 in quarter 1 and $907,500 in quarter 2.

Instructions
Prepare the budgeted income statement for the first 6 months of 2005 and all required supporting budgets by quarters. (*Note*: Use variable and fixed in the selling and administrative expense budget.) Do not prepare the manufacturing overhead budget or the direct materials budget for Dert.

Net income $787,500
Cost per bag $39.00

P9-2A   Greish Inc. is preparing its annual budgets for the year ending December 31, 2005. Accounting assistants furnish the following data.

Prepare sales, production, direct materials, direct labor, and income statement budgets.
(SO 3, 4)

	Product LN 35	Product LN 40
Sales budget:		
Anticipated volume in units	350,000	180,000
Unit selling price	$20	$30
Production budget:		
Desired ending finished goods units	30,000	25,000
Beginning finished goods units	20,000	15,000
Direct materials budget:		
Direct materials per unit (pounds)	2	3
Desired ending direct materials pounds	50,000	20,000
Beginning direct materials pounds	40,000	10,000
Cost per pound	$2	$3
Direct labor budget:		
Direct labor time per unit	0.5	0.75
Direct labor rate per hour	$10	$10
Budgeted income statement:		
Total unit cost	$10	$20

An accounting assistant has prepared the detailed manufacturing overhead budget and the selling and administrative expense budget. The latter shows selling expenses of $560,000 for product LN 35 and $440,000 for product LN 40, and administrative expenses of $420,000 for product LN 35 and $380,000 for product LN 40. Income taxes are expected to be 30%.

(a) Total sales $12,400,000
(b) Required production units:
    LN 35, 360,000
(c) Total cost of direct materials purchases $3,200,000
(d) Total direct labor cost $3,225,000
(e) Net income $2,450,000

Instructions

Prepare the following budgets for the year. Show data for each product. Quarterly budgets should not be prepared.

(a) Sales   (d) Direct labor
(b) Production   (e) Income statement (*Note*: Income taxes are
(c) Direct materials   not allocated to the products.)

Prepare sales and production budgets and compute cost per unit under two plans.
(SO 3, 4)

P9-3A   Hirsch Industries has sales in 2005 of $5,250,000 (750,000 units) and gross profit of $1,587,500. Management is considering two alternative budget plans to increase its gross profit in 2006.

Plan A would increase the selling price per unit from $7.00 to $7.60. Sales volume would decrease by 10% from its 2005 level. Plan B would decrease the selling price per unit by 5%. The marketing department expects that the sales volume would increase by 100,000 units.

At the end of 2005, Hirsch has 75,000 units on hand. If Plan A is accepted, the 2006 ending inventory should be equal to 90,000 units. If Plan B is accepted, the ending inventory should be equal to 100,000 units. Each unit produced will cost $2.00 in direct materials, $1.50 in direct labor, and $0.50 in variable overhead. The fixed overhead for 2006 should be $965,000.

Instructions

(c) Unit cost: Plan A $5.40, Plan B $5.10
(d) Gross profit:
    Plan A $1,485,000
    Plan B $1,317,500

(a) Prepare a sales budget for 2006 under (1) Plan A and (2) Plan B.
(b) Prepare a production budget for 2006 under (1) Plan A and (2) Plan B.
(c) Compute the cost per unit under (1) Plan A and (2) Plan B. Explain why the cost per unit is different for each of the two plans. (Round to two decimals.)
(d) Which plan should be accepted? (*Hint*: Compute the gross profit under each plan.)

Prepare cash budget for 2 months.
(SO 5)

P9-4A   Lorch Company prepares monthly cash budgets. Relevant data from operating budgets for 2006 are:

	January	February
Sales	$360,000	$400,000
Direct materials purchases	100,000	110,000
Direct labor	100,000	115,000
Manufacturing overhead	60,000	75,000
Selling and administrative expenses	75,000	80,000

All sales are on account. Collections are expected to be 60% in the month of sale, 30% in the first month following the sale, and 10% in the second month following the sale. Thirty percent (30%) of direct materials purchases are paid in cash in the month of purchase, and the balance due is paid in the month following the purchase. All other items above are paid in the month incurred. Depreciation has been excluded from manufacturing overhead and selling and administrative expenses.

Other data:

1. Credit sales: November 2005, $200,000; December 2005, $280,000.
2. Purchases of direct materials: December 2005, $90,000.
3. Other receipts: January—Collection of December 31, 2005, interest receivable $3,000;
                    February—Proceeds from sale of securities $5,000.
4. Other disbursements: February—payment of $20,000 for land.

The company's cash balance on January 1, 2006, is expected to be $60,000. The company wants to maintain a minimum cash balance of $50,000.

(a) January:
    collections $320,000
    payments $93,000
(b) Ending cash balance:
    January $55,000
    February $50,000

Instructions

(a) Prepare schedules for (1) expected collections from customers and (2) expected payments for direct materials purchases.
(b) Prepare a cash budget for January and February in columnar form.

P9-5A The budget committee of Ridder Company collects the following data for its Westwood Store in preparing budgeted income statements for July and August 2005.

Prepare purchases and income statement budgets for a merchandiser.
(SO 6)

1. Expected sales: July $400,000, August $450,000, September $500,000.
2. Cost of goods sold is expected to be 60% of sales.
3. Company policy is to maintain ending merchandise inventory at 25% of the following month's cost of goods sold.
4. Operating expenses are estimated to be:

Sales salaries	$30,000 per month
Advertising	4% of monthly sales
Delivery expense	2% of monthly sales
Sales commissions	3% of monthly sales
Rent expense	$3,000 per month
Depreciation	$700 per month
Utilities	$500 per month
Insurance	$300 per month

5. Income taxes are estimated to be 30% of income from operations.

Instructions
(a) Prepare the merchandise purchases budget for each month in columnar form.
(b) Prepare budgeted income statements for each month in columnar form. Show the details of cost of goods sold in the statements.

(a) Purchases: July $247,500
August $277,500
(b) Net income: July $62,650
August $73,500

P9-6A Kurian Industries' balance sheet at December 31, 2005, is presented below.

Prepare budgeted income statement and balance sheet.
(SO 3, 4, 5)

KURIAN INDUSTRIES
Balance Sheet
December 31, 2005

Assets

Current assets		
Cash		$ 7,500
Accounts receivable		82,500
Finished goods inventory (2,000 units)		30,000
Total current assets		120,000
Property, plant, and equipment		
Equipment	$40,000	
Less: Accumulated depreciation	10,000	30,000
Total assets		$150,000

Liabilities and Stockholders' Equity

Liabilities		
Notes payable		$ 25,000
Accounts payable		45,000
Total liabilities		70,000
Stockholders' equity		
Common stock	$50,000	
Retained earnings	30,000	
Total stockholders' equity		80,000
Total liabilities and stockholders' equity		$150,000

Additional information accumulated for the budgeting process is as follows.
Budgeted data for the year 2006 include the following.

	4th Qtr. of 2006	Year 2006 Total
Sales budget (8,000 units at $30)	$70,000	$240,000
Direct materials used	17,000	69,400
Direct labor	8,500	38,600
Manufacturing overhead applied	10,000	54,000
Selling and administrative expenses	18,000	76,000

To meet sales requirements and to have 3,000 units of finished goods on hand at December 31, 2006, the production budget shows 9,000 required units of output. The total unit cost of production is expected to be $18. Kurian Industries uses the first-in, first-out (FIFO) inventory costing method. Selling and administrative expenses include $4,000 for depreciation on equipment. Interest expense is expected to be $3,500 for the year. Income taxes are expected to be 30% of income before income taxes.

All sales and purchases are on account. It is expected that 60% of quarterly sales are collected in cash within the quarter and the remainder is collected in the following quarter. Direct materials purchased from suppliers are paid 50% in the quarter incurred and the remainder in the following quarter. Purchases in the fourth quarter were the same as the materials used. In 2006, the company expects to purchase additional equipment costing $14,000. It expects to pay $8,000 on notes payable plus all interest due and payable to December 31 (included in interest expense $3,500, above). Accounts payable at December 31, 2006, includes amounts due suppliers (see above) plus other accounts payable of $10,700. In 2006, the company expects to declare and pay a $5,000 cash dividend. Unpaid income taxes at December 31 will be $5,000. The company's cash budget shows an expected cash balance of $9,950 at December 31, 2006.

Instructions

Net income $15,750
Total assets $131,950

Prepare a budgeted income statement for 2006 and a budgeted balance sheet at December 31, 2006. In preparing the income statement, you will need to compute cost of goods manufactured (direct materials + direct labor + manufacturing overhead) and finished goods inventory (December 31, 2006).

Problems: Set B

Prepare budgeted income statement and supporting budgets.
(SO 3, 4)

P9-1B   Wahlen Farm Supply Company manufactures and sells a pesticide called Snare. The following data are available for preparing budgets for Snare for the first 2 quarters of 2006.

1. Sales: Quarter 1, 28,000 bags: quarter 2, 40,000 bags. Selling price is $60 per bag.
2. Direct materials: Each bag of Snare requires 4 pounds of Gumm at a cost of $3 per pound and 6 pounds of Tarr at $1.50 per pound.
3. Desired inventory levels:

Type of Inventory	January 1	April 1	July 1
Snare (bags)	8,000	12,000	18,000
Gumm (pounds)	9,000	10,000	13,000
Tarr (pounds)	14,000	20,000	25,000

4. Direct labor: Direct labor time is 15 minutes per bag at an hourly rate of $14 per hour.
5. Selling and administrative expenses are expected to be 15% of sales plus $175,000 per quarter.
6. Income taxes are expected to be 30% of income from operations.

Your assistant has prepared two budgets: (1) The manufacturing overhead budget shows expected costs to be 150% of direct labor cost. (2) The direct materials budget for Tarr shows the cost of Tarr to be $297,000 in quarter 1 and $421,500 in quarter 2.

Instructions

Net income $766,500
Cost per bag $29.75

Prepare the budgeted income statement for the first 6 months and all required supporting budgets by quarters. (*Note:* Use variable and fixed in the selling and administrative expense budget). Do not prepare the manufacturing overhead budget or the direct materials budget for Tarr.

Prepare sales, production, direct materials, direct labor, and income statement budgets.
(SO 3, 4)

P9-2B   Lasorda Inc. is preparing its annual budgets for the year ending December 31, 2006. Accounting assistants furnish the data shown on page 385.

	Product JB 50	Product JB 60
Sales budget:		
Anticipated volume in units	450,000	200,000
Unit selling price	$20	$25
Production budget:		
Desired ending finished goods units	25,000	15,000
Beginning finished goods units	30,000	10,000
Direct materials budget:		
Direct materials per unit (pounds)	2	3
Desired ending direct materials pounds	30,000	15,000
Beginning direct materials pounds	40,000	10,000
Cost per pound	$3	$4
Direct labor budget:		
Direct labor time per unit	0.4	0.6
Direct labor rate per hour	$10	$10
Budgeted income statement:		
Total unit cost	$12	$20

An accounting assistant has prepared the detailed manufacturing overhead budget and the selling and administrative expense budget. The latter shows selling expenses of $660,000 for product JB 50 and $360,000 for product JB 60, and administrative expenses of $540,000 for product JB 50 and $340,000 for product JB 60. Income taxes are expected to be 30%.

Instructions

Prepare the following budgets for the year. Show data for each product. Quarterly budgets should not be prepared.

(a) Sales   (d) Direct labor
(b) Production   (e) Income statement (*Note*: Income taxes are
(c) Direct materials   not allocated to the products.)

(a) Total sales $14,000,000
(b) Required production units:
  JB 50, 445,000
  JB 60, 205,000
(c) Total cost of direct materials purchases $5,120,000
(d) Total direct labor cost $3,010,000
(e) Net income $1,890,000

P9-3B Tick Industries had sales in 2005 of $6,000,000 and gross profit of $1,500,000. Management is considering two alternative budget plans to increase its gross profit in 2006.

Plan A would increase the selling price per unit from $8.00 to $8.40. Sales volume would decrease by 5% from its 2005 level. Plan B would decrease the selling price per unit by $0.50. The marketing department expects that the sales volume would increase by 150,000 units.

At the end of 2005, Tick has 30,000 units of inventory on hand. If Plan A is accepted, the 2006 ending inventory should be equal to 4% of the 2006 sales. If Plan B is accepted, the ending inventory should be equal to 40,000 units. Each unit produced will cost $1.80 in direct labor, $2.00 in direct materials, and $1.20 in variable overhead. The fixed overhead for 2006 should be $1,800,000.

Prepare sales and production budgets and compute cost per unit under two plans.
(SO 3, 4)

Instructions

(a) Prepare a sales budget for 2006 under each plan.
(b) Prepare a production budget for 2006 under each plan.
(c) Compute the production cost per unit under each plan. Why is the cost per unit different for each of the two plans? (Round to two decimals.)
(d) Which plan should be accepted? (*Hint*: Compute the gross profit under each plan.)

(c) Unit cost: Plan A $7.53
  Plan B $6.98
(d) Gross profit:
  Plan A $619,875
  Plan B $468,000

P9-4B Nigh Company prepares monthly cash budgets. Relevant data from operating budgets for 2006 are:

Prepare cash budget for 2 months.
(SO 5)

	January	February
Sales	$350,000	$400,000
Direct materials purchases	120,000	130,000
Direct labor	80,000	100,000
Manufacturing overhead	70,000	75,000
Selling and administrative expenses	79,000	81,000

All sales are on account. Collections are expected to be 50% in the month of sale, 30% in the first month following the sale, and 20% in the second month following the sale. Sixty percent (60%) of direct materials purchases are paid in cash in the month of purchase, and the balance due is paid in the month following the purchase. All other items above are paid in the month incurred except for selling and administrative expenses that include $1,000 of depreciation per month.

Other data:

1. Credit sales: November 2005, $260,000; December 2005, $300,000.
2. Purchases of direct materials: December 2005, $100,000.
3. Other receipts: January—Collection of December 31, 2005, notes receivable $15,000;
   February—Proceeds from sale of securities $6,000.
4. Other disbursements: February—Withdrawal of $5,000 cash for personal use of owner, Dewey Yaeger.

The company's cash balance on January 1, 2006, is expected to be $60,000. The company wants to maintain a minimum cash balance of $50,000.

(a) January:
collections $317,000
payments $112,000
(b) Ending cash balance:
January $52,000
February $50,000

Instructions

(a) Prepare schedules for (1) expected collections from customers and (2) expected payments for direct materials purchases.
(b) Prepare a cash budget for January and February in columnar form.

Prepare purchases and income statement budgets for a merchandiser.
(SO 6)

P9-5B The budget committee of Lococo Company collects the following data for its San Miguel Store in preparing budgeted income statements for May and June 2006.

1. Sales for May are expected to be $600,000. Sales in June and July are expected to be 10% higher than the preceding month.
2. Cost of goods sold is expected to be 75% of sales.
3. Company policy is to maintain ending merchandise inventory at 20% of the following month's cost of goods sold.
4. Operating expenses are estimated to be:

Sales salaries	$30,000 per month
Advertising	5% of monthly sales
Delivery expense	3% of monthly sales
Sales commissions	4% of monthly sales
Rent expense	$5,000 per month
Depreciation	$800 per month
Utilities	$600 per month
Insurance	$500 per month

(a) Purchases:
May $459,000
June $504,900
(b) Net income:
May $28,770
June $34,230

5. Income taxes are estimated to be 30% of income from operations.

Instructions

(a) Prepare the merchandise purchases budget for each month in columnar form.
(b) Prepare budgeted income statements for each month in columnar form. Show in the statements the details of cost of goods sold.

Problems: Set C

Problem Set C is provided at the book's Web site, www.wiley.com/college/weygandt.

▷ BROADENING YOUR PERSPECTIVE

Group Decision Case

BYP 9-1 Peters Corporation operates on a calendar-year basis. It begins the annual budgeting process in late August when the president establishes targets for the total dollar sales and net income before taxes for the next year.

The sales target is given first to the marketing department. The marketing manager formulates a sales budget by product line in both units and dollars. From this budget, sales quotas by product line in units and dollars are established for each of the corporation's sales districts. The marketing manager also estimates the cost of the marketing activities required to support the target sales volume and prepares a tentative marketing expense budget.

The executive vice president uses the sales and profit targets, the sales budget by product line, and the tentative marketing expense budget to determine the dollar amounts that can be devoted to manufacturing and corporate office expense. The executive vice president prepares the budget for corporate expenses. She then forwards to the production department the product-line sales budget in units and the total dollar amount that can be devoted to manufacturing.

The production manager meets with the factory managers to develop a manufacturing plan that will produce the required units when needed within the cost constraints set by the executive vice president. The budgeting process usually comes to a halt at this point because the production department does not consider the financial resources allocated to be adequate.

When this standstill occurs, the vice president of finance, the executive vice president, the marketing manager, and the production manager meet together to determine the final budgets for each of the areas. This normally results in a modest increase in the total amount available for manufacturing costs and cuts in the marketing expense and corporate office expense budgets. The total sales and net income figures proposed by the president are seldom changed. Although the participants are seldom pleased with the compromise, these budgets are final. Each executive then develops a new detailed budget for the operations in his or her area.

None of the areas has achieved its budget in recent years. Sales often run below the target. When budgeted sales are not achieved, each area is expected to cut costs so that the president's profit target can be met. However, the profit target is seldom met because costs are not cut enough. In fact, costs often run above the original budget in all functional areas (marketing, production, and corporate office).

The president is disturbed that Peters has not been able to meet the sales and profit targets. He hired a consultant with considerable experience with companies in Peters's industry. The consultant reviewed the budgets for the past 4 years. He concluded that the product line sales budgets were reasonable and that the cost and expense budgets were adequate for the budgeted sales and production levels.

Instructions

With the class divided into groups, answer the following.

(a) Discuss how the budgeting process employed by Peters Corporation contributes to the failure to achieve the president's sales and profit targets.

(b) Suggest how Peters Corporation's budgeting process could be revised to correct the problems.

(c) Should the functional areas be expected to cut their costs when sales volume falls below budget? Explain your answer. (CMA adapted.)

Managerial Analysis

BYP 9-2 Prasad & Green Inc. manufactures ergonomic devices for computer users. Some of their more popular products include glare screens (for computer monitors), keyboard stands with wrist rests, and carousels that allow easy access to magnetic disks. Over the past 5 years, they experienced rapid growth, with sales of all products increasing 20% to 50% each year.

Last year, some of the primary manufacturers of computers began introducing new products with some of the ergonomic designs, such as glare screens and wrist rests, already built in. As a result, sales of Prasad & Green's accessory devices have declined somewhat. The company believes that the disk carousels will probably continue to show growth, but that the other products will probably continue to decline. When the next year's budget was prepared, increases were built in to research and development so that replacement products could be developed or the company could expand into some other product line. Some product lines being considered are general-purpose ergonomic devices including back supports, foot rests, and sloped writing pads.

The most recent results have shown that sales decreased more than was expected for the glare screens. As a result, the company may have a shortage of funds. Top management has therefore asked that all expenses be reduced 10% to compensate for these reduced sales. Summary budget information is as follows.

Direct materials	$240,000
Direct labor	110,000
Insurance	50,000
Depreciation	90,000
Machine repairs	30,000
Sales salaries	50,000
Office salaries	80,000
Factory salaries (indirect labor)	50,000
Total	$700,000

Instructions

Using the information above, answer the following questions.

(a) What are the implications of reducing each of the costs? For example, if the company reduces direct materials costs, it may have to do so by purchasing lower-quality materials. This may affect sales in the long run.

(b) Based on your analysis in (a), what do you think is the best way to obtain the $70,000 in cost savings requested? Be specific. Are there any costs that cannot or should not be reduced? Why?

Real-World Focus

BYP 9-3   Network Computing Devices Inc. was founded in 1988 in Mountain View, California. The company develops software products such as X-terminals, Z-mail, PC X-ware, and related hardware products. Presented below is a discussion by management in its annual report.

NETWORK COMPUTING DEVICES, INC.
Management Discussion

The Company's operating results have varied significantly, particularly on a quarterly basis, as a result of a number of factors, including general economic conditions affecting industry demand for computer products, the timing and market acceptance of new product introductions by the Company and its competitors, the timing of significant orders from large customers, periodic changes in product pricing and discounting due to competitive factors, and the availability of key components, such as video monitors and electronic subassemblies, some of which require substantial order lead times. The Company's operating results may fluctuate in the future as a result of these and other factors, including the Company's success in developing and introducing new products, its product and customer mix, and the level of competition which it experiences. The Company operates with a small backlog. Sales and operating results, therefore, generally depend on the volume and timing of orders received, which are difficult to forecast. The Company has experienced slowness in orders from some customers during the first quarter of each calendar year due to budgeting cycles common in the computer industry. In addition, sales in Europe typically are adversely affected in the third calendar quarter as many European customers reduce their business activities during the month of August.

Due to the Company's rapid growth rate and the effect of new product introductions on quarterly revenues, these seasonal trends have not materially impacted the Company's results of operations to date. However, as the Company's product lines mature and its rate of revenue growth declines, these seasonal factors may become more evident. Additionally, the Company's international sales are denominated in U.S. dollars, and an increase or decrease in the value of the U.S. dollar relative to foreign currencies could make the Company's products less or more competitive in those markets.

Instructions
(a) Identify the factors that affect the budgeting process at Network Computing Devices, Inc.
(b) Explain the additional budgeting concerns created by the international operations of the company.

Exploring the Web

BYP 9-4   The opportunities for business consulting in the areas of corporate planning, budgeting, and strategy are almost limitless as new, more powerful software continues to be developed. This exercise takes you to the Web site of **CP Corporate Planning**, a European consulting firm.

Address: **www.corporate-planning.com/us/pages/sitemap/sitemap.htm**
        or go to **www.wiley.com/college/weygandt**

Steps: Go to the site above.

Instructions
Choose three case studies, and in each case identify the problem the company faced and how the situation was resolved.

Communication Activity

BYP 9-5   In order to better serve their rural patients, Drs. Ken and Dick Ginavan (brothers) began giving safety seminars. Especially popular were their "emergency-preparedness" talks given to farmers. Many people asked whether the "kit" of materials the doctors recommended for common farm emergencies was commercially available.

After checking with several suppliers, the doctors realized that no other company offered the supplies they recommended in their seminars, packaged in the way they described. Their wives, Nancy and Sue, agreed to make a test package by ordering supplies from various medical supply companies and assembling them into a "kit" that could be sold at the seminars. When these kits proved a runaway success, the sisters-in-law decided to market them. At the advice of their accountant, they organized this venture as a separate company, called Life Protection Products (LPP), with Nancy Ginavan as CEO and Sue Ginavan as Secretary-Treasurer.

LPP soon started receiving requests for the kits from all over the country, as word spread about their availability. Even without advertising, LPP was able to sell its full inventory every month. However, the company was becoming financially strained. Nancy and Sue had about $100,000 in savings, and they invested about half that amount initially. They believed that this venture would allow them to make money. However, at the present time, only about $30,000 of the cash remains, and the company is constantly short of cash.

Nancy Ginavan has come to you for advice. She does not understand why the company is having cash flow problems. She and Sue have not even been withdrawing salaries. However, they have rented a local building and have hired two more full-time workers to help them cope with the increasing demand. They do not think they could handle the demand without this additional help.

Nancy is also worried that the cash problems mean that the company may not be able to support itself. She has prepared the cash budget shown on the next page. All seminar customers pay for their products in full at the time of purchase. In addition, several large companies have ordered the kits for use by employees who work in remote sites. They have requested credit terms and have been allowed to pay in the month following the sale. These large purchasers amount to about 25% of the sales at the present time. LPP purchases the materials for the kits about 2 months ahead of time. Nancy and Sue are considering slowing the growth of the company by simply purchasing less materials, which will mean selling fewer kits.

The workers are paid in cash weekly. Nancy and Sue need about $15,000 cash on hand at the beginning of the month to pay for purchases of raw materials. Right now they have been using cash from their savings, but as noted, only $30,000 is left.

Instructions
Write a response to Nancy Ginavan. Explain why LPP is short of cash. Will this company be able to support itself? Explain your answer. Make any recommendations you deem appropriate.

LIFE PROTECTION PRODUCTS
Cash Budget
For the Quarter Ending June 30, 2006

	April	May	June
Cash balance, beginning	$15,000	$15,000	$15,000
Cash received			
From prior month sales	5,000	7,500	12,500
From current sales	15,000	22,500	37,500
Total cash on hand	35,000	45,000	65,000
Cash payments			
To employees	3,000	3,000	3,000
For products	25,000	35,000	45,000
Miscellaneous expenses	5,000	6,000	7,000
Postage	1,000	1,000	1,000
Total cash payments	34,000	45,000	56,000
Cash balance	$ 1,000	$ 0	$ 9,000
Borrow from savings	$14,000	$15,000	$ 1,000
Borrow from bank?	$ 0	$ 0	$ 5,000

Research Assignment

BYP 9-6 The October 2003 issue of *Inc.* magazine contains an article by Suzanne McGee titled "Breaking Free from Budgets."

Instructions
Read the article and answer the following questions.
(a) What are the deficiencies of a traditional budget according to the proponents of the "Beyond Budgeting Movement"?
(b) Summarize the pros and cons of budgets as perceived by Al Osborne from UCLA. What does he see as the potential benefit of Beyond Budgeting?
(c) What has remained the same and what has changed at Omgeo since it began implementing the principles of Beyond Budgeting?

Ethics Case

BYP 9-7 You are an accountant in the budgetary, projections, and special projects department of National Conductor, Inc., a large manufacturing company. The president, Richard Sheen, asks you on very short notice to prepare some sales and income projections covering the next 2 years of the company's much heralded new product lines. He wants these projections for a series of speeches he is making while on a 2-week trip to eight East Coast brokerage firms. The president hopes to bolster National's stock sales and price.

You work 23 hours in 2 days to compile the projections, hand deliver them to the president, and are swiftly but graciously thanked as he departs. A week later you find time to go over some of your computations and discover a miscalculation that makes the projections grossly overstated. You quickly inquire about the president's itinerary and learn that he has made half of his speeches and has half yet to make. You are in a quandary as to what to do.

Instructions
(a) What are the consequences of telling the president of your gross miscalculations?
(b) What are the consequences of *not* telling the president of your gross miscalculations?
(c) What are the ethical considerations to you and the president in this situation?

Remember to go back to the Navigator box on the chapter-opening page and check off your completed work.

CHAPTER 10

Budgetary Control and Responsibility Accounting

STUDY OBJECTIVES

After studying this chapter,
you should be able to:

1 Describe the concept of budgetary control.

2 Evaluate the usefulness of static budget reports.

3 Explain the development of flexible budgets and the usefulness of flexible budget reports.

4 Describe the concept of responsibility accounting.

5 Indicate the features of responsibility reports for cost centers.

6 Identify the content of responsibility reports for profit centers.

7 Explain the basis and formula used in evaluating performance in investment centers.

 THE NAVIGATOR

THE NAVIGATOR ✔

▶ Scan *Study Objectives* ☐

▶ Read *Feature Story* ☐

▶ Read *Preview* ☐

▶ Read text and answer *Before You Go On*
     p. 403 ☐   p. 411 ☐   p. 416 ☐

▶ Work *Using the Decision Toolkit* ☐

▶ Review *Summary of Study Objectives* ☐

▶ Work *Demonstration Problem* ☐

▶ Answer *Self-Study Questions* ☐

▶ Complete *Assignments* ☐

FEATURE STORY

Trying to Avoid an Electric Shock

Budgets are critical to evaluating an organization's success. They are based on management's expectations of what is most likely to happen in the future. In order to be useful, they must be accurate. But what if management's expectations are wrong? Estimates are never exactly correct, and sometimes, especially in volatile industries, estimates can be "off by a mile."

In recent years the electric utility industry has become very volatile. Deregulation, volatile prices for natural gas, coal, and oil, changes in environmental regulations, and economic swings have all contributed to large changes in the profitability of electric utility companies. This means that for planning and budgeting purposes, utilites must plan and budget based on multiple "what if" scenarios that take into account factors beyond management's control. For example, in recent years, **Duke Energy Corporation**, headquartered in Charlotte, North Carolina, built budgeting and planning models based on three different scenarios of what the future might hold. One scenario assumes that the U.S. economy will slow considerably. A second scenario assumes that the company will experience "pricing pressure" as the market for energy becomes more efficient as a result of more energy being traded in Internet auctions. A third scenario assumes a continuation of the current environment of rapid growth, changing regulation, and large swings in the prices for the fuels the company uses to create energy.

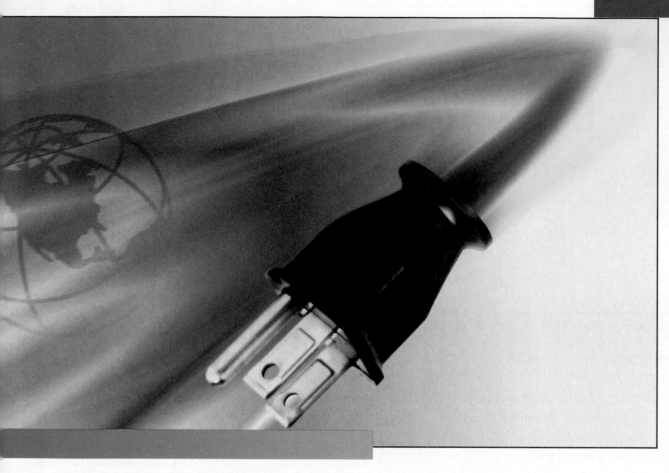

Compounding this budgeting challenge is the fact that changes in many indirect costs can also significantly affect the company. For example, even a tiny change in market interest rates has a huge effect on the company because it has massive amounts of outstanding debt. And finally, as a result of the California energy crisis, there is mounting pressure for government intervention and regulation. This pressure has resulted in setting "rate caps" that limit the amount that utilities and energy companies can charge, thus lowering profits. The bottom line is that for budgeting and planning purposes, utility companies must remain alert and flexible.

THE NAVIGATOR

In contrast to Chapter 9, we now consider how budgets are used by management to control operations. In the Feature Story on **Duke Energy**, we saw that budgeting must take into account factors beyond management's control. This chapter focuses on two aspects of management control: (1) budgetary control and (2) responsibility accounting.

The content and organization of Chapter 10 are as follows.

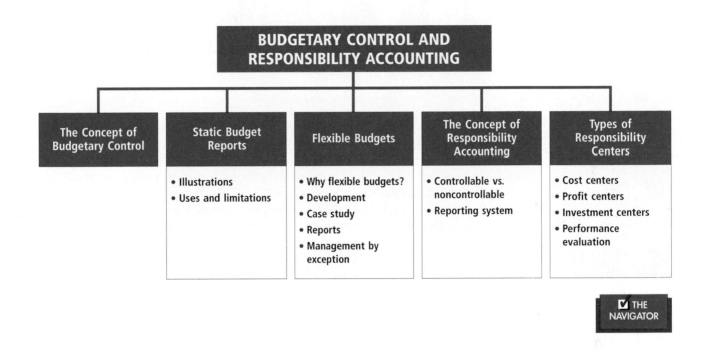

BUDGETARY CONTROL AND RESPONSIBILITY ACCOUNTING

The Concept of Budgetary Control	Static Budget Reports	Flexible Budgets	The Concept of Responsibility Accounting	Types of Responsibility Centers
	• Illustrations • Uses and limitations	• Why flexible budgets? • Development • Case study • Reports • Management by exception	• Controllable vs. noncontrollable • Reporting system	• Cost centers • Profit centers • Investment centers • Performance evaluation

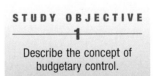

THE NAVIGATOR

The Concept of Budgetary Control

One of management's major functions is to control company operations. Control consists of the steps taken by management to see that planned objectives are met. We now ask: How do budgets contribute to control of operations?

The use of budgets in controlling operations is known as budgetary control. Such control takes place by means of **budget reports** that compare actual results with planned objectives. The use of budget reports is based on the belief that planned objectives lose much of their potential value without some monitoring of progress along the way. Just as your professors give midterm exams to evaluate your progress, so top management requires periodic reports on the progress of department managers toward their planned objectives.

Budget reports provide management with feedback on operations. The feedback for a crucial objective, such as having enough cash on hand to pay bills, may be made daily. For other objectives, such as meeting budgeted annual sales and operating expenses, monthly budget reports may suffice. Budget reports can be prepared as frequently as needed. From these reports, management analyzes any differences between actual and planned results and determines their causes. Management then may take corrective action, or it may decide to modify future plans.

STUDY OBJECTIVE

1

Describe the concept of budgetary control.

Budgetary control involves the following activities.

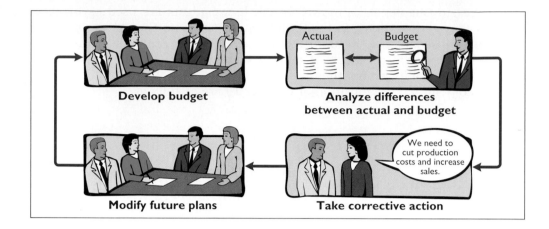

Budgetary control works best when a company has a formalized reporting system. The system should do the following: (1) Identify the name of the budget report, such as the sales budget or the manufacturing overhead budget. (2) State the frequency of the report, such as weekly or monthly. (3) Specify the purpose of the report. And (4) indicate the primary recipient(s) of the report. Illustration 10-2 provides a partial budgetary control system for a manufacturing company. Note the frequency of the reports and their emphasis on control. For example, there is a daily report on scrap and a weekly report on labor.

Illustration 10-2 Budgetary control reporting system

Name of Report	Frequency	Purpose	Primary Recipient(s)
Sales	Weekly	Determine whether sales goals are being met	Top management and sales manager
Labor	Weekly	Control direct and indirect labor costs	Vice president of production and production department managers
Scrap	Daily	Determine efficient use of materials	Production manager
Departmental overhead costs	Monthly	Control overhead costs	Department manager
Selling expenses	Monthly	Control selling expenses	Sales manager
Income statement	Monthly and quarterly	Determine whether income objectives are being met	Top management

Static Budget Reports

You learned in Chapter 9 that the master budget formalizes management's planned objectives for the coming year. When used in budgetary control, each budget included in the master budget is considered to be static. A **static budget** is a projection of budget data **at one level of activity**. Data for different levels of activity are not considered. As a result, actual results are always compared with budget data at the activity level that was used in developing the master budget.

ILLUSTRATIONS

To illustrate the role of a static budget in budgetary control, we will use selected data prepared for Hayes Company in Chapter 9. Budget and actual sales data for the Kitchen-mate product in the first and second quarters of 2005 are as follows.

Illustration 10-3   Budget and actual sales data

Sales	First Quarter	Second Quarter	Total
Budgeted	$180,000	$210,000	$390,000
Actual	179,000	199,500	378,500
Difference	$ 1,000	$ 10,500	$ 11,500

The sales budget report for Hayes Company's first quarter is shown below. The right-most column reports the difference between the budgeted and actual amounts.

Illustration 10-4   Sales budget report—first quarter

HAYES COMPANY
Sales Budget Report
For the Quarter Ended March 31, 2005

Product Line	Budget	Actual	Difference Favorable F Unfavorable U
Kitchen-mate[a]	$180,000	$179,000	**$1,000 U**

[a]In practice, each product line would be included in the report.

Alternative Terminology
The difference between budget and actual is sometimes called a *budget variance.*

The report shows that sales are $1,000 under budget—an unfavorable result. This difference is less than 1 percent of budgeted sales ($1,000 ÷ $180,000 = .0056). Top management's reaction to unfavorable differences is often influenced by the materiality (significance) of the difference. Since the difference of $1,000 is immaterial in this case, we will assume that Hayes Company management takes no specific corrective action.

The budget report for the second quarter is presented in Illustration 10-5. It contains one new feature: cumulative year-to-date information. This report indicates that sales for the second quarter were $10,500 below budget. This is 5 percent of budgeted sales ($10,500 ÷ $210,000). Top management may now conclude that the difference between budgeted and actual sales requires investigation.

Illustration 10-5   Sales budget report—second quarter

HAYES COMPANY
Sales Budget Report
For the Quarter Ended June 30, 2005

Product Line	Second Quarter Budget	Actual	Difference Favorable F Unfavorable U	Year-to-Date Budget	Actual	Difference Favorable F Unfavorable U
Kitchen-mate	$210,000	$199,500	**$10,500 U**	$390,000	$378,500	**$11,500 U**

Management's analysis should start by asking the sales manager the cause(s) of the shortfall. The need for corrective action should be considered. For example, management may decide to spur sales by offering sales incentives to customers or by increasing the advertising of Kitchen-mates. Or, if management concludes that a downturn in the economy is responsible for the lower sales, it may modify planned sales and profit goals for the remainder of the year.

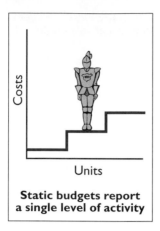

Static budgets report a single level of activity

STUDY OBJECTIVE

3

Explain the development of flexible budgets and the usefulness of flexible budget reports.

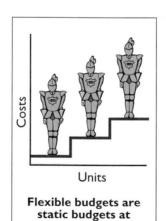

Flexible budgets are static budgets at different activity levels

Illustration 10-6   Static overhead budget

Helpful Hint The static budget is the master budget described in Chapter 9.

USES AND LIMITATIONS

From these examples, you can see that a master sales budget is useful in evaluating the performance of a sales manager. It is now necessary to ask: Is the master budget appropriate for evaluating a manager's performance in controlling costs? Recall that in a static budget, data are not modified or adjusted, regardless of changes in activity. It follows, then, that a static budget is appropriate in evaluating a manager's effectiveness in controlling costs when:

1. The actual level of activity closely approximates the master budget activity level, and/or
2. The behavior of the costs in response to changes in activity is fixed.

A static budget report is, therefore, appropriate for **fixed manufacturing costs** and for **fixed selling and administrative expenses**. But, as you will see shortly, static budget reports may not be a proper basis for evaluating a manager's performance in controlling variable costs.

Flexible Budgets

In contrast to a static budget, which is based on one level of activity, a **flexible budget** projects budget data for various levels of activity. In essence, **the flexible budget is a series of static budgets at different levels of activity**. The flexible budget recognizes that the budgetary process is more useful if it is adaptable to changed operating conditions.

Flexible budgets can be prepared for each of the types of budgets included in the master budget. For example, **Marriott Hotels** can budget revenues and net income on the basis of 60 percent, 80 percent, and 100 percent of room occupancy. Similarly, **American Van Lines** can budget its operating expenses on the basis of various levels of truck miles driven. Likewise, in the Feature Story, **Duke Energy** can budget revenue and net income on the basis of estimated billions of kwh (kilowatt hours) of residential, commercial, and industrial electricity generated. In the following pages, we will illustrate a flexible budget for manufacturing overhead.

WHY FLEXIBLE BUDGETS?

Assume that you are the manager in charge of manufacturing overhead in the Forging Department of Barton Steel. In preparing the manufacturing overhead budget for 2005, you prepare the following static budget based on a production volume of 10,000 units of steel ingots.

BARTON STEEL Manufacturing Overhead Budget (Static) Forging Department For the Year Ended December 31, 2005	
Budgeted production in units (steel ingots)	10,000
Budgeted costs	
Indirect materials	$ 250,000
Indirect labor	260,000
Utilities	190,000
Depreciation	280,000
Property taxes	70,000
Supervision	50,000
	$1,100,000

Fortunately for the company, the demand for steel ingots has increased, and 12,000 units are produced and sold during the year, rather than 10,000. You are elated: Increased sales means increased profitability, which should mean a bonus or a raise for you and the employees in your department. Unfortunately, a comparison of Forging Department actual and budgeted costs has put you on the spot. The budget report is shown below.

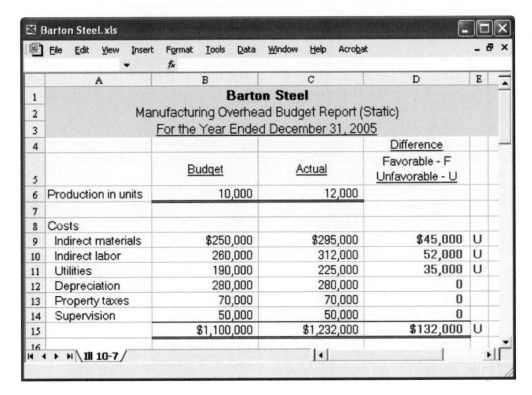

Illustration 10-7 Static overhead budget report

	Budget	Actual	Difference Favorable - F Unfavorable - U	
Barton Steel Manufacturing Overhead Budget Report (Static) For the Year Ended December 31, 2005				
Production in units	10,000	12,000		
Costs				
Indirect materials	$250,000	$295,000	$45,000	U
Indirect labor	260,000	312,000	52,000	U
Utilities	190,000	225,000	35,000	U
Depreciation	280,000	280,000	0	
Property taxes	70,000	70,000	0	
Supervision	50,000	50,000	0	
	$1,100,000	$1,232,000	$132,000	U

This comparison uses budget data based on the original activity level (10,000 steel ingots). It indicates that the Forging Department is significantly **over budget** for three of the six overhead costs. And, there is a total unfavorable difference of $132,000, which is 12 percent over budget ($132,000 ÷ $1,100,000). Your supervisor is very unhappy! Instead of sharing in the company's success, you may find yourself looking for another job. What went wrong?

When you calm down and carefully examine the manufacturing overhead budget, you identify the problem: The budget data are not relevant! At the time the budget was developed, the company anticipated that only 10,000 units of steel ingots would be produced, **not** 12,000 ingots. Comparing actual with budgeted variable costs is meaningless. As production increases, the budget allowances for variable costs should increase proportionately. The variable costs in this example are indirect materials, indirect labor, and utilities.

Analyzing the budget data for these costs at 10,000 units, you arrive at the following per unit results.

Helpful Hint A static budget is not useful for performance evaluation if a company has substantial variable costs.

Illustration 10-8 Variable costs per unit

Item	Total Cost	Per Unit
Indirect materials	$250,000	$25
Indirect labor	260,000	26
Utilities	190,000	19
	$700,000	$70

You then can calculate the budgeted variable costs at 12,000 units as follows.

Illustration 10-9 Budgeted variable costs, 12,000 units

Item	Computation	Total
Indirect materials	$25 × 12,000	$300,000
Indirect labor	26 × 12,000	312,000
Utilities	19 × 12,000	228,000
		$840,000

Because fixed costs do not change in total as activity changes, the budgeted amounts for these costs remain the same. The budget report based on the flexible budget for **12,000 units** of production is shown in Illustration 10-10. (Compare this with Illustration 10-7.)

Illustration 10-10 Flexible overhead budget report

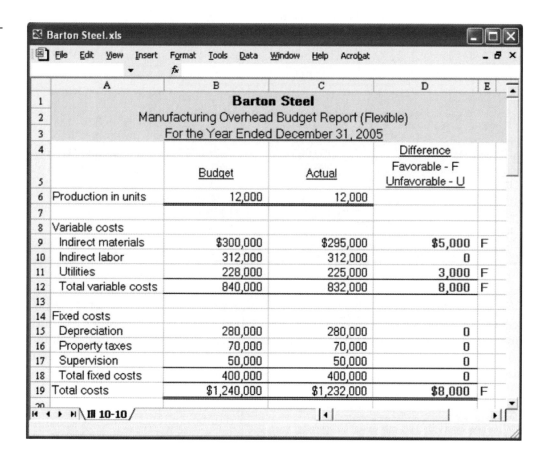

Barton Steel.xls

File Edit View Insert Format Tools Data Window Help Acrobat

Barton Steel
Manufacturing Overhead Budget Report (Flexible)
For the Year Ended December 31, 2005

	Budget	Actual	Difference Favorable - F Unfavorable - U
Production in units	12,000	12,000	
Variable costs			
Indirect materials	$300,000	$295,000	$5,000 F
Indirect labor	312,000	312,000	0
Utilities	228,000	225,000	3,000 F
Total variable costs	840,000	832,000	8,000 F
Fixed costs			
Depreciation	280,000	280,000	0
Property taxes	70,000	70,000	0
Supervision	50,000	50,000	0
Total fixed costs	400,000	400,000	0
Total costs	$1,240,000	$1,232,000	$8,000 F

This report indicates that the Forging Department is below budget—a favorable difference. Instead of worrying about being fired, you may be in line for a bonus or a raise after all! As this analysis shows, the only appropriate comparison is between actual costs at 12,000 units of production and budgeted costs at 12,000 units. Flexible budget reports provide this comparison.

DEVELOPING THE FLEXIBLE BUDGET

The flexible budget uses the master budget as its basis. To develop the flexible budget, management should take the following steps.

1. Identify the activity index and the relevant range of activity.
2. Identify the variable costs, and determine the budgeted variable cost per unit of activity for each cost.

3. Identify the fixed costs, and determine the budgeted amount for each cost.
4. Prepare the budget for selected increments of activity within the relevant range.

The activity index chosen should be one that significantly influences the costs that are being budgeted. For manufacturing overhead costs, for example, the activity index is usually the same as the index used in developing the predetermined overhead rate—that is, direct labor hours or machine hours. For selling and administrative expenses, the activity index usually is sales or net sales.

The choice of the increment of activity is largely a matter of judgment. For example, if the relevant range is 8,000 to 12,000 direct labor hours, increments of 1,000 hours may be selected. The flexible budget is then prepared for each increment within the relevant range.

DECISION TOOLKIT

Decision Checkpoints	Info Needed for Decision	Tool to Use for Decision	How to Evaluate Results
Are the increased costs resulting from increased production reasonable?	Variable costs projected at different levels of production	Flexible budget	After taking into account different production levels, results are favorable if expenses are less than budgeted amounts.

FLEXIBLE BUDGET—A CASE STUDY

To illustrate the flexible budget, we will use Fox Manufacturing Company. Fox's management wants to use a **flexible budget for monthly comparisons** of actual and budgeted manufacturing overhead costs of the Finishing Department. The master budget for the year ending December 31, 2005, shows expected annual operating capacity of 120,000 direct labor hours and the following overhead costs.

Illustration 10-11 Master budget data

Variable Costs		**Fixed Costs**	
Indirect materials	$180,000	Depreciation	$180,000
Indirect labor	240,000	Supervision	120,000
Utilities	60,000	Property taxes	60,000
Total	$480,000	Total	$360,000

The four steps for developing the flexible budget are applied as follows.

STEP 1. **Identify the activity index and the relevant range of activity.** The activity index is direct labor hours. Management concludes that the relevant range is 8,000–12,000 direct labor hours per month.

STEP 2. **Identify the variable costs, and determine the budgeted variable cost per unit of activity for each cost.** There are three variable costs. The variable cost per unit is found by dividing each total budgeted cost by the direct labor hours used in preparing the master budget (120,000 hours). For Fox Manufacturing, the computations are:

Illustration 10-12 Computation of variable costs per direct labor hour

Variable Cost	Computation	Variable Cost per Direct Labor Hour
Indirect materials	$180,000 ÷ 120,000	$1.50
Indirect labor	$240,000 ÷ 120,000	2.00
Utilities	$ 60,000 ÷ 120,000	0.50
Total		$4.00

STEP 3. **Identify the fixed costs, and determine the budgeted amount for each cost.** There are three fixed costs. Since Fox desires **monthly budget data**, the budgeted amount is found by dividing each annual budgeted cost by 12. For Fox Manufacturing, the monthly budgeted fixed costs are: depreciation $15,000, supervision $10,000, and property taxes $5,000.

STEP 4. **Prepare the budget for selected increments of activity within the relevant range.** Management decides to prepare the budget in increments of 1,000 direct labor hours.

The flexible budget is shown in Illustration 10-13.

Illustration 10-13 Flexible monthly overhead budget

Fox Manufacturing Company.xls

	A	B	C	D	E	F
1		**Fox Manufacturing Company**				
2		Flexible Monthly Manufacturing Overhead Budget				
3		Finishing Department				
4		For the Year 2005				
5	Activity level					
6	Direct labor hours	8,000	9,000	10,000	11,000	12,000
7	Variable costs					
8	Indirect materials	$12,000	$13,500	$15,000	$16,500	$18,000
9	Indirect labor	16,000	18,000	20,000	22,000	24,000
10	Utilities	4,000	4,500	5,000	5,500	6,000
11	Total variable costs	32,000	36,000	40,000	44,000	48,000
12	Fixed costs					
13	Depreciation	15,000	15,000	15,000	15,000	15,000
14	Property taxes	10,000	10,000	10,000	10,000	10,000
15	Supervision	5,000	5,000	5,000	5,000	5,000
16	Total fixed costs	30,000	30,000	30,000	30,000	30,000
17	Total costs	$62,000	$66,000	$70,000	$74,000	$78,000

III 10-13

From the budget, the following formula may be used to determine total budgeted costs at any level of activity.

Illustration 10-14 Formula for total budgeted costs

$$\begin{array}{ccccc} \textbf{Fixed} & & \textbf{Variable} & & \textbf{Total} \\ \textbf{Costs} & + & \textbf{Costs*} & = & \textbf{Budgeted} \\ & & & & \textbf{Costs} \end{array}$$

*Total variable cost per unit × activity level.

For Fox Manufacturing, fixed costs are $30,000, and total variable cost per unit is $4.00. Thus, at 9,000 direct labor hours, total budgeted costs are $66,000 [$30,000 + ($4.00 × 9,000)]. Similarly, at 8,622 direct labor hours, total budgeted costs are $64,488 [$30,000 + ($4.00 × 8,622)].

Total budgeted costs can also be shown graphically, as in Illustration 10-15. In the graph, the activity index is shown on the horizontal axis, and costs are indicated on the vertical axis. The graph highlights two activity levels (10,000 and 12,000). As shown, total budgeted costs at these activity levels are $70,000 [$30,000 + ($4.00 × 10,000)] and $78,000 [$30,000 + ($4.00 × 12,000)], respectively.

Helpful Hint Using the data given for the Fox Manufacturing Company, what amount of total costs would be budgeted for 10,600 direct labor hours?
Answer:

Fixed	$30,000
Variable (10,600 × $4)	42,400
Total	$72,400

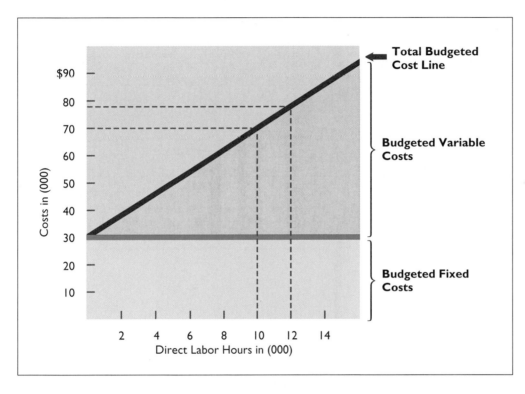

Illustration 10-15
Graphic flexible budget data highlighting 10,000 and 12,000 activity levels

FLEXIBLE BUDGET REPORTS

Flexible budget reports are another type of internal report. The flexible budget report consists of two sections: (1) production data for a selected activity index, such as direct labor hours, and (2) cost data for variable and fixed costs. The report provides a basis for evaluating a manager's performance in two areas: production control and cost control. Flexible budget reports are widely used in production and service departments.

A budget report for the Finishing Department of Fox Company for the month of January is shown in Illustration 10-16 (on page 402). In this month, 9,000 hours were worked. The budget data are therefore based on the flexible budget for 9,000 hours in Illustration 10-13. The actual cost data are assumed.

How appropriate is this report in evaluating the Finishing Department manager's performance in controlling overhead costs? The report clearly provides a reliable basis. Both actual and budget costs are based on the activity level worked during January. Since variable costs generally are incurred directly by the department, the difference between the budget allowance for those hours and the actual costs is the responsibility of the department manager.

Illustration 10-16 Flexible overhead budget report

	A	B	C	D	E
		Fox Manufacturing Company			
1		**Fox Manufacturing Company**			
2		Flexible Manufacturing Overhead Budget Report			
3		Finishing Department			
4		For the Month Ended January 31, 2005			
5				Difference	
6		Budget at	Actual costs at	Favorable - F Unfavorable - U	
7	Direct labor hours (DLH)	9,000 DLH	9,000 DLH		
8					
9	Variable costs				
10	Indirect materials	$13,500	$14,000	$500	U
11	Indirect labor	18,000	17,000	1,000	F
12	Utilities	4,500	4,600	100	U
13	Total variable costs	36,000	35,600	400	F
14					
15	Fixed costs				
16	Depreciation	15,000	15,000	0	
17	Property taxes	10,000	10,000	0	
18	Supervision	5,000	5,000	0	
19	Total fixed costs	30,000	30,000	0	
20	Total costs	$66,000	$65,600	$400	F

Helpful Hint Note that this flexible budget is based on a single cost driver. A more accurate budget often can be developed using the activity-based costing concepts explained in Chapter 4.

In subsequent months, other flexible budget reports will be prepared. For each month, the budget data are based on the actual activity level attained. In February that level may be 11,000 direct labor hours, in July 10,000, and so on.

MANAGEMENT BY EXCEPTION

Management by exception means that top management's review of a budget report is focused either entirely or primarily on differences between actual results and planned objectives. This approach enables top management to focus on problem areas. Management by exception does not mean that top management will investigate every difference. For this approach to be effective, there must be guidelines for identifying an exception. The usual criteria are materiality and controllability.

Materiality

Without quantitative guidelines, management would have to investigate every budget difference regardless of the amount. Materiality is usually expressed as a percentage difference from budget. For example, management may set the percentage difference at 5 percent for important items and 10 percent for other items. All differences either over or under budget by the specified percentage will be investigated. Costs over budget warrant investigation to determine why they were not controlled. Likewise, costs under budget merit investigation to determine whether costs critical to profitability are being curtailed. For example, if maintenance costs are budgeted at $80,000 but only $40,000 is spent, major unexpected breakdowns in productive facilities may occur in the future.

Alternatively, a company may specify a single percentage difference from budget for all items and supplement this guideline with a minimum dollar limit. For example, the exception criteria may be stated at 5 percent of budget or more than $10,000.

Controllability of the Item

Exception guidelines are more restrictive for controllable items than for items that are not controllable by the manager. In fact, there may be no guidelines for noncontrollable items. For example, a large unfavorable difference between actual and budgeted property tax expense may not be flagged for investigation because the only possible causes are an unexpected increase in the tax rate or in the assessed value of the property. An investigation into the difference will be useless: the manager cannot control either cause.

BEFORE YOU GO ON . . .

▶Review It

1. What is the meaning of budgetary control?
2. When is a static budget appropriate for evaluating a manager's effectiveness in controlling costs?
3. What is a flexible budget?
4. How is a flexible budget developed?
5. What are the criteria used in management by exception?

▶Do It

Your roommate asks your help in understanding how total budgeted costs are computed at any level of activity. Compute total budgeted costs at 30,000 direct labor hours, assuming that in the flexible budget graph, the fixed cost line and the total budgeted cost line intersect the vertical axis at $36,000 and that the total budget cost line is $186,000 at an activity level of 50,000 direct labor hours.

Action Plan

• Apply the formula: Fixed costs + Variable costs (Total variable costs per unit × Activity level) = Total budgeted costs.

Solution Using the graph, fixed costs are $36,000, and variable costs are $3 per direct labor hour [($186,000 − $36,000) ÷ 50,000]. Thus, at 30,000 direct labor hours, total budgeted costs are $126,000 [$36,000 + ($3 × 30,000)].

Related exercise material: BE10-3, BE10-4, BE10-5, E10-1, E10-2, E10-3, E10-4, E10-5, and E10-6.

☑ THE NAVIGATOR

The Concept of Responsibility Accounting

Like budgeting, responsibility accounting is an important part of management accounting. **Responsibility accounting** involves accumulating and reporting costs (and revenues, where relevant) on the basis of the manager who has the authority to make the day-to-day decisions about the items. Under responsibility accounting, a manager's performance is evaluated on matters directly under that manager's control. Responsibility accounting can be used at every level of management in which the following conditions exist.

STUDY OBJECTIVE

4

Describe the concept of responsibility accounting.

1. Costs and revenues can be directly associated with the specific level of management responsibility.
2. The costs and revenues are controllable at the level of responsibility with which they are associated.
3. Budget data can be developed for evaluating the manager's effectiveness in controlling the costs and revenues.

Levels of responsibility for controlling costs are depicted in Illustration 10-17.

Illustration 10-17 Responsibility for controllable costs at varying levels of management

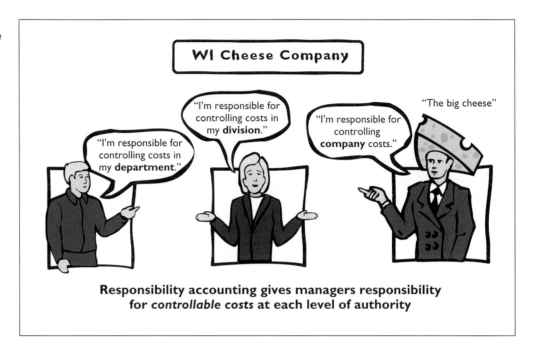

Responsibility accounting gives managers responsibility for *controllable costs* at each level of authority

Helpful Hint All companies use responsibility accounting. Without some form of responsibility accounting, there would be chaos in discharging management's control function.

Under responsibility accounting, any individual who has control and is accountable for a specified set of activities can be recognized as a responsibility center. Thus, responsibility accounting may extend from the lowest level of control to the top strata of management. Once responsibility has been established, the effectiveness of the individual's performance is first measured and reported for the specified activity. It is then reported upward throughout the organization.

Responsibility accounting is especially valuable in a decentralized company. **Decentralization** means that the control of operations is delegated to many managers throughout the organization. The term **segment** is sometimes used to identify an area of responsibility in decentralized operations. Under responsibility accounting, segment reports are prepared periodically such as monthly, quarterly, and annually, to evaluate managers' performance.

Responsibility accounting is an essential part of any effective system of budgetary control. The reporting of costs and revenues under responsibility accounting differs from budgeting in two respects.

1. A distinction is made between controllable and noncontrollable items.
2. Performance reports either emphasize or include only items controllable by the individual manager.

Responsibility accounting applies to both profit and not-for-profit entities. The former seek to maximize net income. The latter wish to minimize the cost of providing services.

Business Insight
Service Company Perspective

Since devising its budgeting and control system, **JKL, Inc.**, a large New York advertising agency, has become aware of which specific customer accounts are unprofitable and the reasons why. As a result, the agency has dropped several unprofitable accounts that otherwise would have gone unnoticed. Account managers now feel responsible for the profitability of their accounts. They carefully monitor actual hours spent on each account to make sure the account is being managed and run as efficiently as possible. For example, an account manager noticed a large amount of supervisory creative time was being spent on one account. Further investigation showed that the supervisors, rather than the creative department, were doing the actual creative work. The account manager pointed this out, and a junior creative team was appointed to the account, saving JKL a great deal of money.

CONTROLLABLE VERSUS NONCONTROLLABLE REVENUES AND COSTS

All costs and revenues are controllable at some level of responsibility within a company. This truth underscores the adage by the CEO of any organization that "the buck stops here." Under responsibility accounting, the critical issue is **whether the cost or revenue is controllable at the level of responsibility with which it is associated**.

A cost over which a manager has control is called a **controllable cost**. From this definition, it follows that:

1. All costs are controllable by top management because of the broad range of its authority.
2. Fewer costs are controllable as one moves down to each lower level of managerial responsibility because of the manager's decreasing authority.

In general, **costs incurred directly by a level of responsibility are controllable at that level**. In contrast, costs incurred indirectly and allocated to a responsibility level are considered to be **noncontrollable costs** at that level.

> **Helpful Hint** Are there more or fewer controllable costs as you move to higher levels of management? Answer: More.

> **Helpful Hint** The longer the time span, the more likely that the cost becomes controllable.

RESPONSIBILITY REPORTING SYSTEM

A **responsibility reporting system** involves the preparation of a report for each level of responsibility in the company's organization chart. To illustrate such a system, we will use the partial organization chart and production departments of Francis Chair Company in Illustration 10-18 (page 406).

The responsibility reporting system begins with the lowest level of responsibility for controlling costs and moves upward to each higher level. The connections between levels are detailed in Illustration 10-19 (on page 407). A brief description of the four reports for Francis Chair Company is as follows.

1. **Report D** is typical of reports that go to managers at the lowest level of responsibility shown in the organization chart—department managers. Similar reports are prepared for the managers of the Fabricating, Assembly, and Enameling Departments.
2. **Report C** is an example of reports that are sent to plant managers. It shows the costs of the Chicago plant that are controllable at the second level of

Illustration 10-18 Partial organization chart

Report A
President sees summary data of vice presidents.

Report B
Vice president sees summary of controllable costs in his/her functional area.

Report C
Plant manager sees summary of controllable costs for each department in the plant.

Report D
Department manager sees controllable costs of his/her department.

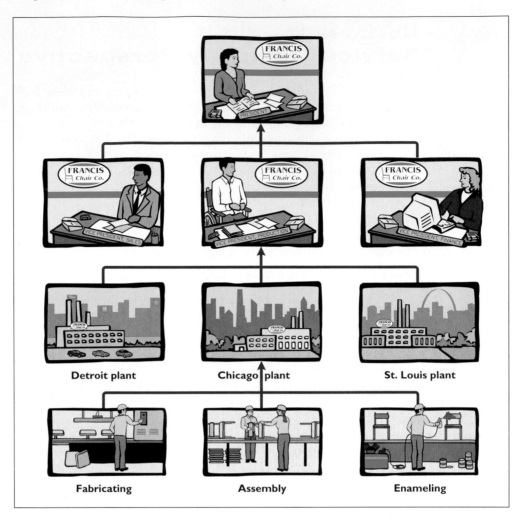

Detroit plant   Chicago plant   St. Louis plant

Fabricating   Assembly   Enameling

responsibility. In addition, Report C shows summary data for each department that is controlled by the plant manager. Similar reports are prepared for the Detroit and St. Louis plant managers.

3. **Report B** illustrates the reports at the third level of responsibility. It shows the controllable costs of the vice president of production and summary data on the three assembly plants for which this officer is responsible.

4. **Report A** is typical of the reports that go to the top level of responsibility—the president. This report shows the controllable costs and expenses of this office and summary data on the vice presidents that are accountable to the president.

A responsibility reporting system permits management by exception at each level of responsibility. And, each higher level of responsibility can obtain the detailed report for each lower level of responsibility. For example, the vice president of production in the Francis Chair Company may request the Chicago plant manager's report because this plant is $5,300 over budget.

This type of reporting system also permits comparative evaluations. In Illustration 10-19, the Chicago plant manager can easily rank the department managers' effectiveness in controlling manufacturing costs. Comparative rankings provide further incentive for a manager to control costs. For example, the Detroit plant manager will want to continue to be No. 1 in the report to the vice president of production. The Chicago plant manager will not want to remain No. 3 in future reporting periods.

Illustration 10-19 Responsibility reporting system

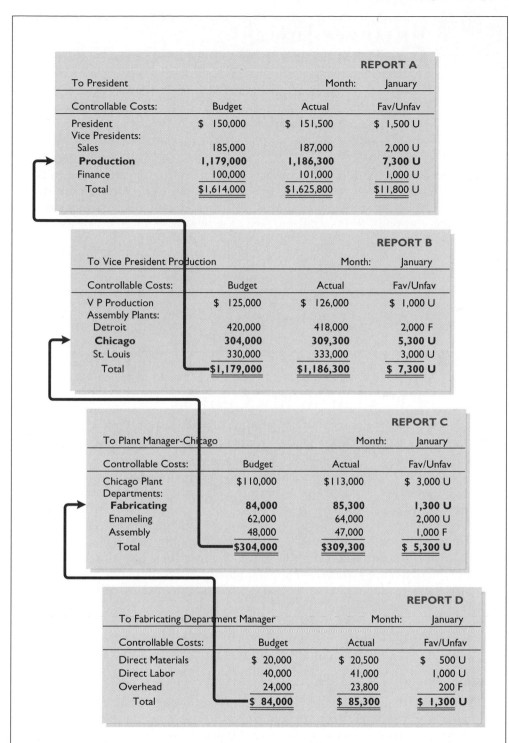

Report A
President sees summary data of vice presidents.

Report B
Vice president sees summary of controllable costs in his/her functional area.

Report C
Plant manager sees summary of controllable costs for each department in the plant.

Report D
Department manager sees controllable costs of his/her department.

Business Insight
e-Business Perspective

In Chapter 1 we discussed enterprise resource planning (ERP) software packages that collect all information regarding the results of the supply chain. A recent innovation is to attach enterprise application systems (EAS) to ERP systems. EAS systems are budgeting and planning tools. By attaching an EAS system called Hyperion Pillar to its ERP system, **Fujitsu Computer Products of America** found that it could more easily compare its budgeted amounts to its actual results. It also reduced its typical time spent on planning and budgeting from 6 to 8 weeks down to 10 to 15 days. Finally, the new system has enabled the company to respond quickly to new developments. For example, recently, the software forewarned the company of a potential oversupply problem, and provided recommendations for changes in staffing and capital needs.

SOURCE: Russ Banham, "Better Budgets," *Journal of Accountancy* (February 2000), p. 37.

Types of Responsibility Centers

There are three basic types of responsibility centers: cost centers, profit centers, and investment centers. These classifications indicate the degree of responsibility the manager has for the performance of the center.

A **cost center** incurs costs (and expenses) but does not directly generate revenues. Managers of cost centers have the authority to incur costs. They are evaluated on their ability to control costs. **Cost centers are usually either production departments or service departments.** The former participate directly in making the product. The latter provide only support services. In a **Ford Motor Company** automobile plant, the welding, painting, and assembling departments are production departments; the maintenance, cafeteria, and human resources departments are service departments. All of them are cost centers.

A **profit center** incurs costs (and expenses) and also generates revenues. Managers of profit centers are judged on the profitability of their centers. Examples of profit centers include the individual departments of a retail store, such as clothing, furniture, and automotive products, and branch offices of banks.

Like a profit center, an **investment center** incurs costs (and expenses) and generates revenues. In addition, an investment center has control over the investment funds available for use. Managers of investment centers are evaluated on both the profitability of the center and the rate of return earned on the funds invested. Investment centers are often associated with subsidiary companies. For example, **General Mills**'s product lines include cereals, helper dinner mixes, fruit snacks, popcorn, and yogurt. And, our Feature Story utility, **Duke Energy**, has operating divisions such as electric utility, energy trading, and natural gas. The manager of the investment center (product line) is able to control or significantly influence investment decisions pertaining to such matters as plant expansion and entry into new market areas. These three types of responsibility centers are depicted in Illustration 10-20 (next page).

The evaluation of a manager's performance in each type of responsibility center is explained in the remainder of this chapter.

Helpful Hint (1) Is the jewelry department of **Marshall Field's** department store a profit center or a cost center? (2) Is the props department of a movie studio a profit center or a cost center? Answers: (1) Profit center. (2) Cost center.

Illustration 10-20   Types of responsibility centers

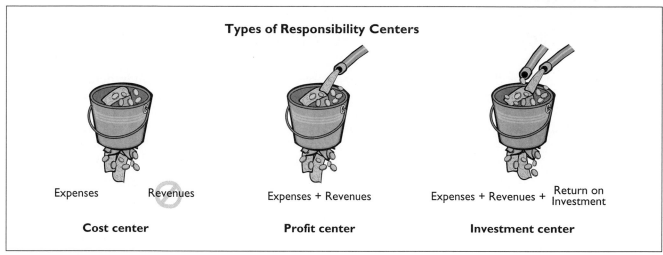

Types of Responsibility Centers

Expenses	Revenues	Expenses + Revenues	Expenses + Revenues + Return on Investment
Cost center		**Profit center**	**Investment center**

RESPONSIBILITY ACCOUNTING FOR COST CENTERS

The evaluation of a manager's performance for cost centers is based on his or her ability to meet budgeted goals for controllable costs. **Responsibility reports for cost centers compare actual controllable costs with flexible budget data.**

A responsibility report is illustrated in Illustration 10-21. The report is adapted from the flexible budget report for Fox Manufacturing Company in Illustration 10-16 on page 402. It assumes that the Finishing Department manager is able to control all manufacturing overhead costs except depreciation, property taxes, and his own monthly salary of $4,000. The remaining $1,000 ($5,000 − $4,000) of supervision costs are assumed to apply to other supervisory personnel within the Finishing Department, whose salaries are controllable by the manager.

STUDY OBJECTIVE

5

Indicate the features of responsibility reports for cost centers.

Illustration 10-21   Responsibility report for a cost center

Fox Manufacturing Company.xls

File   Edit   View   Insert   Format   Tools   Data   Window   Help   Acrobat

Fox Manufacturing Company
Finishing Department
Responsibility Report
For the Month Ended January 31, 2005

Controllable Cost	Budget	Actual	Difference Favorable - F Unfavorable - U	
Indirect materials	$13,500	$14,000	$500	U
Indirect labor	18,000	17,000	1,000	F
Utilities	4,500	4,600	100	U
Supervision	1,000	1,000	0	
	$37,000	$36,600	$400	F

Only controllable costs are included in the report, and no distinction is made between variable and fixed costs. The responsibility report continues the concept of management by exception. In this case, top management may request an explanation of the $1,000 favorable difference in indirect labor and/or the $500 unfavorable difference in indirect materials.

RESPONSIBILITY ACCOUNTING FOR PROFIT CENTERS

To evaluate the performance of a manager of a profit center, detailed information is needed about both controllable revenues and controllable costs. The operating revenues earned by a profit center, such as sales, are controllable by the manager. All variable costs (and expenses) incurred by the center are also controllable by the manager because they vary with sales. However, to determine the controllability of fixed costs, it is necessary to distinguish between direct and indirect fixed costs.

Direct and Indirect Fixed Costs

A profit center may have both direct and indirect fixed costs. **Direct fixed costs** are costs that relate specifically to one center and are incurred for the sole benefit of that center. Examples of such costs include the salaries established by the profit center manager for supervisory personnel and the cost of a timekeeping department for the center's employees. Since these fixed costs can be traced directly to a center, they are also called **traceable costs. Most direct fixed costs are controllable by the profit center manager.**

In contrast, **indirect fixed costs** pertain to a company's overall operating activities and are incurred for the benefit of more than one profit center. Indirect fixed costs are allocated to profit centers on some type of equitable basis. For example, property taxes on a building occupied by more than one center may be allocated on the basis of square feet of floor space used by each center. Or, the costs of a company's human resources department may be allocated to profit centers on the basis of the number of employees in each center. Because these fixed costs apply to more than one center, they are also called **common costs. Most indirect fixed costs are not controllable by the profit center manager.**

Responsibility Report

The responsibility report for a profit center shows budgeted and actual **controllable revenues and costs**. The report is prepared using the cost-volume-profit income statement explained in Chapter 5. In the report:

1. Controllable fixed costs are deducted from contribution margin.
2. The excess of contribution margin over controllable fixed costs is identified as **controllable margin**.
3. Noncontrollable fixed costs are not reported.

The responsibility report for the manager of the Marine Division, a profit center of Mantle Manufacturing Company, is shown in Illustration 10-22 (next page). For the year, the Marine Division also had $60,000 of indirect fixed costs that were not controllable by the profit center manager.

Controllable margin is considered to be the best measure of the manager's performance **in controlling revenues and costs**. This report shows that the manager's performance was below budgeted expectations by 10 percent ($36,000 ÷ $360,000). Top management would likely investigate the causes of this unfavorable result. Note that the report does not show the Marine Division's noncontrollable fixed costs of $60,000. These costs would be included in a report on the profitability of the profit center.

Responsibility reports for profit centers may also be prepared monthly. In addition, they may include cumulative year-to-date results.

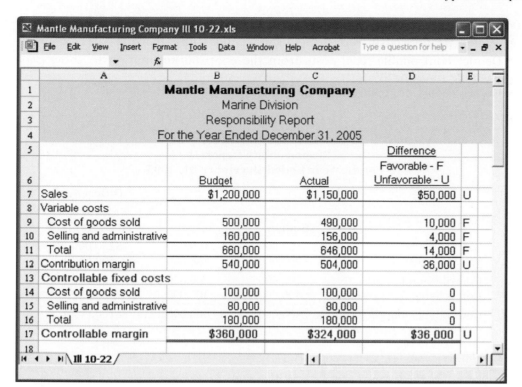

Illustration 10-22 Responsibility report for profit center

Spreadsheet: Mantle Manufacturing Company III 10-22.xls

Mantle Manufacturing Company
Marine Division
Responsibility Report
For the Year Ended December 31, 2005

	Budget	Actual	Difference Favorable - F Unfavorable - U	
Sales	$1,200,000	$1,150,000	$50,000	U
Variable costs				
Cost of goods sold	500,000	490,000	10,000	F
Selling and administrative	160,000	156,000	4,000	F
Total	660,000	646,000	14,000	F
Contribution margin	540,000	504,000	36,000	U
Controllable fixed costs				
Cost of goods sold	100,000	100,000	0	
Selling and administrative	80,000	80,000	0	
Total	180,000	180,000	0	
Controllable margin	$360,000	$324,000	$36,000	U

DECISION TOOLKIT

Decision Checkpoints	Info Needed for Decision	Tool to Use for Decision	How to Evaluate Results
Have the individual managers been held accountable for the costs and revenues under their control?	Relevant costs and revenues, where the individual manager has authority to make day-to-day decisions about the items	Responsibility reports focused on cost centers, profit centers, and investment centers as appropriate	Compare budget to actual costs and revenues for controllable items.

BEFORE YOU GO ON . . .

▶**Review It**

1. What conditions are essential for responsibility accounting?
2. What is involved in a responsibility reporting system?
3. What is the primary objective of a responsibility report for a cost center?
4. How does contribution margin differ from controllable margin in a responsibility report for a profit center?

▶**Do It**

Midwest Division operates as a profit center. It reports the following actual results for the year: Sales $1,700,000, variable costs $800,000, controllable fixed costs $400,000, noncontrollable fixed costs $200,000. Annual budgeted amounts were $1,500,000, $700,000, $400,000, and $200,000, respectively. Prepare a responsibility report for the Midwest Division for December 31, 2005.

Action Plan

- Deduct variable costs from sales to show contribution margin.
- Deduct controllable fixed costs from the contribution margin to show controllable margin.
- Do not report noncontrollable fixed costs.

Solution

MIDWEST DIVISION
Responsibility Report
For the Year Ended December 31, 2005

	Budget	Actual	Difference Favorable F Unfavorable U
Sales	$1,500,000	$1,700,000	$200,000 F
Variable costs	700,000	800,000	100,000 U
Contribution margin	800,000	900,000	100,000 F
Controllable fixed costs	400,000	400,000	–0–
Controllable margin	$ 400,000	$ 500,000	$100,000 F

Related exercise material: BE10-7 and E10-10.

☑ THE
NAVIGATOR

RESPONSIBILITY ACCOUNTING FOR INVESTMENT CENTERS

STUDY OBJECTIVE
7

Explain the basis and formula used in evaluating performance in investment centers.

As explained earlier, an investment center manager can control or significantly influence the investment funds available for use. Thus, the primary basis for evaluating the performance of a manager of an investment center is **return on investment (ROI)**. The return on investment is considered to be a useful performance measurement because it shows the **effectiveness of the manager in utilizing the assets at his or her disposal**.

Return on Investment (ROI)

The formula for computing ROI for an investment center, together with assumed illustrative data, is shown in Illustration 10-23. Both factors in the formula are controllable by the investment center manager. Operating assets consist of current assets and plant assets used in operations by the center and controlled by the manager. Nonoperating assets such as idle plant assets and land held for future use are excluded. Average operating assets are usually based on the cost or book value of the assets at the beginning and end of the year.

Illustration 10-23 ROI
formula

Controllable Margin	÷	Average Operating Assets	=	Return on Investment (ROI)
$1,000,000	÷	$5,000,000	=	20%

Responsibility Report

The scope of the investment center manager's responsibility significantly affects the content of the performance report. Since an investment center is an independent entity for operating purposes, **all fixed costs are controllable by its**

manager. For example, the manager is responsible for depreciation on investment center assets. Therefore, more fixed costs are identified as controllable in the performance report for an investment center manager than in a performance report for a profit center manager. The report also shows budgeted and actual ROI below controllable margin.

To illustrate this responsibility report, we will now assume that the Marine Division of Mantle Manufacturing Company is an investment center. It has budgeted and actual average operating assets of $2,000,000. The manager can control $60,000 of fixed costs that were not controllable when the division was a profit center. The responsibility report is shown in Illustration 10-24.

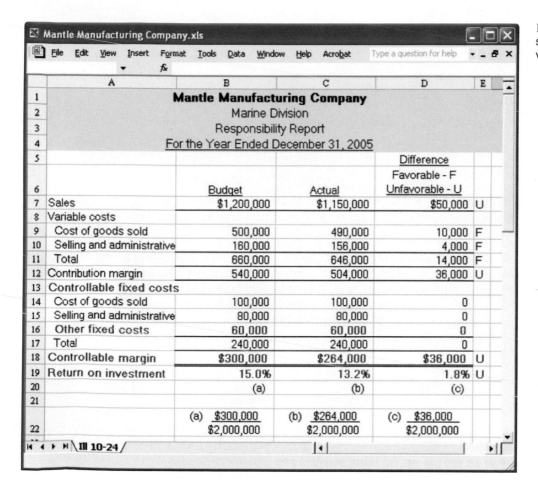

Illustration 10-24 Responsibility report for investment center

The report shows that the manager's performance based on ROI was 12 percent (1.8% ÷ 15%) below budget expectations. Top management would likely want an explanation of the reasons for this unfavorable result.

Judgmental Factors in ROI

The return on investment approach includes two judgmental factors:

1. **Valuation of operating assets.** Operating assets may be valued at acquisition cost, book value, appraised value, or market value. The first two bases are readily available from the accounting records.

2. **Margin (income) measure.** This measure may be controllable margin, income from operations, or net income.

Each of the alternative values for operating assets can provide a reliable basis for evaluating a manager's performance as long as it is consistently applied between reporting periods. However, the use of income measures other than controllable margin will not result in a valid basis for evaluating the performance of an investment center manager.[1]

Improving ROI

The manager of an investment center can improve ROI in two ways: (1) increase controllable margin, and/or (2) reduce average operating assets. To illustrate, we will use the following assumed data for the Laser Division of Berra Manufacturing.

Illustration 10-25
Assumed data for Laser
Division

Sales	$2,000,000
Variable cost	1,100,000
Contribution margin (45%)	900,000
Controllable fixed costs	300,000
Controllable margin (a)	$ 600,000
Average operating assets (b)	$5,000,000
Return on investment (a) ÷ (b)	**12%**

INCREASING CONTROLLABLE MARGIN. Controllable margin can be increased by increasing sales or by reducing variable and controllable fixed costs as follows.

1. **Increase sales 10 percent.** Sales will increase $200,000 ($2,000,000 × .10). Assuming no change in the contribution margin percentage of 45 percent, contribution margin will increase $90,000 ($200,000 × .45). Controllable margin will increase by the same amount because controllable fixed costs will not change. Thus, controllable margin becomes $690,000 ($600,000 + $90,000). The new ROI is 13.8 percent, computed as follows.

Illustration 10-26   ROI
computation—increase in
sales

$$ \text{ROI} = \frac{\text{Controllable margin}}{\text{Average operating assets}} = \frac{\$690,000}{\$5,000,000} = \textbf{13.8\%} $$

An increase in sales benefits both the investment center and the company if it results in new business. It would not benefit the company if the increase was achieved at the expense of other investment centers.

2. **Decrease variable and fixed costs 10 percent.** Total costs will decrease $140,000 [($1,100,000 + $300,000) × .10]. This reduction will result in a corresponding increase in controllable margin. Thus, controllable margin becomes $740,000 ($600,000 + $140,000). The new ROI is 14.8 percent, computed as follows.

Illustration 10-27   ROI
computation—decrease in
costs

$$ \text{ROI} = \frac{\text{Controllable margin}}{\text{Average operating assets}} = \frac{\$740,000}{\$5,000,000} = \textbf{14.8\%} $$

---

[1]Although the ROI approach is often used in evaluating investment performance, it has some disadvantages. The appendix to this chapter illustrates a second method for evaluation referred to as the residual income approach.

This course of action is clearly beneficial when waste and inefficiencies are eliminated. But, a reduction in vital costs such as required maintenance and inspections is not likely to be acceptable to top management.

REDUCING AVERAGE OPERATING ASSETS.   Assume that average operating assets are reduced 10 percent or $500,000 ($5,000,000 × .10). Average operating assets become $4,500,000 ($5,000,000 − $500,000). Since controllable margin remains unchanged at $600,000, the new ROI is 13.3 percent, computed as follows.

$$\text{ROI} = \frac{\text{Controllable margin}}{\text{Average operating assets}} = \frac{\$600,000}{\$4,500,000} = \textbf{13.3\%}$$

Illustration 10-28   ROI computation—decrease in operating assets

Reductions in operating assets may or may not be prudent. It is beneficial to eliminate overinvestment in inventories and to dispose of excessive plant assets. However, it is unwise to reduce inventories below expected needs or to dispose of essential plant assets.

DECISION TOOLKIT

Decision Checkpoints	Info Needed for Decision	Tool to Use for Decision	How to Evaluate Results
Has the investment center performed up to expectations?	Controllable margin (contribution margin minus controllable fixed costs), and average investment center operating assets	Return on investment	Compare actual ROI to expected ROI.

PRINCIPLES OF PERFORMANCE EVALUATION

Performance evaluation is at the center of responsibility accounting. **Performance evaluation** is a management function that compares actual results with budget goals. Performance evaluation involves both behavioral and reporting principles.

Behavioral Principles

The human factor is critical in evaluating performance. Behavioral principles include the following.

1. **Managers of responsibility centers should have direct input into the process of establishing budget goals of their area of responsibility.** Without such input, managers may view the goals as unrealistic or arbitrarily set by top management. Such views adversely affect the managers' motivation to meet the targeted objectives.
2. **The evaluation of performance should be based entirely on matters that are controllable by the manager being evaluated.** Criticism of a manager on matters outside his or her control reduces the effectiveness of the evaluation process. It leads to negative reactions by a manager and to doubts about the fairness of the company's evaluation policies.
3. **Top management should support the evaluation process.** As explained earlier, the evaluation process begins at the lowest level of responsibility and extends upward to the highest level of management. Managers quickly lose

faith in the process when top management ignores, overrules, or bypasses established procedures for evaluating a manager's performance.

4. **The evaluation process must allow managers to respond to their evaluations.** Evaluation is not a one-way street. Managers should have the opportunity to defend their performance. Evaluation without feedback is both impersonal and ineffective.

5. **The evaluation should identify both good and poor performance.** Praise for good performance is a powerful motivating factor for a manager. This is especially true when a manager's compensation includes rewards for meeting budget goals.

Reporting Principles

Performance evaluation under responsibility accounting should be based on certain reporting principles. These principles pertain primarily to the internal reports that provide the basis for evaluating performance. Performance reports should:

1. Contain only data that are controllable by the manager of the responsibility center.
2. Provide accurate and reliable budget data to measure performance.
3. Highlight significant differences between actual results and budget goals.
4. Be tailor-made for the intended evaluation.
5. Be prepared at reasonable intervals.

BEFORE YOU GO ON . . .

▶**Review It**

1. What is the formula for computing return on investment (ROI)?
2. Identify three actions a manager may take to improve ROI.

Using the Decision Toolkit

The manufacturing overhead budget for Reebles Company contains the following items.

Variable costs	
Indirect materials	$25,000
Indirect labor	12,000
Maintenance expenses	10,000
Manufacturing supplies	6,000
Total variable	$53,000
Fixed costs	
Supervision	$17,000
Inspection costs	1,000
Insurance expenses	2,000
Depreciation	15,000
Total fixed	$35,000

The budget was based on an estimated 2,000 units being produced. During November, 1,500 units were produced, and the following costs incurred.

Variable costs

Indirect materials	$25,200
Indirect labor	13,500
Maintenance expenses	8,200
Manufacturing supplies	5,100
Total variable	$52,000

Fixed costs

Supervision	$19,300
Inspection costs	1,200
Insurance expenses	2,200
Depreciation	14,700
Total fixed	$37,400

Instructions

(a) Determine which items would be controllable by Ed Lopat, the production manager. (Assume "supervision" excludes Lopat's own salary.)

(b) How much should have been spent during the month for the manufacture of the 1,500 units?

(c) Prepare a flexible manufacturing overhead budget report for Mr. Lopat.

(d) Prepare a responsibility report. Include only the costs that would have been controllable by Mr. Lopat. In an attached memo, describe clearly for Mr. Lopat the areas in which his performance needs to be improved.

Solution

(a) Ed Lopat should be able to control all the variable costs and the fixed costs of supervision and inspection. Insurance and depreciation ordinarily are not the responsibility of the department manager.

(b) The total variable cost per unit is $26.50 ($53,000 ÷ 2,000). The total budgeted cost during the month to manufacture 1,500 units is variable costs $39,750 (1,500 × $26.50) plus fixed costs ($35,000), for a total of $74,750 ($39,750 + $35,000).

(c)

REEBLES COMPANY
Production Department
Manufacturing Overhead Budget Report (Flexible)
For the Month Ended November 30, 2005

	Budget at 1,500 units	Actual at 1,500 units	Difference Favorable F Unfavorable U
Variable costs			
Indirect materials	$18,750	$25,200	$ 6,450 U
Indirect labor	9,000	13,500	4,500 U
Maintenance	7,500	8,200	700 U
Manufacturing supplies	4,500	5,100	600 U
Total variable	39,750	52,000	12,250 U
Fixed costs			
Supervision	17,000	19,300	2,300 U
Inspection	1,000	1,200	200 U
Insurance	2,000	2,200	200 U
Depreciation	15,000	14,700	300 F
Total fixed	35,000	37,400	2,400 U
Total costs	$74,750	$89,400	$14,650 U

(d) Because a production department is a cost center, the responsibility report should include only the costs that are controllable by the production manager. In this type of report, no distinction is made between variable and fixed costs. Budget data in the report should be based on the units actually produced.

REEBLES COMPANY
Production Department
Manufacturing Overhead Responsibility Report
For the Month Ended November 30, 2005

Controllable Cost	Budget	Actual	Difference Favorable F Unfavorable U
Indirect materials	$18,750	$25,200	$ 6,450 U
Indirect labor	9,000	13,500	4,500 U
Maintenance	7,500	8,200	700 U
Manufacturing supplies	4,500	5,100	600 U
Supervision	17,000	19,300	2,300 U
Inspection	1,000	1,200	200 U
Total	$57,750	$72,500	$14,750 U

To: Mr. Ed Lopat, Production Manager

From: _____, Vice-President of Production

Subject: Performance Evaluation for the Month of November

Your performance in controlling costs that are your responsibility was very disappointing in the month of November. As indicated in the accompanying responsibility report, total costs were $14,750 over budget. On a percentage basis, costs were 26% over budget. As you can see, actual costs were over budget for every cost item. In three instances, costs were significantly over budget (indirect materials 34%, indirect labor 50%, and supervision 14%).

Ed, it is imperative that you get costs under control in your department as soon as possible.

I think we need to talk about ways to implement more effective cost control measures. I would like to meet with you in my office at 9 a.m. on Wednesday to discuss possible alternatives.

Summary of Study Objectives

1   *Describe the concept of budgetary control.* Budgetary control consists of (a) preparing periodic budget reports that compare actual results with planned objectives, (b) analyzing the differences to determine their causes, (c) taking appropriate corrective action, and (d) modifying future plans, if necessary.

2   *Evaluate the usefulness of static budget reports.* Static budget reports are useful in evaluating the progress toward planned sales and profit goals. They are also appropriate in assessing a manager's effectiveness in controlling costs when (a) actual activity closely approximates the master budget activity level, and/or

(b) the behavior of the costs in response to changes in activity is fixed.

3   *Explain the development of flexible budgets and the usefulness of flexible budget reports.* To develop the flexible budget it is necessary to:
(a) Identify the activity index and the relevant range of activity.
(b) Identify the variable costs, and determine the budgeted variable cost per unit of activity for each cost.
(c) Identify the fixed costs, and determine the budgeted amount for each cost.

(d) Prepare the budget for selected increments of activity within the relevant range.

Flexible budget reports permit an evaluation of a manager's performance in controlling production and costs.

4 *Describe the concept of responsibility accounting.* Responsibility accounting involves accumulating and reporting revenues and costs on the basis of the individual manager who has the authority to make the day-to-day decisions about the items. The evaluation of a manager's performance is based on the matters directly under the manager's control. In responsibility accounting, it is necessary to distinguish between controllable and noncontrollable fixed costs and to identify three types of responsibility centers: cost, profit, and investment.

5 *Indicate the features of responsibility reports for cost centers.* Responsibility reports for cost centers compare actual costs with flexible budget data. The reports show only controllable costs, and no distinction is made between variable and fixed costs.

6 *Identify the content of responsibility reports for profit centers.* Responsibility reports show contribution margin, controllable fixed costs, and controllable margin for each profit center.

7 *Explain the basis and formula used in evaluating performance in investment centers.* The primary basis for evaluating performance in investment centers is return on investment (ROI). The formula for computing ROI for investment centers is: Controllable margin ÷ Average operating assets.

☑ THE NAVIGATOR

DECISION TOOLKIT—A SUMMARY

Decision Checkpoints ☑	Info Needed for Decision	Tool to Use for Decision	How to Evaluate Results
Are the increased costs resulting from increased production reasonable?	Variable costs projected at different levels of production	Flexible budget	After taking into account different production levels, results are favorable if expenses are less than budgeted amounts.
Have the individual managers been held accountable for the costs and revenues under their control?	Relevant costs and revenues, where the individual manager has authority to make day-to-day decisions about the items	Responsibility reports focused on cost centers, profit centers, and investment centers as appropriate	Compare budget to actual costs and revenues for controllable items.
Has the investment center performed up to expectations?	Controllable margin (contribution margin minus controllable fixed costs), and average investment center operating assets	Return on investment	Compare actual ROI to expected ROI.

APPENDIX
RESIDUAL INCOME—ANOTHER PERFORMANCE MEASUREMENT

Although most companies use ROI in evaluating their investment performance, ROI has a significant disadvantage. To illustrate, let's look at the Electronics Division of Pujols Manufacturing Company. It has an ROI of 20 percent computed as follows.

STUDY OBJECTIVE
8
Explain the difference between ROI and residual income.

Illustration 10A-1   ROI formula

Controllable Margin	÷	Average Operating Assets	=	Return on Investment (ROI)
$1,000,000	÷	$5,000,000	=	20%

The Electronics Division is considering producing a new product, a GPS satellite tracker (hereafter referred to as Tracker), for its boats. To produce Tracker, operating assets will have to increase $2,000,000. Tracker is expected to generate an additional $260,000 of controllable margin. Illustration 10A-2 shows how Tracker will effect ROI.

Illustration 10A-2 ROI comparison

	Without Tracker	Tracker	With Tracker
Controllable margin (a)	$1,000,000	$ 260,000	$1,260,000
Average operating assets (b)	$5,000,000	$2,000,000	$7,000,000
Return on investment [(a) ÷ (b)]	20%	13%	18%

The investment in Tracker reduces ROI from 20 percent to 18 percent.

Let's suppose that you are the manager of the Electronics Division and must make the decision to produce or not produce Tracker. If you were evaluated using ROI, you probably would not produce Tracker because your ROI would drop from 20 percent to 18 percent. The problem with this ROI analysis is that it ignores an important variable, the minimum rate of return on a company's operating assets. The **minimum rate of return** is the rate at which the Electronics Division can cover its costs and earn a profit. Assuming that the Electronics Division has a minimum rate of return of 10 percent, it should invest in Tracker because its ROI of 13 percent is greater than 10 percent.

Residual Income Compared to ROI

To evaluate performance using the minimum rate of return, companies use the residual income approach. **Residual income** is the income that remains after subtracting from the controllable margin the minimum rate of return on a company's average operating assets. The residual income for Tracker would be computed as follows.

Illustration 10A-3 Residual income formula

Controllable Margin	−	Minimum Rate of Return × Average Operating Assets	=	Residual Income
$260,000	−	10% × $2,000,000	=	$60,000

As shown, the residual income related to the Tracker investment is $60,000. Illustration 10A-4 indicates how residual income changes as the additional investment is made.

Illustration 10A-4 Residual income comparison

	Without Tracker	Tracker	With Tracker
Controllable margin (a)	$1,000,000	$260,000	$1,260,000
Average operating assets × 10% (b)	500,000	200,000	700,000
Residual income [(a) − (b)]	$ 500,000	$ 60,000	**$ 560,000**

This example illustrates how performance evaluation based on ROI can be misleading and can even cause managers to reject projects that would actually increase income for the company. As a result, many companies such as **Coca-Cola**, **Briggs and Stratton**, **Eli Lilly**, and **Siemens AG** use residual income (or a variant often referred to as economic value added) to evaluate investment alternatives and measure company performance.

Residual Income Weakness

It might appear from the above discussion that the goal of any company should be to maximize the total amount of residual income in each division. This goal, however, ignores the fact that one division might use substantially fewer assets to attain the same level of residual income as another division. For example, we know that to produce Tracker, the Electronics Division of Pujols Manufacturing used $2,000,000 of average operating assets to generate $260,000 of controllable margin. Now let's say a different division produced a product called SeaDog, which used $4,000,000 to generate $460,000 of controllable margin, as shown in Illustration 10A-5.

	Tracker	SeaDog
Controllable margin (a)	$260,000	$460,000
Average operating assets × 10% (b)	200,000	400,000
Residual income [(a) − (b)]	$ 60,000	$ 60,000

Illustration 10A-5 Comparison of two products

If the performance of these two investments were evaluated using residual income, they would be considered equal: Both products have the same total residual income. This ignores, however, the fact that SeaDog required **twice** as many operating assets to achieve the same level of residual income.

Summary of Study Objective for Appendix

8 *Explain the difference between ROI and residual income.* ROI is controllable margin divided by average operating assets. Residual income is the income that remains after subtracting the minimum rate of return on a company's average operating assets. ROI sometimes provides misleading results because profitable investments are often rejected when the investment reduces ROI but increases overall profitability.

Glossary

Budgetary control The use of budgets to control operations. (p. 393)

Controllable cost A cost over which a manager has control. (p. 405)

Controllable margin Contribution margin less controllable fixed costs. (p. 410)

Cost center A responsibility center that incurs costs but does not directly generate revenues. (p. 408)

Decentralization Control of operations is delegated to many managers throughout the organization. (p. 404)

Direct fixed costs Costs that relate specifically to a responsibility center and are incurred for the sole benefit of the center. (p. 410)

Flexible budget A projection of budget data for various levels of activity. (p. 396)

Indirect fixed costs Costs that are incurred for the benefit of more than one profit center. (p. 410)

Investment center A responsibility center that incurs costs, generates revenues, and has control over the investment funds available for use. (p. 408)

Management by exception The review of budget reports by top management focused entirely or primarily on differences between actual results and planned objectives. (p. 402)

Noncontrollable costs Costs incurred indirectly and allocated to a responsibility center that are not controllable at that level. (p. 405)

Profit center A responsibility center that incurs costs and also generates revenues. (p. 408)

Residual income The income that remains after subtracting from the controllable margin the minimum rate of return on a company's operating assets. (p. 420)

Responsibility accounting A part of management accounting that involves accumulating and reporting revenues and costs on the basis of the manager who has the authority to make the day-to-day decisions about the items. (p. 403)

Responsibility reporting system The preparation of reports for each level of responsibility in the company's organization chart. (p. 405)

Return on investment (ROI) A measure of management's effectiveness in utilizing assets at its disposal in an investment center. (p. 412)

Segment An area of responsibility in decentralized operations. (p. 404)

Static budget A projection of budget data at one level of activity. (p. 394)

Demonstration Problem

Glenda Company uses a flexible budget for manufacturing overhead based on direct labor hours. For 2005 the master overhead budget for the Packaging Department based on 300,000 direct labor hours was as follows.

Variable Costs		Fixed Costs	
Indirect labor	$360,000	Supervision	$ 60,000
Supplies and lubricants	150,000	Depreciation	24,000
Maintenance	210,000	Property taxes	18,000
Utilities	120,000	Insurance	12,000
	$840,000		$114,000

During July, 24,000 direct labor hours were worked. The company incurred the following variable costs in July: indirect labor $30,200, supplies and lubricants $11,600, maintenance $17,500, and utilities $9,200. Actual fixed overhead costs were the same as monthly budgeted fixed costs.

Instructions

Prepare a flexible budget report for the Packaging Department for July.

Action Plan

- Use budget data for actual direct labor hours worked.
- Classify each cost as variable or fixed.
- Determine the difference between budgeted and actual costs.
- Identify the difference as favorable or unfavorable.
- Determine the difference in total variable costs, total fixed costs, and total costs.

Solution to Demonstration Problem

GLENDA COMPANY
Manufacturing Overhead Budget Report (Flexible)
Packaging Department
For the Month Ended July 31, 2005

Direct labor hours (DLH)	Budget 24,000 DLH	Actual Costs 24,000 DLH	Difference Favorable F Unfavorable U
Variable costs			
Indirect labor	$28,800	$30,200	$1,400 U
Supplies and lubricants	12,000	11,600	400 F
Maintenance	16,800	17,500	700 U
Utilities	9,600	9,200	400 F
Total variable	67,200	68,500	1,300 U

	Budget	**Actual Costs**	**Difference** **Favorable F** **Unfavorable U**
Direct labor hours (DLH)	24,000 DLH	24,000 DLH	
Fixed costs			
Supervision	$ 5,000	$ 5,000	–0–
Depreciation	2,000	2,000	–0–
Property taxes	1,500	1,500	–0–
Insurance	1,000	1,000	–0–
Total fixed	9,500	9,500	–0–
Total costs	$76,700	$78,000	$1,300 U

☑ THE NAVIGATOR

Note: All asterisked Questions, Exercises, and Problems relate to the material contained in the appendix to the chapter.

Self-Study Questions

Self-Study/Self-Test

Answers are at the end of the chapter.

(SO 1) 1. Budgetary control involves all but one of the following:
   (a) modifying future plans.
   (b) analyzing differences.
   (c) using static budgets.
   (d) determining differences between actual and planned results.

(SO 2) 2. A static budget is useful in controlling costs when cost behavior is:
   (a) mixed.   (c) variable.
   (b) fixed.   (d) linear.

(SO 3) 3. At zero direct labor hours in a flexible budget graph, the total budgeted cost line intersects the vertical axis at $30,000. At 10,000 direct labor hours, a horizontal line drawn from the total budgeted cost line intersects the vertical axis at $90,000. Fixed and variable costs may be expressed as:
   (a) $30,000 fixed plus $6 per direct labor hour variable.
   (b) $30,000 fixed plus $9 per direct labor hour variable.
   (c) $60,000 fixed plus $3 per direct labor hour variable.
   (d) $60,000 fixed plus $6 per direct labor hour variable.

(SO 3) 4. At 9,000 direct labor hours, the flexible budget for indirect materials is $27,000. If $28,000 of indirect materials costs are incurred at 9,200 direct labor hours, the flexible budget report should show the following difference for indirect materials:
   (a) $1,000 unfavorable.
   (b) $1,000 favorable.

   (c) $400 favorable.
   (d) $400 unfavorable.

(SO 4) 5. Under responsibility accounting, the evaluation of a manager's performance is based on matters that the manager:
   (a) directly controls.
   (b) directly and indirectly controls.
   (c) indirectly controls.
   (d) has shared responsibility for with another manager.

(SO 4) 6. Responsibility centers include:
   (a) cost centers.
   (b) profit centers.
   (c) investment centers.
   (d) all of the above.

(SO 5) 7. Responsibility reports for cost centers:
   (a) distinguish between fixed and variable costs.
   (b) use static budget data.
   (c) include both controllable and noncontrollable costs.
   (d) include only controllable costs.

(SO 6) 8. In a responsibility report for a profit center, controllable fixed costs are deducted from contribution margin to show:
   (a) profit center margin.
   (b) controllable margin.
   (c) net income.
   (d) income from operations.

(SO 7) 9. In the formula for return on investment (ROI), the factors for controllable margin and operating assets are, respectively:
   (a) controllable margin percentage and total operating assets.

(b) controllable margin dollars and average operating assets.

(c) controllable margin dollars and total assets.

(d) controllable margin percentage and average operating assets.

(SO 7) 10. A manager of an investment center can improve ROI by:

(a) increasing average operating assets.

(b) reducing sales.

(c) increasing variable costs.

(d) reducing variable and/or controllable fixed costs.

*11. In the formula for residual income, the factors for computing residual income are: (SO 8)

(a) contribution margin, controllable margin, and average operating assets.

(b) controllable margin, average operating assets, and ROI.

(c) controllable margin, average operating assets, and minimum rate of return.

(d) controllable margin, ROI, and minimum rate of return.

Questions

1. (a) What is budgetary control?

   (b) Tony Crespino is describing budgetary control. What steps should be included in Tony's description?

2. The following purposes are part of a budgetary reporting system: (a) Determine efficient use of materials. (b) Control overhead costs. (c) Determine whether income objectives are being met. For each purpose, indicate the name of the report, the frequency of the report, and the primary recipient(s) of the report.

3. How may a budget report for the second quarter differ from a budget report for the first quarter?

4. Don Cox questions the usefulness of a master sales budget in evaluating sales performance. Is there justification for Don's concern? Explain.

5. Under what circumstances may a static budget be an appropriate basis for evaluating a manager's effectiveness in controlling costs?

6. "A flexible budget is really a series of static budgets." Is this true? Why?

7. The static manufacturing overhead budget based on 40,000 direct labor hours shows budgeted indirect labor costs of $56,000. During March, the department incurs $65,000 of indirect labor while working 45,000 direct labor hours. Is this a favorable or unfavorable performance? Why?

8. A static overhead budget based on 40,000 direct labor hours shows Factory Insurance $6,500 as a fixed cost. At the 50,000 direct labor hours worked in March, factory insurance costs were $6,200. Is this a favorable or unfavorable performance? Why?

9. Kate Coulter is confused about how a flexible budget is prepared. Identify the steps for Kate.

10. Alou Company has prepared a graph of flexible budget data. At zero direct labor hours, the total budgeted cost line intersects the vertical axis at $35,000. At 10,000 direct labor hours, the line drawn from the total budgeted cost line intersects the vertical axis at $85,000. How may the fixed and variable costs be expressed?

11. The flexible budget formula is fixed costs $40,000 plus variable costs of $3 per direct labor hour. What is the total budgeted cost at (a) 9,000 hours and (b) 12,345 hours?

12. What is management by exception? What criteria may be used in identifying exceptions?

13. What is responsibility accounting? Explain the purpose of responsibility accounting.

14. Ann Wilkins is studying for an accounting examination. Describe for Ann what conditions are necessary for responsibility accounting to be used effectively.

15. Distinguish between controllable and noncontrollable costs.

16. How do responsibility reports differ from budget reports?

17. What is the relationship, if any, between a responsibility reporting system and a company's organization chart?

18. Distinguish among the three types of responsibility centers.

19. (a) What costs are included in a performance report for a cost center? (b) In the report, are variable and fixed costs identified?

20. How do direct fixed costs differ from indirect fixed costs? Are both types of fixed costs controllable?

21. Lori Quan is confused about controllable margin reported in an income statement for a profit center. How is this margin computed, and what is its primary purpose?

22. What is the primary basis for evaluating the performance of the manager of an investment center? Indicate the formula for this basis.

23. Explain the ways that ROI can be improved.

24. Indicate two behavioral principles that pertain to (a) the manager being evaluated and (b) top management.

*25. What is a major disadvantage of using ROI to evaluate investment and company performance?

*26. What is residual income, and what is one of its major weaknesses?

Brief Exercises

BE10-1 For the quarter ended March 31, 2005, Westphal Company accumulates the following sales data for its product, Garden-Tools: $315,000 budget; $304,000 actual. Prepare a static budget report for the quarter.

Prepare static budget report.
(SO 2)

BE10-2 Data for Westphal Company are given in BE10-1. In the second quarter, budgeted sales were $380,000, and actual sales were $386,000. Prepare a static budget report for the second quarter and for the year to date.

Prepare static budget report for 2 quarters.
(SO 2)

BE10-3 In Hinsdale Company, direct labor is $20 per hour. The company expects to operate at 10,000 direct labor hours each month. In January 2005, direct labor totaling $205,000 is incurred in working 10,400 hours. Prepare (a) a static budget report and (b) a flexible budget report. Evaluate the usefulness of each report.

Show usefulness of flexible budgets in evaluating performance.
(SO 3)

BE10-4 Dukane Company expects to produce 1,200,000 units of Product XX in 2005. Monthly production is expected to range from 80,000 to 120,000 units. Budgeted variable manufacturing costs per unit are: direct materials $4, direct labor $6, and overhead $9. Budgeted fixed manufacturing costs per unit for depreciation are $2 and for supervision are $1. Prepare a flexible manufacturing budget for the relevant range value using 20,000 unit increments.

Prepare a flexible budget for variable costs.
(SO 3)

BE10-5 Data for Dukane Company are given in BE10-4. In March 2005, the company incurs the following costs in producing 100,000 units: direct materials $425,000, direct labor $590,000, and variable overhead $915,000. Prepare a flexible budget report for March. Were costs controlled?

Prepare flexible budget report.
(SO 3)

BE10-6 In the Assembly Department of Emil Company, budgeted and actual manufacturing overhead costs for the month of April 2005 were as follows.

Prepare a responsibility report for a cost center.
(SO 5)

	Budget	**Actual**
Indirect materials	$15,000	$14,300
Indirect labor	20,000	20,800
Utilities	10,000	10,750
Supervision	5,000	5,000

All costs are controllable by the department manager. Prepare a responsibility report for April for the cost center.

BE10-7 Advent Manufacturing Company accumulates the following summary data for the year ending December 31, 2005, for its Water Division which it operates as a profit center: sales—$2,000,000 budget, $2,080,000 actual; variable costs—$1,000,000 budget, $1,030,000 actual; and controllable fixed costs—$300,000 budget, $310,000 actual. Prepare a responsibility report for the Water Division.

Prepare a responsibility report for a profit center.
(SO 6)

BE10-8 For the year ending December 31, 2005, Nathan Company accumulates the following data for the Plastics Division which it operates as an investment center: contribution margin—$700,000 budget, $715,000 actual; controllable fixed costs—$300,000 budget, $305,000 actual. Average operating assets for the year were $2,000,000. Prepare a responsibility report for the Plastics Division beginning with contribution margin.

Prepare a responsibility report for an investment center.
(SO 7)

BE10-9 For its three investment centers, Stahl Company accumulates the following data:

Compute return on investment using the ROI formula.
(SO 7)

	I	**II**	**III**
Sales	$2,000,000	$3,000,000	$ 4,000,000
Controllable margin	1,200,000	2,000,000	3,000,000
Average operating assets	6,000,000	8,000,000	10,000,000

Compute the return on investment (ROI) for each center.

BE10-10 Data for the investment centers for Stahl Company are given in BE10-9. The centers expect the following changes in the next year: (I) increase sales 15%; (II) decrease costs $200,000; (III) decrease average operating assets $400,000. Compute the expected return on investment (ROI) for each center. Assume center I has a contribution margin percentage of 80%.

Compute return on investment under changed conditions.
(SO 7)

Compute ROI and residual income.
(SO 8)

*BE10-11 Wasson, Inc. reports the following financial information.

Average operating assets	$3,000,000
Controllable margin	$ 600,000
Minimum rate of return	9%

Compute the return on investment and the residual income.

Compute ROI and residual income.
(SO 8)

*BE10-12 Presented below is information related to the Santa Clara Division of Cut Wood, Inc.

Contribution margin	$1,200,000
Controllable margin	$ 800,000
Average operating assets	$3,200,000
Minimum rate of return	16%

Compute the Santa Clara's return on investment and residual income.

Exercises

Prepare flexible manufacturing overhead budget.
(SO 3)

E10-1 Twyla Company uses a flexible budget for manufacturing overhead based on direct labor hours. Variable manufacturing overhead costs per direct labor hour are as follows.

Indirect labor	$1.00
Indirect materials	0.60
Utilities	0.40

Fixed overhead costs per month are: Supervision $4,000, Depreciation $1,500, and Property Taxes $800. The company believes it will normally operate in a range of 7,000–10,000 direct labor hours per month.

Instructions
Prepare a monthly flexible manufacturing overhead budget for 2005 for the expected range of activity, using increments of 1,000 direct labor hours.

Prepare flexible budget reports for manufacturing overhead costs, and comment on findings.
(SO 3)

E10-2 Using the information in E10-1, assume that in July 2005, Twyla Company incurs the following manufacturing overhead costs.

Variable Costs		**Fixed Costs**	
Indirect labor	$8,700	Supervision	$4,000
Indirect materials	5,300	Depreciation	1,500
Utilities	3,200	Property taxes	800

Instructions
(a) Prepare a flexible budget performance report, assuming that the company worked 9,000 direct labor hours during the month.
(b) Prepare a flexible budget performance report, assuming that the company worked 8,500 direct labor hours during the month.
(c) ▭▭▭▭▷ Comment on your findings.

Prepare flexible selling expense budget.
(SO 3)

E10-3 Vincent Company uses flexible budgets to control its selling expenses. Monthly sales are expected to range from $170,000 to $200,000. Variable costs and their percentage relationship to sales are: Sales Commissions 6%, Advertising 4%, Traveling 3%, and Delivery 2%. Fixed selling expenses will consist of Sales Salaries $32,000, Depreciation on Delivery Equipment $7,000, and Insurance on Delivery Equipment $1,000.

Instructions
Prepare a monthly flexible budget for each $10,000 increment of sales within the relevant range for the year ending December 31, 2005.

E10-4 The actual selling expenses incurred in March 2005 by Vincent Company are as follows.

Variable Expenses		Fixed Expenses	
Sales commissions	$11,000	Sales salaries	$32,000
Advertising	7,000	Depreciation	7,000
Travel	5,100	Insurance	1,000
Delivery	3,500		

Instructions
(a) Prepare a flexible budget performance report for March using the budget data in E10-3, assuming that March sales were $170,000. Expected and actual sales are the same.
(b) Prepare a flexible budget performance report, assuming that March sales were $180,000. Expected sales and actual sales are the same.
(c) ▭▭▭▭▷ Comment on the importance of using flexible budgets in evaluating the performance of the sales manager.

E10-5 Sublette Company's manufacturing overhead budget for the first quarter of 2005 contained the following data.

Variable Costs		Fixed Costs	
Indirect materials	$12,000	Supervisory salaries	$36,000
Indirect labor	10,000	Depreciation	7,000
Utilities	8,000	Property taxes and insurance	8,000
Maintenance	5,000	Maintenance	5,000

Actual variable costs were: indirect materials $13,800, indirect labor $9,600, utilities $8,700, and maintenance $4,200. Actual fixed costs equaled budgeted costs except for property taxes and insurance, which were $8,400.

All costs are considered controllable by the production department manager except for depreciation, and property taxes and insurance.

Instructions
(a) Prepare a flexible manufacturing overhead budget report for the first quarter.
(b) Prepare a responsibility report for the first quarter.

E10-6 As sales manager, Shawn Keyser was given the following static budget report for selling expenses in the Clothing Department of Dunham Company for the month of October.

DUNHAM COMPANY
Clothing Department
Budget Report
For the Month Ended October 31, 2005

	Budget	Actual	Difference Favorable F Unfavorable U
Sales in units	8,000	10,000	2,000 F
Variable expenses			
Sales commissions	$ 2,000	$ 2,600	$ 600 U
Advertising expense	800	850	50 U
Travel expense	4,400	4,900	500 U
Free samples given out	1,600	1,300	300 F
Total variable	8,800	9,650	850 U
Fixed expenses			
Rent	1,500	1,500	–0–
Sales salaries	1,200	1,200	–0–
Office salaries	800	800	–0–
Depreciation—autos (sales staff)	500	500	–0–
Total fixed	4,000	4,000	–0–
Total expenses	$12,800	$13,650	$ 850 U

As a result of this budget report, Shawn was called into the president's office and congratulated on his fine sales performance. He was reprimanded, however, for allowing his costs to get out of control. Shawn knew something was wrong with the performance report that he had been given. However, he was not sure what to do, and comes to you for advice.

Instructions
(a) Prepare a budget report based on flexible budget data to help Shawn.
(b) Should Shawn have been reprimanded? Explain.

Prepare and discuss a responsibility report.
(SO 3, 5)

E10-7 Pronto Plumbing Company is a newly formed company specializing in plumbing services for home and business. The owner, Paul Pronto, had divided the company into two segments: Home Plumbing Services and Business Plumbing Services. Each segment is run by its own supervisor, while basic selling and administrative services are shared by both segments.

Paul has asked you to help him create a performance reporting system that will allow him to measure each segment's performance in terms of its profitability. To that end, the following information has been collected on the Home Plumbing Services segment for the first quarter of 2005.

	Budgeted	Actual
Service revenue	$25,000	$26,000
Allocated portion of:		
Building depreciation	11,000	11,000
Advertising	5,000	4,200
Billing	3,500	3,000
Property taxes	1,200	1,000
Material and supplies	1,500	1,200
Supervisory salaries	9,000	9,400
Insurance	4,000	3,500
Wages	3,000	3,300
Gas and oil	2,700	3,400
Equipment depreciation	1,600	1,300

Instructions
(a) Prepare a responsibility report for the first quarter of 2005 for the Home Plumbing Services segment.
(b) ✏️ Write a memo to Paul Pronto discussing the principles that should be used when preparing performance reports.

State total budgeted cost formulas, and prepare flexible budget graph.
(SO 3)

E10-8 Sherrer Company has two production departments, Fabricating and Assembling. At a department managers' meeting, the controller uses flexible budget graphs to explain total budgeted costs. Separate graphs based on direct labor hours are used for each department. The graphs show the following.

1. At zero direct labor hours, the total budgeted cost line and the fixed cost line intersect the vertical axis at $40,000 in the Fabricating Department and $35,000 in the Assembling Department.
2. At normal capacity of 50,000 direct labor hours, the line drawn from the total budgeted cost line intersects the vertical axis at $160,000 in the Fabricating Department, and $110,000 in the Assembling Department.

Instructions
(a) State the total budgeted cost formula for each department.
(b) Compute the total budgeted cost for each department, assuming actual direct labor hours worked were 53,000 and 47,000, in the Fabricating and Assembling Departments, respectively.
(c) Prepare the flexible budget graph for the Fabricating Department, assuming the maximum direct labor hours in the relevant range is 100,000. Use increments of 10,000 direct labor hours on the horizontal axis and increments of $50,000 on the vertical axis.

Prepare reports in a responsibility reporting system.
(SO 4)

E10-9 Marcum Company's organization chart includes the president; the vice president of production; three assembly plants—Dallas, Atlanta, and Tucson; and two departments within each plant—Machining and Finishing. Budget and actual manufacturing cost data for July 2005 are as follows:

Finishing Department—Dallas: Direct materials $41,000 actual, $45,000 budget; direct labor $83,000 actual, $82,000 budget; manufacturing overhead $51,000 actual, $49,200 budget.

Machining Department—Dallas: Total manufacturing costs $220,000 actual, $214,000 budget.

Atlanta Plant: Total manufacturing costs $424,000 actual, $421,000 budget.

Tucson Plant: Total manufacturing costs $494,000 actual, $499,000 budget.

The Dallas plant manager's office costs were $95,000 actual and $92,000 budget. The vice president of production's office costs were $132,000 actual and $130,000 budget. Office costs are not allocated to departments and plants.

Instructions

Using the format on page 407, prepare the reports in a responsibility system for:

(a) The Finishing Department—Dallas.
(b) The plant manager—Dallas.
(c) The vice president of production.

E10-10   Longhead Manufacturing Inc. has three divisions which are operated as profit centers. Actual operating data for the divisions listed alphabetically are as follows.

Compute missing amounts in responsibility reports for three profit centers, and prepare a report.
(SO 6)

Operating Data	Women's Shoes	Men's Shoes	Children's Shoes
Contribution margin	$250,000	(3)	$170,000
Controllable fixed costs	100,000	(4)	(5)
Controllable margin	(1)	$ 90,000	96,000
Sales	600,000	450,000	(6)
Variable costs	(2)	320,000	250,000

Instructions

(a) Compute the missing amounts. Show computations.
(b) Prepare a responsibility report for the Women's Shoe Division assuming (1) the data are for the month ended June 30, 2005, and (2) all data equal budget except variable costs which are $10,000 over budget.

E10-11   The Green Division of Campana Company reported the following data for the current year.

Compute ROI for current year and for possible future changes.
(SO 7)

Sales	$3,000,000
Variable costs	1,800,000
Controllable fixed costs	600,000
Average operating assets	5,000,000

Top management is unhappy with the investment center's return on investment (ROI). It asks the manager of the Green Division to submit plans to improve ROI in the next year. The manager believes it is feasible to consider the following independent courses of action.

1. Increase sales by $320,000 with no change in the contribution margin percentage.
2. Reduce variable costs by $100,000.
3. Reduce average operating assets by 4%.

Instructions

(a) Compute the return on investment (ROI) for the current year.
(b) Using the ROI formula, compute the ROI under each of the proposed courses of action. (Round to one decimal.)

E10-12   The Medina and Ortiz Dental Clinic provides both preventive and orthodontic dental services. The two owners, Martin Medina and Olga Ortiz, operate the clinic as two separate investment centers: Preventive Services and Orthodontic Services. Each of them is in charge of one of the centers: Martin for Preventive Services and Olga for Orthodontic Services. Each month they prepare an income statement on the two centers to evaluate performance and make decisions about how to improve the operational efficiency and profitability of the clinic.

Prepare a responsibility report for an investment center.
(SO 7)

Recently they have been concerned about the profitability of the Preventive Services operations. For several months it has been reporting a loss. Shown below is the responsibility report for the month of May 2005.

	Actual	Difference from Budget
Service revenue	$ 40,000	$1,000 F
Variable costs:		
Filling materials	5,000	100 U
Novocain	4,000	200 U
Supplies	2,000	250 F
Dental assistant wages	2,500	–0–
Utilities	500	50 U
Total variable costs	14,000	100 U
Fixed costs:		
Allocated portion of receptionist's salary	3,000	200 U
Dentist salary	10,000	500 U
Equipment depreciation	6,000	–0–
Allocated portion of building depreciation	15,000	1,000 U
Total fixed costs	34,000	1,700 U
Operating income (loss)	$(8,000)	$ 800 U

In addition, the owners know that the investment in operating assets at the beginning of the month was $82,400, and it was $77,600 at the end of the month. They have asked for your assistance in evaluating their current performance reporting system.

Instructions
(a) Prepare a responsibility report for an investment center as illustrated in the chapter.
(b) Write a memo to the owners discussing the deficiencies of their current reporting system.

Prepare missing amounts in responsibility reports for three investment centers.
(SO 7)

E10-13 The Transamerica Transportation Company uses a responsibility reporting system to measure the performance of its three investment centers: Planes, Taxis, and Limos. Segment performance is measured using a system of responsibility reports and return on investment calculations. The allocation of resources within the company and the segment managers' bonuses are based in part on the results shown in these reports.

Recently, the company was the victim of a computer virus that deleted portions of the company's accounting records. This was discovered when the current period's responsibility reports were being prepared. The printout of the actual operating results appeared as follows.

	Planes	Taxis	Limos
Service revenue	$?	$500,000	$?
Variable costs	5,500,000	?	320,000
Contribution margin	?	200,000	480,000
Controllable fixed costs	1,500,000	?	?
Controllable margin	?	80,000	240,000
Average operating assets	25,000,000	?	1,600,000
Return on investment	12%	10%	?

Instructions
Determine the missing pieces of information above.

Compare ROI and residual income.
(SO 8)

*E10-14 Presented below is selected information for three regional divisions of Yono Company.

	Divisions		
	North	West	South
Contribution margin	$ 300,000	$ 500,000	$ 400,000
Controllable margin	$ 150,000	$ 400,000	$ 225,000
Average operating assets	$1,000,000	$2,000,000	$1,500,000
Minimum rate of return	13%	16%	10%

Instructions

(a) Compute the return on investment for each division.
(b) Compute the residual income for each division.
(c) Assume that each division has an investment opportunity that would provide a rate of return of 19%.
   (1) If ROI is used to measure performance, which division or divisions will probably make the additional investment?
   (2) If residual income is used to measure performance, which division or divisions will probably make the additional investment?

*E10-15   Presented below is selected financial information for two divisions of Capital Brewery. You are to supply the missing information for the lettered items.

Fill in information related to ROI and residual income.
(SO 8)

	Lager	Lite Lager
Contribution margin	$500,000	$ 300,000
Controllable margin	200,000	(c)
Average operating assets	(a)	$1,000,000
Minimum rate of return	(b)	13%
Return on investment	25%	(d)
Residual income	$ 90,000	$ 200,000

Problems: Set A

P10-1A   Alcore Company estimates that 240,000 direct labor hours will be worked during 2005 in the Assembly Department. On this basis, the following budgeted manufacturing overhead data are computed.

Prepare flexible budget and budget report for manufacturing overhead.
(SO 3)

Variable Overhead Costs		Fixed Overhead Costs	
Indirect labor	$ 72,000	Supervision	$ 72,000
Indirect materials	48,000	Depreciation	36,000
Repairs	24,000	Insurance	9,600
Utilities	38,400	Rent	9,000
Lubricants	9,600	Property taxes	6,000
	$192,000		$132,600

It is estimated that direct labor hours worked each month will range from 18,000 to 24,000 hours.

During January, 20,000 direct labor hours were worked and the following overhead costs were incurred.

Variable Overhead Costs		Fixed Overhead Costs	
Indirect labor	$ 6,200	Supervision	$ 6,000
Indirect materials	3,600	Depreciation	3,000
Repairs	1,600	Insurance	800
Utilities	2,500	Rent	800
Lubricants	830	Property taxes	500
	$14,730		$11,100

Instructions

(a) Prepare a monthly flexible manufacturing overhead budget for each increment of 2,000 direct labor hours over the relevant range for the year ending December 31, 2005.
(b) Prepare a manufacturing overhead budget report for January.
(c) ▭▭▭▭➤ Comment on management's efficiency in controlling manufacturing overhead costs in January.

(a) Total costs: 18,000 DLH, $25,450; 24,000 DLH, $30,250
(b) Budget, $27,050 Actual, $25,830

Prepare flexible budget, budget report, and graph for manufacturing overhead.
(SO 3)

P10-2A Borealis Manufacturing Company produces one product, Kebo. Because of wide fluctuations in demand for Kebo, the Assembly Department experiences significant variations in monthly production levels.

The annual master manufacturing overhead budget is based on 300,000 direct labor hours. In July 27,500 labor hours were worked. The master manufacturing overhead budget for the year and the actual overhead costs incurred in July are as follows.

Overhead Costs	Master Budget (annual)	Actual in July
Variable		
Indirect labor	$ 300,000	$26,000
Indirect materials	210,000	17,000
Utilities	90,000	8,100
Maintenance	60,000	5,400
Fixed		
Supervision	180,000	15,000
Depreciation	120,000	10,000
Insurance and taxes	60,000	5,000
Total	$1,020,000	$86,500

Instructions

(a) Total costs: 22,500 DLH, $79,500; 30,000 DLH, $96,000
(b) Budget $90,500 Actual $86,500

(a) Prepare a monthly flexible overhead budget for the year ending December 31, 2005, assuming monthly production levels range from 22,500 to 30,000 direct labor hours. Use increments of 2,500 direct labor hours.
(b) Prepare a budget performance report for the month of July 2005 comparing actual results with budget data based on the flexible budget.
(c) ▭▭▭▷ Were costs effectively controlled? Explain.
(d) State the formula for computing the total monthly budgeted costs in the Borealis Manufacturing Company.
(e) Prepare the flexible budget graph showing total budgeted costs at 25,000 and 27,500 direct labor hours. Use increments of 5,000 on the horizontal axis and increments of $10,000 on the vertical axis.

State total budgeted cost formula, and prepare flexible budget reports for 2 time periods.
(SO 2, 3)*

P10-3A Chambers Company uses budgets in controlling costs. The May 2005 budget report for the company's Packaging Department is as follows.

CHAMBERS COMPANY
Budget Report
Packaging Department
For the Month Ended May 31, 2005

Manufacturing Costs	Budget	Actual	Difference Favorable F Unfavorable U
Variable costs			
Direct materials	$ 35,000	$ 37,500	$2,500 U
Direct labor	50,000	53,000	3,000 U
Indirect materials	15,000	15,200	200 U
Indirect labor	12,500	13,000	500 U
Utilities	7,500	7,100	400 F
Maintenance	5,000	5,200	200 U
Total variable	125,000	131,000	6,000 U
Fixed costs			
Rent	8,000	8,000	–0–
Supervision	9,000	9,000	–0–
Depreciation	5,000	5,000	–0–
Total fixed	22,000	22,000	–0–
Total costs	$147,000	$153,000	$6,000 U

The monthly budget amounts in the report were based on an expected production of 50,000 units per month or 600,000 units per year.

The company president was displeased with the department manager's performance. The department manager, who thought he had done a good job, could not understand the unfavorable results. In May, 55,000 units were produced.

Instructions
(a) State the total budgeted cost formula.
(b) Prepare a budget report for May using flexible budget data. Why does this report provide a better basis for evaluating performance than the report based on static budget data?
(c) In June, 40,000 units were produced. Prepare the budget report using flexible budget data, assuming (1) each variable cost was 20% less in June than its actual cost in May, and (2) fixed costs were the same in the month of June as in May.

(b) Budget $159,500

(c) Budget $122,000
Actual $126,800

P10-4A Korene Manufacturing Inc. operates the Home Appliance Division as a profit center. Operating data for this division for the year ended December 31, 2005, are shown below.

Prepare responsibility report for a profit center.
(SO 6)

	Budget	Difference from Budget
Sales	$2,400,000	$80,000 U
Cost of goods sold		
Variable	1,200,000	47,000 U
Controllable fixed	200,000	10,000 F
Selling and administrative		
Variable	240,000	8,000 F
Controllable fixed	60,000	6,000 U
Noncontrollable fixed costs	50,000	2,000 U

In addition, Korene Manufacturing incurs $150,000 of indirect fixed costs that were budgeted at $155,000. Twenty percent (20%) of these costs are allocated to the Home Appliance Division. None of these costs are controllable by the division manager.

Instructions
(a) Prepare a responsibility report for the Home Appliance Division (a profit center) for the year.
(b) ▣▣▣▶ Comment on the manager's performance in controlling revenues and costs.
(c) Identify any costs excluded from the responsibility report and explain why they were excluded.

(a) Contribution margin
$119,000 U
Controllable margin
$115,000 U

P10-5A Chudzik Manufacturing Company manufactures a variety of garden and lawn equipment. The company operates through three divisions. Each division is an investment center. Operating data for the Lawnmower Division for the year ended December 31, 2005, and relevant budget data are as follows.

Prepare responsibility report for an investment center, and compute ROI.
(SO 7)

	Actual	Comparison with Budget
Sales	$3,000,000	$150,000 unfavorable
Variable cost of goods sold	1,400,000	100,000 unfavorable
Variable selling and administrative expenses	300,000	50,000 favorable
Controllable fixed cost of goods sold	270,000	On target
Controllable fixed selling and administrative expenses	130,000	On target

Average operating assets for the year for the Lawnmower Division were $5,000,000 which was also the budgeted amount.

Instructions
(a) Prepare a responsibility report (in thousands of dollars) for the Lawnmower Division.
(b) Evaluate the manager's performance. Which items will likely be investigated by top management?
(c) Compute the expected ROI in 2006 for the Lawnmower Division, assuming the following independent changes.
  (1) Variable cost of goods sold is decreased by 15%.
  (2) Average operating assets are decreased by 20%.
  (3) Sales are increased by $500,000 and this increase is expected to increase contribution margin by $200,000.

(a) Controllable margin:
Budget $1,100
Actual $900

Prepare reports for cost centers under responsibility accounting, and comment on performance of managers.
(SO 4)

P10-6A Kojak Company uses a responsibility reporting system. It has divisions in Denver, Seattle, and San Diego. Each division has three production departments: Cutting, Shaping, and Finishing. The responsibility for each department rests with a manager who reports to the division production manager. Each division manager reports to the vice president of production. There are also vice presidents for marketing and finance. All vice presidents report to the president.

In January 2005, controllable actual and budget manufacturing overhead cost data for the departments and divisions were as shown below.

Manufacturing Overhead	Actual	Budget
Individual costs—Cutting Department—Seattle		
Indirect labor	$ 73,000	$ 70,000
Indirect materials	46,700	46,000
Maintenance	20,500	18,000
Utilities	20,100	17,000
Supervision	22,000	20,000
	$ 182,300	$ 171,000
Total costs		
Shaping Department—Seattle	$ 158,000	$ 148,000
Finishing Department—Seattle	210,000	208,000
Denver division	676,000	673,000
San Diego division	722,000	715,000

Additional overhead costs were incurred as follows: Seattle division production manager—actual costs $52,500, budget $51,000; vice president of production—actual costs $65,000, budget $64,000; president—actual costs $76,400, budget $74,200. These expenses are not allocated.

The vice presidents who report to the president, other than the vice president of production, had the following expenses.

Vice president	Actual	Budget
Marketing	$133,600	$130,000
Finance	108,000	105,000

Instructions

(a) (1) $11,300 U
(2) $24,800 U
(3) $35,800 U
(4) $44,600 U

(a) Using the format on page 407, prepare the following responsibility reports.
    (1) Manufacturing overhead—Cutting Department manager—Seattle division.
    (2) Manufacturing overhead—Seattle division manager.
    (3) Manufacturing overhead—vice president of production.
    (4) Manufacturing overhead and expenses—president.
(b) Comment on the comparative performances of:
    (1) Department managers in the Seattle division.
    (2) Division managers.
    (3) Vice presidents.

Compare ROI and residual income.
(SO 8)

*P10-7A Haniwall Industries has manufactured prefabricated houses for over 20 years. The houses are constructed in sections to be assembled on customers' lots. Haniwall expanded into the precut housing market when it acquired Orlando Company, one of its suppliers. In this market, various types of lumber are precut into the appropriate lengths, banded into packages, and shipped to customers' lots for assembly. Haniwall designated the Orlando Division as an investment center.

Haniwall uses return on investment (ROI) as a performance measure with investment defined as average operating assets. Management bonuses are based in part on ROI. All investments are expected to earn a minimum rate of return of 16%. Orlando's ROI has ranged from 20.1% to 23.5% since it was acquired. Orlando had an investment opportunity in 2005 that had an estimated ROI of 19%. Orlando's management decided against the investment because it believed the investment would decrease the division's overall ROI.

Selected financial information for Orlando are presented below. The division's average operating assets were $12,300,000 for the year 2005.

ORLANDO DIVISION
Selected Financial Information
For the Year Ended December 31, 2005

Sales	$26,000,000
Contribution margin	9,100,000
Controllable margin	2,460,000

Instructions
(a) Calculate the following performance measures for 2005 for the Orlando Division.
  (1) Return on investment (ROI).
  (2) Residual income.
(b) ▭▭▭▶ Would the management of Orlando Division have been more likely to accept the investment opportunity it had in 2005 if residual income were used as a performance measure instead of ROI? Explain your answer.

(CMA, adapted)

(a) (2) $492,000

Problems: Set B

P10-1B Oakley Company estimates that 360,000 direct labor hours will be worked during the coming year, 2005, in the Packaging Department. On this basis, the following budgeted manufacturing overhead cost data are computed for the year.

Prepare flexible budget and budget report for manufacturing overhead.
(SO 3)

Fixed Overhead Costs		**Variable Overhead Costs**	
Supervision	$ 90,000	Indirect labor	$144,000
Depreciation	60,000	Indirect materials	90,000
Insurance	30,000	Repairs	54,000
Rent	36,000	Utilities	72,000
Property taxes	18,000	Lubricants	18,000
	$234,000		$378,000

It is estimated that direct labor hours worked each month will range from 27,000 to 36,000 hours.

During October, 27,000 direct labor hours were worked and the following overhead costs were incurred.

Fixed overhead costs: Supervision $7,500, Depreciation $5,000, Insurance $2,470, Rent $3,000, and Property taxes $1,500.

Variable overhead costs: Indirect labor $11,760, Indirect materials, $6,400, Repairs $4,000, Utilities $5,700, and Lubricants $1,640.

Instructions
(a) Prepare a monthly flexible manufacturing overhead budget for each increment of 3,000 direct labor hours over the relevant range for the year ending December 31, 2005.
(b) Prepare a flexible budget report for October.
(c) ▭▭▭▶ Comment on management's efficiency in controlling manufacturing overhead costs in October.

(a) Total costs: DLH 27,000, $47,850; DLH 36,000, $57,300
(b) Total $1,120 U

P10-2B Hindu Company manufactures tablecloths. Sales have grown rapidly over the past 2 years. As a result, the president has installed a budgetary control system for 2005. The following data were used in developing the master manufacturing overhead budget for the Ironing Department, which is based on an activity index of direct labor hours.

Prepare flexible budget, budget report, and graph for manufacturing overhead.
(SO 3)

Variable Costs	**Rate per Direct Labor Hour**	**Annual Fixed Costs**	
Indirect labor	$0.40	Supervision	$30,000
Indirect materials	0.60	Depreciation	18,000
Factory utilities	0.30	Insurance	12,000
Factory repairs	0.20	Rent	24,000

The master overhead budget was prepared on the expectation that 480,000 direct labor hours will be worked during the year. In June, 42,000 direct labor hours were worked. At that level of activity, actual costs were as shown on the next page.

Variable—per direct labor hour: Indirect labor $0.43, Indirect materials $0.58, Factory utilities $0.32, and Factory repairs $0.24.
Fixed: same as budgeted.

Instructions

(a) Prepare a monthly flexible manufacturing overhead budget for the year ending December 31, 2005, assuming production levels range from 35,000 to 50,000 direct labor hours. Use increments of 5,000 direct labor hours.

(b) Prepare a budget performance report for June comparing actual results with budget data based on the flexible budget.

(c) Were costs effectively controlled? Explain.

(d) State the formula for computing the total budgeted costs for Hindu Company.

(e) Prepare the flexible budget graph, showing total budgeted costs at 35,000 and 45,000 direct labor hours. Use increments of 5,000 direct labor hours on the horizontal axis and increments of $10,000 on the vertical axis.

(a) Total costs: 35,000 DLH,
$59,500; 50,000 DLH,
$82,000
(b) Budget $70,000
Actual $72,940

State total budgeted cost formula, and prepare flexible budget reports for 2 time periods.
(SO 2, 3)

P10-3B Yaeger Company uses budgets in controlling costs. The August 2005 budget report for the company's Assembling Department is as follows.

YAEGER COMPANY
Budget Report
Assembling Department
For the Month Ended August 31, 2005

Manufacturing Costs	Budget	Actual	Difference Favorable F Unfavorable U
Variable costs			
Direct materials	$ 48,000	$ 47,000	$1,000 F
Direct labor	66,000	62,700	3,300 F
Indirect materials	24,000	24,200	200 U
Indirect labor	18,000	17,500	500 F
Utilities	15,000	14,900	100 F
Maintenance	9,000	9,200	200 U
Total variable	180,000	175,500	4,500 F
Fixed costs			
Rent	12,000	12,000	–0–
Supervision	17,000	17,000	–0–
Depreciation	7,000	7,000	–0–
Total fixed	36,000	36,000	–0–
Total costs	$216,000	$211,500	$4,500 F

The monthly budget amounts in the report were based on an expected production of 60,000 units per month or 720,000 units per year. The Assembling Department manager is pleased with the report and expects a raise, or at least praise for a job well done. The company president, however, is unhappy with the results for August, because only 58,000 units were produced.

Instructions

(a) State the total monthly budgeted cost formula.

(b) Prepare a budget report for August using flexible budget data. Why does this report provide a better basis for evaluating performance than the report based on static budget data?

(c) In September, 64,000 units were produced. Prepare the budget report using flexible budget data, assuming (1) each variable cost was 10% higher than its actual cost in August, and (2) fixed costs were the same in September as in August.

(b) Budget $210,000

(c) Budget $228,000
Actual $229,050

Prepare responsibility report for a profit center.
(SO 6)

P10-4B Henning Manufacturing Inc. operates the Patio Furniture Division as a profit center. Operating data for this division for the year ended December 31, 2005, are as shown on the next page.

	Budget	Difference from Budget
Sales	$2,500,000	$70,000 F
Cost of goods sold		
Variable	1,300,000	33,000 F
Controllable fixed	200,000	5,000 U
Selling and administrative		
Variable	220,000	7,000 U
Controllable fixed	50,000	2,000 U
Noncontrollable fixed costs	70,000	4,000 U

In addition, Henning Manufacturing incurs $180,000 of indirect fixed costs that were budgeted at $175,000. Twenty percent (20%) of these costs are allocated to the Patio Furniture Division.

Instructions

(a) Prepare a responsibility report for the Patio Furniture Division for the year.

(b) ▭▭▭▭➤ Comment on the manager's performance in controlling revenues and costs.

(c) Identify any costs excluded from the responsibility report and explain why they were excluded.

(a) Contribution margin $96,000 F
Controllable margin $89,000 F

P10-5B Alosio Manufacturing Company manufactures a variety of tools and industrial equipment. The company operates through three divisions. Each division is an investment center. Operating data for the Home Division for the year ended December 31, 2005, and relevant budget data are as follows.

Prepare responsibility report for an investment center, and compute ROI.
(SO 7)

	Actual	Comparison with Budget
Sales	$1,550,000	$100,000 favorable
Variable cost of goods sold	700,000	70,000 unfavorable
Variable selling and administrative expenses	125,000	25,000 unfavorable
Controllable fixed cost of goods sold	170,000	On target
Controllable fixed selling and administrative expenses	100,000	On target

Average operating assets for the year for the Home Division were $2,500,000 which was also the budgeted amount.

Instructions

(a) Prepare a responsibility report (in thousands of dollars) for the Home Division.

(b) Evaluate the manager's performance. Which items will likely be investigated by top management?

(c) Compute the expected ROI in 2006 for the Home Division, assuming the following independent changes to actual data.

   (1) Variable cost of goods sold is decreased by 6%.

   (2) Average operating assets are decreased by 10%.

   (3) Sales are increased by $200,000, and this increase is expected to increase contribution margin by $90,000.

(a) Controllable margin:
Budget $450;
Actual $455

Problems: Set C

Problem Set C is provided at the book's Web site, www.wiley.com/college/weygandt.

BROADENING YOUR PERSPECTIVE

Group Decision Case

BYP 10-1 Z-Bar Pastures is a 400-acre farm on the outskirts of the Kentucky Bluegrass, specializing in the boarding of broodmares and their foals. A recent economic downturn in the thoroughbred industry has led to a decline in breeding activities, and it has made the boarding business extremely competitive. To meet the competition, Z-Bar Pastures planned in 2005 to entertain clients, advertise more extensively, and absorb expenses formerly paid by clients such as veterinary and blacksmith fees.

The budget report for 2005 is presented below. As shown, the static income statement budget for the year is based on an expected 21,900 boarding days at $25 per mare. The variable expenses per mare per day were budgeted: Feed $5, Veterinary fees $3, Blacksmith fees $0.30, and Supplies $0.70. All other budgeted expenses were either semi-fixed or fixed.

During the year, management decided not to replace a worker who quit in March, but it did issue a new advertising brochure and did more entertaining of clients.[2]

Z-BAR PASTURES
Static Budget Income Statement
Year Ended December 31, 2005

	Actual	Master Budget	Difference
Number of mares	52	60	8*
Number of boarding days	18,980	21,900	2,920*
Sales	$379,600	$547,500	$167,900*
Less variable expenses:			
Feed	104,390	109,500	5,110
Veterinary fees	58,838	65,700	6,862
Blacksmith fees	6,074	6,570	496
Supplies	12,954	15,330	2,376
Total variable expenses	182,256	197,100	14,844
Contribution margin	197,344	350,400	153,056*
Less fixed expenses:			
Depreciation	40,000	40,000	–0–
Insurance	11,000	11,000	–0–
Utilities	12,000	14,000	2,000
Repairs and maintenance	10,000	11,000	1,000
Labor	88,000	96,000	8,000
Advertisement	12,000	8,000	4,000*
Entertainment	7,000	5,000	2,000*
Total fixed expenses	180,000	185,000	5,000
Net income	$ 17,344	$165,400	$148,056*

*Unfavorable.

Instructions

With the class divided into groups, answer the following.

(a) Based on the static budget report:
   (1) What was the primary cause(s) of the loss in net income?
   (2) Did management do a good, average, or poor job of controlling expenses?
   (3) Were management's decisions to stay competitive sound?
(b) Prepare a flexible budget report for the year.
(c) Based on the flexible budget report, answer the three questions in part (a) above.
(d) What course of action do you recommend for the management of Z-Bar Pastures?

Managerial Analysis

BYP 10-2 Castle Company manufactures expensive watch cases sold as souvenirs. Three of its sales departments are: Retail Sales, Wholesale Sales, and Outlet Sales. The

[2]Data for this case are based on Hans Sprohge and John Talbott, "New Applications for Variance Analysis," *Journal of Accountancy* (AICPA, New York), April 1989, pp. 137–141.

Retail Sales Department is a profit center. The Wholesale Sales Department is a cost center. Its managers merely take orders from customers who purchase through the company's wholesale catalog. The Outlet Sales Department is an investment center, because each manager is given full responsibility for an outlet store location. The manager can hire and discharge employees, purchase, maintain, and sell equipment, and in general is fairly independent of company control.

Sara Sutton is a manager in the Retail Sales Department. Gilbert Lewis manages the Wholesale Sales Department. Jose Lopez manages the Golden Gate Club outlet store in San Francisco. The following are the budget responsibility reports for each of the three departments.

Budget			
	Retail Sales	**Wholesale Sales**	**Outlet Sales**
Sales	$ 750,000	$ 400,000	$200,000
Variable costs			
Cost of goods sold	150,000	100,000	25,000
Advertising	100,000	30,000	5,000
Sales salaries	75,000	15,000	3,000
Printing	10,000	20,000	5,000
Travel	20,000	30,000	2,000
Fixed costs			
Rent	50,000	30,000	10,000
Insurance	5,000	2,000	1,000
Depreciation	75,000	100,000	40,000
Investment in assets	$1,000,000	$1,200,000	$800,000

Actual Results			
	Retail Sales	**Wholesale Sales**	**Outlet Sales**
Sales	$ 750,000	$ 400,000	$200,000
Variable costs			
Cost of goods sold	195,000	120,000	26,250
Advertising	100,000	30,000	5,000
Sales salaries	75,000	15,000	3,000
Printing	10,000	20,000	5,000
Travel	15,000	20,000	1,500
Fixed costs			
Rent	40,000	50,000	12,000
Insurance	5,000	2,000	1,000
Depreciation	80,000	90,000	60,000
Investment in assets	$1,000,000	$1,200,000	$800,000

Instructions
(a) Determine which of the items should be included in the responsibility report for each of the three managers.
(b) Compare the budgeted measures with the actual results. Decide which results should be called to the attention of each manager.

Real-World Focus

BYP 10-3   Computer Associates International, Inc., the world's leading business software company, delivers the end-to-end infrastructure to enable e-business through innovative technology, services, and education. CA has 19,000 employees worldwide and recently had revenue of over $6 billion.

Presented below is information from the company's annual report.

COMPUTER ASSOCIATES INTERNATIONAL
Management Discussion

The Company has experienced a pattern of business whereby revenue for its third and fourth fiscal quarters reflects an increase over first- and second-quarter revenue. The Company attributes this increase to clients' increased spending at the end of their calendar year budgetary periods and the culmination of its annual sales plan. Since the Company's costs do not increase proportionately with the third- and fourth-quarters' increase in revenue, the higher revenue in these quarters results in greater profit margins and income. Fourth-quarter profitability is traditionally affected by significant new hirings, training, and education expenditures for the succeeding year.

Instructions
(a) Why don't the company's costs increase proportionately as the revenues increase in the third and fourth quarters?
(b) What type of budgeting seems appropriate for the Computer Associates situation?

Exploring the Web

BYP 10-4 Genelle and Doug have recorded the story of their wedding planning. They are on a strict budget and need help in preparing what they call "a somewhat flexible budget."

> *Address:* **www.wednet.com/inspire/wedstory/story1.htm,** *or go to*
> **www.wiley.com/college/weygandt**

Steps
1. Go to Genelle and Doug's Web site, and read about their trials and tribulations in planning a wedding.
2. Review the **Planning and Budgeting** section in "Part 1" of their story. They mention that this is a "somewhat flexible budget" for 250 guests, totalling $7,150. They would like to reduce their total costs to $7,000, if at all possible.

Instructions
Recast Genelle and Doug's budget into a truly flexible budget so that they can see the effects on their total costs of reducing the number of invited guests to 225 or 200.

Communication Activity

BYP 10-5 The manufacturing overhead budget for Dillons Company contains the following items.

Variable costs	
Indirect materials	$28,000
Indirect labor	12,000
Maintenance expense	10,000
Manufacturing supplies	6,000
Total variable	$56,000
Fixed costs	
Supervision	$18,000
Inspection costs	1,000
Insurance expense	2,000
Depreciation	15,000
Total fixed	$36,000

The budget was based on an estimated 2,000 units being produced. During the past month, 1,500 units were produced, and the following costs incurred.

Variable costs		
Indirect materials	$28,200	
Indirect labor	13,500	
Maintenance expense	8,200	
Manufacturing supplies	5,100	
Total variable	$55,000	
Fixed costs		
Supervision	$19,300	
Inspection costs	1,200	
Insurance expense	2,200	
Depreciation	14,700	
Total fixed	$37,400	

Instructions
(a) Determine which items would be controllable by Jeff Howell, the production manager.
(b) How much should have been spent during the month for the manufacture of the 1,500 units?
(c) Prepare a flexible manufacturing overhead budget report for Mr. Howell.
(d) Prepare a responsibility report. Include only the costs that would have been controllable by Mr. Howell. Assume that Mr. Howell's supervision cost was $10,000, both at budget and actual. In an attached memo, describe clearly for Mr. Howell the areas in which his performance needs to be improved.

Research Assignment

BYP 10-6   The February 2000 issue of the *Journal of Accountancy* contains an article by Russ Banham titled "Better Budgets."

Instructions
Read the article and answer the following questions.

(a) Why have some companies decided not to do major overhauls of their budgeting systems after some initial investigations into the possibility? What percentage of companies that attempt overhauls give up before finishing?
(b) What is the "new planning paradigm"?
(c) What does the author argue is the "final link" necessary for successful budgeting and planning?

Ethics Case

BYP 10-7   American Products Corporation participates in a highly competitive industry. In order to meet this competition and achieve profit goals, the company has chosen the decentralized form of organization. Each manager of a decentralized investment center is measured on the basis of profit contribution, market penetration, and return on investment. Failure to meet the objectives established by corporate management for these measures has not been acceptable and usually has resulted in demotion or dismissal of an investment center manager.

An anonymous survey of managers in the company revealed that the managers feel the pressure to compromise their personal ethical standards to achieve the corporate objectives. For example, at certain plant locations there was pressure to reduce quality control to a level which could not assure that all unsafe products would be rejected. Also, sales personnel were encouraged to use questionable sales tactics to obtain orders, including gifts and other incentives to purchasing agents.

The chief executive officer is disturbed by the survey findings. In his opinion such behavior cannot be condoned by the company. He concludes that the company should do something about this problem.

Instructions
(a) Who are the stakeholders (the affected parties) in this situation?
(b) Identify the ethical implications, conflicts, or dilemmas in the above described situation.
(c) What might the company do to reduce the pressures on managers and decrease the ethical conflicts?

(CMA adapted)

Answers to Self-Study Questions
1. c   2. b   3. a   4. d   5. a   6. d   7. d   8. b   9. b   10. d   *11. c

CHAPTER 11

Standard Costs and Balanced Scorecard

STUDY OBJECTIVES

After studying this chapter,
you should be able to:

1 Distinguish between a standard and a budget.

2 Identify the advantages of standard costs.

3 Describe how standards are set.

4 State the formulas for determining direct materials and direct labor variances.

5 State the formulas for determining manufacturing overhead variances.

6 Discuss the reporting of variances.

7 Prepare an income statement for management under a standard costing system.

8 Describe the balanced scorecard approach to performance evaluation.

☑ THE
NAVIGATOR

THE NAVIGATOR ✔

▶ Scan *Study Objectives* ☐

▶ Read *Feature Story* ☐

▶ Read *Preview* ☐

▶ Read text and answer *Before You Go On*
    p. 451 ☐   *p. 455* ☐   *p. 465* ☐

▶ Work *Using the Decision Toolkit* ☐

▶ Review *Summary of Study Objectives* ☐

▶ Work *Demonstration Problem* ☐

▶ Answer *Self-Study Questions* ☐

▶ Complete *Assignments* ☐

FEATURE STORY

Highlighting Performance Efficiency

There's a very good chance that the highlighter you're holding in your hand was made by **Sanford**, a maker of permanent markers and other writing instruments. Sanford, headquartered in Illinois, annually sells hundreds of millions of dollars' worth of ACCENT highlighters, fine-point pens, Sharpie permanent markers, Expo dry-erase markers for overhead projectors, and other writing instruments.

Since Sanford makes literally billions of writing utensils per year, the company must keep tight control over manufacturing costs. A very important part of Sanford's manufacturing process is determining how much direct materials, labor, and overhead should cost. These costs are then compared to actual costs to assess performance efficiency. Raw materials for Sanford's markers include a barrel, plug, cap, ink reservoir, and a nib (tip). These parts are assembled by machine to produce thousands of units per hour. A major component of manufacturing overhead is machine maintenance—some fixed, some variable.

"Labor costs are associated with material handling and equipment maintenance functions. Although the assembly process is highly automated, labor is still required to move raw materials to the machine and to package the finished product. In addition, highly skilled technicians are required to service and maintain each piece of equipment," says Mike Orr, vice president, operations.

Labor rates are predictable because the hourly workers are covered by a union contract. The story is the same with the fringe benefits and some supervisory salaries. Even volume levels are fairly predictable—demand for the product is high—so fixed overhead is efficiently absorbed. Raw material standard costs are based on the previous year's actual prices plus any anticipated inflation. Lately, though, inflation has been so low

that the company is considering any price increase in raw material to be unfavorable because its standards will remain unchanged.

www.sanfordcorp.com

Standards are a fact of life. You met the admission standards for the school you are attending. The vehicle that you drive had to meet certain governmental emissions standards. The hamburgers and salads you eat in a restaurant have to meet certain health and nutritional standards before they can be sold. And, as described in our Feature Story, **Sanford Corp.** develops standards for the costs of its materials, labor, and overhead which it compares with its actual costs. The reason for standards in these cases is very simple: They help to ensure that overall product quality is high. Without standards, quality control is lost.

In this chapter we continue the study of controlling costs. You will learn how to evaluate performance using standard costs and a balanced scorecard.

The content and organization of Chapter 11 are as follows.

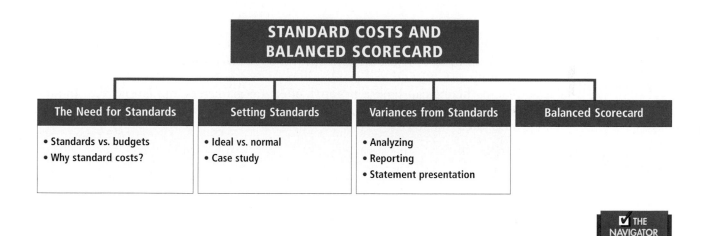

THE NAVIGATOR

The Need for Standards

Standards are common in business. Those imposed by government agencies are often called **regulations**. They include the Fair Labor Standards Act, the Equal Employment Opportunity Act, and a multitude of environmental standards. Standards established internally by a company may extend to personnel matters, such as employee absenteeism and ethical codes of conduct, quality control standards for products, and standard costs for goods and services. In managerial accounting, standard costs are predetermined unit costs, which are used as measures of performance.

We will focus on manufacturing operations in the remainder of this chapter. But you should also recognize that standard costs also apply to many types of service businesses as well. For example, a fast-food restaurant such as **McDonald's** knows the price it should pay for pickles, beef, buns, and other ingredients. It also knows how much time it should take an employee to flip hamburgers. If too much is paid for pickles or too much time is taken to prepare Big Macs, the deviations are noticed and corrective action is taken. Standard costs also may be used in not-for-profit enterprises such as universities, charitable organizations, and governmental agencies.

DISTINGUISHING BETWEEN STANDARDS AND BUDGETS

STUDY OBJECTIVE

1

Distinguish between a standard and a budget.

In concept, **standards** and **budgets** are essentially the same. Both are predetermined costs, and both contribute to management planning and control. There is a difference, however, in the way the terms are expressed. A standard is a **unit** amount. A budget is a **total** amount. Thus, it is customary to state that the standard cost of direct labor for a unit of product is $10. If 5,000 units of the product are produced, the $50,000 of direct labor is the **budgeted** labor cost. A standard is the budgeted cost per unit of product. A standard is therefore concerned with each individual cost component that makes up the entire budget.

There are important accounting differences between budgets and standards. Except in the application of manufacturing overhead to jobs and processes, budget data are not journalized in cost accounting systems. In contrast, as will be illustrated in the appendix to this chapter, standard costs may be incorporated into cost accounting systems. Also, a company may report its inventories at standard cost in its financial statements, but it would not report inventories at budgeted costs.

WHY STANDARD COSTS?

STUDY OBJECTIVE

2

Identify the advantages of standard costs.

Standard costs offer a number of advantages to an organization, as shown in Illustration 11-1. These advantages will be realized only when standard costs are carefully established and prudently used. Using standards solely as a means of placing blame can have a negative effect on managers and employees. In an effort to minimize this effect, many companies offer wage incentives to those who meet their standards.

Illustration 11-1 Advantages of standard costs

Advantages of standard costs

Facilitate management planning

Promote greater economy by making employees more "cost-conscious"

Useful in setting selling prices

Contribute to management control by providing basis for evaluation of cost control

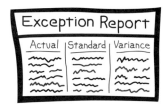

Useful in highlighting variances in management by exception

Simplify costing of inventories and reduce clerical costs

Setting Standard Costs—A Difficult Task

The setting of standard costs to produce a unit of product is a difficult task. It requires input from all persons who have responsibility for costs and quantities. To determine the standard cost of direct materials, management may have to consult purchasing agents, product managers, quality control engineers, and production supervisors. In setting the cost standard for direct labor, pay rate data are obtained from the payroll department, and the labor time requirements may be determined by industrial engineers. The managerial accountant provides important input to management into the standards-setting process by accumulating historical cost data and by knowing how costs respond to changes in activity levels.

To be effective in controlling costs, standard costs need to be current at all times. Thus, standards should be under continuous review. They should be changed whenever it is determined that the existing standard is not a good measure of performance. Circumstances that may warrant revision of a standard include changed wage rates resulting from a new union contract, a change in product specifications, or the implementation of a new manufacturing method.

IDEAL VERSUS NORMAL STANDARDS

Standards may be set at one of two levels: ideal or normal. **Ideal standards** represent optimum levels of performance under perfect operating conditions. **Normal standards** represent efficient levels of performance that are attainable under expected operating conditions.

Some managers believe ideal standards will stimulate workers to ever-increasing improvement. However, most managers believe that ideal standards lower the morale of the entire workforce because they are so difficult, if not impossible, to meet. Very few companies use ideal standards.

Most companies that use standards set them at a normal level. Properly set, normal standards should be **rigorous but attainable**. Normal standards allow for rest periods, machine breakdowns, and other "normal" contingencies in the production process. It will be assumed in the remainder of this chapter that standard costs are set at a normal level.

Helpful Hint When standards are set too high, employees sometimes feel pressure to consider unethical practices to meet these standards.

Business Insight
Management Perspective

Recently a number of organizations, including corporations, consultants, and governmental agencies, agreed to share information regarding performance standards in an effort to create a standard set of measures for thousands of business processes. Having such standards would enable companies to evaluate their performance relative to others with regard to such things as the amount of materials they waste when making a product, or how long it takes to process a purchase order. The group, referred to as the Open Standards Benchmarking Collaborative, includes **IBM**, **Procter and Gamble**, the **U.S. Navy**, and the **World Bank**. Companies that are interested in participating can go to the group's Web site and enter their information.

SOURCE: William M. Bulkeley, "Business, Agencies to Standardize Their Benchmarks," *Wall Street Journal Online* (May 19, 2004).

A CASE STUDY

To establish the standard cost of producing a product, it is necessary to establish standards for each manufacturing cost element—direct materials, direct labor, and manufacturing overhead. The standard for each element is derived from the standard price to be paid and the standard quantity to be used. To illustrate, we will look at a case study of how standard costs are set. In this extended example, we will assume that Xonic, Inc. wishes to use standard costs to measure performance in filling an order for 1,000 gallons of Weed-O, a liquid weed killer.

Direct Materials

The **direct materials price standard** is the cost per unit of direct materials that should be incurred. This standard should be based on the purchasing department's best estimate of the **cost of raw materials**. This is frequently based on current purchase prices. The price standard should also include an amount for related costs such as receiving, storing, and handling. The materials price standard per pound of material for Xonic's weed killer is:

Illustration 11-2 Setting direct materials price standard

Item	Price
Purchase price, net of discounts	$ 2.70
Freight	0.20
Receiving and handling	0.10
Standard direct materials price per pound	**$3.00**

The **direct materials quantity standard** is the quantity of direct materials that should be used per unit of finished goods. This standard is expressed as a physical measure, such as pounds, barrels, or board feet. In setting the standard, management should consider both the quality and quantity of materials required to manufacture the product. The standard should include allowances for unavoidable waste and normal spoilage. The standard quantity per unit for Xonic, Inc. is as follows.

Illustration 11-3 Setting direct materials quantity standard

Item	Quantity (Pounds)
Required materials	3.5
Allowance for waste	0.4
Allowance for spoilage	0.1
Standard direct materials quantity per unit	**4.0**

The standard direct materials cost per unit is the standard direct materials price times the standard direct materials quantity. For Xonic, Inc., the standard direct materials cost per gallon of Weed-O is $12.00 ($3.00 × 4.0 pounds).

Direct Labor

The **direct labor price standard** is the rate per hour that should be incurred for direct labor. This standard is based on current wage rates, adjusted for anticipated changes such as cost of living adjustments (COLAs). The price standard also generally includes employer payroll taxes and fringe benefits, such as paid holidays and vacations. For Xonic, Inc., the direct labor price standard is as follows.

Illustration 11-4 Setting
direct labor price standard

Item	Price
Hourly wage rate	$ 7.50
COLA	0.25
Payroll taxes	0.75
Fringe benefits	1.50
Standard direct labor rate per hour	**$10.00**

The **direct labor quantity standard** is the time that should be required to make one unit of the product. This standard is especially critical in labor-intensive companies. Allowances should be made in this standard for rest periods, cleanup, machine setup, and machine downtime. For Xonic, Inc., the direct labor quantity standard is as follows.

Alternative Terminology The
direct labor quantity standard is
also called the *direct labor
efficiency standard.*

Illustration 11-5 Setting
direct labor quantity
standard

Item	Quantity (Hours)
Actual production time	1.5
Rest periods and cleanup	0.2
Setup and downtime	0.3
Standard direct labor hours per unit	**2.0**

The standard direct labor cost per unit is the standard direct labor rate times the standard direct labor hours. For Xonic, Inc., the standard direct labor cost per gallon of Weed-O is $20 ($10.00 × 2.0 hours).

Manufacturing Overhead

For manufacturing overhead, a **standard predetermined overhead rate** is used in setting the standard. This overhead rate is determined by dividing budgeted overhead costs by an expected standard activity index. For example, the index may be standard direct labor hours or standard machine hours.

As discussed in Chapter 4, many companies employ activity-based costing (ABC) to allocate overhead costs. Because ABC uses multiple activity indices to allocate overhead costs, it results in a better correlation between activities and costs incurred. As a result, the use of ABC can significantly improve the usefulness of a standard costing system for management decision making.

Xonic, Inc. uses standard direct labor hours as the activity index. The company expects to produce 13,200 gallons of Weed-O during the year at normal capacity. Since it takes 2 direct labor hours for each gallon, total standard direct labor hours are 26,400 (13,200 gallons × 2 hours). At this level of activity, overhead costs are expected to be $132,000. Of that amount, $79,200 are variable and $52,800 are fixed. The standard predetermined overhead rates are computed as shown in Illustration 11-6.

Calculating the overhead rate

Overhead ÷ Standard activity index

Illustration 11-6 Computing predetermined
overhead rates

Budgeted Overhead Costs	Amount	÷	Standard Direct Labor Hours	=	Overhead Rate per Direct Labor Hour
Variable	$ 79,200		26,400		**$3.00**
Fixed	52,800		26,400		**2.00**
Total	$132,000		26,400		**$5.00**

The standard manufacturing overhead rate per unit is the predetermined overhead rate times the activity index quantity standard. For Xonic, Inc., which uses direct labor hours as its activity index, the standard manufacturing overhead rate per gallon of Weed-O is $10 ($5 × 2 hours).

Total Standard Cost per Unit

Now that the standard quantity and price have been established per unit of product, the total standard cost can be determined. The total standard cost per unit is the sum of the standard costs of direct materials, direct labor, and manufacturing overhead. For Xonic, Inc., the total standard cost per gallon of Weed-O is $42, as shown on the following standard cost card.

Illustration 11-7   Standard cost per gallon of Weed-O

Product: Weed-O		**Unit Measure: Gallon**	
Manufacturing Cost Elements	Standard Quantity	× Standard Price =	Standard Cost
Direct materials	4 pounds	$ 3.00	$12.00
Direct labor	2 hours	$10.00	$20.00
Manufacturing overhead	2 hours	$ 5.00	$10.00
			$42.00

A standard cost card is prepared for each product. This card provides the basis for determining variances from standards.

Business Insight
Management Perspective

Setting standards can be difficult. Consider **Susan's Chili Factory**, which manufactures and sells chili. The cost of manufacturing Susan's chili consists of the costs of raw materials, labor to convert the basic ingredients to chili, and overhead. We will use materials cost as an example. Three standards need to be developed: (1) What should be the formula (mix) of ingredients for one gallon of chili? (2) What should be the normal wastage (or shrinkage) for the individual ingredients? (3) What should be the standard cost for the individual ingredients that go into the chili?

Susan's Chili Factory also illustrates how standard costs can be used by management in controlling costs. Suppose that summer droughts have reduced crop yields. As a result, prices have doubled for beans, onions, and peppers. In this case, actual costs will be significantly higher than standard costs, which will cause management to evaluate the situation. Management might decide to increase the price charged for a gallon of chili. It might reexamine the product mix to see if other types of ingredients can be used. Or it might curtail production until ingredients can be purchased at or near standard costs. Similarly, assume that poor maintenance caused the onion-dicing blades to become dull. As a result, usage of onions to make a gallon of chili tripled. Because this deviation is quickly highlighted through standard costs, corrective action can be promptly taken.

SOURCE: Adapted from David R. Beran, "Cost Reduction Through Control Reporting," *Management Accounting* (April 1982), pp. 29–33.

BEFORE YOU GO ON . . .

▶**Review It**

1. How do standards differ from budgets?
2. What are the advantages of standard costs to an organization?
3. Distinguish between normal standards and ideal standards. Which standard is more widely used? Why?

▶**Do It**

The management of Arapahoe Company has decided to use standard costs. Management asks you to explain the components used in setting the standard cost per unit for direct materials, direct labor, and manufacturing overhead.

Action Plan

• Differentiate between the two components of each standard: price and quantity.

Solution The standard direct materials cost per unit is the standard direct materials price times the standard direct materials quantity. The standard direct labor cost per unit is the standard direct labor rate times the standard direct labor hours. The standard manufacturing overhead rate per unit is the standard predetermined overhead rate times the activity index quantity standard.

Related exercise material: BE11-2, BE11-3, and E11-1.

 THE NAVIGATOR

Variances from Standards

One of the major management uses of standard costs is to identify variances from standards. **Variances** are the differences between total actual costs and total standard costs. To illustrate, we will assume that in producing 1,000 gallons of Weed-O in the month of June, Xonic, Inc. incurred the following costs.

Direct materials	$13,020
Direct labor	20,580
Variable overhead	6,500
Fixed overhead	4,400
Total actual costs	$44,500

Alternative Terminology In business, the term *variance* is also used to indicate differences between total budgeted and total actual costs.

Illustration 11-8   Actual production costs

Total standard costs are determined by multiplying the units produced by the standard cost per unit. The total standard cost of Weed-O is $42,000 (1,000 gallons × $42). Thus, the total variance is $2,500, as shown below.

Actual costs	$44,500
Less: Standard costs	42,000
Total variance	**$ 2,500**

Illustration 11-9   Computation of total variance

Note that the variance is expressed in total dollars and not on a per unit basis.

When actual costs exceed standard costs, the variance is **unfavorable**. The $2,500 variance in June for Weed-O is unfavorable. An unfavorable variance has a negative connotation. It suggests that too much was paid for one or more of the manufacturing cost elements or that the elements were used inefficiently.

If actual costs are less than standard costs, the variance is **favorable**. A favorable variance has a positive connotation. It suggests efficiencies in incurring manufacturing costs and in using direct materials, direct labor, and manufacturing overhead. However, be careful: A favorable variance could be obtained by using inferior materials. In printing wedding invitations, for example, a favorable variance could result from using an inferior grade of paper. Or, a favorable variance might be achieved in installing tires on an automobile assembly line by tightening only half of the lug bolts. A variance is not favorable if quality control standards have been sacrificed.

ANALYZING VARIANCES

To interpret properly the significance of a variance, you must analyze it to determine the underlying factors. Analyzing variances begins by determining the cost elements that comprise the variance. **For each manufacturing cost element, a total dollar variance is computed. Then this variance is analyzed into a price variance and a quantity variance.** The relationships are shown graphically as follows.

Illustration 11-10 Variance relationships

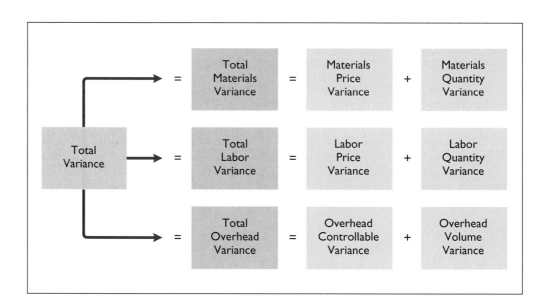

Each of the variances is explained below.

STUDY OBJECTIVE
4
State the formulas for determining direct materials and direct labor variances.

Direct Materials Variances

In completing the order for 1,000 gallons of Weed-O, Xonic used 4,200 pounds of direct materials. These were purchased at a cost of $3.10 per unit. The **total materials variance** is computed from the following formula.

Illustration 11-11 Formula for total materials variance

Actual Quantity **× Actual Price** **(AQ) × (AP)**	−	**Standard Quantity** **× Standard Price** **(SQ) × (SP)**	=	**Total Materials** **Variance** **(TMV)**

For Xonic, Inc., the total materials variance is $1,020 ($13,020 − $12,000) unfavorable as shown below.

$$(4,200 \times \$3.10) \quad (4,000 \times \$3.00) = \$1,020 \text{ U}$$

Next, the total variance is analyzed to determine the amount attributable to price (costs) and to quantity (use). The **materials price variance** is computed from the following formula.[1]

Actual Quantity × Actual Price (AQ) × (AP)	−	Actual Quantity × Standard Price (AQ) × (SP)	=	Materials Price Variance (MPV)

Illustration 11-12 Formula for materials price variance

For Xonic, Inc., the materials price variance is $420 ($13,020 − $12,600) unfavorable as shown below.

$$(4,200 \times \$3.10) - (4,200 \times \$3.00) = \$420 \text{ U}$$

The price variance can also be computed by multiplying the actual quantity purchased by the difference between the actual and standard price per unit. The computation in this case is 4,200 × ($3.10 − $3.00) = $420 U.

The **materials quantity variance** is determined from the following formula.

Helpful Hint The alternative formula is:

$$\boxed{AQ} \times \boxed{AP - SP} = \boxed{MPV}$$

Actual Quantity × Standard Price (AQ) × (SP)	−	Standard Quantity × Standard Price (SQ) × (SP)	=	Materials Quantity Variance (MQV)

Illustration 11-13 Formula for materials quantity variance

For Xonic, Inc., the materials quantity variance is $600 ($12,600 − $12,000) unfavorable, as shown below.

$$(4,200 \times \$3.00) - (4,000 \times \$3.00) = \$600 \text{ U}$$

The price variance can also be computed by applying the standard price to the difference between actual and standard quantities used. The computation in this example is $3.00 × (4,200 − 4,000) = $600 U.

The total materials variance of $1,020 U, therefore, consists of the following.

Helpful Hint The alternative formula is:

$$\boxed{SP} \times \boxed{AQ - SQ} = \boxed{MQV}$$

Materials price variance	$ 420 U
Materials quantity variance	600 U
Total materials variance	**$1,020 U**

Illustration 11-14 Summary of materials variances

A matrix is sometimes used to analyze a variance. **When the matrix is used, the formulas for each cost element are computed first and then the variances.**

---

[1]We will assume that all materials purchased during the period are used in production and that no units remain in inventory at the end of the period.

The completed matrix for the direct materials variance for Xonic, Inc. is shown in Illustration 11-15. The matrix provides a convenient structure for determining each variance.

Illustration 11-15 Matrix for direct materials variances

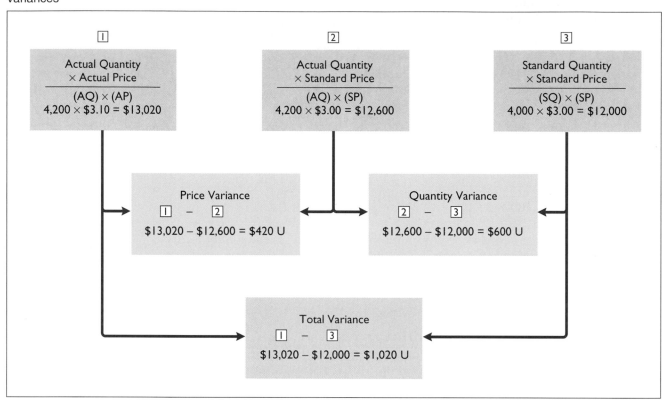

CAUSES OF MATERIALS VARIANCES. What are the causes of a variance? The causes may relate to both internal and external factors. **The investigation of a materials price variance usually begins in the purchasing department.** Many factors affect the price paid for raw materials. These include the delivery method used, availability of quantity and cash discounts, and the quality of the materials requested. To the extent that these factors have been considered in setting the price standard, the purchasing department should be responsible for any variances.

However, a variance may be beyond the control of the purchasing department. Sometimes, for example, prices may rise faster than expected. Moreover, actions by groups over which the company has no control, such as the OPEC nations' oil price increases, may cause an unfavorable variance. There are also times when a production department may be responsible for the price variance. This may occur when a rush order forces the company to pay a higher price for the materials.

The starting point for determining the cause(s) of an unfavorable **materials quantity variance** is in the **production department**. If the variances are due to inexperienced workers, faulty machinery, or carelessness, the production department would be responsible. However, if the materials obtained by the purchasing department were of inferior quality, then the purchasing department should be responsible.

Business Insight
Management Perspective

If purchase price variances are used as a basis for measuring performance, purchasing departments often will continually search for the lowest-cost item. However, this basis can become counterproductive if it leads to late deliveries of the goods or the purchase of inferior-quality goods.

DECISION TOOLKIT

Decision Checkpoints	Info Needed for Decision	Tool to Use for Decision	How to Evaluate Results
Has management accomplished its price and quantity objectives regarding materials?	Actual cost and standard cost of materials	Materials price and materials quantity variances	Positive (favorable) variances suggest that price and quantity objectives have been met.

BEFORE YOU GO ON . . .

▶Review It

1. What are the three main components of the total variance from standard cost?

2. What are the formulas for computing the total, price, and quantity variances for direct materials?

▶Do It

The standard cost of Product XX includes two units of direct materials at $8.00 per unit. During July, 22,000 units of direct materials are purchased at $7.50 and used to produce 10,000 units. Compute the total, price, and quantity variances for materials.

Action Plan

Use the formulas for computing each of the materials variances:

- Total materials variance $= (AQ \times AP) - (SQ \times SP)$
- Materials price variance $= (AQ \times AP) - (AQ \times SP)$
- Materials quantity variance $= (AQ \times SP) - (SQ \times SP)$

Solution Substituting amounts into the formulas, the variances are:

Total materials variance $= (22{,}000 \times \$7.50) - (20{,}000 \times \$8.00) = \$5{,}000$ unfavorable.

Materials price variance $= (22{,}000 \times \$7.50) - (22{,}000 \times \$8.00) = \$11{,}000$ favorable.

Materials quantity variance $= (22{,}000 \times \$8.00) - (20{,}000 \times \$8.00) = \$16{,}000$ unfavorable.

Related exercise material: BE11-4, E11-2, E11-5, and E11-6.

☑ THE NAVIGATOR

Direct Labor Variances

The process of determining direct labor variances is the same as for determining the direct materials variances. In completing the Weed-O order, Xonic, Inc. incurred 2,100 direct labor hours at an average hourly rate of $9.80. The standard hours allowed for the units produced were 2,000 hours (1,000 gallons × 2 hours). The standard labor rate was $10 per hour. The **total labor variance** is obtained from the following formula.

Illustration 11-16 Formula for total labor variance

Actual Hours × Actual Rate (AH) × (AR)	−	Standard Hours × Standard Rate (SH) × (SR)	=	Total Labor Variance (TLV)

The total labor variance is $580 ($20,580 − $20,000) unfavorable, as shown below.

$$(2,100 \times \$9.80) - (2,000 \times \$10.00) = \$580 \text{ U}$$

The formula for the **labor price variance** is:

Illustration 11-17 Formula for labor price variance

Actual Hours × Actual Rate (AH) × (AR)	−	Actual Hours × Standard Rate (AH) × (SR)	=	Labor Price Variance (LPV)

For Xonic, Inc., the labor price variance is $420 ($20,580 − $21,000) favorable as shown below.

$$(2,100 \times \$9.80) - (2,100 \times \$10.00) = \$420 \text{ F}$$

Helpful Hint The alternative formula is:

$$\boxed{AH} \times \boxed{AR - SR} = \boxed{LPV}$$

The labor price variance can also be computed by multiplying actual hours worked by the difference between the actual pay rate and the standard pay rate. The computation in this example is 2,100 × ($10.00 − $9.80) = $420 F.

The **labor quantity variance** is derived from the following formula.

Illustration 11-18 Formula for labor quantity variance

Actual Hours × Standard Rate (AH) × (SR)	−	Standard Hours × Standard Rate (SH) × (SR)	=	Labor Quantity Variance (LQV)

For Xonic, Inc., the labor quantity variance is $1,000 ($21,000 − $20,000) unfavorable:

$$(2,100 \times \$10.00) - (2,000 \times \$10.00) = \$1,000 \text{ U}$$

Helpful Hint The alternative formula is:

$$\boxed{SR} \times \boxed{AH - SH} = \boxed{LQV}$$

The same result can be obtained by multiplying the standard rate by the difference between actual hours worked and standard hours allowed. In this case the computation is $10.00 × (2,100 − 2,000) = $1,000 U.

The total direct labor variance of $580 U, therefore, consists of:

Illustration 11-19   Summary of labor variances

Labor price variance	$ 420 F
Labor quantity variance	1,000 U
Total direct labor variance	**$ 580 U**

These results can also be obtained from the matrix in Illustration 11-20.

Illustration 11-20   Matrix for direct labor variances

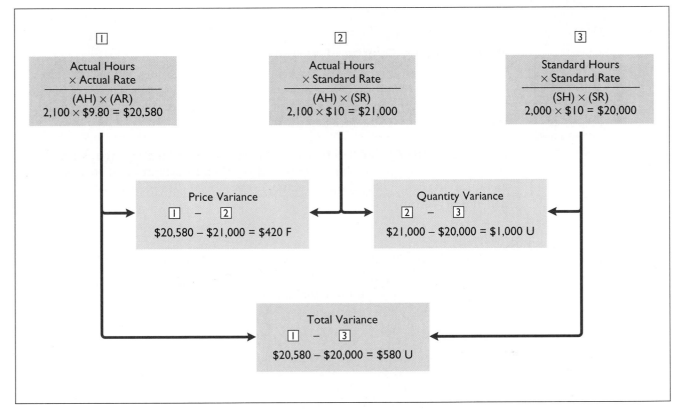

CAUSES OF LABOR VARIANCES.

Labor price variances usually result from two factors: (1) paying workers **higher wages than expected**, and (2) **misallocation of workers**. In companies where pay rates are determined by union contracts, labor price variances should be infrequent. When workers are not unionized, there is a much higher likelihood of such variances. The responsibility for these variances rests with the manager who authorized the wage increase.

Misallocation of the workforce refers to using skilled workers in place of unskilled workers and vice versa. The use of an inexperienced worker instead of an experienced one will result in a favorable price variance because of the lower pay rate of the unskilled worker. An unfavorable price variance would result if a skilled worker were substituted for an inexperienced one. The production department generally is responsible for labor price variances resulting from misallocation of the workforce.

Labor quantity variances relate to the **efficiency of workers**. The cause of a quantity variance generally can be traced to the production department. The causes of an unfavorable variance may be poor training, worker fatigue, faulty machinery, or carelessness. These causes are the responsibility of the **production department**. However, if the excess time is due to inferior materials, the responsibility falls outside the production department.

DECISION TOOLKIT

Decision Checkpoints	Info Needed for Decision	Tool to Use for Decision	How to Evaluate Results
✔	▦ ▦	⚒	👍👎
Has management accomplished its price and quantity objectives regarding labor?	Actual cost and standard cost of labor	Labor price and labor quantity variances	Positive (favorable) variances suggest that price and quantity objectives have been met.

Manufacturing Overhead Variances

The computation of the manufacturing overhead variances is conceptually the same as the computation of the materials and labor variances. However, the task is more challenging for manufacturing overhead because both variable and fixed overhead costs must be considered.

TOTAL OVERHEAD VARIANCE. The **total overhead variance** is the difference between actual overhead costs and overhead costs applied to work done. As indicated earlier, actual manufacturing overhead costs incurred by Xonic were $10,900, as follows.

Illustration 11-21 Actual overhead costs

Variable overhead	$ 6,500
Fixed overhead	4,400
Total actual overhead	**$10,900**

Under a standard costing system, manufacturing overhead costs are applied to work in process on the basis of the **standard hours allowed** for the work done. **Standard hours allowed** are the hours that should have been worked for the units produced. For the 1,000 gallon Weed-O order, the standard hours allowed are 2,000 (1,000 gallons × 2 hours). The predetermined overhead rate is $5 per direct labor hour (see Illustration 11-6 on page 449). Thus, overhead applied is $10,000 (2,000 hours × $5). Note that actual hours of direct labor (2,100) are not used in applying manufacturing overhead.

The formula for the total overhead variance and the calculation for Xonic, Inc. are shown in Illustration 11-22.

Illustration 11-22 Formula for total overhead variance

Actual Overhead	−	Overhead Applied*	=	Total Overhead Variance
$10,900	−	$10,000	=	**$900 U**

*Based on standard hours allowed.

Thus, for Xonic, Inc., the total overhead variance is $900 unfavorable.

The overhead variance is generally analyzed through a price variance and a quantity variance. The name usually given to the price variance is the **overhead controllable variance**, whereas the quantity variance is referred to as the **overhead volume variance**.

OVERHEAD CONTROLLABLE VARIANCE. The **overhead controllable variance** shows whether overhead costs were effectively controlled. To compute this variance, actual overhead costs incurred are compared with budgeted costs for the **standard hours allowed**. The budgeted costs are determined from the flexible manufacturing overhead budget which was presented in Chapter 10. For Xonic the budget formula for manufacturing overhead is variable manufacturing overhead cost of $3 per hour of labor plus fixed manufacturing overhead costs of $4,400. The budget for Xonic, Inc. is as follows.

Alternative Terminology The overhead controllable variance is also called the *budget* or *spending variance.*

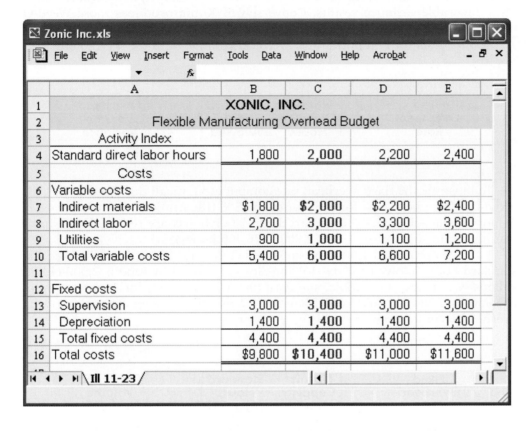

Illustration 11-23 Flexible budget using standard direct labor hours

As shown, the budgeted costs for 2,000 standard hours are $10,400 ($6,000 variable and $4,400 fixed).

The formula for the overhead controllable variance and the calculation for Xonic, Inc. are shown in Illustration 11-24.

Actual Overhead	−	Overhead Budgeted*	=	Overhead Controllable Variance
$10,900	−	$10,400	=	**$500 U**

*Based on standard hours allowed.

Illustration 11-24 Formula for overhead controllable variance

The overhead controllable variance for Xonic, Inc. is $500 unfavorable.

Most controllable variances are associated with variable costs, which are controllable costs. Fixed costs are usually known at the time the budget is prepared. At Xonic, Inc., the variance is accounted for by comparing the actual variable overhead costs ($6,500) with the budgeted variable costs ($6,000).

Management can compare actual and budgeted overhead for each manufacturing overhead cost that contributes to the controllable variance. In addition, cost and quantity variances can be developed for each overhead cost, such as indirect materials and indirect labor.

OVERHEAD VOLUME VARIANCE. The **overhead volume variance** is the difference between normal capacity hours and standard hours allowed times the fixed overhead rate. The overhead volume variance relates to whether fixed costs were under- or over-applied during the year. For example, the overhead volume variance answers the question of whether Xonic effectively used its fixed costs. If Xonic produces less Weed-O than normal capacity would allow, an unfavorable variance results. Conversely, if Xonic produces more Weed-O than what is considered normal capacity, a favorable variance results.

The formula for computing the overhead volume variance is as follows.

Illustration 11-25
Formula for overhead volume variance

$$
\begin{array}{ccc}
\begin{array}{c}\text{Fixed}\\\text{Overhead}\\\text{Rate}\end{array} & \times & \left|\begin{array}{cc}\text{Normal} & \text{Standard}\\\text{Capacity} - & \text{Hours}\\\text{Hours} & \text{Allowed}\end{array}\right| & = & \begin{array}{c}\text{Overhead}\\\text{Volume}\\\text{Variance}\end{array}
\end{array}
$$

To illustrate the fixed overhead rate computation, recall that Xonic Inc. budgeted fixed overhead cost for the year of $52,800 (Illustration 11-6 on page 449). At normal capacity, 26,400 standard direct labor hours are required. The fixed overhead rate is therefore $2 ($52,800 ÷ 26,400 hours).

Xonic Co produced 1,000 units of Weed-O in June. As indicated earlier, the standard hours allowed for the 1,000 gallons produced in June is 2,000 (1,000 gallons × 2 hours). For Xonic, standard direct labor hours for June at normal capacity is 2,200 (26,400 annual hours ÷ 12 months). The computation of the overhead volume variance in this case is as follows.

Illustration 11-26 Computation of overhead volume variance for Xonic Co.

$$
\begin{array}{ccc}
\begin{array}{c}\text{Fixed}\\\text{Overhead}\\\text{Rate}\end{array} & \times & \left|\begin{array}{cc}\text{Normal} & \text{Standard}\\\text{Capacity} - & \text{Hours}\\\text{Hours} & \text{Allowed}\end{array}\right| & = & \begin{array}{c}\text{Overhead}\\\text{Volume}\\\text{Variance}\end{array}\\
\$2 & \times & (2,200 \; - \; 2,000) & = & \$400\ \text{U}
\end{array}
$$

In Xonic's case, a $400 unfavorable volume variance results. The volume variance is unfavorable because Xonic produced only 1,000 gallons rather than the normal capacity of 1,100 gallons in the month of June. As a result, it underapplied fixed overhead for that period.

In computing the overhead variances, it is important to remember the following.

1. Standard hours allowed are used in each of the variances.
2. Budgeted costs for the controllable variance are derived from the flexible budget.
3. The controllable variance generally pertains to variable costs.
4. The volume variance pertains solely to fixed costs.

CAUSES OF MANUFACTURING OVERHEAD VARIANCES. Since the **controllable variance** relates to variable manufacturing costs, the responsibility for the variance rests with the **production department**. The cause of an unfavorable variance may be: (1) **higher than expected use** of indirect materials, indirect labor, and factory supplies, or (2) **increases in indirect manufacturing costs**, such as fuel and maintenance costs.

"What caused manufacturing overhead variances?"

Controllable Variance	Overhead Volume Variance
Production Dept.	Production or Sales Dept.

The **overhead volume variance** is the responsibility of the **production department** if the cause is inefficient use of direct labor or machine breakdowns. When the cause is a **lack of sales orders**, the responsibility rests **outside** the production department.

DECISION TOOLKIT

Decision Checkpoints	Info Needed for Decision	Tool to Use for Decision	How to Evaluate Results
Has management accomplished its price and quantity objectives regarding overhead?	Actual cost and standard cost of overhead	Overhead controllable variance and overhead volume variance	Positive (favorable) variances suggest that price and quantity objectives have been met.

REPORTING VARIANCES

All variances should be reported to appropriate levels of management as soon as possible. The sooner management is informed, the sooner problems can be evaluated and corrective actions taken if necessary.

The form, content, and frequency of variance reports vary considerably among companies. One approach is to prepare a weekly report for each department that has primary responsibility for cost control. Under this approach, materials price variances are reported to the purchasing department, and all other variances are reported to the production department that did the work. The following report for Xonic, Inc., with the materials for the Weed-O order listed first, illustrates this approach.

STUDY OBJECTIVE
6

Discuss the reporting of variances.

XONIC, INC.
Variance Report—Purchasing Department
For Week Ended June 8, 2005

Type of Materials	Quantity Purchased	Actual Price	Standard Price	Price Variance	Explanation
X 100	4,200 lbs.	$3.10	$3.00	$420 U	Rush order
X 142	1,200 units	2.75	2.80	60 F	Quantity discount
A 85	600 doz.	5.20	5.10	60 U	Regular supplier on strike
Total price variance				**$420 U**	

Illustration 11-27
Materials price variance report

The explanation column is completed after consultation with the purchasing department manager.

Variance reports facilitate the principle of "management by exception" explained in Chapter 10. For example, the vice president of purchasing can use the report shown above to evaluate the effectiveness of the purchasing department manager. Or, the vice president of production can use production department variance reports to determine how well each production manager is controlling costs. In using variance reports, top management normally looks for **significant variances**. These may be judged on the basis of some quantitative measure, such as more than 10 percent of the standard or more than $1,000.

Business Insight
e-Business Perspective

Computerized standard cost systems represent one of the most complex accounting systems to develop and maintain. The standard cost system must be fully integrated into the general ledger. It must allow for the creation and timely maintenance of the database of standard usage and costs for every product. It must perform variance computations. And it must also produce variance reports by product, department, or employee. With the increased use of automation and robotics, the computerized standard cost system may even be tied directly into these systems to gather variance information.

STATEMENT PRESENTATION OF VARIANCES

In income statements **prepared for management** under a standard cost accounting system, **cost of goods sold is stated at standard cost and the variances are separately disclosed**, as shown in Illustration 11-28. The statement shown is based entirely on the production and sale of Weed-O. It assumes selling and administrative costs of $3,000. Observe that each variance is shown, as well as the total net variance. In this example, variations from standard costs reduced net income by $2,500.

Illustration 11-28
Variances in income statement for management

XONIC, INC.		
Income Statement		
For the Month Ended June 30, 2005		
Sales		$60,000
Cost of goods sold (at standard)		42,000
Gross profit (at standard)		18,000
Variances		
Materials price	$ 420	
Materials quantity	600	
Labor price	(420)	
Labor quantity	1,000	
Overhead controllable	500	
Overhead volume	400	
Total variance unfavorable		**2,500**
Gross profit (actual)		15,500
Selling and administrative expenses		3,000
Net income		$12,500

In financial statements prepared for stockholders and other external users, standard costs may be used. The costing of inventories at standard costs is in accordance with generally accepted accounting principles when there are no significant differences between actual costs and standard costs. **Hewlett-Packard** and **Jostens, Inc.**, for example, report their inventories at standard costs. However, if there are significant differences between actual and standard costs, inventories and cost of goods sold must be reported at actual costs.

It is also possible to show the variances in an income statement prepared in the variable costing (CVP) format. To do so, it is necessary to analyze the overhead variances into variable and fixed components. This type of analysis is explained in cost accounting textbooks.

Balanced Scorecard

Financial measures (measurement of dollars), such as variance analysis and return on investment (ROI), are useful tools for evaluating performance. However, many companies now supplement these financial measures with nonfinancial measures to better assess performance and anticipate future results. For example, airlines, like **Delta**, **American**, and **United**, use capacity utilization as an important measure to understand and predict future performance. Newspaper publishers, such as the *New York Times* and the *St. Louis Post-Dispatch*, use circulation figures as another measure by which to assess performance. Some key nonfinancial measures used in various industries are listed in Illustration 11-29.

STUDY OBJECTIVE

8

Describe the balanced scorecard approach to performance evaluation.

Illustration 11-29
Nonfinancial measures
used in various industries

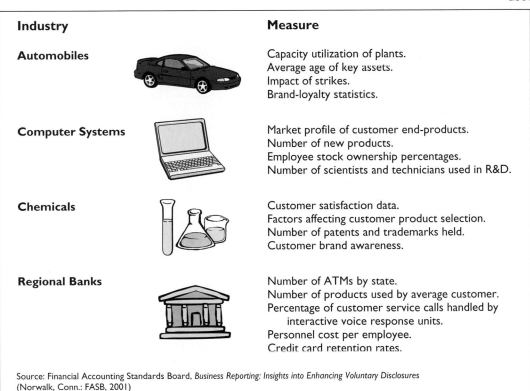

Industry	Measure
Automobiles	Capacity utilization of plants. Average age of key assets. Impact of strikes. Brand-loyalty statistics.
Computer Systems	Market profile of customer end-products. Number of new products. Employee stock ownership percentages. Number of scientists and technicians used in R&D.
Chemicals	Customer satisfaction data. Factors affecting customer product selection. Number of patents and trademarks held. Customer brand awareness.
Regional Banks	Number of ATMs by state. Number of products used by average customer. Percentage of customer service calls handled by interactive voice response units. Personnel cost per employee. Credit card retention rates.

Source: Financial Accounting Standards Board, *Business Reporting: Insights into Enhancing Voluntary Disclosures* (Norwalk, Conn.: FASB, 2001)

Most companies recognize that both financial and nonfinancial measures can provide useful insights into what is happening in the company. As a result, many companies now use a broad-based measurement approach, called the balanced scorecard, to evaluate performance. The **balanced scorecard** incorporates financial and nonfinancial measures in an integrated system that links performance measurement and a company's strategic goals. The balanced scorecard concept is very popular: Nearly 50 percent of the largest companies in the United States including **Unilever**, **Chase**, and **Wal-Mart**, are using this approach.

The balanced scorecard evaluates company performance from a series of "perspectives." The four most commonly employed perspectives are as follows.

1. The **financial perspective** is the most traditional view of the company. It employs financial measures of performance used by most firms.

2. The **customer perspective** evaluates how well the company is performing from the viewpoint of those people who buy and use its products or services. This view measures how well the company compares to competitors in terms of price, quality, product innovation, customer service, and other dimensions.

3. The **internal process perspective** evaluates the internal operating processes critical to success. All critical aspects of the value chain—including product development, production, delivery and after-sale service—are evaluated to ensure that the company is operating effectively and efficiently.

4. The **learning and growth perspective** evaluates how well the company develops and retains its employees. This would include an evaluation of such things as employee skills, employee satisfaction, training programs, and information dissemination.

Within each perspective, the balanced scorecard identifies objectives that will contribute to attainment of strategic goals. Illustration 11-30 shows examples of objectives within each perspective.

Illustration 11-30
Examples of objectives within the four perspectives of balanced scorecard

Financial perspective
  Return on assets
  Net income
  Credit rating
  Share price
  Profit per employee

Customer perspective
  Percentage of customers who would recommend product to a friend
  Customer retention
  Response time per customer request
  Brand recognition
  Customer service expense per customer

Internal process perspective
  Percentage of defect-free products
  Stockouts
  Labor utilization rates
  Waste reduction
  Planning accuracy

Learning and growth perspective
  Percentage of employees leaving in less than one year
  Number of cross-trained employees
  Ethics violations
  Training hours
  Reportable accidents

The objectives are linked across perspectives in order to tie performance measurement to company goals. The financial objectives are normally set first, and then objectives are set in the other perspectives in order to accomplish the financial objectives.

For example, within the financial perspective, a common goal is to increase profit per dollars invested as measured by ROI. In order to increase ROI, a customer perspective objective might be to increase customer satisfaction as measured by the percentage of customers who would recommend the product to a friend. In order to increase customer satisfaction, an internal business process perspective objective might be to increase product quality as measured by the percentage of defect-free units. Finally, in order to increase the percentage of defect-free units, the learning and growth perspective objective might be to reduce factory employee turnover as measured by percentage of employees leaving in under one year.

Illustration 11-31 illustrates this linkage across perspectives.

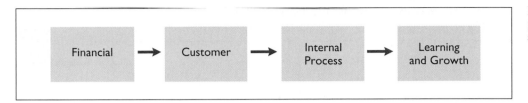

Illustration 11-31 Linked process across balanced scorecard perspectives

Through this linked process, the company can better understand how to achieve its goals and what measures to use to evaluate performance.

In summary, the balanced scorecard does the following:

1. Employs both financial and nonfinancial measures. (For example, ROI is a financial measure; employee turnover is a nonfinancial measure.)
2. Creates linkages so that high-level corporate goals can be communicated all the way down to the shop floor.
3. Provides measurable objectives for such nonfinancial measures as product quality, rather than vague statements such as "We would like to improve quality."
4. Integrates all of the company's goals into a single performance measurement system, so that an inappropriate amount of weight will not be placed on any single goal.

Business Insight
Management Perspective

Many of the benefits of a balanced scorecard approach are evident in the improved operations at **United Airlines**. At the time it filed for bankruptcy in 2002, United had a reputation for some of the worst service in the airline business. But when Glenn Tilton took over as United's Chief Executive Officer in September 2002, he recognized that things had to change.

One thing he did was to implement an incentive program that allows all of United's 63,000 employees to earn a bonus of 2.5 percent or more of their wages if the company "exceeds its goals for on-time flight departures and for customer intent to fly United again." Since instituting this program the company's on-time departures are among the best, its customer complaints have been reduced considerably, and its number of customers who say that they would fly United again is at its highest level ever. While none of these things guarantees that United will survive, these improvements certainly increase its chances.

SOURCE: Susan Carey, "Friendlier Skies: In Bankruptcy, United Airlines Forges a Path to Better Service," *Wall Street Journal Online* (June 15, 2004).

BEFORE YOU GO ON . . .

▶**Review It**

1. What are the formulas for computing the total, price, and quantity variances for direct labor?

2. What are the formulas for computing the total, controllable, and volume variances for manufacturing overhead?

3. How are standard costs and variances reported in income statements prepared for management?

4. What are the basic characteristics of the balanced scorecard?

☑ THE NAVIGATOR

Using the Decision Toolkit

Assume that during the past month **Sanford** produced 10,000 cartons of Liquid ACCENT® highlighters. Liquid ACCENT® offers a translucent barrel and cap with a visible ink supply for see-through color. The special fluorescent ink is fade- and water-resistant. Each carton contains 100 boxes of markers, and each box contains five markers. The markers come in boxes of one of five fluorescent colors—orange, blue, yellow, green, and pink—and in a five-color set.

Assume the following additional facts: The standard cost for one carton of 500 markers is as follows.

Manufacturing Cost Elements	Quantity	×	Price	=	Cost
Direct materials					
Tips (boxes of 500)	500	×	$ 0.03	=	$ 15.00
Translucent barrels and caps (boxes of 500)	500	×	$ 0.09	=	45.00
Fluorescent ink (100 oz. containers)	100 oz.	×	$ 0.32	=	32.00
Total direct materials					92.00
Direct labor	0.25 hours	×	$ 9.00	=	2.25
Overhead	0.25 hours	×	$48.00	=	12.00
					$106.25

During the month, the following transactions occurred in manufacturing the 10,000 cartons of highlighters.

1. Purchased 10,000 boxes of tips for $148,000 ($14.80 per 500 tips); purchased 10,200 boxes of translucent barrels and caps for $453,900 ($44.50 per 500 barrels and caps); and purchased 9,900 containers of fluorescent ink for $328,185 ($33.15 per 100 ounces).

2. All materials purchased during the period were used to make markers during the period.

3. 2,300 direct labor hours were worked at a total labor cost of $20,240 (an average hourly rate of $8.80).

4. Variable manufacturing overhead incurred was $34,600, and fixed overhead incurred was $84,000.

The manufacturing overhead rate of $48.00 is based on a normal capacity of 2,600 direct labor hours. The total budget at this capacity is $83,980 fixed and $40,820 variable.

Instructions
Determine whether Sanford met its price and quantity objectives relative to materials, labor, and overhead.

Solution

To determine whether Sanford met its price and quantity objectives, compute the total variance and the variances for each of the manufacturing cost elements.

Total Variance

Actual cost incurred:		
Direct materials		
Tips	$148,000	
Translucent barrels and caps	453,900	
Fluorescent ink	328,185	
Total direct materials		$ 930,085
Direct labor		20,240
Overhead		118,600
Total actual costs		1,068,925
Standard cost (10,000 × $106.25)		1,062,500
Total variance		$ 6,425 U

Direct Materials Variances

Total	=	$930,085	−	$920,000	= $10,085 U
				(10,000 × $92)	
Price (Tips)	=	$148,000	−	$150,000	= $ 2,000 F
		(10,000 × $14.80)		(10,000 × $15.00)	
Price (Barrels and caps)	=	$453,900	−	$459,000	= $ 5,100 F
		(10,200 × $44.50)		(10,200 × $45.00)	
Price (Ink)	=	$328,185	−	$316,800	= $11,385 U
		(9,900 × $33.15)		(9,900 × $32.00)	
Quantity (Tips)	=	$150,000	−	$150,000	= $ 0
		(10,000 × $15.00)		(10,000 × $15.00)	
Quantity (Barrels and caps)	=	$459,000	−	$450,000	= $ 9,000 U
		(10,200 × $45.00)		(10,000 × $45.00)	
Quantity (Ink)	=	$316,800	−	$320,000	= $ 3,200 F
		(9,900 × $32.00)		(10,000 × $32.00)	

Direct Labor Variances

Total	=	$20,240	−	$22,500	− $ 2,260 F
		(2,300 × $8.80)		(2,500 × $9.00)	
Price	=	$20,240	−	$20,700	= $ 460 F
		(2,300 × $8.80)		(2,300 × $9.00)	
Quantity	=	$20,700	−	$22,500	= $ 1,800 F
		(2,300 × $9.00)		(2,500 × $9.00)	

Overhead Variances

Total	=	$118,600	− $120,000	= $ 1,400 F
		($84,000 + $34,600)	(2,500 × $48)	
Controllable	=	$118,600	− $123,230	= $ 4,630 F
		($84,000 + $34,600)	[(2,500 × $15.70)* + $83,980]	
		*$40,820 ÷ 2,600	= $15.70 per direct labor hour	
Volume	=	$32.30**	× (2,600 − 2,500)	= $ 3,230 U
		**$83,980 ÷ 2,600	= $ 32.30	

Sanford's total variance was an unfavorable $6,425. The unfavorable materials variance outweighed the favorable labor and overhead variances. The primary determinants were an unfavorable price variance for ink and an unfavorable quantity variance for barrels and caps.

THE NAVIGATOR

Summary of Study Objectives

1 *Distinguish between a standard and a budget.* Both standards and budgets are predetermined costs. The primary difference is that a standard is a unit amount, whereas a budget is a total amount. A standard may be regarded as the budgeted cost per unit of product.

2 *Identify the advantages of standard costs.* Standard costs offer a number of advantages. They (a) facilitate management planning, (b) promote greater economy, (c) are useful in setting selling prices, (d) contribute to management control, (e) permit "management by exception," and (f) simplify the costing of inventories and reduce clerical costs.

3 *Describe how standards are set.* The direct materials price standard should be based on the delivered cost of raw materials plus an allowance for receiving and handling. The direct materials quantity standard should establish the required quantity plus an allowance for waste and spoilage.

The direct labor price standard should be based on current wage rates and anticipated adjustments such as COLAs. It also generally includes payroll taxes and fringe benefits. Direct labor quantity standards should be based on required production time plus an allowance for rest periods, cleanup, machine setup, and machine downtime.

For manufacturing overhead, a standard predetermined overhead rate is used. It is based on an expected standard activity index such as standard direct labor hours or standard machine hours.

4 *State the formulas for determining direct materials and direct labor variances.* The formulas for the direct materials variances are:

$$\left(\begin{array}{c}\text{Actual quantity}\\ \times \text{ Actual price}\end{array}\right) - \left(\begin{array}{c}\text{Standard quantity}\\ \times \text{ Standard price}\end{array}\right) = \begin{array}{l}\text{Total}\\ \text{materials}\\ \text{variance}\end{array}$$

$$\left(\begin{array}{c}\text{Actual quantity}\\ \times \text{ Actual price}\end{array}\right) - \left(\begin{array}{c}\text{Actual quantity}\\ \times \text{ Standard price}\end{array}\right) = \begin{array}{l}\text{Materials}\\ \text{price}\\ \text{variance}\end{array}$$

$$\left(\begin{array}{c}\text{Actual quantity}\\ \times \text{ Standard price}\end{array}\right) - \left(\begin{array}{c}\text{Standard quantity}\\ \times \text{ Standard price}\end{array}\right) = \begin{array}{l}\text{Materials}\\ \text{quantity}\\ \text{variance}\end{array}$$

The formulas for the direct labor variances are:

$$\left(\begin{array}{c}\text{Actual hours}\\ \times \text{ Actual rate}\end{array}\right) - \left(\begin{array}{c}\text{Standard hours}\\ \times \text{ Standard rate}\end{array}\right) = \begin{array}{l}\text{Total}\\ \text{labor}\\ \text{variance}\end{array}$$

$$\left(\begin{array}{c}\text{Actual hours}\\ \times \text{ Actual rate}\end{array}\right) - \left(\begin{array}{c}\text{Actual hours}\\ \times \text{ Standard rate}\end{array}\right) = \begin{array}{l}\text{Labor}\\ \text{price}\\ \text{variance}\end{array}$$

$$\left(\begin{array}{c}\text{Actual hours}\\ \times \text{ Standard rate}\end{array}\right) - \left(\begin{array}{c}\text{Standard hours}\\ \times \text{ Standard rate}\end{array}\right) = \begin{array}{l}\text{Labor}\\ \text{quantity}\\ \text{variance}\end{array}$$

5 *State the formulas for determining manufacturing overhead variances.* The formulas for the manufacturing overhead variances are:

$$\left(\begin{array}{c}\text{Actual}\\ \text{overhead}\end{array}\right) - \left(\begin{array}{c}\text{Overhead}\\ \text{applied}\end{array}\right) = \begin{array}{l}\text{Total overhead}\\ \text{variance}\end{array}$$

$$\left(\begin{array}{c}\text{Actual}\\ \text{overhead}\end{array}\right) - \left(\begin{array}{c}\text{Overhead}\\ \text{budgeted}\end{array}\right) = \begin{array}{l}\text{Overhead control-}\\ \text{lable variance}\end{array}$$

$$\left(\begin{array}{c}\text{Fixed}\\ \text{overhead}\\ \text{rate}\end{array}\right) \times \left(\begin{array}{c}\text{Normal} \quad \text{Standard}\\ \text{capacity} - \text{hours}\\ \text{hours} \quad \text{allowed}\end{array}\right) = \begin{array}{l}\text{Overhead}\\ \text{volume}\\ \text{variance}\end{array}$$

6 *Discuss the reporting of variances.* Variances are reported to management in variance reports. The reports facilitate management by exception by highlighting significant differences.

7 *Prepare an income statement for management under a standard costing system.* Under a standard costing system, an income statement prepared for management will report cost of goods sold at standard cost and then disclose each variance separately.

8 *Describe the balanced scorecard approach to performance evaluation.* The balanced scorecard incorporates financial and nonfinancial measures in an integrated system that links performance measurement and a company's strategic goals. It employs four perspectives: financial; customer; internal processes; and learning and growth. Objectives are set within each of these perspectives that link to objectives within the other perspectives.

☑ THE NAVIGATOR

DECISION TOOLKIT—A SUMMARY

Decision Checkpoints	Info Needed for Decision	Tool to Use for Decision	How to Evaluate Results
Has management accomplished its price and quantity objectives regarding materials?	Actual cost and standard cost of materials	Materials price and materials quantity variances	Positive (favorable) variances suggest that price and quantity objectives have been met.
Has management accomplished its price and quantity objectives regarding labor?	Actual cost and standard cost of labor	Labor price and labor quantity variances	Positive (favorable) variances suggest that price and quantity objectives have been met.
Has management accomplished its price and quantity objectives regarding overhead?	Actual cost and standard cost of overhead	Overhead controllable variance and overhead volume variance	Positive (favorable) variances suggest that price and quantity objectives have been met.

APPENDIX
STANDARD COST ACCOUNTING SYSTEM

A **standard cost accounting system** is a double-entry system of accounting. In this system, standard costs are used in making entries, and variances are formally recognized in the accounts. A standard cost system may be used with either job order or process costing. At this point, we will explain and illustrate a **standard cost, job order cost accounting system**. The system is based on two important assumptions: (1) Variances from standards are recognized at the earliest opportunity. (2) The Work in Process account is maintained exclusively on the basis of standard costs. In practice, there are many variations among standard cost systems. The system described here should prepare you for systems you see in the "real world."

> **STUDY OBJECTIVE**
> **9**
> Identify the features of a standard cost accounting system.

Journal Entries

We will use the transactions of Xonic, Inc. to illustrate the journal entries. Note as you study the entries that the major difference between the entries here and those for the job order cost accounting system in Chapter 2 is the **variance accounts**.

1. Purchase raw materials on account for $13,020 when the standard cost is $12,600.

Raw Materials Inventory	12,600	
Materials Price Variance	420	
Accounts Payable		13,020
(To record purchase of materials)		

The inventory account is debited for actual quantities at standard cost. This enables the perpetual materials records to show actual quantities. The price variance, which is unfavorable, is debited to Materials Price Variance.

2. Incur direct labor costs of $20,580 when the standard labor cost is $21,000.

Factory Labor	21,000	
Labor Price Variance		420
Wages Payable		20,580
(To record direct labor costs)		

Like the raw materials inventory account, Factory Labor is debited for actual hours worked at the standard hourly rate of pay. In this case, the labor variance is favorable. Thus, Labor Price Variance is credited.

3. Incur actual manufacturing overhead costs of $10,900.

Manufacturing Overhead	10,900	
Accounts Payable/Cash/Acc. Depreciation		10,900
(To record overhead incurred)		

The controllable overhead variance is not recorded at this time. It depends on standard hours applied to work in process. This amount is not known at the time overhead is incurred.

4. Issue raw materials for production at a cost of $12,600 when the standard cost is $12,000.

Work in Process Inventory	12,000	
Materials Quantity Variance	600	
Raw Materials Inventory		12,600
(To record issuance of raw materials)		

Work in Process Inventory is debited for standard materials quantities used at standard prices. The variance account is debited because the variance is unfavorable. Raw Materials Inventory is credited for actual quantities at standard prices.

5. Assign factory labor to production at a cost of $21,000 when standard cost is $20,000.

Work in Process Inventory	20,000	
Labor Quantity Variance	1,000	
Factory Labor		21,000
(To assign factory labor to jobs)		

Work in Process Inventory is debited for standard labor hours at standard rates. The unfavorable variance is debited to Labor Quantity Variance. The credit to Factory Labor produces a zero balance in this account.

6. Applying manufacturing overhead to production $10,000.

Work in Process Inventory	10,000	
Manufacturing Overhead		10,000
(To assign overhead to jobs)		

Work in Process Inventory is debited for standard hours allowed multiplied by the standard overhead rate.

7. Transfer completed work to finished goods $42,000.

Finished Goods Inventory	42,000	
Work in Process Inventory		42,000
(To record transfer of completed work to finished goods)		

In this example, both inventory accounts are at standard cost.

8. The 1,000 gallons of Weed-O are sold for $60,000.

Accounts Receivable	60,000	
Cost of Goods Sold	42,000	
Sales		60,000
Finished Goods Inventory		42,000
(To record sale of finished goods and the cost of goods sold)		

Cost of Goods Sold is debited at standard cost. Gross profit, in turn, is the difference between sales and the standard cost of goods sold.

9. Recognize unfavorable overhead variances: controllable, $500; volume, $400.

Overhead Controllable Variance	500	
Overhead Volume Variance	400	
Manufacturing Overhead		900
(To recognize overhead variances)		

Prior to this entry, a debit balance of $900 existed in Manufacturing Overhead. This entry therefore produces a zero balance in the Manufacturing Overhead account. The information needed for this entry is often not available until the end of the accounting period.

Ledger Accounts

The cost accounts for Xonic, Inc., after posting the entries, are shown in Illustration 11A-1. Note that six variance accounts are included in the ledger. The remaining accounts are the same as those illustrated for a job order cost system in Chapter 2, in which only actual costs were used.

Illustration 11A-1 Cost accounts with variances

Raw Materials Inventory

(1)	12,600	(4)	12,600	

Materials Price Variance

(1)	420	

Work in Process Inventory

(4)	12,000	(7)	42,000	
(5)	20,000			
(6)	10,000			

Factory Labor

(2)	21,000	(5)	21,000	

Materials Quantity Variance

(4)	600	

Finished Goods Inventory

(7)	42,000	(8)	42,000	

Manufacturing Overhead

(3)	10,900	(6)	10,000	
		(9)	900	

Labor Price Variance

		(2)	420	

Cost of Goods Sold

(8)	42,000	

Labor Quantity Variance

(5)	1,000	

Overhead Controllable Variance

(9)	500	

Overhead Volume Variance

(9)	400	

Helpful Hint All debit balances in variance accounts indicate unfavorable variances; all credit balances indicate favorable variances.

Summary of Study Objective for Appendix

9 *Identify the features of a standard cost accounting system.* In a standard cost accounting system, standard costs are journalized and posted, and separate variance accounts are maintained in the ledger.

Glossary

Balanced scorecard An approach that incorporates financial and nonfinancial measures in an integrated system that links performance measurement and a company's strategic goals. (p. 463)

Customer perspective A viewpoint employed in the balanced scorecard to evaluate the company from the perspective of those people who buy and use its products or services. (p. 463)

Direct labor price standard The rate per hour that should be incurred for direct labor. (p. 448)

Direct labor quantity standard The time that should be required to make one unit of product. (p. 449)

Direct materials price standard The cost per unit of direct materials that should be incurred. (p. 448)

Direct materials quantity standard The quantity of direct materials that should be used per unit of finished goods. (p. 448)

Financial perspective A viewpoint employed in the balanced scorecard to evaluate a company's performance using financial measures. (p. 463)

Ideal standards Standards based on the optimum level of performance under perfect operating conditions. (p. 447)

Internal process perspective A viewpoint employed in the balanced scorecard to evaluate the effectiveness and efficiency of a company's value chain, including product development, production, delivery, and after-sale service. (p. 464)

Labor price variance The difference between the actual hours times the actual rate and the actual hours times the standard rate for labor. (p. 456)

Labor quantity variance The difference between actual hours times the standard rate and standard hours times the standard rate for labor. (p. 456)

Learning and growth perspective A viewpoint employed in the balanced scorecard to evaluate how well a company develops and retains its employees. (p. 464)

Materials price variance The difference between the actual quantity times the actual price and the actual quantity times the standard price for materials. (p. 453)

Materials quantity variance The difference between the actual quantity times the standard price and the standard quantity times the standard price for materials. (p. 453)

Normal standards Standards based on an efficient level of performance that are attainable under expected operating conditions. (p. 447)

Overhead controllable variance The difference between actual overhead incurred and overhead budgeted for the standard hours allowed. (p. 459)

Overhead volume variance The difference between normal capacity hours and standard hours allowed times the fixed overhead rate. (p. 460)

Standard cost accounting system A double-entry system of accounting in which standard costs are used in making entries and variances are recognized in the accounts. (p. 469)

Standard costs Predetermined unit costs which are used as measures of performance. (p. 445)

Standard hours allowed The hours that should have been worked for the units produced. (p. 458)

Standard predetermined overhead rate An overhead rate determined by dividing budgeted overhead costs by an expected standard activity index. (p. 449)

Total labor variance The difference between actual hours times the actual rate and standard hours times the standard rate for labor. (p. 456)

Total materials variance The difference between the actual quantity times the actual price and the standard quantity times the standard price of materials. (p. 452)

Total overhead variance The difference between actual overhead costs and overhead costs applied to work done. (p. 458)

Variances The difference between total actual costs and total standard costs. (p. 451)

Demonstration Problem

Manlow Company makes a cologne called Allure. The standard cost for one bottle of Allure is as follows.

Manufacturing Cost Elements	Standard			
	Quantity	× Price	=	Cost
Direct materials	6 oz.	× $ 0.90	=	$ 5.40
Direct labor	0.5 hrs.	× $12.00	=	6.00
Manufacturing overhead	0.5 hrs.	× $ 4.80	=	2.40
				$13.80

During the month, the following transactions occurred in manufacturing 10,000 bottles of Allure.

1. 58,000 ounces of materials were purchased at $1.00 per ounce.
2. All the materials purchased were used to produce the 10,000 bottles of Allure.
3. 4,900 direct labor hours were worked at a total labor cost of $56,350.
4. Variable manufacturing overhead incurred was $15,000 and fixed overhead incurred was $10,400.

The manufacturing overhead rate of $4.80 is based on a normal capacity of 5,200 direct labor hours. The total budget at this capacity is $10,400 fixed and $14,560 variable.

Instructions
Compute the total variance and the variances for each of the manufacturing cost elements.

Solution to Demonstration Problem

Total Variance

Actual costs incurred	
Direct materials	$ 58,000
Direct labor	56,350
Manufacturing overhead	25,400
	139,750
Standard cost (10,000 × $13.80)	138,000
Total variance	$ 1,750 U

Direct Materials Variances

Total	=	$58,000	−	$54,000	=	$4,000 U
		(58,000 × $1.00)		(60,000 × $0.90)		
Price	=	$58,000	−	$52,200	=	$5,800 U
		(58,000 × $1.00)		(58,000 × $0.90)		
Quantity	=	$52,200	−	$54,000	=	$1,800 F
		(58,000 × $0.90)		(60,000 × $0.90)		

Direct Labor Variances

Total	=	$56,350	−	$60,000	=	$3,650 F
		(4,900 × $11.50)		(5,000 × $12.00)		
Price	=	$56,350	−	$58,800	=	$2,450 F
		(4,900 × $11.50)		(4,900 × $12.00)		
Quantity	=	$58,800	−	$60,000	=	$1,200 F
		(4,900 × $12.00)		(5,000 × $12.00)		

Action Plan
- Check to make sure the total variance and the sum of the individual variances are equal.
- Find the price variance first, then the quantity variance.
- Base budgeted overhead costs on flexible budget data.
- Base overhead applied on standard hours allowed.
- Ignore actual hours worked in computing overhead variances.
- Relate the overhead volume variance solely to fixed costs.

Overhead Variances

Total	=	$25,400	−	$24,000	=	$ 1,400 U
		($15,000 + $10,400)		(5,000 × $4.80)		
Controllable	=	$25,400	−	$24,400	=	$ 1,000 U
		($15,000 + $10,400)		($14,000* + $10,400)		
		*$14,560 ÷ 5,200	=	$2.80; $2.80 × 5,000	=	$14,000
Volume	=	$2.00**	×	(5,200 − 5,000)	=	$ 400 U
		**$10,400 ÷ 5,200	=	$2.00		

Note: All asterisked Questions, Exercises, and Problems relate to material in the appendix to the chapter.

Self-Study Questions

Answers are at the end of the chapter.

(SO 1) 1. Standards differ from budgets in that:
   (a) budgets but not standards may be used in valuing inventories.
   (b) budgets but not standards may be journalized and posted.
   (c) budgets are a total amount and standards are a unit amount.
   (d) only budgets contribute to management planning and control.

(SO 2) 2. The advantages of standard costs include all of the following *except:*
   (a) management by exception may be used.
   (b) management planning is facilitated.
   (c) they may simplify the costing of inventories.
   (d) management must use a static budget.

(SO 3) 3. The setting of standards is:
   (a) a managerial accounting decision.
   (b) a management decision.
   (c) a worker decision.
   (d) preferably set at the ideal level of performance.

(SO 4) 4. Each of the following formulas is correct except:
   (a) Labor price variance = (Actual hours × Actual rate) − (Actual hours × Standard rate).
   (b) Overhead controllable variance = Actual overhead − Overhead budgeted.
   (c) Materials price variance = (Actual quantity × Actual cost) − (Standard quantity × Standard cost).
   (d) Overhead volume variance = Fixed overhead rate × (Normal capacity hours − Standard capacity hours).

(SO 4) 5. In producing product AA, 6,300 pounds of direct materials were used at a cost of $1.10 per pound. The standard was 6,000 pounds at $1.00 per pound. The direct materials quantity variance is:
   (a) $330 unfavorable.
   (b) $300 unfavorable.
   (c) $600 unfavorable.
   (d) $630 unfavorable.

(SO 4) 6. In producing product ZZ, 14,800 direct labor hours were used at a rate of $8.20 per hour. The standard was 15,000 hours at $8.00 per hour. Based on these data, the direct labor:

   (a) quantity variance is $1,600 favorable.
   (b) quantity variance is $1,600 unfavorable.
   (c) price variance is $2,960 favorable.
   (d) price variance is $3,000 unfavorable.

(SO 5) 7. Which of the following is *correct* about overhead variances?
   (a) The controllable variance generally pertains to fixed overhead costs.
   (b) The volume variance pertains solely to variable overhead costs.
   (c) Standard hours actually worked are used in each variance.
   (d) Budgeted overhead costs are based on the flexible overhead budget.

(SO 5) 8. The formula for computing the total overhead variance is:
   (a) actual overhead less overhead applied.
   (b) overhead budgeted less overhead applied.
   (c) actual overhead less overhead budgeted.
   (d) No correct answer given.

(SO 6) 9. Which of the following is *incorrect* about variance reports?
   (a) They facilitate "management by exception."
   (b) They should only be sent to the top level of management.
   (c) They should be prepared as soon as possible.
   (d) They may vary in form, content, and frequency among companies.

(SO 8) 10. Which of the following would *not* be an objective used in the customer perspective of the balanced scorecard approach?
   (a) Percentage of customers who would recommend product to a friend.
   (b) Customer retention.
   (c) Brand recognition.
   (d) Earnings per share.

(SO 9) *11. Which of the following is *incorrect* about a standard cost accounting system?
   (a) It is applicable to job order costing.
   (b) It is applicable to process costing.
   (c) It is a single-entry system.
   (d) It keeps separate accounts for each variance.

Questions

1. (a) "Standard costs are the expected total cost of completing a job." Is this correct? Explain.
   (b) "A standard imposed by a governmental agency is known as a regulation." Do you agree? Explain.

2. (a) Explain the similarities and differences between standards and budgets.
   (b) Contrast the accounting for standards and budgets.

3. Standard costs facilitate management planning. What are the other advantages of standard costs?

4. Contrast the roles of the management accountant and management in setting standard costs.

5. Distinguish between an ideal standard and a normal standard.

6. What factors should be considered in setting (a) the direct materials price standard and (b) the direct materials quantity standard?

7. "The objective in setting the direct labor quantity standard is to determine the aggregate time required to make one unit of product." Do you agree? What allowances should be made in setting this standard?

8. How is the predetermined overhead rate determined when standard costs are used?

9. What is the difference between a favorable cost variance and an unfavorable cost variance?

10. In each of the following formulas, supply the words that should be inserted for each number in parentheses.
    (a) (Actual quantity × (1)) − (Standard quantity × (2)) = Total materials variance
    (b) ((3) × Actual price) − (Actual quantity × (4)) = Materials price variance
    (c) (Actual quantity × (5)) − ((6) × Standard price) = Materials quantity variance

11. In the direct labor variance matrix, there are three factors: (1) Actual hours × Actual rate, (2) Actual hours × Standard rate, and (3) Standard hours × Standard rate. Using the numbers, indicate the formulas for each of the direct labor variances.

12. Keene Company's standard predetermined overhead rate is $8 per direct labor hour. For the month of June, 26,000 actual hours were worked, and 27,500 standard hours were allowed. Normal capacity hours were 28,000. How much overhead was applied?

13. If the $8 per hour overhead rate in question 12 includes $5 variable, and actual overhead costs were $218,000, what is the overhead controllable variance for June? Is the variance favorable or unfavorable?

14. Using the data in questions 12 and 13, what is the overhead volume variance for June? Is the variance favorable or unfavorable?

15. What is the purpose of computing the overhead volume variance? What is the basic formula for this variance?

16. Nancy Morgan does not understand why the overhead volume variance indicates that fixed overhead costs are under- or overapplied. Clarify this matter for Nancy.

17. Mike Darby is attempting to outline the important points about overhead variances on a class examination. List four points that Mike should include in his outline.

18. How often should variances be reported to management? What principle may be used with variance reports?

19. What circumstances may cause the purchasing department to be responsible for both an unfavorable materials price variance and an unfavorable materials quantity variance?

20. What are the four perspectives used in the balanced scorecard? Discuss the nature of each, and how the perspectives are linked.

21. Tom Jones says that the balanced scorecard was created to replace financial measures as the primary mechanism for performance evaluation. He says that it uses only nonfinancial measures. Is this true?

22. What are some examples of nonfinancial measures used by companies to evaluate performance?

23. (a) How are variances reported in income statements prepared for management? (b) May standard costs be used in preparing financial statements for stockholders? Explain.

*24. (a) Explain the basic features of a standard cost accounting system. (b) What type of balance will exist in the variance account when (1) the materials price variance is unfavorable and (2) the labor quantity variance is favorable?

Brief Exercises

BE11-1 Valdez Company uses both standards and budgets. For the year, estimated production of Product X is 500,000 units. Total estimated cost for materials and labor are $1,000,000 and $1,600,000. Compute the estimates for (a) a standard cost and (b) a budgeted cost.

Distinguish between a standard and a budget.
(SO 1)

BE11-2 Hideo Company accumulates the following data concerning raw materials in making one gallon of finished product: (1) Price—net purchase price $3.20, freight-in

Set direct materials standard.
(SO 3)

$0.20 and receiving and handling $0.10. (2) Quantity—required materials 2.6 pounds, allowance for waste and spoilage 0.4 pounds. Compute the following.
(a) Standard direct materials price per gallon.
(b) Standard direct materials quantity per gallon.
(c) Total standard materials cost per gallon.

Set direct labor standard.
(SO 3)

BE11-3 Labor data for making one gallon of finished product in Hideo Company are as follows: (1) Price—hourly wage rate $10.00, payroll taxes $0.80, and fringe benefits $1.20. (2) Quantity—actual production time 1.2 hours, rest periods and clean up 0.25 hours, and setup and downtime 0.15 hours. Compute the following.
(a) Standard direct labor rate per hour.
(b) Standard direct labor hours per gallon.
(c) Standard labor cost per gallon.

Compute direct materials variances.
(SO 4)

BE11-4 Sprague Company's standard materials cost per unit of output is $10 (2 pounds × $5). During July, the company purchases and uses 3,300 pounds of materials costing $16,731 in making 1,500 units of finished product. Compute the total, price, and quantity materials variances.

Compute direct labor variances.
(SO 4)

BE11-5 Talbot Company's standard labor cost per unit of output is $20 (2 hours × $10 per hour). During August, the company incurs 1,900 hours of direct labor at an hourly cost of $9.60 per hour in making 1,000 units of finished product. Compute the total, price, and quantity labor variances.

Compute total overhead variance.
(SO 5)

BE11-6 In October, Russo Company reports 21,000 actual direct labor hours, and it incurs $96,000 of manufacturing overhead costs. Standard hours allowed for the work done is 20,000 hours. The predetermined overhead rate is $5 per direct labor hour. Compute the total overhead variance.

Compute the overhead controllable variance.
(SO 5)

BE11-7 Some overhead data for Russo Company are given in BE11-6. In addition, the flexible manufacturing overhead budget shows that budgeted costs are $4 variable per direct labor hour and $25,000 fixed. Compute the overhead controllable variance.

Compute overhead volume variance.
(SO 5)

BE11-8 Using the data in BE11-6 and BE11-7, compute the overhead volume variance. Normal capacity was 25,000 direct labor hours.

Match balanced scorecard perspectives.
(SO 8)

BE11-9 The four perspectives in the balanced scorecard are (1) financial, (2) customer, (3) internal process, and (4) learning and growth. Match each of the following objectives with the perspective it is most likely associated with: (a) Plant capacity utilization. (b) Employee work days missed due to injury. (c) Return on assets. (d) Brand recognition.

Journalize materials variances.
(SO 9)

*BE11-10 Journalize the following transactions for McBee Manufacturing.
(a) Purchased 6,000 units of raw materials on account for $11,500. The standard cost was $12,000.
(b) Issued 5,600 units of raw materials for production. The standard units were 5,800.

Journalize labor variances.
(SO 9)

*BE11-11 Journalize the following transactions for Worrel Manufacturing.
(a) Incurred direct labor costs of $24,000 for 3,000 hours. The standard labor cost was $24,600.
(b) Assigned 3,000 direct labor hours costing $24,000 to production. Standard hours were 3,100.

Exercises

Compute standard materials costs.
(SO 3)

E11-1 Raul Mondesi manufactures and sells homemade wine, and he wants to develop a standard cost per gallon. The following are required for production of a 50-gallon batch.

3,000 ounces of grape concentrate at $0.04 per ounce
54 pounds of granulated sugar at $0.30 per pound
60 lemons at $0.60 each
50 yeast tablets at $0.25 each
50 nutrient tablets at $0.20 each
2,500 ounces of water at $0.003 per ounce

Raul estimates that 4% of the grape concentrate is wasted, 10% of the sugar is lost, and 20% of the lemons cannot be used.

Instructions
Compute the standard cost of the ingredients for one gallon of wine. (Carry computations to two decimal places.)

E11-2 The standard cost of Product B manufactured by Gomez Company includes three units of direct materials at $5.00 per unit. During June, 27,600 units of direct materials are purchased at a cost of $4.70 per unit, and 27,600 units of direct materials are used to produce 9,000 units of Product B.

Compute materials price and quantity variances.
(SO 4)

Instructions
(a) Compute the materials variance and the price and quantity variances.
(b) Repeat (a), assuming the purchase price is $5.20 and the quantity purchased and used is 26,400 units.

E11-3 Pagley Company's standard labor cost of producing one unit of Product DD is 4 hours at the rate of $12.00 per hour. During August, 40,500 hours of labor are incurred at a cost of $12.10 per hour to produce 10,000 units of Product DD.

Compute labor price and quantity variances.
(SO 4)

Instructions
(a) Compute the total labor variance.
(b) Compute the labor price and quantity variances.
(c) Repeat (b), assuming the standard is 4.2 hours of direct labor at $12.20 per hour.

E11-4 Rapid Repair Services, Inc. is trying to establish the standard labor cost of a typical oil change. The following data have been collected from time and motion studies conducted over the past month.

Compute labor quantity variance.
(SO 3, 4)

Actual time spent on the oil change	1.0 hour
Hourly wage rate	$10
Payroll taxes	10% of wage rate
Setup and downtime	10% of actual labor time
Cleanup and rest periods	30% of actual labor time
Fringe benefits	25% of wage rate

Instructions
(a) Determine the standard direct labor hours per oil change.
(b) Determine the standard direct labor hourly rate.
(c) Determine the standard direct labor cost per oil change.
(d) If an oil change took 1.5 hours at the standard hourly rate, what was the direct labor quantity variance?

E11-5 Kopecky Inc., which produces a single product, has prepared the following standard cost sheet for one unit of the product.

Compute materials and labor variances.
(SO 4)

Direct materials (8 pounds at $2.50 per pound)	$20
Direct labor (3 hours at $12.00 per hour)	$36

During the month of April, the company manufactures 240 units and incurs the following actual costs.

Direct materials purchased and used (1,900 pounds)	$4,940
Direct labor (700 hours)	$8,120

Instructions
Compute the total, price, and quantity variances for materials and labor.

E11-6 The following direct materials and direct labor data pertain to the operations of Batista Manufacturing Company for the month of August.

Compute the materials and labor variances and list reasons for unfavorable variances.
(SO 4, 6)

Costs		Quantities	
Actual labor rate	$13 per hour	Actual hours incurred and used	4,250 hours
Actual materials price	$128 per ton	Actual quantity of materials purchased and used	1,250 tons
Standard labor rate	$12 per hour	Standard hours used	4,300 hours
Standard materials price	$130 per ton	Standard quantity of materials used	1,200 tons

Instructions

(a) Compute the total, price, and quantity variances for materials and labor.
(b) Provide two possible explanations for each of the unfavorable variances calculated above, and suggest where responsibility for the unfavorable result might be placed.

Compute manufacturing overhead variances and interpret findings.
(SO 5)

E11-7   The following information was taken from the annual manufacturing overhead cost budget of Fernetti Company.

Variable manufacturing overhead costs	$33,000
Fixed manufacturing overhead costs	$21,450
Normal production level in labor hours	16,500
Normal production level in units	4,125
Standard labor hours per unit	4

During the year, 4,000 units were produced, 16,100 hours were worked, and the actual manufacturing overhead was $54,000. Actual fixed manufacturing overhead costs equaled budgeted fixed manufacturing overhead costs. Overhead is applied on the basis of direct labor hours.

Instructions

(a) Compute the total, fixed, and variable predetermined manufacturing overhead rates.
(b) Compute the total, controllable, and volume overhead variances.
(c) Briefly interpret the overhead controllable and volume variances computed in (b).

Compute overhead variances.
(SO 5)

E11-8   The loan department of Local Bank uses standard costs to determine the overhead cost of processing loan applications. During the current month a fire occurred, and the accounting records for the department were mostly destroyed. The following data were salvaged from the ashes.

Standard variable overhead rate per hour	$9
Standard hours per application	2
Standard hours allowed	2,000
Standard fixed overhead rate per hour	$6
Actual fixed overhead cost	$13,200
Variable overhead budget based on standard hours allowed	$18,000
Fixed overhead budget	$13,200
Overhead controllable variance	$ 1,500 U

Instructions

(a) Determine the following.
    (1) Total actual overhead cost.
    (2) Actual variable overhead cost.
    (3) Variable overhead cost applied.
    (4) Fixed overhead cost applied.
    (5) Overhead volume variance.
(b) Determine how many loans were processed.

Compute overhead variances.
(SO 5)

E11-9   Manufacturing overhead data for the production of Product H by Rondell Company are as follows.

Overhead incurred for 52,000 actual direct labor hours worked	$213,000
Overhead rate (variable $3; fixed $1) at normal capacity of 54,000 direct labor hours	$4
Standard hours allowed for work done	52,000

Instructions

Compute the total, controllable, and volume overhead variances.

Prepare a variance report for direct labor.
(SO 4, 6)

E11-10   During March 2005, Garner Tool & Die Company worked on four jobs. A review of direct labor costs reveals the following summary data.

Job Number	Actual Hours	Actual Costs	Standard Hours	Standard Costs	Total Variance
A257	220	$ 4,400	225	$4,500	$ 100 F
A258	450	10,350	430	8,600	1,750 U
A259	300	6,150	300	6,000	150 U
A260	115	2,070	110	2,200	130 F
Total variance					$1,670 U

Analysis reveals that Job A257 was a repeat job. Job A258 was a rush order that required overtime work at premium rates of pay. Job A259 required a more experienced replacement worker on one shift. Work on Job A260 was done for one day by a new trainee when a regular worker was absent.

Instructions
Prepare a report for the plant supervisor on direct labor cost variances for March. The report should have columns for (1) Job No., (2) Actual Hours, (3) Standard Hours, (4) Quantity Variance, (5) Actual Rate, (6) Standard Rate, (7) Price Variance, and (8) Explanation.

E11-11   Imperial Landscaping plants grass seed as the basic landscaping for business campuses. During a recent month the company worked on three projects (Ames, Korman, and Stilles). The company is interested in controlling the material costs, namely the grass seed, for these plantings projects.

Prepare a variance report.
(SO 6)

In order to provide management with useful cost control information, the company uses standard costs and prepares monthly variance reports. Analysis reveals that the purchasing agent mistakenly purchased poor-quality seed for the Ames project. The Korman project, however, received higher-than-standard-quality seed that was on sale. The Stilles project received standard-quality seed; however, the price had increased and a new employee was used to spread the seed.

Shown below are quantity and cost data for each project.

Project	Actual Quantity	Actual Costs	Standard Quantity	Standard Costs	Total Variance
Ames	500 lbs.	$1,175	460 lbs.	$1,150	$ 25 U
Korman	400	960	410	1,025	65 F
Stilles	500	1,300	480	1,200	100 U
Total variance					$ 60 U

Instructions
(a) Prepare a variance report for the purchasing department with the following columns: (1) Project, (2) Actual pounds purchased, (3) Actual price, (4) Standard price, (5) Price variance, and (6) Explanation.
(b) Prepare a variance report for the production department with the following columns: (1) Project, (2) Actual pounds, (3) Standard pounds, (4) Standard price, (5) Quantity variance, and (6) Explanation.

E11-12   Carlos Company uses a standard cost accounting system. During January, the company reported the following manufacturing variances.

Prepare income statement for management.
(SO 7)

Materials price variance	$1,250 U	Labor quantity variance	$ 725 U
Materials quantity variance	700 F	Overhead controllable	200 F
Labor price variance	525 U	Overhead volume	1,000 U

In addition, 6,000 units of product were sold at $8.00 per unit. Each unit sold had a standard cost of $6.00. Selling and administrative expenses were $6,000 for the month.

Instructions
Prepare an income statement for management for the month ended January 31, 2005.

E11-13   The following is a list of terms related to performance evaluation.
   (1) Balanced scorecard
   (2) Variance
   (3) Learning and growth perspective
   (4) Nonfinancial measures
   (5) Customer perspective
   (6) Internal process perspective
   (7) Ideal standards
   (8) Normal standards

Identify performance evaluation terminology.
(SO 8)

Instructions
Match each of the following descriptions with one of the terms above.
(a) The difference between total actual costs and total standard costs.
(b) An efficient level of performance that is attainable under expected operating conditions.

(c) An approach that incorporates financial and nonfinancial measures in an integrated system that links performance measurement and a company's strategic goals.

(d) A viewpoint employed in the balanced scorecard to evaluate how well a company develops and retains its employees.

(e) An evaluation tool that is not based on dollars.

(f) A viewpoint employed in the balanced scorecard to evaluate the company from the perspective of those people who buy and use its products or services.

(g) An optimum level of performance under perfect operating conditions.

(h) A viewpoint employed in the balanced scorecard to evaluate the efficiency and effectiveness of the company's value chain.

Journalize entries in a standard cost accounting system.
(SO 9)

*E11-14   Marley Company installed a standard cost system on January 1. Selected transactions for the month of January are as follows.

1. Purchased 18,000 units of raw materials on account at a cost of $4.50 per unit. Standard cost was $4.25 per unit.

2. Issued 18,000 units of raw materials for jobs that required 17,600 standard units of raw materials.

3. Incurred 15,200 actual hours of direct labor at an actual rate of $4.80 per hour. The standard rate is $5.25 per hour. (Credit Wages Payable)

4. Performed 15,200 hours of direct labor on jobs when standard hours were 15,400.

5. Applied overhead to jobs at the rate of 100% of direct labor cost for standard hours allowed.

Instructions
Journalize the January transactions.

Answer questions concerning missing entries and balances.
(SO 4, 5, 9)

*E11-15   Tovar Company uses a standard cost accounting system. Some of the ledger accounts have been destroyed in a fire. The controller asks your help in reconstructing some missing entries and balances.

Instructions
Answer the following questions.

(a) Materials Price Variance shows a $3,000 favorable balance. Accounts Payable shows $128,000 of raw materials purchases. What was the amount debited to Raw Materials Inventory for raw materials purchased?

(b) Materials Quantity Variance shows a $3,000 unfavorable balance. Raw Materials Inventory shows a zero balance. What was the amount debited to Work in Process Inventory for direct materials used?

(c) Labor Price Variance shows a $1,500 unfavorable balance. Factory Labor shows a debit of $150,000 for wages incurred. What was the amount credited to Wages Payable?

(d) Factory Labor shows a credit of $150,000 for direct labor used. Labor Quantity Variance shows a $900 unfavorable balance. What was the amount debited to Work in Process for direct labor used?

(e) Overhead applied to Work in Process totaled $165,000. If the total overhead variance was $1,000 unfavorable, what was the amount of overhead costs debited to Manufacturing Overhead?

(f) Overhead Controllable Variance shows a debit balance of $1,500. What was the amount and type of balance (debit or credit) in Overhead Volume Variance?

Journalize entries for materials and labor variances.
(SO 9)

*E11-16   Data for Kopecky Inc. are given in E11-5.

Instructions
Journalize the entries to record the materials and labor variances.

Journalize overhead variances.
(SO 9)

*E11-17   Data for Rondell Company are given in E11-9.

Instructions

(a) Journalize the incurrence of the overhead costs and the application of overhead to the job, assuming a standard cost accounting system is used.

(b) Prepare the adjusting entry for the overhead variances.

Problems: Set A

P11-1A Inman Corporation manufactures a single product. The standard cost per unit of product is as follows.

Compute variances.
(SO 4, 5)

Direct materials—2 pounds of plastic at $5 per pound	$10
Direct labor—2 hours at $12 per hour	24
Variable manufacturing overhead	12
Fixed manufacturing overhead	6
Total standard cost per unit	$52

The master manufacturing overhead budget for the month based on normal productive capacity of 15,000 direct labor hours (7,500 units) shows total variable costs of $90,000 ($6 per labor hour) and total fixed costs of $45,000 ($3 per labor hour). Normal productive capacity is 15,000 direct labor hours. Overhead is applied on the basis of direct labor hours. Actual costs for November in producing 7,600 units were as follows.

Direct materials (15,000 pounds)	$ 73,500
Direct labor (14,900 hours)	181,780
Variable overhead	88,990
Fixed overhead	44,000
Total manufacturing costs	$388,270

The purchasing department normally buys the quantities of raw materials that are expected to be used in production each month. Raw materials inventories, therefore, can be ignored.

Instructions
Compute all of the materials, labor, and overhead variances.

MPV $1,500 F
LQV $3,600 F
OVV $600 F

P11-2A Soriano Manufacturing Company uses a standard cost accounting system to account for the manufacture of exhaust fans. In July 2005, it accumulates the following data relative to 1,500 units started and finished.

Compute variances, and prepare income statement.
(SO 4, 5, 7)

Cost and Production Data	Actual	Standard
Raw materials		
Units purchased	17,400	
Units used	17,400	18,000
Unit cost	$3.40	$3.00
Direct labor		
Hours worked	2,900	3,000
Hourly rate	$11.80	$12.20
Manufacturing overhead		
Incurred	$87,500	
Applied		$93,750

Manufacturing overhead was applied on the basis of direct labor hours. Normal capacity for the month was 2,800 direct labor hours. At normal capacity, budgeted overhead costs were $20 per labor hour variable and $11.25 per labor hour fixed. Total budgeted fixed overhead costs were $31,500.

Jobs finished during the month were sold for $240,000. Selling and administrative expenses were $25,000.

Instructions
(a) Compute all of the variances for (1) direct materials, (2) direct labor, and (3) manufacturing overhead.
(b) Prepare an income statement for management showing variances. Ignore income taxes.

(a) MQV $1,800 F
    OCV $4,000 F
(b) NI $34,120

P11-3A Kohler Clothiers manufactures women's business suits. The company uses a standard cost accounting system. In March 2005, 11,800 suits were made. The following standard and actual cost data applied to the month of March when normal capacity was 15,000 direct labor hours. All materials purchased were used in production.

Compute and identify significant variances.
(SO 4, 5, 6)

Cost Element	Standard (per unit)	Actual
Direct materials	5 yards at $7.00 per yard	$410,400 for 57,000 yards ($7.20 per yard)
Direct labor	1.0 hours at $12.00 per hour	$125,440 for 11,200 hours ($11.20 per hour)
Overhead	1.0 hours at $9.30 per hour (fixed $6.30; variable $3.00)	$90,000 fixed overhead $42,000 variable overhead

Overhead is applied on the basis of direct labor hours. At normal capacity, budgeted fixed overhead costs were $94,500, and budgeted variable overhead costs were $45,000.

Instructions

(a) MPV $11,400 U
LPV $8,960 F
OVV $20,160 U

(a) Compute the total, price, and quantity variances for (1) materials and (2) labor, and (3) the total, controllable, and volume variances for manufacturing overhead.
(b) ▭▭▭▶ Which of the materials and labor variances should be investigated if management considers a variance of more than 6% from standard to be significant? Discuss the potential causes of this variance.

Answer questions about variances.
(SO 4, 5)

P11-4A Crede Manufacturing Company uses a standard cost accounting system. In 2005, 33,000 units were produced. Each unit took several pounds of direct materials and 1⅓ standard hours of direct labor at a standard hourly rate of $12.00. Normal capacity was 42,000 direct labor hours. During the year, 132,000 pounds of raw materials were purchased at $0.90 per pound. All pounds purchased were used during the year.

Instructions

(a) $0.87

(a) If the materials price variance was $3,960 unfavorable, what was the standard materials price per pound?
(b) If the materials quantity variance was $2,871 favorable, what was the standard materials quantity per unit?

(c) 44,000

(c) What were the standard hours allowed for the units produced?
(d) If the labor quantity variance was $8,400 unfavorable, what were the actual direct labor hours worked?

(e) $11.90

(e) If the labor price variance was $4,470 favorable, what was the actual rate per hour?
(f) If total budgeted manufacturing overhead was $327,600 at normal capacity, what was the predetermined overhead rate per direct labor hour?

(g) $29.967

(g) What was the standard cost per unit of product?
(h) How much overhead was applied to production during the year?

(i) $5,000 F

(i) If the standard fixed overhead rate was $2.50, what was the overhead volume variance?
(j) If the overhead controllable variance was $3,000 favorable, what were the total variable overhead costs incurred? (Assume that the overhead controllable variance relates only to variable costs.)

(k) $988,911

(k) Using selected answers above, what were the total costs assigned to work in process?

Compute variances, prepare an income statement, and explain unfavorable variances.
(SO 4, 5, 7)

P11-5A Hi-Tek Labs performs steroid testing services to high schools, colleges, and universities. Because the company deals solely with educational institutions, the price of each test is strictly regulated. Therefore, the costs incurred must be carefully monitored and controlled. Shown below are the standard costs for a typical test.

Direct materials (1 petrie dish @ $2 per dish)	$ 2.00
Direct labor (0.5 hours @ $20 per hour)	10.00
Variable overhead (0.5 hours @ $8 per hour)	4.00
Fixed overhead (0.5 hours @ $3 per hour)	1.50
Total standard cost per test	$17.50

The lab does not maintain an inventory of petrie dishes. Therefore, the dishes purchased each month are used that month. Actual activity for the month of May 2005, when 2,000 tests were conducted, resulted in the following.

Direct materials (2,020 dishes)	$ 4,242
Direct labor (995 hours)	20,895
Variable overhead	8,100
Fixed overhead	3,400

Monthly budgeted fixed overhead is $3,600. Revenues for the month were $45,000, and selling and administrative expenses were $2,000.

Instructions
(a) Compute the price and quantity variances for direct materials and direct labor, and for overhead the controllable and volume variances.
(b) Prepare an income statement for management.
(c) Provide possible explanations for each unfavorable variance.

(a) MQV $40 U
    LQV $100 F
(b) NI $6,363

*P11-6A   Fayman Manufacturing Company uses standard costs with its job order cost accounting system. In January, an order (Job 84) was received for 3,900 units of Product D. The standard cost of 1 unit of Product D is as follows.

Journalize and post standard cost entries, and prepare income statement.
(SO 4, 5, 7, 9)

Direct materials—1.4 pounds at $4.00 per pound	$ 5.60
Direct labor—1 hour at $9.00 per hour	9.00
Overhead—1 hour (variable $7.40; fixed $10.00)	17.40
Standard cost per unit	$32.00

Overhead is applied on the basis of direct labor hours. Normal capacity for the month of January was 4,500 direct labor hours. During January, the following transactions applicable to Job No. 84 occurred.

1. Purchased 6,200 pounds of raw materials on account at $3.60 per pound.
2. Requisitioned 6,200 pounds of raw materials for production.
3. Incurred 3,700 hours of direct labor at $9.25 per hour.
4. Worked 3,700 hours of direct labor on Job No. 84.
5. Incurred $73,650 of manufacturing overhead on account.
6. Applied overhead to Job No. 84 on the basis of direct labor hours.
7. Transferred Job No. 84 to finished goods.
8. Billed customer for Job No. 84 at a selling price of $250,000.
9. Incurred selling and administrative expenses on account $61,000.

Instructions
(a) Journalize the transactions.
(b) Post to the job order cost accounts.
(c) Prepare the entry to recognize the overhead variances.
(d) Prepare the income statement for management for January 2005.

(a) MPV $2,480 F
    LPV $925 U
(c) OCV $210 F;
    OVV $6,000 U
(d) NI $58,805

Problems: Set B

P11-1B   Ranier Corporation manufactures a single product. The standard cost per unit of product is shown below.

Compute variances.
(SO 4, 5)

Direct materials—1 pound plastic at $7.00 per pound	$ 7.00
Direct labor—1.5 hours at $12.00 per hour	18.00
Variable manufacturing overhead	11.25
Fixed manufacturing overhead	3.75
Total standard cost per unit	$40.00

The predetermined manufacturing overhead rate is $10 per direct labor hour ($15.00 ÷ 1.5). It was computed from a master manufacturing overhead budget based on normal production of 7,500 direct labor hours (5,000 units) for the month. The master budget showed total variable costs of $56,250 ($7.50 per hour) and total fixed overhead costs of $18,750 ($2.50 per hour). Actual costs for October in producing 4,800 units were as follows.

Direct materials (5,100 pounds)	$ 37,230
Direct labor (7,000 hours)	87,500
Variable overhead	56,170
Fixed overhead	19,680
Total manufacturing costs	$200,580

The purchasing department buys the quantities of raw materials that are expected to be used in production each month. Raw materials inventories, therefore, can be ignored.

Instructions
Compute all of the materials, labor, and overhead variances.

MPV $1,530 U
LQV $2,400 F
OVV $750 U

*Compute variances, and
prepare income statement.*
(SO 4, 5, 7)

P11-2B Finley Manufacturing Corporation accumulates the following data relative to jobs started and finished during the month of June 2005.

Costs and Production Data	Actual	Standard
Raw materials unit cost	$2.25	$2.00
Raw materials units used	10,400	10,000
Direct labor payroll	$124,100	$120,000
Direct labor hours worked	14,600	15,000
Manufacturing overhead incurred	$182,500	
Manufacturing overhead applied		$189,000
Machine hours expected to be used at normal capacity		42,500
Budgeted fixed overhead for June		$51,000
Variable overhead rate per hour		$3.00
Fixed overhead rate per hour		$1.20

Overhead is applied on the basis of standard machine hours. Three hours of machine time are required for each direct labor hour. The jobs were sold for $400,000. Selling and administrative expenses were $40,000. Assume that the amount of raw materials purchased equaled the amount used.

(a) MQV $800 U
  LPV $7,300 U
  OCV $3,500 F
(b) NI $30,000

Instructions
(a) Compute all of the variances for (1) direct materials, (2) direct labor, and (3) manufacturing overhead.
(b) Prepare an income statement for management. Ignore income taxes.

Compute and identify significant variances.
(SO 4, 5, 6)

P11-3B Merando Clothiers is a small company that manufactures tall-men's suits. The company has used a standard cost accounting system. In May 2005, 11,200 suits were produced. The following standard and actual cost data applied to the month of May when normal capacity was 14,000 direct labor hours. All materials purchased were used.

Cost Element	Standard (per unit)	Actual
Direct materials	8 yards at $4.50 per yard	$371,050 for 90,500 yards ($4.10 per yard)
Direct labor	1.2 hours at $13.00 per hour	$201,630 for 14,300 hours ($14.10 per hour)
Overhead	1.2 hours at $6.00 per hour (fixed $3.50; variable $2.50)	$49,000 fixed overhead $36,000 variable overhead

Overhead is applied on the basis of direct labor hours. At normal capacity, budgeted fixed overhead costs were $49,000, and budgeted variable overhead was $35,000.

(a) MPV $36,200 F
  LPV $15,730 U
  LQV $11,180 U
  OCV $2,400 U

Instructions
(a) Compute the total, price, and quantity variances for (1) materials and (2) labor, and (3) the total, controllable, and volume variances for manufacturing overhead.
(b) ▭▭▭▶ Which of the materials and labor variances should be investigated if management considers a variance of more than 7% from standard to be significant?

Answer questions about variances.
(SO 4, 5)

P11-4B Harbaugh Manufacturing Company uses a standard cost accounting system. In 2005, 30,000 units were produced. Each unit took several pounds of direct materials and 1½ standard hours of direct labor at a standard hourly rate of $12.00. Normal capacity was 50,000 direct labor hours. During the year, 133,000 pounds of raw materials were purchased at $0.92 per pound. All pounds purchased were used during the year.

(a) $0.96

(b) 4.3 pounds

(f) 6.80 per DLH

(h) $306,000

Instructions
(a) If the materials price variance was $5,320 favorable, what was the standard materials price per pound?
(b) If the materials quantity variance was $3,840 unfavorable, what was the standard materials quantity per unit?
(c) What were the standard hours allowed for the units produced?
(d) If the labor quantity variance was $7,200 unfavorable, what were the actual direct labor hours worked?
(e) If the labor price variance was $9,120 favorable, what was the actual rate per hour?
(f) If total budgeted manufacturing overhead was $340,000 at normal capacity, what was the predetermined overhead rate?
(g) What was the standard cost per unit of product?
(h) How much overhead was applied to production during the year?

(i) If the fixed overhead rate was $2.00, what was the overhead volume variance?
(j) If the overhead controllable variance is $3,000 unfavorable, what were the total variable overhead costs incurred? (Assume that the overhead controllable variance relates only to variable costs.)
(k) Using one or more answers above, what were the total costs assigned to work in process?

(j) $219,000

P11-5B   Farm Labs, Inc. provides mad cow disease testing for both state and federal governmental agricultural agencies. Because the company's customers are governmental agencies, prices are strictly regulated. Therefore, Farm Labs must constantly monitor and control its testing costs. Shown below are the standard costs for a typical test.

Compute variances, prepare an income statement, and explain unfavorable variances.
(SO 4, 5, 7)

Direct materials (2 test tubes @ $1.50 per tube)	$ 3
Direct labor (1 hour @ $25 per hour)	25
Variable overhead (1 hour @ $5 per hour)	5
Fixed overhead (1 hour @ $10 per hour)	10
Total standard cost per test	$43

The lab does not maintain an inventory of test tubes. Therefore, the tubes purchased each month are used that month. Actual activity for the month of November 2005, when 1,500 tests were conducted, resulted in the following:

Direct materials (3,050 test tubes)	$ 4,270
Direct labor (1,600 hours)	36,800
Variable overhead	7,400
Fixed overhead	14,000

Monthly budgeted fixed overhead is $14,000. Revenues for the month were $75,000, and selling and administrative expenses were $4,000.

Instructions
(a) Compute the price and quantity variances for direct materials and direct labor, and for overhead the controllable and volume variances.
(b) Prepare an income statement for management.
(c) Provide possible explanations for each unfavorable variance.

(a) MPV $305 F
    LQV $2,500 U
    OCV $100 F
(b) NI $8,530

*P11-6B   Berman Corporation uses standard costs with its job order cost accounting system. In January, an order (Job No. 12) for 1,950 units of Product B was received. The standard cost of one unit of Product B is as follows.

Journalize and post standard cost entries, and prepare income statement.
(SO 4, 5, 7, 9)

Direct materials	3 pounds at $1.00 per pound	$ 3.00
Direct labor	1 hour at $8.00 per hour	8.00
Overhead	2 hours (variable $4.00 per machine hour;	
	fixed $2.25 per machine hour)	12.50
Standard cost per unit		$23.50

Normal capacity for the month was 4,200 machine hours. During January, the following transactions applicable to Job No. 12 occurred.
1. Purchased 6,250 pounds of raw materials on account at $1.04 per pound.
2. Requisitioned 6,250 pounds of raw materials for Job No. 12.
3. Incurred 2,200 hours of direct labor at a rate of $7.75 per hour.
4. Worked 2,200 hours of direct labor on Job No. 12.
5. Incurred manufacturing overhead on account $25,800.
6. Applied overhead to Job No. 12 on basis of standard machine hours used.
7. Completed Job No. 12.
8. Billed customer for Job No. 12 at a selling price of $70,000.
9. Incurred selling and administrative expenses on account $2,000.

Instructions
(a) Journalize the transactions.
(b) Post to the job order cost accounts.
(c) Prepare the entry to recognize the overhead variances.
(d) Prepare the January 2005 income statement for management.

(a) MPV $250 U
    LPV $550 F

(d) NI $18,650

Problems: Set C

Problem Set C is provided at the book's Web site, www.wiley.com/college/weygandt.

▷ **BROADENING YOUR PERSPECTIVE**

Group Decision Case

BYP 11-1 Agmar Professionals, a management consulting firm, specializes in strategic planning for financial institutions. Tim Agler and Jill Marlin, partners in the firm, are assembling a new strategic planning model for use by clients. The model is designed for use on most personal computers and replaces a rather lengthy manual model currently marketed by the firm. To market the new model Tim and Jill will need to provide clients with an estimate of the number of labor hours and computer time needed to operate the model. The model is currently being test marketed at five small financial institutions. These financial institutions are listed below, along with the number of combined computer/labor hours used by each institution to run the model one time.

Financial Institutions	Computer/Labor Hours Required
Midland National	25
First State	45
Financial Federal	40
Pacific America	30
Lakeview National	30
Total	170
Average	34

Any company that purchases the new model will need to purchase user manuals for the system. User manuals will be sold to clients in cases of 20, at a cost of $300 per case. One manual must be used each time the model is run because each manual includes a nonreusable computer-accessed password for operating the system. Also required are specialized computer forms that are sold only by Agmar. The specialized forms are sold in packages of 250, at a cost of $50 per package. One application of the model requires the use of 50 forms. This amount includes two forms that are generally wasted in each application due to printer alignment errors. The overall cost of the strategic planning model to clients is $12,000. Most clients will use the model four times annually.

Agmar must provide its clients with estimates of ongoing costs incurred in operating the new planning model, and would like to do so in the form of standard costs.

Instructions

With the class divided into groups, answer the following.
(a) What factors should be considered in setting a standard for computer/labor hours?
(b) What alternatives for setting a standard for computer/labor hours might be used?
(c) What standard for computer/labor hours would you select? Justify your answer.
(d) Determine the standard materials cost associated with the user manuals and computer forms for each application of the strategic planning model.

Managerial Analysis

BYP 11-2 Mo Vaughn and Associates is a medium-sized company located near a large metropolitan area in the Midwest. The company manufactures cabinets of mahogany, oak, and other fine woods for use in expensive homes, restaurants, and hotels. Although some of the work is custom, many of the cabinets are a standard size.

One such non-custom model is called Luxury Base Frame. Normal production is 1,000 units. Each unit has a direct labor hour standard of 5 hours. Overhead is applied to production based on standard direct labor hours. During the most recent month, only 900 units were produced; 4,500 direct labor hours were allowed for standard production, but only 4,000 hours were used. Standard and actual overhead costs were as follows.

	Standard (1,000 units)	Actual (900 units)
Indirect materials	$ 12,000	$ 12,300
Indirect labor	48,000	51,000
(Fixed) Manufacturing supervisors salaries	22,000	22,000

	Standard (1,000 units)	Actual (900 units)
(Fixed) Manufacturing office employees salaries	13,000	11,500
(Fixed) Engineering costs	26,000	25,000
Computer costs	10,000	10,000
Electricity	2,500	2,500
(Fixed) Manufacturing building depreciation	8,000	8,000
(Fixed) Machinery depreciation	3,000	3,000
(Fixed) Trucks and forklift depreciation	1,500	1,500
Small tools	700	1,400
(Fixed) Insurance	500	500
(Fixed) Property taxes	300	300
Total	$147,500	$149,000

Instructions

(a) Determine the overhead application rate.
(b) Determine how much overhead was applied to production.
(c) Calculate the controllable overhead variance and the overhead volume variance.
(d) Decide which overhead variances should be investigated.
(e) Discuss causes of the overhead variances. What can management do to improve its performance next month?

Real-World Focus

BYP 11-3   Glassmaster Co. is organized as two divisions and one subsidiary. One division focuses on the manufacture of filaments such as fishing line and sewing thread; the other division manufactures antennas and specialty fiberglass products. Its subsidiary manufactures flexible steel wire controls and molded control panels.

The annual report of Glassmaster provides the following information.

GLASSMASTER COMPANY
Management Discussion

Gross profit margins for the year improved to 20.9% of sales compared to last year's 18.5%. All operations reported improved margins due in large part to improved operating efficiencies as a result of cost reduction measures implemented during the second and third quarters of the fiscal year and increased manufacturing throughout due to higher unit volume sales. Contributing to the improved margins was a favorable materials price variance due to competitive pricing by suppliers as a result of soft demand for petrochemical-based products. This favorable variance is temporary and will begin to reverse itself as stronger worldwide demand for commodity products improves in tandem with the economy. Partially offsetting these positive effects on profit margins were competitive pressures on sales prices of certain product lines. The company responded with pricing strategies designed to maintain and/or increase market share.

Instructions

(a) Is it apparent from the information whether Glassmaster utilizes standard costs?
(b) Do you think the price variance experienced should lead to changes in standard costs for the next fiscal year?

Exploring the Web

BYP 11-4   The Caelus Management System (CMS), is a real-time, fully integrated decision support, operational control, and financial management system.

Address: **www.caelus.com,** *or go to* **www.wiley.com/college/weygandt**

Steps

1. Choose **CMS Product Info** and answer part (a), below.
2. Choose **Standard Cost** and answer parts (b) and (c).

Instructions

(a) List some of the modules that are familiar to you.
(b) What types of decisions does this module of the software support?
(c) Does this product distinguish between fixed and variable costs?

Communication Activity

BYP 11-5   The setting of standards is critical to the effective use of standards in evaluating performance.

Instructions

Explain the following in a memo to your instructor.
(a) The comparative advantages and disadvantages of ideal versus normal standards.
(b) The factors that should be included in setting the price and quantity standards for direct materials, direct labor, and manufacturing overhead.

Research Assignment

BYP 11-6   The June 14, 2004, edition of SmartPros.com contains an article titled "'7 Habits' Author Says Workers Need Four Basic Disciplines of Execution."

Instructions

Read the article at *http://www.smartpros.com/x43931.xml*; answer the following questions.
(a) What are the author's four "disciplines of execution"?
(b) What are some of the potential downfalls of having too many goals, and what are the characteristics of effective goal setting?
(c) What approach for planning does the author suggest?
(d) What are the processes of a good staff meeting?

Ethics Case

BYP 11-7   At Camden Manufacturing Company, production workers in the Painting Department are paid on the basis of productivity. The labor time standard for a unit of production is established through periodic time studies conducted by the Foster Management Department. In a time study, the actual time required to complete a specific task by a worker is observed. Allowances are then made for preparation time, rest periods, and clean-up time. Dan Renfro is one of several veterans in the Painting Department.

Dan is informed by Foster Management that he will be used in the time study for the painting of a new product. The findings will be the basis for establishing the labor time standard for the next 6 months. During the test, Dan deliberately slows his normal work pace in an effort to obtain a labor time standard that will be easy to meet. Because it is a new product, the Foster Management representative who conducted the test is unaware that Dan did not give the test his best effort.

Instructions

(a) Who was benefited and who was harmed by Dan's actions?
(b) Was Dan ethical in the way he performed the time study test?
(c) What measure(s) might the company take to obtain valid data for setting the labor time standard?

Answers to Self-Study Questions

1. c   2. d   3. b   4. c   5. b   6. a   7. d   8. a   9. b   10. d   *11. c

CHAPTER 12

Planning for Capital Investments

STUDY OBJECTIVES

After studying this chapter,
you should be able to:

1 Discuss the capital budgeting evaluation process, and explain what inputs are used in capital budgeting.

2 Describe the cash payback technique.

3 Explain the net present value method.

4 Identify the challenges presented by intangible benefits in capital budgeting.

5 Describe the profitability index.

6 Indicate the benefits of performing a post-audit.

7 Explain the internal rate of return method.

8 Describe the annual rate of return method.

THE NAVIGATOR ✔

▶ Scan *Study Objectives*

▶ Read *Feature Story*

▶ Read *Preview*

▶ Read text and answer *Before You Go On*
    p. 499 ☐   p. 509 ☐

▶ Work *Using the Decision Toolkit*

▶ Review *Summary of Study Objectives*

▶ Work *Demonstration Problem*

▶ Answer *Self-Study Questions*

▶ Complete *Assignments*

FEATURE STORY

Soup Is Good Food

When you hear the word *Campbell's,* what is the first thing that comes to mind? Soup. Campbell's *is* soup. It sells 38 percent of all the soup—including homemade—consumed in the United States.

But can a company survive on soup alone? In an effort to expand its operations and to lessen its reliance on soup, **Campbell Soup Company** in 1990 began searching for an additional line of business. Campbell's management believed it saw an opportunity in convenient meals that were low in fat, nutritionally rich, and had therapeutic value for heart patients and diabetics. This venture would require a huge investment—but the rewards were potentially tremendous.

The initial investment required building food labs, hiring nutritional scientists, researching prototype products, constructing new production facilities, and marketing the new products. Management predicted that with an initial investment of roughly $55 million, the company might generate sales of $200 million per year.

By 1994 the company had created 24 meals, and an extensive field-study revealed considerable health benefits from the products. Unfortunately, initial sales of the new product line, called Intelligent Quisine, were less than stellar. In 1997 a consulting firm was hired to evaluate whether the project should be continued. Product development of the new line was costing $20 million per year—a

sum that some managers felt could be better spent developing new products in other divisions, or expanding overseas operations. In 1998 the project was discontinued.

Campbell's was not giving up on growth, but simply had decided to refocus its efforts on soup. The company's annual report stated management's philosophy: "Soup will be our growth engine." Campbell's is now selling off many of its non-soup businesses, and in a recent year introduced 20 new soup products.

Source: Vanessa O'Connell, "Food for Thought: How Campbell Saw a Break-through Menu Turn into Leftovers," *Wall Street Journal* (October 6, 1998).

www.campbellsoup.com

Companies like **Campbell Soup** must constantly determine how to invest their resources. Other examples: Hollywood studios recently built 25 new sound stage projects to allow for additional filming in future years. **Starwood Hotels and Resorts Worldwide, Inc.** committed a total of $1 billion to renovate its existing hotel properties, while, at roughly the same time, the hotel industry canceled about $2 billion worth of *new* construction. And **Union Pacific Resources Group Inc.** announced that it would cut its planned capital expenditures by 19 percent in order to use the funds to reduce its outstanding debt.

The process of making such capital expenditure decisions is referred to as **capital budgeting**. Capital budgeting involves choosing among various capital projects to find the one(s) that will maximize a company's return on its financial investment. The purpose of this chapter is to discuss the various techniques used to make effective capital budgeting decisions.

The content and organization of this chapter are as follows.

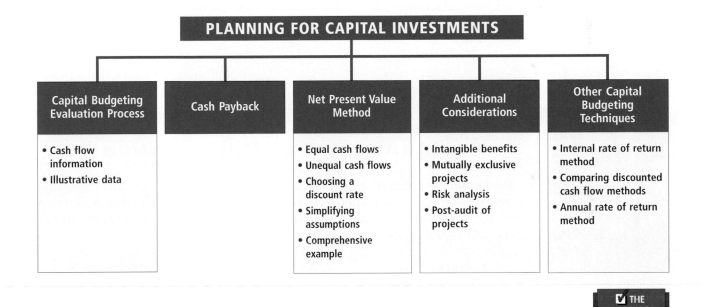

PLANNING FOR CAPITAL INVESTMENTS

Capital Budgeting Evaluation Process	Cash Payback	Net Present Value Method	Additional Considerations	Other Capital Budgeting Techniques
• Cash flow information • Illustrative data		• Equal cash flows • Unequal cash flows • Choosing a discount rate • Simplifying assumptions • Comprehensive example	• Intangible benefits • Mutually exclusive projects • Risk analysis • Post-audit of projects	• Internal rate of return method • Comparing discounted cash flow methods • Annual rate of return method

☑ THE NAVIGATOR

The Capital Budgeting Evaluation Process

Many companies follow a carefully prescribed process in capital budgeting. At least once a year, proposals for projects are requested from each department. The proposals are screened by a capital budgeting committee, which submits its findings to the officers of the company. The officers, in turn, select the projects they believe to be most worthy of funding. They submit this list of projects to the board of directors. Ultimately, the directors approve the capital expenditure budget for the year. This process is shown in Illustration 12-1 (page 492).

The involvement of top management and the board of directors in the process demonstrates the importance of capital budgeting decisions. These decisions often have a significant impact on a company's future profitability. In fact, poor capital

STUDY OBJECTIVE

1

Discuss the capital budgeting evaluation process, and explain what inputs are used in capital budgeting.

Illustration 12-1
Corporate capital budget
authorization process

1. Project proposals are requested from departments, plants, and authorized personnel.	2. Proposals are screened by a capital budget committee.	3. Officers determine which projects are worthy of funding.	4. Board of directors approves capital budget.

budgeting decisions can cost a lot of money, as the **Campbell Soup** Feature Story demonstrated. Such decisions have even led to the bankruptcy of some companies.

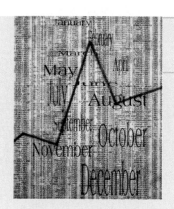
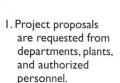

Business Insight
Management Perspective

Monitoring capital expenditure amounts is one way to learn about a company's growth potential. Few companies can grow if they don't make significant capital investments. Here is a list of well-known companies and their amounts and types of capital expenditures in the year 2003.

Company Name	Amount	Type of Expenditures
Campbell Soup Company	$283 million	Acquisitions and plant expansions.
Barrick Gold Corporation	$228 million	Land acquisition and mine expansion.
Dell Computer Corporation	$329 million	Manufacturing and office facilities.
Sears, Roebuck and Co.	$925 million	New stores.
NIKE, Inc.	$186 million	Warehouse locations, management information systems.

CASH FLOW INFORMATION

In this chapter we will look at several methods that help companies make effective capital budgeting decisions. Most of these methods employ **cash flow numbers**, rather than accrual accounting revenues and expenses. Remember from your financial accounting course that accrual accounting records *revenues* and *expenses,* rather than cash inflows and cash outflows. In fact, revenues and expenses measured during a period often differ significantly from their cash flow counterparts. Accrual accounting has advantages over cash accounting in many contexts. **But for purposes of capital budgeting, estimated cash inflows and**

outflows are the preferred inputs. Why? Because ultimately, the value of all financial investments is determined by the value of cash flows received and paid.

Sometimes cash flow information is not available. In this case, adjustments can be made to accrual accounting numbers to estimate cash flow. Often, net annual cash flow is estimated by adding back depreciation expense to net income. Depreciation expense is added back because it is an expense that does not require an outflow of cash. Accordingly, the depreciation expense that is deducted in determining net income is added back to net income to determine net annual cash flow. Suppose, for example, that Reno Company's net income of $13,000 includes a charge for depreciation expense of $26,000. Its estimated net annual cash flow would be $39,000 ($13,000 + $26,000).

Some typical cash outflows and inflows related to equipment purchase and replacement are listed in Illustration 12-2.

Cash Outflows
Initial investment
Repairs and maintenance
Increased operating costs
Overhaul of equipment
Cash Inflows
Sale of old equipment
Increased cash received from customers
Reduced cash outflows related to operating costs
Salvage value of equipment when project is complete

Illustration 12-2 Typical cash flows relating to capital budgeting decisions

These cash flows are the inputs that are considered relevant in capital budgeting decisions.

The capital budgeting decision, under any technique, depends in part on a variety of considerations:

- **The availability of funds**: Does the company have unlimited funds, or will it have to ration capital investments?

- **Relationships among proposed projects**: Are proposed projects independent of each other, or does the acceptance or rejection of one depend on the acceptance or rejection of another?

- **The company's basic decision-making approach**: Does the company want to produce an accept-reject decision, or a ranking of desirability among possible projects?

- **The risk associated with a particular project**: How certain are the projected returns? The certainty of estimates varies with such issues as market considerations or the length of time before returns are expected.

ILLUSTRATIVE DATA

For our initial discussion of quantitative techniques, we will use a continuing example, which will enable us to easily compare the results of the various techniques. Assume that Stewart Soup Company is considering an investment of $130,000 in new equipment. The new equipment is expected to last 10 years. It will have a zero salvage value at the end of its useful life. The annual cash inflows are $200,000, and the annual cash outflows are $176,000. These data are summarized in Illustration 12-3.

Initial investment	$130,000
Estimated useful life	10 years
Estimated salvage value	–0–
Estimated annual cash flows	
Cash inflows from customers	$200,000
Cash outflows for operating costs	176,000
Net annual cash flow	$ 24,000

In the following two sections we will examine two popular techniques for evaluating capital investments: cash payback and the net present value method.

STUDY OBJECTIVE

2

Describe the cash payback technique.

Cash Payback

The **cash payback technique** identifies the time period required to recover the cost of the capital investment from the net annual cash flow produced by the investment. The formula for computing the cash payback period is:

Illustration 12-4 Cash payback formula

Cost of Capital Investment	÷	Net Annual Cash Flow	=	Cash Payback Period

Helpful Hint Net annual cash flow can also be approximated by "Net cash provided by operating activities" from the statement of cash flows.

The cash payback period in the Stewart Soup example is 5.42 years, computed as follows.

$$\$130,000 \div \$24,000 = 5.42 \text{ years}$$

The evaluation of the payback period is often related to the expected useful life of the asset. For example, assume that at Stewart Soup a project is unacceptable if the payback period is longer than 60 percent of the asset's expected useful life. The 5.42-year payback period in this case is a bit over 50 percent of the project's expected useful life. Thus, the project is acceptable.

It follows that when the payback technique is used to decide among acceptable alternative projects, **the shorter the payback period, the more attractive the investment**. This is true for two reasons: (1) The earlier the investment is recovered, the sooner the cash funds can be used for other purposes. (2) The risk of loss from obsolescence and changed economic conditions is less in a shorter payback period.

The computation of the cash payback period above assumes equal net annual cash flows in each year of the investment's life. In many cases, this assumption is not valid. In the case of **uneven** net annual cash flows, the cash payback period is determined when the cumulative net cash flows from the investment equal the cost of the investment. To illustrate, assume that Chan Company proposes an investment in a new Web site that is estimated to cost $300,000. The proposed investment cost, net annual cash flows, cumulative net cash flows, and the cash payback period are shown in Illustration 12-5.

Illustration 12-5 Cash inflow schedule

Year	Investment	Net Annual Cash Flow	Cumulative Net Cash Flow
0	$300,000		
1		$ 60,000	$ 60,000
2		90,000	150,000
3		90,000	240,000
4		120,000	360,000
5		100,000	460,000

Cash payback period = 3.5 years

As indicated from Illustration 12-5, at the end of year 3, cumulative cash inflow of $240,000 is less than the investment cost of $300,000, but at the end of year 4 the cumulative cash inflow of $360,000 exceeds the investment cost. The cash inflow needed in year 4 to equal the investment cost is $60,000 ($300,000 − $240,000). Assuming the cash inflow occurred evenly during year 4, this amount is then divided by the net annual cash flow in year 4 ($120,000) to determine the point during the year when the cash payback occurs. Thus, .50 ($60,000/$120,000), or half of the year, is computed, and the cash payback period is 3.5 years.

The cash payback technique may be useful as an initial screening tool. It also may be the most critical factor in the capital budgeting decision for a company that desires a fast turnaround of its investment because of a weak cash position. It also is relatively easy to compute and understand.

However, cash payback should not ordinarily be the only basis for the capital budgeting decision because it ignores the expected profitability of the project. To illustrate, assume that Projects A and B have the same payback period, but Project A's useful life is double the useful life of Project B. Project A's earning power, therefore, is twice as long as Project B's. A further disadvantage of this technique is that it ignores the time value of money.

Net Present Value Method

Recognition of the time value of money can make a significant difference in the long-term impact of the capital budgeting decision. For example, cash flows that occur early in the life of an investment will be worth more than those that occur later—because of the time value of money. Therefore it is useful to recognize the timing of cash flows when evaluating projects.

Capital budgeting techniques that take into account both the time value of money and the estimated net cash flow from an investment are called **discounted cash flow techniques**. They are generally recognized as the most informative and best conceptual approaches to making capital budgeting decisions. The expected net cash flow used in discounting cash flows consists of the annual net cash flows plus the estimated liquidation proceeds (salvage value) when the asset is sold at the end of its useful life.

The primary discounted cash flow technique is called **net present value**. A second method, discussed later in the chapter, is the **internal rate of return**. At this point, before you read on, **we recommend that you examine Appendix A** (at the end of the book) to review time value of money concepts, upon which these methods are based.

Under the **net present value (NPV) method**, net cash flows are discounted to their present value and then compared with the capital outlay required by the investment. The difference between these two amounts is referred to as **net present value (NPV)**. The interest rate used in discounting the future net cash flows is a rate determined by management. This rate, often referred to as the **discount rate** or required rate of return, is discussed in a later section.

The NVP decision rule is this: **A proposal is acceptable when net present value is zero or positive.** At either of those values, the rate of return on the investment equals or exceeds the discount rate (required rate of return). When net present value is negative, the project is unacceptable. Illustration 12-6 (page 496) shows the net present value decision criteria.

When making a selection among acceptable proposals, **the higher the positive net present value, the more attractive the investment**. The application of this method to two cases is described in the next two sections. In each case, we will assume that the investment has no salvage value at the end of its useful life.

STUDY OBJECTIVE

3

Explain the net present value method.

Illustration 12-6 Net present value decision criteria

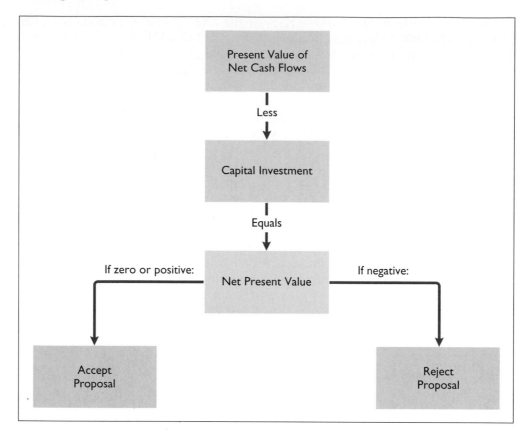

Business Insight
Management Perspective

American Century is an investment company that manages over $100 billion in mutual funds and other types of investments. Investment companies must frequently improve the technology that they use to support the management of investment funds, to be as efficient and cost-effective as possible. As a consequence, during one recent year the company's information technology budget represented 18 percent of the company's revenue. Like most companies, American Century uses a "bottom to top" approach to solicit and evaluate capital investment projects. This means that it requests suggestions from employees at all levels of all areas of the company. It then evaluates these ideas based on their ability to either create revenue, control expenses, or allow the company to differentiate its products from those of its competitors. The projects continue to be evaluated as they are developed, implemented, and used.

SOURCE: Anthony Guerra, "It's Bottoms Up at American Century," *Wall Street and Technology* (March, 2001), p. 12.

EQUAL ANNUAL CASH FLOWS

Stewart's net annual cash flows are $24,000. If we assume this amount **is uniform over the asset's useful life**, the present value of the net annual cash flows can be computed by using the present value of an annuity of 1 for 10 periods (from Table 4, Appendix A). Assuming a discount rate of 12 percent, the present value of net cash flows is computed as shown in Illustration 12-7 (rounded to the nearest dollar).

	Present Value at 12%
Discount factor for 10 periods	5.65022
Present value of net cash flows: $24,000 × 5.65022	**$135,605**

Illustration 12-7 Computation of present value of equal net annual cash flows

The analysis of the proposal by the net present value method is as follows.

	12%
Present value of net cash flows	$135,605
Capital investment	130,000
Net present value	**$ 5,605**

Illustration 12-8 Computation of net present value—equal net annual cash flows

The proposed capital expenditure is acceptable at a required rate of return of 12 percent because the net present value is positive.

UNEQUAL ANNUAL CASH FLOWS

When net annual cash flows are unequal, we cannot use annuity tables to calculate their present value. Instead, tables showing the **present value of a single future amount must be applied to each annual cash flow**. To illustrate, assume that Stewart Soup Company expects the same total net cash flows of $240,000 over the life of the investment. But because of a declining market demand for the new product over the life of the equipment, the net annual cash flows are higher in the early years and lower in the later years. The present value of the net annual cash flows is calculated as follows, using Table 3 in Appendix A.

Helpful Hint The ABC Co. expects equal cash flows over an asset's 5-year useful life. What discount factor should be used in determining present values if management wants (1) a 12% return or (2) a 15% return? Answer: Using Table 4, the factors are (1) 3.60478 and (2) 3.35216.

Year	Assumed Net Annual Cash Flows	Discount Factor 12%	Present Value 12%
	(1)	(2)	(1) × (2)
1	$ 34,000	.89286	$ 30,357
2	30,000	.79719	23,916
3	27,000	.71178	19,218
4	25,000	.63552	15,888
5	24,000	.56743	13,618
6	22,000	.50663	11,146
7	21,000	.45235	9,499
8	20,000	.40388	8,078
9	19,000	.36061	6,852
10	18,000	.32197	5,795
	$240,000		**$144,367**

Illustration 12-9 Computation of present value of unequal annual cash flows

Therefore, the analysis of the proposal by the net present value method is as follows.

	12%
Present value of net cash flows	$144,367
Capital investment	130,000
Net present value	**$ 14,367**

Illustration 12-10 Computation of net present value—unequal annual cash flows

In this example, the present value of the net cash flows is greater than the $130,000 capital investment. Thus, the project is acceptable at a 12 percent required rate of return (discount rate). The difference between the present values using the 12 percent rate under equal cash flows ($135,605) and unequal cash flows ($144,367) is due to the pattern of the flows. Since more money is received sooner under this particular uneven cash flow scenario, its present value is greater.

CHOOSING A DISCOUNT RATE

Now that you understand how the net present value method is applied, it is logical to ask a related question: How is a discount rate (required rate of return) determined in real capital budgeting decisions? In most instances a company uses a discount rate equal to its **cost of capital**—that is, the rate that it must pay to obtain funds from creditors and stockholders.

Helpful Hint Cost of capital is the rate that management expects to pay on all borrowed and equity funds. It does not relate to the cost of funding a *specific* project.

The cost of capital is a weighted average of the rates paid on borrowed funds as well as on funds provided by investors in the company's common stock and preferred stock. If a project is believed to be of higher risk than the company's usual line of business, the discount rate should be increased. That is, the discount rate has two elements, a cost of capital element and a risk element. Often companies assume the risk element is equal to zero.

Using an incorrect discount rate can lead to incorrect capital budgeting decisions. Consider again the Stewart Soup example in Illustration 12-8, where we used a discount rate of 12 percent. Suppose that this discount rate does not take into account the fact that this project is riskier than most of the company's investments. A more appropriate discount rate, given the risk, might be 15 percent. Illustration 12-11 compares the net present values at the two rates. At the higher, more appropriate discount rate of 15 percent, the net present value is negative, and the company should reject the project.

Illustration 12-11 Comparison of net present values at different discount rates

	Present Values at Different Discount Rates	
	12%	**15%**
Discount factor for 10 periods	5.65022	5.01877
Present value of net cash flows:		
$24,000 × 5.65022	$135,605	
$24,000 × 5.01877		$120,450
Capital investment	130,000	130,000
Positive (negative) net present value	**$ 5,605**	**$ (9,550)**

The discount rate is often referred to by alternative names, including the **hurdle rate**, the **required rate of return**, and the **cutoff rate**. Determination of the cost of capital varies somewhat depending on whether the entity is a for-profit or not-for-profit enterprise. Calculation of the cost of capital is discussed more fully in advanced accounting and finance courses.

SIMPLIFYING ASSUMPTIONS

In our examples of the net present value method, we have made a number of simplifying assumptions:

- **All cash flows come at the end of each year.** In reality, cash flows will come at uneven intervals throughout the year. However, it is far simpler to assume that all cash flows come at the end (or in some cases the beginning) of the year. In fact, this assumption is frequently made in practice.

- **All cash flows are immediately reinvested in another project that has a similar return.** In most capital budgeting situations, cash flows are received during each year of a project's life. In order to determine the return on the investment, some assumption must be made about how the cash flows are reinvested in the year that they are received. It is customary to assume that cash flows received are reinvested in some other project of similar return until the end of the project's life.

- **All cash flows can be predicted with certainty.** The outcomes of business investments are full of uncertainty, as the **Campbell Soup** Feature Story shows. There is no way of knowing how popular a new product will be, how long a new machine will last, or what competitors' reactions might be to changes in a product. But, in order to make investment decisions, analysts must estimate future outcomes. In this chapter we have assumed that future amounts are known with certainty.[1] In reality, little is known with certainty. More advanced capital budgeting techniques deal with uncertainty by considering the probability that various outcomes will occur.

BEFORE YOU GO ON . . .

▶Review It

1. What is the cash payback technique? What are its strengths and weaknesses?
2. What is the net present value decision rule to determine whether a project is acceptable?
3. What are common assumptions made in capital budgeting decisions?

▶Do It

Watertown Paper Corporation is considering adding another machine for the manufacture of corrugated cardboard. The machine would cost $800,000. It would have an estimated life of 7 years and a salvage value of $40,000. It is estimated that annual cash inflows would increase by $400,000 and that annual cash outflows would increase by $190,000. Management believes a discount rate of 9 percent is appropriate. Using the net present value technique, should the project be accepted?

Action Plan

- Use the NPV technique to calculate the difference between the present value of net cash flows and the initial investment.
- Accept the project if the net present value is positive.

Solution

Estimated annual cash inflows	$400,000
Estimated annual cash outflows	190,000
Net annual cash flow	$210,000

	Cash Flows	× 9% Discount Factor	= Present Value
Present value of net annual cash flows	$210,000	× 5.03295[a]	= $1,056,920
Present value of salvage value	$ 40,000	× .54703[b]	= 21,881
Present value of net cash flows			1,078,801
Capital investment			800,000
Net present value			$ 278,801

[a]Table 4, Appendix A.
[b]Table 3, Appendix A.

Since the net present value is positive, the project is acceptable.

Related exercise material: BE12-2, BE12-3, BE12-4, BE12-5, E12-1, E12-2, and E12-3.

☑ THE NAVIGATOR

---

[1]One exception is a brief discussion of sensitivity analysis later in the chapter.

COMPREHENSIVE EXAMPLE

Best Taste Foods is considering investing in new equipment to produce fat-free snack foods. Management believes that although demand for fat-free foods has leveled off, fat-free foods are here to stay. The following estimated cost flows, cost of capital, and cash flows were determined in consultation with the marketing, production, and finance departments.

Illustration 12-12   Investment information for Best Taste Foods example

Initial investment	$1,000,000
Cost of equipment overhaul in 5 years	$200,000
Salvage value of equipment in 10 years	$20,000
Cost of capital	15%
Estimated annual cash flows	
Cash inflows received from sales	$500,000
Cash outflows for cost of goods sold	$200,000
Maintenance costs	$30,000
Other direct operating costs	$40,000

Remember that we are using cash flows in our analysis, not accrual revenues and expenses. Thus, for example, the direct operating costs would not include depreciation expense, since depreciation expense does not use cash. Illustration 12-13 presents the computation of the net annual cash flows of this project.

Illustration 12-13   Computation of net annual cash inflow

Cash inflows received from sales	$ 500,000
Cash outflows for cost of goods sold	(200,000)
Maintenance costs	(30,000)
Other direct operating costs	(40,000)
Net annual cash flow	**$ 230,000**

The computation of the net present value for this proposed investment is shown in Illustration 12-14.

Illustration 12-14   Computation of net present value for Best Taste Foods investment

Event	Time Period	Cash Flow	×	15% Discount Factor	=	Present Value
Equipment purchase	0	$1,000,000		1.00000		$(1,000,000)
Equipment overhaul	5	200,000		.49718		(99,436)
Net annual cash flow	1–10	230,000		5.01877		1,154,317
Salvage value	10	20,000		.24719		4,944
Net present value						**$ 59,825**

Because the net present value of the project is positive, the project should be accepted.

DECISION TOOLKIT

Decision Checkpoints	Info Needed for Decision	Tool to Use for Decision	How to Evaluate Results
Should the company invest in a proposed project?	Cash flow estimates, discount rate	Net present = Present value of value net cash flows less capital investment	The investment is financially acceptable if net present value is positive.

Additional Considerations

Now that you understand how the net present value method works, we can add some "additional wrinkles." Specifically, these are: the impact of intangible benefits, a way to compare mutually exclusive projects, refinements that take risk into account, and the need to conduct post-audits of investment projects.

INTANGIBLE BENEFITS

The NPV evaluation techniques employed thus far rely on tangible costs and benefits that can be relatively easily quantified. Some investment projects, especially high-tech projects, fail to make it through initial capital budget screens because only the project's "tangible" benefits are considered. But by ignoring intangible benefits, such as increased quality, improved safety, or enhanced employee loyalty, capital budgeting techniques might incorrectly eliminate projects that could be financially beneficial to the company.

> **STUDY OBJECTIVE**
> **4**
> Identify the challenges presented by intangible benefits in capital budgeting.

To avoid rejecting projects that actually should be accepted, two possible approaches are suggested:

1. Calculate net present value ignoring intangible benefits. Then, if the NPV is negative, ask whether the intangible benefits are worth at least the amount of the negative NPV.
2. Project rough, conservative estimates of the value of the intangible benefits, and incorporate these values into the NPV calculation.

Example

Assume that Berg Company is considering the purchase of a new mechanical robot to be used for soldering electrical connections. The estimates related to this proposed purchase are shown in Illustration 12-15.

Initial investment	$200,000				
Annual cash inflows	$ 50,000				
Annual cash outflows	20,000				
Net annual cash flow	**$ 30,000**				
Estimated life of equipment	10 years				
Discount rate	12%				

	Cash Flows	×	12% Discount Factor	=	Present Value
Present value of net cash flows	$30,000	×	5.65022	=	$169,507
Initial investment					200,000
Net present value					**$ (30,493)**

Illustration 12-15 Investment information for Berg Company example

Based on the negative net present value of $30,493, the proposed project is not acceptable. This calculation, however, ignores important information. First, the company's engineers believe that purchasing this machine will dramatically improve the electrical connections in the company's products. As a result, future warranty costs will be reduced. Also, the company believes that higher quality will translate into higher future sales. Finally, the new machine will be much safer than the previous one.

This new information can be incorporated into the capital budgeting decision in the two ways listed earlier. First, one might simply ask whether the reduced warranty costs, increased sales, and improved safety benefits have an estimated total present value to the company of at least $30,493. If yes, then the project is acceptable.

Alternatively, an estimate of the annual cash flows of these benefits can be made. In our initial calculation, each of these benefits was assumed to have a value of zero. It seems likely that their actual values are much higher than zero. Given the difficulty of estimating these benefits, however, conservative values should be assigned to them. If, after using conservative estimates, the net present value is positive, the project should be accepted.

To illustrate, assume that Berg estimates a sales increase of $10,000 annually as a result of an increase in perceived quality. Berg also estimates that annual cost outflows would be reduced by $5,000 as a result of lower warranty claims, reduced injury claims, and missed work. Consideration of the intangible benefits results in the following revised NPV calculation.

Illustration 12-16 Revised investment information for Berg Company example, including intangible benefits

Initial investment	$200,000			
Annual cash inflows (revised)	$ 60,000			
Annual cash outflows (revised)	15,000			
Net annual cash flow	**$ 45,000**			
Estimated life of equipment	10 years			
Discount rate	12%			

	Cash Flows	× 12% Discount Factor	=	Present Value
Present value of net annual cash flows	$45,000	× 5.65022	=	$254,260
Initial investment				200,000
Net present value				**$ 54,260**

Using these conservative estimates of the value of the additional benefits, it appears that Berg should accept the project.

MUTUALLY EXCLUSIVE PROJECTS

In theory, all projects with positive NPVs should be accepted. However, companies rarely are able to adopt all positive-NPV proposals. First, proposals often are **mutually exclusive**. This means that if the company adopts one proposal, it would be impossible also to adopt the other proposal. For example, a company may be considering the purchase of a new packaging machine and is looking at various brands and models. Only one packaging machine is needed. Once the company has determined which brand and model to purchase, the others will not be purchased—even though they may also have positive net present values.

Even in instances where projects are not mutually exclusive, managers often must choose between various positive-NPV projects because of limited resources. For example, the company might have ideas for two new lines of business, each of which has a projected positive NPV. However, both of these proposals require skilled personnel, and the company determines that it will not be able to find enough skilled personnel to staff both projects. Management will have to choose the project it thinks is a better option.

When choosing between alternative proposals, it is tempting simply to choose the project with the higher NPV. Consider the following example of two mutually exclusive projects. Each is assumed to have a 10-year life and a 12 percent discount rate.

	Project A	Project B
Initial investment	$40,000	$90,000
Net annual cash inflow	10,000	19,000
Salvage value	5,000	10,000
Present value of net cash flows		
($10,000 × 5.65022) + ($5,000 × .32197)	58,112	
($19,000 × 5.65022) + ($10,000 × .32197)		110,574

Illustration 12-17   Investment information for mutually exclusive projects

From the information in Illustration 12-17, the net present values of Project A and Project B are computed in Illustration 12-18.

	Project A	Project B
Present value of net cash flows	$ 58,112	$110,574
Initial investment	40,000	90,000
Net present value	**$18,112**	**$ 20,574**

Illustration 12-18   Net present value computation

Project B has the higher NPV, and so it would seem that the company should adopt B. Note, however, that Project B also requires more than twice the original investment of Project A. In choosing between the two projects, the company should also include in its calculations the amount of the original investment.

One relatively simple method of comparing alternative projects is the **profitability index**. This method takes into account both the size of the original investment and the discounted cash flows. The profitability index is calculated by dividing the present value of net cash flows that occur after the initial investment by the initial investment.

STUDY OBJECTIVE

5

Describe the profitability index.

$$\begin{array}{ccc} \textbf{Present Value of} & & \textbf{Initial} & & \textbf{Profitability} \\ \textbf{Net Cash Flows} & \div & \textbf{Investment} & = & \textbf{Index} \end{array}$$

Illustration 12-19   Formula for profitability index

The profitability index allows comparison of the relative desirability of projects that require differing initial investments. Note that any project with a positive NPV will have a profitability index above 1. The profitability index for each project is calculated below.

$$\textbf{Profitability Index} = \frac{\textbf{Present Value of Net Cash Flows}}{\textbf{Initial Investment}}$$

Project A	Project B
$\dfrac{\$58,112}{\$40,000} = \textbf{1.45}$	$\dfrac{\$110,574}{\$90,000} = \textbf{1.23}$

Illustration 12-20   Calculation of profitability index

In this case the profitability index of Project A exceeds that of Project B. Thus, Project A is more desirable. Again, if these were not mutually exclusive projects, and if resources were not limited, then the company should invest in both projects, since both have positive NPVs. Additional considerations related to preference decisions are discussed in more advanced courses.

DECISION TOOLKIT

Decision Checkpoints	Info Needed for Decision	Tool to Use for Decision	How to Evaluate Results
Which investment proposal should a company accept?	Estimated cash flows and discount rate for each proposal	Profitability index $=$ $\dfrac{\text{Present value of net cash flows}}{\text{Initial investment}}$	The investment proposal with the highest profitability index should be accepted.

RISK ANALYSIS

A simplifying assumption made by many financial analysts is that projected results are known with certainty. In reality, projected results are only estimates based upon the forecaster's belief as to the most probable outcome. One approach for dealing with such uncertainty is **sensitivity analysis**. Sensitivity analysis uses a number of outcome estimates to get a sense of the variability among potential returns. An example of sensitivity analysis was presented in Illustration 12-11, where we illustrated the impact on NPV of different discount rate assumptions. A higher-risk project would be evaluated using a higher discount rate.

Similarly, to take into account that more distant cash flows are often more uncertain, a higher discount rate can be used to discount more distant cash flows. Other techniques to address uncertainty are discussed in advanced courses.

POST-AUDIT OF INVESTMENT PROJECTS

STUDY OBJECTIVE
6
Indicate the benefits of performing a post-audit.

Any well-run organization should perform an evaluation, called a post-audit, of its investment projects after their completion. A post-audit is a thorough evaluation of how well a project's actual performance matches the original projections. An example of a post-audit is seen in the Feature Story about **Campbell Soup**. The original decision to invest in the Intelligent Quisine line was made based on management's best estimates of future cash flows. During the development phase of the project an outside consulting firm was hired to evaluate the project's potential for success. Because actual results during the initial years were far below the estimated results, and because the future also did not look promising, the project was terminated.

Performing a post-audit is important for a variety of reasons. First, if managers know that their estimates will be compared to actual results they will be more likely to submit reasonable and accurate data when they make investment proposals. This clearly is better for the company than for managers to submit overly optimistic estimates in an effort to get pet projects approved. Second, as seen with Campbell Soup, a post-audit provides a formal mechanism by which the company can determine whether existing projects should be supported or terminated. Third, post-audits improve future investment proposals because, by evaluating past successes and failures, managers improve their estimation techniques.

A post-audit involves the same evaluation techniques that were used in making the original capital budgeting decision—for example, use of the NPV method. The difference is that, in the post-audit, actual figures are inserted where known, and estimation of future amounts is revised based on new information. The managers responsible for the estimates used in the original proposal must explain the reasons for any significant differences between their estimates and actual results.

Post-audits are not foolproof. In the case of **Campbell Soup**, some observers suggested that the company was too quick to abandon the project. Industry analysts suggested that with more time and more advertising expenditures, the company might have enjoyed a success.

Business Insight
Management Perspective

Inaccurate trend forecasting and market positioning are more detrimental to capital investment than using the wrong discount rate. **Ampex** patented the VCR, but failed to see its market potential. **Westinghouse** made the same mistake with the flat-screen video display. More often, companies adopt projects or businesses only to discontinue them in response to market changes. **Texas Instruments** announced it would stop manufacturing computer chips, after it had made substantial capital investments that enabled it to become one of the world's leading suppliers. The company has dropped out of some twelve business lines in recent years.

SOURCE: World Research Advisory Inc. (London, August 1998), p. 4.

Other Capital Budgeting Techniques

Some companies use capital budgeting techniques other than, or in addition to, the cash payback and net present value methods. In this section we will briefly discuss these other approaches.

INTERNAL RATE OF RETURN METHOD

The **internal rate of return (IRR) method** differs from the net present value method in that it finds the **interest yield of the potential investment**. The **internal rate of return (IRR)** is the interest rate that will cause the present value of the proposed capital expenditure to equal the present value of the expected net annual cash flows (that is, NPV to equal zero). Note that because it recognizes the time value of money, the internal rate of return method is (like the NPV method) a discounted cash flow technique.

STUDY OBJECTIVE

7

Explain the internal rate of return method.

How does one determine the internal rate of return? One way is to use a financial (business) calculator or computerized spreadsheet to solve for this rate. If a calculator or computer spreadsheet is not employed, a trial-and-error procedure is used.

To illustrate, assume that Stewart Soup Company is considering the purchase of a new front-end loader at a cost of $244,371. Net annual cash flows from this loader are estimated to be $100,000 a year for three years. To determine the internal rate of return on this front-end loader, we find the discount rate that results in a net present value of zero. As shown in Illustration 12-21 (page 506), at a rate of return of 10 percent, Stewart Soup has a positive net present value of $4,315. At a rate of return of 12 percent, it has a negative net present value of $4,188. At an 11 percent rate, the net present value is zero, and therefore this rate is the internal rate of return for this investment.

Illustration 12-21 Estimation of internal rate of return

Year	Annual Cash Flows	Discount Factor 10%	Present Value 10%	Discount Factor 11%	Present Value 11%	Discount Factor 12%	Present Value 12%
1	$100,000	.90909	$ 90,909	.90090	$ 90,090	.89286	$ 89,286
2	$100,000	.82645	82,645	.81162	81,162	.79719	79,719
3	$100,000	.75132	75,132	.73119	73,119	.71178	71,178
			248,686		244,371		240,183
Less: Initial investment			244,371		244,371		244,371
Net present value			$ 4,315		$ –0–		$ (4,188)

An easier approach to solving for the internal rate of return can be used if the net annual cash flows are **equal**, as in the Stewart Soup example. In this special case, we can find the internal rate of return using the following equation.

$$\$244,371 = \$100,000 \times \text{Present value of } \$100,000 \text{ for 3 years at } i \text{ percent}$$

Solving for the interest rate, we find:

$$\frac{\$244,371}{\$100,000} = 2.44371 = \text{Present value of } \$100,000 \text{ for 3 years at } i \text{ percent}$$

We then look up the factor 2.44371 in Table 4 of Appendix A in the 3-period row and find it under 11%. Row 3 is reproduced below for your convenience.

TABLE 4 PRESENT VALUE OF AN ANNUITY OF 1										
(n) Periods	**4%**	**5%**	**6%**	**8%**	**9%**	**10%**	**11%**	**12%**	**15%**	
3	2.77509	2.72325	2.67301	2.57710	2.53130	2.48685	2.44371	2.40183	2.28323	

Recognize that if the cash flows are **uneven**, then a trial-and-error approach or a financial calculator or computerized spreadsheet must be used.

Once we know the internal rate of return, we compare it to management's required rate of return (the discount rate). The IRR decision rule is as follows: **Accept the project when the internal rate of return is equal to or greater than the required rate of return. Reject the project when the internal rate of return is less than the required rate of return.** These relationships are shown graphically in Illustration 12-22 (page 507).

The internal rate of return method is widely used in practice. Most managers find the internal rate of return easy to interpret.

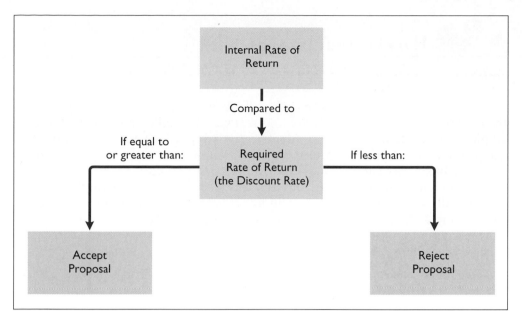

Illustration 12-22   Internal rate of return decision criteria

DECISION TOOLKIT

Decision Checkpoints	Info Needed for Decision	Tool to Use for Decision	How to Evaluate Results
Should the company invest in a proposed project?	Estimated cash flows and the required rate of return (hurdle rate)	Internal rate of return = Interest rate that results in a net present value of zero	If the internal rate of return exceeds the required rate of return for the project, then the project is financially acceptable.

COMPARING DISCOUNTED CASH FLOW METHODS

A comparison of the two discounted cash flow methods—net present value and internal rate of return—is presented in Illustration 12-23. When properly used, either method will provide management with relevant quantitative data for making capital budgeting decisions.

	Net Present Value	**Internal Rate of Return**
1. Objective	Compute net present value (a dollar amount).	Compute internal rate of return (a percentage).
2. Decision rule	If net present value is zero or positive, accept the proposal. If net present value is negative, reject the proposal.	If internal rate of return is equal to or greater than the required rate of return, accept the proposal. If internal rate of return is less than the required rate of return, reject the proposal.

Illustration 12-23   Comparison of discounted cash flow methods

ANNUAL RATE OF RETURN METHOD

STUDY OBJECTIVE
8
Describe the annual rate of return method.

The final capital budgeting technique we will look at is the **annual rate of return method**. It is based directly on accrual accounting data rather than on cash flows. It indicates **the profitability of a capital expenditure** by dividing expected annual net income by the average investment. The formula for computing annual rate of return is shown in Illustration 12-24.

Illustration 12-24 Annual rate of return formula

$$\text{Expected Annual Net Income} \div \text{Average Investment} = \text{Annual Rate of Return}$$

Assume that Reno Company is considering an investment of $130,000 in new equipment. The new equipment is expected to last five years and have zero salvage value at the end of its useful life. The straight-line method of depreciation is used for accounting purposes. The expected annual revenues and costs of the new product that will be produced from the investment are:

Illustration 12-25 Estimated annual net income from Reno Company's capital expenditure

Sales		$200,000
Less: Costs and expenses		
Manufacturing costs (exclusive of depreciation)	$132,000	
Depreciation expense ($130,000 ÷ 5)	26,000	
Selling and administrative expenses	22,000	180,000
Income before income taxes		20,000
Income tax expense		7,000
Net income		$ 13,000

Reno's expected annual net income is $13,000. Average investment is derived from the following formula.

Illustration 12-26 Formula for computing average investment

$$\text{Average investment} = \frac{\text{Original Investment} + \text{Value at End of Useful Life}}{2}$$

The value at the end of useful life is equal to the asset's salvage value, if any. For Reno, average investment is $65,000 [($130,000 + $0) ÷ 2]. The expected annual rate of return for Reno's investment in new equipment is therefore 20 percent, computed as follows.

$$\$13,000 \div \$65,000 = 20\%$$

Management then compares the annual rate of return with its required rate of return for investments of similar risk. The required rate of return is generally based on the company's cost of capital. The decision rule is: **A project is acceptable if its rate of return is greater than management's required rate of return. It is unacceptable when the reverse is true.** When the rate of return technique is used in deciding among several acceptable projects, **the higher the rate of return for a given risk, the more attractive the investment**.

The principal advantages of this method are the simplicity of its calculation and management's familiarity with the accounting terms used in the computation. A major limitation of the annual rate of return method is that it does not consider the time value of money. For example, no consideration is given as to whether cash inflows will occur early or late in the life of the investment. As explained in Appendix A, recognition of the time value of money can make a significant difference between the future value and the discounted present value of an investment. A second disadvantage is that this method relies on accrual accounting numbers rather than expected cash flows.

Helpful Hint A capital budgeting decision based on only one technique may be misleading. It is often wise to analyze an investment from a number of different perspectives.

BEFORE YOU GO ON . . .

▶**Review It**

1. When is a proposal acceptable under (a) the net present value method and (b) the internal rate of return method?
2. How does the internal rate of return method differ from the net present value method?
3. What is the formula for and the decision rule in using the annual rate of return method? What are the drawbacks to the annual rate of return method?

☑ THE NAVIGATOR

Using the Decision Toolkit

Campbell Soup is considering expanding its international presence. It sells 38 percent of the soup consumed in the United States, but only 2 percent of soup worldwide. Thus the company believes that it has great potential for international sales. Recently, 20 percent of Campbell's sales were in foreign markets (and nearly all of that was in Europe). Its goal is to have 30 percent of its sales be in foreign markets. In order to accomplish this goal, the company will have to invest heavily.

In recent years Campbell has spent between $300 and $400 million on capital expenditures. Suppose that Campbell is interested in expanding its South American presence by building a new production facility. After considering tax, marketing, labor, transportation, and political issues, Campbell has determined that the most desirable location is either in Buenos Aires or Rio de Janeiro. The following estimates have been provided (all amounts are stated in U.S. dollars).

	Buenos Aires	Rio de Janeiro
Initial investment	$2,500,000	$1,400,000
Estimated useful life	20 years	20 years
Annual revenues (accrual)	$ 500,000	$ 380,000
Annual expenses (accrual)	$ 200,000	$ 180,000
Annual cash inflows	$ 550,000	$ 430,000
Annual cash outflows	$ 222,250	$ 206,350
Estimated salvage value	$ 500,000	$0
Discount rate	9%	9%

Instructions

Evaluate each of these mutually exclusive proposals employing (1) cash payback, (2) net present value, (3) the profitability index, (4) the internal rate of return, and (5) annual rate of return. Discuss the implications of your findings.

Solution

	Buenos Aires	Rio de Janeiro

(1) Cash payback $\qquad \dfrac{\$2,500,000}{\$327,750} = 7.63$ years $\qquad \dfrac{\$1,400,000}{\$223,650} = 6.26$ years

(2) Net present value
Present value of net cash flows
$327,750 × 9.12855 = $2,991,882 $223,650 × 9.12855 = $2,041,600
$500,000 × 0.17843 =   89,215

                              3,081,097
Less: Initial investment 2,500,000   1,400,000
Net present value $ 581,097 $ 641,600

(3) Profitability index $\qquad \dfrac{\$3,081,097}{\$2,500,000} = 1.23 \qquad \dfrac{\$2,041,600}{\$1,400,000} = 1.46$

(4) Internal rate of return: The internal rate of return can be approximated by experimenting with different discount rates to see which one comes the closest to resulting in a net present value of zero. Doing this, we find that Buenos Aires has an internal rate of return of approximately 12%, while the internal rate of return of the Rio de Janeiro location is approximately 15% as shown below. Rio, therefore, is preferable.

Internal rate of return

Cash Flows	×	12% Discount Factor	=	Present Value	Cash Flows	×	15% Discount Factor	=	Present Value
$327,750 ×		7.46944	=	$2,448,109	$223,650 ×		6.25933	=	$1,399,899
$500,000 ×		0.10367	=	51,835					
				$2,499,944					
Less: Capital investment				2,500,000					1,400,000
Net present value				$ (56)					$ (101)

(5) Annual rate of return

Average investment

$$\frac{(\$2,500,000 + \$500,000)}{2} = \$1,500,000 \qquad \frac{(\$1,400,000 + \$0)}{2} = \$700,000$$

Annual rate of return $\qquad \dfrac{\$300,000}{\$1,500,000} = .20 = 20\% \qquad \dfrac{\$200,000}{\$700,000} = .286 = 28.6\%$

Implications: Although the annual rate of return is higher for Rio de Janeiro, this method has the disadvantage of ignoring time value of money, as well as using accrual numbers rather than cash flows. The cash payback of Rio de Janeiro is also shorter, but this method also ignores the time value of money. Thus, while these two methods can be used for a quick assessment, neither should be relied upon as the sole evaluation tool.

From the net present value calculation it would appear that the two projects are nearly identical in their acceptability. However, the profitability index indicates that the Rio de Janeiro investment is far more desirable because it generates its cash flows with a much smaller initial investment. A similar result is found by using the internal rate of return. Overall, assuming that the company will invest in only one project, it would appear that the Rio de Janeiro project should be chosen.

☑ THE NAVIGATOR

Summary of Study Objectives

1 *Discuss the capital budgeting evaluation process, and explain what inputs are used in capital budgeting.* Project proposals are gathered from each department and submitted to a capital budget committee, which screens the proposals and recommends worthy projects. Company officers decide which projects to fund, and the board of directors approves the capital budget. In capital budgeting, estimated cash inflows and outflows, rather than accrual-accounting numbers, are the preferred inputs.

2 *Describe the cash payback technique.* The cash payback technique identifies the time period required to recover the cost of the investment. The formula when net annual cash flows are equal is: Cost of capital investment divided by estimated net annual cash flow equals cash payback period. The shorter the payback period, the more attractive the investment.

3 *Explain the net present value method.* Under the net present value method, the present value of future cash inflows is compared with the capital investment to determine net present value. The NPV decision rule is: Accept the project if net present value is zero or positive. Reject the project if net present value is negative.

4 *Identify the challenges presented by intangible benefits in capital budgeting.* Intangible benefits are difficult to quantify, and thus are often ignored in capital budgeting decisions. This can result in incorrectly rejecting some projects. One method for considering intangible benefits is to calculate the NPV, ignoring intangible benefits; if the resulting NPV is below zero, evaluate whether the benefits are worth at least the amount of the negative net present value. Alter-

natively, intangible benefits can be incorporated into the NPV calculation, using conservative estimates of their value.

5 *Describe the profitability index.* The profitability index is a tool for comparing the relative merits of alternative capital investment opportunities. It is computed by dividing the present value of net cash flows by the initial investment. The higher the index, the more desirable the project.

6 *Indicate the benefits of performing a post-audit.* A post-audit is an evaluation of a capital investment's actual performance. Post-audits create an incentive for managers to make accurate estimates. Post-audits also are useful for determining whether a project should be continued, expanded, or terminated. Finally, post-audits provide feedback that is useful for improving estimation techniques.

7 *Explain the internal rate of return method.* The objective of the internal rate of return method is to find the interest yield of the potential investment, which is expressed as a percentage rate. The IRR decision rule is: Accept the project when the internal rate of return is equal to or greater than the required rate of return. Reject the project when the internal rate of return is less than the required rate of return.

8 *Describe the annual rate of return method.* The annual rate of return uses accrual accounting data to indicate the profitability of a capital investment. It is obtained by dividing the expected annual net income by the amount of the average investment. The higher the rate of return, the more attractive the investment.

☑ THE NAVIGATOR

DECISION TOOLKIT—A SUMMARY

Decision Checkpoints	Info Needed for Decision	Tool to Use for Decision	How to Evaluate Results
Should the company invest in a proposed project?	Cash flow estimates, discount rate	Net present = Present value of value net cash flows less capital investment	The investment is financially acceptable if net present value is positive.
Which investment proposal should a company accept?	Estimated cash flows and discount rate for each proposal	Profitability = Present value of index <u>net cash flows</u> Initial investment	The investment proposal with the highest profitability index should be accepted.
Should the company invest in a proposed project?	Estimated cash flows and the required rate of return (hurdle rate)	Internal Interest rate that results rate of = in a net present value return of zero	If the internal rate of return exceeds the required rate of return for the project, then the project is financially acceptable.

Glossary

Annual rate of return method The determination of the profitability of a capital expenditure, computed by dividing expected annual net income by the average investment. (p. 508)

Capital budgeting The process of making capital expenditure decisions in business. (p. 491)

Cash payback technique A capital budgeting technique that identifies the time period required to recover the cost of a capital investment from the annual cash inflow produced by the investment. (p. 494)

Cost of capital The average rate of return that the firm must pay to obtain borrowed and equity funds. (p. 498)

Discounted cash flow technique A capital budgeting technique that considers both the estimated net cash flows from the investment and the time value of money. (p. 495)

Discount rate The interest rate used in discounting the future net cash flows to determine present value. (p. 495)

Internal rate of return (IRR) The rate that will cause the present value of the proposed capital expenditure to

equal the present value of the expected net annual cash flows. (p. 505)

Internal rate of return (IRR) method A method used in capital budgeting that results in finding the interest yield of the potential investment. (p. 505)

Net present value (NPV) The difference that results when the original capital outlay is subtracted from the discounted net cash flows. (p. 495)

Net present value (NPV) method A method used in capital budgeting in which net cash flows are discounted to their present value and then compared to the capital outlay required by the investment. (p. 495)

Post-audit A thorough evaluation of how well a project's actual performance matches the projections made when the project was proposed. (p. 504)

Profitability index A method of comparing alternative projects that takes into account both the size of the investment and its discounted future net cash flows. It is computed by dividing the present value of net future cash flows by the initial investment. (p. 503)

Demonstration Problem

Sierra Company is considering a long-term capital investment project called ZIP. ZIP will require an investment of $120,000, and it will have a useful life of 4 years. Annual net income is expected to be $9,000 a year. Depreciation is computed by the straight-line method with no salvage value. The company's cost of capital is 12 percent. (*Hint:* Assume cash flows can be computed by adding back depreciation expense.)

Instructions

(Round all computations to two decimal places.)

(a) Compute the cash payback period for the project. (Round to two decimals.)

(b) Compute the net present value for the project. (Round to nearest dollar.)

(c) Compute the annual rate of return for the project.

(d) Should the project be accepted? Why?

Solution to Demonstration Problem

(a) $120,000 ÷ $39,000, ($9,000 + $30,000), = 3.08 years

(b)

	Present Value at 12%
Discount factor for 4 periods	3.03735
Present value of net cash flows:	
$39,000 × 3.03735	$118,457
Capital investment	120,000
Negative net present value	$ (1,543)

(c) $9,000 ÷ $60,000 ($120,000 ÷ 2) = 15%

(d) The annual rate of return of 15% is good. However, the cash payback period is 77% of the project's useful life, and net present value is negative. The recommendation is to reject the project.

Action Plan

- Calculate the time it will take to pay back the investment: cost of the investment divided by net annual cash flows.
- When calculating NPV, remember that net annual cash flow equals annual net income plus annual depreciation expense.
- Be careful to use the correct discount factor in using the net present value method.
- Calculate the annual rate of return: expected annual net income divided by average investment.

Self-Study Questions

Answers are at the end of the chapter.

(SO 1) 1. Which of the following is *not* an example of a capital budgeting decision?
  (a) Decision to build a new plant.
  (b) Decision to renovate an existing facility.
  (c) Decision to buy a piece of machinery.
  (d) All of these are capital budgeting decisions.

(SO 1) 2. What is the order of involvement of the following parties in the capital budgeting authorization process?
  (a) Plant managers, officers, capital budget committee, board of directors.
  (b) Board of directors, plant managers, officers, capital budget committee.
  (c) Plant managers, capital budget committee, officers, board of directors.
  (d) Officers, plant managers, capital budget committee, board of directors.

(SO 2) 3. What is a weakness of the cash payback approach?
  (a) It uses accrual-based accounting numbers.
  (b) It ignores the time value of money.
  (c) It ignores the useful life of alternative projects.
  (d) Both (b) and (c) are true.

(SO 3) 4. Which is a true statement regarding using a higher discount rate to calculate the net present value of a project?
  (a) It will make it less likely that the project will be accepted.
  (b) It will make it more likely that the project will be accepted.
  (c) It is appropriate to use a higher rate if the project is perceived as being less risky than other projects being considered.
  (d) It is appropriate to use a higher rate if the project will have a short useful life relative to other projects being considered.

(SO 3) 5. A positive net present value means that the:
  (a) project's rate of return is less than the cutoff rate.
  (b) project's rate of return exceeds the required rate of return.
  (c) project's rate of return equals the required rate of return.
  (d) project is unacceptable.

(SO 3) 6. Which of the following is *not* an alternative name for the discount rate?
  (a) Hurdle rate.
  (b) Required rate of return.

(c) Cutoff rate.

(d) All of these are alternative names for the discount rate.

(SO 4)   7. If a project has intangible benefits whose value is hard to estimate, the best thing to do is:

(a) ignore these benefits, since any estimate of their value will most likely be wrong.

(b) include a conservative estimate of their value.

(c) ignore their value in your initial net present value calculation, but then estimate whether their potential value is worth at least the amount of the net present value deficiency.

(d) either (b) or (c) is correct.

(SO 6)   8. A post-audit of an investment project should be performed:

(a) on all significant capital expenditure projects.

(b) on all projects that management feels might be financial failures.

(c) on randomly selected projects.

(d) only on projects that enjoy tremendous success.

9. A project should be accepted if its internal rate   (SO 7) of return exceeds:

(a) zero.

(b) the rate of return on a government bond.

(c) the company's required rate of return.

(d) the rate the company pays on borrowed funds.

10. Which of the following is *incorrect* about the   (SO 8) annual rate of return technique?

(a) The calculation is simple.

(b) The accounting terms used are familiar to management.

(c) The timing of the cash inflows is not considered.

(d) The time value of money is considered.

Questions

1. Describe the process a company may use in screening and approving the capital expenditure budget.

2. What are the advantages and disadvantages of the cash payback technique?

3. Walter Shea claims the formula for the cash payback technique is the same as the formula for the annual rate of return technique. Is Walter correct? What is the formula for the cash payback technique?

4. Two types of present value tables may be used with the discounted cash flow techniques. Identify the tables and the circumstance(s) when each table should be used.

5. What is the decision rule under the net present value method?

6. Discuss the factors that determine the appropriate discount rate to use when calculating the net present value.

7. What simplifying assumptions were made in the chapter regarding calculation of net present value?

8. What are some examples of potential intangible benefits of investment proposals? Why do these intangible benefits complicate the capital budgeting evaluation process? What might happen if intangible benefits are ignored in a capital budgeting decision?

9. What steps can be taken to incorporate intangible benefits into the capital budget evaluation process?

10. What advantages does the profitability index provide over direct comparison of net present value when comparing two projects?

11. What is a post-audit? What are the potential benefits of a post-audit?

12. Identify the steps required in using the internal rate of return method when the net annual cash flows are equal.

13. Waterville Company uses the internal rate of return method. What is the decision rule for this method?

14. What are the strengths of the annual rate of return approach? What are its weaknesses?

15. Your classmate, Kurt Snyder, is confused about the factors that are included in the annual rate of return technique. What is the formula for this technique?

16. Stella Waite is trying to understand the term "cost of capital." Define the term and indicate its relevance to the decision rule under the internal rate of return technique.

Brief Exercises

Compute the cash payback period for a capital investment.
(SO 2)

BE12-1   Marcus Company is considering purchasing new equipment for $450,000. It is expected that the equipment will produce net annual cash flows of $55,000 over its 10-year useful life. Annual depreciation will be $45,000. Compute the cash payback period.

Compute net present value of an investment.
(SO 3)

BE12-2   Nien Company accumulates the following data concerning a proposed capital investment: cash cost $220,000, net annual cash flows $40,000, present value factor of cash inflows for 10 years 5.65 (rounded). Determine the net present value, and indicate whether the investment should be made.

BE12-3 Timo Corporation, an amusement park, is considering a capital investment in a new exhibit. The exhibit would cost $136,000 and have an estimated useful life of 5 years. It will be sold for $70,000 at that time. (Amusement parks need to rotate exhibits to keep people interested.) It is expected to increase net annual cash flows by $25,000. The company's borrowing rate is 8%. Its cost of capital is 10%. Calculate the net present value of this project to the company.

Compute net present value of an investment.
(SO 3)

BE12-4 Michener Bottling Corporation is considering the purchase of a new bottling machine. The machine would cost $200,000 and has an estimated useful life of 8 years with zero salvage value. Management estimates that the new bottling machine will provide net annual cash flows of $35,000. Management also believes that the new bottling machine will save the company money because it is expected to be more reliable than other machines, and thus will reduce downtime. How much would the reduction in downtime have to be worth in order for the project to be acceptable? Assume a discount rate of 9%. (*Hint:* Calculate the net present value.)

Compute net present value of an investment and consider intangible benefits.
(SO 3, 4)

BE12-5 Harry Company is considering two different, mutually exclusive capital expenditure proposals. Project A will cost $395,000, has an expected useful life of 10 years, a salvage value of zero, and is expected to increase net annual cash flows by $70,000. Project B will cost $270,000, has an expected useful life of 10 years, a salvage value of zero, and is expected to increase net annual cash flows by $50,000. A discount rate of 9% is appropriate for both projects. Compute the net present value and profitability index of each project. Which project should be accepted?

Compute net present value and profitability index.
(SO 3, 5)

BE12-6 Martelle Company is performing a post-audit of a project completed one year ago. The initial estimates were that the project would cost $250,000, would have a useful life of 9 years, zero salvage value, and would result in net annual cash flows of $45,000 per year. Now that the investment has been in operation for 1 year, revised figures indicate that it actually cost $260,000, will have a useful life of 11 years, and will produce net annual cash flows of $38,000 per year. Evaluate the success of the project. Assume a discount rate of 10%.

Perform a post-audit.
(SO 6)

BE12-7 Frost Company is evaluating the purchase of a rebuilt spot-welding machine to be used in the manufacture of a new product. The machine will cost $170,000, has an estimated useful life of 7 years, a salvage value of zero, and will increase net annual cash flows by $33,740. What is its approximate internal rate of return?

Calculate internal rate of return.
(SO 7)

BE12-8 Vintech Corporation is considering investing in a new facility. The estimated cost of the facility is $2,045,000. It will be used for 12 years, then sold for $600,000. The facility will generate annual cash inflows of $400,000 and will need new annual cash outflows of $160,000. The company has a required rate of return of 7%. Calculate the internal rate of return on this project, and discuss whether the project should be accepted.

Calculate internal rate of return.
(SO 7)

BE12-9 Engles Oil Company is considering investing in a new oil well. It is expected that the oil well will increase annual revenues by $130,000 and will increase annual expenses by $80,000 including depreciation. The oil well will cost $490,000 and will have a $10,000 salvage value at the end of its 10-year useful life. Calculate the annual rate of return.

Compute annual rate of return
(SO 8)

Exercises

E12-1 Dobbs Corporation is considering purchasing a new delivery truck. The truck has many advantages over the company's current truck (not the least of which is that it runs). The new truck would cost $56,000. Because of the increased capacity, reduced maintenance costs, and increased fuel economy, the new truck is expected to generate cost savings of $8,000. At the end of 8 years the company will sell the truck for an estimated $28,000. Traditionally the company has used a rule of thumb that a proposal should not be accepted unless it has a payback period that is less than 50% of the asset's estimated useful life. Hal Michaels, a new manager, has suggested that the company should not rely solely on the payback approach, but should also employ the net present value method when evaluating new projects. The company's cost of capital is 8%.

Compute cash payback and net present value.
(SO 2, 3)

Instructions

(a) Compute the cash payback period and net present value of the proposed investment.

(b) Does the project meet the company's cash payback criteria? Does it meet the net present value criteria for acceptance? Discuss your results.

Compute cash payback period and net present value.
(SO 2, 3)

E12-2 Jack's Custom Manufacturing Company is considering three new projects, each requiring an equipment investment of $21,000. Each project will last for 3 years and produce the following net annual cash flows.

Year	AA	BB	CC
1	$ 7,000	$ 9,500	$13,000
2	9,000	9,500	10,000
3	15,000	9,500	11,000
Total	$31,000	$28,500	$34,000

The equipment's salvage value is zero, and Jack uses straight-line depreciation. Jack will not accept any project with a cash payback period over 2 years. Jack's required rate of return is 12%.

Instructions

(a) Compute each project's payback period, indicating the most desirable project and the least desirable project using this method. (Round to two decimals and assume in your computations that cash flows occur evenly throughout the year.)

(b) Compute the net present value of each project. Does your evaluation change? (Round to nearest dollar.)

Compute net present value and profitability index.
(SO 3, 5)

E12-3 TLC Corp. is considering purchasing one of two new diagnostic machines. Either machine would make it possible for the company to bid on jobs that it currently isn't equipped to do. Estimates regarding each machine are provided below.

	Machine A	Machine B
Original cost	$78,000	$190,000
Estimated life	8 years	8 years
Salvage value	–0–	–0–
Estimated annual cash inflows	$20,000	$ 40,000
Estimated annual cash outflows	$ 5,000	$ 9,000

Instructions

Calculate the net present value and profitability index of each machine. Assume a 9% discount rate. Which machine should be purchased?

Determine internal rate of return.
(SO 7)

E12-4 Kendra Corporation is involved in the business of injection molding of plastics. It is considering the purchase of a new computer-aided design and manufacturing machine for $425,000. The company believes that with this new machine it will improve productivity and increase quality, resulting in an increase in net annual cash flows of $95,000 for the next 6 years. Management requires a 10% rate of return on all new investments.

Instructions

Calculate the internal rate of return on this new machine. Should the investment be accepted?

Determine internal rate of return.
(SO 7)

E12-5 Summer Company is considering three capital expenditure projects. Relevant data for the projects are as follows.

Project	Investment	Annual Income	Life of Project
22A	$240,000	$15,000	6 years
23A	270,000	24,400	9 years
24A	280,000	21,000	7 years

Annual income is constant over the life of the project. Each project is expected to have zero salvage value at the end of the project. Summer Company uses the straight-line method of depreciation.

Instructions
(a) Determine the internal rate of return for each project. Round the internal rate of return factor to three decimals.
(b) If Summer Company's required rate of return is 11%, which projects are acceptable?

E12-6 Mane Event is considering opening a new hair salon in Pompador, California. The cost of building a new salon is $300,000. A new salon will normally generate annual revenues of $70,000, with annual expenses (including depreciation) of $40,000. At the end of 15 years the salon will have a salvage value of $75,000.

Calculate annual rate of return.
(SO 8)

Instructions
Calculate the annual rate of return on the project.

E12-7 Alameda Service Center just purchased an automobile hoist for $41,000. The hoist has an 8-year life and an estimated salvage value of $3,000. Installation costs and freight charges were $3,300 and $700, respectively. Alameda uses straight-line depreciation.
    The new hoist will be used to replace mufflers and tires on automobiles. Alameda estimates that the new hoist will enable his mechanics to replace five extra mufflers per week. Each muffler sells for $72 installed. The cost of a muffler is $34, and the labor cost to install a muffler is $12.

Compute cash payback period and annual rate of return.
(SO 2, 8)

Instructions
(a) Compute the cash payback period for the new hoist.
(b) Compute the annual rate of return for the new hoist. (Round to one decimal.)

E12-8 Morgan Company is considering a capital investment of $180,000 in additional productive facilities. The new machinery is expected to have a useful life of 6 years with no salvage value. Depreciation is by the straight-line method. During the life of the investment, annual net income and net annual cash flows are expected to be $20,000 and $50,000 respectively. Morgan has a 15% cost of capital rate which is the required rate of return on the investment.

Compute annual rate of return, cash payback period, and net present value.
(SO 2, 3, 8)

Instructions
(Round to two decimals.)
(a) Compute (1) the cash payback period and (2) the annual rate of return on the proposed capital expenditure.
(b) Using the discounted cash flow technique, compute the net present value.

Problems: Set A

P12-1A The Three Stooges partnership is considering three long-term capital investment proposals. Each investment has a useful life of 5 years. Relevant data on each project are as follows.

Compute annual rate of return, cash payback, and net present value.
(SO 2, 3, 8)

	Project Moe	**Project Larry**	**Project Curly**
Capital investment	$150,000	$160,000	$200,000
Annual net income:			
Year 1	13,000	18,000	27,000
2	13,000	17,000	22,000
3	13,000	16,000	21,000
4	13,000	12,000	13,000
5	13,000	9,000	12,000
Total	$ 65,000	$ 72,000	$ 95,000

Depreciation is computed by the straight-line method with no salvage value. The company's cost of capital is 15%. (Assume that cash flows occur evenly throughout the year.)

Instructions
(a) Compute the cash payback period for each project. (Round to two decimals.)
(b) Compute the net present value for each project. (Round to nearest dollar.)
(c) Compute the annual rate of return for each project. (Round to two decimals.) (*Hint*: Use average annual net income in your computation.)
(d) Rank the projects on each of the foregoing bases. Which project do you recommend?

(b) L $(2,368); C $1,407

Compute annual rate of return, cash payback, and net present value.
(SO 2, 3, 8)

P12-2A   Tony Siebers is an accounting major at a midwestern state university located approximately 60 miles from a major city. Many of the students attending the university are from the metropolitan area and visit their homes regularly on the weekends. Tony, an entrepreneur at heart, realizes that few good commuting alternatives are available for students doing weekend travel. He believes that a weekend commuting service could be organized and run profitably from several suburban and downtown shopping mall locations. Tony has gathered the following investment information.

1. Five used vans would cost a total of $75,000 to purchase and would have a 3-year useful life with negligible salvage value. Tony plans to use straight-line depreciation.
2. Ten drivers would have to be employed at a total payroll expense of $48,000.
3. Other annual out-of-pocket expenses associated with running the commuter service would include Gasoline $16,000, Maintenance $4,300, Repairs $5,000, Insurance $5,200, Advertising $2,500.
4. Tony has visited several financial institutions to discuss funding. The best interest rate he has been able to negotiate is 8%. Use this rate for cost of capital.
5. Tony expects each van to make ten round trips weekly and carry an average of six students each trip. The service is expected to operate 30 weeks each year, and each student will be charged $12.00 for a round-trip ticket.

Instructions

(a) (1) $2,000

(a) Determine the annual (1) net income and (2) net annual cash flows for the commuter service.

(b) (1) 2.78 years

(b) Compute (1) the cash payback period and (2) the annual rate of return. (Round to two decimals.)

(c) Compute the net present value of the commuter service. (Round to the nearest dollar.)
(d) What should Tony conclude from these computations?

Compute net present value, profitability index, and internal rate of return.
(SO 3, 5, 7)

P12-3A   Carolina Clinic is considering investing in new heart monitoring equipment. It has two options: Option A would have an initial lower cost but would require a significant expenditure for rebuilding after 4 years. Option B would require no rebuilding expenditure, but its maintenance costs would be higher. Since the option B machine is of initial higher quality, it is expected to have a salvage value at the end of its useful life. The following estimates were made of the cash flows. The company's cost of capital is 11%.

	Option A	Option B
Initial cost	$160,000	$227,000
Annual cash inflows	$ 75,000	$ 80,000
Annual cash outflows	$ 35,000	$ 30,000
Cost to rebuild (end of year 4)	$ 60,000	$ 0
Salvage value	$ 0	$ 12,000
Estimated useful life	8 years	8 years

Instructions

(a) (1) NPV A $6,321
   (3) IRR B 15%

(a) Compute the (1) net present value, (2) profitability index, and (3) internal rate of return for each option. (*Hint:* To solve for internal rate of return, experiment with alternative discount rates to arrive at a net present value of zero.)
(b) Which option should be accepted?

Compute net present value considering intangible benefits.
(SO 3, 4)

P12-4A   Prestige Auto Care is considering the purchase of a new tow truck. The garage doesn't currently have a tow truck, and the $60,000 price tag for a new truck would represent a major expenditure. Jenna Lind, owner of the garage, has compiled the following estimates in trying to determine whether the tow truck should be purchased.

Initial cost	$60,000
Estimated useful life	8 years
Net annual cash flows from towing	$ 8,000
Overhaul costs (end of year 4)	$ 5,000
Salvage value	$15,000

Jenna's good friend, Reid Shaw, stopped by. He is trying to convince Jenna that the tow truck will have other benefits that Jenna hasn't even considered. First, he says, cars that need towing need to be fixed. Thus, when Jenna tows them to her facility her repair revenues will increase. Second, he notes that the tow truck could have a plow mounted on it, thus saving Jenna the cost of plowing her parking lot. (Reid will give her a used plow blade for free if Jenna will plow Reid's driveway.) Third, he notes that the truck will generate goodwill; people who are rescued by Jenna's tow truck will feel grateful and might be more inclined to used her service station in the future, or buy gas there. Fourth, the tow truck will have "Prestige Auto Care" on its doors, hood, and back tailgate—a form of free advertising wherever the tow truck goes. Reid estimates that, at a minimum, these benefits would be worth the following.

Additional annual net cash flows from repair work	$3,000
Annual savings from plowing	500
Additional annual net cash flows from customer "goodwill"	1,000
Additional annual net cash flows resulting from free advertising	500

The company's cost of capital is 9%.

Instructions
(a) Calculate the net present value, ignoring the additional benefits described by Reid. Should the tow truck be purchased?

(b) Calculate the net present value, incorporating the additional benefits suggested by Reid. Should the tow truck be purchased?

(c) Suppose Reid has been overly optimistic in his assessment of the value of the additional benefits. At a minimum, how much would the additional benefits have to be worth in order for the project to be accepted?

(a) NPV $(11,735)

(b) NPV $15,939

P12-5A   Bonita Corp. is thinking about opening a soccer camp in southern California. To start the camp, Bonita would need to purchase land and build four soccer fields and a sleeping and dining facility to house 150 soccer players. Each year the camp would be run for 8 sessions of 1 week each. The company would hire college soccer players as coaches. The camp attendees would be male and female soccer players ages 12–18. Property values in southern California have enjoyed a steady increase in value. It is expected that after using the facility for 20 years, Bonita can sell the property for more than it was originally purchased for. The following amounts have been estimated.

Compute net present value and internal rate of return with sensitivity analysis. (SO 3, 7)

Cost of land	$ 300,000
Cost to build dorm and dining facility	$ 600,000
Annual cash inflows assuming 150 players and 8 weeks	$ 950,000
Annual cash outflows	$ 840,000
Estimated useful life	20 years
Salvage value	$1,500,000
Discount rate	8%

Instructions
(a) Calculate the net present value of the project.

(b) To gauge the sensitivity of the project to these estimates, assume that if only 130 campers attend each week, annual cash inflows will be $800,000 and annual cash outflows will be $770,000. What is the net present value using these alternative estimates? Discuss your findings.

(c) Assuming the original facts, what is the net present value if the project is actually riskier than first assumed, and a 11% discount rate is more appropriate?

(d) Assume that during the first 5 years the annual net cash flows each year were only $45,000. At the end of the fifth year the company is running low on cash, so management decides to sell the property for $1,300,000. What was the actual internal rate of return on the project? Explain how this return was possible given that the camp did not appear to be successful.

(a) NPV $501,822

(d) IRR 12%

Problems: Set B

P12-1B   The partnership of Lou and Bud is considering three long-term capital investment proposals. Relevant data on each project are as follows.

Compute annual rate of return, cash payback, and net present value.
(SO 2, 3, 8)

	Project		
	Brown	**Red**	**Yellow**
Capital investment	$200,000	$225,000	$250,000
Annual net income:			
Year 1	25,000	20,000	26,000
2	16,000	20,000	24,000
3	13,000	20,000	23,000
4	10,000	20,000	22,000
5	8,000	20,000	20,000
Total	$ 72,000	$100,000	$115,000

Salvage value is expected to be zero at the end of each project. Depreciation is computed by the straight-line method. The company's required rate of return is the company's cost of capital which is 12%. (Assume that cash flows occur evenly throughout the year.)

Instructions

(b) NPV B $(584); Y $14,286

(a) Compute the cash payback period for each project. (Round to two decimals.)
(b) Compute the net present value for each project. (Round to nearest dollar.)
(c) Compute the annual rate of return for each project. (Round to two decimals.) (*Hint:* Use average annual net income in your computation.)
(d) Rank the projects on each of the foregoing bases. What project do you recommend?

Compute annual rate of return, cash payback, and net present value.
(SO 2, 3, 8)

P12-2B Jo Quick is managing director of the Tot Lot Day Care Center. Tot Lot is currently set up as a full-time child care facility for children between the ages of 12 months and 6 years. Jo Quick is trying to determine whether the center should expand its facilities to incorporate a newborn care room for infants between the ages of 6 weeks and 12 months. The necessary space already exists. An investment of $20,000 would be needed, however, to purchase cribs, high chairs, etc. The equipment purchased for the room would have a 5-year useful life with zero salvage value.

The newborn nursery would be staffed to handle 11 infants on a full-time basis. The parents of each infant would be charged $125 weekly, and the facility would operate 52 weeks of the year. Staffing the nursery would require two full-time specialists and five part-time assistants at an annual cost of $60,000. Food, diapers, and other miscellaneous supplies are expected to total $6,000 annually.

Instructions

(a) (1) 1,500
(b) (1) 3.64 years

(a) Determine (1) annual net income and (2) net annual cash flows for the new nursery.
(b) Compute (1) the cash payback period for the new nursery and (2) the annual rate of return. (Round to two decimals.)
(c) Compute the net present value of incorporating a newborn care room. (Round to the nearest dollar.) Tot Lot's cost of capital is 10%.
(d) ▱▱▱▭▷ What should Jo Quick conclude from these computations?

Compute net present value, profitability index, and internal rate of return.
(SO 3, 5, 7)

P12-3B Aqua Tech Testing is considering investing in a new testing device. It has two options: Option A would have an initial lower cost but would require a significant expenditure for rebuilding after 5 years. Option B would require no rebuilding expenditure, but its maintenance costs would be higher. Since the option B machine is of initial higher quality, it is expected to have a salvage value at the end of its useful life. The following estimates were provided. The company's cost of capital is 9%.

	Option A	**Option B**
Initial cost	$ 90,000	$170,000
Annual cash inflows	$180,000	$140,000
Annual cash outflows	$160,000	$108,000
Cost to rebuild (end of year 5)	$ 26,500	$ 0
Salvage value	$ 0	$ 27,500
Estimated useful life	8 years	8 years

Instructions

(a) (1) NPV A $3,473
(3) IRR B 12%

(a) Compute the (1) net present value, (2) profitability index, and (3) internal rate of return for each option. (*Hint:* To solve for internal rate of return, experiment with alternative discount rates to arrive at a net present value of zero.)
(b) Which option should be accepted?

P12-4B The Watertown Sanitation Company is considering the purchase of a garbage truck. The $77,000 price tag for a new truck would represent a major expenditure for the company. Kalia Vang, owner of the company, has compiled the following estimates in trying to determine whether the garbage truck should be purchased.

Compute net present value considering intangible benefits.
(SO 3, 4)

Initial cost	$77,000
Estimated useful life	10 years
Net annual cash flows	$12,000
Overhaul costs (end of year 5)	$ 7,000
Salvage value	$15,000

One of the employees is trying to convince Kalia that the truck has other merits that were not considered in the initial estimates. First, the new truck will be more efficient, with lower maintenance and operating costs. Second, it will be safer. Third, it has the ability to handle recycled materials at the same time as trash, thus offering a new revenue source. Estimates of the minimum value of these benefits are as follows.

Annual savings from reduced operating costs	$400
Annual savings from reduced maintenance costs	800
Additional annual net cash savings from reduced employee absence	500
Additional annual net cash inflows from recycling	300

The company's cost of capital is 10%.

Instructions
(a) Calculate the net present value, ignoring the additional benefits. Should the truck be purchased?
(b) Calculate the net present value, incorporating the additional benefits. Should the truck be purchased?
(c) Suppose management has been overly optimistic in the assessment of the value of the additional benefits. At a minimum, how much would the additional benefits have to be worth in order for the project to be accepted?

(a) NPV $(1,828)

(b) NPV $10,461

P12-5B Benjamin Corp. is thinking about opening an ice hockey camp in Idaho. In order to start the camp the company would need to purchase land and build two ice rinks and a dormitory-type sleeping and dining facility to house 200 players. Each year the camp would be run for 8 sessions of 1 week each. The company would hire college hockey players as coaches. The camp attendees would be male and female hockey players ages 12–18. Property values in Idaho have enjoyed a steady increase in recent years. Benjamin Corp. expects that after using the facility for 15 years, the rinks will have to be dismantled, but the land and buildings will be worth more than they were originally purchased for. The following amounts have been estimated.

Compute net present value and internal rate of return with sensitivity analysis.
(SO 3, 7)

Cost of land	$ 300,000
Cost to build dorm and dining hall	$ 600,000
Annual cash inflows assuming 200 players and 8 weeks	$ 920,000
Annual cash outflows	$ 760,000
Estimated useful life	15 years
Salvage value	$1,200,000
Discount rate	11%

Instructions
(a) Calculate the net present value of the project.
(b) To gauge the sensitivity of the project to these estimates, assume that if only 170 campers attend each week, annual cash inflows will be $700,000 and annual cash outflows will be $650,000. What is the net present value using these alternative estimates? Discuss your findings.
(c) Assuming the original facts, what is the net present value if the project is actually riskier than first assumed, and a 15% discount rate is more appropriate?
(d) Assume that during the first 6 years the annual net cash flows each year were only $84,000. At the end of the sixth year the company is running low on cash, so management decides to sell the property for $1,100,000. What was the actual internal rate of return on the project? Explain how this return was possible given that the camp did not appear to be successful.

(a) NPV $501,339

(d) IRR 12%

Problems: Set C

Problem Set C is provided at the book's Web site, www.wiley.com/college/weygandt.

▷ B R O A D E N I N G   Y O U R   P E R S P E C T I V E

Group Decision Case

BYP 12-1 Migami Company is considering the purchase of a new machine. Its invoice price is $117,000, freight charges are estimated to be $3,000, and installation costs are expected to be $5,000. Salvage value of the new machine is expected to be zero after a useful life of 4 years. Existing equipment could be retained and used for an additional 4 years if the new machine is not purchased. At that time, the salvage value of the equipment would be zero. If the new machine is purchased now, the existing machine would be scrapped. Migami accountant, Caitlyn Lahr, has accumulated the following data regarding annual sales and expenses with and without the new machine.

1. Without the new machine, Migami can sell 10,000 units of product annually at a per unit selling price of $100. If the new unit is purchased, the number of units produced and sold would increase by 20%, and the selling price would remain the same.

2. The new machine is faster than the old machine, and it is more efficient in its usage of materials. With the old machine the gross profit rate will be 28.5% of sales, whereas the rate will be 30% of sales with the new machine.

3. Annual selling expenses are $160,000 with the current equipment. Because the new equipment would produce a greater number of units to be sold, annual selling expenses are expected to increase by 10% if it is purchased.

4. Annual administrative expenses are expected to be $100,000 with the old machine, and $112,000 with the new machine.

5. The current book value of the existing machine is $30,000. Migami uses straight-line depreciation.

6. Migami management has a required rate of return of 15% on its investment and a cash payback period of no more than 3 years.

Instructions
With the class divided into groups, answer the following. (Ignore income tax effects.)

(a) Calculate the annual rate of return for the new machine. (Round to two decimals.)
(b) Compute the cash payback period for the new machine. (Round to two decimals.)
(c) Compute the net present value of the new machine. (Round to the nearest dollar.)
(d) On the basis of the foregoing data, would you recommend that Migami buy the machine? Why?

Managerial Analysis

BYP 12-2 Tony Skateboards is considering building a new plant. James Bott, the company's marketing manager, is an enthusiastic supporter of the new plant. Alyssa Minh, the company's chief financial officer, is not so sure that the plant is a good idea. Currently the company purchases its skateboards from foreign manufacturers. The following figures were estimated regarding the construction of a new plant.

Cost of plant	$4,000,000	Estimated useful life	15 years
Annual cash inflows	4,000,000	Salvage value	$2,000,000
Annual cash outflows	3,550,000	Discount rate	11%

James Bott believes that these figures understate the true potential value of the plant. He suggests that by manufacturing its own skateboards the company will benefit from a "buy American" patriotism that he believes is common among skateboarders. He also notes that the firm has had numerous quality problems with the skateboards manufactured by its suppliers. He suggests that the inconsistent quality has resulted in lost sales, increased warranty claims, and some costly lawsuits. Overall, he believes sales will be $200,000 higher than projected above, and that the savings from lower warranty costs and legal costs will be $80,000 per year. He also believes that the project is not as risky as assumed above, and that a 9% discount rate is more reasonable.

Instructions
Answer each of the following questions.

(a) Compute the net present value of the project based on the original projections.
(b) Compute the net present value incorporating James' estimates of the value of the intangible benefits, but still using the 11% discount rate.
(c) Compute the net present value using the original estimates, but employing the 9% discount rate that James suggests is more appropriate.
(d) Comment on your findings.

Real-World Focus

BYP 12-3   Tecumseh Products Company has its headquarters in Tecumseh, Michigan. It describes itself as "a global multinational corporation producing mechanical and electrical components essential to industries creating end-products for health, comfort, and convenience." The following was excerpted from the management discussion and analysis section of a recent annual report.

TECUMSEH PRODUCTS COMPANY
Management Discussion and Analysis
The company has invested approximately $50 million in a scroll compressor manufacturing facility in Tecumseh, Michigan. After experiencing setbacks in developing a commercially acceptable scroll compressor, the Company is currently testing a new generation of scroll product. The Company is unable to predict when, or if, it will offer a scroll compressor for commercial sale, but it does anticipate that reaching volume production will require a significant additional investment. Given such additional investment and current market conditions, management is currently reviewing its options with respect to scroll product improvement, cost reductions, joint ventures and alternative new products.

Instructions
Discuss issues the company should consider and techniques the company should employ to determine whether to continue pursuing this project.

Exploring the Web

BYP 12-4   Campbell Soup Company is an international provider of soup products. Management is very interested in continuing to grow the company in its core business, while "spinning off" those businesses that are not part of its core operation.

Address: www.campbellsoups.com, *or go to* **www.wiley.com/college/weygandt**

Steps
1. Go to the home page of Campbell Soup Company at the address shown above.
2. Choose the current annual report.

Instructions
Review the financial statements and management's discussion and analysis, and answer the following questions.

(a) What was the total amount of capital expenditures in the current year, and how does this amount compare with the previous year?
(b) What interest rate did the company pay on new borrowings in the current year?
(c) Assume that this year's capital expenditures are expected to increase cash flows by $42 million. What is the expected internal rate of return (IRR) for these capital expenditures? (Assume a 10-year period for the cash flows.)

Communication Activity

BYP 12-5 Refer back to Exercise 12-7 to address the following.

Instructions

Prepare a memo to Mary Ann Griffin, your supervisor. Show your calculations from E12-7, (a) and (b). In one or two paragraphs, discuss important nonfinancial considerations. Make any assumptions you believe to be necessary. Make a recommendation based on your analysis.

Research Assignment

BYP 12-6 The May 19, 2004, issue of the *Wall Street Journal* includes an article by John Carreyrou and Jo Wrighton titled "Chunnel Vision: As Eurotunnel Dug Itself a Hole, Its Shareholders Took a Stand" (page A1).

Instructions

Read the article and answer the following questions.

(a) At the time the article was written, what was the selling price of a share of Eurotunnel stock? What was the highest price at which a share ever sold?

(b) When was the first plan for a tunnel between France and England considered and who promoted that project? Why was a previous project halted?

(c) What was the original estimate of the project's cost? What was the actual cost? How many people were predicted to ride the train in the tunnel during its first year? How many actually did? What amount were revenues expected to reach? What amount did they actually reach?

(d) What are some of the causes that are cited as contributing to the tunnel's problems?

Ethics Case

BYP 12-7 Impro Company operates in a state where corporate taxes and workers' compensation insurance rates have recently doubled. Impro's president has just assigned you the task of preparing an economic analysis and making a recommendation relative to moving the entire operation to Missouri. The president is slightly in favor of such a move because Missouri is his boyhood home and he also owns a fishing lodge there.

You have just completed building your dream house, moved in, and sodded the lawn. Your children are all doing well in school and sports and, along with your spouse, want no part of a move to Missouri. If the company does move, so will you because the town is a one-industry community and you and your spouse will have to move to have employment. Moving when everyone else does will cause you to take a big loss on the sale of your house. The same hardships will be suffered by your coworkers, and the town will be devastated.

In compiling the costs of moving versus not moving, you have latitude in the assumptions you make, the estimates you compute, and the discount rates and time periods you project. You are in a position to influence the decision singlehandedly.

Instructions

(a) Who are the stakeholders in this situation?

(b) What are the ethical issues in this situation?

(c) What would you do in this situation?

Answers to Self-Study Questions

1. d   **2.** c   **3.** d   **4.** a   **5.** b   **6.** d   **7.** d   **8.** a   **9.** c   **10.** d

Remember to go back to the Navigator box on the chapter-opening page and check off your completed work.

CHAPTER 13

Statement of Cash Flows

STUDY OBJECTIVES

After studying this chapter,
you should be able to:

1 Indicate the usefulness of the statement of cash flows.

2 Distinguish among operating, investing, and financing activities.

3 Explain the impact of the product life cycle on a company's cash flows.

4 Prepare a statement of cash flows using one of two approaches: (a) the indirect method or (b) the direct method.

5 Use the statement of cash flows to evaluate a company.

 THE NAVIGATOR

THE NAVIGATOR ✔

▶ Scan *Study Objectives* ☐

▶ Read *Feature Story* ☐

▶ Read *Preview* ☐

▶ Read text and answer *Before You Go On*
  p. 531 ☐   p. 535 ☐   p. 543 ☐
  p. 552 ☐   p. 559 ☐

▶ Work *Using the Decision Toolkit* ☐

▶ Review *Summary of Study Objectives* ☐

▶ Work *Demonstration Problem* ☐

▶ Answer *Self-Study Questions* ☐

▶ Complete *Assignments* ☐

FEATURE STORY

I've Got $38 Billion Burning a Hole in My Pocket!

Things move fast in the high technology sector. Very fast. The business story of the turn-of-the-millenium period is surely the explosion of activity in areas such as software, Internet-based services, and high-speed communications.

In today's environment, companies must be ready to respond to changes quickly in order to survive and thrive. They need to produce new products and expand to new markets continually. To do this takes cash—lots and lots of cash. Keeping lots of cash available is a real challenge for a young company. It requires great cash management and careful attention to cash flow.

One technique for cash management that is common in young high-tech companies is paying employees in part through stock options. This frees up cash for business activities, especially in the crucial early phase of the company.

Microsoft, at 29 years of age the great-granddaddy of the software industry, was a pioneer of this and other cash management strategies. By some estimates, more than 1,000 Microsoft employees became millionaires through stock options in the first 20 years of the company's operations.

The story of Microsoft's phenomenal growth—how it was founded in 1975 by Bill Gates and, by 2000, had grown so large and powerful that a U.S. judge ordered it to be broken up—is well-known. But

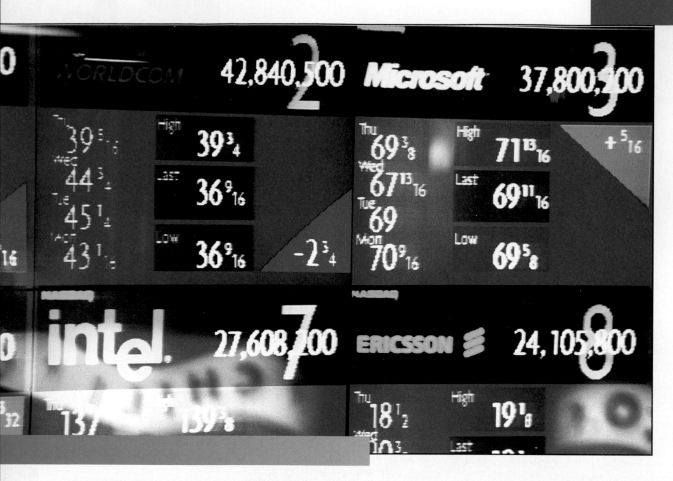

the numbers are nonetheless startling. Seattle-based Microsoft's 2003 statement of cash flows reported cash provided by operating activities in excess of $15 billion. Its cash flow per share, of $1.45, exceeds its earnings per share of $0.92 by more than 50 percent. Its cash and short-term investments amounted to over $49 billion on its balance sheet at its fiscal year-end of June 30, 2003.

That kind of money is astounding, even in this big-money sector. For comparison, consider **Novell, Inc.** Based in Provo, Utah, Novell is an internationally recognized developer of software products, such as NetWare, UnixWare, and Groupwise. Founded in 1983, Novell is younger than Microsoft by 8 years—eons in the computing world. Novell may not be the worldwide household name that Microsoft is, but Novell is certainly a major player. It generated cash from operations of $55 million for the year ending October 31, 2003, down from a high of $145 million in 2000. Still, this is only a drop in the bucket compared with Microsoft's billions.

It is impossible to predict what the future will hold for either of these companies. What effect will the *Antitrust Act* decision have on Microsoft, and on the industry as a whole? How will Novell's recent acquisition of **Cambridge Technology Partners** pan out? Will its reorganization into three segments generate greater efficiencies? Will its newly realigned sales force woo new customers? Will Microsoft's video game console, *Xbox*, meet sales expectations?

Cash management is sure to continue to be an important factor for both companies, and for their ever-growing list of upstart competitors. Beyond that, anything is possible in this sector, where change is the only constant. After all, who could have predicted in 1975 that 19-year-old Bill Gates would become the world's best-known billionaire?

☑ THE NAVIGATOR

On the World Wide Web
Microsoft: www.microsoft.com
Novell: www.novell.com

The balance sheet, income statement, and retained earnings statement do not always show the whole picture of the financial condition of a company or institution. In fact, looking at the financial statements of some well-known companies, a thoughtful investor might ask questions like these: How did **Eastman Kodak** finance cash dividends of $649 million in a year in which it earned only $17 million? How could **United Airlines** purchase new planes that cost $1.9 billion in a year in which it reported a net loss of over $2 billion? Answers to these and similar questions can be found in this chapter, which presents the statement of cash flows.

The content and organization of this chapter are as follows.

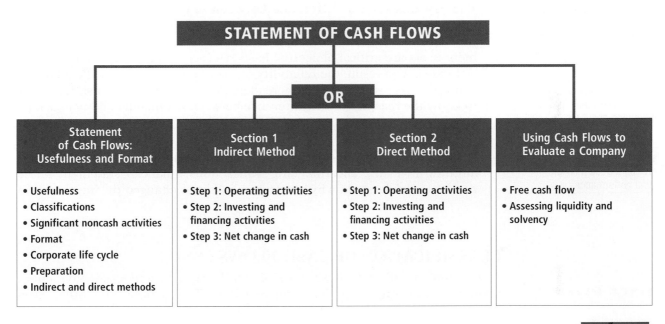

Statement of Cash Flows: Usefulness and Format

The basic financial statements we have presented so far provide only limited information about a company's cash flows (cash receipts and cash payments). For example, comparative balance sheets show the increase in property, plant, and equipment during the year. But they do not show how the additions were financed or paid for. The income statement shows net income. But it does not indicate the amount of cash generated by operating activities. The retained earnings statement shows cash dividends declared but not the cash dividends paid during the year. None of these statements presents a detailed summary of where cash came from and how it was used.

USEFULNESS OF THE STATEMENT OF CASH FLOWS

The **statement of cash flows** reports the cash receipts, cash payments, and net change in cash resulting from operating, investing, and financing activities during a period. The information in a statement of cash flows should help investors, creditors, and others assess:

1. **The entity's ability to generate future cash flows.** By examining relationships between items in the statement of cash flows, investors and others can make predictions of the amounts, timing, and uncertainty of future cash flows better than they can from accrual basis data.

2. **The entity's ability to pay dividends and meet obligations.** If a company does not have adequate cash, it cannot pay employees, settle debts, or pay dividends. Employees, creditors, and stockholders should be particularly interested in this statement; it alone shows the flows of cash in a business.

3. **The reasons for the difference between net income and net cash provided (used) by operating activities.** Net income provides information on the success or failure of a business enterprise. However, some financial statement users are critical of accrual basis net income because it requires many estimates. As a result, the reliability of the number is often challenged. Such is not the case with cash. Many readers of the statement of cash flows want to know the reasons for the difference between net income and net cash provided by operating activities. With such information, they can assess for themselves the reliability of the income number.

4. **The cash investing and financing transactions during the period.** By examining investing and financing transactions, financial statement readers can better understand why assets and liabilities changed during the period.

CLASSIFICATION OF CASH FLOWS

The statement of cash flows classifies cash receipts and cash payments as operating, investing, and financing activities. Transactions and other events characteristic of each kind of activity are described below.

1. **Operating activities** include the cash effects of transactions that create revenues and expenses. They thus enter into the determination of net income.

2. **Investing activities** include (a) acquiring and disposing of investments and property, plant, and equipment, and (b) lending money and collecting the loans.

3. **Financing activities** include (a) obtaining cash from issuing debt and repaying the amounts borrowed, and (b) obtaining cash from stockholders and providing them with a return on their investment.

The category of operating activities is the most important. As noted above, it shows the cash provided by company operations. This source of cash is generally considered to be the best measure of a company's ability to generate sufficient cash to continue as a going concern.

Illustration 13-1 (next page) lists typical cash receipts and cash payments within each of the three classifications. **Study the list carefully.** It will prove very useful in solving homework exercises and problems.

Note the following general guidelines: (1) Operating activities involve income statement items. (2) Investing activities involve cash flows resulting from changes in investments and long-term asset items. (3) Financing activities involve cash flows resulting from changes in long-term liability and stockholders' equity items.

Illustration 13-1 Typical receipts and payments classified by business activity and shown in the statement of cash flows

Types of Cash Inflows and Outflows

Operating activities—Income statement items
Cash inflows:
From sale of goods or services.
From returns on loans (interest received) and on equity securities (dividends received).
Cash outflows:
To suppliers for inventory.
To employees for services.
To government for taxes.
To lenders for interest.
To others for expenses.

Operating activities

Investing activities—Changes in investments and long-term assets
Cash inflows:
From sale of property, plant, and equipment.
From sale of debt or equity securities of other entities.
From collection of principal on loans to other entities.
Cash outflows:
To purchase property, plant, and equipment.
To purchase debt or equity securities of other entities.
To make loans to other entities.

Investing activities

Financing activities—Changes in long-term liabilities and stockholders' equity
Cash inflows:
From sale of common stock.
From issuance of debt (bonds and notes).
Cash outflows:
To stockholders as dividends.
To redeem long-term debt or reacquire capital stock.

Financing activities

Business Insight
Management Perspective

Net income is not the same as net cash provided by operations. The differences are illustrated by the following results from recent annual reports ($ in millions).

Company	Net Income	Net Cash Provided by Operations
Kmart Corporation	$(3,219)	$ 252
Wal-Mart Stores, Inc.	6,671	10,260
JCPenney Company, Inc.	378	1,329
Sears, Roebuck & Co.	1,578	2,467
Target Corporation	1,645	2,863

Note the wide disparity among these companies that all engaged in similar types of retail merchandising.

Some cash flows related to investing or financing activities are classified as operating activities. For example, receipts of investment revenue (interest and dividends) are classified as operating activities. So are payments of interest to lenders. Why? **Because these items are reported in the income statement, where results of operations are shown.**

SIGNIFICANT NONCASH ACTIVITIES

Not all of a company's significant activities involve cash. Examples of significant noncash activities are:

1. Issuance of common stock to purchase assets.
2. Conversion of bonds into common stock.
3. Issuance of debt to purchase assets.
4. Exchanges of plant assets.

Significant financing and investing activities that do not affect cash are not reported in the body of the statement of cash flows. However, these activities are reported in either a **separate schedule** at the bottom of the statement of cash flows or in a **separate note or supplementary schedule** to the financial statements.

The reporting of these noncash activities in a separate schedule satisfies the **full disclosure principle**. In solving homework assignments you should present significant noncash investing and financing activities in a separate schedule at the bottom of the statement of cash flows. (See lower section of Illustration 13-2, at the bottom of this page, for an example.)

FORMAT OF THE STATEMENT OF CASH FLOWS

The general format of the statement of cash flows presents the results of the three activities discussed previously—operating, investing, and financing—plus the significant noncash investing and financing activities. A widely used form of the statement of cash flows is shown in Illustration 13-2.

Illustration 13-2 Format of statement of cash flows

COMPANY NAME Statement of Cash Flows Period Covered		
Cash flows from operating activities		
(List of individual items)	XX	
Net cash provided (used) by operating activities		XXX
Cash flows from investing activities		
(List of individual inflows and outflows)	XX	
Net cash provided (used) by investing activities		XXX
Cash flows from financing activities		
(List of individual inflows and outflows)	XX	
Net cash provided (used) by financing activities		XXX
Net increase (decrease) in cash		XXX
Cash at beginning of period		XXX
Cash at end of period		XXX
Noncash investing and financing activities		
(List of individual noncash transactions)		XXX

The cash flows from operating activities section always appears first. It is followed by the investing activities and the financing activities sections.

BEFORE YOU GO ON . . .

▶Review It

1. Why is the statement of cash flows useful?
2. What are the major classifications of cash flows on the statement of cash flows?
3. What are some examples of significant noncash activities?
4. What is the general format of the statement of cash flows? In what sequence are the three types of business activities presented?

▶Do It

During its first week, Duffy & Stevenson Company had these transactions.

1. Issued 100,000 shares of $5 par value common stock for $800,000 cash.
2. Borrowed $200,000 from Castle Bank, signing a 5-year note bearing 8% interest.
3. Purchased two semi-trailer trucks for $170,000 cash.
4. Paid employees $12,000 for salaries and wages.
5. Collected $20,000 cash for services provided.

Classify each of these transactions by type of cash flow activity.

Action Plan

• Identify the three types of activities used to report cash inflows and outflows.

• Report as operating activities the cash effects of transactions that create revenues and expenses and enter into the determination of net income.

• Report as investing activities transactions that (a) acquire and dispose of investments and productive long-lived assets and (b) lend money and collect loans.

• Report as financing activities transactions that (a) obtain cash from issuing debt and repay the amounts borrowed and (b) obtain cash from stockholders and pay them dividends.

Solution

1. Financing activity   4. Operating activity
2. Financing activity   5. Operating activity
3. Investing activity

Related exercise material: BE13-1, BE13-2, E13-1, and E13-2.

☑ THE NAVIGATOR

THE CORPORATE LIFE CYCLE

All products go through a series of phases called the **product life cycle**. The phases (in order of their occurrence) are often referred to as follows: **introductory phase, growth phase, maturity phase**, and **decline phase**. The introductory phase occurs at the beginning of a company's life, when it is purchasing fixed assets and beginning to produce and sell products. During the growth phase, the company is striving to expand its production and sales. In the maturity phase, sales and production level off. During the decline phase, sales of the product fall due to a weakening in consumer demand.

STUDY OBJECTIVE
3

Explain the impact of the product life cycle on a company's cash flows.

If a company has only one product and that product is nearing the end of its salable life, we could easily say that the company is in the decline phase. Companies generally have more than one product, however, and not all of a company's products are in the same phase of the product life cycle at the same time. Still, we can characterize a company as being in one of the four phases, because the majority of its products are in a particular phase.

Illustration 13-3 shows that the phase a company is in affects its cash flows. In the **introductory phase**, we expect that the company will not be generating positive cash from operations. That is, cash used in operations will exceed cash generated by operations in the introductory phase. Also, the company will be spending considerable amounts to purchase productive assets such as buildings and equipment. To support its asset purchases the company will have to issue stock or debt. Thus, during the introductory phase we expect cash from operations to be negative, cash from investing to be negative, and cash from financing to be positive.

Illustration 13-3 Impact of product life cycle on cash flows

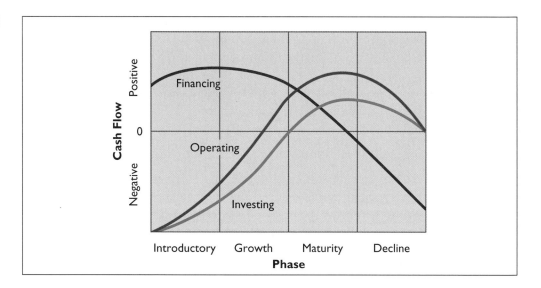

During the **growth phase**, we expect to see the company start to generate small amounts of cash from operations. During this phase, cash from operations on the statement of cash flows will be less than net income on the income statement. One reason income will exceed cash flow from operations during this period is explained by the difference between the cash paid for inventory and the amount expensed as cost of goods sold. Since sales are projected to be increasing, the size of inventory purchases must increase. Thus, less inventory will be expensed on an accrual basis than purchased on a cash basis in the growth phase. Also, collections on accounts receivable will lag behind sales, and accrual sales during a period will exceed cash collections during that period. Cash needed for asset acquisitions will continue to exceed cash provided by operations, requiring that the company make up the deficiency by issuing new stock or debt. Thus, in the growth phase, the company continues to show negative cash from investing and positive cash from financing.

During the **maturity phase**, cash from operations and net income are approximately the same. Cash generated from operations exceeds investing needs. Thus, in the maturity phase the company can actually start to retire debt or buy back stock.

Finally, during the **decline phase**, cash from operations decreases. Cash from investing might actually become positive as the company sells off excess assets. Cash from financing may be negative as the company buys back stock and retires debt.

Consider **Microsoft**: During its early years it had significant product development costs and little revenue. But, an agreement with **IBM** to provide the operating system for IBM PCs gave it a steady source of cash to support growth. Also, one way Microsoft conserved cash was to pay employees with stock options rather than cash. Today Microsoft could be characterized as between the growth and maturity phases. It continues to spend considerable amounts on research and development and investment in new assets. In recent years, however, its cash from operations has exceeded its net income. Also, cash from operations over this period exceeded cash used for investing, and common stock repurchased exceeded common stock issued. For Microsoft, as for any large company, the challenge is to maintain its growth. In the software industry, where products become obsolete very quickly, the challenge is particularly great.

Business Insight
Management Perspective

Listed here are the amounts of net income and cash from operations, investing, and financing during a recent year for some well-known companies. The final column suggests their likely phase in the life cycle based on these figures.

Company ($ in millions)	Net Income	Cash Provided by Operations	Cash Provided (Used) by Investing	Cash Provided (Used) by Financing	Likely Phase in Life Cycle
Amazon.com	$ (567)	$ (120)	$ (253)	$ 107	Introductory
Iomega	(93)	(12)	(5)	(18)	Introductory
Bethlehem Steel	(1,950)	(208)	(42)	244	Early decline
Kellogg	474	1,132	(4,144)	3,040	Late maturity
Southwest Airlines	511	1,485	(998)	1,270	Early maturity
Starbucks	181	461	(433)	15	Late growth

PREPARING THE STATEMENT OF CASH FLOWS

The statement of cash flows is prepared differently from the three other basic financial statements. First, it is not prepared from an adjusted trial balance. The statement requires detailed information concerning the changes in account balances that occurred between two points in time. An adjusted trial balance will not provide the necessary data. Second, the statement of cash flows deals with cash receipts and payments. As a result, the effects of the use of accrual accounting **must be adjusted to determine cash flows**.

The information to prepare this statement usually comes from three sources:

- **Comparative balance sheets.** Information in the comparative balance sheets indicates the amount of the changes in assets, liabilities, and stockholders' equities from the beginning to the end of the period.
- **Current income statement.** Information in this statement helps determine the amount of cash provided or used by operations during the period.
- **Additional information.** Such information includes transaction data that are needed to determine how cash was provided or used during the period.

Preparing the statement of cash flows from these data sources involves three major steps, explained in Illustration 13-4 (page 534).

Illustration 13-4 Three major steps in preparing the statement of cash flows

Step 1: Determine net cash provided/used by operating activities by converting net income from an accrual basis to a cash basis.

Buying & selling goods

This step involves analyzing not only the current year's income statement but also comparative balance sheets and selected additional data.

Step 2: Analyze changes in noncurrent asset and liability accounts and record as investing and financing activities, or as significant non-cash transactions.

Investing   Financing

This step involves analyzing comparative balance sheet data and selected additional information for their effects on cash.

Step 3: Compare the net change in cash on the statement of cash flows with the change in the cash account reported on the balance sheet to make sure the amounts agree.

+ or −

The difference between the beginning and ending cash balances can be easily computed from comparative balance sheets.

INDIRECT AND DIRECT METHODS

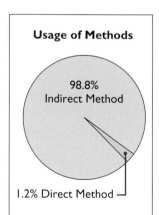

Usage of Methods

98.8% Indirect Method

1.2% Direct Method

In order to perform step 1, **net income must be converted from an accrual basis to a cash basis**. This conversion may be done by either of two methods: (1) the indirect method or (2) the direct method. **Both methods arrive at the same total amount** for "Net cash provided by operating activities." They differ in **how** they arrive at the amount.

The indirect method is used extensively in practice, as shown in the nearby chart.[1] Companies (98.8%) favor the indirect method for two reasons: (1) It is easier and less costly to prepare, and (2) it focuses on the differences between net income and net cash flow from operating activities.

The direct method shows operating cash receipts and payments, making it more consistent with the objective of a statement of cash flows. The FASB has expressed a preference for the direct method, but allows the use of either method.

We describe the use of the two methods in two separate sections. Section 1 (begining on page 535) illustrates the indirect method. Section 2 (begining on page 545) illustrates the direct method. These sections are independent of each other. *Only one or the other* need be covered in order to understand and prepare the statement of cash flows. When you have finished the section assigned by your instructor, turn to the next topic—"Using Cash Flows to Evaluate a Company," on page 555.

---

[1]*Accounting Trends and Techniques—2001* (New York: American Institute of Certified Public Accountants, 2001).

Business Insight
Management Perspective

During the 1990s, analysts increasingly used cash-flow-based measures of income, such as cash flow provided by operations, instead of or in addition to net income. The reason for the change was that they were losing faith in accrual-accounting-based net income numbers. Sadly, these days even cash flow from operations isn't always what it seems to be. For example, in 2002 **WorldCom, Inc.** disclosed that it had improperly capitalized expenses: It moved $3.8 billion of cash outflows from the "Cash from operating activities" section of the cash flow statement to the "Investing activities" section, thereby greatly enhancing cash provided by operating activities. Similarly, in 2002 **Dynegy, Inc.** restated its cash flow statement for 2001 so that $300 million tied to its complex natural gas trading operation was removed from cash flow from operations and instead put into the financing section—a drop of 37% in cash flow from operations.

SOURCE: Henny Sender, "Sadly, These Days Even Cash Flow Isn't Always What It Seems To Be," *Wall Street Journal Online* (May 8, 2002).

BEFORE YOU GO ON . . .

▶Review It

1. What are the phases of the product life cycle, and how do they affect the statement of cash flows?
2. What are the three major steps in the preparation of a statement of cash flows?
3. What is the primary difference between the indirect and direct approaches to the statement of cash flows? Which method is more commonly used in practice?

☑ THE NAVIGATOR

SECTION 1
STATEMENT OF CASH FLOWS—
INDIRECT METHOD

To explain how to prepare a statement of cash flows using the indirect method, we use financial information from Computer Services Company. Illustration 13-5 (page 536) presents Computer Services' current and previous-year balance sheet, its current-year income statement, and related financial information.

STUDY OBJECTIVE

4a

Prepare a statement of cash flows using the indirect method.

Illustration 13-5 Comparative balance sheets, income statement, and additional information for Computer Services Company

COMPUTER SERVICES COMPANY
Comparative Balance Sheets
December 31

Assets	2005	2004	Change in Account Balance Increase/Decrease
Current assets			
Cash	$ 55,000	$ 33,000	$ 22,000 Increase
Accounts receivable	20,000	30,000	10,000 Decrease
Merchandise inventory	15,000	10,000	5,000 Increase
Prepaid expenses	5,000	1,000	4,000 Increase
Property, plant, and equipment			
Land	130,000	20,000	110,000 Increase
Building	160,000	40,000	120,000 Increase
Accumulated depreciation—building	(11,000)	(5,000)	6,000 Increase
Equipment	27,000	10,000	17,000 Increase
Accumulated depreciation—equipment	(3,000)	(1,000)	2,000 Increase
Total	$398,000	$138,000	

Liabilities and Stockholders' Equity	2005	2004	
Current liabilities			
Accounts payable	$ 28,000	$ 12,000	$ 16,000 Increase
Income tax payable	6,000	8,000	2,000 Decrease
Long-term liabilities			
Bonds payable	130,000	20,000	110,000 Increase
Stockholders' equity			
Common stock	70,000	50,000	20,000 Increase
Retained earnings	164,000	48,000	116,000 Increase
Total	$398,000	$138,000	

COMPUTER SERVICES COMPANY
Income Statement
For the Year Ended December 31, 2005

Revenues		$507,000
Cost of goods sold	$150,000	
Operating expenses (excluding depreciation)	111,000	
Depreciation expense	9,000	
Loss on sale of equipment	3,000	
Interest expense	42,000	$315,000
Income before income tax		192,000
Income tax expense		47,000
Net income		$145,000

Additional information for 2005:
1. The company declared and paid a $29,000 cash dividend.
2. Issued $110,000 of long-term bonds in direct exchange for land.
3. A building costing $120,000 was purchased for cash. Equipment costing $25,000 was also purchased for cash.
4. The company sold equipment with a book value of $7,000 (cost $8,000, less accumulated depreciation $1,000) for $4,000 cash.
5. Issued common stock for $20,000 cash.
6. Depreciation expense was comprised of $6,000 for building and $3,000 for equipment.

We will now apply the three steps to the information provided for Computer Services Company.

Step 1: Operating Activities

DETERMINE NET CASH PROVIDED/USED BY OPERATING ACTIVITIES BY CONVERTING NET INCOME FROM AN ACCRUAL BASIS TO A CASH BASIS

To determine net cash provided by operating activities under the indirect method, **net income is adjusted in numerous ways**. A useful starting point is to understand **why** net income must be converted to net cash provided by operating activities. Under generally accepted accounting principles, most companies use the accrual basis of accounting. As you have learned, this basis requires that revenue be recorded when earned and that expenses be recorded when incurred. Earned revenues may include credit sales that have not yet been collected in cash. Expenses incurred may include some items that have not been paid in cash. Thus, under the accrual basis of accounting, net income is not the same as net cash provided by operating activities. Therefore, under the indirect method, net income must be adjusted to convert certain items to the cash basis. The **indirect method** (or reconciliation method) starts with net income and converts it to net cash provided by operating activities. Illustration 13-6 lists the three types of adjustments.

Net Income +/−	Adjustments	=	Net Cash Provided/ Used by Operating Activities
	• Add back noncash expenses, such as depreciation expense, amortization, or depletion.		
	• Deduct gains and add losses that resulted from investing and financing activities.		
	• Analyze changes to noncash current asset and current liability accounts.		

Illustration 13-6 Three types of adjustments to convert net income to net cash provided by operating activities

The three types of adjustments are explained in the next three sections.

DEPRECIATION EXPENSE

Computer Services' income statement reports depreciation expense of $9,000. Although depreciation expense reduces net income, it does not reduce cash. In other words, depreciation expense is a noncash charge. It is added back to net income to arrive at net cash provided by operating activities. Depreciation expense is reported as follows in the statement of cash flows.

Helpful Hint Depreciation is similar to any other expense in that it reduces net income. It differs in that it does not involve a current cash outflow; that is why it must be *added back* to net income to arrive at cash provided by operations.

Illustration 13-7 Adjustment for depreciation

Cash flows from operating activities	
Net income	$145,000
Adjustments to reconcile net income to net cash provided by operating activities:	
Depreciation expense	**9,000**
Net cash provided by operating activities	$154,000

Depreciation and similar noncash charges such as amortization of intangible assets, depletion expense, and bad debt expense are frequently listed in the statement of cash flows as the first adjustment to net income.

LOSS ON SALE OF EQUIPMENT

Computer Services' income statement reports a $3,000 loss on the sale of equipment (book value $7,000, less cash received from sale of equipment $4,000). Illustration 13-1 states that cash received from the sale of plant assets should be reported in the investing activities section. Because of this, **all gains and losses must be eliminated from net income to arrive at cash from operating activities.** In our example, Computer Services Company's loss of $3,000 should not be included in the operating activities section of the statement of cash flows. Illustration 13-8 shows that the $3,000 loss is eliminated by adding $3,000 back to net income to arrive at net cash provided by operating activities.

Illustration 13-8 Adjustment for loss on sale of equipment

Cash flows from operating activities		
Net income		$145,000
Adjustments to reconcile net income to net cash provided by operating activities:		
Depreciation expense	$9,000	
Loss on sale of equipment	**3,000**	12,000
Net cash provided by operating activities		$157,000

If a gain on sale occurs, the gain is deducted from net income in order to determine net cash provided by operating activities. **In the case of either a gain or a loss, the actual amount of cash received from the sale is reported as a source of cash in the investing activities section of the statement of cash flows.**

CHANGES TO NONCASH CURRENT ASSET AND CURRENT LIABILITY ACCOUNTS

A final adjustment in reconciling net income to net cash provided by operating activities involves examining all changes in current asset and current liability accounts. The accrual accounting process records revenues in the period earned and expenses in the period incurred. For example, Accounts Receivable is used to record amounts owed to the company for sales that have been made but cash collections have not yet been received. The Prepaid Insurance account is used to reflect insurance that has been paid for, but which has not yet expired, and therefore has not been expensed. Similarly, the Salaries Payable account reflects salaries expense that has been incurred by the company but has not been paid. As a result, we need to adjust net income for these accruals and prepayments to determine net cash provided by operating activities. Thus we must analyze the change in each current asset and current liability account to determine its impact on net income and cash.

Changes in Noncash Current Assets

The adjustments required for changes in noncash current asset accounts are as follows: **Increases in current asset accounts are deducted from net income, and decreases in current asset accounts are added to net income, to arrive at net cash provided by operating activities.** We can observe these relationships by analyzing the accounts of Computer Services Company.

DECREASE IN ACCOUNTS RECEIVABLE. Computer Services Company's accounts receivable decreased by $10,000 (from $30,000 to $20,000) during the period. For Computer Services Company this means that cash receipts were $10,000 higher than revenues. Illustration 13-9 shows that Computer Services Company had $507,000 in revenues (as reported on the income statement), but it collected $517,000 in cash. As shown in Illustration 13-10, to adjust net income to net cash provided by operating activities, the decrease of $10,000 in accounts receivable is added to net income.

Accounts Receivable

1/1/05	Balance	30,000	**Receipts from customers**	**517,000**
	Revenues	**507,000**		
12/31/05	Balance	20,000		

Illustration 13-9 Analysis of accounts receivable

When the Accounts Receivable balance increases, cash receipts are lower than revenue earned under the accrual basis. Therefore, the amount of the increase in accounts receivable is deducted from net income to arrive at net cash provided by operating activities.

INCREASE IN MERCHANDISE INVENTORY. Computer Services Company's Merchandise Inventory balance increased $5,000 (from $10,000 to $15,000) during the period. The Merchandise Inventory account reflects the difference between the amount of inventory that has been purchased and the amount that has been sold. For Computer Services this means that the cost of merchandise purchased exceeded the cost of goods sold by $5,000. As a result, cost of goods sold does not reflect $5,000 of cash payments made for merchandise. This inventory increase of $5,000 during the period is deducted from net income to arrive at net cash provided by operating activities (see Illustration 13-10, below). If inventory decreases, the amount of the change is added to net income to arrive at net cash provided by operating activities.

INCREASE IN PREPAID EXPENSES. Prepaid expenses increased during the period by $4,000. This means that cash paid for expenses is higher than expenses reported on an accrual basis. Cash payments have been made in the current period, but expenses (as charges to the income statement) have been deferred to future periods. To adjust net income to net cash provided by operating activities, the $4,000 increase in prepaid expenses is deducted from net income (see Illustration 13-10).

Cash flows from operating activities		
Net income		$145,000
Adjustments to reconcile net income to net cash		
provided by operating activities:		
Depreciation expense	$ 9,000	
Loss on sale of equipment	3,000	
Decrease in accounts receivable	**10,000**	
Increase in merchandise inventory	**(5,000)**	
Increase in prepaid expenses	**(4,000)**	13,000
Net cash provided by operating activities		$158,000

Illustration 13-10 Adjustments for changes in current asset accounts

If prepaid expenses decrease, reported expenses are higher than the expenses paid. Therefore, the decrease in prepaid expense is added to net income to arrive at net cash provided by operating activities.

Changes in Current Liabilities

The adjustments required for changes in current liability accounts are as follows: **Increases in current liability accounts are added to net income, and decreases in current liability accounts are deducted from net income, to arrive at net cash provided by operating activities.**

INCREASE IN ACCOUNTS PAYABLE. For Computer Services Company, Accounts Payable increased by $16,000 (from $12,000 to $28,000) during the period. That means the company received $16,000 more in goods than it actually paid for. As shown in Illustration 13-11 (below), to adjust net income to determine net cash provided by operating activities, the $16,000 increase in Accounts Payable is added to net income.

DECREASE IN INCOME TAXES PAYABLE. When a company incurs income tax expense but has not yet paid its taxes, it records income tax payable. A change in the Income Tax Payable account reflects the difference between income tax expense incurred and income tax actually paid. Computer Services' Income Tax Payable account decreased by $2,000. That means the $47,000 of income tax expense reported on the income statement was $2,000 less than the amount of taxes paid during the period of $49,000. As shown in Illustration 13-11, to adjust net income to a cash basis, net income must be reduced by $2,000.

Illustration 13-11 Adjustments for changes in current liability accounts

Cash flows from operating activities		
Net income		$145,000
Adjustments to reconcile net income to net cash provided by operating activities:		
Depreciation expense	$ 9,000	
Loss on sale of equipment	3,000	
Decrease in accounts receivable	10,000	
Increase in merchandise inventory	(5,000)	
Increase in prepaid expenses	(4,000)	
Increase in accounts payable	**16,000**	
Decrease in income tax payable	**(2,000)**	27,000
Net cash provided by operating activities		$172,000

Illustration 13-11 shows that, after starting with net income of $145,000, the sum of all of the adjustments to net income was $27,000. This resulted in net cash provided by operating activities of $172,000.

SUMMARY OF CONVERSION TO NET CASH PROVIDED BY OPERATING ACTIVITIES—INDIRECT METHOD

As shown in the previous illustrations, the statement of cash flows prepared by the indirect method starts with net income. It then adds or deducts items to arrive at net cash provided by operating activities. The required adjustments are of three types: (1) noncash charges such as depreciation, amortization, and depletion; (2) gains and losses on the sale of plant assets; and (3) changes in noncash current asset and current liability accounts. A summary of these changes is provided in Illustration 13-12.

		Adjustment Required to Convert Net Income to Net Cash Provided by Operating Activities
Noncash charges	Depreciation expense	Add
	Patent amortization expense	Add
	Depletion expense	Add
Gains and losses	Loss on sale of plant asset	Add
	Gain on sale of plant asset	Deduct
Changes in current assets and current liabilities	Increase in current asset account	Deduct
	Decrease in current asset account	Add
	Increase in current liability account	Add
	Decrease in current liability account	Deduct

Illustration 13-12 Adjustments required to convert net income to net cash provided by operating activities

Step 2: Investing and Financing Activities

ANALYZE CHANGES IN NONCURRENT ASSET AND LIABILITY ACCOUNTS AND RECORD AS INVESTING AND FINANCING ACTIVITIES, OR AS SIGNIFICANT NONCASH TRANSACTIONS

INCREASE IN LAND. As indicated from the change in the Land account and the additional information, land of $110,000 was purchased through the issuance of long-term bonds. The issuance of bonds payable for land has no effect on cash. But it is a significant noncash investing and financing activity that merits disclosure in a separate schedule.

INCREASE IN BUILDING. As the additional data indicate, a building was acquired for $120,000 cash. This is a cash outflow reported in the investing section.

INCREASE IN EQUIPMENT. The Equipment account increased $17,000. The additional information explains that this was a net increase that resulted from two transactions: (1) a purchase of equipment of $25,000 and (2) the sale for $4,000 of equipment costing $8,000 (accumulated depreciation of $1,000). These transactions are classified as investing activities. Each transaction should be reported separately. Thus the purchase of equipment should be reported as an outflow of cash for $25,000. The sale should be reported as an inflow of cash for $4,000. The T account below shows the reasons for the change in this account during the year.

Helpful Hint The investing and financing activities are measured and reported in the same way under both the direct and indirect methods.

Equipment			
1/1/05 Balance	10,000	Cost of equipment sold	8,000
Purchase of equipment	25,000		
12/31/05 Balance	27,000		

Illustration 13-13 Analysis of equipment

The following entry shows the details of the equipment sale transaction.

Cash	4,000	
Accumulated Depreciation	1,000	
Loss on Sale of Equipment	3,000	
Equipment		8,000

INCREASE IN BONDS PAYABLE. The Bonds Payable account increased $110,000. As indicated in the additional information, land was acquired from the issuance of these bonds. This noncash transaction is reported in a separate schedule at the bottom of the statement.

INCREASE IN COMMON STOCK. The balance sheet reports an increase in Common Stock of $20,000. The additional information section notes that this increase resulted from the issuance of new shares of stock. This is a cash inflow reported in the financing section.

INCREASE IN RETAINED EARNINGS. Retained earnings increased $116,000 during the year. This increase can be explained by two factors: (1) Net income of $145,000 increased retained earnings. (2) Dividends of $29,000 decreased retained earnings. Net income is adjusted to net cash provided by operating activities in the operating activities section. Payment of the dividends is a **cash outflow that is reported as a financing activity**.

STATEMENT OF CASH FLOWS—2005

Using the previous information, we can now prepare a statement of cash flows for 2005 for Computer Services Company as shown in Illustration 13-14.

Illustration 13-14 Statement of cash flows, 2005—indirect method

COMPUTER SERVICES COMPANY
Statement of Cash Flows—Indirect Method
For the Year Ended December 31, 2005

Cash flows from operating activities		
Net income		$ 145,000
Adjustments to reconcile net income to net cash provided by operating activities:		
Depreciation expense	$ 9,000	
Loss on sale of equipment	3,000	
Decrease in accounts receivable	10,000	
Increase in merchandise inventory	(5,000)	
Increase in prepaid expenses	(4,000)	
Increase in accounts payable	16,000	
Decrease in income tax payable	(2,000)	27,000
Net cash provided by operating activities		172,000
Cash flows from investing activities		
Purchase of building	(120,000)	
Purchase of equipment	(25,000)	
Sale of equipment	4,000	
Net cash used by investing activities		(141,000)
Cash flows from financing activities		
Issuance of common stock	20,000	
Payment of cash dividends	(29,000)	
Net cash used by financing activities		(9,000)
Net increase in cash		22,000
Cash at beginning of period		33,000
Cash at end of period		$ 55,000
Noncash investing and financing activities		
Issuance of bonds payable to purchase land		$ 110,000

Step 3: Net Change in Cash

COMPARE THE NET CHANGE IN CASH WITH THE CHANGE IN THE CASH ACCOUNT REPORTED ON THE BALANCE SHEET TO MAKE SURE THE AMOUNTS AGREE

Illustration 13-14 indicates that the net change in cash during the period was an increase of $22,000. This agrees with the change in Cash account reported on the balance sheet in Illustration 13-5.

BEFORE YOU GO ON . . .

▶Review It

1. What is the format of the operating activities section of the statement of cash flows using the indirect method?
2. Where is depreciation expense shown on a statement of cash flows using the indirect method?
3. Where are significant noncash investing and financing activities shown in a statement of cash flows? Give some examples.

▶Do It

Presented below is information related to Reynolds Company. Use it to prepare a statement of cash flows using the indirect method.

REYNOLDS COMPANY Comparative Balance Sheets December 31			
Assets	**2005**	**2004**	**Change Increase/Decrease**
Cash	$ 54,000	$ 37,000	$ 17,000 Increase
Accounts receivable	68,000	26,000	42,000 Increase
Inventories	54,000	–0–	54,000 Increase
Prepaid expenses	4,000	6,000	2,000 Decrease
Land	45,000	70,000	25,000 Decrease
Buildings	200,000	200,000	–0–
Accumulated depreciation—buildings	(21,000)	(11,000)	10,000 Increase
Equipment	193,000	68,000	125,000 Increase
Accumulated depreciation—equipment	(28,000)	(10,000)	18,000 Increase
Total	$569,000	$386,000	
Liabilities and Stockholders' Equity			
Accounts payable	$ 23,000	$ 40,000	$ 17,000 Decrease
Accrued expenses payable	10,000	–0–	10,000 Increase
Bonds payable	110,000	150,000	40,000 Decrease
Common stock ($1 par)	220,000	60,000	160,000 Increase
Retained earnings	206,000	136,000	70,000 Increase
Total	$569,000	$386,000	

REYNOLDS COMPANY
Income Statement
For the Year Ended December 31, 2005

Revenues		$890,000
Cost of goods sold	$465,000	
Operating expenses	221,000	
Interest expense	12,000	
Loss on sale of equipment	2,000	700,000
Income before income taxes		190,000
Income tax expense		65,000
Net income		$125,000

Additional information:

1. Operating expenses include depreciation expense of $33,000 and charges from prepaid expenses of $2,000.
2. Land was sold at its book value for cash.
3. Cash dividends of $55,000 were declared and paid in 2005.
4. Interest expense of $12,000 was paid in cash.
5. Equipment with a cost of $166,000 was purchased for cash. Equipment with a cost of $41,000 and a book value of $36,000 was sold for $34,000 cash.
6. Bonds of $10,000 were redeemed at their book value for cash. Bonds of $30,000 were converted into common stock.
7. Common stock ($1 par) of $130,000 was issued for cash.
8. Accounts payable pertain to merchandise suppliers.

Action Plan

- Determine net cash provided/used by operating activities by adjusting net income for items that did not affect cash.
- Determine net cash provided/used by investing activities and financing activities.
- Determine the net increase/decrease in cash.

Solution

Helpful Hint
1. Determine net cash provided/used by operating activities, recognizing that operating activities generally relate to changes in current assets and current liabilities.
2. Determine net cash provided/used by investing activities, recognizing that investing activities generally relate to changes in noncurrent assets.
3. Determine net cash provided/used by financing activities, recognizing that financing activities generally relate to changes in long-term liabilities and stockholders' equity accounts.

REYNOLDS COMPANY
Statement of Cash Flows—Indirect Method
For the Year Ended December 31, 2005

Cash flows from operating activities		
Net income		$ 125,000
Adjustments to reconcile net income to net cash provided by operating activities:		
Depreciation expense	$ 33,000	
Loss on sale of equipment	2,000	
Increase in accounts receivable	(42,000)	
Increase in inventories	(54,000)	
Decrease in prepaid expenses	2,000	
Decrease in accounts payable	(17,000)	
Increase in accrued expenses payable	10,000	(66,000)
Net cash provided by operating activities		59,000
Cash flows from investing activities		
Sale of land	25,000	
Sale of equipment	34,000	
Purchase of equipment	$(166,000)	
Net cash used by investing activities		(107,000)

(Continued)		
Cash flows from financing activities		
Redemption of bonds	(10,000)	
Sale of common stock	130,000	
Payment of dividends	(55,000)	
Net cash provided by financing activities		65,000
Net increase in cash		17,000
Cash at beginning of period		37,000
Cash at end of period		$ 54,000
Noncash investing and financing activities		
Conversion of bonds into common stock		$ 30,000

Related exercise material: BE13-5, BE13-6, BE13-7, E13-4, E13-5, E13-6, and E13-7.

✓ THE NAVIGATOR

Note: This concludes Section 1 on preparation of the statement of cash flows using the indirect method. Unless your instructor assigns Section 2, you should turn to the concluding section of the chapter, "Using Cash Flows to Evaluate a Company," on page 555.

SECTION 2
STATEMENT OF CASH FLOWS— DIRECT METHOD

To explain and illustrate the direct method, we will use the transactions of Juarez Company for 2005, to prepare a statement of cash flows. Illustration 13-15 presents information related to 2005 for Juarez Company.

STUDY OBJECTIVE

4b

Prepare a statement of cash flows using the direct method.

JUAREZ COMPANY Comparative Balance Sheets December 31			
Assets	**2005**	**2004**	**Change Increase/Decrease**
Cash	$191,000	$159,000	$ 32,000 Increase
Accounts receivable	12,000	15,000	3,000 Decrease
Inventory	170,000	160,000	10,000 Increase
Prepaid expenses	6,000	8,000	2,000 Decrease
Land	140,000	80,000	60,000 Increase
Equipment	160,000	–0–	160,000 Increase
Accumulated depreciation—equipment	(16,000)	–0–	16,000 Increase
Total	$663,000	$422,000	
Liabilities and Stockholders' Equity			
Accounts payable	$ 52,000	$ 60,000	$ 8,000 Decrease
Accrued expenses payable	15,000	20,000	5,000 Decrease
Income taxes payable	12,000	–0–	12,000 Increase
Bonds payable	130,000	–0–	130,000 Increase
Common stock	360,000	300,000	60,000 Increase
Retained earnings	94,000	42,000	52,000 Increase
Total	$663,000	$422,000	

Illustration 13-15 Comparative balance sheets, income statement, and additional information for Juarez Company

JUAREZ COMPANY Income Statement For the Year Ended December 31, 2005		
Revenues		$975,000
Cost of goods sold	$660,000	
Operating expenses (excluding depreciation)	176,000	
Depreciation expense	18,000	
Loss on sale of store equipment	1,000	855,000
Income before income taxes		120,000
Income tax expense		36,000
Net income		$ 84,000

Additional information:
1. In 2005, the company declared and paid a $32,000 cash dividend.
2. Bonds were issued at face value for $130,000 in cash.
3. Equipment costing $180,000 was purchased for cash.
4. Equipment costing $20,000 was sold for $17,000 cash when the book value of the equipment was $18,000.
5. Common stock of $60,000 was issued to acquire land.

To prepare a statement of cash flows under the direct approach, we will apply the three steps outlined in Illustration 13-4 (page 534).

Step 1: Operating Activities

DETERMINE NET CASH PROVIDED/USED BY OPERATING ACTIVITIES BY CONVERTING NET INCOME FROM AN ACCRUAL BASIS TO A CASH BASIS

Under the **direct method**, net cash provided by operating activities is computed by **adjusting each item in the income statement** from the accrual basis to the cash basis. To simplify and condense the operating activities section, **only major classes of operating cash receipts and cash payments are reported**. For these major classes, the difference between cash receipts and cash payments is the net cash provided by operating activities. These relationships are as shown in Illustration 13-16 (next page).

An efficient way to apply the direct method is to analyze the items reported in the income statement in the order in which they are listed. Cash receipts and cash payments related to these revenues and expenses are then determined. The following pages present the adjustments required to prepare a statement of cash flows for Juarez Company using the direct approach.

CASH RECEIPTS FROM CUSTOMERS. The income statement for Juarez Company reported revenues from customers of $975,000. How much of that was cash receipts? To answer that, it is necessary to consider the change in accounts receivable during the year. When accounts receivable increase during the year, revenues on an accrual basis are higher than cash receipts from customers. Operations led to revenues, but not all of these revenues resulted in cash receipts. To determine the amount of cash receipts, the increase in accounts receivable is deducted from sales revenues. On the other hand, there may be a decrease in accounts receivable. That would occur if cash receipts from customers exceeded sales revenues. In that case, the decrease in accounts receivable is added to sales revenues.

Illustration 13-16 Major classes of cash receipts and payments

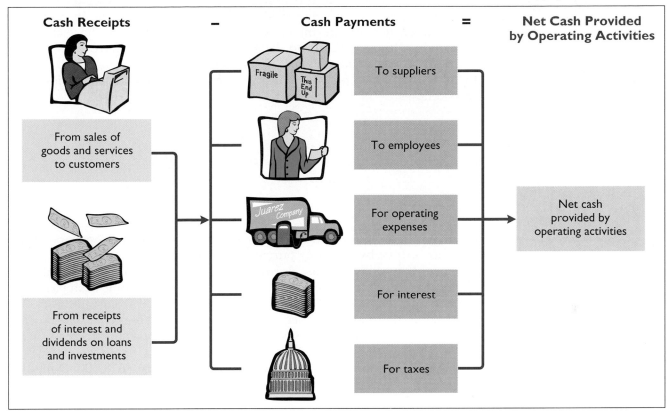

For Juarez Company, accounts receivable decreased $3,000. Thus, cash receipts from customers were $978,000, computed as follows.

Revenues from sales	$ 975,000
Add: Decrease in accounts receivable	3,000
Cash receipts from customers	**$978,000**

Illustration 13-17 Computation of cash receipts from customers

Cash receipts from customers may also be determined from an analysis of the Accounts Receivable account, as shown in Illustration 13-18.

Illustration 13-18 Analysis of accounts receivable

Accounts Receivable

1/1/05	Balance	15,000	**Receipts from customers**	**978,000**
	Revenues from sales	975,000		
12/31/05	Balance	12,000		

The relationships among cash receipts from customers, revenues from sales, and changes in accounts receivable are shown in Illustration 13-19.

Helpful Hint The T account shows that revenue plus decrease in receivables equals cash receipts.

Illustration 13-19 Formula to compute cash receipts from customers—direct method

Cash Receipts from Customers	=	Revenues from Sales	{	+ Decrease in Accounts Receivable or − Increase in Accounts Receivable

CASH PAYMENTS TO SUPPLIERS. Juarez Company reported cost of goods sold of $660,000 on its income statement. How much of that was cash payments to suppliers? To answer that, it is first necessary to find purchases for the year. To find purchases, cost of goods sold is adjusted for the change in inventory. When inventory increases during the year, purchases for the year have exceeded cost of goods sold. As a result, to determine the amount of purchases, the increase in inventory is added to cost of goods sold.

In 2005, Juarez Company's inventory increased $10,000. Purchases are computed as follows.

Illustration 13-20   Computation of purchases

Cost of goods sold	$ 660,000
Add: Increase in inventory	10,000
Purchases	**$670,000**

After purchases are computed, cash payments to suppliers can be determined. This is done by adjusting purchases for the change in accounts payable. When accounts payable increase during the year, purchases on an accrual basis are higher than they are on a cash basis. As a result, to determine cash payments to suppliers, an increase in accounts payable is deducted from purchases. On the other hand, there may be a decrease in accounts payable. That would occur if cash payments to suppliers exceed purchases. In that case, the decrease in accounts payable is added to purchases.

For Juarez Company, cash payments to suppliers were $678,000, computed as follows.

Illustration 13-21   Computation of cash payments to suppliers

Purchases	$ 670,000
Add: Decrease in accounts payable	8,000
Cash payments to suppliers	**$678,000**

Cash payments to suppliers may also be determined from an analysis of the Accounts Payable account as shown in Illustration 13-22.

Illustration 13-22   Analysis of accounts payable

	Accounts Payable			
Payments to suppliers	**678,000**	1/1/05 Balance	60,000
		Purchases	670,000
		12/31/05 Balance	52,000

Helpful Hint The T account shows that purchases plus decrease in accounts payable equals payments to suppliers.

The relationships among cash payments to suppliers, cost of goods sold, changes in inventory, and changes in accounts payable are shown in the following formula.

Illustration 13-23   Formula to compute cash payments to suppliers—direct method

$$
\begin{matrix}
\text{Cash} \\
\text{Payments} \\
\text{to} \\
\text{Suppliers}
\end{matrix}
=
\begin{matrix}
\text{Cost} \\
\text{of} \\
\text{Goods} \\
\text{Sold}
\end{matrix}
\begin{Bmatrix}
\text{+ Increase in Inventory} \\
\text{or} \\
\text{– Decrease in Inventory}
\end{Bmatrix}
\begin{Bmatrix}
\text{+ Decrease in} \\
\text{Accounts Payable} \\
\text{or} \\
\text{– Increase in} \\
\text{Accounts Payable}
\end{Bmatrix}
$$

CASH PAYMENTS FOR OPERATING EXPENSES. Operating expenses of $176,000 were reported on Juarez's income statement. How much of that amount was cash paid for operating expenses? To answer that, we need to adjust this amount for any changes in prepaid expenses and accrued expenses payable. For example, if prepaid expenses increased during the year, cash paid for operating expenses is higher than operating expenses reported on the income statement. To convert operating expenses to cash payments for operating expenses, the increase must be added to operating expenses. On the other hand, if prepaid expenses decrease during the year, the decrease must be deducted from operating expenses.

Operating expenses must also be adjusted for changes in accrued expenses payable. When accrued expenses payable increase during the year, operating expenses on an accrual basis are higher than they are in a cash basis. As a result, to determine cash payments for operating expenses, an increase in accrued expenses payable is deducted from operating expenses. On the other hand, a decrease in accrued expenses payable is added to operating expenses because cash payments exceed operating expenses.

Juarez Company's cash payments for operating expenses were $179,000, computed as follows.

Operating expenses	$ 176,000
Deduct: Decrease in prepaid expenses	(2,000)
Add: Decrease in accrued expenses payable	5,000
Cash payments for operating expenses	**$179,000**

Illustration 13-24 Computation of cash payments for operating expenses

The relationships among cash payments for operating expenses, changes in prepaid expenses, and changes in accrued expenses payable are shown in the following formula.

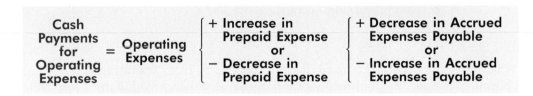

Illustration 13-25 Formula to compute cash payments for operating expenses—direct method

DEPRECIATION EXPENSE AND LOSS ON SALE OF EQUIPMENT. Operating expenses are shown exclusive of depreciation. Depreciation expense in 2005 was $18,000. Depreciation expense is not shown on a statement of cash flows because it is a noncash charge. If the amount for operating expenses includes depreciation expense, operating expenses must be reduced by the amount of depreciation to determine cash payments for operating expenses.

The loss on sale of equipment of $1,000 is also a noncash charge. The loss on sale of equipment reduces net income, but it does not reduce cash. Thus, the loss on sale of equipment is not reported on a statement of cash flows.

Other charges to expense that do not require the use of cash, such as the amortization of intangible assets, depletion expense, and bad debt expense, are treated in the same manner as depreciation.

CASH PAYMENTS FOR INCOME TAXES. Income tax expense reported on the income statement was $36,000. Income taxes payable, however, increased $12,000. This increase means that $12,000 of the income taxes have not been paid. As a result, income taxes paid were less than income taxes reported in the income statement. Cash payments for income taxes were, therefore, $24,000 as shown below.

Illustration 13-26 Computation of cash payments for income taxes

Income tax expense	$ 36,000
Deduct: Increase in income taxes payable	12,000
Cash payments for income taxes	**$24,000**

The relationships among cash payments for income taxes, income tax expense, and changes in income taxes payable are shown in the following formula.

Illustration 13-27 Formula to compute cash payments for income taxes—direct method

$$\begin{matrix} \text{Cash} \\ \text{Payments for} \\ \text{Income Taxes} \end{matrix} = \begin{matrix} \text{Income Tax} \\ \text{Expense} \end{matrix} \begin{cases} + \text{ Decrease in Income Taxes Payable} \\ \qquad\qquad\text{or} \\ - \text{ Increase in Income Taxes Payable} \end{cases}$$

The results of the previous analysis are presented in the operating activities section of the statement of cash flows of Juarez Company in Illustration 13-28.

Illustration 13-28 Operating activities section of the statement of cash flows

Cash flows from operating activities		
Cash receipts from customers		$978,000
Less: Cash payments:		
To suppliers	$678,000	
For operating expenses	179,000	
For income taxes	24,000	881,000
Net cash provided by operating activities		$ 97,000

When the direct method is used, the net cash flows from operating activities as computed under the indirect method must also be provided in a separate schedule (not shown here).

Step 2: Investing and Financing Activities

ANALYZE CHANGES IN NONCURRENT ASSET AND LIABILITY ACCOUNTS AND RECORD AS INVESTING AND FINANCING ACTIVITIES, OR AS SIGNIFICANT NONCASH TRANSACTIONS

INCREASE IN LAND. Land increased $60,000. The additional information section indicates that common stock was issued to purchase the land. The issuance of common stock for land has no effect on cash. But it is a **significant noncash investing and financing transaction**. This transaction requires disclosure in a separate schedule at the bottom of the statement of cash flows.

INCREASE IN EQUIPMENT. The comparative balance sheets show that equipment increased $160,000 in 2005. The additional information in Illustration 13-15 indicates that the increase resulted from two investing transactions: (1) Equipment costing $180,000 was purchased for cash. And (2) equipment costing $20,000 was sold for $17,000 cash when its book value was $18,000. The relevant data for the statement of cash flows is the cash paid for the purchase and the cash proceeds from the sale. For Juarez Company, the investing activities section will show the following: The $180,000 purchase of equipment as an outflow of cash, and the $17,000 sale of equipment also as an inflow of cash. The two amounts **should not be netted. Both individual outflows and inflows of cash should be shown**.

The analysis of the changes in equipment should include the related Accumulated Depreciation account. These two accounts for Juarez Company are shown in Illustration 13-29.

Equipment

1/1/05	Balance	–0–	Cost of equipment sold	20,000
	Cash purchase	**180,000**		
12/31/05	Balance	160,000		

Accumulated Depreciation—Equipment

Sale of equipment	2,000	1/1/05	Balance	–0–
			Depreciation expense	18,000
		12/31/05	Balance	16,000

Illustration 13-29 Analysis of equipment and related accumulated depreciation

INCREASE IN BONDS PAYABLE. Bonds Payable increased $130,000. The additional information in Illustration 13-15 indicated that bonds with a face value of $130,000 were issued for $130,000 cash. The issuance of bonds is a financing activity. For Juarez Company, there is an inflow of cash of $130,000 from the issuance of bonds.

INCREASE IN COMMON STOCK. The Common Stock account increased $60,000. The additional information indicated that land was acquired from the issuance of common stock. This transaction is a **significant noncash investing and financing transaction** that should be reported separately at the bottom of the statement.

INCREASE IN RETAINED EARNINGS. The $52,000 net increase in Retained Earnings resulted from net income of $84,000 and the declaration and payment of a cash dividend of $32,000. **Net income is not reported in the statement of cash flows under the direct method.** Cash dividends paid of $32,000 are reported in the financing activities section as an outflow of cash.

STATEMENT OF CASH FLOWS—2005

The statement of cash flows for Juarez Company is shown in Illustration 13-30.

Illustration 13-30 Statement of cash flows, 2005—direct method

JUAREZ COMPANY
Statement of Cash Flows—Direct Method
For the Year Ended December 31, 2005

Cash flows from operating activities		
Cash receipts from customers		$ 978,000
Less: Cash payments:		
To suppliers	$ 678,000	
For operating expenses	179,000	
For income taxes	24,000	881,000
Net cash provided by operating activities		97,000
Cash flows from investing activities		
Purchase of equipment	(180,000)	
Sale of equipment	17,000	
Net cash used by investing activities		(163,000)
Cash flows from financing activities		
Issuance of bonds payable	130,000	
Payment of cash dividends	(32,000)	
Net cash provided by financing activities		98,000
Net increase in cash		32,000
Cash at beginning of period		159,000
Cash at end of period		$ 191,000
Noncash investing and financing activities		
Issuance of common stock to purchase land		$ 60,000

Step 3: Net Change in Cash

COMPARE THE NET CHANGE IN CASH WITH THE CHANGE IN THE CASH ACCOUNT REPORTED ON THE BALANCE SHEET TO MAKE SURE THE AMOUNTS AGREE

Illustration 13-30 indicates that the net change in cash during the period was an increase of $32,000. This agrees with the change in balances in the cash account reported on the balance sheets in Illustration 13-15.

BEFORE YOU GO ON . . .

▶**Review It**

1. What is the format of the operating activities section of the statement of cash flows using the direct method?
2. Where is depreciation expense shown on a statement of cash flows using the direct method?
3. Where are significant noncash investing and financing activities shown on a statement of cash flows? Give some examples.

▶**Do It**

Presented on the next page is information related to Reynolds Company. Use it to prepare a statement of cash flows using the direct method.

REYNOLDS COMPANY
Comparative Balance Sheets
December 31

Assets	2005	2004	Change Increase/Decrease
Cash	$ 54,000	$ 37,000	$ 17,000 Increase
Accounts receivable	68,000	26,000	42,000 Increase
Inventories	54,000	–0–	54,000 Increase
Prepaid expenses	4,000	6,000	2,000 Decrease
Land	45,000	70,000	25,000 Decrease
Buildings	200,000	200,000	–0–
Accumulated depreciation—buildings	(21,000)	(11,000)	10,000 Increase
Equipment	193,000	68,000	125,000 Increase
Accumulated depreciation—equipment	(28,000)	(10,000)	18,000 Increase
Total	$569,000	$386,000	
Liabilities and Stockholders' Equity			
Accounts payable	$ 23,000	$ 40,000	$ 17,000 Decrease
Accrued expenses payable	10,000	–0–	10,000 Increase
Bonds payable	110,000	150,000	40,000 Decrease
Common stock ($1 par)	220,000	60,000	160,000 Increase
Retained earnings	206,000	136,000	70,000 Increase
Total	$569,000	$386,000	

REYNOLDS COMPANY
Income Statement
For the Year Ended December 31, 2005

Revenues		$890,000
Cost of goods sold	$465,000	
Operating expenses	221,000	
Interest expense	12,000	
Loss on sale of equipment	2,000	700,000
Income before income taxes		190,000
Income tax expense		65,000
Net income		$125,000

Additional information:
1. Operating expenses include depreciation expense of $33,000 and charges from prepaid expenses of $2,000.
2. Land was sold at its book value for cash.
3. Cash dividends of $55,000 were declared and paid in 2005.
4. Interest expense of $12,000 was paid in cash.
5. Equipment with a cost of $166,000 was purchased for cash. Equipment with a cost of $41,000 and a book value of $36,000 was sold for $34,000 cash.
6. Bonds of $10,000 were redeemed at their book value for cash. Bonds of $30,000 were converted into common stock.
7. Common stock ($1 par) of $130,000 was issued for cash.
8. Accounts payable pertain to merchandise suppliers.

Action Plan

- Determine net cash provided/used by operating activities by adjusting each item in the income statement from the accrual basis to the cash basis.
- Determine net cash provided/used by investing activities.
- Determine net cash provided/used by financing activities.
- Determine the net increase/decrease in cash.

Solution

REYNOLDS COMPANY
Statement of Cash Flows—Direct Method
For the Year Ended December 31, 2005

Cash flows from operating activities		
Cash receipts from customers		$848,000[a]
Less: Cash payments:		
To suppliers	$ 536,000[b]	
For operating expenses	176,000[c]	
For interest expense	12,000	
For income taxes	65,000	789,000
Net cash provided by operating activities		59,000
Cash flows from investing activities		
Sale of land	25,000	
Sale of equipment	34,000	
Purchase of equipment	(166,000)	
Net cash used by investing activities		(107,000)
Cash flows from financing activities		
Redemption of bonds	(10,000)	
Sale of common stock	130,000	
Payment of dividends	(55,000)	
Net cash provided by financing activities		65,000
Net increase in cash		17,000
Cash at beginning of period		37,000
Cash at end of period		$ 54,000
Noncash investing and financing activities		
Conversion of bonds into common stock		$ 30,000

Computations:
[a]$848,000 = $890,000 − $42,000
[b]$536,000 = $465,000 + $54,000 + $17,000
[c]$176,000 = $221,000 − $33,000 − $2,000 − $10,000
Technically, an additional schedule reconciling net income to net cash provided by operating activities should be presented as part of the statement of cash flows when using the direct method.

Related exercise material: BE13-9, BE13-10, BE13-11, E13-8, E13-9, E13-10, and E13-11.

Note: This concludes Section 2 on preparation of the statement of cash flows using the direct method. You should now proceed to the concluding section of the chapter, "Using Cash Flows to Evaluate a Company."

Using Cash Flows to Evaluate a Company

Traditionally, the ratios most commonly used by investors and creditors have been based on accrual accounting. Here we introduce cash-based ratios that are gaining increased acceptance among analysts.

FREE CASH FLOW

In the statement of cash flows, cash provided by operating activities is intended to indicate the cash-generating capability of the company. Analysts have noted, however, that **cash provided by operating activities fails to take into account that a company must invest in new fixed assets** just to maintain its current level of operations. Companies also must at least **maintain dividends at current levels** to satisfy investors. A measurement to provide additional insight regarding a company's cash generating ability is free cash flow. **Free cash flow** describes the cash remaining from operations after adjustment for capital expenditures and dividends.

Consider the following example: Suppose that MPC produced and sold 10,000 personal computers this year. It reported $100,000 cash provided by operating activities. In order to maintain production at 10,000 computers, MPC invested $15,000 in equipment. It chose to pay $5,000 in dividends. Its free cash flow was $80,000 ($100,000 − $15,000 − $5,000). The company could use this $80,000 either to purchase new assets to expand the business or to pay an $80,000 dividend and continue to produce 10,000 computers. In practice, free cash flow is often calculated with the formula in Illustration 13-31. Alternative definitions also exist.

Free Cash Flow	=	Cash Provided by Operating Activities	−	Capital Expenditures	−	Cash Dividends

Illustration 13-31   Free cash flow

Illustration 13-32 provides basic information excerpted from the 2003 statement of cash flows of **Microsoft Corporation**.

MICROSOFT CORPORATION
Statement of Cash Flows (partial)
2003

Cash provided by operating activities		$15,797
Cash flows from investing activities		
Additions to property, plant, and equipment	$ (891)	
Purchases of investments	(90,684)	
Sales of investments	84,362	
Cash used by investing activities		(7,213)
Cash paid for dividends on preferred stock		(857)

Illustration 13-32   Microsoft cash flow information ($ in millions)

Microsoft's free cash flow is calculated as shown in Illustration 13-33 (page 556).

Illustration 13-33 Calculation of Microsoft's free cash flow ($ in millions)

Cash provided by operating activities	$15,797
Less: Expenditures on property, plant, and equipment	891
Dividends paid	857
Free cash flow	$14,049

This is a tremendous amount of cash generated in a single year. It is available for the acquisition of new assets, the retirement of stock or debt, or the payment of dividends. It should also be noted that this amount far exceeds Microsoft's 2003 net income of $9,993 million. This lends additional credibility to Microsoft's income number as an indicator of potential future performance. If anything, Microsoft's net income might understate its actual performance.

Oracle Corporation is one of the world's largest sellers of database software and information management services. Like Microsoft, its success depends on continuing to improve its existing products while developing new products to keep pace with rapid changes in technology. Oracle's free cash flow for 2003 was $2,732 million. This is impressive, but significantly less than Microsoft's amazing ability to generate cash.

DECISION TOOLKIT

Decision Checkpoints	Info Needed for Decision	Tool to Use for Decision	How to Evaluate Results
How much cash did the company generate to either expand operations or pay dividends?	Cash provided by operating activities, cash spent on fixed assets, and cash dividends	$$\text{Free cash flow} = \text{Cash provided by operating activities} - \text{Capital expenditures} - \text{Cash dividends}$$	Significant free cash flow indicates greater potential to finance new investment and pay additional dividends.

Business Insight
Management Perspective

Managers in some industries have long suggested that accrual-based income measures understate the true long-term potential of their companies because of what they suggest are excessive depreciation charges. For example, cable companies frequently said that, once they had installed a cable, it would require minimal maintenance and would guarantee the company returns for many years. As a consequence, cable companies, which reported strong operating cash flows but low net income, had high stock prices because investors focused more on their cash flows from operations than on their net income.

A *Wall Street Journal* article suggested, however, that investors have grown impatient with the cable companies and have lost faith in cash flow from operations as an indicator of cable company performance. As it turns out, cable companies have had to make many expensive upgrades to previously installed cable systems. Today, after cable stock prices have fallen dramatically, cable industry analysts emphasize that either free cash flows or net income is a better indicator of a cable TV company's long-term potential than cash provided by operating activities.

SOURCE: Susan Pulliam and Mark Robichaux, "Heard on the Street: Cash Flow Stops Propping Cable Stock," *Wall Street Journal* (January 9, 1997), p. C1.

ASSESSING LIQUIDITY AND SOLVENCY USING CASH FLOWS

Many ratios used by analysts employ accrual-based numbers from the income statement and balance sheet. In this section we focus on ratios that are *cash-based* rather than accrual-based. That is, instead of using numbers from the income statement, these ratios use numbers from the statement of cash flows.

As discussed earlier, many analysts are critical of accrual-based numbers because they feel that the adjustment process allows too much management discretion. These analysts like to supplement accrual-based analysis with measures that use the cash flow statement. One disadvantage of these cash-based measures is that, unlike the more commonly employed accrual-based measures, there are no readily available industry averages for comparison. In the following discussion we use cash flow-based ratios to analyze Microsoft. In addition to the cash flow information provided in Illustration 13-32, we need the following information related to **Microsoft**.

($ in millions)	2003	2002
Current liabilities	$13,974	$12,744
Total liabilities	$18,551	$15,466

Liquidity

Liquidity is the ability of a business to meet its immediate obligations. One commonly used measure of liquidity is the *current ratio*: current assets divided by current liabilities. A disadvantage of the current ratio is that it uses year-end balances of current asset and current liability accounts. These year-end balances may not be representative of the company's position during most of the year.

A ratio that partially corrects this problem is the **current cash debt coverage ratio**. It is computed as cash provided by operating activities divided by average current liabilities. Because cash provided by operating activities involves the entire year rather than a balance at one point in time, it is often considered a better representation of liquidity on the average day. The ratio for **Microsoft Corporation** is calculated as shown in Illustration 13-34, with comparative numbers given for **Oracle**. For comparative purposes, we have also provided each company's current ratio.

Illustration 13-34   Current cash debt coverage ratio

$$\text{Current Cash Debt Coverage Ratio} = \frac{\text{Cash Provided by Operating Activities}}{\text{Average Current Liabilities}}$$

($ in millions)	Current cash debt coverage ratio	Current ratio
Microsoft	$\dfrac{\$15,797}{(\$13,974 + \$12,744)/2} = 1.18$ times	4.22:1
Oracle	.74 times	2.22:1

Microsoft's net cash provided by operating activities is approximately one-fifth greater than its average current liabilities. Oracle's ratio of .74 times, though not a cause for concern, is substantially lower than that of Microsoft. Keep in mind that Microsoft's cash position is extraordinary. For example, many large companies now have current ratios in the range of 1.0. By this standard, Oracle's current ratio of 2.22:1 is respectable. Microsoft's current ratio of 4.22:1 is very strong.

DECISION TOOLKIT

Decision Checkpoints ✔	Info Needed for Decision	Tool to Use for Decision	How to Evaluate Results
Is the company generating sufficient cash provided by operating activities to meet its current obligations?	Cash provided by operating activities and average current liabilities	Current cash debt coverage ratio $=\dfrac{\text{Cash provided by operating activities}}{\text{Average current liabilities}}$	A high value suggests good liquidity. Since the numerator contains a "flow" measure, it provides a good supplement to the current ratio.

Solvency

Solvency is the ability of a company to survive over the long term. A measure of solvency that uses cash figures is the **cash debt coverage ratio**. It is computed as the ratio of cash provided by operating activities to total debt as represented by average total liabilities. This ratio indicates a company's ability to repay its liabilities from cash generated from operations—that is, without having to liquidate productive assets such as property, plant, and equipment. The cash debt coverage ratios for **Microsoft** and **Oracle** for 2003 are given in Illustration 13-35. For comparative purposes, the debt to total assets ratios for each company are also provided.

Illustration 13-35   Cash debt coverage ratio

$$\text{Cash Debt Coverage Ratio} = \frac{\text{Cash Provided by Operating Activities}}{\text{Average Total Liabilities}}$$

($ in millions)	Cash debt coverage ratio	Debt to total assets ratio
Microsoft	$\dfrac{\$15,797}{(\$18,551 + \$15,466)/2} = .93$ times	23%
Oracle	.64 times	43%

Microsoft has relatively few long-term obligations as indicated by its low debt to total assets ratio. Thus, its cash debt coverage ratio is similar to its current cash debt coverage ratio. Obviously, Microsoft is very solvent. Oracle's reliance on debt financing is nearly twice that of Microsoft, as measured by its debt to total assets ratio of 43%. Its cash debt coverage ratio of .64 times is two-thirds as strong as Microsoft's. Neither the cash nor accrual measures suggest any cause for concern for either company.

DECISION TOOLKIT

Decision Checkpoints	Info Needed for Decision	Tool to Use for Decision	How to Evaluate Results
Is the company generating sufficient cash provided by operating activities to meet its long-term obligations?	Cash provided by operating activities and average total liabilities	$$\text{Cash debt coverage ratio} = \frac{\text{Cash provided by operating activities}}{\text{Average total liabilities}}$$	A high value suggests the company is solvent; that is, it will meet its obligations in the long term.

Business Insight
Management Perspective

While **Microsoft**'s cash position is enviable, it does present some challenges. Foremost among these is that management can't find enough ways to spend the cash. For example, unlike computer chip manufacturer **Intel Corporation** (another huge generator of cash), Microsoft has few manufacturing costs, so it cannot spend huge sums on new plant and equipment. Microsoft's management would like to purchase other major software companies, but the federal government won't let it, for fear that it will reduce competition. (For example, the Justice Department blocked Microsoft's proposed purchase of software maker **Intuit**.) Instead, Microsoft is confined to purchasing small software makers with promising new products. Ironically, even this does not use much of its cash because, first, the companies are small, and second, the owners of these small companies prefer to be paid with Microsoft stock rather than cash.

Microsoft's huge holdings of liquid assets could eventually hurt its stock performance. Liquid assets typically provide about a 5% return, whereas Microsoft investors are accustomed to 30% returns. If Microsoft's performance starts to decline because it can't find enough good investment projects, it should distribute cash to its common stockholders in the form of dividends. There's a problem with this plan, though: Bill Gates owns roughly 20% of Microsoft, and the last thing he wants to do is pay personal income tax on billions of dollars of dividend income. In 2003, under severe pressure from stockholders, Microsoft paid its first cash dividend.

SOURCE: David Bank, "Microsoft's Problem Is What Many Firms Just Wish They Had," *Wall Street Journal* (January 17, 1997), p. A9.

BEFORE YOU GO ON . . .

▶Review It

1. What is the difference between cash from operating activities and free cash flow?
2. What does it mean if a company has negative free cash flow?
3. Why might an analyst want to supplement accrual-based ratios with cash-based ratios? What are some cash-based ratios?

☑ THE NAVIGATOR

Using the Decision Toolkit

Intel Corporation is the leading producer of computer chips for personal computers. It makes the hugely successful Pentium chip. Its primary competitor is **AMD** (formerly Advanced Micro Devices). The two are vicious competitors, with frequent lawsuits filed between them. Financial statement data for Intel are provided below.

Instructions

Calculate the following cash-based measures for Intel, and compare them with those for AMD provided on page 561.

1. Free cash flow.
2. Current cash debt coverage ratio.
3. Cash debt coverage ratio.

INTEL CORPORATION
Balance Sheets
December 31, 2003 and 2002
(in millions)

Assets	2003	2002
Current assets	$22,882	$18,925
Noncurrent assets	24,261	25,299
Total assets	$47,143	$44,224
Liabilities and Stockholders' Equity		
Current liabilities	$ 6,879	$ 6,595
Long-term liabilities	2,418	2,161
Total liabilities	9,297	8,756
Stockholders' equity	37,846	35,468
Total liabilities and stockholders' equity	$47,143	$44,224

INTEL CORPORATION
Income Statements
For the Years Ended December 31, 2003 and 2002
(in millions)

	2003	2002
Net revenues	$30,141	$26,764
Expenses	24,500	23,647
Net income	$ 5,641	$ 3,117

INTEL CORPORATION
Statements of Cash Flows
For the Years Ended December 31, 2003 and 2002
(in millions)

	2003	2002
Net cash provided by operating activities	$11,515	$ 9,129
Net cash used for investing activities	(7,090)	(5,765)
Net cash used for financing activities	(3,858)	(3,930)
Net increase (decrease) in cash and cash equivalents	$ 567	$ (566)

Note. Cash spent on property, plant, and equipment in 2003 was $3,656. Cash paid for dividends was $524.

Here are the comparative data for **AMD**:

1. Free cash flow — $275 million
2. Current cash debt coverage ratio .21 times
3. Cash debt coverage ratio .08 times

Solution

1. Intel's free cash flow is $7,335 million ($11,515 − $3,656 − $524). AMD's is actually a negative $275 million. This gives Intel a huge advantage in the ability to move quickly to invest in new projects.

2. The current cash debt coverage ratio for Intel is calculated as follows.

$$\frac{\$11,515}{(\$6,879 + \$6,595)/2} = 1.71 \text{ times}$$

Compared to AMD's value of .21 times, Intel appears to be significantly more liquid.

3. The cash debt coverage ratio for Intel is calculated as follows.

$$\frac{\$11,515}{(\$9,297 + \$8,756)/2} = 1.28 \text{ times}$$

Compared to AMD's value of .08 times, Intel appears to be significantly more solvent.

Summary of Study Objectives

1 *Indicate the usefulness of the statement of cash flows.* The statement of cash flows provides information about the cash receipts, cash payments, and net change in cash resulting from the operating, investing, and financing activities of a company during the period.

2 *Distinguish among operating, investing, and financing activities.* Operating activities include the cash effects of transactions that enter into the determination of net income. Investing activities involve cash flows resulting from changes in investments and long-term asset items. Financing activities involve cash flows resulting from changes in long-term liability and stockholders' equity items.

3 *Explain the impact of the product life cycle on a company's cash flows.* During the introductory stage, cash provided by operating activities and cash from investing are negative, and cash from financing is positive. During the growth stage, cash provided by operating activities becomes positive. During the maturity stage, cash provided by operating activities exceeds investing needs, so the company begins to retire debt. During the decline stage, cash provided by operating activities is reduced, cash from investing becomes positive, and cash from financing becomes more negative.

4a *Prepare a statement of cash flows using the indirect method.* The preparation of a statement of cash flows involves three major steps: (1) Determine net cash provided (used) by operating activities. (2) Determine net cash provided (used) by investing and financing activities.(3) Determine the net increase or decrease in cash. Under the indirect method, accrual-basis net income is adjusted to net cash provided by operating activities.

4b *Prepare a statement of cash flows using the direct method.* The preparation of the statement of cash flows involves three major steps: (1) Determine net cash provided (used) by operating activities. (2) Determine net cash provided (used) by investing and financing activities. (3) Determine the net increase or decrease in cash. The direct method reports cash receipts less cash payments to arrive at net cash provided by operating activities.

5 *Use the statement of cash flows to evaluate a company.* A number of measures can be derived by using information from the statement of cash flows as well as the other required financial statements. Free cash flow indicates the amount of cash a company generated during the current year that is available for the payment of dividends or for expansion. Liquidity can be measured with the current cash debt coverage ratio (cash provided by operating activities divided by average current liabilities). Solvency can be measured by the cash debt coverage ratio (cash provided by operating activities divided by average total liabilities).

DECISION TOOLKIT—A SUMMARY

Decision Checkpoints	Info Needed for Decision	Tool to Use for Decision	How to Evaluate Results
How much cash did the company generate to either expand operations or pay dividends?	Cash provided by operating activities, cash spent on fixed assets, and cash dividends	$\text{Free cash flow} = \text{Cash provided by operating activities} - \text{Capital expenditures} - \text{Cash dividends}$	Significant free cash flow indicates greater potential to finance new investment and pay additional dividends.
Is the company generating sufficient cash provided by operating activities to meet its current obligations?	Cash provided by operating activities and average current liabilities	$\text{Current cash debt coverage ratio} = \dfrac{\text{Cash provided by operating activities}}{\text{Average current liabilities}}$	A high value suggests good liquidity. Since the numerator contains a "flow" measure, it provides a good supplement to the current ratio.
Is the company generating sufficient cash provided by operating activities to meet its long-term obligations?	Cash provided by operating activities and average total liabilities	$\text{Cash debt coverage ratio} = \dfrac{\text{Cash provided by operating activities}}{\text{Average total liabilities}}$	A high value suggests the company is solvent; that is, it will meet its obligations in the long term.

Glossary

Cash debt coverage ratio A cash-basis ratio used to evaluate solvency, calculated as cash provided by operating activities divided by average total liabilities. (p. 558)

Current cash debt coverage ratio A cash-basis ratio used to evaluate liquidity, calculated as cash provided by operating activities divided by average current liabilities. (p. 557)

Direct method A method of determining net cash provided by operating activities by adjusting each item in the income statement from the accrual basis to the cash basis. (p. 546)

Financing activities Cash flow activities that include (a) obtaining cash from issuing debt and repaying the amounts borrowed and (b) obtaining cash from stockholders and providing them with a return on their investment. (p. 528)

Free cash flow Cash provided by operating activities adjusted for capital expenditures and dividends paid. (p. 555)

Indirect method A method of preparing a statement of cash flows in which net income is adjusted for items that do not affect cash, to determine net cash provided by operating activities. (p. 537)

Investing activities Cash flow activities that include (a) acquiring and disposing of investments and property, plant, and equipment using cash and (b) lending money and collecting the loans. (p. 528)

Operating activities Cash flow activities that include the cash effects of transactions that create revenues and expenses and thus enter into the determination of net income. (p. 528)

Product life cycle   A series of phases in a product's sales and cash flows over time; these phases, in order of occurrence, are introductory, growth, maturity, and decline. (p. 531)

Statement of cash flows   A basic financial statement that provides information about the cash receipts and cash payments of an entity during a period, classified as operating, investing, and financing activities, in a format that reconciles the beginning and ending cash balances. (p. 528)

Demonstration Problem

Peachtree

The income statement for Kosinski Manufacturing Company contains the following condensed information.

KOSINSKI MANUFACTURING COMPANY
Income Statement
For the Year Ended December 31, 2005

Revenues		$6,583,000
Operating expenses, excluding depreciation	$4,920,000	
Depreciation expense	880,000	5,800,000
Income before income taxes		783,000
Income tax expense		353,000
Net income		$ 430,000

Included in operating expenses is a $24,000 loss resulting from the sale of machinery for $270,000 cash. Machinery was purchased at a cost of $750,000. The following balances are reported on Kosinski's comparative balance sheet at December 31.

	2005	**2004**
Cash	$672,000	$130,000
Accounts receivable	775,000	610,000
Inventories	834,000	867,000
Accounts payable	521,000	501,000

Income tax expense of $353,000 represents the amount paid in 2005. Dividends declared and paid in 2005 totaled $200,000.

Instructions
(a) Prepare the statement of cash flows using the indirect method.
(b) Prepare the statement of cash flows using the direct method.

Solution to Demonstration Problem

(a)   **KOSINSKI MANUFACTURING COMPANY**
Statement of Cash Flows—Indirect Method
For the Year Ended December 31, 2005

Cash flows from operating activities		
Net income		$ 430,000
Adjustments to reconcile net income to net cash		
provided by operating activities:		
Depreciation expense	$ 880,000	
Loss on sale of machinery	24,000	
Increase in accounts receivable	(165,000)	
Decrease in inventories	33,000	
Increase in accounts payable	20,000	792,000
Net cash provided by operating activities		1,222,000

Action Plan

• Apply the same data to the preparation of a statement of cash flows under both the indirect and direct methods.

• Note the similarities of the two methods: Both methods report the same information in the investing and financing sections.

• Note the differences between the two methods: The cash flows from operating activities sections report different information (but the amount of net cash provided by operating activities is the same for both methods).

Cash flows from investing activities
    Sale of machinery   270,000
    Purchase of machinery   (750,000)

      Net cash used by investing activities   (480,000)

Cash flows from financing activities
    Payment of cash dividends   (200,000)

      Net cash used by financing activities   (200,000)

Net increase in cash   542,000
Cash at beginning of period   130,000

Cash at end of period $ 672,000

(b)   **KOSINSKI MANUFACTURING COMPANY**
            Statement of Cash Flows—Direct Method
            For the Year Ended December 31, 2005

Cash flows from operating activities
    Cash collections from customers $6,418,000*
    Cash payments:
        For operating expenses $4,843,000**
        For income taxes   353,000   5,196,000

        Net cash provided by operating activities   1,222,000

Cash flows from investing activities
    Sale of machinery   270,000
    Purchase of machinery   (750,000)

      Net cash used by investing activities   (480,000)

Cash flows from financing activities
    Payment of cash dividends   (200,000)

      Net cash used by financing activities   (200,000)

Net increase in cash   542,000
Cash at beginning of period   130,000

Cash at end of period $ 672,000

Direct Method Computations:

*Computation of cash collections from customers:
    Revenues per the income statement $6,583,000
    Deduct: Increase in accounts receivable   (165,000)

    Cash collections from customers $6,418,000

**Computation of cash payments for operating
    expenses:
    Operating expenses per the income statement $4,920,000
    Deduct: Loss from sale of machinery   (24,000)
    Deduct: Decrease in inventories   (33,000)
    Deduct: Increase in accounts payable   (20,000)

    Cash payments for operating expenses $4,843,000

☑ THE
NAVIGATOR

Self-Study Questions

Self-Study/Self-Test

Answers are at the end of the chapter.

(SO 1)   1. Which of the following is *incorrect* about the statement of cash flows?
    (a) It is a fourth basic financial statement.

(b) It provides information about cash receipts and cash payments of an entity during a period.

(c) It reconciles the ending cash account balance to the balance per the bank statement.

(d) It provides information about the operating, investing, and financing activities of the business.

(SO 2) 2. The statement of cash flows classifies cash receipts and cash payments by these activities:
(a) operating and nonoperating.
(b) investing, financing, and operating.
(c) financing, operating, and nonoperating.
(d) investing, financing, and nonoperating.

(SO 2) 3. Which is an example of a cash flow from an operating activity?
(a) Payment of cash to lenders for interest.
(b) Receipt of cash from the sale of capital stock.
(c) Payment of cash dividends to the company's stockholders.
(d) None of the above.

(SO 2) 4. Which is an example of a cash flow from an investing activity?
(a) Receipt of cash from the issuance of bonds payable.
(b) Payment of cash to repurchase outstanding capital stock.
(c) Receipt of cash from the sale of equipment.
(d) Payment of cash to suppliers for inventory.

(SO 2) 5. Cash dividends paid to stockholders are classified on the statement of cash flows as:
(a) operating activities.
(b) investing activities.
(c) a combination of (a) and (b).
(d) financing activities.

(SO 2) 6. Which is an example of a cash flow from a financing activity?
(a) Receipt of cash from sale of land.
(b) Issuance of debt for cash.
(c) Purchase of equipment for cash.
(d) None of the above

(SO 2) 7. Which of the following is *incorrect* about the statement of cash flows?
(a) The direct method may be used to report cash provided by operations.
(b) The statement shows the cash provided (used) for three categories of activity.
(c) The operating section is the last section of the statement.
(d) The indirect method may be used to report cash provided by operations.

(SO 3) 8. During the introductory phase of a company's life cycle, one would normally expect to see:
(a) negative cash from operations, negative cash from investing, and positive cash from financing.

(b) negative cash from operations, positive cash from investing, and positive cash from financing.

(c) positive cash from operations, negative cash from investing, and negative cash from financing.

(d) positive cash from operations, negative cash from investing, and positive cash from financing.

Questions 9 and 10 apply only to the indirect method.

9. Net income is $132,000, accounts payable increased $10,000 during the year, inventory decreased $6,000 during the year, and accounts receivable increased $12,000 during the year. Under the indirect method, what is net cash provided by operations? (SO 4a)
(a) $102,000. (c) $124,000.
(b) $112,000. (d) $136,000.

10. Items that are added back to net income in determining cash provided by operations under the indirect method do *not* include: (SO 4a)
(a) depreciation expense.
(b) an increase in inventory.
(c) amortization expense.
(d) loss on sale of equipment.

Questions 11 and 12 apply only to the direct method.

11. The beginning balance in accounts receivable is $44,000, the ending balance is $42,000, and sales during the period are $129,000. What are cash receipts from customers? (SO 4b)
(a) $127,000. (c) $131,000.
(b) $129,000. (d) $141,000.

12. Which of the following items is reported on a cash flow statement prepared by the direct method? (SO 4b)
(a) Loss on sale of building.
(b) Increase in accounts receivable.
(c) Depreciation expense.
(d) Cash payments to suppliers.

13. The statement of cash flows should *not* be used to evaluate an entity's ability to: (SO 5)
(a) earn net income.
(b) generate future cash flows.
(c) pay dividends.
(d) meet obligations.

14. Free cash flow provides an indication of a company's ability to: (SO 5)
(a) generate net income.
(b) generate cash to pay dividends.
(c) generate cash to invest in new capital expenditures.
(d) both (b) and (c).

THE NAVIGATOR

Questions

1. (a) What is a statement of cash flows?
   (b) John Stiller maintains that the statement of cash flows is an optional financial statement. Do you agree? Explain.

2. What questions about cash are answered by the statement of cash flows?

3. Distinguish among the three activities reported in the statement of cash flows.

4. (a) What are the major sources (inflows) of cash in a statement of cash flows?
   (b) What are the major uses (outflows) of cash?

5. Why is it important to disclose certain noncash transactions? How should they be disclosed?

6. Wilma Flintstone and Barny Rublestone were discussing the format of the statement of cash flows of Rock Candy Co. At the bottom of Rock Candy's statement of cash flows was a separate section entitled "Noncash investing and financing activities." Give three examples of significant noncash transactions that would be reported in this section.

7. Why is it necessary to use comparative balance sheets, a current income statement, and certain transaction data in preparing a statement of cash flows?

8. (a) What are the phases of the corporate life cycle?
   (b) What effect does each phase have on the numbers reported in a statement of cash flows?

9. Contrast the advantages and disadvantages of the direct and indirect methods of preparing the statement of cash flows. Are both methods acceptable? Which method is preferred by the FASB? Which method is more popular?

10. When the total cash inflows exceed the total cash outflows in the statement of cash flows, how and where is this excess identified?

11. Describe the indirect method for determining net cash provided (used) by operating activities.

12. Why is it necessary to convert accrual-based net income to cash-basis income when preparing a statement of cash flows?

13. The president of Frogger Company is puzzled. During the last year, the company experienced a net loss of $800,000, yet its cash increased $300,000 during the same period of time. Explain to the president how this could occur.

14. Identify five items that are adjustments to convert net income to net cash provided by operating activities under the indirect method.

15. Why and how is depreciation expense reported in a statement prepared using the indirect method?

16. Why is the statement of cash flows useful?

17. During 2005 Steinbrenner Company converted $1,700,000 of its total $2,000,000 of bonds payable into common stock. Indicate how the transaction would be reported on a statement of cash flows, if at all.

18. Describe the direct method for determining net cash provided by operating activities.

19. Give the formulas under the direct method for computing (a) cash receipts from customers and (b) cash payments to suppliers.

20. Armani Inc. reported sales of $2 million for 2005. Accounts receivable decreased $100,000 and accounts payable increased $300,000. Compute cash receipts from customers, assuming that the receivable and payable transactions related to operations.

21. In the direct method, why is depreciation expense not reported in the cash flows from operating activities section?

22. Give examples of accrual-based and cash-based ratios to measure each of these characteristics of a company:
    (a) Liquidity.
    (b) Solvency.

Brief Exercises

Indicate statement presentation of selected transactions.
(SO 2)

BE13-1   Each of these items must be considered in preparing a statement of cash flows for Jerry Co. for the year ended December 31, 2005. For each item, state how it should be shown in the statement of cash flows for 2005.
(a) Issued bonds for $200,000 cash.
(b) Purchased equipment for $150,000 cash.
(c) Sold land costing $20,000 for $20,000 cash.
(d) Declared and paid a $50,000 cash dividend.

Classify items by activities.
(SO 2)

BE13-2   Classify each item as an operating, investing, or financing activity. Assume all items involve cash unless there is information to the contrary.
(a) Purchase of equipment.   (d) Depreciation.
(b) Sale of building.   (e) Payment of dividends.
(c) Redemption of bonds.   (f) Issuance of capital stock.

BE13-3 The following T account is a summary of the cash account of Elkhart Company.

Identify financing activity transactions.
(SO 2)

Cash (Summary Form)

Balance, Jan. 1	8,000		
Receipts from customers	364,000	Payments for goods	200,000
Dividends on stock investments	6,000	Payments for operating expenses	140,000
Proceeds from sale of equipment	36,000	Interest paid	10,000
Proceeds from issuance of		Taxes paid	8,000
bonds payable	200,000	Dividends paid	50,000
Balance, Dec. 31	206,000		

What amount of net cash provided (used) by financing activities should be reported in the statement of cash flows?

BE13-4

(a) Why is cash from operations likely to be lower than reported net income during the growth phase?
(b) Why is cash from investing often positive during the late maturity phase and during the decline phase?

Answer questions related to the phases of product life cycle.
(SO 3)

BE13-5 Salvador, Inc. reported net income of $2.5 million in 2005. Depreciation for the year was $260,000, accounts receivable decreased $350,000, and accounts payable decreased $280,000. Compute net cash provided by operating activities using the indirect approach.

Compute cash provided by operating activities—indirect method.
(SO 4a)

BE13-6 The net income for Castle Co. for 2005 was $280,000. For 2005 depreciation on plant assets was $60,000, and the company incurred a loss on sale of plant assets of $12,000. Compute net cash provided by operating activities under the indirect method.

Compute cash provided by operating activities—indirect method.
(SO 4a)

BE13-7 The comparative balance sheets for Holders Company show these changes in noncash current asset accounts: accounts receivable decrease $80,000, prepaid expenses increase $18,000, and inventories increase $30,000. Compute net cash provided by operating activities using the indirect method assuming that net income is $200,000.

Compute net cash provided by operating activities—indirect method.
(SO 4a)

BE13-8 The T accounts for Equipment and the related Accumulated Depreciation for Triangle Art Company at the end of 2005 are shown here.

Determine cash received from sale of equipment.
(SO 4a, 4b)

Equipment				**Accumulated Depreciation**			
Beg. bal.	80,000	Disposals	22,000	Disposals	5,500	Beg. bal.	44,500
Acquisitions	41,600					Depr. exp.	12,000
End. bal.	99,600					End. bal.	51,000

In addition, Triangle Art Company's income statement reported a loss on the sale of equipment of $7,500. What amount was reported on the statement of cash flows as "cash flow from sale of equipment"?

BE13-9 Columbia Sportswear Company had accounts receivable of $154,100,000 at January 1, 2003, and $206,000,000 at December 31, 2003. Sales revenues were $951,800,000 for the year 2003. What is the amount of cash receipts from customers in 2003?

Compute receipts from customers—direct method.
(SO 4b)

BE13-10 Boeing Corporation reported income tax expense of $168,000,000 on its 2003 income statement and income taxes payable of $1,134,000,000 at December 31, 2002, and $277,000,000 at December 31, 2003. What amount of cash payments were made for income taxes during 2003? (Ignore deferred taxes.)

Compute cash payments for income taxes—direct method.
(SO 4b)

BE13-11 Drake Corporation reports operating expenses of $75,000 excluding depreciation expense of $15,000 for 2005. During the year prepaid expenses decreased $6,600 and accrued expenses payable increased $4,400. Compute the cash payments for operating expenses in 2005.

Compute cash payments for operating expenses—direct method.
(SO 4b)

BE13-12 During 2003 **Cypress Semiconductor Corporation** reported cash provided by operations of $99,200,000, cash used in investing of $94,600,000, and cash provided in financing of $91,900,000. In addition, cash spent for plant assets during the period

Calculate cash-based ratios.
(SO 5)

was $78,500,000. Average current liabilities were $208,370,000, and average total liabilities were $938,000,000. No dividends were paid. Calculate these values:
(a) Free cash flow.
(b) Current cash debt coverage ratio.

Calculate cash-based ratios.
(SO 5)

BE13-13 Jain Corporation reported cash provided by operating activities of $300,000, cash used by investing activities of $250,000, and cash provided by financing activities of $70,000. In addition, cash spent for capital assets during the period was $200,000. Average current liabilities were $150,000, and average total liabilities were $225,000. No dividends were paid. Calculate these values:
(a) Free cash flow.
(b) Current cash debt coverage ratio.

Calculate cash-based ratios.
(SO 5)

BE13-14 **Alliance Atlantis Communications Inc.** reported a 30% increase in cash flow for its first quarter of 1999-2000. It attributes this increase in cash flow to the overwhelming success of its movie *Austin Powers: The Spy Who Shagged Me*. To date, the film has earned more than $20 million in box office sales. Alliance reported cash provided by operating activities of $234,983,000 and revenues of $163,309,000. An amount of $258,000 was paid for preferred dividends. Cash spent on plant asset additions during the quarter was $4,318,000. Calculate free cash flow.

Exercises

Classify transactions by
type of activity.
(SO 2)

E13-1 Big Salad Corporation had these transactions during 2005.
(a) Issued $50,000 par value common stock for cash.
(b) Purchased a machine for $30,000, giving a long-term note in exchange.
(c) Issued $200,000 par value common stock upon conversion of bonds having a face value of $200,000.
(d) Declared and paid a cash dividend of $18,000.
(e) Sold a long-term investment with a cost of $15,000 for $15,000 cash.
(f) Collected $16,000 of accounts receivable.
(g) Paid $18,000 on accounts payable.

Instructions
Analyze the transactions and indicate whether each transaction resulted in a cash flow from operating activities, investing activities, financing activities, or noncash investing and financing activities.

Classify transactions by
type of activity.
(SO 2)

E13-2 An analysis of comparative balance sheets, the current year's income statement, and the general ledger accounts of Coffee Table Corp. uncovered the following items. Assume all items involve cash unless there is information to the contrary.
(a) Payment of interest on notes payable.
(b) Exchange of land for patent.
(c) Sale of building at book value.
(d) Payment of dividends.
(e) Depreciation.
(f) Receipt of dividends on investment in stock.
(g) Receipt of interest on notes receivable.
(h) Issuance of capital stock.
(i) Amortization of patent.
(j) Issuance of bonds for land.
(k) Purchase of land.
(l) Conversion of bonds into common stock.
(m) Loss on sale of land.
(n) Retirement of bonds.

Instructions
Indicate how each item should be classified in the statement of cash flows using these four major classifications: operating activity (indirect method), investing activity, financing activity, and significant noncash investing and financing activity.

Identify phases of product
life cycle.
(SO 3)

E13-3 The information in the table (page 569) is from the statement of cash flows for a company at four different points in time (A, B, C, and D). Negative values are presented in parentheses.

	Point in Time			
	A	**B**	**C**	**D**
Cash from operations	$ (60,000)	$ 30,000	$120,000	$(10,000)
Cash from investing	(100,000)	25,000	30,000	(40,000)
Cash from financing	70,000	(110,000)	(50,000)	120,000
Net income	(40,000)	10,000	100,000	5,000

Instructions

For each point in time, state whether the company is most likely characterized as being in the introductory phase, growth phase, maturity phase, or decline phase. In each case explain your choice.

E13-4 Poppy Company reported net income of $195,000 for 2005. Poppy also reported depreciation expense of $45,000 and a loss of $5,000 on the sale of equipment. The comparative balance sheet shows a decrease in accounts receivable of $15,000 for the year, a $12,000 increase in accounts payable, and a $4,000 decrease in prepaid expenses.

Prepare the operating activities section—indirect method.
(SO 4a)

Instructions

Prepare the operating activities section of the statement of cash flows for 2005. Use the indirect method.

E13-5 The current sections of DoubleDip Inc.'s balance sheets at December 31, 2004 and 2005, are presented here.

Prepare the operating activities section—indirect method.
(SO 4a)

	2005	**2004**
Current assets		
Cash	$105,000	$ 99,000
Accounts receivable	120,000	89,000
Inventory	148,000	172,000
Prepaid expenses	27,000	22,000
Total current assets	$400,000	$382,000
Current liabilities		
Accrued expenses payable	$ 15,000	$ 5,000
Accounts payable	85,000	92,000
Total current liabilities	$100,000	$ 97,000

DoubleDip's net income for 2005 was $153,000. Depreciation expense was $19,000.

Instructions

Prepare the net cash provided by operating activities section of the company's statement of cash flows for the year ended December 31, 2005, using the indirect method.

E13-6 These three accounts appear in the general ledger of Bosco Corp. during 2005:

Prepare partial statement of cash flows—indirect method.
(SO 4a)

Equipment

Date		Debit	Credit	Balance
Jan. 1	Balance			160,000
July 31	Purchase of equipment	70,000		230,000
Sept. 2	Cost of equipment constructed	53,000		283,000
Nov. 10	Cost of equipment sold		39,000	244,000

Accumulated Depreciation—Equipment

Date		Debit	Credit	Balance
Jan. 1	Balance			71,000
Nov. 10	Accumulated depreciation on equipment sold	30,000		41,000
Dec. 31	Depreciation for year		28,000	69,000

Retained Earnings

Date		Debit	Credit	Balance
Jan. 1	Balance			105,000
Aug. 23	Dividends (cash)	14,000		91,000
Dec. 31	Net income		67,000	158,000

Instructions

From the postings in the accounts (page 569), indicate how the information is reported on a statement of cash flows using the indirect method. The loss on sale of equipment was $3,000. (*Hint:* Purchase of equipment is reported in the investing activities section as a decrease in cash of $70,000.)

Prepare a statement of cash flows—indirect method, and compute cash-based ratios.
(SO 4a, 5)

E13-7   Here are comparative balance sheets for Puffed Up Company:

PUFFED UP COMPANY
Comparative Balance Sheets
December 31

Assets	2005	2004
Cash	$ 63,000	$ 22,000
Accounts receivable	85,000	76,000
Inventories	170,000	189,000
Land	75,000	100,000
Equipment	270,000	200,000
Accumulated depreciation	(66,000)	(32,000)
Total	$597,000	$555,000

Liabilities and Stockholders' Equity	2005	2004
Accounts payable	$ 39,000	$ 47,000
Bonds payable	150,000	200,000
Common stock ($1 par)	216,000	174,000
Retained earnings	192,000	134,000
Total	$597,000	$555,000

Additional information:
1. Net income for 2005 was $98,000.
2. Cash dividends of $40,000 were declared and paid.
3. Bonds payable amounting to $50,000 were redeemed for cash $50,000.
4. Common stock was issued for $42,000 cash.
5. Sales for 2005 were $978,000.

Instructions
(a) Prepare a statement of cash flows for 2005 using the indirect method.
(b) Compute these cash-basis ratios:
    (1) Current cash debt coverage.
    (2) Cash debt coverage.

Compute cash provided by operating activities—direct method.
(SO 4b)

E13-8   Beltless Company completed its first year of operations on December 31, 2005. Its initial income statement showed that Beltless had revenues of $182,000 and operating expenses of $78,000. Accounts receivable and accounts payable at year-end were $60,000 and $18,000, respectively. Assume that accounts payable related to operating expenses. Ignore income taxes.

Instructions
Compute net cash provided by operating activities using the direct method.

Compute cash payments—direct method.
(SO 4b)

E13-9   The 2001 income statement for **McDonald's Corporation** shows cost of goods sold $3,802.1 million and operating expenses (including depreciation expense of $1,086.3 million) $8,370.9 million. The comparative balance sheet for the year shows that inventory increased $6.2 million, prepaid expenses increased $68.9 million, accounts payable (merchandise suppliers) increased $4.6 million, and accrued expenses payable increased $150.3 million.

Instructions
Using the direct method, compute (a) cash payments to suppliers and (b) cash payments for operating expenses.

Compute cash flow from operating activities—direct method.
(SO 4b)

E13-10   The 2005 accounting records of Running on Vapors Transport reveal the transactions and events shown on page 571.

Payment of interest	$ 10,000	Collection of accounts receivable	$192,000
Cash sales	48,000	Payment of salaries and wages	53,000
Receipt of dividend revenue	18,000	Depreciation expense	16,000
Payment of income taxes	12,000	Proceeds from sale of vehicles	812,000
Net income	38,000	Purchase of equipment for cash	22,000
Payment of accounts payable		Loss on sale of vehicles	3,000
for merchandise	110,000	Payment of dividends	14,000
Payment for land	74,000	Payment of operating expenses	28,000

Instructions

Prepare the cash flows from operating activities section using the direct method. (Not all of the items will be used.)

E13-11 The following information is taken from the 2005 general ledger of Lone Ranger Company.

Calculate cash flows—direct method.
(SO 4b)

Rent	Rent expense	$ 35,000
	Prepaid rent, January 1	5,900
	Prepaid rent, December 31	9,000
Salaries	Salaries expense	$ 54,000
	Salaries payable, January 1	10,000
	Salaries payable, December 31	8,000
Sales	Revenue from sales	$180,000
	Accounts receivable, January 1	16,000
	Accounts receivable, December 31	7,000

Instructions

In each case, compute the amount that should be reported in the operating activities section of the statement of cash flows under the direct method.

E13-12 Presented here is 2001 information for **PepsiCo, Inc.** and **The Coca-Cola Company**.

Compare two companies by using cash-based ratios.
(SO 5)

($ in millions)	PepsiCo	Coca-Cola
Cash provided by operations	$ 4,328	$ 5,456
Average current liabilities	6,234	7,614
Average total liabilities	13,702	12,929
Net income	3,568	4,347
Sales	26,971	21,044

Instructions

Using the cash-based ratios presented in this chapter, compare the (a) liquidity and (b) solvency of the two companies.

E13-13 Information for two companies in the same industry, Rita Corporation and Les Corporation, is presented here.

Compare two companies by using cash-based ratios.
(SO 5)

	Rita Corporation	Les Corporation
Cash provided by operating activities	$200,000	$200,000
Average current liabilities	50,000	100,000
Average total liabilities	200,000	250,000
Net earnings	200,000	200,000
Sales	400,000	800,000

Instructions

Using the cash-based ratios presented in this chapter, compare the (a) liquidity and (b) solvency of the two companies.

Problems: Set A

Distinguish among operating, investing, and financing activities.
(SO 2)

P13-1A You are provided with the following transactions that took place during a recent fiscal year.

Transaction	Where Reported on Statement?	Cash Inflow, Outflow, or No Effect?
(a) Recorded depreciation expense on the plant assets.		
(b) Incurred a loss on disposal of plant assets.		
(c) Acquired a building by paying cash.		
(d) Made principal repayments on a mortgage.		
(e) Issued common stock.		
(f) Purchased shares of another company to be held as a long-term equity investment.		
(g) Paid dividends to common stockholders.		
(h) Sold inventory on credit. The company uses a perpetual inventory system.		
(i) Purchased inventory on credit.		
(j) Paid wages to employees.		

Instructions

Complete the table indicating whether each item (1) should be reported as an operating (O) activity, investing (I) activity, financing (F) activity, or as a noncash (NC) transaction reported in a separate schedule, and (2) represents a cash inflow or cash outflow or has no cash flow effect. Assume use of the indirect approach.

Determine cash flow effects of changes in plant asset accounts.
(SO 4)

P13-2A The following selected account balances relate to the plant asset accounts of Trudeau Inc. at year-end.

	2005	2004
Accumulated depreciation—buildings	$337,500	$300,000
Accumulated depreciation—equipment	144,000	96,000
Buildings	750,000	750,000
Depreciation expense	101,500	85,500
Equipment	300,000	240,000
Land	100,000	70,000
Loss on sale of equipment	1,000	0

Additional information:
1. Trudeau purchased $80,000 of equipment and $30,000 of land for cash in 2005.
2. Trudeau also sold equipment in 2005.
3. Depreciation expense in 2005 was $37,500 on building and $64,000 on equipment.

Instructions

(a) Cash proceeds $3,000

(a) Determine the amounts of any cash inflows or outflows related to the plant asset accounts in 2005.
(b) Indicate where each of the cash inflows or outflows identified in (a) would be classified on the statement of cash flows.

Prepare the operating activities section—indirect method.
(SO 4a)

P13-3A The income statement of Kroncke Company is presented on page 573.
Additional information:
1. Accounts receivable decreased $510,000 during the year.
2. Prepaid expenses increased $170,000 during the year.
3. Accounts payable to merchandise suppliers increased $50,000 during the year.
4. Accrued expenses payable increased $165,000 during the year.

KRONCKE COMPANY
Income Statement
For the Year Ended December 31, 2005

Sales		$5,400,000
Cost of goods sold		
Beginning inventory	$1,780,000	
Purchases	3,430,000	
Goods available for sale	5,210,000	
Ending inventory	1,920,000	
Cost of goods sold		3,290,000
Gross profit		2,110,000
Operating expenses		
Selling expenses	400,000	
Administrative expense	525,000	
Depreciation expense	125,000	
Amortization expense	20,000	1,070,000
Net income		$1,040,000

Instructions

Prepare the operating activities section of the statement of cash flows for the year ended December 31, 2005, for Kroncke Company, using the indirect method.

Cash from operating activities
$1,600,000

P13-4A   Data for Kroncke Company are presented in P13-3A.

Prepare the operating activities section—direct method.
(SO 4b)

Instructions

Prepare the operating activities section of the statement of cash flows using the direct method.

Cash from operating activities
$1,600,000

P13-5A   The income statement of Kraemer Inc. reported the following condensed information.

Prepare the operating activities section—direct method.
(SO 2b)

KRAEMER INC.
Income Statement
For the Year Ended December 31, 2005

Revenues	$545,000
Operating expenses	400,000
Income from operations	145,000
Income tax expense	47,000
Net income	$ 98,000

Kraemer's balance sheet contained these comparative data at December 31.

	2005	2004
Accounts receivable	$50,000	$70,000
Accounts payable	30,000	41,000
Income taxes payable	10,000	4,000

Kraemer has no depreciable assets. Accounts payable pertain to operating expenses.

Instructions

Prepare the operating activities section of the statement of cash flows using the direct method.

Cash from operating activities
$113,000

Prepare the operating activities section—indirect method.
(SO 4a)

P13-6A   Data for Kraemer are presented in P13-5A.

Instructions

Prepare the operating activities section of the statement of cash flows using the indirect method.

Cash from operating activities
$113,000

Prepare a statement of cash flows—indirect method, and compute cash-based ratios.
(SO 4a, 5)

P13-7A Here are the financial statements of YoYo Company.

YOYO COMPANY
Comparative Balance Sheets
December 31

Assets		2005		2004
Cash		$ 26,000		$ 33,000
Accounts receivable		28,000		14,000
Merchandise inventory		38,000		25,000
Property, plant, and equipment	$ 70,000		$ 78,000	
Less: Accumulated depreciation	(27,000)	43,000	(24,000)	54,000
Total		$135,000		$126,000

Liabilities and Stockholders' Equity		2005		2004
Accounts payable		$ 31,000		$ 43,000
Income taxes payable		26,000		20,000
Bonds payable		20,000		10,000
Common stock		25,000		25,000
Retained earnings		33,000		28,000
Total		$135,000		$126,000

YOYO COMPANY
Income Statement
For the Year Ended December 31, 2005

Sales		$286,000
Cost of goods sold		194,000
Gross profit		92,000
Selling expenses	$28,000	
Administrative expenses	9,000	37,000
Income from operations		55,000
Interest expense		7,000
Income before income taxes		48,000
Income tax expense		7,000
Net income		$ 41,000

Additional data:
1. Dividends of $36,000 were declared and paid.
2. During the year equipment was sold for $10,000 cash. This equipment cost $15,000 originally and had a book value of $10,000 at the time of sale.
3. All depreciation expense, $8,000, is in the selling expense category.
4. All sales and purchases are on account.
5. Additional equipment was purchased for $7,000 cash.

Instructions
(a) Prepare a statement of cash flows using the indirect method.
(b) Compute these cash-basis measures:
    (1) Current cash debt coverage ratio.
    (2) Cash debt coverage ratio.
    (3) Free cash flow.

(a) Cash from operating activities $16,000

Prepare a statement of cash flows—direct method, and compute cash-based ratios.
(SO 4b, 5)
(a) Cash from operating activities $16,000

P13-8A Data for YoYo Company are presented in P13-7A. Further analysis reveals the following.
1. Accounts payable pertains to merchandise creditors.
2. All operating expenses except for depreciation are paid in cash.

Instructions
(a) Prepare a statement of cash flows using the direct method.

(b) Compute these cash-basis measures:
   (1) Current cash debt coverage ratio.
   (2) Cash debt coverage ratio.
   (3) Free cash flow.

P13-9A   Condensed financial data of George Company follow.

Prepare a statement of cash flows—indirect method.
(SO 4a)

GEORGE COMPANY
Comparative Balance Sheets
December 31

Assets	2005	2004
Cash	$ 92,700	$ 33,400
Accounts receivable	80,800	37,000
Inventories	121,900	102,650
Investments	84,500	107,000
Plant assets	310,000	205,000
Accumulated depreciation	(49,500)	(40,000)
Total	$640,400	$445,050

Liabilities and Stockholders' Equity	2005	2004
Accounts payable	$ 62,700	$ 48,280
Accrued expenses payable	12,100	18,830
Bonds payable	140,000	70,000
Common stock	250,000	200,000
Retained earnings	175,600	107,940
Total	$640,400	$445,050

GEORGE COMPANY
Income Statement Data
For the Year Ended December 31, 2005

Sales		$297,500
Gain on sale of plant assets		5,000
		302,500
Less:		
Cost of goods sold	$99,460	
Operating expenses, excluding depreciation expense	14,670	
Depreciation expense	35,500	
Income taxes	7,270	
Interest expense	2,940	159,840
Net income		$142,660

Additional information:
1. New plant assets costing $141,000 were purchased for cash during the year.
2. Investments were sold at cost.
3. Plant assets costing $36,000 were sold for $15,000, resulting in a gain of $5,000.
4. A cash dividend of $75,000 was declared and paid during the year.

Instructions
Prepare a statement of cash flows using the indirect method.

Cash from operating activities
$117,800

P13-10A   Data for George Company are presented in P13-9A. Further analysis reveals that accounts payable pertain to merchandise creditors.

Prepare a statement of cash flows—direct method.
(SO 4b)

Instructions
Prepare a statement of cash flows for George Company using the direct method.

Cash from operating activities
$117,800

P13-11A   Presented on the next page are the comparative balance sheets for Perry Company at December 31.

Prepare a statement of cash flows—indirect method.
(SO 4a)

PERRY COMPANY
Comparative Balance Sheets
December 31

Assets	2005	2004
Cash	$ 26,000	$ 57,000
Accounts receivable	77,000	64,000
Inventory	192,000	140,000
Prepaid expenses	12,140	16,540
Land	105,000	150,000
Equipment	215,000	175,000
Accumulated depreciation—equipment	(70,000)	(42,000)
Building	250,000	250,000
Accumulated depreciation—building	(70,000)	(50,000)
Total	$737,140	$760,540

Liabilities and Stockholders' Equity		
Accounts payable	$ 63,000	$ 45,000
Bonds payable	235,000	265,000
Common stock, $1 par	280,000	250,000
Retained earnings	159,140	200,540
Total	$737,140	$760,540

Additional information:
1. Operating expenses include depreciation expense $65,000 and charges from prepaid expenses of $4,400.
2. Land was sold for cash at cost.
3. Cash dividends of $74,290 were paid.
4. Net income for 2005 was $32,890.
5. Equipment was purchased for $80,000 cash. In addition, equipment costing $40,000 with a book value of $23,000 was sold for $25,000 cash.
6. Bonds were converted at face value by issuing 30,000 shares of $1 par value common stock.

Cash from operating activities
$53,290

Instructions
Prepare a statement of cash flows for 2005 using the indirect method.

Identify the impact of transactions on ratios.
(SO 5)

P13-12A You are provided with the following transactions that took place during the year.

Transactions	Free Cash Flow ($125,000)	Current Cash Debt Coverage Ratio (0.5 times)	Cash Debt Coverage Ratio (0.3 times)
(a) Recorded cash sales $8,000.			
(b) Purchased inventory for $1,500 cash.			
(c) Purchased new equipment $10,000; signed a short-term note payable for the cost of the equipment.			
(d) Paid a $20,000 cash dividend to common stockholders.			
(e) Acquired a building for $750,000, by signing a mortgage payable for $450,000 and issuing common stock for the balance.			
(f) Made a principal payment on the mortgage currently due, $45,000.			

Instructions

For each transaction listed on page 576, indicate whether it will increase (I), decrease (D), or have no effect (NE) on the ratios.

Problems: Set B

P13-1B You are provided with the following transactions that took place during a recent fiscal year.

Distinguish among operating, investing, and financing activities.
(SO 2)

Transaction	Where Reported on Statement?	Cash Inflow, Outflow, or No Effect?
(a) Recorded depreciation expense on the plant assets.		
(b) Recorded and paid interest expense.		
(c) Recorded cash proceeds from a sale of plant assets.		
(d) Acquired land by issuing common stock.		
(e) Paid a cash dividend to preferred stockholders.		
(f) Distributed a stock dividend to common stockholders.		
(g) Recorded cash sales.		
(h) Recorded sales on account.		
(i) Purchased inventory for cash.		
(j) Purchased inventory on account.		

Instructions

Complete the table indicating whether each item (1) should be reported as an operating (O) activity, investing (I) activity, financing (F) activity, or as a noncash (NC) transaction reported in a separate schedule, and (2) represents a cash inflow or cash outflow or has no cash flow effect. Assume use of the indirect approach.

P13-2B The following account balances relate to the stockholders' equity accounts of Wood Corp. at year-end.

Determine cash flow effects of changes in equity accounts.
(SO 4)

	2005	2004
Common stock, 10,500 and 10,000 shares, respectively, for 2005 and 2004	$160,000	$140,000
Preferred stock, 5,000 shares	125,000	125,000
Retained earnings	300,000	240,000

A small stock dividend was declared and issued in 2005. The market value of the shares was $10,500. Cash dividends were $10,000 in both 2005 and 2004. The common stock has no par or stated value.

Instructions

(a) What was the amount of net income reported by Wood Corp. in 2005?

(b) Determine the amounts of any cash inflows or outflows related to the common stock and dividend accounts in 2005.

(c) Indicate where each of the cash inflows or outflows identified in (b) would be classified on the statement of cash flows.

(a) Net income $80,500

Prepare the operating activities section—indirect method.
(SO 4a)

P13-3B The income statement of Talker Company is presented below.

TALKER COMPANY
Income Statement
For the Year Ended November 30, 2005

Sales		$7,700,000
Cost of goods sold		
Beginning inventory	$1,900,000	
Purchases	4,400,000	
Goods available for sale	6,300,000	
Ending inventory	1,400,000	
Cost of goods sold		4,900,000
Gross profit		2,800,000
Operating expenses		
Selling expenses	450,000	
Administrative expenses	700,000	1,150,000
Net income		$1,650,000

Additional information:
1. Accounts receivable increased $200,000 during the year.
2. Prepaid expenses increased $150,000 during the year.
3. Accounts payable to suppliers of merchandise decreased $340,000 during the year.
4. Accrued expenses payable decreased $100,000 during the year.
5. Administrative expenses include depreciation expense of $110,000.

Instructions
Prepare the operating activities section of the statement of cash flows for the year ended November 30, 2005, for Talker Company, using the indirect method.

Cash from operating activities
$1,470,000

P13-4B Data for Talker Company are presented in P13-3B.

Prepare the operating activities section—direct method.
(SO 4b)

Instructions
Prepare the operating activities section of the statement of cash flows using the direct method.

Cash from operating activities
$1,470,000

Prepare the operating activities section—direct method.
(SO 2b)

P13-5B No Soup Company's income statement contained the condensed information below.

NO SOUP COMPANY
Income Statement
For the Year Ended December 31, 2005

Revenues		$970,000
Operating expenses, excluding depreciation	$624,000	
Depreciation expense	60,000	
Loss on sale of equipment	16,000	700,000
Income before income taxes		270,000
Income tax expense		40,000
Net income		$230,000

No Soup's balance sheet contained these comparative data at December 31.

	2005	2004
Accounts receivable	$65,000	$60,000
Accounts payable	41,000	33,000
Income taxes payable	11,000	7,000

Accounts payable pertain to operating expenses.

Instructions
Prepare the operating activities section of the statement of cash flows using the direct method.

Cash from operating activities
$313,000

P13-6B Data for No Soup Company are presented in P13-5B.

Prepare the operating activities section—indirect method.
(SO 4a)
Cash from operating activities
    $313,000

Instructions

Prepare the operating activities section of the statement of cash flows using the indirect method.

P13-7B Presented below are the financial statements of Newman Company.

Prepare a statement of cash flows—indirect method, and compute cash-based ratios.
(SO 4a, 5)

NEWMAN COMPANY
Comparative Balance Sheets
December 31

Assets	2005	2004
Cash	$ 31,000	$ 20,000
Accounts receivable	38,000	14,000
Merchandise inventory	27,000	20,000
Property, plant, and equipment	60,000	78,000
Accumulated depreciation	(30,000)	(24,000)
Total	$126,000	$108,000

Liabilities and Stockholders' Equity		
Accounts payable	$ 29,000	$ 15,000
Income taxes payable	7,000	8,000
Bonds payable	27,000	33,000
Common stock	18,000	14,000
Retained earnings	45,000	38,000
Total	$126,000	$108,000

NEWMAN COMPANY
Income Statement
For the Year Ended December 31, 2005

Sales		$242,000
Cost of goods sold		175,000
Gross profit		67,000
Selling expenses	$18,000	
Administrative expenses	6,000	24,000
Income from operations		43,000
Interest expense		3,000
Income before income taxes		40,000
Income tax expense		6,000
Net income		$ 34,000

Additional data:

1. Dividends declared and paid were $27,000.
2. During the year equipment was sold for $8,500 cash. This equipment cost $18,000 originally and had a book value of $8,500 at the time of sale.
3. All depreciation expense is in the selling expense category.
4. All sales and purchases are on account.

Instructions

(a) Prepare a statement of cash flows using the indirect method.
(b) Compute these cash-basis measures:
    (1) Current cash debt coverage ratio.
    (2) Cash debt coverage ratio.
    (3) Free cash flow.

(a) Cash from operating activities $31,500

P13-8B Data for Newman Company are presented in P13-7B. Further analysis reveals the information shown on page 580.

Prepare a statement of cash flows—direct method, and compute cash-based ratios.
(SO 4b, 5)

1. Accounts payable pertain to merchandise suppliers.
2. All operating expenses except for depreciation were paid in cash.

Instructions

(a) Cash from operating activities $31,500

(a) Prepare a statement of cash flows for Newman Company using the direct method.
(b) Compute these cash-basis measures:
    (1) Current cash debt coverage ratio.
    (2) Cash debt coverage ratio.
    (3) Free cash flow.

Prepare a statement of cash flows—indirect method.
(SO 4a)

P13-9B Condensed financial data of Elly Inc. follow.

ELLY INC.
Comparative Balance Sheets
December 31

Assets	2005	2004
Cash	$ 97,800	$ 48,400
Accounts receivable	95,800	33,000
Inventories	112,500	102,850
Prepaid expenses	28,400	26,000
Investments	128,000	114,000
Plant assets	270,000	242,500
Accumulated depreciation	(50,000)	(52,000)
Total	$682,500	$514,750

Liabilities and Stockholders' Equity		
Accounts payable	$102,000	$ 67,300
Accrued expenses payable	16,500	17,000
Bonds payable	110,000	150,000
Common stock	220,000	175,000
Retained earnings	234,000	105,450
Total	$682,500	$514,750

ELLY INC.
Income Statement Data
For the Year Ended December 31, 2005

Sales		$392,780
Less:		
Cost of goods sold	$135,460	
Operating expenses, excluding		
depreciation	12,410	
Depreciation expense	46,500	
Income taxes	7,280	
Interest expense	4,730	
Loss on sale of plant assets	7,500	213,880
Net income		$178,900

Additional information:
1. New plant assets costing $85,000 were purchased for cash during the year.
2. Old plant assets having an original cost of $57,500 were sold for $1,500 cash.
3. Bonds matured and were paid off at face value for cash.
4. A cash dividend of $50,350 was declared and paid during the year.

Cash from operating activities $192,250

Instructions
Prepare a statement of cash flows using the indirect method.

Prepare a statement of cash flows—direct method.
(SO 4b)
Cash from operating activities $192,250

P13-10B Data for Elly Inc. are presented in P13-9B. Further analysis reveals that accounts payable pertain to merchandise creditors.

Instructions
Prepare a statement of cash flows for Elly Inc. using the direct method.

P13-11B   The comparative balance sheets for Festivals Company as of December 31 are presented below.

Prepare a statement of cash flows—indirect method.
(SO 4a)

FESTIVALS COMPANY
Comparative Balance Sheets
December 31

Assets	2005	2004
Cash	$ 81,000	$ 45,000
Accounts receivable	49,000	62,000
Inventory	151,450	142,000
Prepaid expenses	15,280	21,000
Land	90,000	130,000
Equipment	228,000	155,000
Accumulated depreciation—equipment	(45,000)	(35,000)
Building	200,000	200,000
Accumulated depreciation—building	(60,000)	(40,000)
Total	$709,730	$680,000

Liabilities and Stockholders' Equity		
Accounts payable	$ 57,730	$ 40,000
Bonds payable	260,000	300,000
Common stock, $1 par	200,000	160,000
Retained earnings	192,000	180,000
Total	$709,730	$680,000

Additional information:
1. Operating expenses include depreciation expense of $42,000 and charges from prepaid expenses of $5,720.
2. Land was sold for cash at book value.
3. Cash dividends of $25,000 were paid.
4. Net income for 2005 was $37,000.
5. Equipment was purchased for $95,000 cash. In addition, equipment costing $22,000 with a book value of $10,000 was sold for $6,000 cash.
6. Bonds were converted at face value by issuing 40,000 shares of $1 par value common stock.

Instructions
Prepare a statement of cash flows for the year ended December 31, 2005, using the indirect method.

Cash from operating activities
$110,000

P13-12B   You are provided with the following transactions that took place during the year.

Identify the impact of transactions on ratios.
(SO 5)

Transactions	Free Cash Flow ($125,000)	Current Cash Debt Coverage Ratio (0.5 times)	Cash Debt Coverage Ratio (0.3 times)
(a) Recorded credit sales $2,500.			
(b) Collected $1,500 owed by customers.			
(c) Paid amount owed to suppliers $2,750.			
(d) Recorded sales returns of $500 and credited the customer's account.			
(e) Purchased new equipment $5,000; signed a long-term note payable for the cost of the equipment.			
(f) Purchased a patent and paid $15,000 cash for the asset.			

Instructions

For each transaction listed on page 581, indicate whether it will increase (I), decrease (D), or have no effect (NE) on the ratios.

Problems: Set C

Problem Set C is provided at the book's Web site, www.wiley.com/college/weygandt.

▷ B R O A D E N I N G   Y O U R   P E R S P E C T I V E

Financial Reporting and Analysis

FINANCIAL REPORTING PROBLEM: *Tootsie Roll Industries, Inc.*

BYP 13-1 The financial statements of **Tootsie Roll Industries** can be found at the company's Web site, www.tootsie.com.

Instructions

Answer the following questions.

(a) What was the amount of net cash provided by operating activities for 2003? For 2002? What were some causes of any significant changes in cash from operations between 2002 and 2003?

(b) What was the amount of increase or decrease in cash and cash equivalents for the year ended December 31, 2003?

(c) Which method of computing net cash provided by operating activities does Tootsie Roll use?

(d) From your analysis of the 2003 statement of cash flows, was the change in accounts receivable a decrease or an increase? Was the change in inventories a decrease or an increase? Was the change in accounts payable a decrease or an increase?

(e) What was the net cash used by investing activities for 2003?

(f) What was the amount of interest paid in 2003? What was the amount of income taxes paid in 2003?

COMPARATIVE ANALYSIS PROBLEM: *Tootsie Roll vs. Hershey Foods*

BYP 13-2 The financial statements of **Hershey Foods** and **Tootsie Roll Industries** can be found at the companies' Web sites, www.hersheys.com and www.tootsie.com.

Instructions

(a) Based on the information in these financial statements, compute these 2003 ratios for each company:
   (1) Current cash debt coverage.
   (2) Cash debt coverage.

(b) What conclusions concerning the management of cash can be drawn from these data?

INTERPRETING FINANCIAL STATEMENTS

BYP 13-3   The incredible growth of **Amazon.com** has put fear into the hearts of traditional retailers. Amazon.com's stock price has soared to amazing levels. However, it is often pointed out in the financial press that the company has never reported a profit for the year. The following financial information is taken from the 2001 financial statements of Amazon.com.

($ in millions)	2001	2000
Current assets	$1,207.9	$ 1,361.1
Total assets	1,637.5	2,135.2
Current liabilities	921.4	975.0
Total liabilities	3,077.5	3,102.4
Cash provided by operations	(119.8)	(130.4)
Capital expenditures	50.3	134.8
Dividends paid	0	0
Net loss	(567.3)	(1,411.3)
Sales	3,122.4	2,762.0

Instructions
(a) Calculate the current ratio and current cash debt coverage ratio for Amazon.com for 2001 and discuss its liquidity.
(b) Calculate the cash debt coverage ratio and the debt to total assets ratio for Amazon.com for 2001 and discuss its solvency.
(c) Calculate free cash flow for Amazon.com for 2001 and discuss its ability to finance expansion from internally generated cash. Thus far Amazon.com has avoided purchasing large warehouses. Instead, it has used those of others. It is possible, however, that in order to increase customer satisfaction the company may have to build its own warehouses. If this happens, how might your impression of its ability to finance expansion change?
(d) Discuss any potential implications of the change in Amazon.com's cash provided by operations and its net loss from 2000 to 2001.
(e) Based on your findings in parts (a) through (d), can you conclude whether or not Amazon.com's amazing stock price is justified?

A GLOBAL FOCUS

BYP 13-4   The statement of cash flows has become a commonly provided financial statement by companies throughout the world. It is interesting to note, however, that its format does vary across countries. The statement of cash flows on page 584 is from the 2001 financial statements of Irish pharmaceutical company **Elan Corporation**.

Instructions
(a) What similarities to U.S. cash flow statements do you notice in terms of general format, as well as terminology?
(b) What differences do you notice in terms of general format, as well as terminology?

ELAN CORPORATION
Consolidated Statement of Cash Flows

		Year Ended 31 December	
		2001	2000
	Notes	$m	$m
Cash Flow from Operating Activities	28(a)	524.6	272.2
Returns on Investments and Servicing of Finance			
Interest received		80.3	111.8
Interest paid		(124.1)	(76.4)
Cash (outflow)/inflow from returns on investments and servicing of finance		(43.8)	35.4
Taxation		(6.5)	(3.6)
Capital Expenditure and Financial Investment			
Additions to property, plant and equipment		(120.8)	(64.4)
Receipts from disposal of property, plant and equipment		2.0	9.8
Payments to acquire intangible assets		(286.7)	(79.5)
Receipts from disposal of intangible assets		11.2	—
Payments to acquire financial current assets		(148.2)	(54.6)
Sale and maturity of financial current assets		143.3	100.1
Payments to acquire financial fixed assets		(624.3)	(411.9)
Receipts from disposal of financial fixed assets		76.2	6.7
Cash outflow from capital expenditure and financial investment		(947.3)	(493.8)
Acquisitions and Disposals			
Cash paid on acquisitions	28(d)	(9.5)	(8.0)
Receipts from part disposal of subsidiary		41.9	—
Cash inflow/(outflow) from acquisitions and disposals		32.4	(8.0)
Cash outflow before use of liquid resources and financing		(440.6)	(197.8)
Management of Liquid Resources	28(b)	106.8	399.1
Financing			
Proceeds from issue of share capital		304.8	76.9
Purchase of treasury shares		—	—
Issue of loan notes		1,185.7	444.1
Repayment of loans		(555.7)	(496.0)
Bank borrowing		342.8	200.0
Cash inflow from financing		1,277.6	225.0
Net increase in cash		943.8	426.3
Reconciliation of Net Cash Flow to Movement in Net Debt			
Increase in cash for the period		943.8	426.3
Cash inflow from movement in liquid resources		(106.8)	(399.1)
		837.0	27.2
Other borrowing		(347.4)	(200.0)
Repayment of loans		557.6	512.4
Issue of loan notes		(1,185.7)	(444.1)
Change in net debt resulting from cash flows		(138.5)	(104.5)
Liquid resources acquired with subsidiary undertaking		—	214.2
Loans acquired with subsidiary undertaking		(0.3)	(363.7)
Non-cash movement — translation differences		(1.4)	(1.1)
Non-cash movement — notes		255.3	(54.4)
Non-cash movement — other		1.1	(1.3)
Decrease/(increase) in net debt	28(c)	116.2	(310.8)

EXPLORING THE WEB

BYP 13-5 *Purpose:* Use the Internet to view SEC filings.

Address: **biz.yahoo.com/i** (*or go to* **www.wiley.com/college/kimmel**)

Steps
1. Enter a company's name.
2. Choose **Quote**. Answer questions (a) and (b).
3. Choose **Profile**.
4. Choose **SEC Filings**. Answer questions (c) and (d).

Instructions
Answer the following questions.

(a) What company did you select?
(b) What is its stock symbol? What is its selling price?
(c) What recent SEC filings are available for your viewing?
(d) Which filing is the most recent? What is the date?

Critical Thinking

GROUP DECISION CASE

BYP 13-6   Rex Nord and Sara Smith are examining the following statement of cash flows for Collector Company for the year ended January 31, 2005.

COLLECTOR COMPANY
Statement of Cash Flows
For the Year Ended January 31, 2005

Sources of cash	
From sales of merchandise	$370,000
From sale of capital stock	420,000
From sale of investment (purchased below)	80,000
From depreciation	55,000
From issuance of note for truck	20,000
From interest on investments	6,000
Total sources of cash	951,000
Uses of cash	
For purchase of fixtures and equipment	340,000
For merchandise purchased for resale	258,000
For operating expenses (including depreciation)	160,000
For purchase of investment	75,000
For purchase of truck by issuance of note	20,000
For purchase of treasury stock	10,000
For interest on note payable	3,000
Total uses of cash	866,000
Net increase in cash	$ 85,000

Rex claims that Collector's statement of cash flows is an excellent portrayal of a superb first year with cash increasing $85,000. Sara replies that it was not a superb first year. Rather, she says, the year was an operating failure, that the statement is presented incorrectly, and that $85,000 is not the actual increase in cash. The cash balance at the beginning of the year was $140,000.

Instructions
With the class divided into groups, answer the following.
(a) With whom do you agree, Rex or Sara? Explain your position.
(b) Using the data provided, prepare a statement of cash flows in proper form using the indirect method. The only noncash items in the income statement are depreciation and the gain from the sale of the investment.

COMMUNICATION ACTIVITY

BYP 13-7 Kyle Benson, the owner-president of Computer Services Company, is unfamiliar with the statement of cash flows that you, as his accountant, prepared. He asks for further explanation.

Instructions

Write him a brief memo explaining the form and content of the statement of cash flows as shown in Illustration 13-14 (page 542).

RESEARCH ASSIGNMENT

BYP 13-8 The March 5, 2002, issue of the *Wall Street Journal* contains an article by Mark Maremont titled "'Cash Flow,' a Highly Touted Measure of Strength, Is Open to Interpretation."

Instructions

Read the article and answer the following questions.

(a) What does the article say is the "conventional wisdom" regarding the measurement of cash flow versus that of net income?
(b) Describe the two methods by which **Tyco** acquires customer contracts.
(c) Explain briefly how it is that the method by which Tyco acquires customer contracts can have a dramatic effect on its reported cash flow.
(d) What measure does Tyco's chief financial officer want investors to focus on, rather than reported earnings?

ETHICS CASE

BYP 13-9 On The Road Again Corp. is a medium-sized wholesaler of automotive parts. It has 10 stockholders who have been paid a total of $1 million in cash dividends for 8 consecutive years. The board's policy requires that, for this dividend to be declared, net cash provided by operating activities as reported in On The Road Again's current year's statement of cash flows must exceed $1 million. President and CEO Willie Nelson's job is secure so long as he produces annual operating cash flows to support the usual dividend.

At the end of the current year, controller Waylon Jennings presents president Willie Nelson with some disappointing news: The net cash provided by operating activities is calculated by the indirect method to be only $970,000. The president says to Waylon, "We must get that amount above $1 million. Isn't there some way to increase operating cash flow by another $30,000?" Waylon answers, "These figures were prepared by my assistant. I'll go back to my office and see what I can do." The president replies, "I know you won't let me down, Waylon."

Upon close scrutiny of the statement of cash flows, Waylon concludes that he can get the operating cash flows above $1 million by reclassifying a $60,000, 2-year note payable listed in the financing activities section as "Proceeds from bank loan—$60,000." He will report the note instead as "Increase in payables—$60,000" and treat it as an adjustment of net income in the operating activities section. He returns to the president, saying, "You can tell the board to declare their usual dividend. Our net cash flow provided by operating activities is $1,030,000." "Good man, Waylon! I knew I could count on you," exults the president.

Instructions

(a) Who are the stakeholders in this situation?
(b) Was there anything unethical about the president's actions? Was there anything unethical about the controller's actions?
(c) Are the board members or anyone else likely to discover the misclassification?

Answers to Self-Study Questions

1. c 2. b 3. a 4. c 5. d 6. b 7. c 8. a 9. d 10. b
11. c 12. d 13. a 14. d

Remember to go back to the Navigator box on the chapter-opening page and check off your completed work.

CHAPTER 14

Financial Statement Analysis: The Big Picture

STUDY OBJECTIVES

After studying this chapter, you should be able to:

1 Describe and apply horizontal analysis.

2 Describe and apply vertical analysis.

3 Identify and compute ratios used in analyzing a company's liquidity, solvency, and profitability.

4 Understand the concept of quality of earnings.

THE NAVIGATOR ✔

▶ Scan *Study Objectives* ☐

▶ Read *Feature Story* ☐

▶ Read *Preview* ☐

▶ Read text and answer *Before You Go On*
      p. 607 ☐   p. 609 ☐

▶ Work *Using the Decision Toolkit* ☐

▶ Review *Summary of Study Objectives* ☐

▶ Work *Demonstration Problem* ☐

▶ Answer *Self-Study Questions* ☐

▶ Complete *Assignments* ☐

FEATURE STORY

Making the Numbers

There it was again, perched atop *Fortune*'s "Most Admired Companies" list for the fifth year in a row. But when the guys who ran **General Electric** went out in public, they didn't exactly get to bask in adulation. Instead, they had to explain how their company was *not* like **Enron**, or **Global Crossing**, or **Tyco**.

At one level, that was a pretty easy argument to make. GE is not about to collapse or to break up. It has tons of cash, and its businesses generate upwards of a billion dollars every month. It is one of only a handful of companies with a triple-A credit rating. It makes real things like turbines and refrigerators that people spend real money to buy.

GE also has an enviable record of pleasing Wall Street. Quarter after quarter, year after year, GE's earnings come gushing in, usually at least 10% higher than the year before, and almost invariably in line with analysts' estimates.

This used to be seen as a good thing. "Making the numbers" became the most watched measure of corporate performance. By missing only once in the past ten years (by a penny, in the fourth quarter of 1997), GE ensured itself a hallowed place in the corporate hall of fame.

But as one analyst noted, "Smoking used to be chic and fashionable and cool; now it's not. The companies that reliably deliver 15 percent earnings growth year after year are the new smokers." All of which means that GE's chief executive, Jeffrey

Immelt, found himself having to tell interviewer after interviewer that no, he's not an earnings cheat.

"Would a miss be more honest?" Immelt asked, with exasperation in his voice. "I think that's terrible. That's where the world has gotten totally turned on its head, where somewhere I'd walk up to a podium and get a Nobel Peace Prize for saying 'I missed my numbers—aren't you proud of me?' "

Source: Adapted from Justin Fox, "What's So Great About GE?" *Fortune* (March 4, 2002), pp. 65–66.

✓ THE NAVIGATOR

On the World Wide Web
General Electric: www.ge.com

As indicated in our Feature Story, even the most admired companies in the United States are under attack regarding their earnings and disclosure practices. A climate of skepticism has caused many companies to lose billions of dollars in market value if there is even the slightest hint that the company is involved in some form of creative accounting. The purpose of this chapter is to explain the importance of **performance measurement** and to highlight the difficulties of developing **high-quality earnings numbers**, given the complexities of modern business transactions.

The content and organization of this chapter are as follows.

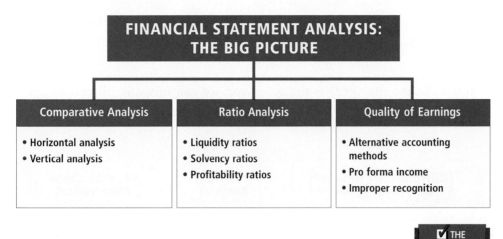

Comparative Analysis

In assessing the financial performance of a company, managers are interested in making comparisons from period to period. We rely on three types of comparisons to improve the decision usefulness of financial information.

1. **Intracompany basis.** Comparisons within a company are often useful to detect changes in financial relationships and significant trends. For example, a comparison of **Kellogg's** current year's cash amount with the prior year's cash amount shows either an increase or a decrease. Likewise, a comparison of Kellogg's year-end cash amount with the amount of its total assets at year-end shows the proportion of total assets in the form of cash.

2. **Intercompany basis.** Comparisons with other companies provide insight into a company's competitive position. For example, Kellogg's total sales for the year can be compared with the total sales of its competitors in the breakfast cereal area, such as **Quaker Oats** and **General Mills**.

3. **Industry averages.** Comparisons with industry averages provide information about a company's relative position within the industry. For example, Kellogg's financial data can be compared with the averages for its industry compiled by financial ratings organizations such as **Dun & Bradstreet**, **Moody's**, and **Standard & Poor's**, or with information provided on the Internet by organizations such as **Yahoo!** on its financial site.

Three basic tools are used in financial statement analysis to highlight the significance of financial statement data:

1. Horizontal analysis
2. Vertical analysis
3. Ratio analysis

In the remainder of this section, we introduce horizontal and vertical analysis. In the next section we review ratio analysis in some detail. Throughout, we will analyze the financial performance of one company, **Kellogg Company**.

HORIZONTAL ANALYSIS

STUDY OBJECTIVE

1

Describe and apply
horizontal analysis.

Horizontal analysis, also known as **trend analysis**, is a technique for evaluating a series of financial statement data over a period of time. Its purpose is to determine the increase or decrease that has taken place, expressed as either an amount or a percentage. For example, here are recent net sales figures (in millions) of **Kellogg Company**:

2003	2002	2001	2000	1999
$8,811.5	$8,304.1	$7,548.4	$6,086.7	$6,156.5

If we assume that 1999 is the base year, we can measure all percentage increases or decreases relative to this base-period amount with the formula shown in Illustration 14-1.

Illustration 14-1 Horizontal analysis—computation of changes since base period

$$\left(\begin{array}{c}\text{Current-Year Amount}\\-\text{Base-Year Amount}\end{array}\right) \div \begin{array}{c}\text{Base-Year}\\\text{Amount}\end{array} = \begin{array}{c}\text{Change Since}\\\text{Base Period}\end{array}$$

For example, we can determine that net sales for Kellogg Company decreased approximately 1.1% [($6,086.7 − $6,156.5) ÷ $6,156.5] from 1999 to 2000. Similarly, we can also determine that net sales increased by 43.1% [($8,811.5 − $6,156.5) ÷ $6,156.5] from 1999 to 2003.

Alternatively, we can express current-year sales as a percentage of the base period. To do so, we would divide the current-year amount by the base-year amount, as shown in Illustration 14-2.

Illustration 14-2 Horizontal analysis—computation of current year in relation to base year

$$\text{Current-Year Amount} \div \begin{array}{c}\text{Base-Year}\\\text{Amount}\end{array} = \begin{array}{c}\text{Current Results in}\\\text{Relation to Base Period}\end{array}$$

Current-period sales expressed as a percentage of the base period for each of the five years, using 1999 as the base period, are shown in Illustration 14-3.

Illustration 14-3 Horizontal analysis of net sales

KELLOGG COMPANY Net Sales (in millions) Base Period 1999				
2003	**2002**	**2001**	**2000**	**1999**
$8,811.5	$8,304.1	$7,548.4	$6,086.7	$6,156.5
143.13%	134.88%	122.61%	99%	100%

The large increase in net sales during 2001 would raise questions regarding possible reasons for such a significant change. Kellogg's 2001 notes to the financial statements explain that "the Company completed its acquisition of

Keebler Foods Company" during 2001. This major acquisition would help explain the increase in sales highlighted by horizontal analysis.

To further illustrate horizontal analysis, we use the financial statements of **Kellogg Company**. Its two-year condensed balance sheets for 2003 and 2002, showing dollar and percentage changes, are presented in Illustration 14-4.

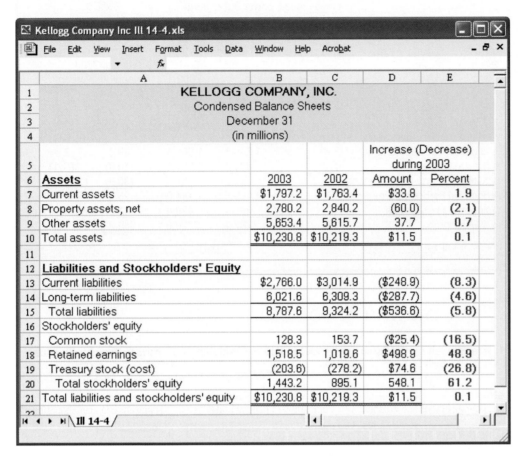

Illustration 14-4   Horizontal analysis of a balance sheet

Helpful Hint It is difficult to comprehend the significance of a change when only the dollar amount of change is examined. When the change is expressed in percentage form, it is easier to grasp the true magnitude of the change.

The comparative balance sheets show that few changes occurred in Kellogg's financial position from 2002 to 2003. In the assets section, current assets increased $33.8 million, or 1.9% ($33.8 ÷ $1,763.4), and property assets (net) decreased $60.0 million, or 2.1%. Other assets increased $37.7, or 0.7%. In the liabilities section, current liabilities decreased $248.9 million, or 8.3%, and long-term liabilities decreased $287.7 million, or 4.6%. In the stockholders' equity section, we find that retained earnings increased $498.9 million, or 48.9%.

Presented in Illustration 14-5 (page 592) is a two-year comparative income statement of Kellogg Company for 2003 and 2002 in a condensed format.

Horizontal analysis of the income statements shows the following changes: Net sales increased $507.4 million, or 6.1% ($507.4 ÷ $8,304.1). Cost of goods sold increased $329.9 million, or 7.2% ($329.9 ÷ $4,569.0). Selling and administrative expenses increased $141.5 million, or 6.4% ($141.5 ÷ $2,227.0). Overall, gross profit increased 4.8% and net income increased 9.2%. The increase in net income can be attributed to the decreases in interest expense and income tax expense.

The measurement of changes from period to period in percentages is relatively straightforward and quite useful. However, complications can result in making the computations. If an item has no value in a base year or preceding year and a value in the next year, no percentage change can be computed. And if a negative amount appears in the base or preceding period and a positive amount exists the following year, no percentage change can be computed.

Illustration 14-5 Horizontal analysis of an income statement

Helpful Hint Note that, in a horizontal analysis, while the amount column is additive (the total is $66.2 million), the percentage column is not additive (9.2% is **not** a total).

Kellogg Company Inc III 14-5.xls

File   Edit   View   Insert   Format   Tools   Data   Window   Help   Acrobat

KELLOGG COMPANY, INC.
Condensed Income Statements
For the Years Ended December 31
(in millions)

	2003	2002	Increase (Decrease) during 2003 Amount	Increase (Decrease) during 2003 Percent
Net sales	$8,811.5	$8,304.1	$507.4	6.1
Cost of goods sold	4,898.9	4,569.0	329.9	7.2
Gross profit	3,912.6	3,735.1	177.5	4.8
Selling and administrative expenses	2,368.5	2,227.0	141.5	6.4
Income from operations	1,544.1	1,508.1	36.0	2.4
Interest expense	371.4	391.2	(19.8)	(5.1)
Other income (expense), net	(3.2)	27.4	(30.6)	(111.7)
Income before income taxes	1,169.5	1,144.3	25.2	2.2
Income tax expense	382.4	423.4	(41.0)	(9.7)
Net income	$787.1	$720.9	$66.2	9.2

III 14-5

DECISION TOOLKIT

Decision Checkpoints	Info Needed for Decision	Tool to Use for Decision	How to Evaluate Results
How do the company's financial position and operating results compare with those of the previous period?	Income statement and balance sheet	Comparative financial statements should be prepared over at least two years, with the first year reported being the base year. Changes in each line item relative to the base year should be presented both by amount and by percentage. This is called horizontal analysis.	Significant changes should be investigated to determine the reason for the change.

VERTICAL ANALYSIS

STUDY OBJECTIVE

2

Describe and apply vertical analysis.

Vertical analysis, also called **common-size analysis**, is a technique for evaluating financial statement data that expresses each item in a financial statement as a percent of a base amount. For example, on a balance sheet we might say that current assets are 22% of total assets (total assets being the base amount). Or on an income statement we might say that selling expenses are 16% of net sales (net sales being the base amount).

Presented in Illustration 14-6 (page 593) is the comparative balance sheet of **Kellogg** for 2003 and 2002, analyzed vertically. The base for the asset items is **total assets**, and the base for the liability and stockholders' equity items is **total liabilities and stockholders' equity**.

In addition to showing the relative size of each category on the balance sheet, vertical analysis may show the percentage change in the individual asset, liability, and stockholders' equity items. In this case, the dollar amount of total assets increased slightly, $11.5 million from 2002 to 2003. The individual assets also changed only slightly. Total liabilities decreased $536.6 million from 2002 to

Illustration 14-6   Vertical analysis of a balance sheet

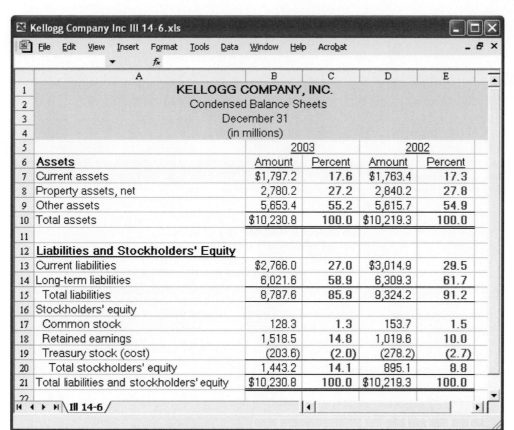

Kellogg Company Inc III 14-6.xls				
	A	B	C	D	E

	A	B	C	D	E
1	**KELLOGG COMPANY, INC.**				
2	Condensed Balance Sheets				
3	December 31				
4	(in millions)				
5		2003		2002	
6	**Assets**	Amount	Percent	Amount	Percent
7	Current assets	$1,797.2	17.6	$1,763.4	17.3
8	Property assets, net	2,780.2	27.2	2,840.2	27.8
9	Other assets	5,653.4	55.2	5,615.7	54.9
10	Total assets	$10,230.8	100.0	$10,219.3	100.0
11					
12	**Liabilities and Stockholders' Equity**				
13	Current liabilities	$2,766.0	27.0	$3,014.9	29.5
14	Long-term liabilities	6,021.6	58.9	6,309.3	61.7
15	Total liabilities	8,787.6	85.9	9,324.2	91.2
16	Stockholders' equity				
17	Common stock	128.3	1.3	153.7	1.5
18	Retained earnings	1,518.5	14.8	1,019.6	10.0
19	Treasury stock (cost)	(203.6)	(2.0)	(278.2)	(2.7)
20	Total stockholders' equity	1,443.2	14.1	895.1	8.8
21	Total liabilities and stockholders' equity	$10,230.8	100.0	$10,219.3	100.0
22					

2003. Total liabilities decreased from 91.2% of total liabilities and stockholders' equity to 85.9% in 2003. Total stockholders' equity increased $548.1 from 2002 to 2003, primarily because of an increase in retained earnings, which increased from 10.0% to 14.8% of total liabilities and stockholders' equity.

Vertical analysis of the comparative income statements of Kellogg, shown in Illustration 14-7, reveals that cost of goods sold **as a percentage of net sales**

Illustration 14-7   Vertical analysis of an income statement

Kellogg Company Inc III 14-7.xls					

	A	B	C	D	E
1	**KELLOGG COMPANY, INC.**				
2	Condensed Income Statements				
3	For the Years Ended December 31				
4	(in millions)				
5		2003		2002	
6		Amount	Percent*	Amount	Percent*
7	Net sales	$8,811.5	100.0	$8,304.1	100.0
8	Cost of goods sold	4,898.9	55.6	4,569.0	55.0
9	Gross profit	3,912.6	44.4	3,735.1	45.0
10	Selling and administrative expenses	2,368.5	26.9	2,227.0	26.8
11	Income from operations	1,544.1	17.5	1,508.1	18.2
12	Interest expense	371.4	4.2	391.2	4.7
13	Other income (expense), net	(3.2)	(0.1)	27.4	0.3
14	Income before income taxes	1,169.5	13.2	1,144.3	13.8
15	Income tax expense	382.4	4.3	423.4	5.1
16	Net income	$787.1	8.9	$720.9	8.7
17	* Numbers have been rounded to total 100%.				

increased slightly from 55.0% to 55.6%, and selling and administrative expenses increased only 0.1%. Net income as a percent of net sales increased from 8.7% to 8.9%. Kellogg's minor increase in net income as a percentage of sales is due primarily to the decrease in income tax expense as a percent of sales.

Vertical analysis also enables you to compare companies of different sizes. For example, one of Kellogg's main competitors is **General Mills**. Using vertical analysis, we can more meaningfully compare the condensed income statements of Kellogg and General Mills, as shown in Illustration 14-8.

Illustration 14-8 Inter-company comparison by vertical analysis

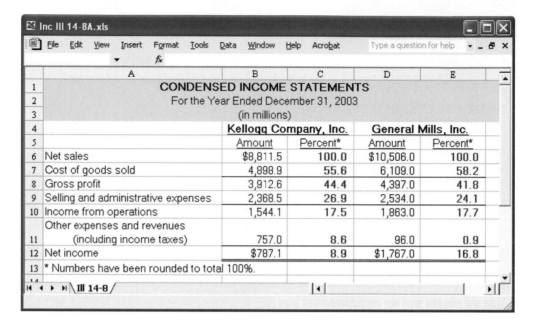

Although Kellogg's net sales are 16% less than those of General Mills, vertical analysis eliminates the impact of this size difference for our analysis. Kellogg has a higher gross profit, 44.4%, compared to 41.8% for General Mills, but Kellogg's selling and administrative expenses are 26.9% of net sales, while those of General Mills are 24.1% of net sales. Looking at income from operations, we see that the companies report similar percentages: Kellogg's income from operations as a percentage of net sales is 17.5%, compared to 17.7% for General Mills.

DECISION TOOLKIT

Decision Checkpoints	Info Needed for Decision	Tool to Use for Decision	How to Evaluate Results
How do the relationships between items in this year's financial statements compare with those of last year or those of competitors?	Income statement and balance sheet	Each line item on the income statement should be presented as a percentage of net sales, and each line item on the balance sheet should be presented as a percentage of total assets or total liabilities and stockholders' equity. These percentages should be investigated for differences either across years in the same company or in the same year across different companies. This is called vertical analysis.	Any significant differences either across years or between companies should be investigated to determine the cause.

Ratio Analysis

Ratios are used for evaluating the financial health and performance of a company. We will provide a comprehensive review of frequently used ratios and discuss some important relationships among them.

The financial information in Illustrations 14-9 through 14-12 will be used to calculate **Kellogg**'s 2003 ratios. You can use these data to review the computations.

STUDY OBJECTIVE

3

Identify and compute ratios used in analyzing a company's liquidity, solvency, and profitability.

Illustration 14-9 Kellogg Company's balance sheet

KELLOGG COMPANY, INC.
Balance Sheets
December 31
(in millions)

Assets	2003	2002
Current assets		
Cash and short-term investments	$ 141.2	$ 100.6
Accounts receivable, net	754.8	741.0
Inventories	649.8	603.2
Prepaid expenses and other current assets	251.4	318.6
Total current assets	$ 1,797.2	$ 1,763.4
Property assets, net	2,780.2	2,840.2
Intangibles and other assets	5,653.4	5,615.7
Total assets	$10,230.8	$10,219.3
Liabilities and Stockholders' Equity		
Current liabilities	$ 2,766.0	$ 3,014.9
Long-term liabilities	6,021.6	6,309.3
Stockholders' equity—common	1,443.2	895.1
Total liabilities and stockholders' equity	$10,230.8	$10,219.3

Illustration 14-10 Kellogg Company's income statement

KELLOGG COMPANY, INC.
Condensed Income Statements
For the Years Ended December 31
(in millions)

	2003	2002
Net sales	$8,811.5	$8,304.1
Cost of goods sold	4,898.9	4,569.0
Gross profit	3,912.6	3,735.1
Selling and administrative expenses	2,368.5	2,227.0
Income from operations	$1,544.1	1,508.1
Interest expense	371.4	391.2
Other income (expense), net	(3.2)	27.4
Income before income taxes	1,169.5	1,144.3
Income tax expense	382.4	423.4
Net income	$ 787.1	$ 720.9

Illustration 14-11 Kellogg Company's statement of cash flows

KELLOGG COMPANY, INC.
Condensed Statements of Cash Flows
For the Years Ended December 31
(in millions)

	2003	2002
Cash flows from operating activities		
Cash receipts from operating activities	$ 8,797.7	$8,325.4
Cash payments for operating activities	7,626.7	7,325.5
Net cash provided by operating activities	1,171.0	999.9
Cash flows from investing activities		
Purchases of property, plant, and equipment	(247.2)	(255.7)
Other investing activities	28.2	66.9
Net cash used in investing activities	(219.0)	(188.8)
Cash flows from financing activities		
Issuance of common stock	31.0	(0.1)
Issuance of debt	773.6	354.9
Reductions of debt	(1,331.6)	(886.6)
Payment of dividends	(412.4)	(412.6)
Net cash provided by (used in) financing activities	(939.4)	(944.4)
Other	28.0	2.1
Increase (decrease) in cash and cash equivalents	40.6	(131.2)
Cash and cash equivalents at beginning of year	100.6	231.8
Cash and cash equivalents at end of year	$ 141.2	$ 100.6

Illustration 14-12 Additional information for Kellogg Company

Additional information

	2003	2002
Average number of shares (millions)	408.8	407.3
Stock price at year-end	$ 37.6	$ 32.8

For analysis of the primary financial statements, ratios can be classified into three types:

1. **Liquidity ratios**: Measures of the short-term ability of the enterprise to pay its maturing obligations and to meet unexpected needs for cash.
2. **Solvency ratios**: Measures of the ability of the enterprise to survive over a long period of time.
3. **Profitability ratios**: Measures of the income or operating success of an enterprise for a given period of time.

As a tool of analysis, ratios can provide clues to underlying conditions that may not be apparent from an inspection of the individual components of a particular ratio. But a single ratio by itself is not very meaningful. Accordingly, in this discussion we use the three comparisons listed below.

1. **Intracompany comparisons** covering two years for Kellogg Company (using comparative financial information from Illustrations 14-9, 14-10, and 14-11).
2. **Intercompany comparisons** using **General Mills** as one of Kellogg's principal competitors.

3. **Industry average comparisons** based on **Reuters** ratios for food processors. For some of the ratios that we use, industry comparisons are not available. (These are denoted "na.")

LIQUIDITY RATIOS

Liquidity ratios measure the short-term ability of the enterprise to pay its maturing obligations and to meet unexpected needs for cash. Short-term creditors such as bankers and suppliers are particularly interested in assessing liquidity. The measures that can be used to determine the enterprise's short-term debt-paying ability are the current ratio, the current cash debt coverage ratio, the receivables turnover ratio, the average collection period, the inventory turnover ratio, and days in inventory.

1. **Current ratio.** The current ratio expresses the relationship of current assets to current liabilities, computed by dividing current assets by current liabilities. It is widely used for evaluating a company's liquidity and short-term debt-paying ability. The 2003 and 2002 current ratios for Kellogg and comparative data are shown in Illustration 14-13.

Illustration 14-13 Current ratio

Ratio	Formula	Indicates:	Kellogg 2003	Kellogg 2002	General Mills 2003	Industry 2003
Current ratio	Current assets / Current liabilities	Short-term debt-paying ability	.65	.58	.92	1.50

What do the measures tell us? **Kellogg's** 2003 current ratio of .65 means that for every dollar of current liabilities, Kellogg has $0.65 of current assets. We sometimes state such ratios as .65:1 to reinforce this interpretation. Kellogg's current ratio—and therefore its liquidity—increased in 2003. It is well below the industry average and that of **General Mills**.

Business Insight
Management Perspective

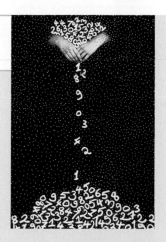

The apparent simplicity of the current ratio can have real-world limitations because adding equal amounts to both the numerator and the denominator causes the ratio to decrease.

Assume, for example, that a company has $2,000,000 of current assets and $1,000,000 of current liabilities; its current ratio is 2:1. If it purchases $1,000,000 of inventory on account, it will have $3,000,000 of current assets and $2,000,000 of current liabilities; its current ratio decreases to 1.5:1. If, instead, the company pays off $500,000 of its current liabilities, it will have $1,500,000 of current assets and $500,000 of current liabilities; its current ratio increases to 3:1. Thus, any trend analysis should be done with care because the ratio is susceptible to quick changes and is easily influenced by management.

2. **Current cash debt coverage ratio.** A disadvantage of the current ratio is that it uses year-end balances of current asset and current liability accounts. These year-end balances may not be representative of the company's current position during most of the year. A ratio that partially corrects for this

problem is the ratio of cash provided by operating activities to average current liabilities, called the **current cash debt coverage ratio**. Because it uses cash provided by operating activities rather than a balance at one point in time, it may provide a better representation of liquidity. Kellogg's current cash debt coverage ratio is shown in Illustration 14-14.

Illustration 14-14 Current cash debt coverage ratio

Ratio	Formula	Indicates:	Kellogg 2003	Kellogg 2002	General Mills 2003	Industry 2003
Current cash debt coverage ratio	Cash provided by operating activities / Average current liabilities	Short-term debt-paying ability (cash basis)	.41	.38	.35	na

Like the current ratio, this ratio increased in 2003 for **Kellogg**. Is the coverage adequate? Probably so. Kellogg's operating cash flow coverage of average current liabilities is higher than that of **General Mills**, and it exceeds a commonly accepted threshold of .40. No industry comparison is available.

3. **Receivables turnover ratio.** Liquidity may be measured by how quickly certain assets can be converted to cash. Low values of the previous ratios can sometimes be compensated for if some of the company's current assets are highly liquid. How liquid, for example, are the receivables? The ratio used to assess the liquidity of the receivables is the **receivables turnover ratio**, which measures the number of times, on average, receivables are collected during the period. The receivables turnover ratio is computed by dividing net credit sales (net sales less cash sales) by average net receivables during the year. The receivables turnover ratio for Kellogg is shown in Illustration 14-15.

Illustration 14-15 Receivables turnover ratio

Ratio	Formula	Indicates:	Kellogg 2003	Kellogg 2002	General Mills 2003	Industry 2003
Receivables turnover ratio	Net credit sales / Average net receivables	Liquidity of receivables	11.8	11.0	8.5	11.2

We have assumed that all **Kellogg**'s sales are credit sales. The receivables turnover ratio for Kellogg rose in 2003. The turnover of 11.8 times compares favorably with the industry median of 11.2, and is much higher than **General Mills**' turnover of 8.5.

Business Insight
Management Perspective

In some cases, the receivables turnover ratio may be misleading. Some companies, especially large retail chains, issue their own credit cards. They encourage customers to use these cards, and they slow their collections in order to earn a healthy return on the outstanding receivables in the form of interest at rates of 18% to 22%. In general, however, the faster the turnover, the greater the reliance that can be placed on the current ratio for assessing liquidity.

4. **Average collection period.**   A popular variant of the receivables turnover ratio converts it into an **average collection period** in days. This is done by dividing the receivables turnover ratio into 365 days. The average collection period for Kellogg is shown in Illustration 14-16.

Illustration 14-16   Average collection period

Ratio	Formula	Indicates:	Kellogg 2003	Kellogg 2002	General Mills 2003	Industry 2003
Average collection period	365 days / Receivables turnover ratio	Liquidity of receivables and collection success	30.9	33.2	42.9	32.6

Kellogg's 2003 receivables turnover of 11.8 times is divided into 365 days to obtain approximately 30.9 days. This means that the average collection period for receivables is about 31 days. Analysts frequently use the average collection period to assess the effectiveness of a company's credit and collection policies. The general rule is that the collection period should not greatly exceed the credit term period (i.e., the time allowed for payment). **General Mills'** average collection period is significantly longer than those of Kellogg and the industry. This difference may be due to less aggressive collection practices, but it is more likely due to a difference in credit terms granted.

5. **Inventory turnover ratio.**   The **inventory turnover ratio** measures the number of times on average the inventory is sold during the period. Its purpose is to measure the liquidity of the inventory. The inventory turnover ratio is computed by dividing the cost of goods sold by the average inventory during the period. Unless seasonal factors are significant, average inventory can be computed from the beginning and ending inventory balances. Kellogg's inventory turnover ratio is shown in Illustration 14-17.

Illustration 14-17   Inventory turnover ratio

Ratio	Formula	Indicates:	Kellogg 2003	Kellogg 2002	General Mills 2003	Industry 2003
Inventory turnover ratio	Cost of goods sold / Average inventory	Liquidity of inventory	7.8	7.8	5.7	6.2

Kellogg's inventory turnover ratio was unchanged in 2003. The turnover ratio of 7.8 times is higher than the industry average of 6.2 and significantly better than **General Mills'** 5.7. Generally, the faster the inventory turnover, the less cash is tied up in inventory and the less the chance of inventory becoming obsolete. Of course, a downside of high inventory turnover is that the company can run out of inventory when it is needed.

6. **Days in inventory.**   A variant of the inventory turnover ratio is the **days in inventory**, which measures the average number of days it takes to sell the inventory. The days in inventory for Kellogg is shown in Illustration 14-18.

Illustration 14-18   Days in inventory

Ratio	Formula	Indicates:	Kellogg 2003	Kellogg 2002	General Mills 2003	Industry 2003
Days in inventory	365 days / Inventory turnover ratio	Liquidity of inventory and inventory management	46.8	46.8	64.0	58.9

Kellogg's 2003 inventory turnover ratio of 7.8 divided into 365 is approximately 46.8 days. An average selling time of 47 days is faster than the industry average and significantly faster than that of **General Mills.** Some of this difference might be explained by differences in product lines across the two companies, although in many ways the types of products of these two companies are quite similar.

Inventory turnover ratios vary considerably among industries. For example, grocery store chains have a turnover of 10 times and an average selling period of 37 days. In contrast, jewelry stores have an average turnover of 1.3 times and an average selling period of 281 days. Within a company there may even be significant differences in inventory turnover among different types of products. Thus, in a grocery store the turnover of perishable items such as produce, meats, and dairy products is faster than the turnover of soaps and detergents.

To conclude, nearly all of these liquidity measures suggest that Kellogg's liquidity increased during 2003. Its liquidity appears acceptable when compared to the industry and to General Mills.

SOLVENCY RATIOS

Solvency ratios measure the ability of the enterprise to survive over a long period of time. Long-term creditors and stockholders are interested in a company's long-run solvency, particularly its ability to pay interest as it comes due and to repay the face value of debt at maturity. The debt to total assets ratio, the times interest earned ratio, and the cash debt coverage ratio provide information about debt-paying ability. In addition, free cash flow provides information about the company's solvency and its ability to pay additional dividends or invest in new projects.

7. **Debt to total assets ratio.** The **debt to total assets ratio** measures the percentage of the total assets provided by creditors. It is computed by dividing total liabilities (both current and long-term) by total assets. This ratio indicates the degree of financial leveraging. It also provides some indication of the company's ability to withstand losses without impairing the interests of its creditors. The higher the percentage of debt to total assets, the greater the risk that the company may be unable to meet its maturing obligations. The lower the ratio, the more equity "buffer" is available to creditors if the company sustains losses. Thus, from the creditors' point of view, a low ratio of debt to total assets is desirable. Kellogg's debt to total assets ratio is shown in Illustration 14-19.

Illustration 14-19 Debt to total assets ratio

Ratio	Formula	Indicates:	Kellogg 2003	Kellogg 2002	General Mills 2003	Industry 2003
Debt to total assets ratio	Total liabilities / Total assets	Percentage of total assets provided by creditors	.86	.91	.77	.54

Kellogg's 2003 ratio of .86 means that creditors have provided financing sufficient to cover 86% of the company's total assets. Alternatively, it says that Kellogg would have to liquidate 86% of its assets at their book value in order to pay off all of its debts. Kellogg's 86% is above the industry average of 54% as well as the 77% ratio of **General Mills.** Kellogg's solvency increased during the year. In that time, Kellogg's use of debt financing changed in two ways: As seen in Illustration 14-4 (page 591), Kellogg increased its equity by 61%, and its debt decreased slightly. Both these factors increased its solvency.

The adequacy of this ratio is often judged in light of the company's earnings. Generally, companies with relatively stable earnings, such as public utilities, have higher debt to total assets ratios than cyclical companies with widely fluctuating earnings, such as many high-tech companies.

Another ratio with a similar meaning is the **debt to equity ratio**. It shows the relative use of borrowed funds (total liabilities) compared with resources invested by the owners. Because this ratio can be computed in several ways, care should be taken when making comparisons. Debt may be defined to include only the noncurrent portion of liabilities, and intangible assets may be excluded from stockholders' equity (which would equal tangible net worth). If debt and assets are defined as above (all liabilities and all assets), then when the debt to total assets ratio equals 50%, the debt to equity ratio is 1 : 1.

8. **Times interest earned ratio.**   The **times interest earned ratio** (also called interest coverage) indicates the company's ability to meet interest payments as they come due. It is computed by dividing income before interest expense and income taxes by interest expense. Note that this ratio uses income before interest expense and income taxes because this amount represents what is available to cover interest. Kellogg's times interest earned ratio is shown in Illustration 14-20.

Illustration 14-20   Times interest earned ratio

Ratio	Formula	Indicates:	Kellogg 2003	Kellogg 2002	General Mills 2003	Industry 2003
Times interest earned ratio	$\dfrac{\text{Net Income} + \text{Interest expense} + \text{Tax expense}}{\text{Interest expense}}$	Ability to meet interest payments as they come due	4.1	3.9	3.4	5.0

For **Kellogg** the 2003 interest coverage was 4.1, which indicates that income before interest and taxes was 4.1 times the amount needed for interest expense. This exceeds the rate for **General Mills**, but it is less than the average rate for the industry. The debt to total assets ratio decreased for Kellogg during 2003, and its times interest earned ratio increased. These ratios indicate that Kellogg is better able to service its debt.

9. **Cash debt coverage ratio.**   The ratio of cash provided by operating activities to average total liabilities, called the **cash debt coverage ratio**, is a cash-basis measure of solvency. This ratio indicates a company's ability to repay its liabilities from cash generated from operating activities without having to liquidate the assets used in its operations. Illustration 14-21 shows Kellogg's cash debt coverage ratio.

Illustration 14-21   Cash debt coverage ratio

Ratio	Formula	Indicates:	Kellogg 2003	Kellogg 2002	General Mills 2003	Industry 2003
Cash debt coverage ratio	$\dfrac{\text{Cash provided by operating activities}}{\text{Average total liabilities}}$	Long-term debt-paying ability (cash basis)	.13	.11	.12	na

An industry average for this measure is not available. **Kellogg**'s .13 is slightly higher than **General Mills**' .12, and it did increase from .11 in 2002. One way of interpreting this ratio is to say that net cash generated from one year of operations would be sufficient to pay off 13% of Kellogg's total liabilities. If 13% of this year's liabilities were retired each year, it would take slightly less than 8 years to retire all of its debt. It would take General Mills slightly more than 8 years to do so. A general rule of thumb is that a measure above .20 is acceptable.

10. **Free cash flow.**   One indication of a company's solvency, as well as of its ability to pay dividends or expand operations, is the amount of excess cash it generated after investing to maintain its current productive capacity and paying dividends. This amount is referred to as **free cash flow**. For example, assume that a company generates $100,000 of cash from operating activities but spends $30,000 to maintain and replace its productive facilities and pays $10,000 in dividends. The company will then have $60,000 to use, either to expand operations or to pay additional dividends. Kellogg's free cash flow is shown in Illustration 14-22.

Illustration 14-22   Free cash flow

| | | | | | Kellogg | | General Mills | Industry |
Ratio	Formula			Indicates:	2003	2002	2003	2003
Free cash flow	Cash provided by operating activities	− Capital expenditures	− Cash dividends	Cash available for paying dividends or expanding operations	$511.4 *(in millions)*	$331.6	$514.0 *(in millions)*	na

Kellogg's free cash flow increased considerably from 2002 to 2003. The free cash flow amounts indicate that Kellogg has the ability to expand operations or pay additional dividends.

PROFITABILITY RATIOS

Profitability ratios measure the income or operating success of an enterprise for a given period of time. A company's income, or the lack of it, affects its ability to obtain debt and equity financing, its liquidity position, and its ability to grow. As a consequence, creditors and investors alike are interested in evaluating profitability. Profitability is frequently used as the ultimate test of management's operating effectiveness.

The relationships among measures of profitability are very important. Understanding them can help management determine where to focus its efforts to improve profitability. Illustration 14-23 diagrams these relationships. Our discussion of **Kellogg**'s profitability is structured around this diagram.

Illustration 14-23
Relationships among profitability measures

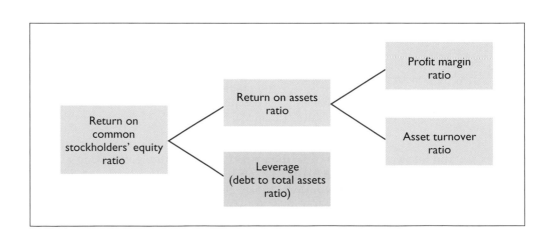

11. **Return on common stockholders' equity ratio.** A widely used measure of profitability from the common stockholder's viewpoint is the **return on common stockholders' equity ratio**. This ratio shows how many dollars of net income were earned for each dollar invested by the owners. It is computed by dividing net income minus any preferred stock dividends—that is, income available to common stockholders—by average common stockholders' equity. The return on common stockholders' equity for Kellogg is shown in Illustration 14-24.

Illustration 14-24 Return on common stockholders' equity ratio

Ratio	Formula	Indicates:	Kellogg 2003	Kellogg 2002	General Mills 2003	Industry 2003
Return on common stockholders' equity ratio	$\dfrac{\text{Net income} - \text{Preferred stock dividends}}{\text{Average common stockholders' equity}}$	Profitability of common stockholders' investment	.67	.82	.24	.24

Kellogg's 2003 rate of return on common stockholders' equity is unusually high at 67%, considering an industry average and **General Mills**' return of 24%. In the subsequent sections we investigate the causes of this high return.

12. **Return on assets ratio.** The return on common stockholders' equity ratio is affected by two factors: the **return on assets ratio** and the degree of leverage. The return on assets ratio measures the overall profitability of assets in terms of the income earned on each dollar invested in assets. It is computed by dividing net income by average total assets. Kellogg's return on assets ratio is shown in Illustration 14-25.

Illustration 14-25 Return on assets ratio

Ratio	Formula	Indicates:	Kellogg 2003	Kellogg 2002	General Mills 2003	Industry 2003
Return on assets ratio	$\dfrac{\text{Net income}}{\text{Average total assets}}$	Overall profitability of assets	.08	.07	.05	.07

Kellogg had an 8% return on assets in 2003. This rate is higher than that of **General Mills** but close to the industry average.

Note that Kellogg's rate of return on stockholders' equity (67%) is substantially higher than its rate of return on assets (8%). The reason is that Kellogg has made effective use of **leverage**. **Leveraging** or **trading on the equity** at a gain means that the company has borrowed money at a lower rate of interest than the rate of return it earns on the assets it purchased with the borrowed funds. Leverage enables management to use money supplied by nonowners to increase the return to owners.

A comparison of the rate of return on assets with the rate of interest paid for borrowed money indicates the profitability of trading on the equity. If you borrow money at 8% and your rate of return on assets is 11%, you are trading on the equity at a gain. Note, however, that trading on the equity is a two-way street: For example, if you borrow money at 11% and earn only 8% on it, you are trading on the equity at a loss.

Kellogg earns more on its borrowed funds than it has to pay in interest. Thus, the return to stockholders exceeds the return on the assets because of the positive benefit of leverage.

13. **Profit margin ratio.** The return on assets ratio is affected by two factors, the first of which is the profit margin ratio. The **profit margin ratio**, or rate of return on sales, is a measure of the percentage of each dollar of sales that results in net income. It is computed by dividing net income by net sales for the period. Kellogg's profit margin ratio is shown in Illustration 14-26.

Illustration 14-26   Profit margin ratio

Ratio	Formula	Indicates:	Kellogg 2003	Kellogg 2002	General Mills 2003	Industry 2003
Profit margin ratio	Net income / Net sales	Net income generated by each dollar of sales	.09	.09	.09	.08

Kellogg's profit margin ratio of 9% was unchanged from 2002 to 2003 and equal to that of **General Mills**. Its profit margin ratio was higher than the industry average of 8%.

High-volume (high inventory turnover) enterprises such as grocery stores and pharmacy chains generally have low profit margins, whereas low-volume enterprises such as jewelry stores and airplane manufacturers have high profit margins.

14. **Asset turnover ratio.** The other factor that affects the return on assets ratio is the asset turnover ratio. The **asset turnover ratio** measures how efficiently a company uses its assets to generate sales. It is determined by dividing net sales by average total assets for the period. The resulting number shows the dollars of sales produced by each dollar invested in assets. Illustration 14-27 shows the asset turnover ratio for Kellogg.

Illustration 14-27   Asset turnover ratio

Ratio	Formula	Indicates:	Kellogg 2003	Kellogg 2002	General Mills 2003	Industry 2003
Asset turnover ratio	Net sales / Average total assets	How efficiently assets are used to generate sales	.86	.81	.60	1.06

The asset turnover ratio shows that in 2003 **Kellogg** generated sales of $0.86 for each dollar it had invested in assets. The ratio increased from 2002 to 2003. Kellogg's asset turnover ratio is below the industry average of 1.06 times but above **General Mills'** ratio of .60.

Asset turnover ratios vary considerably among industries. The average asset turnover for utility companies is .45, for example, while the grocery store industry has an average asset turnover of 3.49.

In summary, Kellogg's return on assets ratio increased from 7% in 2002 to 8% in 2003. Underlying this slight increase was an improvement in the sales-generating efficiency of its assets (as measured by the asset turnover ratio), while the profitability on each dollar of sales (as measured by profit margin ratio) remained unchanged. The combined effects of profit margin and asset turnover on return on assets for Kellogg can be analyzed as shown in Illustration 14-28 on the next page.

Illustration 14-28 Composition of return on assets ratio

Ratios:	Profit Margin	×	Asset Turnover	=	Return on Assets
	$\dfrac{\text{Net Income}}{\text{Net Sales}}$	×	$\dfrac{\text{Net Sales}}{\text{Average Total Assets}}$	=	$\dfrac{\text{Net Income}}{\text{Average Total Assets}}$
Kellogg					
2003	9%	×	.86 times	=	8%
2002	9%	×	.81 times	=	7%

15. **Gross profit rate.** Two factors strongly influence the profit margin ratio. One is the gross profit rate. The **gross profit rate** is determined by dividing gross profit (net sales less cost of goods sold) by net sales. This rate indicates a company's ability to maintain an adequate selling price above its cost of goods sold. As an industry becomes more competitive, this ratio declines. For example, in the early years of the personal computer industry, gross profit rates were quite high. Today, because of increased competition and a belief that most brands of personal computers are similar in quality, gross profit rates have become thin. Gross profit rates should be closely monitored over time. Illustration 14-29 shows Kellogg's gross profit rate.

Illustration 14-29 Gross profit rate

Ratio	Formula	Indicates:	Kellogg 2003	Kellogg 2002	General Mills 2003	Industry 2003
Gross profit rate	$\dfrac{\text{Gross profit}}{\text{Net sales}}$	Margin between selling price and cost of goods sold	.44	.45	.42	.34

Kellogg's gross profit rate decreased slightly from 2002 to 2003.

16. **Earnings per share (EPS).** Stockholders usually think in terms of the number of shares they own or plan to buy or sell. Expressing net income earned on a per share basis provides a useful perspective for determining profitability. **Earnings per share** is a measure of the net income earned on each share of common stock. It is computed by dividing net income by the average number of common shares outstanding during the year. The terms "net income per share" or "earnings per share" refer to the amount of net income applicable to each share of *common stock*. Therefore, when we compute earnings per share, if there are preferred dividends declared for the period, they must be deducted from net income to arrive at income available to the common stockholders. Kellogg's earnings per share is shown in Illustration 14-30.

Illustration 14-30 Earnings per share

Ratio	Formula	Indicates:	Kellogg 2003	Kellogg 2002	General Mills 2003	Industry 2003
Earnings per share (EPS)	$\dfrac{\text{Net income} - \text{Preferred stock dividends}}{\text{Average common shares outstanding}}$	Net income earned on each share of common stock	$1.93	$1.77	$2.43	na

Note that no industry average is presented in Illustration 14-30. Industry data for earnings per share are not reported, and in fact the **Kellogg** and **General Mills** ratios should not be compared. Such comparisons are not meaningful because of the wide variations in the number of shares of outstanding stock among companies. Kellogg's earnings per share increased 16 cents per share in 2003. This represents a 9% increase from the 2002 EPS of $1.77.

17. **Price-earnings ratio.**   The price-earnings ratio is an oft-quoted statistic that measures the ratio of the market price of each share of common stock to the earnings per share. The price-earnings (P-E) ratio is a reflection of investors' assessments of a company's future earnings. It is computed by dividing the market price per share of the stock by earnings per share. Kellogg's price-earnings ratio is shown in Illustration 14-31.

Illustration 14-31 Price-earnings ratio

			Kellogg		General Mills	Industry
Ratio	**Formula**	**Indicates:**	**2003**	**2002**	**2003**	**2003**
Price-earnings ratio	Stock price per share / Earnings per share	Relationship between market price per share and earnings per share	19.5	18.5	19.2	19.1

At the end of 2003 and 2002 the market price of Kellogg's stock was $37.6 and $32.8, respectively. General Mills' stock was selling for $46.6 at the end of 2003.

In 2003 each share of **Kellogg's** stock sold for 19.5 times the amount that was earned on each share. Kellogg's price-earnings ratio is higher than the industry average of 19.1 times, **General Mills'** ratio of 19.2, and its 2002 ratio of 18.5. These higher P-E ratios suggest that the market is slightly more optimistic about Kellogg than about the other companies in the industry. However, it might also signal that its stock is overpriced.

18. **Payout ratio.**   The payout ratio measures the percentage of earnings distributed in the form of cash dividends. It is computed by dividing cash dividends declared on common stock by net income. Companies that have high growth rates are characterized by low payout ratios because they reinvest most of their net income in the business. The payout ratio for Kellogg is shown in Illustration 14-32.

Illustration 14-32 Payout ratio

			Kellogg		General Mills	Industry
Ratio	**Formula**	**Indicates:**	**2003**	**2002**	**2003**	**2003**
Payout ratio	Cash dividends declared on common stock / Net income	Percentage of earnings distributed in the form of cash dividends	.52	.57	.44	.36

The 2003 and 2002 payout ratios for **Kellogg** are comparatively high in relation to that of **General Mills** and the industry average of .36.

Management has some control over the amount of dividends paid each year, and companies are generally reluctant to reduce a dividend below the amount paid in a previous year. Therefore, the payout ratio will actually increase if a company's net income declines but the company keeps its total dividend payment the same. Of course, unless the company returns to its previous level of profitability, maintaining this higher dividend payout ratio is probably not possible over the long run.

Before drawing any conclusions regarding **Kellogg's** dividend payout ratio, we should calculate this ratio over a longer period of time to evaluate any trends, and also try to find out whether management's philosophy regarding dividends has changed recently. The "Selected financial data" section of Kellogg's Management Discussion and Analysis shows that over a 4-year period earnings per share have increased 32.4%, while dividends per share have grown only 1.5%, remaining constant at $1.01 per share for the past 3 years.

Business Insight
Management Perspective

Generally, companies with stable earnings have high payout ratios. For example, a utility such as **Potomac Electric Company** had an 86% payout ratio over a recent five-year period, and **Amoco Corporation** had a 63% payout ratio over the same period. Conversely, a company that is expanding rapidly, such as **Toys 'R' Us**, has never paid a cash dividend.

In terms of the types of financial information available and the ratios used by various industries, what can be practically covered in this textbook gives you only the "Titanic approach": That is, you are seeing only the tip of the iceberg compared to the vast databases and types of ratio analysis that are available on computers. The availability of information is not a problem. The real trick is to be discriminating enough to perform relevant analysis and select pertinent comparative data.

BEFORE YOU GO ON . . .

▶**Review It**

1. What different bases can be used to compare financial information?
2. What is horizontal analysis?
3. What is vertical analysis?
4. Describe ratios that measure liquidity, solvency, and profitability.

Quality of Earnings

In evaluating the financial performance of a company, the quality of a company's earnings is of extreme importance to analysts. A company that has a high **quality of earnings** provides full and transparent information that will not confuse or mislead users of the financial statements. The issue of quality of earnings has taken on increasing importance because recent accounting scandals suggest that some companies are spending too much time managing their income and not enough time managing their business. Here are some of the factors affecting quality of earnings.

STUDY OBJECTIVE
4
Understand the concept of quality of earnings.

ALTERNATIVE ACCOUNTING METHODS

Variations among companies in the application of generally accepted accounting principles may hamper comparability and reduce quality of earnings. For example, one company may use the FIFO method of inventory costing, while another company in the same industry may use LIFO. If inventory is a significant asset to both companies, it is unlikely that their current ratios are comparable. For example, if **General Motors Corporation** had used FIFO instead of LIFO in valuing its inventories, its inventories in a recent year would have been 26% higher, which significantly affects the current ratio (and other ratios as well).

In addition to differences in inventory costing methods, differences also exist in reporting such items as depreciation, depletion, and amortization. Although these differences in accounting methods might be detectable from reading the notes to the financial statements, adjusting the financial data to compensate for the different methods is difficult, if not impossible, in some cases.

PRO FORMA INCOME

Companies whose stock is publicly traded are required to present their income statement following generally accepted accounting principles (GAAP). Many companies also report a second measure of income called pro forma income. **Pro forma income** is a measure that usually excludes items that the company thinks are unusual or nonrecurring. For example, in a recent year, **Cisco Systems** (a high-tech company) reported quarterly net income under GAAP as a quarterly loss of $2.7 billion. However, Cisco also reported pro forma income for the same quarter as a profit of $230 million. This large difference in profits between GAAP income numbers and pro forma income is not unusual these days. For example, during one recent 9-month period the 100 largest firms on the Nasdaq stock exchange reported a total pro forma income of $19.1 billion, but a total loss as measured by GAAP of $82.3 billion—a difference of about $100 billion!

There are no rules as to how to prepare pro forma earnings. Companies have a free rein to exclude any items they deem inappropriate for measuring their performance. Many analysts and investors are critical of the practice of using pro forma income because these numbers often make companies look better than they really are. As noted in the financial press, pro forma numbers might be called EBS, which stands for "earnings before bad stuff." Companies, on the other hand, argue that pro forma numbers more clearly indicate sustainable income because unusual and nonrecurring expenses are excluded. "Cisco's technique gives readers of financial statements a clear picture of Cisco's normal business activities," the company said in a statement issued in response to questions about its accounting.

Recently, regulators stated that they will crack down on companies that use creative accounting to artificially inflate poor earnings results. Stay tuned: Everyone seems to agree that pro forma numbers can be useful if they provide insights into determining a company's sustainable income. However, many companies have abused the flexibility that pro forma numbers allow and have used the measure as a way to put their companies in a good light.

IMPROPER RECOGNITION

Because some managers have felt pressure to continually increase earnings to meet Wall Street's expectations, they have manipulated the earnings numbers to meet these expectations. The most common abuse is the improper recognition of revenue. One practice that companies are using is called channel stuffing. Offering deep discounts on their products to customers, companies encourage their customers to buy early (stuff the channel) rather than later. This lets the company report good earnings in the current period, but it often leads to a disaster in subsequent periods because customers have no need for additional goods. To illustrate, **Bristol-Myers Squibb** recently indicated that it used sales incentives to encourage wholesalers to buy more drugs than needed to meet patients' demands. As a result, the company had to issue revised financial statements showing corrected revenues and income.

Another practice is the improper capitalization of operating expenses. The classic case is **WorldCom**, which capitalized over $7 billion dollars of operating expenses to ensure that it would report positive net income. In other situations, companies fail to report all their liabilities. For example, **Enron** had promised to make payments on certain contracts if financial difficulty developed, but these guarantees were not reported as liabilities. In addition, disclosure was so lacking in transparency that it was impossible to understand what was happening at the company.

BEFORE YOU GO ON . . .

▶**Review It**

1. Explain what is meant by pro forma income.
2. Describe factors that reduce the quality of earnings.
3. Give an example of improper recognition.

☑ THE
NAVIGATOR

Using the Decision Toolkit

In analyzing a company, you should always investigate an extended period of time in order to determine whether the condition and performance of the company are changing. The condensed financial statements of **Kellogg Company** for 2001 and 2000 are presented here.

Kellogg's

KELLOGG COMPANY, INC.
Balance Sheets
December 31
(in millions)

Assets	2001	2000
Current assets		
Cash and short-term investments	$ 231.8	$ 204.4
Accounts receivable, net	762.3	685.3
Inventories	574.5	443.8
Prepaid expenses and other current assets	333.4	283.6
Total current assets	1,902.0	1,617.1
Property assets, net	2,952.8	2,526.9
Intangibles and other assets	5,513.8	742.0
Total assets	$10,368.6	$4,886.0
Liabilities and Stockholders' Equity		
Current liabilities	$ 2,207.6	$2,482.3
Long-term liabilities	7,289.5	1,506.2
Stockholders' equity—common	871.5	897.5
Total liabilities and stockholders' equity	$10,368.6	$4,886.0

Kellogg's KELLOGG COMPANY, INC.
Condensed Income Statements
For the Years Ended December 31
(in millions)

	2001	2000
Net sales	$7,548.4	$6,086.7
Cost of goods sold	4,211.4	3,401.7
Gross profit	3,337.0	2,685.0
Selling and administrative expenses	2,135.8	1,608.7
Nonrecurring charges	33.3	86.5
Income from operations	1,167.9	989.8
Interest expense	351.5	137.5
Other income (expense), net	(23.9)	15.4
Income before income taxes	792.5	867.7
Income tax expense	317.9	280.0
Net income	$ 474.6	$ 587.7

Instructions

Compute the following ratios for Kellogg for 2001 and 2000 and discuss your findings.

1. Liquidity:
   (a) Current ratio.
   (b) Inventory turnover ratio. (Inventory on December 31, 1999, was $503.8 million.)

2. Solvency:
   (a) Debt to total assets ratio.
   (b) Times interest earned ratio.

3. Profitability:
   (a) Return on common stockholders' equity ratio. (Equity on December 31, 1999, was $813.2 million.)
   (b) Return on assets ratio. (Assets on December 31, 1999, were $4,808.7 million.)
   (c) Profit margin ratio.

Solution

1. Liquidity
   (a) Current ratio:

   2001: $\dfrac{\$1,902.0}{\$2,207.6} = .86:1$

   2000: $\dfrac{\$1,617.1}{\$2,482.3} = .65:1$

   (b) Inventory turnover ratio:

   2001: $\dfrac{\$4,211.4}{(\$574.5 + \$443.8)/2} = 8.3 \text{ times}$

   2000: $\dfrac{\$3,401.7}{(\$443.8 + \$503.8)/2} = 7.2 \text{ times}$

We see that between 2000 and 2001 the current ratio and the inventory turnover ratio increased significantly. The faster the inventory turns over (is sold), the more liquid it is. That is, the company can accept a lower current ratio if it can turn over its inventory and receivables more quickly.

2. Solvency
   (a) Debt to total assets ratio:

   2001: $\dfrac{\$9,497.1}{\$10,368.6} = 92\%$

   2000: $\dfrac{\$3,988.5}{\$4,886.0} = 82\%$

   (b) Times interest earned ratio:

   2001: $\dfrac{\$474.6 + \$317.9 + \$351.5}{\$351.5} = 3.3 \text{ times}$

   2000: $\dfrac{\$587.7 + \$280.0 + \$137.5}{\$137.5} = 7.3 \text{ times}$

Kellogg's solvency as measured by the debt to total assets ratio declined in 2001. We also can see that the times interest earned ratio declined.

3. Profitability
   (a) Return on common stockholders' equity ratio:

   2001: $\dfrac{\$474.6}{(\$871.5 + \$897.5)/2} = 54\%$

   2000: $\dfrac{\$587.7}{(\$897.5 + \$813.2)/2} = 69\%$

   (b) Return on assets ratio:

   2001: $\dfrac{\$474.6}{(\$10,368.6 + \$4,886.0)/2} = 6\%$

   2000: $\dfrac{\$587.7}{(\$4,886.0 + \$4,808.7)/2} = 12\%$

   (c) Profit margin ratio:

   2001: $\dfrac{\$474.6}{\$7,548.4} = 6\%$

   2000: $\dfrac{\$587.7}{\$6,086.7} = 10\%$

Kellogg's return on common stockholders' equity ratio declined sharply. This decline was the result of declines in both its return on assets and its profit margin ratios.

THE NAVIGATOR

Summary of Study Objectives

1 *Describe and apply horizontal analysis.* Horizontal analysis is a technique for evaluating a series of data over a period of time to determine the increase or decrease that has taken place, expressed as either an amount or a percentage.

2 *Describe and apply vertical analysis.* Vertical analysis is a technique that expresses each item in a financial statement as a percentage of a relevant total or a base amount.

3 *Identify and compute ratios used in analyzing a company's liquidity, solvency, and profitability.* A sum-

mary of the financial ratios is provided on the back end pages of the book.

4 *Understand the concept of quality of earnings.* A high quality of earnings provides full and transparent information that will not confuse or mislead users of the financial statements. Issues related to quality of earnings are (1) alternative accounting methods, (2) pro forma income, and (3) improper recognition.

THE NAVIGATOR

DECISION TOOLKIT—A SUMMARY

Decision Checkpoints	Info Needed for Decision	Tool to Use for Decision	How to Evaluate Results
How do the company's financial position and operating results compare with those of the previous period?	Income statement and balance sheet	Comparative financial statements should be prepared over at least two years, with the first year reported being the base year. Changes in each line item relative to the base year should be presented both by amount and by percentage. This is called horizontal analysis.	Significant changes should be investigated to determine the reason for the change.
How do the relationships between items in this year's financial statements compare with those of last year or those of competitors?	Income statement and balance sheet	Each line item on the income statement should be presented as a percentage of net sales, and each line item on the balance sheet should be presented as a percentage of total assets or total liabilities and stockholders' equity. These percentages should be investigated for differences either across years in the same company or in the same year across different companies. This is called vertical analysis.	Any significant differences either across years or between companies should be investigated to determine the cause.

Glossary

Asset turnover ratio A measure of how efficiently a company uses its assets to generate sales, computed as net sales divided by average total assets. (p. 604)

Average collection period The average number of days that receivables are outstanding, calculated as receivables turnover divided into 365 days. (p. 599)

Cash debt coverage ratio A cash-basis measure used to evaluate solvency, computed as cash provided by operating activities divided by average total liabilities. (p. 601)

Current cash debt coverage ratio A cash-basis measure of short-term debt-paying ability, computed as cash provided by operating activities divided by average current liabilities. (p. 598)

Current ratio A measure that expresses the relationship of current assets to current liabilities, calculated as current assets divided by current liabilities. (p. 597)

Days in inventory A measure of the average number of days it takes to sell the inventory, computed as inventory turnover divided into 365 days. (p. 599)

Debt to total assets ratio A measure of the percentage of total assets provided by creditors, computed as total liabilities divided by total assets. (p. 600)

Earnings per share The net income earned by each share of common stock, computed as net income less preferred stock dividends divided by the average common shares outstanding. (p. 605)

Free cash flow The amount of cash provided by operating activities after adjusting for capital expenditures and cash dividends paid. (p. 602)

Gross profit rate An indicator of a company's ability to maintain an adequate selling price of goods above their cost, computed as gross profit divided by net sales. (p. 605)

Horizontal analysis A technique for evaluating a series of financial statement data over a period of time to determine the increase (decrease) that has taken place, expressed as either an amount or a percentage. (p. 590)

Inventory turnover ratio A measure of the liquidity of inventory, computed as cost of goods sold divided by average inventory. (p. 599)

Leveraging Borrowing money at a lower rate of interest than can be earned by using the borrowed money; also referred to as trading on the equity. (p. 603)

Liquidity ratios Measures of the short-term ability of the enterprise to pay its maturing obligations and to meet unexpected needs for cash. (p. 596)

Payout ratio A measure of the percentage of earnings distributed in the form of cash dividends, calculated as cash dividends on common stock divided by net income. (p. 606)

Price-earnings ratio A comparison of the market price of each share of common stock to the earnings per share, computed as the market price of the stock divided by earnings per share. (p. 606)

Pro forma income A measure of income that usually excludes items that a company thinks are unusual or nonrecurring. (p. 608)

Profit margin ratio A measure of the net income generated by each dollar of sales, computed as net income divided by net sales. (p. 604)

Profitability ratios Measures of the income or operating success of an enterprise for a given period of time. (p. 596)

Quality of earnings Indicates the level of full and transparent information that is provided to users of the financial statements. (p. 607)

Receivables turnover ratio A measure of the liquidity of receivables, computed as net credit sales divided by average net receivables. (p. 598)

Return on assets ratio An overall measure of profitability, calculated as net income divided by average total assets. (p. 603)

Return on common stockholders' equity ratio A measure of the dollars of net income earned for each dollar invested by the owners, computed as income available to common stockholders divided by average common stockholders' equity. (p. 603)

Solvency ratios Measures of the ability of the enterprise to survive over a long period of time. (p. 596)

Times interest earned ratio A measure of a company's ability to meet interest payments as they come due, calculated as income before interest expense and income taxes divided by interest expense. (p. 601)

Trading on the equity Same as leveraging. (p. 603)

Vertical analysis A technique for evaluating financial statement data that expresses each item in a financial statement as a percent of a base amount. (p. 592)

Demonstration Problem

The comparative balance sheets and income statements for Kellogg Company are presented below.

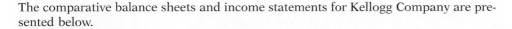

KELLOGG COMPANY, INC. Balance Sheets December 31 (in millions)		
Assets	**2001**	**2000**
Current assets		
Cash and short-term investments	$ 231.8	$ 204.4
Accounts receivable, net	762.3	685.3
Inventories	574.5	443.8
Prepaid expenses and other current assets	333.4	283.6
Total current assets	1,902.0	1,617.1
Property assets, net	2,952.8	2,526.9
Intangibles and other assets	5,513.8	742.0
Total assets	$10,368.6	$4,886.0
Liabilities and Stockholders' Equity		
Current liabilities	$ 2,207.6	$2,482.3
Long-term liabilities	7,289.5	1,506.2
Stockholders' equity—common	871.5	897.5
Total liabilities and stockholders' equity	$10,368.6	$4,886.0

Kellogg's

KELLOGG COMPANY, INC.
Condensed Income Statements
For the Years Ended December 31
(in millions)

	2001	2000
Net sales	$7,548.4	$6,086.7
Cost of goods sold	4,211.4	3,401.7
Gross profit	3,337.0	2,685.0
Selling and administrative expenses	2,135.8	1,608.7
Nonrecurring charges	33.3	86.5
Income from operations	1,167.9	989.8
Interest expense	351.5	137.5
Other income (expense), net	(23.9)	15.4
Income before income taxes	792.5	867.7
Income tax expense	317.9	280.0
Net income	$ 474.6	$ 587.7

Instructions

(a) Prepare a horizontal analysis of the balance sheet and income statement data for Kellogg's using 2000 as a base.

(b) Prepare a vertical analysis of the balance sheet and income statement data for Kellogg's for both years.

Action Plan

- To prepare a horizontal analysis, measure all percentage increases or decreases relative to the base period.

- To prepare a vertical analysis, express each item in the financial statement as a percent of a base amount. Use total assets for balance sheet and net sales for income statement.

Solution to Demonstration Problem

(a)

KELLOGG COMPANY, INC.
Balance Sheets
December 31
(in millions)

Assets	2001	2000	Increase (Decrease) During 2001 Amount	Percent
Current assets				
Cash and short-term investments	$ 231.8	$ 204.4	$ 27.4	13.4
Accounts receivable, net	762.3	685.3	77.0	11.2
Inventories	574.5	443.8	130.7	29.5
Prepaid expenses and other current assets	333.4	283.6	49.8	17.6
Total current assets	1,902.0	1,617.1	284.9	17.6
Property assets, net	2,952.8	2,526.9	425.9	16.9
Intangibles and other assets	5,513.8	742.0	4,771.8	643.1
Total assets	$10,368.6	$4,886.0	$5,482.6	112.2
Liabilities and Stockholders' Equity				
Current liabilities	$ 2,207.6	$2,482.3	(274.7)	(11.1)
Long-term liabilities	7,289.5	1,506.2	5,783.3	384.0
Stockholders' equity—common	871.5	897.5	(26.0)	(2.9)
Total liabilities and stockholders' equity	$10,368.6	$4,886.0	$5,482.6	112.2

KELLOGG COMPANY, INC.
Condensed Income Statements
For the Years Ended December 31
(in millions)

	2001	2000	Increase (Decrease) During 2001 Amount	Percent
Net sales	$7,548.4	$6,086.7	$1,461.7	24.0
Cost of goods sold	4,211.4	3,401.7	809.7	23.8
Gross profit	3,337.0	2,685.0	652.0	24.3
Selling and administrative expenses	2,135.8	1,608.7	527.1	32.8
Nonrecurring charges	33.3	86.5	(53.2)	(61.5)
Income from operations	1,167.9	989.8	178.0	18.0
Interest expense	351.5	137.5	214.0	155.6
Other income (expense), net	(23.9)	15.4	(39.3)	(255.2)
Income before income taxes	792.5	867.7	(75.2)	(8.7)
Income tax expense	317.9	280.0	37.9	13.5
Net income	$ 474.6	$ 587.7	$ (113.1)	(19.2)

(b)

KELLOGG COMPANY, INC.
Balance Sheets
December 31
(in millions)

Assets	2001 Amount	Percent	2000 Amount	Percent
Current assets				
Cash and short-term investments	$ 231.8	2.2	$ 204.4	4.2
Accounts receivable, net	762.3	7.4	685.3	14.0
Inventories	574.5	5.5	443.8	9.1
Prepaid expenses and other current assets	333.4	3.2	283.6	5.8
Total current assets	1,902.0	18.3	1,617.1	33.1
Property assets, net	2,952.8	28.5	2,526.9	51.7
Intangibles and other assets	5,513.8	53.2	742.0	15.2
Total assets	$10,368.6	100.0	$4,886.0	100.0
Liabilities and Stockholders' Equity				
Current liabilities	$ 2,207.6	21.3	$2,482.3	50.8
Long-term liabilities	7,289.5	70.3	1,506.2	30.8
Stockholders' equity—common	871.5	8.4	897.5	18.4
Total liabilities and stockholders' equity	$10,368.6	100.0	$4,886.0	100.0

KELLOGG COMPANY, INC.
Condensed Income Statements
For the Years Ended December 31
(in millions)

	2001		2000	
	Amount	Percent	Amount	Percent
Net sales	$7,548.4	100.0	$6,086.7	100.0
Cost of goods sold	4,211.4	55.8	3,401.7	55.9
Gross profit	3,337.0	44.2	2,685.0	44.1
Selling and administrative expenses	2,135.8	28.3	1,608.7	26.4
Nonrecurring charges	33.3	0.4	86.5	1.4
Income from operations	1,167.9	15.5	989.8	16.3
Interest expense	351.5	4.7	137.5	2.3
Other income (expense), net	(23.9)	(0.3)	15.4	0.3
Income before income taxes	792.5	10.5	867.7	14.3
Income tax expense	317.9	4.2	280.0	4.6
Net income	$ 474.6	6.3	$ 587.7	9.7

Self-Study Questions

Self-Study/Self-Test

Answers are at the end of the chapter.

(SO 1) 1. In horizontal analysis, each item is expressed as a percentage of the:
  (a) net income amount.
  (b) stockholders' equity amount.
  (c) total assets amount.
  (d) base-year amount.

(SO 1) 2. Adams Corporation reported net sales of $300,000, $330,000, and $360,000 in the years 2003, 2004, and 2005, respectively. If 2003 is the base year, what percentage do 2005 sales represent of the base?
  (a) 77%.   (c) 120%.
  (b) 108%.   (d) 130%.

(SO 2) 3. The following schedule is a display of what type of analysis?

	Amount	Percent
Current assets	$200,000	25%
Property, plant, and equipment	600,000	75%
Total assets	$800,000	

  (a) Horizontal analysis.
  (b) Differential analysis.
  (c) Vertical analysis.
  (d) Ratio analysis.

(SO 2) 4. In vertical analysis, the base amount for depreciation expense is generally:
  (a) net sales.
  (b) depreciation expense in a previous year.
  (c) gross profit.
  (d) fixed assets.

5. Which measure is an evaluation of a company's ability to pay current liabilities?   (SO 3)
  (a) Current cash debt coverage ratio.
  (b) Current ratio.
  (c) Both (a) and (b).
  (d) None of the above.

6. Which measure is useful in evaluating the efficiency in managing inventories?   (SO 3)
  (a) Inventory turnover ratio.
  (b) Days in inventory.
  (c) Both (a) and (b).
  (d) None of the above.

7. Which of these is *not* a liquidity ratio?   (SO 3)
  (a) Current ratio.
  (b) Asset turnover ratio.
  (c) Inventory turnover ratio.
  (d) Receivables turnover ratio.

8. Plano Corporation reported net income $24,000; net sales $400,000; and average assets $600,000 for 2005. What is the 2005 profit margin?   (SO 3)
  (a) 6%.   (c) 40%.
  (b) 12%.   (d) 200%.

9. Which situation below might indicate a company has a low quality of earnings?   (SO 4)
  (a) The same accounting principles are used each year.
  (b) Revenue is recognized when earned.
  (c) Maintenance costs are capitalized and then depreciated.
  (d) The financial statements are prepared in accordance with generally accepted accounting principles.

Questions

1. (a) Ilana Hadar believes that the analysis of financial statements is directed at two characteristics of a company: liquidity and profitability. Is Ilana correct? Explain.
   (b) Are short-term creditors, long-term creditors, and stockholders interested in primarily the same characteristics of a company? Explain.

2. (a) Distinguish among the following bases of comparison: intracompany, industry averages, and intercompany.
   (b) Give the principal value of using each of the three bases of comparison.

3. Two popular methods of financial statement analysis are horizontal analysis and vertical analysis. Explain the difference between these two methods.

4. (a) If Belman Company had net income of $380,000 in 2004 and it experienced a 24.5% increase in net income for 2005, what is its net income for 2005?
   (b) If 6 cents of every dollar of Belman's revenue is net income in 2004, what is the dollar amount of 2004 revenue?

5. Name the major ratios useful in assessing (a) liquidity and (b) solvency.

6. Daniel Shapson is puzzled. His company had a profit margin of 10% in 2005. He feels that this is an indication that the company is doing well. Suzie Franklin, his accountant, says that more information is needed to determine the company's financial well-being. Who is correct? Why?

7. What does each type of ratio measure?
   (a) Liquidity ratios.
   (b) Solvency ratios.
   (c) Profitability ratios.

8. What is the difference between the current ratio and working capital?

9. Quick Buys, a retail store, has a receivables turnover ratio of 4.5 times. The industry average is 12.5 times. Does Quick Buys have a collection problem with its receivables?

10. Which ratios should be used to help answer each of these questions?
    (a) How efficient is a company in using its assets to produce sales?
    (b) How near to sale is the inventory on hand?
    (c) How many dollars of net income were earned for each dollar invested by the owners?
    (d) How able is a company to meet interest charges as they fall due?

11. In September 2002 the price-earnings ratio of **General Motors** was 14, and the price-earnings ratio of **Microsoft** was 33. Which company did the stock market favor? Explain.

12. What is the formula for computing the payout ratio? Do you expect this ratio to be high or low for a growth company?

13. Holding all other factors constant, indicate whether each of the following changes generally signals good or bad news about a company.
    (a) Increase in profit margin ratio.
    (b) Decrease in inventory turnover ratio.
    (c) Increase in current ratio.
    (d) Decrease in earnings per share.
    (e) Increase in price-earnings ratio.
    (f) Increase in debt to total assets ratio.
    (g) Decrease in times interest earned ratio.

14. The return on assets for Syed Corporation is 7.6%. During the same year Syed's return on common stockholders' equity is 12.8%. What is the explanation for the difference in the two rates?

15. Which two ratios do you think should be of greatest interest in each of the following cases?
    (a) A pension fund considering the purchase of 20-year bonds.
    (b) A bank contemplating a short-term loan.
    (c) A common stockholder.

16. Merit Grafixx Inc. has net income of $300,000, average shares of common stock outstanding of 50,000, and preferred dividends for the period of $40,000. What is Merit's earnings per share of common stock? Eric Roskopf, the president of Merit Grafixx, believes that the computed EPS of the company is high. Comment.

17. Identify and explain factors that affect quality of earnings.

18. Explain how the choice of one of the following accounting methods over the other raises or lowers a company's net income during a period of continuing inflation.
    (a) Use of FIFO instead of LIFO for inventory costing.
    (b) Use of a 6-year life for machinery instead of a 9-year life.
    (c) Use of straight-line depreciation instead of accelerated declining-balance depreciation.

Brief Exercises

BE14-1 Using these data from the comparative balance sheet of Unisource Company, perform horizontal analysis.

Prepare horizontal analysis.
(SO 1)

	December 31, 2005	December 31, 2004
Accounts receivable	$ 600,000	$ 400,000
Inventory	780,000	600,000
Total assets	3,136,000	2,800,000

Prepare vertical analysis.
(SO 2)

BE14-2 Using the data presented in BE14-1 for Unisource Company, perform vertical analysis. (Round to 2 decimals.)

Calculate percentage of change.
(SO 1)

BE14-3 Net income was $500,000 in 2003, $460,000 in 2004, and $519,800 in 2005. What is the percentage of change from (a) 2003 to 2004, and (b) from 2004 to 2005? Is the change an increase or a decrease?

Calculate net income.
(SO 1)

BE14-4 If Pyramid Company had net income of $672,300 in 2005 and it experienced a 21% increase in net income over 2004, what was its 2004 net income?

Calculate change in net income.
(SO 2)

BE14-5 Vertical analysis (common-size) percentages for Thombet Company's sales, cost of goods sold, and expenses are listed here.

Vertical Analysis	2005	2004	2003
Sales	100.0%	100.0%	100.0%
Cost of goods sold	59.2	62.4	64.5
Expenses	25.0	26.6	27.5

Did Thombet's net income as a percent of sales increase, decrease, or remain unchanged over the 3-year period? Provide numerical support for your answer.

Calculate change in net income.
(SO 1)

BE14-6 Horizontal analysis (trend analysis) percentages for Dunvegan Company's sales, cost of goods sold, and expenses are listed here.

Horizontal Analysis	2005	2004	2003
Sales	96.2%	106.8%	100.0%
Cost of goods sold	102.0	97.0	100.0
Expenses	110.6	95.4	100.0

Explain whether Dunvegan's net income increased, decreased, or remained unchanged over the 3-year period.

Calculate current ratio.
(SO 3)

BE14-7 These selected condensed data are taken from a recent balance sheet of **Bob Evans Farms** (in thousands).

Cash	$ 7,900
Accounts receivable	11,600
Inventories	15,300
Other current assets	9,900
Total current assets	$ 44,700
Total current liabilities	$130,500

What is the current ratio?

Evaluate collection of accounts receivable.
(SO 3)

BE14-8 The following data are taken from the financial statements of Lite Wait Company.

	2005	2004
Accounts receivable (net), end of year	$ 560,000	$ 540,000
Net sales on account	4,800,000	4,100,000
Terms for all sales are 1/10, n/45.		

Compute for each year (a) the receivables turnover ratio and (b) the average collection period. What conclusions about the management of accounts receivable can be drawn from these data? At the end of 2003, accounts receivable was $490,000. (Round to 2 decimals.)

Evaluate management of inventory.
(SO 3)

BE14-9 The following data were taken from the income statements of Menu Masters Company.

	2005	2004
Sales revenue	$6,420,000	$6,240,000
Beginning inventory	960,000	837,000
Purchases	4,640,000	4,661,000
Ending inventory	1,020,000	960,000

Compute for each year (a) the inventory turnover ratio and (b) days in inventory. What conclusions concerning the management of the inventory can be drawn from these data? (Round to 2 decimals.)

BE14-10 **Staples, Inc.** is one of the largest suppliers of office products in the United States. It had net income of $490.2 million and net sales of $13,181.2 million in 2003. Its total assets were $5,721.4 million at the beginning of the year and $6,503.0 million at the end of the year. What is Staples, Inc.'s (a) asset turnover ratio and (b) profit margin ratio? (Round to two decimals.)

Calculate profitability ratios.
(SO 3)

BE14-11 Gem Products Company has stockholders' equity of $400,000 and net income of $56,000. It has a payout ratio of 20% and a return on assets ratio of 16%. How much did Gem Products pay in cash dividends, and what were its average total assets?

Calculate profitability ratios.
(SO 3)

BE14-12 Selected data taken from the 2004 financial statements of trading card company **Topps Company, Inc.** are as follows (in millions).

Net sales for 2004	$297.3
Current liabilities, March 1, 2003	43.4
Current liabilities, February 28, 2004	39.5
Net cash provided by operating activities	12.0
Total liabilities, March 1, 2003	66.2
Total liabilities, February 28, 2004	64.2

Calculate cash-basis liquidity and solvency ratios.
(SO 3)

Compute these ratios at February 28, 2004: (a) current cash debt coverage ratio and (b) cash debt coverage ratio. (Round to 2 decimals.)

Exercises

E14-1 Here is financial information for Canvas Mark Inc.

	December 31, 2005	December 31, 2004
Current assets	$128,000	$100,000
Plant assets (net)	400,000	350,000
Current liabilities	91,000	70,000
Long-term liabilities	144,000	95,000
Common stock, $1 par	150,000	115,000
Retained earnings	143,000	170,000

Prepare horizontal analysis.
(SO 1)

Instructions (Round all computations to 2 decimal places.)
Prepare a schedule showing a horizontal analysis for 2005 using 2004 as the base year.

E14-2 Operating data for Nautilus Corporation are presented here.

	2005	2004
Sales	$800,000	$600,000
Cost of goods sold	500,000	390,000
Selling expenses	120,000	72,000
Administrative expenses	80,000	54,000
Income tax expense	38,400	25,200
Net income	61,600	58,800

Prepare vertical analysis.
(SO 2)

Instructions
Prepare a schedule showing a vertical analysis for 2005 and 2004.

E14-3 The comparative balance sheets of **Philip Morris Companies, Inc.** are presented here.

Prepare horizontal and vertical analyses.
(SO 1, 2)

PHILIP MORRIS COMPANIES, INC.
Comparative Balance Sheets
December 31
($ in millions)

Assets	2003	2002
Current assets	$21,382	$17,441
Property, plant, and equipment (net)	16,067	14,846
Other assets	58,726	55,253
Total assets	$96,175	$87,540

Liabilities and Stockholders' Equity

Current liabilities	$21,393	$19,082
Long-term liabilities	49,705	48,980
Stockholders' equity	25,077	19,478
Total liabilities and stockholders' equity	$96,175	$87,540

Instructions (Round all computations to 2 decimal places.)

(a) Prepare a horizontal analysis of the balance sheet data for Philip Morris using 2002 as a base. (Show the amount of increase or decrease as well.)

(b) Prepare a vertical analysis of the balance sheet data for Philip Morris for 2003.

Prepare horizontal and vertical analyses.
(SO 1, 2)

E14-4 Here are the comparative income statements of Viking Corporation.

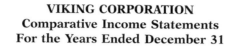

VIKING CORPORATION
Comparative Income Statements
For the Years Ended December 31

	2005	2004
Net sales	$550,000	$550,000
Cost of goods sold	440,000	450,000
Gross profit	$110,000	$100,000
Operating expenses	58,000	55,000
Net income	$ 52,000	$ 45,000

Instructions (Round all computations to 2 decimal places.)

(a) Prepare a horizontal analysis of the income statement data for Viking Corporation using 2004 as a base. (Show the amounts of increase or decrease.)

(b) Prepare a vertical analysis of the income statement data for Viking Corporation for both years.

Compute liquidity ratios and compare results.
(SO 3)

E14-5 **Nordstrom, Inc.** operates department stores in numerous states. Selected financial statement data (in millions) for fiscal year 2004 are presented here.

	End of Year	Beginning of Year
Cash and cash equivalents	$ 476.2	$ 219.3
Accounts receivables (net)	633.9	639.6
Merchandise inventories	901.6	953.1
Other current assets	443.7	276.0
Total current assets	$2,455.4	$2,088.0
Total current liabilities	$1,049.5	$ 885.1

For the year, net credit sales were $6,491.7 million, cost of goods sold was $4,214.0 million, and cash from operations was $573.2 million.

Instructions (Round all computations to 2 decimal places.)

Compute the current ratio, current cash debt coverage ratio, receivables turnover ratio, average collection period, inventory turnover ratio, and days in inventory at the end of the current year.

Perform current ratio analysis.
(SO 3)

E14-6 Gnomes Incorporated had the following transactions involving current assets and current liabilities during February 2005.

Feb.	3	Collected accounts receivable of $15,000.
	7	Purchased equipment for $25,000 cash.
	11	Paid $3,000 for a 3-year insurance policy.
	14	Paid accounts payable of $14,000.
	18	Declared cash dividends, $6,000.

Additional information:

As of February 1, 2005, current assets were $130,000 and current liabilities were $40,000.

Instructions (Round all computations to 2 decimal places.)

Compute the current ratio as of the beginning of the month and after each transaction.

E14-7 Tedd Company has these comparative balance sheet data:

Compute selected ratios.
(SO 3)

TEDD COMPANY
Balance Sheets
December 31

	2005	2004
Cash	$ 20,000	$ 30,000
Receivables (net)	65,000	60,000
Inventories	60,000	50,000
Plant assets (net)	200,000	180,000
	$345,000	$320,000
Accounts payable	$ 50,000	$ 60,000
Mortgage payable (15%)	100,000	100,000
Common stock, $10 par	140,000	120,000
Retained earnings	55,000	40,000
	$345,000	$320,000

Additional information for 2005:
1. Net income was $25,000.
2. Sales on account were $420,000. Sales returns and allowances amounted to $20,000.
3. Cost of goods sold was $198,000.
4. Net cash provided by operating activities was $41,000.

Instructions (Round all computations to 2 decimal places.)
Compute the following ratios at December 31, 2005.
(a) Current.   (e) Days in inventory.
(b) Receivables turnover.   (f) Cash debt coverage.
(c) Average collection period.   (g) Current cash debt coverage.
(d) Inventory turnover.

E14-8 Selected comparative statement data for the giant bookseller **Barnes & Noble** are presented here. All balance sheet data are as of December 31 (in millions).

Compute selected ratios.
(SO 3)

	2003	2002
Net sales	$5,951.0	$5,269.3
Cost of goods sold	4,323.8	3,847.5
Net income	151.9	99.9
Receivables, net	66.5	66.9
Merchandise inventories	1,526.2	1,395.9
Total assets	3,507.3	2,995.4
Total common stockholders' equity	1,259.7	1,027.8

Instructions (Round all computations to 2 decimal places.)
Compute the following ratios for 2003:
(a) Profit margin.
(b) Asset turnover.
(c) Return on assets.
(d) Return on common stockholders' equity.
(e) Gross profit rate.

E14-9 Here is the income statement for Life Style, Inc.

Compute selected ratios.
(SO 3)

LIFE STYLE, INC.
Income Statement
For the Year Ended December 31, 2005

Sales	$400,000
Cost of goods sold	230,000
Gross profit	170,000
Expenses (including $15,000 interest and $24,000 income taxes)	90,000
Net income	$ 80,000

Additional information:
1. Common stock outstanding January 1, 2005, was 30,000 shares, and 40,000 shares were outstanding at December 31, 2005.
2. The market price of Life Style, Inc., stock was $15 in 2005.
3. Cash dividends of $21,000 were paid, $5,000 of which were to preferred stockholders.
4. Cash provided by operating activities was $98,000.

Instructions (Round all computations to 2 decimal places.)
Compute the following measures for 2005.
(a) Earnings per share.
(b) Price-earnings ratio.
(c) Payout ratio.
(d) Times interest earned ratio.

Compute amounts from ratios.
(SO 3)

E14-10 Saylor Corporation experienced a fire on December 31, 2005, in which its financial records were partially destroyed. It has been able to salvage some of the records and has ascertained the following balances.

	December 31, 2005	December 31, 2004
Cash	$ 30,000	$ 10,000
Receivables (net)	72,500	126,000
Inventory	200,000	180,000
Accounts payable	50,000	10,000
Notes payable	30,000	20,000
Common stock, $100 par	400,000	400,000
Retained earnings	113,500	101,000

Additional information:
1. The inventory turnover is 3.6 times.
2. The return on common stockholders' equity is 19%. The company had no additional paid-in capital.
3. The receivables turnover is 9.4 times.
4. The return on assets is 14%.
5. Total assets at December 31, 2004, were $605,000.

Instructions
Compute the following for Saylor Corporation.
(a) Cost of goods sold for 2005.
(b) Net credit sales for 2005.
(c) Net income for 2005.
(d) Total assets at December 31, 2005.

Problems: Set A

Prepare vertical analysis and comment on profitability.
(SO 2, 3)

P14-1A Here are comparative statement data for Here Today Company and Gone Tomorrow Company, two competitors. All balance sheet data are as of December 31, 2005, and December 31, 2004.

	Here Today Company		Gone Tomorrow Company	
	2005	**2004**	**2005**	**2004**
Net sales	$350,000		$1,400,000	
Cost of goods sold	180,000		720,000	
Operating expenses	51,000		278,000	
Interest expense	3,000		10,000	
Income tax expense	11,000		68,000	
Current assets	130,000	$100,000	700,000	$650,000
Plant assets (net)	405,000	270,000	1,000,000	750,000
Current liabilities	60,000	52,000	250,000	275,000
Long-term liabilities	50,000	68,000	200,000	150,000
Common stock	360,000	210,000	950,000	700,000
Retained earnings	65,000	40,000	300,000	275,000

Instructions (Round all computations to 2 decimal places.)

(a) Prepare a vertical analysis of the 2005 income statement data for Today Company and Tomorrow Company.

(a) NI (Today) 30%

(b) ✏➤ Comment on the relative profitability of the companies by computing the return on assets and the return on common stockholders' equity ratios for both companies.

P14-2A The comparative statements of Classic Rock Company are presented here.

Compute ratios from balance sheet and income statement.
(SO 3)

CLASSIC ROCK COMPANY
Income Statements
For the Years Ended December 31

	2005	2004
Net sales	$780,000	$624,000
Cost of goods sold	440,000	405,600
Gross profit	340,000	218,400
Selling and administrative expense	143,880	149,760
Income from operations	196,120	68,640
Other expenses and losses		
Interest expense	9,920	7,200
Income before income taxes	186,200	61,440
Income tax expense	69,000	24,000
Net income	$117,200	$ 37,440

CLASSIC ROCK COMPANY
Balance Sheets
December 31

Assets	2005	2004
Current assets		
Cash	$ 23,100	$ 21,600
Short-term investments	34,800	33,000
Accounts receivable (net)	106,200	93,800
Inventory	116,400	64,000
Total current assets	280,500	212,400
Plant assets (net)	455,300	459,600
Total assets	$735,800	$672,000
Liabilities and Stockholders' Equity		
Current liabilities		
Accounts payable	$168,200	$132,000
Income taxes payable	25,300	24,000
Total current liabilities	193,500	156,000
Bonds payable	132,000	120,000
Total liabilities	325,500	276,000
Stockholders' equity		
Common stock ($10 par)	140,000	150,000
Retained earnings	270,300	246,000
Total stockholders' equity	410,300	396,000
Total liabilities and stockholders' equity	$735,800	$672,000

All sales were on account. Net cash provided by operating activities was $41,000.

Instructions (Round all computations to 2 decimal places.)
Compute the following ratios for 2005.

(a) Earnings per share.
(b) Return on common stockholders' equity.
(c) Return on assets.
(d) Current.
(e) Receivables turnover.
(f) Average collection period.
(g) Inventory turnover.

(h) Days in inventory.
(i) Times interest earned.
(j) Asset turnover.
(k) Debt to total assets.
(l) Current cash debt coverage.
(m) Cash debt coverage.

Perform ratio analysis, and discuss change in financial position and operating results.
(SO 3)

P14-3A The following are condensed balance sheet and income statement data for Juan Valdez Corporation.

JUAN VALDEZ CORPORATION
Balance Sheets
December 31

	2005	2004	2003
Cash	$ 40,000	$ 24,000	$ 20,000
Receivables (net)	120,000	45,000	48,000
Other current assets	80,000	75,000	62,000
Investments	90,000	70,000	50,000
Plant and equipment (net)	603,000	400,000	360,000
	$933,000	$614,000	$540,000
Current liabilities	$ 98,000	$ 75,000	$ 70,000
Long-term debt	250,000	75,000	65,000
Common stock, $10 par	400,000	340,000	300,000
Retained earnings	185,000	124,000	105,000
	$933,000	$614,000	$540,000

JUAN VALDEZ CORPORATION
Income Statements
For the Years Ended December 31

	2005	2004
Sales	$800,000	$750,000
Less: Sales returns and allowances	40,000	50,000
Net sales	760,000	700,000
Cost of goods sold	420,000	400,000
Gross profit	340,000	300,000
Operating expenses (including income taxes)	194,000	225,000
Net income	$146,000	$ 75,000

Additional information:
1. The market price of Juan Valdez's common stock was $5.00, $3.50, and $2.30 for 2003, 2004, and 2005, respectively.
2. You must compute dividends paid. All dividends were paid in cash.

Instructions (Round all computations to 2 decimal places.)
(a) Compute the following ratios for 2004 and 2005.

    (1) Profit margin.
    (2) Gross profit rate.
    (3) Asset turnover.
    (4) Earnings per share.

    (5) Price-earnings.
    (6) Payout.
    (7) Debt to total assets.

(b) ▭▭▭▷ Based on the ratios calculated, discuss briefly the improvement or lack thereof in the financial position and operating results from 2004 to 2005 of Juan Valdez Corporation.

P14-4A Financial information for M. L. Kurt Company is presented here.

M. L. KURT COMPANY
Balance Sheets
December 31

Assets	2005	2004
Cash	$ 50,000	$ 42,000
Short-term investments	80,000	50,000
Receivables (net)	100,000	87,000
Inventories	440,000	300,000
Prepaid expenses	25,000	31,000
Land	75,000	75,000
Building and equipment (net)	570,000	400,000
Total assets	$1,340,000	$985,000

Liabilities and Stockholders' Equity	2005	2004
Notes payable	$ 125,000	$ 25,000
Accounts payable	160,000	90,000
Accrued liabilities	50,000	50,000
Bonds payable, due 2007	200,000	100,000
Common stock, $5 par	500,000	500,000
Retained earnings	305,000	220,000
Total liabilities and stockholders' equity	$1,340,000	$985,000

M. L. KURT COMPANY
Income Statements
For the Years Ended December 31

	2005	2004
Sales	$1,000,000	$940,000
Cost of goods sold	650,000	635,000
Gross profit	350,000	305,000
Operating expenses	235,000	225,000
Net income	$ 115,000	$ 80,000

Additional information:
1. Inventory at the beginning of 2004 was $350,000.
2. Receivables at the beginning of 2004 were $80,000 (net).
3. Total assets at the beginning of 2004 were $1,175,000.
4. No common stock transactions occurred during 2004 or 2005.
5. All sales were on account.

Instructions (Round all computations to 2 decimal places.)
(a) Indicate, by using ratios, the change in liquidity and profitability of the company from 2004 to 2005. (*Note:* Not all profitability ratios can be computed nor can cash-basis ratios be computed.)
(b) Given below are three independent situations and a ratio that may be affected. For each situation, compute the affected ratio (1) as of December 31, 2005, and (2) as of December 31, 2006, after giving effect to the situation. Net income for 2006 was $125,000. Total assets on December 31, 2006, were $1,450,000.

Situation	Ratio
1. 65,000 shares of common stock were sold at par on July 1, 2006.	Return on common stockholders' equity
2. All of the notes payable were paid in 2006.	Debt to total assets
3. The market price of common stock on December 31, 2006, was $6.25. The market price on December 31, 2005, was $5.	Price-earnings

Compute selected ratios, and compare liquidity, profitability, and solvency for two companies.
(SO 3)

P14-5A   Selected financial data for **Black & Decker** and **Snap-On Tools** for 2003 are presented here (in millions).

	Black & Decker	Snap-On Tools
	Income Statement Data for Year	
Net sales	$4,482.7	$2,233.2
Cost of goods sold	2,887.1	1,268.5
Selling and administrative expenses	1,126.0	814.6
Interest expense	35.2	24.4
Other income (expense)	(34.2)	(9.0)
Income tax expense	107.2	38.0
Net income (before irregular items)	$ 293.0	$ 78.7
	Balance Sheet Data (End of Year)	
Current assets	$2,203.0	$1,131.7
Property, plant, and equipment (net)	660.2	328.6
Other assets	1,359.3	678.2
Total assets	$4,222.5	$2,138.5
Current liabilities	$1,312.1	$ 567.2
Long-term debt	2,063.9	560.4
Total stockholders' equity	846.5	1,010.9
Total liabilities and stockholders' equity	$4,222.5	$2,138.5
	Beginning-of-Year Balances	
Total assets	$4,130.5	$1,994.1
Total stockholders' equity	599.6	830.4
Current liabilities	1,453.4	552.4
Total liabilities	3,530.9	1,163.7
	Other Data	
Average receivables (net)	$ 762.1	$ 551.5
Average inventory	717.8	360.5
Net cash provided by operating activities	570.6	177.0

Instructions (Round all computations to 2 decimal places.)
(a) For each company, compute the following ratios.
    (1) Current ratio.
    (2) Receivables turnover.
    (3) Average collection period.
    (4) Inventory turnover.
    (5) Days in inventory.
    (6) Profit margin.
    (7) Asset turnover.
    (8) Return on assets.
    (9) Return on common stockholders' equity.
    (10) Debt to total assets.
    (11) Times interest earned.
    (12) Current cash debt coverage.
    (13) Cash debt coverage.
(b) Compare the liquidity, solvency, and profitability of the two companies.

Problems: Set B

Prepare vertical analysis and comment on profitability.
(SO 2, 3)

P14-1B   Here are comparative statement data for North Company and South Company, two competitors. All balance sheet data are as of December 31, 2005, and December 31, 2004.

	North Company		South Company	
	2005	**2004**	**2005**	**2004**
Net sales	$1,849,035		$539,038	
Cost of goods sold	1,080,490		238,006	
Operating expenses	300,000		82,000	
Interest expense	6,800		1,252	
Income tax expense	52,030		6,650	
Current assets	325,975	$312,410	83,336	$ 79,467
Plant assets (net)	526,800	500,000	139,728	125,812
Current liabilities	66,325	75,815	35,348	30,281
Long-term liabilities	113,990	90,000	29,620	25,000
Common stock, $10 par	500,000	500,000	120,000	120,000
Retained earnings	172,460	146,595	38,096	29,998

Instructions (Round all computations to 2 decimal places.)

(a) Prepare a vertical analysis of the 2005 income statement data for North Company and South Company.

(a) NI (North) 22.2%

(b) ▭▭▭▷ Comment on the relative profitability of the companies by computing the 2005 return on assets and the return on common stockholders' equity ratios for both companies.

P14-2B   The comparative statements of Nathan Hale Company are presented here.

Compute ratios from balance sheet and income statement. (SO 3)

NATHAN HALE COMPANY
Income Statements
For the Years Ended December 31

	2005	**2004**
Net sales	$1,918,500	$1,750,500
Cost of goods sold	1,005,500	996,000
Gross profit	913,000	754,500
Selling and administrative expenses	506,000	479,000
Income from operations	407,000	275,500
Other expenses and losses		
Interest expense	25,000	19,000
Income before income taxes	382,000	256,500
Income tax expense	114,400	77,000
Net income	$ 267,600	$ 179,500

NATHAN HALE COMPANY
Balance Sheets
December 31

Assets	**2005**	**2004**
Current assets		
Cash	$ 60,100	$ 64,200
Short-term investments	54,000	50,000
Accounts receivable (net)	107,800	102,800
Inventory	143,000	115,500
Total current assets	364,900	332,500
Plant assets (net)	625,300	520,300
Total assets	$990,200	$852,800

Liabilities and Stockholders' Equity

Current liabilities		
Accounts payable	$170,000	$145,400
Income taxes payable	43,500	42,000
Total current liabilities	213,500	187,400
Bonds payable	210,000	200,000
Total liabilities	423,500	387,400
Stockholders' equity		
Common stock ($5 par)	280,000	300,000
Retained earnings	286,700	165,400
Total stockholders' equity	566,700	465,400
Total liabilities and stockholders' equity	$990,200	$852,800

All sales were on account. Net cash provided by operating activities for 2005 was $302,000.

Instructions (Round all computations to 2 decimal places.)
Compute the following ratios for 2005.

(a) Earnings per share.
(b) Return on common stockholders' equity.
(c) Return on assets.
(d) Current ratio.
(e) Receivables turnover.
(f) Average collection period.
(g) Inventory turnover.
(h) Days in inventory.
(i) Times interest earned.
(j) Asset turnover.
(k) Debt to total assets.
(l) Current cash debt coverage.
(m) Cash debt coverage.

Perform ratio analysis, and discuss change in financial position and operating results.
(SO 3)

P14-3B Condensed balance sheet and income statement data for Click and Clack Corporation are presented here.

CLICK AND CLACK CORPORATION
Balance Sheets
December 31

	2005	2004	2003
Cash	$ 40,000	$ 20,000	$ 18,000
Receivables (net)	50,000	45,000	48,000
Other current assets	90,000	85,000	64,000
Investments	55,000	70,000	45,000
Plant and equipment (net)	500,000	370,000	258,000
	$735,000	$590,000	$433,000
Current liabilities	$ 85,000	$ 80,000	$ 30,000
Long-term debt	165,000	85,000	20,000
Common stock, $10 par	340,000	300,000	300,000
Retained earnings	145,000	125,000	83,000
	$735,000	$590,000	$433,000

CLICK AND CLACK CORPORATION
Income Statements
For the Years Ended December 31

	2005	2004
Sales	$640,000	$500,000
Less: Sales returns and allowances	40,000	50,000
Net sales	600,000	450,000
Cost of goods sold	425,000	300,000
Gross profit	175,000	150,000
Operating expenses (including income taxes)	121,000	88,000
Net income	$ 54,000	$ 62,000

Additional information:

1. The market price of Click and Clack's common stock was $4.00, $6.00, and $7.95 for 2003, 2004, and 2005, respectively.
2. You must compute dividends paid. All dividends were paid in cash.

Instructions (Round all computations to 2 decimal places.)
(a) Compute the following ratios for 2004 and 2005.
   (1) Profit margin.
   (2) Gross profit.
   (3) Asset turnover.
   (4) Earnings per share.
   (5) Price-earnings.
   (6) Payout.
   (7) Debt to total assets.
(b) Based on the ratios calculated, discuss briefly the improvement or lack thereof in the financial position and operating results from 2004 to 2005 of Click and Clack Corporation.

P14-4B The following financial information is for Azteca Company.

Compute ratios; comment on overall liquidity and profitability.
(SO 3)

AZTECA COMPANY
Balance Sheets
December 31

Assets	2005	2004
Cash	$ 70,000	$ 65,000
Short-term investments	45,000	40,000
Receivables (net)	94,000	90,000
Inventories	230,000	125,000
Prepaid expenses	25,000	23,000
Land	130,000	130,000
Building and equipment (net)	260,000	175,000
Total assets	$854,000	$648,000

Liabilities and Stockholders' Equity	2005	2004
Notes payable	$170,000	$100,000
Accounts payable	45,000	42,000
Accrued liabilities	40,000	40,000
Bonds payable, due 2007	250,000	150,000
Common stock, $10 par	200,000	200,000
Retained earnings	149,000	116,000
Total liabilities and stockholders' equity	$854,000	$648,000

AZTECA COMPANY
Income Statements
For the Years Ended December 31

	2005	2004
Sales	$850,000	$790,000
Cost of goods sold	620,000	575,000
Gross profit	230,000	215,000
Operating expenses	194,000	180,000
Net income	$ 36,000	$ 35,000

Additional information:

1. Inventory at the beginning of 2004 was $115,000.
2. Receivables (net) at the beginning of 2004 were $88,000 (net).

3. Total assets at the beginning of 2004 were $630,000.
4. No common stock transactions occurred during 2004 or 2005.
5. All sales were on account.

Instructions (Round all computations to 2 decimal places.)

(a) Indicate, by using ratios, the change in liquidity and profitability of Azteca Company from 2004 to 2005. (*Note:* Not all profitability ratios can be computed nor can cash-basis ratios be computed.)

(b) Given below are three independent situations and a ratio that may be affected. For each situation, compute the affected ratio (1) as of December 31, 2005, and (2) as of December 31, 2006, after giving effect to the situation. Net income for 2006 was $40,000. Total assets on December 31, 2006, were $900,000.

Situation	Ratio
1. 18,000 shares of common stock were sold at par on July 1, 2006.	Return on common stockholders' equity
2. All of the notes payable were paid in 2006.	Debt to total assets
3. The market price of common stock was $9 and $12.80 on December 31, 2005 and 2006, respectively.	Price-earnings

Compute selected ratios, and compare liquidity, profitability, and solvency for two companies.
(SO 3)

P14-5B   Selected financial data of **Target** and **Wal-Mart** for fiscal year 2004 are presented here (in millions).

	Target Corporation	Wal-Mart Stores, Inc.
	Income Statement Data for Year	
Net sales	$46,781	$256,329
Cost of goods sold	31,790	198,747
Selling and administrative expenses	12,854	44,909
Interest expense	559	996
Other income (expense)	1,382	2,516
Income tax expense	1,119	5,118
Net income	$ 1,841	$ 9,075
	Balance Sheet Data (End of Year)	
Current assets	$12,928	$ 34,421
Noncurrent assets	18,464	70,491
Total assets	$31,392	$104,912
Current liabilities	$ 8,314	$ 37,418
Long-term debt	12,013	23,871
Total stockholders' equity	11,065	43,623
Total liabilities and stockholders' equity	$31,392	$104,912
	Beginning-of-Year Balances	
Total assets	$28,603	$ 94,808
Total stockholders' equity	9,443	39,461
Current liabilities	7,523	32,519
Total liabilities	19,160	55,347
	Other Data	
Average net receivables	$ 5,671	$ 1,412
Average inventory	5,052	25,507
Net cash provided by operating activities	3,160	15,996

Instructions (Round all computations to 2 decimal places.)

(a) For each company, compute the following ratios.

(1) Current.
(2) Receivables turnover.
(3) Average collection period.
(4) Inventory turnover.

(5) Days in inventory.
(6) Profit margin.
(7) Asset turnover.
(8) Return on assets.

(9) Return on common stockholders' equity. (12) Current cash debt coverage.
(10) Debt to total assets. (13) Cash debt coverage.
(11) Times interest earned.

(b) Compare the liquidity, solvency, and profitability of the two companies.

Problems: Set C

Problem Set C is provided at the book's Web site, www.wiley.com/college/weygandt.

▷ **BROADENING YOUR PERSPECTIVE**

Financial Reporting and Analysis

FINANCIAL REPORTING PROBLEM: *Tootsie Roll Industries, Inc.*

BYP 14-1   Your parents are considering investing in **Tootsie Roll Industries** common stock. They ask you, as an accounting expert, to make an analysis of the company for them. Fortunately, the financial statements of Tootsie Roll can be found at the company's Web site, www.tootsie.com.

Instructions (Round all computations to 2 decimal places.)
(a) Make a 5-year trend analysis, using 1999 as the base year, of (1) net revenues and (2) net earnings. Comment on the significance of the trend results.
(b) Compute for 2003 and 2002 the (1) debt to total assets ratio and (2) times interest earned ratio. How would you evaluate Tootsie Roll's long-term solvency?
(c) Compute for 2003 and 2002 the (1) profit margin ratio, (2) asset turnover ratio, (3) return on assets ratio, and (4) return on common stockholders' equity ratio. How would you evaluate Tootsie Roll's profitability? Total assets at December 31, 2001, were $618,676,000, and total stockholders' equity at December 31, 2001, was $508,461,000.
(d) What information outside the annual report may also be useful to your parents in making a decision about Tootsie Roll?

COMPARATIVE ANALYSIS PROBLEM: *Tootsie Roll vs. Hershey Foods*

BYP 14-2   The financial statements of **Hershey Foods** and **Tootsie Roll Industries** can be found at the companies' Web sites, www.hersheys.com and www.tootsie.com.

Instructions (Round all computations to 2 decimal places.)
(a) Based on the information in the financial statements, determine each of the following for each company:
  (1) The percentage increase (i) in net sales and (ii) in net income from 2002 to 2003.
  (2) The percentage increase (i) in total assets and (ii) in total stockholders' equity from 2002 to 2003.
  (3) The earnings per share for 2003.
(b) What conclusions concerning the two companies can be drawn from these data?

INTERPRETING FINANCIAL STATEMENTS

BYP 14-3   The **Coca-Cola Company** and **PepsiCo, Inc.** provide refreshments to every corner of the world. Selected data from the 2003 consolidated financial statements for The Coca-Cola Company and for PepsiCo, Inc., are presented here (in millions).

	Coca-Cola	PepsiCo
Total current assets	$ 8,396	$ 6,930
Total current liabilities	7,886	6,415
Net sales	21,044	26,971
Cost of goods sold	7,762	12,379
Net income	4,347	3,568
Average (net) receivables for the year	2,094	2,681
Average inventories for the year	1,273	1,377
Average total assets	25,874	24,401
Average common stockholders' equity	12,945	10,713
Average current liabilities	7,614	6,234
Average total liabilities	12,929	13,702
Total assets	27,342	25,327
Total liabilities	13,252	13,453
Income taxes	1,148	1,424
Interest expense	178	163
Cash provided by operating activities	5,456	4,328

Instructions (Round all computations to 2 decimal places.)

(a) Compute the following liquidity ratios for 2003 for Coca-Cola and for PepsiCo and comment on the relative liquidity of the two competitors.

(1) Current ratio.   (4) Inventory turnover.
(2) Receivables turnover.   (5) Days in inventory.
(3) Average collection period.   (6) Current cash debt coverage.

(b) Compute the following solvency ratios for the two companies and comment on the relative solvency of the two competitors.

(1) Debt to total assets ratio.
(2) Times interest earned.
(3) Cash debt coverage ratio.

(c) Compute the following profitability ratios for the two companies and comment on the relative profitability of the two competitors.

(1) Profit margin.
(2) Asset turnover.
(3) Return on assets.
(4) Return on common stockholders' equity.

GLOBAL FOCUS

BYP 14-4   The use of railroad transportation has changed dramatically around the world. Attitudes about railroads and railroad usage differ across countries. In England, the railroads were run by the government until recently. Five years ago, **Railtrack Group PLC** became a publicly traded company. The largest railroad company in the United States is **Burlington Northern Santa Fe Railroad Company**. The following data were taken from the 2001 financial statements of each company.

Financial Highlights	Railtrack Group (pounds in millions)		Burlington Northern Santa Fe (dollars in millions)	
	2001	**2000**	**2001**	**2000**
Total current assets	£ 602	£ 1,177	$ 723	$ 976
Total assets	9,443	11,484	24,721	24,375
Current liabilities	2,517	1,314	2,161	2,186
Total liabilities	6,795	8,411	16,872	16,895
Total stockholders' equity	2,648	3,073	7,849	7,480
Sales	2,476		9,208	
Operating costs and other	2,188		7,563	
Interest expense	89		463	
Income tax expense (credit)	(53)		445	
Net income	252		737	
Cash provided by operations	718		2,197	

Instructions (Round all computations to 2 decimal places.)

(a) Calculate the following 2001 liquidity ratios and discuss the relative liquidity of the two companies.

    (1) Current ratio.

    (2) Current cash debt coverage.

(b) Calculate the following 2001 solvency ratios and discuss the relative solvency of the two companies.

    (1) Debt to total assets.

    (2) Times interest earned.

    (3) Cash debt coverage.

(c) Calculate the following 2001 profitability ratios and discuss the relative profitability of the two companies.

    (1) Asset turnover.

    (2) Profit margin.

    (3) Return on assets.

    (4) Return on common stockholders' equity.

(d) What other issues must you consider when comparing these two companies?

EXPLORING THE WEB

BYP 14-5 *Purpose:* To use the Management Discussion and Analysis (MD&A) section of an annual report to evaluate corporate performance for the year.

Addresses: **www.ge.com/investor/** (*or go to* **www.wiley.com/college/weygandt**)

Steps

    1. From General Electric's Web site, choose the most recent annual report.

    2. Choose financial section.

    3. Download annual report.

Instructions

(a) Compare current-year earnings with the previous year's earnings.

(b) What were some of management's explanations for the change in net earnings?

BYP 14-6 *Purpose:* To employ comparative data and industry data to evaluate a company's performance and financial position.

Address: **http://biz.yahoo.com/i** (*or go to* **www.wiley.com/college/weygandt**)

Steps

    (1) Identify two competing companies.

    (2) Go to the above address.

    (3) Type in the first company's name and choose **Search**.

    (4) Choose **Profile**.

    (5) Choose **Key Statistics**.

    (6) Print out the results.

    (7) Repeat steps 3–6 for the competitor.

Instructions

(a) Evaluate the company's liquidity relative to the industry averages and to the competitor that you chose.

(b) Evaluate the company's solvency relative to the industry averages and to the competitor that you chose.

(c) Evaluate the company's profitability relative to the industry averages and to the competitor that you chose.

Critical Thinking

GROUP DECISION CASE

BYP 14-7 You are a loan officer for Premier Bank of Port Washington. Rick Gleason, president of R. Gleason Corporation, has just left your office. He is interested in an 8-year loan to expand the company's operations. The borrowed funds would be used to purchase

new equipment. As evidence of the company's debt-worthiness, Gleason provided you with the following facts.

	2005	2004
Current ratio	3.1	2.1
Asset turnover ratio	2.8	2.2
Cash debt coverage ratio	.1	.2
Net income	Up 32%	Down 8%
Earnings per share	$3.30	$2.50

Rick Gleason is a very insistent (some would say pushy) man. When you told him that you would need additional information before making your decision, he acted offended, and said, "What more could you possibly want to know?" You responded that, at a minimum, you would need complete, audited financial statements.

Instructions
With the class divided into groups, answer the following.
(a) Explain why you would want the financial statements to be audited.
(b) Discuss the implications of the ratios provided for the lending decision you are to make. That is, does the information paint a favorable picture? Are these ratios relevant to the decision?
(c) List three other ratios that you would want to calculate for this company, and explain why you would use each.

COMMUNICATION ACTIVITY

BYP 14-8   M. F. Hoffman is the chief executive officer of Hi-Tech Electronics. Hoffman is an expert engineer but a novice in accounting. Hoffman asks you, as an accounting major, to explain (a) the bases for comparison in analyzing Hi-Tech's financial statements and (b) the limitations, if any, in financial statement analysis.

Instructions
Write a memo to M. F. Hoffman that explains the basis for comparison and the factors affecting quality of earnings.

RESEARCH ASSIGNMENTS

BYP 14-9   The August 21, 2001, issue of the *Wall Street Journal* included an article by Jonathan Weil titled "Companies Pollute Earnings Reports, Leaving P/E Ratios Hard to Calculate."

Instructions
Read the article and answer the following questions.
(a) At the time of the article, what was the overall P-E ratio of the Standard & Poor's 500-stock index of large companies as reported by Thomson Financial/First Call? How did that compare with the long-term historical average?
(b) What earnings measure does Thomson Financial/First Call use to calculate P-E? If, instead, the P-E was measured using earnings as reported under GAAP, what was the P-E for this index? What would this measure suggest about stock prices at the time?
(c) What are "pro forma" earnings? What other names are used for pro forma earnings? Are there any standards or guidelines for determining pro forma income? What justification do companies give for reporting pro forma income?
(d) According to the article, at what point did the use of pro forma earnings "get out of hand"?
(e) What did the article cite as an example of a "start of a backlash" against pro forma earnings measures?

BYP 14-10   The October 15, 2002, issue of the *Wall Street Journal* included an article by Jesse Drucker titled "**Motorola**'s Profit: 'Special' Again?"

Instructions
Read the article and answer the following questions.
(a) For how many consecutive quarters, including the quarter anticipated in the article, has Motorola reported a "special" item on its income statement? What is the total amount of these special charges over this period?

(b) What justification does Motorola give for reporting these charges as special items on its income statement, rather than reporting them as ordinary expenses?

(c) In the second quarter of 2002, what was Motorola's pro forma income, and what was its net income according to generally accepted accounting principles (GAAP)?

(d) According to the article, do Wall Street analysts give more attention to GAAP income or pro forma income? Do analysts agree on how to treat special charges, such as those of Motorola?

ETHICS CASE

BYP 14-11   Grace McQuillan, president of McQ Industries, wishes to issue a press release to bolster her company's image and maybe even its stock price, which has been gradually falling. As controller, you have been asked to provide a list of 20 financial ratios along with some other operating statistics relative to McQ Industries' first-quarter financials and operations.

Two days after you provide the ratios and data requested, you are asked by Minh Ly, the public relations director of McQ, to prove the accuracy of the financial and operating data contained in the press release written by the president and edited by Minh. In the news release, the president highlights the sales increase of 25% over last year's first quarter and the positive change in the current ratio from 1.5:1 last year to 3:1 this year. She also emphasizes that production was up 50% over the prior year's first quarter.

You note that the release contains only positive or improved ratios and none of the negative or deteriorated ratios. For instance, no mention is made that the debt to total assets ratio has increased from 35% to 55%, that inventories are up 89%, and that although the current ratio improved, the current cash debt coverage ratio fell from .15 to .05. Nor is there any mention that the reported profit for the quarter would have been a loss had not the estimated lives of McQ's plant and machinery been increased by 30%. Minh emphasized, "The president wants this release by early this afternoon."

Instructions
(a) Who are the stakeholders in this situation?
(b) Is there anything unethical in president McQ's actions?
(c) Should you as controller remain silent? Does Minh have any responsibility?

Answers to Self-Study Questions
1. d   2. c   3. c   4. a   5. c   6. c   7. b   8. a   9. c

Remember to go back to the Navigator box on the chapter-opening page and check off your completed work.

Time Value of Money

Would you rather receive $1,000 today or a year from now? You should prefer to receive the $1,000 today because you can invest the $1,000 and earn interest on it. As a result, you will have more than $1,000 a year from now. What this example illustrates is the concept of the **time value of money**. Everyone prefers to receive money today rather than in the future because of the interest factor.

Nature of Interest

Interest is payment for the use of another person's money. It is the difference between the amount borrowed or invested (called the **principal**) and the amount repaid or collected. The amount of interest to be paid or collected is usually stated as a rate over a specific period of time. The rate of interest is generally stated as an annual rate.

The amount of interest involved in any financing transaction is based on three elements:

1. **Principal (p)**: The original amount borrowed or invested.
2. **Interest Rate (i)**: An annual percentage of the principal.
3. **Time (n)**: The number of years that the principal is borrowed or invested.

SIMPLE INTEREST

Simple interest is computed on the principal amount only. It is the return on the principal for one period. Simple interest is usually expressed as shown in Illustration A-1.

| Interest | = | **Principal**
p | × | **Rate**
i | × | **Time**
n |

For example, if you borrowed $5,000 for 2 years at a simple interest rate of 12% annually, you would pay $1,200 in total interest computed as follows:

$$\text{Interest} = p \times i \times n$$
$$= \$5,000 \times .12 \times 2$$
$$= \$1,200$$

COMPOUND INTEREST

Compound interest is computed on principal **and** on any interest earned that has not been paid or withdrawn. It is the return on (or growth of) the principal for two or more time periods. Compounding computes interest not only on the principal but also on the interest earned to date on that principal, assuming the interest is left on deposit.

To illustrate the difference between simple and compound interest, assume that you deposit $1,000 in BankOne, where it will earn simple interest of 9 percent per year, and you deposit another $1,000 in CityCorp, where it will earn compound interest of 9 percent per year compounded annually. Also assume that in both cases you will not withdraw any interest until three years from the date of deposit. The computation of interest to be received and the accumulated year-end balances are indicated in Illustration A-2.

	BankOne				CityCorp.		
	Simple Interest Calculation	Simple Interest	Accumulated Year-end Balance		Compound Interest Calculation	Compound Interest	Accumulated Year-end Balance
Year 1	$1,000.00 × 9%	$ 90.00	$1,090.00		Year 1	$1,000.00 × 9%	$ 90.00	$1,090.00
Year 2	$1,000.00 × 9%	90.00	$1,180.00		Year 2	$1,090.00 × 9%	98.10	$1,188.10
Year 3	$1,000.00 × 9%	90.00	$1,270.00		Year 3	$1,188.10 × 9%	106.93	$1,295.03
		$ 270.00				$ 295.03	

$25.03
Difference

Note in the illustration above that simple interest uses the initial principal of $1,000 to compute the interest in all three years. Compound interest uses the accumulated balance (principal plus interest to date) at each year-end to compute interest in the succeeding year—which explains why your compound interest account is larger.

Obviously if you had a choice between investing your money at simple interest or at compound interest, you would choose compound interest, all other things—especially risk—being equal. In the example, compounding provides $25.03 of additional interest income. For practical purposes, compounding assumes that unpaid interest earned becomes a part of the principal, and the accumulated balance at the end of each year becomes the new principal on which interest is earned during the next year.

As can be seen in Illustration A-2, you should invest your money at CityCorp, which compounds interest annually. Compound interest is used in most business situations. Simple interest is generally applicable only to short-term situations of one year or less.

SECTION 1
FUTURE VALUE CONCEPTS

Future Value of a Single Amount

The **future value of a single amount** is the value at a future date of a given amount invested assuming compound interest. For example, in Illustration A-2, $1,295.03 is the future value of the $1,000 at the end of three years at 9% interest. The $1,295.03 could be determined more easily by using the following formula.

STUDY OBJECTIVE

2

Solve for future value of a single amount.

$$FV = p \times (1 + i)^n$$

where

FV = future value of a single amount
p = principal
i = interest rate for one period
n = number of periods

Illustration A-3   Future value computation

The future value of the CityCorp deposit in Illustration A-2 is computed as follows.

$$
\begin{aligned}
FV &= p \times (1 + i)^n \\
&= \$1{,}000 \times (1 + .09)^3 \\
&= \$1{,}000 \times 1.29503 \\
&= \$1{,}295.03
\end{aligned}
$$

The 1.29503 is computed by multiplying $(1.09 \times 1.09 \times 1.09)$. The amounts in this example can be depicted in the following time diagram.

Illustration A-4   Time diagram

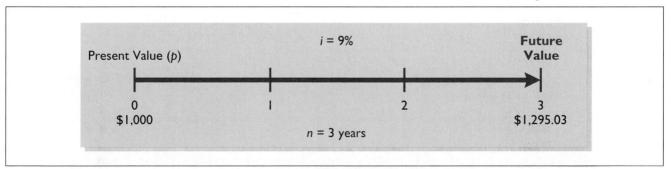

Another method that may be used to compute the future value of a single amount involves the use of a compound interest table. This table shows the future value of 1 for n periods. Table 1, shown at the top of the next page, is such a table.

TABLE 1   Future Value of 1

(n) Periods	4%	5%	6%	8%	9%	10%	11%	12%	15%
1	1.04000	1.05000	1.06000	1.08000	1.09000	1.10000	1.11000	1.12000	1.15000
2	1.08160	1.10250	1.12360	1.16640	1.18810	1.21000	1.23210	1.25440	1.32250
3	1.12486	1.15763	1.19102	1.25971	1.29503	1.33100	1.36763	1.40493	1.52088
4	1.16986	1.21551	1.26248	1.36049	1.41158	1.46410	1.51807	1.57352	1.74901
5	1.21665	1.27628	1.33823	1.46933	1.53862	1.61051	1.68506	1.76234	2.01136
6	1.26532	1.34010	1.41852	1.58687	1.67710	1.77156	1.87041	1.97382	2.31306
7	1.31593	1.40710	1.50363	1.71382	1.82804	1.94872	2.07616	2.21068	2.66002
8	1.36857	1.47746	1.59385	1.85093	1.99256	2.14359	2.30454	2.47596	3.05902
9	1.42331	1.55133	1.68948	1.99900	2.17189	2.35795	2.55803	2.77308	3.51788
10	1.48024	1.62889	1.79085	2.15892	2.36736	2.59374	2.83942	3.10585	4.04556
11	1.53945	1.71034	1.89830	2.33164	2.58043	2.85312	3.15176	3.47855	4.65239
12	1.60103	1.79586	2.01220	2.51817	2.81267	3.13843	3.49845	3.89598	5.35025
13	1.66507	1.88565	2.13293	2.71962	3.06581	3.45227	3.88328	4.36349	6.15279
14	1.73168	1.97993	2.26090	2.93719	3.34173	3.79750	4.31044	4.88711	7.07571
15	1.80094	2.07893	2.39656	3.17217	3.64248	4.17725	4.78459	5.47357	8.13706
16	1.87298	2.18287	2.54035	3.42594	3.97031	4.59497	5.31089	6.13039	9.35762
17	1.94790	2.29202	2.69277	3.70002	4.32763	5.05447	5.89509	6.86604	10.76126
18	2.02582	2.40662	2.85434	3.99602	4.71712	5.55992	6.54355	7.68997	12.37545
19	2.10685	2.52695	3.02560	4.31570	5.14166	6.11591	7.26334	8.61276	14.23177
20	2.19112	2.65330	3.20714	4.66096	5.60441	6.72750	8.06231	9.64629	16.36654

In Table 1, n is the number of compounding periods, the percentages are the periodic interest rates, and the five-digit decimal numbers in the respective columns are the future value of 1 factors. To use Table 1, multiply the principal amount by the future value factor for the specified number of periods and interest rate. For example, the future value factor for two periods at 9 percent is 1.18810. Multiplying this factor by $1,000 equals $1,188.10, which is the accumulated balance at the end of year 2 in the CityCorp example in Illustration A-2. The $1,295.03 accumulated balance at the end of the third year can be calculated from Table 1 by multiplying the future value factor for three periods (1.29503) by the $1,000.

The following demonstration problem illustrates how to use Table 1.

Illustration A-5 Demonstration Problem—
Using Table 1 for FV of 1

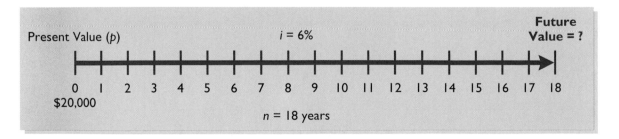

John and Mary Rich invested $20,000 in a savings account paying 6% interest at the time their son, Mike, was born. The money is to be used by Mike for his college education. On his 18th birthday, Mike withdraws the money from his savings account. How much did Mike withdraw from his account?

Answer: The future value factor from Table 1 is 2.85434 (18 periods at 6%). The future value of $20,000 earning 6% per year for 18 years is **$57,086.80** ($20,000 × 2.85434).

Future Value of an Annuity

The preceding discussion involved the accumulation of only a single principal sum. Individuals and businesses frequently encounter situations in which a series of equal dollar amounts are to be paid or received periodically, such as loans or lease (rental) contracts. Such payments or receipts of equal dollar amounts are referred to as **annuities**. The **future value of an annuity** is the sum of all the payments (receipts) plus the accumulated compound interest on them. In computing the future value of an annuity, it is necessary to know (1) the interest rate, (2) the number of compounding periods, and (3) the amount of the periodic payments or receipts.

To illustrate the computation of the future value of an annuity, assume that you invest $2,000 at the end of each year for three years at 5 percent interest compounded annually. This situation is depicted in the time diagram in Illustration A-6.

STUDY OBJECTIVE

3

Solve for future value of an annuity.

Illustration A-6   Time diagram for a three-year annuity

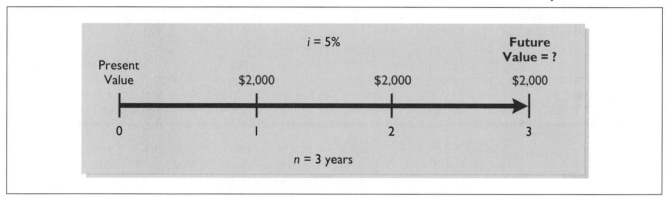

As can be seen in Illustration A-6, the $2,000 invested at the end of year 1 will earn interest for two years (years 2 and 3), and the $2,000 invested at the end of year 2 will earn interest for one year (year 3). However, the last $2,000 investment (made at the end of year 3) will not earn any interest. The future value of these periodic payments could be computed using the future value factors from Table 1 as shown in Illustration A-7.

Year Invested	Amount Invested	×	Future Value of 1 Factor at 5%	=	Future Value
1	$2,000	×	1.10250	=	$ 2,205
2	$2,000	×	1.05000	=	2,100
3	$2,000	×	1.00000	=	2,000
			3.15250		**$6,305**

Illustration A-7   Future value of periodic payments

The first $2,000 investment is multiplied by the future value factor for two periods (1.1025) because two years' interest will accumulate on it (in years 2 and 3). The second $2,000 investment will earn only one year's interest (in year 3) and therefore is multiplied by the future value factor for one year (1.0500). The final $2,000 investment is made at the end of the third year and will not earn any interest. Consequently, the future value of the last $2,000 invested is only $2,000 since it does not accumulate any interest.

This method of calculation is required when the periodic payments or receipts are not equal in each period. However, when the periodic payments (receipts) are the same in each period, the future value can be computed by using a future value of an annuity of 1 table. Table 2, shown on page A-6, is such a table.

TABLE 2   Future Value of an Annuity of 1

(n) Periods	4%	5%	6%	8%	9%	10%	11%	12%	15%
1	1.00000	1.00000	1.00000	1.00000	1.00000	1.00000	1.00000	1.00000	1.00000
2	2.04000	2.05000	2.06000	2.08000	2.09000	2.10000	2.11000	2.12000	2.15000
3	3.12160	3.15250	3.18360	3.24640	3.27810	3.31000	3.34210	3.37440	3.47250
4	4.24646	4.31013	4.37462	4.50611	4.57313	4.64100	4.70973	4.77933	4.99338
5	5.41632	5.52563	5.63709	5.86660	5.98471	6.10510	6.22780	6.35285	6.74238
6	6.63298	6.80191	6.97532	7.33592	7.52334	7.71561	7.91286	8.11519	8.75374
7	7.89829	8.14201	8.39384	8.92280	9.20044	9.48717	9.78327	10.08901	11.06680
8	9.21423	9.54911	9.89747	10.63663	11.02847	11.43589	11.85943	12.29969	13.72682
9	10.58280	11.02656	11.49132	12.48756	13.02104	13.57948	14.16397	14.77566	16.78584
10	12.00611	12.57789	13.18079	14.48656	15.19293	15.93743	16.72201	17.54874	20.30372
11	13.48635	14.20679	14.97164	16.64549	17.56029	18.53117	19.56143	20.65458	24.34928
12	15.02581	15.91713	16.86994	18.97713	20.14072	21.38428	22.71319	24.13313	29.00167
13	16.62684	17.71298	18.88214	21.49530	22.95339	24.52271	26.21164	28.02911	34.35192
14	18.29191	19.59863	21.01507	24.21492	26.01919	27.97498	30.09492	32.39260	40.50471
15	20.02359	21.57856	23.27597	27.15211	29.36092	31.77248	34.40536	37.27972	47.58041
16	21.82453	23.65749	25.67253	30.32428	33.00340	35.94973	39.18995	42.75328	55.71747
17	23.69751	25.84037	28.21288	33.75023	36.97351	40.54470	44.50084	48.88367	65.07509
18	25.64541	28.13238	30.90565	37.45024	41.30134	45.59917	50.39593	55.74972	75.83636
19	27.67123	30.53900	33.75999	41.44626	46.01846	51.15909	56.93949	63.43968	88.21181
20	29.77808	33.06595	36.78559	45.76196	51.16012	57.27500	64.20283	72.05244	102.44358

Illustration A-8 **Demonstration Problem**—Using Table 2 for FV of an annuity of 1

Table 2 shows the future value of 1 to be received periodically for a given number of end-of-period payments. You can see from Table 2 that the future value of an annuity of 1 factor for three periods at 5 percent is 3.15250. The future value factor is the total of the three individual future value factors as shown in Illustration A-7. Multiplying this amount by the annual investment of $2,000 produces a future value of $6,305.

The demonstration problem in Illustration A-8 illustrates how to use Table 2.

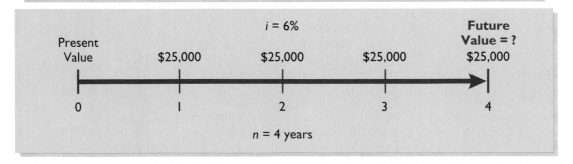

Henning Printing Company knows that in four years it must replace one of its existing printing presses with a new one. To ensure that some funds are available to replace the machine in four years, the company is depositing $25,000 in a savings account at the end of each of the next four years (4 deposits in total). The savings account will earn 6% interest compounded annually. How much will be in the savings account at the end of four years when the new printing press is to be purchased?

Answer: The future value factor from Table 2 is 4.37462 (4 periods at 6%). The future value of $25,000 invested at the end of each year for four years at 6% interest is **$109,365.50** ($25,000 × 4.37462).

SECTION 2
PRESENT VALUE CONCEPTS

Present Value Variables

The **present value**, like the future value, is based on three variables: (1) the dollar amount to be received (future amount), (2) the length of time until the amount is received (number of periods), and (3) the interest rate (the discount rate). The process of determining the present value is referred to as **discounting the future amount**.

In this textbook, present value computations are used in measuring several items. For example, capital budgeting and other investment proposals are evaluated using present value computations. All rate of return and internal rate of return computations involve present value techniques.

STUDY OBJECTIVE

4

Identify the variables fundamental to solving present value problems.

Present Value of a Single Amount

To illustrate present value concepts, assume that you want to invest a sum of money today that will provide $1,000 at the end of one year. What amount would you need to invest today to have $1,000 one year from now? If you want a 10 percent rate of return, the investment or present value is $909.09 ($1,000 ÷ 1.10). The computation of this amount is shown in Illustration A-9.

STUDY OBJECTIVE

5

Solve for present value of a single amount.

Present Value = Future Value ÷ $(1 + i)^1$

$$PV = FV \div (1 + .10)^1$$
$$PV = \$1,000 \div 1.10$$
$$PV = \$909.09$$

Illustration A-9 Present value computation— $1,000 discounted at 10% for one year

The future amount ($1,000), the discount rate (10 percent), and the number of periods (1) are known. The variables in this situation can be depicted in the following time diagram.

Illustration A-10 Finding present value if discounted for one period

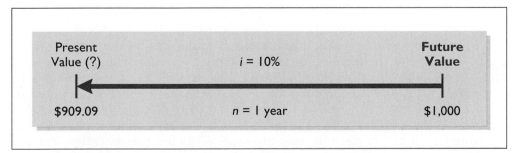

If the single amount of $1,000 is to be received **in two years** and discounted at 10 percent [PV = $1,000 ÷ $(1 + .10)^2$], its present value is $826.45 [($1,000 ÷ 1.10) ÷ 1.10], as shown in Illustration A-11 (page A-8).

Illustration A-11 Finding present value if discounted for two periods

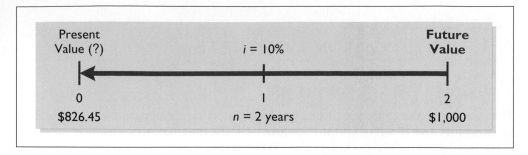

The present value of 1 may also be determined through tables that show the present value of 1 for *n* periods. In Table 3, *n* is the number of discounting periods involved. The percentages are the periodic interest rates or discount rates, and the five-digit decimal numbers in the respective columns are the present value of 1 factors.

TABLE 3   Present Value of 1

(*n*) Periods	4%	5%	6%	8%	9%	10%	11%	12%	15%
1	.96154	.95238	.94340	.92593	.91743	.90909	.90090	.89286	.86957
2	.92456	.90703	.89000	.85734	.84168	.82645	.81162	.79719	.75614
3	.88900	.86384	.83962	.79383	.77218	.75132	.73119	.71178	.65752
4	.85480	.82270	.79209	.73503	.70843	.68301	.65873	.63552	.57175
5	.82193	.78353	.74726	.68058	.64993	.62092	.59345	.56743	.49718
6	.79031	.74622	.70496	.63017	.59627	.56447	.53464	.50663	.43233
7	.75992	.71068	.66506	.58349	.54703	.51316	.48166	.45235	.37594
8	.73069	.67684	.62741	.54027	.50187	.46651	.43393	.40388	.32690
9	.70259	.64461	.59190	.50025	.46043	.42410	.39092	.36061	.28426
10	.67556	.61391	.55839	.46319	.42241	.38554	.35218	.32197	.24719
11	.64958	.58468	.52679	.42888	.38753	.35049	.31728	.28748	.21494
12	.62460	.55684	.49697	.39711	.35554	.31863	.28584	.25668	.18691
13	.60057	.53032	.46884	.36770	.32618	.28966	.25751	.22917	.16253
14	.57748	.50507	.44230	.34046	.29925	.26333	.23199	.20462	.14133
15	.55526	.48102	.41727	.31524	.27454	.23939	.20900	.18270	.12289
16	.53391	.45811	.39365	.29189	.25187	.21763	.18829	.16312	.10687
17	.51337	.43630	.37136	.27027	.23107	.19785	.16963	.14564	.09293
18	.49363	.41552	.35034	.25025	.21199	.17986	.15282	.13004	.08081
19	.47464	.39573	.33051	.23171	.19449	.16351	.13768	.11611	.07027
20	.45639	.37689	.31180	.21455	.17843	.14864	.12403	.10367	.06110

When Table 3 is used, the future value is multiplied by the present value factor specified at the intersection of the number of periods and the discount rate. For example, the present value factor for one period at a discount rate of 10 percent is .90909, which equals the $909.09 ($1,000 × .90909) computed in Illustration A-9. For two periods at a discount rate of 10 percent, the present value factor is .82645, which equals the $826.45 ($1,000 × .82645) computed previously.

Note that a higher discount rate produces a smaller present value. For example, using a 15 percent discount rate, the present value of $1,000 due one year from now is $869.57 versus $909.09 at 10 percent. It should also be recognized that the further removed from the present the future value is, the smaller the present value. For example, using the same discount rate of 10 percent, the present value of $1,000 due in **five** years is $620.92 versus $1,000 due in **one** year is $909.09.

The following two demonstration problems (Illustrations A-12, A-13) illustrate how to use Table 3.

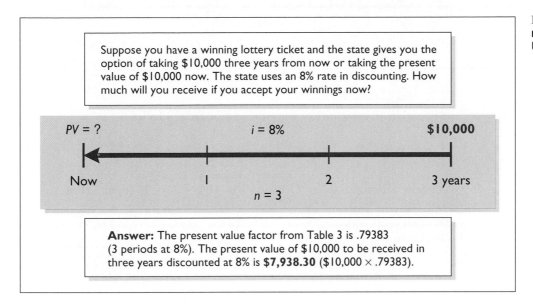

Suppose you have a winning lottery ticket and the state gives you the option of taking $10,000 three years from now or taking the present value of $10,000 now. The state uses an 8% rate in discounting. How much will you receive if you accept your winnings now?

PV = ?   i = 8% $10,000

Now   1   2   3 years

n = 3

Answer: The present value factor from Table 3 is .79383 (3 periods at 8%). The present value of $10,000 to be received in three years discounted at 8% is **$7,938.30** ($10,000 × .79383).

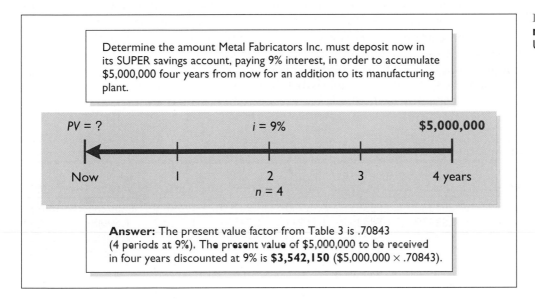

Determine the amount Metal Fabricators Inc. must deposit now in its SUPER savings account, paying 9% interest, in order to accumulate $5,000,000 four years from now for an addition to its manufacturing plant.

PV = ?   i = 9% $5,000,000

Now   1   2   3   4 years

n = 4

Answer: The present value factor from Table 3 is .70843 (4 periods at 9%). The present value of $5,000,000 to be received in four years discounted at 9% is **$3,542,150** ($5,000,000 × .70843).

Present Value of an Annuity

The preceding discussion involved the discounting of only a single future amount. Businesses and individuals frequently engage in transactions in which a series of equal dollar amounts are to be received or paid periodically. Examples of a series of periodic receipts or payments are loan agreements, installment sales, mortgage notes, lease (rental) contracts, and pension obligations. These series of periodic receipts or payments are called **annuities**. In computing the **present value of an annuity**, it is necessary to know (1) the discount rate, (2) the number of discount periods, and (3) the amount of the periodic receipts or payments.

To illustrate the computation of the present value of an annuity, assume that you will receive $1,000 cash annually for three years at a time when the discount rate is 10 percent. This situation is depicted in the time diagram in Illustration A-14.

STUDY OBJECTIVE

6

Solve for present value of an annuity.

Illustration A-14 Time diagram for a three-year annuity

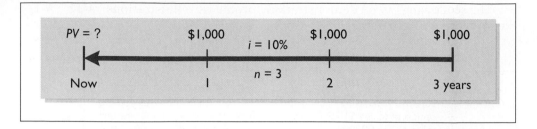

The present value in this situation may be computed as follows.

Illustration A-15 Present value of a series of future amounts computation

Future Amount	×	Present Value of 1 Factor at 10%	=	Present Value
$1,000 (One year away)	×	.90909	=	$ 909.09
1,000 (Two years away)	×	.82645	=	826.45
1,000 (Three years away)	×	.75132	=	751.32
		2.48686		**$2,486.86**

This method of calculation is required when the periodic cash flows are not uniform in each period. However, when the future receipts are the same in each period, there are two other ways to compute present value. First, the annual cash flow can be multiplied by the sum of the three present value factors. In the previous example, $1,000 × 2.48686 equals $2,486.86. Second, annuity tables may be used. As illustrated in Table 4 below, these tables show the present value of 1 to be received periodically for a given number of periods.

TABLE 4 **Present Value of an Annuity of 1**

(n) Periods	4%	5%	6%	8%	9%	10%	11%	12%	15%
1	.96154	.95238	.94340	.92593	.91743	.90909	.90090	.89286	.86957
2	1.88609	1.85941	1.83339	1.78326	1.75911	1.73554	1.71252	1.69005	1.62571
3	2.77509	2.72325	2.67301	2.57710	2.53130	2.48685	2.44371	2.40183	2.28323
4	3.62990	3.54595	3.46511	3.31213	3.23972	3.16986	3.10245	3.03735	2.85498
5	4.45182	4.32948	4.21236	3.99271	3.88965	3.79079	3.69590	3.60478	3.35216
6	5.24214	5.07569	4.91732	4.62288	4.48592	4.35526	4.23054	4.11141	3.78448
7	6.00205	5.78637	5.58238	5.20637	5.03295	4.86842	4.71220	4.56376	4.16042
8	6.73274	6.46321	6.20979	5.74664	5.53482	5.33493	5.14612	4.96764	4.48732
9	7.43533	7.10782	6.80169	6.24689	5.99525	5.75902	5.53705	5.32825	4.77158
10	8.11090	7.72173	7.36009	6.71008	6.41766	6.14457	5.88923	5.65022	5.01877
11	8.76048	8.30641	7.88687	7.13896	6.80519	6.49506	6.20652	5.93770	5.23371
12	9.38507	8.86325	8.38384	7.53608	7.16073	6.81369	6.49236	6.19437	5.42062
13	9.98565	9.39357	8.85268	7.90378	7.48690	7.10336	6.74987	6.42355	5.58315
14	10.56312	9.89864	9.29498	8.24424	7.78615	7.36669	6.98187	6.62817	5.72448
15	11.11839	10.37966	9.71225	8.55948	8.06069	7.60608	7.19087	6.81086	5.84737
16	11.65230	10.83777	10.10590	8.85137	8.31256	7.82371	7.37916	6.97399	5.95424
17	12.16567	11.27407	10.47726	9.12164	8.54363	8.02155	7.54879	7.11963	6.04716
18	12.65930	11.68959	10.82760	9.37189	8.75563	8.20141	7.70162	7.24967	6.12797
19	13.13394	12.08532	11.15812	9.60360	8.95012	8.36492	7.83929	7.36578	6.19823
20	13.59033	12.46221	11.46992	9.81815	9.12855	8.51356	7.96333	7.46944	6.25933

You can see from Table 4 that the present value of an annuity of 1 factor for three periods at 10 percent is 2.48685.[1] This present value factor is the total of the three individual present value factors as shown in Illustration A-15. Applying this amount to the annual cash flow of $1,000 produces a present value of $2,486.85.

The following demonstration problem (Illustration A-16) illustrates how to use Table 4.

Illustration A-16 **Demonstration Problem—** Using Table 4 for PV of an annuity of 1

Steel Products Company has just signed an agreement to purchase equipment for installment payments of $6,000 each, to be paid at the end of each of the next five years. In setting the amount of the payments, the seller used a discount rate of 12%. What is the present value of the installment payments–that is, how much is Steel Products paying for the equipment, and how much is it paying in total interest over the term of the installment contract?

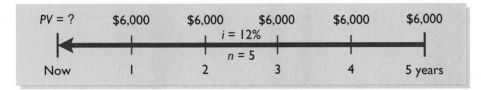

PV = ? $6,000 $6,000 $6,000 $6,000 $6,000

i = 12%

n = 5

Now   1   2   3   4   5 years

Answer: The present value factor from Table 4 is 3.60478 (5 periods at 12%). The present value of five payments of $6,000 each discounted at 12% is **$21,628.68** ($6,000 × 3.60478). Therefore, the cost of the equipment to Steel Products is $21,628.68 and the financing charge (interest) is $8,371.32 [($6,000 × 5) − $21,628.68].

Time Periods and Discounting

In the preceding calculations, the discounting has been done on an annual basis using an annual interest rate. Discounting may also be done over shorter periods of time such as monthly, quarterly, or semiannually. When the time frame is less than one year, it is necessary to convert the annual interest rate to the applicable time frame.

Assume, for example, that the investor in Illustration A-15 received $500 **semiannually** for three years instead of $1,000 annually. In this case, the number of periods becomes six (3 × 2), the discount rate is 5 percent (10% ÷ 2), the present value factor from Table 4 is 5.07569 (6 periods at 5%), and the present value of the future cash flows is $2,537.85 (5.07569 × $500). This amount is slightly higher than the $2,486.86 computed in Illustration A-15 because interest is computed twice during the same year. That is, interest is earned on the first half year's interest.

---

[1]The difference of .00001 between 2.48686 and 2.48685 is due to rounding.

Computing the Present Values in a Capital Budgeting Decision

The decision to make long-term capital investments is best evaluated using discounting techniques that recognize the time value of money. To do this, many companies calculate the present value of the cash flows involved in a capital investment.

To illustrate, Nagel-Siebert Trucking Company, a cross-country freight carrier in Montgomery, Illinois, is considering adding another truck to its fleet because of a purchasing opportunity. Navistar Inc., Nagel-Siebert's primary supplier of overland rigs, is overstocked and offers to sell its biggest rig for $154,000 cash payable upon delivery. Nagel-Siebert knows that the rig will produce a net cash flow per year of $40,000 for 5 years (received at the end of each year), at which time it will be sold for an estimated salvage value of $35,000. Nagel-Siebert's discount rate in evaluating capital expenditures is 10 percent. Should Nagel-Siebert commit to the purchase of this rig?

The cash flows that must be discounted to present value by Nagel-Siebert are as follows.

Cash payable on delivery (now): $154,000.

Net cash flow from operating the rig: $40,000 for 5 years (at the end of each year).

Cash received from sale of rig at the end of 5 years: $35,000.

The time diagrams for the latter two cash flows are shown in Illustration A-17.

Illustration A-17 Time diagrams for Nagel-Siebert Trucking Company

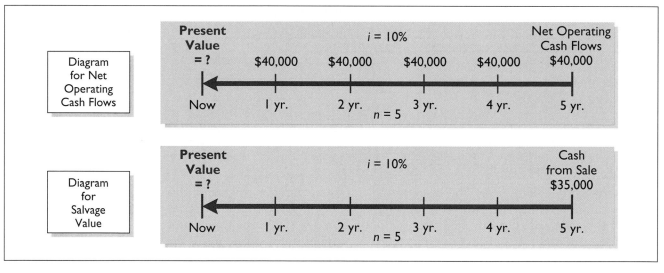

Notice from the diagrams that computing the present value of the net operating cash flows ($40,000 at the end of each year) is **discounting an annuity** (Table 4), while computing the present value of the $35,000 salvage value is **discounting a single sum** (Table 3).

The computation of these present values is shown in Illustration A-18 (page A-13).

Because the present value of the cash receipts (inflows) of $173,363.80 ($151,631.60 + $21,732.20) exceeds the present value of the cash payments

Present Values Using a 10 Percent Discount Rate

Present value of net operating cash flows received annually
over 5 years:

$40,000 × PV of 1 received annually for 5 years at 10%	
$40,000 × 3.79079 =	$151,631.60

Present value of salvage value (cash) to be received in 5 years

$35,000 × PV of 1 received in 5 years at 10%	
$35,000 × .62092 =	21,732.20

Present value of cash **inflows**	173,363.80

Present value cash **outflows** (purchase price due now at 10%):

$154,000 × PV of 1 due now	
$154,000 × 1.00000 =	154,000.00
Net present value	**$ 19,363.80**

(outflows) of $154,000.00, the net present value of $19,363.80 is positive, and **the decision to invest should be accepted**.

Now assume that Nagel-Siebert uses a discount rate of 15 percent, not 10 percent, because it wants a greater return on its investments in capital assets. The cash receipts and cash payments by Nagel-Siebert are the same. The present values of these receipts and cash payments discounted at 15 percent are shown in Illustration A-19.

Present Values Using a 15 Percent Discount Rate

Present value of net operating cash flows received annually
over 5 years at 15%:

$40,000 × 3.35216	$134,086.40

Present value of salvage value (cash) to be received in 5 years
at 15%

$35,000 × .49718	17,401.30

Present value of cash **inflows**	$151,487.70

Present value of cash **outflows** (purchase price due now at 15%):

$154,000 × 1.00000	154,000.00
Net present value	**$ (2,512.30)**

Because the present value of the cash payments (outflows) of $154,000 exceeds the present value of the cash receipts (inflows) of $151,487.70 ($134,086.40 + $17,401.30), the net present value of $2,512.30 is negative, and **the investment should be rejected**.

The above discussion relied on present value tables in solving present value problems. Electronic hand-held calculators may also be used to compute present values without the use of these tables. Some calculators, especially the "business" or "MBA" type calculators, have present value (PV) functions that allow you to calculate present values by merely identifying the proper amount, discount rate, periods, and pressing the PV key.

Summary of Study Objectives

1 *Distinguish between simple and compound interest.* Simple interest is computed on the principal only while compound interest is computed on the principal and any interest earned that has not been withdrawn.

2 *Solve for future value of a single amount.* Prepare a time diagram of the problem. Identify the principal amount, the number of compounding periods, and the interest rate. Using the future value of 1 table, multiply the principal amount by the future value factor specified at the intersection of the number of periods and the interest rate.

3 *Solve for future value of an annuity.* Prepare a time diagram of the problem. Identify the amount of the periodic payments (annuities), the number of compounding periods, and the interest rate. Using the future value of an annuity of 1 table, multiply the amount of the annuity by the future value factor specified at the intersection of the number of periods and the interest rate.

4 *Identify the variables fundamental to solving present value problems.* The following three variables are fundamental to solving present value problems: (1) the future amount, (2) the number of periods, and (3) the interest rate (the discount rate).

5 *Solve for present value of a single amount.* Prepare a time diagram of the problem. Identify the future amount, the number of discounting periods, and the discount (interest) rate. Using the present value of 1 table, multiply the future amount by the present value factor specified at the intersection of the number of periods and the discount rate.

6 *Solve for present value of an annuity.* Prepare a time diagram of the problem. Identify the future amounts (annuities), the number of discounting periods, and the discount (interest) rate. Using the present value of an annuity of 1 table, multiply the amount of the annuity by the present value factor specified at the intersection of the number of periods and the interest rate.

7 *Compute the present values in capital budgeting situations.* Compute the present values of all cash inflows and all cash outflows related to the capital budgeting proposal (an investment-type decision). If the **net** present value is positive, accept the proposal (make the investment). If the **net** present value is negative, reject the proposal (do not make the investment).

Glossary

Annuity   A series of equal dollar amounts to be paid or received periodically. (p. A-5)

Compound interest   The interest computed on the principal and any interest earned that has not been paid or withdrawn. (p. A-2)

Discounting the future amount(s)   The process of determining present value. (p. A-7)

Future value of a single amount   The value at a future date of a given amount invested assuming compound interest. (p. A-3)

Future value of an annuity   The sum of all the payments or receipts plus the accumulated compound interest on them. (p. A-5)

Interest   Payment for the use of another's money. (p. A-1)

Present value   The value now of a given amount to be received in the future assuming compound interest. (p. A-7)

Present value of an annuity   A series of future receipts or payments discounted to their value now assuming compound interest. (p. A-9)

Principal   The amount borrowed or invested. (p. A-1)

Simple interest   The interest computed on the principal only. (p. A-1)

Brief Exercises*

Compute the future value of a single amount.
(SO 2)

BEA-1   Don Smith invested $5,000 at 6% annual interest, and left the money invested without withdrawing any of the interest for 10 years. At the end of the 10 years, Don withdrew the accumulated amount of money.

(a) What amount did Don withdraw assuming the investment earns simple interest?

(b) What amount did Don withdraw assuming the investment earns interest compounded annually?

---

*Use tables to solve the Exercises.

BEA-2   For each of the following cases, indicate (a) to what interest rate columns and (b) to what number of periods you would refer in looking up the future value factor.

1. In Table 1 (future value of 1):

	Annual Rate	Number of Years Invested	Compounded
(a)	6%	5	Annually
(b)	8%	4	Semiannually

2. In Table 2 (future value of an annuity of 1):

	Annual Rate	Number of Years Invested	Compounded
(a)	5%	10	Annually
(b)	4%	6	Semiannually

BEA-3   Porter Company signed a lease for an office building for a period of 10 years. Under the lease agreement, a security deposit of $10,000 is made. The deposit will be returned at the expiration of the lease with interest compounded at 4% per year. What amount will Porter receive at the time the lease expires?

BEA-4   Gordon Company issued $1,000,000, 10-year bonds and agreed to make annual sinking fund deposits of $75,000. The deposits are made at the end of each year into an account paying 6% annual interest. What amount will be in the sinking fund at the end of 10 years?

BEA-5   David and Kathy Hatcher invested $5,000 in a savings account paying 6% annual interest when their daughter, Sue, was born. They also deposited $500 on each of her birthdays until she was 18 (including her 18th birthday). How much will be in the savings account on her 18th birthday (after the last deposit)?

BEA-6   Ron Watson borrowed $20,000 on July 1, 2000. This amount plus accrued interest at 8% compounded annually is to be repaid on July 1, 2005. How much will Ron have to repay on July 1, 2005?

BEA-7   For each of the following cases, indicate (a) to what interest rate columns and (b) to what number of periods you would refer in looking up the discount rate.

1. In Table 3 (present value of 1):

	Annual Rate	Number of Years Involved	Discounts Per Year
(a)	12%	5	Semiannually
(b)	10%	15	Annually
(c)	8%	8	Semiannually

2. In Table 4 (present value of an annuity of 1):

	Annual Rate	Number of Years Involved	Number of Payments Involved	Frequency of Payments
(a)	12%	20	20	Annually
(b)	10%	5	5	Annually
(c)	8%	4	8	Semiannually

BEA-8   (a) What is the present value of $10,000 due 4 periods from now, discounted at 8%? (b) What is the present value of $10,000 to be received at the end of each of 6 periods, discounted at 9%?

BEA-9   Smolinski Company is considering an investment which will return a lump sum of $500,000, 5 years from now. What amount should Smolinski Company pay for this investment to earn a 12% return?

Compute the present value of a single amount investment.
(SO 5)

BEA-10   Pizzeria Company earns 9% on an investment that will return $600,000, 8 years from now. What is the amount Pizzeria should invest now to earn this rate of return?

Compute the present value of an annuity investment.
(SO 6)

BEA-11   Kilarny Company is considering investing in an annuity contract that will return $20,000 annually at the end of each year for 18 years. What amount should Kilarny Company pay for this investment if it earns a 6% return?

Compute the present value of an annuity investment.
(SO 6)

BEA-12   Zarita Enterprises earns 8% on an investment that pays back $110,000 at the end of each of the next 4 years. What is the amount Zarita Enterprises invested to earn the 8% rate of return?

Compute the present value of bonds.
(SO 5, 6)

BEA-13   Hernandez Railroad Co. is about to issue $100,000 of 10-year bonds paying a 10% interest rate, with interest payable semiannually. The discount rate for such securities is 8%. How much can Hernandez expect to receive from the sale of these bonds?

Compute the present value of bonds.
(SO 5, 6)

BEA-14   Assume the same information as BEA-13 except that the discount rate was 10% instead of 8%. In this case, how much can Hernandez expect to receive from the sale of these bonds?

Compute the present value of a note.
(SO 5, 6)

BEA-15   Caledonian Taco Company receives a $50,000, 6-year note bearing interest of 8% (paid annually) from a customer at a time when the discount rate is 9%. What is the present value of the note received by Caledonian?

Compute the present value of bonds.
(SO 5, 6)

BEA-16   Galway Bay Enterprises issued 10%, 7-year, $2,000,000 par value bonds that pay interest semiannually on October 1 and April 1. The bonds are dated April 1, 2005, and are issued on that date. The discount rate of interest for such bonds on April 1, 2005, is 12%. What cash proceeds did Galway Bay receive from issuance of the bonds?

Compute the present value of a machine for purposes of making a purchase decision.
(SO 7)

BEA-17   Barney Googal owns a garage and is contemplating purchasing a tire retreading machine for $14,280. After estimating costs and revenues, Barney projects a net cash flow from the retreading machine of $2,900 annually for 8 years. Barney hopes to earn a return of 11% on such investments. What is the present value of the retreading operation? Should Barney Googal purchase the retreading machine?

Compute the present value of a note.
(SO 6)

BEA-18   Hung-Chao Yu Company issues an 8%, 6-year mortgage note on January 1, 2005 to obtain financing for new equipment. Land is used as collateral for the note. The terms provide for semiannual installment payments of $85,242. What were the cash proceeds received from the issuance of the note?

Compute the maximum price to pay for a machine.
(SO 7)

BEA-19   Ramos Company is considering purchasing equipment. The equipment will produce the following cash flows: Year 1, $30,000; Year 2, $40,000; Year 3, $50,000. Ramos requires a minimum rate of return of 12%. What is the maximum price Ramos should pay for this equipment?

Compute the interest rate on a single amount.
(SO 5)

BEA-20   Kerry Rodriguez invests $3,555.40 now and will receive $10,000 at the end of 12 years. What annual rate of interest will Kerry earn on her investment? (*Hint:* Use Table 3.)

Compute the number of periods of a single amount.
(SO 5)

BEA-21   Maloney Cork has been offered the opportunity of investing $20,462 now. The investment will earn 12% per year and will at the end of that time return Maloney $100,000. How many years must Maloney wait to receive $100,000? (*Hint:* Use Table 3.)

Compute the interest rate on an annuity.
(SO 6)

BEA-22   Annie Dublin purchased an investment of $9,818.15. From this investment, she will receive $1,000 annually for the next 20 years starting one year from now. What rate of interest will Annie's investment be earning for her? (*Hint:* Use Table 4.)

Compute the number of periods of an annuity.
(SO 6)

BEA-23   Andy Sanchez invests $8,863.25 now for a series of $1,000 annual returns beginning one year from now. Andy will earn a return of 5% on the initial investment. How many annual payments of $1,000 will Andy receive? (*Hint:* Use Table 4.)

Standards of Ethical Conduct for Management Accountants

Management accountants have an obligation to the organizations they serve, their profession, the public, and themselves to maintain the highest standards of ethical conduct. In recognition of this obligation, the **Institute of Management Accountants** (formerly the National Association of Accountants), has published and promoted the following standards of ethical conduct for management accountants. Adherence to these standards is integral to achieving the *Objectives of Management Accounting*.

Management accountants shall not commit acts contrary to these standards nor shall they condone the commission of such acts by others within their organizations.

COMPETENCE

Management accountants have a responsibility to:

- Maintain an appropriate level of professional competence by ongoing development of their knowledge and skills.
- Perform their professional duties in accordance with relevant laws, regulations, and technical standards.
- Prepare complete and clear reports and recommendations after appropriate analyses of relevant and reliable information.

CONFIDENTIALITY

Management accountants have a responsibility to:

- Refrain from disclosing confidential information acquired in the course of their work except when authorized, unless legally obligated to do so.
- Inform subordinates as appropriate regarding the confidentiality of information acquired in the course of their work and monitor their activities to assure the maintenance of that confidentiality.
- Refrain from using or appearing to use confidential information acquired in the course of their work for unethical or illegal advantage either personally or through third parties.

INTEGRITY

Management accountants have a responsibility to:

- Avoid actual or apparent conflicts of interest and advise all appropriate parties of any potential conflict.

Source: Institute of Management Accountants, Ethical Standards, SMA 1C (Statement on Management Accounting). Adapted with permission.

- Refrain from engaging in any activity that would prejudice their ability to carry out their duties ethically.
- Refuse any gift, favor, or hospitality that would influence or would appear to influence their actions.
- Refrain from either actively or passively subverting the attainment of the organization's legitimate and ethical objectives.
- Recognize and communicate professional limitations or other constraints that would preclude responsible judgment or successful performance of an activity.
- Communicate unfavorable as well as favorable information and professional judgments or opinions.
- Refrain from engaging in or supporting any activity that would discredit the profession.

OBJECTIVITY

Management accountants have a responsibility to:

- Communicate information fairly and objectively.
- Disclose fully all relevant information that could reasonably be expected to influence an intended user's understanding of the reports, comments, and recommendations presented.

RESOLUTION OF ETHICAL CONFLICT

In applying the standards of ethical conduct, management accountants may encounter problems in identifying unethical behavior or in resolving an ethical conflict. When faced with significant ethical issues, management accountants should follow the established policies of the organization bearing on the resolution of such conflict. If these policies do not resolve the ethical conflict, such practitioners should consider the following courses of action.

- Discuss such problems with the immediate superior except when it appears that the superior is involved, in which case the problem should be presented initially to the next higher managerial level. If a satisfactory resolution cannot be achieved when the problem is initially presented, submit the issues to the next higher managerial level. If the immediate superior is the chief executive officer, or equivalent, the acceptable reviewing authority may be a group such as the audit committee, executive committee, board of directors, board of trustees, or owners. Contact with levels above the immediate superior should be initiated only with the superior's knowledge, assuming the superior is not involved. Except where legally prescribed, communication of such problems to authorities or individuals not employed or engaged by the organization is not considered appropriate.
- Clarify relevant ethical issues by confidential discussion with an objective advisor (e.g., Institute of Management Accountants Ethics Counseling service) to obtain a better understanding of possible courses of action. Consult your own attorney as to legal obligations and rights concerning the ethical conflict.
- If the ethical conflict still exists after exhausting all levels of internal review, there may be no other recourse on significant matters than to resign from the organization and to submit an informative memorandum to an appropriate representative of the organization. After resignation, depending on the nature of the ethical conflict, it may also be appropriate to notify other parties.

CASES FOR
Management
Decision Making

Case

Overview

CASE 1

Greetings Inc. Swims in the Dot-com Sea: Job Order Costing

This case is the first in a series of four cases that presents a business situation in which a traditional retailer decides to employ Internet technology to expand its sales opportunities. It requires the student to employ traditional job order costing techniques and then requests an evaluation of the resulting product costs. (Related to Chapter 2, Job Order Cost Accounting.)

CASE 2

Greetings Inc. Swims in the Dot-com Sea: Activity-based Costing

This case focuses on decision-making benefits of activity-based costing relative to the traditional approach. It also offers an opportunity to discuss the cost/benefit trade-off between simple ABC systems versus refined systems, and the potential benefit of using capacity rather than expected sales when allocating fixed overhead costs. (Related to Chapter 4, Activity-Based Costing.)

CASE 3

Greetings Inc. Swims in the Dot-com Sea: Transfer Pricing Issues

This case illustrates the importance of proper transfer pricing for decision making as well as performance evaluation. The student is required to evaluate profitability using two different transfer pricing approaches and comment on the terms of the proposed transfer pricing agreement. (Related to Chapter 8, Pricing.)

CASE 4

Greetings Inc. Swims in the Dot-com Sea: Capital Budgeting

This case is set in an environment in which the company is searching for new opportunities for growth. It requires evaluation of a proposal based on initial estimates as well as sensitivity analysis. It also requires evaluation of the underlying assumptions used in the analysis. (Related to Chapter 12, Planning for Capital Investments.)

CASE 5

Auburn Circular Club Pro Rodeo Roundup

This comprehensive case is designed to be used as a capstone activity at the end of the course. It deals with a not-for-profit service company. The case involves many managerial accounting issues that would be common for a start-up business. (Related to Chapter 5, Cost-Volume-Profit; Chapter 6, Incremental Analysis; and Chapter 9, Budgetary Planning.)

CASE 6

Sweats Galore

This case focuses on setting up a new business. In planning for this new business, the preparation of budgets is emphasized. In addition, an understanding of cost-volume-profit relationships is required. (Related to Chapter 5, Cost-Volume-Profit, and Chapter 9, Budgetary Planning.)

CASE 7

Armstrong Helmet Company

This comprehensive case involves finding the cost for a given product. In addition, it explores cost-volume-profit relationships. It requires the preparation of a set of budgets. (Related to Chapter 1, Basic Cost Concepts; Chapter 5, Cost-Volume-Profit; Chapter 9, Budgetary Planning; Chapter 10, Budgetary Control and Responsibility Accounting; Chapter 11, Standard Costs and Balanced Scorecard; and Chapter 12, Planning Capital Investments.)

Greetings *Inc.*

Greetings Inc. Swims in the Dot-com Sea: Job Order Costing

Developed by Thomas L. Zeller, Loyola University Chicago, and Paul D. Kimmel, University of Wisconsin– Milwaukee

The Business Situation

Greetings Inc. has operated for many years as a nationally recognized retailer of greeting cards and small gift items. It has 1,500 stores throughout the United States located in high-traffic malls.

During the late 1990s, as the stock price of many other companies soared, Greetings' stock price remained flat. As a result of a heated 1998 shareholders' meeting, the president of Greetings, Robert Burns, came under pressure from shareholders to grow Greetings' stock value. As a consequence of this pressure, in 1999 Mr. Burns called for a formal analysis of the company's options with regard to business opportunities.

Location was the first issue considered in the analysis. Greetings stores are located in high-traffic malls where rental costs are high. The additional rental cost was justified, however, by the revenue that resulted from these highly visible locations. In recent years, though, the intense competition from other stores in the mall selling similar merchandise has become a disadvantage of the mall locations.

Mr. Burns felt that to increase revenue in the mall locations, Greetings would need to attract new customers and sell more goods to repeat customers. In order to do this, the company would need to add a new product line. However, to keep costs down, the product line should be one that would not require much additional store space. In order to improve earnings, rather than just increase revenues, Greetings would have to carefully manage the costs of this new product line.

After careful consideration of many possible products, the company's management found a product that seemed to be a very good strategic fit for its existing products: high-quality unframed and framed prints. The critical element of this plan was that customers would pick out prints by viewing them on wide-screen computer monitors in each store. Orders would be processed and shipped from a central location. Thus, store size would not have to increase at all. To offer these products, Greetings established a new business unit called WallDécor.com. WallDécor is a "profit center"; that is, the manager of the new business unit is responsible for decisions affecting both revenues and costs.

WallDécor was designed to distribute unframed and framed print items to each Greetings store on a just-in-time (JIT) basis. The system works as follows: The WallDécor Web site allows customers to choose from several hundred prints. The print can be purchased in various forms: unframed, framed with a metal frame and no matting, or framed with a wood frame and matting. When a customer purchases an unframed print, it is packaged and shipped the same day from WallDécor. When a customer purchases a framed print, the print is framed at WallDécor and shipped within 48 hours.

Each Greetings store has a computer linked to WallDécor's Web server so Greetings customers can browse the many options to make a selection. Once a selection is made, the customer can complete the order immediately. Store employees are trained to help customers use the Web site and complete the purchase. The advantage to this approach is that each Greetings store, through the WallDécor Web site, can offer a wide variety of prints, yet the individual Greetings stores do not have to hold any inventory of prints or framing materials. About the only cost to the individual store is the computer and high-speed line connection to WallDécor. The advantage to the customer is the wide variety of unframed and framed print items that can be conveniently purchased and delivered to the home or business, or to a third party as a gift.

WallDécor uses a traditional job-order costing system. Operation of WallDécor would be substantially less complicated, and overhead costs would be substantially less, if it sold only unframed prints. Unframed prints require no additional processing, and they can be easily shipped in simple protective tubes. Framing and matting requires the company to have multiple matting colors and frame styles, which requires considerable warehouse space. It also requires skilled employees to assemble the products and more expensive packaging procedures.

Manufacturing overhead is allocated to each unframed or framed print, based on the cost of the print. This overhead allocation approach is based on the assumption that more expensive prints will usually be framed and therefore more overhead costs should be assigned to these items. The predetermined overhead rate is the total expected manufacturing overhead divided by the total expected cost of prints. This method of allocation appeared reasonable to the accounting team and distribution floor manager. Direct labor costs for unframed prints consist of picking the prints off the shelf and packaging them for shipment. For framed prints, direct labor costs consist of picking the prints, framing, matting, and packaging.

The information in Illustration 1-1 on the next page for unframed and framed prints was collected by the accounting and production teams. The manufacturing overhead budget is presented in Illustration 1-2.

Instructions

Use the information in the case and your reading from Chapters 1 and 2 of the text to answer each of the following questions.

1. Define and explain the meaning of a predetermined manufacturing overhead rate that is applied in a job-order costing system.
2. What are the advantages and disadvantages of using the cost of each print as a manufacturing overhead cost driver?
3. Using the information on the next page, compute and interpret the predetermined manufacturing overhead rate for WallDécor.

	Unframed Print	Steel-Framed Print, No Matting	Wood-Framed Print, with Matting
Volume—expected units sold	80,000	15,000	7,000
Cost Elements			
Direct materials			
Print (expected average cost for each of the three categories)	$12	$16	$20
Frame and glass		$4	$6
Matting			$4
Direct labor			
Picking time	10 minutes	10 minutes	10 minutes
Picking labor rate/hour	$12	$12	$12
Matting and framing time		20 minutes	30 minutes
Matting and framing rate/hour		$21	$21

ILLUSTRATION 1-1
Information about prints and framed items for Greetings Inc.

Manufacturing Overhead Budget

Supervisory salaries	$100,000
Factory rent	130,200
Equipment rent (framing and matting equipment)	50,000
Utilities	20,000
Insurance	10,000
Information technology	50,000
Building maintenance	11,000
Equipment maintenance	4,000
Budgeted total manufacturing overhead costs	**$375,200**

ILLUSTRATION 1-2
Manufacturing overhead budget for Greetings Inc.

4. Compute the product cost for the following three items.
   (a) Lance Armstrong unframed print (base cost of print $12).
   (b) John Elway print in steel frame, no mat (base cost of print $16).
   (c) Lambeau Field print in wood frame with mat (base cost of print $20).

5. (a) How much of the total overhead cost is expected to be allocated to unframed prints?
   (b) How much of the total overhead cost is expected to be allocated to steel framed prints?
   (c) How much of the total overhead cost is expected to be allocated to wood framed prints?
   (d) What percentage of the total overhead cost is expected to be allocated to unframed prints?

6. Do you think the amount of overhead allocated to the three product categories is reasonable? Relate your response to this question to your findings in previous questions.

7. Anticipate business problems that may result from allocating manufacturing overhead based on the cost of the prints.

Greetings Inc.

Greetings Inc. Swims in the Dot-com Sea: Activity-based Costing

*Developed by
Thomas L. Zeller,
Loyola University
Chicago, and
Paul D. Kimmel,
University
of Wisconsin–
Milwaukee*

The Business Situation

Mr. Burns, president of Greetings Inc., created the WallDécor unit of Greetings three years ago to increase the company's revenue and profits. Unfortunately, even though WallDécor's revenues have grown quickly, Greetings appears to be losing money on WallDécor. Mr. Burns has hired you to provide consulting services to WallDécor's management. Your assignment is to make WallDécor a profitable business unit.

Your first step is to talk with the WallDécor work force. From your conversations with store managers you learn that the individual Greetings stores are very happy with the WallDécor arrangement. The stores are generating additional sales revenue from the sale of unframed and framed prints. They are especially enthusiastic about this revenue source because the online nature of the product enables them to generate revenue without the additional cost of carrying inventory. WallDécor sells unframed and framed prints to each store at product cost plus 20 percent. A 20 percent mark-up on products is a standard policy of all Greetings intercompany transactions. Each store is allowed to add an additional mark-up to the unframed and framed print items according to market pressures. That is, the selling price charged by each store for unframed and framed prints is determined by each store manager. This policy ensures competitive pricing in the respective store locations, an important business issue because of the intense mall competition.

While the store managers are generally happy with the WallDécor products, they have noted a significant difference in the sales performance of the unframed prints and the framed prints. They find it difficult to sell unframed prints at a competitive price. The price competition in the malls is very intense. On average, stores find that the profits on unframed prints are very low because the cost for unframed prints charged by WallDécor to the Greetings stores is only slightly below what competing stores charge their customers for unframed prints. As a result, the profit margin on unframed prints is very low, and the overall profit earned is small, even with the large volume of prints sold. In contrast, stores make a very good profit on framed prints and still beat the nearest competitor's price by about 15 percent. That is, the mall competitors cannot meet at a competitive price the quality of framed prints provided by the

Greetings stores. As a result, store managers advertise the lowest prices in town for high-quality framed prints. One store manager referred to WallDécor's computer on the counter as a "cash machine" for framed prints and a "lemonade stand" for unframed prints.

In a conversation with the production manager you learned that she believes that the relative profitability of framed and unframed prints is distorted because of improper product costing. She feels that the costs provided by the company's traditional job-order costing system are inaccurate. From the very beginning, she has carefully managed production and distribution costs. She explains, "WallDécor is essentially giving away expensive framed prints, and it appears that it is charging the stores too much for unframed prints." In her office she shows you her own product costing system, which supports her point of view.

Your tour of the information technology (IT) department provided additional insight as to why WallDécor is having financial problems. You discovered that to keep the Web site running requires separate computer servers and several information technology professionals. Two separate activities are occurring in the technology area. First, purchasing professionals and IT professionals spend many hours managing thousands of prints and frame and matting materials. Their tasks include selecting the prints and the types of framing material to sell. They also must upload, manage, and download prints and framing material onto and off of the Web site. The IT staff tells you much of their time is spent with framing and matting material. Only a highly skilled IT professional can properly scan a print and load it up to the site so that it graphically represents what the print will look like when properly matted and framed.

In addition, you discover that a different team of IT professionals is dedicated to optimizing the operating performance of the Web site. These costs are classified as manufacturing overhead because a substantial amount of work is required to keep the site integrated with purchasing and production and to safeguard WallDécor's assets online. Most time-consuming is the effort to develop and maintain the site so that customers can view the prints as they would appear either unframed or framed and matted.

A discussion with the IT professionals suggests that the time spent developing and maintaining the site for the unframed prints is considerably less than that required for the framed prints and in particular for the framed and matted prints. Developing and maintaining a site that can display the unframed prints is relatively straightforward. It becomes more complicated when the site must allow the customer to view every possible combination of print with every type of steel frame, and immensely more complicated when one considers all of the possible wood frames and different matting colors. Obviously, a very substantial portion of the IT professionals' time and resources is required to present the over 1,000 different framing and matting options.

Based on your preliminary findings, you have decided that the company's ability to measure and evaluate the profitability of individual products would be improved if the company employed an activity-based costing (ABC) system. As a first step in this effort, you compiled a list of costs, activities, and values. Your work consisted of taking the original manufacturing overhead cost ($375,200, provided in Case 1) and allocating the costs to activities. You identified four activities: picking prints; inventory selection and management (includes general management and overhead); Web-site optimization; and framing and matting cost (includes equipment, insurance, rent, and supervisor's salary).

The first activity is picking prints. The estimated overhead related to this activity is $30,600. The cost driver for this activity is the number of prints. It is expected that the total number of prints will be 102,000. This is the sum of 80,000 unframed, 15,000 steel-framed, and 7,000 wood-framed.

ILLUSTRATION 2-1
Information for activity 1

Activity	Cost Driver	Estimated Overhead	Expected Use of Cost Driver
Picking prints	Number of prints	$30,600	(80,000 + 15,000 + 7,000) = 102,000 prints

The second activity is inventory selection and management. The estimated overhead related to this activity is $91,700. The cost driver for this activity is the number of components per print item. An unframed print has one component, a steel-framed print has two components (the print and the frame), and a wood-framed print has three components (the print, the mat, and the frame). The total number of components is expected to be 131,000.

ILLUSTRATION 2-2
Information for activity 2

Activity	Cost Driver	Estimated Overhead	Expected Use of Cost Driver
Inventory selection and management	Number of components: Print (1) Print and frame (2) Print, mat, and frame (3)	$91,700	Prints: 80,000 components Print and frame: 15,000 × 2 = 30,000 components Print, mat, and frame: 7,000 × 3 = 21,000 components Total = 131,000 components

The third activity is Web-site optimization. The total overhead cost related to Web-site optimization is expected to be $129,000. It was difficult to identify a cost driver that directly related Web-site optimization to the products. In order to reflect the fact that the majority of the time spent on this activity related to framed prints, you first split the cost of Web-site optimization between unframed prints and framed prints. Based on your discussion with the IT professionals, you determined that they spend roughly one-fifth of their time developing and maintaining the site for unframed prints, and the other four-fifths of their time on framed prints, even though the number of framed prints sold is substantially less than the number of unframed prints. As a consequence, you allocated $25,800 of the overhead costs related to Web-site optimization to unframed prints and $103,200 to framed prints. You contemplated having three categories (unframed, steel-framed, and wood-framed with matting), but chose not to add this additional refinement.

ILLUSTRATION 2-3
Information for activity 3

Activity	Cost Driver	Estimated Overhead	Expected Use of Cost Driver
Web-site optimization:			
Unframed	Number of prints at capacity	$ 25,800	Unframed prints: 100,000 print capacity
Framed	Number of prints at capacity	$103,200	Framed and/or matted prints: 25,000 print capacity (16,000 steel; 9,000 wood)

Once the $129,000 of the third activity was allocated across the two broad product categories, the number of prints at *operating capacity* was used as the cost driver. Note that operating capacity was used instead of expected units sold. The overhead costs related to Web-site optimization are relatively fixed because the employees are salaried. If a fixed cost is allocated using a value that varies from period to period (like expected sales), then the cost per unit will vary from period to period. When allocating fixed costs it is better to use a base that does not vary as much, such as operating capacity. The advantage of using operating capacity as the base is that it keeps the fixed costs per unit stable over time.

The final activity is framing and matting. The expected overhead costs related to framing and matting are $123,900. None of this overhead cost should be allocated to unframed prints. The costs related to framing and matting are relatively fixed because the costs relate to equipment and other costs that do not vary with sales volume. As a consequence, like Web-site optimization, you chose to base the cost driver on levels at operating *capacity*, rather than at the expected sales level. The cost driver is the number of components. Steel-framed prints have two components (the print and frame), and wood-framed prints have three components (the print, mat, and frame). The total components at operating capacity would be steel frame 32,000 or (16,000 × 2) and wood frame 27,000 or (9,000 × 3,000).

Activity	Cost Driver	Estimated Overhead	Expected Use of Cost Driver
Framing and matting cost (equipment, insurance, rent, and supervisory labor)	Number of components at capacity	$123,900	Print and frame: 16,000 × 2 = 32,000 components at capacity Print, mat, and frame: 9,000 × 3 = 27,000 components at capacity Total = 59,000 components

ILLUSTRATION 2-4
Information for activity 4

To summarize, the overhead costs and cost drivers used for each product are expected to be:

Activity	Cost Driver	Unframed	Steel-Framed, No Matting	Wood-Framed, with Matting	Total	Overhead Cost
Picking prints	Number of prints	80,000	15,000	7,000	102,000	$ 30,600
Inventory selection and management	Number of components	80,000	30,000	21,000	131,000	91,700
Web-site optimization	Number of prints at capacity	100,000			100,000	25,800
			16,000	9,000	25,000	103,200
Framing and matting	Number of components at capacity	na	32,000	27,000	59,000	123,900
						$375,200

ILLUSTRATION 2-5
Summary of overhead costs and cost drivers

Instructions

Answer the following questions.

1. Identify two reasons why an activity-based costing system may be appropriate for WallDécor.

2. Compute the activity-based overhead rates for each of the four activities.

3. Compute the product cost for the following three items using ABC. (Review Case 1 for additional information that you will need to answer this question.)
   (a) Lance Armstrong unframed print (base cost of print $12)
   (b) John Elway print in steel frame, no mat (base cost of print $16)
   (c) Lambeau Field print in wood frame with mat (base cost of print $20)

4. In Case 1 for Greetings, the overhead allocations using a traditional volume-based approach were $3.36 for Lance Armstrong, $4.48 for John Elway, and $5.60 for Lambeau Field. The total product costs from Case 1 were Lance Armstrong $17.36, John Elway $33.48, and Lambeau Field $48.10. The overhead allocation rate for unframed prints, such as the unframed Lance Armstrong print in question 3, decreased under ABC compared to the amount of overhead that was allocated under the traditional approach in Case 1. Why is this the case? What are the potential implications for the company?

5. Explain why the overhead cost related to Web-site optimization was first divided into two categories (unframed prints and framed prints) and then allocated based on number of prints.

6. When allocating the cost of Web-site optimization, the decision was made to initially allocate the cost across two categories (unframed prints and framed prints) rather than three categories (unframed prints, steel-framed prints, and wood-framed prints with matting). Discuss the pros and cons of splitting the cost between two categories rather than three.

7. Discuss the implications of using operating *capacity* as the cost driver rather than the expected units sold when allocating fixed overhead costs.

8. (a) Allocate the overhead to the three product categories (unframed prints, steel-framed prints, and wood-framed prints with matting), assuming that the estimate of the expected units sold is correct and the actual amount of overhead incurred equaled the estimated amount of $375,200.
   (b) Calculate the total amount of overhead allocated. Explain why the total overhead of $375,200 was not allocated, even though the estimate of sales was correct. What are the implications of this for management?

Greetings Inc.

Greetings Inc. Swims in the Dot-com Sea: Transfer Pricing Issues

Developed by Thomas L. Zeller, Loyola University Chicago, and Paul D. Kimmel, University of Wisconsin– Milwaukee

The Business Situation

Two years ago, prior to a major capital-budgeting decision (Case 4), Robert Burns, the president of Greetings Inc., faced a challenging transfer pricing issue. He knew that Greetings store managers had heard about the ABC study (see Case 2) and that they knew a price increase for framed items would soon be on the way. In an effort to dissuade him from increasing the transfer price for framed prints, several store managers e-mailed him with detailed analyses showing how framed-print sales had given stores a strong competitive position and had increased revenues and profits. The store managers mentioned, however, that while they were opposed to an increase in the cost of framed prints, they were looking forward to a price decrease for unframed prints.

Management at WallDécor was very interested in changing the transfer pricing strategy. You had reported to them that setting the transfer price based on the product costs calculated by using traditional overhead allocation measures had been a major contributing factor to its non-optimal performance.

Here is a brief recap of what happened during your presentation to Mr. Burns and the WallDécor managers. Mr. Burns smiled during your presentation and graciously acknowledged your excellent activity-based costing (ABC) study and analysis. He even nodded with approval as you offered the following suggestions.

1. WallDécor should decrease the transfer price for high-volume, simple print items.
2. WallDécor should increase the transfer price for low-volume, complex framed print items.
3. Your analysis points to a transfer price that maintains the 20 percent markup over cost.
4. Adoption of these changes will provide WallDécor with an 11 percent return on investment (ROI), beating the required 10 percent expected by Greetings' board of directors.
5. Despite the objections of the store managers, the Greetings stores must accept the price changes.

Finishing your presentation, you asked the executive audience, "What questions do you have?" Mr. Burns responded as follows.

"Your analysis appears sound. However, it focuses almost exclusively on WallDécor. It appears to tell us little about how to move forward and benefit the entire company, especially the Greetings retail stores. Let me explain.

I am concerned about how individual store customers will react to the price changes, assuming the price increase of framed-print items is passed along to the customer. Store managers will welcome a decrease in the transfer price of unframed prints. They have complained about the high cost of prints from the beginning. With a decrease in print cost, store managers will be able to compete against mall stores for print items at a competitive selling price. In addition, the increase in store traffic for prints should increase the sales revenue for related items, such as cards, wrapping paper, and more. These are all low-margin items, but with increased sales volume of prints and related products, revenues and profits should grow for each store.

Furthermore, store managers will be upset with the increase in the cost of framed prints. Framed prints have generated substantial revenues and profits for the stores. Increasing the cost of framed prints to the stores could create one of three problems: First, a store manager may elect to keep the selling price of framed-print items the same. The results of this would be no change in revenues, but profits would decline because of the increase in cost of framed prints.

Second, a store manager may elect to increase the selling price of the framed prints to offset the cost increase. In this case, sales of framed prints would surely decline and so would revenues and profits. In addition, stores would likely see a decline in related sales of other expensive, high-quality, high-margin items. This is because sales data indicate that customers who purchase high-quality, high-price framed prints also purchase high-quality, high-margin items such as watches, jewelry, and cosmetics.

Third, a store manager may elect to search the outside market for framed prints."

Mr. Burns offered you the challenge of helping him bring change to the company's transfer prices so that both business units, Greetings stores and WallDécor, win. From his explanation, you could see and appreciate that setting the transfer price for unframed and framed prints impacts sale revenues and profits for related items and for the company overall. You immediately recognized the error in your presentation by simply providing a solution for WallDécor alone.

You drove home that night thinking about the challenge. You recognized the need and importance of anticipating the reaction of Greetings store customers to changes in the prices of unframed and framed prints. The next day, the marketing team provided you with the following average data.

- For every unframed print sold (assume one print per customer), that customer purchases related products resulting in $4 of additional profit.
- For every framed print sold (assume one print per customer), that customer purchases related products resulting in $8 of additional profit.

- Each Greetings store sets its own selling price for unframed and framed prints. Store managers need this type of flexibility to be responsive to competitive pressures. On average the pricing for stores is as follows: unframed prints $21, steel-framed without matting $50, wood-framed with matting $70.

Instructions

Answer each of the following questions.

1. Prepare for class discussion what you think were the critical challenges for Mr. Burns. Recognize that WallDécor is a profit center and each Greetings store is a profit center.

2. After lengthy and sometimes heated negotiations between WallDécor and the store managers, a new transfer price was determined that calls for the stores and WallDécor to split the profits on unframed prints 30/70 (30% to the store, 70% to WallDécor) and the profits on framed prints 50/50. The following additional terms were also agreed to:

   - "Profits" are defined as the store selling price less the ABC cost.
   - Stores do not share the profits from related products with WallDécor.
   - WallDécor will not seek to sell unframed and framed print items through anyone other than Greetings.
   - WallDécor will work to decrease costs.
   - Greetings stores will not seek suppliers of prints other than WallDécor.
   - Stores will keep the selling price of framed prints as it was before the change in transfer price. On average, stores will decrease the selling price of unframed prints to $20, with an expected increase in volume to 100,000 prints.

   Analyze how WallDécor and the stores benefited from this new agreement. In your analysis, first (a) compute the profits of the stores and WallDécor using traditional amounts related to pricing, cost, and a 20% mark-up on WallDécor costs. Next, (b) compute the profits of the stores and WallDécor using the ABC cost and negotiated transfer price approach. Finally, (c) explain your findings, linking the overall profits for stores and WallDécor.

   The following data apply to this analysis. (Round all calculations to three decimal places.)

	Unframed print	Steel-framed, no matting	Wood-framed, with matting
Average selling price by stores before transfer pricing study	$21	$50	$70
Average selling price by stores after transfer pricing study	$20	$50	$70
Volume at traditional selling price	80,000	15,000	7,000
Volume at new selling price	100,000	15,000	7,000
WallDécor cost (traditional)	$17.36	$33.48	$48.10
ABC cost	$15.258	$39.028	$55.328

3. Review the additional terms of the agreement listed in instruction 2, above. In each case, state whether the item is appropriate, unnecessary, ineffective, or potentially harmful to the overall company.

Greetings Inc.

Greetings Inc. Swims in the Dot-com Sea: Capital Budgeting

*Developed by
Thomas L. Zeller,
Loyola University
Chicago, and
Paul D. Kimmel,
University
of Wisconsin–
Milwaukee*

The Business Situation

Greetings Inc. stores, as well as the WallDécor division, have enjoyed healthy profitability during the last two years. Although the profit margin on prints is often thin, the volume of print sales has been substantial enough to generate 15 percent of Greetings's store profits. In addition, the increased customer traffic resulting from the prints has generated significant additional sales of related non-print products. As a result, the company's rate of return has exceeded the industry average during this two-year period. Greetings's store managers likened the e-business leverage created by WallDécor to a "high-octane" fuel to supercharge the stores' profitability.

This high rate of return (ROI) was accomplished even though WallDécor's venture into e-business proved to cost more than originally budgeted. Why was it a profitable venture even though costs exceeded estimates? Greetings stores were able to generate a considerable volume of business for WallDécor. This helped spread the high e-business operating costs, many of which were fixed, across many unframed and framed prints. This experience taught top management that maintaining an e-business structure and making this business model successful are very expensive and require substantial sales as well as careful monitoring of costs.

WallDécor's success gained widespread industry recognition. The business press documented WallDécor's approach to using information technology to increase profitability. The company's CEO, Robert Burns, has become a frequent luncheon speaker on the topic of how to use information technology to offer a great product mix to the customer and increase shareholder value. From the outside looking in, all appears to be going very well for Greetings stores and WallDécor.

However, the sun is not shining as brightly on the inside at Greetings. The mall stores that compete with Greetings have begun to offer prints at very competitive prices. Although Greetings stores enjoyed a selling price advantage for a few years, the competition eventually responded, and now the pressure on selling price is as intense as ever. The pressure on the stores is heightened by the fact that the company's recent success has led shareholders to expect the stores to generate an above-average rate of return. Mr. Burns is very concerned about how the stores and WallDécor can continue on a path of continued growth.

Fortunately, more than a year ago, Mr. Burns anticipated that competitors would eventually find a way to match the selling price of prints. As a consequence, he formed a committee to explore ways to employ technology to further reduce costs and to increase revenues and profitability. The committee is comprised of store managers and staff members from the information technology, marketing, finance, and accounting departments. Early in the group's discussion, the focus turned to the most expensive component of the existing business model—the large inventory of prints that WallDécor has in its centralized warehouse. In addition, WallDécor incurs substantial costs for shipping the prints from the centralized warehouse to customers across the country. Ordering and maintaining such a large inventory of prints consumes valuable resources.

One of the committee members suggested that the company should pursue a model that music stores have experimented with, where CDs are burned in the store from a master copy. This saves the music store the cost of maintaining a large inventory and increases its ability to expand its music offerings. It virtually guarantees that the store can always provide the CDs requested by customers.

Applying this idea to prints, the committee decided that each Greetings store could invest in an expensive color printer connected to its online ordering system. This printer would generate the new prints. WallDécor would have to pay a royalty on a per print basis. However, this approach does offer certain advantages. First, it would eliminate all ordering and inventory maintenance costs related to the prints. Second, shrinkage from lost and stolen prints would be reduced. Finally, by reducing the cost of prints for WallDécor, the cost of prints to Greetings stores would decrease, thus allowing the stores to sell prints at a lower price than competitors. The stores are very interested in this option because it enables them to maintain their current customers and to sell prints to an even wider set of customers at a potentially lower cost. A new set of customers means even greater related sales and profits.

As the accounting/finance expert on the team, you have been asked to perform a financial analysis of this proposal. The team has collected the information presented in Illustration 4-1.

Available Data	Amount
Cost of equipment (zero residual value)	$800,000
Cost of ink and paper supplies (purchase immediately)	100,000
Annual cash flow savings for WallDécor	175,000
Annual additional store cash flow from increased sales	100,000
Sale of ink and paper supplies at end of 5 years	50,000
Expected life of equipment	5 years
Cost of capital	12%

ILLUSTRATION 4-1
Information about the proposed capital investment project

Instructions

Mr. Burns has asked you to do the following as part of your analysis of the capital investment project.

1. Calculate the net present value using the numbers provided. Assume that annual cash flows occur at the end of the year.

2. Mr. Burns is concerned that the original estimates may be too optimistic. He has suggested that you do a sensitivity analysis assuming all costs are 10% higher than expected and that all inflows are 10% less than expected.

3. Identify possible flaws in the numbers or assumptions used in the analysis, and identify the risk(s) associated with purchasing the equipment.

4. In a one-page memo, provide a recommendation based on the above analysis. Include in this memo: (a) a challenge to store and WallDécor management and (b) a suggestion on how Greetings stores could use the computer connection for related sales.

Auburn Circular Club Pro Rodeo Roundup

Developed by Jessica Johnson Frazier, Eastern Kentucky University, and Patricia H. Mounce, Mississippi College

The Business Situation

When Shelley Jones became president-elect of the Circular Club of Auburn, Kansas, she was asked to suggest a new fund-raising activity for the club. After a considerable amount of research, Shelley proposed that the Circular Club sponsor a professional rodeo. In her presentation to the club, Shelley said that she wanted a fund-raiser that would (1) continue to get better each year, (2) give back to the community, and (3) provide the club a presence in the community. Shelley's goal was to have an activity that would become an "annual community event" and that would break even the first year and raise $5,000 the following year. In addition, based on the experience of other communities, Shelley believed that a rodeo could grow in popularity so that the club would eventually earn an average of $20,000 annually.

A rodeo committee was formed. Shelley contacted the world's oldest and largest rodeo-sanctioning agency to apply to sponsor a professional rodeo. The sanctioning agency requires a rodeo to consist of the following five events: Bareback Riding, Bronco Riding, Steer Wrestling, Bull Riding, and Calf Roping. Because there were a number of team ropers in the area and because they wanted to include females in the competition, members of the rodeo committee added Team Roping and Women's Barrels. Prize money of $3,000 would be paid to winners in each of the seven events.

Members of the rodeo committee contracted with RJ Cattle Company, a livestock contractor on the rodeo circuit, to provide bucking stock, fencing, and chutes. Realizing that costs associated with the rodeo were tremendous and that ticket sales would probably not be sufficient to cover the costs, the rodeo committee sent letters to local businesses soliciting contributions in exchange for various sponsorships. Exhibiting Sponsors would contribute $1,000 to exhibit their products or services, while Major Sponsors would contribute $600. Chute Sponsors would contribute $500 to have the name of their business on one of the six bucking chutes. For a contribution of $100, individuals would be included in a Friends of Rodeo list found in the rodeo programs. At each performance the rodeo announcer would repeatedly mention the names of the businesses and individuals at each level of sponsorship. In addition, large signs and banners with the names of the businesses of the Exhibiting

Sponsors, Major Sponsors, and Chute Sponsors were to be displayed prominently in the arena.

A local youth group was contacted to provide concessions to the public and divide the profits with the Circular Club. The Auburn Circular Club Pro Rodeo Roundup would be held on June 1, 2, and 3. The cost of an adult ticket was set at $8 in advance or $10 at the gate; the cost of a ticket for a child 12 or younger was set at $6 in advance or $8 at the gate. Tickets were not date-specific. Rather, one ticket would admit an individual to one performance of his or her choice—Friday, Saturday, or Sunday. The rodeo committee was able to secure a location through the county supervisor board at a nominal cost to the Circular Club. The arrangement allowed the use of the county fair grounds and arena for a one-week period. Several months prior to the rodeo, members of the rodeo committee had been assured that bleachers at the arena would hold 2,500 patrons. However, on Saturday night there were 1,663 in attendance and all seats were filled. Attendance was 898 Friday and 769 on Sunday.

The following revenue and expense figures relate to the first year of the rodeo.

ILLUSTRATION 5-1
Revenue and expense data, year 1

Receipts		
Contributions from sponsors	$22,000	
Receipts from ticket sales	28,971	
Share of concession profits	1,513	
Sale of programs	600	
Total receipts		$53,084
Expenses		
Livestock contractor	26,000	
Prize money	21,000	
Contestant hospitality	3,341*	
Sponsor signs for arena	1,900	
Insurance	1,800	
Ticket printing	1,050	
Sanctioning fees	925	
Entertainment	859	
Judging fees	750	
Port-a-potties	716	
Rent	600	
Hay for horses and sand for arena	538	
Programs	500	
Western hats to first 500 children	450	
Hotel rooms for stock contractor	325	
Utilities	300	
Interest expense	251	
Miscellaneous fixed costs	105	
Total expenses		61,410
Net loss		$(8,326)

*The club contracted with a local caterer to provide a tent and food for the contestants. The cost of the food was contingent on the number of contestants each evening. Information concerning the number of contestants and the costs incurred are as follows:

	Contestants	Total Cost
Friday	68	$ 998
Saturday	96	1,243
Sunday	83	1,100

On Wednesday after the rodeo, members of the rodeo committee met to discuss and critique the rodeo. Jonathan Edmunds, CPA and President of the Circular Club, commented that the club did not lose money. Rather, Jonathan said, "The club made an investment in the rodeo."

Instructions

Answer each of the following questions.

1. Do you think it was necessary for Shelley Jones to stipulate that she wanted a fund-raiser that would (1) continue to get better each year, (2) give back to the community, and (3) provide the club a presence in the community? Why or why not?

2. What did Jonathan Edmunds mean when he said the club had made an investment in the rodeo?

3. Is Jonathan's comment concerning the investment consistent with Shelley's idea that the club should have a fund-raiser that would (1) continue to get better each year, (2) give back to the community, and (3) provide the club a presence in the community? Why or why not?

4. What do you believe is the behavior of the rodeo expenditures in relation to ticket sales?

5. Determine the fixed and variable cost components of the catering costs using the high-low method.

6. Assume you are elected chair of the rodeo committee for next year. What steps would you suggest the committee take to make the rodeo profitable?

7. Shelley, Jonathan, and Adrian Stein, the Fundraising Chairperson, are beginning to make plans for next year's rodeo. Shelley believes that by negotiating with local feed stores, innkeepers, and other business owners, costs can be cut dramatically. Jonathan agrees. After carefully analyzing costs, Jonathan has estimated that the fixed expenses can be pared to approximately $51,000. In addition, Jonathan has determined that variable costs are 4% of total gross receipts.

   After talking with business owners who attended the rodeo, Adrian is confident that funds solicited from sponsors will increase. Adrian is comfortable in budgeting revenue from sponsors at $25,600. The local youth group is unwilling to provide concessions to the audience unless they receive all of the profits. Not having the personnel to staff the concession booth, members of the Circular Club reluctantly agree to let the youth group have 100 percent of the profits from the concessions. In addition, members of the rodeo committee, recognizing that the net income from programs was only $100, decide not to sell rodeo programs next year. Compute the break-even point in dollars of ticket sales assuming Adrian and Jonathan are correct in their assumptions.

8. Shelley has just learned that you are calculating the break-even point in ticket sales. She is still convinced that the Club can make a profit using the assumptions in number 7 above.

   (a) Calculate the dollars of ticket sales needed in order to earn a target profit of $6,000.

   (b) Calculate the dollars of ticket sales needed in order to earn a target profit of $12,000.

9. Are the facilities at the fairgrounds adequate to handle crowds needed to generate ticket revenues calculated in number 8 above to earn a $6,000 profit? Show calculations to support your answers.

10. Prepare a budgeted income statement for next year using the estimated revenues from sponsors and other assumptions in number 7 above. In addition, use ticket sales based on the target profit of $12,000 estimated in 8(b). The cost of the livestock contractor, prize money, sanctioning fees, entertainment, judging fees, rent, and utilities will remain the same next year (continued on next page).

Changes in expenses include the following: Members of the Club have decided to eliminate all costs related to contestant hospitality by soliciting a tent and food for the contestants and taking care of the "Contestant Hospitality Tent" themselves. The county has installed permanent restrooms at the arena, eliminating the need to rent port-a-potties. The rodeo committee intends to pursue arrangements to have hotel rooms, hay and sand, and children's hats provided at no charge in exchange for sponsorships. The cost of banners varies with the number of sponsors. Signs and More charged the Circular Club $130 for each Exhibiting Sponsor banner and $48 for each Major Sponsor banner. At this time there is no way to know whether additional sponsors will be Exhibiting Sponsors or Major Sponsors. Therefore, for budgeting purposes you should increase the cost of the banners by the percentage increase in sponsor contributions. (*Hint*: Round all calculations to three decimal places.) By checking prices, the Circular Club will be able to obtain insurance providing essentially the same amount of coverage as this year for only $600. For the first rodeo the Club ordered 10,000 tickets. Realizing the constraints on available seating, the Club is ordering only 5,000 tickets for next year, and therefore its costs are reduced 50%. The interest expense for next year will be $300, and miscellaneous fixed costs are to be budgeted at $100.

11. A few members in the Circular Club do not want to continue with the annual rodeo. However, Shelley is insistent that the Club must continue to conduct the rodeo as an annual fund-raiser. Shelley argues that she has spent hundreds of dollars on western boots, hats, and other items of clothing to wear to the rodeo. Are the expenses related to Shelley's purchases of rodeo clothing relevant costs? Why or why not?

12. Rather than hire the local catering company to cater the Contestant Hospitality Tent, members of the Circular Club are considering asking Shady's Bar-B-Q to cater the event in exchange for a $600 Major Sponsor spot. In addition, The Fun Shop, a local party supply business, will be asked to donate a tent to use for the event. The Fun Shop will also be given a $600 Major Sponsor spot. Several members of the Club are opposed to this consideration, arguing that the two Major Sponsor spots will take away from the money to be earned through other sponsors. Adrian Stein has explained to the members that the Major Sponsor signs for the arena cost only $48 each. In addition, there is more than enough room to display two additional sponsor signs. What would you encourage the Club to do concerning the Contestant Hospitality Tent? Would your answer be different if the arena were limited in the number of additional signs that could be displayed? What kind of cost would we consider in this situation that would not be found on a financial statement?

Sweats Galore

*Developed by
Jessica Johnson
Frazier, Eastern
Kentucky
University, and
Patricia H.
Mounce,
Mississippi College*

The Business Situation

After graduating with a degree in business from Eastern University in Campus Town, USA, Michael Woods realized that he wanted to remain in Campus Town. After a number of unsuccessful attempts at getting a job in his discipline, Michael decided to go into business for himself. In thinking about his business venture, Michael determined that he had four criteria for the new business:

1. He wanted to do something that he would enjoy.
2. He wanted a business that would give back to the community.
3. He wanted a business that would grow and be more successful every year.
4. Realizing that he was going to have to work very hard, Michael wanted a business that would generate a minimum net income of $25,000 annually.

While reflecting on the criteria he had outlined, Michael, who had been president of his fraternity and served as an officer in several other student organizations, realized that there was no place in Campus Town to have custom sweatshirts made using a silk-screen process. When student organizations wanted sweatshirts to give to their members or to market on campus, the officers had to make a trip to a city 100 miles away to visit "Shirts and More."

Michael had worked as a part-time employee at Shirts and More while he was in high school and had envisioned owning such a shop. He realized that a sweatshirt shop in Campus Town had the potential to meet all four of his criteria. Michael set up an appointment with Jayne Stoll, the owner of Shirts and More, to obtain information useful in getting his shop started. Because Jayne liked Michael and was intrigued by his entrepreneurial spirit, she answered many of Michael's questions.

In addition, Jayne provided information concerning the type of equipment Michael would need for his business and its average useful life. Jayne knows a competitor who is retiring and would like to sell his equipment. Michael can purchase the equipment at the beginning of 2006, and the owner is willing to give him terms of 50 percent due upon purchase and 50 percent due the quarter following the purchase. Michael decided to purchase the following equipment as of January 1, 2006.

	Cost	Useful Life
Hand-operated press that applies ink to the shirt	$7,500	5 yrs.
Light-exposure table	1,350	10 yrs.
Dryer conveyer belt that makes ink dry on the shirts	2,500	10 yrs.
Computer with graphics software and color printer	3,500	4 yrs.
Display furniture	2,000	10 yrs.
Used cash register	500	5 yrs.

Michael has decided to use the sweatshirt supplier recommended by Jayne. He learned that a gross of good-quality sweatshirts to be silk-screened would cost $1,440. Jayne has encouraged Michael to ask the sweatshirt supplier for terms of 40 percent of a quarter's purchases to be paid in the quarter of purchase, with the remaining 60 percent of the quarter's purchases to be paid in the quarter following the purchase.

Michael also learned from talking with Jayne that the ink used in the silk-screen process costs approximately $0.75 per shirt.

Knowing that the silk-screen process is somewhat labor intensive, Michael plans to hire six college students to help with the process. Each one will work an average of 20 hours per week for 50 weeks during the year. Michael estimates total annual wages for the workers to be $72,000.

In addition, Michael will need one person to take orders, bill customers, and operate the cash register. Cary Sue Smith, who is currently Director of Student Development at Eastern University, has approached Michael about a job in sales. Cary Sue knows the officers of all of the student organizations on campus. In addition, she is very active in the community. Michael thinks Cary Sue can bring in a lot of business. In addition she also has the clerical skills needed for the position. Because of her contacts, Michael is willing to pay Cary Sue $1,200 per month plus a commission of 10 percent of sales. Michael estimates Cary Sue will spend 50 percent of the workday focusing on sales, and the remaining 50 percent will be spent on clerical and administrative duties.

Michael realizes that he will have difficulty finding a person skilled in computer graphics to generate the designs to be printed on the shirts. Jayne recently hired a graphics designer in that position for Shirts and More at a rate of $500 per month plus $0.10 for each shirt printed. Michael believes he can find a university graphics design student to work for the same rate Jayne is paying her designer.

Michael was fortunate to find a commercial building for rent near the university and the downtown area. The landlord requires a one-year lease. Although the monthly rent of $1,000 is more than Michael had anticipated paying, the building is nice, has adequate parking, and there is room for expansion. Michael anticipates that 75 percent of the building will be used in the silk-screen process and 25 percent will be used for sales.

Michael's fraternity brothers have encouraged him to advertise weekly in the Eastern University student newspaper. Upon inquiring, Michael found that a 3" x 3" ad would cost $25 per week. Michael also plans to run a weekly ad in the local newspaper that will cost him $75 per week.

Michael wants to sell a large number of quality shirts at a reasonable price. He estimates the selling price of each customized shirt to be $16. Jayne has suggested that he should ask customers to pay for 70 percent of their purchases in the quarter purchased and pay the additional 30 percent in the quarter following the purchases.

After talking with the insurance agent and the property valuation administrator in his municipality, Michael estimates that the property taxes and insurance on the machinery will cost $2,240 annually; property tax and insurance on display furniture and cash register will total $380 annually.

Jayne reminded Michael that maintenance of the machines is required for the silk-screen process. In addition, Michael realizes that he must consider the cost of utilities. The building Michael wants to rent is roughly the same size as the building occupied by Shirts and More. In addition, Shirts and More sells approximately the same number of shirts Michael plans to sell in his store. Therefore, Michael is confident that the maintenance and utility costs for his shop will be comparable to the maintenance and utility costs for Shirts and More, which are as follows within the relevant range of zero to 8,000 shirts.

	Shirts Sold	Maintenance Costs	Utility Costs
January	2,000	$1,716	$1,100
February	2,110	1,720	1,158
March	2,630	1,740	1,171
April	3,150	1,740	1,198
May	5,000	1,758	1,268
June	5,300	1,818	1,274
July	3,920	1,825	1,205
August	2,080	1,780	1,117
September	8,000	1,914	1,400
October	6,810	1,860	1,362
November	6,000	1,855	1,347
December	3,000	1,749	1,193

Michael estimates the number of shirts to be sold in the first five quarters, beginning January 2006, to be:

First quarter, year 1	8,000
Second quarter, year 1	10,000
Third quarter, year 1	20,000
Fourth quarter, year 1	12,000
First quarter, year 2	18,000

Seeing how determined his son was to become an entrepreneur, Michael's father offered to co-sign a note for an amount up to $20,000 to help Michael open his sweatshirt shop, Sweats Galore. However, when Michael and his father approached the loan officer at First Guarantee Bank, the loan officer asked Michael to produce the following budgets for 2006.

Sales budget
Schedule of expected collections from customers
Shirt purchases budget
Schedule of expected payments for purchases
Silk-screen labor budget
Selling and administrative expenses budget
Silk-screen overhead expenses budget
Budgeted income statement
Cash budget
Budgeted balance sheet

The loan officer advised Michael that the interest rate on a 12-month loan would be 8 percent. Michael expects the loan to be taken out as of January 1, 2006.

Michael has estimated that his income tax rate will be 20 percent. He expects to pay the total tax due when his returns are filed in 2007.

Instructions

Answer the following questions.

1. Do you think it was important for Michael to stipulate his four criteria for the business (see page CA-21), including the goal of generating a net income of at least $25,000 annually? Why or why not?

2. If Michael has sales of $12,000 during January of his first year of business, determine the amount of variable and fixed costs associated with utilities and maintenance using the high-low method for each.

3. Using the format below, prepare a sales budget for the year ending 2006.

SWEATS GALORE
Sales Budget
For the Year Ending December 31, 2006

		Quarter			
	1	2	3	4	Year
Expected unit sales					
Unit selling price	x				
Budgeted sales revenue	$				

4. Prepare a schedule of expected collections from customers.

SWEATS GALORE
Schedule of Expected Collections from Customers
For the Year Ending December 31, 2006

		Quarter		
	1	2	3	4
Accounts receivable 1/1/06	–0–			
First quarter				
Second quarter				
Third quarter				
Fourth quarter				
Total collections				

5. Michael learned from talking with Jayne that the supplier is so focused on making quality sweatshirts that many times the shirts are not available for several days. She encouraged Michael to maintain an ending inventory of shirts equal to 25 percent of the next quarter's sales.

Prepare a shirt purchases budget for shirts using the format provided.

SWEATS GALORE
Shirt Purchases Budget
For the Year Ending December 31, 2006

		Quarter			
	1	2	3	4	Year
Shirts to be silk-screened					
Plus: Desired ending inventory					
Total shirts required					
Less: Beginning inventory					
Total shirts needed					
Cost per shirt					
Total cost of shirt purchases					

6. Prepare a schedule of expected payments for purchases.

SWEATS GALORE
Schedule of Expected Payments for Purchases
For the Year Ending December 31, 2006

		Quarter		
	1	2	3	4
Accounts payable 1/1/06	–0–			
First quarter				
Second quarter				
Third quarter				
Fourth quarter				
Total payments				

7. Prepare a silk-screen labor budget.

SWEATS GALORE
Silk-Screen Labor Budget
For the Year Ending December 31, 2006

	_____	Quarter	_____		
	1	2	3	4	Year

Units to be produced
Silk-screen labor hours per unit
Total required silk-screen labor hours
Silk-screen labor cost per hour
Total silk-screen labor cost

8. Prepare a selling and administrative expenses budget for Sweats Galore for the year ending December 31, 2006.

SWEATS GALORE
Selling and Administrative Expenses Budget
For the Year Ending December 31, 2006

		Quarter			
	1	2	3	4	Year

Variable expenses:
    Sales commissions
Total variable expenses
Fixed expenses:
    Advertising
    Rent
    Sales salaries
    Office salaries
    Depreciation
    Property taxes and insurance
Total fixed expenses
Total selling and
    administrative expenses

9. Prepare a silk-screen overhead expenses budget for Sweats Galore for the year ending December 31, 2006.

SWEATS GALORE
Silk-Screen Overhead Expenses Budget
For the Year Ending December 31, 2006

		Quarter			
	1	2	3	4	Year

Variable expenses:
    Ink
    Maintenance
    Utilities
    Graphics design
Total variable expenses
Fixed expenses:
    Rent
    Maintenance
    Utilities
    Graphics design
    Property taxes and insurance
    Depreciation
Total fixed expenses
Total silk-screen overhead
Direct silk-screen hours
Overhead rate per silk-screen hour

10. Using the information found in the case and the previous budgets, prepare a budgeted income statement for Sweats Galore for the year ended December 31, 2006.

SWEATS GALORE
Budgeted Income Statement
For the Year Ending December 31, 2006

Sales
Cost of goods sold
Gross profit
Selling and administrative expenses
Income from operations
Interest expense
Income before income taxes
Income tax expense
Net income

11. Using the information found in the case and the previous budgets, prepare a cash budget for Sweats Galore for the year ended December 31, 2006.

SWEATS GALORE
Cash Budget
For the Year Ending December 31, 2006

	Quarter			
	1	2	3	4
Beginning cash balance				
Add: Receipts				
Collections from customers				
Total available cash				
Less: Disbursements				
Payments for shirt purchases				
Silk-screen labor				
Silk-screen overhead				
Selling and administrative expenses				
Payment for equipment purchase				
Total disbursements				
Excess (deficiency) of available cash over disbursements				
Financing				
Borrowings				
Ending cash balance				

12. Using the information contained in the case and the previous budgets, prepare a budgeted balance sheet for Sweats Galore for the year ended December 31, 2006.

SWEATS GALORE
Budgeted Balance Sheet
December 31, 2006

Assets

Cash
Accounts receivable
Sweatshirt inventory
Equipment
Less: Accumulated depreciation
Total assets

Liabilities and Owner's Equity

Accounts payable
Notes payable
Interest payable
Taxes payable
Total liabilities
Michael Woods, Capital
Total liabilities and owner's equity

13. (a) Using the information contained in the case and the previous budgets, calculate the estimated contribution margin per unit for 2006.
    (b) Calculate the total estimated fixed costs for 2006 (including interest and taxes). (Hint: Silk-screened labor is a fixed cost.)
    (c) Compute the break-even point in units and dollars for 2006.

14. (a) Michael is very disappointed that he did not have an income of $25,000 for his first year of budgeted operations as he had wanted. How many shirts would Michael have had to sell in order to have had a profit of $25,000? (Ignore changes in income tax expense.)
    (b) Why does Michael's net income differ from his ending cash balance?

15. Do you think it was a good idea to offer Cary Sue a salary plus 10 percent of sales? Why or why not?

Armstrong Helmet Company

*Developed by
Dick Wasson,
Southwestern
College*

The Business Situation

Armstrong Helmet Company manufactures a unique model of bicycle helmet. The company began operations December 1, 2006. Its accountant quit the second week of operations, and the company is searching for a replacement. The company has decided to test the knowledge and ability of all candidates interviewing for the position. Each candidate will be provided with the information below and then asked to prepare a series of reports, schedules, budgets, and recommendations based on that information. The information provided to each candidate is as follows.

Cost items and account balances

Administrative salaries	$15,500
Advertising for helmets	11,000
Cash, December 1	–0–
Depreciation on factory building	1,500
Depreciation on office equipment	800
Insurance on factory building	1,500
Miscellaneous expenses—factory	1,000
Office supplies expense	300
Professional fees	500
Property taxes on factory building	400
Raw materials used	70,000
Rent on production equipment	6,000
Research and development	10,000
Sales commissions	40,000
Utility costs—factory	900
Wages—factory	70,000
Work in process, December 1	–0–
Work in process, December 31	–0–
Raw materials inventory, December 1	–0–
Raw materials inventory, December 31	–0–
Raw material purchases	70,000
Finished goods inventory, December 1	–0–

Production and sales data

Number of helmets produced	10,000
Expected sales in units for December	
($40 unit sales price)	8,000
Expected sales in units for January	10,000
Desired ending inventory	20% of next month's sales
Direct materials per finished unit	1 kilogram
Direct materials cost	$7 per kilogram
Direct labor hours per unit	.35
Direct labor hourly rate	$20

Cash flow data

Cash collections from customers: 75% in month of sale and 25% the following month.

Cash payments to suppliers: 75% in month of purchase and 25% the following month.

Income tax rate: 45%.

Cost of proposed production equipment: $720,000.

Manufacturing overhead and selling and administrative costs are paid as incurred.

Desired ending cash balance: $30,000.

Instructions

Using the data presented above, do the following.

1. Classify the costs as either product costs or period costs using a five-column table as shown below. Enter the dollar amount of each cost in the appropriate column and total each classification.

	Product Costs			
Item	**Direct Materials**	**Direct Labor**	**Manufacturing Overhead**	**Period Costs**

2. Classify the costs as either variable or fixed costs. Assume there are no mixed costs. Enter the dollar amount of each cost in the appropriate column and total each classification. Use the format shown below. Assume that Utility costs—Factory are a fixed cost.

Item	**Variable Costs**	**Fixed Costs**	**Total Costs**

3. Prepare a schedule of cost of goods manufactured for the month of December 2006.
4. Determine the cost of producing a helmet.
5. Identify the type of cost accounting system that Armstrong Helmet Company is probably using at this time. Explain.
6. Under what circumstances might Armstrong use a different cost accounting system?
7. Compute the unit variable cost for a helmet.
8. Compute the unit contribution margin and the contribution margin ratio.
9. Calculate the break-even point in units and in sales dollars.
10. Prepare the following budgets for the month of December 2006.
    (a) Sales.
    (b) Production.
    (c) Direct materials.
    (d) Direct labor.
    (e) Selling and administrative expenses.
    (f) Cash.
    (g) Budgeted income statement.

11. Prepare a flexible budget for manufacturing costs for activity levels between 8,000 and 10,000 units, in 1,000 unit increments.

12. Identify one potential cause of materials, direct labor, and manufacturing overhead variances in the production of the helmet.

13. Determine the cash payback period on the proposed production equipment purchase, assuming a monthly cash flow as indicated in the cash budget (requirement 10f).

PHOTO CREDITS

COMPANY INDEX

A

Advanced Micro Devices (AMD), 303, 305, 560
Alliance Atlantis Communications Inc., 568
Allied Signal, 21
Alstom, 370
Amazon.com, 533, 583
American Airlines, 5, 18, 197, 208, 282, 463
American Century, 496
American Express, 150
American Van Lines, 396
Amoco Corporation, 607
Ampex, 505
Amtrak, 18
Anchor Glass Container Corporation, 46
AOL Time Warner, 18
Armani, 306
Atlantic Network, 366
AT&T, 5, 18, 150, 192

B

Babcock Ice Cream, 371
Ben & Jerry's Homemade, Inc., 93, 95, 99
Bethlehem Steel, 533
Beverly Hills Fan Company, 260
Black & Decker, 626
Blue Cross-Blue Shield, 18
Boeing Corporation, 567
Briggs and Stratton, 421
Bristol-Myers Squibb, 609
Burlington Northeast Santa Fe Railroad Company, 632
Business Systems of America, 61

C

Cambridge Technology Partners, 526
Campbell Soup Company, 5, 489, 491, 492, 499, 504, 505, 509, 523
Caterpillar, 99, 150, 165
Chase, 463
ChevronTexaco, 306
Chiquita Brands International, 21
Cisco Systems, 6, 281, 608
Clark Equipment Company, 146
Clark-Hurth, 146
Coca-Cola Company, 10, 21, 68, 95, 224, 421, 571, 631
Columbia Sportwear Company, 567
Compaq Computer, 1, 3, 10, 17
Consumers Packaging Inc., 46

Cost Technology, 187
Cypress Semiconductor Corporation, 567

D

DaimlerChrysler, 9, 10
Dell Computer, 1, 3, 5, 10, 13, 20, 165, 362
Del Monte Foods Company, 300
Delta Airlines, 463
Digital Equipment, 1
Duke Energy Corporation, 192, 391, 393, 396, 408
Dun & Bradstreet, 589
Dynastar, 229
Dynegy, Inc., 535

E

Eastman Kodak, 527
East Valley Hospital, 186
Elan Corporation, 583
Eli Lilly, 421
Enron, 587, 609
Ethan Allen, 235
E*Trade, 281
ExxonMobil, 52, 95, 306

F

FedEx Corporation, 5, 18, 301
Fidelity Investments, 21
Ford Motor Company, 9, 10, 109, 124, 197, 234, 276, 307, 408
Foundation Software, Inc., 61
Fruit of the Loom Inc., 358
Fujitsu Computer Products of America, 408

G

Ganong Bros. Ltd., 225
General Electric (GE), 6, 508, 587
General Microwave Corporation, 139
General Mills, 95, 156, 408, 589, 594, 596–601, 603, 604, 606
General Motors Corporation, 5, 9, 21, 52, 53, 57, 227, 229, 232, 234, 307, 608, 617
Gibson Greetings, Inc., 227
Glassmaster Co., 487
Global Crossing, 587

H

Harley-Davidson, 165
Hershey Foods Corporation, 98, 582, 631

Hewlett-Packard Company, 2, 150, 165, 187, 227, 233, 243, 276, 462
Hilton Hotels Corporation, 20, 22, 192
H&R Block, 110
Hughes Aircraft, 150

I

IBM, 52, 150, 208, 447, 533
Ideal Manufacturing Company, 186
Inktomi, 263, 265
Intel Corporation, 110, 263, 265, 303, 305, 306, 559, 560
Intuit, 559
Iomega, 533

J

J. C. Penney Company, Inc., 529
JetBlue Airways, 282
Jiffy Lube, 110
JKL, Inc., 405
John Deere Company, 150
Jostens, Inc., 462

K

Kellogg Company, 52, 95, 102–104, 109, 115, 197, 533, 589–592, 595, 597–607, 609
Kinko's Print Shop, 124
Kmart Corporation, 529
Komag, 281

L

Levi Strauss, 307, 348

M

Mahany Welding Supply, 153
Marriott Hotels, 192, 396
Massachusetts General Hospital, 68, 191
Mayo Clinic, 68
McDonald's Corporation, 445, 570
Merck Company, 305, 347
Merrill Lynch, 18, 68
Microsoft Corporation, 525, 533, 555, 557–559, 607, 617
Moody's, 589
Motorola, 634

N

Network Computing Devices Inc., 388
Nike, 192, 227, 281
Nissan Motor, 10
Noratek Solutions, 61